Sommario

Principali strade ed itinerari maritt...
Distanze . . . .
Come servirsi della guida (important...
Scelta di un albergo, di un ristorante
  — Classe e confort — Installazion...
  — Amenità . . . .
  — La Tavola . . . . p. 30
  — La vendita delle bevande alcooliche . . . . p. 31 e 48
  — I Prezzi . . . . p. 31
  — Qualche chiarimento utile . . . . p. 32
Per visitare una città ed i suoi dintorni : p. 33
  — Le Città — Le Curiosità . . . .
  — Le Piante delle città (segni convenzionali) . . . . p. 34
Alberghi autostradali . . . . p. 35
La Grande Londra . . . . p. 44 a 46

                               pagine bordate
                               di rosso
Principali catene alberghiere . . . . p. 606
Segnaletica stradale . . . . p. 607 a 611
Principali compagnie di navigazione . . . . p. 612 a 616
Carte e guide Michelin . . . . consultare le
                               ultime pagine

Nomenclatura delle località citate e carta della regione
Alphabetisches Ortsverzeichnis und Übersichtskarte

ENGLAND AND WALES	49
SCOTLAND	481
NORTHERN IRELAND	553
CHANNEL ISLANDS	563
ISLE OF MAN	572
REPUBLIC OF IRELAND	575

Inhaltsverzeichnis

Hauptverkehrsstraßen und -schiffsverbindungen . . . S. 4 bis 9
Entfernungen . . . . S. 10 und 11
Über den Gebrauch dieses Führers (wichtig) . . . . S. 36 bis 43
Wahl eines Hotels, eines Restaurants :
  — Klasseneinteilung und Komfort — Einrichtung S. 37
  — Annehmlichkeiten . . . . S. 38
  — Küche . . . . S. 39 und 48
  — Ausschank alkoholischer Getränke . . . . S. 39
  — Preise . . . . S. 40
  — Einige nützliche Hinweise . . . . S. 41
Besichtigung einer Stadt und ihrer Umgebung :
  — Städte — Hauptsehenswürdigkeiten . . . . S. 42
  — Stadtpläne (Zeichenerklärung) . . . . S. 43
Autobahn-Rasthäuser . . . . S. 44 bis 46
Groß-London . . . .

                               auf den rot um-
                               randeten Seiten
Die wichtigsten Hotelketten . . . . S. 606
Verkehrszeichen . . . . S. 607 bis 611
Adressen einiger Schiffahrtsgesellschaften . . . . S. 612 bis 616
Michelin-Karten und -Führer . . . . am Ende des
                               Führers

MAJOR ROADS AND PRINCIPAL SHIPPING ROUTES

Motorway and access roads

Road number _ _ _ _ _ _ _ A 4 T 35 N 2

Mileage _ _ _ _ _ _ _ _ _ 20

PRINCIPALES ROUTES ET LIAISONS MARITIMES

Autoroute et accès _ _ _ _ _ _

N° de route _ _ _ _ _ _ _ A 4 T 35 N 2

Distance en miles _ _ _ _ _ _ 20

PRINCIPALI STRADE E ITINERARI MARITTIMI

Autostrada e accessi _ _ _ _ _

Numero di strada _ _ _ _ _ A 4 T 35 N 2

Distanza in miglia _ _ _ _ _ 20

HAUPTVERKEHRSSTRASSEN UND SCHIFFSVERBINDUNGEN

Autobahn mit Anschlußstelle _

Straßennummer _ _ _ _ _ _ A 4 T 35 N 2

Entfernung in Meilen _ _ _ _ _ 20

GREAT BRITAIN : the maps and town plans in the Great Britain Section of this Guide are based upon the Ordnance Survey of Great Britain with the permission of the Controller of Her Majesty's Stationery Office. Crown Copyright reserved.

NORTHERN IRELAND : the maps and town plans in the Northern Ireland Section of this Guide are based upon the Ordnance Survey of Northern Ireland with the sanction of the Controller of H.M. Stationery Office.

REPUBLIC OF IRELAND : the maps and town plans in the Republic of Ireland Section of this Guide are based upon the Ordnance Survey of Ireland by permission of the Government of the Republic, Permit number 4099

4

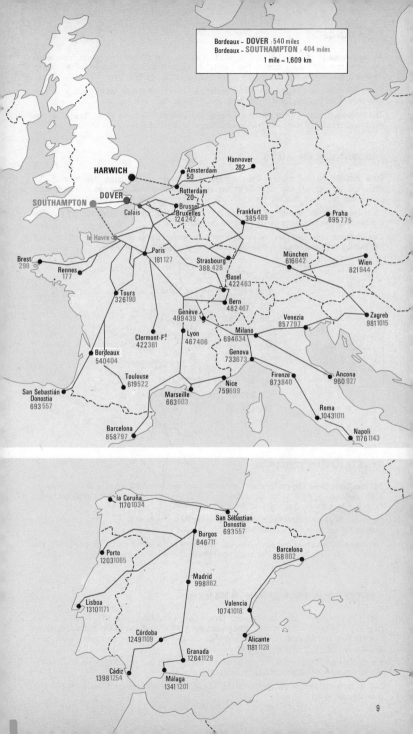

Bordeaux – **DOVER** : 540 miles
Bordeaux – **SOUTHAMPTON** : 404 miles

1 mile = 1,609 km

HARWICH

Amsterdam
50

Hannover
282

SOUTHAMPTON

DOVER

Rotterdam
20

Calais

Brussel
Bruxelles
124 242

Frankfurt
385 489

Praha
695 775

le Havre

Paris
181 127

Strasbourg
388 428

München
616 642

Wien
821 944

Brest
298

Rennes
177

Basel
422 463

Bern
482 467

Tours
326 190

Genève
499 439

Milano
694 634

Venezia
857 797

Zagreb
981 1015

Clermont-Fd
422 361

Lyon
467 406

Genova
733 673

Bordeaux
540 404

Toulouse
619 522

Nice
759 699

Firenze
873 840

Ancona
960 927

San Sebastián
Donostia
693 557

Marseille
663 603

Roma
1043 1011

Barcelona
858 797

Napoli
1176 1143

la Coruña
1170 1034

San Sebastián
Donostia
693 557

Burgos
846 711

Barcelona
858 802

Porto
1203 1065

Madrid
998 862

Lisboa
1310 1171

Valencia
1074 1018

Córdoba
1249 1109

Alicante
1181 1128

Cádiz
1398 1254

Granada
1264 1129

Málaga
1341 1201

9

DISTANCES

All distances in this edition are quoted in miles. The distance is given from each town to its neighbours and to the capital of each region as grouped in the guide. Towns appearing in the charts are preceded by a lozenge ♦ in text.

To avoid excessive repetition some distances have only been quoted once — you may therefore have to look under both town headings.

The mileages quoted are not necessarily the lowest but have been based on the roads which afford the best driving conditions and are therefore the most practical.

DISTANCES EN MILES

Pour chaque région traitée, vous trouverez au texte de chacune des localités sa distance par rapport à la capitale et aux villes environnantes. Lorsque ces villes sont celles des tableaux, leur nom est précédé d'un losange noir ♦.

La distance d'une localité à une autre n'est pas toujours répétée aux deux villes intéressées : voyez au texte de l'une ou de l'autre.

Ces distances ne sont pas nécessairement comptées par la route la plus courte mais par la plus pratique, c'est-à-dire celle offrant les meilleures conditions de roulage.

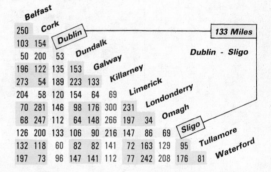

Belfast
250	Cork										
103	154	**Dublin**									
50	200	53	Dundalk								
196	122	135	153	Galway							
273	54	189	223	133	Killarney						
204	58	120	154	64	69	Limerick					
70	281	146	98	176	300	231	Londonderry				
68	247	112	64	148	266	197	34	Omagh			
126	200	133	106	90	216	147	86	69	**Sligo**		
132	118	60	82	82	141	72	163	129	95	Tullamore	
197	73	96	147	141	112	77	242	208	176	81	Waterford

133 Miles

Dublin - Sligo

DISTANZE IN MIGLIA

Per ciascuna delle regioni trattate, troverete nel testo di ogni località la sua distanza dalla capitale e dalle città circostanti. Quando queste città sono comprese nelle tabelle, il loro nome è preceduto da una losanga ♦.

La distanza da una località all'altra non è sempre ripetuta nelle due città interessate : vedere nel testo dell'una o dell'altra.

Le distanze non sono necessariamente calcolate seguendo il percorso più breve, ma vengono stabilite secondo l'itinerario più pratico, che offre cioè le migliori condizioni di viaggio.

ENTFERNUNGSANGABEN IN MEILEN

Die Entfernungen der einzelnen Orte zur Landeshauptstadt und zu den nächstgrößeren Städten in der Umgebung sind im allgemeinen Ortstext angegeben. Die Namen der Städte in der Umgebung, die auf der Tabelle zu finden sind, sind durch eine Raute ♦ gekennzeichnet.

Die Entfernung zweier Städte voneinander können Sie aus den Angaben im Ortstext der einen oder der anderen Stadt ersehen.

Die Entfernungsangaben gelten nicht immer für den kürzesten, sondern für den günstigsten Weg.

442 Miles

Example	Esempio
Exemple	Beispiel
Edinburgh – Southampton	

Cities (diagonal headings): Aberdeen, Ayr, Birmingham, Blackpool, Brighton, Bristol, Cambridge, Cardiff, Carlisle, Coventry, Dover, Dumfries, Dundee, Edinburgh, Glasgow, Inverness, Ipswich, Kingston upon Hull, Leeds, Leicester, Liverpool, London, Manchester, Middlesbrough, Newcastle, Norwich, Nottingham, Oban, Oxford, Plymouth, Portsmouth, Sheffield, Stoke on Trent, Southampton, Swansea, Wick.

Distance chart (each row lists the distances in miles from that town to the towns listed above it):

To \ From	Aberdeen	Ayr	Birmingham	Blackpool	Brighton	Bristol	Cambridge	Cardiff	Carlisle	Coventry	Dover	Dumfries	Dundee	Edinburgh	Glasgow	Inverness
Ayr	196															
Birmingham	442	293														
Blackpool	336	187	130													
Brighton	616	467	180	304												
Bristol	526	377	91	214	157											
Cambridge	500	351	110	221	117	166										
Cardiff	545	396	110	233	191	46	200									
Carlisle	242	93	201	95	375	285	259	304								
Coventry	461	311	18	148	158	96	88	124	219							
Dover	637	488	199	325	84	120	233	259	337	219						
Dumfries	221	59	234	128	408	318	292	337	34	252	396					
Dundee	67	129	375	269	549	459	433	478	252	408	570	154				
Edinburgh	130	81	301	195	475	385	335	404	101	319	459	80	63			
Glasgow	150	35	300	194	474	384	358	403	100	318	458	79	83	46		
Inverness	107	207	468	362	642	552	526	571	268	487	663	247	156	134	172	
Ipswich	553	404	163	274	123	237	54	312	141	126	345	486	388	579	—	—
Kingston upon Hull	397	139	144	250	230	210	155	249	141	121	272	157	231	200	—	61
Leeds	366	216	119	88	262	200	147	229	121	74	272	299	223	188	—	96
Leicester	470	320	43	157	165	121	24	149	228	26	214	403	261	200	—	101
Liverpool	368	219	103	56	277	127	173	155	127	135	318	160	227	131	—	130
London	558	409	122	246	55	121	58	317	355	72	76	301	160	204	416	—
Manchester	409	260	86	51	260	170	155	248	125	132	289	227	132	41	—	202
Middlesbrough	363	214	177	123	319	230	189	319	86	161	485	116	161	227	—	246
Newcastle	331	182	163	90	267	200	122	281	59	160	321	123	183	109	276	109
Norwich	235	349	200	178	286	316	90	264	254	153	153	460	—	190	139	190
Nottingham	527	377	61	173	149	123	61	174	148	43	214	318	361	235	—	—
Oban	432	50	248	170	248	150	235	318	170	223	365	223	141	148	94	74
Oxford	180	294	50	149	88	61	74	149	52	26	132	365	289	326	141	161
Portsmouth	509	360	105	197	73	100	107	268	224	70	59	301	485	428	355	120
Plymouth	641	492	222	329	124	124	161	161	382	236	242	442	516	485	574	—
Sheffield	604	455	48	206	287	133	363	156	139	78	285	396	321	160	258	—
Stoke on Trent	418	89	105	180	122	199	176	91	208	41	254	462	254	345	187	68
Southampton	583	434	79	271	118	79	118	342	80	71	135	209	351	444	275	174
Swansea	397	127	61	41	342	156	342	187	174	105	149	240	149	175	68	41
Wick	542	248	220	161	392	300	227	392	65	190	475	256	269	333	166	251
—	233	46	130	227	136	229	82	333	245	177	333	189	330	186	423	251

Discover
the guide...

To make the most of the guide know how to use it. The Michelin Guide offers in addition to the selection of hotels and restaurants a wide range of information to help you on your travels.

The key to the guide

...is the explanatory chapters which follow.
Remember that the same symbol and character whether in red or black or in bold or light type, have different meanings.

The selection of hotels and restaurants

This book is not an exhaustive list of all hotels but a selection which has been limited on purpose. The final choice is based on regular on the spot enquiries and visits. These visits are the occasion for examining attentively the comments and opinions of our readers.

Town plans

These indicate with precision pedestrian and shopping streets ; major through routes in built up areas ; exact location of hotels whether they be on main or side streets ; post offices ; tourist information centres ; the principal historic buildings and other tourist sights.

For your car

In the text of many towns is to be found a list of agents for the main car manufacturers with their addresses and telephone numbers. Therefore even while travelling you can have your car serviced or repaired.

Your views or comments concerning the above subjects or any others, are always welcome. Your letter will be answered.

Thank you in advance.

Michelin Tyre Public Limited Company
Tourism Department
Lyon Road, HARROW, Middlesex HA1 2DQ

Bibendum wishes you a pleasant journey.

Choosing your hotel or restaurant

We have classified the hotels and restaurants with the travelling motorist in mind. In each category they have been listed in order of preference.

CLASS, STANDARD OF COMFORT

🏨🏨🏨🏨	Luxury in the traditional style	XXXXX
🏨🏨🏨	Top class comfort	XXXX
🏨🏨	Very comfortable	XXX
🏨	Good average	XX
🏠	Quite comfortable	X
🏠	Modest comfort	
🏠	Other recommended accommodation, at moderate prices	
without rest.	The hotel has no restaurant	
	The restaurant has bedrooms	with rm

HOTEL FACILITIES

Hotels in categories 🏨🏨🏨🏨, 🏨🏨🏨, 🏨🏨, usually have every comfort and exchange facilities ; details are not repeated under each hotel.

In other categories, we indicate the facilities available, however, they may not be found in each room.

30 rm	Number of rooms
🛗	Lift (elevator)
▣	Air conditioning
TV	Television in room
🛁wc 🛁	Private bathroom with toilet, private bathroom without toilet
🚿wc 🚿	Private shower with toilet, private shower without toilet
☏	Telephone in room : outside calls connected by the operator
☎	Telephone in room : direct dialling for outside calls
♿	Rooms accessible to the physically handicapped
⚊ ▣	Outdoor or indoor swimming pool
🌳	Garden
🎾	Hotel tennis court
⛳18	Golf course and number of holes
🎣	Fishing available to hotel guests. A charge may be made
🏛	Equipped conference hall (minimum seating : 25)
🚗	Garage available (usually charged for)
Ⓟ	Car park
🐕	Dogs are not allowed
	Where dogs are allowed, they are generally accepted only in bedrooms
May-October	Dates when open, as indicated by the hotelier
season	Probably open for the season - precise dates not available
	Where no date or season is shown, establishments are open all year round
LL35 0SB	Postal code
(T.H.F.)	Hotel Group *(See list at end of the Guide)*

13

Choosing your hotel or restaurant

AMENITY

Your stay in certain hotels will be sometimes particularly agreeable or restful.

Such a quality may derive from the hotel's fortunate setting, its decor, welcoming atmosphere and service.

Such establishments are distinguished in the guide by the symbols shown below.

🏰🏰🏰 ... 🏠	Pleasant hotels
XXXXX ... X	Pleasant restaurants
« Park »	Particularly attractive feature
🦢	Very quiet or quiet, secluded hotel
🦢	Quiet hotel
≤ sea	Exceptional view
≤	Interesting or extensive view

By consulting the maps preceding each geographical area you will find it easier to locate them.

We do not claim to have indicated all the pleasant, very quiet or quiet, secluded hotels which exist.

Our enquiries continue. You can help us by letting us know your opinions and discoveries.

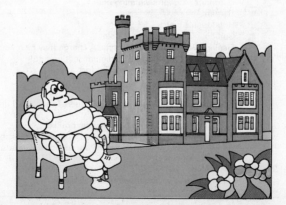

14

CUISINE

The stars for good cooking

We indicate by ❀, ❀❀ or ❀❀❀, establishments where the standard of cooking, whether particular to the country or foreign, deserves to be brought especially to the attention of our readers (see list p. 48 and the maps preceding each geographical area).

In the text of these establishments we show some of the dishes typical of their style of cooking.

❀   **An especially good restaurant in its class**

The star indicates a good place to stop on your journey.

But beware of comparing the star given to a " de luxe " establishment with accordingly high prices, with that of a simpler one, where for a lesser sum one can still eat a meal of quality.

❀❀   **Excellent cooking, worth a detour**

Specialities and wines of first class quality... Do not expect such meals to be cheap.

❀❀❀   **Some of the best cuisine, worth a journey**

Superb food, fine wines, faultless service, elegant surroundings... One will pay accordingly !

M   **The red « M »**

Whilst appreciating the quality of the cooking in restaurants with a star, you may, however, wish to find some serving a perhaps less elaborate but nonetheless always carefully prepared meal.

Certain restaurants seem to us to answer this requirement. We bring them to your attention by marking them with a red « M » in the text of the Guide.

Alcoholic beverages-conditions of sale

The sale of alcoholic drinks is governed in Great Britain and Ireland by licensing laws which vary greatly from country to country.

Allowing for local variances, hotel bars and public houses close during the afternoon and after 11 pm. Hotel residents, however, may buy drinks outside the permitted hours at the discretion of the hotelier.

Children under the age of 14 are not allowed in bars.

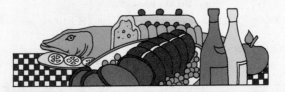

PRICES

Valid for late 1985, the rates shown may be revised if the cost of living changes to any great extent. They are given in the currency of the country. In any event they should be regarded as basic charges.

Your recommendation is self-evident if you always walk into a hotel guide in hand.

Hotels and restaurants whose names appear in bold type have supplied us with their charges in detail and undertaken to abide by them, wherever possible, if the traveller is in possession of this year's guide.

If you think you have been overcharged, let us know. Where no rates are shown it is best to enquire about terms in advance.

Prices are given in £ sterling, except for the Republic of Ireland (Punts)

Where no mention s., t. or st. is shown, prices are subject to the addition of service charge, V.A.T., or both (V.A.T. does not apply in the Channel Islands).

Meals

M 7.00/9.00	**Set meals** — Lunch 7.00, dinner 9.00 — including cover charge, where applicable.
M 11.00/13.00	See page 15.
s. t.	Service only included. — V.A.T. included.
st.	Service and V.A.T. included.
🍾 4.00	Price of 1/2 bottle or carafe of ordinary wine.
M a la carte 14.00/18.00	**A la carte meals** — The prices represent the range of charges for a plain to an elaborate 3 course meal and include a cover charge where applicable.
⌥ 4.00	Charge for full cooked breakfast (i.e. not included in the room rate). Continental breakfast may be available at a lower rate.

Rooms

rm 21.00/38.00	Lowest price 21.00 for a comfortable single and highest price 38.00 for the best double room (including bathroom when applicable).
rm ⌥ 30.00/45.00	Full cooked breakfast is included the price of the room.
suites 100.00/200.00	Lowest and highest prices for a suite comprising bedroom, bathroom and sittingroom.

Short Breaks (see p. 17)

SB 50.00/60.00	Prices indicated are lowest and highest per person for two nights.
🅐 🄰🄴 🄾 **VISA**	Principal **credit cards** accepted by establishments : Access — American Express — Diners Club — Visa (Barclaycard).

A FEW USEFUL DETAILS

Meals

Ask for menus including set meals and a la carte menus with the prices clearly marked if they are not produced automatically.

Hotels

Breakfast is often included in the price of the room, even if it is not required.

Special Rate for "Short Breaks"

Many hotels now offer a special rate for a stay of two nights which includes dinner, room and breakfast usually for a minimum of two people.
It is always advisable to agree terms in advance with a hotelier.

Reservations

Hotels : Reserving in advance, when possible, is advised. Ask the hotelier to provide you, in his letter of confirmation, with all terms and conditions applicable to your reservation.

In seaside resorts especially, reservations usually begin and end on Saturdays.

Certain hoteliers require the payment of a deposit. This constitutes a mutual guarantee of good faith. Deposits, except in special cases, may amount to 10 % of the estimated hotel account.

Restaurants : it is strongly recommended always to book your table well ahead in order to avoid the disappointment of a refusal.

Animals

It is forbidden to bring domestic animals (dogs, cats...) into Great Britain and Ireland.

CAR, TYRES

In the text of many towns are to be found the names of garages or motor agents many of which offer a breakdown service.

The wearing of seat belts is obligatory for drivers and front seat passengers in Great Britain and Ireland.

Motoring organisations

The major motoring organisations in Great Britain are the Automobile Association and the Royal Automobile Club. Each provides services in varying degrees for non-resident members of affiliated clubs.

AUTOMOBILE ASSOCIATION
Fanum House
BASINGSTOKE, Hants., RG21 2EA
✆ (0256) 20123

ROYAL AUTOMOBILE CLUB
RAC House, Lansdowne Rd,
CROYDON, Surrey CR9 2JA
✆ (01) 686 2525

SIGHTS

Star-rating

★★★	Worth a journey
★★	Worth a detour
★	Interesting
AC	Admission charge

Finding the sights

See	Sights in town
Envir.	On the outskirts
Exc.	In the surrounding area
N, S, E, W	The sight lies north, south, east or west of the town
A 22	Go by road A 22, indicated by the same symbol on the Guide map
2 m.	Mileage

TOWNS

✉ York	Post office serving the town
✆ 0225 Bath	STD dialling code (name of exchange indicated only when different from name of the town). Omit 0 when dialling from abroad
401 M 27, ⑩	Michelin map and co-ordinates or fold
West Country G.	See the Michelin Green Guide England : The West Country
pop. 1,057	Population
ECD : Wednesday	Early closing day (shops close at midday)
BX A	Letters giving the location of a place on the town map
⛳ 18	Golf course and number of holes (visitors unrestricted)
☀	Panoramic view, viewpoint
✈	Airport
🚗 ☏ 218	Place with a motorail connection ; further information from telephone number listed
🚢	Shipping line
⛴	Passenger transport only *see list of companies at the end of the Guide*
🛈	Tourist Information Centre

Standard Time

In winter standard time throughout the British Isles is Greenwich Mean Time (G.M.T.). In summer British clocks are advanced by one hour to give British Summer Time (B.S.T.). The actual dates are announced annually but always occur over weekends in March and October.

Seeing a town and its surroundings

TOWN PLANS

Roads

Motorway, dual carriageway
   Interchange : complete, limited, number
Major through route
One-way street - Unsuitable for traffic
Pedestrian street
Pasteur   P   Shopping street - Car park
Gateway - Street passing under arch - Tunnel
Low headroom (16'6" max.) on major through routes
Station and railway
F B   Car ferry - Lever bridge

Sights — Hotels — Restaurants

Place of interest and its main entrance
Interesting place of worship :
   Cathedral, church or chapel
Windmill - Other sights
Castle - Ruins
B   Reference letter locating a sight
Hotel, restaurant with reference letter

Various signs

AGENCE MICHELIN
Tourist Information Centre - Michelin Branch
Hospital - Mosque - Synagogue
Garden, park, wood - Cemetery - Cross
Stadium - Golf course
View - Panorama
Airport - Racecourse
Funicular - Cable-car
Monument, statue - Fountain
Pleasure boat harbour - Lighthouse
Ferry services : passengers and cars
Public buildings located by letter :
C   County Council Offices
H M T   Town Hall - Museum - Theatre
POL.   Police (in large towns police headquarters)
U   University, colleges
Main post office with poste restante, telephone
Golf course (with restrictions for visitors)
Communications tower or mast
Underground station

London

BRENT   S O H O   Borough - Area
Borough boundary - Area boundary

19

Découvrez
le guide...

et sachez l'utiliser pour en tirer le meilleur profit.
Le Guide Michelin n'est pas seulement une
liste de bonnes tables ou d'hôtels, c'est aussi
une multitude d'informations pour faciliter vos
voyages.

La clé du Guide

Elle vous est donnée par les pages explicatives qui suivent.
Sachez qu'un même symbole, qu'un même caractère, en rouge ou en
noir, en maigre ou en gras, n'a pas tout à fait la même signification.

La sélection des hôtels et des restaurants

Ce Guide n'est pas un répertoire complet des ressources hôtelières, il en
présente seulement une sélection volontairement limitée. Cette sélection
est établie après visites et enquêtes effectuées régulièrement sur place.
C'est lors de ces visites que les avis et observations de nos lecteurs sont
examinés.

Les plans de ville

Ils indiquent avec précision : les rues piétonnes et commerçantes,
comment traverser ou contourner l'agglomération, où se situent les
hôtels (sur de grandes artères ou à l'écart), où se trouvent la poste,
l'office de tourisme, les grands monuments, les principaux sites, etc.

Pour votre véhicule

Au texte de la plupart des localités figure une liste de représentants des
grandes marques automobiles avec leur adresse et leur numéro d'appel
téléphonique. En route, vous pouvez ainsi faire entretenir ou dépanner
votre voiture, si nécessaire.

Sur tous ces points et aussi sur beaucoup d'autres, nous souhaitons
vivement connaître votre avis. N'hésitez pas à nous écrire, nous vous
répondrons.

Merci par avance.

Services de Tourisme Michelin
46, avenue de Breteuil, 75341 PARIS CEDEX 07

Bibendum vous souhaite d'agréables voyages.

Le choix d'un hôtel, d'un restaurant

Notre classement est établi à l'usage de l'automobiliste de passage. Dans chaque catégorie les établissements sont cités par ordre de préférence.

CLASSE ET CONFORT

🏨	Grand luxe et tradition	XXXXX
🏨	Grand confort	XXXX
🏨	Très confortable	XXX
🏨	De bon confort	XX
🏠	Assez confortable	X
🏠	Simple mais convenable	
🏠	Autre ressource hôtelière conseillée, à prix modérés	
without rest.	L'hôtel n'a pas de restaurant	
	Le restaurant possède des chambres	with rm

L'INSTALLATION

Les hôtels des catégories 🏨, 🏨, 🏨, possèdent tout le confort et assurent en général le change, les symboles de détail n'apparaissent donc pas au texte de ces hôtels.

Dans les autres catégories, les éléments de confort indiqués n'existent le plus souvent que dans certaines chambres.

30 rm	Nombre de chambres
🛗	Ascenseur
▤	Air conditionné
📺	Télévision dans la chambre
wc 🛁	Salle de bains et wc privés, Salle de bains privée sans wc
wc 🚿	Douche et wc privés, Douche privée sans wc
☎	Téléphone dans la chambre relié par standard
☎	Téléphone dans la chambre, direct avec l'extérieur (cadran)
♿	Chambres accessibles aux handicapés physiques
🏊	Piscine : de plein air ou couverte
🌳	Jardin de repos
🎾	Tennis à l'hôtel
⛳	Golf et nombre de trous
🎣	Pêche ouverte aux clients de l'hôtel (éventuellement payant)
🏛	Salles de conférences (25 places minimum)
🚗	Garage
Ⓟ	Parc à voitures
🐕	Accès interdit aux chiens
	Lorsque les chiens sont acceptés, ils ne le sont que dans les chambres.
May-October	Période d'ouverture communiquée par l'hôtelier
season	Ouverture probable en saison mais dates non précisées
	Les établissements ouverts toute l'année sont ceux pour lesquels aucune mention n'est indiquée
LL35 OSB	Code postal de l'établissement
(T.H.F.)	Chaîne hôtelière (voir liste en fin de guide)

Le choix d'un hôtel, d'un restaurant

L'AGRÉMENT

Le séjour dans certains hôtels se révèle parfois particulièrement agréable ou reposant.

Cela peut tenir d'une part au caractère de l'édifice, au décor original, au site, à l'accueil et aux services qui sont proposés, d'autre part à la tranquillité des lieux.

De tels établissements se distinguent dans le guide par les symboles rouges indiqués ci-après.

🏨🏨🏨 ... 🏠	Hôtels agréables
XXXXX ... X	Restaurants agréables
« Park »	Élément particulièrement agréable
🦮	Hôtel très tranquille ou isolé et tranquille
🦮	Hôtel tranquille
≼ sea	Vue exceptionnelle
≼	Vue intéressante ou étendue

Consultez les cartes placées au début de chacune des régions traitées dans ce guide, elles faciliteront vos recherches.

Nous ne prétendons pas avoir signalé tous les hôtels agréables, ni tous ceux qui sont tranquilles ou isolés et tranquilles.

Nos enquêtes continuent. Vous pouvez les faciliter en nous faisant connaître vos observations et vos découvertes.

LA TABLE

Les étoiles :

Nous marquons par ❀, ❀❀ ou ❀❀❀ les établissements dont la qualité de la table nous a paru mériter d'être signalée spécialement à l'attention de nos lecteurs, qu'il s'agisse de cuisines propres au pays ou étrangères (voir liste p. 48).

Au texte de ces établissements nous indiquons quelques plats caractéristiques du genre de cuisine de la maison.

❀ **Une très bonne table dans sa catégorie**

L'étoile marque une bonne étape sur votre itinéraire.

Mais ne comparez pas l'étoile d'un établissement de luxe à prix élevés avec celle d'une petite maison où à prix raisonnables, on sert également une cuisine de qualité.

❀❀ **Table excellente, mérite un détour**

Spécialités et vins de choix, attendez-vous à une dépense en rapport.

❀❀❀ **Une des meilleures tables, vaut le voyage**

Table merveilleuse, grands vins, service impeccable, cadre élégant... Prix en conséquence.

M **Le « M » rouge**

Tout en appréciant les tables à « étoiles », on peut souhaiter trouver sur sa route un repas plus simple mais toujours de préparation soignée. Certaines maisons nous ont paru répondre à cette préoccupation.

Un « M » rouge les signale à votre attention dans le texte de ce guide.

La vente de boissons alcoolisées

En Grande-Bretagne et en Irlande, la vente de boissons alcoolisées est soumise à des lois pouvant varier d'une région à l'autre.

D'une façon générale, les bars situés dans les hôtels ainsi que les pubs ferment l'après-midi et après 23 heures, les horaires d'ouverture pouvant varier localement.

Néanmoins, l'hôtelier a toujours la possibilité de servir, à sa clientèle, des boissons alcoolisées en dehors des heures légales.

Les enfants au-dessous de 14 ans n'ont pas accès aux bars.

LES PRIX

Les prix que nous indiquons dans ce guide ont été établis en fin d'année 1985. Ils sont susceptibles d'être modifiés si le coût de la vie subit des variations importantes. Ils doivent, en tout cas, être considérés comme des prix de base.

Entrez à l'hôtel le Guide à la main, vous montrerez ainsi qu'il vous conduit là en confiance.

Les hôtels et restaurants figurent en gros caractères lorsque les hôteliers nous ont donné tous leurs prix et se sont engagés à les appliquer aux touristes de passage porteurs de notre guide.

Prévenez-nous de toute majoration paraissant injustifiée. Si aucun prix n'est indiqué, nous vous conseillons de demander les conditions.

Les prix sont indiqués en livres sterling (1 L = 100 pence), sauf en République d'Irlande (Punts).

Lorsque les mentions s.t., ou st. ne figurent pas, les prix indiqués peuvent être majorés d'un pourcentage pour le service, la T.V.A. ou les deux. (La T.V.A. n'est pas appliquée dans les Channel Islands).

Repas

M 7.00/9.00	**Repas à prix fixe** — Déjeuner 7.00, dîner 9.00 y compris le couvert éventuellement.
M 11.00/13.00	Voir page 23.
s. t.	Service compris — T.V.A. comprise.
st.	Service et T.V.A. compris (prix nets).
🍶 4.00	Prix de la 1/2 bouteille ou carafe de vin ordinaire.
M a la carte 14.00/18.00	**Repas à la carte** — Le 1er prix correspond à un repas simple mais soigné, comprenant : petite entrée, plat du jour garni, dessert. Le 2e prix concerne un repas plus complet, comprenant : hors-d'œuvre, plat principal, fromage ou dessert. Ces prix s'entendent couvert compris.
🍽 4.00	Prix du petit déjeuner à l'anglaise, s'il n'est pas compris dans celui de la chambre. Un petit déjeuner continental peut être obtenu à moindre prix.

Chambres

rm 21.00/38.00	Prix minimum 21.00 d'une chambre pour une personne et prix maximum 38.00 de la plus belle chambre occupée par deux personnes.
rm 🍽 30.00/45.00	Le prix du petit déjeuner à l'anglaise est inclus dans le prix de la chambre.
suites 100.00.200.00	Prix minimum et maximum d'un appartement comprenant chambre, salle de bains et salon.

"Short Breaks" (voir p. 25)

SB 50.00/60.00	Prix minimum et maximum par personne pour un séjour de deux nuits.
🚫 AE ⊙ VISA	Principales **cartes de crédit** acceptées par l'établissement : Access (Eurocard) — American Express — Diners Club — Visa (Carte Bleue).

QUELQUES PRÉCISIONS UTILES

Au restaurant

Réclamez les menus à prix fixes et la carte chiffrée s'ils ne vous sont pas présentés spontanément.

A l'hôtel

Le prix du petit déjeuner, même s'il n'est pas consommé, est souvent inclus dans le prix de la chambre.

Conditions spéciales pour "Short Breaks"

De nombreux hôtels proposent des conditions avantageuses pour un séjour de deux nuits ou "Short Break". Ce forfait comprend la chambre, le dîner et le petit déjeuner, en général pour un minimum de deux personnes.

Réservations

Hôtels : Chaque fois que possible, la réservation préalable est souhaitable. Demandez à l'hôtelier de vous fournir dans sa lettre d'accord toutes précisions utiles sur la réservation et les conditions de séjour. Dans les stations balnéaires en particulier, les réservations s'appliquent généralement à des séjours partant d'un samedi à l'autre.

A toute demande écrite il est conseillé de joindre un coupon-réponse international.

Certains hôteliers demandent parfois le versement d'arrhes. Il s'agit d'un dépôt-garantie qui engage l'hôtelier comme le client. Sauf accord spécial le montant des arrhes peut être fixé à 10 % du montant total estimé.

Restaurants : il est vivement recommandé de réserver sa table aussi longtemps que possible à l'avance, de façon à éviter le désagrément d'un refus.

Animaux

L'introduction d'animaux domestiques (chiens, chats…) est interdite en Grande Bretagne et en Irlande.

LA VOITURE, LES PNEUS

Au texte de la plupart des localités figure une liste des garagistes ou concessionnaires automobiles pouvant, éventuellement, vous aider en cas de panne.

En Grande Bretagne et en Irlande, le port de la ceinture de sécurité est obligatoire pour le conducteur et le passager avant.

Automobile Clubs

Les principales organisations de secours automobile dans le pays sont l'Automobile Association et le Royal Automobile Club, toutes deux offrant certains de leurs services aux membres de clubs affiliés.

AUTOMOBILE ASSOCIATION
Fanum House
BASINGSTOKE, Hants., RG21 2EA
☏ (0256) 20123

ROYAL AUTOMOBILE CLUB
RAC House, Lansdowne RD
CROYDON, Surrey CR9 2JA
☏ (01) 686 2525

LES CURIOSITÉS

Intérêt

★★★	Vaut le voyage
★★	Mérite un détour
★	Intéressant
AC	Entrée payante

Situation

See	Dans la ville
Envir.	Aux environs de la ville
Exc.	Excursions dans la région
N, S, E, W	La curiosité est située : au Nord, au Sud, à l'Est, à l'Ouest
A 22	On s'y rend par la route A 22, repérée par le même signe sur le plan du Guide
2 m.	Distance en miles

LES VILLES

✉ York	Bureau de poste dessservant la localité
☎ 0225 Bath	Indicatif téléphonique interurbain suivi, si nécessaire, de la localité de rattachement (De l'étranger, ne pas composer le 0)
401 M 27, ⑩	Numéro des cartes Michelin et carroyage ou numéro du pli
West Country G.	Voir le guide vert Michelin England : The West Country
pop. 1,057	Population
ECD : Wednesday	Jour de fermeture des magasins (après-midi seulement)
BX **A**	Lettres repérant un emplacement sur le plan
⛳18	Golf et nombre de trous
☀, ≼	Panorama, point de vue
✈	Aéroport
🚗 ☎ 218	Localité desservie par train-auto. Renseignements au numéro de téléphone indiqué
⛴	Transports maritimes
⛴	Transports maritimes (pour passagers seulement) *Voir liste des compagnies en fin de guide*
🛈	Information touristique

Heure légale

Les visiteurs devront tenir compte de l'heure officielle en Grande Bretagne : une heure de retard sur l'heure française.

Pour visiter une ville et ses environs

LES PLANS

Voirie

Autoroute, route à chaussées séparées
    échangeur : complet, partiel, numéro
Grande voie de circulation
Sens unique - Rue impraticable
Rue piétonne
Pasteur   Rue commerçante - Parc de stationnement
Porte - Passage sous voûte - Tunnel
Passage bas (inférieur à 16'6'') sur les grandes voies de circulation
Gare et voie ferrée
Bac pour autos - Pont mobile

Curiosités — Hôtels Restaurants

Bâtiment intéressant et entrée principale
Édifice religieux intéressant :
    Cathédrale, église ou chapelle
Moulin à vent - Curiosités diverses
Château - Ruines
Lettre identifiant une curiosité
Hôtel, restaurant. Lettre les identifiant

Signes divers

Information touristique - Agence Michelin
Hôpital - Mosquée - Synagogue
Jardin, parc, bois - Cimetière - Calvaire
Stade - Golf
Aéroport - Hippodrome - Vue - Panorama
Funiculaire - Téléphérique, télécabine
Monument, statue - Fontaine - Port de plaisance - Phare
Transport par bateau :
    passagers et voitures
Bâtiment public repéré par une lettre :
    Bureau de l'Administration du comté
    Hôtel de ville - Musée - Théâtre
    Police (commissariat central) - Université, grande école
Bureau principal de poste restante, téléphone
Golf (réservé)
Tour ou pylône de télécommunications
Station de métro

Londres

BRENT   SOHO   Nom d'arrondissement (borough) - de quartier (area)
Limite de « borough » - d' « area »

Scoprite
la guida...

e sappiatela utilizzare per trarre il miglior vantaggio. La Guida Michelin è un elenco dei migliori alberghi e ristoranti, naturalmente. Ma anche una serie di utili informazioni per i Vostri viaggi !

La " chiave "

Leggete le pagine che seguono e comprenderete !
Sapete che uno stesso simbolo o una stessa parola in rosso o in nero, in carattere magro o grasso, non ha lo stesso significato ?

La selezione degli alberghi e ristoranti

Attenzione ! La guida non elenca tutte le risorse alberghiere. E' il risultato di una selezione, volontariamente limitata, stabilita in seguito a visite ed inchieste effettuate sul posto. E, durante queste visite, amici lettori, vengono tenute in evidenza le Vs. critiche ed i Vs. apprezzamenti !

Le piante di città

Indicano con precisione : strade pedonali e commerciali, il modo migliore per attraversare od aggirare il centro, l'esatta ubicazione degli alberghi e ristoranti citati, della posta centrale, dell'ufficio informazioni turistiche, dei monumenti più importanti e poi altre e altre ancora utili informazioni per Voi !

Per la Vs. automobile

Nel testo di molte località sono elencati gli indirizzi delle principali marche automobilistiche. Così, in caso di necessità, saprete dove trovare il « medico » per la Vs. vettura.

Su tutti questi punti e su altri ancora, gradiremmo conoscere il Vs. parere. Scriveteci e non mancheremo di risponderVi !

Michelin Tyre Public Limited Company
Tourism Department
Lyon Road, HARROW, Middlesex HA1 2DQ

Grazie e buon viaggio.

La scelta di un albergo, di un ristorante

La nostra classificazione è stabilita ad uso dell'automobilista di passaggio. In ogni categoria, gli esercizi vengono citati in ordine di preferenza.

CLASSE E CONFORT

🏨	Gran lusso e tradizione	XXXXX
🏨	Gran confort	XXXX
🏨	Molto confortevole	XXX
🏨	Di buon confort	XX
🏠	Abbastanza confortevole	X
🏠	Semplice ma conveniente	
🏠	Altra risorsa, consigliata per prezzi contenuti	
without rest.	L'albergo non ha ristorante	
	Il ristorante dispone di camere	with rm

INSTALLAZIONI

I 🏨, 🏨, 🏨 offrono ogni confort ed effettuano generalmente il cambio di valute ; per questi alberghi non specifichiamo quindi il dettaglio delle installazioni.

Nelle altre categorie indichiamo gli elementi di confort esistenti, alcune camere possono talvolta esserne sprovviste.

30 rm	Numero di camere
🛗	Ascensore
▤	Aria condizionata
TV	Televisione in camera
🛁wc 🛁	Bagno e wc privati, bagno privato senza wc
🚿wc 🚿	Doccia e wc privati, doccia privata senza wc
☏	Telefono in camera collegato con il centralino
☎	Telefono in camera comunicante direttamente con l'esterno
🔥	Camere d'agevole accesso per i minorati fisici
🏊 🏊	Piscina : all'aperto, coperta
🌳	Giardino da riposo
✻	Tennis appartenente all'albergo
🏌️18	Golf e numero di buche,
🎣	Pesca aperta ai clienti dell'albergo (eventualmente a pagamento)
🏛	Sale per conferenze (minimo 25 posti)
🚗	Garage
Ⓟ	Parcheggio
🐕	E' vietato l'accesso ai cani
	Se i cani sono accetati, lo sono soltanto nelle camere.
May-October	Periodo di apertura comunicato dall'albergatore
season	Possibile apertura in stagione, ma periodo non precisato.
	Gli esercizi senza tali indicazioni sono aperti tutto l'anno.
LL35 0SB	Codice postale dell'esercizio
(T.H.F.)	Catena alberghiera (Vedere la lista alla fine della Guida)

AMENITÀ

Il soggiorno in alcuni alberghi si rivela talvolta particolarmente ameno o riposante.

Ciò può dipendere sia dalle caratteristiche dell'edificio, dalle decorazioni non comuni, dalla sua posizione, dall'accoglienza e dai servizi offerti, sia dalla tranquillità dei luoghi.

Questi esercizi sono così contraddistinti :

🏛	Alberghi ameni
✕	Ristoranti ameni
« Park »	Un particolare piacevole
🍃	Albergo molto tranquillo o isolato e tranquillo
🍃	Albergo tranquillo
⋞ sea	Vista eccezionale
⋞	Vista interessante o estesa

Consultate le carte che precedono ciascuna delle regioni trattate nella guida : sarete facilitati nelle vostre ricerche.

Non abbiamo la pretesa di aver segnalato tutti gli alberghi ameni, nè tutti quelli molto tranquilli o isolati e tranquilli.

Le nostre ricerche continuano. Le potrete agevolare facendoci conoscere le vostre osservazioni e le vostre scoperte.

LA TAVOLA

Le stelle di ottima tavola

Abbiamo contraddistinto con ✿, ✿✿ o ✿✿✿ quegli esercizi che, a nostro parere, meritano di essere segnalati alla vostra attenzione per la qualità della cucina, che può essere tipicamente nazionale o d'importazione (vedere p. 48).

Nel testo di questi esercizi indichiamo alcuni piatti tipici della cucina della casa.

✿ **Un'ottima tavola nella sua categoria.**

La stella indica una tappa gastronomica sul vostro itinerario.

Non mettete però a confronto la stella di un esercizio di lusso, dai prezzi elevati, con quella di un piccolo esercizio dove, a prezzi ragionevoli, viene offerta una cucina di qualità.

✿✿ **Tavola eccellente : merita una deviazione.**

Specialità e vini scelti... Aspettatevi una spesa in proporzione.

✿✿✿ **Una delle migliori tavole : vale il viaggio.**

Tavola meravigliosa, grandi vini, servizio impeccabile, ambientazione accurata... Prezzi conformi.

M **La « M » rossa**

Pur apprezzando le tavole a « stella », si desidera alle volte consumare un pasto più semplice ma sempre accuratamente preparato.

Alcuni esercizi ci son parsi rispondenti a tale esigenza e sono contraddistinti nella guida da una « M » in rosso.

La vendita di bevande alcoliche

In Gran Bretagna e Irlanda la vendita di bevande alcoliche è soggetta a leggi che possono variare da una regione all'altra.

Generalmente i bar degli alberghi, così come i pubs, chiudono il pomeriggio e dopo le ore 23.00 ; gli orari d'apertura possono variare di località in località.

L'albergatore ha tuttavia la possibilità di servire alla clientela bevande alcoliche anche oltre le ore legali.

Ai ragazzi inferiori ai 14 anni è vietato l'accesso ai bar.

I PREZZI

Questi prezzi, redatti alla fine dell'anno 1985, possono venire modificati qualora il costo della vita subisca notevoli variazioni. Essi debbono comunque essere considerati come prezzi base.

Entrate nell'albergo o nel ristorante con la Guida alla mano, dimostrando in tal modo la fiducia in chi vi ha indirizzato.

Gli alberghi e ristoranti figurano in carattere grassetto quando gli albergatori ci hanno comunicato tutti i loro prezzi e si sono impegnati ad applicarli ai turisti di passaggio in possesso della nostra pubblicazione.

Segnalateci eventuali maggiorazioni che vi sembrino ingiustificate. Quando i prezzi non sono indicati, vi consigliamo di chiedere preventivamente le condizioni.

I prezzi sono indicati in lire sterline (1 £ = 100 pence) ad eccezione per la Repubblica d'Irlanda (Punts).

Quando non figurano le lettere **s.**, **t.**, o **st.** i prezzi indicati possono essere maggiorati per il servizio o per l'I.V.A. o per entrambi. (L'I.V.A. non viene applicata nelle Channel Islands).

Pasti

M 7.00/9.00	**Prezzo fisso** — Pranzo 7.00, cena 9.00 compreso il coperto se del caso.
M 11.00/13.00	Vedere p. 31.
s. t.	Servizio compreso. — I.V.A. compresa.
st.	Servizio ed I.V.A. compresi (prezzi netti).
🍷 4.00	Prezzo della mezza bottiglia o di una caraffa di vino.
M a la carte 14.00/18.00	**Alla carta** — Il 1° prezzo corrisponde ad un pasto semplice comprendente : primo piatto, piatto del giorno con contorno, dessert. Il 2° prezzo corrisponde ad un pasto più completo comprendente : antipasto, piatto principale, formaggio e dessert. Questi prezzi comprendono, se del caso, il coperto.
☕ 4.00	Prezzo della prima colazione inglese se non è compreso nel prezzo della camera. Una prima colazione continentale può essere ottenuta a minor prezzo.

Camere

rm 21.00/38.00	Prezzo minimo 21.00 per una camera singola e prezzo massimo 38.00 per la camera più bella per due persone.
rm ☕ 30.00/45.00	Il prezzo della prima colazione inglese è compreso nel prezzo della camera.
suites 100.00/200.00	Prezzo minimo e massimo per un appartamento comprendente camera, bagno e salone.

"Short Breaks" (vedere p. 33)

SB 50.00/60.00	Prezzo minimo e massimo per persona per un soggiorno di due notti.
⬛ AE ⓪ *VISA*	Principali **carte di credito** accettate da un albergo o ristorante : Access (MasterCard) — American Express — Diners Club — Visa (BankAmericard).

La scelta di un albergo, di un ristorante

QUALCHE CHIARIMENTO UTILE

Al ristorante

Chiedete i menu a prezzo fisso e la carta coi relativi prezzi se non vi vengono spontaneamente presentati.

All'albergo

Il prezzo della prima colazione, anche se non viene consumata, è spesso compreso nel prezzo della camera.

Condizioni speciali per "Short Breaks"

Numerosi alberghi propongono delle condizioni vantaggiose per un soggiorno di due notti o "Short Break". Questo forfait comprende la camera, la cena e la colazione del mattino generalmente per un minimo di due persone.

Le prenotazioni

Alberghi : appena possibile, la prenotazione è consigliabile ; chiedete all'albergatore di fornirvi, nella sua lettera di conferma, ogni dettaglio sulla prenotazione e sulle condizioni di soggiorno. Nelle stazioni balneari in particolar modo, le prenotazioni si applicano generalmente a soggiorni che vanno da un sabato all'altro.

Si consiglia di allegare sempre alle richieste scritte di prenotazione un tagliando risposta internazionale.

Alle volte alcuni albergatori chiedono il versamento di una caparra. E' un deposito-garanzia che impegna tanto l'albergatore che il cliente. Salvo accordi speciali, l'ammontare della caparra può venire fissato nella misura del 10 % dell'ammontare totale previsto.

Ristoranti : è sempre consigliabile prenotare con un certo anticipo per evitare uno spiacevole rifiuto all'ultimo momento.

Animali

Non possono accedere in Gran Bretagna e Irlanda animali domestici (cani, gatti...)

L'AUTOMOBILE, I PNEUMATICI

Nel testo di molte località abbiamo elencato gli indirizzi di garage o concessionari in grado di effettuare, eventualmente, il traino o le riparazioni.

In Gran Bretagna e in Irlanda, l'uso della cintura di sicurezza e' obbligatorio per il guidatore e il passeggero che gli siede accanto.

Soccorso automobilistico

Le principali organizzazioni di soccorso automobilistico sono l'Automobile Association ed il Royal Automobile Club : entrambe offrono alcuni loro servizi ai membri dei club affiliati

AUTOMOBILE ASSOCIATION
Fanum House
BASINGSTOKE, Hants, RG21 2EA
☏ (0256) 20123

ROYAL AUTOMOBILE CLUB
RAC House, Lansdowne Rd,
CROYDON, Surrey CR9 2JA
☏ (01) 686 2525

Per visitare una città ed i suoi dintorni

LE CURIOSITÀ

	Grado d'interesse
★★★	Vale il viaggio
★★	Merita una deviazione
★	Interessante
AC	Entrata a pagamento
	Situazione
See	Nella città
Envir.	Nei dintorni della città
Exc.	Nella regione
N, S, E, W	La curiosità è situata : a Nord, a Sud, a Est, a Ovest
A 22	Ci si va per la strada A 22 indicata con lo stesso segno sulla pianta
2 m.	Distanza in miglia

LE CITTÀ

✉ York	Sede dell'ufficio postale
☎ 0225 Bath	Prefisso telefonico interurbano (nome del centralino indicato solo quando differisce dal nome della località). Dall'estero non formare lo 0
401 M 27, ⑩	Numero della carta Michelin e del riquadro o numero della piega
West Country G.	Vedere la Guida Verde Michelin England : The West Country.
pop. 1,057	Popolazione
ECD : Wednesday	Giorno di chiusura settimanale dei negozi (solo pomeriggio)
BX **A**	Lettere indicanti l'ubicazione sulla pianta
18	Golf e numero di buche (accesso consentito a tutti)
✲, ⩤	Panorama, punto di vista
✈	Aeroporto
✆ 218	Località con servizio auto su treno. Informarsi al numero di telefono indicato
⛴	Trasporti marittimi
⛴	Trasporti marittimi (solo passeggeri) *Vedere la lista delle compagnie alla fine della Guida*
i	Ufficio informazioni turistiche

Ora legale

I visitatori dovranno tenere in considerazione l'ora ufficiale in Gran bretagna : un' ora di ritardo sull'ora italiana.

Per visitare una città ed i suoi dintorni

LE PIANTE

Viabilità

Autostrada, strada a carreggiate separate
    svincolo : completo, parziale, numero
Grande via di circolazione
Senso unico - Via impraticabile - Via pedonale
Via commerciale - Parcheggio
Porta - Sottopassaggio - Galleria
Sottopassaggio (altezza inferiore a 16'6") sulle grandi vie di circolazione
Stazione e ferrovia
Battello per auto - Ponte mobile

Curiosità — Alberghi — Ristoranti

Edificio interessante ed entrata principale
Costruzione religiosa interessante :
    Cattedrale, chiesa o cappella
Mulino a vento - Curiosità varie
Castello - Ruderi
Lettera che identifica una curiosità
Albergo, Ristorante. Lettera di riferimento che li identifica sulla pianta

Simboli vari

Centro di distribuzione Michelin
Ufficio informazioni turistiche
Moschea - Sinagoga - Ospedale
Giardino, parco, bosco - Cimitero - Calvario
Stadio - Golf
Vista - Panorama
Aeroporto - Ippodromo
Funicolare - Funivia, Cabinovia
Monumento, statua - Fontana
Porto per imbarcazioni da diporto - Faro
Trasporto con traghetto : passeggeri ed autovetture
Edificio pubblico indicato con lettera :
    Sede dell' Amministrazione di Contea
    Municipio - Museo - Teatro
    Polizia (Questura, nelle grandi città)
    Università, grande scuola
Ufficio centrale di fermo posta, telefono
Golf riservato - Stazione della Metropolitana
Torre o pilone per telecomunicazione

Londra

BRENT SOHO Nome del distretto amministrativo (borough) - del quartiere (area)

Limite del « borough » - di « area »

Der
Michelin-Führer...

Er ist nicht nur ein Verzeichnis guter Restaurants und Hotels, sondern gibt zusätzlich eine Fülle nützlicher Tips für die Reise. Nutzen Sie die zahlreichen Informationen, die er bietet.

Zum Gebrauch dieses Führers

Die Erläuterungen stehen auf den folgenden Seiten.
Beachten Sie dabei, daß das gleiche Zeichen, rot oder schwarz, fett oder dünn gedruckt, verschiedene Bedeutungen hat.

Zur Auswahl der Hotels und Restaurants

Der Rote Michelin-Führer ist kein vollständiges Verzeichnis aller Hotels und Restaurants. Er bringt nur eine bewußt getroffene, begrenzte Auswahl. Diese basiert auf regelmäßigen Überprüfungen durch unsere Inspektoren an Ort und Stelle. Bei der Beurteilung werden auch die zahlreichen Hinweise unserer Leser berücksichtigt.

Zu den Stadtplänen

Sie informieren über Fußgänger- und Geschäftsstraßen, Durchgangs- oder Umgehungsstraßen, Lage von Hotels und Restaurants (an Hauptverkehrsstraßen oder in ruhiger Gegend), wo sich die Post, das Verkehrsamt, die wichtigsten öffentlichen Gebäude und Sehenswürdigkeiten u. dgl. befinden.

Hinweise für den Autofahrer

Bei den meisten Orten geben wir Adresse und Telefonnummer der Vertragshändler der großen Automobilfirmen an. So können Sie Ihren Wagen im Bedarfsfall unterwegs warten oder reparieren lassen.

Ihre Meinung zu den Angaben des Führers, Ihre Kritik, Ihre Verbesserungsvorschläge interessieren uns sehr. Zögern Sie daher nicht, uns diese mitzuteilen... wir antworten bestimmt.

Michelin Tyre Public Limited Company
Tourism Department
Lyon Road, HARROW, Middlesex HA1 2DQ

Vielen Dank im voraus und angenehme Reise !

Wahl eines Hotels, eines Restaurants

Unsere Auswahl ist für Durchreisende gedacht. In jeder Kategorie drückt die Reihenfolge der Betriebe eine weitere Rangordnung aus.

KLASSENEINTEILUNG UND KOMFORT

🏰	Großer Luxus und Tradition	XXXXX
🏯	Großer Komfort	XXXX
🏛	Sehr komfortabel	XXX
🏛	Mit gutem Komfort	XX
🏚	Mit ausreichendem Komfort	X
🏠	Bürgerlich	
🏠	Preiswerte, empfehlenswerte Gasthäuser und Pensionen	
without rest.	Hotel ohne Restaurant	
	Restaurant vermietet auch Zimmer	with rm

EINRICHTUNG

Für die 🏰, 🏯, 🏛 geben wir keine Einzelheiten über die Einrichtung an, da diese Hotels im allgemeinen jeden Komfort besitzen. Außerdem besteht die Möglichkeit, Geld zu wechseln.

In den Häusern der übrigen Kategorien nennen wir die vorhandenen Einrichtungen, diese können in einigen Zimmern fehlen.

30 rm	Anzahl der Zimmer
🛗	Fahrstuhl
🖥	Klimaanlage
📺	Fernsehen im Zimmer
🛁wc 🛁	Privatbad mit wc, Privatbad ohne wc
🚿wc 🚿	Privatdusche mit wc, Privatdusche ohne wc
☎	Zimmertelefon mit Außenverbindung über Telefonzentrale
☎	Zimmertelefon mit direkter Außenverbindung
♿	Für Körperbehinderte leicht zugängliche Zimmer
⚊ ⚊	Freibad, Hallenbad
🌿	Liegewiese, Garten
🎾	Hoteleigener Tennisplatz
⛳18	Golfplatz und Lochzahl
🎣	Angelmöglichkeit für Hotelgäste, evtl. gegen Gebühr
🏛	Konferenzräume (mind. 25 Plätze)
🚗	Garage
Ⓟ	Parkplatz
🐕	Das Mitführen von Hunden ist im ganzen Haus unerwünscht
	Falls Hunde dennoch geduldet werden, dann nur in den Zimmern.
May-October	Öffnungszeit, vom Hotelier mitgeteilt
season	Unbestimmte Öffnungszeit eines Saisonhotels
	Die Häuser, für die wir keine Schließzeiten angeben, sind ganzjährig geöffnet.
LL35 0SB	Angabe des Postbezirks (hinter der Hoteladresse)
(T.H.F.)	Hotelkette *(Liste am Ende des Führers)*

ANNEHMLICHKEITEN

In manchen Hotels ist der Aufenthalt wegen der schönen, ruhigen Lage, der nicht alltäglichen Einrichtung und Atmosphäre und dem gebotenen Service besonders angenehm und erholsam.

Solche Häuser und ihre besonderen Annehmlichkeiten sind im Führer durch folgende Symbole gekennzeichnet :

⋔⋔⋔ ... ⋔	Angenehme Hotels
XXXXX ... X	Angenehme Restaurants
« Park »	Besondere Annehmlichkeit
⤳	Sehr ruhiges, oder abgelegenes und ruhiges Hotel
⤳	Ruhiges Hotel
⇐ sea	Reizvolle Aussicht
⇐	Interessante oder weite Sicht

Die Karten in der Einleitung zu den einzelnen Landesteilen geben Ihnen einen Überblick über die Orte, in denen sich mindestens ein angenehmes, sehr ruhiges Haus befindet.

Wir wissen, daß diese Auswahl noch nicht vollständig ist, sind aber laufend bemüht, weitere solche Häuser für Sie zu entdecken ; dabei sind uns Ihre Erfahrungen und Hinweise eine wertvolle Hilfe.

KÜCHE

Die Sterne für gute Küche

Mit ❀, ❀❀ oder ❀❀❀ kennzeichnen wir die Häuser mit landesüblicher oder ausländischer Küche, deren Qualität wir der Aufmerksamkeit der Leser besonders empfehlen möchten (siehe S. 48).

Für diese Häuser geben wir im Text einige typische Gerichte bürgerlicher Küche an.

❀ **Eine sehr gute Küche : verdient Ihre besondere Beachtung**

Der Stern bedeutet eine angenehme Unterbrechung Ihrer Reise. Vergleichen Sie aber bitte nicht den Stern eines teuren Luxusrestaurants mit dem Stern eines kleinen oder mittleren Hauses, wo man Ihnen zu einem annehmbaren Preis eine ebenfalls vorzügliche Mahlzeit reicht.

❀❀ **Eine hervorragende Küche : verdient einen Umweg**

Ausgesuchte Spezialitäten und Weine... angemessene Preise.

❀❀❀ **Eine der besten Küchen : eine Reise wert**

Ein denkwürdiges Essen, edle Weine, tadelloser Service, gepflegte Atmosphäre... entsprechende Preise.

M **Das rote « M »**

Wir glauben, daß Sie neben den Häusern mit Stern auch solche Adressen interessieren werden, die einfache, aber sorgfältig zubereitete Mahlzeiten anbieten.

Auf solche Häuser weisen wir im Text durch das rote « M » hin.

Ausschank alkoholischer Getränke

In Großbritannien und Irland unterliegt der Ausschank alkoholischer Getränke gesetzlichen Bestimmungen, die in den einzelnen Gegenden verschieden sind.

Im allgemeinen schließen die Hotelbars und Pubs nachmittags sowie nach 23 Uhr ; die genauen Öffnungszeiten sind jedoch örtlich verschieden.

Hotelgästen können alkoholische Getränke jedoch auch außerhalb der Ausschankzeiten serviert werden.

Kindern unter 14 Jahren ist der Zutritt zu den Bars untersagt.

PREISE

Die in diesem Führer genannten Preise wurden uns Ende 1985 angegeben. Sie können sich 1986 erhöhen, wenn die allgemeinen Lebenshaltungskosten steigen. Sie können aber in diesem Fall als Richtpreise angesehen werden.

Halten Sie beim Betreten des Hotels den Führer in der Hand. Sie zeigen damit, daß Sie aufgrund dieser Empfehlung gekommen sind.

Die Namen der Hotels und Restaurants, die ihre Preise genannt haben, sind fett gedruckt. Gleichzeitig haben sich diese Häuser verpflichtet, diese Preise den Benutzern des Michelin-Führers zu berechnen.

Informieren Sie uns bitte über jede unangemessen erscheinende Preiserhöhung. Wenn keine Preise angegeben sind, raten wir Ihnen, sich beim Hotelier danach zu erkundigen.

Die Preise sind in Pfund Sterling angegeben (1 £ = 100 pence) mit Ausnahme der Republik Irland (Punts).

Wenn die Buchstaben s., t., oder st. nicht hinter den angegebenen Preisen aufgeführt sind, können sich diese um den Zuschlag für Bedienung und/oder MWSt erhöhen (keine MWSt auf den Channel Islands).

Mahlzeiten

M 7.00/9.00	**Feste Menupreise** — Mittagessen 7.00, Abendessen 9.00 (inklusive Couvert).
M 11.00/13.00	Siehe Seite 39.
s. t.	Bedienung inbegriffen - MWSt inbegriffen.
st.	Bedienung und MWSt inbegriffen (Inklusivpreise).
⌀ 4.00	Preis für 1/2 Flasche oder eine Karaffe Tafelwein.
M a la carte 14.00/18.00	**Mahlzeiten « à la carte »** — Der erste Preis entspricht einer einfachen aber sorgfältig zubereiteten Mahlzeit, bestehend aus kleiner Vorspeise, Tagesgericht mit Beilage und Nachtisch. Der zweite Preis entspricht einer reichlicheren Mahlzeit mit Vorspeise, Hauptgericht, Käse oder Nachtisch (« couvert » ist in den Preisen enthalten).
⌸ 4.00	Preis des englischen Frühstücks, wenn dieser nicht im Übernachtungspreis enthalten ist. Einfaches, billigeres Frühstück (Continental breakfast) erhältlich.

Zimmer

rm 21.00/38.00	Mindestpreis 21.00 für ein Einzelzimmer und Höchstpreis 38.00 für das schönste Doppelzimmer
rm ⌸ 30.00/45.00	Übernachtung mit englischem Frühstück.
suites 100.00/200.00	Mindest- und Höchstpreis für ein Appartement bestehend aus Wohnzimmer, Schlafzimmer und Bad.

"Short Breaks" (Siehe Seite 41)

SB 50.00/60.00	Mindest- und Höchstpreis pro Person bei einem Aufenthalt von 2 Nächten.
▨ ⁤Æ ⓞ *VISA*	Von Hotels und Restaurants angenommene **Kreditkarten :** Access (MasterCard) — American Express — Diners Club — Visa (BankAmericard).

NÜTZLICHE HINWEISE

Im Restaurant

Verlangen Sie die Karte der Tagesmenus zu Festpreisen und die Speise-
karte, wenn sie Ihnen nicht von selbst vorgelegt werden.

Im Hotel

Im allgemeinen ist das Frühstück (auch wenn es nicht eingenommen
wird) im Zimmerpreis enthalten.

Pauschale für "Short Breaks"

Zahlreiche Hotels bieten Vorzugspreise bei einem Aufenthalt von
2 Nächten ("Short Break"). Diese Pauschalpreise (für mindestens 2 Per-
sonen) umfassen Zimmer, Abendessen und Frühstück.

Zimmerreservierung

Hotels : Es ist ratsam, wenn irgend möglich, die Zimmer reservieren zu
lassen. Bitten Sie den Hotelier, daß er Ihnen in seinem Bestätigungs-
schreiben alle seine Bedingungen mitteilt.

Besonders in Seebädern wird Vollpension im allgemeinen nur wochen-
weise, von Samstag zu Samstag, gewährt.

Bei schriftlichen Zimmerbestellungen empfiehlt es sich, einen Freium-
schlag oder einen internationalen Antwortschein beizufügen.

Einige Hoteliers verlangen eine Anzahlung (etwa 10 % wenn nichts
anderes vereinbart wird) auf den voraussichtlichen Endpreis. Sie ist als
Garantie für beide Seiten anzusehen.

Restaurant : Es empfiehlt sich, Tische immer und so früh wie möglich
vorzubestellen.

Tiere

Das Mitführen von Haustieren (Hunde, Katzen u. dgl.) bei der Einreise in
Großbritannien und Irland ist untersagt.

DAS AUTO, DIE REIFEN

Bei den meisten Orten geben wir Adressen von Kfz-Vertragswerkstätten an ; viele
davon haben einen Abschlepp- bzw. Reparaturdienst.

In Großbritannien und Irland besteht Gurtanlegepflicht für Fahrer und Beifahrer auf
den Vordersitzen.

Automobilclubs

Die wichtigsten Automobilclubs des Landes sind die Automobile Association und
der Royal Automobile Club, die den Mitgliedern der der FIA angeschlossenen Automobilclubs Pannenhilfe leisten und einige ihrer Dienstleistungen anbieten.

AUTOMOBILE ASSOCIATION
Fanum House
BASINGSTOKE, Hants., RG21 2EA
℘ (0256) 20123

ROYAL AUTOMOBILE CLUB
RAC House, Lansdowne Rd
CROYDON, Surrey CR9 2JA
℘ (01) 686 2525

HAUPTSEHENSWÜRDIGKEITEN

Bewertung

★★★	Eine Reise wert
★★	Verdient einen Umweg
★	Sehenswert
AC	Eintritt (gegen Gebühr)

Lage

See	In der Stadt
Envir.	In der Umgebung der Stadt
Exc.	Ausflugsziele
N, S, E, W	Im Norden (N), Süden (S), Osten (E), Westen (W) der Stadt.
A 22	Zu erreichen über die Straße A 22.
2 m.	Entfernung in Meilen

STÄDTE

✉ York	Zuständiges Postamt
✆ 0225 Bath	Vorwahlnummer und evtl. zuständiges Fernsprechamt (bei Gesprächen vom Ausland aus wird die erste Null weggelassen)
101 M 27, ⑩	Nummer der Michelin-Karte und Koordinaten des Gratfeldes oder Faltseite
West Country G.	Siehe auch den grünen Michelinführer "England : The West Country"
pop. 1,057	Einwohnerzahl
ECD : Wednesday	Tag, an dem die Läden nachmittags geschlossen sind
BX **A**	Markierung auf dem Stadtplan
🏌18	Öffentlicher Golfplatz und Lochzahl
☀, ≼	Rundblick, Aussichtspunkt
✈	Flughafen
🚗 ✆ 218	Ladestelle für Autoreisezüge - Nähere Auskünfte unter der angegebenen Telefonnummer
⛴	Autofähre
⛴	Personenfähre *Liste der Schiffahrtsgesellschaften am Ende des Führers*
🛈	Informationsstelle

Uhrzeit

In Großbritannien ist eine Zeitverschiebung zu beachten und die Uhr gegenüber der deutschen Zeit um 1 Stunde zurückzustellen.

STADTPLÄNE

Straßen

Autobahn, Straße mit getrennten Fahrbahnen

Anschlußstelle : Autobahneinfahrt und/oder -ausfahrt, Nummer

Hauptverkehrsstraße

Einbahnstraße - nicht befahrbare Straße

Fußgängerzone

Pasteur   P   Einkaufsstraße - Parkplatz

Tor - Passage - Tunnel

Unterführung (Höhe angegeben bis 16'6") auf Hauptverkehrsstraßen

Bahnhof und Bahnlinie

F B   Autofähre - Bewegliche Brücke

Sehenswürdigkeiten — Hotels — Restaurants

Sehenswertes Gebäude mit Haupteingang

Sehenswerter Sakralbau :

Kathedrale, Kirche oder Kapelle

Windmühle - Sonstige Sehenswürdigkeiten

Schloß - Ruine

B   Referenzbuchstabe einer Sehenswürdigkeit

Hotel, Restaurant - Referenzbuchstabe

Sonstige Zeichen

AGENCE MICHELIN   Informationsstelle - Michelin-Niederlassung

Krankenhaus - Moschee - Synagoge

Garten, Park, Wäldchen - Friedhof - Bildstock

Stadion - Golfplatz

Flughafen - Pferderennbahn - Aussicht - Rundblick

Standseilbahn - Seilschwebebahn

Denkmal, Statue - Brunnen - Jachthafen - Leuchtturm

Schiffsverbindungen : Autofähre

Öffentliches Gebäude, durch einen Buchstaben gekennzeichnet :

C   Sitz der Grafschaftsverwaltung

H   M   T   Rathaus - Museum - Theater

POL   Polizei (in größeren Städten Polizeipräsidium)

U   Universität, Hochschule

Hauptpostamt (postlagernde Sendungen), Telefon

Golfplatz (Zutritt bedingt erlaubt)

Funk-, Fernsehturm - U-Bahnstation

London

BRENT   SOHO   Name des Verwaltungsbezirks (borough) - des Stadtteils (area)

Grenze des „ borough " - des „ area "

MOTORWAY HOTELS

Hotels included in the Guide on, or near the interchanges of motorways and A (M) class roads. See appropriate town for details.

ALBERGHI AUTOSTRADALI

I sottoindicati alberghi, selezionati nella guida, si trovano lungo le autostrade o lungo le strade principali, in prossimità degli svincoli. Per ogni dettaglio vedere la località interessata.

HOTELS D'AUTOROUTE

Les hôtels ci-dessous, sélectionnés dans le guide se trouvent sur les autoroutes ou les routes principales, à proximité des échangeurs. Pour tous détails, voir le nom de la ville.

AUTOBAHN-RASTHÄUSER

Die unten aufgeführten Hotels befinden sich an Autobahnen, Hauptverkehrsstraßen oder in der Nähe von Autobahnauffahrten. Nähere Einzelheiten unter dem Ortstext.

Location	Town	Hotel
M 1		
Scratchwood Service Area	Hendon (L.B. of Barnet)	🏨 Scratchwood TraveLodge
Junction 5 — S : ½ m. on A 41	Watford	🏨 Ladbroke
Junction 6 — NE : 1 m. on A 405 (this hotel also under M 10)	St. Albans	🏨 Noke Thistle
Junction 8 — W : ½ m. on A 4147	Hemel Hempstead	🏨 Post House
Junction 9 — NW : 1 m. on A 5	Flamstead	🏨 Hertfordshire Moat House
Junction 11 — E : ¾ m. on A 505	Luton	🏨 Chiltern
Junction 11 — on A 505	Luton	🏨 Crest
Junction 11 — E : 1 ½ m. on A 505	Luton	⌂ Humberstone
Newport Pagnell Service Area 3	Newport Pagnell	🏨 TraveLodge
Junction 18 — E : ¼ m. on A 428	Rugby (at Crick)	🏨 Post House
Junction 21/21A — NE : 2 ½ m. on A 46	Leicester (at Braunstone)	🏨 Post House
Junction 25 — W : ¼ m. on A 52	Nottingham (at Sandiacre)	🏨 Post House
Junction 25 — S : ½ m. on B 6002	Nottingham (at Long Eaton)	🏨 Novotel Nottingham
Junction 28	South Normanton	🏨 Swallow
Junction 30 — NW : 1 ½ m. on A 616	Renishaw	🏨 Sitwell Arms
Junction 39 — W : ¼ m. on A 636	Wakefield	🏨 Cedar Court
Junction 40 — E : ½ m. on A 638	Wakefield	🏨 Post House
A 1 (M)		
Junction 1, A 638 — N : 2 ½ m. on A 1	Wentbridge (at Barnsdale Bar)	🏠 Doncaster TraveLodge
A 1 (M) via A 66 (M) — E : 2 m. on A 66	Darlington	🏨 Blackwell Grange Moat House
A 1 (M) Junction with A 602 and B 197 — W : 1 ¼ m. on A 602	Hitchin	🏨 Blakemore
A 1 (M) via A 167 — S : ¾ m. by A 167	Darlington (at Coatham Mundeville)	🏨 Hall Garth Country House
A 1 (M) Junction with A 195 — E : ½ m. by A 1231	Washington	🏨 Post House
A 1 (M) Junction A 6 and M 25 (this hotel also under M 25)	South Mimms	🏨 Crest
M 2		
Junction 1 — W : 1 ½ m. on A 2	Shorne	🏨 Inn on the Lake
Junction 3 — N : 1 m. on A 229	Rochester	🏨 Crest
M 3		
Junction 3 — N : 1 m. on A 30	Bagshot	🏠 Cricketer's
Junction 6 — SW : 1 ½ m. at junction A 30 and A 339	Basingstoke	🏨 Crest

M 4

Junction 3 – N : 1 ½ m. off A 312	Heathrow Airport (L.B. of Hillingdon)	Arlington
Junction 4 – S : ½ m. on B 379	Heathrow Airport	Post House
Junction 4 – N : ½ m. on B 379	Heathrow Airport	Holiday Inn
Junction 5 – NW : ¼ m. on A 4	Slough	Holiday Inn
Junction 8-9 – SE : 3 m. by A 308 (M) and A 308	Windsor	Oakley Court
Junction 9 A – NE : ½ m. on Shoppenhangers Rd	Maidenhead	Crest
Junction 11 – N : ½ m. on A 33	Reading	Post House
Junction 15 – N : 2 m. on A 345	Swindon	Post House
Junction 19 – SW : 2 ½ m. by M 32 on A 4174 (this hotel also under M 32)	Bristol (at Hambrook)	Crest
Junction 24 – S : ½ m. on A 48	Newport (Gwent)	Celtic Manor
Junction 24 – E : 1 ½ m. on A 48	Newport (Gwent) (at Langstone)	New Inn Motel
Junction 24 – S : ¼ m. on A 48	Newport (Gwent)	Ladbroke

M 5

Junction 1 – W : 1 m. by A 41	Birmingham (at West Bromwich)	West Bromwich Moat House
Junction 5 – SW : 1 m. on A 38	Droitwich	Château Impney
Junction 11 – E : 1 m. on A 40	Cheltenham	Golden Valley Thistle
Junction 13 – SE : 1 ¾ m. on A 419	Stroud (at Stonehouse)	Stonehouse Court
Junction 14 – SW : 1 ½ m. by A 4509 on A 38	Falfield	Park
Junction 22 – N : 1 m. on A 38	Brent Knoll	Battleborough Grange

M 6

Junction 2 – S : 1 m. on A 46	Coventry (at Walsgrave-on-Sowe)	Crest
Junction 3 – SE : 1 m. on A 444	Coventry (at Longford)	Novotel Coventry
Junction 5	Birmingham (at Castle Bromwich)	Bradford Arms
Junction 7 – N : ¼ m. on A 34	Birmingham (at Great Barr)	Post House
Junction 7 – N : 1 ½ m. on A 34	Walsall	Crest
Junction 12 – E : 2 m. on A 5	Cannock	Roman Way
Junction 13 – N : 1 m. on A 449	Stafford	Garth
Junction 14 – SE : ½ m. on A 5013	Stafford	Tillington Hall
Junction 15 – N : ¼ m. on A 519	Newcastle-under-Lyme	Post House
Junction 15 – N : ¾ m. on A 519	Newcastle-under-Lyme	Clayton Lodge
Junction 15 – NE : 1 ½ m. on A 34	Stoke on Trent	White House
Charnock Richard Service Area	Charnock Richard	TraveLodge
Junction 19 – NE : 2 ½ m. on A 556 (this hotel also under M 56)	Knutsford (at Bucklow Hill)	Swan Inn
Junction 23 – N : ½ m. on A 49	Haydock	Post House
Junction 28 – W : ¼ m. on B 5256	Leyland	Ladbroke
Junction 29 – SE : ¼ m. by A 6	Preston	Novotel
Junction 31 – W : ¼ m. on A 59	Preston (at Samlesbury)	Tickled Trout
Junction 33 – at Junction of A 6 and M 6	Lancaster	Hampson House
Junction 34 – SW : ¼ m. on A 683	Lancaster	Post House
Junction 36 – N : 1 ¼ m. on A 65	Kendal	Crooklands
Junction 44 – N : ¼ m. on A 7	Carlisle (at Kingstown)	Crest
at Tebay West service area	Tebay, Cumbria	Tebay Mountain Lodge

M 8

Junction with M 9 – E : 1 m. on A 8	Edinburgh	Norton House

M 9

Junction with M 8 – E : 1 m. on A 8	Edinburgh	Norton House

M 10

Junction 1 – SW : 1 m. on A 405 (this hotel also under M 1)	St. Albans	Noke Thistle

M 11

Junction 14 with A 604 – NW : 1 ¾ m. on A 604	Cambridge (at Bar Hill)	Cambridgeshire Moat House

M 20

Junction 2 A	**Wrotham Heath**	Post House

M 23

Junction 9 − in Gatwick Airport	**Gatwick**	Gatwick Hilton International
Junction 9 − W : 1 m. on A 23	**Gatwick**	Gatwick Penta
Junction 9 − W : 1 m. on A 23	**Gatwick**	Post House
Junction 9 − W : 1 m. on A 23	**Gatwick**	Gatwick Moat House

M 25

Junction 26 − E : 3 ½ m. by A 121 on B 1393	**Epping**	Post House
Junction 28 − NE : ¾ m. on A 1023	**Brentwood**	Brentwood Moat House
Junction 28 − NE : ¼ m. on A 1023	**Brentwood**	Post House
Junction with A 30 − NW : ½ m. on A 308	**Egham**	Runnymede
Junction A 6 and A 1 (M) (this hotel also under A 1 (M))	**South Mimms**	Crest

M 26

| Junction 2 A | **Wrotham Heath** | Post House |

M 27

| Junction 1 − on A 337 at Junction of A 31 and A 336 | **Cadnam** | Bartley Lodge |
| Junction 12 − N : at junction of A 3 and A 27 | **Portsmouth & Southsea (at Cosham)** | Holiday Inn |

M 32

| Junction 1 − W : ½ m. on A 4174 (this hotel also under M 4) | **Bristol (at Hambrook)** | Crest |

M 40

Junction 2 − E : 1 ¾ m. by A 355 on A 40	**Beaconsfield**	Bellhouse
Junction 4 − on Crest Road	**High Wycombe**	Crest
Junction 7 − W : 2 m. by A 329	**Oxford (at Great Milton)**	with rm Le Manoir aux Quat Saisons

M 54

| Junction 7 − S : 1 m. | **Telford** | Buckatree Hall |

M 55

| Junction 1 − N : ¾ m. | **Preston** | Broughton Park |

M 56

Junction 5 − on Airport Approach Road	**Manchester (at Airport)**	Excelsior
Junction 6 − N : ¼ m. on A 538	**Altrincham**	Four Seasons
Junction 6 − S : 2 m. on A 538	**Wilnslow**	Valley Lodge
Junction 7/8 − SW : 2 m. on A 556 (this hotel also under M 6)	**Knutsford (at Bucklow Hill)**	Swan Inn
Junction 11 − N : ¼ m. on A 56	**Daresbury**	Lord Daresbury
Junction 12 − SE : ½ m. by A 557	**Runcorn**	Crest

M 57

| Junction 2 − E : ½ m. | **Kirkby** | Crest |

M 61

| Junction 5 − NE : 1 m. on A 58 | **Bolton** | Crest |

M 62

| Junction 24 − SE : 1 ½ m. on A 629 | **Huddersfield** | Ladbroke |
| Junction 30 − N : 1 m. on A 639 | **Leeds (at Oulton)** | Crest |

M 63

| Junction 9 − by approach Rd | **Manchester (at Northenden)** | Post House |

M 69

| Junction 1 − NE : 2 ½ m. on A 46 | **Leicester** | Post House |

M 606

| Junction 1 − E : ¼ m. | **Bradford** | Novotel |

MAP OF TOWNS INCLUDED IN THE GUIDE

To keep the full, distinctive flavour of the separate kingdoms, principality, province, republic and islands which go to make up the British Isles, the Guide has been divided into sections each preceded by a separate map.

The maps show the towns and places with establishments included in the Guide, and those particularly selected for their general attractiveness, quiet atmosphere and good food.

A map of Great Britain and the Republic of Ireland at the beginning of the Guide shows major roads and main passenger and car ferry routes.

CARTES DES LOCALITÉS CITÉES

Afin de respecter le caractère propre à chaque Royaume ou Etat composant les Iles Britanniques, ce guide est présenté en six parties, chacune précédée d'une carte de toutes les localités citées.

Ces cartes précisent les lieux où nous recommandons spécialement des établissements hôteliers pour leur agrément, leur tranquillité ou leur bonne cuisine.

Une carte générale de la Grande-Bretagne et de la République d'Irlande figure en outre au début du guide et donne les principales voies de communication terrestres et maritimes.

CARTE DELLE LOCALITÀ COMPRESE NELLA GUIDA

Ogni Reame o Stato che compone le Isole Britanniche mantiene la sua propria personalità; perciò abbiamo ritenuto opportuno presentarli facendo precedere una carta geografica alla nomenclatura di ciascuno di essi.

Queste carte segnalano le località selezionate e, per ognuna di esse, l'eventuale esistenza di esercizi particolarmente raccomandabili per la loro amenità, la loro tranquillità o la loro buona cucina.

Inoltre, una carta generale della Gran Bretagna e della Repubblica d'Irlanda figura all'inizio della Guida ed indica le principali vie di comunicazione terrestri e marittime.

KARTEN MIT DEN ERWÄHNTEN ORTSCHAFTEN

Jedes einzelne der Länder, die unter dem Begriff « Britische Inseln » zusammengefaßt sind, hat seinen eigenen Charakter; wir haben dem Rechnung getragen, indem wir dem Ortsverzeichnis jedes « Landes » eine Übersichtskarte vorangestellt haben.

Auf diesen Karten finden Sie alle im Führer erwähnten Orte, Orte mit besonders angenehmen oder ruhig gelegenen Häusern, sowie solche mit besonders guter Küche.

Eine Gesamtkarte Großbritanniens und der Republik Irland mit den wichtigsten Verkehrsverbindungen (Land- und Seewege) finden Sie in der Einleitung.

TOWNS WITH ESTABLISHMENTS AWARDED ✿✿✿, ✿✿, ✿, M

Localités possédant des établissements à ✿✿✿, ✿✿, ✿, M

Località che possiedono esercizi con ✿✿✿, ✿✿, ✿, M

In folgenden Orten finden sie Häuser mit ✿✿✿, ✿✿, ✿, M

✿✿✿

England and Wales

Bray-on-Thames	Waterside Inn	London	pages bordered in red

✿✿

England and Wales

Ilkley	Box Tree	Oxford	Le Manoir aux Quat'Saisons
London	pages bordered in red	Reading	Chez Nico

✿

England and Wales

Bristol	Les Semailles	Oxford	Petit Blanc
Canterbury	Seventy-Four	Royal Leamington	
Chagford	Gidleigh Park	Spa	Mallory Court
Dartmouth	Carved Angel	Taunton	Castle
Dedham	Le Talbooth	Woburn	Paris House
East Grinstead	Gravetye Manor		
Great Malvern	Croque-en-Bouche	**Scotland**	
Limpsfield	Old Lodge	Fort William	Inverlochy Castle
London	pages bordered in red		
New Milton	Chewton Glen	**Republic of Ireland**	
Oakham	Hambleton Hall	Kenmare	Park
		Navan	Dunderry Lodge

M

England and Wales

Abergavenny	Walnut Tree Inn
Bakewell	Fischers
Bath	Homewood Park
Bath	Hunstrete House
Bath	The Priory
Boroughbridge	Fountain House
Broadway	Buckland Manor
Bromsgrove	Grafton Manor
Chichester	White Horse
Clanfield	Plough
Diss	Salisbury House
Earl Stonham	Mr Underhill's
Eastbourne	Hungry Monk
Flitwick	Flitwick Manor
Fowey	Food for Thought
Fressingfield	Fox and Goose
Glemsford	Weeks
Grasmere	Michael's Nook Country House
Grasmere	White Moss House
Great Dunmow	Starr
Grimsthorpe	Black Horse Inn
Helford	Riverside
Horton	French Partridge
Kintbury	Dundas Arms
Ledbury	Hope End Country House
London	pages bordered in red
Melksham	Beechfield House
Newport	Pantry
Northallerton	McCoys at the Tontine
Padstow	Seafood
Pateley Bridge	Sportsman's Arms
Plymouth	Chez Nous
Pool-in-Wharfedale	Pool Court
Reading	Knights Farm
St. Just	Count House

Shipdham	Shipdham Place
Storrington	Manley's
Sturminster Newton	Plumber Manor
Swansea	Drangway
Tetbury	Calcot Manor
Tetbury	Gibbons
Thornbury	Thornbury Castle
Ullswater	Sharrow Bay Country House
Warwick	Westgate Arms
Waterhouses	Old Beams
Winchester	Old Chesil Rectory
Windermere	Miller Howe
Worcester	Brown's
Wymondham	Adlard's

Scotland

Arisaig	Arisaig House
Glasgow	Poacher's
Gullane	La Potinière
Kilchrenan	Ardanaisaig
Peat Inn	The Peat Inn
Port Appin	Airds
Ullapool	Altnaharrie Inn

Northern Ireland

Portrush	Ramore

Republic of Ireland

Cashel	Chez Hans
Cork	Arbutus Lodge
Cork	Lovetts
Dingle	Doyle's Seafood Bar
Gorey	Marlfield House
Mallow	Longueville House
Moycullen	Drimcong House
Shanagarry	Ballymaloe House

England
and *Wales*

COUNTY ABBREVIATIONS

ABRÉVIATIONS DES COMTÉS

ABBREVIAZIONI DELLE CONTEE

ABKÜRZUNGEN DER GRAFSCHAFTEN

ENGLAND

Avon	Avon	Kent	Kent
Bedfordshire	Beds.	Lancashire	Lancs.
Berkshire	Berks.	Leicestershire	Leics.
Buckinghamshire	Bucks.	Lincolnshire	Lincs.
Cambridgeshire	Cambs.	Merseyside	Merseyside
Cheshire	Cheshire	Norfolk	Norfolk
Cleveland	Cleveland	Northamptonshire	Northants.
Cornwall	Cornwall	Northumberland	Northumb.
Cumbria	Cumbria	North Yorkshire	North Yorks.
Derbyshire	Derbs.	Nottinghamshire	Notts.
Devon	Devon	Oxfordshire	Oxon.
Dorset	Dorset	Shropshire	Salop
Durham	Durham	Somerset	Somerset
East Sussex	East Sussex	South Yorkshire	South Yorks.
Essex	Essex	Staffordshire	Staffs.
Gloucestershire	Glos.	Suffolk	Suffolk
Greater Manchester	Greater Manchester	Surrey	Surrey
Hampshire	Hants.	Tyne and Wear	Tyne and Wear
Hereford and Worcester	Heref. and Worc.	Warwickshire	Warw.
Hertfordshire	Herts.	West Midlands	West Midlands
Humberside	Humberside	West Sussex	West Sussex
Isle of Wight	I. O. W.	West Yorkshire	West Yorks.
		Wiltshire	Wilts.

WALES

Clwyd	Clwyd	Mid Glamorgan	Mid Glam.
Dyfed	Dyfed	Powys	Powys
Gwent	Gwent	South Glamorgan	South Glam.
Gwynedd	Gwynedd	West Glamorgan	West Glam.

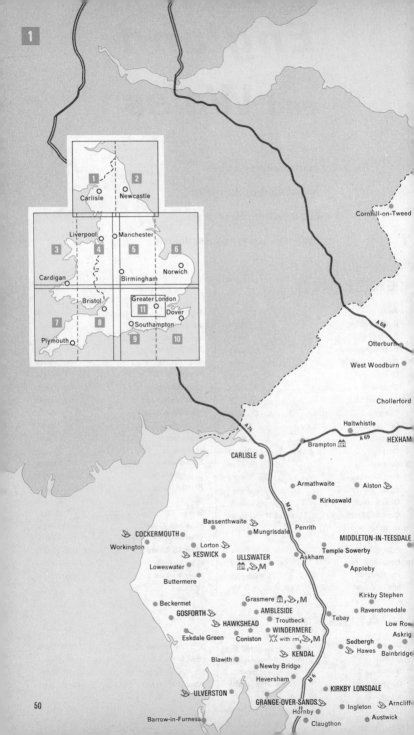

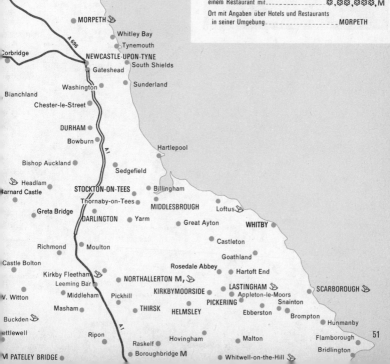

Place with at least :

one hotel or restaurant .... ● Ripon
one pleasant hotel .... 🏠 , ✕ with rm
one quiet, secluded hotel .... ⌒
one restaurant with .... ✿ , ✿✿ , ✿✿✿ , M
See this town for establishments located in its vicinity .... MORPETH

Localité offrant au moins :

une ressource hôtelière .... ● Ripon
un hôtel agréable .... 🏠 , ✕ with rm
un hôtel très tranquille, isolé .... ⌒
une bonne table à .... ✿ , ✿✿ , ✿✿✿ , M
Localité groupant dans le texte les ressources de ses environs .... MORPETH

La località possiede come minimo :

una risorsa alberghiera .... ● Ripon
un albergo ameno .... 🏠 , ✕ with rm
un albergo molto tranquillo, isolato .... ⌒
un'ottima tavola con .... ✿ , ✿✿ , ✿✿✿ , M
La località raggruppa nel suo testo le risorse dei dintorni .... MORPETH

Ort mit mindestens :

einem Hotel oder Restaurant .... ● Ripon
einem angenehmen Hotel .... 🏠 , ✕ with rm
einem sehr ruhigen und abgelegenen Hotel .... ⌒
einem Restaurant mit .... ✿ , ✿✿ , ✿✿✿ , M
Ort mit Angaben über Hotels und Restaurants in seiner Umgebung .... MORPETH

Berwick-upon-Tweed

Bamburgh
Belford
Seahouses
Wooler
Powburn ⌒
Alnwick
Alnmouth
Rothbury

MORPETH ⌒
Whitley Bay
Corbridge
Tynemouth
NEWCASTLE-UPON-TYNE
Gateshead
South Shields
Washington
Sunderland
Blanchland
Chester-le-Street
DURHAM
Bowburn
Hartlepool
Bishop Auckland
Sedgefield
Headlam ⌒
Barnard Castle
STOCKTON-ON-TEES
Billingham
Thornaby-on-Tees
MIDDLESBROUGH
Loftus ⌒
Greta Bridge
DARLINGTON
Yarm
Great Ayton
WHITBY
Richmond
Moulton
Castleton
Castle Bolton
Goathland
Kirkby Fleetham ⌒
Rosedale Abbey
Hartoft End
Leeming Bar
NORTHALLERTON M, ⌒
LASTINGHAM ⌒
W. Witton
Middleham
Pickhill
KIRKBYMOORSIDE
Appleton-le-Moors
SCARBOROUGH ⌒
Masham
PICKERING
Snainton
Buckden ⌒
THIRSK
HELMSLEY
Ebberston
Brompton
ettlewell
Hunmanby
Ripon
Hovingham
Malton
Flamborough
Raskelf
Bridlington
M PATELEY BRIDGE ●
Boroughbridge M
Whitwell-on-the-Hill ⌒

51

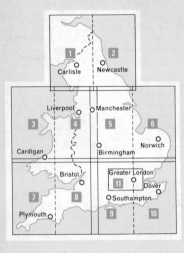

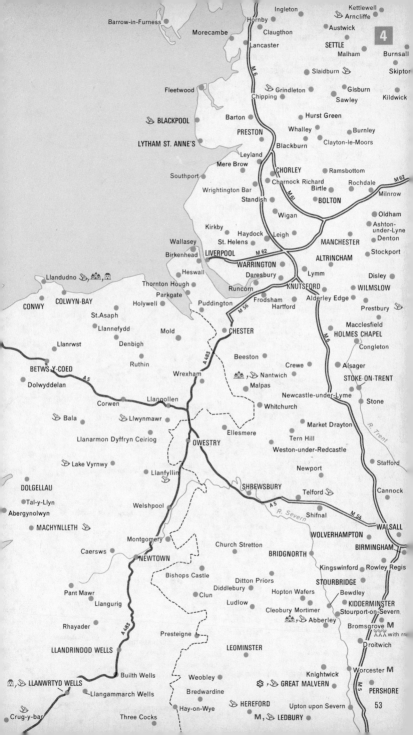

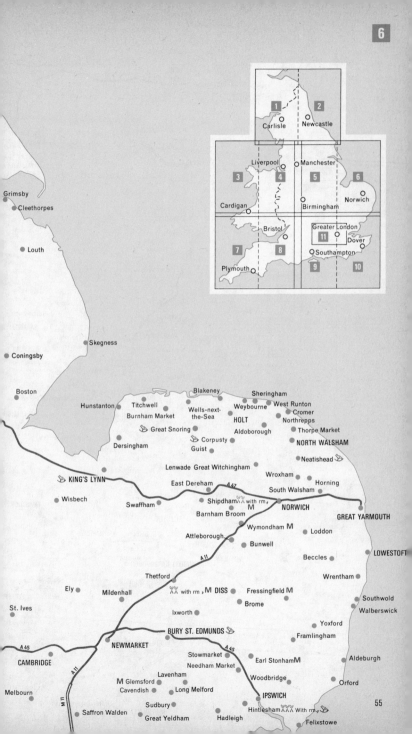

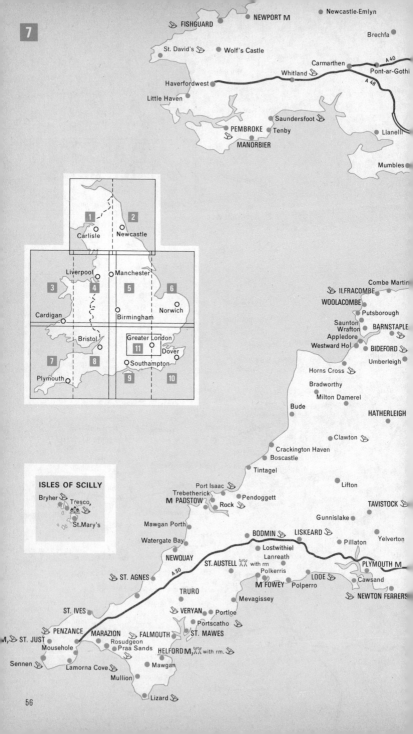

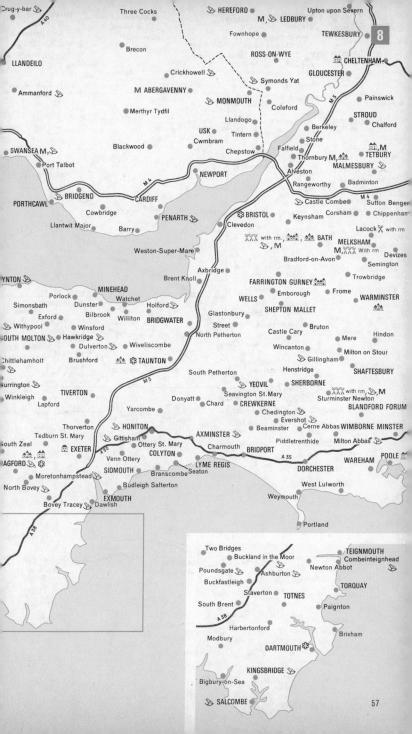

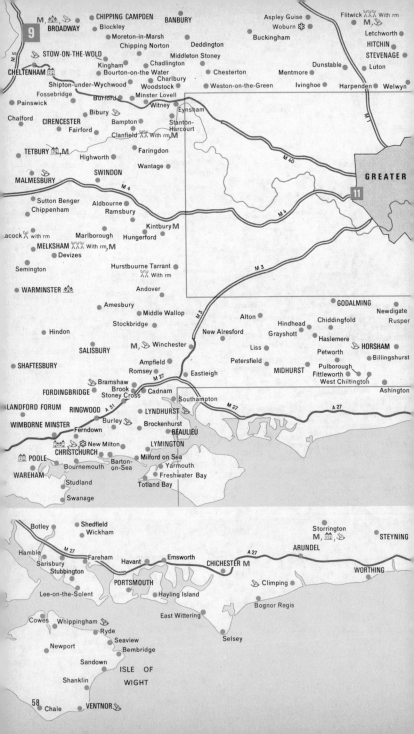

M 11

Sudbury
Hadleigh
IPSWICH
Hintlesham ΛΛΛ With rm
Saffron Walden
Great Yeldham
East Bergholt
Felixstowe
Baldock
THAXTED
Dedham
Manningtree
Harwich and Dovercourt
Clavering
Great Bardfield
COLCHESTER
Bishop's Stortford
Braintree
Coggeshall
Thorpe-le-Soken
Frinton-on-Sea
Great Dunmow M
Felsted
Witham
Clacton-on-Sea
CHELMSFORD
West Mersea
Maldon
South Woodham Ferrers
Burnham-on-Crouch
Rochford
Basildon
LONDON
Southend-on-Sea
North Stifford
Gravesend
A 2
Rochester
Shorne
Herne Bay
Broadstairs
Sittingbourne
Whitstable
RAMSGATE
M 2
Faversham
Sandwich
M 23
CANTERBURY
MAIDSTONE
A 2
Hadlow
Pluckley
Wye
DOVER
Horley
PENSHURST
ASHFORD
EAST GRINSTEAD
Goudhurst
Biddenden
CRAWLEY
ROYAL TUNBRIDGE WELLS
Cranbrook
Hythe
Folkestone
FOREST ROW
Wadhurst
Tenterden
Dymchurch
Cuckfield
Crowborough
Hawkhurst
New Romney
Mayfield
Dallington
Northiam
UCKFIELD
Rushlake Green
Sedlescombe
RYE
Hurstpierpoint
Halland
Battle
A 259
Lewes
HERSTMONCEUX
Hailsham
Bexhill
BRIGHTON AND HOVE
Selmeston
Hastings and St.Leonards
ottingdean
Alfriston
Seaford
EASTBOURNE M

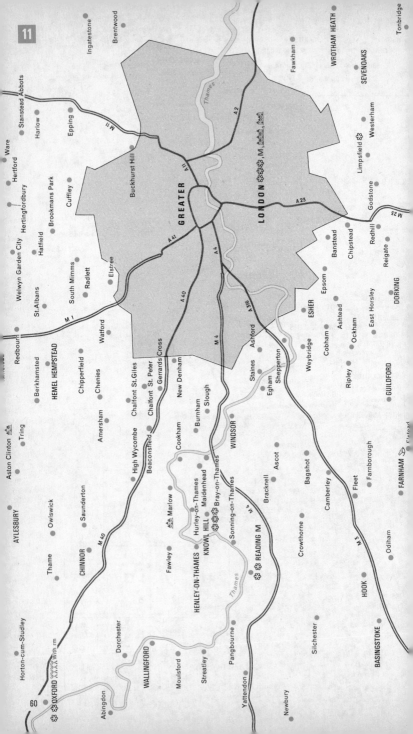

ENGLAND and WALES

Towns

ABBERLEY Heref. and Worc. **403 404** M 27 – pop. 604 – ECD : Wednesday – ✉ Worcester – ☏ 029 921 Great Witley.
◆ London 137 – ◆Birmingham 27 – Worcester 13.

   🏨 **The Elms** ⟊, WR6 6AT, W : 2 m. on A 443 ℰ 666, Telex 337105, ≼, ☞, park, ❊ – 📺 ☎ ℗. ♨, ⚑, 𝔸𝔼 ⓪ 𝘝𝘐𝘚𝘈, ❊
     M 9.50/16.50 **st.** and a la carte ₰ 5.25 – **27 rm** ⬳ 46.00/69.00 **st.** – SB 85.00/93.00 **st.**

ABERAERON Dyfed **403** H 27 – pop. 1 ,445 – ECD : Thursday – ☏ 0545.
Envir. : New Quay (site★) SW : 8 m.
🛈 The Quay ℰ 570602 (summer only).
◆ London 237 – Carmarthen 36 – Fishguard 42 – ◆ Swansea 64.

   🏠 **Feathers Royal,** SA46 0AQ, ℰ 570214, ⬙ – ⌂wc ⋔wc ℗, ♨, ⚑ 𝘝𝘐𝘚𝘈
     closed Christmas – **M** (closed Sunday in winter) 4.50 **st.** (lunch) and a la carte 5.60/9.15 **t.** –
     14 rm ⬳ 17.50/28.00 **st.**

FORD, VOLVO Alban Sq ℰ 570312

ABERDOVEY (ABERDYFI) Gwynedd **403** H 26 – pop. 778 – ECD : Wednesday – ☏ 065 472.
See : Afon Dovey's mouth (site★★).
Envir. : Llanegryn (church★) N : 8 m. – Dolgoch Falls★ NE : 10 m.
🛈 Snowdonia National Park Centre, The Wharf ℰ 321 (summer only).
◆ London 230 – Dolgellau 25 – Shrewsbury 66.

   🏨 **Plas Penhelig** ⟊, LL35 0NA, E : 1 m. by A 493 ℰ 676, ≼, « Terraced gardens », park, ❊ –
     ⌂wc ☎ ℗, ⚑ 𝔸𝔼 ⓪ 𝘝𝘐𝘚𝘈
     closed January and February – **M** 6.95/10.75 **t.** – **11 rm** ⬳ 27.00/36.00 **t.** – SB (except Bank
     Holidays) 36.00/46.00 **st.**

   🏨 **Trefeddian,** Tywyn Rd, LL35 0SB, W : 1 m. on A 493 ℰ 213, ≼ golf course and sea, ⬙, ☞,
     park, ❊ – ▤| 📺 ⌂wc ⋔wc ₺ ⇔ ℗, ⚑
     Easter-October – **M** (buffet lunch Monday to Saturday) 5.60/9.25 **t.** ₰ 2.90 – **46 rm**
     ⬳ 13.50/47.00 **t.** – SB (spring and autumn only) 52.80/68.20 **st.**

   🏠 **Penhelig Arms,** Terrace Rd, LL35 0LT, ℰ 215, Telex 338751, ≼ – 📺 ⌂wc ⋔wc ℗, ⚑ 𝔸𝔼
     ⓪ 𝘝𝘐𝘚𝘈, ❊
     closed Christmas – **M** (bar lunch) a la carte 6.95/8.50 **t.** – **11 rm** ⬳ 15.00/52.00 **t.** – SB
     (weekends only) (October-May) 45.00 **st.**

   🏡 **Harbour,** 17 Glandovey Terr., LL35 0EB, ℰ 250, ≼ – ⋔wc. ⚑ 𝘝𝘐𝘚𝘈. ❊
     March-October – **M** 5.50/9.30 **st.** and a la carte – **6 rm** ⬳ 14.00/28.00 **st.**

   🏡 **Bodfor,** Bodfor Terrace, LL35 0EA, ℰ 475, ≼ – ⋔wc. 𝘝𝘐𝘚𝘈
     closed January and February – **M** (bar lunch)/dinner 6.50 **t.** and a la carte ₰ 2.00 – **15 rm**
     ⬳ 11.00/38.00 **t.** – SB (except July-August) 32.00/36.00 **st.**

   ✕ **Maybank** with rm, LL35 0PT, E : 1 m. on A 493 ℰ 500, ≼ – ⋔wc
     closed February and November – **M** (booking essential)(bar lunch)/dinner a la carte 8.45/9.45 **t.**
     – **6 rm** ⬳ 19.50/33.00 **t.** – SB (except July, August and Bank Holidays) 40.00/45.00 **st.**

ABERGAVENNY (Y-FENNI) Gwent **403** L 28 – pop. 9 ,427 – ECD : Thursday – ☏ 0873.
Envir. : Llanthony Priory★ N : 10 m. – Bwlch (≼★ of the Usk Valley), NW : 9 ½ m.
🛇₈ Llanfoist, ℰ 3171, S : 2 m.
🛈 Brecon Beacons National Park Centre, 2 Lower Monk St. ℰ 3254 (summer only) – at Brecon : Brecon
Beacons National Park, Watton Mount ℰ 0874 (Brecon) 4437 (summer only) – Market Car Park ℰ 0874
(Brecon) 2485 or 5692 (summer only).
◆ London 163 – Gloucester 43 – Newport 19 – ◆Swansea 49.

   🏨 **Angel** (T.H.F.), 15 Cross St., NP7 5EW, ℰ 7121 – 📺 ⌂wc ▧ ℗, ♨, ⚑ 𝔸𝔼 ⓪ 𝘝𝘐𝘚𝘈
     M 4.95/8.75 **st.** and a la carte ₰ 3.25 – ⬳ 5.50 – **29 rm** 35.00/45.00 **st.**

   ⌂ **Park,** 36 Hereford Rd, NP7 5RA, ℰ 3715 – ℗
     7 rm ⬳ 9.50/19.00 **st.**

   ⌂ **Halidon House,** 63 Monmouth Rd, NP7 5HR, ℰ 77855, ⬙, ☞ – ℗. ❊
     closed December – **4 rm** ⬳ 18.00/20.00.

ABERGAVENNY

at Llandewi Skirrid NE : 3 ½ m. by A 465 on B 4521 – ⊠ ✪ 0873 Abergavenny :

✗ **Walnut Tree Inn,** NP7 8AW, ✎ 2797 – **⊕**
closed lunch Monday and Bank Holidays, Sunday, last 2 weeks February and 3 days at Christmas
– **M** a la carte 13.00/20.00 **t.** ⓓ 3.10.

at Llanwenarth NW : 3 m. on A 40 – ⊠ Abergavenny – ✪ 0873 Crickhowell :

🏨 **Llanwenarth Arms,** Brecon Rd, NP7 9SF, ✎ 810550, ≤, ⌕ – ▣ 💺wc ☎ **⊕** 🔊 🖭 ⓪
 𝑽𝑰𝑺𝑨 ⅏
M a la carte 6.95/11.40 **st.** ⓓ 2.10 – **18 rm** ⊑ 28.00/33.00 **st.**

AUSTIN-ROVER, FORD Brecon Rd ✎ 2126   RENAULT 9 Monmouth Rd ✎ 2323
PEUGEOT, TALBOT Penpergwm, Gobion ✎ 087 385
(Gobion) 287

ABERGWAUN = Fishguard.

ABERGWESYN Powys **408** I 27 – see Llanwrtyd Wells.

ABERGYNOLWYN Gwynedd **402 403** I 26 – ⊠ Twywn – ✪ 065 477.
♦London 228 – Dolgellau 12 – Shrewsbury 63.

 ♤ **Dolgoch Falls,** SW : 2 ½ m. on B 4405 ✎ 258, ≤, ☛ – **⊕** 𝑽𝑰𝑺𝑨
 March-October – **6 rm** ⊑ 12.00/24.00 **st.**

ABERHONDDU = Brecon.

ABERLLYNFI = Three Cocks.

ABERMAW = Barmouth.

ABERMULE (ABER-MIWL) Powys **403** K 26 – see Newtown.

ABERPORTH Dyfed **403** G 27 – pop. 1,614 – ECD : Wednesday – ✪ 0239.
See : Site* – Envir. : Llangranog (cliffs*) NE : 4 m.
♦ London 249 – Carmarthen 29 – Fishguard 26.

 🏨 **Penrallt,** SA43 2BS, SW : 1 m. by B 4333 ✎ 810227, ☛, ❃ – ▣ 💺wc 🕮wc ☎ **⊕** 🔊 🖭
 ⓪ 𝑽𝑰𝑺𝑨 ⅏
 closed 23 December-1 January – **M** (bar lunch)/dinner 9.00 **st.** and a la carte ⓓ 3.20 – **17 rm**
 ⊑ 27.50/40.00 **st.**

 🏨 **Highcliffe,** SA43 2DA, ✎ 810534 – ▣ 💺wc **⊕** 🔊 🖭 𝑽𝑰𝑺𝑨
 M (bar lunch)/dinner 12.00 **t.** and a la carte ⓓ 2.45 – **16 rm** ⊑ 15.00/46.00 **t.**

 🏨 **Morlan Motel,** SA43 2EN, ✎ 810611 – ▣ 💺wc **⊕** 🔊 🖭 ⓪ 𝑽𝑰𝑺𝑨
 March-October – **M** (grill rest. only)(bar lunch Monday to Saturday)/dinner 6.75
 st. and a la carte – **16 rm** ⊑ 16.50/26.50 **st.**

 ♤ **Ffynonwen Country** ⌕, SA43 2HT, SE : 1 m. by B 43333 ✎ 810312, ≤ – **⊕**
 12 rm ⊑ 11.00/24.00 **t.**

ABERSOCH Gwynedd **402 403** G 25 – ECD : Wednesday – ⊠ Pwllheli – ✪ 075 881.
Envir. : Llanengan (church* : twin aisles rood screen) W : 2 m. – Hell's Mouth* W : 3 m. – Aber-
daron (site*) W : 10 m. – Braich y Pwll (≤** from 2nd car park) W : 12 m.
🖫 Golf Rd, Pwllheli, ✎ 0758 (Pwllheli) 612520, NE : 7 m. – 🖳 Pwllheli, ✎ 2622.
♦ London 265 – Caernarfon 28 – Shrewsbury 101.

 🏨 **Riverside,** LL53 7HW, ✎ 2419, ≤, 🖾 – ▣ 💺wc 🕮wc **⊕** 𝑽𝑰𝑺𝑨 ⅏
 March-October – **M** (bar lunch)/dinner 15.50 **t.** ⓓ 1.85 – **14 rm** ⊑ 17.00/48.00 **t.** – SB
 55.00/75.00 **st.**

 🏨 **Abersoch Harbour** (Best Western), Long Engan, LL53 7HR, ✎ 2406, ≤ – ▣ 💺wc 🕮wc
 ⊕ 🔊 🖭 ⓪ 𝑽𝑰𝑺𝑨
 March-October – **M** 7.50/15.00 **t.** and a la carte ⓓ 3.00 – **14 rm** ⊑ 20.00/48.00 **t.** – SB
 48.00/60.00 **st.**

 ♤ **Llysfor,** Lôn Garmon, LL53 7AL, ✎ 2248, ☛ – **⊕** 𝑽𝑰𝑺𝑨
 Easter-October – **8 rm** ⊑ 9.50/19.00 **st.**

 ✗✗ **Bronheulog** ⌕ with rm, Lôn Garmon, LL53 7UL, NW : ¾ m. ✎ 2177, ☛ – 💺wc **⊕**
 closed Sunday to Thursday November-February – **M** (closed Sunday to non-residents) (dinner
 only) (booking essential) a la carte 9.80/12.30 ⓓ 2.60 – **4 rm** ⊑ 15.00/30.00 **st.**

 at Bwlchtocyn S : 2 m. – ⊠ Pwllheli – ✪ 075 881 Abersoch :

 🏨 **Porth Tocyn** ⌕, LL53 7BU, ✎ 2966, ≤ Cardigan Bay and mountains, « Country house
 atmosphere », ⊿ heated, ☛, ❃ – ▣ 💺wc ☎ **⊕**
 Easter-early November – **M** (buffet lunch)/dinner 14.50 **t.** ⓓ 3.50 – **17 rm** ⊑ 24.25/57.00 **t.**

ABERTAWE = Swansea.

ABERTEIFI = Cardigan.

ABERYSTWYTH Dyfed **403** H 26 – pop. 8,636 – ECD : Wednesday – ✆ 0970.
See : ≤★ from the National Library – Envir. : Vale of Rheidol★ SE : 6 m.
🛏 Brynmore, ✆ 615104, N : ½ m.
🛈 Eastgate ✆ 612125 and 617911.
♦ London 238 – Chester 98 – Fishguard 58 – Shrewsbury 74.

🏨 **The Groves,** 44-46 North Par., SY23 2NF, ✆ 617623 – 📺 ⌂wc �iwc 🅿. **A** AE ⑩ VISA. ✦
closed Christmas and New Year – **M** (bar lunch)/dinner a la carte 6.50/10.10 **t.** – **12 rm**
☲ 19.00/36.00 **t.** – SB (October-April)(except Bank Holidays) 42.00/50.00 **st.**

🍴 **Four Seasons,** 50-54 Portland St., SY23 2DX, ✆ 612120 – ⌂wc 🅿. **A** VISA
closed 24 December-3 January – **M** (bar lunch Monday to Saturday)/dinner 9.00 **st.** 🍷 2.50 –
16 rm ☲ 15.00/32.50 **st.** – SB (October-March) (except Christmas-New Year) 39.00/41.50 **st.**

at Chancery (Rhydgaled) S : 4 m. on A 487 – ⌧ ✆ 0970 Aberystwyth :

🏨 **Conrah Country** ⬘, SY23 4DF, ✆ 617941, ≤, « 18C country house », 🔲, ✿, park – 📲 📺
⌂wc iwc ☎ 🅿. 🏄. **A** AE ⑩ VISA. ✦
closed 1 week at Christmas – **M** 7.25/10.75 **t.** and a la carte 🍷 2.50 – **22 rm** ☲ 26.00/56.00 **t.** –
SB 58.00/70.00 **st.**

AUSTIN-ROVER-JAGUAR Park Av. ✆ 4841   FORD North Parade ✆ 4171
FIAT Llanfarian ✆ 612311

ABINGDON Oxon. **403 404** Q 28 – pop. 29,130 – ECD : Thursday – ✆ 0235.
🛈 8 Market Pl. ✆ 22711.
♦ London 64 – ♦Oxford 6 – Reading 25.

🏨 **Upper Reaches** (T.H.F.), Thames St., OX14 3JA, ✆ 22311 – 📺 ⌂wc ☎ 🅿. 🏄. **A** AE ⑩
VISA
M 6.95/10.95 **st.** and a la carte 🍷 2.70 – ☲ 5.50 – **20 rm** 45.00/57.00 **st.**
AUSTIN-ROVER Drayton Rd ✆ 22822

ACOCKS GREEN West Midlands **403 404** ⫸ – see Birmingham.

ADLINGTON Lancs. **402 404** M 23 – see Chorley.

AIGBURTH Merseyside – see Liverpool.

ALBRIGHTON Salop **402 403** L 25 – see Shrewsbury.

ALCESTER Warw. **403 404** O 27 – pop. 5,207 – ECD : Thursday – ✆ 0789.
Envir. : Ragley Hall★★ (17C) *AC*, SW : 2 m.
♦London 104 – ♦Birmingham 20 – ♦Coventry 28 – Gloucester 34.

🏨 **Kings Court Motel,** Kings Coughton, B49 5QQ, N : 1 m. on A 435 ✆ 762626 – 📺 ⌂wc 🅿.
A AE ⑩ VISA. ✦
M (grill rest. only) a la carte 6.60/8.65 **t.** – **15 rm** ☲ 18.50/30.00 **t.** – SB (weekends only)
40.00 **st.**

🍴 **Rossini,** 50 Birmingham Rd, on A 435 ✆ 762764, Italian rest. – 🅿. **A** AE ⑩ VISA
closed Sunday, last 2 weeks July and first 2 weeks August – **M** 7.00 **t.** (lunch) and a la carte
7.90/13.40 **t.** 🍷 2.80.

ALDBOROUGH Norfolk **404** X 25 – pop. 461 – ⌧ Norwich – ✆ 0263 Cromer.
Envir. : Blickling Hall★ (Jacobean), S : 5 m. – ♦London 127 – ♦Cambridge 80 – ♦Norwich 18.

🍴 **Old Red Lion,** The Green, NR11 7AA, ✆ 761451 – 🅿. VISA
closed Sunday dinner and Monday – **M** 7.50 **t.** (lunch) and a la carte 11.35/12.75 **t.**

ALDBOURNE Wilts. **403 404** P 29 – pop. 1,479 – ✆ 0672 Marlborough.
♦London 77 – ♦Oxford 36 – ♦Southampton 53 – Swindon 9.

🍴 **Raffles,** 1 The Green, SN8 2BW, ✆ 40700 – **A** AE ⑩ VISA
closed lunch Monday and Saturday, Sunday, last 2 weeks August, 25 to 30 December and
Bank Holidays – **M** a la carte 7.85/15.95 **t.** 🍷 4.00.

ALDEBURGH Suffolk **404** Y 27 – pop. 2,711 – ECD : Wednesday – ✆ 072 885.
🛏 at Thorpeness ✆ 2176, N : 2 ½ m.
🛈 Foundation Office, High St. ✆ 3637 (summer only).
♦ London 97 – ♦Ipswich 24 – ♦Norwich 41.

🏨 **Brudenell** (T.H.F.), The Parade, IP15 5BU, ✆ 2071, ≤ – 📲 📺 ⌂wc ☎ 🅿. 🏄. **A** AE ⑩ VISA
M 6.60/9.00 **st.** and a la carte 🍷 2.50 – **47 rm** 31.00/65.00 **st.**

🏨 **Wentworth,** Wentworth Rd, IP15 5BD, ✆ 2312, ≤ – 📺 ⌂wc iwc 🅿. AE ⑩
closed first 2 weeks January – **M** 8.00/10.00 **t.** and a la carte 🍷 2.25 – **33 rm** ☲ 23.60/59.00 **t.** –
SB 45.00/50.00 **st.**

🏨 **Uplands,** Victoria Rd, IP15 5DX, ✆ 2420, ✿ – 📺 ⌂wc & 🅿. **A** AE ⑩ VISA. ✦
M (dinner only and Sunday lunch)/8.00 **t.** (dinner) and a la carte 🍷 3.00 – **20 rm** ☲ 18.50/39.00 **t.**
– SB (winter only) 42.00/47.00 **st.**

ALDERLEY EDGE Cheshire 402 403 404 N 24 — pop. 4 ,272 — ECD : Wednesday — 🕿 0625.
Envir. : Capesthorne Hall★ (18C) *AC*, S : 4 ½ m.

◆ London 187 — Chester 34 — ◆Manchester 14 — ◆Stoke-on-Trent 25.

　🏨　**De Trafford Arms** (De Vere), Congleton Rd, SK9 7AA, ℰ 583881, Group Telex 629462 — 📶
　　📺 🛏wc ☎ 🅿. 🔲 🆎 🆚🆂🅰
　　M (bar lunch Monday to Saturday)/dinner 8.50 **st.** and a la carte 🍴 3.70 — **36 rm**
　　🖵 37.00/47.00 **st.** — SB (weekends only) 52.00/55.00 **st.**

　🍴🍴　**Mandarin,** 2-3 The Parade, SK9 7JX, ℰ 584434, Chinese rest. — 🆎
　　closed Monday except Bank Holidays — **M** 3.50/11.00 **t.** and a la carte 🍴 2.80.

　🍴　**Octobers,** 47 London Rd, SK9 7JT, ℰ 583942, Bistro — 🔲 🆚🆂🅰
　　M (dinner only) 9.40 **t.** and a la carte 🍴 3.25.

　🍴　**Wizard Country,** Macclesfield Rd, Nether Alderley, SK10 4UB, SE : 1½ m. on B 5087
　　ℰ 584000 — 🅿. 🔲 🆎 🅾 🆚🆂🅰
　　closed Sunday dinner and Monday — **M** (dinner only and Sunday lunch)/dinner 8.50
　　t. and a la carte 🍴 3.00.

AUSTIN-ROVER-JAGUAR　London Rd ℰ 582218　　　　　VOLVO　77 London Rd ℰ 583912
VAUXHALL-OPEL　Knutsford Rd ℰ 582691

ALDRIDGE West Midlands 402 403 404 O 26 — pop. 17 ,549 — ECD : Thursday — ✉ Walsall —
🕿 0922 — ◆London 130 — ◆Birmingham 12 — Derby 32 — ◆Leicester 40 — ◆Stoke-on-Trent 38.

　🏨　**Fairlawns,** 178 Little Aston Rd, WS9 0NU, E : 1 m. on A 454 ℰ 55122, Telex 339873 — 📺
　　🛏wc 🎬wc ☎ 🅿. 🏛. 🔲 🆎 🅾 🆚🆂🅰
　　M *(closed Saturday lunch)* 10.50/8.50 **t.** and a la carte 🍴 2.75 — **30 rm** 🖵 32.50/45.00 **st.** — SB
　　(weekends only) 40.00/45.00 **st.**

ALFRISTON East Sussex 404 U 31 — pop. 811 — ECD : Wednesday — ✉ Polegate — 🕿 0323.

◆ London 66 — Eastbourne 9 — Lewes 10 — Newhaven 8.

　🏨　**Star** (T.H.F.), High St., BN26 5TA, ℰ 870495 — 📺 🛏wc ☎ 🅿. 🔲 🆎 🅾 🆚🆂🅰
　　M 8.75/9.45 **st.** and a la carte 🍴 2.70 — 🖵 5.50 — **32 rm** 35.50/50.50 **st.**

　🏨　**Deans Place,** Polegate, BN26 5TW, ℰ 870248, ≤, 🏊 heated, 🎯, park, 🍴🍴 — 🛏wc ☎ 🅿.
　　🔲 🆚🆂🅰. 🛝
　　closed 28 December-mid February — **M** 6.50/9.50 **t.** — **43 rm** 🖵 24.00/50.00 **t.** — SB (spring and
　　winter only) 48.00/56.00 **st.**

　🍴🍴　**Moonrakers,** High St., BN26 5TD, ℰ 870472
　　closed Sunday, Monday and 6 January-13 February — **M** (dinner only) 12.90 **t.** 🍴 2.80.

ALLESLEY West Midlands 403 404 P 26 — see Coventry.

ALLESTREE Derbs. 402 403 404 P 35 — see Derby.

ALNMOUTH Northumb. 401 402 P 17 — pop. 605 — ECD : Wednesday — 🕿 0665.
◆London 314 — ◆Edinburgh 90 — ◆Newcastle-upon-Tyne 37.

　🏠　**Marine House,** 1 Marine Rd, NE66 2RW, ℰ 830349, ≤, 🎯 — 🎬wc
　　closed December and January — **8 rm** 🖵 17.50/30.00 **t.**

ALNWICK Northumb. 401 402 O 17 — pop. 6 ,972 — ECD : Wednesday — 🕿 0665.

See : Castle★★ (Norman) *AC* — Envir. : Dunstanburgh Castle 14C-15C (ruins, coastal setting★) *AC*,
1 ¼ m. walk from Craster, no cars, NE : 7 ½ m. — Warkworth (castle★ 12C) *AC*, SE : 7 m. — Rothbury
(Cragside gardens★ : rhododendrons) *AC*, SW : 12 m.

📍 Foxton Hall, Alnmouth ℰ 0665 (Alnmouth) 830368, SE : 5 m. — 📍 Swansfield Park, Alnwick
ℰ 602632 — 📍 Marine Rd, Alnmouth ℰ 0665 (Alnmouth) 830370, SE : 5 m.

🖿 The Shambles ℰ 603120/603129 (summer only) — ◆ London 320 — ◆Edinburgh 86 — ◆Newcastle-upon-Tyne 34.

　🏨　**White Swan** (Swallow), Bondgate Within, NE66 1TD, ℰ 602109, Group Telex 53168 — 📺
　　🛏wc ☎ 🅿. 🏛. 🔲 🆎 🅾 🆚🆂🅰
　　M 4.65/7.95 **st.** 🍴 3.50 — **41 rm** 🖵 29.00/45.50 **st.** — SB 60.00 **st.**

　🏠　**Hotspur,** Bondgate Without, NE66 1PR, ℰ 602924 — 📺 🛏wc ☎ 🅿. 🔲 🆚🆂🅰
　　M a la carte 5.60/9.65 **t.** 🍴 2.95 — 🖵 3.50 — **28 rm** 16.00/32.00 **st.**

　🏠　**Bondgate House,** Bondgate Without, NE66 1PN, ℰ 602025 — 📺
　　8 rm 🖵 10.00/20.00 **st.**

FORD　Langy St. ℰ 602294

ALRESFORD Hants. 403 404 Q 30 — see New Alresford.

ALSAGER Cheshire 402 403 404 N 24 — pop. 12 ,944 — ✉ Stoke-on-Trent — 🕿 093 63.
◆ London 180 — Chester 36 — ◆ Liverpool 49 — ◆ Manchester 32 — ◆ Stoke-on-Trent 11.

　🏨　**Manor House,** Audley Rd, ST7 2QQ, SE : ½ m. 🔲 🎬wc ☎ 🅿. 🔲 🆎 🅾 🆚🆂🅰. 🛝
　　M (bar lunch Saturday) 7.55 **t.** (lunch)and a la carte 13.70/16.50 **t.** 🍴 3.25 — **8 rm** 🖵 35.00/42.00 **t.**

AUSTIN-ROVER　Lawton Rd ℰ 2146　　　　　　　　FORD　52 Sandbach Rd South ℰ 3241
CITROEN　Rode Heath ℰ 6226

ALSTON Cumbria [401] [402] M 19 – pop. 1 ,968 – ECD : Tuesday – ✆ 0498.
[i] Railway Station ☎ 81696 – ♦ London 309 – ♦Carlisle 28 – ♦Newcastle-upon-Tyne 45.

🏨 **Lovelady Shield Country House** 🪑, Nenthead Rd, CA9 3LF, E : 2 ½ m. on A 689 ☎ 81203, <, 🌳, ✂ – [TV] 🛁wc 🚿wc [P] [AE] [DC]
Mid March-October – **M** (dinner only and Sunday lunch)/dinner 12.00 **t.** 🍷 3.00 – **12 rm** 🛏 20.00/44.00 **t.**

🏨 **Lowbyer Manor,** Hexham Rd, CA9 3JX, ☎ 81230, 🌳 – 🛁wc 🚿wc [P]. [EA] [AE] [DC] [VISA]. 🐕
closed March – **M** (bar lunch Monday to Saturday)/dinner a la carte approx. 8.60 **t.** 🍷 4.25 – **13 rm** 🛏 24.00/35.00 **t.**

🏨 **High Fell Old Farmhouse** 🪑, CA9 3BP, S : 1 ¾ m. on A 686 ☎ 81597, < – [P]. 🐕
M (booking essential) 17.75 **st.** and a la carte 🍷 3.50 – **5 rm** 🛏 16.50/33.00 **st.**

ALTON Hants. [404] R 30 – pop. 14 ,163 – ECD : Wednesday – ✆ 0420.
⛳9 Old Odiham Rd ☎ 82042, N : 2 m. – ♦ London 53 – Reading 24 – ♦Southampton 29 – Winchester 18.

🏨 **Swan** (Anchor), High St., GU34 1AT, ☎ 83777, Group Telex 858875 – [TV] 🛁wc 🚿wc ☏ [P]. 👥. [EA] [AE] [DC] [VISA]
M (carving rest.)(bar lunch Saturday) 7.35 **t.** 🍷 3.00 – **38 rm** 🛏 40.50/52.00 **t.** – SB (weekends only) 55.00 **st.**

🏨 **Grange,** 17 London Rd, Holybourne, GU34 4EG, ☎ 86565, 🌳 – [TV] 🛁wc 🚿wc ☏ [P]. [EA] [AE] [DC] [VISA]
closed Christmas Day – **M** *(closed Sunday and Bank Holidays)* 7.50 **st.** and a la carte 🍷 2.95 – **13 rm** 🛏 32.50/43.00 **st.**

AUSTIN-ROVER, VAUXHALL Butts Rd ☎ 84141
FORD Ackender Rd ☎ 83993
PEUGEOT, TALBOT Four Marks ☎ 62354

ALTRINCHAM Greater Manchester [402] [403] [404] N 23 – pop. 39 ,528 – ECD : Wednesday – ✆ 061 Manchester – ⛳18 Stockport Rd, Timperley ☎ 928 0761, E : 1 m. on A 160 – ⛳18 Dunham Forest, Oldfield Lane ☎ 928 2605, W : 1 m.
♦ London 191 – Chester 30 – ♦Liverpool 30 – ♦Manchester 8.

🏨 **Cresta Court** (Best Western), Church St., WA14 4DP, on A 56 ☎ 928 8017, Telex 667242 – ⇕ [TV] 🛁wc ☎ [P]. 👥. [EA] [AE] [DC] [VISA]
M a la carte 4.85/9.65 **st.** 🍷 3.15 – **139 rm** 🛏 36.00/52.00 **st.** – SB 50.00/61.00 **st.**

🏨 **George and Dragon** (Greenall Whitley), 22 Manchester Rd, WA14 4PH, on A 56 ☎ 928 9933 – ⇕ [TV] 🛁wc ☏ [P]. [EA] [AE] [DC] [VISA]
M *(closed Sunday dinner)* (bar lunch Monday to Saturday)/dinner 9.50 **st.** and a la carte 🍷 4.00 – **47 rm** 🛏 18.50/47.00 **st.**

🏨 Pelican (Greenall Whitley), Manchester Rd, West Timperley, WA14 5NH, N : 2 m. on A 56 ☎ 962 7414 – [TV] 🚿wc ☏ [P]. 🐕 – **50 rm**.

⌂ **Bollin,** 58 Manchester Rd, WA14 4PJ, on A 56 ☎ 928 2390 – [P]
12 rm 🛏 12.65/22.00 **t.**

at Timperley NE : 2 m. by A 560 on B 5165 – ✉ Altrincham – ✆ 061 Manchester :

XXX **Le Bon Viveur** (at Hare and Hounds H.), Wood Lane, WA15 7LY, on A 560 ☎ 904 0266, French rest. – [P]. [EA] [AE] [DC] [VISA]
closed Saturday lunch, Sunday and Bank Holidays – **M** 12.50/22.00 **t.** 🍷 4.00.

at Hale SE : 1 m. on B 5163 – ✉ Altrincham – ✆ 061 Manchester :

🏨 **Ashley** (De Vere), Ashley Rd, WA15 9SF, ☎ 928 3794, Group Telex 669406 – ⇕ [TV] 🛁wc ☏. 👥. [EA] [AE] [DC] [VISA]
M 6.50/8.25 **st.** 🍷 3.75 – **49 rm** 🛏 38.50/50.00 **st.**

XX Evergreen, 169-171 Ashley Rd, WA15 7EV, ☎ 928 1222, Chinese-Cantonese rest.
M (dinner only).

at Halebarns SE : 3 m. on A 538 – ✉ Altrincham – ✆ 061 Manchester :

🏨 Four Seasons, Hale Rd, WA15 8XW, ☎ 904 0301, Telex 665492 – ⇕ [TV] 🛁wc ☎ [P]. 👥
48 rm.

at Bowdon SW : 1 m. – ✉ Altrincham – ✆ 061 Manchester :

🏨 **Bowdon,** Langham Rd, WA14 2HT, ☎ 928 7121, Telex 668208 – [TV] 🛁wc ☏ [P]. 👥. [EA] [AE] [DC] [VISA]
closed 26 December – **M** 8.50 **st.** and a la carte 🍷 2.50 – **41 rm** 🛏 22.00/48.00 **st.** – SB (weekends only) 46.00 **st.**

🏨 **Bowdon Croft** 🪑, Green Walk, WA14 2SN, ☎ 928 1718, <, «Tastefully furnished 19C house » 🌳 – [TV] 🛁wc ☎ [P]. [EA] [AE]. 🐕
M *(closed lunch to non-residents)* (booking essential) 9.50 **s.** 🍷 3.50 – **8 rm** 🛏 32.50/47.50 **s.**

ALFA-ROMEO Money Ash Rd, Hale Bridge ☎ 928 5980
AUSTIN-ROVER 16 Stockport Rd ☎ 941 4111
AUSTIN-ROVER-DAIMLER-JAGUAR Victoria Rd ☎ 928 7124
FORD 44 Hale Rd Bridge ☎ 928 2275
HONDA, SAAB Bancroft Rd, Hale ☎ 980 8004
NISSAN Manchester Rd ☎ 973 3021
SAAB Bancroft Rd, Hale ☎ 980 8004
TOYOTA Mobberley Rd, Ashley ☎ 928 3112
VAUXHALL-OPEL 276-280 Stockport Rd, Timperley ☎ 980 3212
VOLVO Manchester Rd ☎ 928 2384

ALVESTON Avon **403** **404** M 29 – pop. 3 ,154 – ECD : Wednesday – ✉ Bristol – ☎ 0454 Thornbury.

♦London 127 – ♦Bristol 11 – Gloucester 23 – Swindon 42.

🏨 **Post House** (T.H.F.), Thornbury Rd, BS12 2LL, on A 38 ℘ 412521, Telex 444753, ⅃ heated, ㄅ – 📺 ⌷wc ☏ ⓟ ⚎ 🏊 ⚑ ⚐ ⓪ 𝘝𝘐𝘚𝘈
M 7.50/9.75 **st.** and a la carte ⌙ 2.70 – ⤸ 5.50 – **75 rm** 45.00/51.50 **st.**

🏛 **Alveston House,** BS12 2LJ, on A 38 ℘ 415050, Telex 449212, ⚞ – 📺 ⌷wc ⌑wc ⓟ ⚎ 𝘝𝘐𝘚𝘈 ⚒
M 10.50 **st.** and a la carte ⌙ 3.55 – **17 rm** ⤸ 34.50/42.50 **st.** – SB (weekends only) 57.00 **st.**

AMBLESIDE Cumbria **402** L 20 – pop. 2 ,689 – ECD : Thursday – ☎ 0966.

Envir. : Tarn Hows** (lake) SW : 6 m. by A 593 AY – Langdale Valley** W : 7 m. by B 5343 AY.

🛈 Old Courthouse, Church St. ℘ 33084 and 32582 (summer only).

♦London 278 – ♦Carlisle 47 – Kendal 14.

Plan opposite

🏨 **Kirkstone Foot Country House** ⚘, Kirkstone Pass Rd, LA22 9EH, NE : ¼ m. ℘ 32232, ⚞
 – ⌷wc ⌑wc ⓟ ⚎ ⚑ ⓪ 𝘝𝘐𝘚𝘈   AZ **c**
7 March-9 October – **M** (dinner only) 11.50 **t.** ⌙ 3.50 – **15 rm** ⤸ (dinner included) 26.50/60.00 **t.**

⌂ **Elder Grove,** Lake Rd, LA22 0DB, ℘ 32504 – 📺 ⌷wc ⓟ ⚑ 𝘝𝘐𝘚𝘈   AZ **a**
March-October – **14 rm** ⤸ 17.50/33.00 **t.**

at Waterhead S : 1 m. on A 591 – ✉ ☎ 0966 Ambleside :

🏨 **Regent,** LA22 0ES, ℘ 32254, ⅃ – 📺 ⌷wc ⌑wc ☏ ⓟ ⚑ ⚐ ⓪ 𝘝𝘐𝘚𝘈   BY **e**
closed January – **M** 7.50/13.50 **t.** and a la carte ⌙ 2.75 – **20 rm** ⤸ 35.00/60.00 **t.** – SB
(November-March) 49.95/66.00 **st.**

🏛 **Wateredge,** Borrans Rd, LA22 0EP, ℘ 32332, ≼, « Part 17C Fishermans cottages, lakeside
setting », ⚞ – ⌷wc ⌑wc ⓟ ⚑ 𝘝𝘐𝘚𝘈   BY **o**
closed December-7 February – **M** (bar lunch residents only)/dinner 12.90 **t.** ⌙ 2.80 – **20 rm**
⤸ 16.00/64.00 **t.** – SB (except summer) 52.00/66.00 **st.**

at Rothay Bridge S : ½ m. on A 593 – ✉ ☎ 0966 Ambleside :

🏨 **Rothay Manor,** LA22 0EH, ℘ 33605, ≼, « Elegant Regency interior », ⚞ – 📺 ⌷wc ☏ ⚒
ⓟ ⚑ ⓪ 𝘝𝘐𝘚𝘈 ⚒   BY **r**
closed 5 January-13 February – **M** (buffet lunch Monday to Saturday)/dinner 16.00 **t.** ⌙ 3.00 –
16 rm ⤸ 44.00/70.00 **t.,** **2 suites** 81.00/85.00 **t.** – SB (weekdays only)(November-March)
72.00/81.00 **st.**

🏛 **Riverside H. and Lodge** ⚘, under Loughrigg, LA22 9LJ, ℘ 32395, ⚞ – 📺 ⌷wc ⌑wc
ⓟ ⚑ 𝘝𝘐𝘚𝘈 ⚒   BY **s**
M (bar lunch)/dinner 10.00 **t.** ⌙ 3.25 – **15 rm** ⤸ (dinner included) 38.50/57.00 **t.** –
(November-March) 42.00/57.00 **st.**

⌂ **Borrans Park,** Borrans Rd, LA22 0EN, ℘ 33454, ⚞ – 📺 ⌷wc ⌑wc ⚒ ⓟ ⚑ 𝘝𝘐𝘚𝘈 ⚒
closed 20 to 29 December – **13 rm** ⤸ 14.50/40.00 **st.**   BY **a**

at Clappersgate W : 1 m. on A 593 – ✉ ☎ 0966 Ambleside :

🏛 **Nanny Brow Country House** ⚘, LA23 9NF, ℘ 32036, ≼ Brathay Valley and Langdale,
⚑, ⚞ – 📺 ⌷wc ⌑wc ⓟ ⚑ 𝘝𝘐𝘚𝘈   BY **u**
M (dinner only) 12.50 **st.** ⌙ 2.60 – **19 rm** ⤸ 31.00/45.00 **st.,** **3 suites** 50.00/60.00 **st.** – SB
52.00/75.00 **st.**

at Skelwith Bridge W : 2 ½ m. on A 593 – ✉ ☎ 0966 Ambleside :

🏛 **Skelwith Bridge,** LA22 9NJ, ℘ 32115, ≼, ⚞ – ⌷wc ⓟ ⚑ 𝘝𝘐𝘚𝘈   AY **v**
M (bar lunch Monday to Saturday)/dinner 11.50 **st.** ⌙ 3.00 – **24 rm** ⤸ 14.50/48.00 **st.** – SB
(weekdays only)(November-July) 42.00/56.00 **st.**

at Little Langdale W : 4 ½ m. by A 593 – ✉ ☎ 096 67 Langdale :

🏯 **Three Shires Inn** ⚘, LA22 9NZ, ℘ 215, ≼, ⚞ – ⓟ ⚒   AY **z**
closed mid December-mid January – **M** (bar lunch)/dinner 11.00 **st.** ⌙ 2.80 – **10 rm**
⤸ 15.50/35.00 **st.** – SB (weekdays only)(November-March) 44.00/50.00 **st.**

at Chapel Stile W : 5 m. on B 5343 – ✉ Chapel Stile – ☎ 096 67 Langdale :

🏨 **Pillar** ⚘, Great Langdale, LA22 9JB, ℘ 302, Telex 65188, ⅃, ⚑, park, squash – ▤ rest 📺
☏ ⓟ ⚎ ⚑ ⚐ ⓪ 𝘝𝘐𝘚𝘈 ⚒   AY **c**
M (bar lunch Monday to Saturday)/dinner 15.00 **t.** ⌙ 5.75 – **36 rm** ⤸ 53.00/65.00 **t.,** **18 suites**
77.00 **t.** – SB 79.00/89.00 **st.**

🏛 **Langdales** ⚘, Great Langdale, LA22 9JF, ℘ 253, ⚑, ⚞ – ⌷wc ⌑wc ⓟ   AY **a**
closed 6 January-6 February – **M** (bar lunch Monday to Saturday)/dinner 10.00 **t.** and a la carte
⌙ 3.00 – **20 rm** ⤸ 19.00/44.00 **t.** – SB (winter only) 56.00/58.00 **t.**

at Rydal NW : 1 ½ m. on A 591 – ✉ ☎ 0966 Ambleside :

🏯 **Rydal Lodge,** LA22 9LR, ℘ 33208, ⚞ – ⓟ ⚑ 𝘝𝘐𝘚𝘈   BY **c**
closed January – **8 rm** ⤸ 17.00/39.70 **t.**

FORD   Millans Park ℘ 33033

ZOUCH Leics. **402** **403** **404** P 25 – pop. 9,987 – ECD : Wednesday – © 0530.
urch St. ℰ 415603 (summer only).
Birmingham 29 – ◆Leicester 18 – ◆Nottingham 22.

Crest (Crest), Station Rd, LE6 5GP, ℰ 412833, Group Telex 341629, 🚗 – TV 🛏wc
🅿 🖭 🖳 AE 🆅
unch Saturday) 7.95/10.95 **st.** and a la carte ⏐ 3.00 – ☲ 5.50 – **31 rm** 39.50/49.00 **st.** –
ekends only) 55.00 **st.**

R, SHERPA Bath St. ℰ 412770

Kent **404** W 30 – pop. 45,198 – ECD : Wednesday – © 0233.
field (St. Margaret's Church : memorial tomb★ 17C) NW : 3 m. – Lenham (St. Mary's
dwork★) NW : 9 ½ m.
Kiosk, High St. ℰ 37311 ext 316.
Canterbury 14 – ◆Dover 24 – Hastings 30 – Maidstone 19.

well Manor ৯, Eastwell Park, TN25 4HR, N : 3 m. by A 28 on A 251 ℰ 35751, Telex
1, ≼, « Reconstructed period mansion in formal gardens », ⬡, park, 🎾 – 🖭 TV ☎ 🖳
50/17.00 **st.** and a la carte ⏐ 4.25 – **24 rm** ☲ 48.00/105.00 **st.**, **3 suites** 108.00/130.00 **st.** –
ot weekends) (winter only) 102.00 **st.**

ennington NE : 2 m. on A 28 – ⊠ © 0233 Ashford :

arpoint (Best Western), Canterbury Rd, TN24 9QR, ℰ 36863, 🚗 – TV 🛏wc 🛏wc ☎
🖭 🖳 AE 🆅
la carte 7.70/11.00 **t.** ⏐ 2.50 – **37 rm** ☲ 24.00/45.00 **st.** – SB (weekends only) 44.00/49.00 **st.**

wnsview, Willesborough Rd, TN24 9QP, ℰ 21953, 🚗 – TV 🛏wc 🅿 🖳 🆅
dinner only) 6.50 **st.** and a la carte – **16 rm** ☲ 15.20/30.60 **st.** – SB (except Christmas-New
r and Bank Holidays) 34.60/39.60 **st.**

Mersham SE : 3 m. by A 292 off A 20 – ⊠ Ashford – © 023 372 Aldington :

one Green Hall ৯ with rm, TN25 7HE, S : 1 ¼ m. via Church Rd ℰ 418, « Tastefully
corated Queen Anne house », 🚗, park, 🎾 – 🖭 🛏wc 🅿. – **M** (dinner only and Sunday lunch) (booking essential) 11.00/13.50 **t.** ⏐ 3.00
3 **rm** ☲ 30.00/60.00 **st.**

OVER 20-46 New St. ℰ 20334
Beaver Rd ℰ 35735
ation Rd ℰ 23451
Maidstone Rd ℰ 34177

SKODA, FIAT Chart Rd ℰ 20624
VAUXHALL Faversham Rd ℰ 23173
VOLVO Chart Rd ℰ 35661

RD Surrey **404** S 29 – ECD : Wednesday – © 078 42.
21 – Reading 27.

Terrazza, 45 Church Rd, TW15 2TY, ℰ 44887, Italian rest. – 🖫. 🖳 AE ① 🆅
closed Saturday lunch, Sunday and Bank Holidays – **M** 9.75 **t.** and a la carte 14.15/21.40 **t.**

-ROVER 445 Staines Rd West ℰ 43591
N 594 London Rd ℰ 52125

VAUXHALL Staines Rd ℰ 41901
VW 554 London Rd ℰ 50051

ORD-IN-THE-WATER Derbs – see Bakewell.

NGTON West Sussex **404** S 31 – pop. 1,728 – ECD : Wednesday – ⊠ Pulborough –

50 – ◆Brighton 20 – Worthing 9.

Mill House ৯, Mill Lane, RH20 3BZ, ℰ 892426, 🚗 – TV 🛏wc 🛏wc 🅿. 🖳 AE ① 🆅
M (closed Sunday dinner and Bank Holiday Monday to non-residents) (bar lunch Monday to
Saturday residents only)/dinner 7.50 **t.** and a la carte ⏐ 2.50 – ☲ 4.00 – **10 rm** 17.00/36.00 **t.** –
SB (weekends only) 46.00/49.00 **st.**

EAD Surrey **404** T 30 – © 037 22.
19 – Guildford 15.

Snooty Fox, 21 The Street, KT21 1AA, ℰ 76606 – 🖳 AE ① 🆅
closed Saturday lunch and Sunday – **M** 7.50/12.95 **st.** and a la carte ⏐ 3.95.

N-UNDER-LYNE Greater Manchester **402** **403** **404** N 23 – pop. 43,605 – ECD : Tuesday –
Manchester 7.
209 – ◆Leeds 40 – ◆Manchester 7 – ◆Sheffield 34.

ork House, York Pl., off Richmond St., OL6 7TT, ℰ 330 5899 – TV 🛏wc 🛏wc 🅿 🖳 AE
🆅
closed Bank Holidays – **M** (closed Sunday to non-residents) a la carte 6.90/13.85 **t.** ⏐ 2.50 –
rm ☲ 25.00/40.00 **st.** – SB (weekends only) 40.00/45.00 **st.**

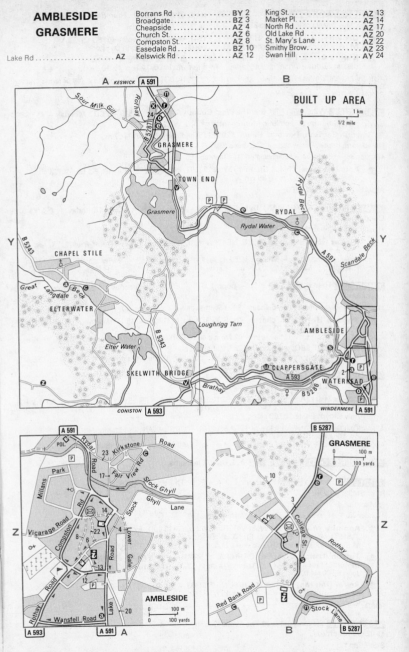

AMBLESIDE
GRASMERE

Lake Rd .... AZ

Borrans Rd .... BY 2
Broadgate .... BZ 3
Cheapside .... AZ 4
Church St. .... AZ 6
Compston St. .... AZ 8
Easedale Rd .... BZ 10
Kelswick Rd .... AZ 12

King St. .... AZ 13
Market Pl. .... AZ 14
North Rd .... AZ 17
Old Lake Rd .... AZ 20
St. Mary's Lane .... AZ 22
Smithy Brow .... AZ 23
Swan Hill .... AY 24

BUILT UP AREA

GRASMERE

AMBLESIDE

Town plans : roads most used by traffic and those on which guide listed hotels
and restaurants stand are fully drawn ; the beginning only of
lesser roads is indicated.

AMERSHAM (Old Town) Bucks. **404** S 28 – pop. 21,326 – ECD : Thursday – ☎ 024 03.
◆London 29 – Aylesbury 16 – ◆Oxford 33.

🏰 **Crown** (T.H.F.), High St., HP7 0DH, ℰ 21541, 🗜 – 📺 ⌂wc 🅿 🖪 AE ⑩ VISA
M 5.95/10.50 **st.** and a la carte ᐀ 2.70 – ☲ 5.00 – **19 rm** 41.00/51.00 **st.**

XX **King's Arms**, High St., HP7 0DJ, ℰ 6333 – 🅿 🖪 AE ⑩ VISA
closed Sunday dinner and Monday – **M** a la carte 10.05/14.25 **t.** ᐀ 3.10.

AUSTIN-ROVER-DAIMLER-JAGUAR London Rd ℰ 5911   TALBOT 4/8 White Lion Rd ℰ 024 04 (Little Chalfont) 4666
RENAULT The Broadway ℰ 4656

AMESBURY Wilts. **403 404** O 30 The West Country G. – pop. 5,519 – ECD : Monday – ☎ 0980.
Envir. : Stonehenge (Megalithic Monument)★★★ AC, W : 2 m.
🇮🇸 Tidworth Garrison, Tidworth, Hants. ℰ 0980 (Stonehenge) 42301 N : 7 m.
🛈 Redworth House, Flower Lane ℰ 22833 and 23255.
◆London 88 – ◆Bristol 52 – ◆Southampton 31 – Taunton 61.

🏛 **Antrobus Arms**, Church St., SP4 7EY, ℰ 23163, 🗜 – 📺 ⌂wc 🅿 🖪 AE ⑩ VISA
closed Christmas Day – **20 rm**

RENAULT High St. ℰ 22525

AMMANFORD (RHYDAMAN) Dyfed **403** I 28 – pop. 5,708 – ECD : Thursday – ✉ ☎ 0269 Llandybie.
◆London 208 – Carmarthen 22 – ◆Swansea 19.

🏛 **Mill at Glynhir** 🐦, SA18 2TE, NE : 3 ¼ m. by A 483 and Glynhir Rd ℰ 850672, 🗜, 🗜 – 📺 ⌂wc ⌂wc 🅿
closed Christmas – **M** 7.50/10.50 **t.** and a la carte ᐀ 2.50 – **9 rm** ☲ 23.00/46.00 **t.** – SB (September-May) 48.00/55.00 **st.**

AMPFIELD Hants. **403 404** P 30 – pop. 1,675 – ECD : Wednesday – ✉ Romsey – ☎ 0794 Braishfield.
◆London 79 – Bournemouth 31 – Salisbury 19 – ◆Southampton 11 – Winchester 7.

🏛 **Potters Heron**, Winchester Rd, SO5 9ZF, on A 31 ℰ 042 15 (Chandlers Ford) 66611 – 📺 ⌂wc ⌂wc 🅿 🛦 🖪 AE VISA 🗜 –
M 7.00/10.50 **t.** and a la carte – **42 rm** ☲ 48.00/60.00 **t.** – SB (weekends only) 50.00/70.00 **st.**

XX **Keats**, SO5 9BQ, on A 31 ℰ 68252, Italian rest. – 🅿 🖪 AE ⑩ VISA
closed Sunday dinner and Monday – **M** 5.90 **t.** (lunch)/dinner a la carte 6.70/11.90 **t.** ᐀ 2.55.

ANDOVER Hants. **403 404** P 30 – pop. 30,632 – ECD : Wednesday – ☎ 0264.
◆London 74 – Bath 53 – Salisbury 17 – Winchester 11.

🏛 **White Hart** (Anchor), Bridge St., SP10 1BH, ℰ 52266 – 📺 ⌂wc ⌂wc 🛦 🅿 🖪 AE ⑩ VISA
M buffet lunch/dinner a la carte 9.20/13.50 **st.** ᐀ 3.00 – **21 rm** ☲ 40.50/53.00 **st.** – SB (weekends only except Easter) 53.00 **st.**

ALFA-ROMEO, FIAT, LANCIA Salisbury Rd ℰ 61166   AUSTIN-ROVER 94 Charlton Rd ℰ 3603
AUDI, VW 50 London St. ℰ 52839   FORD West St. ℰ 51811
AUSTIN-ROVER 278 Weyhill Rd ℰ 3781   VAUXHALL Newbury Rd ℰ 4233

ANDOVERSFORD Glos. **403 404** O 28 – see Cheltenham.

APPLEBY Cumbria **402** M 20 – pop. 2,344 – ECD : Thursday – ☎ 0930.
🇮🇸 ℰ 51432, S : 2 m.
🛈 Moot Hall, Boroughgate ℰ 51177.
◆London 285 – ◆Carlisle 33 – Kendal 24 – ◆Middlesbrough 58.

🏛 **Appleby Manor** (Best Western), Roman Rd, CA16 6JD, E : ½ m. by B 6542 via Station Rd ℰ 51571, ≤, 🗜 – 📺 ⌂wc ⌂wc 🅿 🖪 AE VISA
M (bar lunch)/dinner 10.00 **st.** and a la carte – **19 rm** ☲ 24.00/47.00 **st.** – SB 48.00/74.00 **st.**

🏛 **Tufton Arms**, Market Sq., CA16 6XA, ℰ 51593 – ⌂wc 🅿 🖪 🗜 VISA
M (buffet lunch)/dinner 7.25 **t.** and a la carte ᐀ 2.75 – **18 rm** ☲ 16.50/32.50 **t.** – SB (November-July) 42.00/44.00 **t.**

🏠 **Royal Oak Inn**, Bongate, CA16 6UN, ℰ 51463 – 📺 ⌂wc 🅿 🖪 VISA
M a la carte 5.85/10.25 **t.** ᐀ 13.00/32.00 **t.**

FORD The Sands ℰ 51133   PEUGEOT-TALBOT ℰ 61435

APPLEDORE Devon **403** H 30 The West Country G. – pop. 2,180 – ECD : Wednesday – ✉ ☎ 023 72 Bideford.
See : Site★.
◆London 235 – Bideford 4 – Exeter 47 – ◆Plymouth 62.

🏠 **Seagate**, The Quay, EX39 1QS, ℰ 72589 – 📺 ⌂wc 🖪 AE ⑩ VISA
M (bar lunch)/dinner 6.75 **t.** and a la carte ᐀ 2.80 – **9 rm** ☲ 20.00/40.00 **t.**

APPLETON-LE-MOORS North Yorks. – pop. 166 – ☎ 075
◆London 245 – ◆Middlesbrough 37 – ◆Scarborough 27 – York 33.

🏛 **Dweldapilton Hall** 🐦, YO6 6TF, ℰ 227, 🗜 – 🗐 📺 🖪
closed January – **M** (bar lunch)/dinner 8.50 **t.** and a la SB (October-April) 46.00 **st.**

ARDSLEY South Yorks. – see Barnsley.

ARMATHWAITE Cumbria **401 402** L 19 – ✉ Carlisle – ☎ 069 9
◆London 305 – ◆Carlisle 10 – Penrith 12.

🏠 **Fox and Pheasant**, CA4 9PY, ℰ 400, ≤ – 📺 ⌂wc 🅿
M (bar lunch)/dinner 7.75 **st.** and a la carte ᐀ 1.80 – **7 rm** ☲

ARMITAGE Staffs. **402 403 404** O 25 – see Rugeley.

ARNCLIFFE North Yorks. **402** N 21 – pop. 67 – ✉ Skipton – ☎ 0
◆London 232 – Kendal 41 – ◆Leeds 41 – Preston 50 – York 52.

🏠 **Amerdale House** 🐦, BD23 5QE, ℰ 250, ≤, 🗜 – ⌂wc 🅿 🖪
April-October – **M** (bar lunch)/dinner 10.00 **st.** ᐀ 3.00 – **9** 44.00/50.00 **st.**

ARUNDEL West Sussex **404** S 31 – pop. 2,595 – ECD : Wednesday
See : Castle★ (keep 12C, ≤★ 119 steps, State apartments★) AC – St. N Fitzalan chapel★ 14C).
Envir. : Bignor (Roman Villa : mosaics★★ AC) NW : 7 m.
🛈 61 High St. ℰ 882268.
◆London 58 – ◆Brighton 21 – ◆Southampton 41 – Worthing 9.

🏛 **Norfolk Arms**, 22 High St., BN18 9AD, ℰ 882101 – 📺 ⌂wc 🐦 🅿
M 6.45/9.45 **t.** and a la carte – **34 rm** ☲ 26.00/42.00 **st.** – SB 52.00/68.

🏠 **Swan**, 29 High St., BN18 9AG, ℰ 882314 – ⌂wc ⌂wc. 🖪 AE ⑩ V
M (grill rest. only) a la carte 3.65/9.15 **t.** ᐀ 2.50 – **10 rm** ☲ 25.00/30.00 except Christmas) 42.00/65.00 **st.**

at Burpham NE : 3 m. by A 27 – ✉ 0903 Arundel :

🏠 **Burpham Country** 🐦, Old Down, BN18 9RJ, ℰ 882160, ≤, 🗜 – 🅿
6 rm ☲ 15.00/35.00 **t.**

at Crossbush E : 1 m. on A 27 – ✉ 0903 Arundel :

🏛 **Howards**, BN18 9PQ, ℰ 882655 – 📺 ⌂wc ☎ 🅿 🖪 AE ⑩ VISA 🗜
closed Christmas Day – **M** (carving rest.) 6.50/7.50 **t.** – **9 rm** ☲ 28.00/38.0 only) 47.50/61.00 **st.**

at Walberton W : 3 m. by A 27 on B 2132 – ✉ Arundel – ☎ 0243 Yapton

🏛 **Avisford Park**, Yapton Lane, BN18 0LS, ℰ 551215, ≤, 🗜 heated, 🗜, 🗜 – 📺 ⌂wc ☎ 🅿 🛦 🖪 VISA
M (buffet lunch)/dinner 12.75 **st.** and a la carte ᐀ 2.75 – **84 rm** ☲ 38.5 64.00/70.00 **st.** – SB (weekends only) 75.00/85.00 **st.**

ASCOT Berks. **404** R 29 – pop. 17,930 (inc. Sunningdale) – ECD : Wednesda
🇮🇸 Downshire, Easthampstead Park ℰ 0344 (Bracknell) 424066, W : 4 m.
◆London 36 – Reading 15.

🏛 **Berystede** (T.H.F.), Bagshot Rd, Sunninghill, SL5 9JH, S : 1 ¼ m. on A 847017, 🗜 heated, 🗜 – 📺 ⌂wc 🅿 🖪 AE ⑩ VISA
M 8.95/12.50 **st.** and a la carte ᐀ 2.70 – ☲ 5.00 – **88 rm** 47.50/57.00 **st.**

AUSTIN-ROVER Ascot Motor Works ℰ 20324   CITROEN Lyndhurst Rd, Sou

ASHBURTON Devon **403** I 32 The West Country G. – pop. 3,610 – ECD : W
◆London 220 – Exeter 20 – ◆Plymouth 23.

🏛 **Holne Chase** 🐦, Two Bridges Rd, TQ13 7NS, NW : 3 m. on B 335 gate) 471, ≤, 🗜, 🗜, park – ⌂wc ⌂wc 🐦 🅿 🖪 AE ⑩ VISA
M 7.75/12.50 **st.** ᐀ 2.50 – **15 rm** ☲ 18.00/47.50 **st.** – SB (except Chri 47.00/55.00 **st.**

🏛 **Dartmoor Motel**, Peartree Cross, TQ13 7JW, W : ½ m. ℰ 52232 – 🖪 VISA, 🗜
closed 25 and 26 December – **M** 5.00/5.50 **t.** and a la carte – **22 rm** (October-April except Christmas) 38.85/40.85 **st.**

XX **Country Garden**, 22 East St., TQ13 7AZ, ℰ 53431
M (dinner only).

COLT 6 East St. ℰ 52215

ASHBY DE ...
🇮🇸 13-15 Lower ...
◆London 119 ...
🏛 Roya...
⌂wc ...
M (ba...
SB (w...
AUSTIN-ROV...

ASHFORD...
Envir. : Hot...
Church : wo...
🛈 Informatio...
◆London 56 ...
🏛 Eas...
9662...
🅿 ...
M (b...
SB ...
at ...
🏛 Sp...
🅿 ...
M ...
🏠 De...
Ye...
a...
XX S...
c...
AUSTI...
CITROE...
FORD...
RENAU...

ASHP...
◆Lond...
XX ...
c...
AUSTI...
CITRO...

ASHF...
ASHI...
☎ 0903 ...
◆Londo...
🏛 ...

ASHI...
☎ 06...
◆London...
🏛 ...
70

ASKHAM Cumbria 401 402 L 20 – pop. 387 – ECD : Thursday – ✉ Penrith – ☎ 093 12 Hackthorpe.

See : Lowther (Wildlife Park★) *AC*.

♦London 288 – ♦Carlisle 23 – Kendal 28.

🏠 **Queen's Head Inn**, CA10 2PF, ✆ 225, « Miniature model railway » – **P**. ✿
   M (bar lunch)/dinner 12.50 **t**. – **6 rm** ⌿ 17.50/35.00 **st**.

ASKRIGG North Yorks. 402 N 21 – pop. 404 – ✉ Leyburn – ☎ 0969 Wensleydale.

♦London 251 – Kendal 32 – ♦Leeds 70 – York 63.

🏠 **King's Arms**, Market Sq., DL8 3HQ, ✆ 50258 – 📺 ⇔wc 🛢wc. ◪ *VISA*
   M (bar lunch)/dinner 9.25 **t**. ⚬ 2.75 – **10 rm** ⌿ 21.50/41.00 **t**. – SB (except July-August) 42.00/52.00 **st**.

✕ **Rowan Tree**, DL8 3HT, ✆ 50536
   closed Tuesday and Wednesday September-December, Sunday, Monday, January and February
   – **M** (dinner only)(booking essential) 10.95 **t**.

ASPLEY GUISE Beds. 404 S 27 – pop. 2,296 – ✉ ☎ 0908 Milton Keynes.

♦London 50 – Bedford 12 – Luton 15 – Northampton 22.

🏛 **Holt**, The Square, MK17 8DW, ✆ 583652, 🌸 – 📺 ⇔wc **P**. ◪ 🄰🄴 ⓪ *VISA*. ✿
   M 11.95 **t**. and a la carte ⚬ 3.00 – **19 rm** ⌿ 40.00/60.00 **st**. – SB (weekends only) 30.00/40.00 **st**.

ASTON CLINTON Bucks. 404 R 28 – pop. 3,671 – ECD : Wednesday – ✉ ☎ 0296 Aylesbury.

♦London 42 – Aylesbury 4 – ♦Oxford 26.

🏯 **Bell Inn**, HP22 5HP, ✆ 630252, Telex 83252, « Courtyard and gardens » – ▤ rest 📺 ☎ **P**.
   ⚬. ◪ *VISA*
   M (closed Sunday dinner and Monday to non-residents) a la carte 26.00/40.00 **st**. ⚬ 3.00 –
   21 rm 44.00/77.00 **st**., **5 suites** 77.00/86.00 **st**.

ATTLEBOROUGH Norfolk 404 X 26 – pop. 6,322 – ECD : Wednesday – ☎ 0953.

♦London 94 – ♦Cambridge 47 – ♦Norwich 15.

🏠 **Sherbourne**, Norwich Rd, NR17 2JX, NE : ½ m. ✆ 452129, 🌸 – 📺 ⇔wc 🛢 **P**. ◪ 🄰🄴 ⓪
   VISA. ✿
   M (closed Sunday and Monday to non-residents) (buffet lunch)/dinner 12.50 **t**. and a la carte
   ⚬ 2.80 – **5 rm** ⌿ 18.00/42.00 **t**. – SB (except Christmas and New Year) 42.00/55.00 **st**.

🏠 **Griffin**, Church St., NR17 2AH, ✆ 452149 – 📺 ✿
   M (closed Sunday dinner) (bar lunch Monday to Saturday)/dinner 8.50 **st**. and a la carte ⚬ 2.75
   – **7 rm** ⌿ 14.00/22.00 **st**.

AUSTWICK North Yorks. 402 M 21 – pop. 478 – ✉ Lancaster (Lancs.) – ☎ 046 85 Clapham.

♦London 237 – Kendal 26 – Lancaster 23 – ♦Leeds 47.

🏠 **Traddock** ⟨S⟩, LA2 8BY, ✆ 224, 🌸 – ⇔wc 🛢wc **P**. ✿
   Easter-October – **M** (dinner only)(booking essential) 7.50 **t**. – **12 rm** ⌿ 14.50/30.00 **t**.

AVENING Glos. 403 404 N 28 – see Tetbury.

AVON Hants. – see Ringwood.

AXBRIDGE Somerset 403 L 30 The West Country G. – pop. 1,724 – ECD : Wednesday – ☎ 0934.

See : Site★★ – King John's Hunting Lodge★*AC* – St. John the Baptist Church★.

Envir. : The Cheddar Gorge★★ (The Gorge★★ - Jacob's Ladder⋲★*AC* - The Caves★★*AC*) –
St. Andrews Church★, SE : 1 ½ m.

♦London 142 – ♦Bristol 17 – Taunton 31 – Weston-Super-Mare 10.

✕ **Oak House** with rm, The Square, BS26 2AP, ✆ 732444 – 📺 ⇔wc. ◪ 🄰🄴 ⓪ *VISA* ✿
   M (closed Sunday dinner to non-residents) 10.95 **t**. and a la carte ⚬ 3.80 – **11 rm**
   ⌿ 25.00/39.50 **t**. – SB (weekends only) 56.00 **st**.

AXMINSTER Devon 403 L 31 – pop. 4,457 – ECD : Wednesday – ☎ 0297.

🛈 Old Court House, Church St. ✆ 34386 (summer only).

♦London 156 – Exeter 27 – Lyme Regis 5.5 – Taunton 22 – Yeovil 24.

🏠 **Woodbury Park Country House** ⟨S⟩, Woodbury Cross, EX13 5TL, SE :1½ m. on A 35
   ✆ 33010, ⋲, ◲ heated, 🌸, park – ⇔wc 🛢 **P**. ◪ 🄰🄴 ⓪ *VISA*
   M (bar lunch)/dinner 4.50 **t**. and a la carte 5.75/10.35 **t**. – **8 rm** ⌿ 21.00/32.00 **t**.

   at Hawkchurch NE : 4 ½ m. by A 35 off B 3165 – ✉ Axminster – ☎ 029 77 Hawkchurch :

🏛 **Fairwater Head** ⟨S⟩, EX13 5TX, S : ¾ m. ✆ 349, ⋲ Axe Vale, 🌸 – ⇔wc **P**. ◪ ⓪ *VISA*. ✿
   closed January-mid March – **M** (bar lunch)/dinner 9.50 **st**. ⚬ 2.70 – **14 rm** ⌿ 25.00/45.00 **st**. –
   SB 53.00/58.00 **st**.

AYLESBURY Bucks. **404** R 28 – pop. 51,999 – ECD : Thursday – ✆ 0296.

Envir. : Waddesdon Manor (Rothschild Collection★★★) *AC*, NW : 5 ½ m. – Ascott House★★ (Rothschild Collection★★) and gardens★ *AC*, NE : 8 ½ m. – Stewkley (St. Michael's Church★ 12C) NE : 12 m.

🏕 Weston Turville, New Rd ♒ 24084, SE : 2 ½ m.

🛈 County Hall, Walton St. ♒ 5000.

◆London 46 – ◆Birmingham 72 – Northampton 37 – ◆Oxford 22.

 🏨 **Bell** (T.H.F.), Market Sq., HP20 1TX, ♒ 82141 – 📺 🛏wc ☎. 🔂 🄰🄴 ⓞ 𝘝𝘐𝘚𝘈
  M 7.95/9.50 **st.** and a la carte ⓘ 2.70 – 🖃 5.50 – **17 rm** 35.50/45.00 **st.**

 ✕ **Pebbles,** 1 Pebble Lane, HP20 2JH, ♒ 86622 – 🔂 🄰🄴 𝘝𝘐𝘚𝘈
  closed Saturday lunch, Sunday and 25-26 December – **M** 10.00/18.00 **st.** and a la carte ⓘ 3.00.

 at Weston Turville SE : 3 ½ m. by A 413 on B 4544 – ✉ Aylesbury – ✆ 029 661 Stoke Mandeville :

 🏨 **Five Bells,** 40 Main St., HP22 5RW, ♒ 3131 – 📺 🛏wc ☎ ⓟ. 🔂 ⓞ 𝘝𝘐𝘚𝘈. 🛱
  M 12.00 **t.** and a la carte ⓘ 2.35 – **17 rm** 🖃 30.00/45.00 **t.** – SB (weekends only) 45.00/50.00 **st.**

 ✕✕ **Chequers Inn,** Church Lane, by Bate's Lane, ♒ 3298 – ⓟ. 🔂 🄰🄴 ⓞ 𝘝𝘐𝘚𝘈
  closed Saturday lunch, Sunday dinner and Bank Holidays – **M** 9.00 **t.** (lunch)/dinner a la carte approx. 13.25 **t.**

 at Stoke Mandeville S : 3 ¼ m. by A 413 on A 4010 – ✉ Aylesbury – ✆ 029 661 Stoke Mandeville :

 🏨 **Belmore,** Risborough Rd, HP22 5UT, ♒ 2258, ⌁ heated, 🐎 – 📺 🛏wc ⊛ ₺ ⓟ. 🔂 🄰🄴 ⓞ 𝘝𝘐𝘚𝘈. 🛱
  closed 9 days at Christmas – **M** (dinner only) (residents only) 5.90 **s.** ⓘ 2.50 – 🖃 3.10 – **15 rm** 22.00/36.00 **s.**

AUSTIN-ROVER-DAIMLER-JAGUAR Buckingham Rd ♒ 84071
MERCEDES-BENZ Bicester Rd ♒ 81641
RENAULT Little Kimble ♒ 029 661 (Stoke Mandeville) 2239

VAUXHALL-OPEL 143 Cambridge St. ♒ 82321
VOLVO Stocklake ♒ 35331

BABBACOMBE Devon **403** J 32 – see Torquay.

BACKFORD CROSS Cheshire **402** **403** L 24 – see Chester.

BADMINTON Avon **403** **404** N 29 The West Country G. – pop. 283 – ✆ 045 423 Didmarton.

See : Badminton House★ *AC*.

◆London 114 – ◆Bristol 19 – Gloucester 26 – Swindon 33.

 🏨 **Petty France,** GL9 1AF, NW : 3 m. on A 46 ♒ 361, 🐎 – 📺 🛏wc 🛏wc ⊛ ⓟ. 🔂 🄰🄴 ⓞ 𝘝𝘐𝘚𝘈
  M 10.50 **t.** and a la carte ⓘ 3.40 – 🖃 3.75 – **16 rm** 26.50/50.00 **st.** – SB (except Christmas) 60.00 **st.**

 ✕✕✕ **Bodkin House,** Petty France, GL9 1AF, NW : 3 m. on A 46 ♒ 310, « Tastefully furnished former coaching inn » – ⓟ. 🔂 🄰🄴 𝘝𝘐𝘚𝘈
  closed Sunday dinner, Monday and first 2 weeks August – **M** a la carte 10.60/17.40 **t.** ⓘ 2.45.

BAE COLWYN = Colwyn Bay.

BAGSHOT Surrey **404** R 29 – pop. 4,239 – ECD : Wednesday – ✆ 0276.

◆London 37 – Reading 17 – ◆Southampton 49.

 🏨🏨 **Pennyhill Park** 🍴, College Ride, GU19 5ET, off A 30 ♒ 71774, ≤, ⌁ heated, 🏕, 🐎, 🐎, park, 🛱 – 📺 ☎ ⓟ. 🔂 🔂 🄰🄴 ⓞ 𝘝𝘐𝘚𝘈. 🛱
  M 15.95 **t.** (lunch) and a la carte 15.65/19.70 **t.** ⓘ 3.75 – 🖃 6.50 – **50 rm** 55.00/95.00 **t.**, **1 suite** 95.00/125.00 **st.** – SB (weekends only) 95.00 **st.**

 🏨 **Cricketer's,** London Rd, GU19 5HR, N : ½ m. on A 30 ♒ 73196, 🐎 – 📺 🛏wc ⊛ ⓟ
  M (grill rest. only) – **29 rm**.

BAILDON West Yorks. **402** O 22 – pop. 14,901 – ✆ 0274 Bradford.

◆London 217 – Bradford 5 – ◆Leeds 13.

 ✕✕ **White House,** Hawksworth Rd, Baildon Moor, BD17 6BQ, ♒ 591176, ≤ – ⓟ. 🔂 🄰🄴 ⓞ 𝘝𝘐𝘚𝘈
  M *(closed Sunday)* (dinner only) (booking essential) a la carte 9.60/16.75 **t.**

BAINBRIDGE North Yorks. **402** N 21 – pop. 474 – ECD : Wednesday – ✉ Leyburn – ✆ 0969 Wensleydale.

◆London 249 – Kendal 31 – ◆Leeds 68 – York 61.

 🏨 **Rose and Crown,** DL8 3EE, ♒ 50225 – 📺 🛏wc 🛏wc ⓟ. 🔂 𝘝𝘐𝘚𝘈
  M (bar lunch)/dinner a la carte 6.85/9.50 **t.** ⓘ 1.65 – **13 rm** 🖃 18.00/36.00 **t.** – SB (November-23 March) 33.00/39.00 **st.**

BAKEWELL Derbs. 402 403 404 O 24 – pop. 3,839 – ECD : Thursday – ☎ 062 981.
Envir. : Chatsworth★★★ : site★★, house★★★ (Renaissance) garden★★★ *AC*, NE : 2 ½ m. – Haddon Hall★★ (14C-16C) *AC*, SE : 3 m.

🚉 Station Rd ℰ 2307.

🏢 Old Market Hall, Bridge St. ℰ 3227.

♦London 160 – Derby 26 – ♦Manchester 37 – ♦Nottingham 33 – ♦Sheffield 17.

🏨 Rutland Arms, The Square, DE4 1BT, ℰ 2872 – 📺 ➚wc ☎ 🅿 – **36 rm**.

🏠 **Milford House,** Mill St., DE4 1DA, ℰ 2130, 🚗 – ➚wc 🅿 . 🎾
April-October and weekends in November, February and March – **11 rm** ☲ 16.40/37.35 t.

🍴🍴 **Fischer's,** Bath St., DE4 1BX, ℰ 2687 – ▩ *AE* *VISA*
closed Saturday lunch, Sunday dinner, Monday, 25 August-9 September and 1 to 7 January –
M (restricted lunch) 9.00 t. and a la carte 12.75/18.65 t. ⬧ 2.90.

at Hassop N : 3 ½ m. by A 619 on B 6001 – ✉ Bakewell – ☎ 062 987 Great Longstone :

🏰 **Hassop Hall** 🦢, DE4 1NS, ℰ 488, ≼, « Part 16C hall », 🚗, park, 🎾 – 🍽 📺 🅿 . ▩ *AE* ⓪ *VISA*. 🎾
closed 3 days at Christmas – **M** *(closed Monday lunch and Sunday dinner)* 8.50/15.50 **st.**
⬧ 3.95 – ☲ 5.00 – **12 rm** 38.50/68.50 **st.**, **1 suite** 95.00/145.00 **st.** – SB (November-March) 98.00/131.00 **st.**

at Ashford-in-the-Water NW : 1 ¾ m. by A 6 and A 6020 on B 6465 – ✉ ☎ 062 981 Bakewell :

🍴🍴 **Riverside Country House** with rm, DE4 1QF, ℰ 4275, 🚗 – 📺 ➚wc 🏧wc 🅿 . ▩ *AE* *VISA*. 🎾
M *(closed Sunday dinner)* (dinner only and Sunday lunch) 19.50 t. ⬧ 3.80 – **4 rm** ☲ 38.00/45.00 t. – SB (except Christmas and Bank Holidays) 70.00/75.00 **st.**

BALA Gwynedd 402 403 J 25 – pop. 1,852 – ECD : Wednesday – ☎ 0678.
See : Site★.
Envir. : SW : Road ★ from Pandy to Dinas Mawddwy.

🚉 Penlan ℰ 520359.

🏢 Snowdonia National Park Visitor Centre, High St. ℰ 520367 (summer only).

♦London 216 – Chester 46 – Dolgellau 18 – Shrewsbury 52.

🏰 **Palé Hall** 🦢, Llandderfel, LL23 7PS, E : 4 ¾ m. by A 494 on B 4401 ℰ 067 83 (Llandderfel) 285, ≼, ⚲, 🚗, park – 🍽 🅿 . ▩ *AE* ⓪ *VISA*. 🎾
M 8.75/14.00 t. and a la carte – **17 rm** ☲ 34.50/86.00 t., **2 suites** 69.00 t..

🏨 **White Lion Royal** (Greenall Whitley), 66 High St., LL23 7AE, ℰ 520314 – ➚wc ☎ 🅿 . ▩ *AE* ⓪ *VISA*
M 6.00/7.50 st. ⬧ 3.60 – **22 rm** ☲ 25.00/35.00 **st.** – SB 48.00/54.00 **st.**

🏨 **Bala Lake** 🦢, LL23 7YF, SW : 1 ¼ m. by B 4391 on B 4403 ℰ 520344, ≼, ☴, 🚉 – 📺 🏧wc 🅿 . ▩ *AE* ⓪ *VISA*
M 7.00/8.50 st. ⬧ 3.20 – **13 rm** ☲ 23.00/40.00 st., **1 suite** – SB (October-March) 44.00/50.00 **st.**

🏨 **Plas Coch,** High St., LL23 7AB, ℰ 520309 – ➚wc 🍽 🅿 . ▩ *AE* ⓪ *VISA*
closed Christmas Day – **M** (bar lunch)/dinner 6.50 t. ⬧ 2.50 – **10 rm** ☲ 27.00/32.00 **st.** – SB (September-May) 40.00/43.00 **st.**

🏠 **Plas Teg,** 45 Tegid St., LL23 7EN, ℰ 520268, 🚗 – 🅿
7 rm ☲ 8.75/17.50 **s.**

VOLVO High St. ℰ 520210

BALDOCK Herts. 404 T 28 – pop. 6,703 – ECD : Thursday – ☎ 0462.
Envir. : Ashwell (St. Mary's Church★ 14C : Medieval graffiti) NE : 4 ½ m.

♦London 42 – Bedford 20 – ♦Cambridge 21 – Luton 15.

🏨 **Butterfield House,** 4 Hitchin St., SG7 6AE, ℰ 892701, 🚗 – 📺 ➚wc ☎ 🅿 . ▩ *AE* *VISA*. 🎾
M (dinner only Monday to Thursday)(weekends by arrangement) 7.50 **s.** and a la carte ⬧ 2.00 – ☲ 1.75 – **13 rm** 22.00/30.00 **s.**

COLT High St. ℰ 893305

BAMBER BRIDGE Lancs. 402 M 22 – see Preston.

BAMBURGH Northumb. 401 402 O 17 – pop. 567 – ECD : Wednesday – ☎ 066 84.
See : Castle★★ (12C-18C) *AC*.

🚉 Bamburgh Castle ℰ 378.

♦London 337 – ♦Edinburgh 77 – ♦Newcastle-upon-Tyne 51.

🏨 **Lord Crewe Arms,** Front St., NE69 7BL, ℰ 243 – 📺 ➚wc 🅿
Easter-October – **M** (bar lunch)/dinner 10.50 t. ⬧ 2.90 – **25 rm** ☲ 18.50/39.00 t. – SB 43.00/53.00 **st.**

🏠 **Sunningdale,** 21-23 Lucker Rd, NE69 7BS, ℰ 334 – ➚wc 🅿
April-October – **18 rm** ☲ 10.00/26.00.

BAMPTON Oxon. 403 404 P 28 – pop. 1,948 – ✪ 0993 Bampton Castle.

♦London 75 – ♦Oxford 18 – Swindon 18.

↑ **University Farm,** Lew, OX8 2AU, NE : 2 m. on A 4095 ✆ 850297, ⇌ – ⊟wc ⑂wc ℗. ⚐
closed Christmas and first 3 weeks January – **6 rm** ⊏⊐ 20.00/28.00 t.

BANBURY Oxon. 403 404 P 27 – pop. 37,463 – ECD : Tuesday – ✪ 0295.

Envir. : Upton House (pictures★★★, porcelain★★) *AC*, NW : 7 m. – East Adderbury (St. Mary's Church : corbels★) SE : 3½ m. – Broughton Castle (great hall★, white room : 1599 plaster ceiling★★) and St. Mary's Church (memorial tombs★) *AC*, SW : 3½ m. – Wroxton (thatched cottages★) NW : 3 m. – Farnborough Hall (interior plasterwork★) *AC*, NW : 6 m.

🖥 Cherwell Edge, Chacombe ✆ 711591, NE : 4 m.

🛈 8 Horsefair ✆ 59855.

♦London 76 – ♦Birmingham 40 – ♦Coventry 25 – ♦Oxford 23.

🏨 **Whately Hall** (T.H.F.), Horsefair, by Banbury Cross, OX16 0AN, ✆ 3451, Telex 837149, « Part 17C hall », ⇌ – ☰ ⓣⓥ ℗. 🅰. 🔁 🄰🄴 ⑳ 𝗩𝗜𝗦𝗔
M 6.50/8.75 **st.** and a la carte ⑁ 3.25 – ⊏⊐ 5.50 – **72 rm** 40.00/47.50 **st.**

🏨 **Banbury Moat House** (Q.M.H) Oxford Rd, OX16 9AH, ✆ 59361 – ⓣⓥ ⊟wc ☎ ℗. 🅰. 🔁 🄰🄴 ⑳ 𝗩𝗜𝗦𝗔
M (bar lunch)/dinner 15.00 **st.** and a la carte ⑁ 2.50 – **30 rm** ⊏⊐ 36.00/50.00 **st.** – SB (except Christmas) 51.00/57.00 **st.**

🏠 **Lismore,** 61 Oxford Rd, OX16 9AJ, ✆ 62105, ⇌ – ⓣⓥ ⊟wc ℗. 🔁 𝗩𝗜𝗦𝗔
M (dinner only) 7.75 **t.** and a la carte ⑁ 3.00 – **14 rm** ⊏⊐ 13.00/35.00 **t.** – SB (weekends only) (November-June) 40.00 **st.**

🏠 **White Lion,** 64 High St., OX16 8JW, ✆ 4358 – ⓣⓥ ⑂. 🔁 🄰🄴 ⑳ 𝗩𝗜𝗦𝗔
M 6.50 **st.** (lunch) and a la carte 7.15/10.00 **t.** ⑁ 2.25 – **15 rm** ⊏⊐ 25.50/37.50 **st.** – SB (weekends only) 44.00 **st.**

↑ **Tredis,** 15 Broughton Rd, OX16 9QB, ✆ 4632, ⇌
6 rm ⊏⊐ 10.00/17.00.

at Bloxham SW : 4¼ m. on A 361 – ✉ ✪ 0295 Banbury :

🏠 **Olde School,** Church St., OX15 4ET, ✆ 720369 – ⓣⓥ ⊟wc ⑂wc ⊛ ℗. 🅰. 🔁 🄰🄴 ⑳ 𝗩𝗜𝗦𝗔. ⚐
M 8.50/10.50 **t.** and a la carte ⑁ 3.00 – ⊏⊐ 4.50 – **16 rm** 20.00/45.00 **st.** – SB (weekends only) (except Bank Holidays) 48.00/52.00 **st.**

at Wroxton NW : 3 m. by A 41 on A 422 – ✉ Banbury – ✪ 029 573 Wroxton St. Mary :

🏨 Wroxton House, Silver St., OX15 6PZ, ✆ 482, ⇌ – ⓣⓥ ⊟wc ⑂wc ☎ ℗
15 rm.

AUSTIN-ROVER Southam Rd ✆ 51551
DAIHATSU Hook Norton ✆ 0608 (Hook Norton) 737641
FIAT, SAAB 21-27 Broad St. ✆ 50733
FORD 98 Warwick Rd ✆ 67711
PEUGEOT, TALBOT Thorpe Rd, Middleton Cheney ✆ 710325

PEUGEOT-TALBOT Southam Rd ✆ 53511
RENAULT 9/16 Southam Rd ✆ 50141
VAUXHALL-OPEL 8 Middleton Rd ✆ 3551
VOLVO Main Rd, Middleton Cheney ✆ 710233
VW, AUDI George St. ✆ 65432

BANGOR Gwynedd 402 403 H 24 – pop. 12,126 – ECD : Wednesday – ✪ 0248.

Envir. : Bethesda (slate quarries★) SE : 5 m. – Nant Francon Pass★★ SE : 9 m.

🖥 St. Deiniol ✆ 353098.

🛈 Texaco Service Station, Beach Rd ✆ 352786 – Town Hall ✆ 2463 (Easter-September).

♦London 247 – Birkenhead 68 – Holyhead 23 – Shrewsbury 83.

🏠 **Ty-Uchaf,** Tal-y-Bont, LL57 3UR, SE : 2 m. by A 5122 ✆ 352219 – ⓣⓥ ⊟wc ⑂wc ⊛ ℗. 🔁 𝗩𝗜𝗦𝗔. ⚐
closed first 2 weeks January – **M** *(closed Sunday and Bank Holidays)* (bar lunch)/dinner 10.00 **t.** and a la carte ⑁ 3.00 – **9 rm** ⊏⊐ 15.00/24.00 **t.**

BANSTEAD Surrey 404 T 30 – pop. 35,360 (inc. Tadworth) – ECD : Wednesday – ✉ Tadworth – ✪ 073 73 Burgh Heath.

🖥 Sandy Lane, Kingswood, Tadworth ✆ 0737 (Mogador) 832188, S : 3 m.

♦London 17 – ♦Brighton 39.

🏨 **Pickard Motor** (Best Western) without rest., Brighton Road, KT20 6BW, S : 1½ m. on A 217 ✆ 53355, Telex 929908 – ⓣⓥ ⊟wc ☎ ℗. 🅰. 🔁 🄰🄴 ⑳ 𝗩𝗜𝗦𝗔
⊏⊐ 3.50 – **44 rm** 33.00/50.00 **st.**

BARFORD Warw. 403 404 P 27 – see Warwick.

BARFORD ST. MARTIN Wilts. 403 404 O 30 – see Salisbury.

BAR HILL Cambs. 404 U 27 – see Cambridge.

BARKSTON Lincs. 402 404 S 25 – see Grantham.

BARMOUTH (ABERMAW) Gwynedd 🗺️🗺️ H 25 – pop. 2 ,142 – ECD : Wednesday – ☎ 0341.
See : Site★★ – Panorama walk★★.
🛈 The Old Library ℰ 280787 (summer only).
◆London 231 – Chester 74 – Dolgellau 10 – Shrewsbury 67.

🏛 **Ty'r Craig Castle,** Llanaber Rd, LL42 1YN, on A 496 ℰ 280470, ≤ – 📺 🛏wc 🛏wc 🅿. ▦
 🆅🅸🆂🅰 ⌕
 March-September – **M** 7.00 t. (dinner) and a la carte ↓ 3.00 – **12 rm** ⊑ 20.00/32.00 t. – SB
 (spring and autumn only) 38.00 **st.**

⌂ **Bryn Melyn** ⌕, Panorama Rd, LL42 1DQ, ℰ 280556, ≤ Mawddach estuary and mountains
 – 🛏wc 🅿. ▦
 Easter-October – **9 rm** ⊑ 17.00/27.50 **st.**

AUSTIN-ROVER, DAIMLER-JAGUAR Park Rd ℰ   COLT Smithy Garage ℰ 034 17 (Dyffryn) 279
280449

BARNARD CASTLE Durham 🗺️ O 20 – pop. 6 ,075 – ECD : Thursday – ☎ 0833 Teesdale.
See : Bowes Museum★★ *AC* – Castle★ (ruins 12C-14C).
Envir. : Raby Castle★ (14C) *AC*, NE : 6 m.
🏌 Harmire Rd ℰ 37237.
🛈 43 Galgate ℰ 38481.
◆London 258 – ◆Carlisle 63 – ◆Leeds 68 – ◆Middlesbrough 31 – ◆Newcastle-upon-Tyne 39.

🏛 **Kings Head,** 14 Market Pl., DL12 8ND, ℰ 38356 – 📺 🛏wc ☎ 🅿. ⌕
 20 rm, 1 suite.

XX **Blagraves House,** 34-36 The Bank, DL12 8PN, ℰ 37668, « 15C town house » – 🅰🅴 🆅🅸🆂🅰
 closed Sunday, Monday and first 2 weeks February – **M** (dinner only) 13.00 t. ↓ 2.95.

FORD, AUSTIN-ROVER 19 Galgate ℰ 37129   VAUXHALL Newgate ℰ 38352

BARNBY MOOR Notts. 🗺️🗺️🗺️ Q 23 – pop. 268 – ECD : Wednesday – ✉ ☎ 0777 Retford.
◆London 151 – ◆Leeds 44 – Lincoln 27 – ◆Nottingham 31.

🏨 **Ye Olde Bell** (T.H.F.), DN22 8QS, ℰ 705121, « 16C coaching inn », 🎠 – 📺 🛏wc ⊛ 🅿.
 🅰 🅰🅴 🅾 🆅🅸🆂🅰
 M 6.25/9.50 **st.** and a la carte ↓ 2.70 – ⊑ 5.50 – **58 rm** 35.50/43.00 **st.**

BARNHAM BROOM Norfolk 🗺️ X 26 – pop. 541 – ✉ Norwich – ☎ 060 545.
🏌 Barnham Broom Hotel ℰ 393.
◆London 109 – East Dereham 10 – ◆Norwich 10.

🏨 **Barnham Broom H. Golf and Country Club** (Best Western) ⌕, NR9 4DD, NE : 1 m.
 ℰ 393, ≤, 🏊, 🏌, 🎣, 🎾, squash – 📺 🛏wc ☎ ㅎ 🅿. 🅰 ▦ 🅰🅴 🅾 🆅🅸🆂🅰
 M 6.50/9.00 **st.** and a la carte ↓ 3.50 – **40 rm** ⊑ 36.50/48.00 **st.** – SB 56.00/60.00 **st.**

BARNSDALE BAR West Yorks. 🗺️🗺️ Q 23 – see Wentbridge.

BARNSLEY South Yorks. 🗺️🗺️ P 23 – pop. 76 ,783 – ECD : Thursday – ☎ 0226.
🏌 Wakefield Rd, Staincross ℰ 382856, N : 4 m.
🛈 Civic Hall, Eldon St. ℰ 206757.
◆London 177 – ◆Leeds 21 – ◆Manchester 36 – ◆Sheffield 15.

🏛 **Queens,** Regent St., S70 2HY, ℰ 284192 – 📺 🛏wc ⊛. 🅰 ▦ 🅰🅴 🅾 🆅🅸🆂🅰
 M 3.95/6.45 **st.** ↓ 2.65 – **37 rm** ⊑ 29.00/39.00 **st.** – SB (weekends only) 49.90 **st.**

☆ **Royal,** Church St., S70 2AD, ℰ 203658 – 📺 🅿. ▦ 🅰🅴 🅾 🆅🅸🆂🅰
 M *(closed Sunday dinner)* 5.65/9.00 t. and a la carte ↓ 2.50 – **17 rm** ⊑ 22.50/38.00 t.

 at Ardsley E : 2 ½ m. on A 635 – ✉ ☎ 0226 Barnsley :

🏨 **Ardsley House** (Best Western), Doncaster Rd, S71 5EH, ℰ 289401, Telex 547762, 🎠 – 📺
 ☎ 🅿. 🅰 ▦ 🅰🅴 🅾 🆅🅸🆂🅰
 M 7.00/8.50 **t.** – ⊑ 5.00 – **62 rm** 35.00/48.00 **t.** – SB (weekends only) 44.00 **st.**

AUSTIN-ROVER Claycliff Rd, Barkgreen ℰ 299891   RENAULT Doncaster Rd ℰ 291554
CITROEN The Cross, Silkstone ℰ 790636   TALBOT, FIAT, PEUGEOT Stairfoot ℰ 206675
FORD Dodworth Rd ℰ 205741   VAUXHALL-OPEL New St. ℰ 289181
HONDA Doncaster Rd ℰ 287417   VW, AUDI Huddersfield Rd ℰ 299494
LADA Wakefield Rd ℰ 243228

Pour vos déplacements en Grande-Bretagne :

– cinq cartes détaillées n^{os} 🔢 🔢 🔢 🔢 🔢 à 1/400 000

– utilisez-les conjointement avec ce guide,

 un souligné rouge signale toutes les localités citées dans ce guide.

BARNSTAPLE Devon **403** H 30 The West Country G. – pop. 24,490 – ECD : Wednesday – ✿ 0271.

See : Site★★ – The Long Bridge★.

Envir. : Arlington Court★★ *AC* The Carriage Collection★, NE : 8 m. on A 39.

🛈 Holland St. ✆ 72742.

♦London 222 – Exeter 40 – Taunton 51.

🏨 **Imperial** (T.H.F.), Taw Vale Par., EX32 8NB, ✆ 45861 – |\$| 📺 ⇌wc ☎ 🅿. 🏄 🔼 AE ⓪ VISA
   M (bar lunch Monday to Saturday)/dinner 8.95 **st.** and a la carte 🍴 2.70 – ⇌ 5.50 – **56 rm** 32.00/43.00 **st.**

🏨 **Royal and Fortescue**, Boutport St., EX31 1HG, ✆ 42289, Telex 42551 – |\$| 📺 ⇌wc 🅿. 🔼 AE ⓪ VISA 🕅
   M 3.50/6.90 **t.** and a la carte 🍴 2.50 – **61 rm** ⇌ 15.50/31.00 – SB 39.10/54.05 **st.**

🏨 **North Devon Motel**, Taw Vale, EX32 8NJ, ✆ 72166 – 📺 ⇌wc ☎ 🅿. 🏄
   26 rm

XX **Lynwood House**, Bishops Tawton Rd, EX32 9DZ, on A 377 ✆ 43695, Seafood – 🅿. 🔼 AE ⓪ VISA
   closed Saturday lunch and Sunday – **M** a la carte 6.95/19.20 **t.** 🍴 2.85.

at Bishop's Tawton S : 2 m. on A 377 – ✉ ✿ 0271 Barnstaple :

🏨 **Downrew House** 🦢, EX32 0DY, SE : 1 ½ m. on Chittlehampton Rd ✆ 42497, ≤, « Country house atmosphere », ⬚ heated, 🐎, park, 🎾 – 📺 ⇌wc 🅿 🕅
   Mid March-December – **M** (bar lunch)/dinner 14.50 🍴 1.50 – **14 rm** ⇌ 33.00/72.00 – SB (except Christmas) 56.00/62.70.

AUSTIN-ROVER-DAIMLER-JAGUAR Boutport St. ✆ 73232
BMW Abbey Rd ✆ 74070
DAIHATSU Newport Rd ✆ 45363

FIAT, TOYOTA, VOLVO Pottington Industrial Estate, Pillandway ✆ 76551
FORD New Rd ✆ 74173
VAUXHALL-OPEL 42 Boutport St. ✆ 74366

BARROW-IN-FURNESS Cumbria **402** K 21 – pop. 50,174 – ✿ 0229.

♦London 295 – Kendal 34 – Lancaster 47.

🏨 **Victoria Park**, Victoria Rd, LA14 5JX, ✆ 21159 – 📺 ⇌wc 🛉wc ☎ 🅿. 🏄 🔼 AE ⓪ VISA
   M 7.50/9.50 **st.** and a la carte 🍴 2.35 – **40 rm** ⇌ 30.00/46.00 **st.** – SB (weekends only) 40.00/50.00 **st.**

BARRY (BARRI) South Glam. **403** K 29 – pop. 44,443 – ECD : Wednesday – ✿ 0446.

🛈 Barry Island ✆ 747111 (summer only).

♦London 167 – ♦Cardiff 10 – ♦Swansea 39.

🏨 **Mount Sorrel**, Porthkerry Rd, CF6 8AY, ✆ 740069 – 📺 ⇌wc 🛉wc ☎ 🅿. 🔼 AE ⓪ VISA
   M 4.65/8.75 **t.** and a la carte 🍴 2.90 – **37 rm** ⇌ 27.75/37.00 **t.** – SB (weekends only) 37.50/39.50 **st.**

AUSTIN-ROVER-DAIMLER-JAGUAR Brook St. ✆ 734365

BARTON Lancs. **402** L 22 – pop. 2,055 – ✉ Preston – ✿ 0772 Broughton.

♦London 228 – ♦Blackpool 18 – Lancaster 16 – Preston 4.5.

🏨 **Barton Grange** (Best Western), Garstang Rd, PR3 5AA, ✆ 862551, Telex 67392, 🔲, 🐎, 🎾 – |\$| 📺 ⇌wc 🛉wc ☎ 🅿. 🏄 🔼 AE ⓪ VISA 🕅
   M (closed Saturday lunch and Sunday dinner) 6.25/8.95 **st.** and a la carte 🍴 3.00 – **65 rm** ⇌ 22.50/42.00 **st.** – SB 49.50/52.00 **st.**

BARTON ON SEA Hants. **403** **404** P 31 – pop. 3,590 – ✿ 0425 New Milton.

♦London 101 – Bournemouth 11 – ♦Southampton 23.

↑ **Gainsborough**, 39 Marine Drive East, BH25 7DX, ✆ 610541, ≤ – 🅿
   9 rm ⇌ 14.00/28.00 **st.**

BARWICK Somerset **403** **404** M 31 – see Yeovil.

BASFORD Staffs. – see Stoke-on-Trent.

BASILDON Essex **404** V 29 – pop. 94,800 – ECD : Wednesday – ✿ 0268.

🛈 Kingswood ✆ 3297.

♦London 30 – Chelmsford 17 – Southend-on-Sea 13.

🏨 **Crest** (Crest), Cranes Farm Rd, SS14 3DG, NW : 2 ¼ m. by A 176 off A 1235 ✆ 3955, Telex 995141 – 📺 ⇌wc ☎ 🅿. 🏄 🔼 AE ⓪ VISA 🕅
   M approx. 11.50 **st.** – ⇌ 5.25 – **116 rm** 45.00/55.00 **st.** – SB (weekends only) 51.00 **st.**

AUSTIN-ROVER Southern Hay ✆ 22661
FORD Cherrydown ✆ 22741

NISSAN Nethermayne ✆ 22261
VAUXHALL-OPEL High Rd, Laindon ✆ 42481

🏠 Bishopswood, Bishopswood Lane 🖉 073 56 (Tadley) 5213, N : 6 m. off A 340 Z.

♦London 55 – Reading 17 – ♦Southampton 31 – Winchester 18.

BASINGSTOKE

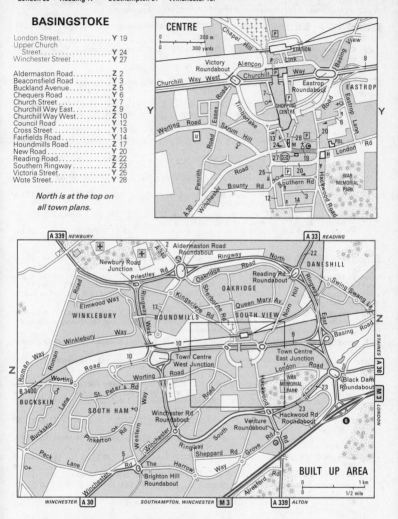

London Street	Y 19
Upper Church	
Street	Y 24
Winchester Street	Y 27
Aldermaston Road	Z 2
Beaconsfield Road	Y 3
Buckland Avenue	Z 5
Chequers Road	Y 6
Church Street	Y 7
Churchill Way East	Y 8
Churchill Way West	Z 10
Council Road	Y 12
Cross Street	Y 13
Fairfields Road	Y 14
Houndmills Road	Z 17
New Road	Y 20
Reading Road	Z 22
Southern Ringway	Z 23
Victoria Street	Y 25
Wote Street	Y 28

*North is at the top on
all town plans.*

🏛️ **Crest** (Crest), Grove Rd, RG21 3EE, SW : 1 m. junction A 339 and A 30 🖉 468181, Telex
858501 – 📺 🛏️wc 📞 ♿ 🅿️ 🏢 🔺 AE ⓓ VISA   Z e
M approx. 11.50 **st.** – 🍽️ 5.75 – **86 rm** 48.00/57.00 **st.** – SB (weekends only) 51.00 **st.**

🏛️ **Ladbroke** (Ladbroke), Aldermaston Roundabout, Ringway North, RG24 9NV, N : 2 m. junction A 339 and A 340 🖉 20212, Telex 858223 – 📶 📺 🛏️wc 📞 🅿️ 🏢 🔺 AE ⓓ VISA   Z a
M (carving rest.) 8.00/11.00 **t.** 🍷 3.50 – 🍽️ 5.50 – **108 rm** 35.00/65.00 **t.** – SB (weekends only)
50.00/60.00 **st.**

🏛️ **Red Lion** (Anchor) 24 London St., RG21 1NY, 🖉 28525, Telex 859504 – 📶 📺 🛏️wc 🛁wc 📞
🅿️ 🏢 🔺 AE ⓓ VISA   Y c
M (carving rest.) 6.95 **st.** 🍷 3.00 – **63 rm** 🍽️ 48.50/54.00 **st.** – SB (weekends only) 49.00 **st.**

at Oakley W : 5 m. on B 3400 –Z – 📮 🔔 0256 Basingstoke :

🏨 **Beach Arms**, Andover Rd, RG23 7EP, on B 3400 🖉 780210, 🚲 – 📺 🛏️wc 📞 🅿️ 🔺 AE VISA
M (bar lunch Saturday) 7.00 **st.** and a la carte 🍷 2.50 – **17 rm** 🍽️ 41.00/50.00 **st.** – SB 44.00 **st.**

BASINGSTOKE

AUDI, VW London Rd ✆ 24444
AUSTIN-ROVER-DAIMLER Houndmills ✆ 65991
AUSTIN-ROVER-JAGUAR New Rd ✆ 24561
BEDFORD, VAUXHALL-OPEL West Ham ✆ 62551

FIAT, LANCIA, ALFA-ROMEO London Rd ✆ 55221
FORD Lower Wote St. ✆ 3561
TALBOT Eastdrop Roundabout ✆ 65454
VOLVO London Rd ✆ 66111

BASLOW Derbs. 402 408 404 P 24 – pop. 1 ,205 – ECD : Wednesday – ✉ Bakewell – ✆ 024 688.
♦London 161 – Derby 27 – ♦Manchester 35 – ♦Sheffield 13.

🏠 **Cavendish,** DE4 1SP, on A 619 ✆ 2311, Telex 547150, ≼, « Tasteful decor », ➪, 🍽 – 📺 ☎
🅿. 🆎 ⓪ 💳. ⚘
M a la carte 13.80/21.45 **t.** 🍸 3.50 – ⊑ 6.10 – **23 rm** 45.00/55.00 **t.**

BASSENTHWAITE Cumbria 401 402 K 19 – pop. 533 – ✆ 059 681 Bassenthwaite Lake.
♦London 300 – ♦Carlisle 24 – Keswick 7.

🏠 **Armathwaite Hall** ⚲, CA12 4RE, W : 1 ½ m. on B 5291 ✉ Keswick ✆ 551, ≼ Bassenthwaite
Lake, « Part 18C mansion in extensive grounds », 🔲, ➪, 🍽, park, ⚲, squash – 🖭 📺 ☎
⊂➪ 🅿. 🔼 🆎 ⓪. ⚘
closed January and February – **M** a la carte 13.75/17.75 **t.** – **40 rm** ⊑ 30.00/70.00 **t.**

🏠 **Pheasant Inn,** CA13 9YE, SW : 3 ¼ m. by B 5291 off A 66 ✉ Cockermouth ✆ 234, « 16C
inn », 🍽 – ⊏wc 🅿. ⚘
closed Christmas Day – **M** 6.50/10.20 **st.** and a la carte 🍸 2.25 – **20 rm** ⊑ 23.00/48.00 **st.** – SB
(mid November-mid March) 50.00/60.00 **st.**

🏠 **Overwater Hall** ⚲, CA5 1HH, NE : 2 ¼ m. on Uldale Rd ✉ Ireby ✆ 566, ≼, 🍽, park – 📺
⊏wc 🅿. 🔼 💳
closed 24 December-21 February – **M** (bar lunch residents only)/dinner 10.50 **t.** 🍸 2.90 – **13 rm**
⊑ 20.00/34.00 **t.** – SB (October-June) 42.00/46.00 **st.**

🏠 **Castle Inn,** CA12 4RG, W : 1 m. at junction A 591 and B 5291 ✉ Keswick ✆ 401, ≼,
🔼 heated, 🍽, ⚲ – 📺 ⊏wc 🅿. 🔼 💳
closed 2 weeks mid November and 1 week at Christmas – **M** 6.50/10.00 **st.** 🍸 2.75 – **20 rm**
⊑ 30.00/50.00 **st.** – SB (weekends only)(November-July) 114.00 **st.**

BATH Avon 403 404 M 29 **The West Country** G. – pop. 84 ,283 – ECD : Monday and Thursday –
✆ 0225 – See : Site★★★ : Royal Crescent★★★ (N° 1 Royal Crescent★★AC) V – Circus★★★ V –
Museum of costume★★★AC V M2 – Royal Photographic Society National Centre of Photogra-
phy★★AC V M3 – Roman Baths★★AC (Pump Room★AC) X D – Holburne of Menstrie Museum★★AC
V M1 – Pulteney Bridge★ X – Assembly Rooms★AC V M2 – Bath Abbey★ X B – Camden Works
Museum★AC V M4 – Bath Carriage Museum★AC V M5.

Envir. : Lansdown Crescent★★ (Somerset Place★) Y – at Claverton, E : 2 ½ m. by A36 Y American
Museum★★AC - Claverton Pump★AC – Camden Crescent★ V – Beckford Tower and Museum AC
(prospect★) Y M6 – Dyrham Park★AC, N : 8 m. by A 46 Y.

📗, 📗 Tracy Park, Bath Rd, Wick ✆ 027 582 (Abson) 2251, N : 5 m. by Lansdown Rd Y – 📗 Lansdown
✆ 22138, NW : 3 m. by Lansdown Rd Y.

🅱 Abbey Churchyard ✆ 62831/60521 – ♦London 119 – ♦Bristol 13 – ♦Southampton 63 – Taunton 49.

Plans opposite

🏠 **Royal Crescent,** 16 Royal Crescent, BA1 2LS, ✆ 319090, Telex 444251, ≼, « Tastefully
restored Georgian town houses », 🍽 – 🖭 📺 ☎ 🅿. 🆎 ⓪ 💳. ⚘   V u
M 23.00/29.00 **st.** 🍸 5.80 – ⊑ 8.00 – **45 rm** 65.00/110.00 **st.**, **7 suites** 165.00/250.00 **st.** – SB
(not weekends)(December-mid March) 115.00/265.00 **st.**

🏠 **The Priory,** Weston Rd, BA1 2XT, ✆ 331922, Telex 44612, ≼, 🔼 heated, 🍽 – 📺 ☎ 🅿. 🔼
🆎 ⚘   Y c
closed first 2 weeks January – **M** a la carte 13.00/23.00 **s.** 🍸 3.75 – ⊑ 3.50 – **21 rm** 42.00/96.00 **s.**
– SB (November-March) 117.30/136.00 **st.**

🏠 **Francis** (T.H.F.), Queen Sq., BA1 2HH, ✆ 24257, Telex 449162 – 🖭 📺 & 🅿. 🚹. 🔼 🆎 ⓪
💳   X o
M 7.95/10.95 **st.** and a la carte 🍸 2.80 – ⊑ 5.50 – **90 rm** 47.50/59.00 **st.**, **1 suite**.

🏠 **Ladbroke Beaufort** (Ladbroke), Walcot St., BA1 5BJ, ✆ 63411, Telex 449519 – 🖭 📺 🅿.
🚹. 🔼 🆎 ⓪ 💳   V i
M a la carte lunch/dinner 10.00 **t.** 🍸 3.70 – ⊑ 6.50 – **123 rm** 24.00/71.50 **st.** – SB (weekends
only) 65.50/91.50 **st.**

🏠 **Six Kings Circus** without rest, 6 The Circus, BA1 2EW, ✆ 28288, « Georgian town house »,
🍽 – ☎ 🅿. 💳. ⚘   V n
closed last week December and first 2 weeks January – **6 rm** ⊑ 60.00/95.00 **st.**

🏠 **Lansdown Grove** (Best Western), Lansdown Rd, BA1 5EH, ✆ 315891, 🍽 – 🖭 📺 ⊏wc ☎
🅿. 🚹. 🔼 🆎 ⓪ 💳   Y o
M (buffet lunch Monday to Saturday)/dinner 12.50 **t.** and a la carte – **42 rm** ⊑ 35.00/60.00 **t.** –
SB (weekends only) 61.00/68.00 **st.**

🏠 **Pratt's,** South Par., BA2 4AB, ✆ 60441, Telex 47439 – 🖭 📺 ⊏wc ☎. 🚹. 🔼 🆎 ⓪ 💳
M (bar lunch Monday to Saturday)/dinner 12.95 **st.** 🍸 3.75 – **46 rm** ⊑ 32.00/48.00 **st.** – SB
(except Christmas) 56.00/68.00 **st.**   X r

🏠 **Apsley House,** 141 Newbridge Hill, BA1 3PT, ✆ 336966, Telex 44821, 🍽 – 📺 ⊏wc ☎ 🅿.
🔼 🆎 💳. ⚘   Y e
M (buffet lunch)/dinner 15.95 **st.** 🍸 2.95 – **7 rm** ⊑ 50.00/75.00 **st.** – SB (November-March)
70.00/85.00 **st.**

BATH

Gay Street . . . . **V** 23
Green Street . . . . **VX** 27
Milsom Street . . . . **V** 33
New Bond Street . . . . **X** 36

Ambury . . . . **X** 2
Avon Street . . . . **X** 3
Barton Street . . . . **X** 4
Beckford Road . . . . **V** 6
Belvedere . . . . **X** 9
Broad Quay . . . . **X** 10
Broad Street . . . . **V** 10
Charles Street . . . . **X** 12
Charlotte Street . . . . **X** 14
Cheap Street . . . . **X** 15
Churchill Bridge . . . . **X** 17
Claverton Street . . . . **X** 18
Cleveland Place . . . . **V** 19
Corn Street . . . . **X** 20
Darlington Street . . . . **V** 22
George Street . . . . **V** 24
Gt. Pulteney Street . . . . . . **V** 25
Gt. Stanhope Street . . . . . **X** 26
High Street . . . . **X** 28
Lower Borough Walls . . . . . **X** 30
Manvers Street . . . . **X** 31
Midland Bridge Road . . . . . **X** 32
Monmouth Place . . . . **X** 34
Newark Street . . . . **X** 35
New King Street . . . . **X** 37
Nile Street . . . . **X** 38
Orange Grove . . . . **X** 39
Pierrepont Street . . . . **X** 42
Pines Way . . . . **X** 43
Queen Square . . . . **VX** 44
Rossiter Road . . . . **X** 45
St. James' Parade . . . . **X** 46
Southgate . . . . **X** 48
Stanley Road . . . . **X** 49
Union Street . . . . **X** 53
Upper Borough Walls . . . . . **X** 54
Westgate Buildings . . . . . . **X** 56

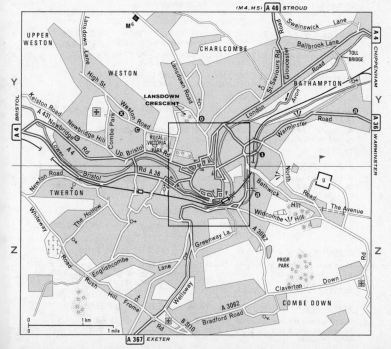

🏨 **Gainsborough,** Weston Lane, BA1 4AB, ✆ 311380, 🚗 – 📺 ⌸wc �📵wc ☎ 🄿. 🔼 🄰🄴 🆅🄸🅂🄰
Y x
closed Christmas and first 2 weeks January – **M** (bar lunch)/dinner 9.00 t. ⌸ 2.00 – **14 rm**
⌷ 18.00/41.00 t. – SB 49.00/54.00 st.

🏨 **Redcar,** 27 Henrietta St., BA2 6LR, ✆ 65432 – 📺 ⌸wc ☎ 🄿. 🏌. 🔼 🄰🄴 🅸 🆅🄸🅂🄰. 🕸 V a
M 8.50/9.50 st. and a la carte ⌸ 3.50 – ⌷ 5.25 – **31 rm** 36.00/47.00 st. – SB (weekends only)
60.00/66.00 st.

🏨 **Number Nine,** 9 Miles Building, George St., BA1 2QS, ✆ 25462, 🚗 – 📺 ⌸wc �📵wc ☎. 🄰🄴
🄾🄳 🆅🄸🅂🄰. 🕸 V c
closed January – **M** *(closed Sunday and Monday)* (dinner only) 15.00 – **8 rm** ⌷ 45.00/75.00 t.,
1 suite.

🏠 **Villa Magdala** without rest., Henrietta Rd, BA2 6LX, ✆ 66329, 🚗 – 📺 ⌸wc �📵wc 🄿. 🕸
closed Christmas – **17 rm** ⌷ 22.00/40.00 st. V e

🏠 **Paradise House** without rest., 86-88 Holloway, BA2 4PX, ≤, 🚗 – 📺 ⌸wc. 🔼
🆅🄸🅂🄰 X c
closed December-mid February – **9 rm** ⌷ 20.00/39.00 st.

🏠 **Oldfields** without rest., 102 Wells Rd, BA2 3AL, ✆ 317984, 🚗 – 📺 �📵wc 🄿. 🆅🄸🅂🄰. 🕸 X s
closed mid December-mid January – **14 rm** ⌷ 17.50/38.00 st.

🏠 **Sydney Gardens** without rest., Sydney Rd, BA2 6NT, ✆ 64818, 🚗 – 📺 ⌸wc 🄿. 🔼 🆅🄸🅂🄰
closed Christmas – **7 rm** ⌷ 25.00/45.00 st. Y i

🏠 **North Parade,** 10 North Par., BA2 4AL, ✆ 63384 – 📺 ⌸wc ☎. 🔼 🄰🄴 🄾🄳 🆅🄸🅂🄰 X n
closed 2 weeks Christmas-New Year – **M** (dinner only) 6.50 t. and a la carte ⌸ 2.20 – **17 rm**
⌷ 18.00/45.00 t. – SB (November-March)(except Bank Holidays) 38.00/50.00 st.

↑ **Holly Villa,** 14 Pulteney Gdns, BA2 4HG, ✆ 310331, 🚗 – 🕸 Z a
5 rm ⌷ 12.00/20.00 st.

↑ **Lynwood,** 6-7 Pulteney Gdns., BA2 4HG, ✆ 26410 – 📺 �📵. 🔼 🄰🄴 🄾🄳 🆅🄸🅂🄰 X v
14 rm ⌷ 14.75/20.00 st.

XXX **Popjoy's,** Beau Nash's House, Sawclose, BA1 1EU, ✆ 60494, « Former residence of Beau
Nash » – 🔼 🆅🄸🅂🄰 X z
closed Sunday, Monday and 3 weeks after Christmas – **M** (dinner only) a la carte approx. 12.50 t.
⌸ 2.70.

XX **The Hole in the Wall** with rm, 16 George St., BA1 2EN, ✆ 25242, « Converted Georgian
kitchen and coal hole » – 📺 ⌸wc ☎. 🔼 🄰🄴 🄾🄳 🆅🄸🅂🄰. 🕸 V v
closed 2 weeks after Christmas – **M** *(closed Sunday lunch)* 21.00 st. (dinner) and a la carte
⌸ 3.00 – ⌷ 4.50 – **8 rm** 40.00/70.00 st. – SB (November-March) 98.00/118.00 st.

XX **Clos du Roy,** 7 Edgar Buildings, George St., BA1 2EE, ✆ 64356 – 🔼 🄰🄴 🄾🄳 🆅🄸🅂🄰 V r
closed Monday and 2 weeks January-February – **M** 9.50/19.50 t. and a la carte ⌸ 4.20.

XX **Rajpoot,** 4 Argyle St., BA2 4BE, ✆ 66833, Indian rest. – 🔼 🄰🄴 🄾🄳 🆅🄸🅂🄰 VX s
closed 25 and 26 December – **M** 8.95/10.50 st. and a la carte ⌸ 4.95.

X **Flowers,** 27 Monmouth St, BA1 2AP, ✆ 313774 – 🔼 🄰🄴 🄾🄳 🆅🄸🅂🄰 X a
closed Sunday and 2 weeks Christmas-New Year – **M** 7.50/13.50 t. ⌸ 3.25.

X **Eastern Eye,** 11 Argyle St., BA2 4BQ, ✆ 22323, Indian rest. VX x

X **Chikako's,** Theatre Royal, Saw Close, BA1 1ET, ✆ 64125, Japanese rest. – 🔼 🆅🄸🅂🄰 X e
M 10.00 t. and a la carte ⌸ 2.25.

X **Ainslie's,** 12 Pierrepont St., BA1 1LA, Bistro – 🔼 🄰🄴 🄾🄳 🆅🄸🅂🄰 X u
closed Sunday lunch and 25-26 December – **M** (bar lunch)/dinner a la carte 10.60/12.10 t.
⌸ 2.55.

at Bathampton E : 2 ½ m. on A 36 – ⌧ ☯ 0225 Bath :

🏠 **Orchard House,** Warminster Rd, BA2 6XG, ✆ 66115 – 📺 ⌸wc 🄿. 🔼 🄰🄴 🄾🄳 🆅🄸🅂🄰 Y a
M (dinner only) 8.50 t. ⌸ 2.50 – **12 rm** ⌷ 34.00/38.00 t. – SB (November-February)
42.00/44.00 st.

at Bathford E : 3 ½ m. by A 4 off A 363 – Y – ⌧ ☯ 0225 Bath :

↑ **Eagle House,** Church St., BA1 7RS, ✆ 859946, « Georgian house », 🚗 – 📺 ⌸wc 🄿
closed first 2 weeks February – ⌷ 1.70 – **6 rm** 23.50/32.00 st.

at Freshford S : 7 ½ m. on A 36 – Y – ⌧ Bath – ☯ 022 122 Limpley Stoke :

🏨 **Homewood Park** 🕸, Hinton Charterhouse, BA3 6BB, S : 1 ½ m. on A 36 ✆ 3731, ≤,
« Tastefully converted country house », 🚗, park, ⚒ – 📺 ☎ 🄿. 🏌. 🔼 🄰🄴 🄾🄳 🆅🄸🅂🄰. 🕸
closed 23 December-14 January – **M** 15.00 st. (lunch) and a la carte approx. 20.00 st. ⌸ 3.50 –
⌷ 5.00 – **15 rm** 40.00/85.00 st. – SB (weekdays only)(November-March) 75.00 st.

at Woolverton (Somerset) S : 10 m. on A 36 – Y – ⌧ Bath – ☯ 0373 Frome :

🏠 **Woolverton House,** BA3 6QS, ✆ 830415, 🚗 – 📺 ⌸wc 🄿. 🔼 🆅🄸🅂🄰
M 14.00 st. and a la carte ⌸ 2.50 – **8 rm** ⌷ 25.00/36.00 st. – SB (weekdays only)(November-
March) 45.00 st.

at Hunstrete W : 8 ½ m. by A 4 – Y – and A 39 off A 368 – ⊠ Pensford – ☎ 076 18 Compton Dando :

🏰 **Hunstrete House** ⌂, BS18 4NS, ✆ 578, Telex 449540, ≼, « Country house atmosphere and gardens », ⌧ heated, park, ✾ – 📺 ☎ & 🅿, 🔏, 🆔 ⓪ VISA, ✄
M (restricted lunch in summer Monday to Saturday) 14.00/22.00 **s.** ⓵ 4.00 – ⌷ 4.00 – **21 rm** 70.00/115.00 **s.**, **1 suite** 135.00/180.00 **s.**.

AUSTIN-ROVER-DAIMLER-JAGUAR Newbridge Rd ✆ 312774
BMW Wellsway ✆ 29187
CITROEN, DAIHATSU Prior Park Rd ✆ 29552
FIAT, ALFA ROMEO Margarets Buildings, Circus Pl. ✆ 27328

FORD 5/10 James St. West ✆ 61636
NISSAN Lower Bristol Rd ✆ 25864
VAUXHALL, BEDFORD Rush Hill ✆ 833338
VAUXHALL Upper Bristol Rd ✆ 22131
VOLVO Bathwick Hill ✆ 65814

BATTISBOROUGH CROSS Devon – see Newton Ferrers.

BATTLE East Sussex 404 V 31 – pop. 4 ,662 – ☎ 042 46.

See : Abbey★ (11C-14C) *AC* (site of the Battle of Hastings 1066).

🛈 88 High St. ✆ 3721.

◆London 55 – ◆Brighton 34 – Folkestone 43 – Maidstone 30.

🏰 **Netherfield Place Country House** ⌂, TN33 9PP, NW : 1 ¾ m. by A 2100 on Netherfield Rd ✆ 4455, ≼, « Gardens », park – 📺 ⌂wc ☎ 🅿, 🔏 🆔 ⓪ VISA, ✄
M 13.50 **t.** (dinner) and a la carte 11.15/17.15 ⓵ 3.50 – **11 rm** ⌷ 30.00/75.00 **t.**

🏰 **George,** 23 High St., TN33 0EA, ✆ 4466 – 📺 ⌂wc ☎ 🅿, 🔏 🆔 ⓪ VISA
closed Christmas – **M** (closed Sunday lunch) 5.95 **t.** ⓵ 2.95 – ⌷ 3.95 – **20 rm** 19.75/29.50 **st.**

↑ **Little Hemingfold Farmhouse** ⌂, Telham, TN33 0TT, SE : 1 ¾ m. on B 2100 ✆ 2910, ≼, « Lakeside setting », ⌦, 🍴, park – 📺 ⌂wc 🅿
12 rm ⌷ (dinner included) 25.00/60.00.

XX **Boxers,** 31 Mount St., TN33 0EG, ✆ 2132 – 🅿, 🔏 🆔 VISA
closed Sunday, Monday, 10 September-1 October and 23 to 30 December – **M** 5.50/10.75 **t.** and a la carte ⓵ 2.40.

X **Blacksmiths,** 43 High St., TN33 0EE, ✆ 3200 – 🔏 VISA
closed Saturday lunch, Monday and 10 to 24 October – **M** 6.90/9.90 **t.** and a la carte.

AUSTIN-ROVER High St. ✆ 2425
CITROEN Ninfield ✆ 0424 (Ninfield) 892278
CITROEN Whatlington ✆ 042 487 (Sedlescombe) 307

FORD Upper Lake ✆ 3155
RELIANT, SKODA ✆ 0424 (Ninfield) 892286
VAUXHALL-OPEL Battle Hill ✆ 2286

BAWTRY South Yorks. 402 403 404 Q 23 – pop. 2 ,677 – ⊠ ☎ 0302 Doncaster.

🛝 Hoveringham, Austerfield Park, Cross Lane ✆ 710841, NE : 2 m. off A 614.

◆London 158 – ◆Leeds 39 – Lincoln 32 – ◆Nottingham 36 – ◆Sheffield 29.

🏰 Crown (Anchor), High St., DN10 6JW, ✆ 710341, Telex 547089, ⌦ – 📺 ⌂wc ☎ 🅿, 🔏
57 rm.

BAYCLIFF Cumbria 402 K 21 – see Ulverston.

BEACONSFIELD Bucks. 404 S 29 – pop. 13 ,397 – ECD : Wednesday and Saturday – ☎ 049 46.

◆London 26 – Aylesbury 19 – ◆Oxford 32.

🏰 **Bellhouse** (De Vere), Oxford Rd, HP9 2XE, E : 1 ¾ m. on A 40 ✆ 0753 (Gerrard'sCross) 887211, Telex 848719 – 🕴 📺 ⌂wc ☎ 🅿, 🔏, 🔏 🆔 ⓪ VISA
M 8.75/9.90 **st.** and a la carte ⓵ 4.00 – **120 rm** ⌷ 55.00/72.00 **st.** – SB (weekends only) 63.50 **st.**

🏰 **Crest** (Crest), Aylesbury End, HP9 1LW, ✆ 71211 – 📺 ⌂wc ☎ 🅿, 🔏 🆔 ⓪ VISA
M (buffet lunch)/dinner approx. 11.50 **t.** – ⌷ 5.75 – **38 rm** 45.00/55.00 **st.** – SB (weekends only) 55.00 **st.**

XX **Santella,** 43 Aylesbury End, HP9 1LV, ✆ 6806, Italian rest. – 🔏 🆔 ⓪ VISA
closed Sunday – **M** 6.75 **t.** (lunch) and a la carte 12.00/15.75 **t.** ⓵ 2.75.

XX **La Lanterna,** 57 Wycombe End, HP9 1LX, ✆ 5210, Italian rest. – 🆔 ⓪ VISA
M 6.95 **t.** (lunch) and a la carte 8.30/15.30 **t.** ⓵ 3.50.

MERCEDES-BENZ, TOYOTA 55 Station Rd ✆ 2141   VAUXHALL-OPEL Penn Rd, Knotty Green ✆ 3730

BEADLAM North Yorks. – see Helmsley.

BEAMINSTER Dorset 403 L 31 The West Country G. – pop. 2 ,338 – ECD : Wednesday – ☎ 0308.

◆London 149 – Dorchester 19 – Exeter 40 – Taunton 31.

X **Nevitt's Eating House,** 57 Hogshill St., DT8 3AG, ✆ 862600 – VISA
M (dinner only and Sunday lunch)/dinner 10.50 **t.** ⓵ 3.00.

BEARSTED Kent 404 V 30 – see Maidstone.

BEAULIEU Hants. **403 404** P 31 – pop. 1 ,027 – ECD : Tuesday and Saturday – ⊠ Brockenhurst – ✆ 0590 – **See** : Beaulieu Abbey★ (ruins 13C) : Palace House★ 14C, National Motor Museum★★, Buckler's Hard Maritime Museum *AC*.

🇿 John Montagu Building ℰ 612345 — ◆London 102 – Bournemouth 24 – ◆Southampton 13 – Winchester 23.

⚓ Montagu Arms, Palace Lane, SO4 7ZL, ℰ 612324, « Part 18C inn », ⚔ – 📺 🅟 ⚞ 🄰🄴 ⓞ **VISA**
M 9.75/15.75 **st.** and a la carte 🍴 3.50 – **26 rm** ⚏ 39.50/70.00 **st.** – SB (November-June except Bank Holidays) 63.25/69.75 **st.**

at Bucklers Hard S : 2 ½ m. – ⊠ Brockenhurst – ✆ 059 063 Bucklers Hard :

🏨 **Master Builder's House,** SO4 7XB, ℰ 253, ≼, ⚔ – 📺 🛏wc ⊛ 🕭 🅟. 🅰. ⚞ 🄰🄴 ⓞ **VISA**
M 10.00 **t.** and a la carte 🍴 3.10 – **23 rm** ⚏ 30.00/49.00 **st.** – SB 56.00 **st.**

BEAUMARIS Gwynedd **402 403** H 24 – pop. 1 ,413 – ECD : Wednesday – ✆ 0248.
See : Castle★ (13C) *AC* – **Envir.** : Menai Strait★ (Channel, Menai Suspension Bridge ≼★ SW : 4 ½ m. – Bryn Celli Du (burial chamber★) SW : 8 m.

🇫 Baron Hill ℰ 810231, NW : 1 m. – ◆London 253 – Birkenhead 74 – Holyhead 25.

🏨 **Bulkeley Arms,** 19 Castle St., LL58 8AW, ℰ 810415, ≼ Menai Strait, ⚔ – 📳 📺 🛏wc
🛏wc ☎ 🅟. ⚞ 🄰🄴 ⓞ **VISA**
M 8.00/10.00 **st.** 🍴 2.50 – **41 rm** ⚏ 23.50/49.00 **st.**, **2 suites** 55.00 **st.** – SB 45.00/59.95 **st.**

🏡 **Liverpool Arms** without rest., Castle St., LL58 8BA, ℰ 810362 – 📺 🛏wc 🛏wc 🅟. ⚞ **VISA**
closed 24 to 30 December – **10 rm** ⚏ 20.00/40.00.

🏡 **Bishopsgate House,** 54 Castle St., LL58 8AB, ℰ 810302 – 📺 🛏wc 🅟. ⚞ **VISA**
April-December – **M** 4.95/12.00 **t.** and a la carte 🍴 3.75 – **10 rm** ⚏ 17.00/34.00 **t.** – SB 45.00 **st.**

BECCLES Suffolk **404** Y 26 – pop. 10 ,677 – ECD : Wednesday – ✆ 0502.
🇿 The Quay, Fen Lane ℰ 713196 (summer only).
◆London 113 – Great Yarmouth 15 – ◆Ipswich 40 – ◆Norwich 18.

🏨 **Waveney House** ⟆, Puddingmoor, NR34 9PL, ℰ 712270 – 📺 🛏wc 🛏wc ⊛ 🅟 – **13 rm**.

AUSTIN-ROVER Beccles Rd. Barnby ℰ 050 276   VAUXHALL-OPEL Station Rd ℰ 717023
(Barnby) 204

BECKERMET Cumbria **402** J 20 – ECD : Tuesday and Thursday – ⊠ ✆ 094 684.
◆London 326 – ◆Carlisle 45 – Kendal 62 – Workington 17.

🏡 **Royal Oak** without rest., CA21 2XB, ℰ 551 – 📺 🛏wc ☎ 🅟
8 rm ⚏ 18.00/40.00 **st.** – SB (weekends only) 38.00 **st.**

BEDDGELERT Gwynedd **402 403** H 24 – pop. 646 – ECD : Wednesday – ✆ 076 686.
Envir. : NE : Llyn Dinas valley★★ – Llyn Gwynant valley★ – **Exc.** : Blaenau Ffestiniog (site : slate quarries★) E : 14 m. by Penrhyndeudraeth.
◆London 249 – Caernarfon 13 – Chester 73.

🏨 **Royal Goat,** LL55 4YE, ℰ 224, ⟋ – 📳 🛏wc ⊛ 🅟. ⚞ 🄰🄴 ⓞ **VISA**
M 7.50/10.00 **st.** and a la carte 🍴 3.50 – **22 rm** ⚏ 22.00/40.00 **t.** – SB (November-April) 50.00/54.00 **st.**

🏡 **Tanronen,** LL55 4YB, ℰ 347 – 🅟. ⚞ **VISA**
M (bar lunch Monday to Saturday)/dinner 7.75 **st.** 🍴 3.00 – **9 rm** ⚏ 12.50/25.00 **st.** – SB 38.00 **st.**

BEDFORD Beds. **404** S 27 – pop. 75 ,632 – ECD : Thursday – ✆ 0234.
See : Embankment★ – Cecil Higgins Art Gallery (porcelain★ 18C).
Envir. : Elstow (Abbey Church★ 11C, Moot Hall : John Bunyan Museum *AC*) S : 1 ¼ m. – Ampthill (Houghton House : site★, ≼★) S : 5 m. – Old Warden (St. Leonard's Church : woodwork★ – Aeroplane Museum, near Biggleswade Aerodrome : the Shuttleworth collection★ *AC*) SE : 7 ½ m.
🇫 Bedford and County, Green Lane, Clapham ℰ 52617, N : 2 m. on A 6 – 🇫 Bedfordshire, Biddenham ℰ 53241, NE : 1 m. on A 428.
🇿 10 St. Paul's Sq. ℰ 215226.
◆London 59 – ◆Cambridge 31 – Colchester 70 – ◆Leicester 51 – Lincoln 95 – Luton 20 – ◆Oxford 52 – Southend-on-Sea 85.

🏨 **Bedford Swan** (Mt. Charlotte), The Embankment, MK40 1RW, ℰ 46565 – 📺 🛏wc ⊛ 🅟. 🅰
84 rm.

🏡 **De Parys,** 41 de Parys Av., MK40 2UA, ℰ 52121, ⚔ – 📺 🛏wc 🛏wc 🅟. 🅰. ⚞ 🄰🄴 ⓞ **VISA**
closed 1 week at Christmas – **M** (bar lunch)/dinner 7.75 **st.** 🍴 3.20 – **33 rm** ⚏ 23.00/40.00 **st.** – SB (weekends only) 42.00/57.00 **st.**

🏡 **Shakespeare,** 27 Shakespeare Rd, MK40 2DX, ℰ 213147, ⚔ – 📺 🛏wc 🛏wc 🅟. ⚞ 🄰🄴
VISA. ⟆⟆
M *(closed Saturday lunch and Sunday dinner)* 8.50 **t.** and a la carte 🍴 3.50 – **18 rm**
⚏ 29.50/38.50 **t.**

⋔ **Edwardian House,** 15 Shakespeare Rd, MK40 2DZ, ℰ 45281 – 📺 🛏wc 🛏wc 🅟. 🄰🄴 ⓞ.
⟆⟆
16 rm ⚏ 17.00/36.00 **s.**

at Houghton Conquest S : 6 ½ m. by A 6 – ⊠ ✿ 0234 Bedford :

XX **Knife and Cleaver,** MK45 3LA, ✐ 740387 – **P** **A5** **VISA**
closed Sunday – **M** a la carte 9.75/12.75 **t.** ▯ 3.25.

at Turvey W : 7 m. on A 428 – ⊠ Bedford – ✿ 023 064 Turvey :

XX **Laws** with rm, MK43 8DB, ✐ 213, ✿ – **⊡** ⇌wc **P.** **A5** **VISA.** ✽
closed Sunday, Christmas and Bank Holidays – **M** *(closed Monday and Saturday lunch)* a la
carte 11.45/13.50 **t.** ▯ 3.90 – **5 rm** ⊒ 33.00/45.00 **st.**

at Clapham NW : 2 m. on A 6 – ⊠ ✿ 0234 Bedford :

🏛 **Woodlands Manor,** Green Lane, MK41 6EP, ✐ 63281, Telex 825007, ✿ – **⊡** **☎** **P.** ⚐. **A5**
AE **VISA.** ✽
M *(closed Saturday lunch April-October)* 13.25 **t.** and a la carte ▯ 4.50 – ⊒ 5.50 – **21 rm**
40.00/69.00 **t.** – SB (weekends only) 53.70 **st.**

MICHELIN Branch, Hammond Rd, Elms Farm Industrial Estate, MK41 0LG, ✐ 213491

AUDI, MERCEDES-BENZ, VAUXHALL-OPEL Bar-
ker's Lane ✐ 50011
AUSTIN-ROVER-DAIMLER-JAGUAR 120 Golding-
ton Rd ✐ 55221
BMW, ROLLS ROYCE-BENTLEY Shuttleworth Rd,
Goldington ✐ 60412

FORD 8/10 The Broadway ✐ 58391
FORD Hudson Rd ✐ 40041
HONDA, VOLVO Windsor Rd ✐ 45454
NISSAN 180 Goldington Rd ✐ 60121
RENAULT 87 High St., Clapham ✐ 54257
SAAB Station Rd, Oakley ✐ 023 02 (Oakley) 3118

BEESTON Cheshire **402** **403** **404** L 24 – pop. 221 – ⊠ Tarporley – ✿ 0829 Bunbury.
♦London 186 – Chester 15 – ♦Liverpool 40 – Shrewsbury 32.

XXX **Wild Boar Inn** (Embassy) with rm, CW6 9NW, on A 49 ✐ 260309, Telex 61455, ✿ – **⊡**
⇌wc **☎** **P.** **A5** **AE** **①** **VISA.** ✽
closed 27 to 31 December – **M** 10.75/15.00 **st.** and a la carte ▯ 3.00 – ⊒ 5.00 – **30 rm**
31.00/40.00 **st.** – SB 56.00 **st.**

XXX **Rembrandt,** Whitchurch Road, Spurstow, CW6 9PD, on A 49 ✐ 260281 – **P.** **A5** **①** **VISA**
closed Sunday dinner, Monday and Bank Holidays – **M** 9.75 **st.** and a la carte.

BEESTON Notts. **402** **403** **404** Q 25 – see Nottingham.

BELBROUGHTON Heref. and Worc. **403** **404** N 26 – see Stourbridge (West Midlands).

BELFORD Northumb. **401** **402** O 17 – pop. 943 – ECD : Thursday – ✿ 066 83.
♦London 335 – ♦Edinburgh 71 – ♦Newcastle-upon-Tyne 49.

🏠 Blue Bell, Market Pl., NE70 7NE, ✐ 543, ✿ – **⊡** ⇌wc **☎** **P.** – **15 rm.**

BELPER Derbs. **402** **403** **404** P 24 – pop. 17,328 – ⊠ ✿ 077 382.
♦London 141 – Derby 8 – ♦Manchester 55 – ♦Nottingham 17.

XX **Remy's,** 84 Bridge St., DE5 1AZ, ✐ 2246, French rest. – **AE** **①** **VISA**
closed Sunday dinner, Monday, 2 weeks January and 3 weeks August – **M** 11.95 **t.** ▯ 3.00.

BEMBRIDGE I.O.W. **403** **404** Q 31 – see Wight (Isle of).

BENLLECH Gwynedd **402** **403** H 24 – pop. 1,948 – ECD : Thursday – ✿ 0248 Tynygongl.
♦London 258 – Caernarfon 17 – Chester 70 – Holyhead 22.

🏠 **Rhostrefor,** Amlwch Rd, LL74 8SR, on A 5025 ✐ 852347, ⬚, ✿ – **⊡** ⇌wc 🛁wc **P.** **A5** ·
M (bar lunch)/dinner 12.00 **t.** and a la carte ▯ 2.65 – **15 rm** ⊒ 16.00/32.00 **t.** – SB (October-May)
38.00/42.00 **st.**

BEPTON West Sussex – see Midhurst.

BERKELEY Glos. **403** **404** M28 – pop. 1,498 – ECD : Wednesday – ✿ 0453 Dursley.
♦London 129 – ♦Bristol 20 – ♦Cardiff 50 – Gloucester 18.

🏠 **Old School House,** Canonbury St., GL13 9BG, ✐ 811711 – **⊡** ⇌wc 🛁wc ✆ **P.** **A5** **VISA.**
✽
M *(closed Monday lunch)* a la carte lunch/dinner 12.50 **st.** ▯ 2.75 – **7 rm** ⊒ 23.00/35.00 **st.** –
SB (weekends only) 52.00 **st.**

BERKHAMSTED Herts **404** S 28 – pop. 16,874 – ECD : Wednesday and Saturday – ✿ 044 27.
ℹ Library, Kings Rd ✐ 4545.
♦London 33 – Luton 16 – ♦Oxford 35.

🏠 **Hamberlin's** ॐ without rest., Tring Rd, Northchurch, HP4 3TL, NW : 1 ½ m. on A 41
✐ 75100, ✿ – 🛁wc **P.** **A5** **①** **VISA**
closed 1 week at Christmas – **15 rm** ⊒ 25.00/35.00 **st.**

🏠 **Swan,** 139 High St., HP4 3HH, ✐ 71451, Telex 82257 – **⊡** ⇌wc **☎** **P.** **A5** **VISA**
M *(closed Sunday dinner)* 10.00 **t.** and a la carte ▯ 3.50 – **16 rm** ⊒ 25.00/42.00 **st.** – SB
(weekends only) 50.00/55.00 **st.**

BERKSWELL West Midlands 🅐🅐🅑 P 26 — see Coventry.

BERWICK-UPON-TWEED Northumb. 🅐🅐🅑 O 16 — pop. 12 ,772 — ECD : Thursday — ☎ 0289.

See : City Walls★ 16C.

Envir. : Norham Castle★ (12C) SW : 7 m.

🔘 Goswick, Beal ℰ 87256, S : 5 m. — 🔘 Magdalene Fields ℰ 305109.

🅘 Castlegate Car Park ℰ 307187 (summer only).

◆London 349 — ◆Edinburgh 57 — ◆Newcastle-upon-Tyne 63.

🏨 **King's Arms,** 43 Hide Hill, TD15 1EJ, ℰ 307454, Telex 8811232 — 📺 🚽wc 📶wc 📞. 🔙 🅰🅴 ⓪ 𝘝𝘐𝘚𝘈
M 5.50 **st.** (lunch) and a la carte 10.90/11.65 **st.** ⬧ 2.50 — **36 rm** ⛛ 32.00/48.00 **st.** — SB (weekends only)(not summer) 52.00 **st.**

🏠 **Turret House,** Etal Rd, TD15 2EG, S : ¾ m. by A 1167 on B 6354 ℰ 307344, 🌳 — 📺 🚽wc
📞 🅿 🔙 🅰🅴 ⓪ 𝘝𝘐𝘚𝘈
M 4.75/9.75 **st.** ⬧ 3.50 — **10 rm** ⛛ 28.75/45.00 **st.** — SB (weekends only) 44.00/50.00 **st.**

AUSTIN-ROVER Tweedside Trading Estate ℰ 307561
RENAULT Golden Sq. ℰ 307371
VAUXHALL 12 Silver St. ℰ 307436
VOLVO Tweed St. ℰ 307537

BETWS-Y-COED Gwynedd 🅐🅑🅑 I 24 — pop. 654 — ECD : Thursday — ☎ 069 02.

Envir. : Fairy Glen and Conway Falls★ *AC*, SE : 2 m. — Swallow Falls★ *AC*, NW : 2 m. — Nanty-gwryd valley★ W : by Capel Curig.

🔘 ℰ 556, ½ m. off A 5.

🅘 Royal Oak Stables ℰ 426665 (summer only).

◆London 226 — Holyhead 44 — Shrewsbury 62.

🏨 **Royal Oak,** Holyhead Rd, LL24 0AY, ℰ 219 — 📺 🚽wc 📞 🅿 🔙 🅰🅴 ⓪ 𝘝𝘐𝘚𝘈 ✂
closed 25-26 December — **M** 6.00/14.00 **t.** ⬧ 3.25 — **21 rm** ⛛ 37.00/50.00 **t.**

🏠 **Waterloo,** LL24 0AR, on A 5 ℰ 411 — 📺 🚽wc 📞 🅿. ✂
28 rm.

🏡 **Park Hill,** Llanrwst Rd, LL24 0HD, NE : 1 m. by A 5 on A 470 ℰ 540, ≤ Vale of Conwy, 🔲, 🌳
— 🚽wc 📶wc 🅿 🔙 🅰🅴 ⓪ 𝘝𝘐𝘚𝘈
closed December and January — **11 rm** ⛛ 15.00/38.00 **t.**

at Pont-y-Pant SW : 4 ½ m. on A 470 — 🖂 ☎ 069 06 Dolwyddelan :

🏠 **Plas Hall,** LL25 0PJ, ℰ 206, 🎣, 🌳 — 📺 🚽wc 📞 ⅙ 🅿. 🔙 🅰🅴 ⓪ 𝘝𝘐𝘚𝘈 ✂
closed 25 and 26 December — **M** (lunch by arrangement) 5.95/7.95 **t.** and a la carte ⬧ 3.20 —
16 rm ⛛ 35.00/50.00 **t.**

BEVERLEY Humberside 🅐🅑🅑 S 22 — pop. 19 ,368 — ECD : Thursday — 🖂 ☎ 0482 Kingston-upon-Hull.

See : Minster★★ 13C-15C — St. Mary's Church★ 14C-15C.

🔘 Walkington Rd ℰ 867190.

🅘 30 Market Pl. ℰ 867430.

◆London 188 — ◆Kingston-upon-Hull 8 — ◆Leeds 52 — York 29.

🏨 **Beverley Arms** (T.H.F.), North Bar Within, HU17 8DD, ℰ 869241, Telex 597568 — 🛗 📺
🚽wc 📞 🅿. 🔙 🅰🅴 ⓪ 𝘝𝘐𝘚𝘈
M 7.00/9.50 **st.** and a la carte ⬧ 2.70 — ⛛ 5.50 — **61 rm** 38.50/49.50 **st.**

🏠 **Lairgate,** 30 Lairgate, HU17 8EP, ℰ 882141 — 📺 🚽wc 📶wc 📞 🅿. 🔙 𝘝𝘐𝘚𝘈
closed 26 December — **M** 5.50/8.50 **t.** and a la carte ⬧ 3.00 — **24 rm** ⛛ 21.00/37.00 **t.** — SB
(weekends only)(October-March) 42.00/45.00 **st.**

🏡 King's Head, Market Pl., HU17 9AH, ℰ 869241, Telex 527568 — 🅿 — **9 rm**.

at Tickton NE : 3 ½ m. by A 1035 — 🖂 Kingston-upon-Hull — ☎ 0401 Leven :

🏨 **Tickton Grange,** HU17 9SH, ℰ 43666, 🌳 — 📺 🚽wc 📶wc 📞 🅿. ⅗ 🔙 🅰🅴 ⓪ 𝘝𝘐𝘚𝘈 ✂
M a la carte lunch/dinner 16.50 **t.** — ⛛ 4.50 — **15 rm** 36.00/48.00 **t.** — SB (weekends only)
54.00/68.00 **st.**

AUSTIN-ROVER 20 Norwood ℰ 867922
FORD Wednesday Market ℰ 868311
VAUXHALL-OPEL Swinemoor Lane ℰ 882207

BEWDLEY Heref. and Worc. 🅐🅐🅑 N 26 — pop. 8 ,696 — ECD : Wednesday — ☎ 0299.

🅘 The Library, Load St. ℰ 403303.

◆London 140 — ◆Birmingham 20 — Worcester 16.

🏠 **Black Boy,** Kidderminster Rd, DY12 1AG, ℰ 402119, 🌳 — 📺 🚽wc 📶 🅿. 🔙 🅰🅴 𝘝𝘐𝘚𝘈
M 7.50 **t.** (dinner) and a la carte ⬧ 3.00 — **25 rm** ⛛ 15.50/38.00 **t.** — SB (weekends only)
29.50/39.50 **t.**

✕✕ **Bailiff's House,** 68 High St., DY12 2DJ, ℰ 402691, « 17C Bailiff's House » — 🔙 🅰🅴 𝘝𝘐𝘚𝘈
closed Saturday lunch, Sunday dinner and Monday — **M** 13.50/15.50 **t.** ⬧ 2.95.

BEXHILL East Sussex ⁴⁰⁴ V 31 – pop. 34 ,625 – ECD : Wednesday – ✆ 0424.

🏌 Cooden Beach ℰ 042 43 (Cooden) 2040.

🛈 De La Warr Pavilion, Marina ℰ 212023.

◆London 66 – ◆ Brighton 32 – Folkestone 42.

🏨 **Cooden Beach** (Best Western), Cooden Sea Rd, Cooden Beach, TN39 4TT, W : 2 m. on B 2182 ℰ 04243 (Cooden) 2281, Telex 95489, ⏋ heated, ⇌ – 📺 ⇐ 🅿 ⚓ 🔄 AE ⓿ 𝗩𝗜𝗦𝗔
M 10.50 st. (dinner) and a la carte 🍴 3.00 – **30 rm** ⎅ 28.50/49.50 **st.**

AUDI, VW   King Offa Way ℰ 212255
AUSTIN-ROVER-DAIMLER-JAGUAR   57-69 London Rd ℰ 212000
FIAT, MAZDA   Holliers Hill ℰ 213577
FORD ℰ 212727

HONDA   Sackville Rd ℰ 221330
RENAULT   London Rd ℰ 210485
TOYOTA   Holliers Hill ℰ 213577
VAUXHALL-OPEL   Dorset Rd ℰ 211212

BIBURY Glos. ⁴⁰³ ⁴⁰⁴ O 28 – pop. 603 – ECD : Wednesday – ✉ Cirencester – ✆ 028 574.

See : Arlington Row★ 17C.

◆London 86 – Gloucester 26 – ◆Oxford 30.

🏨 **Swan,** GL7 5NW, ℰ 204, « Garden and trout stream », ⯏ – 📺 ⌂wc ☎ 🅿 🔄 𝗩𝗜𝗦𝗔
M 10.25/13.75 **t.** 🍴 3.00 – **23 rm** ⎅ 30.50/52.50 **t.** – SB (November-March) 52.50/57.50 **st.**

🏨 **Bibury Court** ⯏, GL7 5NT, ℰ 337, ≼, « Tudor mansion », ⯏, ⇌, park – ⌂wc 🅿 🔄 AE ⓿ 𝗩𝗜𝗦𝗔
closed 1 week at Christmas – **M** (bar lunch)/dinner a la carte 9.00/13.55 **t.** 🍴 2.50 – ⎄ 3.00 – **16 rm** 22.00/42.00 **t.**, **1 suite** 52.00 **t.** – SB (November-March) 54.00/58.00 **st.**

BIDDENDEN Kent ⁴⁰⁴ V 30 – pop. 2 ,229 – ✉ Ashford – ✆ 0580.

◆London 51 – Folkestone 29 – Hastings 23 – Maidstone 14.

XX **Ye Maydes,** 13-15 High St., TN27 8AL, ℰ 291306 – 🔄 AE
closed Sunday, Monday, last week January, last 2 weeks August, first week November and Bank Holidays – **M** 6.55/14.00 **t.** and a la carte 🍴 2.80.

XX **West House,** 28 High St., TN27 8AH, ℰ 291341, Italian rest. – 🅿 🔄 𝗩𝗜𝗦𝗔
closed Sunday, Monday except Bank Holidays, 2 weeks April, 2 weeks August and 1 week November – **M** 7.50/10.50 **t.** and a la carte 🍴 2.50.

BIDEFORD Devon ⁴⁰³ H 30 **The West Country G.** – pop. 13 ,826 – ECD : Wednesday – ✆ 023 72.

See : The Bridge★★ – Burton Art Gallery★AC.

Envir. : Clovelly★★, W : 11 m. – Great Torrington : Dartington Glass★AC, SE : 7 m. – at Hartland (≼★★★) Church★ Quay★ (≼★★), W : 12 m. – at Thornbury, Devon Museum of Mechanical Music★AC, S : 15 m.

⛴ to the Isle of Lundy (Lundy Co.) 2-3 Weekly (2 h 30 mn).

🛈 The Quay ℰ 77676 (summer only).

◆London 231 – Exeter 43 – ◆Plymouth 58 – Taunton 60.

🏨 Durrant House, Heywood Rd, Northam, EX39 3QB, N : 1 m. on A 386 ℰ 72361, ⏋ heated – 📺 ⌂wc ☎ 🅿 🔄 AE ⓿ 𝗩𝗜𝗦𝗔
50 rm ⎅ 29.50/43.50 **t.** – SB (weekends only) (winter only) 55.00 **st.**

🏨 **Yeoldon House** (Best Western) ⯏, Durrant Lane, Northam, EX39 2RL, N : 1 ½ m. by A 386 ℰ 74400, ≼ Torridge estuary, « Country house atmosphere », ⇌ – 📺 ⌂wc 🍴wc 🅿 🔄 AE ⓿ 𝗩𝗜𝗦𝗔. ✎
closed 24 December-10 January – **M** (bar lunch)/dinner 10.50 **t.** 🍴 3.50 – **10 rm** ⎅ 29.75/53.00 **t.** – SB 49.50/74.00 **st.**

🏠 **Beaconside House** ⯏, Landcross, EX39 5JL, S : 3 m. by A 386 on A 388 ℰ 77205, ≼, ⏋, ⇌, park, ✎ – 📺 ⌂wc 🅿 🔄 ⓿
M (bar lunch Monday to Saturday)/dinner 8.50 **t.** 🍴 2.55 – **9 rm** ⎅ 15.00/34.00 – SB (September-June) 36.00/46.00 **st.**

🏠 **Riversford** ⯏, Limers Lane, Northam, EX39 2RG, N : 1 m. by A 386 ℰ 74239, ≼, ⇌ – 📺 ⌂wc 🅿 🔄 AE ⓿
M 5.20/8.50 **t.** and a la carte – **17 rm** ⎅ 15.50/38.00 **t.** – SB (weekends only)(October-May except December and New Year) 44.50/55.00 **st.**

XX Gray's, 4 Fore St., Northam, EX39 1AW, N : 1 ¾ m. by A 386 ℰ 6371.

at Instow N : 3 m. on A 39 – ✉ Bideford – ✆ 0271 Instow :

🏨 **Commodore,** Marine Par., EX39 4JN, ℰ 860347, ≼ Taw and Torridge estuaries, ⇌ – 📺 🅿 ⚓ 🔄 AE 𝗩𝗜𝗦𝗔. ✎
M 6.50/10.00 **t.** and a la carte 🍴 5.20 – **20 rm** ⎅ 31.00/56.00 **t.**

at Eastleigh NE : 2 ½ m. by A 39 (via Old Barnstaple Road) – ✉ Bideford – ✆ 0271 Instow :

⌂ **Pines,** EX39 4PA, ℰ 860561, ≼, ⇌ – 🅿 🔄 𝗩𝗜𝗦𝗔. ✎
March-October – **7 rm** ⎅ 9.00/20.00 **st.**

AUSTIN-ROVER   6 Queen St. ℰ 73304
PEUGEOT-TALBOT   Bridgeland St. ℰ 72016
RENAULT   Kingsley Rd ℰ 72546

SAAB, HYUNDAI   Meddon St. ℰ 72467
VAUXHALL-OPEL, BEDFORD   Handy Cross ℰ 72282

BIDFORD-ON-AVON Warw. 🔢🔢 O 27 – pop. 2,748 – ECD : Thursday – ✉ Alcester – ☎ 0789.

♦London 103 – ♦Birmingham 25 – ♦Coventry 27 – ♦Oxford 50 – Worcester 22.

🏠 **White Lion** (Best Western), High St., B50 4BQ, ℰ 773309 – 📺 🛏wc. 🔊 🗚
M (bar lunch Monday to Saturday)/dinner a la carte 10.90/15.30 t. ⓙ 3.30 – ♐ 1.50 – **15 rm**
17.00/40.00 t. – SB (except Easter and Bank Holidays) 42.00/46.00 t.

BIGBURY-ON-SEA Devon 🔢 I 33 – pop. 559 – ECD : Thursday – ✉ Kingsbridge – ☎ 054 881.

♦London 196 – Exeter 42 – ♦Plymouth 17.

🏠 **Henley**, Folly Hill, TQ7 4AR, ℰ 240, ≤, 🌫 – 🛏wc 🅿
Easter-September – **M** (bar lunch)/dinner 7.00 t. ⓙ 1.50 – **9 rm** ♐ 11.00/26.00 t.

🏠 **Seagulls**, TQ7 4AR, ℰ 331, ≤ Bigbury Bay and Bolt Head, 🌫 – 🛏wc 🛏wc. 🔊 *VISA*
Easter-mid October – **M** (bar lunch)/dinner 9.00 **st.** ⓙ 1.80 – **10 rm** ♐ 16.00/36.00 st.

BILBROOK Somerset 🔢 J 30 – ✉ Minehead – ☎ 0984 Washford.

♦London 181 – Minehead 5 – Taunton 19.

🏠 **Dragon House**, TA24 6HQ, ℰ 40215, « Part 18C house with gardens » – 📺 🛏wc 🛏wc 🅿.
🔊 🗚 ⑩ *VISA*
M 9.75 t. and a la carte ⓙ 2.60 – **10 rm** ♐ 19.50/32.75 t. – SB 28.25/31.50 st.

🏠 **Bilbrook Lawns**, TA24 6HE, ℰ 40331, 🌫 – 📺 🛏wc 🅿. 💥
M a la carte 6.35/10.70 t. ⓙ 2.75 – **13 rm** ♐ 13.50/30.00 t. – SB (except Christmas) 32.00/36.00 st.

BILLESLEY Warw. – see Stratford-upon-Avon.

BILLINGHAM Cleveland 🔢 Q 20 – pop. 36,855 – ✉ ☎ 0642 Stockton-on-Tees.

🏌 Sandy Lane ℰ 554494.

♦London 255 – ♦Middlesbrough 3 – Sunderland 26.

🏠 **Billingham Arms Thistle** (Thistle), Town Sq., TS23 2HD, ℰ 553661, Group Telex 587746 –
📺 🛏wc 🛏wc 🌫 🅿. 🔊. 🔊 🗚 ⑩ *VISA*
M 6.85/10.00 t. and a la carte ⓙ 3.00 – ♐ 5.25 – **63 rm** 31.00/52.00 t.

AUSTIN-ROVER Wolviston Rd ℰ 553959   RENAULT Central Garage ℰ 553071
FORD The Green ℰ 550415

BILLINGSHURST West Sussex 🔢 S 30 – pop. 4,877 – ECD : Wednesday – ☎ 040 381.

♦London 45 – ♦Brighton 24 – Guildford 20 – ♦Portsmouth 39.

✕✕ **The Jennie Wren**, Pulborough Rd, RH14 9EU, S : ½ m. on A 29 ℰ 2571 – 🅿. 🔊 🗚 ⑩ *VISA*
closed Saturday lunch, Sunday dinner, 2 weeks February and Bank Holidays – **M** a la carte
8.75/12.30 t. ⓙ 3.15.

AUSTIN-ROVER-JAGUAR 62 High St. ℰ 2022   PEUGEOT-TALBOT Five Oaks ℰ 2075
FORD High St. ℰ 2537
MERCEDES-BENZ, PORSCHE, SCIMITAR High St.
ℰ 3341

BINGLEY West Yorks. 🔢 O 22 – pop. 18,954 – ECD : Tuesday – ✉ ☎ 0274 Bradford.

♦London 204 – Bradford 6 – Skipton 13.

🏠 **Bankfield** (Embassy), Bradford Rd, BD16 1TV, SE : 1 ½ m. on A 650 ℰ 567123, 🌫 – 📺
🛏wc 🅿. 🔊. 🔊 🗚 ⑩ *VISA*. 💥
M (carving rest.) 8.25 **st.** and a la carte ⓙ 2.75 – ♐ 5.00 – **65 rm** 36.50/48.50 st. – SB
52.00/55.00 **st.**

SCIMITAR Park Rd ℰ 563556

BIRKENHEAD Merseyside 🔢🔢 K 23 – pop. 99,075 – ECD : Thursday – ☎ 051 Liverpool.

🏌 Arrowe Park, Woodchurch ℰ 677 1527 – 🏌 Prenton, Golf Links Rd ℰ 608 1053.

⛴ to Liverpool (Merseyside Transport) frequent services daily (7-8 mn).

🛈 Central Library, Borough Rd ℰ 652 6106/7/8.

♦London 222 – ♦Liverpool 2.

Plan : see Liverpool p. 3

🏨 Bowler Hat, 2 Talbot Rd, Oxton, L43 2HH, ℰ 652 4931, Telex 628761, 🌫 – 📺 ☎ 🅿. 🔊
29 rm. 1 suite.   AX

ALFA-ROMEO Watermound ℰ 630 1844   MAZDA Albion St., Wallasey ℰ 638 2234
AUSTIN-ROVER Park Rd North ℰ 647 9445   NISSAN Hoylake Rd ℰ 678 1060
COLT New Chester Rd ℰ 645 1025   RENAULT Borough Rd ℰ 608 9121
FIAT Claughton Firs ℰ 653 8555   VAUXHALL-OPEL 6 Woodchurch Rd ℰ 652 2366
LANCIA Watermound ℰ 638 0046

BIRMINGHAM West Midlands **403 404** O 26 – pop. 1,013,995 – ECD : Wednesday – ✪ 021.

See : Museum and Art Gallery★★ JZ **M1** – Museum of Science and Industry★ JY **M2** – Cathedral (stained glass windows★ 19C) KYZ **E**.

ᚒ Cocks Moor Woods, Alcester Rd South, King's Heath ℰ 444 2062, S : 6 ½ m. by A 435 FX – ᚒ Edgbaston, Church Rd ℰ 454 1736, S : 1 m. FX – ᚒ Pype Hayes, Eachelhurst Rd, Walmley ℰ 361 1014, NE : 7 ½ m. DT – ᚒ Warley, Lightwoods Hill, ℰ 429 2440, W : 5 m. BU.

✈ Birmingham Airport : ℰ 767 7153, E : 6 ½ m. by A 45 DU.

🖪 2 City Arcade ℰ 643 2514 – National Exhibition Centre ℰ 780 4141 – Birmingham Airport ℰ 767 7145.

✦London 122 – ✦Bristol 91 – ✦Liverpool 103 – ✦Manchester 86 – ✦Nottingham 50.

Town plans : Birmingham pp. 2-7
Except where otherwise stated see pp. 6 and 7

🏨 **Albany** (T.H.F.), Smallbrook, Queensway, B5 4EW, ℰ 643 8171, Telex 337031, ≼, ◲, squash – 🛗 🗏 📺 ☎ ⟨, 🚗 ⚠ 匝 ① **VISA**
JKZ **a**
M 8.25 **st**. and a la carte 🍷 2.70 – ⊆ 5.50 – **254 rm** 47.50/57.00 **st**., **8 suites**.

🏨 **Plough and Harrow** (Crest), 135 Hagley Rd, Edgbaston, B16 8LS, W : 1 ½ m. on A 456 ℰ 454 4111, Telex 338074, 🚗 – 🛗 🗏 📺 ☎ 🚗 🚗 匝 ① **VISA**
p. 4 EX **a**
⊆ 6.50 – **44 rm** 65.00/75.00 **st**., **3 suites** – SB (weekends only) 92.00 **st**.

🏨 **Holiday Inn**, Central Sq., Holliday St., B1 1HH, ℰ 643 2766, Telex 337272, ≼, ◲ – 🛗 🗏 📺 ☎ ⟨, 🚗 匝 ① **VISA** 🎾
JZ **z**
M 8.95/9.45 **t**. and a la carte 🍷 3.00 – ⊆ 5.25 – **304 rm** 45.00/55.00, **4 suites** 120.00/205.00.

🏨 **Midland** (Best Western), 128 New St., B2 4JT, ℰ 643 2601, Telex 338419 – 🛗 🗏 rest 📺 🚗 匝 ① **VISA** 🎾
KZ **r**
M 12.50 **t**. and a la carte 🍷 2.75 – **107 rm** ⊆ 27.50/66.00 **st**., **1 suite** 71.50/104.50 **st**. – SB 44.00/63.80 **st**.

🏨 **Strathallan Thistle** (Thistle), 225 Hagley Rd, Edgbaston, B16 9RY, W : 2 m. on A 456 ℰ 455 9777, Telex 336680 – 🛗 📺 ☎ 🚗 🚗 匝 ① **VISA**
p. 4 EX **i**
M 6.95/10.50 **t**. and a la carte 🍷 2.50 – ⊆ 5.50 – **164 rm** 43.50/70.00 **t**., **4 suites** 85.00 **t**.

🏨 **Grand** (Q.M.H.), Colmore Row, B3 2DA, ℰ 236 7951, Telex 338174 – 🛗 📺 🚗 匝 ① **VISA** closed 4 days at Christmas – **M** 8.50 **st**. and a la carte 🍷 3.10 – **145 rm** ⊆ 44.50/55.00 **st**., **3 suites** 95.00 **st**. – SB (weekends only) 52.00 **st**.
JKY **c**

🏨 **Royal Angus Thistle** (Thistle), St. Chad's, Queensway, B4 6HY, ℰ 236 4211, Telex 336889 – 🛗 📺 🚗 🚗 匝 ① **VISA** 🎾
KY **s**
M 9.00/11.00 **t**. and a la carte 🍷 2.75 – ⊆ 5.25 – **139 rm** 43.50/70.00 **t**., **1 suite**.

🏨 **Apollo**, Hagley Rd, Edgbaston, B16 9RA, W : 2 ¼ m. on A 456 ℰ 455 0271, Telex 336759 – 🛗 🗏 rest 📺 🖃wc 🚗 🚗 🚗 匝 ① **VISA** 🎾
p. 4 EX **o**
M 9.05/11.70 **st**. and a la carte 🍷 2.75 – ⊆ 4.95 – **130 rm** 33.50/46.75 **s**., **3 suites** 69.00/76.00 **s**. – SB (weekends only) 60.00 **st**.

🏨 **Birmingham International**, New St., B2 4RX, ℰ 643 2747, Telex 338331 – 🛗 🗏 rest 📺 🖃wc ☎ 🚗
KZ **x**
198 rm, **4 suites**.

🏨 **Asquith House**, 19 Portland Rd, off Hagley Rd, Edgbaston, B16 9HN, W : 2 m. by A 456 ℰ 454 5282, 🚗 – 📺 🖃wc 🖫wc 🚗 🚗 匝 ⚠
p. 4 EX **c**
closed 1 week at Christmas – **M** (residents only)(lunch by arrangement) 12.00/16.00 **st**. 🍷 2.20 – **10 rm** ⊆ 24.05/38.95 **st**. – SB (weekends only) 60.00/70.00 **st**.

🏨 **Berrow Court** 🐾, Berrow Drive off Westfield Rd, Edgbaston, B15 3UD, W : 3 m. by A 456 ℰ 454 1488, « Country house atmosphere », 🚗 – 🚗 匝 **VISA**
p. 4 EX **e**
closed 24 December-2 January – **M** (closed Saturday and Sunday) (dinner only)(residents only) 5.80 **st**. – **16 rm** ⊆ 21.30/30.45 **st**.

🏨 **Hagley Court**, 229 Hagley Rd, Edgbaston, B16 9RP, W : 2 m. on A 456 ℰ 454 6514 – 📺 🖃wc 🖫wc 🚗 🚗 **VISA**. 🎾
p. 4 EX **s**
closed Christmas – **M** (closed Friday to Sunday) (dinner only) 8.25 **st**. and a la carte 🍷 2.50 – **24 rm** ⊆ 20.00/37.00 **st**.

🏨 **Cobden**, 166-174 Hagley Rd, Edgbaston, B16 9NZ, W : 2 m. on A 456 ℰ 454 6621, Group Telex 339715, 🚗 – 🛗 📺 🖃wc 🖫wc 🚗 🚗 🚗 匝 **VISA**
p. 4 EX **n**
closed Christmas – **M** 4.50/7.50 **st**. (unlicensed) 🚗 – **210 rm** ⊆ 20.00/39.50 **st**.

🏨 **Norfolk**, 257-267 Hagley Rd, Edgbaston, B16 9NA, W : 2 ¼ m. on A 456 ℰ 454 8071, Group Telex 339715, 🚗 – 🛗 📺 🖃wc 🖫wc 🚗 🚗 🚗 匝 **VISA**
p. 4 EX **u**
closed Christmas – **M** 4.50/7.50 **st**. (unlicensed) – **175 rm** ⊆ 19.50/38.50 **st**.

XXX **Jonathans'**, 16-20 Wolverhampton Rd, B68 0LH, W : 4 m. by A 456 ℰ 429 3757, English rest., « Victoriana », 🚗 – 🚗 匝 ① **VISA**
p. 2 BU **e**
closed Saturday lunch – **M** a la carte 10.70/21.10 **t**. 🍷 2.60.

XX **Sloans**, Chad Sq., off Harborne Rd, Edgbaston, B15 3TQ, ℰ 455 6697, Seafood – 🚗 匝 ① **VISA**
p. 4 EX **v**
closed Saturday lunch, Sunday, last 2 weeks July and Bank Holidays – **M** 7.50/21.00 **t**. and a la carte.

XX **Rajdoot**, 12-22 Albert St., B4 7UD, ℰ 643 8805, Indian rest. – 🚗 匝 ① **VISA**
KZ **c**
closed lunch Sunday and Bank Holidays – **M** 4.50/10.00 **t**. and a la carte 🍷 2.70.

P.T.O. →

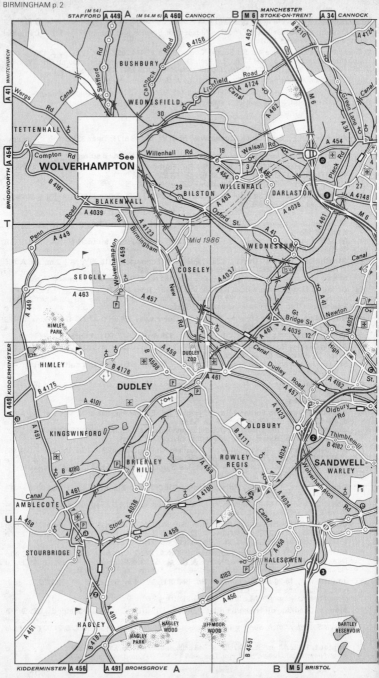

BIRMINGHAM AND WOLVERHAMPTON
ENLARGED AREA

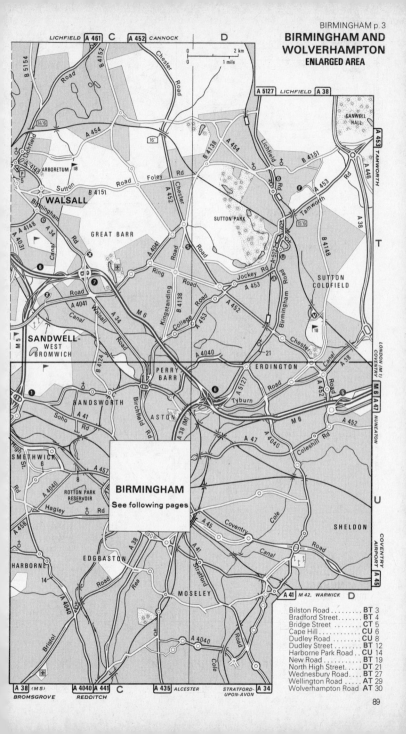

Bilston Road	**BT** 3
Bradford Street	**BT** 4
Bridge Street	**CT** 5
Cape Hill	**CU** 6
Dudley Road	**CU** 8
Dudley Street	**BT** 12
Harborne Park Road	**CU** 14
New Road	**BT** 19
North High Street	**DT** 21
Wednesbury Road	**BT** 27
Wellington Road	**AT** 29
Wolverhampton Road	**AT** 30

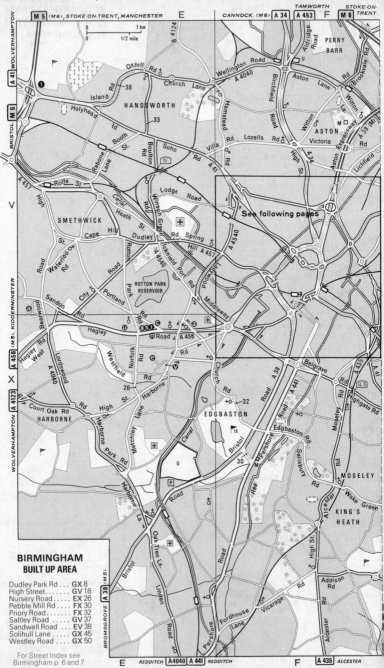

See following pages

BIRMINGHAM
BUILT UP AREA

Dudley Park Rd ... GX 8
High Street .... GV 16
Nursery Road .... EX 26
Pebble Mill Rd .... FX 30
Priory Road .... FX 32
Saltley Road ..... GV 37
Sandwell Road ... EV 38
Solihull Lane .... GX 45
Westley Road .... GX 50

For Street Index see
Birmingham p. 6 and 7

90

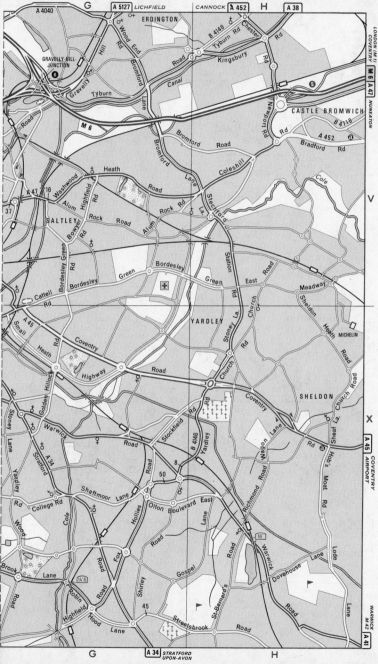

Bull Ring Centre . . . . p. 6 KZ
Corporation St. . . . . p. 6 KY
New St. . . . . p. 6 KZ

Adderley St. . . . . p. 7 LZ
Addison Rd . . . . p. 4 FX
Albert St. . . . . p. 6 KZ
Alcester Rd . . . . p. 4 FX
Alcester St. . . . . p. 7 LZ
Aldridge Rd . . . . p. 4 FV
Alum Rock Rd . . . . p. 5 GV
Aston Expressway . . . . p. 4 FV
Aston Lane . . . . p. 4 FV

Aston Rd. St. . . . . p. 6 KY
Avenue Rd . . . . p. 7 LY
Bagot St. . . . . p. 6 KY
Bath Row . . . . p. 6 JZ
Bearwood Rd . . . . p. 4 EV
Belgrave Rd . . . . p. 4 FX
Bell Barn Rd . . . . p. 6 JZ
Birchfield Rd . . . . p. 4 FV
Bishopsgate St. . . . . p. 6 JZ
Booth St. . . . . p. 4 EV
Bordesley Green . . . . p. 5 GV
Bordesley Green Rd . . . . p. 5 GV
Boulton Rd . . . . p. 4 EV

Bowyer Rd . . . . p. 5 GV
Bradford Rd . . . . p. 5 HV
Bradford St. . . . . p. 6 KZ
Bristol Rd . . . . p. 4 EX
Bristol St. . . . . p. 6 JZ
Broad St. . . . . p. 6 JZ
Bromford Lane . . . . p. 5 GV
Bromford Rd . . . . p. 5 HV
Bromsgrove St. . . . . p. 6 KZ
Brook Lane . . . . p. 5 GX
Brook St. . . . . p. 6 JY 2
Brookvale Rd . . . . p. 4 FV
Bull Ring . . . . p. 6 KZ 3

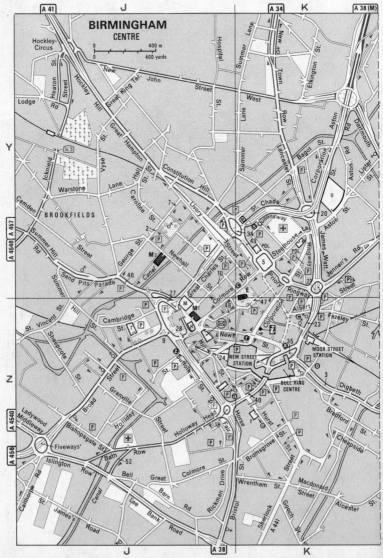

Bull Ring Centre . . . . p. 6 **KZ**
Calthorpe Rd. . . . . p. 6 **JZ**
Cambridge St. . . . . p. 6 **JZ**
Camden St. . . . . p. 6 **JY**
Camp Hill . . . . p. 7 **LZ**
Cape Hill . . . . p. 4 **EV**
Caroline St. . . . . p. 6 **JY**
Cattell Rd. . . . . p. 5 **GV**
Cheapside. . . . . p. 6 **KZ**
Chester St. . . . . p. 7 **LY**
Church Lane . . . . p. 4 **EV**
Church Rd EDGBASTON . . p. 4 **FX**
Church Rd SHELDON . . . . . . p. 5 **HX**

Church Rd YARDLEY . . . p. 5 **HX**
City Rd . . . . p. 4 **EV**
Coleshill Rd. . . . . p. 5 **HV**
College Rd. . . . . p. 5 **GX**
Colmore Circus . . . . p. 6 **KY** 5
Colmore Row . . . . p. 6 **JY**
Constitution Hill . . . . p. 6 **JY**
Corporation St. . . . . p. 6 **KZ**
Court Oak Rd . . . . p. 4 **EX**
Coventry Rd . . . . p. 7 **LZ** 6
Cox St. . . . . p. 6 **JY** 7
Curzon St. . . . . p. 7 **LY**
Dartmouth St. . . . . p. 6 **KY**
Digbeth . . . . p. 6 **KZ**
Dovehouse Lane . . . . p. 5 **HX**
Dudley Park Rd. . . . . . . p. 5 **GX** 8
Dudley Rd . . . . p. 4 **EV**
East Meadway . . . . p. 5 **HV**
Easy Row . . . . p. 6 **JZ**
Edgbaston Rd. . . . . p. 4 **FX**
Edmund St. . . . . p. 6 **JY** 10
Elkington St. . . . . p. 6 **KY**
Fazeley St. . . . . p. 6 **KZ**
Fiveways . . . . p. 6 **JZ**
Fordhouse Lane . . . . p. 4 **FX**
Fox Hollies Rd. . . . . p. 5 **GX**
George St. . . . . p. 6 **JY**
Golden Hillock Rd . . . . p. 5 **GX**
Gooch St. . . . . p. 6 **KZ**
Gospel Lane . . . . p. 5 **HX**
Granville St. . . . . p. 6 **JZ**
Gravelly Hill. . . . . p. 5 **GV**
Gravelly Hill Junction. . . . . p. 5 **GV**
Great Barr St. . . . . p. 7 **LZ**
Great Charles St. . . . . p. 6 **JY**
Great Colmore St. . . . . p. 6 **JZ**
Great Hampton St. . . . . p. 6 **JY**
Great King Ter. . . . . p. 6 **JY**
Great Lister St. . . . . p. 7 **LY**
Hagley Rd . . . . p. 4 **EX**
Hagley Rd West . . . . p. 4 **EX**
Hall St. . . . . p. 6 **JY**
Hampstead Rd. . . . . p. 4 **FV**
Harborne Lane . . . . p. 4 **EX**
Harborne Park Rd. . . . . p. 4 **EX**
Harborne Rd . . . . p. 4 **EX**
Heath Mill Lane . . . . p. 7 **LZ**
Heath St. . . . . p. 4 **EV**
Heaton St. . . . . p. 6 **JY**
Highfield Rd . . . . p. 5 **GX**
Highfield Rd . . . . p. 5 **GX**
Highgate Rd . . . . p. 4 **FX**
High St. ASTON . . . . p. 4 **FV**
High St. BORDESLEY . . . . p. 7 **LZ** 14
High St. DERITEND. . . . . . p. 7 **LZ**
High St. HARBORNE. . . . . p. 4 **EX**
High St. KING'S HEATH . . p. 4 **FX**
High St. SALTLEY . . . . . p. 5 **GV** 16
High St. SMETHWICK. . . . p. 4 **EV**
Hill St. . . . . p. 6 **JZ**
Hob's Moat Rd . . . . p. 5 **HX**
Hockley Circus . . . . p. 6 **JY**
Hockley Hill. . . . . p. 6 **JY**
Holliday St. . . . . p. 6 **JZ**
Holloway Circus . . . . . . p. 6 **JZ** 18
Holloway Head. . . . . p. 6 **JZ**
Holyhead Rd . . . . p. 4 **EV**
Horse Fair . . . . p. 6 **JZ**
Hospital St. . . . . p. 6 **JY**
Hurst St. . . . . p. 6 **KZ**
Icknield Port Rd . . . . p. 4 **EV**
Icknield St. . . . . p. 6 **JY**
Island Rd . . . . p. 4 **EV**
Islington Row . . . . p. 6 **JZ**
James Watt Ringway . . . p. 6 **KY**
Jennen's Rd . . . . p. 6 **KY**
Kingsbury Rd . . . . p. 5 **HV**
Ladywood Middleway . . . . p. 4 **EV**
Lancaster Circus . . . . . p. 6 **KY** 20
Lancaster St. . . . . p. 6 **KY**
Lawley St. . . . . p. 7 **LY**
Lee Bank Rd . . . . p. 6 **JZ**
Lichfield Rd. . . . . p. 4 **FV**
Linden Rd . . . . p. 4 **EX**
Lister St. . . . . p. 6 **KY**
Livery St. . . . . p. 6 **JY**
Lode Lane . . . . p. 5 **HX**
Lodge Rd. . . . . p. 4 **EV**
Lordswood Rd . . . . p. 4 **EX**
Lozells Rd . . . . p. 4 **FV**
Macdonald St. . . . . p. 6 **KZ**
Masshouse Circus . . . . p. 6 **KY** 21
Metchley Lane . . . . p. 4 **EX**

Moor St. Ringway . . . . . p. 6 **KZ** 23
Moseley Rd. . . . . p. 4 **FX**
Navigation St. . . . . p. 6 **JZ** 24
Nechell's Parkway . . . . . p. 7 **LY**
Newhall St. . . . . p. 6 **JY**
New John St. West . . . . . . p. 6 **JY**
Newport St. . . . . p. 5 **HV**
New St. . . . . p. 6 **JZ**
New Town Row . . . . p. 6 **KY**
Norfolk Rd . . . . p. 4 **EX**
Nursery Rd . . . . p. 4 **EX** 26
Oak Tree Lane. . . . . p. 4 **EX**
Olton Bd East . . . . p. 5 **GX**
Oxhill Rd . . . . p. 4 **EV**
Paradise Circus . . . . . . p. 6 **JY** 27
Paradise St. . . . . p. 6 **JZ** 28
Pebble Mill Rd . . . . p. 4 **FX** 30
Pershore Rd . . . . p. 4 **FX**
Portland Rd . . . . p. 4 **EV**
Priory Ringway . . . . p. 6 **KY**
Priory Rd . . . . p. 4 **FX** 32
Prospect Row . . . . p. 7 **LY**
Rabone Lane. . . . . p. 4 **EV**
Richmond Rd . . . . p. 5 **HX**
Rickman Drive . . . . p. 6 **JZ**
Robin Hood Lane . . . . p. 5 **GX**
Rolfe St. . . . . p. 4 **EV**
Rookery Rd . . . . p. 4 **EV** 33
Rotton Park Rd . . . . p. 4 **EV**
Rupert St. . . . . p. 7 **LY**
St. Bernard's Rd . . . . p. 5 **HX**
St. Chads Circus . . . . . p. 6 **KY** 34
St. Chads Ringway . . . . . . p. 6 **KY**
St. James's Rd . . . . p. 6 **JZ**
St. Martin's Circus . . . . p. 6 **KZ** 35
St. Vincent St. . . . . p. 6 **JZ**
Salisbury Rd . . . . p. 4 **FX**
Saltley Rd . . . . p. 5 **GV** 37
Sandon St. . . . . p. 4 **EV**
Sand Pits Parade . . . . p. 6 **JY**
Sandwell Rd . . . . p. 4 **EV** 38
Sandy Lane . . . . p. 7 **LZ**
Shaftmoor Lane . . . . p. 5 **GX**
Sheaf Lane . . . . p. 5 **HX**
Sheepcote St. . . . . p. 6 **JZ**
Sheldon Heath Rd . . . . . . p. 5 **HX**
Sherlock St. . . . . p. 6 **KZ**
Shirley Rd . . . . p. 5 **GX**
Smallbrook Ringway . . . p. 6 **KZ** 40
Small Heath Highway . . . . p. 5 **GX**
Snow Hill Ringway . . . . p. 6 **KY** 43
Soho Rd. . . . . p. 4 **EV**
Solihull Lane . . . . p. 5 **GX** 45
Spring Hill . . . . p. 4 **EV**
Station Rd . . . . p. 5 **HV**
Stechford Lane. . . . . p. 5 **HV**
Steelhouse Lane . . . . p. 6 **KY**
Stockfield Rd . . . . p. 5 **GX**
Stoney La. MOSELEY . . . p. 5 **GX**
Stoney La. SHELDON . . . p. 5 **HX**
Stratford Pl. . . . . p. 7 **LZ**
Stratford Rd. . . . . p. 5 **GX**
Streetsbrook Rd . . . . p. 5 **HX**
Suffolk St. . . . . p. 6 **JZ**
Summer Hill Rd, St. . . . . . p. 6 **JY**
Summer Lane . . . . p. 6 **KY**
Summer Row . . . . p. 6 **JY** 46
Temple Row . . . . p. 6 **KZ** 47
Tyburn Rd . . . . p. 5 **GV**
Vauxhall Rd . . . . p. 7 **LY**
Vicarage Rd . . . . p. 4 **FX**
Victoria Rd . . . . p. 4 **FV**
Villa Rd. . . . . p. 4 **FV**
Vyse St. . . . . p. 6 **JY**
Wagon Lane . . . . p. 5 **HX**
Wake Green Rd . . . . p. 4 **FX**
Warstone Lane . . . . p. 6 **JY**
Warwick Rd . . . . p. 5 **GX**
Washwood Heath Rd . . . . p. 5 **GV**
Waterloo Rd . . . . p. 4 **EV**
Waterloo St. . . . . p. 6 **JZ** 48
Watery Lane . . . . p. 7 **LZ**
Wellington Rd . . . . p. 4 **FV**
Westfield Rd . . . . p. 4 **EX**
Westley Rd . . . . p. 5 **GX** 50
Wheeley's Lane . . . . . . p. 6 **JZ** 52
Winson Green Rd. . . . . . . p. 4 **EV**
Witton Lane . . . . p. 4 **FV**
Witton Rd . . . . p. 4 **FV**
Wood End Rd . . . . p. 5 **GV**
Wrentham St . . . . p. 6 **KZ**
Yardley Rd . . . . p. 5 **HX**
Yardley Wood Rd . . . . . . p. 5 **GX**

XX **Dynasty,** 93-103 Hurst St., B5 4TE, *ℰ* 622 1410, Chinese rest. – **⚫ AE ⓞ VISA**　　　KZ **e**
　　　M 10.50 **t.** (dinner) and a la carte ⌀ 2.60.

XX **Lorenzo,** 3 Park St., Digbeth, B5 5JD, *ℰ* 643 0541, Italian rest. – **⚫ AE ⓞ VISA**　　KZ **o**
　　　closed Saturday lunch, Monday dinner, Sunday, 3 weeks July-August and Bank Holidays – **M**
　　　a la carte 9.30/14.40 **t.** ⌀ 3.10.

X **Pinocchio's,** 8 Chad Sq., off Harborne Rd, B15 3TQ, W : 2¾ m. by A 456 *ℰ* 454 8672, Italian
　　　rest. – **⚫ AE ⓞ VISA**　　　　　　　　　　　　　　　　　　　　　p. 4　EX **v**
　　　closed Sunday – **M** 5.75 **t.** (lunch) and a la carte 9.40/13.00 **t.** ⌀ 2.50.

MICHELIN Branch, Valepits Rd, Garretts Green, B33 0YD, *ℰ* 784 7900 p. 5 HX

AUSTIN-ROVER 9-14 Dozells St. *ℰ* 643 5111	FORD Long Acre, Aston *ℰ* 327 4791
AUSTIN-ROVER Bristol St. *ℰ* 622 1122	FORD 221 High St., Digbeth *ℰ* 632 6756
AUSTIN-ROVER Essex St. *ℰ* 622 2851	MAZDA Rookery Rd, Handsworth *ℰ* 554 9333
AUSTIN-ROVER-DAIMLER-JAGUAR 22 Berkeley St.	MERCEDES-BENZ Charles Henry St. *ℰ* 622 3031
ℰ 643 7901	NISSAN 4 Birmingham Rd *ℰ* 358 7011
AUSTIN-ROVER-JAGUAR Aston Hall Rd, Aston *ℰ*	PEUGEOT, TALBOT Summer Lane, Newtown *ℰ*
328 0833	359 4848
AUSTIN-ROVER 71 Aston Rd North, Aston *ℰ*	RENAULT 1300 Bristol Rd South *ℰ* 475 5241
359 2011	TALBOT, PEUGEOT Charlotte St. *ℰ* 236 4382
CITROEN Barnes Hill, Weoley Castle *ℰ* 427 5231	TALBOT 30 High St, Deriford *ℰ* 772 4388
COLT 266 Broad St., *ℰ* 643 6508	TOYOTA 138 Soho Hill, Handsworth *ℰ* 554 6311
COLT 205 Lozells Rd *ℰ* 551 7717	VOLVO Bristol St. *ℰ* 622 4491
FORD 156/182 Bristol St. *ℰ* 622 2777	VW, AUDI Digbeth *ℰ* 643 7341

Except where otherwise stated see pp. 2 and 3

at Streetly N : 7 m. on A 452 – ⊠ Sutton Coldfield – ✪ 021 Birmingham :

🏠 **Parson and Clerk** (Golden Oak) *without rest.,* Chester Rd North, B73 6SP, S : 1 ½ m. on A
　　　452 *ℰ* 353 1747 – **tv 🛏wc ☎ Ⓟ. ⚫ AE VISA. 🎨**　　　　　　　　　　CT **s**
　　　30 rm ⌧ 28.75/34.50 **st.**

at Walmley NE : 6 m. by B 4148 – ⊠ Sutton Coldfield – ✪ 021 Birmingham :

🏛 **Penns Hall** (Embassy) 🌳, Penns Lane, B76 8LH, *ℰ* 351 3111, Telex 335789, ⌇, 🏛 – **🛗 tv**
　　　☎ Ⓟ. 🚗. ⚫ AE ⓞ VISA. 🎨　　　　　　　　　　　　　　　　　　　DT **v**
　　　closed Bank Holidays – **M** *(closed Sunday dinner to non-residents)* (bar lunch Saturday) a la
　　　carte 13.25/18.50 **st.** ⌀ 2.75 – ⌧ 5.00 – **115 rm** 45.00/52.00, **5 suites** – SB 55.00 **st.**

BMW Jockey Rd, Boldmere *ℰ* 354 8131	NISSAN 504-508 College Rd, Erdington *ℰ* 373 2542
CITROEN Old Kingsbury Rd, Minworth *ℰ* 351 4367	SAAB Eachelhurst Rd, Erdington *ℰ* 351 1027
DAIHATSU, FIAT, LANCIA 35 Sutton New Rd,	TALBOT, PEUGEOT Newport Rd, Castle Bromwich
Erdington *ℰ* 350 1301	*ℰ* 747 4712
FORD Kingsbury Rd, Erdington *ℰ* 382 1111	VAUXHALL 364 Chester Rd, Castle Bromwich *ℰ*
HONDA Bromford Lane *ℰ* 328 4211	747 4601

at Castle Bromwich NE : 6 m. by A 47 – ⊠ ✪ 021 Birmingham :

🏛 Bradford Arms Motel, Chester Rd, B36 0AG, *ℰ* 747 0227 – **tv 🛏wc ☎ Ⓟ. ⚫ AE ⓞ VISA**
　　　closed 3 days at Christmas – **M** (grill rest. only) – **30 rm** ⌧ 27.50/32.00 **st.**　　　p. 5　HV **a**

at Sutton Coldfield NE : 8 m. by A 38 – ⊠ Sutton Coldfield – ✪ 021 Birmingham :

🏛 **Belfry** (De Vere) 🌳, Lichfield Rd, Wishaw, B76 9PR, E : 3 m. on A 446 *ℰ* 0675 (Curd-
　　　worth) 70301, Telex 338848, ≼, 🏊, 🏌, park, 🎾, squash – 🛏 rest **tv ☎ Ⓟ. 🚗. ⚫ AE ⓞ**
　　　VISA　　　　　　　　　　　　　　　　　　　　　　　　by A 38　DT
　　　M 7.95/9.95 **st.** and a la carte ⌀ 3.50 – **168 rm** ⌧ 53.50/80.00 **st.** – SB (weekends only) 73.00 **st.**

🏛 **Moor Hall** (Best Western) 🌳, Moor Hall Drive, Four Oaks, B75 6LN, NE : 1 m. by A 453
　　　ℰ 308 3751, Telex 335127, 🏛 – **tv 🛏wc 🕸 Ⓟ. 🚗. ⚫ AE ⓞ VISA. 🎨**　　　　DT **r**
　　　M 10.95/16.50 **st.** ⌀ 2.75 – **50 rm** ⌧ 40.00/48.00 **t.** – SB (weekends only) 48.00/55.00 **st.**

🏠 **Standbridge,** 138 Birmingham Rd, B72 1LY, *ℰ* 354 3007, 🎨 – 🛏 Ⓟ　　　　DT **a**
　　　closed 26 May-2 June and Christmas-New Year – **9 rm** ⌧ 13.75/26.50 **st.**

XX **Le Bon Viveur,** 65 Birmingham Rd, B72 1QF, *ℰ* 355 5836 – **⚫ AE ⓞ VISA**　　　DT **u**
　　　closed Saturday lunch, Sunday, Monday and August – **M** a la carte 9.95/13.95 **t.** ⌀ 2.75.

XX La Gondola, Mere Green Precinct, 304 Lichfield Rd, B74 2UW, N : 2 m. on A 5127 *ℰ* 308 6782,
　　　Italian rest.　　　　　　　　　　　　　　　　　　　　　　　　DT **o**

AUSTIN-ROVER Maney Corner *ℰ* 354 7601	RENAULT 62 Chester Rd *ℰ* 352 0022
AUSTIN-ROVER 10 Birmingham Rd *ℰ* 355 5537	VOLVO 127 Chester Rd *ℰ* 353 3191
DAIHATSU 35 Sutton New Rd *ℰ* 350 1301	VW, AUDI 45-51 Kings Rd *ℰ* 355 1261

at National Exhibition Centre E : 9 ½ m. on A 45 – DU – ⊠ ✪ 021 Birmingham :

🏛 **Birmingham Metropole,** Blackfirs Lane, Bickenhill, B40 1PP, *ℰ* 780 4242, Telex 336129, ≼,
　　　squash – 🛗 ▤ **tv ☎ 🕸 Ⓟ. 🚗. ⚫ AE ⓞ VISA**
　　　M a la carte 10.70/22.50 **t.** ⌀ 3.75 – ⌧ 4.00 – **501 rm** 49.50/75.00 **st.**, **9 suites** 180.00/210.00 **st.**

🏛 **Warwick** , Blackfirs Lane, Bickenhill, B40 1PP, *ℰ* 780 4242, Telex 336129, squash – 🛗 ▤ **tv**
　　　🛏wc **☎ Ⓟ. 🚗. ⚫ AE ⓞ VISA**
　　　Exhibitions only – **M** (rest. see **Birmingham Metropole H.**) – ⌧ 4.00 – **200 rm** 44.00/65.00 **st.**

🏛 **Arden Motel,** Coventry Rd, Bickenhill, B92 0EH, S : ½ m. on A 45 ⊠ Solihull
　　　ℰ 067 55 (Hampton-in-Arden) 3221, Telex 337766 – 🛗 **tv 🛏wc 🕸 Ⓟ. 🚗. ⚫ AE ⓞ VISA**
　　　closed 3 days at Christmas – **M** 7.50/10.50 **t.** and a la carte ⌀ 2.40 – ⌧ 3.50 – **46 rm**
　　　23.00/36.00 **st.** – SB (weekends only) (April-June) 45.50 **st.**

at Acocks Green SE : 4 ½ m. on A 41 – DU – ✉ ☎ 021 Birmingham :

Kerry House, 946 Warwick Rd, B27 6QG, ✆ 707 0316 – TV ⋒wc P
23 rm ☕ 17.25/26.00 **t.**

ALFA-ROMEO 683 Stratford Rd, Sparkhill ✆ 778 1295
AUSTIN-ROVER 884 Warwick Rd ✆ 706 8271
AUSTIN-ROVER Warwick Rd, Tyseley ✆ 706 4331
CITROEN 2 Warwick Rd ✆ 707 3122
DAIHATSU, SKODA 1520 Stratford Rd, Hall Green ✆ 744 1144
FIAT, LANCIA, LOTUS, SAAB 979 Stratford Rd, Hall Green ✆ 778 2323
FSO 438 Stratford Rd, Spartihill ✆ 773 8646
LADA 723-725 Stratford Rd, Sparkhill ✆ 777 6164
RENAULT High St., Bordesley ✆ 773 8251
TOYOTA, RELIANT 32-38 Coventry Rd, Bordesley ✆ 772 5916
VAUXHALL 291 Shaftmoor Lane, Hall Green ✆ 777 1074
VAUXHALL-OPEL 870 Stratford Rd, Sparkhill ✆ 777 3361

at Sheldon SE : 6 m. on A 45 – HX – ✉ ☎ 021 Birmingham :

Wheatsheaf (Golden Oak), 2225 Coventry Rd, B26 3EH, ✆ **743 2021** – ▤ rest TV ⋒wc ☎ P. ♿. AE VISA. p. 5 HX **a**
M 6.00/6.50 **t.** and a la carte 🍷 3.75 – **84 rm** ☕ 33.00/42.00 **st.**

AUSTIN-ROVER, FORD 1652 Coventry Rd ✆ 706 1688
CITROEN The Radleys ✆ 743 5621
PEUGEOT-TALBOT 2119 Coventry Rd ✆ 742 5533

at Birmingham Airport SE : 7 m. on A 45 – DU – ✉ ☎ 021 Birmingham :

Excelsior (T.H.F.), Coventry Rd, Elmdon, B26 3QW, ✆ 743 8141, Telex 338005 – |‡| TV P. ♿. AE ⓓ VISA
M 6.55/10.50 **st.** and a la carte 🍷 4.00 – ☕ 5.50 – **141 rm** 39.00/48.50 **st.**

AUSTIN-ROVER Station Rd, Marston Green ✆ 779 2261
FIAT Station Rd, Marston ✆ 779 5140
NISSAN 120-126 Alcester Rd, Moseley ✆ 449 4751

at Northfield SW : 6 m. by A 38 – CU – ✉ ☎ 021 Birmingham :

Norwood, 87 Bunbury Rd, B31 2ET, ✆ 475 3262 – P
closed 1 week at Christmas – **12 rm** ☕ 11.00/33.00 **st.**

AUSTIN-ROVER 428 Redditch Rd, Kings Norton ✆ 458 4031
AUSTIN-ROVER Alcester Rd, Moseley, Kings Heath, ✆ 449 6115
CITROEN Hallan St., Balsall Heath, Kings Heath ✆ 440 4606
FORD 82 St. Mary's Row, Moseley, Kings Heath ✆ 449 3771
NISSAN 57 Walkers Heath Rd ✆ 451 1411
SKODA 307 Northfield Rd, Harborne, Kings Heath ✆ 427 4050
VAUXHALL 16 Ryland St., Edgbaston, Kings Heath ✆ 455 7171

at Smethwick W : 3 ½ m. by A 456 – ✉ ☎ 021 Birmingham :

Franzl's, 151 Milcote Rd, Bearwood, B67 5BN, ✆ 429 7920, Austrian rest. – VISA
closed Sunday, Monday, first 3 weeks August and 1 week after Christmas – **M** (dinner only) a la carte 8.10/11.45 **t.** 🍷 3.10. p. 4 EV **a**

at West Bromwich NW : 6 m. on A 41 – ✉ West Bromwich – ☎ 021 Birmingham :

West Bromwich Moat House (Q.M.H.) Birmingham Rd, B70 6RS, SW : 1 m. by A 41 ✆ 553 6111, Telex 336232 – |‡| ▤ rest TV ⛀wc ☎ P. ♿. AE ⓓ VISA BU **c**
M 8.75/9.25 **st.** and a la carte 🍷 3.60 – **179 rm** ☕ 40.50/53.50 **st.** – SB (weekends only) 40.00 **st.**

AUSTIN-ROVER High St. ✆ 553 0778
FERRARI, FIAT Birmingham Rd ✆ 553 7509
FORD 377 High St. ✆ 553 1881
VAUXHALL-OPEL Spon Lane ✆ 553 3777
VOLVO 127 Hill Top ✆ 502 3802

at Great Barr NW : 6 m. on A 34 – ✉ Great Barr – ☎ 021 Birmingham :

Post House (T.H.F), Chapel Lane, B43 7BG, ✆ 357 7444, Telex 338497, heated – ▤ rest TV ⛀wc ☎ P. ♿. AE ⓓ VISA CT **x**
M 6.50/23.00 **st.** and a la carte 🍷 2.70 – ☕ 5.50 – **204 rm** 38.00/45.00 **st.**

Barr (De Vere), Pear Tree Drive, Newton Rd, B43 6HS, W : 1 m. by A 4041 ✆ 357 1141, Telex 336406, – TV ⛀wc ☎ P. ♿. AE ⓓ VISA. CT **z**
closed 24 to 26 December – **M** 6.50/7.00 **st.** and a la carte 🍷 4.00 – **111 rm** ☕ 36.50/47.00 **st.** – SB (weekends only) 72.00 **st.**

BIRTLE Greater Manchester 402 ㉒ 404 ⑩ – ✉ Bury – ☎ 061 Manchester.
♦London 217 – Bolton 10 – ♦Manchester 11.

Normandie , Elbut Lane, BL9 6UT, ✆ 764 3869 – |‡| TV ⛀wc ⋒wc ☎ P. AE ⓓ VISA
M *(closed Saturday lunch and Sunday)* 13.50 **t.** (dinner) and a la carte – ☕ 4.50 – **17 rm** 31.00/37.00 **t.**

BISHOP AUCKLAND Durham 401 402 P 20 – pop. 23 ,560 – ECD : Wednesday – ☎ 0388.
♦London 253 – ♦Carlisle 73 – ♦Middlesbrough 24 – ♦Newcastle-upon-Tyne 28 – Sunderland 25.

Park Head, New Coundon, DL14 8AL, NE : 1¾ m. by A 689 on A 688 ✆ 661727 – TV ⛀wc ⋒wc ☎ P. AE ⓓ VISA
M (carving rest. Sunday) a la carte lunch/dinner 10.50 **t.** 🍷 2.50 – **12 rm** ☕ 25.00/35.00 **st.** – SB (weekends only) 38.50/50.50 **st.**

BISHOP'S CASTLE Salop **403** L 26 – pop. 1,810 – ✆ 0588.
◆London 182 – ◆Birmingham 71 – Shrewsbury 24.

🏰 **Castle,** Market Sq., SY9 5DG, ✆ 638403 – **Ⓟ. 🅰 AE ⓞ**
M a la carte 5.60/8.10 **t. – 7 rm** 🖙 15.50/26.00 **t. –** SB 36.00/38.00 **st.**

BISHOP'S STORTFORD Herts. **404** U 28 – pop. 22,535 – ECD : Wednesday – ✆ 0279.
✈ Stansted Airport : ✆ 502380, Telex 81102, NE : 3 ½ m.
🛈 Council Offices, The Causeway ✆ 55261 ext 251.
◆London 34 – ◆Cambridge 27 – Chelmsford 19 – Colchester 33.

🏨 **Foxley,** Foxley Drive, Stanstead Rd, CM23 2EB, N : ¾ m. on A 1184 ✆ 53977, ☎ – 📺 ➪wc
Ⓟ. 🅰 AE VISA
M a la carte 6.35/12.95 **t.** ♨ 3.50 – **12 rm** 🖙 30.00/45.00 **st.**

🏠 **Brook House,** 29 Northgate End, CM23 2LD, ✆ 57892, ☎ – 📺 ➪wc 🛁wc **Ⓟ. ✖**
24 rm.

AUSTIN-ROVER-DAIMLER-JAGUAR 123-129 South
St. ✆ 58441
CITROEN Dunmow Rd ✆ 54335
DAIHATSU, LANCIA London Rd ✆ 54181
FORD London Rd ✆ 52214

PEUGEOT-TALBOT 26 Northgate End ✆ 53494
RENAULT Northgate End ✆ 53127
VAUXHALL-OPEL, VOLVO The Causeway ✆ 52304
VW, AUDI Dane St. ✆ 54680

BISHOP'S TAWTON Devon **403** H 30 – see Barnstaple.

BLACKBURN Lancs. **402** M 22 – pop. 109,564 – ECD : Thursday – ✆ 0254.
📷 Beardwood Brow, ✆ 51122 – 📷 Pleasington ✆ 21028, W : 3 m.
🛈 Town Hall ✆ 55201 ext 214 and 53277.
◆London 228 – ◆Leeds 47 – ◆Liverpool 39 – ◆Manchester 24 – Preston 11.

🏨 **Blackburn Moat House** (Q.M.H.), Yew Tree Drive, Preston New Rd, BB2 7BE, NW : 2 m. at
junction A 677 and A 6119 ✆ 64441, Telex 63271, 🏊 heated – 🛗 📺 ➪wc ☎ **Ⓟ. 🅰 🅰 AE**
ⓞ VISA
M 6.95/7.95 **st.** and a la carte ♨ 3.25 – **98 rm** 🖙 35.00/46.00 **st., 2 suites** 55.00 **st. –** SB
(weekends only) 46.00 **st.**

🏠 **Woodlands,** 363 Preston New Rd, BB2 7AA, NW : 1 ¼ m. on A 677 ✆ 691122 – 📺 ➪wc **Ⓟ**
M (Greek rest.) – **14 rm**.

AUSTIN-ROVER-DAIMLER-JAGUAR Park Rd ✆
662721
CITROEN Whalley New Rd ✆ 661616
FIAT 52/56 King St. ✆ 52981
FORD Montague St. ✆ 57021

RENAULT Gt. Harwood ✆ 886590
TOYOTA Accrington Rd ✆ 57333
VAUXHALL Quarry St., Eanam ✆ 51191
VAUXHALL-OPEL Montague St. ✆ 53885
VW, AUDI 854 Whalley New Rd ✆ 48091

BLACKPOOL Lancs. **402** K 22 – pop. 146,297 – ECD : Wednesday – ✆ 0253.
See : Illuminations★★ (late September and early October) – Tower★ (❋★) AC AY A.
📷 Blackpool North Shore, Devonshire Rd ✆ 52054, N : 1 ½ m. from main station BY – 📷 Blackpool
Park, Stanley Park ✆ 33960, E : 1 ½ m. BY – 📷 Poulton-le-Fylde, Myrtle Farm, Breck Rd ✆ 0253
(Poulton) 893150, E : 3 m. by A 586 BY.
🛈 1 Clifton St. ✆ 21623 and 25212 (weekdays only) – 87a Coronation St. ✆ 21891.
◆London 246 – ◆Leeds 88 – ◆Liverpool 56 – ◆Manchester 51 – ◆Middlesbrough 123.

Plan opposite

🏩 **Imperial,** North Shore, North Promenade, FY1 2HB, ✆ 23971, Telex 677376, ≼, 🔲 – 🛗 📺
☎ **Ⓟ. 🅰 🅰 AE ⓞ VISA**
AY c
M (carving rest.) 7.50/8.50 **st.** ♨ 2.50 – **159 rm** 🖙 44.00/62.00 **st., 7 suites** 100.00 **st. –** SB
62.00 **st.**

🏩 **Pembroke,** North Promenade, FY1 2JQ, ✆ 23434, Telex 677469, ≼, 🔲 – 🛗 📺 ☎ **Ⓟ. 🅰 🅰**
AE ⓞ VISA
AY x
M (carving lunch) 8.00/9.00 **t.** and a la carte ♨ 3.75 – **201 rm** 🖙 43.75/62.50 **t., 6 suites**
135.00/225.00 **t. –** SB 57.00/79.00 **st.**

🏨 **Savoy,** Queens Promenade, FY2 9SJ, ✆ 52561, Telex 67570 – 🛗 📺 ➪wc 🛁wc ☎ **Ⓟ. 🅰.**
🅰 AE ⓞ VISA
AY a
M 4.50/7.75 **st.** and a la carte ♨ 2.40 – **127 rm** 🖙 19.00/38.00 **st. –** SB (weekends only)
46.00/50.00 **st.**

🏨 **New Clifton,** Talbot Sq., FY1 1ND, ✆ 21481, Group Telex 67415 – 🛗 📺 ➪wc ☎. 🅰 🅰
AE ⓞ VISA
AY n
M 5.50/6.50 **t.** and a la carte ♨ 1.50 – **78 rm** 🖙 33.00/49.50 **t., 1 suite** 80.00 **t. –** SB (weekends
only) 49.00/55.00 **st.**

🏠 **Warwick** (Best Western), 603-609 New South Promenade, FY4 1NG, ✆ 42192, 🔲 – 📺
➪wc **Ⓟ. 🅰 🅰 AE ⓞ VISA**
BZ u
M (bar lunch)/dinner 8.00 **st.** ♨ 2.60 – **52 rm** 🖙 20.50/44.00 **st.**

🏠 **Mimosa** without rest., 24a Lonsdale Rd, FY1 6EE, ✆ 41906 – 📺 ➪wc 🛁wc **Ⓟ. 🅰 AE VISA**
✖
BZ c
closed 22 December-2 January – **15 rm** 🖙 15.00/23.50.

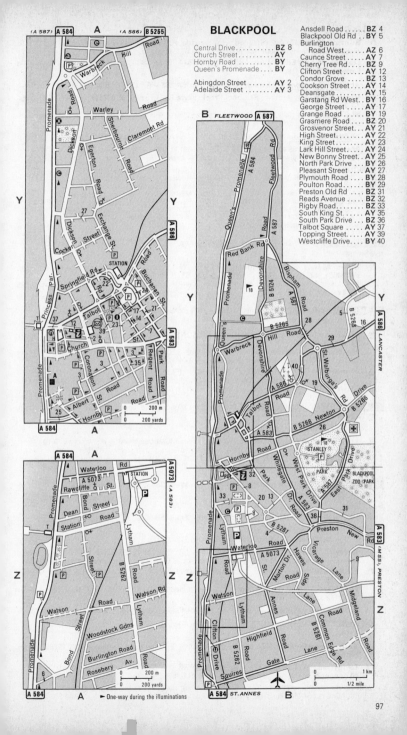

BLACKPOOL

Central Drive . . . . BZ 8
Church Street . . . . AY
Hornby Road . . . . BY
Queen's Promenade . . . . BY

Abingdon Street . . . . AY 2
Adelaide Street . . . . AY 3

Ansdell Road . . . . BZ 4
Blackpool Old Rd . . BY 5
Burlington
Road West . . . . . . AZ 6
Caunce Street . . . . . . AY 7
Cherry Tree Rd . . . . . BZ 9
Clifton Street . . . . . . AY 12
Condor Grove . . . . . BZ 13
Cookson Street . . . . . AY 14
Deansgate . . . . AY 15
Garstang Rd West . . BY 16
George Street . . . . . . AY 17
Grange Road . . . . . . BY 19
Grasmere Road . . . . BZ 20
Grosvenor Street . . . AY 21
High Street . . . . AY 22
King Street . . . . AY 23
Lark Hill Street . . . . . AY 24
New Bonny Street . . . AY 25
North Park Drive . . . BY 26
Pleasant Street . . . . . AY 27
Plymouth Road . . . . BY 28
Poulton Road . . . . . . BY 29
Preston Old Rd . . . . BZ 31
Reads Avenue . . . . . BZ 32
Rigby Road . . . . BZ 33
South King St. . . . . . AY 35
South Park Drive . . . BZ 36
Talbot Square . . . . . . AY 37
Topping Street. . . . . . AY 39
Westcliffe Drive. . . . . BY 40

► One-way during the illuminations

97

↑ **Sunray**, 42 Knowle Av., off Queens Promenade, FY2 9TQ, ℰ 51937 – 🖵 ⋔wc 🅿   BY **c**
closed Christmas and New Year – **9 rm** ⊊ 13.00/26.00 **st.**

↑ **Denely**, 15 King Edward Av., FY2 9TA, ℰ 52757 – ⋔ 🅿. ⁓   AY **e**
9 rm ⊊ 8.75/21.00 **st.**

at Little Thornton NE : 5 m. by A 586 – BY – off A 588 – ✉ 🅗 0253 Blackpool :

XX **River House** 🍃 with rm, Skippool Creek, Wyre Rd, FY5 5LF, ℰ 883497, ≼, 🕱 – 🖵 ☎ 🅿.
🔼 🗚
M (booking essential) 7.50 **t.** and a la carte ⏽ 2.50 – **4 rm** ⊊ 23.00/37.00 **t.** – SB (weekends only) 50.00 **st.**

at Little Singleton NE : 6 m. by A 586 – BY – on A 585 – ✉ 🅗 0253 Blackpool :

🏛 **Mains Hall** 🍃, 86 Mains Lane, FY6 7LE, ℰ 885130, 🕱 – ⊖wc ⋔wc 🅿. ⊚
M (closed Sunday) (dinner only) 8.50 **t.** ⏽ 2.00 – **7 rm** ⊊ 16.50/35.00 **st.**

ALFA-ROMEO, DAIHATSU St. Annes Rd ℰ 402671
AUSTIN-ROVER, DAIMLER-JAGUAR Vicarage Lane
ℰ 67811
AUSTIN-ROVER Cherry Tree Rd ℰ 67811
AUSTIN-ROVER 159 Devonshire Rd ℰ 34301
BMW Bloomfield Rd ℰ 402541
COLT 234 Talbot Rd ℰ 26688
FIAT 79/83 Breck Rd, Poulton-le-Fylde ℰ 882571

FORD Whitegate Drive ℰ 63333
HONDA Devonshire Rd ℰ 35816
MERCEDES-BENZ Church St. ℰ 22257
MERCEDES-BENZ Church St. ℰ 28436
PEUGEOT-TALBOT Squires Gate Lane ℰ 45544
TOYOTA 145/147 Dickson Rd ℰ 21469
VW, AUDI Central Drive ℰ 401228

BLACKWOOD (COED-DUON) Gwent 🗠🗠🗠 K 29 – pop. 13 ,255 – ECD : Thursday – 🅗 0495.

♦London 158 – ♦Cardiff 15 – Newport 13.

🏛 **Maes Manor** 🍃, Maesrudded, NP2 0AG, N : 1 ¼ m. by A 4048 turning at Rock Inn
ℰ 224551, 🕱, park – 🖵 ⊖wc ⋔ ☎ 🅿. ⛴. 🔼 🗚 ⊚ 𝕍𝕀𝕊𝔸
M (closed Sunday dinner to non-residents) (bar lunch Saturday) a la carte 11.50/15.00 **t.** ⏽ 3.25
– **24 rm** ⊊ 24.00/39.50 **t.**

BLAKENEY Norfolk 🗠🗠🗠 X 25 – pop. 1 ,559 – ECD : Wednesday – ✉ Holt – 🅗 0263 Cley.

♦London 127 – King's Lynn 37 – ♦Norwich 28.

🏛 **Blakeney** (Best Western), The Quay, NR25 7NE, ℰ 740797, ≼, 🔲, 🕱 – 🖵 ⊖wc ☎ 🅿.
⛴. 🔼 🗚 ⊚ 𝕍𝕀𝕊𝔸
M (bar lunch Monday to Saturday)/dinner 9.50 **st.** and a la carte ⏽ 3.00 – **52 rm**
⊊ 18.00/74.00 **st.** – SB (except Bank Holidays) 44.00/82.00 **st.**

🏛 **Manor,** The Quay, NR25 7ND, ℰ 740376, 🕱 – 🖵 ⊖wc ⅄ 🅿
closed 2 to 26 December – **M** (buffet lunch Monday to Saturday)/dinner 13.30 **st.** ⏽ 2.40 –
22 rm ⊊ 21.00/60.00 **st.** – SB (winter and spring only) 30.00/52.00 **st.**

BLANCHLAND Northumb. 🗠🗠🗠 🗠🗠🗠 N 19 – ECD : Monday and Tuesday – ✉ Consett (Durham)
– 🅗 043 475.

♦London 298 – ♦Carlisle 47 – ♦Newcastle-upon-Tyne 24.

🏛 **Lord Crewe Arms** 🍃, DH8 9SP, ℰ 251, « Part 13C abbey », 🕱 – ⊖wc ⋔wc ☎ 🅿. ⛴.
closed Monday to Thursday from February-mid March and January – **M** (bar lunch Monday to Saturday)/dinner 11.00 **st.** ⏽ 3.75 – **15 rm** ⊊ 30.00/45.00 **st.** – SB (except Bank Holidays) 60.00/69.00 **st.**

BLANDFORD FORUM Dorset 🗠🗠🗠 🗠🗠🗠 N 31 The West Country G. – pop. 7 ,249 – ECD : Wednesday – 🅗 0258 Blandford.

See : Site★.

Envir. : Royal Blandford Signals Museum★AC, NE : 2 m. off B 3082.

🛈 West St. ℰ 51989 (summer only).

♦London 124 – Bournemouth 17 – Dorchester 17 – Salisbury 24.

🏛 **Crown** 1 West St., DT11 7AJ, ℰ 56626, 🕱 – 🖵 ⊖wc ☎ 🅿. 🔼 🗚 ⊚ 𝕍𝕀𝕊𝔸
M 8.00/10.00 **st.** and a la carte ⏽ 2.95 – **28 rm** ⊊ 30.00/50.00 **t.** – SB (weekends only) 54.00 **st.**

XX **La Belle Alliance** with rm, Portman Lodge, Whitecliff, Mill St., DT11 7PB, ℰ 52842 – 🖵
⊖wc 🅿. 🔼 🗚 𝕍𝕀𝕊𝔸
M (closed Sunday dinner) (lunch by arrangement) a la carte 8.85/12.60 **st.** ⏽ 2.50 – **4 rm**
⊊ 22.00/33.00 **st.** – SB 48.00/56.00 **st.**

at Pimperne NE : 2 ½ m. on A 354 – ✉ 🅗 0258 Blandford Forum :

⌂ Anvil, DT11 8UQ, ℰ 53431, ⬛ heated – ⊖wc ⋔wc 🅿
8 rm.

at Tarrant Monkton NE : 5 ½ m. by A 354 – ✉ Blandford Forum – 🅗 025 889 Tarrant
Hinton :

XX **Langtons,** DT11 8RX, ℰ 225 – 🅿. 🔼 🗚 ⊚ 𝕍𝕀𝕊𝔸
M (dinner only and Sunday lunch) a la carte 8.00/9.75 **t.** ⏽ 2.50.

AUSTIN-ROVER Mill St. ℰ 52457
FERRARI, JAGUAR, LANCIA Pimperne ℰ 51211

RENAULT St. Leonards Av. ℰ 52311

BLAWITH Cumbria – pop. 101 – ✉ Ulverston – ✪ 022 985 Lowick Bridge.
♦London 290 – ♦Carlisle 66 – Kendal 28 – Lancaster 43.

🏠 **Highfield,** LA12 8EG, on A 5084 ♒ 238, ≼, 🏡 – 📺 ⌂wc 🛁wc 🅿. ⚠ 𝘝𝘐𝘚𝘈
　M (bar lunch)/dinner 9.50 t. and a la carte ▯ 2.95 – **11 rm** ⌂ 26.50/55.00 t. – SB 45.00/50.00 t.

BLOCKLEY Glos. 𝟜𝟘𝟛 𝟜𝟘𝟜 O 27 – pop. 1,729 – ECD : Thursday – ✉ Moreton-in-Marsh –
✪ 0386.
♦London 89 – ♦Birmingham 40 – Gloucester 29 – ♦Oxford 33.

🏠 **Lower Brook House** 🏡, Lower St., GL56 9DS, ♒ 700286, « Converted 17C cottages », 🏡
　– ⌂wc 🛁wc 🅿. ⚠
　closed January – **M** (bar lunch in summer)/dinner 13.50 t. ▯ 2.50 – **8 rm** ⌂ 35.00/71.00 t. – SB
　(weekends only) (winter only) 65.00 **st.**

BLOFIELD Norfolk 𝟜𝟘𝟜 Y 26 – see Norwich.

BLOXHAM Oxon. 𝟜𝟘𝟛 𝟜𝟘𝟜 P 28 – see Banbury.

BLUE ANCHOR Somerset – see Minehead.

BLUNDELLSANDS Merseyside 𝟜𝟘𝟚 𝟜𝟘𝟛 K 23 – see Liverpool.

BLUNSDON Wilts. 𝟜𝟘𝟛 𝟜𝟘𝟜 O 29 – see Swindon.

BLYTH Notts. 𝟜𝟘𝟚 𝟜𝟘𝟛 𝟜𝟘𝟜 Q 23 – pop. 1,897 – ECD : Wednesday – ✉ Worksop – ✪ 090 976.
♦London 154 – ♦Leeds 41 – Lincoln 29 – ♦Nottingham 31 – ♦Sheffield 21.

🏠 Fourways, High St., S81 8EW, ♒ 235 – 🅿 – **9 rm.**

BODINNICK-BY-FOWEY Cornwall – see Fowey.

BODMIN Cornwall 𝟜𝟘𝟛 F 32 The West Country G. – pop. 11,992 – ECD : Wednesday – ✪ 0208.
See : St. Petroc Church★ – **Envir.** : Lanhydrock★★*AC*, S : 3 m. – Bodmin Moor★★ – St. Endellion
Church★★, NW : 12 m. – Pencarrow House★*AC*, NW : 4 m. – Cardinham Church★, NE : 5 m. –
Blisland★ (Church★), NE : 6 m. – St. Mabyn Church★, N : 6 m. – St. Tudy★, N : 8 m.
🛈 Shire House, Mount Folly Sq. ♒ 4159.
♦London 273 – Exeter 63 – Penzance 47 – ♦Plymouth 30.

🏠 **Westberry,** Rhind St., PL31 2EL, ♒ 2772 – 📺 ⌂wc 🛁wc ☎ 🅿. ⚠ ① 𝘝𝘐𝘚𝘈
　closed 1 week at Christmas – **M** *(closed lunch Saturday and Sunday)* (bar lunch)/dinner 6.50 t.
　and a la carte ▯ 2.30 – **23 rm** ⌂ 14.00/27.00 t. – SB (weekends only) (September-May)
　40.00/50.00 **st.**

　at Tredethy N : 5 m. by A 389 off B 3266 – ✉ Bodmin – ✪ 020 884 St. Mabyn :

🏛 **Tredethy Country** 🏡, PL30 4QS, ♒ 262, ≼, « Country house atmosphere », ⊻ heated,
　🏡, park – ⌂wc 🛁wc 🅿. ⚠
　closed 1 week at Christmas – **M** 6.00/7.50 t. ▯ 2.10 – **11 rm** ⌂ 17.00/46.00 t. – SB (winter
　only) 42.00 **st.**

BOGNOR REGIS West Sussex 𝟜𝟘𝟜 R 31 – pop. 50,323 – ECD : Wednesday – ✪ 0243.
🛈 1-2 Place St-Maur des Fossés, Belmont St. ♒ 823140.
♦London 65 – ♦Brighton 29 – ♦Portsmouth 24 – ♦Southampton 37.

🏛 Royal Norfolk (Best Western), The Esplanade, PO21 2LH, ♒ 826222, ≼, ⊻ heated, 🏡, ✹ –
　⌂ 📺 🅿. 🛄 – **52 rm.**
🏠 **Steyne House,** 10 West St., PO21 1UF, ♒ 828476 – 📺 🅿. 𝘝𝘐𝘚𝘈
　7 rm ⌂ 8.50/24.00 s.

AUSTIN-ROVER 65 Aldwick Rd ♒ 864041
AUSTIN-ROVER, FORD Lennox St. ♒ 864641
PEUGEOT-TALBOT 131 Elmer Rd, Middleton-on-Sea
♒ 024 369 (Middleton-on-Sea) 2432

VW, AUDI 126 Felpham Way ♒ 024 369 (Middleton-
on-Sea) 3185

BOLTON Greater Manchester 𝟜𝟘𝟚 𝟜𝟘𝟜 M 23 – pop. 143,960 – ECD : Wednesday – ✪ 0204.
Envir. : Hall I'Th'Wood★ (16C) *AC*, N : 1½ m.
🛝 Bolton Municipal, Links Rd, Lostock ♒ 42336 – 🛝 Dunscar, Longworth Lane, Bromley Cross
♒ 53321, N : 3 m. off A 666 – 🛝 Lostock Park, ♒ 43067, W : 3½ m.
🛈 Town Hall, ♒ 22311 ext 211/485 and 384174.
♦London 214 – Burnley 19 – ♦Liverpool 32 – ♦Manchester 11 – Preston 23.

🏛 **Crest** (Crest), Beaumont Rd, BL3 4TA, SW : 2½ m. on A 58 ♒ 651511, Telex 635527 – 📺
　⌂wc ☎ 🅿. 🛄. ⚠ 𝘈𝘌 ① 𝘝𝘐𝘚𝘈
　M approx. 11.50 **st.** – ⌂ 5.75 – **100 rm** 44.50/54.50 **st.** – SB (weekends only) 51.00 **st.**

🏛 Pack Horse (De Vere), Bradshawgate, BL1 1DP, ♒ 27261, Telex 635168 – ⌂ 📺 ⌂wc ☎. 🛄.
　⚠ 𝘈𝘌 𝘝𝘐𝘚𝘈
　M (carving rest.) 9.95/11.50 **st.** ▯ 3.10 – **78 rm.**

at Egerton N : 3 ½ m. by A 673 on A 666 – ✉ ⊛ 0204 Bolton :

🏨 **Egerton House** 🌙, Blackburn Rd, BL7 9PL, ☏ 57171, <, 🌲, park – [TV] 🛁wc ☎ [P]. [A] [AE] [D]. ⊘
closed 1 January – **M** *(closed lunch Saturday)* 4.95 **t.** (lunch) and a la carte 7.90/20.35 **t.** 🍷 2.30 – **25 rm** ☕ 42.00/54.00 **st.**

at Bromley Cross N : 4 m. by A 676 – ✉ ⊛ 0204 Bolton :

🏨 **Last Drop Village,** Hospital Rd, PL7 9PZ, ☏ 591131, Telex 635322, [≈], 🌲 – [TV] 🛁wc ☎ [P]. 👥. [A] [AE] [D] [VISA]
M 8.00/9.00 **t.** and a la carte 🍷 5.00 – **80 rm** ☕ 29.00/56.00 **t.**, **3 suites** 60.00/80.00 **t.** – SB (weekends only) 52.00/60.00 **st.**

AUSTIN-ROVER-DAIMLER-JAGUAR Manchester Rd ☏ 32241
COLT 154/160 Crook St. ☏ 24686
FORD 54/56 Higher Bridge St. ☏ 24474
HYUNDAI, SUBARU Thynne St. ☏ 32511
OPEL Halliwell Rd ☏ 26566
PEUGEOT-TALBOT, CITROEN, LANCIA Bradshawgate ☏ 31323
TOYOTA Radcliffe Rd ☏ 382234
VW, AUDI Blackburn Rd ☏ 31464
VW, AUDI St. Helens Rd ☏ 62131

BOLTON ABBEY North Yorks. [402] O 22 – pop. 122 – ✉ Skipton – ⊛ 075 671.
See : Bolton Priory★ (ruins) and woods (the Strid★ and nature trails in upper Wharfedale).
◆London 216 – Harrogate 18 – ◆Leeds 23 – Skipton 6.

🏨 **Devonshire Arms** 🌙, BD21 6AJ, on A 59 at Bolton Bridge ☏ 441, Telex 51218, <, « Restored former coaching inn », 🎣 – [TV] ☎ ♿ [P]. 👥. [A] [AE] [D] [VISA]
M (buffet lunch)/dinner a la carte 9.65/16.00 **st.** 🍷 4.00 – **38 rm** ☕ 48.00/68.00 **st.**

BONCHURCH I.O.W. [403] [404] Q 32 – see Wight (Isle of) : Ventnor.

BONTDDU Gwynedd [402] [403] I 25 – see Dolgellau.

BONT-FAEN = Cowbridge.

BOOTLE Merseyside [402] ㉜ [403] ② – see Liverpool.

BOREHAM STREET East Sussex [404] V 31 – see Herstmonceux.

BOROUGHBRIDGE North Yorks. [402] P 21 – pop. 1,835 – ECD : Thursday – ⊛ 090 12.
[i] Fishergate (summer only).
◆London 216 – ◆Leeds 26 – ◆Middlesbrough 35 – York 17.

🏨 **Crown,** Horsefair, YO5 9LB, ☏ 2328, Telex 57906 – [⇕] [TV] ♿ [P]. 👥. [A] [AE] [D] [VISA]
M 7.95/11.50 **t.** and a la carte 🍷 3.50 – **43 rm** ☕ 37.00/60.00 **t.**, **1 suite** 70.00/150.00 **t.** – SB (weekends only) 57.00/62.00 **st.**

🏨 **Three Arrows** (Embassy) 🌙, Horsefair, YO5 9LL, ☏ 2245, 🌲, park – [TV] 🛁wc ☎ [P]. [A] [AE] [D] [VISA]. ⊘
M 7.00/10.00 **st.** and a la carte 🍷 2.75 – ☕ 5.00 – **17 rm** 34.00/43.50 **st.** – SB 53.00/62.00 **st.**

⌂ **Farndale,** Horsefair, YO5 9AH, ☏ 3463 – 🛁wc 🚿wc [P]
closed 24 December-1 January – **13 rm** ☕ 9.50/23.00 **st.**

XXX **Fountain House,** St. James Sq., YO5 9AR, ☏ 2241 – [P]. [A] [AE] [D] [VISA]
closed Sunday, Monday and last 2 weeks June – **M** (dinner only) 12.50 **t.** and a la carte 12.05/18.25 **t.** 🍷 3.00.

BORROWDALE Cumbria [402] K 20 – see Keswick.

BOSCASTLE Cornwall [403] F 31 The West Country G. – ⊛ 084 05.
See : Site★.
◆London 260 – Bude 14 – Exeter 59 – ◆Plymouth 43.

🏨 **Riverside,** The Harbour, PL35 0HE, ☏ 216 – 🛁wc 🚿wc [P]. [A]. ⊘
closed December and January – **M** a la carte 6.95/10.20 **t.** 🍷 2.65 – **10 rm** ☕ 18.50/27.00 **t.**

🏨 Bottreaux House, PL35 0BG, on B 3266 ☏ 231 – [TV] 🛁wc 🚿wc [P]. [A] [VISA]
M (bar lunch)/dinner 10.00 **t.** 🍷 2.50 – **7 rm**.

⌂ St. Christopher's Country House, High St., PL35 0BD, S : ½ m. by B 3266 ☏ 412 – 🚿wc [P]
8 rm.

⌂ **Valency House,** The Harbour, PL35 0HD, ☏ 288, 🌲 – [P]. [A] [AE] [VISA]. ⊘
closed Christmas – **7 rm** ☕ 10.00/20.00 **st.**

BOSHAM West Sussex [404] R 31 – see Chichester.

BOSTON Lincs. 402 404 T 25 — pop. 33,908 — ECD : Thursday — ☎ 0205.

See : St. Botolph's Church★★ 14C — ⌐ Cowbridge, Horncastle Rd ℘ 62306, N : 2 m. on B 1183.

🛈 28 South St. ℘ 56656 (summer only) — ◆London 122 — Lincoln 35 — ◆Nottingham 55.

🏠 **New England** (Anchor), 49 Wide Bargate, PE21 6SH, ℘ 65255 — 📺 ➰wc ☎. 🖪 AE ⑩ VISA. ✆
    closed 25 and 26 December — **M** (carving rest.) 8.80 **t.** ▮ 3.00 — **25 rm** ☲ 25.00/45.00 **t.** — SB (weekends only) 49.00/53.00 **st.**

AUSTIN-ROVER-DAIMLER Wide Bargate ℘ 66677	PEUGEOT, TALBOT Grantham Rd ℘ 69020
BMW, NISSAN ℘ 63851	TOYOTA Tawney St. ℘ 68626
COLT, LADA, RELIANT Frith Rd ℘ 62230	VAUXHALL Butterwick ℘ 760421
FIAT London Rd ℘ 55500	VOLVO West St. ℘ 69288
FORD 57 High St. ℘ 60404	VW, AUDI-NSU ℘ 63867

BOTALLACK Cornwall — see St. Just.

BOTLEY Hants. 403 404 Q 31 — pop. 2,156 — ECD : Thursday — ✉ Hedge End, Southampton — ☎ 048 92 — ◆London 83 — ◆Portsmouth 17 — ◆Southampton 6 — Winchester 11.

🏠 **Botleigh Grange** ⌂, Grange Rd, Hedge End, SO3 2GA, W : 1 m. on A 334 ℘ 5611, ≼, ⌐, ✿, park — ▤ 📺 ➰wc ▥wc ☎. 🖪 🖪 AE ⑩ VISA
    M 3.00/12.00 **st.** and a la carte — **45 rm** ☲ 34.00/55.00 **s.** — SB (weekends only) 45.00 **st.**

XX **Cobbett's**, 15 The Square, SO3 2EA, ℘ 2068 — ℗. 🖪 AE VISA
    closed Saturday and Monday lunch, Sunday, 2 weeks in Summer, 2 weeks in winter and Bank Holidays — **M** 8.25 **t.** (lunch) and a la carte 13.00/20.15 **t.** ▮ 4.00.

AUDI, VW Shamblehurst Lane ℘ 3434	AUSTIN-ROVER-DAIMLER-JAGUAR Southampton Rd ℘ 5111

BOTTESFORD Leics. 402 404 R 25 — pop. 2,085 — ECD : Wednesday — ☎ 0949.

◆London 116 — Grantham 75 — Lincoln 26 — ◆ Leicester 32 — ◆ Nottingham 18.

XX **Thatch**, 26 High St., NG13 0AA, ℘ 42330 — ℗. 🖪 AE ⑩ VISA
    closed Sunday — **M** 7.95/9.95 **t.** and a la carte ▮ 3.05.

BOURNE Lincs. 402 404 S 25 — pop. 7,672 — ECD : Wednesday — ☎ 077 833 Witham-on-the-Hill.

◆London 101 — ◆Leicester 42 — Lincoln 35 — ◆Nottingham 42.

🏠 **Toft House,** Main Rd, Toft, PE10 0JT, SW : 3 m. on A 6121 ℘ 614, ✿, squash — 📺 ➰wc ▥wc ℗. VISA. ✆
    M (closed Sunday dinner) 4.40/7.50 **t.** and a la carte ▮ 2.40 — **10 rm** ☲ 20.00/30.00.

AUSTIN-ROVER Thurlby Rd ℘ 2892	FORD Spalding Rd ℘ 4464
AUSTIN-ROVER North St. ℘ 2129	NISSAN Rippingale ℘ 07785 (Dowsby) 777

BOURNE END Herts. 404 S 28 — see Hemel Hempstead.

BOURNEMOUTH Dorset 403 404 O 31 The West Country G. — pop. 142,829 — ECD : Wednesday and Saturday — ☎ 0202 — **See :** Museums★ AC DX, DZ **M.**

⌐ Meyrick Park ℘ 20862 CY — ⌐ Queen's Park, Queen's Park South Drive ℘ 36198, NE : 2 m. CV.

✈ Hurn Airport : ℘ 578646, Telex 41345, N : 5 m. by Hurn Rd DV.

🛈 Westover Rd ℘ 291715 and 290883 — ◆London 114 — ◆Bristol 76 — ◆Southampton 34.

Plans on following pages

🏰 **Carlton**, Meyrick Rd, East Overcliff, BH1 3DN, ℘ 22011, Telex 41244, ≼, ⊿ heated, ✿ — ▯
    📺 ☎ & ⇔ ℗. 🖪. 🖪 AE ⑩ VISA   EZ **a**
    M 9.00/12.00 **t.** and a la carte ▮ 3.45 (see also La Causerie below) — ☲ 6.00 — **55 rm** 47.00/83.00 **t.**, **4 suites** 130.00 **t.** — SB (October-March) 90.00/108.00 **st.**

🏰 **Royal Bath** (De Vere), Bath Rd, BH1 2EW, ℘ 25555, Telex 41375, ≼, ⊿ heated, ✿ — ▯ 📺 & ⇔ ℗. 🖪 🖪 AE ⑩ VISA. ✆   DZ **a**
    M 9.50/15.00 **t.** and a la carte ▮ 3.75 (see also The Royal Grill below) — **133 rm** ☲ 52.00/85.00 **st.** — SB (weekends only) 100.00/105.00 **st.**

🏰 **Palace Court**, Westover Rd, BH1 3BZ, ℘ 27681, Telex 418451, ≼ — ▯ 📺 ☎ ℗. 🖪. 🖪 AE ⑩ VISA   DZ **c**
    M 8.50/10.50 **t.** and a la carte ▮ 4.00 (see also La Taverna below) — **103 rm** ☲ 37.00/59.50 **t.**

🏰 **Highcliff** (Best Western), 105 St. Michael's Rd, West Cliff, BH2 5DU, ℘ 27702, Telex 417153, ≼, ⊿ heated, ✿, ✗ — ▯ 📺 ☎ ℗. 🖪 🖪 AE ⑩ VISA   CZ **z**
    M 7.50/12.00 **st.** and a la carte ▮ 3.00 — **99 rm** ☲ 35.00/95.00 **st.** — SB 60.00/75.00 **st.**

🏰 **Marsham Court** (De Vere), Russell Cotes Rd, East Cliff, BH1 3AB, ℘ 22111, Group Telex 41420, ≼, ⊿ heated — ▯ 📺 ☎ ℗. 🖪 🖪 AE ⑩ VISA ✆   DZ **e**
    M 8.50/10.50 **st.** and a la carte ▮ 3.50 — **80 rm** ☲ 35.00/55.00 **st.** — SB 63.50/66.50 **st.**

🏠 **Cliff End,** Manor Rd, East Cliff, BH1 3EX, ℘ 309711, ⊿ heated, ✿ — ▯ 📺 ➰wc ▥wc ☎ ℗   CX **v**
    M 5.95/7.95 **st.** ▮ 3.20 — **40 rm** ☲ 24.50/49.00 **st.** — SB (September-May) 45.80/47.80 **st.**

🏠 **Crest** (Crest), Meyrick Rd, The Lansdowne, BH1 2PR, ℘ 23262, Telex 41232 — ▯ 📺 ➰wc ☎ ℗. 🖪 🖪 AE ⑩ VISA   DY **a**
    M approx. 10.85 **st.** — ☲ 5.75 — **102 rm** 46.50/56.50 **st.** — SB (weekends only) 67.00 **st.**

BUILT UP AREA

0 ——— 1 km
0 ——— 1/2 mile

BEAR CROSS

KINSON

WALLISDOWN

MOORDOWN

REDHILL PARK

WINTON

MEYRICK PARK

POOLE

WESTBOURNE

BRANKSOME PARK

COMPTON ACRES GARDENS

Lilliput

BOURNEMOUTH

Old Christchurch Road . . . . . **DY**
Square (The) . . . . **CY** 60
Westover Road . . . . **DZ** 73

Archway Road . . . . **AX** 2
Boscombe Cliff Road . . . . **CX** 6
Boscombe Overcliff Road . . . **DX** 7
Boscombe Spa Road . . . . **CX** 8
Branksome Wood Road . . . . **CY** 10
Clarendon Road . . . . **BX** 12
Commercial Road . . . . **CY** 13
Durley Road . . . . **CZ** 15
Ensbury Park Road . . . . **BV** 16
Exeter Road . . . . **CDZ** 17
Fir Vale Road . . . . **DY** 18
Gervis Place . . . . **DY** 20

Gloucester Road . . . . **DV** 21
Hinton Road . . . . **DZ** 25
Lansdowne (The) . . . . **DY** 26
Lansdowne
    Road . . . . **DY** 27
Leicester Road . . . . **AX** 29
Leven Avenue . . . . **BX** 30
Madeira Road . . . . **DY** 32
Manor Road . . . . **EY** 34
Meyrick Road . . . . **EYZ** 35
Owls Road . . . . **CX** 36
Pinecliff Road . . . . **AX** 37
Post Office Road . . . . **CY** 41
Priory Road . . . . **CZ** 43
Queen's Road . . . . **BX** 44
Richmond Hill . . . . **CY** 45
Richmond Park Road . . . . . . **CV** 46
Russell Cotes Road . . . . **DZ** 47
St. Michael's Road . . . . **CZ** 48

St. Paul's Road . . . . **EY** 49
St. Peter's Road . . . . **DY** 50
St. Stephen's Road . . . . **CY** 51
St. Swithuns Road
    South . . . . **EY** 52
Saxonbury Road . . . . **EV** 53
Seabourne Road . . . . **DV** 54
Seamoor Road . . . . **BX** 55
Sea View Road . . . . **AV** 56
Southbourne Grove . . . . **DX** 57
Southbourne Overcliff
    Drive . . . . **DX** 59
Suffolk Road . . . . **CY** 61
Surrey Road . . . . **BX** 62
Triangle (The) . . . . **CY** 63
Upper Hinton Road . . . . **DZ** 64
Wessex Way . . . . **BX** 66
West Cliff Promenade . . . . . . **CZ** 67
Western Road . . . . **AX** 72

*Town plans : the names of main shopping streets are indicated in red
at the beginning of the list of streets.*

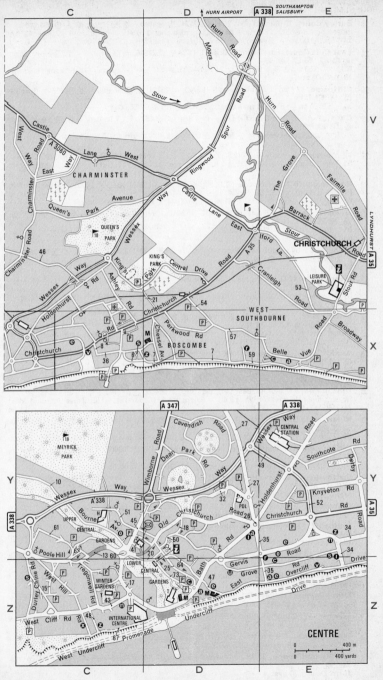

🏨 **Burley Court,** 29 Bath Rd, BH1 2NP, ℰ 22824, ⚊ heated – 🛎️ 📺 🛏️wc ☎ & 🅿️ 🔼 𝑉𝐼𝑆𝐴
closed first 3 weeks January – **M** (bar lunch)/dinner 8.50 **st.** and a la carte ▯ 2.90 – **41 rm**
⚏ 17.50/48.00 **st.** – SB (weekends only)(November-mid May) 42.00/47.00 **st.**
DY **i**

🏨 **East Cliff Court,** East Overcliff Drive, BH1 3AN, ℰ 24545, ⋟, ⚊ heated – 🛎️ 📺 🛏️wc 🗄️wc
☎ 🅿️ ⚄ 🔼 𝐴𝐸 𝑉𝐼𝑆𝐴 ⚘
M 8.00/10.50 **s.** ▯ 3.20 – **69 rm** ⚏ 24.50/84.00 **t.** – SB (weekends only except Bank Holidays)
46.00/60.00 **st.**
EZ **v**

🏨 **Cliffeside,** 32 East Overcliff Drive, BH1 3AQ, ℰ 25724, ⋟, ⚊ heated – 🛎️ 📺 🛏️wc 🗄️wc
🅿️ ⚄ 🔼 𝑉𝐼𝑆𝐴
M 5.75/8.95 **st.** ▯ 1.85 – **64 rm** ⚏ 20.00/58.00 **t.** – SB 38.00/55.00 **st.**
EZ **v**

🏨 **Chesterwood,** East Overcliff Drive, BH1 3AR, ℰ 28057, ⋟, ⚊ heated – 🛎️ 📺 🛏️wc 🗄️wc
🅿️ ⚄ ⓘ 𝑉𝐼𝑆𝐴
closed January and February – **M** 5.00/7.00 **st.** ▯ 2.70 – **54 rm** ⚏ 16.50/46.00 **st.** – SB (winter
only) 36.00/43.00 **st.**
EZ **i**

🏨 **Winterbourne,** Priory Rd, BH2 5GJ, ℰ 24927, ⋟, ⚊ heated – 🛎️ 📺 🛏️wc 🗄️wc 🅿️ 🔼 𝑉𝐼𝑆𝐴
M (bar lunch)/dinner 7.50 **st.** ▯ 4.40 – **41 rm** ⚏ 18.00/47.00 **st.** – SB (October-April)
37.00/43.00 **st.**
CZ **n**

🏨 **Bournemouth Moat House** (Q.M.H.), Knyveton Rd, BH1 3QQ, ℰ 293311, ⚊ heated – 🛎️
📺 🛏️wc ☎ 🅿️ ⚄ 🔼 𝐴𝐸 ⓘ 𝑉𝐼𝑆𝐴
M 7.00/9.00 **st.** and a la carte – **151 rm** ⚏ 30.00/44.00 **st.** – SB 49.50/52.50 **st.**
CX **e**

🏨 **Queens,** Meyrick Rd, Eastcliff, BH1 3DL, ℰ 24415, Group Telex 418297 – 🛎️ 📺 🛏️wc ☎ 🅿️
⚄ 🔼 𝑉𝐼𝑆𝐴
M 6.00/9.50 **t.** ▯ 2.60 – **110 rm** ⚏ 20.00/50.00 **t.** – SB (October-April except Easter, Christmas
and Bank Holidays) 49.00 **st.**
EYZ **r**

🏨 **Ladbroke Savoy** (Ladbroke), West Hill Rd, West Cliff, BH2 5EJ, ℰ 294241, ⋟, ⚊ heated, ⚞
– 🛎️ 📺 🛏️wc ☎ & 🅿️ ⚄
88 rm.
CZ **x**

🏨 **Heathlands,** 12 Grove Rd, East Cliff, BH1 3AY, ℰ 23336, ⚊ heated – 🛎️ 📺 🛏️wc ☎ & 🅿️.
⚄ 🔼 𝐴𝐸 ⓘ 𝑉𝐼𝑆𝐴
M (restricted lunch Monday to Saturday)/dinner 8.00 **st.** ▯ 3.25 – **116 rm** ⚏ 20.00/54.00 **st.** –
SB 42.50/45.00 **st.**
EZ **c**

🏨 **Durley Hall,** 7 Durley Chine Rd, Westcliff, BH2 5JS, ℰ 766886, ⚊ heated, ⚞ – 🛎️ 📺
🛏️wc ☎ 🅿️. 🔼 𝐴𝐸 ⓘ 𝑉𝐼𝑆𝐴
M (bar lunch)/dinner 9.00 **t.** and a la carte ▯ 2.75 – **81 rm** ⚏ 20.00/60.00 **t.** – SB (except Easter,
July, August, Christmas and New Year) 34.00/52.00 **st.**
CZ **s**

🏨 **Anglo-Swiss,** 16 Gervis Rd, East Cliff, BH1 3EQ, ℰ 24794, ⚊ heated, ⚞ – 🛎️ 📺 🛏️wc ☎
🅿️ 🔼 𝐴𝐸 ⓘ 𝑉𝐼𝑆𝐴
M (bar lunch in summer)/dinner 8.50 **t.** ▯ 3.25 – **63 rm** ⚏ 20.00/64.00 **t.** – SB (weekends
only)(September-June) 42.50/48.00 **st.**
EY **e**

🏨 **Hinton Firs,** 9 Manor Rd, East Cliff, BH1 3HB, ℰ 25409, ⚊ heated – 🛎️ 📺 🛏️wc 🅿️. ⚘
M (bar lunch)/dinner 6.75 **st.** ▯ 2.40 – **56 rm** ⚏ 13.00/50.00 **st.** – SB (November-mid May)
34.00/43.00 **st.**
EY **n**

🏨 **Miramar,** 19 Grove Rd, East Overcliff, BH1 3AL, ℰ 26581, ⋟, ⚞ – 🛎️ 📺 🛏️wc 🗄️wc ☎ 🅿️
🔼 𝐴𝐸 ⓘ 𝑉𝐼𝑆𝐴
M 5.50/8.50 ▯ 3.50 – **42 rm** ⚏ 21.50/49.00 – SB (weekends only) (October-April) 47.20/71.20 **st.**
DZ **u**

🏨 **Cliff House,** 113 Alumhurst Rd, Alum Chine, BH4 8HS, ℰ 763003, ⋟ – 🛎️ 📺 🛏️wc 🗄️wc &
🅿️. ⚘
April-October – **M** (dinner only) 7.00 **st.** ▯ 1.50 – **10 rm** ⚏ 15.50/46.00 **st.**
BX **s**

🏨 **Cottonwood,** 79 Grove Rd, East Cliff, BH1 3AP, ℰ 23183, ⋟, – 🛎️ 📺 🛏️wc 🗄️wc 🅿️. 𝑉𝐼𝑆𝐴
M (bar lunch Monday to Saturday)/dinner 6.35 **t.** ▯ 2.75 – **30 rm** ⚏ 13.50/45.00 – SB (October-
April) (except Christmas and Bank Holidays) 35.00/39.00 **st.**
EY **s**

🏨 **Chinehead,** 31 Alumhurst Rd, BH4 8EN, ℰ 761693 – 🛏️wc 🅿️. 𝑉𝐼𝑆𝐴
M (dinner only) 5.50 **st.** ▯ 2.60 – **27 rm** ⚏ 10.00/45.00 **st.**
BX **n**

⌂ **Alumcliff,** 121 Alumhurst Rd, Alum Chine, BH4 8HS, ℰ 764777, ⋟ – 🛏️wc 🗄️wc 🅿️. 🔼 𝐴𝐸
𝑉𝐼𝑆𝐴
16 rm ⚏ 18.40/39.10 **t.**
BX **a**

⌂ **Valberg,** 1A Wollstonecraft Rd, Boscombe, BH5 1JQ, ℰ 34644, ⚞ – 🗄️wc 🅿️
10 rm ⚏ 12.00/20.00 **s.**
CX **s**

⌂ **Naseby Nye,** 10 Byron Rd, Boscombe Overcliff, BH5 1JD, ℰ 34079, ⚞ – 🛏️wc 🅿️
13 rm ⚏ 11.50/19.00 **t.**
DX **z**

⌂ **Tudor Grange,** 31 Gervis Rd, BH1 3EE, ℰ 291472, ⚞ – 🅿️
12 rm ⚏ 10.50/28.00 **st.**
EY **o**

⌂ **Mariners,** 22 Clifton Rd, Southbourne, BH6 3PA, ℰ 420851 – 🛏️wc 🅿️
March-October – **15 rm** ⚏ 7.50/15.00 **s.**
EX **c**

⌂ **Wood Lodge,** 10 Manor Rd, East Cliff, BH1 3EY, ℰ 290891, ⚞ – 🛏️wc 🗄️wc 🅿️. ⚘
Easter-October – **16 rm** ⚏ 10.25/34.00 **t.**
EY **z**

⌂ **Southwood Lodge,** 36-38 Southwood Av., Southbourne, BH6 3QB, ℰ 422213 – 🗄️wc 🅿️.
𝑉𝐼𝑆𝐴 ⚘
31 rm ⚏ 8.50/20.50 **st.**
DX **r**

XXX La Causerie (at Carlton H.), Meyrick Rd, East Overcliff, BH1 3DN, ✆ 22011, Telex 41244 – ℗
EZ a

XXX The Royal Grill (at Royal Bath H.), Bath Rd, BH1 2EW, ✆ 25555, Telex 41375 – ℗
DZ a

XX La Taverna (at Palace Court H.), Westover Rd, BH1 3BZ, ✆ 27681, Telex 418451 – ℗. ⒶⒺ
ⓄⓋ𝑉𝐼𝑆𝐴
DZ c
closed Sunday – M 12.50 t. and a la carte 🍴 4.00.

XX Provence, 91 Belle Vue Rd., Southbourne, BH6 3DH, ✆ 424421, French rest. – ⒶⒺ Ⓞ 𝑉𝐼𝑆𝐴
closed Sunday and late July-early August – M (dinner only) a la carte 16.40/18.80.
EX a

X Sophisticats, 43 Charminster Rd, BH8 8UE, ✆ 291019
BV a
M (closed Sunday, Monday, 2 weeks January, last week June and last week October) (dinner only) a la carte 10.35/12.55 t.

X Crust, The Square, BH2 5AE, ✆ 21430 – ⒶⒺ Ⓞ 𝑉𝐼𝑆𝐴
CY o
M 5.25 t. (lunch) and a la carte 7.35/10.95 t. 🍴 2.75.

ALFA-ROMEO, VOLVO 33 R. L. Stephenson Av. ✆ 763344
AUSTIN-ROVER 235 Castle Lane West, Redhill ✆ 510201
AUSTIN-ROVER 14 Carbery Row ✆ 423243
BENTLEY, ROLLS ROYCE Ringwood Rd ✆ 570575
BMW Exeter Rd ✆ 24433
CITROEN, PEUGEOT, TALBOT 43 Holdenhurst Rd ✆ 26566
DAIMLER-JAGUAR 38 Poole Hill ✆ 25405

FORD Poole Rd ✆ 762442
LANCIA 318/320 Holdenhurst Rd ✆ 33304
MERCEDES BENZ Wallisdown Rd ✆ 525111
PEUGEOT 25/27 Palmerston Rd, Boscombe ✆ 37206
PORSCHE 382/386 Charminster Rd ✆ 510252
VAUXHALL 521 Christchurch Rd ✆ 35362
VAUXHALL Castle Lane West ✆ 526434
VAUXHALL 984 Christchurch Rd ✆ 423201
VAUXHALL-OPEL Poole Rd ✆ 763361

BOURTON-ON-THE-WATER Glos. 403 404 O 28 – pop. 2,538 – ECD : Saturday – ✆ 0451 Cotswold.

♦London 91 – ♦Birmingham 47 – Gloucester 24 – ♦Oxford 36.

🏠 Old Manse, Sherborne St., GL54 2BX, ✆ 20642, 🌸 – 📺 ⇔wc ⓟ. ⒶⒺ 𝑉𝐼𝑆𝐴. ⚘
closed 2 weeks January – M 7.50/9.25 t. and a la carte 🍴 3.85 – ⚊ 2.50 – 9 rm 20.50/47.00 t. – SB (winter only) 53.00/66.00 st.

🏠 Old New Inn, High St., GL54 2AF, ✆ 20467, « Bourton model village », 🌸 – 🚗 ⓟ. ⒶⒺ 𝑉𝐼𝑆𝐴
closed Christmas day – M 6.00/9.20 st. 🍴 2.50 – 24 rm ⚊ 17.50/39.00 st.

🏠 Brookside, Riverside, GL54 2BS, ✆ 20371, 🌸 – 📺 ⇔wc 🅼wc ⓟ. ⒶⒺ Ⓞ 𝑉𝐼𝑆𝐴
M 6.50 t. and a la carte 🍴 2.90 – 10 rm ⚊ 15.00/36.00 t. – SB 45.00/50.00 st.

X Rose Tree, Riverside, GL54 2BX, ✆ 20635 – ⒶⒺ Ⓞ 𝑉𝐼𝑆𝐴
closed Sunday dinner, Tuesday-Saturday lunch October-April, Monday and mid January-mid February – M (bar lunch Tuesday to Saturday)/dinner 15.95 t. 🍴 3.25.

FORD Lansdowne Rd ✆ 20366   SKODA Fossway ✆ 20132

BOVEY TRACEY Devon 403 I 32 The West Country G. – pop. 3,434 – ECD : Wednesday – ✉ Newton Abbot – ✆ 0626 – See : St. Peter, St. Paul and St. Thomas of Canterbury Church★.
🅱 Lower Car Park ✆ 832047 (summer only).
♦London 214 – Exeter 14 – ♦Plymouth 32.

🏠 Prestbury Country House 🦢, Brimley Lane, Brimley, TQ13 9JS, SW : 1 m. by A 382 ✆ 833246, ≤, « Country house atmosphere », 🌸 – ⇔wc 🅼wc ⓟ. ⒶⒺ 𝑉𝐼𝑆𝐴. ⚘
March-October – M (bar lunch)/dinner 10.50 st. 🍴 2.50 – 8 rm ⚊ 19.00/44.00 st.

🏠 Coombe Cross, Coombe Cross, TQ13 9EY, ✆ 832476, 🌸 – 📺 ⇔wc ⓟ. ⒶⒺ Ⓞ 𝑉𝐼𝑆𝐴
M (closed Monday) (bar lunch)/dinner 9.95 t. 🍴 2.70 – 23 rm ⚊ 23.95/39.90 – SB 40.00/50.00 st.

🏠 Front House, East St., TQ13 9EL, ✆ 832202, ⅃, 🌸 – 🅼wc ⓟ
April-October – 6 rm ⚊ 11.00/20.00 st.

BOWBURN Durham 401 402 P 19 – pop. 3,748 – ✆ 0385 Durham.
♦London 265 – Durham 3 – ♦Middlesbrough 20.

🏠 Bowburn Hall, DH6 5NT, E : 1 m. ✆ 770311, 🌸 – 📺 ⇔wc ⓟ. ⒶⒺ Ⓞ 𝑉𝐼𝑆𝐴
M 9.00 st. 🍴 3.50 – 20 rm ⚊ 29.00/35.00 st.

BOWDON Greater Manchester 402 403 404 M 23 – see Altrincham.

BOWNESS-ON-WINDERMERE Cumbria 402 L 20 – see Windermere.

BRACKNELL Berks. 404 R 29 – pop. 52,257 – ECD : Wednesday – ✆ 0344.
🅱 Central Library, Town Sq., ✆ 423149.
♦London 35 – Reading 11.

🏨 Ladbroke (Ladbroke), Bagshot Rd, RG12 3QJ, S : 2 m. on A 322 ✆ 424801, Telex 848058 – 🛗
📺 ⇔wc ♨ ⚬ ⓟ. 🎱. ⒶⒺ Ⓞ 𝑉𝐼𝑆𝐴
M (closed Saturday lunch) (buffet lunch)/dinner 10.95 t. and a la carte 🍴 3.90 – ⚊ 5.50 – 115 rm 48.50/60.00 t. – SB (weekends only) 57.00 st.

BRADFIELD COMBUST Suffolk – see Bury St. Edmunds.

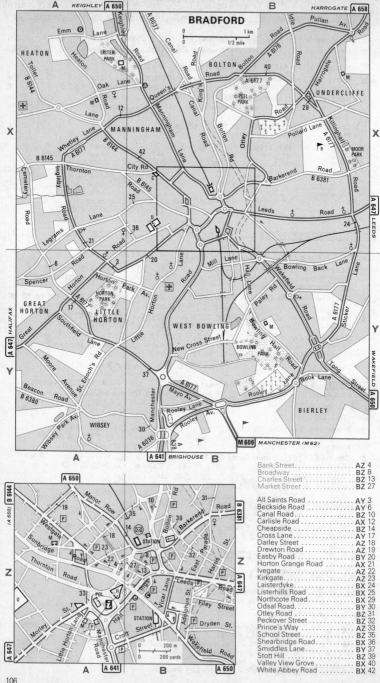

BRADFORD

1 km
1/2 mile

Bank Street	AZ 4
Broadway	BZ 8
Charles Street	BZ 13
Market Street	BZ 27
All Saints Road	AY 3
Beckside Road	AY 6
Canal Road	BZ 10
Carlisle Road	AX 12
Cheapside	BZ 14
Cross Lane	AY 17
Darley Street	AZ 18
Drewton Road	AZ 19
Easby Road	BY 20
Horton Grange Road	AX 21
Ivegate	AZ 22
Kirkgate	AZ 23
Laisterdyke	BX 24
Listerhills Road	BX 25
Northcote Road	BX 29
Odsal Road	BY 30
Otley Road	BZ 31
Peckover Street	BZ 32
Prince's Way	AZ 33
School Street	BZ 35
Shearbridge Road	BZ 36
Smiddles Lane	BY 37
Stott Hill	BZ 39
Valley View Grove	BX 40
White Abbey Road	BX 42

BRADFORD West Yorks. 402 O 22 – pop. 293 ,336 – ECD : Wednesday – ☎ 0274.

🏠 West Bradford, Chellow Grange, Haworth Rd ℰ 427671, NW : 3 m. by A 6144 AX – 🏠 Hawksworth Lane, Guiseley ℰ 0943 (Guiseley) 75570, N : 8 m. by A 6037 BX – 🏠 Bradford Moor, Scarr-Hall, Pollard Lane ℰ 638313 BX – 🏠 East Bierley, South View Rd ℰ 681023, SE : 4 m. on plan of Leeds BX.

✈ Leeds and Bradford Airport : ℰ 0532 (Rawdon) 503431, NE : 6 m. by A 658 BX.

🛈 Central Library, Princes Way ℰ 753678 – City Hall ℰ 763678.

♦ London 212 – ♦Leeds 9 – ♦Manchester 39 – ♦Middlesbrough 75 – ♦Sheffield 45.

Plan of Enlarged Area : see Leeds

Plan opposite

🏨 **Stakis Norfolk Gardens** (Stakis), Hall Ings, BD1 5SH, ℰ 734734, Telex 517573 – 🛗 ▤ rest
　📺 & 🅿. 🔬 🔼 🆎 ⓪ 𝖵𝖨𝖲𝖠　　　　　　　　　　　　　　　　　　　　　　　　　　BZ e
　M 8.00/10.00 t. and a la carte ⓘ 3.50 – ヱ 3.75 – **126 rm** 45.00/60.00 t., **3 Suites** 80.00 t.

🏨 **Victoria** (T.H.F.), Bridge St., BD1 1JX, ℰ 728706, Telex 517456 – 🛗 📺 ➯wc ⋔wc ☎ 🅿.
　🔬 🔼 🆎 ⓪ 𝖵𝖨𝖲𝖠　　　　　　　　　　　　　　　　　　　　　　　　　　　　　　BZ c
　M (carving rest.) 8.25 **st.** ⓘ 2.75 – ヱ 5.50 – **59 rm** 36.00/45.50 **st.**

🏨 **Novotel Bradford,** Euroway Trading Estate, Merrydale Rd, BD4 6SA, S : 3 ½ m. by A 641
　and A 6117 off M 606 ℰ 683683, Telex 517312, ⊿ heated – 🛗 📺 ➯wc ⋔wc ☎ 🅿. 🔼 🆎
　⓪ 𝖵𝖨𝖲𝖠　　　　　　　　　　　　　　　　　　　　　　on plan of Leeds AX a
　M 7.50 **st.** and a la carte ⓘ 3.20 – ヱ 4.50 – **136 rm** 36.00/44.00 **st.**

🏠 **Cartwright,** 308 Manningham Lane, BD8 7AX, ℰ 499908 – 📺 ➯wc ⋔wc 🅿. 𝖵𝖨𝖲𝖠. ⋇
　M (closed Saturday lunch and Sunday dinner) 5.20/7.50 **st.** and a la carte ⓘ 2.50 – **12 rm**
　ヱ 25.00/34.00 **st.** – SB (weekends only) 37.00 **st.**　　　　　　　　　　　BX a

⌂ **Maple Hill** 🐾, 3 Park Drive, Heaton, BD9 4DP, ℰ 44061, ☞ – 📺 🅿　　　　　　AX o
　10 rm ヱ 12.50/25.00 s.

　at Thornton W : 5 ¼ m. on B 6145 – AX – ✉ ☎ 0274 Bradford :

XXX **Cottage,** 869 Thornton Rd, BD13 3NW, W : 1 m. on B 6145 ℰ 832752 – 🅿. 🔼 🆎 ⓪ 𝖵𝖨𝖲𝖠
　closed Saturday lunch and Sunday – **M** 10.50 (dinner) and a la carte ⓘ 4.50.

AUSTIN-ROVER-DAIMLER-JAGUAR　Canal Rd ℰ
　733488
AUSTIN-ROVER 38 Manningham Lane ℰ 732444
BMW Oak Lane ℰ 495521
CITROEN Whetley Hill ℰ 495543
COLT St. Enoch's Rd ℰ 722234
FIAT Keighley Rd, Frizinghall ℰ 490031
FORD 44 Bowland St. ℰ 725131
FORD 146/148 Tong St. ℰ 681601

MERCEDES-BENZ Thornton Rd ℰ 494122
NISSAN 88 Thornton Rd ℰ 727302
NISSAN, PORSCHE, VAUXHALL-OPEL Parry Lane
　ℰ 392321
POLONEZ, FSO 341 Leeds Rd ℰ 726812
SAAB Apperley Lane, Yeadon ℰ 0532 (Leeds) 502231
VOLVO 221 Sunbridge Rd ℰ 721720
VW, AUDI-NSU Ingleby Rd ℰ 494100

BRADFORD-ON-AVON Wilts. 403 404 N 29 The West Country G. – pop. 8 ,921 – ECD : Wednesday – ☎ 022 16.

See : Site★★ – Saxon Church of St. Lawrence★★ – Bridge★.

Envir. : Great Chalfield Manor★ AC (Church★), NE : 2 m. – Westwood Manor★AC, SW : 1 ½ m.

🛈 Waterlands, 34 Silver St. ℰ 2495.

♦London 118 – ♦ Bristol 24 – Salisbury 35 – Swindon 33.

🏨 **Leigh Park,** Leigh Road West, BA15 2RA, NE : 1 m. by A 363 and B 3109 on B 3105 ℰ 3433,
　☞, ⋇ – 📺 ➯wc ⋔wc 🅿. 🔬 🔼 𝖵𝖨𝖲𝖠. ⋇
　closed 25 and 26 December – **M** (closed Saturday) (lunch by arrangement) 5.75/9.50 t. ⓘ 2.25
　– **20 rm** ヱ 21.50/38.00 t.

🏨 **Swan,** 1 Church St., BA15 1LN, ℰ 2224 – 📺 ➯wc ⋔wc 🅿. 🔼 ⓪ 𝖵𝖨𝖲𝖠
　M (closed Sunday dinner) a la carte 6.65/13.10 **st.** ⓘ 3.40 – **13 rm** ヱ 23.50/38.00 **st.** – SB
　(except summer)(weekends only) 45.00 **st.**

BRADFORD-ON-TONE Somerset 403 K 30 – see Taunton.

BRADWORTHY Devon 403 G 31 – pop. 821 – ECD : Wednesday – ✉ Holsworthy – ☎ 040 924.

♦London 251 – Barnstaple 27 – Exeter 50 – ♦Plymouth 47.

🏨 **Lake Villa** 🐾, EX22 7SQ, E : ½ m. ℰ 342, ☞, ⋇ – 📺 ➯wc ⋔wc 🅿. ⋇
　M (booking essential) (bar lunch)/dinner 9.50 t. ⓘ 2.25 – **7 rm** ヱ 12.00/28.00 **st.** – SB
　(October-March) 36.00/40.00 **st.**

BRAINTREE Essex 404 V 28 – pop. 30 ,975 – ECD : Thursday – ☎ 0376.

♦London 45 – ♦Cambridge 38 – Chelmsford 12 – Colchester 15.

🏨 **White Hart,** Bocking End, CM7 6AB, ℰ 21401 – 📺 ➯wc ⋔wc 🅿. 🔬 🔼 🆎 ⓪ 𝖵𝖨𝖲𝖠
　M a la carte 7.25/9.60 **t.** ⓘ 2.20 – **35 rm** ヱ 28.00/48.00 **t.** – SB (weekends only) 56.00 **st.**

ALFA-ROMEO Bocking ℰ 26604
FORD Rayne Rd ℰ 21202
MAZDA Rayne Rd ℰ 42159

VAUXHALL-OPEL 277/281 Rayne Rd ℰ 21456
VOLVO Skitts Hill ℰ 47797

BRAITHWAITE Cumbria 401 402 K 20 – see Keswick.

BRAMBER West Sussex – see Steyning.

BRAMHOPE West Yorks. 402 P 22 – see Leeds.

BRAMLEY Surrey 404 S 30 – see Guildford.

BRAMPTON Cambs. 404 T 27 – pop. 4 ,339 – ECD : Tuesday and Saturday – ⊠ ✪ 0480 Huntingdon.

♦London 67 – Bedford 19 – Huntingdon 2.

🏨 **Brampton,** PE18 8NH, W : 1 ½ m. at junction A 1 and A 604 ✆ 810434 – 📺 🛏wc 🕾 🅿. �. ⚑ 🆑 ⓞ 𝘝𝘐𝘚𝘈
M 8.45/8.65 **st.** and a la carte ⏐3.00 – **17 rm** ⊊ 38.50/54.00 **st.** – SB (weekends only) 56.00/60.00 **st.**

CITROEN Huntingdon Rd ✆ 53132

BRAMPTON Cumbria 401 402 L 19 – pop. 3 ,686 – ECD : Thursday – ✪ 069 77.
Envir. : Lanercost : Priory★ (14C ruins) *AC*, NE : 3 m. – Bewcastle (churchyard Runic Cross★ 8C) N : 12 m.
🛇 Talkin Tarn ✆ 2255, SE : 1 m. on B 6413.
🖪 Moot Hall, Market Place ✆ 3433 (summer only).
♦ London 317 – ♦Carlisle 9 – ♦Newcastle-upon-Tyne 49.

🏨 **Farlam Hall** 🦢, CA8 2NG, SE : 2 ¾ m. on A 689 ✆ 069 76 (Hallbankgate) 234, ≼, « Gardens » – 📺 🛏wc 🕿wc 🅿. ⚑ 🆑 𝘝𝘐𝘚𝘈 ✀
closed Monday and Tuesday November-December, February and first 2 weeks in November –
M (dinner only) 14.50 **t.** – **13 rm** ⊊ (dinner included) 42.00/84.00 **t.** – SB (October-April except Easter) 66.00/76.00 **st.**

🏠 Howard Arms, Front St., CA8 1NG, ✆ 2357 – 📺 🛏wc 🕿wc
11 rm.

BRAMSHAW Hants. 403 404 P 31 – pop. 611 – ECD : Tuesday – ⊠ Lyndhurst – ✪ 0703 Southampton.

♦London 93 – Salisbury 13 – ♦Southampton 11 – Winchester 21.

🏠 **Bramble Hill** 🦢, Bramble Hill, SO4 7JG, W : ½ m. ✆ 813165, ≼, « Former hunting lodge », 🌹, park – 🛏wc 🅿. ⚑ 𝘝𝘐𝘚𝘈
M *(closed Sunday dinner)* (bar lunch)/dinner a la carte 8.70/14.25 **t.** ⏐2.50 – **16 rm** ⊊ 18.50/45.00 **t.** – SB (weekdays only)(October-June) 40.00/60.00 **st.**

BRANDON Warw. 403 404 P 26 – see Coventry.

BRANSCOMBE Devon 403 K 32 **The West Country** G. – pop. 506 – ECD : Thursday – ⊠ Seaton – ✪ 029 780.

♦London 167 – Exeter 20 – Lyme Regis 11.

🏨 **Ye Olde Masons Arms,** EX12 3DJ, ✆ 300, « 14C inn », 🌹 – 🛏wc 🅿. ⚑ 𝘝𝘐𝘚𝘈
M (bar lunch Monday to Saturday)/dinner 13.00 **t.** ⏐3.20 – **20 rm** ⊊ 16.00/48.00 – SB (November-March) 47.30/51.60 **st.**

BRANSTON Lincs 402 404 S 24 - see Lincoln.

BRANSTON Staffs. – see Burton-upon-Trent.

BRAUNSTONE Leics. 402 403 404 Q 26 – see Leicester.

BRAY-ON-THAMES Berks. 404 R 29 – pop. 9 ,427 – ⊠ ✪ 0628 Maidenhead.
♦London 34 – Reading 13.

🏨 **Monkey Island,** SL6 2EE, SE : 1 m. by Monkey Island Lane ✆ 23400, ≼, « Island in River Thames », 🦢, 🌹, park – 📺 🛏wc 🕾 🅿. ⚑ 🆑 ⓞ 𝘝𝘐𝘚𝘈 ✀
M 12.50/15.00 **st.** ⏐3.75 – **25 rm** ⊊ 55.00/60.00 **st.** – SB (weekends only) 70.00/90.00 **st.**

🏠 **Chauntry House,** High St., SL6 2AB, ✆ 73991, 🌹 – 📺 🛏wc 🕾 🅿. ⚑ 🆑 ⓞ 𝘝𝘐𝘚𝘈
M *(closed Friday, Saturday and Sunday)* (dinner only) 11.50 **st.** – **9 rm** ⊊ 42.50/56.00 **st.**

XXXX ✿✿✿ **Waterside Inn,** Ferry Rd, SL6 2AT, ✆ 20691, Telex 8813079, ≼, French rest., « Thames-side setting », 🌹 – 🅿. ⚑ 🆑 ⓞ 𝘝𝘐𝘚𝘈 ✀
closed Tuesday lunch, Sunday dinner 20 October-Easter, Monday, 26 December-February and Bank Holidays – **M** 20.00/33.00 **st.** and a la carte
Spec. Huitres tièdes en feuilleté au vinaigre de framboises (Oct-March), Caneton croisé challandais aux clous de girofle et au miel (Oct.-March), Tarte citron et délice au cassis.

XX **Hind's Head,** High St., SL6 2AB, ✆ 26151, English rest., 🌹 – 🅿. ⚑ 🆑 ⓞ 𝘝𝘐𝘚𝘈
M *(closed Sunday dinner)* 17.50/20.50 **st.**

BRECHFA Dyfed **403** H 28 – ⊠ Carmarthen – ☎ 026 789.

♦London 223 – Carmarthen 11 – ♦Swansea 30.

※※ **Ty Mawr** ⌕ with rm, Abergorlech Rd, SA32 7RA, ℰ 332, ➘, 🍴 – ⌐wc **P**. **☒** **①** **VISA**
closed 3 weeks February and 1 week November – **M** (closed Sunday and Monday to non-
residents) (bar lunch residents only)/dinner 8.95 **st**. and a la carte – **5 rm** ⊊ 23.10/42.00 **st**. –
SB 55.00/58.00 **st**.

BRECON (ABERHONDDU) Powys **403** J 28 – pop. 7,166 – ECD : Wednesday – ☎ 0874.

See : Cathedral★ 13C.

Envir. : Bwlch (≤★ of the Usk Valley), SE : 8 ½ m. – Road★ from Brecon to Hirwaun – Road★ from
Brecon to Merthyr Tydfil – Craig-y-Nos (Dan-yr-Ogof Caves★), SW : 18 m.

🛈 Watton Mount ℰ 4437 (summer only) – Market Car Park ℰ 2485 and 5692 (summer only).

♦London 171 – ♦Cardiff 40 – Carmarthen 31 – Gloucester 65.

🏠 Wellington, The Bulwark, LD3 7AD, ℰ 5225 – **TV** ⌐wc ☎. **☒** **AE** **VISA**. ⅏
21 rm ⊊ 20.00/38.00 **st**. – SB 23.75/25.75 **st**.

BREDWARDINE Heref. and Worc. **403** L 27 – pop. 177 – ⊠ Hereford – ☎ 098 17 Moccas.

♦London 150 – Hereford 12 – Newport 51.

🏠 **Red Lion**, HR3 6BU, ℰ 303, ➘, 🍴 – ⌐wc **P**. **☒** **AE** **①** **VISA**. ⅏
M (bar lunch)/dinner 12.00 **s**. ⅃ 2.50 – **10 rm** ⊊ 11.50/40.00 **t**. – SB (July-March) 30.00/45.00 **st**.

BRENDON Devon **403** I 30 – see Lynton.

BRENT KNOLL Somerset **403** L 30 – pop. 1,092 – ECD : Wednesday and Saturday – ⊠ High-
bridge – ☎ 0278 Bridgwater.

🛈 Brent Knoll Picnic Area (M5 Southbound) ℰ Edingworth (093 472) 466 (summer only).

♦London 151 – ♦Bristol 33 – Taunton 21.

🏠 **Battleborough Grange**, Bristol Rd, TA9 4HJ, on A 38 ℰ 760208, 🍴 – **TV** ⌐wc 🏧wc **P**.
☒ **AE** **①** **VISA**. ⅏
M (lunch by arrangement)/dinner 7.50 **t**. and a la carte ⅃ 2.90 – **11 rm** ⊊ 21.00/35.00 **t**. – SB
(weekends only)(October-March) 42.00 **st**.

BRENTWOOD Essex **404** V 29 – pop. 51,212 – ECD : Thursday – ☎ 0277.

🖈 King George's playing fields, Ingrave Rd ℰ 218850.

♦London 22 – Chelmsford 11 – Southend-on-Sea 21.

🏨 **Brentwood Moat House** (Q.M.H.), London Rd, CM14 4NR, SW : 1 ¼ m. on A 1023
ℰ 225252, Telex 995182, 🍴 – **TV** & **P**. 🏧. **☒** **AE** **①** **VISA** ⅏
M a la carte 14.90/19.45 **t**. ⅃ 2.95 – ⊊ 5.25 – **37 rm** 48.00/55.00 **st**.

🏨 **Post House** (T.H.F.), Brook St., CM14 5NF, SW : 1 ¾ m. on A 1023 ℰ 210888, Telex 995379,
🛁 heated – 📶 **TV** ⌐wc ☎ & **P**. **☒** **☒** **AE** **①** **VISA**
M 8.00/10.00 **st**. and a la carte ⅃ 3.20 – ⊊ 5.50 – **120 rm** 45.00/52.50 **st**.

AUDI, VW, DAIMLER-JAGUAR 2 Brook St. ℰ 216161
AUSTIN-ROVER Ingrave Rd ℰ 221401
FORD Brook St. ℰ 215544

NISSAN 110 Shenfield Rd, Shenfield ℰ 222424
RENAULT Shenfield ℰ 218686
VAUXHALL-OPEL Brook St. ℰ 233131

BRERETON Cheshire – see Holmes Chapel.

BRIDGEND (PEN-Y-BONT) Mid Glam. **403** J 29 – pop. 31,008 – ECD : Wednesday – ☎ 0656
Pencoed.

♦London 177 – ♦Cardiff 20 – ♦Swansea 23.

🏨 Heronston, Ewenny, CF35 5AW, S : 2 m. on B 4265 ℰ 68811, Telex 498232, **☒** – **TV** ⌐wc ☎
P. 🏧
40 rm.

at Coychurch (Llangrallo) E : 2 ¼ m. by A 473 – ⊠ ☎ 0656 Bridgend :

※※※ **Coed-y-Mwstwr** ⌕ with rm, CF35 6AF, N : 1 m. ℰ 860621, ≤, 🛁 heated, 🍴, park, ⅏ –
TV ⌐wc ☎ **P**. **☒** **AE** **①** **VISA**. ⅏
closed 25 to 27 December – **M** (closed Sunday dinner) 13.95 **t**. and a la carte ⅃ 2.95 – ⊊ 6.50
– **15 rm** 28.50/52.00 **t**.

MICHELIN Branch, Brackla Industrial Estate, CF31 2BD, ℰ 62343

N'oubliez pas qu'il existe des limitations de vitesse au Royaume Uni en dehors de
celles mentionnées sur les panneaux.

– 60 mph (= 96 km/h) sur route.

– 70 mph (= 112 km/h) sur route à chaussées séparées et autoroute.

BRIDGNORTH Salop 403 404 M 26 – pop. 10,332 – ECD : Thursday – ✪ 074 62.

Envir. : Claverley (Parish church : wall paintings★ 13C-15C) E : 5 m. – Much Wenlock : Wenlock priory★ (ruins 11C) *AC*, NW : 8 ½ m.

◪ Stanley Lane ♒ 3315, N : 1 m.

🛈 Bridgnorth Library, Listley St. ♒ 3358.

♦London 146 – ♦Birmingham 26 – Shrewsbury 20 – Worcester 29.

    🏠 **Falcon,** St. John St., Low Town, WV15 6AG, ♒ 3134 – 📺 ⌂wc 🅿. 🔼 AE ⓪ VISA
    M *(closed Sunday dinner to non-residents)* (bar lunch Saturday) 8.00/12.00 **t.** and a la carte ▮ 4.20 – **16 rm** ⤶ 22.50/38.00 **st.**

    ↑ **Croft,** St. Mary's St., WV16 4DW, ♒ 2416 – ⌂wc 🛏wc. 🔼 VISA
    7 rm ⤶ 14.00/30.00 **st.**

    at Worfield NE : 4 m. by A 454 – ✉ Bridgnorth – ✪ 074 64 Worfield :

    🏠 **Old Vicarage** ⬥, WV15 5JZ, ♒ 498, 🐴 – 📺 ⌂wc 🛏wc 🅿. 🔼 AE ⓪ VISA
    M (booking essential) 9.95/12.50 **st.** and a la carte ▮ 3.45 – **10 rm** ⤶ 31.50/42.50 **st.** – SB (except Bank Holidays) 53.00 **st.**

AUSTIN-ROVER-DAIMLER-JAGUAR 52 West Castle St. ♒ 2207

RENAULT Northgate ♒ 3332
VW, AUDI Hollybush Rd ♒ 4343

BRIDGWATER Somerset 403 L 30 The West Country G. – pop. 30,782 – ECD : Thursday – ✪ 0278.

See : Site★ – Castle St.★ – St. Mary's★ – Admiral Blake Museum★ *AC*.

Envir. : Stogursey Priory Church★★, NW : 14 m. by A 39 – Westonzoyland Church★★, SE : 3 m. – North Petherton Church Tower★★, S : 3 m.

◪ Enmore Park ♒ 027 867 (Spaxton) 481, W : 3 m.

🛈 Town Hall, High St. ♒ 427652/424391 ext 419 (summer only).

♦London 160 – ♦Bristol 39 – Taunton 11.

    🏠 **Watergate,** 10-11 West Quay, TA6 3DB, ♒ 423847 – 📺 🛏wc. 🔼 AE ⓪ VISA ⬥
    M *(closed Sunday to non-residents)* 6.00/8.50 **t.** and a la carte ▮ 3.00 – **8 rm** ⤶ 20.00/32.00 **t.**

    ✗ **Old Vicarage** with rm, 45 St. Mary St., TA6 3EQ, ♒ 458891, 🐴 – 📺 ⌂wc 🅿. 🔼 AE VISA.
    ⬥
    closed Sunday and 26 December-6 January – **M** 4.45 **t.** (lunch) and a la carte 7.30/8.80 **t.** – **10 rm** ⤶ 21.50/29.00 **t.**

    at West Huntspill N : 6 m. on A 38 – ✉ Highbridge – ✪ 0278 Burnham-on-Sea :

    🏠 **Sundowner,** 74 Main Rd, TA9 3QU, on A 38 ♒ 784766 – ⌂wc 🛏 🅿. 🔼 AE ⓪ VISA
    M (bar lunch Monday to Saturday)/dinner 9.95 **t.** and a la carte ▮ 2.85 – **7 rm** ⤶ 14.00/29.50 **t.** – SB 40.00 **st.**

    ✗✗ **Huntspill Villa** with rm, 82 Main Rd, TA9 3QX, ♒ 782291 – 📺 ⌂wc 🅿. 🔼 AE ⓪ VISA. ⬥
    M *(closed lunch Monday and Saturday and Sunday)* a la carte 8.80/13.80 **t.** ▮ 2.45 – **6 rm** ⤶ 21.50/33.00 **t.** – SB 48.00/52.00 **st.**

    at Chilton Polden NE : 6 ¼ m. by A 39 – ✉ ✪ 0278 Bridgwater :

    ✗ **Wilton Farmhouse,** 9 Goose Lane, TA7 9ED, ♒ 722134 – 🅿. ⓪ VISA
    closed Sunday and Monday – **M** (lunch by arrangement)/dinner 9.50 **t.** ▮ 2.75.

AUSTIN-ROVER Market St. ♒ 422125
BMW High St., Cannington ♒ 652228
CITROEN Main Rd, Cannington ♒ 0278 (Combwich) 652233

FORD 37 Frian St. ♒ 451332
RENAULT 52 Eastover ♒ 422218
VOLVO Bristol Rd ♒ 455333

BRIDLINGTON Humberside 402 T 21 – pop. 28,426 – ECD : Thursday – ✪ 0262.

See : Priory Church★ 12C-15C.

Envir. : Burton Agnes Hall★ (Elizabethan) *AC*, SW : 6 m.

◪ Belvedere ♒ 72092, S : 1 ½ m. on A 165 – ◪ Flamborough Head ♒ 850333, NE : 5 m.

🛈 Garrison St. ♒ 673474 and 679626.

♦ London 236 – ♦Kingston-upon-Hull 29 – York 41.

    🏨 **Expanse,** North Marine Drive, YO15 2LS, ♒ 675347, ≤ – 🛗 📺 ⌂wc 📞 🅿. 🔼 AE ⓪ VISA.
    ⬥
    M 4.25/7.00 **t.** ▮ 2.95 – **49 rm** ⤶ 20.00/41.00 **t.** – SB 47.50/52.00 **st.**

    🏠 **Monarch,** South Marine Drive, YO15 3JJ, ♒ 674447, ≤ – 🛗 ⌂wc 📞 🅿. 🔼 AE ⓪ VISA. ⬥
    April-October – **M** (bar lunch Monday to Saturday)/dinner 7.50 **st.** and a la carte ▮ 2.70 –
    44 rm ⤶ 16.00/37.00 **st.** – SB 35.00/47.00 **st.**

    ✗✗ **Old Cooperage,** 91-93 High St., Old Town, YO16 4PN, ♒ 675190 – 🔼 VISA
    closed lunch Saturday and Monday and Sunday – **M** a la carte 9.50/13.50 **t.** ▮ 3.50.

FORD Hamilton Rd ♒ 675336
NISSAN Quay Rd ♒ 670331
TALBOT 74 Pessingby Rd ♒ 678141

VAUXHALL-OPEL 52-60 Quay Rd ♒ 672022
VOLVO Pinfold Lane ♒ 670351

BRIDPORT Dorset **403** L 31 The West Country G. – pop. 10 ,615 – ECD : Thursday – ⊙ 0308.

Envir. : Parnham House★★ *AC*, N : 6 m. on A 3066.

🏌 Bridport and West Dorset, West Bay ✆ 22597, S : 1 ½ m.

🛈 32 South St. ✆ 24901 (summer only).

♦London 150 – Exeter 38 – Taunton 33 – Weymouth 19.

🏠 **Roundham House,** Roundham Gdns, West Bay Rd, DT6 4BD, ✆ 22753, ✐ – ⌂wc ▥wc
     P. ▣. ⅙
     9 rm ⊇ 15.50/29.00 t.

🏠 **Britmead House,** 154 West Bay Rd, DT6 4EG, S : 1 m. by B 3157 ✆ 22941 – 📺 ⌂wc **P**.
     ▣ *VISA*
     closed January – **8 rm** ⊇ 11.00/27.50 t.

     at Nettlecombe NE : 4 m. off A 3066 – ⊠ Bridport – ⊙ 030 885 Powerstock :

🏨 **Marquis of Lorne** ⌂, DT6 3SY, ✆ 236, ✐ – ▥wc **P**. ⅙
     M 6.00/7.50 t. and a la carte ⅙ 2.95 – **6 rm** ⊇ 12.00/30.00 t. – SB (October-March) 27.90/35.00 st.

     at Shipton Gorge SE : 3 m. off A 35 – ⊠ ⊙ 0308 Bridport :

XX **Innsacre Farmhouse** ⌂ with rm, Shipton Lane, DT6 4LJ, N : 1 m. ✆ 56137, ✐ – **P**. ▣ Æ
     ⓪ *VISA*
     M 7.25/11.25 t. ⅙ 2.50 – **5 rm** ⊇ 14.00/28.00 st. – SB 45.50/50.50 st.

     at West Bexington SE : 7 ½ m. by B 3157 – ⊠ Bridport – ⊙ 0308 Burton Bradstock :

🏠 **Manor,** Beach Rd, DT2 9DF, ✆ 897616, ≤, ✐ – 📺 ⌂wc **P**. ▣ Æ *VISA*
     M 8.95/9.95 t. ⅙ 2.50 – **11 rm** ⊇ 18.00/34.50 t. – SB (except Christmas) 43.00/50.00 st.

     at West Bay S : 1 ½ m. on B 3157 – ⊠ ⊙ 0308 Bridport :

🏠 **Haddon House,** DT6 4EN, ✆ 23626 – 📺 ⌂wc ▥wc **P**. ▣ Æ ⓪ *VISA*
     M 8.00/11.00 t. – **13 rm** ⊇ 26.50/38.50 t.

     at Chideock W : 3 m. on A 35 – ⊠ Bridport – ⊙ 029 789 Chideock :

🏠 **Chideock House,** Main St., DT6 6JN, ✆ 242 – ⌂wc **P**. ▣ Æ ⓪ *VISA*
     M *(closed Monday lunch)* 9.50/13.50 t. and a la carte ⅙ 2.50 – **9 rm** ⊇ 21.00/30.00 t. – SB
     45.00/50.00 st.

BRIGHTON AND HOVE East Sussex **404** T 31 – pop. 200 ,168 (inc. Hove) – ECD : Wednesday
and Thursday – ⊙ 0273 – **See :** Royal Pavilion★ (interior★★) *AC* CZ – Aquarium★ *AC* CZ **A** –
Booth Museum (bird collection)★ BV **M** – Preston Manor (Chinese collection★) BV **D** – The Lanes
CZ – **Envir. :** Stanmer Park (site★) N : 3 ½ m. by A 27 CV – Clayton (church of St. John the Baptist :
frescoes★ 14C) N : 6 m. by A 23 BV.

🏌 East Brighton, Roedean ✆ 604838 CV – 🏌 Hollingbury Park, Ditchling Rd ✆ 552010 BV – 🏌 Dyke,
Dyke Rd ✆ 079 156 (Poynings) 296, N : by Dyke Rd BV – 🏌 Dyke Rd ✆ 556482 BV.

✈ Shoreham Airport : ✆ 079 17 (Shoreham-by-Sea) 2304 W : 8 m. by A 27 A.

🛈 Marlborough House, 54 Old Steine ✆ 23755 – Sea Front, Kings Rd ✆ 23755 (summer only).

🛈 at Hove : Town Hall, Norton Rd ✆ 775400.

♦London 53 – ♦Portsmouth 48 – ♦Southampton 61.

Plans on following pages

🏨 **Brighton Metropole,** Kings Rd, BN1 2FU, ✆ 775432, Telex 877245, ≤ – ▐ ▤ rest 📺 ☎ **P**.
     ▨ ▣ Æ ⓪ *VISA*   BZ **s**
     M 11.95 t. and a la carte ⅙ 5.00 – ✑ 4.90 – **349 rm** 45.00/80.00 t., **16 suites** 138.00/240.00 t. –
     SB (weekends only) 55.00/65.00 st.

🏨 **Wheeler's Sheridan** without rest., 64 King's Rd, BN1 1NA, ✆ 23221, ≤ – ▐ 📺 ▣ Æ ⓪
     VISA. ⅙   BZ **e**
     closed 25 and 26 December – **58 rm** ⊇ 35.00/55.00 st., **2 suites** 75.00/85.00 st.

🏨 **Old Ship,** King's Rd, BN1 1NR, ✆ 29001, Telex 877101, ≤ – ▐ 📺 ⌂wc ▨ ⟷ ▨. ▣ Æ
     ⓪ *VISA*. ⅙   CZ **n**
     M a la carte 11.85/15.00 t. – **153 rm** ⊇ 43.00/55.00 st., **1 suite** 75.00 st. – SB (weekends
     only)(except Easter) 67.50/71.50 st.

🏨 **Royal Crescent,** Marine Par., BN2 1AX, ✆ 606311, Telex 87253, ≤ – ▐ 📺 ⌂wc ▨. ▨
     54 rm, 4 suites   CV **a**

🏨 **Topps,** 17 Regency Sq., BN1 2FG, ✆ 729334 – 📺 ⌂wc ▥wc ☎. ▣ Æ ⓪ *VISA*. ⅙   BZ **i**
     closed January – **M** *(closed Sunday and Wednesday)* (dinner only) a la carte 7.60/9.70 st.
     ⅙ 1.80 – **7 rm** ⊇ 27.50/55.00 st.

🏨 **Granville,** 125 King's Rd, BN1 2FA, ✆ 733516, Telex 878149, ≤ – 📺 ⌂wc ▥wc ☎. ▣ Æ
     ⓪ *VISA*   BZ **n**
     M 6.95/12.95 t. and a la carte ⅙ 2.50 – ✑ 3.70 – **28 rm** 34.00/95.00 t. – SB (except Bank
     Holidays) 68.50/100.00 st.

🏨 **The Twenty One,** 21 Charlotte St., BN2 1AG, ✆ 686450 – 📺 ▥wc. ▣ Æ ⓪ *VISA*   CV **i**
     closed mid December-January – **M** *(closed Sunday and Bank Holidays)* (dinner only, residents
     only) 18.40 st. ⅙ 3.80 – **6 rm** ⊇ 20.00/38.00 st.

🏠 **Marina House,** 8 Charlotte St., BN2 1AG, ✆ 605349 – 📺 ▥wc   CV **n**
     10 rm ⊇ 10.50/27.00 st.

111

BRIGHTON AND HOVE

Churchill Square
Shopping Centre .... **BYZ**
London Road .... **CX**
North Street .... **CZ**
Western Road .... **ABY**

Adelaide Crescent .... AY 2
Brunswick Place .... AY 4
Brunswick Square .... AYZ 5
Carlton Terrace .... AV 6
Chatham Place .... BX 7

Denmark Road .... BY 8
East Street .... CZ 9
Eastern Road .... CX 10
Gladstone Terrace .... CX 12
Gloucester Place .... CY 13
Gloucester Road .... CY 14
Goldsmid Road .... BX 15

Grand Junction Road ..... CZ 16
Hollingbury Park Av. ..... BV 17
Hollingdean Road .... AV 18
Hove Street .... AV 19
Market Place .... CX 20
Marlborough Place .... CY 21
Montpelier Place .... BY 22

Old Steine .... CZ 23
Pavillon Parade .... CZ 26
Richmond Place .... CY 27
Richmond Terrace .... CX 28
St. George's Place .... CY 30
St. Peter's Place .... CX 31
Terminus Road .... BCX 32

Upper Lewes Road .... CX 33
Upper North Street .... BY 34
Victoria Road .... AV 36
Warren Road .... CV 37
Waterloo Place .... CX 39
Wellington Road .... AV 40
York Place .... CY 42

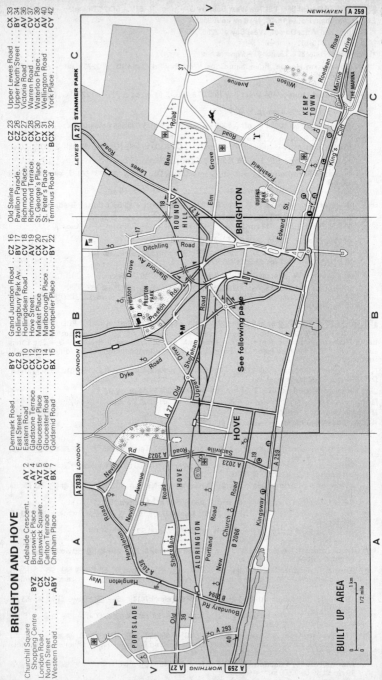

BUILT UP AREA

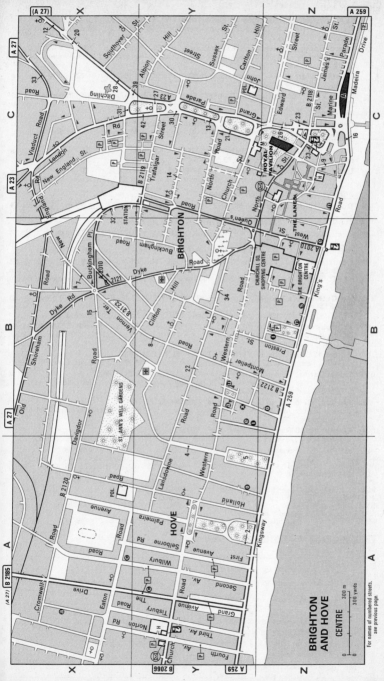

BRIGHTON AND HOVE
CENTRE

For names of numbered streets,
see previous page.

0   300 m
0   300 yards

113

XX **La Marinade,** 77 St. Georges Rd, Kemp Town, BN2 1EF, ℰ 600992 – 🍽. 🔳 AE ⓪ VISA
closed Sunday dinner, 19 August-4 September and 25-26 December – **M** 6.00 **t.** (lunch) and a
la carte 8.75/14.25 **t.** ⵊ 2.50.　　　　　　　　　　　　　　　　　　　　　　　　CV **c**

XX **Chardonnay,** 33 Chesham Rd, Kemp Town, ℰ 672733, French rest. – 🔳 AE ⓪ VISA　　CV **e**
closed Saturday lunch, Monday dinner, Sunday, 2 weeks February and 1 week September – **M**
5.95/8.50 **t.** and a la carte ⵊ 3.75.

XX **French Cellar,** 37 New England Rd, BN1 4GG, ℰ 603643, French rest. – 🔳 ⓪ VISA　　CX **a**
closed Sunday and August – **M** (dinner only) 15.75 **t.** ⵊ 1.80.

XX **Dolce Vito,** 106c Western Rd, Corner of Bedford Pl., BN1 2AA, ℰ 737200, Italian rest. – 🔳
AE ⓪ VISA　　　　　　　　　　　　　　　　　　　　　　　　　　　　　　　　　　　　BY **u**
M a la carte 9.45/12.25 **t.** ⵊ 3.35.

X **Orchard,** 33 Western St., BN1 2PG, ℰ 776618 – 🔳 AE ⓪ VISA　　　　　　　　　　BZ **o**
closed Sunday dinner, Monday and 23 to 30 December – **M** (dinner only and Sunday lunch)
7.00/10.00 **t.** ⵊ 3.00.

X **Foggs,** 5 Little Western St., BN1 2PU, ℰ 735907 – 🔳 AE VISA　　　　　　　　　　BY **a**
M (dinner only) a la carte 8.15/10.70 **t.** ⵊ 2.45.

X **Le Grandgousier,** 15 Western St., BN1 2PG, ℰ 772005, French rest. – AE　　　　　BY **x**
closed Saturday lunch, Sunday and 23 December-3 January – **M** 9.15 **st.** (wine included).

at Hove – ✉ Hove – ☎ 0273 Brighton :

🏨 **Dudley** (T.H.F.), Lansdowne Pl., BN3 1HQ, ℰ 736266, Telex 87537 – 🛗 📺 🅿. 🎱. 🔳 AE ⓪
VISA　　　　　　　　　　　　　　　　　　　　　　　　　　　　　　　　　　　　　　AY **o**
M 8.95/10.00 **st.** ⵊ 2.60 – ⌷ 5.50 – **80 rm** 45.50/58.00 **st.**, **2 suites.**

🏨 **Sackville** (Best Western), 189 Kingsway, BN3 4GU, ℰ 736292, Telex 877830, ≼ – 🛗 📺
🛏wc ☎ ⇦. 🎱. 🔳 AE ⓪ VISA　　　　　　　　　　　　　　　　　　　　　　　　　AV **n**
M 8.50/10.25 **st.** ⵊ 3.20 – **45 rm** ⌷ 37.95/68.00 **st.** – SB (weekends only) 60.00/66.00 **st.**

🏨 **Courtlands,** 19-27 The Drive, BN3 3JE, ℰ 731055, Telex 87574 – 🛗 📺 🛏wc 🛁wc 📞 🅿. 🔳
AE ⓪ VISA　　　　　　　　　　　　　　　　　　　　　　　　　　　　　　　　　　　AY **c**
M 9.00/12.00 **t.** and a la carte ⵊ 3.25 – **60 rm** ⌷ 40.00/55.00 **st.** – SB (weekends only except
Bank Holidays) 55.00/65.00 **st.**

🏨 **St. Catherine's Lodge,** Kingsway, BN3 2RZ, ℰ 778181, Telex 877073 – 🛗 📺 🛏wc 📞. 🔳
AE ⓪ VISA　　　　　　　　　　　　　　　　　　　　　　　　　　　　　　　　　　　AV **a**
M 5.25/8.25 **st.** and a la carte ⵊ 2.90 – **53 rm** ⌷ 28.00/49.00 **st.** – SB 47.00/56.00 **st.**

🏨 **Whitehaven,** 34 Wilbury Rd, BN3 3JP, ℰ 778355, ≼ – 📺 🛏wc 🛁wc ☎ 🔳 AE ⓪ VISA. ✷
M (bar lunch)/dinner 8.50 **st.** and a la carte – **17 rm** ⌷ 37.00/47.00 **st.** – SB (weekends only)
50.00 **st.**　　　　　　　　　　　　　　　　　　　　　　　　　　　　　　　　　　AX **c**

XXX **Eaton,** 13 Eaton Gdns, BN3 3TN, ℰ 738921 – 🅿. 🔳 AE ⓪ VISA　　　　　　　　AX **a**
closed Sunday dinner, Good Friday and Christmas Day – **M** 9.50/13.00 **t.** and a la carte ⵊ 3.75.

XX **Hove Manor,** 5 Hove Manor Par., Hove St., ℰ 730850. 🔳 AE ⓪ VISA　　　　　　AV **c**
closed Sunday dinner, Monday, 1 to 8 January and September – **M** (booking essential)
6.75/8.75 **t.** and a la carte ⵊ 3.30.

X **Fig Leaf,** 37 Waterloo St., BN3 1AY, ℰ 732383 – 🍽. 🔳 VISA　　　　　　　　　　BY **i**
closed Sunday, Monday, first 2 weeks September and 23 December-8 January – **M** (dinner
only) 10.95 **t.** ⵊ 2.50.

X **Lawrence,** 40 Waterloo St., BN3 1AY, ℰ 772922 – 🔳 AE VISA　　　　　　　　　　BY **e**
closed Sunday, 2 weeks July and Christmas – **M** (dinner only) 15.00 (wine included) **st.**

ALFA-ROMEO Old Shoreham Rd, Portslade ℰ 411020	MAZDA 42/43 George St. ℰ 681766
AUDI, VW Old Shoreham Rd, Portslade ℰ 422552	MAZDA 373 Kingsway, Hove ℰ 413833
AUSTIN-ROVER-DAIMLER-JAGUAR 200 DYKE Rd ℰ 553061	MERCEDES-BENZ Victoria Rd ℰ 414911
	NISSAN 21/29 Preston Rd ℰ 685985
AUSTIN-ROVER 233 Preston Rd ℰ 553021	RENAULT Stephenson Rd ℰ 692111
AUSTIN-ROVER 1a Lewes Rd ℰ 604131	SKODA, TALBOT Longridge Av., Saltdean ℰ 31061
BMW Sillwood St. ℰ 27991	TALBOT 270-272 Old Shoreham Rd ℰ 737555
FIAT, LANCIA 100 Lewes Rd ℰ 603244	VAUXHALL-OPEL Old Shoreham Rd, Portslade ℰ 422552
FORD 90/96 Preston Rd ℰ 550211	VOLVO Bedford Place ℰ 203487

BRIMSCOMBE Glos. 🔢🔢🔢 N 28 – see Stroud.

Camping or Caravanning in France ?

Your holiday will be more enjoyable if you use the Michelin Guide

"Camping Caravaning France"

It includes :

　– A comprehensive selection of sites classified according to the nature
　　and comfort of their amenities

　– Notes on charges, local rules and conditions, insurances etc...

　– Location maps

The Guide is revised annually - get this year's edition.

BRISTOL Avon **408** **404** M 29 The West Country G. – pop. 413,861 – ECD : Wednesday and Saturday – ☺ 0272.

See : Site★★★ – Clifton Suspension Bridge★★★ AY – Cabot Tower Area★★ (The Georgian House★★★AC CZ – Red Lodge★AC DZ **D**) – St. Nicholas Church Museum★★AC DZ **M1** – Theatre Royal★★ DZ **T** – Quakers Friars★★AC EZ **K** – St. Mary Redcliffe Church★★ DZ – Industrial Museum★★AC AY **M2** – S.S Great Britain ★★ AC AY **A** – Bristol Zoological Garden★★AC AY – Clifton Roman Catholic Cathedral off SS Peter and Paul★★ AY B – Cathedral★ DZ – Lord Mayors Chapel★AC DZ **E** – City Museum and Art Gallery★AC CZ **M** – John Wesleys New Room★AC DZ **G**.

Envir. : Blaise Castle House Museum★AC AX **M3** Blaise Hamlet★, NW : 5 m. by B4057 AX – at Chew Magna★ Stanton Drew Stone Circles★AC, S : 8 m. by A37 BY.

🛏 Carsons Rd, Mangotsfield ☎ 565501, NE : 6 m. by B 4465 BX – 🛏 Bristol and Clifton, Beggar Bush Lane ☎ 393474 by A369 AY.

✈ Bristol Airport : ☎ 027 587 (Lulsgate) 4441/6, SW : 7 m. by A 38 AY.

🚗 ☎ 291001 ext 2479.

🛈 Colston House, Colston St. ☎ 293891 – Watershed, 1 Canons Rd ☎ 214272 (summer only).

♦London 121 – ♦Birmingham 91.

Plans on following pages

🏨 **Holiday Inn**, Lower Castle St., Old Market, BS1 3AD, ☎ 294281, Telex 449720, ☒ – 📶 🆃🆅 ☎ 🕭 ℗ 🅰 – **284 rm**. EZ **s**

🏨 **Grand** (Mt. Charlotte), Broad St., BS1 2EL, ☎ 291645, Telex 449889 – 📶 🆃🆅 ☎. 🅰 🖭 🖼 ⓪ **VISA** DZ **a**
M 10.00/12.00 **t**. and a la carte – **179 rm** ⌑ 49.00/60.00 **st.**, **3 suites** 75.00/100.00 **st.** – SB (weekends only) 50.00/52.00 **st.**

🏨 **Ladbroke Dragonara** (Ladbroke), Redcliffe Way, BS1 6NJ, ☎ 20044, Telex 449240 – 📶 🆃🆅 ☎ ♿ ℗ 🅰 🖭 🖼 🖭 ⓪ **VISA** DEZ **n**
M (bar lunch Saturday) a la carte 13.40/19.95 **st.** ◊ 3.70 – ⌑ 5.95 – **201 rm** 54.50/66.00 **st.**, **2 suites** 85.00/105.00 **st.** – SB (weekends only) 63.90 **st.**

🏨 **Unicorn** (Rank), Prince St., BS1 4QF, ☎ 294811, Telex 44315 – 📶 🆃🆅 ☎ ℗ 🅰 🖭 🖼 ⓪ **VISA**
M (closed Saturday lunch) 5.75/8.25 **t**. and a la carte ◊ 2.75 – ⌑ 4.95 – **192 rm** 34.50/48.00 **t.**, **2 suites** 67.50/75.00 **t.** – SB (weekends only) 61.00/69.00 **st.** DZ **i**

🏦 **St. Vincent Rocks** (Anchor), Sion Hill, Clifton, BS8 4BB, ☎ 739251, Telex 858875 – 🆅
🛏wc 🛁wc ⊛ ℗ 🅰 🖭 🖼 ⓪ **VISA** AY **c**
M (closed Saturday lunch) 8.90/15.00 **t**. and a la carte ◊ 3.00 – **46 rm** ⌑ 44.00/55.00 **t.** – SB (weekends only) 56.00/59.00 **st.**

🏦 **Avon Gorge** (Mt. Charlotte), Sion Hill, Clifton, BS8 4LD, ☎ 738955, Telex 444237, ← – 📶 🆃🆅
🛏wc ⊛. 🅰 🖭 ⓪ **VISA** AY **x**
M 7.95 **t**. and a la carte ◊ 3.50 – **81 rm** ⌑ 35.00/52.50 **t.**, **2 suites** 65.00/140.00 **st.** – SB (weekends only) 48.00/50.00 **st.**

🏠 **Westbury Park**, 37 Westbury Rd, BS9 3AU, ☎ 620465 – 🆅 🛏wc ℗ AX **r**
M a la carte lunch/dinner 6.95 **t**. – **9 rm** ⌑ 18.50/32.50 **st.**

🏠 **Oakfield**, 52-54 Oakfield Rd, Clifton, BS8 2BG, ☎ 735556 – ℗ AY **n**
closed 23 December-1 January – **27 rm** ⌑ 13.00/21.00 **st.**

XXX **Harvey's**, 12 Denmark St., BS1 5DQ, ☎ 277665 – ▤. 🖭 🖼 ⓪ **VISA** DZ **c**
closed Saturday lunch, Sunday and Bank Holidays – **M** 10.25 (lunch) and a la carte 14.00/19.55 **t.**

XX ⊛ **Les Semailles**, 9 Druid Hill, Stoke Bishop, BS9 1EW, ☎ 686456, French rest. – 🖭 🖼 **VISA**
closed Sunday, Monday, last 2 weeks July, 25 December-6 January and Bank Holidays AX **a**
(booking essential) 9.00 **st.** (lunch) and a la carte 14.40/21.10 **st.**
Spec. Gâteau de homard et beurre de vanille (Summer), Galette d'aile de canard de barbarie aux épices et poires, Mousse glacée de carottes et mangue au fruit de la passion.

XX **Barbizon**, 43 Corn St., BS1 1HT, ☎ 22658, French rest. – 🖭 ⓪ **VISA** DZ **x**
closed Saturday lunch and Sunday – **M** 8.60 **t**. (lunch) and a la carte 11.50/14.45 **t.** ◊ 3.00.

XX **Rajdoot**, 83 Park St., BS1 5PJ, ☎ 28033, Indian rest. – 🖭 🖼 ⓪ **VISA** CZ **u**
closed lunch Sunday and Bank Holidays and 25-26 December – **M** 10.00 **t**. and a la carte ◊ 3.00.

XX **Du Gourmet**, 43 Whiteladies Rd, BS8 2LS, ☎ 736230 – 🖭 🖼 ⓪ **VISA** AY **v**
closed Sunday, Monday and 26 December-1 January – **M** a la carte 10.85/16.15 ◊ 2.70.

X **Bistro Twenty One**, 21 Cotham Road, Kingsdown, BS6 5TZ, ☎ 421744 AY **z**
closed Sunday, Monday, 10 days Easter, August and 10 days at Christmas – **M** (booking essential)(dinner only) a la carte 9.85/12.25 **t.** ◊ 2.75.

X **La Taverna Dell'Artista**, 33 King St., BS1 4EF, ☎ 297712, Italian rest. – 🖭 **VISA** DZ **s**
closed Sunday and Monday – **M** a la carte 5.40/11.40 **t.** ◊ 2.50.

X **Ganges**, 368 Gloucester Rd, Horfield, BS7 8TP, ☎ 45234, Indian rest. – 🖭 🖼 ⓪ **VISA** AX **e**
closed 25 and 26 December – **M** 5.00/10.50 **t**. and a la carte ◊ 2.20.

at Hambrook NE : 5 ½ m. by A 4174 – ⊠ ☺ 0272 Bristol :

🏦 **Crest** (Crest), Filton Rd, BS16 1QX, ☎ 564242, Telex 449376, ⚕, park – 📶 ▤ rest 🆃🆅 🛏wc ☎ ♿ ℗ 🅰 🖭 🖼 **VISA**. ⚘ BX **o**
M approx. 11.50 **st.** – ⌑ 6.25 – **151 rm** 51.00/59.00 **st.** – SB (weekends only) 63.00 **st.**

115

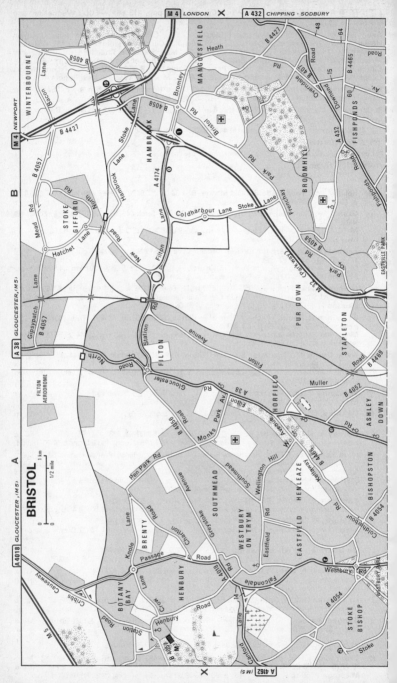

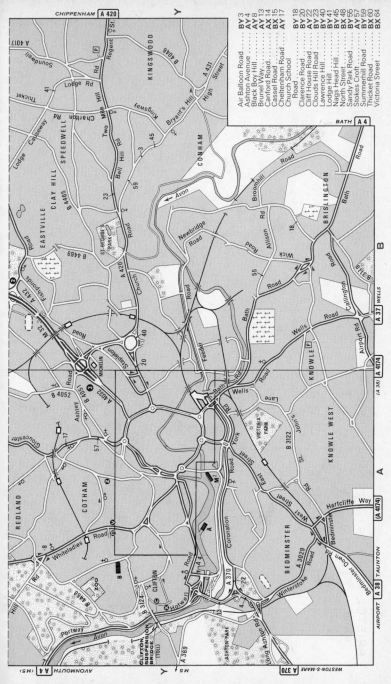

Air Balloon Road	BY 3
Ashton Avenue	AY 4
Black Boy Hill	AY 8
Brunel Way	AY 13
Canford Road	AX 14
Cassel Road	BX 15
Cheltenham Road	AY 17
Church School	
Road	BY 18
Clarence Road	BY 20
Cliff House Road	AY 22
Clouds Hill Road	BY 23
Lawrence Hill	BY 40
Lodge Hill	BY 41
Nags Head Hill	BX 45
North Street	BX 48
Sandy Park Road	BY 55
Stokes Croft	AY 57
Summerhill Road	BY 59
Thicket Road	BX 60
Victoria Street	BX 64

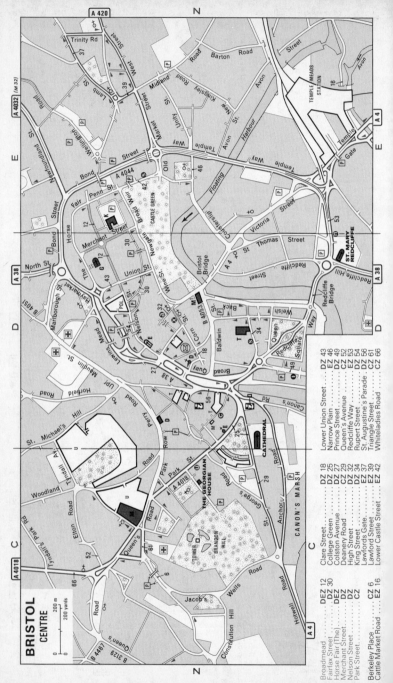

BRISTOL
CENTRE

0   200 m
0   200 yards

Broadmead	DEZ 12	
Fairfax Street	DEZ 30	
Horse Fair (The)	DEZ	
Merchant Street	DZ	
Nelson Street	DZ	
Park Street	CZ	

Berkeley Place	CZ 6	
Cattle Market Road	EZ 16	

Clare Street	DZ 18
College Green	DZ 25
Colston Avenue	CZ 27
Deanery Road	CZ 29
High Street	DZ 32
King Street	DZ 34
Lawfords Gate	EZ 37
Lawford Street	EZ 39
Lower Castle Street	EZ 42

Lower Union Street	DZ 43
Narrow Plain	EZ 46
Prince Street	DZ 49
Queen's Avenue	CZ 52
Redcliffe Way	DZ 53
Rupert Street	DZ 54
St. Augustine's Parade	DZ 56
Triangle Street	CZ 61
Whiteladies Road	CZ 66

118

at Winterbourne N : 6 ¾ m. by M 32 on B 4058 – BX – ✉ Bristol – ☎ 0454 Winterbourne :

XXX **Grange** ♨ with rm, Northwoods, BS17 1RP, NW : 2 m. by B 4057 on B 4427 ☏ 777333, Telex 449205, ≤, ☂, park – 🅃🅅 ⇌wc ☎ 🅿. 🄰 🄰🄴 ⓪ 🆅🅸🆂🅰
M 10.00/13.50 **t.** and a la carte – ⌕ 5.00 – **32 rm** 43.00/55.00 **t.**, **4 suites** 65.00/75.00 **t.** – SB (weekends only) 60.00 **st.**

MICHELIN Branch, Pennywell Rd, BS5 0UB, ☏ 559802 BY

AUSTIN-ROVER 74-80 Staple Hill Rd ☏ 654776
AUSTIN-ROVER-DAIMLER-JAGUAR, ROLLS
ROYCE 11/15 Merchants Rd, Clifton ☏ 730361
BMW 33 Zetland Rd ☏ 428333
CITROEN, FIAT 724 Fishponds Rd ☏ 657247
FIAT 168/176 Coronation Rd ☏ 631101
FORD 175/185 Muller Rd, Horfield ☏ 513333
FORD College Green ☏ 293881
FORD Church Rd ☏ 556381
FORD 135 High St. ☏ 670011

MAZDA, ALFA ROMEO 676 Fishponds Rd ☏ 655439
MERCEDES-BENZ 20 Whitehouse St. ☏ 669331
PEUGEOT-TALBOT 84 Downend Rd ☏ 567088
RENAULT Vale Lane ☏ 665070
RENAULT Station Rd, Kingswood ☏ 569911
RENAULT Marlborough St. ☏ 421816
TOYOTA Gloucester Rd, Patchway ☏ 693704
VAUXHALL-OPEL, BEDFORD Gloucester Rd ☏ 694331
VOLVO Berkeley Pl. ☏ 277355

BRIXHAM Devon 🔟🔟🔟 J 32 The West Country G. – pop. 15,171 – ECD : Wednesday – ☎ 080 45.
Envir. : Berry Head★ (≤★★★), E : 2 m.
🛈 The Old Market House, The Quay ☏ 2861/8444.
♦London 230 – Exeter 30 – ♦Plymouth 32 – Torquay 8.

🏛 **Quayside,** 41-49 King St., TQ5 9TJ, ☏ 55751, ≤ harbour – 🅃🅅 ⇌wc ☎ 🅿. 🄰 🄰🄴 ⓪ 🆅🅸🆂🅰
M (bar lunch Monday to Saturday)/dinner 10.50 **t.** and a la carte ░ 3.85 – **32 rm** ⌕ 22.00/58.00 **t.** – SB (except Bank Holidays) 46.00/77.00 **st.**

🏠 **Smuggler's Haunt,** 1 Church Hill East, TQ5 8HH, ☏ 3050 – ⇌wc. 🄰 🄰🄴 🆅🅸🆂🅰
M 3.55/8.50 **t.** and a la carte ░ 2.40 – **14 rm** ⌕ 13.75/24.75 **t.**

AUSTIN-ROVER Milton St. ☏ 2474
FORD Churston Ferrers ☏ 0803 (Churston) 842245
RENAULT New Rd ☏ 2266

BROADSTAIRS Kent 🔟🔟🔟 Y 29 – pop. 21,551 (inc. St. Peter's) – ECD : Wednesday – ☎ 0843 Thanet.
See : Bleak House (stayed in by Charles Dickens) *AC*.
🛈 Pierremont Hall, 67 High St. ☏ 68399.
♦London 78 – ♦Dover 21 – Maidstone 47.

🏛 **Castlemere,** 15 Western Esplanade, CT10 1TD, ☏ 61566, ≤, ☂ – 🅃🅅 ⇌wc ⑃wc ☎ 🅿. 🄰 🆅🅸🆂🅰
M *(closed for lunch November-April)* (bar lunch)/dinner 9.00 **st.** ░ 2.70 – **38 rm** ⌕ 21.00/44.00 **st.** – SB (weekends only except Bank Holidays) 48.00/55.00 **st.**

🏠 **Royal Albion,** Albion St., CT10 1LU, ☏ 68071, Telex 965761, ≤, ☂ – 🅃🅅 ⇌wc ⑃wc ☎ 🅿. 🄰. 🄰 🄰🄴 ⓪ 🆅🅸🆂🅰
M 8.00/8.50 **st.** and a la carte ░ 2.50 – **20 rm** ⌕ 33.00/55.00 **st.** – SB (except July and August) 47.50/69.00 **st.**

↑ **Bay Tree,** 12 Eastern Esplanade, CT10 1DR, ☏ 62502, ≤ – 🅿. ⌘
9 rm ⌕ 9.50/22.00 **s.**

↑ **Keston Court,** 14 Ramsgate Rd, CT10 1PS, ☏ 62401 – 🅿. 🄰🄴 ⌘
9 rm ⌕ 9.00/19.00.

XX **Marchesi,** 18 Albion St., CT10 1LU, ☏ 62481, ≤ – 🅿. 🄰 🄰🄴 ⓪ 🆅🅸🆂🅰
closed 26 to 28 December – **M** 6.50/8.50 **t.** and a la carte ░ 2.50.

AUDI, VW St. Peter's Rd ☏ 62333
PEUGEOT-TALBOT Ramsgate Rd ☏ 63531
RENAULT Oscar Rd ☏ 62568

BROADSTONE Dorset 🔟🔟🔟 🔟🔟🔟 O 31 – see Wimborne Minster.

BROADWATER Herts. – see Stevenage.

BROADWAY Heref. and Worc. 🔟🔟🔟 🔟🔟🔟 O 27 – pop. 1,931 – ECD : Thursday – ☎ 0386.
🛈 The Green ☏ 852937 (summer only).
♦London 93 – ♦Birmingham 36 – Cheltenham 15 – Worcester 22.

🏛🏛 **Lygon Arms,** High St., WR12 7DU, ☏ 852255, Telex 338260, « Part 15C inn », ☂, ⌘ – 🅃🅅 ☎ ⅊ ⇌ 🅿. 🄰. 🄰 🄰🄴 ⓪ 🆅🅸🆂🅰
M 11.00/18.00 **t.** and a la carte ░ 3.25 – ⌕ 5.50 – **61 rm** 70.00/115.00 **t.**, **4 suites** 135.00/150.00 **t.** – SB (November-March) 98.00 **st.**

🏛 **Broadway,** The Green, WR12 7AA, ☏ 852401, ☂ – 🅃🅅 ⇌wc ☎ 🅿. 🄰 🄰🄴 ⓪ 🆅🅸🆂🅰 ⌘
M 7.50/10.50 **t.** and a la carte ░ 2.50 – **24 rm** ⌕ 34.00/64.00 **st.** – SB (weekends only) (winter only) 50.00/68.00 **st.**

🏠 **Collin House** ♨, Collin Lane, WR12 7PB, NW : 1 ¼ m. by A 44 ☏ 858354, ≤, « Country house atmosphere », ⌓ heated, ☂ – ⇌wc 🅿. 🄰 🆅🅸🆂🅰 ⌘
closed 24 to 26 December – **M** (bar lunch Monday to Saturday)/dinner a la carte 10.00/12.75 **t.** – **7 rm** ⌕ 35.00/53.00 **t.** – SB (winter only) 63.00/68.00 **st.**

↑ **Halfway House,** 89 High St., WR12 7AL, ℘ 852237 – **ℙ**
5 rm ⊊ 15.00/30.00 **s.**

↑ **Westdon,** Station Rd, WR12 7DE, ℘ 858821, 🚗 – **ℙ**. ℅
6 rm ⊊ 12.00/26.00 **st.**

XX **Hunters Lodge,** High St., WR12 7DT, ℘ 853247, 🚗 – **ℙ**. 🔳 🄰🄴 ⓪ *VISA*
closed Sunday dinner, Monday, first 2 weeks January and first 2 weeks August – **M** 6.75 **t.**
(lunch) and a la carte 11.75/14.45 **t.** ▯ 2.80.

at Willersley N : 2 m. on A 46 – ⊠ ✿ 0386 Broadway :

🏛 **Old Rectory** ⊗ without rest., Church St., WR12 7PM, ℘ 853729, 🚗 – 🔳 ⌷wc ⋔wc **ℙ**.
🔳 *VISA*. ℅
5 rm ⊊ 29.00/49.00 **t.**

at Willersey Hill (Glos.) E : 2 m. by A 44 – ⊠ ✿ 0386 Broadway :

🏛 **Dormy House,** WR12 7LF, ℘ 852711, Telex 338275, 🚗 – 🔳 ☎ **ℙ**. 🔬 🔳 🄰🄴 ⓪ *VISA*
M 10.50/14.50 **t.** and a la carte ▯ 6.25 – **48 rm** ⊊ 39.00/83.00 **t.** – SB (weekends only) (except
Easter) 95.00 **st.**

at Buckland (Glos.) SW : 2 ¼ m. by A 46 – ⊠ ✿ 0386 Broadway :

🏛 **Buckland Manor** ⊗, WR12 7LY, ℘ 852626, « Country house atmosphere », 🛏 heated, 🚗,
park, ℅ – 🔳 ☎ **ℙ**. 🔳 ⓪ *VISA*. ℅
closed 3 weeks January-February – **M** a la carte 13.80/20.00 **t.** ▯ 2.85 – **11 rm** ⊊ 80.00/115.00 **t.**

AUSTIN-ROVER Willersley ℘ 852338

BROCKENHURST Hants. �403 �404 P 31 – pop. 2 ,939 – ECD : Wednesday – ✿ 0590 Lymington.
♦London 99 – ♦Bournemouth 17 – ♦Southampton 14 – Winchester 27.

🏛 **Ladbroke Balmer Lawn** (Ladbroke), Lyndhurst Rd, SO4 7ZB, ℘ 23116, ≼, 🛏 heated, 🚗, ℅,
squash – 📳 🔳 ⌷wc ⊛ **ℙ**. 🔬
60 rm

🏛 **Carey's Manor,** Lyndhurst Rd, SO4 7RH, ℘ 23551, Telex 47442, Dancing Friday and Saturday, 🔳, 🚗 – 🔳 ⌷wc ☎ ♿ **ℙ**. 🔬 🔳 🄰🄴 ⓪ *VISA*. ℅
M 7.75/11.75 **t.** and a la carte ▯ 2.95 – **57 rm** ⊊ 43.95/67.90 **t.** – SB (except Bank Holidays)
63.70/79.70 **st.**

🏛 **Forest Park,** Rhinefield Rd, SO4 7NG, ℘ 22844, Group Telex 477802, 🛏 heated, 🚗, ℅ –
🔳 ⌷wc ⊛ **ℙ**. 🔬 🔳 🄰🄴 ⓪ *VISA*
M 5.25/9.95 **t.** and a la carte – **34 rm** ⊊ 32.00/46.00 **t.** – SB 54.00/66.00 **st.**

🏛 **Whitley Ridge** ⊗, Beaulieu Rd, SO4 7QL, E : 1 m. on B 3055 ℘ 22354, ≼, 🚗, ℅ – ⌷wc
⋔wc **ℙ**. 🔳 🄰🄴 ⓪ *VISA*. ℅
closed January – **M** (bar lunch)(residents only)/dinner 9.50 **t.** and a la carte ▯ 3.25 – **14 rm**
⊊ 29.00/46.00 **t.** – SB 52.00/57.00 **st.**

🏛 **Watersplash,** The Rise, SO4 7ZP, ℘ 22344, 🛏 heated, 🚗 – ⌷wc ♿ **ℙ**. 🔬 🔳
M 5.95/9.95 **t.** ▯ 3.00 – **26 rm** ⊊ 22.00/44.00 **t.** – SB (except summer) 44.00/50.00 **st.**

XX **Le Poussin,** 57-59 Brookley Rd, SO4 7RB, ℘ 23063, French rest. – 🔳 *VISA*
closed lunch Sunday and Monday, 27 January-5 February – **M** (booking essential) 7.95/
15.95 **t.** and a la carte ▯ 3.25.

AUSTIN-ROVER Sway Rd ℘ 23344   SAAB, HONDA 24 Brookley Rd ℘ 23464

BROME Suffolk �404 X 26 – pop. 265 – ⊠ ✿ 0379 Eye.
♦London 86 – ♦Cambridge 50 – ♦Ipswich 20 – ♦Norwich 22.

🏛 **Oaksmere** ⊗, IP23 8AJ, ℘ 870326, « Part 16C country house », 🚗, park – 🔳 ⋔wc **ℙ**. 🔳
🄰🄴 ⓪ *VISA*
M a la carte 10.70/15.40 **t.** ▯ 3.95 – **5 rm** ⊊ 29.00/48.00 **st.** – SB (weekends only) 55.00/65.00 **st.**

BROMLEY CROSS Greater Manchester �402 �404 M 23 – see Bolton.

BROMPTON BY SAWDON North Yorks. �402 S 21 – pop. 1 ,827 – ⊠ ✿ 0723 Scarborough.
♦London 242 – ♦Kingston-upon-Hull 44 – Scarborough 8 – York 31.

XX **Brompton Forge,** YO13 9DP, ℘ 85409 – **ℙ**
closed lunch Friday and Saturday, Sunday dinner, Monday, Tuesday and 2 weeks February –
M 7.50 **t.** ▯ 3.10.

BROMSGROVE Heref. and Worc. �403 �404 N 26 – pop. 24 ,576 – ECD : Thursday – ✿ 0527.
🛈 47/49 Worcester Rd ℘ 31809.
♦London 117 – ♦Birmingham 14 – ♦Bristol 71 – Worcester 13.

🏛 **Perry Hall** (Embassy), 13 Kidderminster Rd, B61 7JN, ℘ 31976, 🚗 – 🔳 ⌷wc ⋔wc ⊛ **ℙ**.
🔬 🔳 🄰🄴 ⓪ *VISA*. ℅
M 7.00 **st.** and a la carte ▯ 2.75 – ⊊ 5.00 – **53 rm** 35.25/43.50 **st.** – SB 51.00 **st.**

🏛 **Pine Lodge,** 85 Kidderminster Rd, B61 9AB, W : 1 m. on A 448 ℘ 33033, 🛏 heated, 🚗 – 🔳
⌷wc ☎ **ℙ**. 🔳 *VISA*. ℅
M (grill rest. only) 5.50/6.50 **t.** and a la carte ▯ 2.80 – **21 rm** ⊊ 25.00/34.00 **t.**

XXX **Grafton Manor** ⊗ with rm, Grafton Lane, B61 7HA, SW : 1 ¾ m. by Worcester Rd (A 38) ℰ 31525, « 16C and 18C manor », ⬎, ☞, park – 📺 ⌂wc ☎ 🅿. 🔼 AE ⑩ VISA. ⁑
M (dinner only and Sunday lunch)/dinner 17.75 t. 🍴 2.90 – ⊆ 5.25 – **5 rm** 46.00/75.00 t., **1 suite** 55.00/100.00 t.

AUSTIN-ROVER 52 Birmingham Rd ℰ 72212
LADA Windsor St. ℰ 75210
PEUGEOT-TALBOT 12/14 Old Birmingham Rd ℰ 72552

RENAULT 17-21 Worcester Rd ℰ 79898
VAUXHALL-OPEL 137 Birmingham Rd ℰ 71244

BROOK Hants. 403 404 P 31 – ECD : Tuesday – ⊠ Lyndhurst – ✆ 0703 Southampton.
⏺₈, ⏺₈ Bramshaw ℰ 813433.
♦London 92 – Bournemouth 24 – ♦Southampton 14.

🏠 **Bell,** SO4 7HE, ℰ 812214, ⏺₈, ☞ – 📺 ⌂wc 🅿. 🔼 AE ⑩ VISA
M 7.50/8.75 t. and a la carte 🍴 2.80 – **12 rm** ⊆ 24.00/48.00 t. – SB (November-February) 50.00 st.

BROOKMANS PARK Herts. 404 T 28 – pop. 4,020 – ✆ 0707 Potters Bar.
♦London 21 – Luton 21.

XX **Villa Rosa,** 3 Great North Rd, SE : 1 ¾ m. on A 1000 ℰ 51444, Italian rest. – 🅿. 🔼 AE ⑩ VISA
closed Saturday lunch and Sunday – **M** a la carte 8.15/11.75 t. 🍴 2.95.

BROUGHTON Lancs. 402 L 22 – see Preston.

BROXTED Essex – see Thaxted.

BRUSHFORD Somerset 403 J 30 – pop. 486 – ⊠ ✆ 0398 Dulverton.
♦London 195 – Exeter 24 – Minehead 18 – Taunton 24.

🏛 **Carnarvon Arms,** TA22 9AE, ℰ 23302, ⬎ heated, ⬎, ☞, park, ⁖ – ⌂wc 🅿
closed 9 to 21 February – **M** 5.50/11.00 st. and a la carte 🍴 2.65 – **27 rm** ⊆ 18.50/49.00 st. – SB (April-October) 51.50/58.00 st.
🏠 **Three Acres Captain's Country** ⊗, TA22 9AR, ℰ 23426, ☞ – ⌂wc 🅿
M 6.00/10.00 t. 🍴 2.00 – **7 rm** ⊆ 16.00/32.00 t.

BRUTON Somerset 403 404 M 30 – pop. 1,759 – ✆ 0749.
♦London 118 – ♦Bristol 27 – Bournemouth 44 – Salisbury 35 – Taunton 36.

XX **Grants** with rm, High St., BA10 0EQ, ℰ 813395 – ⌂wc. 🔼 VISA ⁑
M *(closed Sunday dinner, Tuesday and 27 January-12 February)* (dinner only and Sunday lunch) a la carte 9.75/11.75 t. 🍴 2.40 – **3 rm** ⊆ 14.00/24.00 t.
X **Clogs,** 95 High St., ℰ 812255, Dutch Indonesian rest.
closed Sunday, 1 week April, 1 week September and 25-26 December – **M** (dinner only)(booking essential) a la carte 10.30/12.20 t. 🍴 2.90.

BRYHER Cornwall 403 ㉚ – see Scilly (Isles of).

BRYNBUGA = Usk.

BUCKDEN North Yorks. 402 N 21 – pop. 223 – ⊠ Skipton – ✆ 075 676 Kettlewell.
♦London 241 – Kendal 47 – ♦Leeds 44 – Preston 55 – York 63.

↑ **Low Greenfield** ⊗, Langstrothdale Chase, Greenfield, BD23 5JN, NW : 6 m. on Hawes Rd ℰ 858, ≤, ⬎, ☞
Easter-October – **6 rm** ⊆ 14.40/28.80 st.

BUCKFASTLEIGH Devon 403 I 32 The West Country G. – pop. 2,355 – ECD : Wednesday – ✆ 0364.
See : Buckfast Abbey (the Sacrament Chapel★).
♦London 223 – Exeter 23 – ♦Plymouth 20.

↑ **Furzeleigh Mill,** Dart Bridge, TQ11 0JP, NE : ¾ m. on old A 38 ℰ 43476, ☞ – ⌂wc 🅿
17 rm.

BUCKHURST HILL Essex 404 ㊵ – pop. 11,147 – ECD : Wednesday – ✆ 01 London.
♦London 13 – Chelmsford 25.

Plan : see Greater London (North-East)

🏛 **Roebuck** (T.H.F.), North End, IG9 5QY, ℰ 505 4636 – 📺 ⌂wc ☞ 🅿. 🔼. 🔼 AE ⑩ VISA
M 7.00/9.00 st. and a la carte 🍴 2.70 – ⊆ 5.50 – **23 rm** 38.50/48.00 st.
GU **u**

BUCKINGHAM Bucks. **403 404** Q 27 – pop. 6,439 – ECD : Thursday – ✪ 0280.

Envir. : Claydon House★ (Rococo interior★★ : Chinese Room★★ staircase★★★, Florence Nightingale Museum) *AC*, SE : 8 m. – Stowe School 18C (south front★, Marble Saloon★, park : monuments★ 18C, ≼★ from the Lake Pavilions) *AC*.

♦London 64 – ♦Birmingham 61 – Northampton 20 – ♦Oxford 25.

🏨 **White Hart** (T.H.F.), Market Sq., MK18 1NL, ℰ 815151 – 🔟 ♒wc 🎧 🅿. ♨. 🔼 AE ⓪ VISA
M 7.50/17.00 **st.** and a la carte ≬ 2.70 – ⊡ 5.50 – **19 rm** 36.00/45.00 **st.**

AUSTIN-ROVER Motorworks ℰ 812121   VAUXHALL-OPEL School Lane ℰ 814242

BUCKLAND Glos. **403 404** O 27 – see Broadway (Heref. and Worc.).

BUCKLAND IN THE MOOR Devon The West Country G. – pop. 93 – ✉ ✪ 0364 Ashburton.

♦London 225 – Exeter 25 – ♦Plymouth 28.

🏠 **Buckland Hall** ⧖, TQ13 7HL, ℰ 52679, ≼ countryside and Holne Moor, ⚘, park – ♒wc 🅿. 🔼 AE VISA. ❄
M (restricted lunch) 4.00/7.50 **t.** and a la carte ≬ 1.50 – **6 rm** ⊡ 17.50/35.00 **t.** – SB (October-June) 40.00/50.00 **st.**

BUCKLERS HARD Hants. **403 404** P 31 – see Beaulieu.

BUCKLOW HILL Cheshire **402 403 404** M 24 – see Knutsford.

BUDE Cornwall **403** G 31 The West Country G. – pop. 2,679 – ECD : Thursday – ✪ 0288.
See : The breakwater★★ – ≼ from Compass Point★.

Envir. : Poughill★ (Church★★), N : 2 ½ m. – at Poundstock★ (≼★★, church★★, Gildhouse★), S : 4 ½ m. – Morwenstowe Church★ (cliffs★★), N : 11 m. – Stratton Church★, E : 1 ½ m. – Launcells Church★, E : 3 m. – Kilkhampton Church★, NE : 5 ½ m. – Jacobstowe Church★, S : 7 m.

🇹 Burn View ℰ 2006 – 🇹 Holsworthy ℰ 0409 (Holsworthy) 253177, E : 8 ½ m.
🇿 The Crescent car park ℰ 4240 (summer only) – A 39, Stamford Hill, Stratton ℰ 3781 (summer only).

♦London 252 – Exeter 51 – ♦Plymouth 44 – Truro 53.

🏨 **Strand** (T.H.F.), The Strand, EX23 8RA, ℰ 3222 – 📶 🔟 ♒wc 🎧 🅿. 🔼 AE ⓪ VISA
M (bar lunch)/dinner 8.50 **st.** and a la carte ≬ 2.70 – ⊡ 5.50 – **40 rm** 30.50/45.00 **st.**

🏨 **Hartland**, Hartland Terr., EX23 8JY, ℰ 2509, ≼, ⚏ heated – 📶 🔟 ♒wc 📶wc 🅿
Easter-September – **M** 6.90/7.50 **t.** and a la carte ≬ 2.50 – **30 rm** ⊡ 18.40/46.00 **t.**

🏠 **Camelot**, Downs View, EX23 8RS, ℰ 2361 – ♒wc 📶wc 🅿. 🔼 VISA. ❄
March-October – **M** (bar lunch)/dinner 8.95 **st.** ≬ 2.95 – **13 rm** ⊡ 26.00/48.00 **st.**

🏠 **Bude Haven,** Flexbury Av., EX23 8NS, ℰ 2305, ⚘ – ♒wc 📶wc 🅿. 🔼 VISA
closed mid December-mid January – **M** (bar lunch)/dinner 5.75 **st.** ≬ 2.10 – **10 rm** ⊡ 11.50/27.00 **st.** – SB (weekdays only)(except July and August) 29.00/36.00 **st.**

↑ **Meva Gwin**, Upton, EX23 0LY, S : 1 ¼ m. on coast rd ℰ 2347, ≼ – ♒wc 🅿. ❄
Late March-early October – **13 rm** ⊡ 9.20/24.75 **st.**

↑ **Teeside**, 2 Burn View, EX23 8BY, ℰ 2351 – ❄
March-October – **6 rm** ⊡ 7.00/17.00 **s.**

AUSTIN-ROVER Bencoolen Rd ℰ 2146   FORD, POLSKI-FIAT Bencoolen Rd ℰ 4616

BUDLEIGH SALTERTON Devon **403** K 32 The West Country G. – pop. 4,346 – ECD : Thursday – ✪ 039 54.
🇿 Rolle Mews Car Park, Fore St. ℰ 5275 (summer only).

♦London 215 – Exeter 16 – ♦Plymouth 55.

🏠 **Southlands**, 9 Marine Par., EX9 6NS, ℰ 3497, ≼ – ♒wc 🅿 – **20 rm**.

↑ **Long Range,** 5 Vales Rd, EX9 6HS, ℰ 3321, ⚘ – 🔟 🅿. ❄
closed winter – **9 rm** ⊡ 11.00/29.00 **t.**

AUSTIN-ROVER 10-12 High St. ℰ 2277

BUILTH WELLS (LLANFAIR-YM-MUALLT) Powys **403** J 27 – pop. 2,225 – ✪ 0982.

♦London 197 – Brecon 22 – ♦Cardiff 63 – ♦Swansea 63 – Shrewsbury 70.

🏠 **Caer Beris Manor** ⧖, Garth Rd, LD2 3NP, W : ¾ m. by A 483 ℰ 552601, ≼, « 19C mock-tudor house », ⚲, park – ♒wc 🅿. 🔼 AE ⓪ VISA. ❄
M 4.95/7.50 **t.** and a la carte ≬ 1.95 – **14 rm** ⊡ 10.00/40.00 **st.**

🏠 **Llanfair**, 1, The Strand, LD2 3BG, ℰ 553253, ⚘ – 🔟 🅿. VISA. ❄
March-October – **8 rm** ⊡ 8.75/20.00 **s.**

BUNWELL Norfolk **404** X 26 – pop. 797 – ECD : Monday and Wednesday – ✪ 095 389.

♦London 102 – ♦Cambridge 51 – ♦Norwich 16.

🏠 **Bunwell Manor** ⧖, Bunwell St., NR16 1QU, NW : 1 m. ℰ 317, ⚘ – 🔟 ♒wc 📶wc 🅿. 🔼 AE VISA
M (bar lunch)/dinner 9.00 **t.** and a la carte ≬ 2.25 – **11 rm** ⊡ 20.00/40.00 **t.** – SB 40.00/44.00 **st.**

[BURFORD] Oxon. [403] [404] P 28 – pop. 1,371 – ECD : Wednesday – ⊛ 099 382.

See : St. John's Church★ 12C-14C.

Envir. : Swinbrook (church : Fettiplace Monuments★) E : 3 ½ m. – Cotswold Wildlife Park★ *AC*, S : 2 m. – Northleach : SS. Peter and Paul's Church : South Porch and the brasses★ (Perpendicular) NW : 7 ½ m.

[i] The Brewery, Sheep St. ☎ 3590.

♦London 76 – ♦Birmingham 55 – Gloucester 32 – ♦Oxford 20.

🏨🏨 **Bay Tree,** Sheep St., OX8 4LW, ☎ 3137, 🌳 – [TV] 🛁wc 🚗 🅿. [S] [AE] ⊙ [VISA]. 🚫
M 6.50/10.75 **t.** 🍷 2.95 – **22 rm** ☕ 24.00/54.00 **t.** – SB (November-April) 40.00/70.00 **st.**

🏨🏨 **Inn For All Seasons,** The Barringtons, OX8 4TN, W : 3 ¼ m. on A 40 ☎ 045 14 (Windrush) 324, 🌳 – [TV] 🛁wc ☎ 🅿. [S] [AE] [VISA]. 🚫
closed 20 December-4 January – **M** *(closed Sunday lunch)* (bar lunch)/dinner 11.50 **t.** and a la carte 🍷 3.50 – **9 rm** ☕ 28.00/45.00 **t.** – SB (except September) 57.00/67.00 **st.**

🏨 **Golden Pheasant,** High St., OX8 4RJ, ☎ 3223 – [TV] 🛁wc 🚿wc ☎ 🅿. [S] [VISA]
M 7.50/10.50 **st.** – **12 rm** ☕ 20.00/40.00 **st.** – SB 37.50/63.50 **st.**

🏨 **Lamb Inn,** Sheep St., OX8 4LR, ☎ 3155, 🌳 – 🛁wc 🅿
M *(closed Sunday dinner to non-residents)* (bar lunch Monday to Saturday)/dinner 14.00 **t.** 🍷 2.50 – **13 rm** ☕ 19.00/48.00 **t.** – SB (November-March) 50.00/60.00 **st.**

🏨 **Corner House,** High St., OX8 4RJ, ☎ 3151 – 🛁wc 🚿wc
March-mid November – **M** *(closed Sunday lunch)* 4.25/6.00 **t.** and a la carte 🍷 1.60 – **9 rm** ☕ 18.00/32.00 **t.**

🏨 **Highway,** High St., OX8 4RG, ☎ 2136 – [TV] 🛁wc 🚿wc 🅿. [S] [AE] ⊙ [VISA]
M (bar lunch)/dinner 9.00 **t.** and a la carte 🍷 3.05 – **10 rm** ☕ 18.00/40.00 **st.** – SB 51.00/65.00 **st.**

[BURGHFIELD] Berks. [403] [404] Q 29 – see Reading.

[BURLEY] Hants. [403] [404] O 31 – pop. 1,492 – ECD : Wednesday – ✉ Ringwood – ⊛ 042 53.

⛳[9] ☎ 2431.

♦London 102 – Bournemouth 17 – ♦Southampton 17 – Winchester 30.

🏨 **Moorhill House** 🐴, BH24 4AG, ☎ 3285, [swimming pool], 🌳 – 🛁wc 🚿wc 🅿. [S] [AE] ⊙ [VISA]
M (bar lunch)/dinner 11.00 **s.** and a la carte 🍷 2.75 – **24 rm** ☕ 26.00/44.00 **st.** – SB 49.00/57.00 **st.**

🏨 **Tree House,** The Cross, Ringwood Rd, BH24 4BA, ☎ 3448, 🌳 – [TV] 🚿wc 🅿. [S] [AE] ⊙ [VISA]
M (bar lunch)/dinner 6.50 **st.** and a la carte 🍷 2.75 – **8 rm** ☕ 21.00/37.00 **t.** – SB (except summer) 42.00/49.00 **st.**

[BURN BRIDGE] North Yorks. – see Harrogate.

[BURNHAM] Bucks. [404] S 29 – ECD : Thursday – ⊛ 062 86.

♦London 33 – ♦Oxford 37 – Reading 17.

🏨🏨 **Grovefield** 🐴, Taplow Common Rd, SL1 8LP, ☎ 3131, 🌳 – [lift] [TV] 🛁wc ☎ 🅿. [conference] [S] [AE] ⊙ [VISA]
M *(closed Sunday dinner to non-residents and Saturday lunch)* 9.50/11.00 **t.** and a la carte 🍷 2.25 – **31 rm** ☕ 49.00 **st.** – SB (weekends only) (except Easter) 110.00/120.00 **st.**

CITROEN 46/48 High St. ☎ 5255 VAUXHALL-OPEL 71 Stomp Rd ☎ 4994

[BURNHAM MARKET] Norfolk [404] W 25 – pop. 943 – ⊛ 0328 Fakenham.

♦London 128 – ♦Cambridge 71 – ♦Norwich 36.

🍴 **Fishes,** Market Pl., PE31 8HE, ☎ 738588, Seafood – [S] [AE] ⊙ [VISA]
closed Sunday dinner October-June, Monday, 24 to 26 December and 13 to 30 January – **M** 6.25 **t.** (lunch) and a la carte 9.45/13.95 **t.**

[BURNHAM-ON-CROUCH] Essex [404] W 29 – pop. 6,268 – ECD : Wednesday – ⊛ 0621 Maldon.

♦London 52 – Chelmsford 19 – Colchester 32 – Southend-on-Sea 25.

🍴🍴 **Contented Sole,** 80 High St., CM0 8AA, ☎ 782139
closed Sunday, Monday, 20 July-5 August and 22 December-21 January – **M** 5.25 **s.** (lunch) and a la carte 10.00/13.75 🍷 2.35.

🍴 **Boozles,** 4 Station Rd, CM0 8BG, ☎ 783167 – [S] [VISA]
closed Sunday dinner, Monday and 26 to 30 December – **M** 6.50 **t.** (lunch) and a la carte 7.95/10.85 **t.** 🍷 2.25.

AUSTIN-ROVER, FORD Station Rd ☎ 782130

[BURNLEY] Lancs. [402] N 22 – pop. 76,365 – ⊛ 0282.

Envir. : Towneley Hall★ (16C-18C) SE : 1 m.

⛳[18] Towneley, Towneley Park, Todmorden Rd ☎ 38473, E : 1 ½ m. – ⛳[18] Glen View ☎ 21045 – ⛳[18] Marsden Park, Townhouse Rd, Walton Lane, Nelson ☎ 0282 (Nelson) 67525, N : 4 m. – ⛳[18] Marsden Heights, Brierfield, Nelson ☎ 0282 (Nelson) 64583, N : 2 m.

♦London 236 – Bradford 32 – ♦Leeds 37 – ♦Liverpool 55 – ♦Manchester 25 – ♦Middlesbrough 104 – Preston 22 – ♦Sheffield 68.

🏨 **Oaks** (Best Western), Colne Rd, Reedley, BB10 2LF, NE : 2½ m. on A 56 ℰ 414141, 🔟, 🛲 –
📺 🚗wc ☎ 🅿 ⚒ 🔼 AE ⓪ 𝘝𝘐𝘚𝘈
M 5.95/13.75 **t.** and a la carte ▲ 3.25 – **32 rm** ⇆ 38.50/59.50 **st.** SB (weekends only)
52.50/63.00 **st.**

🏨 **Rosehill House,** Rosehill Av., Manchester Rd, BB11 2PW, ℰ 53931, 🛲 – 📺 🚗wc 🔥wc
🅿. 🔼 AE 𝘝𝘐𝘚𝘈
M a la carte 7.35/11.95 **st.** ▲ 3.25 – **20 rm** ⇆ 28.00/38.00 **st.**

AUSTIN-ROVER Todmorden Rd ℰ 36131
DATSUN Accrington Rd ℰ 27328
FIAT, FSO Manchester Rd ℰ 26020

RENAULT Trafalgar St. ℰ 33311
VAUXHALL Accrington Rd ℰ 27321

BURNSALL North Yorks. 𝟰𝟬𝟮 O 21 – pop. 116 – ECD : Monday and Thursday – ⊠ Skipton –
☎ 075 672 – ◆London 223 – Bradford 26 – ◆Leeds 29.

🏯 **Red Lion,** BD23 6BU, ℰ 204 – 🚗wc 🔥wc 🅿. 🛲
M (bar lunch Monday to Saturday)/dinner 6.50 **t.** – **12 rm** ⇆ 20.00/46.00 **t.**

🏠 **Manor House,** BD23 6BW, ℰ 231, 🔦, 🛲 – 🅿
March-October – **7 rm** ⇆ 13.00/20.00 **st.**

BURPHAM West Sussex 𝟰𝟬𝟰 S 30 – see Arundel.

BURRINGTON Devon – pop. 482 – ECD : Saturday – ☎ 0769 High Bickington.
◆London 260 – Barnstaple 14 – Exeter 28 – Taunton 50.

🏨 **Northcote Manor** (Best Western) 🔦, EX37 9LZ, NW : 1 m. ℰ 60501, ≼, 🛲 – 📺 🚗wc ☜
🅿. 🔼 AE ⓪ 𝘝𝘐𝘚𝘈. 🕉
16 March-4 November and Christmas – **M** (bar lunch)/dinner 12.00 **st.** ▲ 3.00 – **11 rm**
⇆ 25.00/50.00 **st.** – SB 58.00/64.00 **st.**

BURTON-UPON-TRENT Staffs. 𝟰𝟬𝟮 𝟰𝟬𝟯 𝟰𝟬𝟰 O 25 – pop. 59,040 – ECD : Wednesday – ☎ 0283.
🛈 Town Hall, King Edward Square ℰ 45454.
◆London 128 – ◆Birmingham 29 – ◆Leicester 27 – ◆Nottingham 27 – Stafford 27.

🏠 **Edgecote,** 179 Ashby Rd, DE15 0LB, SE : 1 m. on A 50 ℰ 68966, 🛲 – 🅿
11 rm ⇆ 11.75/20.25 **st.**

at Rolleston on Dove N : 4 m. by A 38 – ⊠ ☎ 0283 Burton-upon-Trent :

✕✕✕ **Brookhouse Inn** 🔦 with rm, Brookside, DE13 9AA, ℰ 814188, Telex 913001, 🛲 – 📺
🚗wc ☜ 🅿. 🔼 AE ⓪ 𝘝𝘐𝘚𝘈. 🕉
closed 24 December-5 January and Bank Holidays – **M** (closed Saturday lunch and Sunday)
5.55 **t.** (lunch) and a la carte 12.35/16.75 **t.** ▲ 2.65 – **16 rm** ⇆ 36.00/60.00 **st.** – SB (weekends
only) 64.00 **st.**

at Newton Solney NE : 3 m. by A 50 on B 5008 – ⊠ ☎ 0283 Burton-upon-Trent :

🏨 **Newton Park** (Embassy) 🔦, DE15 0SS, ℰ 703568, ≼, 🛲 – 📺 🚗wc ☜ 🅿. ⚒ 🔼 AE ⓪
𝘝𝘐𝘚𝘈
closed 24 to 27 December – **M** (closed Saturday lunch and Sunday dinner to non-residents)
6.00/9.00 **st.** ▲ 4.45 – ⇆ 4.50 – **26 rm** 31.50/39.00 **st.** – SB 50.00 **st.**

at Branston SW : 1 ½ m. on A 5121 – ⊠ ☎ 0283 Burton-upon-Trent :

🏠 **Riverside** 🔦, Riverside Dr., off Warren Lane, DE14 3EP, ℰ 63117, 🛲 – 📺 🚗wc ☜ 🅿. 🔼
𝘝𝘐𝘚𝘈
M (closed Saturday lunch) a la carte 7.75/14.80 **t.** ▲ 2.95 – **22 rm** ⇆ 29.50/40.50 **st.** – SB
(weekends only) 39.00/44.00 **st.**

ALFA-ROMEO Station Rd ℰ 813593
AUSTIN-ROVER-JAGUAR Moor St. ℰ 45353
CITROEN Tollgate ℰ 212454
DAIHATSU Main St. ℰ 716302
FIAT Derby Rd ℰ 64891
FORD Horninglow St. ℰ 61081
LADA Woodside Rd ℰ 760363

NISSAN Scalpcliffe Rd ℰ 66677
PEUGEOT, TALBOT Derby Rd ℰ 65432
RENAULT 118 Horninglow Rd ℰ 67811
SUBARU Main St. ℰ 217513
VAUXHALL-OPEL 12 Lichfield St. ℰ 61655
VOLVO New St. ℰ 31331
VW, AUDI Tutbury Rd ℰ 31336

BURY ST. EDMUNDS Suffolk 𝟰𝟬𝟰 W 27 – pop. 30,563 – ECD : Thursday – ☎ 0284.
See : St. Mary's Church★ 15C (the Angel roof★★) – **Envir. :** Ickworth House★ (18C) AC, SW : 3 m.
🛈 Lark Valley, Fornham St. Martin ℰ 63426, off A 134 on B 1106.
🛈 Abbey Gardens, Angel Hill ℰ 64667 (summer only).
◆London 79 – ◆Cambridge 27 – ◆Ipswich 26 – ◆Norwich 41.

🏨 **Angel,** 3 Angel Hill, IP33 1LT, ℰ 3926, Telex 81630 – 📺 ☎ 🅿. ⚒ 🔼 AE ⓪ 𝘝𝘐𝘚𝘈
M a la carte 12.75/15.75 **t.** ▲ 3.10 – ⇆ 5.00 – **38 rm** 40.00/50.00 **st.** – **2 suites** 60.00/70.00 **t.**

🏨 **Suffolk** (T.H.F.), 38 The Buttermarket, IP33 1DC, ℰ 3995 – 📺 🚗wc ☜ 🅿. 🔼 AE ⓪ 𝘝𝘐𝘚𝘈
M 4.95/7.50 **st.** and a la carte ▲ 2.75 – ⇆ 5.50 – **41 rm** 35.50/45.00 **st.**

✕ **Bradleys,** St. Andrews St. South, ℰ 703825 – 𝘝𝘐𝘚𝘈
closed Sunday, Monday, 2 weeks summer and 2 weeks Christmas – **M** (lunch by arrangement)
10.50 **t.** and a la carte 12.30/18.70 **t.** ▲ 2.95.

at Bradfield Combust SE : 4 ½ m. on A 134 – ⊠ Bury St. Edmunds – ☺ 028 486 Sickles-mere :

XX **Bradfield House,** Sudbury Rd, IP30 0LR, ℰ 301, ⇴ – ℗ 〽 ⓪ 𝗩𝗜𝗦𝗔
closed Sunday dinner and Monday – **M** a la carte 10.65/14.55 **t.** ▲ 3.50.

at Whepstead S : 4 ½ m. by A 143 on B 1066 – ⊠ Bury St. Edmunds – ☺ 028 486 Sickles-mere :

⌂ **Hammonds** ⟲, Bull Lane, Pinford End, IP29 5NU, by Hawkstead rd and Pinford End rd
ℰ 8867, ⇴, ⇴ – ⇾wc ℗
5 rm ⟷ 19.00/50.00.

AUSTIN-ROVER 76 Risbygate St. ℰ 31015
FIAT, LANCIA Mildenhall Rd ℰ 3280
FORD 5 Fornham Rd ℰ 2332
RENAULT Bury Rd, Horringer ℰ 028 488 (Horringer) 362

VAUXHALL-OPEL Cotton Lane ℰ 5621
VOLVO, NISSAN Out Risbygate ℰ 62444
VW, AUDI Northern Way ℰ 63441

BUTTERMERE Cumbria 🅰🅾🅱 K 20 – pop. 194 – ⊠ Cockermouth – ☺ 059 685.

See : Lake★.

♦London 306 – ♦Carlisle 35 – Kendal 43.

🏠 **Bridge,** CA13 9UZ, ℰ 252, ⇴ – ⇾wc ℿwc ℗
closed mid December-mid January – **M** (bar lunch Monday to Saturday)/dinner 9.50 **t.** ▲ 3.15
– **19 rm** ⟷ (dinner included) 24.00/58.00 **t.**

BUXTON Derbs. 🅰🅾🅱 🅰🅾🅴 O 24 – pop. 19 ,502 – ECD : Wednesday – ☺ 0298.

Envir. : Tideswell (Parish Church★ 14C) NE : 9 m.

🅱 Buxton and High Peak, Townend ℰ 3453, NE : on A 6 – 🅱 Cavendish, Gadley Lane ℰ 3494, ¾ m. Buxton Station.

🇮 The Cresent ℰ 5106.

♦London 172 – Derby 38 – ♦Manchester 25 – ♦Stoke-on-Trent 24.

🏨 **Lee Wood** (Best Western), 13 Manchester Rd, SK17 6TQ, on A 5002 ℰ 3002, Telex 669848, ⇴ – ⁆ ⓉⓋ ⇾wc ℿwc ☎ ℗ ▲ 🅽 〽 ⓪ 𝗩𝗜𝗦𝗔
closed 24 to 27 December – **M** 8.00/10.50 **t.** and a la carte ▲ 2.50 – **41 rm** ⟷ 30.00/44.00 **t.** – SB 54.00/59.00 **st.**

⌂ **Hartington,** 18 Broad Walk, SK17 6JR, ℰ 2638 – ⇾wc ℿwc ⅙. 🅽 ⁒
closed last week October and 24 December-3 January – **17 rm** ⟷ 20.00/30.00 **t.**

AUDI, VW 3 The Front ℰ 2903
FORD 127 London Rd ℰ 3816
HONDA, SAAB Leek Rd ℰ 2494

RENAULT The Old Court House ℰ 3947
VAUXHALL-OPEL Leek Rd ℰ 3466

BWLCHTOCYN Gwynedd 🅰🅾🅱 🅰🅾🅳 G 25 – see Abersoch.

CADNAM Hants. 🅰🅾🅳 🅰🅾🅴 P 31 – pop. 1 ,882 – ECD : Wednesday – ☺ 0703 Southampton.

♦London 91 – Salisbury 16 – ♦Southampton 8 – Winchester 19.

🏠 **Bartley Lodge** ⟲, Lyndhurst Rd, SO4 2NR, on A 337 ℰ 812248, ⇴, ⫽, ⇴ – ⓉⓋ ⇾wc ℿwc
℗ 〽 𝗩𝗜𝗦𝗔
M *(closed Sunday dinner)* 7.95/10.95 **t.** and a la carte ▲ 2.20 – **13 rm** ⟷ 22.00/38.50 **st.** – SB (October-March) 55.00/59.00 **st.**

CAERDYDD = Cardiff.

CAERFFILI = Caerphilly.

CAERFYRDDIN = Carmarthen.

CAERGYBI = Holyhead.

CAERNARFON Gwynedd 🅰🅾🅱 🅰🅾🅳 H 24 – pop. 9 ,271 – ECD : Thursday – ☺ 0286 Llanwnda.

See : Castle★★★ 13C-14C (Royal Welsh Fusiliers Regimental museum★) *AC* – City walls★.

Envir. : SE : Snowdon (ascent and ✲★★★) 1 h 15 mn by Snowdon Mountain Railway (*AC*) from Llanberis (Pass★★) SE : 13 m. – Dinas Dindle★ SW : 5 m.

🇮 The Slate Quay ℰ 2232 (summer only).

♦London 249 – Birkenhead 76 – Chester 68 – Holyhead 30 – Shrewsbury 85.

🏨 **The Stables,** Llanwnda, LL54 5SD, SW : 3 ½ m. by A 487 on A 499 ℰ 830711, ⫽, ⇴ – ⓉⓋ
⇾wc ☜ ℗ 🅽 〽 𝗩𝗜𝗦𝗔
M 6.75/9.00 **t.** and a la carte ▲ 3.25 – **12 rm** ⟷ 26.00/44.00 **t.** – SB (weekends only) 55.00/65.00 **st.**

CAERPHILLY (CAERFFILI) Mid Glam. **403** K 29 – pop. 28 ,681 – ECD : Wednesday – ✆ 0222.
See : Castle** 13C.
🛈 Park Lane ✆ 863378 (summer only).
♦London 157 – ♦Cardiff 8 – Newport 11.

Hotels and restaurants see : *Cardiff* S : 8 m., *Newport (Gwent)* E : 11 m.

CAERSWS Powys **403** J 26 – ECD : Thursday – ✉ Newtown – ✆ 068 684.
♦London 202 – Aberystwyth 38 – Newtown 6.

🏨 **Maesmawr Hall** ⌂, SY17 5SF, E : 1 m. on A 489 ✆ 255, ≤, « 16C manor house in large garden », ⌂, park – 🚪wc 🏧wc 🅿. ⚠ ⬛ 𝗩𝗜𝗦𝗔
M 6.50/8.50 and a la carte – **19 rm** ⊐ 22.50/47.00 t. – SB 34.50/46.75 st.

AUSTIN-ROVER Central Garage ✆ 345   VOLVO Trefeglwys ✆ 055 16 (Trefeglwys) 202

CALCOT Glos. – see Tetbury.

CAMBERLEY Surrey **404** R 29 – pop. 45 ,108 – ECD : Wednesday – ✆ 0276.
Envir. : Sandhurst (Royal Military Academy : Royal Memorial Chapel*) NW : 1 ½ m.
♦London 40 – Reading 13 – ♦Southampton 48.

🏨 **Frimley Hall** (T.H.F.), off Portsmouth Rd via Lime Av., GU15 2BG, E : ¾ m. off A 325 ✆ 28321, Telex 858446, ⟵ – 📺 🅿. ⚠ ⬛ ⬛ ⓪ 𝗩𝗜𝗦𝗔
M 8.50/11.50 **st.** and a la carte 👙 3.50 – ⊐ 5.50 – **66 rm** 41.50/51.50 **st.**

✗ **Villa Romana,** 20 Park St., GU15 3PL, ✆ 24370, Italian rest. – ⬛ ⬛ ⓪ 𝗩𝗜𝗦𝗔
closed Sunday – **M** a la carte 8.25/12.00 **t.** 👙 2.50.

AUSTIN-ROVER London Rd ✆ 63443

CAMBRIDGE Cambs. **404** U 27 – pop. 87 ,111 – ECD : Thursday – ✆ 0223.
See : Colleges Quarter*** : King's College** (King's Chapel***) Z – Queens' College** (Cloister Court) Z – St. John's College** (Gateway*) Y – Fitzwilliam Museum** AC Z M1 – Trinity College** (Wren Library**, Chapel*, Great Court and Gate*) Y – Holy Sepulchre* (12C round church) Y E – Senate House* Z S – The Backs* YZ – Jesus College (Chapel*) Y K – Christ's College (Gatehouse) YZ A.
Envir. : Anglesey Abbey 12C (interior** and park* AC) NE : 6 m. by A 1303 X and B 1102.
🛏 Cambridgeshire Hotel, Bar Hill ✆ 0954 (Crafts Hill) 80555, NW : 5 ½ m. by A 1307 X.
✈ Cambridge Airport : ✆ 61133, E : 2 m. on A 1303 X.
🛈 Wheeler St. ✆ 358977 or 353363 (weekends).
♦London 55 – ♦Coventry 88 – ♦Kingston-upon-Hull 137 – ♦Ipswich 54 – ♦Leicester 74 – ♦Norwich 61 – ♦Nottingham 88 – ♦Oxford 100.

Plan opposite

🏨 **Garden House** (Best Western), Granta Pl., off Mill Lane, CB2 1RT, ✆ 63421, Telex 81463, ≤, ⟵ – 🛗 📺 ☎ 🅿. ⚠ ⬛ ⬛ 𝗩𝗜𝗦𝗔 ⬚   Z n
M 12.50/15.00 **t.** and a la carte – ⊐ 4.00 – **117 rm** 45.00/70.00 **t.** – SB (weekends only) 67.50/98.50 **st.**

🏨 **University Arms,** Regent St., CB2 1AD, ✆ 351241, Telex 817311 – 🛗 📺 ☎ 🅿. ⚠ ⬛ ⬛ ⓪ 𝗩𝗜𝗦𝗔   Z e
M 6.60/8.70 **st.** and a la carte – **113 rm** ⊐ 33.00/47.00 **st.** – SB (weekends only) (October-May) 49.80/53.00 **st.**

🏨 **Gonville,** Gonville Pl., CB1 1LY, ✆ 66611 – 🛗 📺 🚪wc ⊞ 🅿. ⚠ ⬛ 𝗩𝗜𝗦𝗔   Z r
closed 3 days at Christmas – **M** 6.50/8.90 **st.** and a la carte 👙 3.45 – **62 rm** ⊐ 33.00/47.00 **st.** – SB (weekends only) (October-May) 53.00 **st.**

🏨 **Blue Boar** (T.H.F.), 17 Trinity St., CB2 1TB, ✆ 63121 – 📺 🚪wc ⊞. ⚠ ⬛ ⬛ ⓪ 𝗩𝗜𝗦𝗔   Y s
M *(closed Monday lunch)* 8.50/8.75 **st.** and a la carte 👙 2.70 – ⊐ 5.50 – **48 rm** 37.50/48.50 **st.**

🏨 **Arundel House,** 53 Chesterton Rd, CB4 3AN, ✆ 67701 – 📺 🚪wc 🏧wc ☎ 🅿. ⚠ ⬛ ⬛ 𝗩𝗜𝗦𝗔   Y u
closed Christmas – **M** 6.25/8.25 **t.** and a la carte 👙 1.60 – ⊐ 1.85 – **72 rm** 18.50/43.50 **t.** – SB (weekends only) (April-October) 43.00/47.00 **st.**

🏨 **Centennial,** 63-69 Hills Rd, CB2 1PG, ✆ 314652 – 🚪wc 🏧 🅿. ⚠ ⬛ ⬛ ⓪ 𝗩𝗜𝗦𝗔 ⬚   X x
closed 24 December-2 January – **M** 5.50/6.50 **t.** and a la carte 👙 2.25 – **22 rm** ⊐ 23.50/33.00 **t.** – SB (weekends only) (November-March) 33.00/71.10 **st.**

🏠 **Ashley,** 74 Chesterton Rd, CB4 1ER, ✆ 350059, ⟵ – 📺 🏧wc ☎ 🅿. ⚠ 𝗩𝗜𝗦𝗔   Y o
closed 25 and 26 December – **10 rm** ⊐ 16.50/27.50 **st.**

🏠 **May View,** 12 Park Par., CB5 8AL, ✆ 66018   Y v
closed 15 December-2 January – **6 rm** ⊐ 14.00/24.00 **st.**

🏠 **Helen,** 167-169 Hills Rd, CB2 2RJ, ✆ 246465 – 📺 🏧wc ☎ 🅿. ⚠ 𝗩𝗜𝗦𝗔   X c
closed 10 December-10 January – **24 rm** ⊐ 14.00/35.00 **st.**

✗✗ **Cambridge Lodge** with rm, 139 Huntingdon Rd, CB3 0DQ, ✆ 352833, Telex 817438, ⟵ – 📺 🚪wc 🏧wc 🅿. ⚠ ⬛ ⓪ 𝗩𝗜𝗦𝗔   X i
M *(closed Saturday lunch)* 7.95/15.00 **t.** and a la carte 👙 2.65 – **11 rm** ⊐ 38.00/45.00 **t.**

CAMBRIDGE

Grafton Centre . . . . . **Y**
Lion Yard Centre . . . **Z**
Market Hill . . . . **Z** 18
Market Street . . . . . **Y** 19
Petty Cury . . . . **Z** 27
St. Andrew's St. . . . . **Z** 28
Sidney Street . . . . . **Y** 32
Trinity Street . . . . . . **Y** 36

Bridge Street . . . . . **Y** 2
Corn Exchange St. . **Z** 6
Downing Street . . . . **Z** 7
Free School Lane . . . **Z** 12
Hobson Street . . . . . **Y** 14

King's Parade . . . . . . **Z** 15
Madingley Road . **X, Y** 16
Magdalene St. . . . . . **Y** 17
Milton Road . . . . **Y** 20
Newmarket Road . . **Y** 21
Northampton Street **Y** 22
Parker Street . . . . . **Z** 23
Peas Hill . . . . **Z** 25
Pembroke Street . . . **Z** 26
St. John's Street . . . . **Y** 29
Short Street . . . . **Y** 30
Tennis Court Road . **Z** 35
Trumpington Road . **Z** 37
Wheeler Street . . . . . **Z** 39

COLLEGES

CHRIST'S _____ **Y A**
CHURCHILL _____ **X B**
CLARE _____ **Z B**
CORPUS CHRISTI _____ **Z G**
DARWIN _____ **Z D**
DOWNING _____ **Z E**
EMMANUEL _____ **Z F**
FITZWILLIAM HOUSE ___ **X G**
GONVILLE AND CAIUS _ **Y G**
HARVEY COURT _____ **Z K**
HUGHES HALL _____ **Z J**
JESUS _____ **Y K**
KING'S _____ **Z**
LUCY CAVENDISH _____ **Y O**
MAGDALENE _____ **Y N**

NEW HALL _____ **X D**
NEWNHAM _____ **X E**
PEMBROKE _____ **Z N**
PETERHOUSE _____ **Z O**
QUEENS' _____ **Z Q**
RIDDLEY HALL _____ **Z R**
ST-CATHARINE'S _____ **Z U**
ST-EDMUNDS HOUSE ___ **Y Y**
ST-JOHN'S _____ **Y F**
SELWYN _____ **X P**
SIDNEY SUSSEX _____ **Y P**
TRINITY _____ **Y V**
TRINITY HALL _____ **Y V**
WESTMINSTER _____ **Y W**
WOLFSON _____ **X U**

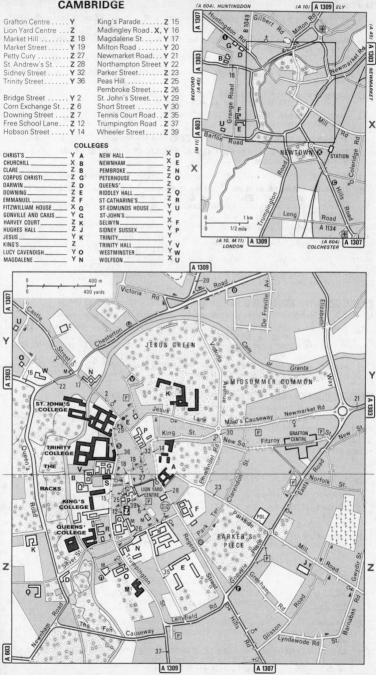

at Impington N : 2 m. on B 1049 at junction of A 45 – X – ⊠ Cambridge – ☻ 022 023
Histon :

🏨 **Post House** (T.H.F.), Lakeview, Bridge Rd, CB4 4PH, ✆ 7000, Telex 817123, 🏊, 🚗 – 🔟 ☎ ⬢ 🄿 ⚖ 🅰️ 🆚🆂🄰
M 10.70/12.95 **st.** and a la carte ⧍ 2.70 – ☲ 5.50 – **120 rm** 46.00/57.50 **st.**

at Fowlmere S : 8 ¾ m. by A 1309 – X – and A 10 on B 1368 – ⊠ Royston – ☻ 076 382
Fowlmere :

XX **Chequers Inn,** High St., SG8 7SR, ✆ 369 – 🄿 🄰 🅰️ ⓞ 🆅🄸🅂🄰
closed 25 and 26 December – **M** a la carte 12.55/20.85 **st.**

XX **Swan House Inn,** High St., SG8 7SR, ✆ 444 – 🄿 🄰 🅰️ ⓞ 🆅🄸🅂🄰
closed Sunday dinner and 25-26 December – **M** 9.50 **t.** ⧍ 2.75.

at Madingley W : 4 ½ m. by A 1303 – X – ⊠ ☻ 0954 Madingley :

XX **Three Horseshoes,** High Street, CB3 8AB, ✆ 210221, 🚗 – 🄿 🄰 🅰️ ⓞ 🆅🄸🅂🄰
M a la carte 14.35/17.35 **st.** ⧍ 2.95.

at Bar Hill NW : 5 ½ m. by A 1307 – X – on A 604 – ⊠ Bar Hill – ☻ 0954 Crafts Hill :

🏨 **Cambridgeshire Moat House** (Q.M.H.), Huntingdon Rd, CB3 8EU, ✆ 80555, Telex 817141, 🏊, ⛴, ☂, ✕, squash – 🔟 ➳wc ☎ & 🄿 ⚖ 🄰 🅰️ ⓞ 🆅🄸🅂🄰
M 9.80 **t.** and a la carte ⧍ 3.35 – **100 rm** ☲ 42.50/56.00 **t.** – SB (except weekdays July-September) 56.00/66.00 **t.**

ALFA-ROMEO, HYUNDAI, SUZUKI Babraham Rd ✆ 247072
AUSTIN-ROVER-DAIMLER-JAGUAR 400 Newmarket Rd ✆ 65111
BEDFORD, OPEL-VAUXHALL 137 Histon Rd ✆ 66751
CITROEN Newmarket Rd, Duxford ✆ 832136
HONDA Cheddars Lane ✆ 359151

MERCEDES-BENZ 121/129 Perne Rd ✆ 247268
NISSAN 315 Mill Rd ✆ 242222
RENAULT 217 Newmarket Rd ✆ 351616
TOYOTA 1 Union Lane ✆ 356225
VAUXHALL-OPEL Elizabeth Way ✆ 321321
VOLVO Harston ✆ 870123
VW, AUDI 383 Milton Rd ✆ 354472

CANNOCK Staffs. 🄸🄾🄶 🄸🄾🄷 🄸🄾🄸 N 25 – pop. 54 ,503 – ECD : Thursday – ☻ 054 35.
◆London 135 – ◆Birmingham 20 – Derby 36 – ◆Leicester 51 – Shrewsbury 32 – ◆Stoke-on-Trent 28.

🏨 **Roman Way,** Watling St., Hatherton, WS11 1SH, SW : 1 ¼ m. by A 460 on A 5 ✆ 72121 – 🔟 ➳wc 🏿wc ☎ 🄿 ⚖ 🄰 🅰️ ⓞ 🆅🄸🅂🄰
M *(closed Saturday lunch)* 6.25 **t.** (lunch) and a la carte 7.60/11.35 **t.** – **24 rm** ☲ 28.50/39.00 **t.** – SB (weekends only) 27.50/39.50 **st.**

🏨 **Hollies,** Hollies Av., off Hednesford St., WS11 1DW, ✆ 3151, 🚗 – 🔟 🄿 🄰 🅰️ ⓞ 🆅🄸🅂🄰 ⚘
M *(closed Sunday dinner)* 6.50/8.50 **st.** and a la carte ⧍ 3.50 – **6 rm** ☲ 18.00/26.00 **st.**

CANTERBURY Kent 🄸🄾🄸 X 30 – pop. 34 ,546 – ECD : Thursday – ☻ 0227.
See : Christ Church Cathedral★★★ (Norman crypt★★, Bell Harry Tower★★, Great Cloister★★, ≤★ from Green Court) Y – King's School★ Y B – Mercery Lane★ Y – Weavers★ (old houses) Y D.
Envir. : Patrixbourne (St. Mary's Church : south door★) SE : 3 m. by A 2 Z.
🄱 13 Longmarket CTI 2JS ✆ 66567.
◆London 59 – ◆Brighton 76 – ◆Dover 15 – Maidstone 28 – Margate 17.

Plan opposite

🏨 **County,** High St., CT1 2RX, ✆ 66266, Telex 965076 – 🛗 ▤ rest 🔟 ☎ ⇔ 🄿 ⚖ 🄰 🅰️ ⓞ 🆅🄸🅂🄰 ⚘
Y n
M 8.00/11.50 **t.** and a la carte – ☲ 5.50 – **74 rm** 38.50/52.00 **t.**, **1 suite** 100.00 **t.**

🏨 **Chaucer** (T.H.F.), Ivy Lane, CT1 1TT, ✆ 464427, Telex 965096 – 🔟 ➳wc ☎ 🄿 ⚖ 🄰 🅰️ ⓞ 🆅🄸🅂🄰
Z c
M 6.25/8.50 **st.** and a la carte ⧍ 2.80 – ☲ 5.50 – **43 rm** 36.50/48.50 **st.**, **1 suite**.

🏨 **Falstaff,** 8-12 St. Dunstan's St., CT2 8AF, ✆ 462138 – 🔟 ➳wc ☎ 🄿 🄰 🅰️ ⓞ 🆅🄸🅂🄰 ⚘
M 7.25 **st.** (lunch) and a la carte 7.70/12.20 **st.** ⧍ 4.35 – **16 rm** ☲ 40.00/50.00 **st.** – SB (weekends only) 60.00/80.00 **st.**
Y a

🏨 **Canterbury,** 71 New Dover Rd, CT1 3DY, ✆ 450551, Telex 965386 – 🛗 🔟 ➳wc 🏿wc ☎ 🄿 🄰 🅰️ ⓞ 🆅🄸🅂🄰
Z u
M 6.00/8.00 **t.** and a la carte ⧍ 3.00 – **28 rm** ☲ 30.00/38.00 **st.**

🏨 **Victoria,** 59 London Rd, CT2 7JY, ✆ 459333, 🚗 – 🔟 ➳wc 🏿wc ☎ 🄿 🄰 🅰️ ⓞ 🆅🄸🅂🄰 ⚘
closed Christmas – **M** *(closed Sunday)* (bar lunch)/dinner 6.00 **t.** and a la carte ⧍ 3.00 – **23 rm** ☲ 16.00/38.00 **t.**
Y i

🏨 **Pointers,** 1 London Rd, CT2 8LR, ✆ 456846 – 🔟 ➳wc 🏿 ☎ 🄿 🄰 🅰️ ⓞ 🆅🄸🅂🄰
Y e
closed 24 December-mid January – **M** (dinner only) 9.00 **t.** ⧍ 2.70 – **14 rm** ☲ 18.00/38.00 **t.** – SB 42.00/44.00 **st.**

🏨 **Ebury,** 65-67 New Dover Rd, CT1 3DX, ✆ 68433, 🚗 – 🔟 ➳wc 🏿wc ☎ 🄿 🄰 🅰️ 🆅🄸🅂🄰 ⚘
Z r
closed 1 to 14 January – **M** *(closed Sunday)* (bar lunch)/dinner 8.00 **t.** ⧍ 2.50 – **15 rm** ☲ 25.00/45.00 **t.** – SB (except Sunday) 37.50/45.00 **st.**

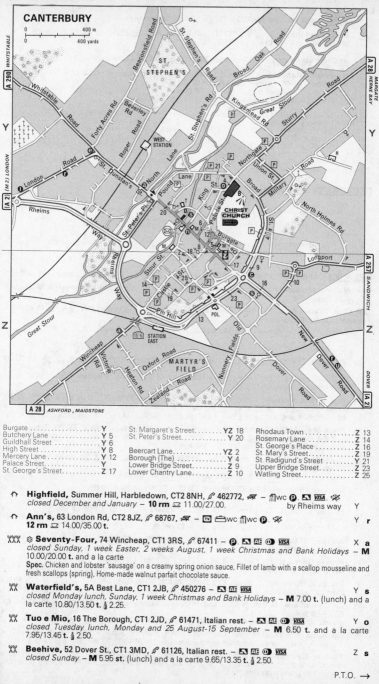

CANTERBURY

Burgate	Y
Butchery Lane	Y 5
Guildhall Street	Y 6
High Street	Y 8
Mercery Lane	Y 12
Palace Street	Y
St. George's Street	Z 17

St. Margaret's Street	YZ 18
St. Peter's Street	Y 20
Beercart Lane	YZ 2
Borough (The)	Y 4
Lower Bridge Street	Z 9
Lower Chantry Lane	Z 10

Rhodaus Town	Z 13
Rosemary Lane	Z 14
St. George's Place	Z 16
St. Mary's Street	Z 19
St. Radigund's Street	Y 21
Upper Bridge Street	Z 23
Watling Street	Z 25

↑ **Highfield,** Summer Hill, Harbledown, CT2 8NH, ℰ 462772, �というwc 🅿 🔊 VISA ⚘
closed December and January – **10 rm** ⇌ 11.00/27.00. by Rheims way   Y

↑ **Ann's,** 63 London Rd, CT2 8JZ, ℰ 68767, 🌲 – TV ⇌wc 🃕wc 🅿 ⚘   Y **r**
12 rm ⇌ 14.00/35.00 t.

XXX ❀ **Seventy-Four,** 74 Wincheap, CT1 3RS, ℰ 67411 – 🅿 🔊 AE ① VISA   X **a**
closed Sunday, 1 week Easter, 2 weeks August, 1 week Christmas and Bank Holidays – **M**
10.00/20.00 t. and a la carte
Spec. Chicken and lobster 'sausage' on a creamy spring onion sauce, Fillet of lamb with a scallop mousseline and fresh scallops (spring), Home-made walnut parfait chocolate sauce.

XX **Waterfield's,** 5A Best Lane, CT1 2JB, ℰ 450276 – 🔊 AE VISA   Y **s**
closed Monday lunch, Sunday, 1 week Christmas and Bank Holidays – **M** 7.00 t. (lunch) and a la carte 10.80/13.50 t. 🍷 2.25.

XX **Tuo e Mio,** 16 The Borough, CT1 2JD, ℰ 61471, Italian rest. – 🔊 AE ① VISA   Y **o**
closed Tuesday lunch, Monday and 25 August-15 September – **M** 6.50 t. and a la carte 7.95/13.45 t. 🍷 2.50.

XX **Beehive,** 52 Dover St., CT1 3MD, ℰ 61126, Italian rest. – 🔊 AE ① VISA   Z **s**
closed Sunday – **M** 5.95 st. (lunch) and a la carte 9.65/13.35 t. 🍷 2.50.

P.T.O. →

CANTERBURY

at Fordwich NE : 3 m. by A 28 – Y – ✉ ✪ 0227 Canterbury :

🏨 George and Dragon, King St., CT2 0DB, ☎ 710661, 🌭 – ⊡ ⇔wc 🅿 🅿 ⊠ 🅰🅴 ⓞ 𝘝𝘐𝘚𝘈
M (grill rest. only) – **13 rm** ☞ 17.50/34.00 t.

at Chartham Hatch W : 3 ¼ m. by A 28 – Z – ✉ ✪ 0227 Canterbury :

🏨 **Howfield Manor** 🦢, Howfield Lane, CT4 7HQ, SE : 1 m. ☎ 738294, « Country house atmosphere », 🌭 – ⇔wc 🎱wc 🅿 ⊠ 🅰🅴 𝘝𝘐𝘚𝘈 🛇
closed mid December-mid January – **M** (dinner only) (booking essential) 13.00 **st.** – **5 rm** ☞ 30.00/48.00 **st.** – SB (November-mid March) 52.00/63.00 **st.**

AUSTIN-ROVER-DAIMLER-JAGUAR 5 Rose Lane and 28/30 St. Peters St. ☎ 66161	PEUGEOT, TALBOT The Pavillon ☎ 51791
BMW Vauxhall Rd ☎ 54341	RENAULT Northgate ☎ 65561
COLT 1/3 Park Rd ☎ 75114	SUBARU Castle Row ☎ 53810
FIAT, CITROEN, ROLLS ROYCE 41 St. Georges Pl. ☎ 66131	TOYOTA Union St. ☎ 61993
	VAUXHALL-OPEL Ashford Rd, Chartham ☎ 731331
FORD 23 Lower Bridge St. ☎ 51777	VOLVO Mill Rd, Sturry ☎ 710481
NISSAN Island Rd ☎ 710431	VW-AUDI Vauxhall Rd Industrial Estate ☎ 57611

CARBIS BAY Cornwall 🲃🲄🲅 D 33 – see St. Ives.

---

*During the season, particularly in resorts, it is wise to book in advance.
However, if you find you cannot take up a hotel booking you have made,
please let the hotel know immediately.
If you are writing to a hotel abroad enclose an International Reply Coupon
(available from Post Offices.)*

CARDIFF (CAERDYDD) South Glam. 🲃🲄🲅 K 29 – pop. 262 ,313 – ECD : Wednesday – ✪ 0222.

See : National Museum★★ BY **M** – Llandaff Cathedral★ AY **B** – St. Fagan's Castle (Folk Museum)★ AC, by St. Fagans Rd. AY.

🛫 Cardiff-Wales Airport ☎ 0446 (Rhoose) 711911 (day) 711914 (night) SW : 8 m. by A 48 AZ – Terminal : Central Bus Station.

🏢 3 Castle St. ☎ 27281 – ◆London 155 – ◆Birmingham 110 – ◆Bristol 46 – ◆Coventry 124.

Plans on following pages

🏨🏨 **Park** (Mt. Charlotte), Park Pl., CF1 3UD, ☎ 383471, Telex 497195 – 🛗 ⊡ ☎ 🅿 ⚼ ⊠ 🅰🅴 𝘝𝘐𝘚𝘈
BZ **c**
M 7.50/8.75 **st.** and a la carte 🍴 3.35 – **108 rm** ☞ 46.75/57.75 **st.**, **6 suites** 60.50/71.50 **st.** – SB (weekends only) 48.00/50.00 **st.**

🏨🏨 **Inn on the Avenue**, Circle Way East, Llanedeyrn, CF3 7XF, NE : 3 m. on A 48 ☎ 732520, Telex 497582, 🔲 – 🛗 ⊡ ☎ 🅿 ⚼ ⊠ 🅰🅴 ⓞ 𝘝𝘐𝘚𝘈 🛇
AY **n**
M 8.00/9.50 **t.** and a la carte 🍴 2.85 – **140 rm** ☞ 43.00/52.00 **st.** – SB (weekends only) 52.00 **st.**

🏨 Post House (T.H.F.), Church Rd, Pentwyn, CF2 7XA, NE : 4 m. on A 48 ☎ 731212, Telex 497633
on A 48 AY
– 🛗 ⊡ ⇔wc 👦 🅿 ⚼ ⊠ 🅰🅴 ⓞ 𝘝𝘐𝘚𝘈
M 8.50/9.50 **st.** and a la carte 🍴 2.75 – **150 rm**.

🏨 Crest (Crest), Westgate St., CF1 1JB, ☎ 388681, Telex 497258 – 🛗 ⊡ ⇔wc ☎ 🅿 ⚼ ⊠
BZ **i**
🅰🅴 ⓞ 𝘝𝘐𝘚𝘈
M approx. 11.50 **st.** – ☞ 5.75 – **160 rm** 40.00/53.00 **st.**, **1 suite** – SB (weekends only) 55.00 **st.**

🏨 Beverley, 75 Cathedral Rd, CF1 9PG, ☎ 43443 – ⊡ ⇔wc 🎱wc 👦 🅿
AZ **o**
18 rm

🏨 **Ferrier's**, 130-132 Cathedral Rd, CF1 9LQ, ☎ 383413 – ⊡ 🎱 🅿 ⊠ 🅰🅴 ⓞ 𝘝𝘐𝘚𝘈
AY **e**
closed 2 weeks at Christmas – **M** (closed dinner Saturday and Sunday and Friday) (bar lunch)/dinner a la carte 4.85/7.85 **t.** 🍴 2.00 – **27 rm** ☞ 16.00/32.50 **t.**

🏚 **Abbey**, 151 Cathedral Rd, CF1 9PJ, ☎ 390896 – ⊡ 🎱wc. ⊠ 𝘝𝘐𝘚𝘈
AY **o**
27 rm ☞ 15.00/40.00 **t.**

🏚 **Preste Gaarden**, 181 Cathedral Rd, CF1 9PN, ☎ 28607 – ⊡. 🛇
AY **x**
10 rm ☞ 12.00/20.00 **st.**

🏚 **Princes**, 10 Princes St., Roath, CF2 3PR, ☎ 491732 – 🛇
AY **r**
6 rm ☞ 12.00/18.00 **st.**

XX **La Chaumière**, 44 Cardiff Rd, Llandaff (behind Maltsters Arms), CF5 2XX, ☎ 555319 – 🅿
AY **a**
⊠ 🅰🅴 ⓞ 𝘝𝘐𝘚𝘈
closed dinner Sunday and Monday – **M** a la carte approx. 11.85 **t.** 🍴 3.00.

X **Gibson's**, 8 Romilly Crescent, Canton, CF1 9NR, ☎ 41264, Bistro – ⊠ 🅰🅴 ⓞ 𝘝𝘐𝘚𝘈
AZ **a**
closed Sunday, 1 week Christmas and Bank Holidays – **M** 11.50/13.95 **t.** and a la carte 🍴 3.00.

X **Blas-ar-Gymru**, 48 Crwys Rd, CF2 4NN, ☎ 382132 – ⊠ 🅰🅴 ⓞ 𝘝𝘐𝘚𝘈
BY **z**
closed Saturday lunch, Sunday, 6 to 20 January and Bank Holidays – **M** (booking essential) 12.75/12.95 **t.** and a la carte.

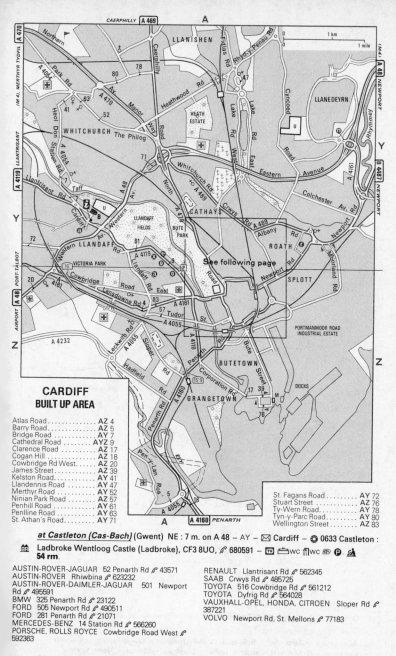

CARDIFF
BUILT UP AREA

Atlas Road . . . . AZ 4
Barry Road . . . . AZ 5
Bridge Road . . . . AY 7
Cathedral Road . . . . AYZ 9
Clarence Road . . . . AZ 17
Cogan Hill . . . . AZ 18
Cowbridge Rd West. . . . . . AZ 20
James Street . . . . AZ 39
Kelston Road . . . . AY 41
Llandennis Road . . . . AY 47
Merthyr Road . . . . AY 52
Ninian Park Road . . . . AY 57
Penhill Road . . . . AY 61
Penlline Road . . . . AY 63
St. Athan's Road. . . . . AY 71

St. Fagans Road . . . . AY 72
Stuart Street . . . . AZ 76
Ty-Wern Road. . . . . AY 78
Tyn-y-Parc Road. . . . . AY 80
Wellington Street . . . . AZ 83

at Castleton (Cas-Bach) (Gwent) NE : 7 m. on A 48 – AY – ⊠ Cardiff – ☎ 0633 Castleton :

🏨 Ladbroke Wentloog Castle (Ladbroke), CF3 8UO, ℰ 680591 – 📺 ⇌wc flllwc ☜ 🅿 🔏 **54 rm**.

AUSTIN-ROVER-JAGUAR 52 Penarth Rd ℰ 43571
AUSTIN-ROVER Rhiwbina ℰ 623232
AUSTIN-ROVER-DAIMLER-JAGUAR 501 Newport Rd ℰ 495591
BMW 325 Penarth Rd ℰ 23122
FORD 505 Newport Rd ℰ 490511
FORD 281 Penarth Rd ℰ 21071
MERCEDES-BENZ 14 Station Rd ℰ 566260
PORSCHE, ROLLS ROYCE Cowbridge Road West ℰ 592363

RENAULT Llantrisant Rd ℰ 562345
SAAB Crwys Rd ℰ 485725
TOYOTA 516 Cowbridge Rd ℰ 561212
TOYOTA Dyfrig Rd ℰ 564028
VAUXHALL-OPEL, HONDA, CITROEN Sloper Rd ℰ 387221
VOLVO Newport Rd, St. Mellons ℰ 77183

Plans de ville : Les rues sont sélectionnées en fonction de leur importance pour la circulation et le repérage des établissements cités. Les rues secondaires ne sont qu'amorcées.

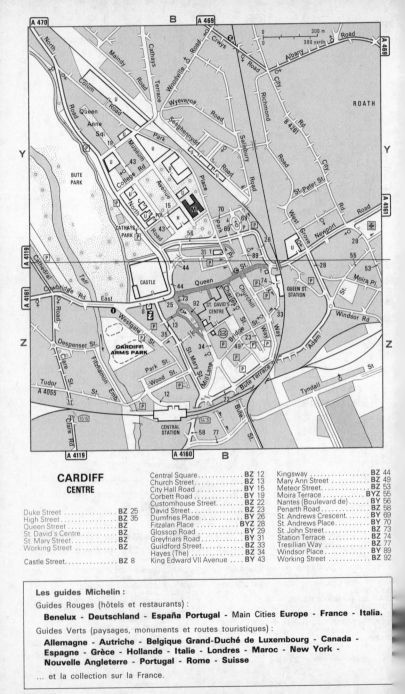

CARDIFF
CENTRE

Duke Street .... **BZ** 25
High Street .... **BZ** 35
Queen Street .... **BZ**
St. David's Centre .... **BZ**
St. Mary Street .... **BZ**
Working Street .... **BZ**

Castle Street .... **BZ** 8

Central Square .... **BZ** 12
Church Street .... **BZ** 13
City Hall Road .... **BY** 15
Corbett Road .... **BY** 19
Customhouse Street .... **BZ** 22
David Street .... **BZ** 23
Dumfries Place .... **BY** 26
Fitzalan Place .... **BYZ** 28
Glossop Road .... **BY** 29
Greyfriars Road .... **BY** 31
Guildford Street .... **BZ** 33
Hayes (The) .... **BZ** 34
King Edward VII Avenue .... **BY** 43

Kingsway .... **BZ** 44
Mary Ann Street .... **BZ** 49
Meteor Street .... **BZ** 53
Moira Terrace .... **BYZ** 55
Nantes (Boulevard de) .... **BY** 56
Penarth Road .... **BZ** 58
St. Andrews Crescent .... **BY** 69
St. Andrews Place .... **BY** 70
St. John Street .... **BZ** 73
Station Terrace .... **BZ** 74
Tresillian Way .... **BZ** 77
Windsor Place .... **BY** 89
Working Street .... **BZ** 92

Les guides Michelin :

Guides Rouges (hôtels et restaurants) :

Benelux - Deutschland - España Portugal - Main Cities **Europe - France - Italia.**

Guides Verts (paysages, monuments et routes touristiques) :

Allemagne - Autriche - Belgique Grand-Duché de Luxembourg - Canada - Espagne - Grèce - Hollande - Italie - Londres - Maroc - New York - Nouvelle Angleterre - Portugal - Rome - Suisse

... et la collection sur la France.

CARDIGAN (ABERTEIFI) Dyfed 408 G 27 – pop. 3 ,815 – ECD : Wednesday – ☎ 0239.
Envir. : Mwnt (site★) N : 6 m. – Gwbert-on-Sea (cliffs ≤★) NW : 3 m. – Cilgerran (castle★ 13C) *AC* SE : 4 m.

🛏 Gwbert-on-Sea ♐ 612035, NW : 3 m.

🎫 3 Heathfield Pendre ♐ 613230 (summer only).

♦London 250 – Carmarthen 30 – Fishguard 19.

❌ **Rhyd-Garn-Wen** 🦢 with rm, SA43 3NW, SW : 2 ¾ m. by A 487 on Cilgerran rd ♐ 612742, 🍴 – 🛁wc ❷ ⚑ 🛉
Easter-September – **M** (dinner only)(booking essential) 12.50 ↕ 2.85 – **3 rm** ⌑ (dinner included) 32.00/62.00.

   at Gwbert-on-Sea NW : 3 m. on B 4548 – ✉ ☎ 0239 Cardigan :

🏨 **Cliff** 🦢, SA43 1PP, ♐ 613241, Telex 48440, ≤ bay and countryside, ↴ heated, 🛉, 🦢, 🍴, squash – 🛁wc ⏀wc ⚑ 🛁 🅿 ⦿ *VISA*
M (bar lunch Monday to Saturday)/dinner 9.00 **st.** and a la carte ↕ 2.75 – **70 rm** ⌑ 23.00/60.00 **st.** – SB (weekends only) (October-March) 56.00/62.00 **st.**

AUSTIN-ROVER Aberystwyth Rd ♐ 612365   FIAT St. Dogmaels ♐ 612025

CARLISLE Cumbria 401 402 L 19 – pop. 72 ,206 – ECD : Thursday – ☎ 0228.
See : Castle★ (12C) *AC* AY – Cathedral★ 12C-14C AY E.

🛏 Aglionby ♐ 022 872 (Scotby) 303 E : 2 m. by A 69 BY – 🛏 Stoneyholme ♐ 34856 E : 1 m. by St. Aidan's Rd BY.

✈ ♐ 022 873 (Crosby-on-Eden) 641, Telex 64476 by A 7 BY and B 6264 – Bus Station , Lowther Street.

🚉 ♐ 44711.

🎫 The Old Town Hall, Greenmarket ♐ 25517.

♦London 317 – ♦Blackpool 95 – ♦Edinburgh 101 – ♦Glasgow 100 – ♦Leeds 124 – ♦Liverpool 127 – ♦Manchester 122 – ♦Newcastle-upon-Tyne 59.

Plan on next page

🏨 **Cumbrian,** Court Sq., CA1 1QY, ♐ 31951, Telex 64287 – 🛗 📺 🛁wc ☎ ⚑ 🛁 🅿 ⦿ *VISA*
BZ **u**
M 8.25/8.95 **st.** and a la carte ↕ 2.95 – ⌑ 5.25 – **70 rm** 37.00/52.00 **st.** – SB (weekends only) 54.00/58.00 **st.**

🏨 **Swallow Hilltop** (Swallow), London Rd, CA1 2PQ, SE : 1 m. on A 6 ♐ 29255, Telex 64292 – 🛗 📺 🛁wc ☎ ⚑ ⦿ *VISA*
by A 6 BZ
M (bar lunch)/dinner 8.75 **st.** and a la carte ↕ 3.40 – **110 rm** ⌑ 26.50/52.00 **st.** – SB 49.00/62.00 **st.**

🏨 **Ladbroke Crown and Mitre** (Ladbroke), English St., CA3 8HZ, ♐ 25491, Telex 64183 – 🛗 📺 🛁wc ☎ ⚑ 🛁 🅿 🛁 🅿 ⦿ *VISA*
BY **a**
M (bar lunch)/dinner 9.00 **st.** and a la carte ↕ 3.70 – ⌑ 6.00 – **94 rm** 30.00/42.00 **t.**

🏨 **Cumbria Park,** 32 Scotland Rd, CA3 9DG, N : 1 m. on A 7 ♐ 22887 – 🛁wc ⏀wc ⚑ 🛁 *VISA*. 🛉
by A 7 BY
closed 25 and 26 December – **M** *(closed Sunday dinner)* (bar lunch Monday to Saturday)/dinner 7.50 **st.** ↕ 2.50 – **35 rm** ⌑ 24.00/34.00 **t.**

   at Kingstown N : 3 m. at junction 44 of A 7 – BY – and M 6 – ✉ ☎ 0228 Carlisle :

🏨 **Crest** (Crest), Kingstown, CA4 0HR, ♐ 31201, Telex 64201 – 📺 🛁wc ☎ ⚑ 🛁 🅿 🛁 🅿 ⦿ *VISA*. 🛉
M approx. 11.50 **st.** – ⌑ 5.75 – **98 rm** 45.00/55.00 **st.** – SB (weekends only) 59.00 **st.**

   at Crosby-on-Eden NE : 4 ½ m. by A 7 – BY – on B 6264 – ✉ Carlisle – ☎ 022 873 Crosby-on-Eden :

❌❌ **Crosby Lodge** 🦢 with rm, CA6 4QZ, ♐ 618, ≤, « 18C country mansion », 🍴 – 🛁wc ⏀wc ⚑ 🛁 🅿 ⦿ *VISA*. 🛉
closed 24 December-21 January – **M** *(closed Sunday dinner)* 9.50/15.00 **t.** and a la carte ↕ 3.00 – **11 rm** ⌑ 36.50/58.00 **t.** – SB (weekends only) (October-March) 55.00 **st.**

   at Faugh E : 8 ¼ m. by A 69 – BY – ✉ Carlisle – ☎ 022 870 Hayton :

🏨 **String of Horses Inn,** Heads Nook, CA9 9EG, ♐ 297, « Elaborately furnished 17C inn », ↴ heated – 🍽 rest 📺 🛁wc ⏀wc ☎ ⚑ 🛁 🅿 ⦿ *VISA*. 🛉
M 11.75 **t.** (dinner) and a la carte ↕ 2.75 – **13 rm** ⌑ 37.00/64.00 **t.** – SB 43.50/69.35 **st.**

   at Wetheral SE : 6 ¼ m. by A 6 – BZ – on B 6233 – ✉ Carlisle – ☎ 0228 Wetheral :

🏨 **Crown** (Best Western), CA8 8BD, ♐ 61888, Telex 64175, 🍴 – 📺 🛁wc ☎ ⚑ 🛁 🅿 🛁 🅿 ⦿ *VISA*
M (bar lunch Saturday)/dinner 13.00 **t.** and a la carte ↕ 3.50 – **50 rm** ⌑ 44.00/64.00 **st.** – SB (weekends only) 63.00/67.00 **st.**

♨ **Killoran** 🦢, The Green, CA4 8ET, ♐ 60200, 🍴 – ⏀ ⚑
9 rm.

❌❌ **Fantails,** The Green, CA4 8ET, ♐ 60239 – ⚑ 🛁 🛁 ⦿ *VISA*
closed Sunday, Monday, February, 26 December and 1 January – **M** a la carte 6.85/14.00 **t.** ↕ 3.75.

133

CARLISLE

Botchergate .... **BZ**
Castle Street .... **BY 6**
English Street .... **BY 13**
Scotch Street .... **BY 19**

Annetwell Street .... **AY 2**

Bridge Street .... **AY 3**
Brunswick Street .... **BZ 4**
Caldcotes .... **AY 5**
Charlotte Street .... **AZ 7**
Chiswick Street .... **BY 8**
Church Street .... **AY 10**
Eden Bridge .... **BY 12**
Lonsdale Street .... **BY 14**
Lowther Street .... **BY 15**

Port Road .... **AY 16**
St. Aidan's Road .... **BY 17**
St. Nicholas Street .... **BZ 18**
Spencer Street .... **BY 20**
Tait Street .... **BZ 21**
Victoria Viaduct .... **ABZ 24**
West Tower Street .... **BY 26**
West Walls .... **ABY 27**
Wigton Road .... **AZ 29**

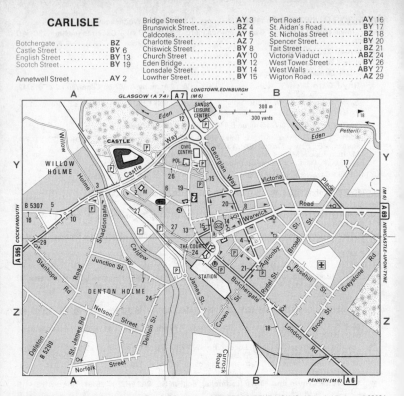

AUSTIN-ROVER-DAIMLER-JAGUAR Rosehill Estate ✆ 24387
CITROEN, SAAB Willowholme Estate ✆ 26617
COLT ✆ 27287
FIAT Church St., Caldewgate ✆ 25092
FORD Warwick Circus ✆ 24234
LADA Cecil St. ✆ 25051

MERCEDES-BENZ, VOLVO Victoria Viaduct ✆ 28234
NISSAN Lowther St. ✆ 31469
PEUGEOT-TALBOT Kingstown Estate ✆ 38444
RENAULT Church St. ✆ 22423
VAUXHALL-OPEL Viaduct Estate ✆ 29401
VOLVO Victoria Viaduct ✆ 28234
VW, AUDI-NSU Lowther St. ✆ 26104

CARLYON BAY Cornwall **403** F 33 – see St. Austell.

CARMARTHEN (CAERFYRDDIN) Dyfed **403** G 28 – pop. 13,860 – ECD : Thursday – ✆ 026 723 (4 and 5 fig.) or 0267 (6 fig.) – ⌐ Blaenycoed Rd ✆ 87214, NW : 4 m.

🇧 Lammas St. ✆ 231557 (summer only) – ◆London 220 – Fishguard 45 – ◆Swansea 27.

  🏨 **Ivy Bush Royal** (T.H.F.), 11-13 Spilman St., SA31 1LG, ✆ 235111, Telex 48520 – 🛗 📺 ⌐wc
    🛅wc ☎ 🅿 🕿 🔄 AE ⓪ VISA
    M 7.00/9.50 **st.** and a la carte ⌐ 2.95 – ⌐ 5.50 – **80 rm** 32.00/41.00 **st.**

  ✗ **Hoi San**, 15 Queen St., SA31 1JT, Chinese-Cantonese rest. – 🔄 AE ⓪ VISA
    closed 3 days at Christmas – **M** (restricted lunch) a la carte 5.85/13.50 **t.**

AUSTIN-ROVER, LAND-ROVER, SHERPA Pensarn Rd ✆ 5252
FIAT Pensarn ✆ 6633

FORD The Bridge ✆ 6482
HONDA, TOYOTA Priory St. ✆ 4171
NISSAN Penguin Court ✆ 7356

CARTMEL Cumbria **402** L 21 – see Grange-over-Sands.

CAS-BACH = Castleton.

CAS-BLAIDD = Wolf's Castle.

CASNEWYDD-AR-WYSG = Newport.

CASTELL NEWYDD EMLYN = Newcastle Emlyn.

CASTERTON Cumbria – see Kirkby Lonsdale.

134

CASTLE ACRE Norfolk 404 W 25 – pop. 777 – ✪ 076 05.

See : Priory★★ (ruins 11C - 14C) *AC*.

♦London 101 – King's Lynn 20 – ♦Norwich 31.

Hotels see : King's Lynn NW : 20 m., *Swaffam* S : 4 m.

CASTLE BOLTON North Yorks. 402 O 21 – pop. 57 – ☒ Leyburn – ✪ 0969 Wensleydale.

♦London 253 – Kendal 37 – ♦ Middlesbrough 43 – York 54.

✗ **Bolton Castle**, DL8 4ET, ✆ 23408 – ℗. ⏶ 🅰🅴 🆅🅸🆂🅰
closed dinner Tuesday-Wednesday November-May and Sunday, Monday and 2 to 17 February
– **M** 6.00/9.25 **t.** and lunch a la carte ⑂ 3.20.

CASTLE BROMWICH West Midlands 403 404 O 26 – see Birmingham.

CASTLE CARY Somerset 403 404 M 30 – pop. 2 ,599 – ECD : Thursday – ✪ 0963.

♦London 125 – ♦Bristol 28 – Taunton 31 – Yeovil 13.

🏨 George, Market Pl., BA7 7AH, ✆ 50761 – 📺 ⌷wc ㎡wc ☎ ℗. ⏶ 🅰🅴 ⓪ 🆅🅸🆂🅰
closed 24 to 26 December – **17 rm** ⌿ 25.00/35.00 **t.**

CASTLE COMBE Wilts. 403 404 N 29 The West Country G. – pop. 347 – ☒ Chippenham –
✪ 0249 – See : Site★★.

♦London 110 – ♦Bristol 23 – Chippenham 6.

🏨 **Manor House** (Best Western) 🛇, SN14 7HR, ✆ 782206, « Part 14C manor house in park »,
⏃ heated, 🛇, ☂, ⚒ – 📺 ℗. ⏶ 🅰🅴 ⓪ 🆅🅸🆂🅰
M 9.00/15.50 **t.** and a la carte – **33 rm** ⌿ 38.00/82.00 **st.** – SB (November-March) (except
Christmas week) 75.00/80.00 **st.**

🏠 Castle, SN14 7HN, ✆ 782461 – ⌷wc ㎡wc
9 rm.

CASTLE DONINGTON Leics. 402 403 404 P 25 – pop. 5 ,854 – ☒ ✪ 0332 Derby.

🛪 East Midlands, ✆ 810621, Telex 37543.

♦London 123 – ♦Birmingham 38 – ♦Leicester 23 – ♦Nottingham 13.

🏨 **Donington Manor,** High St., DE7 2PP, ✆ 810253, Telex 377208 – 📺 ⌷wc ㎡wc ☎ ℗. 🈁.
🅰🅴 ⓪ 🆅🅸🆂🅰 ⚒
closed 26 to 31 December – **M** a la carte 6.80/10.30 **st.** ⑂ 3.00 – **38 rm** ⌿ 28.00/46.00 **st.**

VAUXHALL-OPEL Station Rd ✆ 810221

CASTLETON Derbs. 402 403 404 O 23 – pop. 881 – ECD : Wednesday – ☒ Sheffield (South
Yorks.) – ✪ 0433 Hope Valley – Envir. : Blue John Caverns★ *AC*, W : 1 m.

♦London 173 – ♦Manchester 27 – ♦Sheffield 16.

🍴 **Ye Olde Nag's Head,** Cross St., S30 2WH, ✆ 20248 – ℗. ⏶ 🅰🅴 ⓪ 🆅🅸🆂🅰. ⚒
M a la carte 10.40/13.70 **t.** – **7 rm** ⌿ 14.50/32.00 **t.**

CASTLETON (CAS-BACH) Gwent 403 K 29 – see Cardiff (South Glam.).

CASTLETON North Yorks. 402 R 20 – ☒ Whitby – ✪ 0287.

♦London 258 – ♦Middlesbrough 18 – York 61.

🍴 **Moorlands,** High St., YO21 2DB, ✆ 60206, ⪡ – ㎡wc ℗
Easter-October – **M** (bar lunch Monday to Saturday)/dinner a la carte 10.50/12.50 **st.** – **10 rm**
⌿ 14.00/32.00 **st.** – SB 44.00/48.00 **st.**

CAVENDISH Suffolk 404 V 27 – pop. 973 – ☒ Sudbury – ✪ 0787 Glemsford.

♦London 66 – ♦Cambridge 29 – ♦Ipswich 28.

🍴🍴 **Alfonso's** with rm, The Green, CO10 8BB, ✆ 280372, Italian rest. – ㎡wc ℗. ⏶ 🅰🅴 ⓪. ⚒
M (closed Monday lunch and Sunday dinner) a la carte 8.40/12.00 **t.** ⑂ 3.50 – **5 rm**
⌿ 17.00/29.00 **st.**

CAWSAND Cornwall 403 H 33 – ☒ ✪ 0752 Plymouth.

♦London 253 – ♦Plymouth 10 – Truro 53.

🏠 Criterion 🛇, Garrett St., PL10 1PD, ✆ 822244, ⪡ Plymouth Sound, « Converted fishermen's
cottages » – 📺 ㎡wc
M (bar lunch)/dinner 9.50 **t.** ⑂ 2.65 – **8 rm** ⌿ 14.50/35.00 **t.**

CERNE ABBAS Dorset 403 404 M 31 The West Country G. – pop. 573 – ✪ 030 03.

See : Site★.

♦ London 137 – Dorchester 8 – Salisbury 49 – Yeovil 16.

🍴🍴 **Old Market House,** 25 Long St., DT2 7JG, ✆ 680 – ⏶ 🅰🅴
M 8.95/9.95 **t.** and a la carte ⑂ 3.25.

135

CHADLINGTON Oxon. [403] [404] P 28 – pop. 749 – ☎ 060 876.
♦London 74 – Cheltenham 32 – ♦Oxford 18 – Stratford-upon-Avon 25.

🏠 **Chadlington House,** OX7 3LZ, ☎ 437, 🌳 – 🛁wc 🚿wc 🅿. 💳 VISA. 🚫🐕
closed January and February – **M** (bar lunch)/dinner 10.50 **t.** 🍷 3.00 – **10 rm** ☕ 18.00/50.00 **t.** – SB 49.00/55.00 **st.**

CHAGFORD Devon [403] I 31 The West Country G. – pop. 1 ,400 – ECD : Wednesday – ☎ 064 73.
Envir. : Castle Drogo★ *AC*, NE : 2 m.
♦London 218 – Exeter 17 – ♦Plymouth 28.

🏠 ❀ **Gidleigh Park** 🐦, TQ13 8HH, NW : 2 m. by Gidleigh Rd ☎ 2367, ≤, « Country house atmosphere », 🌳, park – 📺 ☎ 🅿. 💳 AE VISA
M (booking essential) 15.00/24.00 **s.** and a la carte 🍷 4.50 – ☕ 4.50 – **12 rm** 60.00/110.00 **s.**
Spec. Salad of mixed lettuce and sautéed duck foie gras walnut oil dressing, Rack of English lamb with rosemary sauce, Apple tart with Devon cream.

🏠 **Teignworthy Country House** 🐦, Frenchbeer, TQ13 8EX, SW : 2 ½ m. by Fernworthy Rd, off Thornworthy Rd ☎ 3355, ≤, « Country house atmosphere », 🌳, park, 🎾 – 📺 🛁wc ☎ 🅿. 🚫🐕
M 19.50 **t.** (dinner) and a la carte 9.50/20.50 **t.** 🍷 4.00 – **9 rm** ☕ 42.50/67.00 **t.**

🏠 **Thornworthy House** 🐦, Thornworthy, TQ13 8EY, SW : 3 m. by Fernworthy Rd on Thornworthy Rd ☎ 3297, ≤, « Country house atmosphere », 🌳, park, 🎾 – 🛁wc 🅿
closed January-March – **M** (bar lunch)/dinner 10.00 **s.** – **5 rm** ☕ (dinner included) 30.00/52.00 **s.**

at Sandypark NE : 1 ½ m. – ✉ ☎ 064 73 Chagford :

🏠 **Mill End** 🐦, TQ13 8JN, on A 382 ☎ 2282, « Country house with water mill », 🎣, 🌳 – 📺 🛁wc ☎ 🚗 🅿. 💳 AE ⓓ VISA
closed 15 to 28 December – **M** (lunch by arrangement) 10.50/13.00 **t.** 🍷 3.50 – **16 rm** ☕ 38.50/60.00 **t.** – SB (November-March) 50.00/63.00 **st.**

🏠 **Great Tree** 🐦, Sandy Park, TQ13 8JS, on A 382 ☎ 2491, ≤, « Country house atmosphere », 🌳, park – 📺 🛁wc 🅿. 💳 AE ⓓ VISA
closed 27 December-31 January – **M** 6.50/12.50 **t.** 🍷 2.50 – **14 rm** ☕ 26.00/65.00 **t.** – SB (winter only) 50.00/65.00 **st.**

at Easton Cross NE : 1 ½ m. – ✉ ☎ 064 73 Chagford :

🏠 **Easton Court,** TQ13 8JL, on A 382 ☎ 3469, « 15C thatched house », 🌳 – 🛁wc 🚿wc 🅿. 💳 AE ⓓ VISA
M (bar lunch)/dinner 14.50 **t.** 🍷 3.00 – **8 rm** ☕ 25.00/48.00 **t.** – SB (November-May) (except Easter, Christmas and Bank Holidays) 54.00/58.00 **st.**

RENAULT New St. ☎ 2226

CHALE I.O.W. – see Wight (Isle of).

CHALFONT ST. GILES Bucks. [404] S 29 – pop. 5 ,216 – ☎ 024 07.
See : Milton's Cottage *AC*.
♦London 26 – Aylesbury 18.

🍴🍴 Le Relais, London Rd, HP8 4NJ, ☎ 2590 – 🅿. 💳 AE ⓓ VISA
closed Monday lunch and Sunday dinner.

AUSTIN-ROVER London Rd ☎ 3045

CHALFONT ST. PETER Bucks. [404] S 29 – pop. 19 ,447 – ☎ 024 07 Chalfont St. Giles.
♦London 22 – ♦Oxford 37.

🍺 Greyhound Inn, High St., SL9 9QL, ☎ 0753 (Gerrard's Cross) 883404 – 📺 🅿. 🚫🐕 – **7 rm**.

NISSAN High St. ☎ 028 13 (Gerrards Cross) 885581

CHALFORD Glos. [403] [404] N 28 – pop. 4 ,125 – ✉ Stroud – ☎ 0453 Brimscombe.
♦London 105 – ♦Bristol 40 – Gloucester 14 – Swindon 22.

🏠 **Springfield House,** London Rd, GL6 8NW, on A 419 ☎ 883555, 🌳 – 📺 🛁wc ☎ 🅿. 💳 AE ⓓ VISA
closed January – **M** 5.50/7.75 **st.** and a la carte 🍷 2.75 – **6 rm** ☕ 25.00/38.00 **st.** – SB (except Christmas) 44.00 **st.**

CHANCERY (RHYDGALED) Dyfed [403] H 26 – see Aberystwyth.

CHAPEL-EN-LE-FRITH Derbs. [402] [403] [404] O 24 – pop. 7 ,090 – ✉ Stockport (Cheshire) – ☎ 0298 – ⛳18 Manchester Rd ☎ 812118.
♦ London 176 – ♦ Manchester 22 – Derby 42 – ♦ Sheffield 24.

🍺 **King's Arms,** Market Place, SK12 6EN, ☎ 812105 – 📺 🅿. 💳 AE ⓓ VISA
M 6.00 **t.** and a la carte 🍷 1.80 – **11 rm** ☕ 12.50/23.00 **t.** – SB (except Bank Holidays) 30.00 **st.**

CHAPEL STILE Cumbria [402] K 20 – see Ambleside.

CHARD Somerset 403 L 31 The West Country G. – pop. 9,357 – ECD : Wednesday – ✆ 046 06.
Envir. : Ilminster★ St. Mary's Church★★, N ; 5 m. – Cricket St. Thomas Wildlife park★, E : 3 m. –
Forde Abbey★, SE : 4 m. – Barrington Court★AC, NE : 8 m. – Clapton Court Gardens★AC, E :
11 m.

♦London 180 – Exeter 31 – ♦Southampton 85 – Taunton 16.

  🏠 George, 15 Fore St., TA20 1PH, ✆ 3413 – 📺 ⇌wc �🛏wc 🅿. ⚲ – **20 rm**.

CHARLBURY Oxon. 403 404 P 28 – pop. 2,637 – ✆ 0608.

♦London 72 – ♦Birmingham 50 – ♦Oxford 15.

  🏨 **Bell at Charlbury** (Best Western), Church St., OX7 3AP, ✆ 810278 – 📺 ⇌wc ☎ 🅿. ◨ AE
    ⓪ VISA
    M 9.50/10.95 t. and a la carte ⑃ 3.65 – **13 rm** ⌁ 27.50/48.00 t. – SB (except Christmas week)
    56.00/83.00 st.

CHARLESTOWN Cornwall 403 F 33 – see St. Austell.

CHARLTON West Sussex 404 R 31 – see Chichester.

CHARMOUTH Dorset 403 L 31 – pop. 1,121 – ECD : Thursday – ✉ Bridport – ✆ 0297.

♦London 157 – Dorchester 22 – Exeter 31 – Taunton 27.

  🏠 **White House,** 2 Hillside, The Street, DT6 6PJ, ✆ 60411 – 📺 ⇌wc 🅿. ◨ VISA
    M 10.50 st. and a la carte ⑃ 2.80 – **7 rm** ⌁ 15.50/35.00 st. – SB 40.00/44.00 st.

  🏠 **Fernhill,** Fernhill, DT6 6BX, W : ¾ m. by A 35 on A 3052 ✆ 60492, ⊿ heated, 🐾 – ⇌wc
    🛏wc 🅿. ◨ VISA
    M (bar lunch)/dinner 9.25 t. and a la carte – **15 rm** ⌁ 18.00/48.00 t. – SB 45.00/57.00 st.

  ↑ **Newlands House,** Stonebarrow Lane, DT6 6RA, ✆ 60212, 🐾 – 📺 ⇌wc 🛏wc 🅿
    February-September – **9 rm** ⌁ 11.00/28.00 st.

  ↑ **Hensleigh,** Lower Sea Lane, Bridport, DT6 6LW, ✆ 60830 – 📺 ⇌wc 🛏wc 🅿
    March-October – **10 rm** ⌁ 12.00/26.00 st.

  ↑ **Sea Horse,** Higher Sea Lane, DT6 6BB, ✆ 60414, ≤, 🐾 – ⇌wc 🅿
    April-October – **10 rm** ⌁ 11.50/31.50 t.

CHARNOCK RICHARD Lancs. 402 404 M 23 – pop. 2,000 – ECD : Wednesday – ✆ 0257
Coppull – 🛦 Duxbury Park, Chorley ✆ 025 72 (Chorley) 65380, E : 2 m.

♦London 215 – ♦Liverpool 26 – ♦Manchester 24 – Preston 10.

  🏨 **TraveLodge** (T.H.F.) without rest., Mill Lane, PR7 5LR, on M 6 ✆ 791746, Telex 67315 – 📺
    ⇌wc ☎ ⓖ 🅿. ◨ AE ⓪ VISA
    103 rm 29.00/37.00 st.

CHARTHAM HATCH Kent 404 X 30 – see Canterbury.

CHEDINGTON Dorset – pop. 96 – ✉ Beaminster – ✆ 093 589 Corscombe.

♦ London 148 – Dorchester 17 – Taunton 25.

  🏨 Chedington Court ⑊, DT8 3HY, ✆ 265, ≤ countryside, « Country house in landscaped gar-
    dens », park – 📺 ⇌wc ☎ 🅿. ⚲. ⅍ – **8 rm**.

CHELMSFORD Essex 404 V 28 – pop. 91,109 – ECD : Wednesday – ✆ 0245.

♦London 33 – ♦Cambridge 46 – ♦Ipswich 40 – Southend-on-Sea 19.

  🏨 South Lodge (Best Western), 196 New London Rd, CM2 0AR, ✆ 264564, Telex 99452, 🐾 –
    📺 ⇌wc ☎ 🅿. ⚲ – **41 rm**.

  🏠 **County,** 29 Rainsford Rd, CM1 2QA, ✆ 266911 – 📺 ⇌wc 🛏wc ☎ 🅿. ◨ AE ⓪ VISA
    closed 27 to 31 December – **M** 6.50/8.00 t. and a la carte ⑃ 3.95 – **52 rm** ⌁ 23.00/57.50 t.

  ↑ **Oaklands,** 240 Springfield Rd, CM2 6BP, ✆ 352004, 🐾 – 🛏wc 🅿. ⅍
    8 rm ⌁ 14.00/28.00 s.

  ↑ **Tanunda,** 217-219 New London Rd, CM2 0AJ, ✆ 354295, 🐾 – 📺 ⇌wc 🛏wc 🅿
    closed 1 week at Christmas – **20 rm** ⌁ 16.00/32.00 st.

    at Great Baddow SE : 3 m. by A 130 – ✉ ✆ 0245 Chelmsford :

  XXX **Pontlands Park** ⑊ with rm, West Hanningfield Rd, CM2 8HR, ✆ 76444, Telex 995411, ≤,
    ◨, 🐾, park – 📺 ⇌wc ☎ 🅿. ⚲. ◨ AE ⓪ VISA ⅍
    closed first week January – **M** (closed lunch Monday and Saturday and Sunday dinner)
    9.00/13.00 t. and a la carte ⑃ 3.50 – ⌁ 5.00 – **8 rm** 38.00/65.00 st. – SB (weekends only)
    82.50 st.

    at High Easter NW : 10 m. by A 414 and A 1060 – ✉ Chelmsford – ✆ 024 531 Good Easter :

  XX **Punch Bowl,** CM1 4QW, ✆ 222 – 🅿. ◨ AE ⓪ VISA
    closed Sunday dinner and Monday – **M** (lunch by arrangement Tuesday to Saturday) 8.00/15.50
    t. and a la carte ⑃ 3.00.

AUSTIN-ROVER, RENAULT 74 Main Rd, Broomfield   RENAULT Southend Rd, Sandon ✆ 71113
✆ 440571   VAUXHALL Eastern Approach ✆ 466333
CITROEN, LANCIA Galley Wood ✆ 268366   VAUXHALL-OPEL Moulsham Lodge ✆ 351611
FORD 39 Robjohns Rd ✆ 264111   VOLVO Colchester Rd, Springfield ✆ 468151
NISSAN, PEUGEOT-TALBOT Bridge St. ✆ 421233

CHELTENHAM Glos. 🗺️403 404 N 28 – pop. 87,188 – ECD : Wednesday and Saturday – ✆ 0242.

See : Pittville Park★ A – Municipal Art Gallery and Museum★ B **M.**

Envir. : Elkstone (Parish Church : doorway★ and arches★ 12C) SE : 7 m. by A 435 A – Sudeley Castle★ (12C - 15C) *AC*, NE : 6 m. by A 46. A.

🛫 Cleeve Hill ✆ 024 267 (Bishop's Cleeve) 2025, N : 3 m. by A 46. A.

🅑 Municipal Offices, The Promenade ✆ 522878.

◆London 99 – ◆Birmingham 48 – ◆Bristol 40 – Gloucester 9 – ◆Oxford 43.

Plan opposite

🏨 **Queen's** (T.H.F.), Promenade, GL50 1NN, ✆ 514724, Telex 43381, 🍴 – 📶 📺 🅿️ 🔥 🚗 🆎 ① 🆅🆂🅰️   **B n**
  M 8.95/12.50 **st.** and a la carte ₰ 2.90 – ⊑ 5.50 – **77 rm** 46.00/57.00 **st.**

🏨 **Golden Valley Thistle** (Thistle), Gloucester Rd, GL51 0TS, W : 2 m. on A 40 ✆ 32691, Telex 43410, 🍴 – 📶 📺 🅿️ 🔥 🚗 🆎 🆅🆂🅰️   by A 40   A
  M 8.25/10.75 **t.** and a la carte ₰ 3.40 – ⊑ 5.50 – **99 rm** 45.00/70.00 **t.**

🏨 **Carlton,** Parabola Rd, GL50 3AQ, ✆ 514453, 🍴 – 📶 📺 🛏️wc 🅿️ 🔥 🚗 🆎 ① 🆅🆂🅰️
  M 7.00/9.00 **st.** and a la carte – **49 rm** 33.50/48.00 **st.** – SB (weekends only) 51.00 **st.**
                                                                          B r

🏨 **Wyastone,** Parabola Rd, GL50 3BG, ✆ 45549 – 📺 🛏️wc 🛏️wc 🍴 🅿️ 🔥 🆎 ① 🆅🆂🅰️ 🚭
  M *(closed Sunday to non-residents)* 8.00 **st.** and a la carte ₰ 3.15 – ⊑ 3.00 – **13 rm**
  30.00/44.00 **st.** – SB 55.00/60.00 **st.**   **B e**

🛏️ **Abbottslee,** Priory Walk, GL52 6DU, ✆ 515255 – 🅿️ 🚭   **C a**
  closed 3 days at Christmas – **6 rm** ⊑ 10.00/19.00 **s.**

🛏️ **Willoughby,** 1 Suffolk Sq., GL50 2DR, ✆ 522798, 🍴 – 🛏️wc 🅿️   **B o**
  closed 2 weeks Christmas and New Year – **9 rm** ⊑ 12.50/24.50 **st.**

🛏️ **Hollington House,** 115 Hales Rd, GL52 6ST, ✆ 519718 – 📺 🛏️wc 🅿️   **A s**
  6 rm ⊑ 14.00/30.00 **t.**

🍴🍴 **Twelve,** 12 Suffolk Par., GL50 2AB, ✆ 584544 – 🔦 🆅🆂🅰️   **B i**
  closed Sunday dinner, Monday and first 2 weeks January – **M** 6.25 **t.** (lunch) and a la carte
  10.35/11.65 **t.** ₰ 2.40.

🍴 **La Ciboulette,** 24 Suffolk Rd, GL50 2AQ, ✆ 573449 – 🔦 🆎 🆅🆂🅰️   **B c**
  closed Sunday, Monday, Easter week, 3 weeks August and 1 week at Christmas – **M** 8.20 **t.**
  (lunch) and a la carte 11.90/18.80 **t.** ₰ 2.50.

🍴 **Mayflower,** 32 Clarence St., GL50 3NX, ✆ 522426, Chinese rest. – 🆎 ①   **C e**
  closed Sunday lunch and Christmas – **M** 9.50 **t.** (dinner) and a la carte.

at Southam NE : 3 m. on A 46 – A – ✉️ ✆ 0242 Cheltenham :

🏨 **De La Bere** (Best Western), GL52 3NH, ✆ 37771, Telex 43232, « Tudor manor house », ⏚ heated, 🍴, park, 🎾 squash – 📺 🅿️ 🔥 🆎 ① 🆅🆂🅰️
  M 8.00/12.00 **t.** and a la carte ₰ 2.90 – ⊑ 4.00 – **31 rm** 32.00/70.00 **st.** – SB (except Christmas)
  70.00/80.00 **st.**

at Cleeve Hill NE : 4 m. on A 46 – A – ✉️ Cheltenham – ✆ 024 267 Bishop's Cleeve :

🏨 **Rising Sun,** GL52 3PX, ✆ 2002, ≤, 🍴 – 📺 🛏️wc 🛏️wc 🅿️ 🚭
  13 rm.

🍴🍴🍴 **Malvern View** with rm, GL52 3PR, ✆ 2017, ≤ Malvern hills, 🍴 – 📺 🛏️wc 🛏️wc 🔦 🆅🆂🅰️ 🚭
  closed Christmas-New Year – **M** *(closed Sunday to non - residents)* (dinner only) 13.50 **st.**
  ₰ 3.75 – **6 rm** ⊑ 28.50/39.50 **st.** – SB (weekends only) (October-March) 57.50 **st.**

at Andoversford SE : 6 m. on A 40 – A – ✉️ ✆ 0242 Cheltenham :

🛏️ **Old Cold Comfort,** Kilkenny, GL54 4LR, SW : 1 ½ m. on A 436 ✆ 820349, 🍴 – 🅿️ 🚭
  6 rm ⊑ 20.00/28.00 **st.**

at Shurdington SW : 3 ¾ m. on A 46 – A – ✉️ ✆ 0242 Cheltenham :

🏨 **Greenway** 🦢, GL51 5UG, ✆ 862352, Telex 437216, ≤, « Country house, gardens », park –
  📺 🛏️wc 🅿️ 🔦 🆎 ① 🆅🆂🅰️ 🚭
  M *(closed lunch Saturday and Bank Holiday Mondays)* (Sunday dinner residents only)
  13.00/20.00 **st.** ₰ 2.75 – ⊑ 3.00 – **11 rm** 55.00/90.00 **t.** – SB (weekends only) (winter only)
  52.00/88.00 **st.**

ALFA-ROMEO High St, Prestbury ✆ 44247
AUSTIN-ROVER Princess Elizabeth Way ✆ 520441
CITROEN, PEUGEOT-TALBOT 16/28 Bath Rd ✆ 515391
COLT 60/66 Fairview Rd ✆ 513880
FORD 71/93 Winchcombe St. ✆ 527061
HONDA 172 Leckhampton Rd ✆ 524348
LADA, YUGO, ALFA-ROMEO Stoke Orchard ✆ 024 268 (Combe Hill) 428
LANCIA Swindon Rd ✆ 32167
MAZDA Bath Rd ✆ 523879

PEUGEOT-TALBOT Charlton Kings ✆ 521131
RENAULT Montpellier Spa Rd ✆ 521651
RENAULT Montpellier Spa Rd ✆ 521121
ROLLS ROYCE-BENTLEY Rutherford Way ✆ 515374
SAAB, SUZUKI High St., Prestbury ✆ 44247
TOYOTA 38 Suffolk Rd ✆ 527778
VAUXHALL-OPEL 379 High St. ✆ 522666
VAUXHALL-OPEL Albion St. ✆ 525252
VOLVO Bishops Cleeve ✆ 674851
VW, AUDI North St. ✆ 515301

CHELTENHAM

High Street . . . . **BC**
Pittville Street . . . . **C** 26
Portland Street . . . . **C** 27
Promenade (The) . . . . **BC** 28
Winchcombe Street . . . . . . **C** 38

Ambrose Street . . . . **C** 2
Berkeley Street . . . . **C** 4
Clarence Road . . . . **C** 5

Clarence Street . . . . **BC** 6
Crescent Terrace . . . . **B** 7
Deep Street . . . . **A** 9
Dunalley Street . . . . **C** 10
Henrietta Street . . . . **C** 13
High Street
 (PRESTBURY) . . . . **A** 14
Keynsham Road . . . . **C** 15
Knapp Road . . . . **B** 16
Montpellier Avenue . . . . . . **B** 17
Montpellier Walk . . . . **C** 18

Norwood Road . . . . **B** 21
Oriel Road . . . . **B** 22
Parabola Road . . . . **B** 23
Park (The) . . . . **B** 24
Park Place . . . . **C** 25
Regent Street . . . . **C** 29
Royal Well Road . . . . **BC** 30
St. George's Place . . . . **B** 32
St. Margaret's Road . . . . . . **C** 33
Sandford Mill Road . . . . . . **C** 34
Sandford Terrace . . . . **C** 35
Thatcham Lane . . . . **A** 36

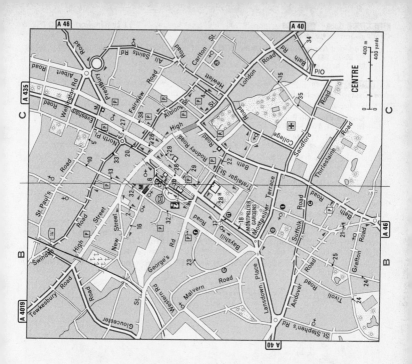

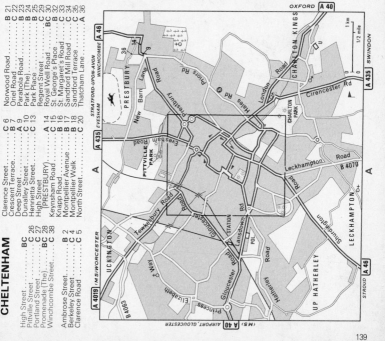

CHENIES Bucks. 404 S 28 – pop. 2,240 – ECD : Thursday – ⊠ Rickmansworth – ☎ 092 78
Chorleywood – ♦London 30 – Aylesbury 18 – Watford 7.

🏛 **Bedford Arms Thistle** (Thistle), WB3 6EQ, ℰ 3301, Telex 893939, « 16C inn », ⇗ – 📺 🅿.
🔄 AE ⓪ VISA
M a la carte 15.50/17.50 t. ᵬ 5.00 – ⇌ 6.50 – **10 rm** 45.50/64.50 t.

CHEPSTOW Gwent 403 404 M 29 – pop. 9,039 – ECD : Wednesday – ☎ 029 12.

See : Castle★ (stronghold) *AC*.

🛈 The Gatehouse, High St. ℰ 3772 (summer only) – ♦London 131 – ♦Bristol 17 – ♦Cardiff 28 – Gloucester 34.

🏠 **Castle View**, 16 Bridge St., NP6 5EZ, ℰ 70349, ⇗ – 📺 🔄wc ☎. 🔄 AE ⓪ VISA
M 10.50 st. ᵬ 3.50 – **10 rm** ⇌ 27.50/43.50 st. – SB 52.00/57.00 st.

🏠 **George** (T.H.F.), Moor St., NP6 5DB, ℰ 5363 – 📺 🔄wc ☜ 🅿. 🔄 AE ⓪ VISA
M (buffet lunch)/dinner 8.95 st. and a la carte ᵬ 2.70 – ⇌ 5.50 – **15 rm** 35.00/43.00 st.

AUSTIN-ROVER Station Rd ℰ 3159
FORD Newport Rd ℰ 8155
PEUGEOT, TALBOT Tutshill ℰ 3131
VAUXHALL-OPEL St. Lawrence Rd ℰ 3889

CHESTER Cheshire 402 403 L 24 – pop. 80,154 – ECD : Wednesday – ☎ 0244.

See : Cathedral★★ 14C-16C (choir stalls and misericords★★) – St. John's Church★ 12C **D** – The
Rows★ – City Walls★ – Grosvenor Museum (Roman gallery★) **M1**.

Envir. : Upton (Chester Zoo★★) *AC*, N : 3 m. by A 5116.

🅘 Upton-by-Chester, Upton Lane ℰ 381183, by A 5116 – 🅘 Vicars Cross, Littleton ℰ 335174, E :
2 m. by A 51 – 🅘 Helsby, Tower's Lane ℰ 092 82 (Helsby) 2021, NE : 8 m. by A 56 – 🅘 Ellesmere
Port, Chester Rd ℰ 051 (Liverpool) 339 7689, N : 9 m. by A 5116 on A 41.

🛈 Town Hall, Northgate St. ℰ 40144 ext 2111/2250 – Chester Visitor Centre, Vicars Lane ℰ 313126.

♦London 207 – Birkenhead 17 – ♦Birmingham 91 – ♦Liverpool 119 – ♦Manchester 40 – Preston 52 – ♦Sheffield 76
– ♦Stoke-on-Trent 38.

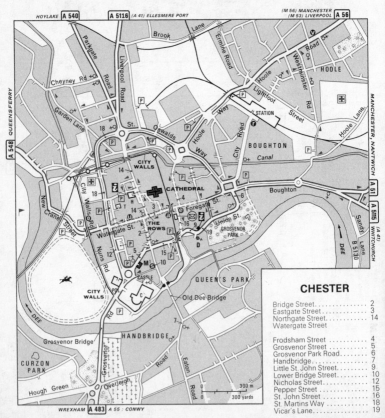

CHESTER

Bridge Street............. 2
Eastgate Street........... 3
Northgate Street.......... 14
Watergate Street

Frodsham Street........... 4
Grosvenor Street.......... 5
Grosvenor Park Road....... 6
Handbridge................ 7
Little St. John Street.... 9
Lower Bridge Street....... 10
Nicholas Street........... 12
Pepper Street............. 15
St. John Street........... 16
St. Martins Way........... 18
Vicar's Lane.............. 19

🏛 **Chester Grosvenor,** Eastgate St., CH1 1LT, ℰ 24024, Telex 61240 – 🕭 🗏 rest 📺 ☎ ໒ **P**
    a
🏛 🔼 **Æ ⑩ VISA** ⅏
closed 25 and 26 December – **M** 7.95/13.50 **t.** and a la carte ᐅ 3.60 – ⌒ 7.50 – **108 rm**
52.00/100.00 **t.**, **5 suites** 125.00/200.00 **t.** – SB (weekends only) 85.00/95.00 **st.**

🏛 **Queen** (T.H.F.), City Rd, CH3 3AH, ℰ 28341, Telex 617101, 🚗 – 🕭 📺 ⑩ 🔼 🔼 **Æ ⑩ VISA** ⅍
    M (bar lunch Saturday) 7.00/9.00 **st.** and a la carte ᐅ 2.70 – ⌒ 5.50 – **91 rm** 37.00/47.00 **st.**

🏛 **Mollington Banastre** (Best Western), Parkgate Rd, CH16NN, NW : 2 m. on A 540
    ℰ 851471, Telex 61686 – 🕭 📺 ⤳wc ☜ **P** 🔼 🔼 **Æ ⑩ VISA**
    M 11.50 **t.** (dinner) and a la carte ᐅ 3.85 – **70 rm** ⌒ 48.00/65.00 **st.** – SB 60.00/90.00 **st.**

🏛 **Post House** (T.H.F.), Wrexham Rd, CH4 9DL, S : 2 m. on A 483 ℰ 674111, Telex 61450, 🚗 –
    📺 ⤳wc ☜ **P** 🔼 🔼 **Æ ⑩ VISA**
    M (buffet lunch Monday to Saturday)/dinner 9.50 **st.** and a la carte ᐅ 2.65 – ⌒ 5.50 – **62 rm**
    38.00/47.50 **st.**, **1 suite**.

🏛 **Blossoms,** St. John St., CH1 1HL, ℰ 23186, Telex 61113 – 🕭 📺 ⤳wc ☜ **P** 🔼 🔼 **Æ ⑩**
    VISA
    e
    M (carving lunch) 8.00/9.00 **st.** and a la carte – **71 rm** ⌒ 40.00/66.00 **st.**, **1 suite** 90.00 **st.** – SB
    (except Christmas and New Year) 56.00/68.00 **st.**

🏠 **Chester Court,** 48 Hoole Rd, CH2 3NL, ℰ 20779 – 📺 ⤳wc ╫wc **P** 🔼 🔼 **Æ ⑩ VISA**
    v
    M (dinner only) 9.50 **t.** ᐅ 3.50 – **20 rm** ⌒ 24.00/34.00 **t.**

🏠 **City Walls,** City Walls Rd, CH1 2LU, ℰ 313416 – 🕭 📺 ⤳wc. 🔼 **VISA**
    o
    M *(closed Sunday and Monday)* (dinner only)(carving table) 8.00 **t.** and a la carte ᐅ 2.50 – ⌒
    3.00 – **17 rm** 24.00/33.00 **t.** – SB (weekdays only) (September-May except Christmas)
    40.50/45.00 **st.**

🏠 **Gloster Lodge** without rest., 44 Hoole Rd, CH2 3NL, ℰ 48410 – 📺 ⤳wc **P**
    v
    closed 24 to 27 December – **8 rm** ⌒ 19.50/30.00 **st.**

⚐ **Ye Olde King's Head,** 48-50 Lower Bridge St., CH1 1RS, ℰ 24855, « 16C inn » – 🔼 **Æ ⑩**
    VISA ⅍
    s
    closed 25 to 27 December – **M** 4.50/6.00 **t.** ᐅ 2.80 – **11 rm** ⌒ 14.00/27.00 **t.** – SB 36.00/42.00 **st.**

⚐ **Redland,** 64 Hough Green, CH4 8JY, SW : 1 m. on A 549 ℰ 671024, « Victorian town house »
    – ╫wc **P**.
    closed January and February – **10 rm** ⌒ 13.00/29.00 **st.**

⚐ **Green Bough,** 60 Hoole Rd, CH2 3NL, ℰ 26241 – 📺 ⤳wc ╫wc **P** 🔼 **VISA** ⅍
    i
    closed first 2 weeks March and 23 December-1 January – **11 rm** ⌒ 14.50/30.00 **t.**

✗ **Pippa's,** 58 Watergate St., CH1 2LA, ℰ 313721 – 🔼 **Æ ⑩ VISA**
    u
    closed Sunday, 1 week at Christmas and Bank Holiday Mondays – **M** 10.50 **t.** and a la carte
    ᐅ 3.50.

at Backford Cross N : 4 ½ m. by A 5116 junction A 41 and A 5117 – ⊠ Chester – ✆ 0244
Great Mollington :

🏛 **Ladbroke** (Ladbroke), CH1 6PE, ℰ 851551, Telex 61552 – 📺 ⤳wc ☎ ໒ **P** 🔼 🔼 **Æ ⑩**
    VISA
    M *(closed Saturday lunch)* (buffet lunch)/dinner 10.95 **t.** ᐅ 4.00 – ⌒ 6.00 – **121 rm** 44.25/54.00 **t.**,
    1 suite 54.25/64.00 **t.** – SB (weekends only) 59.00/65.00 **st.**

at Christleton E : 2 m. on A 41 – ⊠ ✆ 0244 Chester :

🏛 **Abbots Well** (Embassy), Whitchurch Rd, CH3 5QL, ℰ 332121, Telex 61561, 🚗 – 📺 ⤳wc
    ☜ **P** 🔼 🔼 **Æ ⑩ VISA** ⅍
    M (bar lunch Saturday) 7.00/10.00 **st.** and a la carte ᐅ 2.80 – ⌒ 5.00 – **127 rm** 38.50/49.50 **st.** –
    SB 59.00 **st.**

MICHELIN Branch, Sandycroft Industrial Estate, Glendale Av., Sandycroft, Deeside, CH5 2QP, ℰ
537373 by A 548

AUSTIN-ROVER Victoria Rd ℰ 381246
BMW Chester Rd ℰ 311404
CITROEN Border House ℰ 672977
COLT Chester Rd ℰ 534347
DAIMLER-JAGUAR, ROLLS ROYCE 8 Russell St. ℰ
25262
FIAT Sealand Rd ℰ 374440
FORD Bridge Gate ℰ 20444
FORD Station Rd ℰ 813414

NISSAN Hamilton Pl. ℰ 317661
PEUGEOT-TALBOT Station Rd, Queensferry ℰ
813414
SAAB Western Av. ℰ 375744
TOYOTA Welsh Rd ℰ 813633
VAUXHALL-OPEL Broughton ℰ 24611
VAUXHALL-OPEL 21/25 Garden Lane ℰ 46955
VAUXHALL-OPEL, BEDFORD Parkgate Rd ℰ 372666
VOLVO, MERCEDES-BENZ 36 Tarvin Rd ℰ 47441

CHESTERFIELD Derbs. **402 403 404** 🄿 24 – pop. 73 ,352 – ECD : Wednesday – ✆ 0246.

Envir. : Chatsworth★★★ : site★★, house★★★ (Renaissance), garden★★★ *AC*, W : 7 m. – Hardwick
Hall★★ 16C (Tapestries and embroideries★★) *AC*, SE : 8 m. – Bolsover Castle★ (17C) *AC*, E : 6 m. –
Worksop (Priory Church : Norman nave★) NE : 14 m.

🄻🄸 Tapton Park, Murray House, Crow Lane, Tapton ℰ 73887.

🄸 The Peacock Tourist Information and Heritage Centre, Low Pavement ℰ 207777 and 207778.

◆London 152 – Derby 24 – ◆Nottingham 25 – ◆Sheffield 12.

🏛 **Chesterfield** (Best Western), Malkin St., S41 7UA, ℰ 71141, Telex 547492 – 🕭 📺 ☎ 🚗
    P 🔼 🔼 **Æ ⑩ VISA** ⅍
    M 7.95 **t.** and a la carte ᐅ 2.85 – **61 rm** ⌒ 35.00/54.00 **t.** – SB (weekends only) 47.50/55.00 **st.**

🏠 **Portland,** West Bars, S40 1AY, ℰ 34502 – 📺 ⤳wc ☜ **P** 🔼 ⑩ **VISA**
    M a la carte 6.90/10.50 **t.** ᐅ 2.75 – **24 rm** ⌒ 23.00/40.00 **t.** – SB (weekends only) 40.00 **st.**

CHESTERFIELD

AUSTIN-ROVER 221 Sheffield Rd ℰ 77241
CITROEN, HONDA, AUDI Sheffield Rd ℰ 451611
FIAT 300 Northwingfield Rd ℰ 850686
FORD Chatsworth Rd ℰ 76341
NISSAN Ringwood Rd ℰ 77386
OPEL, FIAT Chesterfield Rd, Staveley ℰ 473286
PEUGEOT-TALBOT, SIMCA 361 Sheffield Rd ℰ 450383

PORSCHE, AUDI-VW Broombank Rd ℰ 451611
RENAULT Chesterfield Rd ℰ 473286
SAAB Sheffield Rd ℰ 451800
VAUXHALL 464 Chatsworth Rd ℰ 79201
VOLVO Whittington Moor ℰ 453655

CHESTER-LE-STREET Durham 401 402 P 19 – pop. 34,776 – ECD : Wednesday – ☎ 0385.

Envir. : Lumley Castle★ (14C), E : 1 m. – Beamish (North of England open Air Museum★) *AC*, NW : 3 m – ◆London 275 – Durham 7 – ◆Newcastle-upon-Tyne 8.

🏠 **Lumley Castle,** DH3 4NX, E : 1 m. on B 1284 ℰ 891111, Telex 537433, « 13C castle », 🐎, park – 📺 📶wc 📶wc ☎ 🅿. 🅰. 🔼 🅰🅴 ⑩ *VISA*
M 7.25/10.00 st. and a la carte ≬ 3.75 – **54 rm** ⥮ 37.50/72.00 st., **1 suite** 99.00 st. – SB (weekends only) 32.00/50.00 st.

MICHELIN Branch, Drum Rd, DH3 2AF, ℰ 091 (Tyneside) 410 7762

AUSTIN-ROVER Newcastle Rd ℰ 882267
COLT Picktree Lane ℰ 882761
FIAT Peton Rd ℰ 881813

FORD 187 Front St. ℰ 884221
RENAULT Durham Rd, Birtley ℰ (091) 4103485
VAUXHALL Hopgarth ℰ 886111

CHESTERTON Oxon. 403 404 Q 28 – pop. 1,120 – ✉ ☎ 0869 Bicester.

◆London 65 – Northampton 33 – ◆Oxford 13.

XX **Woods,** Bignell View, OX6 8UE, on A 4095 ℰ 241444, 🐎 – 🅿. 🔼 🅰🅴 ⑩ *VISA*
closed Saturday lunch, Sunday dinner and Monday – **M** 17.75 t. ≬ 2.50.

CHICHESTER West Sussex 404 R 31 – pop. 26,050 – ECD : Thursday – ☎ 0243.

See : Cathedral★ 11C-15C BZ **A** – Market Cross★ BZ **B** – Envir. : Fishbourne Roman Palace (mosaics★) *AC* W : 2 m. AZ **R** – Goodwood House★ (18C) *AC*, NE : 4 m. by A 27 AY and A 285.

🛈 The Council House, St. Peter's Market, West St. ℰ 775888.

◆London 69 – ◆Brighton 31 – ◆Portsmouth 18 – ◆Southampton 30.

CHICHESTER

East Street	BZ
North Street	BYZ
South Street	BZ
Birdham Road	AZ 2
Bognor Road	AZ 3
Chapel Street	BY 6
Chichester Arundel Road	AY 7

Fishbourne Road	AZ 8
Florence Road	AZ 10
Hornet (The)	BZ 12
Kingsham Road	BZ 13
Lavant Road	AY 14
Little London	BY 15
Market Road	BZ 16
Northgate	BY 17
North Pallant	BZ 19
Priory Lane	BY 20
St. James's	AZ 21

St. John's Street	BZ 23
St. Martin's Square	BY 24
St. Pancras	BY 25
St. Paul's Road	BY 27
Sherborne Road	AZ 28
Southgate	BZ 29
South Pallant	BZ 31
Spitalfield Lane	BY 32
Stockbridge Road	AZ 33
Tower Street	BY 35
Westhampnett Road	AYZ 36

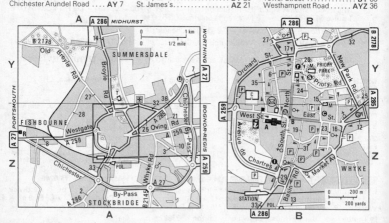

🏠 **Dolphin and Anchor** (T.H.F.), West St., PO19 1QE, ℰ 785121 – 📺 📶wc ☎. 🅰. 🔼 🅰🅴 ⑩ *VISA*
M 7.95/9.25 t. and a la carte ≬ 2.75 – ⥮ 5.50 – **54 rm** 38.50/49.50 st.
BZ **a**

🏠 **Chichester Lodge,** Westhampnett Roundabout, PO19 4UL, on A 27 ℰ 786351, 🐎 – 📺 📶wc 📶 🅿. 🅰. 🔼 🅰🅴 *VISA*
closed Christmas – **M** 8.00/10.00 t. and a la carte ≬ 2.90 – **43 rm** ⥮ 40.00/50.00 t. – SB 73.00/79.00 st.
AY **u**

142

🏠 **Bedford** without rest., Southgate, PO19 1DP, ☎ 785766 – 📺 ⒨. 🅿 🅰🅴 ⓪ 𝗩𝗜𝗦𝗔   BZ **i**
27 rm ⥮ 17.50/35.00 **st.**

🏠 **Ship**, North St., PO19 1NH, ☎ 782028, Telex 957141 – 🔣 📺 ⌂wc ☎ 🅿 🅰🅴 ⓪ 𝗩𝗜𝗦𝗔. ⚡
M (carving lunch) 7.00/8.50 **t.** and a la carte – **36 rm** ⥮ 22.00/44.00 **t.** – SB (except Bank
Holidays) 54.00/56.00 **st.**   BY **r**

XX **Clinchs'** with rm, 4 Guildhall St., PO19 1NJ, ☎ 789915, « Tastefully furnished town house »
– 📺 ⌂wc ⒨wc ☎ 🅿 🅰🅴 ⓪ 𝗩𝗜𝗦𝗔. ⚡   BY **s**
M (closed Sunday dinner) (dinner only) 13.50 **t.** ⅃ 3.75 – **7 rm** ⥮ 40.00/50.00 **st.**

XX **Christopher's**, 149 St. Pancras, PO19 1SH, ☎ 788724 – 🅰🅴 ⓪ 𝗩𝗜𝗦𝗔   BZ **e**
closed Sunday, Monday, 3 weeks October and 1 week at Christmas – **M** 5.25/10.50 **t.** and a la
carte ⅃ 3.60.

XX **Little London**, 38 Little London, PO19 1PL, ☎ 784899 – 🅰🅴 ⓪ 𝗩𝗜𝗦𝗔   BZ **c**
closed Sunday and Monday – **M** 5.95/8.90 **t.** and a la carte ⅃ 3.10.

at Chilgrove N : 6 ½ m. by A 286 – AY – on B 2141 – ✉ Chichester – ☎ 024 359 East
Marden :

XX **White Horse Inn**, 1 High St., PO18 9HX, ☎ 219 – 🅿 🅰🅴 ⓪ 𝗩𝗜𝗦𝗔
closed Sunday, Monday, February and last week October – **M** 11.95/14.95 **t.** ⅃ 2.75.

at Charlton N : 6 ¼ m. by A 286 – AY – ✉ Chichester – ☎ 024 363 Singleton :

🏡 **Woodstock House**, PO18 0HU, ☎ 666, 🚗 – ⌂wc ⒨wc 🅿 ⚡
March-October – **M** (dinner only) 9.00 ⅃ 3.00 – **11 rm** ⥮ 16.00/38.00 **t.** – SB 48.00/56.00 **st.**

at Goodwood NE : 3 ½ m. by A 27 AY on East Dean Rd – ✉ ☎ 0243 Chichester :

🏠 **Goodwood Park** (Best Western), PO18 0QB, ☎ 775537, Telex 869173, 🚗 – 📺 ⌂wc ☎ ♿
🅿 🅰🅴 ⓪ 𝗩𝗜𝗦𝗔
M 9.50/12.50 **t.** and a la carte ⅃ 2.80 – ⥮ 4.95 – **50 rm** 43.50/55.50 **st.**, **5 suites** 80.00 **st.** – SB
(weekends only) 58.00/70.00 **st.**

at Bosham W : 4 m. by A 27 – AZ – ✉ ☎ 0243 Chichester :

🏠 **Millstream** (Best Western), Bosham Lane, PO18 8HL, ☎ 573234, « Tasteful decor », 🚗 –
📺 ⌂wc ☎ 🅿 🅰🅴 ⓪ 𝗩𝗜𝗦𝗔
M 9.00 **t.** and a la carte ⅃ 2.50 – **22 rm** ⥮ 32.00/58.00 **t.** – SB (except Christmas) 60.00/80.00 **st.**

AUSTIN-ROVER-DAIMLER-JAGUAR   Westhamp-   RENAULT   113 The Hornet ☎ 782293
nett Rd ☎ 781331   VAUXHALL-OPEL, CITROEN, TOYOTA, VOLVO 55
FIAT, LANCIA Northgate ☎ 784844   Fishbourne Rd ☎ 782241
FORD   The Hornet ☎ 788100   VW, AUDI   51/54 Bognor Rd ☎ 787684
NISSAN   Delling Lane, Bosham ☎ 573271

CHIDDINGFOLD Surrey 🄌🄍🄎 S 30 – pop. 2 ,209 – ☎ 042 879 Wormley.
♦London 45 – ♦Brighton 40 – Guildford 12.

XXX **Crown Inn** with rm, The Green, Petworth Rd, GU8 4TS, ☎ 2255, « 13C inn » – 📺 ⌂wc ☎
🅿 🅰🅴 ⓪ 𝗩𝗜𝗦𝗔
closed Christmas Night and 2 to 16 January – **M** (closed Monday and Tuesday after Bank
Holidays) 12.00 **t.** and a la carte ⅃ 3.75 – ⥮ 3.00 – **4 rm** 30.00/65.00 **t.**

CHIDDINGSTONE Kent 🄌🄍🄎 U 30 – see Penshurst.

CHIDEOCK Dorset 🄌🄍🄏 L 31 – see Bridport.

CHILGROVE West Sussex 🄌🄍🄎 R 31 – see Chichester.

CHILLINGTON Devon 🄌🄍🄏 I 33 – see Kingsbridge.

CHILTON POLDEN Somerset – see Bridgwater.

CHINNOR Oxon. 🄌🄍🄎 R 28 – pop. 5 ,432 – ☎ 0844 Kingston Blount.
♦London 45 – ♦Oxford 19.

XX **Cricket's**, 4 Keen's Lane, OX9 4PF, ☎ 53566 – ♿ 🅿 🅰🅴 𝗩𝗜𝗦𝗔
closed Tuesday lunch, Sunday dinner, Monday, 2 weeks August, 26 to 30 December and
1 January – **M** 12.00 **t.** ⅃ 2.95.

at Sprigg's Alley E : 2 m. – ✉ Chinnor – ☎ 024 026 Radnage :

X **Sir Charles Napier**, by Bledlow Ridge Rd ☎ 3011, 🚗 – 🅿 🅰🅴 ⓪
closed 3 days September and 3 days Christmas – **M** (closed Sunday dinner and Monday)
(booking essential) 9.00/10.00 **t.** and a la carte ⅃ 2.50.

CHIPPENHAM Wilts. 403 404 N 29 The West Country G. – pop. 21,325 – ECD : Wednesday –
🌀 0249 – See : Yelde Hall★*AC* – Envir. : Biddestone★, W : 4 ½ m. – Sheldon Manor★*AC*, W :
1 ½ m. – Bowood House★*AC* (Library ≤★ of the Park), SE : 5 m.

🃏 Malmesbury Rd ✆ 652040, N : 1 m.

🛈 The Neeld Hall, High St. ✆ 657733.

♦London 106 – ♦Bristol 27 – ♦Southampton 64 – Swindon 21.

　🏨 **Angel** (Norfolk Cap.), 8 Market Pl., SN15 3HD, ✆ 652615, Group Telex 23241 – 📺 🛏wc ☎
　　P. 🅰️ 🔼 🆎 ⓪ **VISA**
　　M a la carte 6.60/10.50 **st.** 🍷 2.50 – **45 rm** ☐ 27.00/40.00 **st.** – SB 50.00/55.00 **st.**

FIAT New Rd ✆ 652215　　　　　　　　　　　　VAUXHALL-OPEL 16/17 The Causeway ✆ 654321
FORD Cocklebury Rd ✆ 653255　　　　　　　　VOLVO Malmesbury Rd ✆ 652016
RENAULT London Rd ✆ 6551131

CHIPPERFIELD Herts. 404 @ – pop. 1,764 – ECD : Wednesday – ✉ 🌀 092 77 Kings Langley.

♦ London 27 – Hemel Hempstead 5 – Watford 6.

　🏨 **Two Brewers Inn** (T.H.F.), The Common, WD4 9BS, ✆ 65266 – 📺 🛏wc ☎ **P**. 🔼 🆎 ⓪
　　VISA
　　M 8.50/11.25 **st.** and a la carte 🍷 2.70 – ☐ 5.50 – **20 rm** 41.00/51.50 **st.**

CHIPPING Lancs. 402 M 22 – pop. 1,376 – ✉ Preston – 🌀 099 56.

♦London 233 – Lancaster 30 – ♦Leeds 54 – ♦Manchester 40 – Preston 12.

　🏨 Gibbon Bridge ⑤, PR3 2TQ, E : 1 m. on Clitheroe Rd ✆ 277, ≤, 🍴 – 📺 🛏wc **P**. 🔼 **VISA**. 🎾
　　6 rm ☐ 20.00/40.00 **t.** – SB (except Christmas) 36.00 **st.**

CHIPPING CAMPDEN Glos. 403 404 O 27 – pop. 1,936 – ECD : Thursday – 🌀 0386 Evesham.
See : High Street★ – Envir. : Hidcote Manor Garden★ *AC*, NE : 2 ½ m.

🛈 Woolstaplers Hall Museum, High St. ✆ 840289 (summer only).

♦London 93 – Cheltenham 21 – ♦Oxford 37 – Stratford-upon-Avon 12.

　🏨 **King's Arms,** The Square, GL55 6AW, ✆ 840256, 🍴 – 🛏wc. 🔼 **VISA**
　　M (bar lunch) 12.60 **st.** 🍷 3.65 – **14 rm** ☐ 20.00/48.00 **st.** – SB (weekends only)
　　(winter only) 48.50/56.00 **st.**

　🏨 **Noel Arms,** High St., GL55 6AT, ✆ 840317 – 🛏wc 🍴wc **P**. 🔼. 🎾
　　M 7.00/9.50 **t.** and a la carte 🍷 2.85 – **19 rm** ☐ 30.50/39.50 **t.** – SB (November-April)
　　91.00/109.00 **st.**

　✕ **Caminetto,** Wool Market House, High St., GL55 6AG, ✆ 840934, Italian rest. – 🔼 🆎 ⓪
　　VISA
　　closed Sunday and 3 weeks September – **M** (dinner only) a la carte 6.90/13.40 **t.** 🍷 3.20.

　　at Mickleton N : 3 ¼ m. by B 4035 and B 4081 on A 46 – ✉ Chipping Campden – 🌀 038 677
　　Mickleton :

　🏨 **Three Ways,** Chapel Lane, GL55 6SB, ✆ 231 – 📺 🛏wc 🍴 🔥 **P**. 🅰️ 🔼 🆎 ⓪ **VISA**
　　M (bar lunch Monday to Saturday)/dinner 12.50 **st.** 🍷 2.95 – **37 rm** ☐ 28.00/52.00 **st.** – SB
　　(weekdays only)(October-March) 52.00/58.00 **st.**

AUSTIN-ROVER High St. ✆ 840213　　　　　　FORD Mickleton ✆ 038 677 (Mickleton) 270
CITROEN Sheep St. ✆ 840221

CHIPPING NORTON Oxon. 403 404 P 28 – pop. 5,003 – ECD : Thursday – 🌀 0608.

🛈 22 New St. ✆ 41320.

♦London 77 – ♦Birmingham 44 – Gloucester 36 – ♦Oxford 21.

　🏨 **White Hart** (T.H.F.), High St., OX7 5AD, ✆ 2572 – 📺 🛏wc ☎ **P**. 🔼 🆎 ⓪ **VISA**
　　M (bar lunch Monday to Saturday)/dinner 9.00 **st.** and a la carte 🍷 2.70 – ☐ 5.00 – **21 rm**
　　33.50/43.00 **st.**

　✕✕ **La Madonette,** 7 Horse Fair, OX7 5AL, ✆ 2320 – 🔼 ⓪ **VISA**
　　closed Sunday, Monday, mid July-mid August and 25-26 December – **M** (dinner only) 17.50 **t.**
　　and a la carte 9.60/14.50 **t.** 🍷 2.50.

AUSTIN-ROVER London Rd ✆ 2014　　　　　　VAUXHALL-OPEL Burford Rd ✆ 2461

CHIPSTEAD Surrey 404 T 30 – pop. 7,177 (inc. Hooley and Woodmansterne) – 🌀 073 75 Down-
land.

♦London 15 – Reigate 6.

　✕✕✕ **Dene Farm,** Outwood Lane, CR3 3NP, on B 2032 ✆ 52661, 🍴 – **P**. 🔼 🆎 ⓪ **VISA**
　　closed Saturday lunch, Sunday dinner, Monday, first 2 weeks August, first 2 weeks January
　　and Bank Holidays – **M** 11.75 **t.** and a la carte.

BMW Outwood Lane ✆ 56221

CHITTLEHAMHOLT Devon 403 I 31 – pop. 259 – ✉ Umberleigh – 🌀 076 94.

♦London 216 – Barnstaple 14 – Exeter 28 – Taunton 45.

　🏨 **Highbullen** ⑤, EX37 9HD, ✆ 561, ≤, ⊿ heated, 🔲, 🐾, 🎣, 🎿, park, 🎾, squash – 📺
　　🛏wc **P**. 🎾
　　M (bar lunch)/dinner 10.50 **st.** 🍷 2.95 – ☐ 1.50 – **30 rm** 23.50/47.00 **st.**

CHOLLERFORD Northumb. [401] [402] N 18 – ✉ Hexham – ⊛ 043 481 Humshaugh.
♦London 303 – ♦Carlisle 36 – ♦Newcastle-upon-Tyne 21.

🏨 **George** (Swallow), NE46 4EW, ☎ 205, Group Telex 53168, ⋞, « Riverside gardens », 🏊, 🎣 – [TV] 🛁wc 📞 [P]. 🏃. [CB] [AE] [DC] [VISA]
M 7.00/10.00 **st.** and a la carte 🍷 3.50 – **54 rm** 🛏 36.00/50.00 **st.** – SB 56.00/64.00 **st.**

CHORLEY Lancs. [402] [404] M 23 – pop. 33 ,465 – ECD : Wednesday – ⊛ 025 72.
♦London 222 – ♦Blackpool 30 – ♦Liverpool 32 – ♦Manchester 26.

at Whittle-le-Woods N : 2 m. on A 6 – ✉ ⊛ 025 72 Chorley :

🏨 **Shaw Hill Country Club** 🌿, Preston Road, PR6 7PP, ☎ 69221, ⋞, ⛳18 – [TV] 🛁wc 📞 [P]. 🏃. [CB] [AE] [DC] [VISA]
M 12.50/10.00 **st.** and a la carte 🍷 2.60 – **22 rm** 🛏 40.00/60.00 **t.** – SB (except Christmas) 70.00/90.00 **st.**

at Adlington S : 3 m. on A 6 – ✉ Chorley – ⊛ 0257 Adlington :

🏨 **Gladmar** 🌿, Railway Rd, PR6 9RH, ☎ 480398, 🌳 – [TV] 🛁wc 🚿wc 📞 [P]. [CB]. 🚫
closed Christmas Day and New Years Day – **M** (bar lunch)/dinner 8.50 **st.** and a la carte 🍷 2.60 – **13 rm** 🛏 21.00/32.00 **st.**

CHRISTCHURCH Dorset [403] [404] O 31 – pop. 32 ,854 – ECD : Wednesday – ⊛ 0202.
See : Site★ – Priory★ – Envir. : Hengistbury Head★ (⋞★★), SW : 4 m. by B 3059.
ℹ 30 Saxon Sq. ☎ 471780 – ♦London 111 – Bournemouth 6 – Salisbury 26 – ♦Southampton 24 – Winchester 39.

🏨 King's Arms, Castle St., BH23 1DT, ☎ 484117 – [lift] [TV] 🛁wc 🚿wc 📞 [P]. 🏃. 🚫 – **32 rm.**

🏠 **Park House,** 48 Barrack Rd, BH23 1PF, ☎ 482124, 🌳 – [P]. [CB] [VISA]. 🚫
closed Christmas and New Year – **9 rm** 🛏 12.50/30.00 **t.**

🍴 **Splinters,** 12 Church St., BH23 1BW, ☎ 483454 – [AE] [DC] [VISA]
closed Sunday and 25-26 December – **M** (dinner only) a la carte 9.75/13.00 **t.** 🍷 2.50.

at Mudeford SE : 2 m. – ✉ ⊛ 0202 Christchurch :

🏨 **Avonmouth** (T.H.F.), BH23 3NT, ☎ 483434, ⋞ Christchurch harbour, 🏊 heated, 🌳 – [TV] 🛁wc 📞 [P]. 🏃. [CB] [AE] [DC] [VISA]
M (buffet lunch Monday to Saturday)/dinner 8.75 **st.** and a la carte 🍷 2.80 – 🛏 5.50 – **41 rm** 33.50/53.00 **st.**

🏠 **The Pines,** 39 Mudeford, BH23 3NQ, ☎ 475121 – [TV] 🚿wc [P]
13 rm 🛏 12.50/33.00 **st.**

CITROEN Barrack Rd ☎ 479351
FIAT Highcliffe ☎ 042 52 (Highcliffe) 72333
FORD Lyndhurst Rd ☎ 042 52 (Highcliffe) 71371
VW, AUDI 105 Summerford Rd ☎ 476871

CHRISTLETON Cheshire [402] [403] L 24 – see Chester.

CHURCH STRETTON Salop [403] L 26 – pop. 2 ,932 – ECD : Wednesday – ⊛ 0694.
⛳18 Links Rd ☎ 722281.
ℹ Church St. ☎ 722535 (summer only) – ♦London 166 – ♦Birmingham 46 – Hereford 39 – Shrewsbury 14.

🏨 **Stretton Hall** 🌿, Old Shrewsbury Rd, All Stretton, SY6 6HG, NE : 1 m. on B 4370 ☎ 723224, « Country house atmosphere », 🌳 – [TV] 🛁wc 📞 [P]. [CB] [AE] [DC] [VISA]
M 8.50/12.00 **t.** and a la carte 🍷 1.75 – **12 rm** 🛏 27.00/40.00 **t.** – SB (weekends only) (October-March) 50.00 **st.**

🏨 **Sandford,** Watling St. South, SY6 7BG, ☎ 722131, 🌳 – 🛁wc 🚿wc [P]. 🏃. [CB] [VISA]
M 4.75/6.00 **t.** and a la carte 🍷 2.50 – **24 rm** 🛏 15.50/31.00 **t.** – SB (except Christmas) 36.50/39.50 **st.**

🏠 **Mynd House,** Ludlow Rd, Little Stretton, SY6 6RB, SW : 1 m. on B 4370 ☎ 722212, ⋞, 🌳 – 🛁wc 🚿 [P]. [CB] [VISA]
closed 18 December-January – **13 rm** 🛏 11.50/29.50 **t.**

CHURT Surrey [404] R 30 – see Farnham.

CIRENCESTER Glos. [403] [404] O 28 – pop. 13 ,491 – ECD : Thursday – ⊛ 0285.
See : Parish Church★ (Perpendicular) – Corinium Museum★ – Envir. : Chedworth (Roman Villa ★) *AC*, **N : 7 m.**
⛳18 Cheltenham Rd ☎ 2465, N 1 ½ m.
ℹ Corn Hall, Market Pl. ☎ 4180 – ♦London 97 – ♦Bristol 37 – Gloucester 19 – ♦Oxford 37.

🏨 **King's Head** (Best Western), 24 Market Pl., GL7 2NR, ☎ 3322, Telex 43470 – [lift] [TV] [P]. 🏃. [CB] [AE] [DC] [VISA]
closed 27 to 30 December – **M** 8.25/10.05 **st.** and a la carte 🍷 4.25 – **70 rm** 🛏 40.50/54.00 **st.** – SB 42.00/66.00 **st.**

🏨 **Fleece,** Market Pl., GL7 4NZ, ☎ 68507 – [TV] 🛁wc 📞 [P]. [CB] [AE] [DC] [VISA]
closed 24 to 26 December – **M** 5.50/7.50 **t.** and a la carte 🍷 2.75 – 🛏 4.25 – **19 rm** 37.50/45.00 **t.** – SB (weekends only) 51.50 **st.**

🏨 **Corinium Court,** 12 Gloucester St., GL7 2DG, ☎ 4499 – [TV] 🛁wc 🚿wc [P]. [CB] [AE] [DC] [VISA]
M 6.50/11.00 **t.** and a la carte 🍷 2.75 – **8 rm** 🛏 30.00/42.50 **t.** – SB (October-May) 60.00/80.00 **st.**

🏛 **Raydon House,** 1-3 The Avenue, GL7 1EH, ℰ 3485 – 🛏wc **P.** 🔄 *VISA* 🕸
closed 25 December-2 January – **M** (bar lunch)/dinner 7.50 **st.** and a la carte 🍴 2.50 – **15 rm**
🖃 13.00/33.00 **st.** – SB (October-February) 36.00/40.00 **st.**

🏠 **La Ronde,** 52-54 Ashcroft Rd, GL7 1QX, ℰ 4611 – 🕸
10 rm 🖃 14.50/26.50 **t.**

🏠 **Wimborne,** 91 Victoria Rd, GL7 1ES, ℰ 3890 – **P.** 🕸
7 rm 🖃 16.00/17.00 **st.**

at Ewen SW : 3 ¼ m. by A 429 – ⊠ Cirencester – 🕾 028 577 Kemble :

🏛 **Wild Duck Inn,** GL7 6BY, ℰ 364, 🍴 – 📺 🛏wc **P.** 🔄 AE ⑩ *VISA*
M 9.50 **t.** and a la carte 🍴 2.75 – 🖃 3.50 – **7 rm** 29.00/38.00 **t.** – SB 60.00 **st.**

at Stratton NW : 1 ¼ m. on A 417 – ⊠ 🕾 0285 Cirencester :

🏨 **Stratton House,** Gloucester Rd, GL7 2LE, ℰ 61761, 🍴 – 📺 🛏wc 🚿wc **P.** 🍴. 🔄 AE
⑩ *VISA*
M 7.00/9.50 **st.** and a la carte 🍴 2.65 – **26 rm** 🖃 28.50/42.00 **st.** – SB (except Christmas)
51.50/56.50 **st.**

AUSTIN-ROVER Tetbury Rd ℰ 2614
CITROEN Perrotts Brook ℰ 028 583 (North Cerney)
219
COLT Love Lane ℰ 5799

NISSAN Chesterton Lane ℰ 2196
PEUGEOT-TALBOT Victoria Rd ℰ 3460
RENAULT Gloucester Rd ℰ 68007
VAUXHALL-OPEL Lovelane Trading Estate ℰ 3314

CLACTON-ON-SEA Essex 👁👁👁 X 28 – pop. 39,618 – ECD : Wednesday – 🕾 0255.
See : Sea front (gardens)★.
🛈 Town Hall, Station Rd ℰ 425501 ext 200 – Central Seafront, Marine Parade ℰ 423400 (summer only).
♦London 71 – Chelmsford 38 – Colchester 16.

🏛 **Kings Cliff,** 55 Kings Par., Esplanade, Holland-on-Sea, CO15 5JB, NE : 1 ½ m. ℰ 812343, ≼
– 📺 🛏wc **P.** 🔄 *VISA*. 🕸
M 5.00/7.00 and a la carte 🍴 1.25 – **13 rm** 🖃 21.00/36.00 **t.**

AUSTIN-ROVER 107 Old Rd ℰ 424128
BEDFORD, OPEL-VAUXHALL 65 High St. ℰ 420444

CITROEN 67 Frinton Rd ℰ 812205
FORD St John's Rd ℰ 425487

CLANFIELD Oxon. 👁👁👁 👁👁👁 P 28 – pop. 822 – ECD : Wednesday and Saturday – 🕾 036 781.
♦London 76 – ♦Oxford 20 – Swindon 17.

🍴🍴 **Plough** with rm, Bourton Rd, OX8 2RB, on A 4095 ℰ 222, « Small Elizabethan manor house »,
🍴 – 📺 🛏wc 🚿wc 🕾 **P.** 🔄 AE ⑩ *VISA*. 🕸
M (booking essential) 10.00/22.95 **t.** 🍴 2.75 – **8 rm** 🖃 45.00/75.00 **t.**

CLAPHAM Beds. 👁👁👁 S 27 – see Bedford.

CLAPPERSGATE Cumbria – see Ambleside.

CLAUGHTON Lancs. 👁👁👁 M 21 – pop. 121 – ⊠ Lancaster – 🕾 0468 Hornby.
♦London 254 – Kendal 25 – Lancaster 6 – ♦Leeds 63.

🏨 **Old Rectory,** LA2 9LA, on A 683 ℰ 21455, 🍴 – 📺 🛏wc **P.** 🔄 *VISA*. 🕸
M *(closed Sunday)* (restricted lunch)/dinner 14.50 **t.** 🍴 3.00 – **7 rm** 🖃 27.50/37.50 **t.**

CLAVERDON Warw. 👁👁👁 👁👁👁 O 27 – see Henley-in-Arden.

CLAVERING Essex 👁👁👁 U 28 – pop. 1,076 – 🕾 079 985.
♦London 44 – ♦Cambridge 25 – Colchester 44 – Luton 29.

🍴 **Cricketers,** CB11 4QT, ℰ 442 – **P.** 🔄 *VISA*
M 7.50/11.50 **t.** and a la carte 🍴 2.00.

CLAWTON Devon 👁👁👁 H 31 – pop. 300 – ⊠ Holsworthy – 🕾 040 927 North Tamerton.
♦London 240 – Exeter 39 – ♦Plymouth 36.

🏠 **Court Barn** 🌸, EX22 6PS, W : ½ m. ℰ 219, « Gardens » – 🛏wc 🚿wc **P.** 🔄 *VISA*
closed 10 to 24 December and 27 December-11 January – **M** (dinner only) 8.75 **t.** and a la carte
🍴 2.25 – **8 rm** 🖃 14.35/37.50 **t.** – SB (October-May) 37.00/40.00 **st.**

CLAYGATE Surrey 👁👁👁 @ – see Esher.

CLAYTON-LE-MOORS Lancs 👁👁👁 M 22 – pop. 5,484 – ECD : Wednesday – ⊠ 🕾 0254 Accrington.
♦London 232 – Blackburn 3.5 – Lancaster 37 – ♦Leeds 44 – Preston 14.

🏨 **Dunkenhalgh,** Blackburn Rd, BB5 5RP, W : 1 ½ m. on A 678 ℰ 398021, Telex 63282, 🍴, park
– 📺 🛏wc 🕾 **P.** 🍴. 🔄 AE ⑩ *VISA*
M (bar lunch Saturday) 6.25/9.50 **t.** and a la carte 🍴 3.50 – **50 rm** 🖃 37.00/47.00 **t.**, **2 suites**
44.00/56.00 **st.** – SB (weekends only) 45.00 **st.**

CLAYWORTH Notts. 402 404 R 23 – pop. 275 – ⊠ ✆ 0777 Retford.
♦London 150 – ♦Leeds 49 – Lincoln 26 – ♦Nottingham 38 – ♦Sheffield 29.

🏠 **Royston Manor** ⌖, St. Peters Lane, DN22 9AA, ✆ 817484, ≼, – ⊡ ⇔wc ∭wc ☎ Ⓟ.
🄰🄴 ⓪ 𝘝𝘐𝘚𝘈
M *(closed Saturday lunch)* 5.50/11.50 **st.** ‖ 3.00 – **12 rm** ⊡ 23.00/38.00 **st.** – SB (weekends only) 44.00/54.00 **st.**

CLEETHORPES Humberside 402 404 U 23 – pop. 33,238 – ECD : Thursday – ✆ 0472.
🄵 43 Alexandra Rd ✆ 697472.
♦London 171 – Boston 49 – Lincoln 38 – ♦Sheffield 77.

Plan : see Grimsby

🏠 **Kingsway**, Kingsway, DN35 0AE, ✆ 601122, ≼ – ▐⫶ ⊡ ⇔wc ⊛ ⫘ Ⓟ. 🄰 🄰🄴 ⓪ 𝘝𝘐𝘚𝘈.
⌖   BZ **a**
closed 25 and 26 December – **M** 6.75/8.50 **st.** and a la carte ‖ 3.25 – **55 rm** ⊡ 28.00/50.00 **st.**
– SB (weekends only) 55.00 **st.**

🏠 **Wellow**, Kings Rd, DN35 0AQ, ✆ 695589 – ⊡ ⇔wc ⊛ Ⓟ   Y
10 rm.

CITROEN 76-80 Brereton Av. ✆ 56417   LANCIA 421 Grimsby Rd ✆ 698991

CLEEVE HILL Glos. 403 404 N 28 – see Cheltenham.

CLEOBURY MORTIMER Salop 403 404 M 26 – pop. 1,883 – ✆ 0299.
♦London 147 – ♦Birmingham 29 – Shrewsbury 35.

🏠 **Redfern,** Lower St., DY14 8AA, ✆ 270395, Telex 335176 – ⊡ ⇔wc ∭wc ☎ Ⓟ. 🄰 🄰🄴 ⓪
𝘝𝘐𝘚𝘈
M 4.00/8.75 **st.** and a la carte ‖ 2.75 – **11 rm** ⊡ 23.00/35.00 **st.** – SB 44.00/48.00 **st.**

CLEVEDON Avon 403 L 29 The West Country G. – pop. 17,875 – ECD : Wednesday – ✆ 0272.
See : Site★ (≼ from park benches★★) – Clevedon Court★ *AC.*
♦London 138 – ♦Bristol 15 – Taunton 34.

🏠 Walton Park, 1 Wellington Terr., BS21 7BL, ✆ 874253, ≼, 🐾 – ▐⫶ ⊡ ⇔wc ⫘ Ⓟ. 🄰
35 rm.

AUSTIN-ROVER Old Church Rd ✆ 872201

CLIFFORD CHAMBERS Warw. – see Stratford-upon-Avon.

CLIMPING West Sussex 404 S 31 – pop. 925 – ⊠ Littlehampton – ✆ 0903 Arundel.
♦London 64 – Bognor Regis 5 – ♦ Brighton 23.

🏠 **Bailiffscourt** ⌖, Climping St., BN17 5RW, ✆ 723511, Telex 877870, « Reconstructed
medieval house », ⏄, 🐾, park, ✾ – ⊡ ⇔wc ☎ Ⓟ. 🄰 🄰🄴 ⓪ 𝘝𝘐𝘚𝘈
M 18.50 **st.** – **20 rm** ⊡ 50.00/80.00 **st.**

CLOWNE Derbs. 402 403 404 Q 24 – pop. 6,846 – ECD : Wednesday – ✆ 0246 Chesterfield.
♦London 156 – Derby 40 – Lincoln 35 – ♦Nottingham 30 – ♦Sheffield 12.

🏠 **Van Dyk,** Worksop Rd, S43 4TD, N : ¾ m. on A 619 ✆ 810219 – ⊡ ⇔wc ∭wc ⊛ Ⓟ. 🄰.
🄰 🄰🄴 𝘝𝘐𝘚𝘈
M *(closed Sunday dinner)* (lunch residents only) 9.75 **t.** and a la carte ‖ 2.50 – **16 rm**
⊡ 26.00/44.00 **t.**

CLUN Salop 403 KL 26 – pop. 817 – ⊠ Craven Arms – ✆ 058 84.
♦London 178 – ♦Birmingham 60 – Shrewsbury 29.

🛏 Sun Inn, High St., SY7 8JB, ✆ 559 – ∭wc Ⓟ. 🄰. ✾
M (bar lunch) – **7 rm** ⊡ 10.00/26.00 **st.**

COATHAM MUNDEVILLE Durham 402 P 20 – see Darlington.

COBHAM Surrey 404 S 30 – pop. 13,920 – ECD : Wednesday – ✆ 093 26.
Envir. : Wisley gardens★★ *AC*, SW : 4 m. by A 3 AZ.
♦London 24 – Guildford 10.

Plan : see Greater London (South-West)

🏠 Ladbroke Seven Hills (Ladbroke), Seven Hills Rd South, KT11 1EW, W : 1 ½ m. by A 245
✆ 4471, Telex 929196, ⏄ heated, 🐾, park, ✾, squash – ▐⫶ ⊡ ⇔wc ☎ Ⓟ. 🄰. ✾
92 rm.   by A 3   AZ

✕✕ **San Domenico,** Portsmouth Rd, KT11 1EL, SW : 1 m. on A 3 ✆ 3006, Italian rest., 🐾 – Ⓟ.
🄰 🄰🄴 ⓪ 𝘝𝘐𝘚𝘈   by A 3   AZ
closed Sunday dinner and Bank Holidays – **M** a la carte 11.55/15.85 **t.** ‖ 2.75.

AUDI-VW 42 Portsmouth Rd ✆ 4493   BMW 22 Portsmouth Rd ✆ 7141
AUSTIN-ROVER Stoke Rd ✆ 4244

COCKERMOUTH Cumbria **401 402** J 20 – pop. 7 ,074 – ECD : Thursday – ✪ 0900.
🛈 Riverside Car Park, Market St. ♪ 822634 (summer only) – ◆London 306 – ◆Carlisle 25 – Keswick 13.

🏠 **Trout,** Crown St., CA13 0EJ, ♪ 823591, ⬍, 🐎 – 🖵 ⌂wc ⊓wc ☎ 🅿. ☒ VISA
closed Christmas Day – **M** 6.00/10.00 **t.** and a la carte ⊢ 3.00 – **16 rm** ⌂ 24.00/37.00 **t.** – SB (weekends only) 42.00/43.00 **st.**

🏠 **Wordsworth,** Main St., CA13 9JS, ♪ 822757 – 🖵 ⌂wc ⊓wc 🅿. ☒ VISA ⋇
M (bar lunch)/dinner 8.00 **t.** ⊢ 3.00 – **18 rm** ⌂ 16.00/33.00 **st.** – SB (weekends only) 29.50/32.50 **st.**

at Great Broughton W : 2 ¾ m. by A 66 – ✉ ✪ 0900 Cockermouth :

🏠 **Broughton Craggs** ⬍, CA13 0XW, ♪ 824400, 🐎 – 🖵 ⌂wc ☎ 🅿. ☒ AE VISA ⋇
M 5.75/9.75 **t.** and a la carte ⊢ 3.00 – **10 rm** ⌂ 25.00/38.00 **t.** – SB (weekends only except Bank Holidays) 39.00/42.50 **st.**

BMW, VOLVO Derwent St. ♪ 823666   FORD Lorton St. ♪ 822033

COED-DUON = Blackwood.

COGGESHALL Essex **404** W 28 – pop. 3 ,505 – ECD : Wednesday – ✉ Colchester – ✪ 0376.
◆London 49 – Braintree 6 – Chelmsford 16 – Colchester 9.

🏠 **White Hart,** Market End, CO6 1NH, ♪ 61654, « Part 14C Guild Hall » – 🖵 ⌂wc ⊓wc ☎
🅿. ☒ AE ① VISA ⋇
closed August – **M** (closed Friday dinner) (bar lunch Monday to Saturday)/dinner a la carte 10.95/25.00 **t.** ⊢ 3.25 – **18 rm** ⌂ 35.00/50.00 **st.**

COLCHESTER Essex **404** W 28 – pop. 87 ,476 – ECD : Thursday – ✪ 0206.
See : Roman Walls★ – Envir. : Layer Marney (Marney Tower★ 16C) SW : 7 m. – ⭧ Birch Grove, Layer Rd ♪ 020 634 (Layer-de-la-Haye) 276, S : 2 m.
🛈 Town Hall, High St. ♪ 46379 and 712233.
◆London 58 – ◆Cambridge 48 – ◆Ipswich 18 – Luton 76 – Southend-on-Sea 41.

🏠 **George** (Q.M.H.), 116 High St., CO1 1TD, ♪ 578494 – 🖵 ⌂wc ☎ 🅿. ⌖. ☒ AE ① VISA
M (carving rest.) 7.75 **st.** ⊢ 2.75 – **47 rm** ⌂ 35.00/45.00 **st.** – SB (weekends only) 50.00/60.00 **st.**

🏠 **Rose and Crown,** East Gates, CO1 2TZ, ♪ 866677, « Part 15C inn » – 🖵 ⌂wc ☎ 🅿. ☒
AE ① VISA
M 8.95 **st.** and a la carte ⊢ 2.75 – **28 rm** ⌂ 23.50/39.50 **st.**

✗ **Wm. Scraggs,** 2 North Hill, CO1 1DZ, ♪ 41111, Seafood – ☒ AE VISA
closed Sunday and Bank Holidays – **M** (bar lunch)/dinner a la carte 8.05/11.80 **t.** ⊢ 3.00.

✗ **Bistro 9,** 9 North Hill, CO1 1OZ, ♪ 576466 – ☒ VISA
closed Sunday, Monday and 24 to 31 December – **M** 5.00 **t.** (lunch) and a la carte 6.45/8.60 **t.** ⊢ 2.60.

at Marks Tey W : 5 m. by A 12 on B 1408 – ✉ ✪ 0206 Colchester :

🏠 **Marks Tey,** London Rd, CO6 1DU, ♪ 210001, Telex 987176 – 🖵 ⌂wc ☎ 🅿. ⌖. ☒ AE ①
VISA
M 7.25 **st.** and a la carte ⊢ 3.45 – **106 rm** ⌂ 35.00/45.00 **st.** – SB (weekends only) 39.50 **st.**

at Nayland (Suffolk) NW : 6 m. by A 134 – ✉ Colchester – ✪ 0206 Nayland :

✗✗ **Bear Country House** with rm, Bear St., CO6 1NH, ♪ 262204, ⬍, 🐎 – 🖵 ⌂wc 🅿. ☒ VISA
closed Monday, Monday, 2 weeks August-September and first 2 weeks January – **M** (dinner only) 10.95 **t.** and a la carte ⊢ 3.50 – **4 rm** ⌂ 28.00/40.00 **t.**

MICHELIN Branch, Gosbecks Rd, CO1 1XB, ♪ 578451/4

AUDI, FERRARI, PORSCHE, MERCEDES-BENZ, VW
Auto Way, Ipswich Rd ♪ 48141
AUSTIN-ROVER East Gates ♪ 867484
AUSTIN-ROVER Cowdray Av. ♪ 576291
AUSTIN-ROVER-DAIMLER-JAGUAR Elmstead Rd
♪ 862811
CITROEN Butt Rd ♪ 576803
FIAT, TOYOTA Gosbecks Rd ♪ 576455

FORD Magdalen St. ♪ 71171
HONDA, LADA, RELIANT ♪ 867298
NISSAN 78 Military Rd ♪ 577295
RENAULT Ipswich Rd ♪ 68555
TALBOT, PEUGEOT, ALFA-ROMEO Wimpole Rd ♪
570197
VAUXHALL-OPEL Ipswich Rd ♪ 844422
VOLVO, BMW 10 Osborne St. ♪ 577287

COLEBROOK Devon – see Plymouth.

COLEFORD Glos. **403 404** M 28 – pop. 8 ,246 – ECD : Thursday – ✉ Gloucester – ✪ 0594.
Dean – ⭧ Coalway Rd ♪ 0594 (Dean) 32583, ½ m. on Parkend Rd.
◆London 143 – ◆ Bristol 28 – Gloucester 19 – Newport 29.

🏠 **Speech House** (T.H.F.), Forest of Dean, GL16 7EL, NE : 3 m. on B 4226 ♪ 22607, 🐎 – 🖵
⌂wc ☎ 🅿. ☒ AE ① VISA
M (bar lunch Monday to Saturday)/dinner a la carte 9.80/14.80 **st.** ⊢ 2.70 – ⌂ 5.50 – **13 rm** 38.50/46.00 **st.**

🏠 **Lambsquay** ⬍, Perrygrove Rd, GL16 8QB, S : 1 m. on B 4228 ♪ 33127, 🐎 – 🖵 ⌂wc 🅿.
☒ VISA
closed December-February – **M** (closed Sunday dinner) 7.50/9.00 ⊢ 3.00 – **9 rm** ⌂ 28.00/46.00 – SB 28.50/34.25 **st.**

AUSTIN-ROVER, LAND ROVER-RANGE ROVER
Market Pl. ♪ 32468

FORD High St ♪ 32747
NISSAN ♪ 33517

COLESHILL Warw. **403 404** O 26 – pop. 6,038 – ECD : Monday and Thursday – ⊠ Birmingham – ☎ 0675.

♦London 113 – ♦Birmingham 8 – ♦Coventry 11.

🏨 **Swan** (Golden Oak), High St., B46 3BL, ℰ 62212 – 📺 🍴wc ☎ 🅿 🛄 🔊 🆎 VISA. 🕸
M 6.00/6.50 **t.** and a la carte 🍷 3.75 – **34 rm** ⊇ 27.00/38.00 **st.**

🏨 **Coleshill**, 152 High St., B46 3BG, ℰ 65527 – 📺 ➡wc 🅿 🔊 🆎 ① VISA. 🕸
M *(closed Saturday lunch)* 7.50/9.50 **t.** and a la carte 🍷 3.25 – **15 rm** ⊇ 38.00/46.00 **t.** – SB (weekends only) 54.00 **st.**

✗ **Blythe's,** 19 High St., B46 1AY, ℰ 62266 – 🅿 🔊 🔊 VISA
closed Sunday, Monday, 2 weeks August-September, 2 to 9 January and Bank Holidays –
M a la carte lunch/dinner 14.50 **t.** 🍷 2.90.

COLLYWESTON Northants. **402 404** S 26 – see Stamford (Lincs.).

COLWALL Heref. and Worc. – see Great Malvern.

COLWYN BAY (BAE COLWYN) Clwyd **402 403** I 24 – pop. 27,002 – ECD : Wednesday – ☎ 0492.

See : Zoo★.

Envir. : Bodnant gardens★★ *AC*, SW : 6 m.

🏌 Abergele and Pensarn, Tan-y-Goppa Rd, Abergele ℰ 0745 (Abergele) 824034, E : 6 m. – 🏌,🏌 Old Colwyn, Woodland Av. ℰ 515581.

🎫 Prince of Wales Theatre ℰ 30478 – Colwyn Bay Hotels and Guest Houses Association ℰ 515719 (summer only).

♦London 237 – Birkenhead 50 – Chester 42 – Holyhead 41.

🏨 **Norfolk House,** 36 Princes Drive, LL29 8PF, ℰ 31757, 🌴 – 🎐 📺 ➡wc 🍴wc 🕸 🅿 🛄 🔊 🆎 ① VISA
M (bar lunch Monday to Saturday)/dinner a la carte 5.95/8.95 **st.** 🍷 3.50 – **27 rm** ⊇ 27.50/38.00 **st.** – SB (weekends only) 45.00 **st.**

🏠 **Hopeside,** 63-67 Prince's Drive, West End, LL29 8PW, ℰ 33244 – 📺 ➡wc 🍴wc 🕸 🅿 🔊 🆎 VISA
closed 2 weeks Christmas and New Year – **M** *(closed Sunday lunch)* (bar lunch)/dinner a la carte 7.00/10.00 **t.** 🍷 1.80 – **19 rm** ⊇ 22.00/38.00 **st.** – SB 45.00/50.00 **st.**

🏠 **Lyndale,** 410 Abergele Rd, Old Colwyn, LL29 9AB, E : 1¾ m. on A 547 ℰ 515429 – 📺 ➡wc 🍴wc ☎ 🅿 🔊 VISA
M (bar lunch Monday to Saturday)/dinner 7.50 **st.** and a la carte 🍷 3.25 – **14 rm** ⊇ 20.00/35.00 **st.** – SB 42.00/50.00 **st.**

at Penmaenhead E : 2¼ m. on A 547 – ⊠ ☎ 0492 Colwyn Bay :

🏨 **Hotel 70°** (Best Western), Old Colwyn, LL29 9LD, ℰ 516555, Telex 61362, ≤ – 📺 ☎ 🅿 🛄 🔊 🆎 ① VISA
M 10.85/16.85 🍷 3.50 – **41 rm** ⊇ 35.00/60.00 **st.**, **1 suite** 80.00/100.00 **st.** – SB 56.00/65.00 **st.**

at Rhos-on-Sea (Llandrillo-yn-Rhos) NW : 1 m. – ⊠ ☎ 0492 Colwyn Bay :

🏠 **Ashmount,** College Av., LL28 4NT, ℰ 45479 – 📺 ➡wc 🍴wc ☎ 🚲 🅿 🔊 🆎 ① VISA
M 4.50/7.00 **st.** and a la carte 🍷 2.75 – **18 rm** ⊇ 17.30/31.00 **st.** – SB 39.00/42.00 **st.**

🏠 **Cabin Hill,** 12 College Av., LL28 4NT, ℰ 44568 – 🍴wc. 🕸
March-October – **10 rm** ⊇ 11.00/26.00 **st.**

AUSTIN-ROVER 394 Abergele Rd ℰ 515292
FORD Conwy Rd ℰ 2201
PEUGEOT 268 Conwy Rd ℰ 44278

PORSCHE, MERCEDES-BENZ Abergele Rd ℰ 30456
VAUXALL Conwy Rd ℰ 30271
VW, AUDI Penrhyn Av. ℰ 46722

COLYFORD Devon – see Colyton.

COLYTON Devon **403** K 31 The West Country G. – pop. 2,435 – ☎ 0297.

See : Site★ – St. Andrew's Church★ – ♦London 160 – Exeter 23 – Lyme Regis 7.

🏠 **Grove,** South St., EX13 6ER, ℰ 52438, 🌴 – 🍴wc 🅿
7 rm ⊇ 7.75/20.00 **st.**

at Colyford S : 1 m. by B 3161 on A 3052 – ⊠ ☎ 0297 Colyton :

🏰 **Old Manor** 🕸, Swan Hill Rd, EX13 6QQ, ℰ 52862, ≤, « Converted 15C manor house », 🌴, 🕸 – ➡wc 🅿. 🕸
March-October – **M** (bar lunch)/dinner 10.50 **t.** 🍷 2.80 – **11 rm** ⊇ 14.50/44.00.

COMBEINTEIGNHEAD Devon – ⊠ Newton Abbot – ☎ 062 687 Shaldon.

♦London 219 – Exeter 19 – ♦Plymouth 34 – Torquay 10.

🏠 **Netherton House** 🕸, TQ12 4RN, W : ¾ m. by B 3195 ℰ 3251, 🏊 heated, 🌴, park – 📺 ➡wc 🅿 🔊 🆎 VISA
M (bar lunch)/dinner 12.95 **t.** 🍷 2.95 – **10 rm** ⊇ 16.00/44.00 **t.** – SB 53.00/68.00 **st.**

COMBE MARTIN Devon 408 H 30 The West Country G. – pop. 2,279 – ECD : Wednesday – ⊠ Ilfracombe – ☎ 027 188.

🖪 Sea Cottage, Cross St. ℰ 3319 (summer only).

♦London 218 – Exeter 56 – Taunton 58.

🏛 **Coulsworthy Country House** ⤳, EX34 0PD, SE : 2 ½ m. by A 399 on road to Hunters Inn ℰ 2463, ⩿, ⽞ heated, 🐎, ⅍ – 📺 ➬wc ⅏wc ℗
closed 9 December-6 February – **M** (closed Sunday dinner) (bar lunch Monday to Saturday)/dinner 12.50 **st.** – **10 rm** ⊑ 16.00/56.00 **st.**

⚲ **Brittania,** Moory Meadow, Seaside, EX34 0DG, ℰ 2294 – ℗
10 rm ⊑ 13.00/26.00 **st.**

※※ **La Gallerie** with rm, Victoria St., EX34 0JT, ℰ 2566, « Antique collection » – ℗. 🌅 AE ⓪ VISA
closed Sunday to Tuesday November-Easter – **M** (dinner only) 9.50 **t.** and a la carte 11.30/14.90 **t.** ⅃ 2.90 – **3 rm** ⊑ 10.50/21.00 **st.** – SB (weekends only)(November-Easter) 39.00 **st.**

AUSTIN-ROVER Borough Rd ℰ 2391   VAUXHALL-OPEL Borough Rd ℰ 3257

COMPTON Surrey 404 S 30 – see Guildford.

CONGLETON Cheshire 402 408 404 N 24 – pop. 23,482 – ECD : Wednesday – ☎ 0260.

🖪 Town Hall, High St. ℰ 271095.

♦London 183 – ♦Liverpool 50 – ♦Manchester 25 – ♦Sheffield 46 – ♦Stoke-on-Trent 13.

🏛 Lion and Swan, Swan Bank, CW12 1JR, ℰ 273115, « 16C inn » – 📺 ➬wc ⅏wc ☎ ℗
13 rm.

CONINGSBY Lincs. 402 404 T 24 – pop. 4,277 – ☎ 0526.

♦London 134 – ♦Leicester 61 – Lincoln 29 – ♦Nottingham 54.

※※ Ratty's, 43 High St., LN4 4RB, ℰ 42285, 🐎 – ℗.

CONISTON Cumbria 402 K 20 – pop. 1,713 – ☎ 0966.

🖪 1 Yewdale Rd ℰ 41533 (summer only).

♦London 285 – ♦Carlisle 55 – Kendal 22 – Lancaster 42.

🏛 **Sun** ⤳, LA21 8HQ, ℰ 41248, ⩿, 🐎 – ⅏wc ℗. 🌅 VISA
closed January and February – **M** (bar lunch)/dinner 12.50 **t.** ⅃ 3.50 – **10 rm** ⊑ 27.00/48.00 **t.** – SB (November-March) 60.00/65.00 **st.**

AUSTIN-ROVER Broughton Rd ℰ 41253

CONSTANTINE BAY Cornwall 408 E 32 – see Padstow.

CONWY Gwynedd 402 408 I 24 – pop. 3,649 – ECD : Wednesday – ☎ 049 263.

See : Site★★ – Castle★★ (13C) AC – St. Mary's Church★ 14C.

Envir. : Sychnant Pass★ W : 2 ½ m.

🛤 Penmaenmawr ℰ 0492 (Penmaenmawr) 623330 W : 4 m.

🖪 Snowdonia National Park, Visitor Centre, Castle St. ℰ 2248.

♦London 241 – Caernarfon 22 – Chester 46 – Holyhead 37.

🏛 **Bryn Cregin Garden,** Ty Mawr Rd, Deganwy, LL31 9UR, NE : 2 m. by A 55 on A 546 ℰ 0492 (Deganwy) 85266, ⩿, 🐎 – 📺 ➬wc ⅏wc ☎ ℗. 🌅 AE ⓪ VISA. ⅍
closed January – **M** (closed Sunday dinner to non-residents and Monday lunch) (bar lunch)/dinner 9.50 **t.** and a la carte ⅃ 3.65 – **16 rm** ⊑ 20.00/42.00 **t.**. **1 suite** 37.00/45.00 **t.** – SB 46.00/60.00 **st.**

🏛 **Sychnant Pass,** Sychnant Pass Rd, LL32 8BJ, SW : 1 ¾ m. ℰ 6868, 🐎 – 📺 ➬wc ⅏wc ⤳ ℗. 🌅 AE ⓪ VISA
February-October and Christmas – **M** 6.00/13.00 **st.** ⅃ 2.65 – **10 rm** ⊑ 25.00/45.00 **st.**

🏛 **Castle** (T.H.F.), High St., LL32 8DB, ℰ 2324 – 📺 ➬wc ⬚ ℗. 🌅 AE ⓪ VISA
M 6.50/9.00 **st.** and a la carte ⅃ 2.70 – ⊑ 5.50 – **25 rm** 32.00/45.00 **st.**

🏛 **Castle Bank,** Mount Pleasant, LL32 8NY, ℰ 3888, ⩿ – 📺 ⅏wc ℗. ⅍
closed February-mid March and 25-26 December – **M** (closed dinner Sunday to Wednesday in winter) (lunch by arrangement) 6.00/10.00 **t.** ⅃ 3.00 – **9 rm** ⊑ 15.00/32.00 **t.** – SB (October-mid May) 40.00/42.00 **st.**

⚲ **Llys Gwilym,** 3 Mountain Rd (off Cadnant Park), LL32 8PU, ℰ 2351 – ⅍
6 rm ⊑ 9.00/16.00.

at Roewen S : 3 m. by B 5106 – ⊠ Conwy – ☎ 049 267 Twyn-y-Groes :

⚲ **Tir-y-Coed** ⤳, LL32 8TP, ℰ 219, ⩿, 🐎 – 📺 ➬wc ⅏wc ℗
March-October – **8 rm** ⊑ 14.50/31.00 **t.**

at Tal-y-Bont S : 5 ¾ m. on B 5106 – ⊠ Conwy – ☎ 049 269 Dolgarrog :

🏛 **Lodge,** LL32 8YX, ℰ 766 – 📺 ➬wc ⤳ ℗. 🌅 AE ⓪ VISA
M 5.50/10.50 **t.** and a la carte ⅃ 3.00 – **10 rm** ⊑ 25.00/40.00 **t.** – SB (except Christmas and New Year) 45.00/55.00 **st.**

COOKHAM Berks. 👁️👁️👁️ R 29 – pop. 5 ,865 – ECD : Wednesday and Thursday – ✉️ Maidenhead – ☎ 062 85 Bourne End.

Envir. : Cliveden House★ 19C (Park★★) *AC* SE : 2 m.

🏌️ Winter Hill, Grange Lane ℰ 27613.

♦London 32 – High Wycombe 7 – Reading 16.

  ✕ **Cookham Tandoori**, High St., SL6 9SL, ℰ 22584 – 🔥 AE ⓪ VISA
    closed 25 and 26 December – **M** a la carte 9.65/16.40 **t.**

CITROEN High St. ℰ 22984

COPDOCK Suffolk 👁️👁️👁️ X 27 – see Ipswich.

COPTHORNE West Sussex 👁️👁️👁️ T 30 – see Crawley.

CORBRIDGE Northumb. 👁️👁️👁️ 👁️👁️👁️ N 19 – pop. 2 ,757 – ECD : Thursday – ☎ 043 471.

Envir. : Corstopitum Roman Fort★ *AC*, NW : 1 ½ m.

🛈 Vicar's Pele Tower, Market Pl. ℰ 2815 (summer only).

♦London 300 – Hexham 3 – ♦Newcastle-upon-Tyne 18.

  🏨 **Riverside**, Main St., NE45 5LE, ℰ 2942 – 🏠wc ⓟ
    closed December and January – **M** (booking essential)(dinner only) 9.25 **st.** 🍷 3.20 – **11 rm**
    ⬜ 16.00/28.25 **st.** – SB (October-May) 31.00/36.00 **st.**

  ✕✕✕ **Ramblers Country House**, Tinklers Bank, Farnley, NE45 5RN, S : 1 m. on Riding Mill Rd
    ℰ 2424, German rest. – ⓟ 🔥 AE ⓪ VISA
    closed Sunday and Monday – **M** (dinner only) 8.95 **t.** and a la carte 🍷 2.45.

AUSTIN-ROVER Main St. ℰ 2068   SUBARU Stagshaw ℰ 043 472 (Great Whittington) 216

CORNHILL-ON-TWEED Northumb. 👁️👁️👁️ 👁️👁️👁️ N 17 – pop. 312 – ECD : Thursday – ☎ 0890 Coldstream.

♦London 345 – ♦Edinburgh 49 – ♦Newcastle-upon-Tyne 59.

  🏠 **Coach House**, Crookham, TD12 4TD, E : 4 m. on A 697 ℰ 089 082(Crookham) 293, 🌳 –
    🛏️wc ⅙ ⓟ
    closed January and February – **11 rm** ⬜ 12.00/30.00 **st.**

CORPUSTY Norfolk 👁️👁️👁️ X 25 – pop. 1 ,234 – ✉️ Heydon – ☎ 026 387 Saxthorpe.

♦London 134 – ♦Cambridge 77 – ♦Norwich 16.

  🏨 **Cropton Hall** 🦢, NR11 6RX, S : 1 m. on Heydon Rd ℰ 869, 🏊, 🌳 – 📺 🛏️wc 🏠wc ⓟ
    M 3.95/6.95 **t.** 🍷 2.00 – **8 rm** ⬜ 19.50/37.00 **t.** – SB (except Easter, Christmas and New Year)
    35.00/41.00 **st.**

CORRIS Gwynedd 👁️👁️👁️ 👁️👁️👁️ I 26 – see Machynlleth (Powys).

CORSE LAWN Heref. and Worc. – see Tewkesbury (Glos.).

CORSHAM Wilts. 👁️👁️👁️ 👁️👁️👁️ N 29 The West Country G. – pop. 11 ,259 – ECD : Wednesday – ☎ 0249.

See : Corsham Court★★★*AC*.

🛈 Methuen Arms Hotel, High St. ℰ 714867.

♦London 110 – ♦Bristol 22 – Swindon 25.

  🏨🏨 **Rudloe Park**, Leafy Lane, SN13 0PA, ℰ 0225 (Bath) 810555, ≤, 🌳 – 📺 🛏️wc ⊛ ⓟ. 🏌️.
    🔥 AE ⓪ VISA 🍴
    closed first 2 weeks January – **M** 9.50/11.50 **t.** and a la carte 🍷 3.25 – **8 rm** ⬜ 35.00/65.00 **t.** –
    SB 64.50/74.50 **t.**

  ✕ **Weavers Loft**, 1 High St., SN13 0ES, ℰ 713982 – 🔥 ⓪ VISA
    closed Sunday dinner, Monday and first 2 weeks November – **M** (dinner only and Sunday
    lunch) 6.75/12.75 **t.** and a la carte 🍷 2.50.

CORTON Wilts. 👁️👁️👁️ 👁️👁️👁️ N 30 – see Warminster.

CORWEN Clwyd 👁️👁️👁️ 👁️👁️👁️ J 25 – pop. 2 ,187 – ECD : Wednesday – ✉️ ☎ 049 084 Llandrillo.

♦London 202 – Aberystwyth 64 – Chester 32 – Holyhead 67 – Shrewsbury 41.

  🏠 **Tyddyn Llan**, LL21 0ST, SW : 5 m. by A 5 on B 4401 ℰ 264, 🌳 – 🛏️wc ⓟ. 🔥 VISA
    closed February – **6 rm** ⬜ 16.50/17.50 **t.**

COSHAM Hants. 👁️👁️👁️ 👁️👁️👁️ Q 31 – see Portsmouth and Southsea.

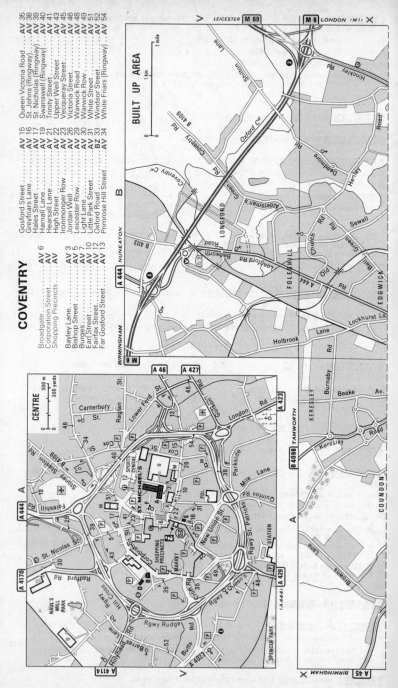

COVENTRY

Broadgate	AV 6
Corporation Street	AV
Shopping Precincts	AV
Bayley Lane	AV 3
Bishop Street	AV 5
Burges	AV 7
Earl Street	AV 10
Fairfax Street	AV 12
Far Gosford Street	AV 13
Gosford Street	AV 15
Greyfriars Lane	AV 16
Hales Street	AV 17
Harnall Lane	AV 19
Hearsall Lane	AV 21
High Street	AV 22
Ironmonger Row	AV 23
Jordan Well	AV 26
Leicester Row	AV 29
Little Park Street	AV 30
Oxford Road	AV 31
Primrose Hill Street	AV 34
Queen Victoria Road	AV 35
St. Johns (Ringway)	AV 38
St. Nicholas (Ringway)	AV 39
Swanswell (Ringway)	AV 40
Trinity Street	AV 41
Upper Well Street	AV 43
Vecqueray Street	AV 45
Victoria Street	AV 46
Warwick Road	AV 48
White Street	AV 49
Winde Street	AV 51
White Friars Street	BZ 52
White Friars Street (Ringway)	AV 54

BUILT UP AREA

CENTRE

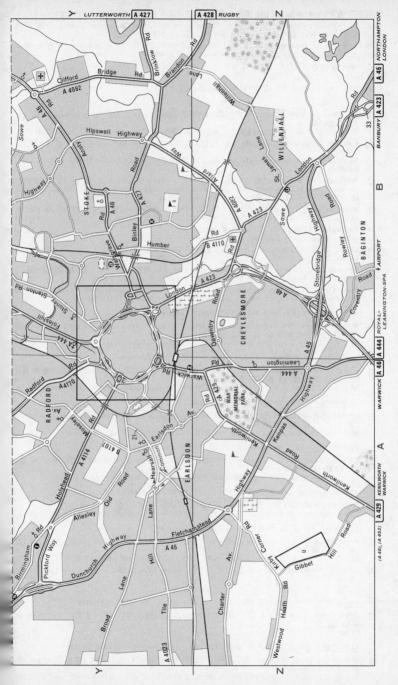

See : St. Michael's Cathedral★★★ (1962) : tapestry★★★ AV – Old Cathedral★ (ruins) AV **A** – St. John's Church★ 14C-15C AV **B** – Old houses★ 16C-17C AV **DEF**.

🖼 Brandon Wood, Brandon Lane ♗ 0203 (Wolston) 543141,SE : 6 m. by A 428 BY – ⛳ Sphinx, Siddeley Av.♗ 458890 BY – ⛳ The Grange, Copsewood ♗ 451465, E : 3 m. on A 428 BY.

✈ Coventry Airport : ♗ 301717, S : 3 ½ m. by Coventry Rd BZ.

🛈 36 Broadgate ♗ 20084 and 51717.

♦London 100 – ♦Birmingham 18 – ♦Bristol 96 – ♦Nottingham 52.

Plans on preceding pages

🏨 **De Vere** (De Vere), Cathedral Sq., CV1 5RP, ♗ 51851, Telex 31380 – 🛗 ⊟ rest 📺 ☎ 🅿 ᴁ. 🔄 ᴀᴇ ⓞ 𝐕𝐈𝐒𝐀 AV **n**
M 7.00/9.00 **st.** and a la carte ᐟ 3.25 – **209 rm** ⇆ 49.50/66.50 **st., 10 suites** 61.50/87.50 **st.**

🏨 **Leofric** (Embassy), Broadgate, CV1 1LZ, ♗ 21371, Telex 311193 – 🛗 📺 ☎. ᴁ. 🔄 ᴀᴇ ⓞ 𝐕𝐈𝐒𝐀 ⅀ AV **c**
M (closed Saturday lunch) 9.50 **st.** and a la carte ᐟ 2.75 – ⇆ 5.00 – **91 rm** 43.00/53.00 **st., 6 suites.**

🏨 **Hylands,** 153 Warwick Rd, CV3 6AU, ♗ 501600 – ⊟ rest 📺 ⇱wc ⊛ 🅿 ᴁ. 🔄 ᴀᴇ ⓞ 𝐕𝐈𝐒𝐀 closed 25 and 26 December – **M** (closed Saturday lunch) (carving rest.) 8.25 **t.** and a la carte – **56 rm** ⇆ 32.75/43.00 **st.** – SB (weekends only) 39.00 **st.** AYZ **z**

🏠 **Merrick Lodge,** 80-82 St. Nicholas St., CV1 4BP, ♗ 553940 – 📺 🛉wc 🅿. 🔄 ᴀᴇ ⓞ 𝐕𝐈𝐒𝐀 ⅀ AV **a**
M 6.50/8.50 **st.** and a la carte ᐟ 5.50 – **14 rm** ⇆ 25.00/36.00 **st.**

↑ **Fairlight,** 14 Regent St., CV1 3EP, ♗ 24215 AV **i**
closed 24 December-2 January – **11 rm** ⇆ 9.50/17.00 **st.**

↑ **Croft,** 23 Stoke Green, off Binley Rd, CV3 1FP, ♗ 457846, 🐖 – 🛉 🅿 BY **x**
12 rm ⇆ 14.50/29.50 **t.**

XX **Grandstand,** Coventry City F.C., King Richard St., CV2 4FW, ♗ 27053 – 🅿. 🔄 ᴀᴇ ⓞ 𝐕𝐈𝐒𝐀 BY **a**
closed Saturday and Sunday – **M** (lunch only) a la carte 8.50/13.15 ᐟ 2.50.

X **Herbs** with rm, 28 Lower Holyhead Rd, CV1 3AU, ♗ 555654, Vegetarian rest. – ⅀ AV **o**
M (closed Sunday) (dinner only) a la carte 5.50/6.15 **t.** – **8 rm** ⇆ 12.00/19.50 **t.**

at Longford N : 4 m. on A 444 – ✉ ✆ 0203 Coventry :

🏨 **Novotel Coventry,** Wilsons Lane, CV6 6HL, ♗ 365000, Telex 31545, ⊒ heated, squash – 🛗 ⊟ rest 📺 ⇱wc ☎ ᕼ 🅿. ᴁ. 🔄 ᴀᴇ ⓞ 𝐕𝐈𝐒𝐀 BV **v**
M 7.40/8.00 **st.** and a la carte ᐟ 3.50 – ⇆ 4.50 – **100 rm** 38.50/45.50 **st.**

at Walsgrave on Sowe NE : 3 m. on A 46 – ✉ ✆ 0203 Coventry :

🏨 **Crest** (Crest), Hinckley Rd, CV2 2HP, NE : ½ m. on A 46 ♗ 613261, Telex 311292 – 🛗 ⊟ rest 📺 ⇱wc ⊛ ᕼ 🅿. ᴁ. 🔄 ᴀᴇ ⓞ 𝐕𝐈𝐒𝐀 ⅀ BX **e**
M approx. 11.50 **st.** – ⇆ 5.75 – **152 rm** 45.00/55.00 **st., 2 suites** 55.00 **st.**

at Brandon E : 6 m. on A 428 – BZ – ✉ ✆ 0203 Coventry :

🏨 **Brandon Hall** (T.H.F.) ⑊, Main St., CV8 3FW, ♗ 542571, Telex 31472, 🐖, park, squash – 📺 ⇱wc ⊛ 🅿. ᴁ. 🔄 ᴀᴇ ⓞ 𝐕𝐈𝐒𝐀
M 5.95/9.75 **st.** and a la carte ᐟ 2.80 – ⇆ 5.50 – **67 rm** 35.00/45.50 **st.**

at Willenhall SE : 3 m. on A 423 – ✉ ✆ 0203 Coventry :

🏨 **Chace Crest** (Crest), London Rd, CV3 4EQ, ♗ 303398, Telex 311993, 🐖 – 📺 ⇱wc ⊛ 🅿. ᴁ. 🔄 ᴀᴇ ⓞ 𝐕𝐈𝐒𝐀 ⅀ BZ **u**
M approx. 11.50 **st.** – ⇆ 4.95 – **68 rm** 43.00/52.00 **st.** – SB (weekends only) 55.00 **st.**

at Berkswell W : 6 ½ m. on A 4023 – AY – ✉ ✆ 0203 Coventry :

XXX **Nailcote Hall,** CV7 7DE, S : 1 ½ m. on A 4023 ♗ 466174, 🐖 – 🅿. 🔄 ᴀᴇ ⓞ. ⅀
closed Sunday – **M** 8.50 **t.** (lunch) and a la carte 10.05/14.75 **t.** ᐟ 2.85 – **4 rm** ⇆ 45.00/75.00 **t.**

at Allesley NW : 3 m. on A 4114 – ✉ ✆ 0203 Coventry :

🏨 **Post House** (T.H.F.), Rye Hill, CV5 9PH, ♗ 402151, Telex 31427 – 🛗 ⊟ rest 📺 ⇱wc ☎ 🅿. ᴁ. 🔄 ᴀᴇ ⓞ 𝐕𝐈𝐒𝐀 AXY **s**
M (carving rest.) 6.50/7.00 **st.** and a la carte ᐟ 2.70 – ⇆ 5.50 – **196 rm** 37.50/44.50 **st.**

🏨 **Allesley,** Birmingham Rd, CV5 9GT, ♗ 403272, Group Telex 312549 – 📺 ⇱wc 🛉wc ⊛ 🅿. ᴁ. ⅀ AY **r**
37 rm.

at Keresley NW : 3 m. on B 4098 – AX – ✉ Coventry – ✆ 020 333 Keresley :

🏨 **Royal Court,** Tamworth Rd, CV7 8JG, ♗ 4171, Group Telex 312549, 🐖 – 🛗 📺 ⇱wc 🛉wc ⊛ ᕼ 🅿. ᴁ. ⅀
99 rm.

at Meriden NW : 6 m. by A 45 on B 4102 – AX – ✉ Coventry – ✆ 0676 Meriden :

🏨 **Manor** (De Vere), Main Rd, CV7 7NH, ♗ 22735, Telex 311011, ⊒ heated, 🐖 – 📺 ⇱wc ⊛ 🅿. ᴁ. 🔄 ᴀᴇ ⓞ 𝐕𝐈𝐒𝐀
M 7.95/12.95 **st.** and a la carte ᐟ 2.95 – **32 rm** ⇆ 41.50/58.00 **st.** – SB (weekends only) 60.00 **st.**

AUSTIN-ROVER Lockhurst Lane ☎ 88851
AUSTIN-ROVER, LAND ROVER-RANGE ROVER
Kenpas Highway ☎ 411515
BMW 138 Sutherland Av. ☎ 461441
CITROEN 105 Foleshill Rd ☎ 26417
FIAT 324 Station Rd Balsall Common ☎ 0676
(Berkswell) 33145
HONDA 207 Wheelwright Lane, Exhall ☎ 364004

NISSAN 149 Far Gosford St. ☎ 24552
PEUGEOT-TALBOT 136 Daventry Rd ☎ 503522
RELIANT, SKODA 142 Lower Ford St. ☎ 20475
RENAULT 181-6 Walsgrave Rd ☎ 458600
TOYOTA Bennetts Rd, Keresley ☎ 334204
VAUXHALL-OPEL Raglan St. ☎ 25361
VW, AUDI Spon End ☎ 56325

COWBRIDGE (BONT-FAEN) South Glam. 🔢 J 29 – pop. 3 ,525 – ECD : Wednesday – ☎ 044 63.
Envir. : Old Beaupré Castle★ 14C, SE : 3 m.
♦London 169 – ♦Cardiff 12 – ♦Swansea 27.

🏨 Bear, High St., CF7 7AF, ☎ 4814 – 📺 ➡wc ☎ 🅿. 🔏
31 rm

✗ Basil's Brasserie, 2 Eastgate, CF7 7DG, ☎ 3738, Bistro – 🅿. 🔼 𝖵𝖨𝖲𝖠
closed Sunday, Monday, 2 weeks August and 1 week Christmas – **M** (bar lunch)/dinner a la
carte 9.15/10.45 t.

COWES I.O.W. 🔢 🔢 PQ 31 – see Wight (Isle of).

COYCHURCH (LLANGRALLO) Mid Glam. 🔢 J 29 – see Bridgend.

CRACKINGTON HAVEN Cornwall 🔢 G 31 The West Country G. – ECD : Tuesday – ✉ Bude –
☎ 084 03 St. Gennys.
♦London 262 – Bude 11 – Truro 42.

🏨 Crackington Manor ⤸, EX23 0JG, ☎ 397, 🏊 heated, 🐾 – ➡wc 🅿. 🔼 🅰🅴 𝖵𝖨𝖲𝖠
closed January and February – **M** (bar lunch)/dinner a la carte 🛇 2.40 – **15 rm**
⊑ 21.45/53.00 t. – SB (except summer and Bank Holidays) 36.00/40.00 st.

🏨 Coombe Barton, EX23 0JG, ☎ 345, ≤ – ➡wc 🅿. 🔼 𝖵𝖨𝖲𝖠
March-October – **M** (bar lunch)/dinner 8.50 t. and a la carte 🛇 2.80 – **9 rm** ⊑ 15.75/33.00 t. –
SB 35.00/41.00 t.

CRANBROOK Kent 🔢 V 30 – pop. 3 ,593 – ECD : Wednesday – ☎ 0580.
Envir. : Sissinghurst : castle★ 16C (≤★, 78 steps), gardens★★ AC NE : 1 ½ m.
📗 Benenden Rd ☎ 712833.
🛈 Vestry Hall, Stone St. ☎ 712538 (summer only).
♦London 53 – Hastings 19 – Maidstone 15.

🏨 Willesley, Angley Rd, TN17 2LE, N : ¾ m. on B 2189 at junction with A 229 ☎ 713555, 🐾 –
📺 ➡wc ☎ 🅿. 🔼 🅰🅴 ⓞ 𝖵𝖨𝖲𝖠
closed first week February – **M** 6.75/10.50 st. and a la carte 🛇 3.50 – **16 rm** ⊑ 33.00/48.00 st. –
SB (weekends only)(mid October-April) 52.00/54.00 st.

🏨 Kennel Holt ⤸, Flishinghurst, TN17 2PT, NW : 2 ¼ m. by A 229 on A 262 ☎ 712032, ≤,
« Country house atmosphere and gardens » – 📺 ➡wc 🅿
closed 21 December-26 January – **M** (dinner only) 15.00 t. – **7 rm** ⊑ 19.00/52.00 t.

AUSTIN-ROVER Cranbrook Rd, Staplehurst ☎
892093

FORD Stone St. ☎ 712121
RENAULT Wisley Pound ☎ 713262

CRANTOCK Cornwall 🔢 E 32 – see Newquay.

CRAWLEY West Sussex 🔢 T 30 – pop. 80 ,113 – ECD : Wednesday – ☎ 0293.
📗 Cottesmore, Buchan Hill ☎ 28256, S : 4 m. on plan of Gatwick Z – 📗 Gatwick Manor ☎ 24470,
N : 5 m. on plan of Gatwick Y.
♦London 33 – ♦Brighton 21 – Lewes 23 – Royal Tunbridge Wells 23.

Plan of Enlarged Area : see Gatwick

Plan on next page

🏨 George (T.H.F.), High St., RH10 1BS, ☎ 24215, Telex 87385 – 📺 ➡wc ☎ 🅿. 🔏. 🔼 🅰🅴 ⓞ
𝖵𝖨𝖲𝖠   BY o
M 8.50/10.25 st. and a la carte 🛇 2.70 – ⊑ 5.50 – **76 rm** 43.00/51.50 st.

🏨 Crest (Crest), Langley Drive, Tushmore Roundabout, RH11 7SX, ☎ 29991, Telex 877311 – 📲
📺 ➡wc ☎ 🅿. 🔏. 🔼 🅰🅴 ⓞ 𝖵𝖨𝖲𝖠   BY n
M approx. 11.50 st. – ⊑ 5.75 – **231 rm** 46.50/56.50 st. – SB (weekends only) 55.00 st.

🏨 Goffs Park, 45-47 Goffs Park Rd, RH11 8AX, ☎ 35447, Group Telex 87415, 🐾 – 📺 ➡wc
🍴wc ☎ 🅿. 🔼 🅰🅴 ⓞ 𝖵𝖨𝖲𝖠   AZ s
M 6.25/7.25 t. and a la carte 🛇 3.75 – **47 rm**.

🏨 Grange, 15 Brighton Rd, RH10 6AE, ☎ 35191 – 📺 🍴wc ☎ 🅿. 🔼 🅰🅴 ⓞ 𝖵𝖨𝖲𝖠. 🔏   BZ a
closed 2 weeks at Christmas – **M** (dinner only) 7.40 t. 🛇 2.25 – **39 rm** ⊑ 32.45/46.20 t.

155

Broad Walk	**BY** 2	Caffins Close	**BY** 4	Queensway	**BY** 24
High Street	**BY**	College Road	**BY** 6	Southgate Road	**BZ** 28
Queens Square	**BY** 22	Drake Road	**BY** 12	Station Road	**BY** 30
The Broadway	**BY**	Exchange Road	**BZ** 15	The Boulevard	**BY** 32
The Martlets	**BY**	Hunter Road	**BZ** 18	Titmus Drive	**BZ** 34
		Livingstone Road	**BZ** 19	West Street	**ABZ** 42
Buckmans Road	**AY** 3	Orchard Street	**BY** 19	Woolborough Road	**BY** 45

CRAWLEY

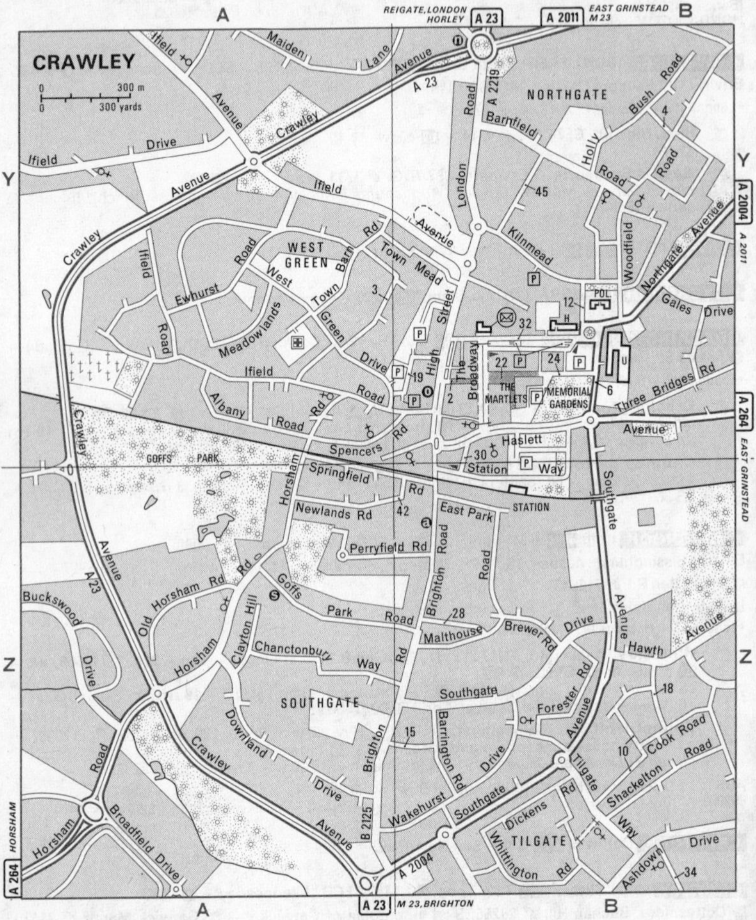

at Copthorne NE : 4 ½ m. on A 264 – BY – ⊠ Crawley – ☎ 0342 Copthorne :

Copthorne, Copthorne Rd, RH10 3PG, ☎ 714971, Telex 95500, ☞, park, squash – 📺 ☎ ⅙ ℗

223 rm. 10 suites.

at Pound Hill E : 3 m. by A 264 – BY – on B 2036 – ⊠ ☎ 0293 Crawley :

Barnwood, Balcombe Rd, RH10 4RU, ☎ 882709, ☞ – 📺 Ⓦc ☎ ℗ ⚠ AE ⓄⒹ VISA ≉
closed 1 week at Christmas – **M** *(closed lunch Saturday and Sunday)* (grill rest. only)(bar
lunch)/dinner 11.50 **st**. ⅙ 2.60 – **30 rm** ⊆ 30.00/40.00 **t**.   see plan of Gatwick **Z a**

AUSTIN-ROVER Copthorne ☎ 713933
BEDFORD, OPEL-VAUXHALL Fleming Way ☎ 29771
CITROEN 163/165 Three Bridges Rd ☎ 25533
FORD Worth Park Av., Three Bridges ☎ 28381
PEUGEOT-TALBOT Barton ☎ 543232

RENAULT Orchard St. ☎ 23323
SAAB Turners Hill ☎ 715467
SKODA Balcombe Rd ☎ 882620
VW, AUDI Overdene Way ☎ 515551

🚗 *To go a long way quickly, use Michelin maps at a scale of 1:1 000 000.*

156

CREWE Cheshire 402 403 404 M 24 – pop. 59 ,097 – ECD : Wednesday – ✆ 0270.
Envir. : Sandbach (Two Crosses★ 7C, in Market Place) NE : 10 m.
🚗 ☎ 214343.
🚩 Delamere House, Delamere St., ☎ 583191.
♦London 174 – Chester 24 – ♦Liverpool 49 – ♦Manchester 36 – ♦Stoke-on-Trent 15.

- 🏨 **Crewe Arms** (Embassy), Nantwich Rd, CW1 1DW, ☎ 213204 – 📺 ➪wc ☎ 🅿 🛎 📶 AE
  ① VISA ✣
  M (carving rest.) 8.25 **st.** and a la carte ₪ 2.50 – ➩ 5.00 – **36 rm** 33.00/40.50 **st.** – SB (weekends only) 48.00 **st.**

ALFA-ROMEO Newcastle Rd ☎ 665138
AUSTIN-ROVER Hough ☎ 841320
AUSTIN-ROVER High St. ☎ 256521
CITROEN Woolstanwood ☎ 213495
FIAT, NISSAN Cross Green ☎ 583437
LADA Stewart St. ☎ 67560

MAZDA West St. ☎ 214317
PEUGEOT, TALBOT 613 Crewe Rd, Wistaston ☎ 664111
VOLVO Earle St. ☎ 587711
VW, AUDI Oak St. ☎ 213241

CREWKERNE Somerset 403 L 31 The West Country G. – pop. 6 ,018 – ECD : Thursday – ✆ 0460.
♦London 145 – Exeter 38 – ♦Southampton 81 – Taunton 20.

- 🏠 Old Parsonage, 55-59 Barn St., TA18 8BP, ☎ 73516 – 📺 ➪wc 🍴wc 🅿 – **10 rm**.

  at Haselbury Plucknett NE : 2 ¾ m. by A 30 on A 3066 – ✉ ✆ 0460 Crewkerne :

- ↥ **Oak House,** North St., TA18 7RB, ☎ 73625, « 16C thatched cottage », 🥀 – 🅿
  Easter-October – **7 rm** ➩ 13.00/30.00 **st.**

CRICCIETH Gwynedd 402 403 H 25 – pop. 1 ,535 – ECD : Wednesday – ✆ 076 671.
See : Castle ⪦★★ AC.
🏨 Ednyfed Hill ☎ 2154.
♦London 249 – Caernarfon 17 – Shrewsbury 85.

- 🏨 Bron Eifion Country House ⌂, LL52 0SA, W : ½ m. on A 497 ☎ 2385, ⪦, « 19C country house in large garden », park – ➪wc 🍴wc ☎ 🅿 – **24 rm**.
- 🏠 **Plas Isa,** Porthmadog Rd, LL52 0HP, ☎ 2443 – 📺 ➪wc 🍴wc ☎ 🅿 📶 AE ① VISA ✣
  M (bar lunch)/dinner 8.00 **t.** and a la carte ₪ 2.75 – **12 rm** ➩ 18.50/37.00 – SB (October-May) 48.00 **st.**
- ↥ **Glyn-y-Coed,** Portmadoc Rd, LL52 0HL, ☎ 2870 – 🅿
  closed Christmas and New Year – **10 rm** ➩ 10.00/20.00 **t.**
- ✗ **Moelwyn** with rm, 27-29 Mona Terr., LL52 0HG, ☎ 2500, ⪦ – 📶 VISA ✣
  April-October – **M** (closed Monday lunch) 9.95 **t.** (dinner) and a la carte 7.35/11.20 **t.** ₪ 3.00 –
  8 rm ➩ 9.50/19.00 **t.**

AUDI, MERCEDES-BENZ, VW Caernarfon Rd ☎ 2516
FIAT Ala Rd, Pwllheli ☎ 612827

VOLVO Llanystumdwy ☎ 2733

CRICK Northants. 403 404 Q 26 – see Rugby.

CRICKHOWELL Powys 403 K 28 – pop. 1 ,979 – ECD : Wednesday – ✆ 0873.
Envir. : Tretower Court and Castle★, NW : 2 ½ m.
♦London 169 – Abergavenny 6 – Brecon 14 – Newport 25.

- 🏨 **Gliffaes Country House** ⌂, NP8 1RH, W : 3 ¾ m. by A 40 ☎ 0874 (Bwlch) 730371, ⪦,
  « Garden », ⛳, park, ✣ – ➪wc 🍴wc ☎ 🅿 📶 VISA ✣
  closed January-mid March – **M** 6.00/9.00 **st.** – **19 rm** ➩ 18.50/50.00 **st.** – SB 28.50/38.00 **st.**
- 🏠 **Bear,** High St., NP8 1BW, ☎ 810408, 🥀 – ➪wc 🍴wc 🅿 📶
  M (closed Sunday) (bar lunch)/dinner a la carte 10.20/12.00 **t.** ₪ 3.50 – **12 rm** ➩ 20.15/34.50 **t.**

CROMER Norfolk 404 X 25 – pop. 4 ,197 – ECD : Wednesday – ✆ 0263.
♦London 132 – ♦Norwich 23 – Peterborough 76.

- 🏠 **Craigside,** St. Mary's Rd, NR27 9DJ, ☎ 511025, ⛲ heated, 🥀 – 📺 🍴 🅿 📶 ① VISA
  M (bar lunch)/dinner 10.00 **st.** ₪ 2.50 – **22 rm** ➩ 15.00/32.00 **st.** – SB 28.00/34.00 **st.**

CROOKLANDS Cumbria 402 L 21 – see Kendal.

CROSBY-ON-EDEN Cumbria 401 402 L 29 – see Carlisle.

CROSSBUSH West Sussex – see Arundel.

CROWBOROUGH East Sussex 404 U 30 – pop. 17 ,008 – ECD : Wednesday – ✆ 089 26.
♦London 45 – ♦Brighton 25 – Maidstone 26.

- 🏨 Crest, Beacon Rd, TN6 1AD, on A 26 ☎ 2772 – 📟 📺 ➪wc 🍴wc 📺 🅿 🛎 – **30 rm**.

AUSTIN-ROVER Beacon Rd ☎ 2777
FORD Crowborough Hill ☎ 2175

TALBOT Church Rd ☎ 3424

CROWTHORNE Berks. **404** R 29 – pop. 19,166 – ECD : Wednesday – ✉ ✆ 0344.
♦London 42 – Reading 15.

🏨 **Waterloo** (Anchor), Dukes Ride, RG11 7NW, on B 3348 ℰ 777711, Telex 848139, ⚗ – 📺
☐wc ⋔wc ☎ ℗. ♨. ⚠ ᴁ ⓞ 𝗩𝗜𝗦𝗔
M *(closed lunch Saturday and Bank Holidays)* 8.45/10.50 **t.** and a la carte ⌕ 3.00 – **58 rm**
⊊ 47.00/53.00 – SB (weekends only) 56.00 **st.**

CROXDALE Durham – see Durham.

CRUDWELL Wilts. **403 404** N 29 – see Malmesbury.

CRUG-Y-BAR Dyfed **403** I 27 – ECD : Saturday – ✉ Llanwrda – ✆ 055 83 Talley.
♦London 213 – Carmarthen 26 – ♦Swansea 36.

🏠 **Glanrannell Park** ⑤, SA19 8SA, SW : ½ m. by B 4302 ℰ 230, <, ⌕, ⚗, park – ☐wc ℗
April-October – **M** *(closed Sunday lunch)* (bar lunch)/dinner 8.50 **t.** ⌕ 3.00 – **8 rm**
⊊ 15.00/33.00 **t.**

CUCKFIELD West Sussex **404** T 30 – pop. 2,650 – ECD : Wednesday – ✆ 0444 Haywards
Heath.
♦London 40 – ♦Brighton 15.

🏨 **Ockenden Manor,** Ockenden Lane, RH17 5LD, ℰ 416111, « Part 16C manor », ⚗ – 📺
☐wc ☎ ℗. ⚠ ᴁ ⓞ 𝗩𝗜𝗦𝗔. ⚘
M 9.25/15.00 **t.** and a la carte – ⊊ 5.25 – **10 rm** 30.00/80.00 **t.**, **2 suites** 70.00/80.00 **t.**.

CUFFLEY Herts. **404** T 28 – pop. 4,875 – ECD : Thursday – ✆ 0707 Potter's Bar.
♦London 16 – ♦Cambridge 44 – Luton 26.

🏨 **Ponsbourne** ⑤, Ponsbourne Park, Newgate St., SG13 8QZ, N : 3 m. by B 157 ℰ 875221,
Telex 299912, <, ⌕, ⚗, park, ☎ ℗ ⚠ ᴁ ⓞ 𝗩𝗜𝗦𝗔
M *(closed Sunday dinner to non-residents)* 11.00/13.00 **t.** and a la carte – **32 rm** ⊊ 30.00/50.00 **t.**

CUMNOR Oxon. **403 404** P 28 – see Oxford.

CWMBRAN Gwent **403** K 29 – pop. 44,592 – ECD : Wednesday – ✆ 063 33.
🏌 Greenmeadow, Treherbert Rd ℰ 69321 – ♦London 149 – ♦Bristol 35 – ♦Cardiff 17 – Newport 5.

🏨 **Commodore,** Mill Lane, Llan-yr-Afon, NP44 8SN, ℰ 4091 – 🛗 📺 ☎ ℗ ☐wc ⋔wc ☎ ℗. ♨. ⚠
ᴁ ⓞ 𝗩𝗜𝗦𝗔
M 7.95/9.50 **st.** and a la carte ⌕ 3.75 – **60 rm** ⊊ 25.00/45.00 **st.** – SB (weekends only)
48.00/54.00 **st.**

DALLINGTON East Sussex **404** V 31 – pop. 286 – ✉ Heathfield – ✆ 042 482 Brightling.
♦London 59 – ♦Brighton 26 – Hastings 14 – Maidstone 34.

✕ **Little Byres,** Christmas Farm, Battle Rd, TN21 9LE, on B 2096 ℰ 230 – ℗. ⚠
closed Sunday dinner and January – **M** (dinner only and Sunday lunch) 8.00/11.00 **t.** ⌕ 2.70.

DARESBURY Cheshire **402 403 404** M 23 – pop. 353 – ✉ ✆ 0925 Warrington.
♦London 197 – Chester 16 – ♦Liverpool 22 – ♦Manchester 25.

🏨 **Lord Daresbury** (De Vere), Chester Rd, WA4 4BB, on A 56 ℰ 67331, Telex 629330, ⚠,
squash – ♨. ☎ ℗. ♨. ⚠ ᴁ ⓞ 𝗩𝗜𝗦𝗔
M 10.00 **st.** and a la carte ⌕ 3.50 – **141 rm** ⊊ 49.00/59.00 **st.**, **3 suites** 69.00 **st.** – SB (weekends
only) 65.50/69.50 **st.**

DARLINGTON Durham **402** P 20 – pop. 85,519 – ECD : Wednesday – ✆ 0325.
🏌 Blackwell Grange, Briar Close ℰ 464464, S : 1 m. on A 66 – 🏌 Stressholme, Snipe Lane,
ℰ 461002, S : 2 m. – ✈ Tees-side Airport : ℰ 332811, E : 6 m. by A 67.
🛈 District Library, Crown St. ℰ 469858.
♦London 251 – ♦Leeds 61 – ♦Middlesbrough 14 – ♦Newcastle-upon-Tyne 35.

🏨 **Blackwell Grange Moat House** (Q.M.H.) ⑤, Blackwell Grange, DL3 8QH, SW : 2 m. on
A 66 ℰ 460111, Telex 587272, ⚗, ⚘ – 🛗 📺 ☎ ℗ ♨. ⚠ ᴁ ⓞ
M *(closed Saturday lunch)* 8.50/10.50 **st.** and a la carte ⌕ 3.25 – **98 rm** ⊊ 36.50/48.00 **st.**,
2 suites 65.00/70.00 **st.** – SB (weekends only) 45.00/56.00 **st.**

🏨 **King's Head** (Swallow), Priestgate, DL1 1NW, ℰ 467612 – 🛗 📺 ☐wc ☎ ℗. ♨. ⚠ ᴁ ⓞ
𝗩𝗜𝗦𝗔
M 6.50/9.00 **st.** and a la carte ⌕ 3.50 – **86 rm** ⊊ 36.50/49.00 **st.** – SB 46.00/56.00 **st.**

🏨 **Stakis White Horse** (Stakis), Harrowgate Hill, DL1 3AD, N : 2 ¼ m. on A 167 ℰ 487111 – 🛗
📺 ☎ ℗. ♨. ⚠ ᴁ ⓞ 𝗩𝗜𝗦𝗔
M (bar lunch Saturday)/a la carte 4.80/12.35 **t.** ⌕ 3.25 – **40 rm** ⊊ 35.00/45.00 **st.**

✕✕ **Bishop's House,** 38 Coniscliffe Rd, DL3 7RG, ℰ 286666 – ⚠ ᴁ 𝗩𝗜𝗦𝗔
closed Saturday lunch, Sunday, last week June, first week July and 24 December-3 January –
M 7.50/11.85 **t.** ⌕ 3.60.

at Coatham Mundeville N : 4 m. by A 167 – ⊠ Darlington – ✪ 0325 Aycliffe :

🏛 **Hall Garth Country House** ⌂, DL1 3LU, ℰ 313333, « Country house atmosphere »,
⅃ heated, 🐾, ✗ – 📺 ⊖wc ⊪wc ☎ 🅿 🔄 AE ⓞ 𝘝𝘐𝘚𝘈
closed 22 December-2 January – **M** *(closed Sunday dinner)* 10.70/13.95 t. ⅃ 2.50 – ⌐ 3.25 –
20 rm 31.00/50.00 t., **2 suites** – SB (weekends only) 98.90/108.90 **st.**

at Tees-side Airport E : 5 ½ m. by A 67 – ⊠ ✪ 0325 Darlington :

🏛 **St. George** (Mt. Charlotte), DL2 1RH, ℰ 332631, Telex 58664, squash – 📺 ⊖wc ☜ 🅿 🔄
🔄 AE ⓞ 𝘝𝘐𝘚𝘈
M 6.00/9.00 **st.** and a la carte ⅃ 3.15 – **58 rm** ⌐ 31.25/49.00 **st.**, **1 suite** 86.00 **st.** – SB (weekends
only) 44.00/50.60 **st.**

at Neasham SE : 6 ½ m. by A 66 off A 167 – ⊠ ✪ 0325 Darlington :

🏛 **Newbus Arms** ⌂, DL2 1PE, W : ½ m. ℰ 721071, 🐾, squash – 📺 ⊖wc ☎ 🅿 🔄 🔄 AE
ⓞ 𝘝𝘐𝘚𝘈
M 12.75 t. and a la carte ⅃ 3.00 – **15 rm** ⌐ 31.00/39.00 t. – SB (weekends only) 44.00 **st.**

at Stapleton S : 3 m. by A 66 – ⊠ ✪ 0325 Darlington :

✗ **Bridge Inn**, DL2 2QQ, ℰ 50106 – 🅿 🔄 AE ⓞ 𝘝𝘐𝘚𝘈
closed Saturday lunch, Sunday dinner and Monday – **M** (lunch by arrangement) 6.50/17.50 t.
and a la carte ⅃ 3.00.

CITROEN 163 Northgate ℰ 468753
FIAT Woodland Rd ℰ 483251
FORD St. Cuthberts Way ℰ 467581
LADA Albert Rd ℰ 485759
RENAULT, HONDA Chestnut St. ℰ 485141
TOYOTA Neasham Rd. ℰ 482141

VAUXHALL Chestnut St. ℰ 466155
VAUXHALL-OPEL Whessoe Rd ℰ 466044
VW, AUDI 28/56 West Auckland Rd, Faverdale ℰ
53737
YUGO Haughton Rd ℰ 463384

DARTINGTON Devon 📖 I 32 – see Totnes.

DARTMOUTH Devon 📖 J 32 The West Country G. – pop. 5,282 – ECD : Wednesday and
Saturday – ✪ 080 43.

See : Site★★ (≼★) – Dartmouth Castle (≼★★★) *AC*.

Envir. : Start Point (≼★), S : 15 m. including 1 m. on foot.

🚩 Royal Avenue Gardens ℰ 4224 (summer only).

♦London 236 – Exeter 36 – ♦Plymouth 35.

🏛 **Dart Marina** (T.H.F.), Sandquay, TQ6 9PH, ℰ 2580, ≼ – 📺 ⊖wc ☜ 🅿 🔄 AE ⓞ 𝘝𝘐𝘚𝘈
M 10.30/15.00 **st.** and a la carte ⅃ 2.70 – ⌐ 5.50 – **35 rm** 33.00/47.50 **st.**

🏛 **Royal Castle**, 11 The Quay, TQ6 9PS, ℰ 2397 – 📺 ⊖wc ⟵. 🔄 𝘝𝘐𝘚𝘈
M a la carte 4.45/6.70 **st.** ⅃ 3.15 – **20 rm** ⌐ 23.95/59.00 **st.** – SB (except Christmas)
49.95/59.95 **st.**

↑ **Townstal Farm**, Townstal Rd, TQ6 9HY, N : 1 m. on A 379 ℰ 2300, 🐾 – 🅿
7 rm ⌐ 10.00/22.00 **st.**

✗✗ ✿ **Carved Angel**, 2 South Embankment, TQ6 9BH, ℰ 2465, ≼
closed Sunday dinner, Monday and January – **M** 21.00 **st.** (dinner) and a la carte ⅃ 3.50
Spec. Provençal fish soup, Salmon in pastry with ginger and currants (April-August), Summer pudding (June-
August).

at Strete SW : 6 m. on A 379 – ⊠ Dartmouth – ✪ 080 427 Stoke Fleming :

✗ **Laughing Monk**, TQ6 0RN, ℰ 770639 – 🅿 🔄 AE ⓞ 𝘝𝘐𝘚𝘈
closed Sunday and 2 weeks January – **M** (dinner only) (booking essential) a la carte 8.50/10.50 t.
⅃ 2.50.

DAWLISH Devon 📖 J 32 The West Country G. – pop. 8,030 – ECD : Thursday and Saturday –
✪ 0626.

🏌 Warren ℰ 862255, E : 1 ½ m.

🚩 The Lawn ℰ 863589.

♦London 215 – Exeter 13 – ♦Plymouth 40 – Torquay 11.

🏛 **Langstone Cliff** ⌂, Dawlish Warren, EX7 0NA, N : 2 m. by A 379 ℰ 865155, ⅃ heated, 🔄,
🐾, ☜ – ✢ 📺 ⊖wc ☜ ⅓ 🅿 🔄 🔄 AE ⓞ 𝘝𝘐𝘚𝘈
M 6.00/8.50 **st.** ⅃ 3.20 – **70 rm** ⌐ 20.00/48.00 **st.** – SB 54.00/60.00 **st.**

↑ **Lynbridge**, 8 Barton Villas, The Bartons, EX7 9QJ, ℰ 862352, 🐾 – 🅿 ✗
Easter-October – **8 rm** ⌐ 8.50/18.00 **st.**

DEDDINGTON Oxon. 📖📖 Q 28 – pop. 1,617 – ✪ 0869.

♦London 72 – ♦Birmingham 46 – ♦Coventry 33 – ♦Oxford 18.

↑ **Maunds Farm**, High St., OX5 4SL, ℰ 38569, 🐾 – 🅿 ✗
closed Christmas – **8 rm** ⌐ 9.00/18.00 **st.**

DEDHAM Essex **404** W 28 – pop. 1,905 – ECD : Wednesday – ✉ ✪ 0206 Colchester.
🛈 Countryside Centre, Duchy Barn, The Drift ✆ 323447 (summer only).
♦London 63 – Chelmsford 30 – Colchester 8 – ♦Ipswich 12.

🏨 **Maison Talbooth** ⟡ without rest., Stratford Rd, CO7 6HW, W : ½ m. ✆ 322367, ≼, 🚗 –
📺 **P**. 🔃 🄰🄴 ⓞ **VISA**. ✠
⟐ 4.00 – **10 rm** 60.00/95.00 st., **1 suite** 105.00 st.

✕✕✕ ✿ **Le Talbooth**, Gun Hill, CO7 6HP, W : 1 m. ✆ 323150, Group Telex 987083, ≼, « Tudor
house on riverside », 🚗 – 📺 **P**. 🔃 🄰🄴 ⓞ **VISA**
M 11.25 **t.** (lunch) and a la carte 14.50/18.00 **t.** 🛈 3.60
Spec. Soufflé Talbooth, Game (September-February), Strawberry mille feuille.

✕✕ **Dedham Vale** with rm, Stratford Rd, CO7 6HW, W : ¾ m. ✆ 322273, Group Telex 987083, ≼,
🚗 – 📺 ⇌wc ☎ **P**. 🔃 🄰🄴 ⓞ **VISA**. ✠
M (smörgasbord lunch)/dinner a la carte 11.25/14.50 **t.** 🛈 4.10 – ⟐ 3.50 – **6 rm** 40.00/70.00. st.

DENBIGH (DINBYCH) Clwyd **402 403** J 24 – pop. 7,710 – ECD : Thursday – ✪ 074 578 Llanynys.
♦London 217 – Chester 29 – Shrewsbury 55.

🏨 **Bryn Morfydd** ⟡, Llanrhaedr, LL16 4NP, SE : 3 ¼ m. by A 525 ✆ 280, ≼ Vale of Clwyd,
🌊 heated, 🌲, 🚲, park, ✠ – 📺 ⇌wc 𝔪wc **P**. 🔃 🄰🄴 ⓞ **VISA**. ✠
M 4.50/8.50 **st.** and a la carte 🛈 4.15 – **29 rm** ⟐ 25.00/35.00 **st.** – SB 45.00 **st.**

DENHOLME West Yorks. **402** 0 22 – pop. 2,369 – ✉ ✪ 0274 Bradford.
♦London 220 – Burnley 22 – ♦Leeds 17 – ♦Manchester 39.

🏨 **Five Flags**, Manywell Heights, BD13 5EA, N : 1 m. on A 629 ✆ 834188, 🚗 – 📺 ⇌wc 𝔢
P. 🛆 🔃 🄰🄴 ⓞ **VISA**. ✠
M 5.75/8.95 and a la carte – **26 rm** ⟐ 24.00/48.00 **t.**, **2 suites** – SB (weekends only)
30.00/60.00 **st.**

DENTON Greater Manchester **402 403 404** N 23 – pop. 37,784 – ECD : Tuesday – ✉ ✪ 061
Manchester.
♦London 204 – ♦Manchester 6 – ♦Sheffield 34.

🏨 **Old Rectory** ⟡, Meadow Lane, Haughton Green, M34 1GD, S : 2 m. by A 6017 ✆ 336 7516,
Telex 668615, 🚗 – 📺 ⇌wc ☎ **P**. 🔃 **VISA**. ✠
closed 1 week at Christmas and Bank Holidays – **M** (closed Saturday lunch and Sunday) a la
carte 7.75/10.50 **st.** 🛈 2.50 – **26 rm** ⟐ 32.00/45.00 **st.** – SB (weekends only) 60.00/80.00 **st.**

DERBY Derbs. **402 403 404** P 25 – pop. 218,026 – ECD : Wednesday – ✪ 0332.
Envir. : Kedleston Hall★★ (18C) **AC**, NW : 5 m. by Kedleston Rd ✕ – Melbourne (St. Michael's
Church : Norman nave★) S : 8 m. by A 514 ✕.
🏌 Allestree Park, ✆ 550616, N : 2 m. on A 6 ✕ – 🏌 Mickleover,✆ 513339, W : 3 m. by A 38 ✕ – 🏌
Breadsall Priory, Moor Rd, Morley ✆ 832235, NE : 3 m. off A 38 ✕.
✈ East Midlands, Castle Donington ✆ 810621, Telex 37543, SE : 12 m. by A6 ✕.
🛈 Reference Library, The Wardwick ✆ 31111 ext 2185/6 or 46124 (evenings and Saturday).

♦London 132 – ♦Birmingham 40 – ♦Coventry 49 – ♦Leicester 29 – ♦Manchester 62 – ♦Nottingham 16 – ♦Sheffield
47 – ♦Stoke-on-Trent 35.

Plan opposite

🏨 **Midland,** Midland Rd, DE1 2SQ, ✆ 45894, 🚗 – 📺 ⇌wc ☎ **P**. 🛆. 🔃 🄰🄴 ⓞ **VISA**   Z i
M 7.00/10.50 **t.** and a la carte – **62 rm** ⟐ 23.50/43.00 **st.**

🏨 **Pennine** (De Vere), Macklin St., DE1 1LF, ✆ 41741, Telex 377545 – 📱 📺 ⇌wc 𝔪wc 𝔢. 🛆.
🔃 🄰🄴 **VISA**   Z e
M (buffet lunch) 5.50/7.50 **t.** and a la carte 🛈 3.25 – **96 rm** ⟐ 37.50/47.50 **st.**

🏨 **Gables,** 119 London Rd, DE1 2QR, ✆ 40633 – 📺 𝔪wc **P**. 🔃 **VISA**. ✠   Z o
closed 1 week at Christmas – **M** 5.50/7.50 **t.** and a la carte 🛈 4.00 – **54 rm** ⟐ 18.50/48.00 **t.**

✕✕ **La Gondola,** 220 Osmaston Rd, DE3 8JX, ✆ 32895, Italian rest. Dancing (Saturday) – **P**. 🔃
🄰🄴 ⓞ **VISA**   X c
closed Sunday dinner – **M** 4.90/7.25 **st.** and a la carte 🛈 3.00.

at Allestree N : 2 m. on A 6 – ✕ – ✉ – ✪ 0332 Derby :

✕✕✕ **Palm Court,** Duffield Rd, DE3 1ET, ✆ 558107 – **P**. 🔃 🄰🄴 ⓞ **VISA**
closed Sunday dinner – **M** 7.25/8.95 **t.** and a la carte 🛈 3.50.

at Shelton Lock S : 3 ½ m. on A 514 – ✕ – ✉ ✪ 0332 Derby :

✕✕ **Golden Pheasant,** 221 Chellaston Rd, DE2 9EE, ✆ 700112 – **P**. 🔃 🄰🄴 ⓞ **VISA**
closed Sunday dinner and Bank Holidays – **M** 6.00/8.00 **st.** and a la carte 🛈 3.30.

at Littleover SW : 2 ½ m. on A 5250 – ✉ ✪ 0332 Derby :

🏨 **Crest** (Crest), Pasture Hill, DE3 7BA, ✆ 514933, Telex 377081, 🚗 – 📺 ⇌wc ☎ 🛆 **P**. 🛆.
🔃 🄰🄴 ⓞ **VISA**   X a
M approx. 11.50 **st.** – ⟐ 5.75 – **66 rm** 47.00/57.00 **st.** – SB (weekends only) 63.00 **st.**

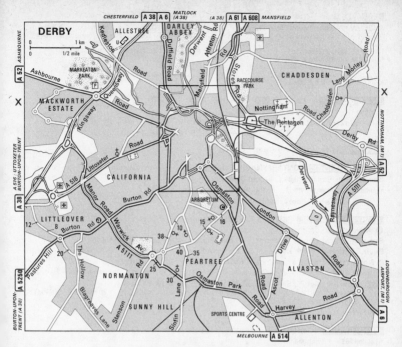

DERBY

Corn Market . . . . Z 13
Iron Gate . . . . Y 23
Shopping Centre . . . . Z
Victoria Street . . . . Z 39

Albert Street . . . . Z 2
Babington Lane . . . . Z 3
Bold Lane . . . . Y 4
Bradshaw Way . . . . Z 5
Carrington Street . . . . Z 6
Cathedral Road . . . . Y 7
Chain Lane . . . . X 8
Charnwood Street . . . . Z 9
Church Street . . . . X 10
Corden Avenue . . . . X 12
Corporation Street . . . . YZ 14
Dairy House Road . . . . X 15
Douglas Street . . . . X 16
Duffield Road . . . . Y 17
East Street . . . . Z 18
Full Street . . . . Y 19
Hillsway . . . . X 20
Jury Street . . . . Y 24
Kenilworth Avenue . . . . X 25
King Street . . . . Y 26
Market Place . . . . YZ 27
Midland Road . . . . Z 28
Mount Street . . . . Z 29
Newdigate Street . . . . X 30
Normanton Road . . . . Z 31
Queen Street . . . . Y 32
St. Mary's Gate . . . . Z 33
St. Peter's Street . . . . Z 34
St. Thomas Road . . . . X 35
Sacheveral Street . . . . Z 36
Stafford Street . . . . Z 37
Upper Dale Road . . . . X 38
Walbrook Road . . . . X 40
Wardwick . . . . Z 41

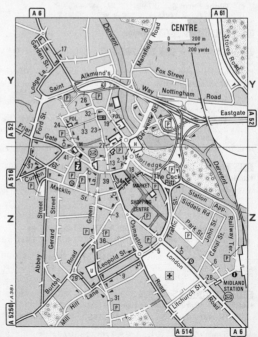

CENTRE

DERBY

AUDI, VW 29-33 Ashbourne Rd ☎ 31282
AUSTIN-ROVER Derwent St. ☎ 31166
AUSTIN-ROVER 152/160 Burton Rd ☎ 43224
BMW King St. ☎ 369511
CITROEN Alfreton Rd ☎ 381502
FORD Normanton Rd ☎ 40271
MAZDA Nottingham Rd ☎ 666101
NISSAN Burton Rd ☎ 369723

PEUGEOT-TALBOT Ascot Drive ☎ 361626
RENAULT 1263 London Rd, Alvaston ☎ 71847
SAAB Uttoxeter Rd ☎ 513943
TOYOTA St. Alkmunds Way ☎ 49536
VAUXHALL-OPEL Pentagon Island, Nottingham Rd
☎ 362661
VOLVO Kedleston Rd ☎ 32625

DERSINGHAM Norfolk **402** **404** V 25 – pop. 3 ,263 – ✪ 0485.
♦London 110 – ♦Cambridge 53 – ♦Norwich 46.

↑ **Westdene House,** 60 Hunstanton Rd, PE31 6HQ, ☎ 40395, ✿ – **ℙ**. ⚘
March-October – **5 rm** ⌿ 12.50/27.00.

DEVERON Cornwall – see Truro.

DEVIL'S BRIDGE (PONTARFYNACH) Dyfed **403** I 26 – ✉ Aberystwyth – ✪ 097 085 Ponterwyd.
See : Nature Trail (Mynach Falls and Devil's Bridge)★★.
♦London 230 – Aberystwyth 12 – Shrewsbury 66.

Hotels see : Aberystwyth W : 12 m.

DEVIZES Wilts. **403** **404** O 29 The West Country G. – pop. 12 ,430 – ECD : Wednesday –
✪ 0380.
See : Site★ – St. John's Church★★ – Market Place★ – Devizes Museum★ AC.
Envir. : Potterne : Porch House★★, S : 2 m. on A 360.
🛅 North Wilts., Bishop's Cannings ☎ 038 086 (Cannings) 627, N : 5 m.
🖪 Canal Centre, Couch Lane ☎ 71069 (summer only) – ♦London 98 – ♦Bristol 38 – Salisbury 25 – Swindon 19.

🏨 **Bear,** Market Pl., SN10 1HS, ☎ 2444 – 📺 ⌿wc ☎ **ℙ**. 🄰🄴 *VISA*
closed 25 and 26 December – **M** 9.00/11.50 t. and a la carte ⋔ 2.95 – **26 rm** ⌿ 24.00/45.00 t. –
SB (weekends only) 56.00 **st.**

FORD New Park St. ☎ 3456   PEUGEOT ☎ 038 081 (Lavington) 2336

DIDDLEBURY Salop **403** L 26 – pop. 526 – ✉ Craven Arms – ✪ 058 476 Munslow.
♦ London 169 – ♦ Birmingham 46.

↑ **Glebe Farm** ⌂, SY7 9DH, ☎ 221, ✿ – **ℙ**. ⚘
closed first 2 weeks June and November-March – **7 rm** ⌿ 15.00/52.00 **st.**

DINBYCH-Y-PSYGOD = Tenby.

DISLEY Cheshire **402** **403** **404** N 23 – pop. 3 ,425 – ECD : Wednesday – ✉ Stockport –
✪ 066 32.
🛅 Stanley Hall Lane ☎ 2071 – ♦London 187 – Chesterfield 35 – ♦Manchester 12.

🏨 **Moorside** (Best Western) ⌂, Mudhurst Lane, Higher Disley, SK12 2AP, SE : 2 m. ☎ 4151,
Telex 665170, ≼ – 📺 ⌿wc ☏ **ℙ**. 🄰, 🄰🄴 ⓪ *VISA*
M 7.25/11.50 **st.** and a la carte ⋔ 2.95 – ⌿ 5.00 – **41 rm** 30.00/45.00 t., **1 suite** 70.00/90.00 **st.** –
SB (weekends only) 50.00/65.00 **st.**

✗ **The Ginnel,** 3 Buxton Old Rd, SK12 2BB, ☎ 4494 – 🄰 🄰🄴 ⓪ *VISA*
closed Sunday dinner, Monday and 1 to 6 January – **M** (dinner only and Sunday lunch)/dinner
a la carte 10.25/13.90 t. ⋔ 2.50.

MAZDA Fountain Sq. ☎ 2327   RENAULT 159 Buxton Rd ☎ 2105

DISS Norfolk **404** X 26 – pop. 5 ,463 – ECD : Tuesday – ✉ ✪ 0379.
♦London 98 – ♦Ipswich 25 – ♦Norwich 21 – Thetford 17.

✗✗ **Salisbury House** with rm, 84 Victoria Rd, IP22 3JG, ☎ 4738, « Victorian house with period
furniture, garden » – 📺 ⌿wc **ℙ**
closed 1 week spring, 1 week autumn, 2 weeks at Christmas and Bank Holidays – **M** (closed
Sunday and Monday) (lunch by arrangement)/dinner 16.50 t. ⋔ 4.00 – **3 rm** ⌿ 40.00/45.00 t.

at Scole E : 2 m. by A 1066 on A 143 – ✉ ✪ 0379 Diss :

🏨 **Scole Inn** (Best Western), Main St., IP21 4DR, ☎ 740481, « 17C inn » – 📺 ⌿wc ☎ **ℙ**. 🄰.
🄰 🄰🄴 ⓪ *VISA*
M 8.00 t. and a la carte 9.25/11.40 t. ⋔ 2.25 – **20 rm** ⌿ 26.00/40.00 t. – SB 44.00/48.00 **st.**

AUSTIN-ROVER Victoria Rd ☎ 3141   VAUXHALL-OPEL 142/144 Victoria Rd ☎ 2241
FORD Park Rd ☎ 2311

DITTON PRIORS Salop **403** **404** M 26 – pop. 550 – ✉ Bridgnorth – ✪ 074 634.
♦London 154 – ♦Birmingham 34 – Ludlow 13 – Shrewsbury 21.

✗✗ **Howard Arms** ⌂ with rm, WV16 6SQ, ☎ 200, ✿ – **ℙ**. ⚘
closed Sunday dinner, Monday, 2 weeks August and 2 weeks September – **M** (dinner only and
Sunday lunch) 15.50 t. ⋔ 3.50 – **2 rm** ⌿ 18.00/30.00 t.

DODDISCOMBSLEIGH Devon – see Exeter.

DOLGELLAU Gwynedd **402 403** I 25 – pop. 2 ,261 – ECD : Wednesday – ✆ 0341.

Envir. : N : Precipice walk★★, Torrent walk★, Rhaiadr Ddu (Black waterfalls★), Coed-y-Brenin Forest★ – E : Bwlch Oerddrws★ on road★ from Cross Foxes Hotel to Dinas Mawddwy – S : Cader Idris (road★★ to Cader Idris : Cregenneu lakes) – Tal-y-Llyn Lake★★.

🛢 Pencefn Rd ✆ 422603.

🛈 Snowdonia National Park Visitor Centre, The Bridge ✆ 422888 (summer only).

◆London 221 – Birkenhead 72 – Chester 64 – Shrewsbury 57.

🏠 **Golden Lion Royal**, Lion St., LL40 1DG, ✆ 422579, 🚗 – 📺 ⌷wc ℗
    28 rm. 1 suite.

🏠 **Royal Ship**, Queen Sq., LL40 1AR, ✆ 422209 – ▯ ⌷wc ℗. 🔼 *VISA*
    M 4.75/8.25 **t.** and a la carte – **23 rm** ⊡ 12.50/34.00 **t.** – SB 37.50/45.00 **st.**

at Penmaenpool W : 2 m. on A 493 – ✉ ✆ 0341 Dolgellau :

✗ **George III** with rm, LL40 1YD, ✆ 422525, ≼ Mawddach estuary and mountains – 📺 ⌷wc
    ℗. 🔼 🔼 *VISA*
    closed Christmas and New Year – **M** *(closed Sunday dinner to non-residents)* (bar lunch Monday to Saturday)/dinner a la carte 8.75/19.80 **t.** – **12 rm** ⊡ 16.50/50.00 **t.** – SB (November-April) 40.00/63.80 **st.**

at Bontddu W : 5 m. on A 496 – ✉ Dolgellau – ✆ 034 149 Bontddu :

🏛 **Bontddu Hall**, LL40 2SU, ✆ 661, ≼ Mawddach estuary and mountains, « Victorian mansion in large gardens » – 📺 ⌷wc ⌷wc ☎ ℗ 🔼 🔼 ① *VISA*
    Easter-September – **M** (buffet lunch)/dinner a la carte 9.80/13.80 **t.** – **23 rm** ⊡ 23.50/55.00 **t.,**
    2 suites 65.00 **t.** – SB 65.00/71.00 **st.**

✗✗ **Borthwnog Hall** with rm, LL40 2TT, E : 1 m. on A 496 ✆ 271, ≼, « Part Regency house on banks of Mawddach estuary », 🚗, park – ℗ ⫸
    M *(closed Sunday, Monday and 24 December-1 January to non-residents)* (booking essential) (lunch by arrangement to non-residents)/dinner 7.50 **t.** and a la carte – **3 rm** ⊡ 18.50/31.50 **t.**
    – SB (November-May except Bank Holidays) 37.95/46.50 **st.**

AUSTIN-ROVER Arran Rd ✆ 422631   PEUGEOT-TALBOT Bontddu ✆ 49278
NISSAN Bala Rd ✆ 422681

DOLWYDDELAN Gwynedd **402 403** I 24 – pop. 480 – ECD : Thursday – ✆ 069 06.

◆London 232 – Holyhead 51 – Dolgellau 24 – LLandudno 27.

🏠 **Elen's Castle**, LL25 0EJ, on A 470 ✆ 207, ≼, 🔾, 🚗 – ⌷wc ⌷wc ℗
    April-September – **M** (bar lunch)/dinner 6.50 **t.** 🍷 1.30 – **10 rm** ⊡ 13.70/33.40 **t.** – SB 35.80/39.80 **st.**

DONCASTER South Yorks. **402 403 404** Q 23 – pop. 74 ,727 – ECD : Thursday – ✆ 0302.

🛢 Crookhill Park, Conisbrough ✆ 0709 (Rotherham) 862979, W : 3 m. on A 630.

🛈 Central Library, Waterdale ✆ 734309.

◆London 173 – ◆Kingston-upon-Hull 46 – ◆Leeds 30 – ◆Nottingham 46 – ◆Sheffield 19.

🏛 **Danum** (Swallow), High St., DN1 1DN, ✆ 62261, Telex 547533 – ▯ 📺 ⌷wc ⌷wc ☜ ℗. 🏛.
    🔼 🔼 ① *VISA*
    M 7.25/8.95 **st.** and a la carte 🍷 3.40 – **66 rm** ⊡ 27.00/49.50 **st., 2 suites** 45.00/60.00 **st.** – SB
    42.00 **st.**

🏛 **Grand St. Leger** (Best Western), Bennethorpe, DN3 6AX, S : 1 ½ m. on A 638 ✆ 64111 – 📺
    ⌷wc ⌷wc ☎ ℗. 🏛 – **14 rm.**

🏛 **Earl of Doncaster** (Anchor), Bennethorpe, DN2 6AD, SE : ½ m. on A 638 ✆ 61371, Telex
    547923 – ▯ 📺 ⌷wc ☜ ℗. 🏛 – **53 rm.**

🏠 **Punch's** (Embassy), Bawtry Rd, Bessacarr, DN4 7BS, SE : 3 m. on A 638 ✆ 535235 – 📺
    ⌷wc ☜ ℗. 🏛. 🔼 🔼 ① *VISA*. ✄
    M *(closed Saturday lunch and Sunday dinner to non-residents)* 8.00 **st.** and a la carte 🍷 2.50 –
    ⊡ 5.00 – **25 rm** 24.75/42.00 **st.** – SB (weekends only) 43.00 **st.**

🛏 **Ashlea**, 81 Thorne Rd, DN1 2ES, ✆ 63374 – 📺 ⌷wc ℗. 🔼. ✄
    8 rm ⊡ 11.00/25.00 **st.**

at Rossington S : 6 m. on A 638 – ✉ ✆ 0302 Doncaster :

🏠 **Mount Pleasant**, Great North Rd, DN11 0HP, on A 638 ✆ 868219, 🚗 – 📺 ⌷wc ⌷wc ☜
    ℗. 🏛. 🔼. ✄
    closed Christmas Day – **M** 8.25/8.95 **t.** 🍷 2.30 – **28 rm** ⊡ 13.50/38.00 **t.** – SB (weekends only)
    38.00/46.00 **st.**

at Sprotbrough W : 3 ½ m. by A 630 – ✉ ✆ 0302 Doncaster :

✗✗ **Edelweiss**, 4 Main St., DN5 7PJ, ✆ 853923 – 🔼 🔼 ① *VISA*
    closed Monday – **M** (dinner only) 10.50 **t.** and a la carte 🍷 3.50.

BMW Wheatley Hall Rd ✆ 69191   TOYOTA Thorne Rd, Hatfield ✆ 840348
LANCIA Springwell Lane ✆ 854674   VW, AUDI York Rd Roundabout ✆ 64141
RENAULT Selby Rd, Thorne ✆ 0405 (Thorne) 8121100

DONHEAD ST. ANDREW Wilts. – see Shaftesbury (Dorset).

DONYATT Somerset 403 L 37 – pop. 311 – ⊠ ✆ 046 05 Ilminster.
♦London 147 – Exeter 33 – Taunton 11 – Yeovil 17.

  ✗ **Thatchers Pond,** TA19 0RG, ✆ 3210, ☞ – ➋. 🅰 𝖵𝖨𝖲𝖠
    closed Sunday dinner, Monday, January and February – **M** (buffet/bar lunch)/dinner 9.00 **t.**

DORCHESTER Dorset 403 404 M 31 The West Country G. – pop. 13,734 – ECD : Thursday – ✆ 0305.

See : Site★ – Dorset County Museum★ AC – Envir. : Bere Regis : St. John the Baptist Church★★★, NE : 11 m. by A 35 – Maiden Castle★★ (≼★) AC, SW : 2 m. by A 354 – Puddletown Church★, NE : 5 m. by A 35 – Athelhampton★ AC, NE : 6 m. on A 35 – Moreton Church★, E : 10 m.

🛐 Came Down ✆ 030 581 (Upwey) 2531, S : 2 m.

🆔 Antelope Yard, South St. ✆ 67992.

♦London 135 – Bournemouth 27 – Exeter 53 – ♦Southampton 53.

  🏨 **King's Arms,** 30 High East St., DT1 1HF, ✆ 65353 – 📺 ⇔wc ☎ ➋. 🅰. 🔼 🄰🄴 𝖵𝖨𝖲𝖠
    M 5.25/9.50 **st.** and a la carte 🯄 4.00 – **27 rm** � 28.00/42.50 **st.** – SB (weekends only)(October-May) 40.00/45.00 **st.**

  🏨 **Casterbridge** without rest., 49 High East St., ✆ 64043 – 📺 ⇔wc 🛗wc. 🔼 🄰🄴 ➊ 𝖵𝖨𝖲𝖠 ✗
    closed 25 and 26 December – **15 rm** ⊑ 20.00/40.00 **t.**

  at Owermoigne SE : 7 m. by A 352 – ⊠ Dorchester – ✆ 0305 Warmwell :

  🏨 **Owermoigne Moor Country House** ⬎, 32 Moreton Rd, DT2 8DX, N : 1 ½ m. ✆ 852663, ≼, ☞, park – ➋
    M (lunch by arrangement) 7.50/10.00 **st.** – **6 rm** ⊑ 15.00/25.00 **st.**

AUSTIN-ROVER 21/26 Trinity St. ✆ 63031
BMW North Sq. ✆ 67411
CITROEN, LAND ROVER, PEUGEOT, TALBOT, RANGE ROVER Puddletown ✆ 84456
FIAT, LANCIA, MERCEDES-BENZ Trinity St. ✆ 64494

FORD Prince of Wales Rd ✆ 62211
NISSAN London Rd ✆ 66066
VAUXHALL 6 High East St. ✆ 63913
VOLVO Bridport Rd ✆ 65555

DORCHESTER Oxon. 403 404 Q 29 – pop. 1,045 – ✆ 0865 Oxford.

See : Abbey Church★ 14C.

♦London 51 – Abingdon 6 – ♦Oxford 8 – Reading 17.

  🏨 **White Hart,** 26 High St., OX9 8HN, ✆ 340074, « Tastefully converted 17C coaching inn » –
    📺 ⇔wc ☎ ➋. 🔼 🄰🄴 ➊ 𝖵𝖨𝖲𝖠 ✗
    M 15.50 **t.** and a la carte 🯄 4.00 – **16 rm** ⊑ 48.40/66.75 **st.** – SB (weekends only) 73.00/84.00 **st.**

  🏨 **George,** High St., OX9 8HH, ✆ 340404 – 📺 ⇔wc ☎ ➋. 🔼 🄰🄴 ➊ 𝖵𝖨𝖲𝖠 ✗
    closed 25 to 30 December – **M** 7.50/10.00 **t.** and a la carte 🯄 2.10 – **17 rm** ⊑ 31.00/43.00 **t.** – SB (weekends only) 52.50/58.50 **st.**

DORKING Surrey 404 T 30 – pop. 14,602 – ECD : Wednesday – ✆ 0306.

Envir. : Box Hill ≼★★ NE : 2 ½ m. – Polesden Lacey★★ (19C) AC, NW : 4 ½ m.

♦London 26 – ♦Brighton 39 – Guildford 12 – Worthing 33.

  🏩 **Burford Bridge** (T.H.F.), Box Hill, RH5 6BX, N : 1 ½ m. on A 24 ✆ 884561, Telex 859507, ⬎ heated, ☞ – 📺 ➋. 🅰. 🔼 🄰🄴 ➊ 𝖵𝖨𝖲𝖠
    M 12.00/14.50 **st.** and a la carte 🯄 4.00 – ⊑ 5.50 – **48 rm** 48.50/64.50 **st.**

  🏨 **White Horse** (T.H.F.), High St., RH4 1BE, ✆ 881138, ⬎ heated – 📺 ⇔wc ☎ ➋. 🅰. 🔼 🄰🄴 ➊ 𝖵𝖨𝖲𝖠
    M a la carte 8.80/15.55 **st.** 🯄 2.70 – ⊑ 5.50 – **68 rm** 37.50/48.50 **st.**

  🏨 **Punch Bowl** (Anchor), Reigate Rd, RH4 1QB, ✆ 889335 – 📺 ⇔wc ☎ ➋. 🔼 🄰🄴 ➊ 𝖵𝖨𝖲𝖠
    M (carving rest.) 9.25 **t.** 🯄 3.00 – **29 rm** ⊑ 25.00/48.00 **t.** – SB (weekends only) 49.00 **st.**

  ✗ **Le Bistro,** 84 South St., RH4 2EZ, ✆ 883239, French rest. – 🔼 🄰🄴 ➊ 𝖵𝖨𝖲𝖠
    closed Saturday lunch, Sunday, 25 to 27 December, 1 to 3 January and Bank Holidays – **M** 7.50 **st.** (lunch) and a la carte 9.30/15.80 **st.** 🯄 3.30.

  at Peaslake SW : 8 m. by A 25 – ⊠ Guildford – ✆ 0306 Dorking :

  🏨 **Hurtwood Inn** (T.H.F.), Walking Bottom, GU5 9RR, ✆ 730851, ☞ – 📺 ⇔wc ☎ ➋. 🔼 🄰🄴 ➊ 𝖵𝖨𝖲𝖠
    M 7.95 **st.** (dinner) and a la carte 🯄 2.70 – ⊑ 5.50 – **18 rm** 33.50/45.00 **st.**

  at Gomshall W : 5 ½ m. on A 25 – ⊠ Guildford – ✆ 048 641 Shere :

  🏦 **Black Horse Inn,** Station Rd, GU5 9NP, on A 25 ✆ 2242, ☞ – ➋ ➊ 𝖵𝖨𝖲𝖠 ✗
    M (closed Sunday dinner and Monday) (bar lunch Tuesday to Saturday)/dinner a la carte 5.35/11.75 **t.** 🯄 2.70 – **6 rm** ⊑ 16.10/32.20 **t.**

  at Shere W : 6 ¼ m. by A 25 – ⊠ Guildford – ✆ 048 641 Shere :

  ✗✗ **La Chaumiere,** Gomshall Lane, GU5 9HE, ✆ 2168 – ➋. 🔼 🄰🄴 ➊ 𝖵𝖨𝖲𝖠
    M 7.50 **t.** (lunch) and a la carte 11.15/13.75 **t.** 🯄 3.50.

AUSTIN-ROVER 105 South St. ✆ 882244
RENAULT 40 West St ✆ 886080

VAUXHALL-OPEL Reigate Rd ✆ 885022

DORMINGTON Heref. and Worc. – see Hereford.

DOVER Kent **404** Y 30 – pop. 33,461 – ECD : Wednesday – ✆ 0304.

See : Castle★★ 12C (≼★) *AC* Y.

Envir. : Barfreston (Norman Church★ 11C : carvings★★) NW : 6 ½ m. by A 2 Z – Bleriot Memorial E : 1 ½ m. Z **A**.

⚓ Shipping connections with the Continent : to France (Boulogne) (Sealink) (Townsend Thoresen) (Hoverspeed) – to France (Calais) (Sealink) (Hoverspeed) (Townsend Thoresen) – to France (Dunkerque West) (Sealink) – to Belgium (Oostende) (Sealink) – to Belgium (Zeebrugge) (Townsend Thoresen).

⚓ to Belgium (Oostende) (Sealink, Jetfoil).

🛈 Townwall St. ✆ 205108.

♦London 76 – ♦Brighton 84.

DOVER

Bench Street	**Y** 3
Biggin Street	**Y** 4
Cannon Street	**Y** 5
High Street	**Y**
King Street	**Y** 13
Pencester Road	**Y**
Barton Road	**Y** 2
Charlton Green	**Y** 6
Crabble Hill	**Z** 7
Eaton Road	**Z** 10
Ladywell Park Street	**Y** 15
London Road	**Y** 17
New Bridge	**Y** 18
Priory Road	**Y** 19
Priory Street	**Y** 20
Sandwich Road	**Z** 21
Tower Street	**Z** 24
Worthington Street	**Y** 25

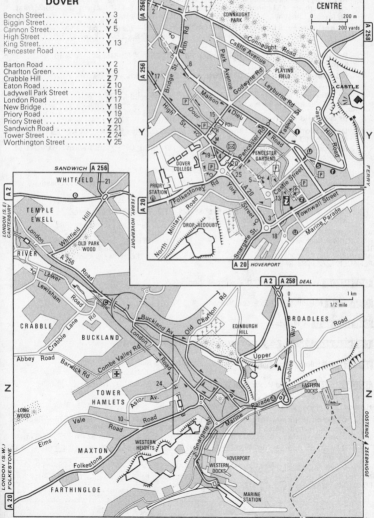

Dover Moat House (Q.M.H.), Townwall St., CT16 1SZ, ☏ 203270, Telex 96458, ⬜ – ⬛ ▦
▦ ☎ ♦ 🅿. 🕭. 🔲 ⬛ AE ⑩ *VISA*   Y z
M a la carte 8.40/14.80 **st.** 🍷 1.75 – ⌁ 4.50 – **80 rm** 39.00/49.00 **st.** – SB (weekends only)
55.00 **st.**

White Cliffs, Seafront, CT17 9BW, ☏ 203633, Telex 965422, ≼ – ⬛ ▦ 🛏️wc ⋔wc ☎ 🚗,
🔲 ⬛ AE ⑩ *VISA*   Y a
closed 25 and 26 December – **M** 5.40/6.75 **t.** and a la carte 🍷 3.75 – **62 rm** ⌁ 25.00/45.00 **t.** –
SB (weekends only) (October-May) 40.00 **st.**

St. James, 2 Harold St., CT16 1SF, ☏ 204579 – ▦ 🛏️wc ⋔wc 🚗. 🔲 ⬛ AE ⑩ *VISA*   Y i
M (lunch by arrangement) a la carte 6.30/8.75 **t.** 🍷 2.80 – **16 rm** ⌁ 13.00/30.00 **st.** – SB
(October-March) 36.00 **st.**

Cliffe Court, 25-26 East Cliff, Marine Par., CT16 1LU, ☏ 211001, ≼ – ▦ 🛏️wc ⋔wc 🅿. 🔲
⬛ AE ⑩ *VISA*. ℅   Z a
M 5.50/5.90 **t.** and a la carte 🍷 2.50 – **26 rm** ⌁ 19.00/31.00 **st.** – SB 46.00/48.00 **st.**

Mildmay, 78 Folkestone Rd, CT17 9SF, ☏ 204278 – ▦ 🛏️wc 🅿. 🔲 ⬛ AE ⑩ *VISA*. ℅   Y n
closed January – **M** (dinner only) a la carte approx. 8.70 **t.** 🍷 3.50 – **21 rm** ⌁ 24.50/36.00 **st.** –
SB (except Christmas, New Year and Bank Holidays) 34.00/40.00 **st.**

Hubert House, 9 Castle Hill Rd, CT16 1QW, ☏ 202253 – ▦ ⋔ 🅿. 🔲 ⬛ ⑩ *VISA*   Y s
closed October – **M** *(closed Sunday)* (dinner only) 6.75 **t.** 🍷 2.50 – **8 rm** ⌁ 18.00/25.00 **st.** –
SB 38.00 **st.**

Beulah House, 94 Crabble Hill, London Rd, CT17 0SA, ☏ 824615, ☞ – 🚗 🅿. ℅   Z c
8 rm ⌁ 12.00/20.00 **s.**

Number One, 1 Castle St., CT16 1QH, ☏ 202007 – ▦ ⋔wc 🚗. *VISA*. ℅   Y u
5 rm ⌁ 15.00/22.00 **st.**

St. Martins, 17 Castle Hill Rd, CT16 1QW, ☏ 205938 – ▦ ⋔. ℅   Y r
closed Christmas – **9 rm** ⌁ 15.00/25.00 **st.**

at Whitfield N : 3 ½ m. on A 256 – ✉ ✪ 0304 Dover :

Dover Motel, Singledge Lane, CT16 3LF, ☏ 821222, Telex 965866 – ▦ rest ▦ 🛏️wc ☎ ♦.
🅿. 🕭. 🔲 ⬛ AE ⑩ *VISA*   Z o
M 8.95/11.65 **t.** and a la carte 🍷 3.75 – ⌁ 3.95 – **67 rm** 35.00/45.00 **st.**, **1 suite** 50.00/60.00 **st.** –
SB (weekends only) (October-June) 50.00/60.00 **st.**

at St. Margaret's Bay NE : 4 m. by A 258 – Z – and B 2058 – ✉ ✪ 0304 Dover :

Granville ℁, Hotel Rd, off Granville Rd, CT15 6OX, ☏ 852212, ≼ sea and coastline, ☞ –
🛏️wc 🅿. 🔲 ⬛ AE ⑩ *VISA*
M 6.00/7.00 **st.** and a la carte 🍷 2.20 – ⌁ 3.60 – **20 rm** 12.00/28.00 **t.**

Cliffe Tavern, High St., CT15 6AT, ☏ 852749 – ▦ 🛏️wc 🅿. 🔲 ⬛ AE ⑩ *VISA*
M a la carte 4.25/9.45 **t.** – ⌁ 3.00 – **12 rm** 15.00/44.00 **t.**

AUSTIN-ROVER Woolcomber St. ☏ 201904
NISSAN Woolcomber St. ☏ 206518
NISSAN Cherry Tree Av. ☏ 206682
RELIANT South Rd ☏ 206160
RENAULT London Rd, River ☏ 74155

RENAULT 6/12 Folkestone Rd ☏ 201760
TOYOTA Eric Rd, Buckland ☏ 201235
VAUXHALL Castle St. ☏ 203001
VW, AUDI 1 Crabble Hill ☏ 206710

DOWNTON Wilts. 🔢 🔢 O 31 – see Salisbury.

DRAYTON Norfolk 🔢 X 25 – see Norwich.

DRENEWYDD = Newtown.

DRENEWYDD YN NOTAIS (NOTTAGE) Mid Glam. – see Porthcawl.

DRIFFIELD Humberside 🔢 S 21 – see Great Driffield.

DROITWICH Heref. and Worc. 🔢 🔢 N 27 – pop. 18,025 – ECD : Thursday – ✪ 0905.
🔎 Heritage Way ☏ 774312.
♦London 129 – ♦Birmingham 20 – ♦Bristol 66 – Worcester 6.

Château Impney, WR9 0BN, NE : 1 m. on A 38 ☏ 774411, Group Telex 336673, « Reproduction 16C French château », ☞, park, ℅ – ⬛ ▦ 🅿. 🕭. 🔲 ⬛ AE ⑩ *VISA*
closed Christmas – **M** 9.00/11.00 **st.** and a la carte 🍷 5.25 – ⌁ 5.95 – **67 rm** 59.95/64.95 **st.**

Raven, St. Andrews Rd, WR9 8DV, ☏ 772224, Group Telex 336673, ☞ – ⬛ ▦ 🅿. 🕭. 🔲 ⬛ AE
⬜ *VISA*
closed Christmas – **M** 9.00/11.00 **st.** and a la carte 🍷 5.25 – ⌁ 5.95 – **55 rm** 44.95/64.95 **st.**

AUSTIN-ROVER St. Georges Sq. ☏ 775123
FORD 141-149 Worcester Rd ☏ 772132

RENAULT Cutnall Green ☏ 029 923 (Cutnall Green)
344

Do not use yesterday's maps for today's journey.

DRONFIELD Derbs. 402 403 404 P 24 – pop. 22,641 – ECD : Wednesday – ✉ Sheffield (South Yorks) – ☎ 0246.

◆ London 158 – Derby 30 – ◆ Nottingham 31 – ◆ Sheffield 6.

☎ **Manor,** 10-15 High St., S18 6PY, ☎ 413971 – 📺 ♨wc 🅿. 🔄 🄰🄴 𝗩𝗜𝗦𝗔
M *(closed Monday lunch, Sunday dinner and Bank Holidays to non-residents)* (bar lunch)/ dinner 8.50 **t.** and a la carte ♨ 2.75 – **10 rm** ⚏ 27.50/35.00 **t.**

DULVERTON Somerset 403 J 30 The West Country G. – pop. 1,301 – ECD : Thursday – ☎ 0398.

See : Site★ – Envir. : Tarr Steps★★, NW : 6 m. by B 3223.

◆ London 198 – Barnstaple 27 – Exeter 26 – Minehead 18 – Taunton 21.

🏠 **Ashwick House** ⚘, TA22 9QD, NW : 4 ¼ m. by B 3223 ☎ 23868, ≤, « Country house atmosphere », 🌳 – 📺 ♨wc 🅿. ⚶
M *(closed Sunday and Monday to non-residents)* (dinner only and Sunday lunch) 8.50 **t.** ♨ 3.00 – **6 rm** ⚏ 30.00/54.00 **t.** – SB 45.50/50.50 **st.**

DUNCHURCH Warw. 403 404 Q 26 – pop. 2,409 – ✉ ☎ 0788 Rugby.

◆ London 90 – ◆ Coventry 12 – ◆ Leicester 24 – Northampton 26.

🏠 **Dun Cow,** The Green, CV22 6NJ, ☎ 810233, « 16C inn » – 📺 ♨wc ♨wc ☎ 🅿. 🔄 🄰🄴 ⓪ 𝗩𝗜𝗦𝗔
M 6.95/7.95 **st.** ♨ 4.00 – **23 rm** ⚏ 35.00/55.00 **st.** – SB (weekends only) 55.00/85.00 **st.**

VW, AUDI Coventry Rd ☎ 815044

DUNSTABLE Beds. 404 S 28 – pop. 48,436 – ECD : Thursday – ☎ 0582.

See : Priory Church of St. Peter (West front★).

Envir. : Whipsnade Park★ (zoo) ≤★★ AC, S : 3 m.

🔥 Tilsworth, Dunstable Rd ☎ 0525 (Leighton Buzzard) 210721, N : 2 m. on A 5.

🛈 The Library, Vernon Pl. ☎ 608441/2 – ◆ London 40 – Bedford 24 – Luton 4.5 – Northampton 35.

🏠 **Old Palace Lodge,** Church St., LU5 4RP, ☎ 62201 – 📳 ▤ rest 📺 🅿. 🔄 🄰🄴 ⓪ 𝗩𝗜𝗦𝗔. ⚶
M 14.50 **t.** (dinner) and a la carte ♨ 3.00 – ⚏ 4.50 – **33 rm** 38.00/44.00 **st.** – SB (weekends only) 52.00 **st.**

🏠 **Highwayman,** London Rd, LU6 3DX, SE : 1 m. on A 5 ☎ 61999 – 📺 ♨wc ♨wc 📠 🅿. 🔄 🄰🄴 ⓪ 𝗩𝗜𝗦𝗔
closed 4 days at Christmas – **M** (buffet lunch Monday to Saturday) 7.85 **st.** (dinner) and a la carte ♨ 1.95 – **26 rm** ⚏ 28.00/36.00 **st.**

AUSTIN-ROVER London Rd ☎ 696111   RENAULT 3 Tring Rd ☎ 63231
FORD 55 London Rd ☎ 67811   VW, AUDI Common Rd, Kensworth ☎ 872182

DUNSTER Somerset 403 J 30 The West Country G. – pop. 793 – ECD : Wednesday – ✉ Minehead – ☎ 064 382 – See : Site★★ – Castle★★ AC (upper rooms ≤★ from window) – Dunster Castle Water Mill★ AC – Dovecote★ – St. Georges Church★.

Envir. : Cleeve Abbey★★ AC, SE : 5 m. on A 39 – Wheddon Cross (Vantage Point★), SW : 6 m.

◆ London 184 – ◆ Bristol 61 – Exeter 40 – Taunton 22.

🏠 **Luttrell Arms** (T.H.F.), 36 High St., TA24 6SG, ☎ 821555, 🌳 – 📺 ♨wc 📠. 🔄 🄰🄴 ⓪ 𝗩𝗜𝗦𝗔
M 6.50/9.00 **st.** and a la carte ♨ 2.70 – ⚏ 5.50 – **21 rm** 36.50/49.50 **st.**

🏠 **Exmoor House,** 12 West St., TA24 6SN, ☎ 821268, 🌳 – 📺 ♨wc. 🔄 🄰🄴 ⓪ 𝗩𝗜𝗦𝗔
M (dinner only and Sunday lunch) 4.50/9.25 **t.** ♨ 2.40 – **6 rm** ⚏ 23.50/37.00 **t.** – SB 44.00/52.00 **st.**

DURHAM Durham 401 402 P 19 – pop. 38,105 – ECD : Wednesday – ☎ 0385.

See : Cathedral★★★ (Norman) (Chapel of the Nine Altars★★) B – University (Gulbenkian Museum of Art and Archaeology★★ AC) by Elvet Hill Rd A – Castle★ (Norman chapel★) AC B.

🔥 Low Job's Hill, Crook ☎ 0388 (Bishop Auckland) 762429, SW : 10 m. by A 690 A – 🔥 South Moor, The Middles, Craghead ☎ 0207 (Stanley) 32848, NW : 8 m. by Framwelgate Peth A and B 6532 – 🔥 Durham City, Littleburn, Langley Moor ☎ 780806 by Potters Bank A.

🛈 13 Claypath ☎ 43720/47641.

◆ London 267 – ◆ Leeds 77 – ◆ Middlesbrough 23 – Sunderland 12.

Plan on next page

🏠 **Royal County** (Swallow), Old Elvet, DH1 3JN, ☎ 66821, Group Telex 538238 – 📳 📺 ⚶ 🅿.
🔄 🄰🄴 𝗩𝗜𝗦𝗔   B a
M 7.50/10.50 **st.** and a la carte ♨ 3.40 – **120 rm** ⚏ 43.00/54.00 **st.** – SB (weekends only) 58.00/64.00 **st.**

🏠 **Three Tuns** (Swallow), New Elvet, DH1 3AQ, ☎ 64326, Group Telex 538238 – 📺 ♨wc 📠
🔄 🄰🄴 ⓪ 𝗩𝗜𝗦𝗔   B e
M 7.00/8.75 **st.** ♨ 3.40 – **54 rm** ⚏ 42.00/48.50 **st.** – SB 55.00/64.00 **st.**

at Croxdale S : 3 m. by A 1050 on A 167 – B – ✉ ☎ 0385 Durham :

🏠 **Bridge,** DH1 3SP, ☎ 780524, Telex 538156 – 📺 ♨wc 📠 🅿. 🔄 🄰🄴 ⓪ 𝗩𝗜𝗦𝗔 ⚶
M a la carte 6.60/9.70 **st.** ♨ 2.75 – **46 rm** ⚏ 16.50/38.00 **st.** – SB 39.75/51.00 **st.**

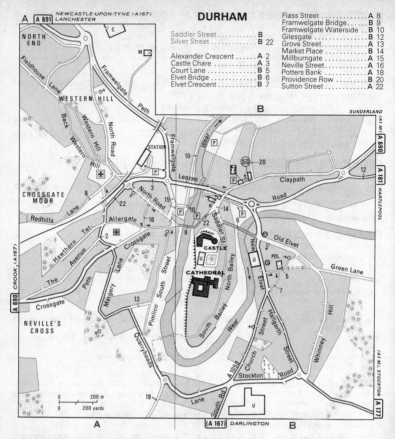

DURHAM

Saddler Street . . . . B
Silver Street . . . . B 22

Alexander Crescent . . . . . . A 2
Castle Chare . . . . A 3
Court Lane . . . . B 5
Elvet Bridge . . . . B 6
Elvet Crescent . . . . B 7

Flass Street . . . . A 8
Framwelgate Bridge . . . . . . B 9
Framwelgate Waterside . . . B 10
Gilesgate . . . . B 12
Grove Street . . . . A 13
Market Place . . . . B 14
Millburngate . . . . A 15
Neville Street . . . . A 16
Potters Bank . . . . A 18
Providence Row . . . . B 20
Sutton Street . . . . A 22

ALFA-ROMEO 81 New Elvet ✆ 47777
AUSTIN-ROVER 74 New Elvet ✆ 47278
AUSTIN-ROVER Gilesgate Moor ✆ 67231
CITROEN Croxdale ✆ 0388 (Spennymoor) 814671
FORD Nevilles Cross ✆ 46655

RENAULT Langley Moor ✆ 69666
VAUXHALL Claypath ✆ 42511
VOLVO Sawmills Lane ✆ 780866
VW, AUDI 20 Alma Rd, Gilesgate Moor ✆ 67215
YUGO Pity Me ✆ 44000

DYMCHURCH Kent 404 W 30 – pop. 3,327 – ✿ 0303 Hythe.
◆London 72 – ◆Brighton 65 – ◆Dover 19.

↑ **Chantry,** Sycamore Gdns, TN29 0LA, ✆ 873137, 昴 – 🛏wc **P**. ⅌
March-October – **8 rm** ⊒ 11.50/31.00 st.

EAGLESCLIFFE Cleveland 402 P 20 – see Stockton-on-Tees.

EARL SHILTON Leics. 403 404 Q 26 – pop. 16,484 – ECD : Wednesday – ⊠ Leicester – ✿ 0455.
◆London 107 – ◆Birmingham 35 – ◆Coventry 16 – ◆Leicester 9 – ◆Nottingham 35.

🏠 **Fernleigh,** 32 Wood St., LE9 7ND, ✆ 47011 – 📺 ⋔wc ☎ **P**. ⟁ 𝘝𝘐𝘚𝘈
M 4.95/6.95 st. and a la carte ⓙ 4.00 – **13 rm** ⊒ 23.00/30.00 t.

EARL STONHAM Suffolk 404 X 27 – ⊠ Stowmarket – ✿ 0449 Stonham.
◆London 81 – ◆Cambridge 47 – ◆Ipswich 10 – ◆Norwich 33.

XX **Mr. Underhill's,** IP14 5DW, Junction of A 140 and A 1120 ✆ 711206 – **P**. ⟁ 𝘝𝘐𝘚𝘈
closed Saturday lunch, Sunday, Monday and Bank Holidays – **M** (lunch by arrangement)
(booking essential) 13.00/16.95 t. ⓙ 4.00.

EAST BERGHOLT Suffolk **404** X 28 – pop. 2,757 – ✉ ✪ 0206 Colchester (Essex).

♦London 59 – Colchester 9 – ♦Ipswich 8.5.

XX **Fountain House,** The Street, CO7 6TB, ℰ 298232 – ℗. 🄫 VISA
closed Sunday dinner, Monday and 2 weeks January – **M** 7.95/9.95 t.

EASTBOURNE East Sussex **404** U 31 – pop. 86,715 – ECD : Wednesday – ✪ 0323.

See : Grand Parade★ X – Envir. : Beachy Head★ (cliff), ≫★ SW : 3 m. Z – Seven Sisters★ (cliffs)
from Birling Gap, SW : 5 m. Z – Charleston Manor★ *AC*, W : 8 m. by A 259 Z – W : scenic road
from Eastdean by A 259 Z up to Wilmington by Westdean – Wilmington : The Long Man★ :
prehistoric giant figure, NW : 7 m. by A 27 Y.

🏊, 🏊 Royal Eastbourne, Paradise Drive ℰ 30412 Z – 🏊 Eastbourne Downs, East Dean Rd ℰ 20827 Z.

🛈 3 Cornfield Terr. ℰ 27474/21333 ext 1105 – Seafront, Grand Parade ℰ 27474 (summer only) – Terminus Rd,
Precinct, ℰ 27474 – at Pevensey, Castle Car Park, High St. ℰ 0323 (Eastbourne) 761444 (summer only).

♦London 68 – ♦Brighton 25 – ♦Dover 61 – Maidstone 49.

Plan on next page

🏰 **Grand** (De Vere), King Edward's Par., BN21 4EQ, ℰ 22611, Telex 87332, ≤, ⊴ heated, ⚞ –
│✿│ TV 🕿 ♿ ⅍ 🄫 AE ⓄD VISA   Z **x**
M 13.50 **st.** (dinner) and a la carte 21.50/29.50 **st.** – **178 rm** ⇆ 55.00/105.00 **st.**, **15 suites**
105.00/185.00 **st.** – SB (weekends only) 95.00/145.00 **st.**

🏰 **Cavendish** (De Vere), 37-40 Grand Par., BN21 4DH, ℰ 27401, Telex 87579, ≤ – │✿│ TV 🕿 ♿
⅍ 🄫 AE VISA   X **r**
M 7.00/12.00 **st.** and a la carte 🛇 2.95 – **114 rm** ⇆ 41.00/72.00 **st.**, **4 suites** 84.00/104.00 **st.** –
SB 78.00/84.00 **st.**

🏰 **Queen's** (De Vere), Marine Par., BN21 3DY, ℰ 22822, Telex 877736, ≤ – │✿│ TV 🕿 ℗ ⅍ 🄫
AE ⓄD VISA   V **e**
M 9.00/10.50 **t.** and a la carte – **108 rm** ⇆ 37.00/64.00 **st.**, **2 suites** 71.00 **st.** – SB (weekends
only) 74.00 **st.**

🏰 **Hydro,** Mount Rd, BN20 7HZ, ℰ 20643, ≤, ⊴ heated, ⚞ – │✿│ TV ℗ ⅍ 🄫 VISA   Z **e**
M 5.50/7.50 **t.** 🛇 2.50 – **100 rm** ⇆ 18.50/47.00 **t.** – SB (weekends only) (November-March)
45.00/49.00 **st.**

🏛 **Lansdowne** (Best Western), King Edward's Par., BN21 4EE, ℰ 25174, ≤ – │✿│ TV ⌷wc ⓜwc
⚞ ♦. 🄫 AE ⓄD VISA   Z **z**
closed 1 to 12 January – **M** (bar lunch)/dinner 8.25 **st.** and a la carte 🛇 3.00 – **136 rm**
⇆ 22.00/55.00 **st.** – SB (except summer) 35.00/49.50 **st.**

🏛 **Wish Tower** (T.H.F.), King Edward's Par., BN21 4EB, ℰ 22676, ≤ – │✿│ TV ⌷wc ⚞ ♦. 🄫 AE
ⓄD VISA   Z **r**
M (bar lunch Monday to Saturday)/dinner 9.50 **st.** and a la carte 🛇 3.00 – ≈ 5.50 – **73 rm**
31.00/43.00 **st.**

🏛 **Chatsworth,** Grand Par., BN21 3YR, ℰ 30327, ≤ – │✿│ TV ⌷wc ⓜwc ⚞. 🄫 AE VISA   X **n**
closed January-mid March – **M** (buffet lunch Monday to Saturday)/dinner 7.70 **t.** 🛇 5.00 –
45 rm ⇆ 23.00/49.20 **t.** – SB (except Bank Holidays) 50.00/55.00 **st.**

🏛 **Sandhurst,** Grand Par., BN21 4DJ, ℰ 27868, ≤ – │✿│ TV ⌷wc ⓜwc ⚞. 🄫 AE ⓄD VISA   X **o**
M 5.50/6.95 **t.** 🛇 2.25 – **64 rm** ⇆ 18.50/55.00 **t.**

🏛 **Princes,** 12-20 Lascelles Terr., BN21 4BL, ℰ 22056 – │✿│ TV ⌷wc 🕿. ⅍ 🄫 AE ⓄD VISA
closed January-mid March – **M** (bar lunch in summer)/dinner 7.25 **t.** and a la carte 🛇 2.65 –
51 rm ⇆ 16.50/32.50 **t.**, **1 suite** – SB (except summer) 39.00/45.00 **st.**   X **z**

🏛 **Farrar's,** 3-5 Wilmington Gdns, BN21 4JN, ℰ 23737, ⚞ – │✿│ TV ⌷wc ⓜwc ℗. 🄫 AE VISA
M a la carte lunch/dinner 7.50 **t.** 🛇 2.25 – **42 rm** ⇆ 19.50/46.00 **t.** – SB (November-April)
38.00/44.00 **st.**   X **s**

🏛 **Mandalay,** 16 Trinity Trees, BN21 3LE, ℰ 29222 – TV ⌷wc ⓜwc ℗. 🄫 VISA. ≫
M *(closed dinner to non-residents, Sunday and Bank Holidays)* (chinese rest.) (bar lunch)/dinner
12.00 **t.** 🛇 3.95 – **12 rm** ⇆ 14.00/36.00 **t.**, **1 suite** – SB (October-May) 30.00/33.00 **st.**   V **v**

🏛 **Oban,** King Edward's Par., BN21 4DS, ℰ 31581 – │✿│ TV ⌷wc ⓜwc   X **a**
April-October – **M** 4.50/7.00 **t.** 🛇 2.50 – **31 rm** ⇆ 14.00/30.00 **t.** – SB 36.00/44.00 **t.**

🛖 **Traquair,** 25 Hyde Gdns, BN21 4PX, ℰ 25198 – TV ⓜwc   V **x**
11 rm ⇆ 12.50/28.00 **t.**

🛖 **Hanburies,** 4 Hardwick Rd, BN21 4NY, ℰ 30698 – TV ⌷wc. ≫   X **c**
14 rm ⇆ 13.00/31.00 **t.**

🛖 **Orchard House,** 10 Old Orchard Rd, BN21 1DB, ℰ 23682 – TV ⌷wc ⓜwc. ≫   V **o**
7 rm ⇆ 13.00/38.00 **t.**

🛖 **Nirvana,** 32 Redoubt Rd, BN22 7DL, ℰ 22603 – ≫   V **n**
closed last 2 weeks October – **9 rm** ⇆ 8.00/18.00 **st.**

XX **Crimples Flemish Room,** 42-44 Meads St., BN20 7RG, ℰ 26805 – 🄫 VISA   Z **a**
closed Sunday dinner, Monday, 1 week March, 2 weeks October and 25-26 December –
M 8.75 **t.** and a la carte 🛇 2.25.

X **Byron's,** 6 Crown St., Old Town, BN21 1NX, ℰ 20171 – AE ⓄD VISA   Z **s**
closed Saturday lunch, Sunday, 1 week at Christmas and Bank Holidays – **M** a la carte
9.45/13.25 **t.** 🛇 2.25.

X **Brown's,** 17 Carlisle Rd, BN21 4BT, ℰ 28837, Bistro – 🄫 AE ⓄD VISA   X **e**
*closed Sunday except lunch in Summer, Monday, 1 week August, 1 week November, 1 week
January and Bank Holidays* – **M** 8.70/13.00 **t.** and a la carte 🛇 2.80.

EASTBOURNE

Arndale Centre V
Grove Road V
South Street V
Terminus Road V

Ashford Road .... V 2
Bedfordwell Road .... V 3
Church Street .... Z 4
Cornfield Road .... V 5
Devonshire Place .... X 6
Gildredge Road .... V 7
Hailsham Road .... Y 8
High Street .... Z 9
Lewes Road .... Y 13
Lismore Road .... V 14
North Street .... V 15

Polegate By-Pass .... Y 18
Royal Parade .... Z 20
St. Anthony's Avenue .... Y 21
Station Road .... Y 24

Susan's Road .... V 25
The Goffs .... Z 26
Trinity Trees .... V 27
Upperton Road .... V, Z 28

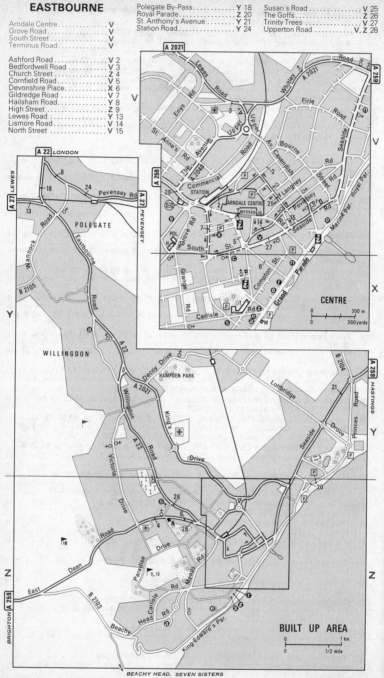

CENTRE

0   300 m
0   300 yards

BUILT UP AREA

0   1 km
0   1/2 mile

BEACHY HEAD, SEVEN SISTERS

170

at Willingdon N : 2 ¾ m. on A 22 – ⊠ ☺ 0323 Eastbourne :

🏠 **Chalk Farm** ॐ, Coopers Hill, BN20 9JD, ℰ 503800, ≤, ☞ – ⌂wc ℗. 🖾. ⅋⅋   Y **a**
M *(closed Sunday dinner and Monday)* 6.25/9.50 **t.** ♟ 3.00 – **8 rm** ☲ 14.50/33.00 **t.**

at Stone Cross N : 4 m. by A 259 on B 2104 (Hailsham Rd) – Y – ⊠ Pevensey – ☺ 0323
Hailsham :

🏛 **Glyndley Manor** ॐ, Hailsham Rd, BN24 5BS, NW : 1 ¾ m. on B 2104 ℰ 843737, ≤, ⅃
heated, ॐ, ☞, park, ⅋ – 🖵 ⌂wc ⏁wc ☎ ℗. 🅰. 🖾 🝏 ⓞ 𝚅𝙸𝚂𝙰
M 8.00/11.00 **t.** and a la carte ♟ 3.50 – **20 rm** ☲ 35.00/56.00 **t.** – SB (weekends only)
72.00/80.00 **st.**

at Pevensey NE : 5 m. by A 259 – Y – on A27 – ⊠ ☺ 0323 Eastbourne :

🏠 **Priory Court,** Castle Rd., BN22 5LG, ℰ 763150, ☞ – 🖵 ⌂wc ℗. 🖾 🝏 ⓞ 𝚅𝙸𝚂𝙰 ⅋⅋
M (buffet lunch)/dinner 8.75 **t.** and a la carte ♟ 2.95 – ☲ 2.50 – **12 rm** 21.00/52.00 **st.** – SB
(except weekends) 42.50/52.50 **st.**

at Jevington NW : 6 m. by A 259 – Z – on B 2105 – ⊠ ☺ 032 12 Polegate :

⅋⅋ **Hungry Monk,** The Street, BN26 5QF, ℰ 2178 – ℗
closed 24 to 26 December – **M** (dinner only and Sunday lunch) (booking essential) 10.60/11.50 **t.**

at Wilmington NW : 6 ½ m. by A 22 on A 27 – Y – ⊠ ☺ 032 12 Polegate :

⌂ **Crossways,** BN26 5SG, ℰ 2455, ☞ – ⌂wc ℗
10 rm ☲ 11.00/24.00 **st.**

AUSTIN-ROVER, ROLLS ROYCE Meads Rd ℰ 30201
CITROEN, SAAB 8-14 Seaside ℰ 640139
FIAT Ashford Rd ℰ 640101
FORD Lottbridge Drove ℰ 37171
LADA, SUBARU Susans Rd ℰ 639589
NISSAN 46 Pevensey Rd ℰ 37339

PEUGEOT-TALBOT East Dean ℰ 3053
RELIANT, SKODA Pevensey Bay Rd ℰ 761150
RENAULT 18 Lottbridge Drove ℰ 37233
VAUXHALL, RELIANT 336/8 Seaside ℰ 30663
VW, AUDI Burlington Rd ℰ 640114

EAST BUCKLAND Devon 🔢 I 30 – see South Molton.

EAST CHINNOCK Somerset – see Yeovil.

EAST DEREHAM Norfolk 🔢 W 25 – pop. 11,798 – ☺ 0362 Dereham.
♦London 109 – ♦Cambridge 57 – King's Lynn 27 – ♦Norwich 16.

🏛 **Phoenix** (T.H.F.), Church St., NR19 1DL, ℰ 2276 – 🖵 ⌂wc ☏ ℗. 🅰. 🖾 🝏 ⓞ 𝚅𝙸𝚂𝙰
M 5.75/7.75 **st.** and a la carte ♟ 2.70 – ☲ 5.50 – **28 rm** 33.00/43.00 **st.**

🏠 **King's Head,** 42 Norwich St., NR19 1AD, ℰ 3842, ⅋ – 🖵 ⌂wc ⏁wc ℗. 🖾 🝏 ⓞ 𝚅𝙸𝚂𝙰
M 8.00/10.50 **t.** and a la carte ♟ 2.35 – **15 rm** ☲ 20.50/32.00 **t.** – SB (weekends only)
45.00/50.00 **st.**

AUSTIN-ROVER Two Oaks Garage Beetley ℰ 860219
AUSTIN-ROVER Norwich Rd ℰ 2293

FORD High St. ℰ 2281

EAST GRINSTEAD West Sussex 🔢 T 30 – pop. 23,867 – ECD : Wednesday – ☺ 0342.
Envir. : Hever Castle★ (13C-20C) and gardens★★ *AC*, NE : 10 m.

♦London 32 – ♦Brighton 29 – Eastbourne 33 – Lewes 21 – Maidstone 32.

🏛 **Felbridge,** London Rd, RH19 2BH, NW : 1 ½ m. on A 22 ℰ 26992, Telex 95156, ⅃ heated, 🖾,
☞ – 🖵 ⌂wc ☏ ℗. 🅰. 🖾 🝏 ⓞ 𝚅𝙸𝚂𝙰
M *(closed Saturday lunch)* (carving lunch)/dinner 11.50 **st.** ♟ 3.85 – **48 rm** ☲ 41.25/55.00 **st.** –
SB (weekends only) 57.20 **st.**

⅋⅋ **Woodbury House** with rm, Lewes Rd, RH19 3UD, SE : ½ m. on A 22 ℰ 313657, ☞ – 🖵
⏁wc ☎ ℗. 🖾 🝏 ⓞ 𝚅𝙸𝚂𝙰 ⅋⅋
closed 25 and 26 December – **M** *(closed Sunday dinner to non-residents)* 7.50/8.50 **t.** and a la
carte ♟ 2.70 – **7 rm** ☲ 25.00/45.00 **t.**

at Gravetye SW : 4 ½ m. by B 2110 – ⊠ East Grinstead – ☺ 0342 Sharpthorne :

🏛🏛 ☺ **Gravetye Manor** ॐ, RH19 4LJ, ℰ 810567, Telex 957239, ≤, «16C Manor house with
gardens and grounds by William Robinson », ॐ, park – 🖵 ℗. ⅋⅋
M (booking essential) a la carte 18.00/29.30 **s.** ♟ 5.60 – ☲ 6.00 – **14 rm** 55.00/100.00 **s.**
Spec. Parfait of chicken livers, Best end of lamb marinated in herbs with garlic sauce (March-August), Reuble
torte.

AUSTIN-ROVER King St. ℰ 24666

FORD 220 London Rd ℰ 24344

EAST HORSLEY Surrey 🔢 S 30 – pop. 5,864 – ECD : Thursday – ⊠ Leatherhead – ☺ 048 65.
♦London 29 – Guildford 7.

🏛 **Thatchers** (Best Western), Epsom Rd, KT13 6DB, on A 246 ℰ 4291, ⅃ heated, ☞ – 🖵 ☎
℗. 🅰. 🖾 🝏 ⓞ 𝚅𝙸𝚂𝙰 ⅋⅋
M 10.50/19.50 **t.** and a la carte ♟ 3.50 – ☲ 5.25 – **29 rm** 45.00/56.00 **st.** – SB (weekends only)
60.00/70.00 **st.**

EASTLEIGH Devon 🔢 H 30 – see Bideford.

EASTLEIGH Hants. 408 P 31 – pop. 58,585 – ECD : Wednesday – ✆ 0703.

🏛 Town Hall Centre, Leigh Rd ✆ 614646 ext 3067.

♦London 74 – Winchester 8 – ♦Southampton 4.

🏨 **Crest** (Crest), Leigh Rd, SO5 5PG, ✆ 619700, Telex 47606 – 📶 🍴 rest 📺 ☎ & 🅿 . 🦺 . 🔼 🆎 ⓘ 🆅🆂🅰 . ✂

  M approx. 11.50 **st.** – � 5.75 – **120 rm** 51.00/61.00 **st.** – SB (weekends only) 59.00 **st.**

EAST MOLESEY Surrey 404 ⊛ – see Esher.

EASTON CROSS Devon 408 I 31 – see Chagford.

EASTON GREY Wilts. 408 404 N 29 – see Malmesbury.

EAST PRESTON West Sussex 404 S 31 – see Worthing.

EAST WITTERING West Sussex 404 R 31 – pop. 3,503 – ✆ 0243 Chichester.

♦London 74 – ♦Brighton 37 – ♦Portsmouth 25.

🍴 **Clifford's Cottage,** Bracklesham Lane, Bracklesham Bay, PO20 8JF, E : ¼ m. by B 2179 on B 2198 ✆ 670250 – 🅿 . 🔼 🆎 ⓘ 🆅🆂🅰
  closed Sunday dinner, Monday October-Easter, first week January and first 2 weeks November – **M** (lunch by arrangement) 6.75/9.50 **st.** and a la carte 🍷 2.80.

EBBERSTON North Yorks. 402 S 21 – pop. 425 – ✉ ✆ 0723 Scarborough.

♦London 243 – Scarborough 9 – York 31.

🏠 **Foxholm,** YO13 9NJ, off A 170 ✆ 85550, ☞ – 🏠wc 🅿
  April-October – **10 rm** ⊏ 17.50/42.00 **t.**

EDWALTON Notts. 402 408 404 Q 25 – see Nottingham.

EDWINSTOWE Notts. 402 408 404 Q 24 – pop. 4,870 – ✉ ✆ 0623 Mansfield.

♦London 154 – Derby 31 – Lincoln 26 – ♦Nottingham 21 – ♦Sheffield 25.

🍴🍴 **Maid Marian,** 8-10 Church St., NG21 9QA, ✆ 822266 – 🅿 . 🔼 🆎 ⓘ 🆅🆂🅰
  closed Sunday dinner, Monday and 25 to 30 December – **M** (dinner only and Sunday lunch) a la carte 6.40/10.70 **t.** 🍷 3.50.

EGERTON Greater Manchester 402 ② 408 ② 404 ⑨ – see Bolton.

EGHAM Surrey 404 S 29 – pop. 21,337 – ECD : Thursday – ✆ 0784.

♦London 29 – Reading 21.

🏨 **Runnymede,** Windsor Rd, TW20 0AG, on A 308 ✆ 36171, Telex 934900, ≤ – 📶 📺 ☎ 🅿 . 🦺 . 🔼 🆎 ⓘ 🆅🆂🅰
  M (Dancing Friday and Saturday) 8.00/9.50 **st.** and a la carte 🍷 3.10 – ⊏ 2.00 – **124 rm** 43.50/70.00 **st.** – SB (weekends only) 60.00/122.75 **st.**

🏨 **Great Fosters,** Stroude Rd, TW20 9UR, S : 1 ¼ m. by B 388 ✆ 33822, Telex 944441, ≤, « Elizabethan mansion with extensive gardens », 🔼 heated, park, ☜ – 📺 🅿 . 🦺 . 🔼 🆎 ⓘ 🆅🆂🅰 . ✂
  M 9.50/13.00 **t.** and a la carte 🍷 2.55 – **44 rm** ⊏ 39.50/71.50 **t.**, **2 suites** 75.50 **t.**

🍴🍴🍴 **Bailiwick,** Wick Rd, Englefield Green, TW20 0HN, SW : 2 ½ m. by A 30 ✆ 32223 – 🔼 🆎 ⓘ 🆅🆂🅰
  closed Sunday dinner – **M** a la carte 11.80/19.45 **t.** 🍷 3.00.

🍴🍴 **La Bonne Franquette,** 5 High St., TW20 9EA, ✆ 33206, ☞ – 🅿 . 🔼 🆎 ⓘ 🆅🆂🅰
  closed Saturday lunch and Bank Holidays – **M** 12.50 **t.** (lunch) and a la carte 14.40/20.50 **t.** 🍷 3.25.

🍴 **Trattoria il Borgo,** 15 The Precinct, ✆ 33544, Italian rest. – 🔼 🆎 🆅🆂🅰
  closed Sunday and Bank Holidays – **M** a la carte 8.00/13.75 **t.** 🍷 3.00.

AUSTIN-ROVER The Causeway ✆ 36191   PEUGEOT-TALBOT 186 High St. ✆ 38787
FERRARI Egham-by-pass ✆ 36431

EGLWYSFACH Dyfed 408 I 26 – see Machynlleth (Powys).

ELLESMERE Salop 402 408 L 25 – pop. 2,474 – ECD : Thursday – ✆ 069 171.

♦London 181 – Chester 24 – Shrewsbury 17 – ♦Stoke-on-Trent 33.

🏠 **Grange** ☜, Grange Rd, SY12 9DE, N : 1 m. on A 528 ✆ 2735, ☞ – 📺 🏠wc ☎ & 🅿 . 🔼 ⓘ 🆅🆂🅰
  M (bar lunch Monday to Saturday)/dinner 10.00 **t.** 🍷 2.50 – **15 rm** ⊏ 18.00/37.00 **t.** – SB (October-May) (except Christmas-New Year) 45.00/48.00 **st.**

ELSTEAD Surrey 404 R 30 – pop. 2,633 – ✆ 0252.

♦London 43 – Guildford 9 – ♦Portsmouth 41.

🍴🍴🍴 **Bentleys,** Elstead Mill, GU8 6LE, on B 3001 ✆ 702310, « Converted watermill », ☞ – 📶 🅿 . 🔼 🆎 ⓘ 🆅🆂🅰
  closed Sunday dinner – **M** 7.50 **t.** (lunch) and a la carte 12.75/18.00 **t.** 🍷 2.70.

ELSTREE Herts 404 T 29 – pop. 5,296 – ✪ 01 London.
◆London 18 – Luton 20.

ⅩⅩⅩ Battleaxes (T.H.F.), Butterfly Lane, NW : 2 m. by A 411 and Aldenham Rd ℰ 953 1049 – 🄿.

ELY Cambs. 404 U 26 – pop. 9,006 – ECD : Tuesday – ✪ 0353.
See : Cathedral★★ 11C-16C (Norman nave★★★, lantern★★★).
📷 Ely City, Cambridge Rd ℰ 2751.
🅉 Public Library, Palace Green ℰ 2062 – ◆London 74 – ◆Cambridge 16 – ◆Norwich 60.

🏨 **Lamb** (Q.M.H.), 2 Lynn Rd, CB7 4EJ, ℰ 3574 – 📺 🛁wc 🕭 🄿. 🔄 AE Ⓞ VISA
M 6.50 **st.** and a la carte 🍴 4.00 – **32 rm** 🛏 29.00/38.00 **st.** – SB (weekends only) 48.00 **st.**

🏨 **Fenlands Lodge,** Soham Rd, Stuntney, CB7 5TR, SE : 3 m. on A 142 ℰ 67047, 🍴 – 📺
🛁wc 🕿 🄿. 🔄 AE Ⓞ VISA
M 6.90/9.20 **t.** and a la carte 🍴 2.50 – **9 rm** 🛏 30.00/40.00.

Ⅹ **Old Fire Engine House,** 25 St. Mary's St., CB7 4ER, ℰ 2582, English rest. – 🄿
closed Sunday dinner, 2 weeks at Christmas and Bank Holidays – **M** a la carte 8.20/10.50 **t.**
🍴 3.20.

Ⅹ **Peking Duck,** 26 Fore Hill, CB7 4AF, ℰ 2948, Chinese rest. – AE
closed Tuesday lunch, Monday and 25-26 December – **M** 10.50 **t.** and a la carte.

AUSTIN-ROVER Lynn Rd ℰ 2981
CITROEN, PEUGEOT, TALBOT St. Mary's St. ℰ 2952
FORD Station Rd ℰ 61181

NISSAN 64 St. Mary's St. ℰ 2300
VOLVO The Slade, Witcham ℰ 778403
VW, AUDI 16-18 St. Mary's St. ℰ 61272

EMBOROUGH Somerset 403 404 M 30 – pop. 163 – ✉ Bath (Avon) – ✪ 0761 Stratton-on-the-Fosse.
◆London 127 – ◆Bristol 15 – Taunton 33.

🏨 **Court,** Lynch Hill, BA3 4SA, E : ¼ m. on B 3139 ℰ 232237, 🍴, ⅩⅩ – 📺 🛁wc 🍴wc 🄿. 🔄
VISA
closed 24 December-12 January – **M** *(closed Monday and Saturday lunch and Sunday to non-residents)* 9.75 **t.** (dinner) and a la carte 🍴 2.50 – **9 rm** 🛏 25.00/37.50 **t.** – SB (weekends only) 44.50/49.50 **st.**

EMSWORTH Hants. 404 R 31 – pop. 17,604 (inc. Southbourne) – ECD : Wednesday – ✪ 0243.
◆London 75 – ◆Brighton 37 – ◆Portsmouth 10.

🏨 **Brookfield,** 93-95 Havant Rd, PO10 7LF, ℰ 373363, 🍴 – 📺 🛁wc 🕿 🄿. 🔼 🔄 AE Ⓞ VISA
🍴
M 6.50 **t.** and a la carte 🍴 2.40 – **31 rm** 🛏 24.00/32.00 – SB (weekends only)(October-March)
40.00 **st.**

Ⅹ **36 North Street,** 36 North St., PO10 7DG, ℰ 375592 – 🔄 AE Ⓞ VISA
closed Sunday, Monday and 21 December-21 January – **M** (dinner only) a la carte 11.40/16.85 **t.**
🍴 2.70.

EPPING Essex 404 U 28 – pop. 10,148 – ECD : Wednesday – ✪ 0378.
See : Forest★ – Envir. : Waltham Abbey (Abbey★) W : 6 m.
◆London 20 – ◆Cambridge 40 – Chelmsford 18.

🏨 **Post House** (T.H.F.), High Rd, Bell Common, CM16 4DG, S : ¾ m. on B 1393 ℰ 73137, Telex
81617, 🍴 – 📺 🛁wc 🕿 🄿. 🔄 AE Ⓞ VISA
M 6.95/9.40 **st.** and a la carte 🍴 3.15 – 🛏 5.50 – **82 rm** 43.00/50.50 **st.**

RENAULT High Rd ℰ 72266

EPSOM Surrey 404 ⑳ – pop. 65,830 (inc. Ewell) – ECD : Wednesday – ✪ 037 27.
Envir. : Chessington Zoo★ AC, NW : 3 ½ m.
📷 Longdown Lane South, Epsom Downs ℰ 21666 – ◆London 17 – Guildford 16.

↑ **White House,** Downshill Rd, KT18 5HW, ℰ 22472, 🍴 – 🛁wc 🄿. 🍴
10 rm 🛏 15.50/29.50 **s.**

AUSTIN-ROVER 4 Church St. ℰ 26611
CITROEN Walton-on-the-Hill ℰ 073 781 (Tadworth)
3811
FORD East St. ℰ 26246
MAZDA 5 Ruxley Lane, Ewell ℰ 01 393 0202

PEUGEOT, TALBOT 38 Upper High St. ℰ 25611
RENAULT 1/3 Dorking Rd ℰ 28391
VAUXHALL 48 Upper High St. ℰ 25920
VW, AUDI Reigate Rd ℰ 073 73 (Burgh Heath) 60111

ESHER Surrey 404 S 29 – pop. 46,688 (inc. Molesey) – ECD : Wednesday – ✪ 0372.
📷 Moore Place, Portsmouth Rd ℰ 63533 BZ – 📷 Sandown Park, More Lane ℰ 65921 BZ.
◆London 20 – ◆Portsmouth 58.

Plan : see Greater London (South-West)

ⅩⅩ **Good Earth,** 14-16 High St., KT10 9RT, ℰ 62489, Chinese rest. – 🍽. 🔄 AE Ⓞ VISA   BZ **e**
closed 24 to 27 December – **M** 15.95 and a la carte 2.80.

ⅩⅩ **Le Pierrot,** 63 High St., KT10 9RQ, ℰ 63191, French rest. – 🍽. 🔄 AE Ⓞ VISA   BZ **o**
closed Saturday lunch, Sunday, 25-26 December and Bank Holidays – **M** 6.50/9.45 **t.** and a la carte 🍴 3.00.

at East Molesey N : 2 m. by A 309 – ⊠ East Molesey – ✪ 01 London :

XX **Vecchia Roma,** 55-57 Bridge Rd, KT9 2ER, ℰ 979 5490, Italian rest. – ᴀᴥ ⓞ 𝘝𝘐𝘚𝘈   BZ **n**
   closed Saturday lunch – **M** 8.25/12.50 **t.** and a la carte ⓙ 3.95.

XX **Le Chien Qui Fume,** 107 Walton Rd, KT8 0DR, ℰ 979 7150, French rest. – ᴀᴥ ᴀᴇ ⓞ 𝘝𝘐𝘚𝘈
   closed Sunday, 3 weeks August and Bank Holidays – **M** 6.50 **t.** /dinner a la carte 12.20/29.80 **t.**
   ⓙ 2.80.   BZ **c**

XX **Lantern,** 20 Bridge Rd, KT8 9AH, ℰ 979 1531, French rest. – ᴀᴥ ᴀᴇ ⓞ 𝘝𝘐𝘚𝘈   BZ **i**
   closed Sunday, August and Bank Holidays – **M** (lunch by arrangement)/dinner 14.50 **t.** and a
   la carte ⓙ 2.70.

at Claygate SE : 1 m. by A 244 – ⊠ ✪ 0372 Esher

X **Reads,** 4 The Parade, ℰ 65105 – ᴀᴥ ᴀᴇ ⓞ 𝘝𝘐𝘚𝘈   BZ **r**
   closed Sunday and Monday – **M** a la carte 8.30/11.95 **t.** ⓙ 2.75.

AUSTIN-ROVER 94 Hare Lane, Claygate ℰ 62996   VAUXHALL Kingston By-Pass, Hinchley Wood ℰ 01
                                                      (London) 398 0123

ESKDALE GREEN Cumbria 🗺️**402** K 20 – pop. 457 – ECD : Wednesday and Saturday – ⊠ Holm-
rook – ✪ 094 03.
♦London 312 – ♦Carlisle 59 – Kendal 60.

🏚 **Bower House Inn** ⒮, CA19 1TD, W : ¾ m. ℰ 244, ⌖, – 📺 ⌂wc ⓟ
   closed 24 to 26 December – **M** (bar lunch)/dinner 14.50 **t.** ⓙ 3.00 – **15 rm** ⊏⊐ 21.50/55.00 **t.**

ETON Berks. 🗺️**404** S 29 – see Windsor.

ETTINGTON Warw. 🗺️**403 404** P 27 – see Stratford-upon-Avon.

EVERSHOT Dorset 🗺️**403 404** M 31 – pop. 224 – ⊠ Dorchester – ✪ 093 583.
♦London 149 – Bournemouth 39 – Dorchester 12 – Salisbury 53 – Taunton 30 – Yeovil 10.

🏨 **Summer Lodge** ⒮, Summer Lane, DT2 0JR, ℰ 424, « Country house atmosphere »,
   ᙭ heated, ⌖ – ⌂wc ⓟ ᴀᴥ 𝘝𝘐𝘚𝘈
   closed December-January – **M** *(closed lunch to non-residents)* (dinner only) 14.50 **t.** ⓙ 2.95 –
   9 rm ⊏⊐ 30.00/70.00 **t.** – SB (February-May and October-November) 70.00/80.00 **st.**

EVESHAM Heref. and Worc. 🗺️**403 404** O 27 – pop. 15,069 – ECD : Wednesday – ✪ 0386.
🛈 The Almonry Museum, Abbey Gate ℰ 6944.
♦London 99 – ♦Birmingham 30 – Cheltenham 16 – ♦Coventry 32.

🏨 **Evesham,** Coopers Lane, off Waterside (A 44), WR11 6DA, ℰ 49111, Telex 339342, ⌖ – 📺
   ⌂wc 🛏wc 🐾 ⓟ 🚿 ᴀᴥ ᴀᴇ ⓞ 𝘝𝘐𝘚𝘈
   closed 25 and 26 December – **M** (buffet lunch) a la carte 7.50/12.80 **st.** ⓙ 2.90 – **34 rm**
   ⊏⊐ 30.00/50.00 **st.** – SB (weekends only) 46.00/72.00 **st.**

🏚 **Waterside,** 56-59 Waterside (A 44), WR11 6JZ, ℰ 2420 – 📺 ⌂wc 🛏wc ⓟ ᴀᴥ ᴀᴇ 𝘝𝘐𝘚𝘈
   M 5.50 **t.** (lunch) and a la carte 6.90/9.50 **t.** – **12 rm** ⊏⊐ 21.00/38.00 **t.** – SB 49.75/54.75 **st.**

AUSTIN-ROVER Abbey Rd ℰ 6173   NISSAN Cheltenham Rd ℰ 47103
BEDFORD, VAUXHALL-OPEL 70 High St. ℰ 2614 PEUGEOT-TALBOT Broadway Rd ℰ 6441
BMW, VW, AUDI Harvington ℰ 870612   RENAULT Pershore ℰ 0386 (Pershore) 2167
FIAT 3 Cheltenham Rd ℰ 2301   RENAULT 123 Pershore Rd, Hampton ℰ 45072
FORD Market Pl. ℰ 2525   SKODA Sedgeberrow ℰ 881208

EWEN Glos. 🗺️**403 404** O 28 – see Cirencester.

EXETER Devon 🗺️**403** J 31 The West Country G. – pop. 88,235 – ✪ 0392.
See : Site★★ – Cathedral★★ AZ **A** – Maritime Museum★★*AC* AZ – Royal Albert Memorial
Museum★*AC* AZ **M2.**
Envir. : Killerton House★★*AC*, N : 7 m. by B 3181 BY – Crediton (Holy Cross Church★), NW : 8 m. by
A 377 AY – Cullompton★, St. Andrews Church★, NE : 14 m. by B 3181 BY.
🏌 Downes Crediton ℰ 036 32 (Crediton) 3991, NW : 7 ½ m. by A 377 AY.
🛫 Exeter Airport : ℰ 67433, Telex 42648, E : 5 m. by A 30 BY – Terminal : St. David's and Central
Stations.
🛈 Civic Centre, Dix's Field ℰ 72434 – Exeter Services Area (M 5) Sandygate, ℰ 37581 (summer only).
♦London 201 – Bournemouth 83 – ♦Bristol 83 – ♦Plymouth 46 – ♦Southampton 110.

Plan opposite

🏩 **Buckerell Lodge** (Crest), Topsham Rd, EX2 4SQ, SE : 1 m. on B 3182 ℰ 52451, Telex 42410,
   ⌖ – 📺 ⌂wc 📞 ⅙ ⓟ ᴀᴥ ᴀᴇ ⓞ 𝘝𝘐𝘚𝘈 🍴   BY **a**
   M approx. 11.50 **st.** – ⊏⊐ 5.75 – **54 rm** 44.50/54.50 **st.** – SB (weekends only) 63.00 **st.**

🏩 **White Hart,** 65-66 South St., EX1 1EE, ℰ 79897, « Part 14C inn » – 📱 📺 ⌂wc 🛏wc 🐾 ⓟ
   🚿 ᴀᴥ ᴀᴇ ⓞ 𝘝𝘐𝘚𝘈 🍴   AZ **n**
   closed 24-26 December – **M** 5.75 **t.** (lunch) and a la carte 9.50/18.50 **t.** – **61 rm** ⊏⊐ 24.00/50.00 **t.**
   – SB (weekends only) 25.00/35.00 **st.**

EXETER

Bedford Street . . . . **AZ** 3
Fore Street . . . . **AZ**
High Street . . . . **AZ**
Shopping Precinct . . . . **AZ**

Alphington Road . . . . **AZ** 2
Blackall Road . . . . **AZ** 4
Buddle Lane . . . . **AY** 5
Butts Road . . . . **BY** 6
Commins Road . . . . **BZ** 8
Edmund Street . . . . **AZ** 9

East Wonford Hill . . . . **BY** 10
Frog Street . . . . **AZ** 12
Ladysmith Road . . . . **BZ** 16
Little John's Cross Hill . . . . . **AY** 17
Loongbrook Street . . . . **AZ** 18
Magdalen Street . . . . **AZ** 19
Marsh Barton Road . . . . **AY** 20
Mount Pleasant Road . . . . . . **BY** 21
New Bridge Street . . . . **AZ** 22
North Street . . . . **AZ** 23
North Street
   HEAVITREE . . . . **BY** 24
Okehampton Road . . . . **AZ** 26
Old Tiverton Road . . . . **BZ** 27

Paris Street . . . . **BZ** 28
Prince Charles Road . . . . **BY** 30
Prince of Wales Road . . . . . . **AY** 31
Richmond Road . . . . **AZ** 32
St. Andrew's Road . . . . **AY** 33
South Street . . . . **AZ** 34
Southernhay East . . . . **ABZ** 35
Southernhay West . . . . **AZ** 36
Sweetbriar Lane . . . . **BY** 38
Trusham Road . . . . **AZ** 39
Union Road . . . . **AY** 41
Western Way . . . . **AZ** 42
Whipton Lane . . . . **BY** 43
Wonford Street . . . . **BY** 45

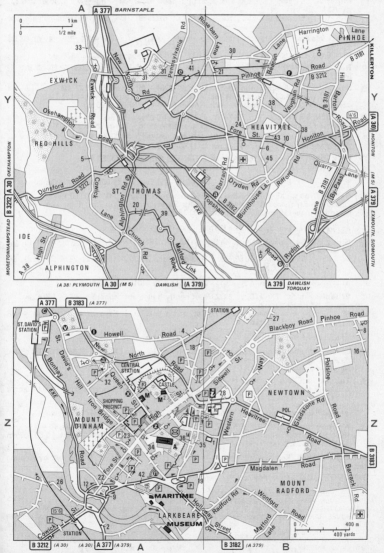

🏨 **Royal Clarence** (Norfolk Cap.), Cathedral Yard, EX1 1HD, ℰ 58464, Group Telex 23241 – 📶
📺 🛁wc 🚿wc ☎. 🛃 🔼 🅰🄴 ⓞ *VISA*
AZ **z**
M 6.50/8.50 **t.** and a la carte ≬ 2.90 – **62 rm** ⟤ 35.20/52.00 **st.**, **1 suite** 69.00 **st.** – SB 51.00/54.50 **st.**

🏨 **Rougemont** (Mt. Charlotte), Queen St., EX4 3SP, ℰ 54982, Telex 42455 – 📶 📺 🛁wc 🚿
🅿. 🛃 🔼 🅰🄴 ⓞ *VISA*
AZ **x**
M 7.35/7.75 **st.** and a la carte ≬ 3.90 – **63 rm** ⟤ 32.50/42.50 **st.** – SB (weekends only) 46.00/52.00 **st.**

🏨 **Exeter Moat House** (Q.M.H.), 398 Topsham Rd., EX2 6HE, S : 2 ½ m. at junction of A 379 and B 3182 ℰ 039 287 (Topsham) 5441 – 📺 🛁wc ☎ 🅿. 🛃 🔼 🅰🄴 ⓞ *VISA*
BY **o**
M 6.95 **t.** and a la carte ≬ 2.75 – **44 rm** ⟤ 25.00/41.00 **st.** – SB 46.00/52.00 **st.**

🏨 **Imperial,** St. David's Hill, EX4 4JX, ℰ 211811, Telex 42551, 🚗 – 📺 🛁wc 🚿wc 🚿 🚘 🅿.
🛃 🔼 🅰🄴 ⓞ *VISA*
AZ **v**
M 5.25/8.95 **t.** and a la carte ≬ 2.60 – **25 rm** ⟤ 18.00/39.00 **t.** – SB (weekends only)(except summer) 45.00 **st.**

🏨 **Great Western,** St. David's Station Approach, EX4 4NU, ℰ 74039 – 📺 🛁wc 🚿 🅿. 🔼 🅰🄴
ⓞ *VISA*
AZ **c**
M 4.25/6.95 **t.** ≬ 2.60 – **42 rm** ⟤ 16.50/31.00 **t.** – SB (weekends only) 40.00/48.00 **st.**

🏨 **Red House,** 2 Whipton Village Rd, EX4 8AR, ℰ 56104 – 📺 🛁wc 🚿wc 🅿. 🔼 🅰🄴 ⓞ *VISA*
BY **r**
M 5.35/8.50 **t.** and a la carte ≬ 2.30 – **13 rm** ⟤ 14.00/30.00 **t.**

🏨 **St. Andrews,** 28 Alphington Rd, EX2 8HN, ℰ 76784 – 📺 🛁wc 🅿. 🔼 🅰🄴 *VISA*
AY **a**
closed 1 week at Christmas – **M** (bar lunch)/dinner a la carte 7.85/10.45 **t.** ≬ 2.80 – **16 rm** ⟤ 21.00/35.00 **t.** – SB (weekends only) (November-March) 37.70/45.90 **st.**

🏨 **Bystock,** 6-8 Bystock Terr., EX4 4HY, ℰ 72709 – 📺 🛁wc 🚿wc. 🔼 *VISA*
AZ **a**
M (closed Sunday) (bar lunch)/dinner 7.50 **t.** and a la carte – **24 rm** ⟤ 16.00/33.00 **t.**

↑ **Sylvania House,** 64 Pennsylvania Rd, EX4 6DF, ℰ 75583 – 🚿wc 🅿. *VISA*. 🎇
AY **e**
closed 14 December-1 January – **8 rm** ⟤ 11.50/30.00 **t.**

↑ **Park View,** 8 Howell Rd, EX4 4LG, ℰ 71772 – 📺 🛁wc 🚿wc 🅿. 🔼 *VISA*
AZ **i**
15 rm ⟤ 13.80/25.00 **t.**

at Huxham N : 5 m. by A 377 – AY – off A 396 – ✉ Exeter – ☎ 039 284 Stoke Canon :

✕✕ **Barton Cross,** EX5 4EJ, ℰ 245, « Part 16C thatched cottage », 🚗 – 🅿. 🔼 *VISA*
closed Sunday dinner, Monday, first 2 weeks September and 2 to 15 January – **M** (booking essential)/dinner 10.85 **t.** and a la carte 11.30/13.70 **t.** ≬ 2.45.

at Pinhoe NE : 3 m. by B 3212 on B 3181 – BY – ✉ ☎ 0392 Exeter :

🏨 **Gipsy Hill** 🌳, Gipsy Hill Lane, via Station Rd, EX1 3RN, ℰ 65252, 🚗 – 📺 🛁wc 🚿 🅿. 🛃.
🔼 🅰🄴 ⓞ *VISA*
M (closed Sunday dinner) 6.50/8.50 **t.** and a la carte ≬ 2.75 – **19 rm** ⟤ 29.50/39.50 **t.** – SB (weekends only) 49.50 **st.**

at Whimple NE : 9 m. by A 30 – BY – ✉ Exeter – ☎ 0404 Whimple :

🏨 **Woodhayes** 🌳, EX5 2TD, ℰ 822237, « Country house atmosphere », 🚗 – 📺 🛁wc 🚿
🚘 🅿. 🔼 🅰🄴 *VISA*. 🎇
M (lunch by arrangement) 12.00/17.00 **st.** and a la carte – **7 rm** ⟤ 40.00/65.00 **st.** – SB (November-March) 67.50 **st.**

at Kennford S : 5 m. on A 38 – AY – ✉ ☎ 0392 Exeter :

🏨 Ladbroke Mercury Motor Inn (Ladbroke), Kennford Services, EX6 7UX, ℰ 832121 – 📺 🛁wc
🚿 🕭 🅿. 🛃
M (grill rest. only) – **61 rm**.

🏨 **Fairwinds,** EX6 7UD, ℰ 832911 – 📺 🛁wc 🚿wc 🅿. 🔼 *VISA*. 🎇
closed 12 to 31 December – **M** (closed Sunday and Bank Holidays) (bar lunch)/dinner 8.35 **t.** ≬ 2.00 – **8 rm** ⟤ 18.00/35.00 **t.** – SB 38.00/42.00 **st.**

at Doddiscombsleigh SW : 7 ½ m. by A 38 – AY – ✉ Exeter – ☎ 0647 Christow :

✿ **Nobody Inn** 🌳, EX6 7PS, ℰ 52394, « 16C inn », 🚗 – 🛁wc 🚿wc 🅿. 🔼 *VISA*. 🎇
M (closed dinner Sunday and Monday) (bar lunch)/dinner a la carte 7.50/10.50 **t.** ≬ 2.80 – **7 rm** ⟤ 10.00/28.00 **t.**

MICHELIN Branch, Kestrel Way, Sowton Industrial Estate, EX2 7LH, ℰ 77246/7/8/9 by Honiton Road BY

ALFA-ROMEO, LADA, SUZUKI Hennock Rd, Marsh Barton ℰ 37337
AUSTIN-ROVER 55 Sidwell St. ℰ 78342
AUSTIN-ROVER 84-88 Sidwell St. ℰ 54923
AUSTIN-ROVER-DAIMLER-JAGUAR, ROLLS ROYCE, LAND ROVER-RANGE ROVER Marsh Barton Rd ℰ 37152
BMW Pinhill, Pinhoe ℰ 69595
CITROEN, FIAT, MERCEDES-BENZ Trusham Rd, Marsh Barton ℰ 77311

COLT 66 Polsloe Rd ℰ 57990
FORD 9 Marsh Barton Rd ℰ 50141
MAZDA Alphinbrook Rd ℰ 57737
NISSAN Honiton Rd ℰ 68187
RENAULT Summerland St. ℰ 77225
TOYOTA 37 Marsh Green Rd, Marsh Barton ℰ 34761
VAUXHALL-OPEL, BEDFORD 8 Marsh Barton Rd, Marsh Barton Trading Estsate ℰ 34851
VOLVO Longbrook Terr. ℰ 215691
VW, AUDI Haven Rd ℰ 30321

EXFORD Somerset **403** J 30 The West Country G. − pop. 409 − ECD : Thursday − ⊠ Minehead − ☻ 064 383.

See : Exmoor National Park★★ − Church★.

Envir. : Dunkery Beacon★★★ (≤★★★), N : 4 ½ m − Winsford★, SE : 8 m. − at Oare, Doone Valley★, NW : 8 m. plus 6 m. return on foot − Luccombe★ (Church★), NE : 9 m.

♦London 194 − Exeter 35 − Minehead 13 − Taunton 32.

🏠 **Crown,** TA24 7PP, ℰ 554 − 📺 ⇔wc **P.** 🔼 AE VISA
M 5.95/12.95 t. and a la carte ⌀ 3.00 − **18 rm** ⊒ (dinner included) 34.00/42.00 t. − SB (weekends only) (January-February and May-July) 68.00 **st.**

EXMOUTH Devon **403** J 32 The West Country G. − pop. 28 ,037 − ECD : Wednesday − ☻ 0395.

Envir. : A La Ronde★ AC, N : 2 m. − Bicton★, The Gardens★ AC, NE : 8 m.

🄱 Alexandra Terr. ℰ 263744 (summer only).

♦London 210 − Exeter 11.

🏨 **Imperial** (T.H.F.), The Esplanade, EX8 2SW, ℰ 274761, ≤, ⊒ heated, ✿, ✾ − ⧈ 📺 **P.** 🔼 AE ① VISA
M (buffet lunch Monday to Saturday)/dinner 8.95 **t.** and a la carte ⌀ 2.70 − ⊒ 5.50 − **58 rm** 34.50/51.50 **st.**

🏠 **Royal Beacon,** The Beacon, EX8 2AF, ℰ 264886, ≤ − ⧈ ▤ rest 📺 ⇔wc ⇐ **P.** 🔼 AE ① VISA
M 6.50/8.00 **st.** and a la carte ⌀ 3.60 − **35 rm** − SB (October to March) 45.00/50.00 **st.**

🏠 **Devoncourt** ❦, 16 Douglas Av., EX8 2EX, by Rolle Rd ℰ 272277, ≤, ⊒ heated, 🔼, ✿, ✾ − ⧈ 📺 ⇔wc ☜ **P.** 🔼 AE VISA
M 5.50/6.50 **t.** and a la carte ⌀ 2.50 − **68 rm** ⊒ 26.50/72.00 **t.** − SB (weekends only)(October-April) 40.80/44.50 **st.**

🏠 **Balcombe House** ❦, 7 Stevenstone Rd, EX8 2EP, NE : 1 m. by A 376 ℰ 266349, ✿ − 📺 �fireplacewc ⌀ **P.** ✾
April-October − **M** (bar lunch)/dinner 8.00 **t.** ⌀ 2.00 − **12 rm** ⊒ 16.85/35.70 **t.** − SB 42.70/45.80 **st.**

at Lympstone N : 3 m. by A 376 − ⊠ ☻ 0395 Exmouth

XXX **River House,** The Strand, EX8 5EY, ℰ 265147, ≤ Exe Estuary − 🔼 AE VISA
closed Sunday dinner, Monday, 25 to 27 December and 1-2 January − **M** (booking essential) a la carte 9.80/17.60 **t.** ⌀ 3.15.

AUSTIN-ROVER The Parade ℰ 72258   VAUXHALL-OPEL Salterton Rd ℰ 264366
RENAULT 4 Church Rd ℰ 263888

EYAM Derbs. **403 404** O 24 − pop. 923 − ⊠ Sheffield (South Yorks.) − ☻ 0433 Hope Valley.

See : Celtic Cross★ 8C.

♦London 163 − Derby 29 − ♦Manchester 32 − ♦Sheffield 12.

🏠 **Miners Arms,** Water Lane, S30 1RG, ℰ 30853 − **P.** ✾
closed Monday lunch, Sunday dinner and Christmas Day − **M** (restricted lunch)/dinner 11.00 **t.** ⌀ 2.95 − **4 rm** ⊒ 18.00/22.00 **t.**

EYNSHAM Oxon. **403 404** P 28 pop. 4 ,339 − ☻ 0865 Oxford.

♦London 65 − ♦Birmingham 65 − Gloucester 40 − Northampton 43.

XX **Edward's,** 4 Lombard St., OX8 1HT, ℰ 880777 − 🔼 VISA
closed Saturday lunch, Sunday dinner, 28 March and 24 to 28 December − **M** a la carte 7.75/11.75 **t.** ⌀ 2.15.

FADMOOR North Yorks. − see Kirkbymoorside.

FAIRFORD Glos. **403 404** O 28 − pop. 2 ,408 − ECD : Saturday − ☻ 0285 Cirencester.

See : St. Mary's Church (stained glass windows★★ 15C-16C).

♦London 99 − ♦Bristol 46 − Gloucester 28 − ♦Oxford 27.

🏠 **Hyperion,** London Rd, GL7 4AH, ℰ 712349 − 📺 ⇔wc ☎ **P.** 🔼 AE ① VISA
M (bar lunch)/dinner 10.00 **t.** and a la carte ⌀ 2.30 − **23 rm** ⊒ 25.00/39.00 **t.** − SB (except Christmas and Bank Holidays) 52.00 **st.**

🏠 Bull, Market Pl., GL7 4AA, ℰ 712535, ➘, ✿ − 📺 ⇔wc **P.** − **17 rm**.

AUSTIN-ROVER The Bridge ℰ 712222   RENAULT ℰ 712219

FALFIELD Avon **403 404** M 29 − pop. 657 − ☻ 0454.

♦London 129 − ♦Bristol 16 − Gloucester 18 − Newport 30.

🏠 **Park,** GL12 8DR, S : 1 m. on A 38 ℰ 260550, ✿ − 📺 ⇔wc ⌀wc ☞ **P.** 🔼 AE ① VISA
M (closed Sunday) a la carte 9.25/18.00 **t.** ⌀ 3.00 − ⊒ 4.50 − **10 rm** 25.00/40.00 **st.** − SB 60.00 **st.**

FALLOWFIELD Greater Manchester **402** ⑱ **403** ③ **404** ⑩ − see Manchester.

FALMOUTH Cornwall **403** E 33 The West Country G. – pop. 17,810 – ECD : Wednesday – ✪ 0326.

See : Site★★ – Pendennis Castle★ (≼★★)*AC* B.

Envir. : Glendurgan Garden★★*AC*, S : 3½ m. by Swanpool Rd A – Helston Flora Day Flurry Dance★★, SW : 11 m. by A 39 A – Mawnan Parish Church★, (≼★★), SW : 4 m. by Trescobeas Rd A – at Gweek, Seal Sanctuary★, setting★*AC*, SW : 8 m. by A 39 A – Carn Brea (≼★), NW : 9 m. by A 39 A – at Wendron, Poldark Mine★, W : 9 m. by A 39 A – at Culdrose, Cornwall Aero Park★*AC*, SW : 10 m. by A 39 A – at Redruth, Tolgus Tin Streaming★*AC*, NW : 11 m. by A 39 A.

🅱 Swanpool Rd 🖋 311262 A – 🅱 Budock Vean Hotel 🖋 0326 (Mawnan Smith) 250288, SW : 7 m. by Trescobeas Rd A.

🅱 Town Hall, The Moor 🖋 312300.

♦London 308 – Penzance 26 – ♦Plymouth 65 – Truro 11.

Plan opposite

🏨 **Falmouth,** TR11 4NZ, 🖋 312671, Telex 45262, ≼, 🛴 heated, 🚗 – 🛗 TV 🅿 ⬛ 🔼 AE ⓞ VISA
   closed Christmas – **M** 6.50/10.50 **st.** and a la carte ⑃ 2.75 – **85 rm** ⌷ 24.00/80.00 **st.** – SB (weekends only) 56.00/64.00 **st.**
   B **x**

🏨 **Royal Duchy,** Cliff Rd, TR11 4NX, 🖋 313042, ≼, 🚗 – 🛗 TV 🅿 🔼 AE ⓞ VISA
   M 4.95/7.00 **st.** and a la carte ⑃ 3.40 – **38 rm** ⌷ 20.35/73.70 **t.** – SB 38.00/50.00 **st.**
   B **a**

🏨 **Greenbank,** Harbourside, TR11 2SR, 🖋 312440, Telex 45240, ≼ harbour – 🛗 TV ⌷wc ☎ ⇔ 🅿 🔼 AE ⓞ VISA
   closed 24 December-14 January – **M** 7.50/11.50 **t.** and a la carte – **43 rm** ⌷ 29.00/60.00 **t.** – SB (weekends only) 58.00/64.00 **st.**
   A **a**

🏨 **Green Lawns,** Western Terr., TR11 4QJ, 🖋 312734, Telex 45169 – TV ⌷wc �filwc ☏ 🅿 ⬛ 🔼 AE ⓞ VISA
   M 7.00/9.00 **t.** ⑃ 2.50 – **42 rm** ⌷ 17.25/49.45 **t.** – SB (October-May) 51.35/61.70 **st.**
   A **i**

🏨 **St. Michaels,** Sea Front, Gyllyngvase Beach, TR11 4NB, 🖋 312707, Telex 45540, ≼, 🔼, 🗝, 🚗 – TV ⌷wc ⓕⓘⓛwc ☎ 🅿 🔼 AE ⓞ VISA
   M 5.75/11.25 **t.** and a la carte ⑃ 2.50 – **75 rm** ⌷ 25.00/59.00 **t.** – SB (November-mid April) 46.00/50.00 **st.**
   A **z**

🏨 **Falmouth Beach,** Gyllyngvase Beach, Seafront, TR11 4NA, 🖋 318084, Telex 45540, ≼ – 🛗 TV ⌷wc ⓕⓘⓛwc ☎ 🅿 🔼 AE ⓞ VISA
   M (bar lunch)/dinner 14.50 **t.** ⑃ 2.50 – **67 rm** ⌷ 24.00/57.00 **t.** – SB (November-mid April) 45.00/50.00 **st.**
   A **r**

🏠 **Penmere Manor** (Best Western) 🗝, Mongleath Rd, TR11 4PN, 🖋 314545, Telex 45266, 🛴 heated, 🚗 – TV ⌷wc ⓕⓘⓛwc ⬛ 🅿 🔼 AE ⓞ VISA, 🗝
   closed 21 to 27 December – **M** (bar lunch)/dinner 11.00 **st.** ⑃ 2.80 – **29 rm** ⌷ 25.50/46.00 **st.** – SB 54.00/65.00 **st.**
   A **e**

🏠 **Crill House** 🗝, Golden Bank, TR11 5BL, SW : 2 ½ m. by Swanpool Rd 🖋 312994, 🛴 heated, 🚗 – ⌷wc 🅿 🔼 VISA
   by Boslowick Rd A
   April-mid October – **M** (bar lunch)/dinner 8.50 **st.** and a la carte ⑃ 3.50 – **11 rm** ⌷ 20.00/48.00 **st.** – SB (mid October-March) 50.00/58.00 **st.**

🏠 **Carthion,** Cliff Rd, TR11 4AP, 🖋 313669, ≼, 🚗 – TV ⌷wc ⓕⓘⓛwc 🅿 🔼 AE ⓞ VISA
   March-October – **M** (bar lunch)/dinner 8.50 **t.** ⑃ 2.30 – **18 rm** ⌷ 14.25/55.70 **t.**
   B **v**

🏠 **Broadmead,** 68 Kimberley Park Rd, TR11 2DD, 🖋 315704 – TV ⌷wc ⬛ 🔼 VISA
   closed Christmas and New Year – **M** (bar lunch) (booking essential)/dinner 8.00 **t.** ⑃ 3.00 – **15 rm** ⌷ 14.00/50.00 **t.** – SB 40.00/55.00 **st.**
   A **u**

⋔ **Rosemullion,** Gyllyngvase Hill, TR11 4DF, 🖋 314690 – ⌷wc ⓕⓘⓛwc 🅿 🗝
   May-October – **14 rm** ⌷ 10.35/20.70 **t.**
   B **c**

⋔ **Gyllyngvase House,** Gyllyngvase Rd, TR11 4DJ, 🖋 312956, 🚗 – ⌷wc 🅿 VISA, 🗝
   April-October – **16 rm** ⌷ 11.50/27.60 **t.**
   B **s**

⋔ **Cotswold House,** 49 Melvill Rd, TR11 4DF, 🖋 312077 – ⌷wc ⓕⓘⓛ 🅿 🗝
   April-October – **11 rm** ⌷ 8.50/22.00.
   B **o**

⋔ **Tresillian House,** 3 Stracey Rd, TR11 4DW, 🖋 312425 – TV ⌷wc ⓕⓘⓛwc 🅿 🗝
   March-October – **12 rm** ⌷ 13.75/29.50 **t.**
   A **n**

at Mawnan Smith SW : 5 m. by Trescobeas Rd – A – off B 3291 – ✉ ✪ 0326 Falmouth :

🏨 **Meudon** 🗝, TR11 5HT, E : ½ m. 🖋 250541, Telex 45478, « ≼ Terraced gardens » – TV ☎ 🅿 🔼 AE ⓞ VISA
   Mid February-mid November – **M** 12.50 **t.** (dinner) and a la carte 11.00/13.00 **t.** ⑃ 3.00 – **30 rm** ⌷ 30.00/68.00 **t.** – SB (except summer) 72.00/79.20 **st.**

🏨 **Budock Vean** 🗝, TR11 5LG, 🖋 250288, ≼, 🔼, 🅱, 🚗, park, 🗝 – 🛗 ☎ 🅿 ⬛ 🔼 AE ⓞ VISA, 🗝
   M 10.00/15.00 **t.** and a la carte ⑃ 3.75 – **50 rm** ⌷ 30.00/80.00 **t.** – SB (weekends only) (October-April) 70.00/90.00 **st.**

🏨 **Nansidwell Country House** 🗝, TR11 5HU, E : ¼ m. on Mawnan Church rd 🖋 250340, ≼, « Gardens », park, 🗝 – ⌷wc 🅿
   20 rm.

🏠 **Trelawne** 🗝, Maenporth Rd, TR11 5HS, E : ¾ m. 🖋 250226, 🔼, 🚗 – TV ⌷wc ⓕⓘⓛwc 🅿 🔼 ⓞ VISA
   April-October – **M** (bar lunch)/dinner 9.50 **t.** ⑃ 2.50 – **16 rm** ⌷ 19.00/54.00 **t.**

BMW Falmouth Rd, Penryn 🖋 032 67 (Penryn) 2641   TOYOTA North Parade 🖋 313029
FORD Ponsharden 🖋 72011

FALMOUTH

Church Street .... **B**
High Street .... **A**
Market Street .... **A** 33

Arwenack Street .... **B** 2
Avenue Road .... **A** 3
Beacon Road .... **A** 4
Belmont Road .... **A** 7
Berkeley Vale .... **A** 8

Boscawen Road .... **A** 9
Budock Terrace .... **A** 13
Conway Road .... **A** 14
De Pass Road .... **B** 15
Emslie Road .... **A** 18
Fenwick Road .... **A** 19
Glasney Road .... **A** 20
Grovehill Crescent ..... **B** 23
Gyllyngvase Hill .... **A** 24
Gyllyngvase Road ...... **A** 25
Kimberley Place .... **A** 28
Langton Road .... **A** 29

Madeira Walk .... **A** 30
Marlborough
  Crescent .... **A** 34
Park Terrace .... **A** 35
Pendennis Road .... **B** 38
Swanpool Road .... **A** 39
Symons Hill .... **A** 40
Tredova Crescent ...... **A** 43
Trescobeas Road .... **A** 44
Wellington Terrace ..... **A** 45
Windsor Terrace .... **A** 48
Wodehouse Terrace .... **A** 49

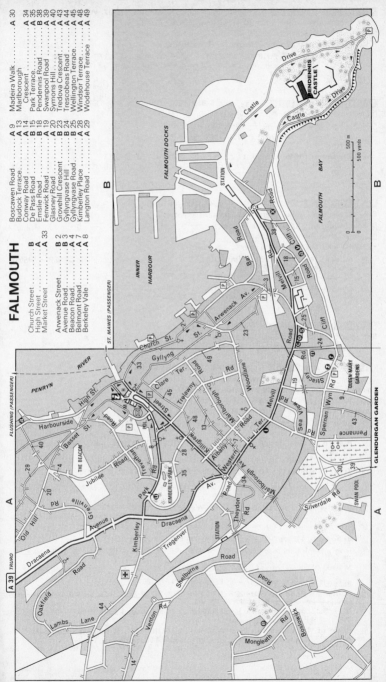

FAREHAM Hants. 408 404 Q 31 – pop. 55 ,563 (inc. Portchester) – ECD : Wednesday – ✆ 0329.
Envir. : Porchester castle★ (ruins 3C - 12C), Keep ≼★ *AC*, SE : 2 ½ m.
🖥 Ferneham Hall, Osborn Rd ☎ 221342.
◆London 77 – ◆Portsmouth 9 – ◆Southampton 13 – Winchester 19.

   🏨 **Red Lion,** East St., PO16 0BN, ☎ 239611 – 📺 🚻wc ☎ 🅿. 🔬. 🔼 Æ ⑩ 𝘝𝘐𝘚𝘈 ❄
     M 5.50/7.50 **st.** and a la carte ∬ 3.50 – **33 rm** ⊒ 24.00/44.00 **st.** – SB (weekends only)(except
     summer) 50.00/60.00 **st.**

AUSTIN-ROVER West St. ☎ 231511   PEUGEOT-TALBOT Newgate Lane ☎ 282811

FARINGDON Oxon. 408 404 P 29 – pop. 4 ,646 – ECD : Thursday – ✆ 0367.
🖥 Car Park, Southampton St. ☎ 22191 (summer only).
◆London 79 – ◆Bristol 55 – ◆Oxford 17 – Reading 34.

   🏠 **Bell,** Market Pl., SN7 7HP, ☎ 20534 – 📺 🚻wc 🅿
     11 rm.

   ✗ **Restaurant 1645,** 23 Market Sq., SN7 7HP, ☎ 20678 – 🔼 ⑩ 𝘝𝘐𝘚𝘈
     closed Saturday lunch, Sunday and Bank Holidays – **M** 6.50 **t.** (lunch) and a la carte 9.30/14.40 **t.**
     ∬ 3.00.

TOYOTA Church St. ☎ 22070   PEUGEOT, TALBOT Marlborough St. ☎ 21212

FARNBOROUGH Hants. 404 R 30 – pop. 48 ,063 – ECD : Wednesday – ✆ 0252.
See : St. Michael's Abbey church★ 19C (Imperial crypt *AC*).
🏌 Southwood, Ively Rd ☎ 548700, W : 1 m.
🖥 Country Library, Pinehurst Av. ☎ 513838.
◆London 41 – Reading 17 – ◆Southampton 44 – Winchester 33.

   🏨 **Queens** (Anchor), Lynchford Rd, GU14 6AZ, S : 1 ½ m. on Farnborough Rd (A 325) ☎ 545051,
     Group Telex 858875 – 📺 🚻wc ☎ 🅿. 🔬. 🔼 Æ ⑩ 𝘝𝘐𝘚𝘈
     M 8.25 **t.** and a la carte ∬ 3.00 – **79 rm** ⊒ 45.00/52.00 **t.** – SB (weekends only) 52.00/59.00 **st.**

   🏠 **Falcon,** 68 Farnborough Rd, GU14 6TH, S : ¾ m. on A 325 ☎ 545378 – 📺 🚻wc 🅿. ❄
     M (bar lunch Saturday and Sunday) 7.50/8.50 **st.** ∬ 2.60 – **25 rm** ⊒ 28.00/40.00 **st.**

FORD Elles Rd ☎ 544344

FARNE ISLANDS Northumb. 401 402 P 17.
See : Islands★★ (Sea Bird Sanctuary and grey seals, by boat from Seahouses *AC*).
   Hotels see : Bamburgh.

FARNHAM Surrey 404 R 30 – pop. 34 ,541 – ECD : Wednesday – ✆ 0252.
See : Castle keep 12C (square tower★) *AC*.
Envir. : Birdworld★ (zoological bird gardens) *AC*, SW : 3 ½ m.
🖥 Locality Office, South St. ☎ 048 68 (Godalming) 4104 ext 554.
◆London 45 – Reading 22 – ◆Southampton 39 – Winchester 28.

   🏨 **Bush** (Anchor), The Borough, GU9 7NN, ☎ 715237, Telex 858764, 🌳 – 📺 🚻wc ☎ 🅿. 🔬.
     65 rm.

   🏠 **Bishop's Table** (Best Western), 27 West St., GU9 7DR, ☎ 715545, 🌳 – 📺 🚻wc ☎. 🔼 Æ
     ⑩ 𝘝𝘐𝘚𝘈
     M 7.50/9.50 **t.** and a la carte – **16 rm** ⊒ 28.00/41.00 **t.** – SB (weekends only) 42.00 **st.**

   🏠 **Trevena House** ⟨⟩, Alton Rd, GU10 5ER, SW : 1 ¾ m. on A 31 ☎ 716908, ≼, ⌇ heated, 🌳,
     ❄ – 📺 🚻wc 🛗wc 🅿. 🔼 ⑩ 𝘝𝘐𝘚𝘈. ❄
     closed Sunday, Christmas and New Year – **M** (dinner only) a la carte 8.60/11.30 **t.** ∬ 3.00 –
     19 rm ⊒ 29.50/48.00 **st.** – SB 49.00/58.00 **st.**

   ✗ **Brasserie,** Lion and Lamb Courtyard, West St., GU9 7LL, ☎ 715434 – 🔼 Æ ⑩ 𝘝𝘐𝘚𝘈
     closed Monday dinner, Sunday, 1 week August-September and 1 week Christmas – **M** (res-
     tricted a la carte lunch)/dinner 13.95 **t.** ∬ 3.95.

   at Seale E : 4 m. on A 31 – ✉ Farnham – ✆ 025 18 Runfold :

   🏨 **Hog's Back** (Embassy), GU10 1EX, on A 31 ☎ 2345, ≼, 🌳 – 📺 🚻wc ☎ ♿ 🅿. 🔬. 🔼 Æ
     ⑩ 𝘝𝘐𝘚𝘈. ❄
     M 10.00 **st.** and a la carte ∬ 3.00 – ⊒ 5.00 – **50 rm** 40.00/48.50 **st.** – SB 55.00 **st.**

   at Churt S : 5 ¾ m. on A 287 – ✉ Farnham – ✆ 025 125 Frensham :

   🏯 **Frensham Pond** ⟨⟩, GU10 2QB, N : 1 ½ m. by A 287 ☎ 3175, Telex 858610, ≼, « Lake-side
     setting », 🌳 – 📺 🅿. 🔬. 🔼 Æ ⑩ 𝘝𝘐𝘚𝘈. ❄
     M 11.50/12.50 **t.** and a la carte ∬ 3.50 – **19 rm** ⊒ 44.00/54.00 **t.**, **1 suite** 75.00 **t.** – SB (weekends
     only except Bank Holidays) 70.00 **st.**

   🏠 **Pride of the Valley Inn** (Best Western) ⟨⟩, GU10 2LE, E : 1 ½ m. via Hale House Lane
     ☎ 042 873 (Hindhead) 5799, 🌳 – 📺 🚻wc ☎ 🅿. 🔼 Æ ⑩ 𝘝𝘐𝘚𝘈
     M 8.50/9.50 **t.** and a la carte ∬ 2.65 – **10 rm** ⊒ 38.00/48.00 **st.**, **1 suite** 60.00 **st.** – SB
     66.00/70.00 **st.**

AUSTIN-ROVER East St. ☎ 716201   VW, AUDI West St. and Crondall Lane ☎ 715616
MERCEDES-BENZ 48/50 Shortheath Rd ☎ 716266

FARRINGTON GURNEY Avon **403 404** M 30 – pop. 587 – ⊠ Bristol – ✪ 0761 Temple Cloud.

♦London 132 – Bath 13 – ♦Bristol 12 – Wells 8.

🏨 **Country Ways** 🐾, Marsh Lane, BS18 5TT, ☞ 52449, ☞ – ▣ ⌁wc ☏ 🅿. 🔼 AE ⑩ VISA. 🎇
closed 20 December-5 January and February – **M** (closed Sunday dinner) (bar lunch) (residents only)/dinner 12.50 **st.** ⋔ 2.50 – **6 rm** ⥰ 25.35/42.35 **st.** – SB (weekends only) 52.00/57.20 **st.**

XX **Old Parsonage** with rm, Main St., BS18 5UB, ☞ 52211, ☞ – ⌁wc 🅿. 🎇
closed 28 March and 25-26 December – **M** (closed Sunday dinner and Monday to non-residents) (booking essential) a la carte 10.00/13.55 **t.** ⋔ 2.80 – **3 rm** ⥰ 17.50/35.00 **t.**

at Ston Easton S : 1 ¼ m. on A 37 – ⊠ Bath – ✪ 076 121 Chewton Mendip :

🏛 **Ston Easton Park** 🐾, BA3 4DF, ☞ 631, ≤, « Palladian country house », ☞, park – ▣ ☎ 🅿. 🔼 AE ⑩ VISA. 🎇
M 14.00 **t.** (lunch) and a la carte 19.00/25.00 **t.** ⋔ 3.25 – ⥰ 5.00 – **20 rm** 50.00/140.00 **st.** – SB (weekdays only) (November-March) 110.00/140.00 **t.**

FAR SAWREY Cumbria **402** L 20 – see Hawkshead.

FAUGH Cumbria – see Carlisle.

FAVERSHAM Kent **404** W 30 – pop. 15,914 – ECD : Thursday – ✪ 0795.
🖪 Fleur de Lis Heritage Centre, 13 Preston St. ☞ 534542.

♦London 52 – ♦Dover 26 – Maidstone 21 – Margate 25.

XX **Reads**, Painters Forstal, ME13 0EE, SW : 2 ¼ m. by A 2 ☞ 535344 – 🅿. AE ⑩ VISA
closed Sunday, first 2 weeks August and Bank Holidays – **M** 9.00 **t.** (lunch) and a la carte 12.85/15.95 **t.** ⋔ 2.50.

FAWKHAM Kent – ✪ 0474 Ash Green.

♦London 22 – Maidstone 16.

🏨 **Brands Hatch Place**, DA3 8NQ, ☞ 872239, 🔲, ☞, squash – ▣ ⌁wc ☎ 🅿. 🛆. 🔼 AE ⑩ VISA. 🎇
M 11.50/15.00 **t.** and a la carte ⋔ 4.00 – ⥰ 4.75 – **20 rm** 42.00/58.00 **st.** – SB (weekends only) (except Christmas) 99.00 **st.**

FAWLEY Bucks. **404** R 29 – pop. 369 – ECD : Wednesday – ⊠ Henley-on-Thames (Oxon.) – ✪ 049 163 Turville Heath.

♦London 45 – ♦Oxford 25 – Reading 12.

X **Walnut Tree**, Fawley Green, RG9 6JE, ☞ 360 – 🅿. 🔼 VISA
closed Christmas Day – **M** a la carte 7.60/11.05 **t.**

FELINDRE FARCHOG (VELINDRE) Dyfed **403** F 27 – see Newport (Dyfed).

FELINHELI = Port Dinorwic.

FELIXSTOWE Suffolk **404** Y 28 – pop. 24,207 – ECD : Wednesday – ✪ 0394.
⚓ Shipping connections with the Continent : to Belgium (Zeebrugge) (Townsend Thoresen).
🚢 to Harwich (Orwell & Harwich Navigation Co.) 5-8 daily (15 mn).
🖪 91 Undercliffe Rd West ☞ 282126 and 282122 – ♦London 84 – ♦Ipswich 11.

🏨 **Orwell Moat House** (Q.M.H.), Hamilton Rd, IP11 7DX, ☞ 285511, ☞ – 🛗 ▣ ☎ 🅿. 🛆. 🔼 AE ⑩ VISA
M 8.50/10.50 **t.** and a la carte ⋔ 4.00 – ⥰ 5.00 – **58 rm** 36.00/45.00 **st.** – SB (weekends only) 57.50/65.00 **st.**

AUSTIN-ROVER Crescent Rd ☞ 283221

FELSTED Essex **404** V 28 – pop. 2,509 – ✪ 0371 Great Dunmow.
♦London 44 – ♦Cambridge 30 – Colchester 18 – Chelmsford 11.

XX **Boote House**, Chelmsford Rd, CM6 3DH, ☞ 820279 – 🔼 AE ⑩ VISA
closed Sunday dinner, Monday, Tuesday , 2 weeks February and 2 weeks August – **M** (dinner only and Sunday lunch)/dinner a la carte 8.75/16.20 **t.** ⋔ 3.20.

FERNDOWN Dorset **403 404** O 31 – pop. 23,921 – ECD : Wednesday – ✪ 0202.
♦London 108 – Bournemouth 6 – Dorchester 27 – Salisbury 23.

🏨 **Dormy** (De Vere), New Rd, BH22 8ES, on A 347 ☞ 872121, Telex 418301, 🔲, ☞, squash – 🛗 ≡ rest ▣ ☎ ⅙ 🅿. 🛆. 🔼 AE ⑩ VISA
M 9.50/12.00 **t.** and a la carte – **94 rm** ⥰ 45.00/70.00 **st.** – SB (weekends only) 85.00/90.00 **st.**

🏨 **Coach House Motel**, Wimbourne Rd, Tricketts Cross, BH22 9NW, on A 31 ☞ 871222 – ▣ 🅿wc 🅿. 🔼 AE ⑩ VISA
M (bar lunch)/dinner 8.00 **st.** ⋔ 2.95 – **44 rm** ⥰ 25.00/42.00 **st.** – SB (weekends only) 49.00/53.00 **st.**

AUSTIN-ROVER 553 Ringwood Rd ☞ 872212
COLT Victoria Rd ☞ 871131
RENAULT Ringwood Rd ☞ 893589

TOYOTA Ringwood Rd ☞ 872201
VAUXHALL-OPEL Wimborne Rd East ☞ 872055

FINDON West Sussex **404** S 31 − see Worthing.

FISHBOURNE I.O.W. **403 404** Q 31 Shipping Services : see Wight (Isle of).

FISHGUARD (ABERGWAUN) Dyfed **403** F 28 − pop. 2 ,903 − ECD : Wednesday − ✪ 0348.
Envir. : Porthgain (cliffs ※★★★) SW : 10 m. − Goodwick (≤★★) NW : 1 ½ m. − Strumble Head
(≤★★ from the lighthouse) NW : 5 m. − Trevine (≤★★) SW : 8 m. − Bryn Henllan (site★) NE : 5 m.
🚢 to Ireland (Rosslare) (Sealink) 1-2 daily (3 h 30 mn).
🛈 Town Hall 🕿 873484 (summer only).
♦London 265 − ♦Cardiff 114 − Gloucester 176 − Holyhead 169 − Shrewsbury 136 − ♦Swansea 76.

🏠 **Cartref,** High St., SA65 9AW, 🕿 872430 − 🛏wc 🛁wc. 🅿 *VISA* 🍴
   M *(closed Sunday)* (bar lunch)/dinner 7.50 **t.** ⅃ 2.50 − **13 rm** ⥮ 14.50/31.00 **t.** − SB (weekends
   only)(winter only) 39.00/49.00 **st.**

🏠 **Blair Athol,** Windy Hall, SA65 9DP, 🕿 873147 − 🅿
   closed February − **M** (dinner only)(booking essential) a la carte 5.35/9.90 **t.** − **9 rm**
   ⥮ 10.00/20.00 **t.**

   at Llanychaer SE : 2 ¼ m. on B 4313 − ✉ Fishguard − ✪ 034 882 Puncheston :

✕ **Penlan Oleu** 🐾 with rm, SA65 9TL, SE : 2 m. by B 4313 off Puncheston rd 🕿 314, ≤,
   « Converted farmhouse », 🌾 − 🛏wc 🅿 *VISA*
   M *(closed Sunday lunch)* (booking essential) a la carte 9.00/11.00 **t.** ⅃ 2.50 − **3 rm**
   ⥮ 15.00/30.00 **st.**

   at Goodwick (Wdig) NW : 1 ½ m. − ✉ ✪ 0348 Fishguard :

🏨 **Fishguard Bay,** Quay Rd, SA64 0BT, 🕿 873571, ⤓ heated, park − 📶 🛏wc ⅙ 🅿 🎿 🝗 🅰🅴
   VISA
   M 6.00/7.50 **t.** and a la carte ⅃ 2.50 − **62 rm** ⥮ 24.00/40.00 **st.** − SB (weekends only)
   (November-May) 45.00/50.00 **st.**

AUSTIN-ROVER West St. 🕿 872253

FITTLEWORTH West Sussex **404** S 31 − pop. 895 − ECD : Wednesday − ✉ Pulborough −
✪ 079 882.
♦London 52 − ♦Brighton 28 − Chichester 15 − Worthing 17.

🏠 **Swan,** Lower St., RH20 1EN, 🕿 429, 🌾 − 🛁 🅿 🝗 🅰🅴 ① *VISA*
   M 6.50/7.95 **t.** ⅃ 3.00 − **7 rm** ⥮ 20.00/40.00 **st.** − SB 45.00 **st.**

FLAMBOROUGH Humberside **402** T 21 − pop. 1 ,588 − ECD : Wednesday − ✪ 0262 Bridlington.
♦London 240 − ♦Kingston-upon-Hull 34 − Scarborough 18 − York 45.

🏛 **Timoneer Country Manor** 🐾, South Landing, YO15 1AG, 🕿 850219, 🌾 − 📺 🛏wc 🛁wc
   🅿 🝗 🅰🅴 ① *VISA*
   M a la carte 9.30/13.95 **t.** ⅃ 3.50 − **10 rm** ⥮ 23.65/42.50 **t.** − SB (except Bank Holidays) 49.50 **st.**

FLAMSTEAD Herts. **404** S 28 − pop. 1 ,407 − ✉ St. Albans − ✪ 0582 Luton.
♦London 32 − Luton 5.

🏨 **Hertfordshire Moat House** (Q.M.H.), London Rd, AL3 8HH, on A 5 🕿 840840 − 📺 🛏wc
   🝗 🎿 🅰🅴 ① *VISA*
   M (bar lunch Saturday)/dinner 10.50 **st.** and a la carte ⅃ 3.50 − **97 rm** ⥮ 43.00/48.00 **st.** − SB
   (except weekdays September-June) 50.00/55.00 **st.**

FLEET Hants. **404** R 30 − pop. 27 ,406 − ECD : Wednesday − ✪ 025 14.
♦London 46 − Guildford 14 − Reading 16 − ♦Southampton 42.

🏨 **Lismoyne,** Church Rd, GU13 8NA, 🕿 28555, 🌾 − 📺 🛏wc 🛁wc 🍸 🅿 🝗 🅰🅴 ① *VISA*
   M 7.00/8.00 **st.** and a la carte ⅃ 3.30 − **40 rm** ⥮ 24.00/44.00 **st.**

AUSTIN-ROVER 66 Albert St. 🕿 3303

FLEETWOOD Lancs. **402** K 22 − pop. 27 ,899 − ECD : Wednesday − ✪ 039 17.
⛳ Fleetwood, Princes Way 🕿 3661, W : from Promenade.
🚢 to the Isle of Man : Douglas (Isle of Man Steam Packet Co.) June-September, 2-3 weekly (3 h).
🛈 Marine Hall, The Esplanade 🕿 71141/70547 (summer only).
♦London 245 − ♦Blackpool 10 − Lancaster 28 − ♦Manchester 53.

🏨 **North Euston,** The Esplanade, FY7 6BN, 🕿 6525 − 📶 📺 🛏wc 🛁wc 🍸 🅿 🎿 🝗 🅰🅴 ①
   VISA
   M 5.75/9.50 **t.** ⅃ 2.65 − **57 rm** ⥮ 22.00/38.00 **t.**

FORD West View 🕿 2292

182

♦London 45 – Bedford 13 – Luton 12 – Northampton 28.

XXX **Flitwick Manor** ⚓ with rm, Church Rd, off Dunstable Rd, MK45 1AE, ✆ 712242, Telex 825562, ≤, « 18C manor house », ☞, ✗ – ☎ ☐wc ╫wc ☎ ℗ ⚠ AE ⓪ VISA ✗
closed 25-27 December – **M** (Seafood) 13.00 **t.** and a la carte ↓ 3.50 – **7 rm** ☑ 50.00/95.00 **st.**

FOLKESTONE Kent **404** X 30 – pop. 42 ,949 – ECD : Wednesday and Saturday – ✆ 0303.
See : Site★ – Envir. : The Warren★ (cliffs) E : 2 m. by A 20 X – Acrise Place★ *AC*, NW : 6 m. by A 260 X – ⏸ Sene Valley , Folkestone and Hythe,Sene, ✆ 68513, N : 2 m. from Hythe on B 2065, W : by A 259 X.
🛳 Shipping connections to France (Boulogne) and Belgium (Oostende) (Sealink).
🇿 Harbour St. ✆ 58594 – Pedestrian Precinct, Sandgate Rd ✆ 53840 (summer only).
♦London 76 – ♦Brighton 76 – ♦Dover 8 – Maidstone 33.

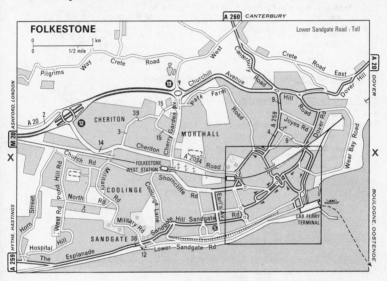

Guildhall Street . . . . Y 22
Rendezvous Street. . . . . YZ
Sandgate Road . . . . Z
Tontine Street . . . . Y

Ashford Road . . . . X 2
Ashley Avenue . . . . X 3
Black Bull Road . . . . . . X, Y 4
Bouverie Place. . . . . Z 6
Bouverie Road East . . . . Z 7
Bradstone Road . . . . Y 8
Canterbury Road. . . . . . . X 9
Castle Road . . . . Z 12
Cheriton Place. . . . . Z 13
Cheriton High Street . . . X 14
Cherry Garden Lane . . . X 15
Clifton Crescent. . . . . . . Z 16
Clifton Road. . . . . Z 17
Durlocks (The). . . . . Y 20
Grace Hill . . . . Y 21
Harbour Street. . . . . Z 24
Harbour App. Road. . . . Z 25
Langhorne Gardens . . . Z 27
Manor Road. . . . . Z 28
Marine Terrace . . . . Z 29
Morrison Road . . . . Y 31
North Street . . . . Y 32
Radnor Bridge Road. . . . Y 33
Remembrance (Road of). Z 34
Ryland Place . . . . Y 35
Sandgate High Street . . X 36
Shorncliffe Road . . . . . . Z 37
Tilekiln Lane . . . . X 39
Trinity Gardens . . . . Y 41
Victoria Grove . . . . Y 43
Wear Bay Road . . . . Y 44
West Terrace . . . . Z 45

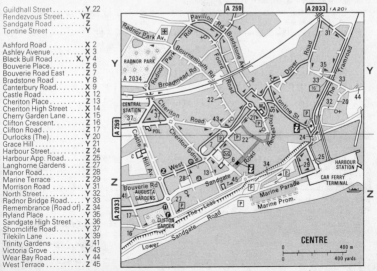

🏛 **Burlington,** Earl's Av., CT20 2HR, ☎ 55301, ≼, ♨ – 📶 📺 ⇌wc ☜ 🅿 ♨ 🔊 🇦🇪 ⓞ 𝘝𝘐𝘚𝘈.
            X s
    M 8.50/10.25 **t.** and a la carte – **57 rm** ⟷ 30.00/50.00 **t.** – SB 49.00/59.00 **st.**

🏛 **Clifton** (T.H.F.), The Leas, CT20 2EB, ☎ 41231, ≼, ♨ – 📶 📺 ⇌wc ☜. 🔊
            Z r
    59 rm.

🏛 **Banque** without rest., 4 Castle Hill Av., CT20 2QT, ☎ 53797 – 📺 ⇌wc. 🔊 🇦🇪 ⓞ 𝘝𝘐𝘚𝘈
    12 rm ⟷ 16.00/32.00 **t.**
            Z z

XX **Emilio's Portofino,** 124a Sandgate Rd, CT20 2BT, ☎ 55762, Italian rest. – 🔊 🇦🇪 ⓞ 𝘝𝘐𝘚𝘈
    closed Monday and Bank Holidays – **M** 6.50 **t.** (lunch) and a la carte 9.00/14.15 **t.** ♨ 2.40.   Z a

XX **La Tavernetta,** Leaside Court, Clifton Gdns, CT20 2EY, ☎ 54955, Italian rest. – 🔊 🇦🇪 ⓞ
    𝘝𝘐𝘚𝘈
            Z n
    closed Sunday and Bank Holidays – **M** 6.20 **t.** (lunch) and a la carte 8.45/12.40 ♨ 3.05.

X **Paul's,** 2a Bouverie Rd West, CT20 2RX, ☎ 59697 – 🔊 𝘝𝘐𝘚𝘈
            Z e
    closed Sunday, 1 week summer and 25-26 December – **M** a la carte approx. 9.25 **t.** ♨ 2.75.

AUSTIN-ROVER 141/143 Sandgate Rd ☎ 55101
CITROEN, FIAT, ROLLS ROYCE, VAUXHALL Caesars
Way, Cheriton ☎ 76431
COLT 1/3 Park Rd ☎ 75114
FORD 104 Foord Rd ☎ 41234

NISSAN Shorncliffe Industrial Estate ☎ 39656
PEUGEOT, TALBOT Cheriton Rd ☎ 76959
RENAULT Sandgate Rd ☎ 55331
VAUXHALL Sandgate Rd ☎ 53103
VOLVO Park Farm Industrial Estate ☎ 42027

FONTMELL MAGNA Dorset 403 404 N 30 – see Shaftesbury.

FORDINGBRIDGE Hants. 403 404 O 31 – pop. 3 ,026 – ECD : Thursday – ✆ 0425.
See : St. Mary's Church★ 13C.

Envir. : Breamore House★ (Elizabethan) *AC*, N : 2 m.

♦London 101 – Bournemouth 17 – Salisbury 11 – Winchester 30.

XX **Hour Glass,** Salisbury Rd, Burgate, SP6 1LX, N : 1 m. on A 338 ☎ 52348, « 14C thatched
    cottage » – 🅿 🔊 🇦🇪 ⓞ 𝘝𝘐𝘚𝘈
    closed Sunday and Monday – **M** 6.75/14.50 **st.** and a la carte ♨ 3.35.

    at Stuckton SW : 1 m. by B 3078 – ✉ ✆ 0425 Fordingbridge :

X **Three Lions Inn,** Stuckton Rd, SP6 2HF, ☎ 52489 – 🅿
    *closed February, 31 March-7 April, 2 weeks July-August, 1 week November and 24 to
    31 December* – **M** *(closed Tuesday lunch, Sunday dinner and Monday)* (booking essential) a la
    carte 7.50/17.15 **t.** ♨ 2.75.

FORDWICH Kent 404 X 30 – see Canterbury.

FOREST ROW East Sussex 404 U 30 – pop. 3 ,842 – ECD : Wednesday – ✆ 034 282.
🏌 Royal Ashdown Forest ☎ 2018.

♦London 35 – ♦Brighton 26 – Eastbourne 30 – Maidstone 32.

🏛 **Chequers Inn,** The Square, RH19 5ES, ☎ 4394 – 📺 ⇌wc ☎ 🅿 🔊 🇦🇪 ⓞ 𝘝𝘐𝘚𝘈 ✂
    M 9.85 **t.** and a la carte ♨ 3.75 – **4 rm** 17.00/25.00 **t.**

🏛 **Brambletye,** The Square, RH18 5EZ, ☎ 4144, Telex 8952645 – 📺 ⇌wc ☎ 🅿 🔊 🇦🇪 ⓞ
    𝘝𝘐𝘚𝘈 ✂
    M 3.95/13.95 **t.** and a la carte ♨ 1.85 – **12 rm** ⟷ 25.00/37.50 **t.** – SB (weekends only)(October-
    June) 33.50/40.00 **st.**

    at Wych Cross S : 2 ½ m. on A 22 – ✉ ✆ 034 282 Forest Row :

🏛 **Roebuck** (Embassy), RH18 5JL, ☎ 3811, Telex 957088, ♨ – 📺 ⇌wc ☜ 🅿 ♨ 🔊 🇦🇪 ⓞ
    𝘝𝘐𝘚𝘈 ✂
    M 9.00 **st.** and a la carte ♨ 2.25 – ⟷ 5.00 – **31 rm** 33.00/42.00 **st.** – SB (weekends only) 52.00 **st.**

AUDI, VW 92-93 Hartfield Rd ☎ 3055

FOSSEBRIDGE Glos. 403 404 O 28 – pop. 1 ,706 – ✉ ✆ 028 572.
♦London 88 – Gloucester 23 – ♦Oxford 31 – Swindon 21.

♨ **Fossebridge Inn,** GL54 3JS, ☎ 310, ♨ – ⇌wc 🅿 🔊 🇦🇪 ⓞ 𝘝𝘐𝘚𝘈 ✂
    M a la carte 6.50/8.50 **t.** ♨ 3.00 – **10 rm** ⟷ 31.50/42.00 **t.** – SB (mid October-May) 47.00/52.50 **st.**

FOWEY Cornwall 403 G 32 The West Country G. – pop. 2 ,092 – ECD : Wednesday – ✆ 072 683.
See : Site★★ – 🅸 Albert Quay ☎ 3320.

♦London 277 – Newquay 24 – ♦Plymouth 34 – Truro 22.

🏛 Fowey ⚓, The Esplanade, PL23 1HX, ☎ 2551, ≼ Fowey estuary and Polruan, ♨ – 📶 📺
    ⇌wc 🁢wc 🅿 ♨ – **20 rm**.

🏛 **Marina,** The Esplanade, PL23 1HY, ☎ 3315, ≼ Fowey river and harbour – ⇌wc. 🔊 🇦🇪 ⓞ
    𝘝𝘐𝘚𝘈 ✂
    M (dinner only April to October) a la carte 8.80/11.55 **st.** ♨ 2.50 – **13 rm** ⟷ 18.20/48.40 **st.**

XX **Food for Thought,** 4 Town Quay, PL23 1AT, ℰ 2221, ⪡ – ☒ _VISA_
closed Monday to Friday lunch, Sunday dinner, January and February – **M** (booking essential)
a la carte 11.05/17.65 **t.** ᐟ 2.95.

XX **Cordon Bleu,** 3 The Esplanade, PL23 1HY, ℰ 2359 – ☒ AE ⓞ _VISA_
closed Monday to Wednesday November-March and Sunday – **M** (dinner only) (booking
essential) a la carte 6.80/10.15 **t.** ᐟ 2.25.

X **Al Fresco,** The Esplanade, PL23 1JA, ℰ 3249, ⪡, Seafood – **P.** ☒ AE ⓞ _VISA_
closed Sunday October-May, Monday except Bank Holidays and 1 week at Christmas – **M**
(booking essential) a la carte 8.40/12.35 **t.** ᐟ 2.15.

at Golant N : 3 m. by B 3269 – ⊠ ✪ 072 683 Fowey :

🏠 **Cormorant** ⪢, PL23 1LL, ℰ 3426, ⪡ river Fowey, ☒, ⇸ – ☒ ⌷wc **P.** _VISA_
M (bar lunch)/dinner 14.00 **t.** and a la carte ᐟ 3.45 – **10 rm** ⊑ 25.50/44.00 **t.**

at Bodinnick-by-Fowey E : ¼ m. via car ferry – ⊠ Fowey – ✪ 072 687 Polruan :

🏠 **Old Ferry Inn,** PL23 1LY, ℰ 237, ⪡ Fowey estuary and town, « Part 16C inn » – ⌷wc **P.**
VISA
closed Christmas – **M** _(closed October-March)_ (bar lunch)/dinner 10.50 **t.** ᐟ 3.15 – **12 rm**
⊑ 16.50/37.00 **t.**

FOWLMERE Cambs. ⬛⓪⬛ U 27 – see Cambridge.

FOWNHOPE Heref. and Worc. ⬛⓪⬛ ⬛⓪⬛ M 27 – pop. 1,362 – ⊠ Hereford – ✪ 043 277.
♦London 132 – ♦Cardiff 46 – Hereford 6 – Gloucester 27.

🏠 **Green Man Inn,** HR1 4PE, ℰ 243 – ☒ ⌷wc ⊞wc **P.**
M (bar lunch)/dinner 12.00 **t.** and a la carte – **12 rm** ⊑ 16.00/26.50 **t.** – SB (October-April)
37.00 **st.**

🏠 **Bowens Farmhouse,** HR1 4PS, on B 4224 ℰ 430, ⇸ – ⌷wc ⊞ **P.** ⪥
closed 15 December-1 February – **10 rm** ⊑ 14.00/31.00 **t.**

FRAMFIELD East Sussex ⬛⓪⬛ U 31 – see Uckfield.

FRAMLINGHAM Suffolk ⬛⓪⬛ X 27 – pop. 1,830 – ECD : Wednesday – ⊠ Woodbridge – ✪ 0728.
See : Castle ramparts★ (Norman ruins) _AC._
♦London 92 – ♦Ipswich 19 – ♦Norwich 42.

🏠 **Crown** (T.H.F.), Market Hill, IP13 9AN, ℰ 723521, « 16C inn » – ☒ ⌷wc ☎ **P.** ☒ AE ⓞ
VISA
M (buffet lunch)/dinner 12.10 **st.** and a la carte ᐟ 2.70 – **17 rm** 34.50/45.00 **st.**

X **Market Place,** 18 Market Hill, IP13 9BB, ℰ 724275. ☒ _VISA_
closed Sunday, Monday and January – **M** (restricted lunch) a la carte 8.25/11.20 **t.** ᐟ 2.40.

FORD   Market Hill ℰ 723215

FRESHFORD Avon – see Bath.

FRESHWATER BAY I.O.W. ⬛⓪⬛ ⬛⓪⬛ P 31 – see Wight (Isle of).

FRESSINGFIELD Suffolk ⬛⓪⬛ X 26 – pop. 831 – ⊠ Diss – ✪ 037 986.
♦London 103 – ♦Ipswich 30 – ♦Norwich 23.

X **Fox and Goose,** IP21 5PB, ℰ 247 – **P.** ☒ AE ⓞ _VISA_
closed Tuesday – **M** (booking essential) 14.00 **t.** and a la carte ᐟ 2.70.

FRIETH Bucks. – see Henley-on-Thames (Oxon.).

FRINTON-ON-SEA Essex ⬛⓪⬛ X 28 – pop. 12,507 (inc. Walton) – ECD : Wednesday – ✪ 025 56.
♦London 72 – Chelmsford 39 – Colchester 17.

🏠 **Maplin,** Esplanade, CO13 9EL, ℰ 3832, ⪡, ⩒ heated – ☒ ⌷wc ☎ **P.** ☒ AE ⓞ _VISA_
closed January – **M** 8.75/11.00 **st.** and a la carte ᐟ 3.00 – **11 rm** ⊑ 21.00/45.00 **st.**

🏠 **Uplands,** 41 Hadleigh Rd, CO13 9HQ, ℰ 4889, ⇸ – **P.**
closed January – **8 rm** ⊑ 11.50/23.00 **s.**

AUSTIN-ROVER Connaught Av. ℰ 4311
FIAT, VOLVO 132 Connaught Av. ℰ 4341
FORD Connaught Av. ℰ 77137

PEUGEOT, TALBOT Thorpe Rd ℰ 4383
TOYOTA Frinton Rd, Kirby Cross ℰ 4141

FRODSHAM Cheshire ⬛⓪⬛ ⬛⓪⬛ ⬛⓪⬛ L 24 – pop. 9,143 – ⊠ Warrington – ✪ 0928.
♦London 203 – Chester 11 – ♦Liverpool 21 – ♦Manchester 29 – ♦Stoke on Trent 42.

🏠 **Old Hall,** Main St., WA6 7AB, ℰ 32052 – ☒ ⌷wc ☎. ☒ AE ⓞ _VISA_
M 5.95 **t.** (lunch) and a la carte 8.50/12.00 **t.** ᐟ 3.50 – **17 rm** ⊑ 30.00/40.00 **st.**, **1 suite** 40.00/50.00
st.

FROME Somerset **403 404** N 30 The West Country G. – pop. 19 ,678 – ECD : Thursday – ☎ 0373.

Envir. : Farleigh Hungerford Castle★*AC*, (St. Leonards Chapel★), N : 11 m. by A 361 and A 36 – Longleat House★★★*AC*, SE : 7 m.

🛈 Cattle Market Car Park ✆ 67271 (summer only).

♦London 115 – ♦Bristol 28 – ♦Southampton 51 – Taunton 43.

🏠 **Mendip Lodge,** Bath Rd, BA11 2HP, N : ½ m. on A 361 ✆ 63223, ≼, 🐎 – 📺 🛏wc ☎ 🅿.
🛄 🔄 Ⓐ Ⓔ ⑩ 𝘝𝘐𝘚𝘈
M (buffet lunch)/dinner 10.00 **st.** and a la carte ⬧ 4.50 – ⥮ 3.50 – **40 rm** 31.50/48.00 **st.** – SB (weekends only) (except Bank Holidays) 57.00/60.00 **st.**

FULWOOD Lancs. **402** L M 22 – see Preston.

GAINSBOROUGH Lincs. **402 404** R 23 – pop. 20 ,326 – ECD : Wednesday – ☎ 0427.

See : Old Hall★★ (15C) *AC*.

🛈 Trinity Centre, Trinity St. ✆ 617242.

♦London 150 – Lincoln 19 – ♦Nottingham 42 – ♦Sheffield 34.

Hotels and Restaurant see : Bawtry NW : 12 m., *Scunthorpe* NE : 17 m.

AUSTIN-ROVER North St. ✆ 2251   TALBOT North St. ✆ 2505
FORD Trinity St. ✆ 3146   VAUXHALL-OPEL 35 Trinity St. ✆ 611570

GANAREW Heref. and Worc. – see Monmouth (Gwent).

GARFORTH West Yorks. **402** P 22 – see Leeds.

🐎   *Pas de publicité payée dans ce guide.*

GATESHEAD Tyne and Wear **401 402** P 19 – pop. 91 ,429 – ECD : Wednesday – ☎ 091 Tyneside.

🏌 Ravensworth, Mossheaps, Wrekenton ✆ 487 6014 – 🏌 Whickham, Hollinside Park ✆ 4887309, SW : 5 m.

🛈 Central Library, Prince Consort Rd ✆ 4773478.

♦London 282 – Durham 16 – ♦Middlesbrough 38 – ♦Newcastle-upon-Tyne 1 – Sunderland 11.

Plan : see Newcastle-upon-Tyne

🏠 **Springfield** (Embassy), Durham Rd, NE9 5BT, S : ½ m. on A 6127 ✆ 477 4121 – 📺 🛏wc ☎
🅿 🛄 🔄 Ⓐ Ⓔ ⑩ 𝘝𝘐𝘚𝘈 ✀   BX **s**
M 8.00 **st.** and a la carte ⬧ 3.00 – ⥮ 5.00 – **40 rm** 34.00/46.00 **st.** – SB (weekends only) 49.00 **st.**

🏠 **Five Bridges** (Swallow), High West Street, NE8 1PE, ✆ 477 1105, Telex 53534 – 🛗 📺
🛏wc ☎ 🅿 🛄 🔄 Ⓐ Ⓔ ⑩ 𝘝𝘐𝘚𝘈   CZ **r**
M 9.25 **st.** (dinner) and a la carte 10.75/16.95 **st.** ⬧ 3.40 – **104 rm** ⥮ 35.50/45.00 **st.** – SB (weekends only) 42.00 **st.**

🏠 **Eslington Villa,** 8 Station Rd, Low Fell, NE9 6DR, ✆ 487 6017 – 📺 🛏wc 🌀wc ☎ 🅿. ✀
M *(closed Sunday)* 5.75 **t.** (lunch) and a la carte 8.35/17.50 **t.** ⬧ 3.00 – **8 rm** ⥮ 24.50/31.50 **t.**
                                                                            by A 6127   BX

AUDI, VW Bensham Rd ✆ 784545   FORD Eslington Park ✆ 607464
AUSTIN-ROVER Low Fell ✆ 4872118   TOYOTA St. James Sq. ✆ 784333

GATWICK AIRPORT West Sussex **404** T 30 – ✉ West Sussex – ☎ 0293 Gatwick.

✈ ✆ 0293 (Crawley) 28822 and ✆ 01 (London) 668 4211.

♦ London 29 – ♦Brighton 28.

Plan opposite

🏩 **Gatwick Hilton International,** Gatwick Airport, RH6 0LL, ✆ 518080, Telex 877021, 🔲 –
🛗 🍽 📺 ☎ ⛐ 🅿 🛄 🔄 Ⓐ Ⓔ ⑩ 𝘝𝘐𝘚𝘈   Y **u**
M 25.00/30.00 **t.** and a la carte ⬧ 4.50 – ⥮ 6.00 – **333 rm** 65.00/80.00 **t.**, **13 suites** 135.00/225.00 **t.**

🏨 **Gatwick Penta,** Povey Cross Rd ✉Horley (Surrey), RH6 0BE, ✆ 785533, Telex 87440, 🐎 –
🛗 🍽 📺 ☎ ⛐ 🅿 🛄 🔄 Ⓐ Ⓔ ⑩ 𝘝𝘐𝘚𝘈   Y **a**
M 8.50/10.95 **st.** and a la carte ⬧ 4.50 – ⥮ 5.85 – **260 rm** 56.00/67.00 **st.**, **4 suites** 75.00/105.00 **st.**

🏨 **Post House** (T.H.F.), Povey Cross Rd ✉Horley (Surrey), RH6 0BA, ✆ 771621, Telex 877351, 🌊 heated – 🛗 📺 ⛐ 🅿 🛄 🔄 Ⓐ Ⓔ ⑩ 𝘝𝘐𝘚𝘈   Y **c**
M 10.50/10.75 **st.** and a la carte ⬧ 2.70 – ⥮ 6.00 – **148 rm** 46.00/57.00 **st.**

🏠 Gatwick Moat House (Q.M.H.), Longbridge Roundabout ✉Horley (Surrey), RH6 0AB, ✆ 785599, Telex 877138 – 🛗 🍽 📺 🛏wc ☎ ⛐ 🅿 🛄 🔄 Ⓐ Ⓔ ⑩ 𝘝𝘐𝘚𝘈   Y **e**
⥮ 5.25 – **121 rm** 42.50/55.00 **st.**, **4 suites**.

🏠 Gatwick Concorde (Q.M.H.), Church Rd, Lowfield Heath, RH11 0PQ, ✆ 33441, Telex 87287 –
🛗 📺 🛏wc ☎ 🅿 🛄   Y **x**
92 rm, **3 suites**.

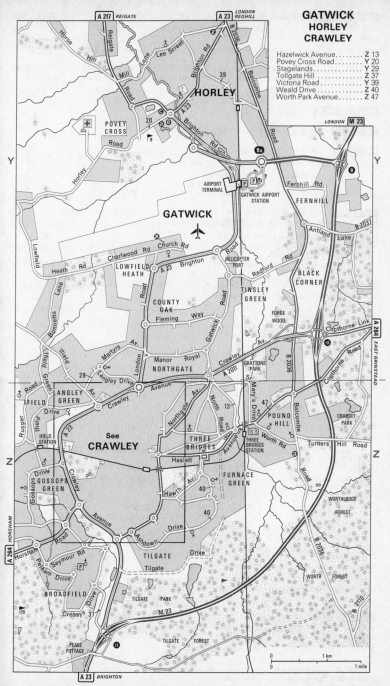

Hazelwick Avenue........ Z 13
Povey Cross Road........ Y 20
Stagelands.............. Y 29
Tollgate Hill........... Z 37
Victoria Road........... Y 39
Weald Drive............. Z 40
Worth Park Avenue....... Z 47

See CRAWLEY

GERRARDS CROSS Bucks. 404 S 29 – pop. 19,447 (inc. Chalfont St. Peter) – ECD : Wednesday – ☻ 0753.

♦London 22 – Aylesbury 22 – ♦Oxford 36.

🏛 **Bull** (De Vere), Oxford Rd, SL9 7PA, on A 40 ℰ 885995, Group Telex 847747, ☞ – 📺 ⌂wc ☻ 🅿. 🏖. 🔼 🅰🅴 ⓪ 🆅🆂🆘. 🕸
M 14.00/15.00 st. and a la carte ⓵ 4.00 – **40 rm** ☷ 60.00/75.00 st. – SB (weekends only) 78.00 st.

🏠 Ethorpe, Packhorse Rd, FL9 8HX, ℰ 882039, ☞ – 📺 ⌂wc ☎ 🅿 – **28 rm**.

BMW 31-33 Station Rd ℰ 888321   TALBOT Oxford Rd ℰ 882545

GIGGLESWICK North Yorks. – see Settle.

GILLAN Cornwall 403 E 33 The West Country G. – see Helford.

GILLINGHAM Dorset 403 404 N 30 – pop. 5.379 – ☻ 074 76.

♦London 116 – Bournemouth 34 – ♦Bristol 46 – ♦Southampton 52.

🏛 **Stock Hill House** ♨, Wyke, SP8 5NR, W : 1 ½ m. on B 3081 ℰ 3626, « Victorian country house », 🔼, ☞, park – 📺 ⌂wc ⌂wc ☎ 🅿. 🕸
closed 15 January-15 February – **M** 8.00/14.00 t. – **7 rm** ☷ 35.00/60.00 t.

GISBURN Lancs. 402 N 22 – pop. 435 – ECD : Wednesday – ✉ Clitheroe – ☻ 020 05.

🏌 Ghyll, Ghyll Brow, Barnoldswick ℰ 0282 (Earby) 842466, SE : 5 ½ m.

♦London 243 – ♦Manchester 37 – Preston 25.

🏛 **Stirk House**, BB7 4LJ, SW : 1 m. on A 59 ℰ 581, Telex 635238, 🔼, ☞, squash – 📺 ⌂wc ☎ 🅿. 🏖. 🔼 🅰🅴 ⓪ 🆅🆂🆘. 🕸
M 8.75 st. (dinner) and a la carte 8.75/13.75 t. ⓵ 3.25 – **50 rm** ☷ 29.00/44.00 st. – SB 50.00 st.

GITTISHAM Devon 403 K 31 – pop. 233 – ECD : Thursday – ✉ ☻ 0404 Honiton.

♦London 164 – Exeter 14 – Sidmouth 9 – Taunton 21.

🏛 **Combe House** ♨, EX14 0AD, ℰ 2756, ≼, « Country house atmosphere », ☞, park – 📺 ⌂wc 🅿. 🔼 🅰🅴 ⓪ 🆅🆂🆘
M (bar lunch Monday to Saturday)/dinner approx. 15.50 st. ⓵ 2.95 – **12 rm** ☷ 25.00/68.00 st. – SB (2 January-31 March and November-22 December) 37.00/51.00 st.

🔫 *Michelin non applica targhe pubblicitarie agli alberghi e ristoranti segnalati in Guida.*

GLASTONBURY Somerset 403 L 30 The West Country G. – pop. 6,751 – ECD : Wednesday – ☻ 0458.

See : Site★★★ – Abbey★★★AC – St. John the Baptist Church★★ – Somerset Rural Life Museum★★AC – Glastonbury Tor★ (≼★★★).

🛈 1 Marchant's Buildings, Northload St. ℰ 32954 (summer only).

♦London 136 – ♦Bristol 26 – Taunton 22.

🏠 **George and Pilgrims**, 1 High St., BA6 9DP, ℰ 31146, « Part 15C inn » – 📺 ⌂wc 🛁wc ☎. 🔼 🅰🅴 ⓪ 🆅🆂🆘. 🕸
M 11.50 t. (dinner) and a la carte ⓵ 2.95 – **14 rm** ☷ 30.00/54.00 t. – SB 60.00/70.00 st.

🏯 **Hawthorns**, Northload St., BA6 9JJ, ℰ 31255 – 🛁wc. 🔼 🅰🅴 ⓪ 🆅🆂🆘. 🕸
closed 1 week January – **M** (buffet lunch)/dinner a la carte 7.85/10.90 t. ⓵ 3.00 – **12 rm** ☷ 13.00/17.00 t. – SB 30.00/42.00 st.

XX **No 3**, 3 Magdalene St., BA6 9EW, ℰ 32129, ☞ – 🅿. 🅰🅴 ⓪ 🆅🆂🆘
closed Sunday dinner, Monday and first 2 weeks February – **M** (dinner only and Sunday lunch) (booking essential) 18.00 t.

AUSTIN-ROVER Street Rd ℰ 32137   RENAULT Beckery Rd ℰ 32741

GLEMSFORD Suffolk 404 W 27 – pop. 2,406 – ✉ ☻ 0787.

♦London 145 – ♦Cambridge 32 – Colchester 21 – ♦Ipswich 28.

XX **Weeks**, 31 Egremont St., CO10 7SA, ℰ 281573 – 🅿
closed Sunday, Monday, 24 December-1 January and Bank Holidays – **M** (dinner only) (booking essential) 14.50 t. ⓵ 2.20.

GLOUCESTER Glos. 403 404 N 28 – pop. 106,526 – ECD : Thursday – ☻ 0452.

See : Cathedral★★ 12C-14C (Great Cloister★★★ 14C) Y – Bishop Hooper's Lodging (Folk Museum)★ 15C Y M.

🏌, 🏌 Gloucester Hotel and Country Club, Matson Lane ℰ 25653, S : 2 m. Z.

🛈 St Michael's Tower, The Cross ℰ 421188.

♦London 106 – ♦Birmingham 52 – ♦Bristol 38 – ♦Cardiff 66 – ♦Coventry 57 – Northampton 83 – ♦Oxford 48 – ♦Southampton 98 – ♦Swansea 92 – Swindon 35.

GLOUCESTER

Eastgate Shopping
  Centre . . . . Y
Eastgate Street . . . . Y 10
Northgate Street . . . . Y 16
Southgate Street . . . . Y

Barnwood By-Pass . . . . Z 3
Black Dog Way . . . . Y 5
Commercial Road . . . . Z 6
Cotteswold Road . . . . Z 9
Derby Road . . . . Y 12
Great Western Road . . . . . Y 13
Heathville Road . . . . Y 14
King Edward's Avenue . . . Z 14
Lower Westgate Street . . . Z 15
Parkend Road . . . . Z 17
Parliament Street . . . . Y 18
Pitt Street . . . . Y 19
Quay Street . . . . Y 20
Royal Oak Road . . . . Y 21
St. Aldate Street . . . . Y 22
St. Johns Lane . . . . Y 23
Southern Avenue . . . . Y 24
Spa Road . . . . Y 26
Stroud Road . . . . Z 28
Tredworth Road . . . . Z 30
Worcester Street . . . . Y 31

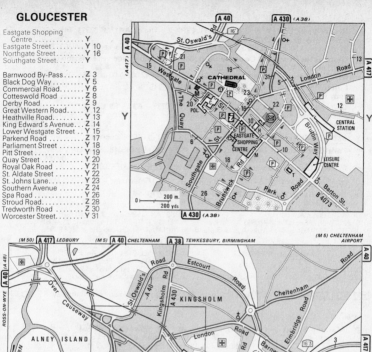

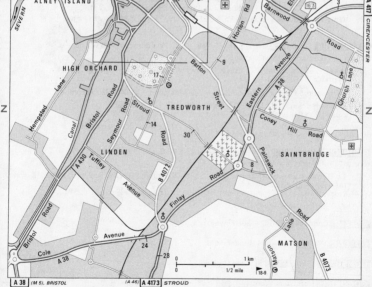

Benutzen Sie auf Ihren Reisen in Europa
die **Michelin-Länderkarten** 1 : 1 000 000.

🏨 **Crest** (Crest), Crest Way, Barnwood, GL4 7RX, E : 3 m. on A 417 𝒫 63311, Telex 437273 – 📺
🛏wc ⊛ 🕭 🅿. 🚲. 🔼 🖭 ⓞ 𝒱𝒾𝒮𝒜. 🛰   by A 417   Z
M approx. 11.50 **st.** – 🗜 5.75 – **100 rm** 47.50/57.50 **st.** – SB (weekends only) 63.00 **st.**

🏨 **Gloucester Hotel and Country Club** (Embassy), Robinswood Hill, Matson Lane, GL4 9EA,
SE : 3 m. by B 4073 𝒫 25653, 🖼 – 📺 🛏wc 🕿 🕭 🅿. 🚲. 🔼 🖭 ⓞ 𝒱𝒾𝒮𝒜   Z c
M 7.50/9.00 **st.** and a la carte 🍷 2.75 – 🗜 5.00 – **74 rm** 42.00/54.00 **st.** – SB 62.00 **st.**

↥ **Lulworth**, 12 Midland Rd, GL1 4UF, 𝒫 21881 – 📺 🅿   Z e
8 rm 🗜 10.00/20.00.

✕ **College Green,** 7-11 College St., GL1 2NE, 𝒫 20739 – 🔼 🖭 ⓞ 𝒱𝒾𝒮𝒜   Y a
closed dinner Monday and Tuesday, Sunday and Bank Holidays – **M** 7.30 (lunch) and a la
carte 9.15/13.00 **st.** 🍷 2.50.

at Upton St. Leonards SE : 3 ½ m. on B 4073 – 🖂 ✪ 0452 Gloucester :

🏨 **Tara** (Best Western), Upton Hill, GL4 8DE, 𝒫 67412, Telex 449848, ≼ Severn Valley, 🔟 heated,
🎋 – 📺 🛏wc 🎐wc ⊛ 🅿. 🚲. 🔼 🖭 ⓞ 𝒱𝒾𝒮𝒜. 🛰   by B 4073   Z
M 9.95 **t.** (dinner) and a la carte 🍷 2.85 – 🗜 5.00 – **22 rm** 30.00/72.00 **t.**

at Minsterworth W : 5 m. by A 40 on A 48 – Z – 🖂 Gloucester – ✪ 045 275 Minsterworth :

↥ **Severn Bank,** Main Rd, GL2 8JH, 𝒫 357, 🎋 – 📺 🅿. 🛰
closed 24 and 25 December – **6 rm** 🗜 10.00/25.00 **s.**

AUDI, VW Eastern Av. 𝒫 25177
AUSTIN-ROVER Mercia Rd 𝒫 416565
BEDFORD, PANTHER LIMA, VAUXHALL Shepherd
Rd, Cole Av. 𝒫 26711
BMW Kingsholm Rd 𝒫 23456
CITROEN 143 Westgate St. 𝒫 23252
FORD Bristol Rd 𝒫 21731
LADA Painswick Rd 𝒫 29866
LANCIA, DAIHATSU, FIAT Bristol Rd 𝒫 29755

NISSAN Eastern Av. 𝒫 423691
PEUGEOT, TALBOT London Rd 𝒫 24081
RENAULT St. Oswalds Rd 𝒫 35051
SAAB Montpelier 𝒫 22404
TOYOTA London Rd 𝒫 21555
VAUXHALL-OPEL Cole Av. 𝒫 26711
VAUXHALL-OPEL Priory Rd 𝒫 24912
VOLVO 100 Eastgate St. 𝒫 25291
VW, AUDI Eastern Av. 𝒫 25177

GOATHLAND North Yorks. 🄴🄾🄶 R 20 – pop. 442 – ECD : Wednesday and Saturday – 🖂 ✪ 0947
Whitby.
◆London 248 – ◆Middlesbrough 36 – York 38.

🏨 **Mallyan Spout** ⌔, YO22 5AN, 𝒫 86206, 🎋 – 📺 🛏wc 🅿. 🖭 ⓞ 𝒱𝒾𝒮𝒜
closed December and January – **M** (bar lunch)/dinner 9.00 **t.** and a la carte 🍷 2.80 – **22 rm**
🗜 15.00/38.00 **t.** – SB (except Easter and Bank Holidays) 49.50/57.20 **st.**

↥ **Whitfield House** ⌔, Darnholm, YO22 5LA, NW : ¾ m. 𝒫 86215, 🎋 – 🎐wc
11 rm 🗜 11.00/25.00 **se.**

GODALMING Surrey 🄴🄾🄸 S 30 – pop. 18 ,758 – ECD : Wednesday – ✪ 048 68.
◆London 38 – Guildford 5 – ◆Southampton 51.

↥ **Meads,** 65 Meadrow, GU7 3HS, N : ½ m. on A 3100 𝒫 21800 – 🎐wc 🅿. 🖭 𝒱𝒾𝒮𝒜
14 rm 🗜 13.00/22.00 **t.**

at Hascombe SE : 3 ½ m. on B 2130 – 🖂 Godalming – ✪ 048 632 Hascombe :

✕ **White Horse,** GU8 4JA, 𝒫 258, Bistro, 🎋 – 🅿. 🔼 🖭 𝒱𝒾𝒮𝒜
closed Sunday dinner – **M** 8.50/17.00 **t.** and a la carte 🍷 3.50.

NISSAN The Wharf 𝒫 5201
RENAULT Farncombe 𝒫 7743

VAUXHALL Ockford Rd 𝒫 5666

GODSTONE Surrey 🄴🄾🄸 T 30 – pop. 2 ,567 – ✪ 0342 South Godstone.
◆London 22 – ◆Brighton 36 – Maidstone 28.

✕✕ **La Bonne Auberge,** Tilburstow Hill, South Godstone, RH9 8JY, S : 2 ¼ m. 𝒫 892318, French
rest., 🎋 – 🅿. 🔼 🖭 𝒱𝒾𝒮𝒜
closed Sunday dinner and Monday – **M** 16.00/19.00 **st.** and a la carte 🍷 2.95.

VAUXHALL Eastbourne Rd 𝒫 842000

GOLANT Cornwall 🄴🄾🄳 G 32 – see Fowey.

GOLCAR West Yorks. – see Huddersfield.

GOMSHALL Surrey 🄴🄾🄸 S 30 – see Dorking.

GOODRICH Heref. and Worc. 🄴🄾🄳 🄴🄾🄸 M 28 – see Ross-on-Wye.

GOODWICK (WDIG) Dyfed 🄴🄾🄳 F 27 – see Fishguard.

GOODWOOD West Sussex 🄴🄾🄸 R 31 – see Chichester.

GORLESTON-ON-SEA Norfolk 🄴🄾🄸 Z 26 – see Great Yarmouth.

[GOSFORTH] Cumbria [402] J 20 – pop. 1,701 – ✉ Seascale – ☏ 094 05.
Envir. : E : Wast Water★, Wasdale Head (site★).
⛳18 Seascale, The Banks ☎ 0940 (Seascale) 28202 or 28800, SW : 3 m. by B 5344.
♦London 314 – Kendal 62 – Workington 20.

🏡 **Gosforth Hall,** CA20 1AZ, ☎ 322, 🏊, 🌳 – [TV] 🛁wc [P]. 🚫🐕
M (bar lunch)/dinner 8.95 **t.** and a la carte 🍷 2.00 – **12 rm** ☕ 16.50/27.00 **t.**, **1 suite** 50.00 **t.** – SB (weekends only) 40.00 **st.**

at Wasdale Head NE : 9 m. – ✉ Gosforth – ☏ 094 06 Wasdale :

🏠 **Wasdale Head Inn** 🔇, CA20 1EX, ☎ 229, < Wasdale Head – 🛁wc 🚿wc 📞 [P]. [Access] [VISA]
closed 15 November-28 December – **M** (bar lunch)/dinner 10.45 **t.** 🍷 2.75 – **10 rm** ☕ 22.00/44.00 **t.**

[GOSFORTH] Tyne and Wear [401] [402] P 18 – see Newcastle-upon-Tyne.

[GOUDHURST] Kent [404] V 30 – pop. 2,673 – ECD : Wednesday – ✉ Cranbrook – ☏ 0580.
♦London 45 – Hastings 22 – Maidstone 13.

🏘 Star and Eagle, High St., TN17 1AB, ☎ 211512, « 14C inn » – [TV] 🛁wc 📞 [P]
11 rm.

🏡 **Green Cross,** Station Road, TN17 1HA, W : 1 m. on A 262 ☎ 211200, 🌳 – [P]. [Access] [AE] [DC]
M a la carte 5.00/9.75 **t.** 🍷 3.00 – **6 rm** ☕ 16.00/26.00 **t.** – SB (except Christmas week) 37.00/40.00 **st.**

[GOVETON] Devon [403] I 33 – see Kingsbridge.

[GRANGE-IN-BORROWDALE] Cumbria [402] K 20 – see Keswick.

[GRANGE-OVER-SANDS] Cumbria [402] L 21 – pop. 3,864 – ECD : Thursday – ☏ 044 84.
Envir. : Cartmel (Priory Church★ 12C chancel★★) NW : 3 m.
⛳18 Meathop Rd ☎ 3180, ½ m. Grange Station – ⛳9 Grange Fell, Cartmell Rd ☎ 2536.
[i] Victoria Hall, Main St. ☎ 4026 (summer only).
♦London 268 – Kendal 13 – Lancaster 24.

🏘 **Graythwaite Manor** 🔇, Fernhill Rd, LA11 7JE, ☎ 2001, < gardens and sea, « Extensive flowered gardens », park, 🎾 – [TV] 🛁wc 📞 🚗 [P]. [Access] [VISA]. 🚫🐕
M *(closed 25 and 26 December to non-residents)* 6.50/12.50 **t.** 🍷 2.50 – **24 rm** ☕ (dinner included) 29.00/66.00 **st.** – SB (November-March except Christmas-New Year) 42.00/52.00 **st.**

🏘 Cumbria Grand, Lindale Rd, LA11 6EN, ☎ 2331, <, 🌳, park, 🎾 – ⇅ [TV] 🛁wc 📞 ♿ [P]. 👥 🚫🐕 – **120 rm.**

🏠 **Netherwood** 🔇, Lindale Rd, LA11 6ET, ☎ 2552, <, 🌳 – 🛁wc 🚗 [P]. 👥
M 4.80/7.30 **st.** 🍷 2.50 – **23 rm** ☕ 16.00/37.00 **st.** – SB (November-March) 43.00/47.50 **st.**

⌂ **Somerset House,** Kents Bank Rd, LA11 7EY, ☎ 2631 – 🚫🐕
March-October – **8 rm** ☕ 12.95/21.90.

at Witherslack NE : 5 m. by B 5277 off A 590 – ✉ ☏ 044 852 Witherslack :

🍴🍴 **Old Vicarage** 🔇 with rm, Church Rd, LA11 6RS, ☎ 381, 🌳 – [TV] 🛁wc 🚿wc 📞 [P]. [Access] [AE] [DC] [VISA]. 🚫🐕
closed 1 week at Christmas – **M** (dinner only)(booking essential) 14.50 **t.** 🍷 3.00 – **7 rm** ☕ 35.00/59.00 **t.** – SB (November-March) 55.00/65.00 **st.**

at Kents Bank SW : 1 ¾ m. by B 5277 – ✉ ☏ 044 84 Grange-over-Sands :

⌂ **Kents Bank,** 96 Kentsford Rd, LA11 7BB, ☎ 2054, < – 🛁wc [P]. [Access] [VISA]
8 rm ☕ 15.00/30.00 **t.**

at Cartmel NW : 3 m. – ✉ Grange-over-Sands – ☏ 044 854 Cartmel :

🏠 **Aynsome Manor** 🔇, LA11 6HH, NE : ½ m. ☎ 276, « Country house atmosphere », 🌳 – 🛁wc [P]. [Access] [AE] [VISA]
closed 2 to 23 January – **M** *(closed Sunday dinner)* (dinner only and Sunday lunch)/dinner 11.65 **t.** 🍷 2.80 – **13 rm** ☕ (dinner included) 29.50/63.15 **t.** – SB (November-mid May) 44.00/46.00 **st.**

🏡 **Priory,** The Square, LA11 6QB, ☎ 267 – 🛁wc [P]. [Access]
accomodation available June-December only – **M** *(closed Monday lunch)* (restricted lunch)/dinner 10.90 **t.** 🍷 3.60 – **11 rm** ☕ 15.50/34.80 **t.** – SB (weekdays only) 49.50/52.80 **st.**

⌂ **Ivy House,** Aynsome Rd, LA11 6HF, ☎ 543, 🌳 – [TV] 🛁wc 🚿wc [P]. 🚫🐕
April-November – **6 rm** ☕ 21.00/33.00 **t.**

🍴🍴 **Uplands** 🔇 with rm, Haggs Lane, LA11 6HD, SE : 1 m. ☎ 248, <, 🌳 – [TV] 🚿wc 📞 [P]. [Access] [AE]
closed January – **M** 8.00/14.50 **t.** 🍷 4.00 – **4 rm** ☕ 45.00/84.00 **t.**

BMW Lindale Corner ☎ 3751
FORD, SUBARU Lindale Corner ☎ 2282
VW, AUDI Lindale ☎ 4242

GRANTHAM Lincs. **402** **404** S 25 – pop. 30,700 – ECD : Wednesday – ✆ 0476.

See : St. Wulfram's Church★ 13C.

Envir. : Belton House★ (Renaissance) *AC* NE : 2 m. – Belvoir Castle 19C (interior★) W : 8 m. – ⟦18⟧
Stoke Rochford, Great North Rd ✆ 045 683 (Great Ponton) 275, S : 6 m. on A 1.

🛈 The Guildhall Yard, St. Peters Hill ✆ 66444 (summer only).

♦London 113 – ♦Leicester 31 – Lincoln 29 – ♦Nottingham 24.

🏨 **George** (Best Western), High St., NG31 6NN, ✆ 63286, Telex 378121 – 🗺 🛏wc 🝔wc 🕾 🅿.
🛦 🖭 🖭 *VISA*
closed 3 days at Christmas – **M** 7.50/10.95 **t.** and a la carte 🛦 3.25 – **43 rm** 🖙 35.00/55.00 **t.** –
SB (weekends only) 54.00/56.00 **st.**

🏨 **Angel and Royal** (T.H.F.), 4 High St., NG31 6PN, ✆ 65816, « 13C stone walled restaurant
and bar » – 🗺 🛏wc 🝔 🅿. 🛦 🖭 🖭 *VISA*
M 5.25/8.75 **st.** and a la carte 🛦 2.70 – 🖙 5.50 – **32 rm** 34.50/44.00 **st.**

🏨 **King's**, 130 North Par., NG31 8AU, ✆ 65881 – 🗺 🛏wc 🝔wc 🝔 🅿. 🖭 🖭 *VISA*
M 6.25/7.25 **st.** and a la carte 🛦 2.45 – **16 rm** 🖙 19.00/36.00 **st.** – SB (weekends only)
40.00/45.00 **st.**

🍴 **Premier**, 2-6 North Par., NG31 8AN, ✆ 77855 – 🖭 🖭 🖭 *VISA*
closed Tuesday lunch, Sunday dinner, Monday, 2 weeks August and 2 weeks January – **M**
6.95/14.50 **t.** and a la carte 10.80/21.50 **t.**

at Barkston N : 3 ¾ m. on A 607 – ✉ Grantham – ✆ 0400 Loveden :

🍴 **Barkston House** with rm, NG32 2NH, ✆ 50555, 🖛 – 🗺 🛏wc 🝔 🅿. 🖭 🖭 *VISA*
closed Christmas – **M** *(closed Saturday lunch, dinner Sunday and Monday and Bank Holidays)*
a la carte 8.15/12.50 **t.** – **2 rm** 🖙 25.00/35.00 **t.** – SB (weekends only) 50.00 **st.**

AUSTIN-ROVER 12 North St. ✆ 61066	RENAULT London Rd ✆ 61338
FORD 30/40 London Rd ✆ 65195	TOYOTA Great Ponton ✆ 047 683 261
NISSAN Barrowby High Rd ✆ 64443	VOLVO Barrowby Rd ✆ 4114
PEUGEOT-TALBOT 66 London Rd ✆ 62595	VW, AUDI, SUBARU Spittlegate ✆ 66416

GRAPPENHALL Cheshire – see Warrington.

GRASMERE Cumbria **402** K 20 – ECD : Thursday – ✆ 096 65.

🛈 Red Bank Rd.

♦London 282 – ♦Carlisle 43 – Kendal 18.

Plans : see Ambleside

🏨 **Wordsworth**, LA22 9SW, ✆ 592, Telex 65329, 🗺, 🖛 – 🛗 ▤ rest 🗺 🛦 🅿. 🛦 🖭 🖭
VISA. 🛠   BZ **s**
M 14.50 **t.** (dinner) and a la carte 13.40/15.75 **t.** 🛦 2.95 – **35 rm** 🖙 29.00/78.00 **t.** – SB
(November-March) 75.00/83.00 **t.**

🏨 **Michaels Nook Country House** 🛦, LA22 9RP, ✆ 496, Group Telex 65329, ≼ mountains
and countryside, « Antiques and gardens » – 🗺 🛏wc 🝔 🅿. 🛠   AY **n**
M (booking essential) 18.00/24.00 **t.** 🛦 2.75 – **11 rm** 🖙 (dinner included) 65.00/150.00 **t.**, **2 suites**
160.00/180.00 **t.** – SB (weekdays only)(November-March except Christmas) 88.00 **st.**

🏨 **Swan** (T.H.F.), LA22 9RF, on A 591 ✆ 551, ≼, 🖛 – 🗺 🛏wc 🝔 🅿. 🖭 🖭 🖭 *VISA*   AY **r**
M 7.50/11.00 **st.** and a la carte 🛦 2.70 – 🖙 5.50 – **41 rm** 38.50/51.00 **st.**

🏨 **Gold Rill Country House** 🛦, Langdale Rd, LA22 9PU, ✆ 486, ≼, 🛣 heated, 🖛 – 🗺
🛏wc 🝔 🅿. 🖭 🖭 🖭 *VISA*. 🛠   BZ **c**
closed 27 January-24 February – **M** (bar lunch)/dinner 11.25 **t.** 🛦 2.50 – **17 rm** 🖙 35.00/78.00 **t.**,
1 suite – SB (November-April) 50.00 **st.**

🏨 **White Moss House**, Rydal Water, LA22 9SE, S : 1 ½ m. on A 591 ✆ 295, 🖛 – 🗺 🛏wc
🅿. 🛠   BY **e**
Mid March-early November – **M** (dinner only) (booking essential) 16.00 **t.** 🛦 2.75 – **6 rm**
🖙 (dinner included) 48.50/91.00 **t.** – SB (weekdays only in March, April and November) 85.00 **st.**

🏨 **Rothay Garden**, Broadgate, LA22 9RH, ✆ 334, 🖛 – 🗺 🛏wc 🝔 🅿. 🖭 *VISA*   AY **e**
closed December and January – **M** (bar lunch)/dinner 11.00 **t.** 🛦 2.50 – **16 rm** 🖙 27.50/70.00 **t.**
– SB (February, March and November) 49.80/63.00 **st.**

🏨 **Oak Bank**, Broadgate, LA22 9TA, ✆ 217, 🖛 – 🗺 🛏wc 🝔wc 🅿. 🖭 *VISA*   BZ **e**
Mid February-mid November – **M** (bar lunch)/dinner 10.00 **st.** 🛦 2.50 – **14 rm** 🖙 18.00/44.00 **st.**
– SB (weekdays only)(winter only) 40.00 **st.**

🏨 **Grasmere**, Broadgate, LA22 9TA, ✆ 277, 🖛 – 🛏wc 🝔wc 🅿. 🖭 *VISA*   BZ **i**
March-November – **M** (bar lunch)/dinner 10.00 **t.** 🛦 2.20 – **12 rm** 🖙 15.00/40.00 **t.**

🏨 **How Foot Lodge** without rest., Town End, LA22 9SQ, on A 591 ✆ 366, ≼, 🖛 – 🛏wc 🝔wc
🅿. 🛠   AY **v**
March-mid November – **6 rm** 🖙 28.00/32.00 **st.**

🏠 **Bridge House** 🛦, Stock Lane, LA22 9SN, ✆ 425, 🖛 – 🛏wc 🅿. 🖭 *VISA*. 🛠   BZ **n**
March-mid November – **12 rm** 🖙 (dinner included) 20.00/49.00 **t.**

🏠 **Titteringdales** 🛦, Pye Lane, LA22 9RQ, ✆ 439, 🖛 – 🝔wc 🅿   AY **x**
April-October – **7 rm** 🖙 16.50/28.00 **st.**

🏠 **Rothay Lodge** 🛦, White Bridge, LA22 9RH, ✆ 341, 🖛 – 🅿. 🛠   AY **o**
closed Christmas – **6 rm** 🖙 11.00/22.00 **st.**

GRASSINGTON North Yorks. ⁴⁰² O 21 – pop. 1,220 – ECD : Thursday – ⊠ Skipton – ☎ 0756.
♦London 240 – Bradford 30 – Burnley 28 – ♦Leeds 37.

🏨 **Wilson Arms** (Best Western), Station Rd, Threshfield, BD23 5EL, SW : ½ m. on B 6265
  ✆ 752666, ☞ – 🖨 🗏 rest 📺 🖨wc ☎ ⇔ 🅿 ⚠ 🗛 ⓐ 𝘝𝘐𝘚𝘈
  closed January – **M** 7.00/10.00 t. ↓ 2.75 – **25 rm** ⪫ 30.00/56.00 t. – SB 50.00/67.00 st.

🕿 **Grassington House**, BD23 5AQ, ✆ 752406 – ⊓wc 🅿
  April-October – **M** (closed lunch Monday and Friday) (bar lunch)/dinner 7.00 s. – **18 rm**
  ⪫ 14.50/28.00 s.

GRAVESEND Kent ⁴⁰⁴ V 29 – pop. 53,450 – ECD : Wednesday – ☎ 0474.
⇔ to Tilbury (Sealink) frequent services daily (5 mn).
🖪 10 Parrock St. ✆ 337600/64422.
♦London 25 – ♦Dover 54 – Maidstone 16 – Margate 53.

🏨 **Tollgate Moat House** (Q.M.H.), Watling St., DA13 9RA, S : 2 m. at junction A 2 and A 227
  ✆ 357655, Telex 966227 – 📺 🖨wc ☎ & 🅿 ⚠ 🗛 ⓐ 𝘝𝘐𝘚𝘈
  M 6.00/10.00 t. and a la carte ↓ 2.60 – **114 rm** ⪫ 32.50/45.00 st.

🏨 **Overcliffe**, 16 The Overcliffe, DA11 0EF, ✆ 22131 – 📺 ⊓wc 🕮 🅿 ⚠ 🗛 ⓐ 𝘝𝘐𝘚𝘈
  M (closed lunch Saturday and Sunday) 6.50/10.00 t. and a la carte ↓ 2.30 – **19 rm**
  ⪫ 28.50/35.00 t. – SB (weekends only) 45.00/55.00 st.

AUSTIN-ROVER The Grove ✆ 22111
CITROEN, RELIANT Rochester Rd ✆ 65211
FIAT 50 Singlewell Rd ✆ 66148
FORD 1/3 Pelham Rd ✆ 64411
PEUGEOT, TALBOT Vale Rd ✆ 69943

RENAULT West St. ✆ 67801
SKODA Meopham ✆ 813562
TOYOTA High St., Northfleet ✆ 57481
VAUXHALL Overcliffe ✆ 63566
VW-AUDI Old Rd West ✆ 57925

GRAVETYE East Sussex – see East Grinstead.

GRAYSHOTT Hants. ⁴⁰⁴ R 30 – pop. 2,048 – ⊠ Hindhead (Surrey) – ☎ 042 873 Hindhead.
♦London 47 – Chichester 23 – Farnham 9 – Guildford 14 – ♦Portsmouth and Southsea 31.

✗ **Woods**, Headley Rd, GU26 6LB, ✆ 5555 – 🗛 🗛 ⓐ 𝘝𝘐𝘚𝘈
  closed Sunday and Monday – **M** (dinner only) a la carte 14.30/15.95 t. ↓ 2.40.

HONDA Headley Rd ✆ 4222

LANCIA, MASSERATI, SUBARU Headley Rd ✆ 5363

GREAT AYTON North Yorks. ⁴⁰² Q 20 – pop. 4,690 – ⊠ ☎ 0642 Middlesbrough.
♦London 245 – ♦Leeds 63 – ♦Middlesbrough 7 – York 48.

✗✗✗ **Ayton Hall** 🕭 with rm, Low Green, TS9 6BW, ✆ 723595, « Tasteful decor », ☞, ✗ – 📺
  🖨wc ☎ ⇔ 🅿 🗛 𝘝𝘐𝘚𝘈 ✣
  M 7.95/11.95 t. and a la carte ↓ 3.75 – **5 rm** ⪫ 45.00/69.00 t. – SB 75.00/80.00 st.

GREAT BADDOW Essex ⁴⁰⁴ V 28 – see Chelmsford.

GREAT BARDFIELD Essex ⁴⁰⁴ V 28 – pop. 1,030 – ⊠ Braintree – ☎ 0371 Great Dunmow.
♦London 49 – ♦Cambridge 30 – Chelmsford 20 – Colchester 26.

✗ **Corn Dolly**, High St., CM7 4SP, ✆ 810554, English rest.

GREAT BARR West Midlands ⁴⁰³ ⁴⁰⁴ O 26 – see Birmingham.

GREAT BROUGHTON Cumbria ⁴⁰¹ ⁴⁰² J 19 – see Cockermouth.

GREAT DRIFFIELD Humberside ⁴⁰² S 21 – pop. 8,970 – ECD : Wednesday – ⊠ York – ☎ 0377.
🖫 Driffield, Sunderlandwick ✆ 43116.
♦London 201 – ♦Kingston-upon-Hull 21 – Scarborough 22 – York 29.

🏨 **Bell** (Best Western), 46 Market Pl., YO25 7AP, ✆ 46661, squash – 📺 🖨wc ☎ & 🅿 ⚠ 🗛
  🗛 ⓐ
  M (buffet lunch)/dinner a la carte 8.50/11.85 t. ↓ 2.95 – **14 rm** ⪫ 29.90/39.10 st. – SB (weekends
  only) 50.00 st.

at Nafferton NE : 2 ½ m. on A 166 – ⊠ ☎ 0377 Great Driffield :

🏠 **Wold House** 🕭, Wold Rd, YO25 0LD, ✆ 44242, 🏊 heated, ☞ – 🖨wc ⊓wc 🅿 ✣
  M (bar lunch)/dinner 7.50 st. ↓ 3.00 – **13 rm** ⪫ 17.50/30.00 st. – SB 50.00/53.00 st.

Cet ouvrage n'est pas un répertoire de tous les hôtels et restaurants,
ni même de tous les bons hôtels et restaurants de Grande-Bretagne et d'Irlande.

Comme nous cherchons à rendre service à tous les touristes,
nous sommes amenés à indiquer des établissements
de toutes les classes et à n'en citer que quelques-uns de chaque sorte.

GREAT DUNMOW Essex **404** V 28 – pop. 4,026 – ECD : Wednesday – ✆ 0371.

♦London 42 – ♦Cambridge 27 – Chelmsford 13 – Colchester 24.

🏨 **Saracen's Head** (T.H.F.), High St., CM6 1AG, ℰ 3901 – 📺 ⇔wc ☎ 🅿 🎦 ⚠ AE ⓞ VISA
M 9.00/9.25 **st.** and a la carte ⓘ 2.70 – ⇆ 5.50 – **24 rm** 40.00/50.50 **st.**

XXX **Starr,** Market Pl., CM6 1AX, ℰ 4321 – 🅿 ⚠ ⓞ VISA
closed Saturday lunch, Sunday dinner, first 3 weeks August and 25 December-9 January – **M**
12.95 **t.** (lunch) and a la carte 13.95/19.80 **t.** ⓘ 3.25.

BMW The Downs, 81 High St. ℰ 2884

GREAT MALVERN Heref. and Worc. **403** **404** N 27 – pop. 30,153 – ECD : Wednesday –
✆ 068 45.

See : Priory Church★ 11C B **B.**

🛈 Winter Gdns, Grange Rd ℰ 2700.

♦London 127 – ♦Birmingham 34 – ♦Cardiff 66 – Gloucester 24.

Plan opposite

🏨 **Foley Arms** (Best Western), Worcester Rd, WR14 4QS, ℰ 3397, Group Telex 437269, ≤, 🐎
– 📺 ⇔wc 🛁wc ☎ 🅿 🎦 ⚠ AE ⓞ VISA   B **a**
M 6.65/9.75 **st.** and a la carte ⓘ 2.75 – **26 rm** ⇆ 32.50/46.50 **st.** – SB 44.00/48.00 **st.**

🏨 **Mount Pleasant,** Belle Vue Terr., WR14 4PZ, ℰ 61837, ≤, 🐎 – 📺 ⇔wc 🛁wc 🅿 🎦 ⚠
AE ⓞ VISA 🐎   B **e**
M 6.95/12.00 **st.** ⓘ 2.50 – ⇆ 4.50 – **14 rm** 28.00/36.00 **t.** – SB (except Christmas and New Year)
52.00/62.00 **st.**

🏨 **Cotford,** Graham Rd, WR14 2JW, ℰ 2427, 🐎 – 📺 ⇔wc 🛁wc 🅿 ⚠ VISA   B **o**
M (dinner only and Sunday lunch)/dinner 7.50 **st.** ⓘ 3.00 – **14 rm** ⇆ 15.00/34.00 **st.**

🏨 **Montrose,** 23 Graham Rd, WR14 2HU, ℰ 2335, 🐎 – 🛁wc 🅿 ⚠ VISA   B **i**
M (dinner only) 7.50 **st.** ⓘ 2.55 – **14 rm** ⇆ 17.50/30.00 **st.** – SB (November-March)
35.00/39.00 **st.**

⌂ **Fromefield,** 147 Barnards Green Rd, WR14 3LT, ℰ 62466, 🐎 – ⋇   B **r**
7 rm ⇆ 12.50/28.35 **st.**

⌂ **Bredon,** 34 Worcester Rd, WR14 4AA, ℰ 5323, ≤ – 📺 ⇔wc 🛁wc ☎ 🅿 ⚠ AE VISA   B **u**
closed 25 December-1 January – **9 rm** ⇆ 16.00/40.00 **t.**

⌂ **Sidney House,** 40 Worcester Rd, WR14 4AA, ℰ 4994, ≤ – 📺 🅿 ⚠ AE ⓞ VISA   B **s**
6 rm ⇆ 11.00/25.00 **s.**

XX **Walmer Lodge** with rm, 49 Abbey Rd, WR14 3HH, ℰ 4139, 🐎 – ⇔wc 🛁wc 🅿 ⋇   A **n**
closed Sunday, Christmas and New Year – **M** *(closed Bank Holidays)* (dinner only) (booking
essential) a la carte 7.90/9.50 ⓘ 2.80 – **8 rm** ⇆ 16.10/29.90 **t.**

at Welland SE : 4 ½ m. by A 449 on A 4104 – ✉ Great Malvern – ✆ 0684 Hanley Swan :

🏨 **Holdfast Cottage** 🌲, WR13 6NA, W : ¾ m. ℰ 310288, « 17C country cottage », 🐎 –
⇔wc 🛁wc 🅿   A **x**
M (bar lunch, residents only)/dinner 9.75 **t.** ⓘ 3.75 – **9 rm** ⇆ 18.00/38.00 **t.** – SB (mid October-
April) 45.00/48.00 **st.**

at Malvern Wells S : 2 m. on A 449 – ✉ ✆ 068 45 Great Malvern :

🏨 **Cottage in the Wood** 🌲, Holywell Rd, WR14 4LG, ℰ 3487, ≤ Severn and Evesham Vales,
🐎 – 📺 ⇔wc 🅿 ⚠ VISA ⋇   A **z**
closed 24 to 29 December – **M** 7.00/14.00 **st.** and a la carte ⓘ 3.90 – ⇆ 4.00 – **20 rm**
38.00/68.00 **st.** – SB 42.50/82.50 **st.**

XX ✿ **Croque-en-Bouche,** 221 Wells Rd, WR14 4NF, ℰ 65612 – ⚠ VISA   A **u**
closed Sunday to Tuesday and Christmas – **M** (dinner only) (booking essential) 18.80 **st.** ⓘ 3.00.
Spec. White fish and Lovage soup, Ceviche of salmon and scallops, Ragoût of venison with a parsnip purée.

at Colwall S : 3 ¼ m. by A 449 on B 4218 – ✉ Great Malvern – ✆ 0684 Colwall :

🏨 **Colwall Park,** Walwyn Rd, WR13 6QG, ℰ 40206 – 📺 ⇔wc 🛁wc ☎ 🅿 🎦 ⚠ AE VISA
M 6.50/9.50 **t.** ⓘ 2.75 – **14 rm** ⇆ 28.50/47.50 **t.** – SB (except Easter, Christmas and Bank
Holidays) 57.00 **st.**   A **r**

at Wynds Point S : 4 m. on A 449 – ✉ Great Malvern – ✆ 0684 Colwall :

🏨 **Malvern Hills,** British Camp, WR13 6DW, ℰ 40237, 🐎 – 📺 ⇔wc 🅿 ⚠ AE ⓞ   A **s**
M 7.50/7.95 **st.** and a la carte ⓘ 2.50 – **15 rm** ⇆ 22.00/45.00 **st.** – SB (except Christmas and
Bank Holidays) 55.00/60.00 **st.**

at West Malvern W : 2 m. on B 4232 – ✉ ✆ 068 45 Great Malvern :

🕊 **Broomhill,** West Malvern Rd, WR14 4AY, ℰ 64367, ≤ hills and countryside, 🐎 – ⇔wc
🛁wc 🅿   A **v**
March-October – **M** (bar lunch)/dinner 7.00 **t.** – **10 rm** ⇆ 15.00/31.00 **t.** – SB (except summer)
30.50/37.00 **st.**

AUSTIN-ROVER Newtown Rd ℰ 3301   VAUXHALL-OPEL Linktop ℰ 3336
CITROEN 62 Court Rd ℰ 3391   VOLVO Pickersleigh Rd ℰ 61498
FORD 203-5 Worcester Rd ℰ 69111   VW, AUDI Worcester Rd ℰ 3601

GREAT MALVERN

Church Street .... B
Wells Road .... B

Albert Road North .... B 2
Albert Road South .... B 3
Blackmore
  Park Road .... A 5
Clerkenwell Crescent ..... B 6
Cockshot Road .... B 8
Court Road .... B 12
Croft Bank .... A 13
Happy Valley
  off St. Ann's Road ..... B 15
Imperial Road .... B 16
Jubilee Drive .... A 17
Lygon Bank .... B 18
Madresfield Road .... B 20
Moorlands Road .... B 22
North Malvern Road ...... B 23
Orchard Road .... B 24
Richmond Road .... B 26
Upper Welland
  Road .... A 27
Walwyn Road .... A 29
Wells Road .... A 30

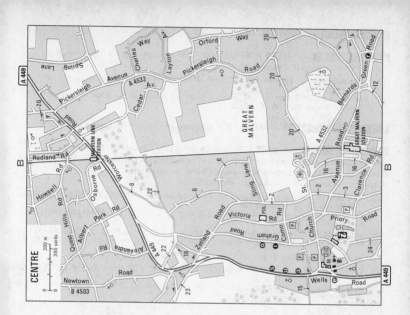

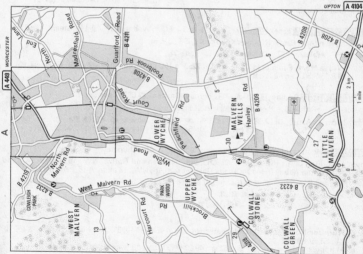

Town plans

roads most used
by traffic and those
on which guide listed
hotels and restaurants
stand are fully drawn ;
the beginning only
of lesser roads
is indicated.

GREAT MILTON Oxon. 🟧🟧🟧 🟧🟧🟧 Q 28 – see Oxford.

GREAT SNORING Norfolk 🟧🟧🟧 W 25 – pop. 180 – ✉ Fakenham – ☻ 032 872 Walsingham.
◆London 115 – ◆Cambridge 68 – ◆Norwich 28.

  🏠 **Old Rectory** ⚲, Barsham Rd, NR21 0HP, ℰ 597, « Country house atmosphere », ⚞ – 📺
    ⛱wc 🅿. 🆎 ⓪. ✼
    closed 25 and 26 December – **M** (booking essential) 10.00/11.00 **t**. – **6 rm** ⍈ 25.00/45.00 **t**. –
    SB (November-March) 58.00/72.00 **st**.

GREAT WITCHINGHAM Norfolk 🟧🟧🟧 X 25 – see Lenwade - Great Witchingham.

GREAT YARMOUTH Norfolk 🟧🟧🟧 Z 26 – pop. 54 ,777 – ECD : Thursday – ☻ 0493.
  🚢 Shipping connections with the Continent : to The Netherlands (Scheveningen) (Norfolk Line).
  🅱 1 South Quay ℰ 856100 ext 345 – Marine Parade ℰ 842195 (summer only).
◆London 126 – ◆Cambridge 81 – ◆Ipswich 53 – ◆Norwich 20.

  🏨 **Carlton** (Mt. Charlotte), 1-5 Kimberley Terr., Marine Par., NR30 3JE, ℰ 855234, Telex 97249
    – 🛗 📺 ⟵ 🅿. 🅰. 🔼 🆎 ⓪ 𝘝𝘐𝘚𝘈
    M (bar lunch Monday to Saturday)/dinner 7.95 **st**. and a la carte 🍴 4.05 – **94 rm** ⍈ 26.50/42.50 **s**..
    5 suites 47.50/125.00 **t**.

  🏨 **Star** (Q.M.H.), 24 Hall Quay, NR30 1HG, ℰ 842294 – 🛗 📺 ⛱wc ⟵ 🅿. 🅰. 🔼 🆎 ⓪ 𝘝𝘐𝘚𝘈
    M 6.20 **st**. and a la carte 🍴 3.50 – **42 rm** ⍈ 32.50/45.00 **st**. – SB (weekends only) 44.00/70.00 **st**.

  at Gorleston-on-Sea S : 3 m. on A 12 – ✉ ☻ 0493 Great Yarmouth :

  🏨 **Cliff** (Best Western), Cliff Hill, NR31 6DH, ℰ 662179, ⚞ – 📺 ⛱wc 🔥wc ☎ 🅿. 🔼 🆎 ⓪
    𝘝𝘐𝘚𝘈
    M 6.50/9.00 **t**. and a la carte 🍴 3.75 – **30 rm** ⍈ 28.00/48.50 **t**. – SB (weekends only)
    44.00/50.00 **st**.

AUSTIN-ROVER North Quay ℰ 4266
CITROEN Main Rd, Repps ℰ 069 27 (Potter Heigham) 271/256
FORD South Gates Rd ℰ 844922

FORD 134 Lowestoft Rd, Gorleston-on-Sea ℰ 664151
RENAULT Drudge Rd ℰ 664158
VW, AUDI-NSU South Denes Rd ℰ 857711

GREAT YELDHAM Essex 🟧🟧🟧 V 27 – pop. 1 ,440 – ECD : Wednesday – ✉ Halstead – ☻ 0787.
Envir. : Hedingham Castle (Norman Keep★) AC, SE : 2 ½ m.
◆London 56 – ◆Cambridge 27 – Chelmsford 23 – Colchester 21.

  XX **White Hart**, Poole St., CO9 4HJ, ℰ 237250, « 15C timbered inn », ⚞ – 🅿. 🔼 🆎 ⓪ 𝘝𝘐𝘚𝘈
    M 8.95/9.50 **t**. and a la carte 🍴 2.60.

GRETA BRIDGE Durham 🟧🟧 O 20 – ✉ Barnard Castle – ☻ 0833 Teesdale.
◆London 253 – ◆Carlisle 63 – ◆Leeds 63 – ◆Middlesbrough 32.

  🏨 **Morritt Arms**, DL12 9SE, ℰ 27232, ⚲, ⚞ – 📺 ⛱wc ⟵ 🅿. 🔼 ⓪ 𝘝𝘐𝘚𝘈
    M 8.50/14.50 **st**. 🍴 3.50 – **23 rm** ⍈ 20.00/45.00 **t**. – SB (November-April) 45.00/62.00 **st**.

GRIMSBY Humberside 🟧🟧🟧 🟧🟧🟧 T 23 – pop. 91 ,532 – ECD : Thursday – ☻ 0472.
Envir. : Thornton Curtis (St. Lawrence's Church★ : Norman and Gothic) NW : 16 m. by A 18 Y and
B 1211 – Thornton Abbey (ruins 14C) : the Gatehouse★ AC, NW : 18 m. by A 18 Y and B 1211.
  ✈ Humberside Airport : ℰ 0652 (Barnetby) 688456, W : 13 m. by A 8 Y.
  🅱 Central Library, Town Hall Square ℰ 53123.
◆London 172 – Boston 50 – Lincoln 36 – ◆Sheffield 75.

Plan opposite

  🏨 **Humber Royal** (Crest), Littlecoates Rd, DN34 4LX, ℰ 50295, Telex 527776, ≼ – 🛗 📺 🅿.
    🅰. 🔼 🆎 ⓪ 𝘝𝘐𝘚𝘈 ✼   Y c
    M approx. 11.50 **st**. – ⍈ 5.75 – **52 rm** 49.00/59.00 **st**. – SB (weekends only) 59.00 **st**.

  🏨 **Crest** (Crest), St. James Sq., DN31 1EP, ℰ 59771, Telex 527741 – 🛗 📺 ⛱wc 🅿. 🅰.
    🆎 ⓪ 𝘝𝘐𝘚𝘈 ✼   AZ n
    M approx. 10.85 **st**. – ⍈ 5.75 – **131 rm** 43.00/53.00 **st**. – SB (weekends only) 57.00 **st**.

  XX **Regines**, 2 Osborne St., ℰ 56737 – 🔼 🆎 𝘝𝘐𝘚𝘈   AZ **a**
    closed Monday lunch, Sunday, first 2 weeks February and first 2 weeks August – **M** 7.95/
    8.95 **t**. and a la carte 🍴 3.25.

AUSTIN-ROVER 166/168 Hainton Av. ℰ 52461
AUSTIN-ROVER 415 Victoria St. ℰ 56161
FIAT, SUBARU Wellowgate ℰ 55951
FORD Corporation Rd ℰ 58941
FSO, MAZDA Rendel St. ℰ 362021
HONDA Alexandra Rd ℰ 58625
MERCEDES-BENZ Bradley Cross Rd ℰ 79274
NISSAN 210/212 Victoria St. ℰ 53572 and 41281

PEUGEOT, TALBOT Park St. ℰ 46011
RENAULT Chelmsford Av. ℰ 70111
SAAB Heneage Rd ℰ 48527
SKODA, ALFA ROMEO Rendel St. ℰ 57362
TOYOTA Cromwell Rd ℰ 52191
VAUXHALL-OPEL 123 Cromwell Rd ℰ 46066
VAUXHALL-OPEL Brighowgate ℰ 58486
VW, AUDI Doughty Rd ℰ 45131

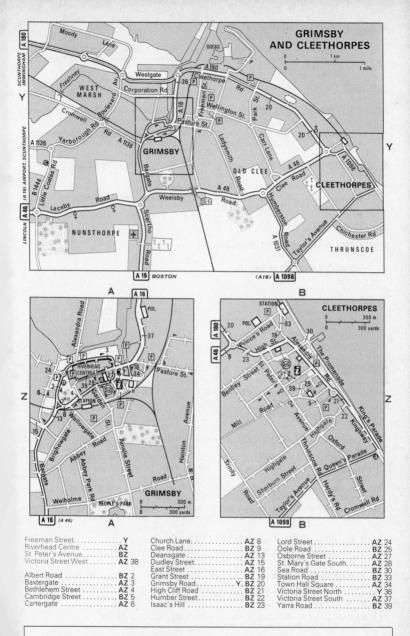

GRIMSBY AND CLEETHORPES

CLEETHORPES

GRIMSBY

Freeman Street . . . . **Y**	Church Lane . . . . **AZ** 8	Lord Street . . . . **AZ** 24
Riverhead Centre . . . . **AZ**	Clee Road . . . . **BZ** 9	Oole Road . . . . **BZ** 25
St. Peter's Avenue . . . . **BZ**	Deansgate . . . . **AZ** 13	Osborne Street . . . . **AZ** 27
Victoria Street West . . . . **AZ** 38	Dudley Street . . . . **AZ** 15	St. Mary's Gate South . . . . **AZ** 28
	East Street . . . . **AZ** 16	Sea Road . . . . **BZ** 30
Albert Road . . . . **BZ** 2	Grant Street . . . . **BZ** 19	Station Road . . . . **BZ** 33
Baxtergate . . . . **AZ** 3	Grimsby Road . . . . **Y, BZ** 20	Town Hall Square . . . . **AZ** 34
Bethlehem Street . . . . **AZ** 4	High Cliff Road . . . . **BZ** 21	Victoria Street North . . . . **Y** 36
Cambridge Street . . . . **BZ** 5	Humber Street . . . . **BZ** 22	Victoria Street South . . . . **AZ** 37
Cartergate . . . . **AZ** 6	Isaac's Hill . . . . **BZ** 23	Yarra Road . . . . **BZ** 39

Für Ihre Reisen in Großbritannien

– 5 Karten (Nr. **401**, **402**, **403**, **404**, **405**) im Maßstab 1:400 000
– Die auf den Karten rot unterstrichenen Orte sind im Führer erwähnt,
  benutzen Sie deshalb Karten und Führer zusammen.

197

GRIMSTHORPE Lincs. 402 404 S 25 – ⊠ Bourne – ✪ 077 832 Edenham.

♦London 105 – Lincoln 43 – ♦Nottingham 38.

XX **Black Horse Inn** with rm, PE10 0LY, ✆ 247, English rest. – ⊟wc 🅿. 🔼 AE VISA
closed Sunday, Christmas-New Year and Bank Holidays – **M** 10.95/12.95 **t.** and a la carte ⑃ 4.40
– ⊊ 6.00 – **4 rm** 35.00/45.00 **t.**

GRIMSTON Norfolk – see Kings Lynn.

GRINDLEFORD Derbs. 402 403 404 P 24 – ⊠ Sheffield (South Yorks.) – ✪ 0433 Hope Valley.

♦London 165 – Derby 31 – ♦Manchester 34 – ♦Sheffield 10.

🏛 **Maynard Arms,** Main Rd, S30 1HP, ✆ 30321, ≼, 🐎 – 📺 ⊟wc ☎ 🅿. 🔼 AE ① VISA
M 6.45/10.50 **t.** ⑃ 2.50 – **13 rm** ⊊ 30.00/42.00 **t.** – SB 46.00/55.00 **st.**

GRINDLETON Lancs. 402 M 22 – pop. 1,451 (inc. West Bradford) – ⊠ ✪ 020 07 Bolton-by-Bowland.

♦London 241 – ♦Blackpool 38 – Lancaster 25 – ♦Leeds 45 – ♦Manchester 33.

🏠 **Harrop Fold Farm** ⯾, Harrop Fold, BB7 4PJ, N : 2 ¾ m. by Slaidburn Rd ✆ 600, ≼, « 17C
Longhouse », ⯅ – 📺 ⊟wc 🅿. 🔼 VISA ⯾
M (dinner only) 15.00 **st.** and a la carte ⑃ 2.85 – **8 rm** ⊊ 17.00/37.00 **st.** – SB (except
Christmas-New Year) 54.00/56.00 **st.**

GRIZEDALE Cumbria 402 K 20 – see Hawkshead.

LES GUIDES VERTS MICHELIN

Paysages, monuments
Routes touristiques
Géographie, Économie
Histoire, Art
Itinéraires de visite
Plans de villes et de monuments.

GUILDFORD Surrey 404 S 30 – pop. 61,509 – ECD : Wednesday – ✪ 0483.

See : Cathedral★ (1961) Z A.

Envir. : Clandon Park★★ (Renaissance House) AC, E : 3 m. by A 246 Z.

🛈 Civic Hall, London Rd ✆ 575857.

♦London 33 – ♦Brighton 43 – Reading 27 – ♦Southampton 49.

Plan opposite

🏛 **Angel** (T.H.F.), High St., GU1 3DR, ✆ 64555, « 16C coaching inn » – 📺 ⊟wc 🈂. 🔼 🔼 AE
① VISA   Y a
M 10.50/11.50 **st.** and a la carte ⑃ 2.60 – ⊊ 5.50 – **27 rm** 40.00/50.00 **st.**, **2 suites.**

🏠 **Quinns** without rest., 78 Epsom Rd, GU1 2BX, ✆ 60422, 🐎 – 📺 🍴wc 🅿. 🔼 AE ① VISA
11 rm ⊊ 21.00/44.00 **st.**   Z e

XX **Three Kingdoms,** 14 Park St., GU1 4XB, ✆ 61458, Chinese rest. – 🔼 AE ① VISA   Y u
closed 25 to 27 December – **M** 6.50/12.50 **t.** and a la carte.

X **Café de Paris,** 35 Castle St., GU1 2HS, ✆ 34896, French rest. – 🔼 AE ① VISA   Y c
closed Saturday lunch, Monday dinner, Sunday and Bank Holidays – **M** 8.75/9.75 **t.** and a la
carte 14.70/19.00 **t.** ⑃ 2.70.

at West Clandon NE : 5 m. by A 246 on A 247 – Z – ⊠ ✪ 0483 Guildford :

XXX **Onslow Arms Inn,** The Street, GU4 7TE, ✆ 222447 – 🅿. 🔼 AE ① VISA
closed Sunday dinner and Monday – **M** 9.95 **t.** (lunch) and a la carte 13.25/21.50 **t.** ⑃ 3.85.

at Bramley S : 3 m. on A 281 – Z – ⊠ ✪ 0483 Guildford :

🏛 **Bramley Grange,** High St., GU5 0BL, ✆ 893434, 🐎 – 📺 ⊟wc 🈂 🅿. 🔼 AE ① VISA. ⯾
M a la carte 13.60/18.50 **t.** – ⊊ 4.75 – **21 rm** 40.00/70.00 **st.** – SB (weekends only)(November-
April) 70.00/80.00 **st.**

XX **La Baita,** High St., GU5 0HB, ✆ 893392, Italian rest. – 🅿. 🔼 AE ① VISA
closed Sunday – **M** a la carte 11.95/16.90 **t.**

at Compton SW : 4 m. by A 3100 on B 3000 – Z – ⊠ Guildford – ✪ 048 68 Godalming :

XX Withies Inn, Withies Lane, GU3 1JA, ✆ 21158, 🐎 – 🅿.

AUSTIN-ROVER, JAGUAR, ROLLS ROYCE Wood-
bridge Rd ✆ 69231
BEDFORD, VAUXHALL-OPEL Woking Rd ✆ 37731
BMW Moorfield Rd ✆ 502211

FORD Woodbridge Meadow ✆ 60601
MERCEDES-BENZ Aldershot Rd ✆ 60751
RENAULT Walnut Tree Close ✆ 577371
TOYOTA Pitch Pl. Worplesdon ✆ 234242

GUILDFORD

Friary Centre............. **Y**
High Street............... **Y**
Market Street............ **Y 18**
North Street............. **Y**

Bedford Road............ **Y 2**
Bridge Street............ **Y 3**
Castle Street............ **Y 5**
Chertsey Street.......... **Y 6**
College
  Road Link.............. **Y 7**
Commercial Road......... **Y 8**
Eastgate Gardens......... **Y 9**
Friary Bridge............ **Y 12**
Ladymead................ **Z 13**
Leapale Lane............ **Y 15**
Leapale Road............ **Y 16**
Leas Road............... **Y 17**
Mary Road.............. **Y 19**
Midleton Road........... **Y 20**
Millbrook............... **Y 21**
New Inn Lane............ **Z 22**
One Tree
  Hill Road.............. **Z 24**
Onslow Street........... **Y 25**
Park Street............. **Y 27**
Quarry Street........... **Y 28**
Stoughton Road.......... **Z 30**
Trood's Lane............ **Z 31**
Tungsgate.............. **Y 33**
Warwick's Bench......... **Y 34**
Woodbridge Road........ **Z 37**

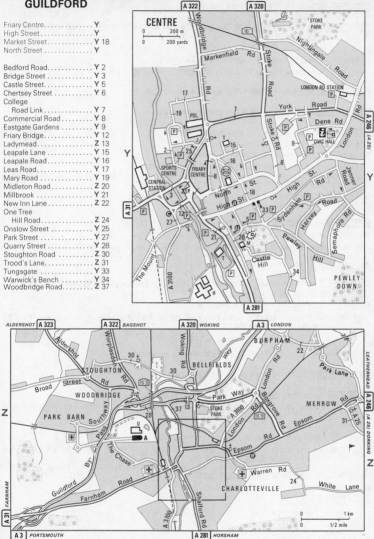

GUIST Norfolk **404** W 25 – pop. 209 – ⊠ Fakenham – ☎ 036 284 Foulsham.

♦London 119 – ♦Cambridge 67 – King's Lynn 29 – ♦Norwich 20.

XX   **Tollbridge,** Dereham Rd, NR20 5NU, S : ½ m. on B 1110 ℰ 359, ≤, « Attractive setting on banks of River Wensum », 🍴 – **℗**. **VISA**
closed Sunday, Monday, 3 weeks January and first 10 days October – **M** (booking essential) 7.50 **t.** (lunch) and a la carte 9.25/11.20 **t.** 🍷 2.40.

AUSTIN-ROVER Norwich Rd ℰ 0328 (Fakenham) 2266
PEUGEOT-TALBOT Hempton Rd ℰ 0328 (Fakenham) 3331

VAUXHALL-OPEL Greenway Lane ℰ 0328 (Fakenham) 2200

GULWORTHY Devon 🔢 H 32 – see Tavistock.

GUNNISLAKE Cornwall 🔢 H 32 The West Country G. – pop. 2 ,154 – ECD : Wednesday – ✆ 0822 Tavistock.
Envir. : Cotehele House★★*AC*, SW : 2 ½ m.
♦London 244 – Bude 37 – Exeter 43 – ♦Plymouth 20 – Tavistock 5.

   ☎ Cornish Inn, The Square, PL18 9BW, ℰ 832475 – ⌐wc 🅿 – **9 rm**.

GWBERT-ON-SEA Dyfed 🔢 F 27 – see Cardigan.

HACKNESS North Yorks. 🔢 S 21 – see Scarborough.

HADLEIGH Suffolk 🔢 W 27 – pop. 5 ,858 – ✆ 0473.
🛈 Topliss Hall ℰ 822922.
♦London 72 – ♦Cambridge 49 – Colchester 17 – ♦Ipswich 10.

   ✗ **Weavers,** 25-27 High St., IP7 5AG, ℰ 827247 – 🔶 𝘝𝘐𝘚𝘈
     closed Sunday, Monday, 2 weeks July and 25 December-2 January – **M** (dinner only) a la carte
     7.55/10.95 t. ⓵ 2.90.

AUSTIN-ROVER 115 High St. ℰ 823286   RENAULT 272 London Rd ℰ 554563
PEUGEOT, TALBOT 132 High St. ℰ 823525

HADLOW Kent 🔢 V 30 – pop. 2 ,655 – ⊠ Tonbridge – ✆ 0732.
♦London 34 – Maidstone 10 – Royal Tunbridge Wells 9.

   ✗✗ **La Cremaillère,** The Square, TN11 0DD, ℰ 851489, French rest. – 🔶 𝔸𝔼 ⓞ 𝘝𝘐𝘚𝘈
     closed lunch Saturday and Sunday, 1 week January, 1 week spring, 1 week summer and Bank
     Holidays – **M** (booking essential) 10.75 t. ⓵ 1.95.

HAILSHAM East Sussex 🔢 U 31 – pop. 12 ,774 – ECD : Thursday – ⊠ ✆ 0323.
🛈 Area Library, Western Rd ℰ 840604.
♦London 57 – ♦Brighton 23 – Eastbourne 7 – Hastings 20.

   🏨 **Boship Farm,** BN27 4DT, NW : 3 m. by A 295 on A 22 ℰ 844826, ⌂ heated, 🐾, ✗ – 📺
     ⌐wc ☎ 🅿 ♿ 🔶 𝔸𝔼 ⓞ 𝘝𝘐𝘚𝘈
     M 5.75 t. (lunch) and a la carte 8.95/13.40 t. – **47 rm** ⇌ 34.50/38.00 t. – SB 52.00/66.00 st.

HALE Greater Manchester 🔢🔢🔢 M 23 – see Altrincham.

HALEBARNS Greater Manchester – see Altrincham.

HALIFAX West Yorks. 🔢 O 22 – pop. 76 ,675 – ECD : Thursday – ✆ 0422.
🛈 Halifax Bradley Hall, Holywell Green ℰ 0422 (Elland) 74108 – 🛈 West End, Highroad Well
ℰ 53608, N : 3 m – 🛈 Ryburn, Norland ℰ 831355, S : 3 m.
🛈 The Piece Hall ℰ 68725.
♦London 205 – Bradford 8 – Burnley 21 – ♦Leeds 15 – ♦Manchester 28.

   🏰 **Holdsworth House,** Holmfield, HX2 9TG, N : 3 m. by A 629 ℰ 240024, Telex 51574, « Part
     17C house » – 📺 ☎ 🅿 ♿ 🔶 𝔸𝔼 ⓞ 𝘝𝘐𝘚𝘈
     closed 23 December-2 January – **M** (closed Saturday lunch and Sunday) a la carte
     14.75/16.50 st. ⓵ 4.00 – **40 rm** ⇌ 37.50/45.00 st. – SB (weekends only) 60.00/70.00 st.

AUSTIN-ROVER-DAIMLER-JAGUAR Huddersfield   RENAULT Hope St. ℰ 59442
Rd ℰ 65944   VAUXHALL Northgate ℰ 62851
FIAT, CITROEN Queens Rd ℰ 67711   VAUXHALL-OPEL 7 Horton St. ℰ 65846
FIAT, POLSKI Rochdale Rd ℰ 65036   VOLVO 354 Pellon Lane ℰ 61961
FORD Skircoat Rd ℰ 65790   VW, AUDI Denholme Gate Rd, Hipperholme ℰ
HONDA Boothtown ℰ 67516   205611
PEUGEOT-TALBOT Skircoat Rd ℰ 53701

HALLAND East Sussex 🔢 U 31 – ECD : Wednesday – ⊠ Lewes – ✆ 082 584.
♦London 48 – ♦Brighton 16 – Eastbourne 16 – Royal Tunbridge Wells 19.

   🏨 **Halland Forge,** BN8 6PW, on A 22 ℰ 456, 🐾 – 📺 ⌐wc ⌐wc ☎ 🅿 🔶 𝔸𝔼 ⓞ 𝘝𝘐𝘚𝘈. ✗
     M 7.50/9.50 t. and a la carte ⓵ 2.90 – ⇌ 5.00 – **20 rm** 29.50/37.00 t. – SB 53.00/56.00 st.

HALSE TOWN Cornwall 🔢 D 33 – see St. Ives.

HALTWHISTLE Northumb. 🔢🔢 M 19 – pop. 3 ,522 – ✆ 0498.
🛈 Sycamore St. ℰ 20351 (summer only).
♦London 335 – ♦Carlisle 22 – ♦Newcastle 37.

   ↑ **Ashcroft,** NE49 0DA, ℰ 20213, 🐾 – 🅿 ✗
     closed 24 December-6 January – **8 rm** ⇌ 8.00/16.00 s.

HAMBLE Hants. 403 404 Q 31 – pop. 2,936 – ✪ 0703 Southampton.

◆London 88 – ◆Portsmouth 20 – ◆Southampton 7 – Winchester 22.

　XX　**Beth's,** The Quay, ✆ 454314, ≼ – �& AE ⓞ VISA
　　closed Sunday and first 2 weeks January – **M** 8.25 **t.** and a la carte 12.35/16.05 **t.** ⓵ 2.80.

PEUGEOT-TALBOT　Hamble Lane ✆ 453757

HAMBLETON Leics. – see Oakham.

HAMBROOK Avon 403 404 M 29 – see Bristol.

HANDFORTH Cheshire 402 403 404 N 23 – see Wilmslow.

HANLEY Staffs. 402 403 404 N 24 – see Stoke-on-Trent.

HARBERTONFORD Devon 403 I 32 – pop. 970 – ✉ Totnes – ✪ 080 423.

◆London 228 – Exeter 28 – ◆Plymouth 24 – Torquay 13.

　XX　**Hungry Horse,** Old Rd, TQ9 7TA, ✆ 441 – ⓟ. 🚙 AE ⓞ VISA
　　closed Sunday, Monday, 2 weeks February and 10 days June – **M** (dinner only) a la carte
　　11.20/13.85 **t.**

HARLECH Gwynedd 402 403 H 25 – pop. 1,292 – ECD : Wednesday – ✪ 0766.

See : Castle★★ (13C) AC, site and ≼ from the castle★.

Envir. : Llanbedr (Cwm Bychan★) S : 3 ½ m. – Vale of Ffestiniog★ NE : 9 m.

🛆 Royal St. David's ✆ 780203.

🇧 Snowdonia National Park Visitor Centre, High St. ✆ 780658 (summer only).

◆London 241 – Chester 72 – Dolgellau 21.

　🏨　**Maes-y-Neuadd** ⌖, Talsarnau, LL47 6YA, NE : 3 ½ m. by B 4573 ✆ 780200, ≼, « Part 14C
　　country house », ⟍, ⚘, park – 🅣🆅 ⌷wc ⓟ. 🚙 AE ⓞ VISA
　　closed 3 to 26 December – **M** (lunch by arrangement) 7.75/10.50 **st.** ⓵ 2.50 – **14 rm**
　　⊇ 25.00/58.00 **st.** – SB (October-April except Bank Holidays) 50.00/56.50 **st.**
　🏠　**Noddfa,** Lower Rd, LL46 2UB, ✆ 780043, ≼ – ⌷wc ⓟ. 🚙 VISA
　　April-October – **M** (bar lunch)/dinner 6.50 **st.** and a la carte ⓵ 3.25 – **7 rm** ⊇ 12.00/26.00 **st.**
　X　**The Cemlyn,** High St., LL46 2YA, ✆ 780425, ≼ Harlech Castle, Cardigan Bay and Lleyn
　　Peninsula – AE ⓞ
　　April-December – **M** (closed Sunday to Thursday October-December) (lunch by arrange-
　　ment)/dinner 8.50 **t.**

HARLOW Essex 404 U 28 – pop. 79,150 – ECD : Wednesday – ✪ 0279.

◆London 22 – ◆Cambridge 37 – ◆Ipswich 60.

　🏨　**Green Man** (Anchor), Mulberry Green, Old Harlow, CM17 0ET, E : 2 ¼ m. by A 414 and B 183
　　✆ 442521, Group Telex 817972 – 🅣🆅 ⌷wc ☎ ⓟ. 🛆. 🚙 AE ⓞ VISA
　　M (closed Saturday lunch) 8.45/12.00 **st.** and a la carte ⓵ 3.00 – **55 rm** ⊇ 43.00/53.00 **st.** – SB
　　(weekends only) 49.00 **st.**

HARNHAM Wilts. 403 404 O 30 – see Salisbury.

HARPENDEN Herts. 404 S 28 – pop. 28,589 – ECD : Wednesday – ✪ 058 27.

◆London 32 – Luton 6.

　🏨🏨　**Harpenden Moat House** (Q.M.H.), 18 Southdown Rd, AL5 1PE, ✆ 64111, ⚘ – 🅣🆅 ⓟ. 🛆.
　　🚙 AE ⓞ VISA
　　M 9.75/13.50 **t.** and a la carte ⓵ 6.00 – ⊇ 4.50 – **35 rm** 34.50/46.50 **t.**
　🏨　**Glen Eagle,** 1 Luton Rd, AL5 2PX, ✆ 60271 – 🅸🅣🆅 ⌷wc ☎ ⓟ. 🛆.
　　51 rm.

FORD, RELIANT, RENAULT, SCIMITAR　Southdown　　　　VAUXHALL-OPEL　17 Luton Rd ✆ 67776
Rd ✆ 5217　　　　　　　　　　　　　　　　　　　　　　VOLVO　Station Rd ✆ 64311
RENAULT　74 High St. ✆ 4545

HARROGATE North Yorks. 402 P 22 – pop. 63,637 – ECD : Wednesday – ✪ 0423.

See : Harlow Car gardens★★ by B 6162 AZ.

Envir. : Fountains Abbey★★★ (ruins 12C-13C, floodlit in summer), Studley Royal Gardens★★ –
Fountains Hall★ (17C) AC, NW : 9 m. by A 61 AY.

🛆 Oakdale, off Kent Rd ✆ 67126 AY – 🛆 Crimple Valley, Hookstone Wood Rd ✆ 883485 by
A 661 CZ.

🇧 Royal Baths Assembly Rooms, Crescent Rd ✆ 65912.

◆London 211 – Bradford 18 – ◆Leeds 15 – ◆Newcastle-upon-Tyne 76 – York 22.

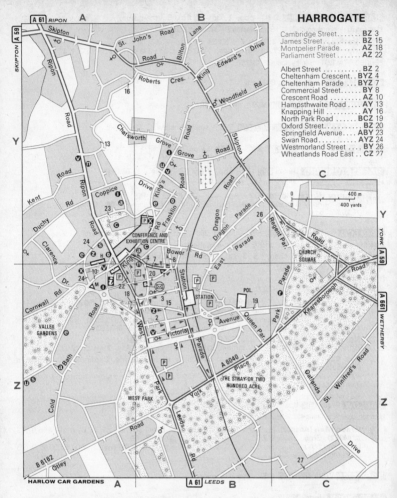

Cambridge Street	**BZ** 3
James Street	**BZ** 15
Montpelier Parade	**AZ** 18
Parliament Street	**AZ** 22

Albert Street	**BZ** 2
Cheltenham Crescent	**BYZ** 4
Cheltenham Parade	**BYZ** 7
Commercial Street	**BY** 8
Crescent Road	**AZ** 10
Hampsthwaite Road	**AY** 13
Knapping Hill	**AY** 16
North Park Road	**BCZ** 19
Oxford Street	**BZ** 20
Springfield Avenue	**ABY** 23
Swan Road	**AYZ** 24
Westmorland Street	**BY** 26
Wheatlands Road East	**CZ** 27

Majestic (T.H.F.), Ripon Rd, HG1 2HU, ℰ 68972, Telex 57918, ⬚, ⟰, ℁, squash – ⬚ 📺 ☎
🅿 ⅍ 🔼 ﹨ 🄰🄴 ⓪ 𝘝𝘐𝘚𝘈
M 8.75/10.25 **st.** and a la carte ⅄ 2.70 – ⅏ 5.50 – **160 rm** 43.00/51.50 **st.**, **10 suites**.
AY **c**

Harrogate International (Best Western), Kings Rd, HG1 1XX, ℰ 500000, Telex 57575, ⇐ –
⬚ ▤ rest 📺 ☎ ⅋ 🅿 ⅍ 🔼 🄰🄴 ⓪ 𝘝𝘐𝘚𝘈
M 6.00/7.50 **st.** and a la carte ⅄ 3.50 – **214 rm** ⅏ 48.50/75.00 **st.**, **9 suites** 90.00 **st.** – SB
52.00/58.00 **st.**
BY **n**

Crown (T.H.F.), Crown Pl., HG1 2RZ, ℰ 67755, Telex 57652 – ⬚ 📺 ☎ ⅋ 🅿 ⅍ 🔼 ﹨ 🄰🄴 ⓪ 𝘝𝘐𝘚𝘈
M 7.25/11.00 **st.** and a la carte ⅄ 2.70 – ⅏ 5.50 – **122 rm** 41.50/49.50 **st.**, **6 suites**. AZ **i**

Old Swan (Norfolk Cap.), Swan Rd, HG1 2SR, ℰ 500055, Telex 57922, ⟰, park, ℁ – ⬚ 📺
☎ ⅋ 🅿 ﹨ 🄰🄴 ⓪ 𝘝𝘐𝘚𝘈
M 8.00/10.50 **st.** and a la carte ⅄ 3.75 – **137 rm**, **10 suites**.
AY **e**

Studley, Swan Rd, HG1 2SE, ℰ 60425, Telex 57506 – ⬚ ▤ rest 📺 ⌂wc ☎ ☏ 🅿 ﹨ 🄰🄴 ⓪
𝘝𝘐𝘚𝘈 ⅏⅍
M a la carte 7.80/12.15 **t.** ⅄ 2.60 – **39 rm** ⅏ 42.00/56.00 **st.**, **1 suite** 70.00/75.00 **st.** – SB (week-
ends only) 55.00 **st.**
AZ **x**

Balmoral, 16-18 Franklin Mount, HG1 5EJ, ℰ 58208, « Comfortably furnished house » – 📺
⌂wc ☎ 🅿 ﹨ 🄰🄴 ⓪
M (lunch by arrangement) 7.00/13.50 **t.** ⅄ 3.00 – **14 rm** ⅏ 30.00/42.00 **t.**, **1 suite** 70.00 **t.** – SB
(weekends only) 54.00 **st.**
BY **v**

🏛 **Hospitality Inn** (Mt. Charlotte), Prospect Pl., West Park, HG1 1LB, 🕿 64601, Telex 57530 – ▮
📺 📥wc 🕿 🅿
71 rm, **2 suites**.
BZ **v**

🏛 **St. George** (Swallow), 1 Ripon Rd, HG1 2SY, 🕿 61431, Telex 57995 – ▮ 📺 📥wc 📠 🅿 🛗
🔼 🆎 ⓪ 𝗩𝗜𝗦𝗔
M (buffet lunch)/dinner 9.25 **st.** and a la carte ▮ 3.40 – **84 rm** ⇆ 44.00/62.00 **st.** – SB 62.00 **st.**
AY **o**

🏛 **Grants**, 3-7 Swan Rd, HG1 2QL, 🕿 60666 – ▮ ▤ rest 📺 📥wc ⋔wc 🕿 🛗 🅿 🔼 🆎 ⓪ 𝗩𝗜𝗦𝗔
🛠
closed 1 to 8 January – **M** (bar lunch)/dinner 7.95 **t.** and a la carte ▮ 2.65 – **17 rm**
⇆ 35.00/55.00 **t.** – SB 48.50/59.00 **st.**
AY **s**

🏠 **Russell**, 29-35 Valley Drive, HG2 0JN, 🕿 509866 – ▮ 📺 📥wc ⋔wc 📠 🔼 🆎 ⓪ 𝗩𝗜𝗦𝗔
closed 27 to 30 December – **M** (closed Sunday and Monday to non-residents) (dinner only)
11.25 **st.** and a la carte ▮ 3.00 – **34 rm** ⇆ 25.95/48.50 **st.**, **2 suites** 59.50/63.50 **st.** – SB
55.50/61.00 **st.**
AZ **e**

🏠 **Green Park**, Valley Drive, HG2 0JT, 🕿 504681 – ▮ 📺 📥wc ⋔wc 📠 🅿 🛗 🔼 🆎 ⓪ 𝗩𝗜𝗦𝗔
M (bar lunch)/dinner 8.25 **t.** and a la carte – **44 rm** ⇆ 27.00/44.00 **t.** – SB (weekends only)
45.00/49.50 **st.**
AZ **a**

🏠 **Fern**, Swan Rd, HG1 2SS, 🕿 523866, Telex 57583 – 📺 📥wc 🕿 🛗 🔼 🆎 ⓪ 𝗩𝗜𝗦𝗔 🛠
M (lunch residents only) 7.95/12.95 **st.** ▮ 2.55 – **28 rm** ⇆ 32.95/51.95 **st.** – SB (except summer)
39.95 **st.**
AY **z**

🏠 **Italia**, 53 King's Rd, HG1 5HJ, 🕿 67404 – 📺 📥wc ⋔ 🅿 🛗 🆎 ⓪ 𝗩𝗜𝗦𝗔 🛠
M (bar lunch)/dinner 8.00 **t.** and a la carte ▮ 3.00 – **25 rm** ⇆ 23.00/39.00 **t.** – SB 45.00 **st.**
BY **u**

🏠 **White House**, 10 Park Par., HG1 5AH, 🕿 501388 – 📺 📥wc ⋔wc 🕿 🅿 🔼 🆎 ⓪ 𝗩𝗜𝗦𝗔
M 5.00/10.00 **st.** and a la carte ▮ 2.75 – **15 rm** ⇆ 32.00/43.00 **st.** – SB 35.00/45.00 **st.**
CZ **r**

🏠 **Gables**, 2 West Grove Rd, HG1 2AD, 🕿 55625 – 📺 📥wc ⋔wc. 🛠
M (bar lunch)/dinner 7.50 **st.** – **9 rm** ⇆ 19.50/39.00 **st.** – SB (weekends only) 50.00 **st.**
BY **i**

🏠 **Woodhouse**, 7 Spring Grove, HG1 2HS, 🕿 60081 – 📺 📥wc ⋔wc. 🛠
closed 24 December-2 January – **7 rm** ⇆ 11.00/25.00 **st.**
AY **a**

🏠 **Stoney Lea**, 13 Spring Grove, HG1 2HS, 🕿 501524 – 📺 📥wc ⋔wc 🅿 🛠
6 rm ⇆ 15.00/26.00 **st.**
AY **i**

🏠 **Alexa House**, 26 Ripon Rd, HG2 2JJ, 🕿 501988 – 📺 📥wc ⋔wc 🛗 🅿 🛠
closed 1 week at Christmas – **15 rm** ⇆ 12.50/29.00 **st.**
AY **n**

🏠 **Garden House**, 14 Harlow Moor Drive, HG2 0JX, 🕿 503059 – 📺 📥wc ⋔wc
8 rm ⇆ 13.00/28.00 **st.**
AZ **u**

🏠 **Oakfield**, 32-34 Kings Rd, HG1 5JW, 🕿 67516 – 📺 📥wc 🅿 🔼 🆎 ⓪ 𝗩𝗜𝗦𝗔 🛠
13 rm ⇆ 15.00/34.00 **st.**
BY **c**

🏠 **Abbey Lodge**, 29-31 Ripon Rd, HG1 2JL, 🕿 69712 – ⋔wc 🅿 🛠
closed Christmas – **8 rm** ⇆ 11.00/25.00 **st.**
AY **v**

🏠 **Alvera Court**, 76 Kings Rd, HG1 5JX, 🕿 55735 – 📺 📥wc ⋔wc ⋔ 🅿 🛠
11 rm ⇆ 15.00/34.00 **st.**
BY **e**

🏠 **Alexandra Court**, 8 Alexandra Rd, HG1 5JS, 🕿 502764 – 📺 ⋔wc 🅿
12 rm ⇆ 15.00/35.00 **st.**
BY **o**

🏠 **Wessex**, 22-23 Harlow Moor Drive, HG2 0JY, 🕿 65890 – ⋔wc. 🔼 𝗩𝗜𝗦𝗔 🛠
closed December – **14 rm** ⇆ 16.00/31.50 **t.**
AZ **s**

✕✕ **Shabab**, 1 John St., HG1 1JZ, 🕿 500250, Indian rest. – 🔼 🆎 ⓪ 𝗩𝗜𝗦𝗔
closed Sunday lunch and Christmas Day.
BZ **z**

✕✕ **Oliver**, 24 King's Rd, HG1 5JW, 🕿 68600 – 🔼 🆎 𝗩𝗜𝗦𝗔
closed Sunday and Bank Holidays – **M** (dinner only) 7.50 **t.** and a la carte.
BY **a**

✕ **Burdekins**, 21 Cheltenham Cres., HG1 1DH, 🕿 502610 – 🔼 🆎 𝗩𝗜𝗦𝗔
M (dinner only) a la carte 7.30/9.85 **t.** ▮ 2.55.
BYZ **n**

✕ **Drum and Monkey**, 5 Montpellier Gardens, HG1 2TF, 🕿 502650, Seafood – 🔼 𝗩𝗜𝗦𝗔
closed Sunday and 24 December-2 January – **M** (booking essential) a la carte 9.00/13.80 **t.**
AZ **v**

at Burn Bridge S : 4 m. by A 61 – BZ – ✉ 🕿 0423 Harrogate :

✕✕ **Roman Court**, 55 Burn Bridge Rd, HG3 1PB, 🕿 879933, Italian rest. – 🅿 🔼 🆎 𝗩𝗜𝗦𝗔
closed Sunday – **M** (dinner only) 8.25 **t.** and a la carte.

at Markington NW : 8 ¾ m. by A 61 – AY – ✉ 🕿 0423 Harrogate :

🏛 **Hob Green** 🛠, HG3 3PJ, SW : ½ m. 🕿 770031, Telex 57780, ≼, « Country house in extensive
parkland », 🌳, park – 📺 📥wc 🕿 🅿 🔼 🆎 ⓪ 𝗩𝗜𝗦𝗔 🛠
closed February – **M** (buffet lunch Monday to Saturday)/dinner 15.00 **t.** ▮ 3.00 – **11 rm**
⇆ 40.00/60.00 **t.** – SB (October-March) 65.00/70.00 **st.**

AUSTIN-ROVER-DAIMLER-JAGUAR, ROLLS
ROYCE 91 Leeds Rd 🕿 871263
FIAT Leeds Rd, Panna 🕿 879236
CITROEN, LANCIA Cheltenham Mount 🕿 68151
FORD Station Par. 🕿 88593

PEUGEOT-TALBOT, VAUXHALL-OPEL West Park 🕿
504601
RENAULT Pannal 🕿 879231
VOLVO East Parade 🕿 64567
VW, AUDI-NSU Ripon Rd 🕿 55141

HARTFORD Cheshire 402 403 404 M 24 – pop. 4 ,000 – ۞ 0606 Northwich.

🏠 Delamere Forest ✏ 0606 (Sandiway) 882807, SW : 2 m.

♦London 188 – Chester 15 – ♦Liverpool 31 – ♦Manchester 25.

🏛 Hartford Hall, School Lane, CW8 1PW, ✏ 75711, 🚗 – 📺 ➰wc 🕿 ℗ – **21 rm, 1 suite**.

AUDI, VW Station Rd, Northwich ✏ 0606 (Northwich) 6061
CITROEN Manchester Rd, Northwich ✏ 0606 (Northwich) 3816
FORD Chesterway, Northwich ✏ 0606 (Northwich) 6141

RENAULT Runcorn Rd, Barnton ✏ 0606 (Northwich) 77137
PEUGEOT-TALBOT 322 Chester Rd ✏ 0606 (Sandiway) 888188
VAUXHALL-OPEL 9 London Rd, Northwich ✏ 0606 (Northwich) 3434

HARTLEPOOL Cleveland 402 Q 19 – pop. 91 ,749 – ECD : Wednesday – ۞ 0429.

🏠 Seaton Carew, Tees Rd ✏ 66249.

✈ Teesside Airport ✏ 0325 (Darlington) 332811, SW : 20 m.

🛈 Leisure and Amenities Dept., Civic Centre ✏ 66522 ext 375 – Victoria Terr., Hartlepool Docks ✏ 74922 (summer only).

♦London 263 – Durham 19 – ♦Middlesbrough 9 – Sunderland 21.

🏛 Grand, Swainson St., TS24 8AA, ✏ 66345 – 🕿 📺 ➰wc ☎. 🅿 – **44 rm**.

AUSTIN-ROVER 128/130 York Rd ✏ 66393
AUSTIN-ROVER York Rd ✏ 74431
CITROEN Casebourne Rd ✏ 33031

FORD Stockton Rd ✏ 64311
LADA York Rd ✏ 67881

HARTOFT END North Yorks. 402 R 21 – pop. 62 – ✉ Pickering – ۞ 075 15 Lastingham.

♦London 243 – Scarborough 26 – York 32.

🏠 Blacksmith's Arms, YO18 8EN, ✏ 331 – 📺 🅿wc ℗. 𝘝𝘐𝘚𝘈
M (bar lunch)/dinner 12.00 t. and a la carte 🍷 3.00 – **12 rm** 🛏 18.00/36.00 t. – SB (October-March) 45.00 st.

HARWICH and DOVERCOURT Essex 404 X 28 – pop. 17 ,245 – ECD : Wednesday – ۞ 025 55 (4 fig.) or 0255 (6 fig.).

🚢 Shipping connections with the Continent : to Germany (Hamburg) (DFDS Seaways) – to Denmark (Esbjerg) (DFDS Seaways) – from Parkeston Quay to The Netherlands (Hoek van Holland) (Sealink) – to Sweden (Göteborg) (DFDS Seaways) – to Norway (Kristiansand) (Fred Olsen Lines KDS) summer only – 🚢 to Felixstowe (Orwell & Harwich Navigation Co.) 5-8 daily (15 mn).

🛈 Parkeston Quay ✏ 506139 (summer only) – ♦London 78 – Chelmsford 41 – Colchester 20 – ♦Ipswich 23.

🏛 Tower, Main Road, CO12 3PJ, ✏ 504952 – 📺 ➰wc 🅿wc ℗. 🅰 🅰🅴 ⓞ 𝘝𝘐𝘚𝘈
M 6.00 t. (lunch) and a la carte 9.75/15.75 t. 🍷 3.00 – **15 rm** 🛏 25.00/44.00 t.

🏛 Cliff, Marine Par., CO12 3RD, ✏ 503345, Telex 987372, ≼ – 📺 ➰wc 🅿wc ℗. 🅰. 🅰 🅰🅴 ⓞ 𝘝𝘐𝘚𝘈
M 5.50/6.50 st. and a la carte 🍷 2.60 – **33 rm** 🛏 21.00/39.00 t. – SB (weekends only) 40.00/55.00 st.

XX Pier at Harwich, The Quay, CO12 3HH, ✏ 503363, ≼, Seafood – 🅰 🅰🅴 ⓞ 𝘝𝘐𝘚𝘈
closed 25 to 27 December – M 7.75 st. (lunch) and a la carte 8.40/13.25 t. 🍷 3.10.

HASCOMBE Surrey – see Godalming.

HASELBURY PLUCKNETT Somerset 403 L 31 – see Crewkerne.

HASLEMERE Surrey 404 R 30 – pop. 10 ,544 – ECD : Wednesday – ۞ 0428.
Envir. : Petworth House★★★ 17C (paintings★★★ and carved room★★★) AC, SE : 11 m.

♦London 47 – ♦Brighton 46 – ♦Southampton 44.

🏨 Lythe Hill 🦢, Petworth Rd, GU27 3BQ, E : 1 ½ m. on B 2131 ✏ 51251, Telex 858402, ≼, 🦢, 🌳, park, 🎾 – 📺 🕿 ℗. 🅰. 🅰 🅰🅴 ⓞ 𝘝𝘐𝘚𝘈
M 10.75/12.75 st. and a la carte 🍷 3.75 – 🛏 4.50 – **36 rm** 36.00/63.00 st., **11 suites** 72.50/110.00 st. – SB (except Easter, Christmas, New Year and Bank Holidays) 67.00/72.00 st.

XXX Auberge de France (at Lythe Hill H.), Petworth Rd, GU27 3BQ, E : 1 ½ m. on B 2131 ✏ 51251, Telex 858402, ≼, French rest., 🚗 – ℗. 🅰 🅰🅴 ⓞ 𝘝𝘐𝘚𝘈
closed Tuesday lunch, Monday and 21 to 31 December – M a la carte 15.50/20.75 st. 🍷 3.75.

XX Morels, 25 Lower St., GU27 2NY, ✏ 51462, French rest. – 🅰 🅰🅴 ⓞ 𝘝𝘐𝘚𝘈
closed Saturday lunch, Sunday, Monday, 3 weeks February-March and 3 weeks September-October – M 12.00/17.00 t. and a la carte 🍷 2.75.

X Shrimptons, 2 Grove Cottages, Midhurst Rd, Kingsley Green, GU27 3AL, SW : 1 ¼ m. on A 286 ✏ 3539 – 🅰 🅰🅴 ⓞ 𝘝𝘐𝘚𝘈
closed Sunday dinner, Monday, 26 December and 1 January – M a la carte 10.60/16.20 t. 🍷 4.00.

AUSTIN-ROVER Grayswood Rd ✏ 2303
FORD Farnham Lane ✏ 3222
PEUGEOT-TALBOT High St. ✏ 52552

VAUXHALL-OPEL West St. ✏ 3333
VW, AUDI Hindhead Rd ✏ 53811

HASSOP Derbs. – see Bakewell.

See : Norman Castle (ruins) ❋❋★★ *AC* BZ – Alexandra Park★ AY – White Rocks gardens ⩽★ ABZ – Public Museum and Art Gallery (Pottery★, Durbar Hall★) BZ **M.**

🔟 Beauport Park, St. Leonards, ✆ 52977, NW : 3 m. by B 2159 AY.

🅱 4 Robertson Terr. ✆ 424242 – The Fishmarket ✆ 425641 (summer only).

♦London 65 – ♦Brighton 37 – Folkestone 37 – Maidstone 34.

HASTINGS AND ST. LEONARDS

King's Road	....	**AZ** 22
London Road	....	**AZ**
Norman Road	....	**AZ**
Queen's Road	....	**BZ**
Robertson Street	....	**BZ** 27
Wellington Place	....	**BZ** 35

Bourne (The)	....	**BY** 4
Cambridge Gardens	....	**BZ** 5
Castle Street	....	**BZ** 7
Castle Hill Road	....	**BZ** 8
Cornwallis Gardens	....	**BZ** 9
Cornwallis Terrace	....	**BZ** 10
Denmark Place	....	**BZ** 13
Dorset Place	....	**BZ** 15
Gensing Road	....	**AZ** 16
George Street	....	**BY** 18

Grosvenor Crescent	....	**AY** 19
Harold Place	....	**BZ** 20
Marine Court	....	**AZ** 23
Rock-a-Nore Road	....	**BY** 30
St. Helen's Park Road	......	**BY** 31
Sedlescombe Road South	..	**AY** 32
Silchester Road	....	**AZ** 33
Warrior Square	....	**AZ** 34
Wellington Square	....	**BZ** 36
White Rock Road	....	**BZ** 38

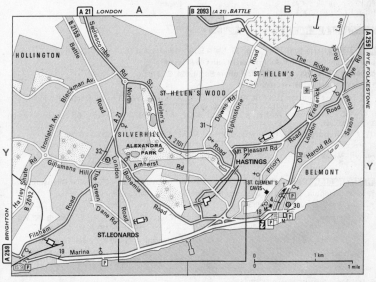

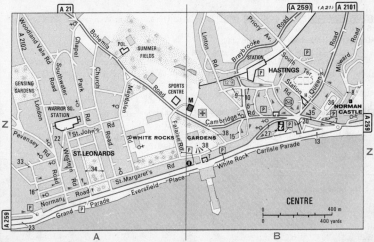

🏨 **Beauport Park** 🐦, Battle Rd, TN38 8EA, NW : 3 ½ m. at junction A 2100 and B 2159 ✆ 51222, Telex 957126, ≤, « Formal garden », 🏊 heated, park, 🎾 – ▤ rest 📺 🛁wc ☎ [P]. 🏇. [CB] [AE] [D] [VISA] on B 2159 AY
M 7.75/9.50 **t.** and a la carte 🍷2.75 – **23 rm** ☕ 35.00/48.00 **t.** – SB (weekends only) 49.90/55.90 **st.**

⌂ Chimes, 1 St. Matthews Gdns, Silverhill, TN38 0TS, ✆ 434041, 🌳 – 📺 🛁wc AY **a**
9 rm.

XX **Röser's,** 64 Eversfield Pl., TN37 6DB, ✆ 712218 – [CB] [AE] [D] [VISA] BZ **i**
closed Saturday lunch, Sunday and first 2 weeks January – **M** 7.75/9.25 **t.** and a la carte 🍷2.85.

X **Coach House,** 60a All Saints St., Old Town, TN34 3BN, ✆ 428080 – [CB] [AE] [VISA] BY **e**
closed Monday lunch – **M** 5.25 (lunch) and a la carte 7.30/10.80 🍷3.50.

AUSTIN-ROVER Sedlescombe Rd North ✆ 754444
CITROEN London Rd ✆ 427746
DAF, VOLVO 100 Battle Rd ✆ 423451
FIAT, COLT, LANCIA, MAZDA West Marina ✆ 433533
FORD Bohemia Rd ✆ 422727
NISSAN Bexhill Rd ✆ 431276
PEUGEOT, TALBOT Sedlescombe Rd North ✆ 440511
RENAULT 109/111 Sedlescombe Rd North ✆ 432982
VAUXHALL 36/39 Western Rd, St. Leonards ✆ 424545

HATCH BEAUCHAMP Somerset [403] K 30 – see Taunton.

HATFIELD Herts. [404] T 28 – pop. 33,174 – ECD : Monday and Thursday – ☎ 070 72.
See : Hatfield House★★★ *AC* (gardens★ and Old Palace★).
⛳18 Bedwell Park, Essendon ✆ 0707 (Potters Bar) 42624, E : 3 m.
♦London 27 – Bedford 38 – ♦Cambridge 39.

🏨 **Comet** (Embassy), 301 St. Albans Rd West, AL10 9RH, SW : 1 m. by A 1057 at junction with A 1 and A 414 ✆ 65411 – 📺 🛁wc ☎ [P]. [CB] [AE] [D] [VISA]. 🐕
M (carving rest.) 12.75 **st.** 🍷2.50 – ☕ 5.00 – **57 rm** 25.50/46.00 **st.** – SB (weekends only) 49.00 **st.**

XXX **Salisbury,** 15 The Broadway, Old Hatfield, AL9 5JB, ✆ 62220 – [CB] [AE] [D] [VISA]
closed Saturday lunch, Sunday dinner and Monday – **M** 10.50/18.00 **t.** and a la carte.

ALFA-ROMEO, HONDA, TALBOT, PEUGEOT By-Pass ✆ 64521
AUSTIN-ROVER 1 Great North Rd ✆ 64366
LANCIA 42 Beaconsfield Rd ✆ 71226

HATHERLEIGH Devon [403] H 31 – pop. 1,355 – ECD : Wednesday – ✉ ☎ 0837 Okehampton.
⛳18 at Okehampton, Tors Rd, ✆ 0837 (Okehampton) 2113, SE : 7 m.
♦London 230 – Exeter 29 – ♦Plymouth 38.

🏨 **George,** Market St., EX20 3JN, ✆ 810454, « 15C inn », 🏊 heated – 🛁wc 🚿wc [P]. [CB] [VISA]
M (bar lunch)/dinner a la carte 11.20/15.90 **t.** 🍷3.50 – ☕ 4.50 – **12 rm** 18.00/29.00 **t.**

at Sheepwash NW : 4 ½ m. by A 3072 – ✉ Beaworthy – ☎ 040 923 Black Torrington :

🏨 **Half Moon Inn,** The Square, EX21 5NE, ✆ 376, « 17C inn », 🐟 – 📺 🛁wc [P]. [CB] [VISA]
March-October – **M** (bar lunch)/dinner 9.00 **t.** 🍷2.60 – **14 rm** ☕ 17.50/38.00 **t.** – SB 50.00/59.00 **st.**

FORD The Industrial Estate ✆ 810661

HATHERSAGE Derbs. [402] [403] [404] P 24 – pop. 1,966 – ECD : Wednesday – ✉ Sheffield (South Yorks.) – ☎ 0433 Hope Valley.
♦London 165 – ♦Manchester 33 – ♦Sheffield 10.

🏨 **George,** Main Rd, S30 1BB, ✆ 50436 – 📺 🛁wc ☎ [P]. [CB] [AE] [D] [VISA]
M a la carte 7.85/15.60 **st.** – **18 rm** ☕ 35.00/47.50 **st.** – SB (weekends only) 51.00/55.00 **st.**

⌂ **Highlow Hall** 🐦, S30 1AX, S : 1 ½ m. by B 6001 on Abney Rd ✆ 50393, ≤, 🌳 – [P]
Easter-October – **6 rm** ☕ 16.00/24.00 **t.**

AUSTIN-ROVER Main Rd ✆ 50341

HAVANT Hants. [404] R 31 – pop. 50,098 – ECD : Wednesday – ☎ 0705.
♦London 70 – ♦Brighton 39 – ♦Portsmouth 9 – ♦Southampton 22.

🏨 **Bear,** 15 East St., PO9 1AA, ✆ 486501 – [lift] 📺 🛁wc 🚿wc ☎ [P]. 🏇. [CB] [AE] [D] [VISA]
M 6.75/8.75 **st.** and a la carte – **35 rm** ☕ 32.00/44.00 **t.** – SB (weekends only) 50.00 **st.**

FORD New Rd ✆ 482161

Ne confondez pas :

Confort des hôtels : 🏨🏨 ... 🏨, 🏨, ⌂
Confort des restaurants : XXXXX X
Qualité de la table : ✿✿✿, ✿✿, ✿, **M**

[HAVERFORDWEST] (HWLFFORDD) Dyfed [403] F 28 – pop. 13,572 – ECD : Thursday – ☎ 0437.
Envir. : SW : Martin's Haven ※★★ – St. Ann's Head★★ by Dale ←★.
[i] Pembrokeshire Coast National Park Centre, 40 High St. ☎ 3110 (summer only).
♦London 250 – Fishguard 15 – ♦Swansea 57.

- **Mariners,** Mariners Sq., SA61 2DU, ☎ 3353 – [TV] 🛁wc 🚿wc ☎ [P]. [S] [AE] [O] [VISA]
closed Christmas Night-29 December – **M** (bar lunch)/dinner 8.00 **st.** and a la carte 🍷 2.90 – **28 rm** ☕ 19.00/37.00 **st.** – SB (weekends only) 45.00 **st.**
- **Pembroke House,** 6 Spring Gdns, SA61 2EN, ☎ 3652 – [TV] 🛁wc 🚿wc ☎ [P]. [S] [AE] [O] [VISA]
M (bar lunch)/dinner 5.85 **t.** and a la carte 🍷 2.85 – **23 rm** ☕ 15.85/30.00 **t.** – SB 35.00/38.00 **st.**
- **Elliotts Hill** 🐦, Crow Hill Rd, SA62 6HT, NW : 1 ½ m. on B 4330 ☎ 2383, 🌳, 🎾 – [P]. [VISA]
M 6.50 **t.** (dinner) and a la carte 🍷 2.00 – **18 rm** ☕ 14.00/28.00 – SB (weekends only) (except mid July-mid September) 30.00/35.00 **st.**

AUSTIN-ROVER-DAIMLER-JAGUAR Salutation Sq. ☎ 4511
FORD Dew St. ☎ 3772
RENAULT Fishguard Rd ☎ 2468
SAAB Johnston ☎ 0437 (Johnston) 890 377
VAUXHALL-OPEL Bridgend Sq. ☎ 2717

[HAWES] North Yorks [402] N 21 – pop. 1,177 – ☎ 096 97.
[i] National Park Centre, Station Yard ☎ 450 (summer only).
♦London 253 – Kendal 27 – ♦Leeds 72 – ♦York 65.

- **Simonstone Hall** 🐦, Simonstone, DL8 3LY, N : 1 ½ m. on Muker rd ☎ 255, ←, « Country house atmosphere », 🌳 – 🛁wc [P]. [S] [O]
M (bar lunch)/dinner 10.95 **t.** 🍷 3.00 – **10 rm** ☕ 19.75/47.00 **t.** – SB (November-mid April) (except Easter, Christmas and New Year) 50.50/55.00 **st.**
- **Stone House** 🐦, Sedbusk, DL8 3PT, N : 1 m. by Muker rd on Askrigg rd ☎ 571, 🌳 – [TV] 🚿wc [P]. [VISA]
April-10 November, Christmas, New Year and weekends by arrangement in winter – **M** (dinner only) 8.95 **t.** 🍷 2.60 – **12 rm** ☕ 17.50/37.00 **t.**
- 🍴🍴 **Cockett's** with rm, Market Place, DL8 3RD, ☎ 312 – [TV] 🚿wc. [S] [VISA]. 🐕
Mid March-mid November and 2 weeks Christmas – **M** (dinner only)(booking essential) 14.50 **t.** 🍷 3.00 – **7 rm** ☕ 25.00/33.00 **t.**

[HAWKCHURCH] Devon [403] L 31 – see Axminster.

[HAWKHURST] Kent [404] V 30 – pop. 3,192 – ECD : Wednesday – ☎ 058 05.
Envir. : Bedgebury Pinetum★ *AC*, NW : 2 m.
⛳ High St. ☎ 2396.
♦London 47 – Folkestone 34 – Hastings 14 – Maidstone 19.

- **Tudor Arms** (Best Western), Rye Rd, TN18 5DA, E : 1 ½ m. on A 268 ☎ 2312, Telex 945003, ←, « Gardens » – [TV] 🛁wc 🚿wc [P]. [S] [AE] [O] [VISA]
M 7.50/8.00 **st.** and a la carte 🍷 3.00 – **13 rm** ☕ 19.00/46.00 **st.** – SB (weekends only except Easter) 45.00/62.00 **st.**
- 🍴🍴 **Osborn House,** Highgate, TN18 4AG, ☎ 3265 – [S] [AE] [VISA]
closed Sunday, Wednesday and January – **M** (dinner only) 20.00 **t.** and a la carte 11.10/13.25 **t.** 🍷 2.75.

AUSTIN-ROVER Horns Rd ☎ 2020
FORD Winchester Rd ☎ 3313
TALBOT, PEUGEOT Rye Rd ☎ 3151

[HAWKRIDGE] Somerset [403] J 30 – ✉ Dulverton – ☎ 064 385 Winsford.
♦London 203 – Exeter 32 – Minehead 17 – Taunton 32.

- **Tarr Steps** 🐦, TA22 9PY, NE : 1 ½ m. ☎ 293, ←, 🎣, 🌳, park – 🛁wc [P]. [AE] [VISA]
Mid March-mid November – **M** (bar lunch Monday to Saturday)/dinner 9.50 **t.** 🍷 2.00 – **15 rm** ☕ 19.50/41.50 **t.**

[HAWKSHEAD] Cumbria [402] L 20 – pop. 660 – ECD : Thursday – ✉ Ambleside – ☎ 096 66.
[i] Brown Cow Laithe ☎ 525 (summer only).
♦London 283 – ♦Carlisle 52 – Kendal 19.

- Tarn Hows 🐦, LA22 0PR, NW : 1 ½ m. on Ambleside rd ☎ 330, ←, 🏊 heated, 🌳, park, 🎾 – 🛁wc ☎ [P]
25 rm.
- **Highfield House** 🐦, Hawkshead Hill, LA22 0PN, W : ½ m. on B 5285 ☎ 344, ←, 🌳 – [TV] 🛁wc [P]
12 rm ☕ 12.00/28.00 **t.**

at Far Sawrey SE : 2 ½ m. on B 5285 – ✉ Ambleside – ☎ 096 62 Windermere :

- **West Vale,** LA22 0LQ, ☎ 2817, ← – 🚿wc [P]. 🐕
8 rm ☕ 10.00/23.00 **t.**

at Grizedale SW : 2 ¾ m. – ✉ Ambleside – ☎ 096 66 Hawkshead :

- **Ormandy** 🐦, LA22 0QH, ☎ 532 – 🚿wc [P]. 🐕
closed January and February – **M** *(closed Wednesday lunch)* (restricted lunch) (booking essential) a la carte 5.30/10.35 🍷 2.90 – **6 rm** ☕ 17.00/30.00 **st.**

HAWORTH West Yorks. 402 O 22 – pop. 5,041 – ECD : Tuesday – ⊠ Keighley – ☎ 0535.
See : Brontë Parsonage Museum★ *AC*.
🖪 2/4 West Lane ☎ 42329 – ◆London 213 – Burnley 22 – ◆Leeds 22 – ◆Manchester 34.

　🏦　**Old White Lion,** 6 West Lane, BD22 8DU, ☎ 42313 – ⇔wc �fflwc 🅿 🖪 Æ ⓸ VISA
　　　M *(closed Sunday dinner)* (bar lunch)/dinner 6.75 **t.** and a la carte ⓵ 3.45 – **11 rm**
　　　⊐ 17.50/31.00 **t.** – SB (weekends only) (except Bank Holidays) 31.75/34.75 **st.**

HAYDOCK Merseyside 402 403 404 M 23 – pop. 17,372 – ⊠ Newton-Le-Willows – ☎ 0942
Ashton-in-Makerfield.
◆London 198 – ◆Liverpool 17 – ◆Manchester 18.

　🏯　**Post House** (T.H.F.), Lodge Lane, WA12 0JG, NE : 1 m. on A 49 ☎ 717878, Telex 677672 – 🕍
　　　📺 ☎ ⅋ 🅿 ⬭ 🖪 Æ ⓸ VISA
　　　M 5.65/8.50 **st.** and a la carte ⓵ 2.70 – ⊐ 5.50 – **98 rm** 43.00/51.00 **st.**

HAYLING ISLAND Hants. 404 R 31 – pop. 12,410 – ECD : Wednesday – ☎ 0705.
🖪 32 Seafront ☎ 467111 (summer only) – ◆London 77 – ◆Brighton 45 – ◆Southampton 28.

　🏦　**Post House** (T.H.F.), Northney Rd, PO11 0NQ, ☎ 465011, Telex 86620, ≤, ⤬ heated – 📺
　　　⇔wc ☞ 🅿 ⬭ 🖪 Æ ⓸ VISA
　　　M 6.95/9.95 **st.** and a la carte ⓵ 2.70 – ⊐ 5.50 – **96 rm** 42.00/49.50 **st.**

　🏠　**Newtown House,** Manor Rd, PO11 0QR, ☎ 466131, ⤬ heated, ⤭, ⅋ – 📺 ⇔wc ⓯wc ☞
　　　🅿 🖪 Æ ⓸ VISA ⅌
　　　closed 24 December-2 January – **M** 6.25/8.00 **t.** and a la carte ⓵ 3.00 – **28 rm** ⊐ 30.00/50.00 **t.**
　　　– SB (weekends only) 50.00/55.00 **t.**

HAY-ON-WYE Powys 403 K 27 – pop. 1,578 – ECD : Tuesday – ☎ 0497.
🖪 Car Park ☎ 820144 (summer only) – ◆London 154 – Brecon 16 – Hereford 21 – Newport 62.

　🏠　**Old Black Lion,** 26 Lion St., HR3 5AD, ☎ 820841 – 📺 ⇔wc ⓯wc 🅿 🖪
　　　M a la carte 6.50/11.00 **t.** ⓵ 3.00 – **10 rm** ⊐ 13.90/33.90 **st.** – SB 48.90 **st.**

AUSTIN-ROVER Church St. ☎ 820404　　　　　　FORD Ford St. ☎ 820548

HEADLAM Durham – pop. 48 – ⊠ Gainford – ☎ 0325 Darlington.
◆London 247 – Middlesbrough 25 – ◆Newcastle-upon-Tyne 44.

　🏦　**Headlam Hall** ⑊, DL2 3HA, ☎ 730238, ≤, « Part Jacobean mansion », ⤭, park, ⅋ – 📺
　　　⇔wc ⓯wc ☎ 🅿 🖪 VISA
　　　closed 24 December-2 January – **M** *(closed Sunday dinner to non-residents)* (dinner only)
　　　14.50 **t.** and a la carte ⓵ 2.50 – **13 rm** ⊐ 30.00/55.00 **st.** – SB (weekends only) (October-July)
　　　45.00/65.00 **st.**

HEALD GREEN Greater Manchester 402 403 404 N 23 – see Manchester.

HEATHROW AIRPORT – see Hillingdon (Greater London).

HEDDONS MOUTH Devon 403 I 30 – see Lynton.

HELFORD Cornwall 403 E 33 – ⊠ Helston – ☎ 032 623 Manaccan.
◆London 324 – Falmouth 15 – Penzance 22 – Truro 27.

　XX　**Riverside** with rm, TR12 6JU, ☎ 443, ≤, « Converted cottages in picturesque setting », ⤭
　　　– 📺 ⇔wc 🅿
　　　Mid March-October – **M** *(closed lunch to non-residents)* (booking essential)/dinner 25.00 **st.**
　　　⓵ 4.00 – **6 rm** 40.00/65.00 **st.**

　　　at Gillan S : 3 m. – ⊠ Helston – ☎ 032 623 Manaccan :

　🏯　**Tregildry** ⑊, TR12 6HG, ☎ 378, ≤, ⤭ – 🅿 🖪 VISA
　　　Easter-mid October – **M** (bar lunch)/dinner 7.50 **t.** ⓵ 2.75 – **13 rm** ⊐ 17.50/45.00 **t.**

HELMSLEY North Yorks. 402 Q 21 – pop. 1,399 – ECD : Wednesday – ☎ 0439.
See : Castle★ (ruins 12C) *AC* – **Envir. :** Rievaulx Abbey★★ (ruins 12C-13C) *AC*, NW : 2 ½ m. –
Byland Abbey★ (ruins 12C) SW : 6 m. by Ampleforth.
🖪 9 Church St. ☎ 70401 – ◆London 234 – ◆Middlesbrough 29 – York 24.

　🏯　**Black Swan** (T.H.F.), Market Pl., YO6 5BJ, ☎ 70466, « 16C inn », ⤭ – 📺 🖪 Æ ⓸ VISA
　　　M 7.50/11.00 **st.** and a la carte ⓵ 2.70 – ⊐ 5.50 – **37 rm** 38.50/53.00 **st.**

　🏦　**Feversham Arms** (Best Western), 1 High St., YO6 5AG, ☎ 70766, ⤭, ⅋ – 📺 ⇔wc ☞
　　　🅿 ⬭ 🖪 Æ ⓸ VISA
　　　M (bar lunch Monday to Saturday)/dinner 10.00 **t.** and a la carte ⓵ 3.00 – **15 rm** ⊐ 34.00/44.00 **t.**
　　　– SB (except Easter, Christmas and Bank Holidays) 48.00/58.00 **st.**

　🏯　**Crown,** Market Sq., YO6 5BJ, ☎ 70297, ⤭ – ⓯wc ⇦ 🅿 🖪 VISA
　　　M 4.75/8.25 **t.** ⓵ 1.85 – **15 rm** ⊐ 18.00/40.00 **t.** – SB (mid October-mid May) (except Bank
　　　Holidays) 42.00/47.00 **st.**

　🏯　**Feathers,** Market Pl., YO6 5BH, ☎ 70275 – ⇔wc ⓯wc 🅿 🖪 Æ ⓸ VISA
　　　M 7.50/10.25 **st.** and a la carte ⓵ 2.85 – **18 rm** ⊐ 16.00/38.00 **st.** – SB (October-March)
　　　38.00/44.00 **st.**

at Beadlam E : 3 m. on A 170 – ⊠ York – ☻ 0439 Helmsley :

⌂ Omega Barn, High Lane, YO6 5SY, ℰ 71254 – 🎿 ℗. ℀ – **8 rm**.

at Nawton E : 3 ¼ m. on A 170 – ⊠ York – ☻ 0439 Helmsley :

⌂ **Plumpton Court,** High St., YO6 5TT, ℰ 71223, 🍴 – ℗. ℀
closed December and January – **6 rm** ⌑ 11.00/18.00 **st.**

at Nunnington SE : 6 ¼ m. by A 170 off B 1257 – ⊠ York – ☻ 043 95 Nunnington :

XX **Ryedale Lodge** ⌑ with rm, YO6 5XB, W : 1 m. ℰ 246, ≤, « Converted railway station »,
🗝, 🍴 – 📺 ⌑wc ☏ ℗. 🅂 𝒱𝒮𝒜. ℀
closed 1 to 21 January – **M** (dinner only) 15.75 **t.** ⌑ 3.25 – **7 rm** ⌑ 32.50/47.00 **t.** – SB (except
Bank Holidays) 65.00/70.00 **st.**

HEMEL HEMPSTEAD Herts. 🛤🛤 S 28 – pop. 80 ,110 – ECD : Wednesday – ☻ 0442.
🛤 Little Hay, Little Hay Farm, Bovington ℰ 833798 off A 41 at Box Lane.
🛈 Pavilion, Marlowes ℰ 64451 – ♦London 30 – Aylesbury 16 – Luton 10 – Northampton 46.

🏛 **Post House** (T.H.F.), Breakspear Way, HP2 4UA, E : 2 ½ m. by A 414 on A 4147 ℰ 51122,
Telex 826902, 🍴 – 🛗 📺 ⌑wc ☏ ℗. 🄰. 🅂 🅰🄴 ⑩ 𝒱𝒮𝒜
M 5.95/8.95 **st.** and a la carte ⌑ 2.70 – ⌑ 5.50 – **107 rm** 41.50/49.50 **st.**

X **Casanova,** 75 Waterhouse St., HP2 1AT, ℰ 47482, Italian rest. – 🅂 🅰🄴 ⑩ 𝒱𝒮𝒜
closed Saturday lunch, Sunday, 26 December and Bank Holidays – **M** a la carte 8.50/13.55 **t.**
⌑ 2.75.

at Bourne End W : 2 ¼ m. on A 41 – ⊠ Hemel Hempstead – ☻ 044 27 Berkhamsted :

🏛 **Hemel Hempstead Moat House** (Q.M.H.), London Rd, HP1 2RJ, ℰ 71241 – 📺 ⌑wc ☏
℗. 🄰. 🅂 🅰🄴 ⑩ 𝒱𝒮𝒜
M 7.25 **st.** and a la carte ⌑ 3.50 – **40 rm** ⌑ 35.75/42.50 **st.** – SB (weekends only) 48.00/59.00 **st.**

AUSTIN-ROVER-JAGUAR London Rd ℰ 42841   FORD Redbourne Rd ℰ 63013
BEDFORD, FIAT, VAUXHALL-OPEL Two Waters Rd   PEUGEOT-TALBOT High St. ℰ 54561
ℰ 51212   TOYOTA Queensway ℰ 51466

HENDY-GWYN = Whitland.

HENLADE Somerset – see Taunton.

HENLEY-IN-ARDEN Warw. 🛤🛤 O 27 – pop. 2 ,636 – ECD : Thursday – ☻ 056 42.
♦London 104 – ♦Birmingham 15 – Stratford-upon-Avon 8 – Warwick 8.5.

🏛 **Yew Trees,** 154 High St., B95 5BN, ⊠ Solihull ℰ 4636, Telex 334264, ⌸ heated, 🍴 – 📺
⌑wc ☏ ℗. 🅂 🅰🄴 ⑩ 𝒱𝒮𝒜
M a la carte 11.30/16.20 **t.** – **8 rm** ⌑ 35.00/68.00 **t.** – SB (weekends only) 56.00/74.00 **st.**

⌂ **Ashleigh House,** Whitley Hill, B95 5DL, E : 1 ¾ m. on B 4095 ℰ 2315, 🍴 – 📺 🎿wc ℗. ℀
8 rm ⌑ 13.00/35.00 **st.**

XX **Beaudesert,** Birmingham Rd, B95 5QR, ⊠ Solihull N : 1 m. on A 34 ℰ 2675 – ℗. 🅂 🅰🄴 ⑩
𝒱𝒮𝒜
closed Sunday dinner and Monday – **M** (dinner only and Sunday lunch)/dinner 11.00
t. and a la carte ⌑ 3.00.

XX **Le Filbert Cottage,** 64 High St., B95 5BX, ℰ 2700, French rest. – 🅂 🅰🄴 ⑩ 𝒱𝒮𝒜
closed Sunday, 26 December, 1 January and Bank Holidays – **M** 7.50/19.50 **t.** and a la carte
⌑ 2.20.

at Claverdon E : 3 m. on B 4095 – ⊠ Henley-in-Arden – ☻ 092 684 Claverdon :

🏛 Ardencote Country, Star Lane, CV35 8HW, N : ½ m. by Lyle Green ℰ 3111, 🗝, 🍴, ℀ – 📺
⌑wc ℗ – **5 rm**.

HENLEY-ON-THAMES Oxon. 🛤 R 29 – pop. 10 ,910 – ECD : Wednesday – ☻ 0491.
Envir. : Greys Court★ *AC*, NW : 2 ½ m. – 🛤 Huntercombe, Nuffield ℰ 641207, W : 6 m. on A 423.
🛈 Town Hall, Market Place ℰ 578034 – ♦London 40 – ♦Oxford 23 – Reading 9.

🏛 **Red Lion,** Hart St., RG9 2AR, ℰ 572161, ≤ – 📺 ⌑wc ☏ ℗. 🅂 🅰🄴 𝒱𝒮𝒜. ℀
M 7.50/8.00 **st.** and a la carte ⌑ 2.50 – **28 rm** ⌑ 25.00/60.00 **st.** – SB (weekends only)
(November-April) 55.00 **st.**

⌂ **Thamesmead House,** Remenham Lane, RG9 2LR, E : ½ m. by A 423 ℰ 574745 – 🎿wc ℗.
🅰🄴 ⑩ 𝒱𝒮𝒜
8 rm ⌑ 15.00/35.00 **st.**

XX **Flohr's** with rm, 15 Northfield End, RG9 2JG, ℰ 573412 – 🅂 🅰🄴 ⑩ 𝒱𝒮𝒜
M *(closed Sunday dinner)* a la carte 9.50/16.70 **st.** – **8 rm** ⌑ 21.50/39.50 **st.**

XX Gaylord Tandoori, 60 Bell St., RG9 2BN, ℰ 575157, Indian rest.

at Frieth (Bucks.) NE : 7 ½ m. by A 4155 – ⊠ Henley-on-Thames – ☻ 0494 High Wycombe :

X **Yew Tree,** RG9 6RJ, ℰ 882330 – ℗. 🅰🄴 ⑩ 𝒱𝒮𝒜
M (booking essential) 8.50/8.95 **t.** and a la carte.

BMW 49 Station Rd ℰ 577933   FIAT 66 Bell St. ℰ 573077

HENSTRIDGE Somerset [403] [404] M 31 – pop. 1,334 – ECD : Thursday – ✉ Templecombe – ☎ 0963 Stalbridge.

♦London 125 – Bournemouth 33 – Dorchester 20 – Salisbury 32 – Yeovil 11.

🏠 Keyham House 🐕, BA8 0QZ, ☎ 62253, 🌳 – 🚿wc 🅿
6 rm.

HEREFORD Heref. and Worc. [403] L 27 – pop. 48,277 – ECD : Thursday – ☎ 0432.

See : Cathedral★★ 12C-13C (the Mappa Mundi★ 13C) A **A** – The Old House★ 17C A **B**.

Envir. : Abbey Dore★ (12C-17C) SW : 12 m. by A 465 B.

⛳18 Herefordshire, Raven's Causeway, Wormsley ☎ 71219, NW : 6 m. by A 438 B.

ℹ Shirehall, 1a St. Owen St. ☎ 268430.

♦London 133 – ♦Birmingham 51 – ♦Cardiff 56.

HEREFORD

Broad Street .... A 7
Commercial Street ...... A 13
High Street .... A 19
High Town .... A 20

Bath Street .... A 2
Belmont Road .... B 5
Blue School Street ...... A 6
Castle Street .... A 9

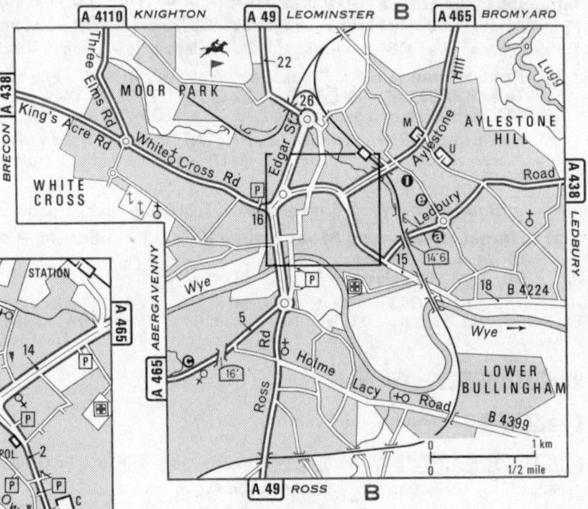

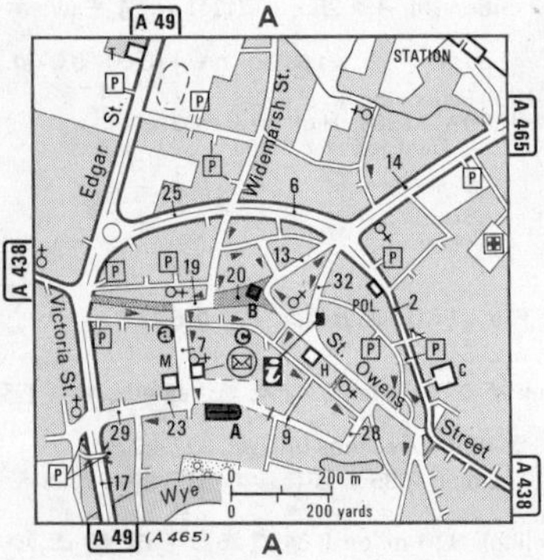

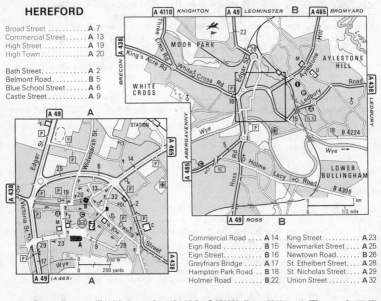

Commercial Road ..... A 14
Eign Road .... B 15
Eign Street .... B 16
Greyfriars Bridge ..... A 17
Hampton Park Road .. B 18
Holmer Road .... B 22
King Street .... A 23
Newmarket Street .... A 25
Newtown Road .... B 26
St. Ethelbert Street .... A 28
St. Nicholas Street .... A 29
Union Street .... A 32

🏨 **Green Dragon** (T.H.F.), Broad St., HR4 9BG, ☎ 272506, Telex 35491 – 🛗 📺 🚗. 🏛. [AE] [VISA] — A **a**
M 6.25/11.50 **st.** 🍷 2.70 – ☕ 5.50 – **88 rm** 37.50/45.00 **st.**, **1 suite**.

🏨 **Hereford Moat House** (Q.M.H.), Belmont Rd, HR2 7BP, SW : 1 ½ m. on A 465 ☎ 54301 – 📺 🛁wc ☎ ♿ 🅿. 🏛. [AE] [VISA] — B **c**
M *(closed lunch Saturday and Bank Holidays)* 6.00/8.00 **t.** and a la carte 🍷 4.00 – **32 rm** ☕ 36.00/46.00 **st.** – SB (weekends only) 50.00 **st.**

🏠 **Litchfield Lodge,** 32 Bodenham Rd, HR1 2TS, ☎ 273258 – 📺 🛁wc 🚿wc 🅿. [AE] [VISA]. 🐕 — B **e**
closed 1 week at Christmas – **M** *(closed Sunday)* (lunch by arrangement)/dinner a la carte 7.25/9.00 **st.** 🍷 3.50 – **11 rm** ☕ 18.00/33.00 **st.**

🏠 **Somerville,** 12 Bodenham Rd, HR1 2TS, ☎ 273991, 🌳 – 📺 🚿wc 🅿 — B **i**
10 rm ☕ 13.00/30.00 **st.**

🏠 **Ferncroft,** 144 Ledbury Rd, HR1 2TB, ☎ 265538, 🌳 – 📺 🚿wc 🅿. [VISA]. 🐕 — B **a**
closed mid December-mid January – **11 rm** ☕ 13.00/35.00 **st.**

🍴 **Effy's,** 96 East St., HR1 2LW, ☎ 59754 – [AE] [VISA] — A **c**
closed Sundays and Bank Holidays – **M** (buffet lunch in summer)/dinner 13.50 **t.** and a la carte 🍷 4.00.

at Lugwardine E : 2 ½ m. on A 438 – B – ✉ ☎ 0432 Hereford :

🏨 Newcourt Park 🐕, HR1 4DP, ☎ 850752, ⩤, « Country house atmosphere », 🌳 – 🛁wc 🅿
9 rm.

at Dormington E : 5 ¼ m. on A 438 – B – ✉ ☎ 0432 Hereford :

🏠 **Dormington Court,** HR1 4DA, ☎ 850370, 🏊, 🌳 – 📺 🅿. [AE] [VISA]
M 9.50 **st.** 🍷 2.75 – **6 rm** ☕ 15.00/24.00 **st.** – SB (except Easter, Christmas and Bank Holidays) 33.00/36.00 **st.**

at Much Birch S : 5 ½ m. on A 49 – B – ⊠ Hereford – 🕿 0981 Golden Valley :

🏠 **Pilgrim,** HR2 8HJ, on A 49 ⋒ 540742, 🛋 – 📺 ⌂wc ⋔wc ☎ 🅿. ☒ 🆎 ⓪ 𝘝𝘐𝘚𝘈
　　M 8.95 **t.** and a la carte ⓘ 2.95 – **15 rm** ⌸ 35.00/50.00 **t.** – SB (weekends only) 60.00 **st.**

ALFA ROMEO, SUBARU Conningsby St. ⋒ 253471	LANCIA, HYUNDAI Whitestone ⋒ 850464
AUSTIN-ROVER-DAIMLER-JAGUAR-LAND ROVER	NISSAN Muchgowarne ⋒ 053186 (Bosbury) 605
91/97 Widemarsh St. ⋒ 267611	PEUGEOT 101/105 St. Owen St. ⋒ 276268
AUSTIN-ROVER Callow G 92 ⋒ 273074	RELIANT Bridge St. ⋒ 272341
BEDFORD, OPEL-VAUXHALL Blackfriars St. ⋒	RENAULT Whitecross Rd ⋒ 272589
267441	SKODA ⋒ 272341
BMW White Cross Rd ⋒ 272589	TALBOT Blue School St. ⋒ 272354
CITROEN 38 St. Martin St. ⋒ 272545	TOYOTA Mill St. ⋒ 269255
DAF, LADA, SAAB Kings Acre Rd ⋒ 266974	VOLVO 14-15 Commercial Rd ⋒ 276275
FIAT Bath St. ⋒ 274134	VW, AUDI Harrow Rd ⋒ 59234
FORD Commercial Rd ⋒ 276494	

HERNE BAY Kent 🔢 X 29 – pop. 26 ,523 – ECD : Thursday – 🕿 0227.
Envir. : Reculver (church twin towers★ *AC*) E : 3 m.
🛈 William St. ⋒ 66031.
♦London 63 – ♦Dover 24 – Maidstone 32 – Margate 13.

　　✗ **L'Escargot,** 22 High St., CT6 5LH, ⋒ 372876 – ☒ 𝘝𝘐𝘚𝘈
　　　closed lunch Saturday and Bank Holidays – **M** 10.80 **t.** and a la carte ⓘ 2.50.

HERSTMONCEUX East Sussex 🔢 U 31 – pop. 2 ,246 – 🕿 032 181 (4 fig.) or 0323 (6 fig.).
See : Castle 15C (home of the Royal Greenwich Observatory) site and grounds★★ *AC*.
Envir. : Michelham Priory (site★) *AC*, SW : 6 m.
♦London 63 – Eastbourne 12 – Hastings 14 – Lewes 16.

　　✗✗ **Sundial,** Gardner St., BN27 4LA, ⋒ 832217, French rest., « Converted 16C cottage », 🛋 –
　　　🅿. 🆎 𝘝𝘐𝘚𝘈
　　　closed Sunday dinner, Monday, mid August-first week September and 25 December-20 January
　　　– **M** 9.50/13.50 **t.** and a la carte ⓘ 3.25.

　　at Boreham Street SE : 2 m. on A 271 – ⊠ 🕿 0323 Herstmonceux :

🏠 **White Friars** (Best Western), Boreham St., BN27 4SE, ⋒ 832355, 🛋 – 📺 ⌂wc ☎ 🅿. ☒
　　🆎 ⓪ 𝘝𝘐𝘚𝘈
　　closed 2 to 23 January – **M** (closed Sunday dinner and Monday to non-residents) 10.50
　　st. and a la carte – **22 rm** ⌸ 22.00/53.00 **st.** – SB 46.00/76.00 **st.**

AUSTIN-ROVER Boreham St. ⋒ 832353　　　　　　FIAT Cowbeech ⋒ 833321

HERTFORD Herts. 🔢 T 28 – pop. 21 ,350 – ECD : Thursday – 🕿 0992.
🛈 Vale House, 43 Cowbridge ⋒ Bishop' Stortford (0279) 55261 ext 487.
♦London 24 – ♦Cambridge 35 – Luton 26.

　　✗✗ **Marquee,** 1 Bircherley Green, SG14 1BN, ⋒ 558999, ⪡ – ☒ 🆎 ⓪ 𝘝𝘐𝘚𝘈
　　　closed Good Friday and Christmas Day – **M** 7.50 **t.** (lunch) and a la carte 11.50/23.00 **t.** ⓘ 3.50.

ALFA ROMEO Templefields Industrial Estate ⋒	PEUGEOT-TALBOT North Rd ⋒ 53044
Harlow (0279) 21215	VW, AUDI Wych Elm ⋒ 21461
AUSTIN-ROVER First Av. ⋒ Harlow (0279) 27541	

HERTINGFORDBURY Herts. 🔢 T 28 – pop. 658 – ⊠ 🕿 0992 Hertford.
♦London 26 – Luton 18.

🏠 **White Horse Inn** (T.H.F.), Hertingfordbury Rd, SG14 2LB, ⋒ 56791, 🛋 – 📺 ⌂wc ☎ 🅿.
　　☒ 🆎 ⓪ 𝘝𝘐𝘚𝘈
　　M 10.45/10.95 **st.** and a la carte ⓘ 2.70 – ⌸ 5.50 – **30 rm** 40.00/50.50 **st.**

HESWALL Merseyside 🔢 🔢 K 24 – pop. 31 ,037 – ECD : Wednesday – ⊠ Wirral – 🕿 051
Liverpool.
♦London 223 – Birkenhead 6.5 – Chester 12 – ♦Liverpool 9 – ♦Manchester 48.

　　✗✗ **Les Bougies,** 106 Telegraph Rd, L60 0AQ, ⋒ 342 6673 – 🅿. ☒ 🆎 𝘝𝘐𝘚𝘈
　　　closed Sunday, Monday, August, Christmas and Bank Holidays – **M** (dinner only)(booking
　　　essential) a la carte 9.35/12.65 **t.** ⓘ 2.30.

HETHERSETT Norfolk 🔢 X 26 – see Norwich.

HEVERSHAM Cumbria 🔢 L 21 – pop. 741 – ECD : Thursday and Saturday – ⊠ 🕿 044 82
Milnthorpe.
♦London 259 – Kendal 6 – Lancaster 15.

🏠 **Blue Bell,** The Princes' Way, LA7 7EF, on A 6 ⋒ 3159, 🛋 – 📺 ⌂wc ⋔wc 🅿. ☒ 🆎 𝘝𝘐𝘚𝘈
　　🌸
　　M (closed 25 and 26 December) 6.00/11.00 **st.** and a la carte – **28 rm** ⌸ 19.00/37.00 **st.** – SB
　　(October-June) 42.00/44.00 **st.**

HEXHAM Northumb. 401 402 N 19 − pop. 8 ,914 − ECD : Thursday − ⊙ 0434.

See : Abbey Church★ 13C − Envir. : Hadrian's Wall★★ with its forts and milecastles (Chesters Fort★, museum *AC*) NW : 5 ½ m. − Housesteads Fort★★, museum *AC*, NW : 14 m. − Derwent Reservoir (site★) SE : 7 m. − Vindolanda★ (fort and town) *AC*, NW : 14 ½ m.

🛏 Spital Park 𝒫 603072.

🛈 The Manor Office, Hallgate 𝒫 605225.

♦London 304 − ♦Carlisle 37 − ♦Newcastle-upon-Tyne 21.

🏠 **County,** Priestpopple, NE46 1PS, 𝒫 602030 − 📺 🛤wc. 🔼 🆎 𝑽𝑰𝑺𝑨
M 6.50/14.00 **t.** and a la carte ⌆ 2.70 − **10 rm** � 18.00/31.00 **s.** − SB (weekends only) (November-Easter) 40.00 **st.**

🏠 **Beaumont,** Beaumont St., NE46 3LT, 𝒫 602331 − 📺 🛤wc. 🔼 🆎 ⓪ 𝑽𝑰𝑺𝑨. ⟡
closed 25 December and 1 January − **M** 4.95/6.95 **t.** and a la carte ⌆ 2.25 − **22 rm** ⊳ districts 20.00/31.00 **st.** − SB (weekends only) (October-March) 42.00 **st.**

✗ **Pine Kitchen,** Battle Hill, NE46 1BB, 𝒫 606688 − 🔼 🆎 ⓪ 𝑽𝑰𝑺𝑨
closed 26 December and 6 to 12 January − **M** a la carte 5.20/14.80 **t.** ⌆ 2.95.

at Wall N : 4 m. on A 6079 − ✉ Hexham − ⊙ 043 481 Humshaugh :

🏠 **Hadrian,** NE46 4EE, 𝒫 232, 🚗 − 📺 🛏wc 🛤 ⓟ
M 6.50 **st.** (lunch) and a la carte 7.40/12.10 **st.** ⌆ 2.85 − **9 rm** districts 21.00/38.00 **st.** − SB 46.00 **st.**

AUSTIN-ROVER Alemouth Rd 𝒫 605151
FIAT Tyne Mills 𝒫 603013
FORD Priestpopple 𝒫 603516
MAZDA Tynemills 𝒫 605544
NISSAN Haugh Lane 𝒫 604527
RENAULT West Rd 𝒫 603861

SAAB 𝒫 602184
SUZUKI Priestpopple 𝒫 603615
VAUXHALL Parkwell 𝒫 602411
VOLVO Gilesgate 𝒫 605825
VW, AUDI Station Garage 𝒫 602170

HEYSHAM Lancs. 402 L 21 − ECD : Wednesday − ⊙ 0524.

⛴ to the Isle of Man : Douglas (Isle of Man Steam Packet Co.) summer 2-5 daily; winter 7-10 weekly (3 h 45 mn day) (7 h 5 mn night). − Lancaster 8.

♦London 251 − ♦Blackpool 33 − ♦Carlisle 74 − Lancaster 8.

↟ **Carr Garth,** 18 Bailey Lane, LA3 2PS, 𝒫 51175, 🚗 − ⓟ
Easter-October − **10 rm** districts 9.00/16.00.

HIGHAM Derbs. 402 403 404 P 24 − pop. 4 ,803 (inc. Shirland) − ✉ ⊙ 0773 Alfreton.

♦London 147 − Derby 16 − ♦Nottingham 20 − ♦Sheffield 20.

🏠 Higham Farm, Main Rd, DE5 6EH, on B 6013 𝒫 833812, ⚲ − 📺 🛏wc 🛤wc ☎ ⓟ − **12 rm**.

HIGH EASTER Essex 404 V 28 − see Chelmsford.

HIGHWORTH Wilts. 403 404 0 29 − pop. 8 ,020 − ⊙ 0367 Faringdon.

♦London 88 − Gloucester 33 − ♦Oxford 25 − Swindon 5.

✗✗ **Inglesham Forge,** SN4 7QY, N : 2 ½ m. on A 361 𝒫 52298 − ⓟ. 🔼 🆎 ⓪ 𝑽𝑰𝑺𝑨
closed lunch Monday and Saturday, Sunday, last 2 weeks August, 25 to 30 December and Bank Holidays − **M** a la carte 10.55/17.10 **t.** ⌆ 3.10.

HIGH WYCOMBE Bucks. 404 R 29 − pop. 69 ,575 − ECD : Wednesday − ⊙ 0494.

Envir. : Hughenden Manor★ (site★, Disraeli Museum) *AC*, N : 1 m. − West Wycombe (Manor House★ 18C, *AC*, St. Lawrence's Church : from the tower 74 steps, *AC*, ✳★) NW : 2 ½ m.

🛈 Council Offices, Queen Victoria Rd 𝒫 26100.

♦London 34 − Aylesbury 17 − ♦Oxford 26 − Reading 18.

🏨 **Crest** (Crest), Crest Rd, HP11 1TL, SW : 1 ½ m. by A 404 𝒫 442100, Telex 83626 − 📺 🛏wc ☎ ⅋ ⓟ. 🏋 🔼 🆎 ⓪ 𝑽𝑰𝑺𝑨. ⟡
M approx. 11.50 **st.** − districts 5.25 − **108 rm** 52.00/62.00 **st.** − SB (weekends only) 55.00 **st.**

MICHELIN Branch, Thomas Rd, Wooburn Green, HP10 0PE, 𝒫 06285 (Bourne End) 27472

TOYOTA Littleworth Rd, Downley 𝒫 35811
VAUXHALL-OPEL London Rd 𝒫 30021

VAUXHALL-OPEL West Wycombe Rd 𝒫 32545

HINDHEAD Surrey 404 R 30 − pop. 6 ,174 − ECD : Wednesday − ⊙ 042 873.

See : Devil's Punch Bowl (✳★).

♦London 46 − Guildford 12 − ♦Portsmouth 28.

🏠 **Hindhead Motor** (Best Western) without rest., GU26 6TF, on A 3 Portsmouth Rd 𝒫 6666 − 📺 🛏wc ☎ ⓟ. 🏋 🔼 🆎 ⓪ 𝑽𝑰𝑺𝑨
districts 2.95 − **16 rm** 25.00/36.00 **t.**

HINDON Wilts. 403 404 N 30 − pop. 489 − ECD : Saturday − ✉ Salisbury − ⊙ 074 789.

♦London 107 − Bath 28 − Bournemouth 40 − Salisbury 15.

🏠 **Lamb at Hindon,** SP3 6DP, 𝒫 225, 🚗 − 🛏wc ⓟ. 🔼
closed 25 and 26 December − **M** 8.00/10.50 **t.** ⌆ 3.00 − **16 rm** districts 16.00/48.00 **st.** − SB (November-March) (except Easter, Christmas and New Year) 37.80/41.40 **st.**

212

HINTLESHAM Suffolk ⁴⁰⁴ X 27 – pop. 554 – ✪ 047 387.
♦London 76 – Colchester 18 – ♦Ipswich 5.

XXX **Hintlesham Hall** 🍃 with rm, IP8 3NS, ℰ 268, ≤, « Georgian country house with 16C origins », 🐾, park, ℀ – 📺 🅿 🛎 🔼 ⚠ ⓞ 𝐕𝐈𝐒𝐀. ℀
M (closed Saturday lunch) 13.50/20.00 st. and a la carte ⓐ 3.95 – ☲ 3.00 – **10 rm** 38.00/95.00 st. – SB (October-June) 65.00/100.00 st.

HITCHIN Herts. ⁴⁰⁴ T 28 – pop. 33,480 – ECD : Wednesday – ✪ 0462.
🅱 Library, Paynes Park ℰ 34738 and 50133 – ♦London 40 – Bedford 14 – ♦Cambridge 26 – Luton 9.

🏛 **Sun**, Sun St., SG5 1AF, ℰ 36411 – 📺 ☐wc 🅿 🛎 🔼 ⚠ ⓞ 𝐕𝐈𝐒𝐀. ℀
M (carving rest.) 5.25 t. ⓐ 2.85 – **32 rm** ☲ 23.50/43.50 t.

⌂ **Lord Lister**, Park St., SG4 9AH, ℰ 32712 – 📺 🛏 🅿 🔼 ⚠ ⓞ 𝐕𝐈𝐒𝐀. ℀
15 rm ☲ 20.00/40.00 t.

at Little Wymondley SE : 2 ½ m. on A 602 – ✉ Hitchin – ✪ 0438 Stevenage :

🏛 **Blakemore**, SG4 7JJ, ℰ 355821, Telex 825479, ☐ heated, 🐾 – 🛎 📺 ☐wc ☎ 🅿 🔼 ⚠ ⓞ 𝐕𝐈𝐒𝐀. ℀
M 8.00 t. and a la carte ⓐ 3.00 – **70 rm** ☲ 35.00/45.00 t. – SB (weekends only) 70.00/80.00 st.

XX **Redcoats Farmhouse** 🍃 with rm, Redcoats Green, SG4 7JL, S : ½ m. by A 602 ℰ 729500, Telex 83343, 🐾 – 📺 🛏wc 🅿 🔼 ⚠ ⓞ 𝐕𝐈𝐒𝐀. ℀
closed 1 week Christmas – **M** (closed Sunday and Bank Holidays) 16.50 t. and a la carte 12.75/17.25 t. ⓐ 2.75 – **10 rm** ☲ 18.50/45.00 t. – SB (weekends only) 55.00/60.00 st.

AUSTIN-ROVER Queen St. ℰ 50311   CITROEN High St., Graveley ℰ 0438 (Stevenage) 316177

HOLFORD Somerset ⁴⁰³ K 30 – pop. 266 – ✉ Bridgwater – ✪ 027 874.
Envir. : Stogursey Priory Church★★, W : 4 ½ m. – ♦London 171 – ♦Bristol 48 – Minehead 15 – Taunton 22.

🏛 **Combe House** 🍃, TA5 1RZ, SW : 1 m. ℰ 382, « Country house atmosphere », 🔼, 🐾, ℀ – 📺 ☐wc 🅿 🔼 ⚠ 𝐕𝐈𝐒𝐀
February-October – **M** (bar lunch)/dinner 8.00 t. ⓐ 2.90 – **16 rm** ☲ 16.50/35.00 t. – SB (October-April) (except Bank Holidays) 38.00/41.50 st.

🏛 **Alfoxton Park** 🍃, TA5 1SG, W : 1 ½ m. ℰ 211, ≤, ☐ heated, 🐾, park, ℀ – 📺 ☐wc 🅿. ℀
18 rm.

HOLMES CHAPEL Cheshire ⁴⁰² ⁴⁰³ ⁴⁰⁴ M 24 – pop. 4,672 – ✉ Crewe – ✪ 0477.
♦London 181 – Chester 25 – ♦Liverpool 41 – ♦Manchester 24 – ♦Stoke-on-Trent 20.

🏛 **Holly Lodge**, 70 London Rd, CW4 7AS, on A 50 ℰ 37033 – 📺 ☐wc ☎ 🖐 🅿 🔼 ⚠ ⓞ 𝐕𝐈𝐒𝐀
M (closed Saturday lunch and Sunday dinner) 4.75/8.50 t. and a la carte ⓐ 2.60 – **33 rm** ☲ 16.00/36.00 t. – SB (weekends only) 46.50 st.

🏛 **Old Vicarage**, Knutsford Rd, Cranage, CW4 8EF, NW : ½ m. on A 50 ℰ 32041 – 📺 ☐wc ☎ 🅿 🔼 ⚠ ⓞ 𝐕𝐈𝐒𝐀. ℀
M 7.50/9.50 t. and a la carte ⓐ 3.80 – **8 rm** ☲ 36.50/46.00 t. – SB (weekends only) 42.00/79.50 st.

at Twemlow Green NE : 1 ¾ m. on A 535 – ✉ ✪ 0477 Holmes Chapel :

XXX **Yellow Broom**, Macclesfield Rd, CW4 8BL, ℰ 33289 – 🅿 🔼 ⚠ 𝐕𝐈𝐒𝐀
closed Sunday dinner, Monday and first 2 weeks August – **M** (dinner only and Sunday lunch) (booking essential) 15.00 t. ⓐ 2.50.

at Brereton SE : 2 m. on A 50 – ✉ Sandbach – ✪ 0477 Holmes Chapel :

🏛 **Bear's Head**, Newcastle Rd, CW11 9RS, ℰ 35251, 🐾, ℀ – 📺 ☐wc 🛏wc ☎ 🅿 🔼 ⚠ ⓞ 𝐕𝐈𝐒𝐀. ℀
M (closed Sunday dinner to non-residents and Bank Holidays) 6.45/10.50 t. and a la carte ⓐ 3.50 – **21 rm** ☲ 30.50/39.50 st. – SB (weekends only) 48.00 st.

HOLT Norfolk ⁴⁰⁴ X 25 – pop. 2,502 – ECD : Thursday – ✪ 026 371.
♦London 124 – King's Lynn 34 – ♦Norwich 22.

⌂ **Lawns**, 26 Station Rd, NR25 6BS, ℰ 3390, 🐾 – 🅿
10 rm ☲ 12.00/30.00.

at Thornage SW : 2 ¾ m. on B 1110 – ✉ Holt – ✪ 0263 Melton Constable :

X **Black Boys** with rm, NR25 7QG, ℰ 861218 – ☐wc 🅿 🔼 ⚠ 𝐕𝐈𝐒𝐀. ℀
March-November – **M** (closed Sunday and Monday) (dinner only) a la carte 11.45/14.50 t. ⓐ 3.00 – **2 rm** ☲ 28.00/44.00 st. – SB 60.00/65.00 st.

HOLYHEAD (CAERGYBI) Gwynedd ⁴⁰² ⁴⁰³ G 24 – pop. 12,569 – ECD : Tuesday – ✪ 0407.
Envir. : South Stack (cliffs★) W : 3 ½ m. – Rhosneigr (site★) SE : 13 m.
⛴ to Ireland (Dun Laoghaire) (Sealink) summer 2-4 daily; winter 2 daily (3 h 30 mn) – to Ireland (Dublin) (B & I Line) 1-2 daily (3 h 30 mn).
🅱 Marine Sq., Salt Island Approach ℰ 2622 (summer only).
♦London 269 – Birkenhead 94 – ♦Cardiff 215 – Chester 88 – Shrewsbury 105 – ♦Swansea 190.

Hotel see : Trearddur Bay S : 2 ½ m.

HOLY ISLAND Northumb. 401 402 O 16 – pop. 190 – ✪ 0289 Berwick-upon-Tweed.
See : Castle (16C) ≤★★ AC – Priory★ (ruins 12C) AC.
♦London 342 – Berwick-upon-Tweed 13 – ♦Newcastle-upon-Tyne 59.

   Hotels see : Berwick-upon-Tweed NW : 13 m.

HOLYWELL (TREFFYNNON) Clwyd 402 403 K 24 – pop. 11 ,101 – ECD : Wednesday – ✪ 0352.
🛈 Little Chef Services, A 55 ✆ 780144 (summer only).
♦London 217 – Chester 19 – ♦Liverpool 34.

   🏠 **Stamford Gate,** Halkyn Rd, CH8 7SJ, ✆ 712942 – 📺 🖵wc 🅿. 🔼 🗚🖃 ⓞ �. 🛠
   M 4.50/6.50 **t.** and a la carte 🍴 2.60 – **12 rm** ⊇ 20.00/32.00 **st.**

HONITON Devon 403 K 31 The West Country G. – pop. 6 ,490 – ECD : Thursday – ✪ 0404.
See : All Hallows Museum★AC – Envir. : Farway Countryside Park (≤★) AC, S : 3 m.
🛈 Angel Hotel car park, High St. ✆ 3716 (summer only).
♦London 186 – Exeter 17 – ♦Southampton 93 – Taunton 18.

   🏠 **Deer Park** ⟨, EX14 0PG, ✆ 2064, ≤, 🏊 heated, 🐾, 🎿, park, 🎾, squash – 🍽 rest 📺
   🖵wc ☎ 🅿. 🖧 🔼 🗚🖃 ⓞ �CСА. 🛠
   M 6.00/13.00 **st.** and a la carte 🍴 3.50 – **31 rm** ⊇ 27.50/70.00 **st.** – SB (weekends only)
   60.00/70.00 **st.**

   at Stockland NE : 8 ½ m. by A 30 – pop. 6 ,627 – ⊠ Honiton – ✪ 040 486 Upottery :

   🏠 **Snodwell Farm** ⟨, Stockland Hill, EX14 9HZ, ✆ 263, 🏊, 🎿, – 🖵wc 🖩🅿. �CСА. 🛠
   M *(closed Sunday dinner and Monday to non-residents)* (bar lunch)/dinner 8.00 **t.** and a la
   carte 🍴 2.00 – **11 rm** ⊇ 20.00/30.00 **st.** – SB 60.00 **st.**

   at Wilmington E : 3 ½ m. on A 35 – ⊠ Honiton – ✪ 040 483 Wilmington :

   🏠 **Home Farm,** EX14 9JR, on A 35 ✆ 278, « Converted 16C thatched farm house », 🎿 –
   🖵wc 🅿. 🔼 �CСА.
   closed January-7 March and 28 to 31 December – **M** 6.75/9.50 **st.** and a la carte 🍴 2.75 – **14 rm**
   ⊇ 16.00/37.00 **st.** – SB 42.00/55.00 **st.**

HOOK Hants. 404 R 30 – pop. 2 ,562 – ECD : Wednesday – ✪ 025 672.
♦London 47 – Reading 13 – ♦Southampton 35.

   ⌂ **Oaklea,** London Rd, RG27 9LA, ✆ 2673, 🎿 – 🅿
   10 rm ⊇ 16.50/33.00 **st.**

   at Rotherwick NW : 2 m. by A 32 – ⊠ Basingstoke – ✪ 025 072 Hook :

   🏰 **Tylney Hall** ⟨, RG27 9AJ, S : 1 m. ✆ 4881, Telex 859864, « 19C mansion in extensive
   gardens », park, 🎾 – 🛎 📺 ☎ 🅿. 🖧 🔼 🗚🖃 ⓞ �CСА. 🛠
   M 12.00/17.00 **st.** and a la carte 🍴 4.50 – **37 rm** ⊇ 61.00/110.00 **st.**. **8 suites** 154.00/187.00 **st.** –
   SB (weekends only) 90.00/140.00 **st.**

HOPE COVE Devon 403 I 33 – see Salcombe.

HOPTON WAFERS Salop 403 404 M 26 – pop. 948 – ⊠ Kidderminster – ✪ 0299 Cleobury
Mortimer.
♦London 150 – ♦Birmingham 32 – Shrewsbury 38.

   ✗ **Crown Inn,** DY14 0NB, on A 4117 ✆ 270372 – 🅿. 🔼 �CСА.
   closed Sunday dinner and Monday except Bank Holidays – **M** 11.00 **t.** and a la carte
   11.00/13.50 **t.** 🍴 2.70.

HORLEY Surrey 404 T 30 – pop. 17 ,700 – ECD : Wednesday – ✪ 029 34 (4 and 5 fig.) or 0293
(6 fig.).
♦London 27 – ♦Brighton 26 – Royal Tunbridge Wells 22.

Plan : see Gatwick

   🏰 **Chequers Thistle** (Thistle), Brighton Rd, RH6 8PH, ✆ 786992, Telex 877550, 🏊 heated – 📺
   🖵wc ☎ 🕭 🅿. 🖧 🔼 🗚🖃 ⓞ �CСА
   M 7.25/9.50 **t.** and a la carte 🍴 3.00 – ⊇ 5.25 – **78 rm** 44.00/56.00 **t.**   Y z

AUSTIN-ROVER Massetts Rd ✆ 5176   RENAULT 61 Brighton Rd ✆ 72566
FORD Hookwood Rd ✆ 2257
PEUGEOT Keppers Corner, Burstow ✆ 0342 (Cop-
thorne) 712017

HORNBY Lancs. 402 M 21 – pop. 1 ,808 – ✪ 0468.
♦London 257 – Kendal 20 – Lancaster 9.

   🏛 **Castle,** Main St., LA2 8JT, ✆ 21204 – 📺 🖵wc 🖩wc 🅿. 🔼 �CСА. 🛠
   M (bar lunch)/dinner 10.00 **t.** and a la carte 🍴 2.50 – **12 rm** ⊇ 16.00/35.00 **t.** – SB (except
   Christmas and Bank Holidays) 75.00/85.00 **st.**

214

HORNCASTLE Lincs. 402 404 T 24 – pop. 4,194 – ECD : Wednesday – ✆ 065 82.
♦London 140 – Lincoln 21.

  XX **Magpies,** 73 East St., LN9 6AA, on A 158 ✆ 7004 – ◪
    closed Sunday dinner and Monday – **M** (lunch by arrangement Tuesday to Saturday)
    6.50/12.00 **t.** ⌀ 3.20.

AUSTIN-ROVER Spilsby Rd ✆ 2391   LANCIA Lincoln Rd ✆ 7667

HORNING Norfolk 404 Y 25 – pop. 1,033 – ECD : Wednesday – ✉ Norwich – ✆ 0692.
♦London 122 – Great Yarmouth 17 – ♦Norwich 11.

  🏨 **Petersfield House** ⌂, Lower St., NR12 8PF, ✆ 630741, ☞ – TV ⌷wc ☎ Ⓟ. ◪ 🅐🅔 ①
    VISA
    M 7.00/9.00 **t.** and a la carte ⌀ 2.95 – **16 rm** ⊐ 24.00/38.00 **t.** – SB 53.00 **st.**

HORNS CROSS Devon 403 H 31 – ECD : Wednesday – ✉ Bideford – ✆ 023 75.
♦London 237 – Barnstaple 15 – Exeter 48.

  🏨 **Foxdown Manor** ⌂, Foxdown, EX39 5PJ, S : 1 m. ✆ 325, ≤, « Country house atmosphere »,
    ⬱ heated, ☞, park, ❦ – TV ⌷wc �🌡wc ☎. ◪ 🅐🅔 **VISA**
    closed January and February – **M** 5.50/9.75 **t.** and a la carte ⌀ 2.75 – **7 rm** ⊐ 15.25/49.00 **t.** –
    SB 50.00/60.00 **st.**

  🏠 **Hoops Inn,** EX39 5DJ, W : ¾ m. on A 39 ✆ 222, ☞ – TV ⌷wc ☎ Ⓟ
    M (bar lunch)/dinner 8.75 **t.** and a la carte ⌀ 2.75 – **14 rm** ⊐ 13.50/35.00 **t.** – SB (November-
    March) 44.00 **st.**

HORSFORTH West Yorks. 402 P 22 – see Leeds.

HORSHAM West Sussex 404 T 30 – pop. 38,356 – ECD : Monday and Thursday – ✆ 0403.
♦London 39 – ♦Brighton 23 – Guildford 20 – Lewes 25 – Worthing 20.

  🏠 **Ye Olde King's Head,** 35 Carfax, RH12 1EG, ✆ 53126 – TV ⌷wc �🌡wc ☎ Ⓟ. ◪ 🅐🅔 **VISA**
    M 6.00/8.50 **t.** ⌀ 2.25 – **41 rm** ⊐ 31.00/49.00 **t.** – SB (weekends only) 48.00 **st.**

  at Lower Beeding SE : 3 ½ m. on A 281 – ✉ Horsham – ✆ 040 376 Lower Beeding :

  🏨🏨 **South Lodge** ⌂, Brighton Rd, RH13 6PS, on A 281 ✆ 711, Telex 877765, ≤, ❦, ☞, park,
    ❦ – TV ☎ Ⓟ. ◪ 🅐🅔 ① **VISA**
    M 11.75/22.50 **t.** and a la carte ⌀ 3.60 – ⊐ 5.00 – **25 rm** 49.00/85.00 **t.**, **2 suites** 125.00 **t.** – SB
    (weekends only) 99.00 **st.**

  XXX **Cisswood House** with rm, Sandygate Lane, RH13 6NF, ✆ 216, ☞ – TV ⌷wc ☎ Ⓟ. ◪ 🅐🅔
    ① **VISA**. ❦
    closed Christmas and New Year – **M** *(closed Saturday lunch, Sunday and Monday to non-
    residents)* a la carte 12.05/14.40 **t.** ⌀ 3.25 – ⊐ 4.00 – **8 rm** 35.00/50.00 **st.**

AUSTIN-ROVER Springfield Rd ✆ 54311   TOYOTA Slinfold ✆ 790766
CITROEN Guildford Rd ✆ 61393   VAUXHALL-OPEL, VW, AUDI Plummers Plain ✆
FIAT Brighton Rd ✆ 65637   76466
FORD The Bishopric ✆ 54331   VAUXHALL-OPEL Broadbridge Heath ✆ 56464
PEUGEOT-TALBOT North St. ✆ 62655   VOLVO Guildford Rd ✆ 56381
RENAULT 108 Crawley Rd ✆ 61146

HORSHAM ST. FAITH Norfolk 404 X 25 – see Norwich.

HORTON Dorset 403 404 O 31 – see Wimborne Minster.

HORTON Northants. 404 R 27 – ✉ ✆ 0604 Northampton.
♦London 66 – Bedford 18 – Northampton 6.

  XX **French Partridge,** Newport Pagnell Rd, NN7 2AP, ✆ 870033 – Ⓟ
    closed Sunday, Monday, 2 weeks Easter, mid July-first week August and 2 weeks at Christmas
    – **M** (dinner only) (booking essential) 15.00 **st.** ⌀ 3.20.

HORTON-CUM-STUDLEY Oxon. 403 404 Q 28 – ECD : Wednesday – ✉ Oxford – ✆ 086 735
Stanton St. John – ♦London 57 – Aylesbury 23 – ♦Oxford 7.

  🏨 **Studley Priory** ⌂, OX9 1AZ, ✆ 203, « Converted priory in park », ☞, ❦ – TV ⌷wc
    ⌷wc ☎ Ⓟ. ⌂. ◪ 🅐🅔 ① **VISA**. ❦
    closed 2 to 17 January – **M** 12.00 **st.** and a la carte ⌀ 3.25 – **19 rm** ⊐ 40.00/88.00 **st.** – SB
    (October-April) 80.00/100.00 **st.**

HOUGHTON CONQUEST Beds. 404 S 27 – see Bedford.

HOVE East Sussex 404 T 31 – see Brighton and Hove.

HOVINGHAM North Yorks. 402 R 21 – pop. 310 – ECD : Thursday – ✉ York – ✆ 065 382.
♦London 235 – ♦Middlesbrough 36 – York 25.

  🏨 **Worsley Arms,** YO6 4LA, ✆ 234, ☞ – ⌷wc ⇦ Ⓟ. ◪ **VISA**
    closed 24 to 26 December – **M** 9.00/12.00 **t.** ⌀ 2.50 – ⊐ 5.00 – **14 rm** 24.00/44.50 **t.** – SB
    (November-March) (except Easter, Christmas and New Year) 55.00/70.00 **st.**

HOWDEN Humberside 402 R 22 – pop. 3,227 – ECD : Thursday – ✆ 0430.
See : St. Peter's Church★ 12C-14C.
◆London 196 – ◆Kingston-upon-Hull 23 – ◆Leeds 37 – York 22.

　🏠 **Bowmans**, Bridgegate, DN14 7JG, ℰ 30805 – 📺 ➡wc 📻 🅿. 🔙 AE ⓞ VISA. ⋇
　　M *(closed Saturday lunch and Sunday dinner)* 8.60 **t.** and a la carte ⑃ 3.60 – **13 rm**
　　⊊ 26.05/42.00 **t.**

HOWEY Powys – see Llandrindod Wells.

HOWTOWN Cumbria – see Ullswater.

HUDDERSFIELD West Yorks. 402 404 O 23 – pop. 147,825 – ECD : Wednesday – ✆ 0484.
🏌 Thick Hollins Hall, Meltham ℰ 850227, SW : 5 m. – 🏌 Bradley Park, off Bradley Rd ℰ 39988
– 🏌 Longley Park, Maple St., off Somerset Rd ℰ 22304.
🖪 3-5 Albion St. ℰ 22133 ext 313/685 and 32177 (Saturday only).
◆London 191 – Bradford 11 – ◆Leeds 15 – ◆Manchester 25 – ◆Sheffield 26.

　🏛 **Ladbroke** (Ladbroke), Ainley Top, HD3 3RH, NW : 2 ½ m. at junction A 629 and A 640
　　ℰ 0422 (Elland) 75431, Telex 517346 – 🛗 🗏 rest 📺 ☎ 🅿. 🔙 – **119 rm**.

　🏦 **George** (T.H.F.), St. George's Sq., HD1 1JA, ℰ 25444 – 🛗 📺 ➡wc 📻 🅿. 🔙 AE ⓞ VISA
　　M 7.25/10.00 **st.** and a la carte ⑃ 2.70 – ⊊ 5.50 – **62 rm** 35.50/40.00 **st.**

　🏠 **Cote Royd**, 7 Halifax Rd, HD3 3AN, ℰ 547588, 🔲, ⋇ – 📺 ➡wc 🍴wc ☎ 🅿. 🔙 AE ⓞ
　　VISA. ⋇
　　closed 25 December-1 January – **M** *(closed dinner Friday, Saturday and Sunday)* (dinner only)
　　(residents only) 8.50 **st.** and a la carte ⑃ 3.00 – **21 rm** ⊊ 29.50/38.00 **st.**

　🏠 **Huddersfield**, 37-47 Kirkgate, HD1 1QT, ℰ 512111 – 🛗 📺 ➡wc 🍴wc ☎. 🔙 AE ⓞ VISA
　　M (restricted lunch Saturday and Sunday) 3.50/6.50 **st.** and a la carte ⑃ 3.00 – **21 rm**
　　⊊ 21.50/39.00 **st., 1 suite** 33.00/60.00 **st.**

　✗✗ Shabab, 37-39 New St., HD1 2BG, ℰ 49514, Indian rest..

　at Golcar W : 3 ½ m. by A 62 on B 6111 – ✉ ✆ 0484 Huddersfield :

　✗ **Weaver's Shed**, Knowl Rd, HD7 4AN, via Scar Lane ℰ 654284, « Converted 18C woollen
　　mill » – 🅿
　　closed Saturday lunch, Sunday dinner, Monday, first 2 weeks January and last 2 weeks July –
　　M a la carte 10.00/12.95 **t.** ⑃ 2.90.

　at Outlane NW : 4 m. on A 640 – ✉ Huddersfield – ✆ 0422 Elland :

　🏦 **Old Golf House**, New Hey Rd, HD3 3YP, ℰ 79311 – 📺 ➡wc 📻 🅿. 🔙 AE ⓞ VISA. ⋇
　　closed Christmas Day – **M** *(closed Saturday lunch)* 7.30/9.70 **t.** and a la carte ⑃ 2.90 – **29 rm**
　　⊊ 24.00/58.00 **t.**

ALFA-ROMEO, PEUGEOT, TALBOT　Northgate ℰ
20822
AUSTIN-ROVER-DAIMLER-JAGUAR　Southgate ℰ
35341
BMW　Somerset Rd ℰ 515515
FORD　Southgate ℰ 29675

RENAULT　Northgate ℰ 35251
SAAB　Kirkheaton ℰ 29754
TOYOTA　Fartown ℰ 514514
VAUXHALL-OPEL　386 Leeds Rd ℰ 23191
VOLVO　Northgate ℰ 31362
VW, AUDI　Bradford Rd ℰ 42001

HULL Humberside 402 S 22 – see Kingston-upon-Hull.

HUNGERFORD Berks. 403 404 P 29 – pop. 4,488 – ECD : Thursday – ✆ 0488.
Envir. : Littlecote House★ *AC*, NW : 3 ½ m.
🏌 West Berkshire, Chaddleworth ℰ 048 82 (Chaddleworth) 574, N : 2 ½ m.
◆London 74 – ◆Bristol 57 – ◆Oxford 28 – Reading 26 – ◆Southampton 46.

　🏦 **Bear** (Best Western), 17 Charnham St., RG17 0EL, on A 4 ℰ 82512, Telex 477575, 🐎 – 📺
　　➡wc 🍴wc 📻 🅿. 🔙 AE ⓞ VISA. ⋇
　　M *(closed 25 and 26 December)* 16.95/18.95 **t.** and a la carte ⑃ 3.80 – ⊊ 4.25 – **28 rm**
　　30.00/45.00 **st.** – SB (weekends only) 52.00/57.50 **st.**

BMW　Bath Rd ℰ 82772

PEUGEOT-TALBOT　Bath Rd ℰ 82033

HUNMANBY North Yorks. 402 T 21 – pop. 2,623 – ✆ 0723 Scarborough.
◆London 198 – ◆Kingston-upon-Hull 40 – Scarborough 9 – York 41.

　🏠 **Wrangham House**, 10 Stonegate, YO14 0NS, ℰ 891333, 🐎 – 📺 ➡wc 🍴wc 🅿. 🔙 VISA.
　　⋇
　　closed December and January – **M** (dinner only) 9.00 **t.** ⑃ 2.65 – **9 rm** ⊊ 22.00/33.00 **t.** – SB
　　(October-May) (except Bank Holidays) 45.00 **st.**

HUNSTANTON Norfolk 402 404 V 25 – pop. 3,990 – ECD : Thursday – ✆ 048 53.
🏌 ℰ 2811, E : ½ m. – 🖪 The Green ℰ 2610 – ◆London 120 – ◆Cambridge 60 – ◆Norwich 45.

　🏦 Le Strange Arms, Golf Links Lane, PE36 6JJ, N : 1 m. by A 149 ℰ 34411, ≤, 🐎 – 📺 ➡wc
　　🍴wc ☎ 🅿. 🔙 – **32 rm**.

　⤒ **Claremont**, 35 Greevegate, PE36 6AF, ℰ 33171 – ⋇
　　February-October – **7 rm** ⊊ 9.00/18.00 **st.**

AUSTIN-ROVER　12 Lynn Rd ℰ 33435

CITROEN, FORD　Westgate ℰ 2508

HUNSTRETE Avon 403 404 M 29 – see Bath.

HUNTINGDON Cambs. 404 T 26 – pop. 14 ,395 – ECD : Wednesday – ✆ 0480.
See : Cromwell Museum – All Saint's Church (interior★).
Envir. : Hinchingbrooke House★ (Tudor mansion-school) W : 1 m. – Ramsey (Abbey Gatehouse★ 15C) NE : 11 ½ m.
🧗 St. Ives ♟ 64459, E : 5 m.
♦London 69 – Bedford 21 – ♦Cambridge 16.

  🏨 **Old Bridge,** 1 High St., PE18 6TQ, ♟ 52681, Telex 32706 – 📺 🚿wc ☎ 🅿. 🔼 🅰🅴 ⓪ VISA
    M a la carte 15.65/20.30 **st.** – **22 rm** ⚏ 42.00/65.50 **st.**

  🏨 **George** (T.H.F.), George St., PE18 6AB, ♟ 53096 – 📺 🚿wc ☜ 🅿. 🔬 🔼 🅰🅴 ⓪ VISA
    M 5.95/8.75 **st.** and a la carte ▯ 2.70 – ⚏ 5.50 – **24 rm** 36.50/45.00 **st.**

AUSTIN-ROVER-LAND ROVER 1-3 Hartford Rd ♟   BMW, VAUXHALL-OPEL Ring Rd ♟ 52694
56441

HURLEY-ON-THAMES Berks. 404 R 29 – ECD : Wednesday – ✉ Maidenhead – ✆ 062 882
Littlewick Green.
♦London 38 – ♦Oxford 26 – Reading 12.

  🏨 **Ye Olde Bell,** High St., SL6 5NB, ♟ 5881, Telex 847035, « Part 12C inn », 🛋 – 📺 🚿wc ☎
    🅿. 🔼 🅰🅴 ⓪ VISA
    M 12.50/20.00 **t.** and a la carte ▯ 3.50 – ⚏ 4.95 – **24 rm** 35.00/60.00 **st.**

HURSTBOURNE TARRANT Hants. 403 404 P 30 – pop. 709 – ✉ Andover – ✆ 026 476.
♦London 77 – ♦Bristol 77 – ♦Oxford 38 – ♦Southampton 33.

  ✕✕ **Esseborne Manor** 🦌 with rm, SP11 0ER, NE : 1 ½ m. on A 343 ♟ 444, 🛋, ✗ – 📺 🚿wc
    🕿 🅿. 🔼 🅰🅴 ⓪ VISA ✗
    M (closed Sunday dinner to non-residents) (lunch by arrangement) a la carte 12.00/14.60 **t.**
    ▯ 3.00 – **6 rm** ⚏ 39.50/55.00 **st.** – SB (October-April) 67.00 **st.**

HURST GREEN Lancs. 402 M 22 – ✉ Whalley – ✆ 025 486 Stonyhurst.
♦London 236 – Blackburn 12 – Burnley 13 – Preston 12.

  🏚 **Shireburn Arms** 🦌, Whalley Rd, BB6 9QJ, ♟ 518, 🛋 – 📺 🚿wc 🅿. 🔼 VISA
    M 5.00/11.00 **st.** and a la carte ▯ 2.80 – **11 rm** ⚏ 18.00/38.00 **st.** – SB (weekends only)
    40.00/47.00 **st.**

HURSTPIERPOINT West Sussex 404 T 31 – pop. 11 ,913 (inc. Keymer) – ✉ Hassocks – ✆ 0273
Brighton.
♦London 45 – ♦Brighton 8.

  ✕ **Barron's,** 120 High St., BN6 9PX, ♟ 832183 – 🔼 🅰🅴 VISA
    closed Sunday – **M** (dinner only) a la carte 15.00 **st.** ▯ 2.50.

HUSBANDS BOSWORTH Leics. 403 404 Q 26 – pop. 889 – ✉ Lutterworth – ✆ 0858 Market
Harborough.
♦London 88 – ♦Birmingham 40 – ♦Leicester 14 – Northampton 17.

  ✕✕ **Fernie Lodge,** Berridges Lane, LE17 6LE, ♟ 880551 – 🅿. 🔼 VISA
    closed Saturday lunch, Sunday dinner, Monday and Bank Holidays – **M** (booking essential)
    6.75/11.95 **st.** ▯ 4.50.

HUTTON-LE-HOLE North Yorks. 402 R 21 – see Lastingham.

HUXHAM Devon – see Exeter.

HWLFFORDD = Haverfordwest.

HYTHE Kent 404 X 30 – pop. 13 ,118 – ECD : Wednesday – ✆ 0303.
See : St. Leonard's Church (≼★ from the churchyard) – Canal.
🧗 Hythe Imperial, Princes Parade ♟ 67441.
♦London 68 – Folkestone 6 – Hastings 33 – Maidstone 31.

  🏨 **Imperial** (Best Western) 🦌, Princes Par., CT21 6AE, ♟ 67441, Telex 965082, ≼, 🔲, 🧗, 🛋,
    ✗, squash – 📳 📺 🅿. 🔬 🔼 🅰🅴 ⓪ VISA ✗
    M 10.00/13.50 **t.** and a la carte ▯ 3.00 – **83 rm** ⚏ 35.00/80.00 **t.**, **5 suites** 80.00/120.00 **t.** – SB
    (weekends only) (except Bank Holidays) 60.00/100.00 **st.**

  🏨 **Stade Court** (Best Western), West Par., CT21 6DT, ♟ 68263, Telex 965082, ≼ – 📳 📺 🚿wc
    📺wc 🕿 🅿. 🔼 🅰🅴 ⓪ VISA
    M 7.50/10.50 **st.** and a la carte – **32 rm** ⚏ 26.50/45.00 **st.** – SB 49.00/56.00 **st.**

AUSTIN-ROVER 6/12 East St. ♟ 69335   PEUGEOT-TALBOT The Green ♟ 60511
FORD Stade St. ♟ 67726   SAAB 215 Seabrook Rd ♟ 38467

IBSLEY Hants. 403 404 O 31 – see Ringwood.

IDE HILL Kent – see Sevenoaks.

IGHTHAM Kent – see Wrotham Heath.

ILFRACOMBE Devon 403 H 30 The West Country G. – pop. 9 ,966 – ECD : Thursday – ☎ 0271.
See : Capstone Hill★ (≤★) – Hillsborough (≤★★) – St. Nicholas' Chapel AC (≤★).
ᵣ₈ Hele Bay ✆ 62176, E : 1 m.
Access to Lundy Island from Hartland Point by helicopter ✆ 062 882 (Littlewick Green) 3431.
🛈 The Promenade ✆ 63001.
◆London 223 – Exeter 54 – Taunton 61.

 🏠 **St. Helier,** Hillsborough Rd, EX34 9QQ, ✆ 64906, ♨ – ⇌wc ℗. *VISA*
  May-September – **M** (dinner only) 6.50 **st.** ▯ 2.80 – **25 rm** ⊑ 18.00/27.00 **st.**

 🏠 Torrs, Torrs Park, EX34 8AY, ✆ 62334 – ⇌wc ℟wc ℗. ⚡ Æ ⓞ *VISA*
  March-October – **M** (bar lunch) – **17 rm** ⊑ 17.00/39.00 **t.** – SB 32.00/37.00 **st.**

 at Lee W : 3 ¼ m. by B 3231 – ✉ ☎ 0271 Ilfracombe :

 🏨 **Lee Bay** (Best Western) ⌕, EX34 8LP, ✆ 63503, ≤, ⤓ heated, ⌕, ☞, park – ⓣⱽ ⇌wc ℗.
  ⚡ Æ ⓞ *VISA*
  M (buffet lunch)/dinner 10.50 **t.** ▯ 3.00 – **48 rm** ⊑ 30.00/60.00 – SB 65.55/74.90 **st.**

 🏠 Lee Manor ⌕, EX34 8LR, ✆ 63920, ☞, park – ⓣⱽ ⇌wc ℟wc ℗
  12 rm.

PEUGEOT, TALBOT West Down ✆ 63104   RENAULT Northfield Rd ✆ 62075

ILKLEY West Yorks. 402 O 22 – pop. 13 ,060 – ECD : Wednesday – ☎ 0943.
ᵣ₉ Ben Rhydding, High Wood ✆ 608759.
🛈 Station Rd ✆ 602319.
◆London 210 – Bradford 13 – Harrogate 17 – ◆Leeds 16 – Preston 46.

 🏨 **Rombalds,** 11 West View, Wells Rd, LS29 9JG, ✆ 603201, Telex 51593 – ⓣⱽ ⇌wc ℟wc ☎
  ℗. ⚡ Æ ⓞ *VISA*
  M (closed Saturday lunch to non-residents) 8.30/16.50 **t.** and a la carte ▯ 3.60 – **18 rm**
  ⊑ 36.00/55.00 **t.**, **2 suites** 72.00/96.00 **t.** – SB (weekends only) 60.00/66.00 **st.**

 🏠 **Grove,** 66 The Grove, LS29 9PA, ✆ 600298 – ⓣⱽ ⇌wc ℟wc ℗. ⚡ *VISA*
  closed mid December-mid January – **M** (residents only) 6.00/7.50 **t.** ▯ 3.00 – **6 rm**
  ⊑ 20.00/36.00 **t.**

 🏠 **Moorview,** 104 Skipton Rd, LS29 9HE, W : ¼ m. on A 65 ✆ 600156, ≤, ☞ – ⓣⱽ ℟wc ℗
  ⌕
  10 rm ⊑ 18.00/30.00 **st.**

 XXX ❀❀ **Box Tree,** 35-37 Church St., LS29 9DR, ✆ 608484, « Ornate decor » – ⚡ Æ ⓞ *VISA*
  closed Sunday, Monday, 25-26 December and 1 January – **M** (dinner only) (booking essential)
  a la carte 16.35/19.75 **t.**
  Spec. La salade de pigeonneau fumé au vinaigrette a l'orange, Noisette d'agneau Edward VII, Timbale de fraises
  "Box Tree".

AUSTIN-ROVER, ROLLS ROYCE-BENTLEY Ben   PEUGEOT-TALBOT Skipton Rd ✆ 608966
Rhydding ✆ 603261   VAUXHALL-OPEL Bradford Rd. Menston ✆ 0943
AUSTIN-ROVER Skipton Rd ✆ 607606   (Menston) 76122

IMPINGTON Cambs. – see Cambridge.

INGATESTONE Essex 404 V 28 – pop. 6 ,150 – ECD : Wednesday – ☎ 0277.
◆London 27 – Chelmsford 6.

 XXX **Furze Hill,** Ivy Barn Lane, Margaretting, CM4 0EW, NE : 2 ¼ m. by A 12 ✆ 353040, Dancing
  (Saturday), ⤓ heated, ☞, ⌘ – ℗. ⚡ Æ ⓞ *VISA*
  closed Sunday dinner and Monday – **M** 6.25/13.50 **st.** and a la carte ▯ 2.85.

INGLETON North Yorks. 402 M 21 – pop. 1 ,769 – ✉ Carnforth – ☎ 0468.
🛈 Community Centre car park ✆ 41049/41280.
◆London 266 – Kendal 21 – Lancaster 18 – ◆Leeds 53.

 🏠 **Oakroyd,** Main St., LA6 3HJ, ✆ 41258, ☞ – ⓣⱽ ℗
  7 rm ⊑ 8.50/19.00 **t.**

INSTOW Devon 403 H 30 – see Bideford.

IPWICH

Butter Market.............. X 9
Carr Street X
Corn Hill .... X 16
Tavern Street.............. X
Westgate Street.......... X 52

Argyle Street .... X 2
Back Hamlet.............. Z 3
Birkfield Drive .... Z 5
Bond Street .... X 6
Bridgwater Road .... Z 7
Chevallier Street......... Y 13
College Street .... X 15
Dogs Head Street .... X 18
Ellenbrook Road .... Z 19
Falcon Street .... X 21
Fore Hamlet .... X 22
Franciscan Way.......... X 24
Friars Street .... X 25
Grove Lane.............. YZ 28
Handford Road .... X, Y 30
Lloyds Avenue........... X 31
Lower Orwell Street ..... X 32
Northgate Street......... X 33
Orwell Place .... X 34
Queen Street .... X 37
St. Helen's Street ..... X, Y 39
St. Margarets Street .... X 40
St. Nicholas Street ..... X 41
St. Peter's Street .... X 42
Salthouse Street .... X 43
Silent Street .... X 44
Sprite's Lane .... Z 45
Upper Brook Street...... X 48
Upper Orwell Street ..... X 49
Waterworks Street ...... X 51
Yarmouth Road .... Y 54

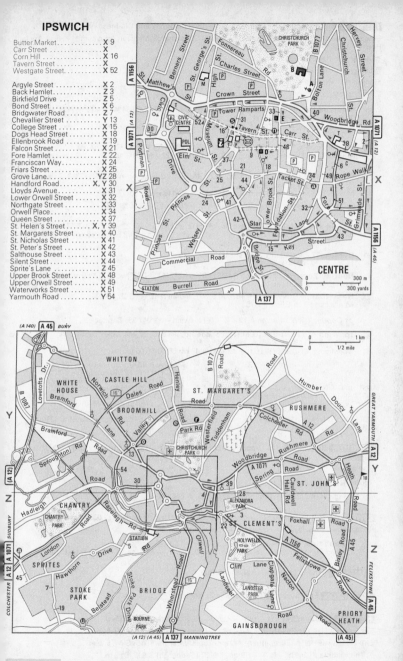

Red Lion

If the name of the hotel
is not in bold type,
on arrival ask the hotelier his prices.

IPSWICH Suffolk 404 X 27 – pop. 129,661 – ECD : Monday and Wednesday – ☎ 0473.

See : St. Margaret's Church (the roof★) X **A** – Christchurch Mansion (museum★) X **B** – Ancient House★ 16C X **D** – Pykenham House★ 16C X **E**.

⌗ Rushmere Heath ♗ 77109 Y.

🛈 Town Hall, Princes St. ♗ 58070.

♦London 76 – ♦Norwich 43.

Plan on preceding page

🏨 **Belstead Brook** ♨, Belstead Rd, IP2 9HB, SW : 2 ½ m. ♗ 684241, Telex 987674, ☞, park – 📺 🅿. 🏖 🖻 AE ① VISA ♺   Z u
M a la carte 14.10/17.20 **st.** – ♎ 4.95 – **32 rm** 41.00/55.00 **st.** – SB (weekends only) 38.00/60.00 **st.**

🏨 **Marlborough,** Henley Rd, IP1 3SP, ♗ 57677, ☞ – 📺 🅿. 🏖 🖻 AE ① VISA   Y e
M 9.75/11.50 **t.** and a la carte 🍷 4.50 – ♎ 5.00 – **22 rm** 38.00/45.00 **t.** – SB (weekends only) (except Easter) 60.00 **st.**

🏛 **Post House** (T.H.F.), London Rd, IP2 0UA, SW : 2 ¼ m. on A 12 ♗ 212313, Telex 987150, ♒ heated – 📺 🖻wc 🕿 🅿. 🏖 🖻 AE ①   Z a
M 8.50/10.50 **st.** and a la carte 🍷 2.70 – ♎ 5.50 – **118 rm** 39.00/47.00 **st.**

🏚 **Great White Horse,** Tavern St., IP1 3AH, ♗ 56558 – 📺 🖻wc ☎. 🏖   X n
52 rm.

🏤 **Crown and Anchor,** Westgate St., IP1 3EQ, ♗ 58506 – 📺 🖻wc 🕿 🅿. 🖻 AE ① VISA
closed 23 to 31 December – **M** (grill rest. only) a la carte 4.90/8.50 **t.** – **55 rm** ♎ 30.00/45.00 **t.** – SB (weekends only) 48.00/52.00 **st.**   X s

🏠 **Gables,** 17 Park Rd, IP1 3SX, ♗ 54252, ☞ – 🅿   Y r
12 rm ♎ 12.00/24.00 **st.**

🏠 **Bentley Tower,** 172 Norwich Rd, IP1 2PY, ♗ 212142 – 📺 🍴wc 🅿. 🖻 AE ① VISA ♺   Y o
9 rm ♎ 20.00/32.00 **st.**

XX **Rajasthan,** 6 Orwell Pl., IP4 1BB, ♗ 51397, Indian rest. – 🖻 AE ① VISA   X a
M a la carte 7.15/8.95 **t.** 🍷 2.75.

at Copdock SW : 4 m. on A 12 – Z – ✉ Ipswich – ☎ 047 386 Copdock :

🏛 **Ipswich Moat House** (Q.M.H.), London Rd, IP8 3JD, ♗ 444, Telex 987207, ☞ – 📺 🖻wc 🕿 🅿. 🏖 🖻 AE ① VISA ♺
M (carving rest.) 9.00/14.00 **t.** – ♎ 4.50 – **47 rm** 36.00/46.00 **t.**

ALFA-ROMEO Rushmore Rd ♗ 622790	MAZDA, POLSKI Fuchsia Lane ♗ 74535
AUDI, VW 88 Princes St. ♗ 214231	MERCEDES-BENZ Raneleigh Rd ♗ 221388
AUSTIN-ROVER 935 Woodbridge Rd ♗ 76929	PEUGEOT-TALBOT, VOLVO Derby Rd ♗ 70101
AUSTIN-ROVER Barrack Lane ♗ 54202	RENAULT 301/305 Norwich Rd ♗ 43021
AUSTIN-ROVER Felixstowe Rd ♗ 75431	SAAB Dales Rd ♗ 42547
BMW West End Rd ♗ 212456	SKODA West End Rd ♗ 55461
CITROEN Norwich Rd ♗ 55173	TOYOTA 301/5 Woodbridge Rd ♗ 76927
FIAT, LANCIA Burrel Rd ♗ 210321	VAUXHALL-OPEL Knightsdale Rd ♗ 43044
FORD Princes St. ♗ 55401	

IVINGHOE Bucks. 404 S 28 – pop. 2,517 (inc. Pitstone) – ✉ Leighton Buzzard – ☎ 0296 Cheddington.

⌗ ♗ 668696.

♦London 42 – Aylesbury 9 – Luton 11.

XXX King's Head (T.H.F.), Station Rd, LU7 9EB, ♗ 668388 – 🖵 🅿.

IXWORTH Suffolk 404 W 27 – pop. 2,121 – ✉ Bury St. Edmunds – ☎ 0359 Pakenham.

♦London 85 – ♦Cambridge 35 – ♦Ipswich 25 – ♦Norwich 36.

X **Theobalds,** 68 High St., IP31 2HJ, ♗ 31707 – 🖻 VISA
closed Sunday dinner, Monday and 1 to 10 January – **M** a la carte 11.00/13.65 **t.** 🍷 2.50.

JAMESTON Dyfed 403 F 29 – see Manorbier.

JEVINGTON East Sussex 404 U 31 – see Eastbourne.

KENDAL Cumbria 402 L 21 – pop. 23,710 – ECD : Thursday – ☎ 0539.

See : Abbot Hall Art Gallery (Museum of Lakeland Life and Industry★) AC.

Envir. : Levens Hall★ (Elizabethan) AC and Topiary Garden★ AC, SW : 5 ½ m.

⌗ The Heights ♗ 24079 – ⌗ The Riggs ♗ 0587 (Sedbergh) 20993, E : 9 m.

🛈 Town Hall, Highgate ♗ 25758.

♦London 270 – Bradford 64 – Burnley 63 – ♦Carlisle 49 – Lancaster 22 – ♦Leeds 72 – ♦Middlesbrough 77 – ♦Newcastle-upon-Tyne 104 – Preston 44 – Sunderland 88.

🏨 **Woolpack** (Swallow), Stricklandgate, LA9 4ND, 𝒫 23852, Group Telex 53168 – 📺 ➪wc
🏮wc ☎ 🄿. 🎿. 🔼 🄰🄴 🄾 𝘝𝘐𝘚𝘈
M 6.50/9.50 **st.** and a la carte 🍷 3.40 – **57 rm** ⊐ 38.00/49.50 **st.** – SB 62.00 **st.**

🏠 **Garden House** 🦢, Fowling Lane, LA9 6PH, by A 685 𝒫 31131, 🚗 – 📺 ➪wc 🏮wc ☎ 🄿.
🔼 𝘝𝘐𝘚𝘈. 🍽
closed 1 to 14 January – **M** *(closed Sunday lunch)* (bar lunch)/dinner 10.50 **st.** 🍷 2.90 – **5 rm**
⊐ 27.00/39.00 **st.** – SB 39.00/52.00 **st.**

XX **Castle Dairy**, 26 Wildman St., LA9 6EN, 𝒫 21170, English rest., « Part 13C and 16C »
closed Sunday to Tuesday – **M** (booking essential)(dinner only) 12.00 🍷 2.30.

at Crooklands S : 6 ¼ m. on A 65 – ✉ Milnthorpe – ☎ 044 87 Crooklands :

🏨 **Crooklands** (Best Western), LA7 7NW, N : 1 ¼ m. on A 65 𝒫 432, 🔦 – 📺 ➪wc ☎ 🄿. 🎿.
🔼 🄰🄴 🄾 𝘝𝘐𝘚𝘈
M (bar lunch Monday to Saturday)/dinner 11.95 **t.** and a la carte 🍷 3.90 – **15 rm** ⊐ 33.00/48.00 **t.**
– SB (except Easter and Christmas) 50.00/94.00 **st.**

at Underbarrow W : 3 ½ m. on Crosthwaite rd – ✉ Kendal – ☎ 044 88 Crosthwaite :

🏠 **Greenriggs Country House** 🦢, LA8 8HF, E : ½ m. 𝒫 387, ≼, « Country house atmosphere », 🚗 – ➪wc 🄿
closed weekdays November-December, January and February – **M** (bar lunch)/dinner 12.25 **t.**
🍷 2.00 – **13 rm** ⊐ 24.00/36.00 **t.**

ALFA-ROMEO, FORD, MERCEDES BENZ Ings 𝒫   PEUGEOT Kirkland 𝒫 28822
0539 (Staveley) 821442   RENAULT Kirklands 𝒫 22211
AUSTIN-ROVER Sandes Av. 𝒫 28800   VAUXHALL Sandes Av. 𝒫 24420
FIAT 113 Stricklandgate 𝒫 20967   VOLVO Station Rd 𝒫 31313
FORD Mintsfeet Rd South 𝒫 23534   VW, AUDI-NSU, PORSCHE Longpool 𝒫 24331

KENILWORTH Warw. �403 �404 P 26 – pop. 18 ,782 – ECD : Monday and Thursday – ☎ 0926.
See : Castle★ (12C) *AC.*
🏌 Crew Lane 𝒫 54296.
🛈 Library, 11 Smalley Pl. 𝒫 52595.
♦London 102 – ♦Birmingham 19 – ♦Coventry 5 – Warwick 5.

🏨 **De Montfort** (De Vere), The Square, CV8 1ED, 𝒫 55944, Telex 311012 – 🛗 📺 ☎ 🄿. 🎿. 🔼
🄰🄴 🄾 𝘝𝘐𝘚𝘈
M 8.50/9.75 **st.** and a la carte 🍷 3.35 – **95 rm** ⊐ 45.50/63.00 **st.**, **1 suite** – SB (weekends only)
60.00/62.00 **st.**

🏠 **Clarendon House,** 6-8 High St., Old Town, CV8 1LZ, 𝒫 54694 – 📺 ➪wc 🏮wc 🄿. 🔼 𝘝𝘐𝘚𝘈
M (bar lunch Monday to Saturday)/dinner 9.00 **st.** and a la carte 🍷 3.50 – **23 rm**
⊐ 25.00/45.00 **st.** – SB (weekends only) 45.00/50.00 **st.**

⌂ **Enderley**, 20 Queens Rd, CV8 1JQ, 𝒫 55388
5 rm ⊐ 9.50/18.00 **st.**

XX **Diment**, 121-123 Warwick Rd, CV8 1HP, 𝒫 53763 – 🄿. 🔼 🄰🄴 🄾 𝘝𝘐𝘚𝘈
closed Saturday lunch, Sunday, Monday, first 3 weeks August and Bank Holidays – **M** 5.50/10.95
t. and a la carte 🍷 2.90.

XX **Bosquet**, 97a Warwick Rd, CV8 1HP, 𝒫 52463 – 🄰🄴 𝘝𝘐𝘚𝘈
closed Sunday, 3 weeks July-August, 24 December-2 January and Bank Holidays – **M** (lunch
by arrangement) 10.50 **t.** and a la carte 🍷 2.90.

X **Ana's Bistro,** 121-123 Warwick Rd, CV8 1HP, 𝒫 53763, Bistro – 🄿. 🔼 🄰🄴 🄾 𝘝𝘐𝘚𝘈
closed Sunday, Monday, first 3 weeks August and Bank Holidays – **M** (dinner only) a la carte
5.05/8.20 **t.** 🍷 2.15.

ALFA-ROMEO, LANCIA Station Rd 𝒫 53073

KENNFORD Devon �403 J 32 – see Exeter.

KENNINGTON Kent �404 W 30 – see Ashford.

KENTS BANK Cumbria �402 L 21 – see Grange-over-Sands.

KERESLEY West Midlands �403 �404 P 26 – see Coventry.

KESWICK Cumbria �402 K 20 – pop. 4 ,777 – ECD : Wednesday – ☎ 0596.
See : Derwent Water★★ Y.
Envir. : Castlerigg (stone circle) ✳★ E : 2 m. Y **A.**
🏌 Threlkeld Hall 𝒫 059 683 (Threlkeld) 324, E : 4 m. by A 66 Y.
🛈 Moot Hall, Market Sq. 𝒫 72645.
♦London 294 – ♦Carlisle 31 – Kendal 30.

KESWICK

Main Street . . . . **Z**
Station Street . . . . **Z**

Bank Street . . . . **Z** 2
Borrowdale Road . . . . . **Z** 3
Brackenrigg Drive . . . . **Z** 5
Brundholme Road . . . . **Y** 6
Chestnut Hill . . . . **Z** 8
Church Street . . . . **Z** 10
Crosthwaite Road . . . . **Y** 12
Derwent Street . . . . . . **Z** 13
High Hill . . . . **Z** 14
Manor Brow . . . . **Y** 17
Market Square . . . . . . **Z** 18
Otley Road . . . . **Z** 20
Police Station
  Court . . . . **Z** 22
Ratcliffe Place . . . . **Z** 23
St. Herbert
  Street . . . . **Z** 24
Station Street . . . . **Z** 26
The Crescent . . . . **Z** 27
The Hawthorns . . . . . . **Y** 29
The Headlands . . . . . . **Z** 31
Tithebarn Street . . . . . **Z** 32

*North is at the top
on all town plans.*

*Les plans de villes
sont disposés
le Nord en haut.*

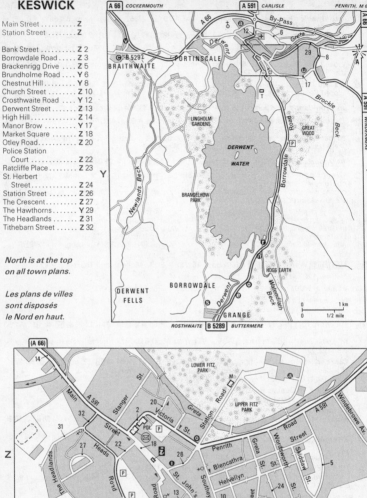

CENTRE

🏨 **Keswick** (T.H.F.) 🐟, Station Rd, CA12 4NQ, ✆ 72020, Telex 64200, 🍴 – 📶 📺 🚗 🅿. 🏧. ◪ ʌᴇ ① 𝗩𝗜𝗦𝗔
  M (bar lunch Monday to Saturday)/dinner 10.00 **st.** and a la carte ⌀ 2.95 – ⊊ 5.50 – **64 rm** **Z a**
  33.50/45.50 **st.**

🏨 Royal Oak, Station St., CA12 5HH, ✆ 72965 – 📶 📺 🛁wc ☎ 🅿   **Z i**
  43 rm.

🏨 **Underscar** 🐟, Applethwaite, CA12 4PH, N : 1 ½ m. by A 591 ✆ 72469, Telex 64354, ≼
  Derwent Water and mountains, 🍴, park – 📺 🛁wc 🚿wc 🅿. ◪ ʌᴇ ⊬ᴂ   by A 591   **Y**
  closed December – **M** 8.50/16.50 **t.** and a la carte ⌀ 3.50 – ⊊ 3.50 – **18 rm** 40.00/85.00 **t.** – SB
  (winter only) 50.00/80.00 **st.**

222

🏨 **Walpole,** Station Rd, CA12 4NA, ☎ 72072 – [TV] 🛁wc 🚿wc Ⓟ — Z **o**
M 4.50/8.50 **t.** 🍷 2.85 – **17 rm** 🛏 13.75/32.50 **t.**

🏨 Grange Country House 🐎, Manor Brow, Ambleside Rd, CA12 4BA, ☎ 72500, ⋞, 🌳 – [TV] 🛁wc 🚿wc Ⓟ. 💳 [VISA] — Y **u**
Restricted service November-February – **10 rm** 🛏 13.50/30.00 **t.**

🏨 **Lyzzick Hall** 🐎, Under Skiddaw, CA12 4PY, NW : 2 ½ m. on A 591 ☎ 72277, ⋞, 🏊 heated, 🌳 – 🚿 Ⓟ. 🚫 — by A 591 Y
April-October – **M** (dinner only) 8.50 **st.** 🍷 2.50 – **18 rm** 🛏 14.00/34.50 **st.**

🏨 **Highfield,** The Heads, CA12 5ER, ☎ 72508, ⋞ – 🚿wc Ⓟ — Z **r**
Easter-October – **M** (dinner only) 7.00 **t.** 🍷 2.50 – **19 rm** 🛏 10.50/27.00 **t.**

⌂ **Lairbeck** 🐎, Vicarage Hill, CA12 5QB, ☎ 73373, 🌳 – 🛁wc Ⓟ. 🚫 — Y **a**
12 rm 🛏 12.00/35.00 **t.**

⌂ **Gale** 🐎, Underskiddaw, CA12 4PL, NW : 1 ¾ m. by A 591 ☎ 72413, ⋞, 🌳 – Ⓟ. 🚫 — by A 591 Y
March-November – **13 rm** 🛏 12.00/24.00 **st.**

at Borrowdale S : 3 ¼ m. on B 5289 – ✉ Keswick – 📞 059 684 Borrowdale :

🏨 **Lodore Swiss** 🐎, CA12 5UX, ☎ 285, Group Telex 64305, ⋞ Derwent Water and mountains, 🏊 heated, [🏊], 🌳, park, 🎾, squash – ⇅ [TV] ☏ 🚗 Ⓟ. [AE]. 🚫 — Y **n**
20 March-9 November – **M** 12.00 **t.** (dinner) and a la carte – **72 rm** 🛏 31.00/62.00 **t.**, **1 suite** 105.00 **t.**

🏨 **Borrowdale,** CA12 5UY, ☎ 224, ⋞, 🌳 – [TV] 🛁wc Ⓟ. 💳 [VISA] — Y **o**
closed 22 December-5 February – **M** (bar lunch Monday to Saturday)/dinner 10.90 **t.** 🍷 2.90 – **35 rm** 🛏 (dinner included) 30.50/65.60 **t.** – SB (weekdays only) (November-April) 55.60 **st.**

🏨 **Mary Mount Country House** 🐎, CA12 5UU, ☎ 223, Group Telex 64305, ⋞ Derwent Water and mountains, 🌳, park – [TV] 🛁wc ☏ Ⓟ. [AE]. 🚫 — Y **r**
closed 17 November-27 December – **M** (bar lunch)/dinner 9.50 **t.** 🍷 2.70 – **15 rm** 🛏 27.00/44.00 **t.** – SB (3 January-24 March) 46.00/54.00 **st.**

⌂ Leathes Head 🐎, CA12 5UY, ☎ 247, ⋞, 🌳 – 🛁wc 🚿wc Ⓟ. 🚫 — Y **e**
13 rm.

at Grange-in-Borrowdale S : 4 ¾ m. by B 5289 – ✉ Keswick – 📞 059 684 Borrowdale :

🏨 **Borrowdale Gates Country House** 🐎, CA12 5UQ, ☎ 204, ⋞, 🌳 – [TV] 🛁wc Ⓟ. 💳 [AE] [DC] [VISA] — Y **s**
M (bar lunch)/dinner 9.95 **st.** 🍷 1.95 – **20 rm** 🛏 (dinner included) 16.00/58.00 **st.** – SB (weekends only) 45.00/51.00 **st.**

at Rosthwaite S : 6 m. on B 5289 – Y – ✉ Keswick – 📞 059 684 Borrowdale :

🏨 **Scafell** 🐎, CA12 5XB, ☎ 208, 🌳 – 🛁wc Ⓟ
closed January – **M** (bar lunch Monday to Saturday)/dinner 11.00 **t.** – **20 rm** 🛏 18.50/41.00 **t.** – SB (November-April) 33.00/60.00 **st.**

⌂ **Royal Oak** 🐎, CA12 5XB, ☎ 214 – 🛁wc Ⓟ. 💳
closed 1 to 27 December – **12 rm** 🛏 15.00/30.00 **t.**

at Seatoller S : 8 m. on B 5289 – Y – ✉ Keswick – 📞 059 684 Borrowdale :

⌂ **Seatoller House,** Borrowdale, CA12 5XN, ☎ 218, ⋞ Borrowdale, 🌳 – 🚿wc Ⓟ
April-October – **9 rm** 🛏 (dinner included) 18.50/34.00 **t.**

at Braithwaite W : 2 m. on A 66 – ✉ Keswick – 📞 059 682 Braithwaite :

🏨 **Ivy House,** CA12 5SY, ☎ 338 – [TV] 🛁wc Ⓟ. 💳 [VISA]. 🚫 — Y **c**
March-23 November – **M** 10.75 **t.** 🍷 2.85 – **8 rm** 🛏 19.25/38.50 **t.**

🏨 **Middle Ruddings,** CA12 5RY, on A 66 ☎ 436, 🌳 – [TV] 🛁wc Ⓟ. 💳 — Y **v**
closed 7 January - Easter – **M** (bar lunch)/dinner 10.50 **st.** 🍷 2.75 – **15 rm** 🛏 15.00/37.00 **t.**

at Thornthwaite W : 3 ½ m. by A 66 – ✉ Keswick – 📞 059 682 Braithwaite :

🏨 **Thwaite Howe** 🐎, CA12 5SA, ☎ 281, ⋞ Skiddaw and Derwent Valley, 🌳 – [TV] 🛁wc Ⓟ. 🚫 — Y **i**
March-October – **M** (lunch by arrangement) 5.50/8.50 **t.** 🍷 2.50 – **8 rm** 🛏 26.00/42.00 **t.** – SB 48.00 **st.**

AUSTIN-ROVER High Hill ☎ 72768
FIAT Lake Rd ☎ 72064
FORD Tithe Barn St. ☎ 72386

KETTLEWELL North Yorks. [402] N 21 – pop. 361 (inc. Starbotton) – ECD : Tuesday and Thursday – ✉ Skipton – 📞 075 676.
♦London 237 – Bradford 33 – ♦Leeds 40.

🏨 **Racehorses,** Town Foot, BD23 5QZ, ☎ 233 – 🛁wc 🚿wc Ⓟ. 💳
M (bar lunch Monday to Saturday)/dinner 9.75 **t.** 🍷 2.95 – **14 rm** 🛏 18.00/40.00 **t.** – SB (November-March except Christmas and New Year) 45.00/50.00 **st.**

Ne voyagez pas aujourd'hui avec une carte d'hier.

KEYNSHAM Avon [403] [404] M 29 – pop. 16,452 – ECD : Wednesday – ✉ Bristol – ☎ 027 56.
♦London 127 – Bath 8 – ♦Bristol 4.

🏨 **Grange,** 42 Bath Rd, BS18 1SN, ☎ 69181 – [TV] 🛁wc 🚿wc Ⓟ. 💳 VISA. 🐕
M a la carte 4.25/8.15 **t.** 🍷 2.15 – **31 rm** ☕ 23.00/40.00 **t.** – SB (weekends only) 48.40/56.50 **st.**

KEYSTON Cambs. [404] S 26 – pop. 252 (inc. Bythorn) – ✉ Huntingdon – ☎ 080 14 Bythorn.
♦London 75 – ♦Cambridge 29 – Northampton 24.

🍴🍴 **Pheasant Inn,** Village Loop Rd, PE18 0RE, ☎ 241 – Ⓟ. 💳 [AE] ⓓ VISA
closed 3 days at Christmas – **M** 9.75/15.75 **st.** 🍷 6.25.

KIDDERMINSTER Heref. and Worc. [403] [404] N 26 – pop. 50,385 – ECD : Wednesday – ☎ 0562.
[i] Library, Market St. ☎ 752832.
♦London 139 – ♦Birmingham 17 – Shrewsbury 34 – Worcester 15.

🏨 **Gainsborough House** (Best Western), Bewdley Hill, DY11 6BS, SW : 1 m. on A 456 ☎ 754041, Telex 333058, 🌳 – [TV] 🛁wc ☎ Ⓟ. 🏢. 💳 [AE] ⓓ VISA
closed 25 December-2 January – **M** 5.00/7.50 **t.** and a la carte 🍷 3.00 – **42 rm** ☕ 30.50/41.85 **t.** – SB (weekends only) 42.50 **st.**

at Stone SE : 2 ½ m. on A 448 – ✉ Kidderminster – ☎ 056 283 Chaddesley Corbett :

🏨 Stone Manor, DY10 4PJ, ☎ 555, Telex 335661, ←, 🏊 heated, 🌳, park, 🎾 – [TV] Ⓟ. 🏢. 🐕
22 rm.

ALFA-ROMEO Mill St. ☎ 3708
AUSTIN-ROVER Churchfields ☎ 69159
BMW Mustow Green ☎ 056 283 (Chaddesley Corbett) 435
CITROEN, FIAT Worcester Rd ☎ 2202
FORD Worcester Rd ☎ 752661
LADA Plimsoll St. ☎ 2145
RENAULT High St. ☎ 0299 (Cleobury Mortimer) 270352
VOLVO Stourport Rd ☎ 515832
VW, AUDI Worcester Rd ☎ 745056

KIDLINGTON Oxon. [403] [404] Q 28 – see Oxford.

KILDWICK North Yorks. [402] O 22 – ✉ Keighley – ☎ 0535 Cross Hills.
♦London 226 – Burnley 15 – ♦Leeds 23.

🏨 **Kildwick Hall** 🐦, BD20 9AE, ☎ 32244, ←, « Jacobean manor house », 🌳 – [TV] Ⓟ. 💳 [AE] ⓓ VISA
M (grill rest. lunch Monday to Saturday) 8.95/12.95 **st.** and a la carte 🍷 3.85 – ☕ 4.95 – **12 rm** 30.00/80.00 **st.** – SB 67.90 **st.**

KILSBY Northants. [403] [404] Q 26 – see Rugby (Warw.).

KINGHAM Oxon. [403] [404] P 28 – pop. 576 – ECD : Wednesday – ☎ 060 871.
♦London 81 – Gloucester 32 – ♦Oxford 25.

🏨 **Mill** 🐦, OX7 6UH, ☎ 8188, 🌳 – [TV] 🛁wc 🚿wc ☎ Ⓟ. 💳 [AE] ⓓ VISA. 🐕
M 6.95/9.75 **st.** 🍷 4.10 – **20 rm** ☕ 25.00/45.00 **t.** – SB 58.00/64.00 **st.**

⌂ **Conygree Gate,** Church St., OX7 6YA, ☎ 389, 🌳 – Ⓟ. 🐕
March-October – **6 rm** ☕ 13.00/26.00 **st.**

KINGSBRIDGE Devon [403] I 33 The West Country G. – pop. 4,164 – ECD : Thursday – ☎ 0548.
See : Site★ – Boat Trip to Salcombe★★ *AC*.
[i] The Quay ☎ 3195 (summer only).
♦London 236 – Exeter 36 – ♦Plymouth 20 – Torquay 21.

🏨 **Crabshell Motor Lodge** without rest., Embankment Rd, TQ7 1JZ, ☎ 3301, ← – [TV] 🛁wc Ⓟ. 💳 [AE] ⓓ VISA
☕ 3.50 – **24 rm** 19.50/29.50 **t.**

🏨 **Vineyard,** Embankment Rd, TQ7 1JN, ☎ 2520, 🌳 – 🛁wc 🚿wc Ⓟ. 💳 VISA
Easter-October – **M** (bar lunch)/dinner 9.00 **t.** – **11 rm** ☕ 25.20/33.60 **t.**

at Loddiswell N : 3 ½ m. by B 3196 – ✉ ☎ 0548 Kingsbridge :

🍴🍴 **Lavinia's,** TQ7 4ED, N : 1 m. ☎ 550306, 🌳 – Ⓟ. 💳 VISA
Easter-October – **M** *(closed Sunday and Monday)* (dinner only)/a la carte 17.00/20.00 **st.**

at Goveton NE : 2 ½ m. by A 381 – ✉ ☎ 0548 Kingsbridge :

🏨 **Buckland-Tout-Saints** (Best Western) 🐦, TQ7 2DS, ☎ 3055, Telex 42513, ←, « Queen Anne mansion », 🌳, park – [TV] 🛁wc 🚿wc ☎ Ⓟ. 💳 [AE] ⓓ VISA
closed January – **M** 15.00/20.00 **st.** and a la carte 🍷 6.50 – **13 rm** ☕ 40.00/76.00 **st.** – SB 76.00/86.00 **st.**

at Chillington SE : 5 m. on A 379 – ✉ Kingsbridge – ☎ 054 853 Frogmore :

🏨 **Oddicombe House,** TQ7 2JD, ☎ 234, 🏊, 🌳 – 🛁wc Ⓟ
April-October – **M** (bar lunch residents only, Monday to Saturday)/dinner 9.00 **t.** and a la carte 🍷 3.70 – **10 rm** ☕ 16.50/44.00 **t.** – SB 47.00/58.00 **st.**

at Thurlestone W : 4 m. by A 381 – ⊠ ✪ 0548 Kingsbridge :

🏨 **Thurlestone** (Best Western) ⊗, TQ7 3NN, ℰ 560382, ≤, ⊒ heated, ⊠, ऺ, ☞, park, ⅍,
squash – ⧉ 🅃 ☎ ❷. 🄰. ◪ ꬃ ⓞ 𝑽𝑰𝑺𝑨. ⅍
closed 1 January-6 February – **M** (bar lunch)/dinner 12.00 **st.** and a la carte ▮ 3.50 – **68 rm**
⊊ 26.00/84.00 **st.** – SB (October-May) 68.00/92.00 **st.**

🏠 Furzey Close ⊗, TQ7 3NP, ℰ 560333, ≤, ☞ – 🅃 ꬃwc ﹟wc ❷
April-September – **10 rm**.

AUSTIN-ROVER The Quay ℰ 2323

KING'S LYNN Norfolk 🄾🄾🄶 🄾🄾🄶 V 25 – pop. 37,323 – ECD : Wednesday – ✪ 0553.
See : St. Margaret's Church★ (17C, chancel 13C) – St. Nicholas' Chapel★ (Gothic).
Envir. : Houghton Hall★★ (18C) *AC*, NE : 15 m. – Sandringham House★ and park★★ *AC*, NE : 6 m.
🛈 Saturday Market Place ℰ 63044 – ◆London 103 – ◆Cambridge 45 – ◆Leicester 75 – ◆Norwich 44.

🏨 **Duke's Head** (T.H.F.), Tuesday Market Pl., PE30 1JS, ℰ 774996, Telex 817349 – ⧉ 🅃 ꬃwc
☜ ❷. 🄰. ◪ ⓞ 𝑽𝑰𝑺𝑨
M 8.95 **st.** and a la carte ▮ 2.70 – ⊊ 5.50 – **72 rm** 36.50/47.50 **st.**

🏠 **Stuart House**, 35 Goodwins Rd, PE30 5QX, ℰ 772169, ☞ – 🅃 ꬃwc ☎ ❷. 🄰 ◪ 𝑽𝑰𝑺𝑨. ⅍
closed 22 December-5 January – **M** (bar lunch)/dinner 13.00 **t.** and a la carte ▮ 2.75 – **21 rm**
⊊ 17.50/42.00 **t.** – SB (weekends only)(October-March) 38.00/44.00 **st.**

🏠 **Russet House**, 53 Goodwins Rd, PE30 5PE, ℰ 773098, ☞ – 🅃 ꬃwc ❷. ⅍
closed 24 December-1 January – **11 rm** ⊊ 17.00/29.50 **t.**

at Grimston NE : 6 ¼ m. by A 148 – ⊠ Kings Lynn – ✪ 0485 Hillington :

🏨 **Congham Hall** ⊗, Lynn Rd, PE32 1AH, ℰ 600250, ≤, « Country house atmosphere »,
⊒ heated, ☞, park, ⅍ – 🅃 ꬃwc ☜ ❷. 🄰 ◪ ⓞ 𝑽𝑰𝑺𝑨. 🄰
closed 29 December-6 January – **M** *(closed lunch Saturday and Bank Holidays and Sunday
dinner to non-residents)* 10.00/25.00 **t.** ▮ 3.50 – ⊊ 2.00 – **11 rm** 46.00/58.00 **t.**, **1 suite**
70.00/90.00 **t.** – SB (weekends only) 95.00/115.00 **st.**

AUSTIN-ROVER-DAIMLER-JAGUAR,   ROLLS
ROYCE-BENTLEY Church St. ℰ 763133
PEUGEOT-TALBOT Lynn Rd, Heacham ℰ 0485
(Heacham) 70243

RELIANT, MAZDA Valingers Rd ℰ 772255
RENAULT Hardwick Rd ℰ 772644
TOYOTA Tottenhill ℰ 810306
VAUXHALL-OPEL North St. ℰ 773861

KINGSTON-UPON-HULL Humberside 🄾🄾🄶 S 22 – pop. 322,144 – ECD : Monday and Thursday
– ✪ 0482 Hull :
Envir. : Burton Constable Hall★ (16C) *AC*, NE : 8 m. by A 165 Z – ᴛᴳ Springhead Park, Willerby Rd
ℰ 656309, W : by Spring Bank West Z – ᴛᴳ Sutton Park, Salthouse Rd ℰ 74242, E : 3 m. Z.
✈ Humberside Airport : ℰ 0652 (Barnetby) 688456, S : 19 m. by A 63 Z and A 15 via Humber
Bridge – Terminal : Coach Service – ⸺ Shipping connections with the Continent : to The
Netherlands (Rotterdam) and Belgium (Zeebrugge) (North Sea Ferries).
🛈 Central Library, Albion St. ℰ 223344 – Corporation Rd, King George Dock, Hedon Rd ℰ 702118.
◆London 183 – ◆Leeds 61 – ◆Nottingham 94 – ◆Sheffield 68.

Plan on next page

🏨 Stakis Paragon (Stakis), Paragon St., HU1 3PJ, ℰ 26462, Telex 52431 – ⧉ ▤ rest 🅃 ꬃwc
☎. 🄰. ◪ ⓞ 𝑽𝑰𝑺𝑨 – **125 rm**.   Y e

⅍⅍ **Cerutti's**, 10 Nelson St., HU1 1XE, ℰ 28501, Seafood – ❷. 🄰   Y o
closed Saturday lunch, Sunday, 1 week at Christmas and Bank Holidays – **M** a la carte
9.00/15.35 **t.** ▮ 3.45.

at North Ferriby W : 7 m. on A 63 – Z – ⊠ Kingston-upon-Hull – ✪ 0482 Hull :

🏨 **Crest** (Crest), Ferriby High Rd, HU14 3LG, ℰ 645212, Telex 52558 – 🅃 ꬃwc ☎ ❷. 🄰. 🄰
◪ ⓞ 𝑽𝑰𝑺𝑨. ⅍
M approx. 11.50 **st.** – ⊊ 5.75 – **102 rm** 44.00/47.00 **st.** – SB (weekends only) 59.00 **st.**

at Willerby NW : 5 m. by A 63 – Z – off A 164 – ⊠ Kingston-upon-Hull – ✪ 0482 Hull :

🏨 **Willerby Manor**, Well Lane, HU10 6ER, ℰ 652616, Telex 52659, ☞ – 🅃 ꬃwc ☜ ❷. 🄰.
🄰 𝑽𝑰𝑺𝑨
M *(closed Saturday lunch and Sunday dinner)* 7.00/8.00 **t.** ▮ 3.00 – ⊊ 3.75 – **41 rm** 32.50/46.95 **t.**
– SB (weekends only) 45.00 **st.**

at Little Weighton NW : 11 m. by A 164 – Z – ⊠ Cottingham – ✪ 0482 Hull :

🏨 **Rowley Manor** ⊗, HU20 3XR, SW : ½ m. by Rowley Rd ℰ 848248, ≤, ☞ – 🅃 ꬃwc ﹟wc
☜ ❷. 🄰 ◪ ⓞ 𝑽𝑰𝑺𝑨
M (dinner only and Sunday lunch) a la carte 8.75/12.80 **st.** ▮ 2.75 – **15 rm** ⊊ 23.50/50.00 **st.** –
SB (weekends only) 46.50/60.00 **st.**

ALFA-ROMEO, LANCIA Calvert Lane ℰ 572444
AUSTIN-ROVER Boothferry Rd ℰ 506911
BMW 54 Anlaby Rd ℰ 25071
COLT 32 Princes Av. ℰ 42739
DAIHATSU, SAAB Anlaby Rd ℰ 23773
FIAT Holderness High Rd ℰ 701785
FIAT 96 Boothferry Rd ℰ 506976
FORD 172 Anlaby Rd ℰ 25732

HONDA 576 Springbank West ℰ 51250
MAZDA 300/2 Boothferry Rd, Hessle ℰ 645283
MERCEDES-BENZ 170 Aulaby Rd ℰ 20370
NISSAN Witham ℰ 24131
TALBOT Anlaby Rd ℰ 23631
TOYOTA Clarence St. ℰ 20039
VAUXHALL-OPEL 230/6 Anlaby Rd ℰ 23681
VW, AUDI 1/13 Boothferry Rd ℰ 649124

KINGSTON-UPON-HULL

Carr Lane . . . . **Y**
George Street . . . . **X**
Jameson Street . . . . **XY**
King Edward Street . . . . . . **Y** 19
Paragon Street . . . . **Y** 29
Prospect Street . . . . **X**
Whitefriargate . . . . **Y** 49

Albion Street . . . . **X** 2
Bond Street . . . . **X** 3
Caroline Street . . . . **X** 6
Commercial Road . . . . **Y** 8
County Road North . . . . . . **Z** 9
Dock Office Row . . . . **X** 10
Dock Street . . . . **X** 12
Fairfax Avenue . . . . **Z** 13
Ferensway . . . . **XY** 14
Great Union Street . . . . . . **X** 15
Grimston Street . . . . **X** 16
Humber Dock Street . . . . . **Y** 17
Jarratt Street . . . . **X** 18
Lockwood Street . . . . **X** 21
Lowgate . . . . **Y** 23
Market Place . . . . **Y** 24
Maybury Road . . . . **Z** 25
Prince's Avenue . . . . **Z** 31
Prince's Dock Street . . . . . **Y** 32
Queen's Road . . . . **Z** 33
Queen Street . . . . **Y** 35
Queen's Dock Avenue . . . . **X** 36
Reform Street . . . . **X** 37
St. Mark's Street . . . . **X** 40
Sculcoates Bridge . . . . **X** 42
Southcoates Avenue . . . . . **Z** 43
Southcoates Lane . . . . **Z** 44
Waterhouse Lane . . . . **Y** 47
Wilberforce Drive . . . . **X** 50
Worship Street . . . . **X** 52

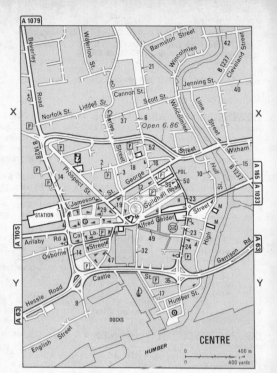

CENTRE

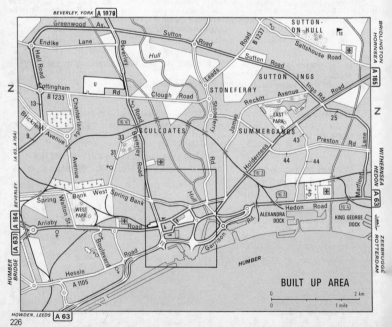

BUILT UP AREA

226

KINGSTOWN Cumbria − see Carlisle.

KINGSWINFORD West Midlands 403 404 N 26 − ECD : Thursday − ✿ 0384.
♦London 135 − ♦Birmingham 14 − Stafford 22 − Worcester 32.

Plan : see Birmingham p. 2

🏨 **Summerhill House** (Golden Oak), Swindon Rd, DY6 9XA, ℰ 295254, ㆟ − ➩wc 🅰 🅿 🔊
🔼 VISA ⌾
AU **a**
M *(closed Saturday lunch)* 6.00/6.50 **t.** and a la carte ⌀ 3.75 − **10 rm** ⌷ 21.50/27.50 **st.**

KINTBURY Berks. 403 404 P 29 − pop. 2,034 − ✉ Newbury − ✿ 0488.
♦London 73 − Newbury 6 − Reading 23.

XX **Dundas Arms** with rm, Station Rd, RG15 0UT, ℰ 58263, ≼, ㆟ − 📺 ➩wc ☎ 🅿 🔊 🔼 ⑩
VISA ⌾
closed Christmas and New Year − **M** *(closed Sunday and Monday)* (booking essential) 8.50 **t.**
(lunch) and a la carte 14.50/17.50 **t.** ⌀ 3.00 − **6 rm** ⌷ 32.00/38.00 **t.**

KINVER Staffs. 403 404 N 26 − see Stourbridge (West Midlands).

KIRKBY Merseyside 402 403 L 23 − pop. 52,825 − ECD : Wednesday − ✿ 051 Liverpool.
🏌 Liverpool Municipal, Ingoe Lane ℰ 546 5435.
🅱 Municipal Buildings, Cherryfield Drive ℰ 548 6555.
♦London 214 − ♦ Blackpool 54 − ♦Liverpool 7 − ♦Manchester 31.

🏨 **Crest** (Crest), East Lancs Rd, Knowsley, Prescot, L34 9HA, S : 1 ½ m. at junction A 580 and
A 5207 ℰ 546 7531, Telex 629769 − 📺 ➩wc 🅰 🅿 🔊. 🔼 🔼 🔊 ⑩ VISA ⌾
M approx. 10.85 **st.** − ⌷ 5.75 − **50 rm** 41.00/50.00 **st.** − SB (weekends only) 51.00 **st.**

KIRKBY FLEETHAM North Yorks. − pop. 406 (inc. Fencote) − ✉ ✿ 0609 Northallerton.
♦London 236 − ♦Leeds 46 − ♦Middlesbrough 31 − ♦Newcastle-upon-Tyne 51 − York 37.

🏨 **Kirkby Fleetham Hall** ⌾, DL7 0SU, N : 1 m. ℰ 748226, ≼, « Georgian country house »,
㆟, park − 📺 ➩wc ☎ 🅿 🔊 🔼 VISA ⌾
M (dinner only and Sunday lunch) 13.50 **st.** − **15 rm** ⌷ 43.00/69.00 **st.**

KIRKBY LONSDALE Cumbria 402 M 21 − pop. 1,557 − ECD : Wednesday − ✉ Carnforth −
✿ 0468.
🏌 Casterton Rd ℰ 71429, 1 m. on Sedbergh Rd.
🅱 18 Main St. ℰ 71603.
♦London 259 − ♦Carlisle 62 − Kendal 13 − Lancaster 17 − ♦Leeds 58.

🏨 **Royal,** Main St., Market Sq., LA6 2AE, ℰ 71217 − 📺 ➩wc 🅿 🔊 🔼 ⑩ VISA
closed first 2 weeks January − **M** (bar lunch)/dinner 10.50 **st.** and a la carte ⌀ 2.95 − **22 rm**
⌷ 20.00/45.00 **st.** − SB (October-March except Christmas) 45.00/50.00 **st.**

at Casterton NE : 1 ¼ m. on A 683 − ✉ ✿ 0468 Kirkby Lonsdale :

🏨 **Pheasant Inn,** LA6 2SD, ℰ 71230 − 📺 ➩wc 🅿
M (bar lunch Monday to Saturday)/dinner 15.00 **t.** ⌀ 3.00 − **14 rm** ⌷ 19.50/32.00 **t.** − SB
90.00/95.00 **st.**

KIRKBYMOORSIDE North Yorks. 402 R 21 − pop. 2,227 − ECD : Thursday − ✿ 0751.
🏌 Manor Vale ℰ 31525.
♦London 244 − Scarborough 26 − York 33.

🏨 **George and Dragon,** 17 Market Pl., YO6 6AA, ℰ 31637, ㆟ − 📺 ➩wc 🍴wc ☎ 🅿 🔊 VISA
⌾
closed 24 to 26 December − **M** 6.00/12.00 and a la carte ⌀ 3.10 − **23 rm** ⌷ 10.00/36.00.

at Fadmoor N : 2 ½ m. − ✉ York − ✿ 0751 Kirkbymoorside :

X **Plough Inn,** YO6 6HY, ℰ 31515 − 🅿
closed Sunday, Monday, 1 week February, 1 week May and 1 week October − **M** (dinner only)
(booking essential) a la carte 8.40/9.50 **st.** ⌀ 2.20.

NISSAN Pickering Rd ℰ 31551   VAUXHALL-OPEL Piercy End ℰ 31434
RENAULT New Rd ℰ 31401

KIRKBY STEPHEN Cumbria 402 M 20 − pop. 1,518 − ECD : Thursday − ✿ 0930.
Envir. : Brough (Castle ruins 12C-14C : keep ⁂* *AC*) N : 4 m.
🅱 Bank House, 22 Market St. ℰ 71804.
♦London 285 − ♦Carlisle 48 − Kendal 24.

🏨 **King's Arms,** Market Sq., CA17 4QN, ℰ 71378, ㆟ − 🅿 🔊 VISA
closed Christmas Day − **M** (bar lunch Monday to Saturday)/dinner 10.00 **t.** and a la carte ⌀ 3.00
− **9 rm** ⌷ 15.50/35.00 **t.** − SB (October-May except Bank Holidays) 38.00 **st.**

[KIRKOSWALD] Cumbria [401] [402] L 19 – pop. 730 – ✉ Penrith – ☎ 076 883 Lazonby.

♦London 300 – ♦Carlisle 23 – Kendal 41 – Lancaster 58.

🏠 **Prospect Hill** 🐦, CA10 1ER, N : ¾ m. ☎ 500, ←, « Converted 18C farm buildings », 🌳 – 🛁wc Ⓟ. [CB] [AE] [DC] [VISA]. ✈
closed February – **M** (lunch by arrangement) 7.00/15.00 **t.** 🍷 3.20 – **10 rm** ☕ 14.50/40.00 **t.**

[KIRTON] Notts. – see Ollerton.

[KNAPTON] Norfolk – see North Walsham.

[KNARESBOROUGH] North Yorks. [402] P 21 – pop. 12,910 – ECD : Thursday – ☎ 0423 Harrogate.

⛳18 Boroughbridge Rd ☎ 863219, N : 1 ½ m.

[i] Market Place ☎ 866886 (summer only).

♦London 217 – Bradford 21 – Harrogate 3 – ♦Leeds 18 – York 18.

🏨 **Dower House,** Bond End, HG5 9AL, ☎ 863302, 🌳 – [TV] 🛁wc 🚿wc ☎ Ⓟ. [CB] [VISA]. ✈
closed 25 and 26 December – **M** *(closed Saturday lunch)* 13.30 **t.** (dinner) and a la carte 🍷 3.25 – **20 rm** ☕ 25.00/45.00 **t.**, **1 suite** 52.00/60.00 **t.** – SB (weekends only) (November-April) 54.00 **st.**

🍴🍴 **Schwallers,** 6-8 Bond End, HG5 9AQ, ☎ 863899 – [CB] [VISA]
closed Monday lunch, Tuesday and 9 to 25 February – **M** (booking essential)(dinner only and lunch Sunday and summer)/dinner 11.50 **t.** and a la carte 🍷 2.40.

FORD York Place ☎ 862291

[KNIGHTWICK] Heref. and Worc. [403] [404] M 27 – pop. 82 – ECD : Wednesday – ✉ Worcester – ☎ 0886.

♦London 132 – Hereford 20 – Leominster 18 – Worcester 8.

🏠 Talbot, WR6 5PH, on B 4197 ☎ 21235, 🎣, squash – 🛁wc 🚿wc Ⓟ. [CB] [VISA]
M *(closed dinner Sunday and Monday)* (bar lunch Monday to Saturday) – **9 rm**.

[KNOWLE] West Midlands [403] [404] O 26 – pop. 16,850 – ECD : Thursday – ✉ Solihull – ☎ 056 45.

♦London 108 – ♦Birmingham 9 – ♦Coventry 10 – Warwick 11.

🏠 **Greswolde Arms** (Golden Oak), High St., B93 OLP, ☎ 2711 – [TV] 🚿wc ☎ Ⓟ. 🏛. [CB] [AE] [VISA]. ✈
M *(closed Saturday lunch and Sunday dinner)* 7.00 (dinner) and a la carte 🍷 2.60 – **18 rm** ☕ 24.00/38.00.

🍴🍴 **Florentine,** 15 Kenilworth Rd, B93 0JB, ☎ 6449, Italian rest. – [CB] [AE] [DC] [VISA]
closed Monday lunch, Sunday and Bank Holidays – **M** 6.00 **t.** (lunch) and a la carte 8.50/11.60 **t.**

AUSTIN-ROVER 25 Station Rd ☎ 4221
NISSAN Four Ashes Rd ☎ 560 5118
VAUXHALL Grange Rd, Dorridge ☎ 6131

[KNOWL HILL] Berks. [404] R 29 – ✉ Twyford – ☎ 062 882 Littlewick Green.

♦London 38 – Maidenhead 5 – Reading 8.

🍴🍴 **Bird in Hand,** Bath Rd, RG10 9UP, ☎ 2781, 🌳 – Ⓟ. [CB] [AE] [DC] [VISA]
M 7.95/10.50 **t.** and a la carte 🍷 3.00.

at Warren Row NW : 1 m. – ✉ Knowl Hill – ☎ 062 882 Littlewick Green :

🍴🍴 **Warrener,** Wargrave, RG10 8QS, ☎ 2803 – Ⓟ. [CB] [AE] [DC] [VISA]
closed Saturday lunch, Sunday, Monday, first week April and last week August – **M** 12.50 **t.** (lunch) and a la carte 15.25/20.00 **t.** 🍷 3.00.

[KNUTSFORD] Cheshire [402] [403] [404] M 24 – pop. 13,628 – ECD : Wednesday – ☎ 0565.

Envir. : Tatton Hall★ (Georgian) and gardens★★ *AC*, N : 2 m. – Jodrell Bank (Concourse building-radiotelescope *AC*) SE : 8 ½ m.

⛳18 Mere Golf ☎ 0565 (Bucklow Hill) 830155, NW : 3 m. on A 50.

[i] Council Offices, Toft Rd ☎ 2611.

♦London 187 – Chester 25 – ♦Liverpool 33 – ♦Manchester 18 – ♦Stoke-on-Trent 30.

🏨 **Cottons,** Manchester Rd, WA16 0SU, NE : 1 ½ m. on A 50 ☎ 50333, Telex 669931, 🏊 – [lift] [TV] 🛁wc ☎ ♿ Ⓟ. 🏛. [CB] [AE] [DC] [VISA]
M 7.00/13.00 **t.** and a la carte 🍷 3.35 – **62 rm** ☕ 46.00/56.00 **t.**, **9 suites** 58.00/65.00 **t.** – SB (weekends only) 63.00 **st.**

🏨 **Royal George,** King St., WA16 6EE, ☎ 4151 – [lift] [TV] 🛁wc ☎ Ⓟ. [CB] [AE] [DC] [VISA]. ✈
closed Christmas Day – **M** (grill rest. only) 4.00 **st.** – **31 rm** ☕ 28.00/43.00 **st.**

🏠 **Longview,** 55 Manchester Rd, WA16 0LX, ☎ 2119 – [TV] 🚿wc Ⓟ
closed Christmas-New Year – **14 rm** ☕ 17.00/25.50 **st.**

XXX **La Belle Epoque** with rm, 60 King St., WA16 6ED, 𝒫 3060, « Art nouveau » – 📺 ⌂wc 🅿.
🔝 🅰🅴 ⓄⒹ 𝘝𝘐𝘚𝘈. 𝔛
closed Sunday, first week January and Bank Holidays – **M** (dinner only) (booking essential) a
la carte 11.75/15.50 t. ⋔ 2.50 – 🖙 3.50 – **5 rm** 25.00/35.00 st.

X **David's Place,** 10 Princess St., WA16 6DD, 𝒫 3356 – 🔝 🅰🅴 ⓄⒹ 𝘝𝘐𝘚𝘈
closed Sunday and Bank Holidays – **M** 9.95 t. (dinner) and a la carte ⋔ 2.90.

at Lower Peover S : 3 ½ m. by A 50 on B 5081 – ✉ Knutsford – ☎ 056 581 Lower Peover :

X **Bells of Peover, The Cobbles,** 𝒫 2269, 🌳 – 🅿.

at Bucklow Hill NW : 3 ½ m. at junction A 556 and A 5034 – ✉ Knutsford – ☎ 0565
Bucklow Hill :

🏛 **Swan Inn** (De Vere), Chester Rd, WA16 6RD, 𝒫 830295, Telex 666911 – 📺 ⌂wc 🏛wc ☎
🅿. 🔝. 🔝 🅰🅴 ⓄⒹ 𝘝𝘐𝘚𝘈
M 7.00/8.50 st. and a la carte ⋔ 3.50 – **70 rm** 🖙 42.00/52.00 st. – SB (weekends only)
60.00/65.00 st.

ALFA-ROMEO, LANCIA London Rd, Allostock 𝒫   RENAULT Toft Rd 𝒫 4294
056 581 (Lower Peover) 2899   VOLVO Park Lane, Pickmere 𝒫 056 589 (Pickmere)
FORD Garden Rd 𝒫 4141   3254

LACOCK Wilts. 🔢🔢 N 29 The West Country G. – pop. 1 ,289 – ✉ Chippenham – ☎ 024 973.
See : Site* – Lacock Village : High St.*, St. Cyriac Church*, Fox Talbot Museum of Photography*AC – Lacock Abbey*AC.
♦London 109 – Bath 16 – ♦Bristol 30 – Chippenham 3.

X **Sign of the Angel** with rm, 6 Church St., SN15 2LA, 𝒫 230, English rest., « 14C inn in
National Trust village », 🌳 – ⌂wc
closed lunch Saturday and Bank Holidays, Sunday dinner and 22 December-5 January – **M**
12.50/16.50 st. and a la carte ⋔ 4.00 – **6 rm** 🖙 30.00/50.00 st. – SB (November-March) 70.00 st.

LAKE VYRNWY Powys 🔢🔢 J 25 – ☎ 069 173 Llanwddyn.
♦London 204 – Chester 52 – Llanfyllin 10 – Shrewsbury 40.

🏛 **Lake Vyrnwy** ⤡, SY10 0LY, ✉ Llanwddyn via Oswestry, Salop 𝒫 244, ≤ Lake Vyrnwy,
« Country house atmosphere », 🥄, 🌳, park, 𝔛 – ⌂wc ⌦ 🅿. 𝔛
closed February – **M** (buffet lunch Monday to Saturday)/dinner 8.75 st. ⋔ 2.50 – **28 rm**
🖙 16.00/58.00 st. – SB 55.00/60.00 st.

LAMORNA COVE Cornwall 🔢 D 33 – ECD : Thursday – ✉ ☎ 0736 Penzance.
Envir. : Land's End** W : 7 ½ m.
♦London 323 – Penzance 5 – Truro 31.

🏛 **Lamorna Cove** ⤡, TR19 6XH, 𝒫 731411, ≤, ⍐ heated, 🌳 – 🛗 📺 ⌂wc 🏛wc ☎ 🅿. 🔝 🅰🅴
ⓄⒹ 𝘝𝘐𝘚𝘈
closed December-mid February – **M** 6.75/9.75 t. and a la carte ⋔ 3.50 – **18 rm** 🖙 21.50/32.00 t.
– SB (except summer) 49.00/65.00 st.

LAMPETER (LLANBEDR PONT STEFFAN) Dyfed 🔢 H 27 – pop. 1 ,908 – ECD : Wednesday –
☎ 0570.
🛏 Cilgwyn, Llangybi 𝒫 057 045 (Llangybi) 286, NE : 4 m. off A 485.
♦London 223 – Brecon 41 – Carmarthen 22 – ♦Swansea 50.

🏛 **Black Lion Royal,** High St., SA48 7BG, 𝒫 422172 – 📺 ⌂wc 🅿. 🔝 𝘝𝘐𝘚𝘈
M *(closed Sunday lunch and Sunday dinner to non-residents)* 6.50 t. and a la carte – **15 rm**
🖙 15.50/30.00 t. – SB 36.00/41.50 st.

LAMPHEY Dyfed – see Pembroke.

LANCASTER Lancs. 🔢 L 21 – pop. 43 ,902 – ECD : Wednesday – ☎ 0524.
🛈 7 Dalton Sq. 𝒫 32878.
♦London 252 – ♦Blackpool 26 – Bradford 62 – Burnley 44 – ♦Leeds 71 – ♦Middlesbrough 97 – Preston 26.

🏛 **Post House** (T.H.F.), Waterside Park, Caton Rd, LA1 3RA, NE : 1 ¼ m. on A 683 𝒫 65999,
Telex 65363, 🔲, 🥄 – 🛗 📺 ☎ 🅿. 🔝. 🔝 🅰🅴 ⓄⒹ 𝘝𝘐𝘚𝘈
M 8.90/11.50 st. and a la carte ⋔ 2.80 – 🖙 5.50 – **117 rm** 41.00/51.50 st.

🏛 **Hampson House,** Hampson Lane, LA2 0JB, S : 5 m. by A 6, ✉ Galgate 𝒫 751158, 🌳 – 📺
⌂wc 🅿. 𝘝𝘐𝘚𝘈. 𝔛
M (bar lunch)/dinner a la carte 5.50/10.50 t. ⋔ 2.40 – **13 rm** 🖙 16.00/32.00 st.

ALFA-ROMEO, DAIHATSU, LADA Scotsforth Rd 𝒫   FORD Parliament St. 𝒫 63553
62939   HYUNDAI, PONY Brookhouse 𝒫 0524 (Caton) 770501
AUSTIN-ROVER King St. 𝒫 32233   PEUGEOT-TALBOT Bulk Rd 𝒫 63373

LANGSTONE Gwent 🔢 L 29 – see Newport.

LANREATH Cornwall 403 G 32 – pop. 449 – ⊠ Looe – ✪ 0503.
♦London 269 – ♦Plymouth 26 – Truro 34.

🏠 **Punch Bowl Inn,** PL13 2NX, ✆ 20218, 舞 – 📺 🗂wc 🕅 🅿. 🅰 VISA
April-December – **M** 7.50 **t.** (dinner) and a la carte 🍴 2.40 – **18 rm** ⊊ 9.70/34.40 **t.**

LAPFORD Devon 408 I 31 – pop. 875 – ECD : Wednesday – ⊠ Crediton – ✪ 036 35.
♦London 218 – Exeter 17 – ♦Plymouth 63 – Taunton 54.

↑ **Nymet Bridge House** ⑤, EX17 6QX, NW : 1 ½ m. by A 377 ✆ 334, 舞 – 🗂wc 🅿. ⌘
closed Christmas – **5 rm** ⊊ 11.00/24.00.

LARKFIELD Kent 404 V 30 – see Maidstone.

LASTINGHAM North Yorks. 402 R 21 – pop. 108 – ECD : Wednesday – ⊠ York – ✪ 075 15.
♦London 244 – Scarborough 26 – York 32.

🏠 **Lastingham Grange** ⑤, YO6 6TH, ✆ 345, ≼, « Country house atmosphere », 舞 – 📺
🗂wc 🅿. AE ①
closed mid December-February – **M** (bar lunch Monday to Saturday)/dinner 11.50 **t.** 🍴 2.50 –
12 rm ⊊ 30.75/61.00 **t.** – SB 70.75/77.75 **st.**

at Hutton-Le-Hole W : 2 m. – ⊠ York – ✪ 075 15 Lastingham :

↑ **Barn,** YO6 6UA, ✆ 311 – 🗂wc 🅿. ⌘
March-October – **9 rm** ⊊ 10.00/25.00 **t.**

LAVENHAM Suffolk 404 W 27 – pop. 1,658 – ECD : Wednesday – ⊠ Sudbury – ✪ 0787.
See : SS. Peter and Paul's Church : the Spring Parclose★ (Flemish).
♦London 66 – ♦Cambridge 39 – Colchester 22 – ♦Ipswich 19.

🏨 **Swan** (T.H.F.), High St., CO10 9QA, ✆ 247477, « Part 14C timbered inn », 舞 – 📺 🅿. 🅰. 🅰
AE ① VISA
M 7.75/11.50 **st.** and a la carte 🍴 3.50 – ⊊ 5.50 – **42 rm** 38.50/51.50 **st.**

PEUGEOT, TALBOT Sudbury Rd ✆ 247228

LEAMINGTON SPA Warw. 403 404 P 27 – see Royal Leamington Spa.

LEDBURY Heref. and Worc. 403 404 M 27 – pop. 4,985 – ECD : Wednesday – ✪ 0531.
See : Church Lane★.
Envir. : Birtsmorton Court★ (15C) AC, SE : 7 m.
🛈 St. Katherine's, High St. ✆ 2461.
♦London 119 – Hereford 14 – Newport 46 – Worcester 16.

🏠 **Feathers,** High St., HR8 1DS, ✆ 5266, « Heavily timbered 16C inn », squash – 📺 🗂wc 🅿.
🅰 AE ①
M (buffet lunch)/dinner 9.00 **st.** and a la carte 🍴 2.40 – **11 rm** ⊊ 32.00/45.00 **st.** – SB (October-
April) 60.00 **st.**

🏠 **Royal Oak,** The Southend, HR8 2EY, ✆ 2110 – 🅿. 🅰 VISA. ⌘
M (buffet lunch)/dinner a la carte approx. 5.85 **t.** – **8 rm** ⊊ 13.50/37.50 **t.** – SB (October-Easter
except Christmas) 34.00/55.00 **st.**

at Wellington Heath N : 2 m. by B 4214 – ⊠ ✪ 0531 Ledbury :

🏠 **Hope End Country House** ⑤, Hope End, HR8 1JQ, N : ¾ m. ✆ 3613, « Country house
atmosphere », 舞, park – 🗂wc 🏤 🅿. 🅰 VISA. ⌘
March-November – **M** (dinner only) (booking essential) 16.50 **st.** 🍴 3.00 – **7 rm**
⊊ 33.50/61.00 **st.** – SB 71.00/90.00 **st.**

AUSTIN-ROVER New St. ✆ 2233   FORD New St. ✆ 2261

LEE Devon 408 H 30 – see Ilfracombe.

LEEDS West Yorks. 402 P 22 – pop. 445,242 – ECD : Wednesday – ✪ 0532.
See : St. John's Church★ 17C DZ A.
Envir. : Temple Newsam House★ 17C (interior★★) AC, E : 4 m. CX D – Kirkstall Abbey★ (ruins 12C)
AC, NW : 3 m. BV.

📷₁₈, 📷₁₈ The Lady Dorothy Wood, The Lord Irwin, Temple Newsam Rd, Halton ✆ 645624, E : 3 m. CX –
📷₁₈ Gotts Park, Armley Ridge Rd, ✆ 638232, W : 2 m. BV – 📷₁₈ Horsforth, Layton Rise ✆ 586819, NW :
6 m. BV – 📷₁₈ Middleton Park Municipal, Town St., Middleton ✆ 700449, S : 3 m. CX.

✈ Leeds and Bradford Airport : ✆ 0532 (Rawdon) 503431, NW : 8 m. by A 65 and A 658 BV.
🛈 Central Library, Calverley St. ✆ 462454.
♦London 204 – ♦Liverpool 75 – ♦Manchester 43 – ♦Newcastle-upon-Tyne 95 – ♦Nottingham 74.

Plans on following pages

🏛 Ladbroke Dragonara (Ladbroke), Neville St., LS1 4BX, ℰ 442000, Telex 557143 – 📶 🔲 🔲 ☎
🔥 🍴 🏛.
234 rm.
DZ r

🏛 Queen's (T.H.F.), City Sq., LS1 1PL, ℰ 431323, Telex 55161 – 📶 🔲 ⌂wc 🐾. 🏛. 🔼 AE ⓪
VISA
DZ a
M 8.50/9.50 st. and a la carte 🍷 4.00 – ☲ 5.50 – 198 rm 42.00/56.00 st.

🏛 Metropole (T.H.F.), King St., LS1 2HQ, ℰ 450841, Telex 557755 – 📶 🔲 ⌂wc 🐾 🅿. 🏛. 🔼
AE ⓪ VISA
CZ o
M (carving rest.) 8.25 st. and a la carte 🍷 2.70 – ☲ 5.50 – 110 rm 37.00/45.00 st.

🏛 Merrion, Merrion Centre, 17 Wade Lane, LS2 8NH, ℰ 439191, Telex 55459 – 📶 🔲 ⌂wc ☎
🅿. 🏛. 🔼 AE ⓪ VISA. 🌿
DZ x
M 7.50/9.50 st. and a la carte 🍷 3.25 – ☲ 5.25 – 120 rm 44.00/57.00 st. – SB (weekends only)
57.00/62.00 st.

↑ Aragon 🌮, 250 Stainbeck Lane, LS7 2PS, ℰ 759306, 🌳 – 🔲 ⌂wc ⌂wc 🅿. 🔼 ⓪ VISA
closed Christmas – 11 rm ☲ 12.95/25.80 s.
CV c

↑ Pinewood, 78 Potternewton Lane, LS7 3LW, ℰ 622561, 🌳 – 🍴 🅿. 🔼. 🌿
closed 1 week Christmas – 11 rm ☲ 16.00/32.00 t.
AY s

↑ Ash Mount, 22 Wetherby Rd., Oakwood, LS8 2QD, ℰ 654263 – 🅿. 🌿
closed 1 week Christmas – 14 rm ☲ 13.25/23.00 st.
CV u

↑ Highfield, 79 Cardigan Rd, LS6 1EB, ℰ 752193 – 🅿
10 rm ☲ 10.50/19.00 t.
AY x

XXX Gardini's Terrazza, Minerva House, 16 Greek St., LS1 5RU, ℰ 432880, Italian rest. – 🔳
CDZ n

XXX Mandalay, 8 Harrison St., LS1 6PA, ℰ 446453, Indian rest. – 🔳
DZ e

XX Embassy, 333 Roundhay Rd, LS8 4HT, NE : 2 ½ m. by A 58 ℰ 490562 – 🅿. 🔼 AE ⓪ VISA
closed Sunday, 1 week January, 2 weeks August-September and Bank Holidays – M (dinner
only) 11.20 t. and a la carte 🍷 2.75.
BY v

XX Shabab, 2 Eastgate, LS2 7JL, ℰ 468988, Indian rest. – 🔳
DZ v

at Seacroft NE : 5 ½ m. at junction of A 64 and A 6120 – ✉ ✪ 0532 Leeds :

🏛 Stakis Windmill (Stakis), Ring Rd, LS14 5QP, ℰ 732323 – 📶 🔳 rest 🔲 ⌂wc 🐾 🔥 🅿. 🏛.
🔼 AE ⓪ VISA
CV a
M (grill rest. only) 4.95/8.00 t. and a la carte – 40 rm ☲ 42.00/50.00 t.

at Garforth E : 6 m. at junction of A 63 and A 642 – CV – ✉ ✪ 0532 Leeds :

🏛 Ladbroke (Ladbroke), Wakefield Rd, LS25 1LH, ℰ 866556, Telex 556324 – 🔲 ⌂wc ☎ 🔥
🅿. 🏛. 🔼 AE ⓪ VISA
M (closed Saturday lunch) (carving rest.) 8.50/10.65 t. 🍷 3.70 – ☲ 5.50 – 142 rm 42.00/56.00 t.
– SB (weekends only) 39.50/57.00 st.

at Oulton SE : 6 ¼ m. at junction of A 639 and A 642 – ✉ ✪ 0532 Leeds :

🏛 Crest (Crest), The Grove, LS26 8EJ, ℰ 826201, Telex 557646 – 🔲 ⌂wc 🐾 🔥 🅿. 🔼 AE ⓪
VISA. 🌿
CX z
M approx. 11.50 st. – ☲ 5.75 – 40 rm 46.00/56.00 st. – SB (weekends only) 51.00 st.

at Liversedge SW : 9 m. on A 62 – BX – ✉ Liversedge – ✪ 0924 Heckmondwike :

XX Lillibet's with rm, Ashfield House, 64 Leeds Rd, WF15 6HX, ℰ 404911, 🌳 – 🔲 ⌂wc 🍴wc
🐾 🅿. 🔼 AE ⓪ VISA. 🌿
closed Sunday, 2 weeks July, 25 December-2 January and Bank Holidays – M (dinner only)
11.95 t. 🍷 3.50 – 7 rm ☲ 25.00/45.00 st.

at Horsforth NW : 5 m. by A 65 off A 6120 – ✉ ✪ 0532 Leeds :

XXX Low Hall, Calverley Lane, LS18 4EF, ℰ 588221, « Elizabethan manor », 🌳 – 🅿. 🔼 VISA
closed Saturday lunch, Sunday, Monday, 25 to 30 December and Bank Holidays – M 7.95/15.00
st. and a la carte 🍷 2.85.
BV a

XX Roman Garden, Hall Lane, Hall Park, LS18 5JY, ℰ 587962, ≼, Italian rest. – 🅿. 🔼 AE VISA
closed Saturday lunch, Sunday and Monday – M 11.25 t. (dinner) and a la carte 🍷 3.30.
BV i

at Bramhope NW : 8 m. on A 660 – BV – ✉ ✪ 0532 Leeds :

🏛 Post House (T.H.F.), Otley Rd, LS16 9JJ, ℰ 842911, Telex 556367, ≼ – 📶 🔳 rest 🔲 ⌂wc
🐾 🔥 🅿. 🏛. 🔼 AE ⓪ VISA
M 7.00 (lunch) and a la carte 9.40/16.15 st. 🍷 2.70 – ☲ 5.50 – 120 rm 43.00/51.50 st.

🏛 Parkway (Embassy), Otley Rd, LS16 8AG, S : 2 m. on A 660 ℰ 672551, 🌳 – 🔲 ⌂wc 🐾
🅿. 🏛. 🔼 AE ⓪ VISA. 🌿
M (closed Saturday lunch) (Sunday residents only) 9.00 st. and a la carte 🍷 2.75 – ☲ 5.00 –
39 rm 30.00/50.00 st. – SB (weekends only) 55.00 st.

MICHELIN Branch, Gelderd Rd, LS12 6EU, ℰ 793911 BX

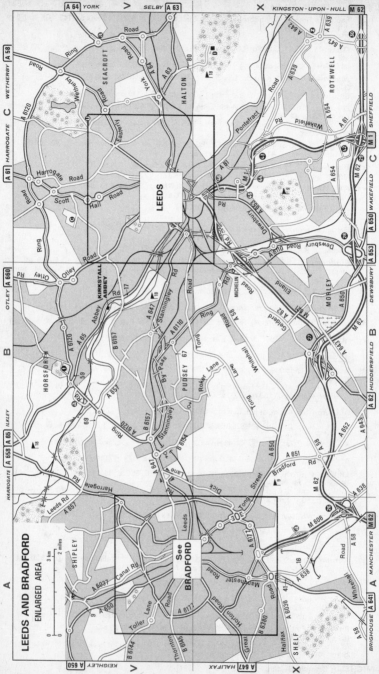

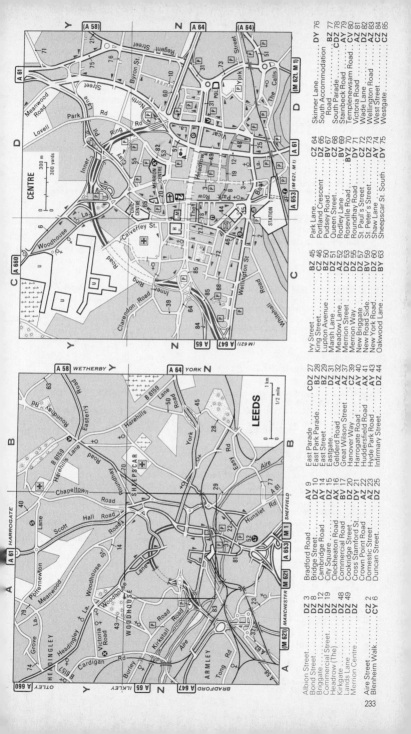

Albion Street.............DZ 3
Bond Street.............DZ 8
Brigate.............DZ 12
Commercial Street.............DZ 19
Headrow (The).............DZ
Kirkgate.............DZ 48
Lands Lane.............DZ 49
Merrion Centre.............DZ

Aire Street.............CZ 2
Blenheim Walk.............CY 6

Bradford Road.............AV 9
Bridge Street.............DZ 10
Cambridge Road.............DZ 14
City Square.............DZ 15
Cleckheaton Road.............AX 16
Gelderd Road.............BV 17
Commercial Road.............BV 17
Cookridge Street.............DZ 20
Cross Stamford St.............DY 21
Crown Point Road.............DZ 22
Domestic Street.............AZ 23
Duncan Street.............DZ 25

East Parade.............CDZ 27
East Park Parade.............BZ 28
East Street.............DZ 29
Eastgate.............DZ 31
Gelderd Road.............AZ 32
Great Wilson Street.............CZ 37
Hanover Way.............CZ 39
Harrogate Road.............AY 40
Harehills Road.............AX 41
Hyde Park Road.............AY 43
Infirmary Street.............DZ 44

Ivy Street.............BZ 45
King Street.............CZ 46
Lupton Avenue.............BZ 50
Marsh Lane.............DZ 51
Meadow Lane.............AZ 52
Merrion Street.............DZ 53
Merrion Way.............DZ 55
New Briggate.............DZ 57
New Road Side.............BV 59
New York Lane.............DZ 60
Oakwood Lane.............BY 63

Park Lane.............CZ 64
Portland Crescent.............DZ 65
Pudsey Road.............AZ 67
Queen Street.............CZ 68
Rodley Lane.............BV 69
Roseville Road.............BYZ 70
Roundhay Road.............DY 71
St. Paul's Street.............CZ 72
St. Peter's Street.............DZ 73
Shaw Lane.............AY 74
Sheepscar St. South.............DY 75

Skinner Lane.............DY 76
South Accommodation Road.............BZ 77
South Parade.............CZ 78
Stainbeck Road.............AV 79
Templenewsam Road.............AV 80
Victoria Road.............DY 81
Wade Lane.............DZ 82
Wellington Road.............AZ 83
West Street.............AY 84
Westgate.............CZ 85

LEEDS

LEEDS

AUSTIN-ROVER Town St., Stanningley ✆ 571811
AUSTIN-ROVER Water Lane ✆ 438091
AUSTIN-ROVER-DAIMLER-JAGUAR, ROLLS
ROYCE-BENTLEY Roseville Rd ✆ 432731
AUSTIN-ROVER Breary Lane, Bramhope ✆ 0532
(Arthington) 842696
BMW Sheepscar Way ✆ 620641
FORD 83 Roseville Rd ✆ 455955
FORD Aberford Rd ✆ 863261
FORD Whitehall Rd ✆ 634222
LADA, ALFA-ROMEO Domestic St. ✆ 468141
MAZDA York Rd ✆ 480093
NISSAN Meadow Rd ✆ 444531

NISSAN, PORSCHE, SAAB Apperley Lane, Yeadon
✆ 0532 (Rawdon) 502231
PEUGEOT South Milford ✆ 0977 (South Milford)
682714
PEUGEOT-TALBOT Wike Ridge Lane ✆ 661129
RENAULT Regent St. ✆ 430837
TOYOTA Low Rd ✆ 702341
TOYOTA Regent St. ✆ 444223
VAUXHALL 123 Hunslet Rd ✆ 439911
VAUXHALL-OPEL Armley Rd ✆ 434554
VOLVO Wellington Rd ✆ 436412
VW, AUDI Gelderd Rd ✆ 633431

LEEMING BAR North Yorks. 402 P 21 – pop. 1 ,468 – ECD : Wednesday – ✉ Northallerton –
✆ 0677 Bedale.

♦London 235 – ♦Leeds 44 – ♦Middlesborough 30 – ♦Newcastle-upon-Tyne 52 – York 37.

  🏠 **White Rose,** DL7 9AY, ✆ 22707 – 📺 ⌷wc �𝄐wc 🅿. 🅰 ⒶⒺ ⑩ 𝗩𝗜𝗦𝗔
    M 8.95 st. (dinner) and a la carte 🍷 2.75 – **12 rm** ☎ 14.75/27.50 st. – SB (weekends only)
    (October-March) 32.00 st.

LEE-ON-THE-SOLENT Hants. 403 404 Q 31 – pop. 7 ,068 – ECD : Thursday – ✆ 0705.

♦London 81 – ♦Portsmouth 13 – ♦Southampton 15 – Winchester 23.

  🏠 **Belle Vue,** 39 Marine Par. East, PO13 2BW, ✆ 550258 – 📺 ⌷wc �𝄐wc 🅿. 🅰 𝗩𝗜𝗦𝗔
    closed 25 and 26 December – **M** (carving rest.) a la carte approx. 7.95 t. 🍷 2.70 – **32 rm**
    ⌷ 24.50/40.00 t. – SB 43.50 st.

NISSAN High St. ✆ 551785

LEICESTER Leics. 402 403 404 Q 26 – pop. 324 ,394 – ECD : Monday and Thursday – ✆ 0533.

See : Museum of local archaeology, Jewry Wall and baths★ AC BY M1 – Museum and Art Gallery★
CY M2 – St. Mary de Castro's Church★ 12C BY A.

🏌 Leicestershire, Evington Lane ✆ 738825 E : 2 m. AY – 🏌 Western Park, Scudamore Rd ✆ 876158,
W : 4 m. AY – 🏌 Cambridge Rd, Whetstone ✆ 861424 by A 426 AZ.

✈ East Midlands Airport : Castle Donington ✆ 0332 (Derby) 810621, NW : 22 m. by A 50 AX and
M1.

🛈 12 Bishop St. ✆ 556699.

♦London 107 – ♦Birmingham 43 – ♦Coventry 24 – ♦Nottingham 26.

Plans on following pages

  🏨 **Holiday Inn,** 129 St. Nicholas Circle, LE1 5LX, ✆ 531161, Telex 341281, 🔲 – 🛗 🔳 📺 ☎ ㉫
    🅿 🅰 🅰 ⒶⒺ ⑩ 𝗩𝗜𝗦𝗔   BY c
    M a la carte 8.20/23.45 st. 🍷 3.95 – ⌷ 5.15 – **188 rm** 36.00/50.00 s., **1 suite** 120.00 s.

  🏨 **Grand** (Embassy), 73 Granby St., LE1 6ES, ✆ 555599 – 🛗 📺 🅿 🅰 🅰 ⒶⒺ ⑩ 𝗩𝗜𝗦𝗔 ⌷⌷
    M (carving rest.) 8.25 st. 🍷 2.75 – ⌷ 5.00 – **93 rm** 40.00/46.75 st. – SB (weekends only)   CY o
    55.00 st.

  🏨 **Belmont** (Best Western), De Montfort St., LE1 7GR, ✆ 544773, Telex 34619 – 🛗 📺 ⌷wc ☎
    🅿 🅰 ⒶⒺ ⑩ 𝗩𝗜𝗦𝗔   CY c
    closed 23 December-3 January – **M** (closed Saturday lunch, Sunday dinner and Bank Holidays)
    7.50/8.00 st. and a la carte 🍷 4.50 – **60 rm** ⌷ 25.00/53.00 st. – SB (weekends only) 45.00/60.00 st.

  🏨 **Eaton Bray,** Abbey St., LE1 3TE, ✆ 50666, Telex 342434 – 🛗 📺 ⌷wc �𝄐wc ⌷ 🅿. 🅰 🅰
    ⒶⒺ ⑩ 𝗩𝗜𝗦𝗔   CX a
    M (closed Sunday and Bank Holidays) (carving rest.) 5.95 st. and a la carte 🍷 2.35 – **72 rm**
    ⌷ 17.00/36.95 st. – SB 35.90/48.85 st.

  🏨 **Ladbroke International** (Ladbroke), Humberstone Rd, LE5 3AT, ✆ 20471, Telex 341460 –
    🛗 🔳 rest. 📺 ⌷wc ☎ 🅿. 🅰 🅰 ⒶⒺ ⑩ 𝗩𝗜𝗦𝗔   CX n
    closed Christmas Day – **M** a la carte lunch/dinner 9.25 st. – ⌷ 4.75 – **220 rm** 35.00/45.00 st.
    – SB (weekends only) 58.00 st.

  ↑ **Scotia,** 10 Westcotes Drive, LE3 0QR, ✆ 549200   AY e
    closed Christmas – **15 rm** ⌷ 14.00/24.00 st.

  ↑ **Burlington,** 3 Elmfield Av., Stoneygate, LE2 1RB, ✆ 705112 – 📺 �𝄐 🅿. 🅰 ⌷⌷   AY a
    17 rm ⌷ 13.00/25.00 t.

  ↑ **Rowans,** 290 London Rd, LE2 2AG, ✆ 705364, ⌷ – 𝄐 🅿. 🅰   AY i
    closed 23 December-2 January – **15 rm** ⌷ 15.50/25.00 st.

  ✕✕ **Water Margin,** 76-78 High St., ✆ 56422, Chinese-Cantonese rest. – 🔳   BY x

  at Rothley N : 5 m. by A 6 – AX – on B 5328 – ✉ ✆ 0533 Leicester :

  🏨 **Rothley Court** (Best Western) ⌷, West End Lane, LE7 7LG, W : ½ m. on B 5328 ✆ 374141,
    Telex 341995, ⌷, « Part 12C house and chapel », ⌷ – 📺 ☎ 🅿. 🅰 🅰 ⒶⒺ ⑩ 𝗩𝗜𝗦𝗔
    closed 25 and 26 December – **M** (closed Saturday lunch) 10.50/15.50 t. 🍷 4.50 – **34 rm**
    ⌷ 46.00/65.00 t. – SB (weekends only) 70.00/84.00 st.

  ↑ **Limes,** 35 Mount Sorrel Lane, LE7 7PS, ✆ 302531 – 𝄐wc 🅿. ⌷⌷
    10 rm ⌷ 11.50/21.00 s.

LEICESTER
BUILT UP AREA

Middleton Street . . . . **AZ** 43
Upperton Road . . . . **AY** 69
Uppingham Road . . . . **AX** 70

Walnut Street . . . . **AY** 72
Woodville Road . . . . **AX** 77
Wyngate Drive . . . . **AY** 78

Belgrave Road . . . . **AX** 3
Braunstone Avenue . . . . **AY** 9
Bull Head Street . . . . **AZ** 12
Chapel Lane . . . . **AY** 16
Fosse Road North . . . . **AX** 23
Henley Road . . . . **AX** 27
Humberstone Road . . . . **AX** 31
Knighton Lane East . . . . **AY** 34
Knighton Road . . . . **AY** 35
Lansdowne Road . . . . **AY** 36
Little Glen Road . . . . **AZ** 38
Marfitt Street . . . . **AX** 42

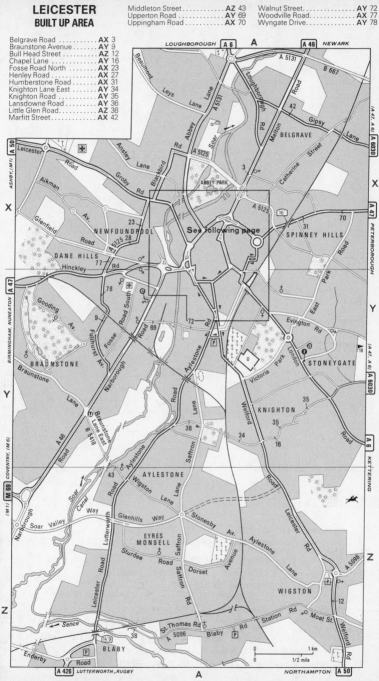

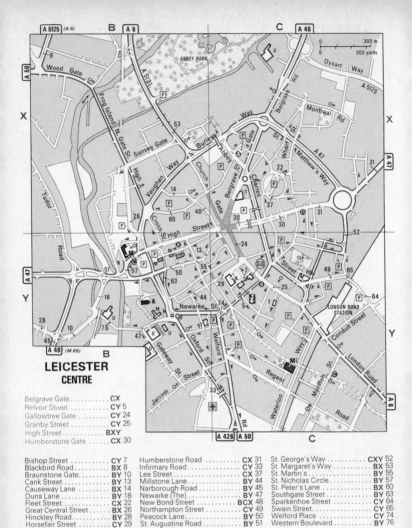

LEICESTER
CENTRE

Belgrave Gate	**CX**
Relvoir Street	**CY** 5
Gallowtree Gate	**CY** 24
Granby Street	**CY** 25
High Street	**BXY**
Humberstone Gate	**CX** 30

Bishop Street	**CY** 7	Humberstone Road	**CX** 31	St. George's Way	**CXY** 52
Blackbird Road	**BX** 8	Infirmary Road	**CY** 33	St. Margaret's Way	**BX** 53
Braunstone Gate	**BY** 10	Lee Street	**CX** 37	St. Martin's	**BX** 55
Cank Street	**BY** 13	Millstone Lane	**BY** 44	St. Nicholas Circle	**BX** 57
Causeway Lane	**BX** 14	Narborough Road	**BY** 45	St. Peter's Lane	**BX** 60
Duns Lane	**BY** 18	Newarke (The)	**BY** 47	Southgate Street	**BY** 63
Fleet Street	**CX** 22	New Bond Street	**BCX** 48	Sparkenhoe Street	**CY** 64
Great Central Street	**BX** 26	Northampton Street	**CY** 49	Swain Street	**CY** 65
Hinckley Road	**BY** 28	Peacock Lane	**BY** 50	Welford Place	**CY** 74
Horsefair Street	**CY** 29	St. Augustine Road	**BY** 51	Western Boulevard	**BY** 76

at Oadby SE : 3 ¼ m. by A 6 on A 5096 – AY – ⊠ ✆ 0533 Leicester :

🏦 **Leicestershire Moat House** (Q.M.H.), Wigston Rd, LE2 5QE, ✆ 719441 – 🛗 📺 🚽wc ☎
🅿 🏛. 🔌 🅰🅴 ⑩ 𝗩𝗜𝗦𝗔
M 5.50/6.50 t. and a la carte – **29 rm** ⊠ 36.50/46.50 t.

at Whetstone S : 5 ½ m. by A 426 – AZ – ⊠ – ✆ 0533 Leicester :

XXX **Old Vicarage,** 123 Enderby Rd, LE8 3JH, ✆ 771195 – 🅿
closed Saturday lunch, Sunday and Bank Holidays – **M** a la carte 8.00/11.60 ⏐ 3.00.

at Braunstone SW : 2 m. on A 46 – ⊠ ✆ 0533 Leicester :

🏛 **Post House** (T.H.F.), Braunstone Lane East, LE3 2FW, ✆ 896688, Telex 341009 – 🛗 📺
🚽wc ☎ 🛦 🅿 🏛. 🔌 🅰🅴 ⑩ 𝗩𝗜𝗦𝗔   AY **u**
M *(closed Saturday lunch)* 6.50/8.95 **st.** and a la carte ⏐ 2.70 – ⊠ 5.50 – **172 rm** 40.00/46.00 **st.**

at Narborough SW : 6 m. by A 46 – AZ – on B 4114 – ⊠ ✆ 0533 Leicester :

🏠 **Charnwood,** 48 Leicester Rd, LE9 5DF, ✆ 862218, 🐎 – 📺 🚽wc 🅿. ✂
23 rm.

236

at Leicester Forest East W : 3 m. on A 47 – AY – ⊠ ☎ 0533 Leicester :

🏨 **Leicester Forest Moat House** (Q.M.H.), Hinckley Rd, LE3 3GH, ✆ 394661 – 📺 ⇔wc ☎ 🅿 🛅 📼 ⴊ ⓪ 📶 ✄
closed 25 to 31 December – **M** 6.70/8.50 **st.** and a la carte ⌁ 3.25 – **30 rm** ⊐ 36.00/42.00 **st.**

ALFA-ROMEO 2 Saxby St. ✆ 543300	NISSAN Abbey Lane ✆ 666861
AUDI, VW Dover St. ✆ 556262	NISSAN Conduit St. ✆ 544301
AUSTIN-ROVER Leicester Rd ✆ 881601	PEUGEOT, TALBOT Stoneygate Rd ✆ 700521
AUSTIN-ROVER Parker Drive ✆ 352587	PORSCHE, ALFA-ROMEO Coventry Rd at Narbo-
AUSTIN-ROVER 60/62 North Gate St. ✆ 28612	rough ✆ 848270
CITROEN 135/137 Queens Rd ✆ 709523	RENAULT, ROLLS ROYCE Welford Rd ✆ 548757
CITROEN, SUZUKI Lee Circle ✆ 25285	SKODA 252 Loughborough Rd ✆ 661135
FORD Belgrave Gate ✆ 50111	TALBOT 91 Abbey Lane ✆ 61501
FORD Welford Rd ✆ 706215	VAUXHALL-OPEL Evington ✆ 730421
HONDA 7 Pike St. ✆ 56281	VAUXHALL-OPEL Aylestone Rd ✆ 547515
LADA Uppingham Rd ✆ 418544	VOLVO 459 Aylestone Rd ✆ 831052

LEIGH Greater Manchester **402 403 404** M 23 – pop. 42,627 – ECD : Wednesday – ☎ 0942.
🛆 Kenyon Hall, Culcheth ✆ 092 576 (Culcheth) 3130, S : by A 574.
♦London 205 – ♦Liverpool 25 – ♦Manchester 12 – Preston 25.

🏨 **Greyhound** (Embassy), Warrington Rd, WN7 3XQ, S : 1 m. at junction A 580 and A 574
✆ 671256 – ⋮⋮ 📺 ⇔wc ☎ 🅿 🛅 📼 ⴊ ⓪ 📶
M *(closed Sunday dinner to non-residents)* 7.95 **st.** and a la carte ⌁ 2.25 – ⊐ 5.00 – **54 rm**
38.50/44.00 **st.** – SB (weekends only) 45.00 **st.**

AUSTIN-ROVER Wigan Rd ✆ 671131	NISSAN 39 Plank Lane ✆ 673334
FIAT Small Brook Lane, Atherton ✆ 882201	VAUXHALL-OPEL Wigan Rd ✆ 602931
FORD Brown St. Nth ✆ 673401	VAUXHALL-OPEL 196 Chapel St. ✆ 671326

LENWADE-GREAT WITCHINGHAM Norfolk **404** X 25 – ECD : Wednesday – ⊠ ☎ 0605 Norwich.
♦London 121 – Fakenham 14 – ♦Norwich 10.

🏛 **Lenwade House** ⤸, Fakenham Rd, NR9 5QP, ✆ 872288, ≼, « Country house atmosphere »,
⤴ heated, ⤳, ⛳, park, ⚡ squash – 📺 ⇔wc 🜚 🅿 🛅 📼 ⓪ 📶
M *(closed Sunday lunch)* 6.95/8.95 **t.** and a la carte ⌁ 2.30 – ⊐ 3.50 – **13 rm** 23.20/32.90 **t.** –
SB (weekends only) (October-May) 49.00 **st.**

LEOMINSTER Heref. and Worc. **403** L 27 – pop. 8,637 – ECD : Thursday – ☎ 0568.
See : Priory Church★ 14C (the north aisle★ 12C).
Envir. : Berrington Hall★ (Georgian) *AC*, N : 3 m. – Croft Castle★ (15C) *AC*, NW : 6 m.
🛈 School Lane ✆ 2291.
♦London 141 – ♦Birmingham 47 – Hereford 13 – Worcester 26.

🏨 **Talbot** (Best Western), West St., HR6 8EP, ✆ 2121 – 📺 ⇔wc 🜚wc 🅿 🛅 📼 ⴊ ⓪ 📶
M 8.00/12.00 **t.** ⌁ 2.45 – **28 rm** ⊐ 21.00/47.50 **t.**, **1 suite** 65.00/77.00 **t.** – SB 45.00/54.00 **st.**

🏛 **Royal Oak**, South St., HR6 8JA, ✆ 2610 – 📺 ⇔wc 🅿 🛅 📼 ⓪ 📶
M 6.75/8.00 **st.** and a la carte ⌁ 3.00 – **16 rm** ⊐ 19.50/52.50 **st.** – SB 38.00/48.00 **st.**

at Stoke Prior SE : 2 m. by A 44 – ⊠ ☎ 0568 Leominster :

✗ **Wheelbarrow Castle**, HR6 0NB, ✆ 2219 – 🅿 📼 ⴊ 📶
M a la carte 8.00/12.00 **t.** ⌁ 2.00.

AUSTIN-ROVER South St. ✆ 2545	RENAULT West St. ✆ 2562
FORD 3-4 Etnam St. ✆ 2060	TALBOT, VAUXHALL-OPEL The Bargates ✆ 2337

LETCHWORTH Herts. **404** T 28 – pop. 31,146 – ECD : Wednesday – ☎ 046 26 (4 and 5 fig.) or
0462 (6 fig.).
♦London 40 – Bedford 22 – ♦Cambridge 22 – Luton 14.

🏨 **Letchworth Hall** ⤸, Letchworth Lane, SG6 3NP, S : 1 m. by A 505 ✆ 683747, Telex 825740,
≼, Dancing (Saturday), ⤳ – 📺 ⇔wc ☎ 🅿 🛅 📼 ⴊ ⓪ 📶 ✄
M 7.50 **t.** and a la carte ⌁ 3.00 – **42 rm** ⊐ 38.00/50.00 **st.**

🏨 **Broadway**, The Broadway, SG6 3NZ, ✆ 685651 – ⋮⋮ 📺 ⇔wc ☎ 🅿 🛅 📼 ⴊ ⓪ 📶 ✄
closed Christmas and New Year – **M** (carving rest.) 5.25 **t.** ⌁ 2.65 – **37 rm** ⊐ 29.50/39.50 **t.**

AUSTIN-ROVER Works Rd ✆ 73161	HONDA Norton Way North ✆ 78191
FORD 18/22 Station Rd ✆ 3722	VW, AUDI Norton Way North ✆ 6341

LEWES East Sussex **404** U 31 – pop. 14,499 – ECD : Wednesday – ☎ 0273.
See : Norman Castle (ruins) site and ≼★, 45 steps, *AC* – Anne of Cleves' House (1559) *AC*.
Envir. : Glynde Place (pictures★) *AC*, E : 3 ½ m. – Firle Place★ (mansion 15C-16C) *AC*, SE : 4 ½ m.
– Ditchling Beacon ≼★ W : 7 ½ m. – Glyndebourne Opera Festival (May-August) *AC*, E : 3 m.
🛆 Chapel Hill ✆ 473245, Opp. Junction Cliffe High/South St.
🛈 Lewes House, 32 High St. ✆ 471600.
♦London 53 – Brighton 8 – Hastings 29 – Maidstone 43.

🏠 **Shelleys** (Mt. Charlotte), High St., BN7 1XS, ✆ 472361, 🎨 – 📺 ➡wc �🛁wc ☎ 🅿
21 rm.

✕✕ **Trumps**, 19-20 Station St., BN7 2DB, ✆ 473906 – � 🎨 ⓞ 𝘝𝘐𝘚𝘈
closed Monday and 1 January – **M** 11.95 **t.** ≬ 3.50.

✕ **Kenwards**, Pipe Passage, 151a High St., BN7 1XU, ✆ 472343 – 🎨
closed Sunday, Monday, 1 week spring, 1 week November and Christmas – **M** (dinner only)
(booking essential) a la carte 11.50/13.00 **st.** ≬ 3.60.

AUSTIN-ROVER   Brooks Rd ✆ 3186
BMW   Western Rd ✆ 3221

FORD   Station St. ✆ 4461
RENAULT   96/106 Malling St. ✆ 77131

LEYLAND Lancs. 402 L 22 – pop. 36,694 – ECD : Wednesday – 🕾 077 44.

◆London 220 – ◆Liverpool 31 – ◆Manchester 32 – Preston 6.

🏠 **Ladbroke** (Ladbroke), Leyland Way, PR5 2JX, E : ¾ m. on B 5256 ✆ 422922, Telex 677651 –
📺 ➡wc ☎ 🛁 🅿. 🛁.
M (carving rest.) – **93 rm**.

AUSTIN-ROVER   Preston Rd ✆ 52311
FORD   Towngate ✆ 21766

PEUGEOT, TALBOT   Golden Hill Lane ✆ 23416
SKODA   Wigan Rd ✆ 21546

LICHFIELD Staffs. 402 403 404 O 25 – pop. 25,408 – ECD : Wednesday – 🕾 054 32 (5 fig.) and
0543 (6 fig.).

See : Cathedral★★ 12C-14C.

🖪 9 Breadmarket St. ✆ 52109.

◆London 128 – ◆Birmingham 16 – Derby 23 – ◆Stoke-on-Trent 30.

🏠 **George** (Embassy), Bird St., WS13 6PR, ✆ 414822 – 📺 ➡wc �🛁wc ☎ 🅿. 🛁. 🔳 🎨 ⓞ 𝘝𝘐𝘚𝘈.
🍴.
M 8.00/9.00 **st.** and a la carte ≬ 2.50 – ⌖ 5.00 – **40 rm** 33.00/53.00 **st.** – SB (weekends only)
49.00 **st.**

🏠 **Swan** (Embassy) without rest., Bird St., WS13 6PW, ✆ 414851 – 📺 ➡wc ☜ 🅿. 🛁. 🔳 🎨
ⓞ 𝘝𝘐𝘚𝘈. 🍴.
closed Friday, Saturday and Sunday – ⌖ 5.00 – **31 rm** 31.00/42.00 **st.**

🏠 **Little Barrow**, Beacon St., WS13 7AR, ✆ 414500 – 📺 ➡wc ⚙wc ☎ 🅿. 🔳 🎨 ⓞ 𝘝𝘐𝘚𝘈. 🍴.
M 6.50/9.00 **t.** and a la carte ≬ 3.50 – **24 rm** ⌖ 30.00/38.00 **t.**

🏛 **Oakleigh House**, 25 St. Chad's Rd, WS13 7LZ, ✆ 22688, 🎨 – 📺 ➡wc ⚙wc 🅿. 🔳. 🍴.
closed 1 week at Christmas – **M** *(closed Sunday and Monday)* (dinner only) 11.50
st. and a la carte ≬ 3.00 – **11 rm** ⌖ 15.00/30.00 **st.**

🏛 **Angel Croft**, 3 Beacon St., WS13 7AA, ✆ 58737, 🎨 – 📺 ⚙wc ☎ 🅿. 🔳 ⓞ 𝘝𝘐𝘚𝘈. 🍴.
closed 25 and 26 December – **M** *(closed Sunday dinner)* 10.00/12.00 **t.** ≬ 3.00 – **21 rm**
⌖ 26.00/46.00 **st.**

⚲ **Gaialands** 🍴, 9 Gaiafields Rd, off Bulldog Lane, WS13 7LT, ✆ 23764, 🎨 – 🅿. 🍴.
5 rm ⌖ 12.00/25.00 **s.**

✕✕ **Champs Elysées**, Minster House, Minster Pool Walk, ✆ 53788, French rest. – 🔳 🎨 ⓞ
𝘝𝘐𝘚𝘈
closed Saturday lunch, Sunday and last 2 weeks July – **M** 5.95/13.50 **t.** ≬ 3.50.

✕ **Thrales**, 40-44 Tamworth St. (corner of Backcester Lane), ✆ 55091
closed Sunday dinner and 5 days at Christmas – **M** (dinner only and Friday lunch) 6.90/10.90
st. and a la carte.

AUSTIN-ROVER   St. John St. ✆ 51451
FORD   Birmingham Rd ✆ 53566

MAZDA   Birmingham Rd ✆ 53571

LIFTON Devon 403 H 32 – pop. 966 – ECD : Tuesday – 🕾 0566.

🖪 Launceston, St. Stephen ✆ 0566 (Launceston) 3442, W : 5 m.

◆London 238 – Bude 24 – Exeter 37 – Launceston 4 – ◆Plymouth 32.

🏠 **Arundell Arms** (Best Western), Fore St., PL16 0AA, on A 30 ✆ 84666, ⚘, 🎨 – 📺 ➡wc
⚙wc ☎ 🅿. 🛁. 🔳 🎨 ⓞ 𝘝𝘐𝘚𝘈
closed 22 to 27 December – **M** 7.75/13.00 **t.** and a la carte ≬ 3.50 – **27 rm** ⌖ 23.50/54.00 **t.** –
SB (October-May) 58.00/64.00 **st.**

LILLIPUT Dorset – see Poole.

LIMPSFIELD Surrey 404 U 30 – pop. 3,325 – ✉ 🕾 088 33 Oxted.

◆London 24 – ◆Brighton 40 – Maidstone 25.

✕✕ 🕸 **Old Lodge**, High St., RH8 0DR, ✆ 2996 – 🅿. 🔳 🎨 ⓞ 𝘝𝘐𝘚𝘈
closed Saturday lunch, Sunday dinner, Monday, 28 March and first 2 weeks January – **M**
15.00/17.50 **st.** ≬ 3.75
Spec. Quenelles de volaille sauce au roquefort, Ragoût de ris de veau et d'écrevisses sauce au poivre rose, Soufflé
glacé au chocolat et à la menthe.

See : Cathedral★★★ 11C-15C (Angel Choir★★, Library : Magna Carta *AC*) Y – Jew's House★★ 12C Y
– Castle★ (11C) *AC* Y – Newport Arch★ (Roman) Y E – Stonebow and Guildhall★ 15C-16C Z S.

Envir. : Doddington Hall★ (Elizabethan) *AC*, SW : 7 m. by A 15 Z and A 46 – 🚌 Carholme ✆ 23725,
1 m. from town centre – ✈ Humberside Airport : ✆ 0652 (Barnetby) 688456, N : 32 m. by A 15 Y.

🛈 9 Castle Hill ✆ 29828 – 21 The Cornhill ✆ 32151 ext 504/5 – ◆London 140 – Bradford 81 – ◆Cambridge 94 –
◆Kingston-upon-Hull 44 – ◆Leeds 73 – ◆Leicester 53 – ◆Norwich 104 – ◆Nottingham 38 – ◆Sheffield 48 – York 82.

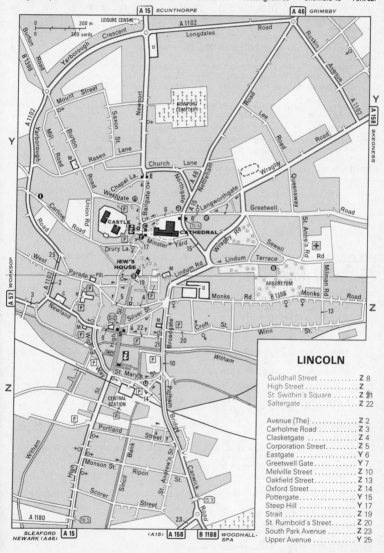

LINCOLN

Guildhall Street . . . . Z 8
High Street . . . . Z
St. Swithin's Square . . . . . . Z 21
Saltergate . . . . Z 22

Avenue (The) . . . . Z 2
Carholme Road . . . . Z 3
Clasketgate . . . . Z 4
Corporation Street . . . . Z 5
Eastgate . . . . Y 6
Greetwell Gate . . . . Y 7
Melville Street . . . . Z 10
Oakfield Street . . . . Z 13
Oxford Street . . . . Z 14
Pottergate . . . . Y 15
Steep Hill . . . . Y 17
Strait . . . . Z 19
St. Rumbold's Street . . . . . . Z 20
South Park Avenue . . . . Z 23
Upper Avenue . . . . Y 25

🏨🏨 **White Hart** (T.H.F.), Bailgate, LN1 3AR, ✆ 26222, Telex 56304, « Antique furniture » – 📶 📺
⟷ 🅿 ⬛ 🔄 ⁙ AE ⓭ VISA
M 6.95/10.50 **st.** and a la carte ⬧ 4.00 – ⊡ 6.00 – **51 rm** 45.00/55.50 **st.**, **8 suites**. Y **c**

🏨🏨 **Eastgate Post House** (T.H.F.), Eastgate, LN2 1PN, ✆ 20341, Telex 56316, 🚗 – 📶 📺 ☎ 👓
🅿 🔄 ⬛ AE ⓭ VISA
M 6.50/8.80 **st.** and a la carte ⬧ 2.70 – ⊡ 5.50 – **71 rm** 41.50/51.50 **st.** Y **a**

🏛 **D'Isney Place** without rest., Eastgate, LN2 4AA, 🕿 38881, ⚎ – 🖵 ⇱wc 🏨wc 🕿. 🔼 AE ⓪ VISA
　Y e
　17 rm ⟱ 30.00/40.00 **t.**

🏛 **Hillcrest,** 15 Lindum Terr., LN2 5RT, 🕿 26341, ≤, ⚎ – 🖵 🏨wc Ⓟ. 🔼 VISA
　Y o
　M *(closed Sunday dinner)* (bar lunch)/dinner a la carte 5.90/8.60 **t.** ⓵ 3.25 – **15 rm**
　⟱ 17.00/34.50 **t.** – SB (weekends only) (spring and autumn) 31.00/34.00 **st.**

🏛 **Castle,** Westgate, LN1 3AS, 🕿 38801 – 🖵 ⇱wc 🏨wc Ⓟ. 🔼 AE ⓪ VISA
　Y n
　M a la carte 8.00/10.85 **t.** ⓵ 2.30 – **21 rm** ⟱ 30.00/40.00 **st.** – SB (weekends only) 42.00/46.00 **st.**

🏛 **Grand,** St. Mary's St., LN5 7EP, 🕿 24211 – 🖵 ⇱wc 🏨wc ⚏ Ⓟ. 🔼 AE ⓪ VISA
　Z u
　M 5.60/7.10 **t.** and a la carte ⓵ 2.40 – **50 rm** ⟱ 28.50/42.00 **t.** – SB (weekends only) 48.00 **st.**

🏠 **Carline,** 3 Carline Rd, LN1 4NI, 🕿 30422 – 🖵 ⇱wc 🏨 Ⓟ
　Y i
　closed Christmas – **6 rm** ⟱ 8.50/21.00 **s.**

🏠 **Tennyson,** 7 South Park Avenue, LN5 8EN, 🕿 21624 – 🖵 ⇱wc 🏨wc Ⓟ. 🔼 VISA. ⌘
　Z
　closed 1 week at Christmas – **8 rm** ⟱ 18.00/30.00 **st.**
　by A 158

XX **White's** with rm, **Jews House,** 15 The Strait, LN2 1JD, 🕿 24851, « 12C town house »
　YZ s
　2 rm.

XX **Harveys,** 1 Exchequer Gate, Castle Sq., LN2 1PZ, 🕿 21886 – 🔼 VISA
　Y r
　closed Sunday lunch and 1 to 6 January – **M** (restricted a la carte lunch)/dinner 15.50 **t.** ⓵ 3.00.

　at Branston SE : 3 m. on B 1188 – Z – ✆ 0522 Lincoln :

🏰 **Moor Lodge,** LN4 1HU, 🕿 791366 – 🖵 ⇱wc Ⓟ. 🏨. 🔼 AE ⓪ VISA
　M *(closed Saturday lunch)* 6.75/8.75 **t.** and a la carte ⓵ 3.25 – **25 rm** ⟱ 28.00/45.00 **t.** – SB
　45.00/55.00 **st.**

MICHELIN Branch, Tritton Rd, LN6 7RX, 🕿 684023 by A 1180 Z

AUSTIN-ROVER　Outer Circle Rd 🕿 35771
BMW　South Park Av. 🕿 21345
CITROEN　300 Wragby Rd 🕿 31195
DAIMLER-JAGUAR　300 Wragby Rd 🕿 31195
FIAT　316-322 Wragby Rd 🕿 34805
FORD　Wragby Rd 🕿 30101
HONDA, LANCIA　Wragby Rd 🕿 31735
LADA, MAZDA　Newark Rd, North Hykeham 🕿 681242

NISSAN　148 Newark Rd 🕿 42281
RENAULT　25 Wragby Rd 🕿 21252
SAAB　247 Lincoln Rd 🕿 681463
TALBOT, PEUGEOT　477 High St. 🕿 29131
TOYOTA　Newark Rd 🕿 692805
VAUXHALL　Outer Circle Rd 🕿 31785
VOLVO　314 Wragby Rd 🕿 29462/3
VW, AUDI　223 Newark Rd 🕿 31881

LISKEARD Cornwall 403 G 32 The West Country G. – pop. 6,213 – ECD : Wednesday – ✆ 0579.
See : Church★ – Envir. : St. Neot★ (Church★★), NW : 5 m.
◆London 261 – Exeter 59 – ◆Plymouth 18 – Truro 37.

🏛 **Country Castle** ⌂, Station Rd, PL14 4EB, SW : ¾ m. by B 3254 🕿 42694, 🔄, ⚎ – 🖵
　⇱wc 🏨wc ⚏ Ⓟ. 🔼 VISA
　closed November – **M** 8.50 **t.** (dinner) and a la carte ⓵ 2.75 – **11 rm** ⟱ 15.50/40.00 **t.** – SB
　(October-March) 44.00/49.00 **st.**

🏛 **Lord Eliot,** Castle St., PL14 3AU, 🕿 42717 – ⇱wc 🏨wc Ⓟ
　M (restricted lunch) a la carte 5.50/8.50 **t.** and a la carte ⓵ 3.00 – **16 rm** ⟱ 20.00/34.00 **t.**

　at St. Keyne S : 3 ½ m. on B 3254 – ✉ ✆ 0579 Liskeard :

🏛 **Old Rectory** ⌂, PL14 4RL, 🕿 42617, ⚎ – ⇱wc 🏨wc Ⓟ. 🔼 VISA
　M (dinner only) 8.00 **t.** ⓵ 2.60 – **9 rm** ⟱ 13.00/29.50 **t.**

LISS Hants. 404 R 30 – pop. 5,489 – ✆ 0730 – ◆London 57 – ◆Portsmouth 22 – Reading 34.

XX **Le Papillon,** 94 Station Rd., GU33 7AQ, 🕿 893363 – 🔼 AE ⓪ VISA
　closed Sunday and Monday – **M** (lunch by arrangement)/dinner 14.00 **t.** ⓵ 2.75.

LITTLE HAVEN Dyfed 403 E 28 – ECD : Thursday – ✉ Haverfordwest – ✆ 043 783 Broad Haven.
◆London 258 – Haverfordwest 8.

🏛 **Haven Fort,** Settlands Hill, SA62 3LA, 🕿 401, ≤ St. Brides Bay, ⚎ – ⇱wc 🏨wc Ⓟ. ⌘
　March-mid October – **M** (bar lunch)/dinner 9.95 **t.** and a la carte ⓵ 2.00 – **15 rm** ⟱ 17.90/36.00 **t.**

🏠 **Pendyffryn,** SA62 3LA, 🕿 337, ≤ – 🖵 Ⓟ. ⌘
　Easter-mid October – **7 rm** ⟱ 10.50/17.00.

LITTLE KELYNACK Cornwall – see St. Just.

LITTLE LANGDALE Cumbria 402 K 20 – see Ambleside.

LITTLEOVER Derbs. 402 403 404 P 25 – see Derby.

LITTLE SINGLETON Lancs. – see Blackpool.

LITTLE THORNTON Lancs. 402 L 22 – see Blackpool.

LITTLE WEIGHTON Humberside 402 S 22 – see Kingston-upon-Hull.

LITTLE WYMONDLEY Herts. 404 T 28 – see Hitchin.

LIVERPOOL Merseyside 402 403 L 23 – pop. 538,809 – ECD : Wednesday – ✪ 051.

See : Walker Art Gallery★★ CY **M1** – City of Liverpool Museums★ CY **M2** – Anglican Cathedral★ (1904) CZ **A** – Roman Catholic Cathedral★ (1967) DZ **B**.

Envir. : Knowsley Safari Park★★ *AC*, NE : 8 m. by A 57 BX – Speke Hall★ (16C) *AC*, SE : 7 m. by A 561 BX.

🏌 Dunnings Bridge Rd, Bootle ✆ 928 1371, N : 5 m. by A 5036 AV – 🏌 Allerton Park ✆ 428 1046, S : 5 m. by B 5180 BX – 🏌 Childwall, Naylor's Rd, Gateacre ✆ 487 9982, E : 7 m. by B 5178 BX.

✈ Liverpool Airport : ✆ 494 0066, Telex 629323, SE : 6 m. by A 561 BX – **Terminal : Pier Head**.

🚢 to Ireland (Dublin) (B & I Line) 1 nightly (8 h 45 mn) – to Belfast (Belfast Car Ferries) 1 daily (9 h).

🚢 to Birkenhead (Merseyside Transport) frequent services daily (7-8 mn) – to Wallasey (Merseyside Transport) frequent services daily (7-8 mn).

🛈 29 Lime St. ✆ 709 3631 and 8681.

♦London 219 – ♦Birmingham 103 – ♦Leeds 75 – ♦Manchester 35.

Town plans : Liverpool pp. 2-5

🏨 **Holiday Inn,** Paradise St., L1 8JD, ✆ 709 0181, Telex 627270, 🏊 – 🛗 🍴 📺 ☎ 🕭 🅿 ⚒ 🏊
AE ⓘ VISA
CZ n
M 5.50/8.00 t. and a la carte 🛈 3.00 – **253 rm** 🛏 48.00/65.00 t., **7 suites** 74.00/165.00 st. – SB (weekends only) 56.90/66.90 st.

🏨 **Atlantic Tower Thistle** (Thistle), 30 Chapel St., L3 9RE, ✆ 227 4444, Telex 627070, ← – 🛗
🍴 📺 ☎ 🅿 ⚒ 🏊 AE ⓘ VISA 🍽
CY r
M 7.45/9.50 t. and a la carte 🛈 2.85 – 🛏 5.50 – **226 rm** 45.00/70.00 t., **10 suites** 85.00 t.

🏨 **St. George's** (T.H.F.), St. John's Precinct, Lime St., L1 1NQ, ✆ 709 7090, Telex 627630 – 🛗
📺 ☎ 🕭 🅿 ⚒ 🏊 AE ⓘ VISA
CY v
M (carving rest.) 5.00/8.25 **st**. and a la carte 🛈 2.70 – 🛏 5.50 – **155 rm** 42.00/50.50 st., **3 suites**.

🏨 **Crest** (Crest), Lord Nelson St., L3 5QB, ✆ 709 7050, Telex 627954 – 🛗 📺 🛁wc ☎ 🅿 ⚒
🏊 AE ⓘ VISA 🍽
CY i
M approx. 10.85 **st**. – 🛏 5.75 – **165 rm** 43.00/53.00 st., **1 suite** – SB (weekends only) 55.00 st.

🏨 **Green Park,** 4-6 Green Bank Drive, Sefton Park, L17 1AN, SE : 2 ½ m. by A 562 ✆ 733 3382,
🍴 – 📺 🛁wc 🍴wc ☎ 🅿 🏊 AE VISA
BX u
M (bar lunch)/dinner 5.25 **st**. and a la carte 🛈 2.30 – **24 rm** 🛏 20.00/35.00 st.

XXX Ristorante del Secolo, First Floor, 36-40 Stanley St., L2 6AL, ✆ 236 4004, Italian rest. CY x

XXX Churchill's, Churchill House, Tithebarn St., L2 2PB, ✆ 227 3877 – 🏊 AE ⓘ VISA CY a
closed Saturday lunch and Sunday – **M** 7.55/8.95 t. and a la carte.

XX **Jenny's Seafood,** Old Ropery, Fenwick St., L2 7NT, ✆ 236 0332, Seafood – 🍴 🏊 AE ⓘ
VISA
CZ e
closed Saturday lunch, Monday dinner, Sunday, 25 December-3 January and Bank Holidays –
M 8.75 t. and a la carte 🛈 2.50.

at Bootle N : 5 m. by A 565 – AV – ✉ ✪ 051 Liverpool :

🏨 **Park,** Park Lane West, L30 3SU, on A 5036 ✆ 525 7555, Telex 629772 – 🛗 📺 🛁wc 🍴wc ☎
🅿 ⚒ 🏊 AE ⓘ VISA
M 5.50 **st**. and a la carte 🛈 4.90 – **60 rm** 🛏 32.50/44.00 st.

at Blundellsands N : 6 ½ m. by A 565 – AV – ✉ ✪ 051 Liverpool :

🏨 Blundellsands, The Serpentine South, L23 6TN, ✆ 924 6515 – 🛗 📺 🛁wc 🍴 🅿 ⚒
44 rm.

at Aigburth SE : 4 m. on A 561 – BX – ✉ ✪ 051 Liverpool :

🏨 **Grange,** 14 Holmefield Rd, L19 3PG, ✆ 427 2950, 🍴 – 📺 🛁wc ☎ 🅿 🏊 AE ⓘ VISA 🍽
M (dinner only and Sunday lunch) 6.00/9.75 t. and a la carte 🛈 3.50 – **25 rm** 🛏 20.00/38.00 t.

X L'Alouette, 2 Lark Lane, L17, ✆ 727 2142, French rest. BX n

AUSTIN-ROVER 72/74 Coronation Rd ✆ 924 6411
RENAULT Edge Lane ✆ 228 4737
BMW Scotland Rd ✆ 207 7213
BMW Aigburth Rd ✆ 427 8086
CITROEN Speke Rd ✆ 427 6464
CITROEN 607 West Derby Rd ✆ 228 3670
FIAT East Prescot Rd ✆ 228 9151
FIAT Long Lane ✆ 523 4040
FIAT, DAIHATSU, HONDA, PEUGEOT Long Lane ✆ 523 3737
FORD Linacre Lane ✆ 922 0070
FORD Prescot St. ✆ 260 9898
FORD Speke Hall Rd ✆ 486 2233
HONDA Berry St. ✆ 709 4207
LADA Long Lane ✆ 523 3737
MAZDA Longmore Lane ✆ 525 6900
NISSAN Coronation Rd ✆ 924 6575

NISSAN Allerton Rd ✆ 727 2386
PEUGEOT-TALBOT Edge Lane ✆ 924 4210
PEUGEOT-TALBOT Ullet Rd ✆ 727 1414
RENAULT, NISSAN Queen's Drive ✆ 523 9779
SAAB 574 Aigburth Rd ✆ 427 3500
SKODA Durning Rd ✆ 263 7374
SKODA Bridge Rd ✆ 928 2515
TOYOTA Gale Rd ✆ 546 8228
TOYOTA 1 Aigburth Rd ✆ 727 2204
TOYOTA Coronation Rd ✆ 924 9101
VAUXHALL-OPEL 215 Knowsley Rd ✆ 922 7585
VAUXHALL-OPEL Speke Hall Rd ✆ 486 8846
VAUXHALL-OPEL Derby Rd ✆ 933 7575
VOLVO Fox St. ✆ 207 4364
VW, AUDI Moor Lane, Thornton ✆ 931 2861
VW, AUDI Edge Lane ✆ 228 0919

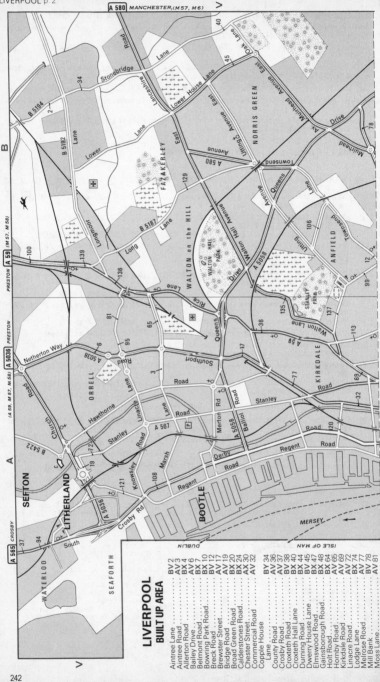

LIVERPOOL
BUILT UP AREA

Aintree Lane	BV 2
Aintree Road	AV 3
Allerton Road	BX 4
Bailey Drive	AV 6
Belmont Road	BX 7
Bowring Park Road	BV 10
Breck Road	BX 12
Brewster Street	AV 17
Bridge Green Road	AV 19
Broad Green Road	BX 20
Calderstones Road	BX 24
Chester Street	AX 30
Commercial Road	AV 32
Copple House		
Lane	BY 34
County Road	AV 36
Crosby Road	BV 38
Croxteth Road	BX 40
Croxteth Hall Lane	BX 44
Durning Road	BX 45
Dwerry House Lane	BX 47
Elmswood Road	BX 48
Gainsborough Road	BX 64
Holt Road	BX 64
Hornby Road	AV 65
Kirkdale Road	AV 69
Linacre Road	AV 72
Lodge Lane	BX 74
Melrose Road	AV 77
Mill Bank	BV 78
Moss Lane	AV 81

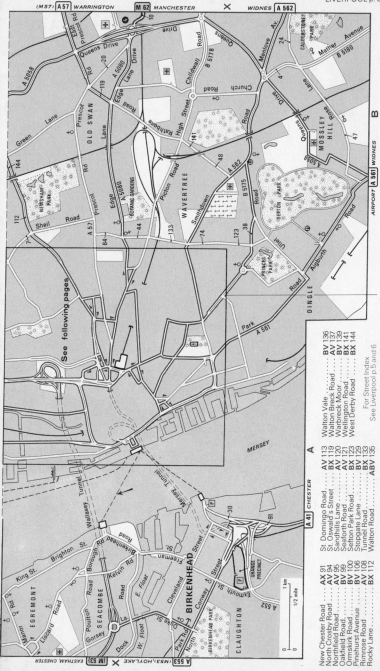

(M57) A57 WARRINGTON   M62 MANCHESTER   ✕ WIDNES A562

A41 CHESTER   A

A553 (M53) HOYLAKE   ✕ EASTHAM, CHESTER

AIRPORT A561 WIDNES

B

See following pages

MERSEY

EGREMONT

SEACOMBE

BIRKENHEAD

CLAUGHTON

BIRKENHEAD PARK

GRANGE PRECINCT

Mersey Tunnel

Wallasey Tunnel

NEWSHAM PARK

OLD SWAN

WAVERTREE

BOTANIC GARDENS

MOSSLEY HILL

SEFTON PARK

PRINCES PARK

DINGLE

CALDERSTONES PARK

1 km
1/2 mile

243

New Chester Road .... **AX** 91
North Crosby Road .... **AX** 94
Northfield Road .... **AV** 95
Oakfield Road .... **BV** 99
Ormskirk Road .... **BV** 100
Pinehurst Avenue .... **BV** 106
Rimrose Road .... **AV** 108
Rocky Lane .... **BX** 112

St. Domingo Road .... **AV** 113
St. Oswald's Street .... **BX** 119
Sandhills Lane .... **AV** 120
Seaforth Road .... **AV** 121
Sefton Park Road .... **BX** 123
Strongate Lane .... **BV** 129
Tunnel Road .... **BX** 133
Walton Road .... **ABV** 135

Walton Vale .... **BV** 136
Walton Breck Road .... **AV** 137
Warbreck Moor .... **BV** 139
Wellington Road .... **BX** 141
West Derby Road .... **BX** 144

For Street Index
See Liverpool p 5 and 6

LIVERPOOL
CENTRE

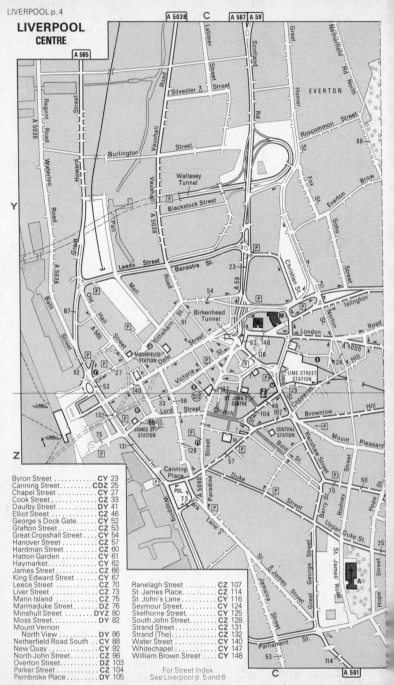

Byron Street	CY	23
Canning Street	CDZ	25
Chapel Street	CY	27
Cook Street	CZ	33
Daulby Street	DY	41
Elliot Street	CZ	46
George's Dock Gate	CY	52
Grafton Street	CZ	53
Great Crosshall Street	CY	54
Hanover Street	CZ	57
Hardman Street	CZ	60
Hatton Garden	CY	61
Haymarket	CY	62
James Street	CZ	66
King Edward Street	CY	67
Leece Street	CZ	70
Liver Street	CZ	73
Mann Island	CZ	75
Marmaduke Street	DZ	76
Minshull Street	DYZ	80
Moss Street	DY	82
Mount Vernon North View	DY	86
Netherfield Road South	CY	88
New Quay	CY	92
North John Street	CZ	96
Overton Street	DZ	103
Parker Street	CZ	104
Pembroke Place	DY	105
Ranelagh Street	CZ	107
St. James Place	CZ	114
St. John's Lane	CZ	116
Seymour Street	CY	124
Skelhorne Street	CZ	125
South John Street	CZ	128
Strand Street	CZ	131
Strand (The)	CZ	132
Water Street	CY	140
Whitechapel	CY	147
William Brown Street	CY	148

For Street Index
See Liverpool p. 5 and 6

244

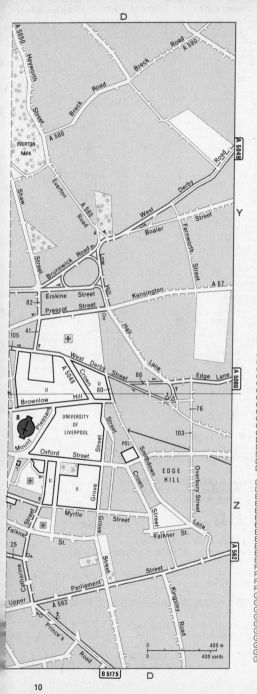

STREET INDEX

Church St.	p. 4	CZ
Bold St.	p. 4	CZ
Lime St.	p. 4	CY
London Rd.	p. 4	CY
Lord St.	p. 4	CY
Parker St.	p. 4	CZ 104
Ranelagh St.	p. 4	CZ 107
Renshaw St.	p. 4	CZ
St. Johns Centre	p. 4	CY

Aigburth Rd	p. 3	BX 2
Aintree Lane	p. 2	BV 2
Aintree Rd	p. 2	AV 3
Allerton Rd.	p. 3	BX 4
Bailey Drive	p. 2	AV 6
Balliol Rd	p. 2	AV
Bath St.	p. 4	CY
Belmont Rd	p. 3	BX 7
Berry St.	p. 4	CZ
Birkenhead Rd	p. 3	AX
Blackstock St.	p. 4	CY
Boaler St.	p. 5	DY
Bold St.	p. 4	CZ
Borough Rd	p. 3	AX
Bowring Park Rd	p. 3	BX 10
Breck Rd.	p. 5	DY
Brewster St.	p. 2	AV 17
Bridge Rd.	p. 2	AV 19
Brighton St.	p. 3	AX
Broad Green Rd	p. 3	BX 20
Brownlow Hill	p. 4	CZ
Brunswick Rd	p. 5	DY
Burlington St.	p. 4	CY
Byron St.	p. 4	CY 23
Calderstones Rd.	p. 3	BX 24
Canning Pl.	p. 4	CZ
Canning St.	p. 5	DZ 25
Catharine St.	p. 5	DZ
Chapel St.	p. 4	CY 27
Chester St.	p. 3	AX 30
Childwall Rd	p. 3	BX
Christian St.	p. 4	CY
Church Rd	p. 3	BX
Church Rd LITHERLAND	p. 2	AV
Church St.	p. 4	CZ
Cleveland St.	p. 3	AX
Commercial Rd.	p. 2	AV 32
Conway St.	p. 3	AX
Cook St.	p. 4	CZ 33
Copperas Hill	p. 4	CZ
Copple House Lane	p. 2	BV 34
County Rd	p. 2	AV 36
Crosby Rd	p. 2	AV 37
Crown St.	p. 5	DZ
Croxteth Rd	p. 3	BX 38
Croxteth Hall Lane	p. 2	BV 40
Dale St.	p. 4	CY
Daulby St.	p. 5	DY 41
Derby Rd	p. 2	AV
Duke St. BIRKENHEAD	p. 4	CZ
	p. 3	AX
Durning Rd	p. 3	BX 44
Dwerry House Lane	p. 2	BV 45
East Lancashire Rd	p. 2	BV
East Prescot Rd	p. 3	BX
Edge Lane	p. 3	BX
Edge Lane Drive	p. 3	BX
Elliot St.	p. 4	CZ 46
Elmswood Rd	p. 3	BX 47
Erskine St.	p. 5	DY
Everton Brow	p. 4	CY
Everton Rd	p. 5	DY
Exmouth St.	p. 3	AX
Falkner St.	p. 5	DZ
Farnworth St.	p. 5	DY
Fox St.	p. 4	CY
Freeman St.	p. 3	AX
Gainsborough Rd	p. 3	BX 48
George's Dock Gate	p. 4	CY 52
Gorsey Lane.	p. 3	AX
Grafton St.	p. 4	CZ 53
Great Crosshall St.	p. 4	CY 54
Great George St.	p. 4	CZ
Great Homer St.	p. 4	CY
Great Howard St.	p. 4	CY
Green Lane	p. 3	BX
Grove St.	p. 5	DZ

Concluded on next page

STREET INDEX TO LIVERPOOL TOWN PLANS (concluded)

Hall Lane . . . . p. 5 DY
Hanover St. . . . . p. 4 CZ 57
Hardman St. . . . . p. 4 CZ 60
Hatton Garden . . . . p. 4 CY 61
Haymarket. . . . . p. 4 CY 62
Hawthorne Rd. . . . . p. 2 AV
Heyworth St. . . . . p. 5 DY
High St. . . . . p. 3 BX
Holt Rd. . . . . p. 3 BX 64
Hope St. . . . . p. 4 CZ
Hornby Rd . . . . p. 2 AV 65
Islington. . . . . p. 4 CY
Jamaica St. . . . . p. 4 CY
James St. . . . . p. 4 CZ 66
Kelvin Rd . . . . p. 3 AX
Kensington . . . . p. 5 DY
King St. . . . . p. 3 AX
King Edward St. . . . . p. 4 CY 67
Kingsley Rd . . . . p. 5 DZ
Kingsway . . . . p. 3 AX
Kirkdale Rd . . . . p. 2 AV 69
Knowsley Rd . . . . p. 2 AV
Latimer St. . . . . p. 4 CY
Leece St. . . . . p. 4 CZ 70
Leeds St. . . . . p. 4 CY
Lime St. . . . . p. 4 CY
Linacre Rd . . . . p. 2 AV 72
Linacre Lane . . . . p. 2 AV
Liscard Rd . . . . p. 3 AX
Liver St. . . . . p. 4 CZ 73
Lodge Lane . . . . p. 3 BX 74
London Rd . . . . p. 4 CY
Long Lane . . . . p. 2 BV
Longmoor Lane . . . . p. 2 BV
Lord St. . . . . p. 4 CZ
Lower House Lane . . . . . . p. 2 BV
Lower Lane . . . . p. 2 BV
Low Hill . . . . p. 5 DY
Manor Rd. . . . . p. 3 AX
Mann Island . . . . p. 4 CZ 75
Marmaduke St. . . . . p. 5 DZ 76
Marsh Lane . . . . p. 2 AV
Mather Av. . . . . p. 3 BX
Melrose Rd . . . . p. 2 AV 77
Menlove Av. . . . . p. 3 BX
Merton Rd . . . . p. 2 AV
Mill Bank . . . . p. 2 BV 78
Minshull St. . . . . p. 5 DY 80
Moss Lane . . . . p. 2 AV 81
Moss St. . . . . p. 5 DY 82

Mount Pleasant . . . . . . p. 4 CZ
Mount Vernon
  North View . . . . p. 5 DY 86
Muirhead Av. . . . . p. 2 BV
Muirhead Av. E. . . . . p. 2 BV
Myrtle St. . . . . p. 5 DZ
Netherfield Rd N. . . . . . . p. 4 CY
Netherfield Rd S. . . . . . . p. 4 CY 88
Netherton Way . . . . p. 2 AV
New Chester Rd . . . . . . p. 3 AX 91
New Quay . . . . p. 4 CY 92
North Crosby Rd. . . . . . . p. 2 AV 94
Northfield Rd . . . . p. 2 AV 95
North John St. . . . . p. 4 CZ 96
Norton St. . . . . p. 4 CY
Oakfield Rd . . . . p. 2 BV 99
Oak Lane . . . . p. 2 BV
Old Hall St. . . . . p. 4 CY
Ormskirk Rd . . . . p. 2 BV 100
Overbury St. . . . . p. 5 DZ
Overton St. . . . . p. 5 DZ 103
Oxford St. . . . . p. 5 DZ
Pall Mall . . . . p. 4 CY
Paradise St. . . . . p. 4 CZ
Parker St. . . . . p. 4 CZ 104
Park Lane . . . . p. 4 CZ
Park Rd. . . . . p. 3 AX
Park Rd North . . . . p. 3 AX
Parliament St. . . . . p. 4 CZ
Pembroke Pl. . . . . p. 5 DY 105
Picton Rd. . . . . p. 3 BX
Pinehurst Av. . . . . p. 2 BV 106
Poulton Rd. . . . . p. 3 AX
Prescot Rd. . . . . p. 3 BX
Prescot St. . . . . p. 5 DY
Prince's Rd . . . . p. 5 DZ
Queens Drive . . . . p. 3 BX
Queensway . . . . p. 3 AX
Ranelagh St. . . . . p. 4 CZ 107
Rathbone Rd . . . . p. 3 BX
Regent Rd . . . . p. 2 AV
Renshaw St. . . . . p. 4 CZ
Rice Lane . . . . p. 2 AV
Rimrose Rd . . . . p. 2 AV 108
Rocky Lane . . . . p. 3 BX 112
Rodney St. . . . . p. 4 CZ
Roscommon St. . . . . p. 4 CY
Rose Lane . . . . p. 3 BX
St. Domingo Rd . . . . p. 2 AV 113
St. James Pl. . . . . p. 4 CZ 114

St. James Rd . . . . p. 4 CZ
St. James St. . . . . p. 4 CZ
St. John's Lane . . . . p. 4 CY 116
St. Johns Centre . . . . . . p. 4 CY
St. Oswald's St. . . . . . . p. 3 BX 119
Sandhills Lane . . . . p. 2 AV 120
Scotland Rd . . . . p. 4 CY
Seaforth Rd . . . . p. 2 AV 121
Sefton Park Rd . . . . p. 3 BX 123
Seymour St. . . . . p. 4 CY 124
Shaw St. . . . . p. 5 DY
Sheil Rd . . . . p. 3 BX
Silvester St. . . . . p. 4 CY
Skelhorne St. . . . . p. 4 CY 125
Smithdown Lane . . . . . . p. 5 DZ
Smithdown Rd . . . . p. 3 BX
Soho St. . . . . p. 4 CY
South Crosby Rd . . . . . . p. 2 AV
South John St. . . . . p. 4 CZ 128
Southport Rd . . . . p. 2 AV
Stanley Rd . . . . p. 2 AV
Stonebridge Lane . . . . . p. 2 BV
Stopgate Lane . . . . p. 2 BV 129
Strand St. . . . . p. 4 CZ 131
Strand (The) . . . . p. 4 CZ 132
Tithebarn St. . . . . p. 4 CY
Townsend Av. . . . . p. 2 BV
Townsend Lane . . . . p. 2 BV
Tunnel Rd . . . . p. 3 BX 133
Ullet Rd . . . . p. 3 BX
Upper Duke St. . . . . p. 4 CZ
Upper Parliament St. . . p. 5 DZ
Utting Av. . . . . p. 2 BV
Utting Av. E. . . . . p. 2 BV
Vauxhall Rd . . . . p. 4 CY
Victoria St. . . . . p. 4 CY
Walton Lane . . . . p. 2 AV
Walton Rd . . . . p. 2 AV 135
Walton Vale . . . . p. 2 BV 136
Walton Breck Rd . . . . . p. 2 BV 137
Walton Hall Av. . . . . . . p. 2 BV
Wapping . . . . p. 4 CZ
Warbreck Moor . . . . . . p. 2 BV 139
Water St. . . . . p. 4 CY 140
Waterloo Rd . . . . p. 4 CY
Wellington St. . . . . p. 3 BX 141
West Derby Rd . . . . p. 3 BX 144
West Derby St. . . . . p. 5 DY
Whitechapel . . . . p. 4 CY 147
William Brown St. . . . . . p. 4 CY 148

Si vous écrivez à un hôtel à l'étranger,
joignez à votre lettre un coupon-réponse international.
(disponible dans les bureaux de poste).

LIVERSEDGE West Yorks. **402** O 22 – see Leeds.

LIZARD Cornwall **403** E 34 The West Country G. – ✆ 0326 The Lizard.
See : Lizard Peninsula★★.

Envir. : Kynance Cove★★★, NW : 1 ½ m. – Landewednack★, Church★, E : ½ m. – Cury★, Church★,
N : 6 ½ m. – Cadgwith★, SE : 4 m. – Ruan Minor (Church★), NE : 4 m. – Gunwalloe Fishing Cove★,
NW : 9 m. – Mawgan In Meneage Church★, N : 10 m.

♦London 326 – Penzance 24 – Truro 29.

 🏨 **Housel Bay** ⌕, Housel Cove, TR12 7PG, ℰ 290417, ≤ Housel Cove, ☞ – 🚽wc 🛎wc 🅿.
  🔽 🅰🅴
  M (bar lunch)/dinner 11.00 t. ₺ 2.50 – **22 rm** � 18.00/50.00 t.

 ⌂ **Parc Brawse House** ⌕, Penmenner Rd, TR12 7NR, ℰ 290466, ≤, ☞ – 🅿
  March-October – **6 rm** ⊇ 13.00/23.00.

 ⌂ **Penmenner House** ⌕, Penmenner Rd, TR12 7NR, ℰ 290370 – 🛎wc 🅿
  April-October – **8 rm** ⊇ 11.00/24.00 t.

LLANARMON DYFFRYN CEIRIOG Clwyd **402 403** K 25 – pop. 137 – ✉ Llangollen – ✆ 069 176.
♦London 196 – Chester 33 – Shrewsbury 32.

 🏨 **Hand,** LL20 7LD, ℰ 666, ⌣, ☞, ※ – 🚽wc 🅿. 🔽 🅰🅴 **VISA**
  M (bar lunch Monday to Saturday)/dinner 10.50 t. ₺ 2.75 – **13 rm** ⊇ 29.00/46.00 t. – SB
  63.00/70.00 st.

 🏨 **West Arms,** LL20 7LD, ℰ 665, ⌣, ☞ – 🚽wc 🛎 🅿. 🔽 🅰🅴 ⓘ **VISA**. ※
  M (bar lunch)/dinner 10.50 t. ₺ 2.90 – **12 rm** ⊇ 17.00/37.00 t. – SB (October-May)
  48.00/60.00 st.

LLANBEDR Gwynedd 402 403 H 25 – pop. 486 – ECD : Wednesday – ☎ 034 123.

♦London 262 – Holyhead 54 – Shrewsbury 100.

🏨 **Pensarn Hall** ⬙, LL45 2HS, N : ¾ m. on A 496 ℰ 236, ≼, 🐴 – 🆃🆅 ⊟wc ❶. ❊
M (dinner only) 7.50 **t.** and a la carte – **7 rm** ⪜ 14.50/27.00 **t.** – SB (winter and spring only) 35.00 **st.**

🏠 **Ty Mawr** ⬙, LL45 2HH, ℰ 440, 🐴 – 🆃🆅 ⊟wc ▥wc ❶
M 8.50 **t.** and a la carte ▮ 2.50 – **10 rm** ⪜ 13.00/32.00 **t.**

LLANBEDR PONT STEFFAN = Lampeter.

LLANBERIS Gwynedd 403 H 24 – pop. 1,809 – ECD : Wednesday – ☎ 0286.

🅩 Old Station car park ℰ 870765.

♦London 243 – Caernarfon 7 – Chester 65 – Shrewsbury 78.

🏠 **Pen y Gwryd** ⬙, Nant Gwynant, LL55 4NT, SE : 6 m. via Pass of Llanberis ℰ 870211, ≼ – ❶
closed mid November-1 January and weekdays January-February – **M** (buffet lunch)/dinner 7.50 – **21 rm** ⪜ 10.90/23.80.

❌❌ **Y Bistro**, 43-45 High St., LL55 4EU, ℰ 871278 – 🄰🄴 ① 𝘝𝘐𝘚𝘈
closed Sunday, 2 weeks January and 25-26 December – **M** (lunch by arrangement) (booking essential) a la carte 11.50/15.00 **t.**

LLANDEILO Dyfed 403 I 28 – pop. 1,598 – ECD : Thursday – ☎ 0558.

Envir. : Talley (abbey and lakes★) N : 7 m.

🛇 Glynhir, Llandybie nr. Ammanford ℰ 0269 (Llandybie) 850472.

♦London 218 – Brecon 34 – Carmarthen 15 – ♦Swansea 25.

🏛 **Cawdor Arms,** Rhosmaen St., SA19 6EN, ℰ 823500, « Tasteful decor » – 🆃🆅 ⊟wc ▥wc ❊ ❶. 🄰🄴 ① 𝘝𝘐𝘚𝘈
M 10.00/13.50 **t.** and a la carte ▮ 3.75 – **17 rm** ⪜ 29.50/49.50 **t.** – SB (September-June) 54.00 **st.**

at Rhosmaen N : 1 m. on A 40 – ⊠ ☎ 0558 Llandeilo :

❌ **Plough Inn**, SA19 6NP, ℰ 823431, Italian rest. – ❶. 🄰🄵 𝘝𝘐𝘚𝘈
closed Sunday, first week November and Christmas Day – **M** a la carte 7.75/16.80 **t.** ▮ 3.00.

AUSTIN-ROVER   28 Rhosmaen St. ℰ 823221

LLANDEWI SKIRRID Gwent – see Abergavenny.

LLANDOGO Gwent 403 404 L 28 – ECD : Thursday – ⊠ Monmouth – ☎ 0594 Dean.

♦London 140 – ♦Bristol 26 – Gloucester 43 – Newport 25.

🏠 **Old Farmhouse**, NP5 4TL, on A 466 ℰ 530303 – 🆃🆅 ⊟wc ❶. 🄰🄵 𝘝𝘐𝘚𝘈
M (bar lunch Monday to Saturday)/dinner 6.95 **t.** and a la carte ▮ 2.50 – **24 rm** ⪜ 20.00/30.00 **t.** – SB (October-June) 36.00 **st.**

LLANDRILLO-YN-RHOS (RHOS-ON-SEA) Clwyd – see Colwyn Bay.

LLANDRINDOD WELLS Powys 403 J 27 – pop. 4,232 – ECD : Wednesday – ☎ 0597.

🛇 ℰ 2010, E : 1 m.

🅩 Rock Park Spa ℰ 2600.

♦London 204 – Brecon 29 – Carmarthen 60 – Shrewsbury 58.

🏠 **Griffin Lodge,** Temple St., LD1 5HF, ℰ 2432 – ▥wc ❶. 🄰🄵 🄰🄴
closed January – **M** 4.55 **t.** and a la carte ▮ 2.15 – **8 rm** ⪜ 13.00/29.00 **t.**

at Howey S : 1 ½ m. on A 483 – ⊠ ☎ 0597 Llandrindod Wells :

🏠 **Corven Hall** ⬙, LD1 5RE, S : ½ m. by A 483 on Hundred House rd ℰ 3368, 🐴 – ▥wc ❶
7 rm ⪜ 8.00/18.00 **st.**

LLANDUDNO Gwynedd 402 403 I 24 – pop. 13,202 – ECD : Wednesday except summer – ☎ 0492.

See : Great Orme's Head (≼★★ from the summit) by Ty-Gwyn Rd A – Tour of the Great Orme's Head★★.

🛇 Rhos-on-Sea Residential, Penryn Bay ℰ 49641 by A 546 B.

🅩 Chapel St. ℰ 76413 – Arcadia Theatre ℰ 76413 ext 264 (summer only) – Kiosk, North Promenade ℰ 76572 (summer only).

♦London 243 – Birkenhead 55 – Chester 47 – Holyhead 43.

Gloddaeth Street . . . . A 5
Mostyn Street. . . . . B
Upper Mostyn Street. . . . . A 15

Chapel Street . . . . A 3
Deganwy Avenue . . . . A 4
Llewelyn Avenue . . . . A 6
Maelgwyn Road. . . . . A 7
North Parade . . . . AB 8
Oxford Road . . . . B 10
Trinity Square . . . . B 12
Tudno Street . . . . A 13
Vaughan Street . . . . B 16

Bodysgallen Hall ⚘, LL30 1RS, SE : 2 ½ m. by B 5115 ℘ 0492 (Deganwy) 84466, Telex 617163, ≤ gardens and mountains, « Part 17 C and 18 C hall with terraced gardens », park, ✗ — 📺 ☎ 🅿. ⚒. ◪ 🆎 ⓘ 𝗩𝗜𝗦𝗔. ✘ — by B 5115 B
M 8.30/16.50 **t.** and a la carte ♠ 3.30 — ⌷ 4.00 — **19 rm** 40.00/80.00 **st.**, **9 suites** 60.00/80.00 **st.** — SB (November-April) (except Bank Holidays) 90.00 **st.**

Empire, 73 Church Walks, LL30 2HE, ℘ 79955, Telex 617161, ◪ — 🛗 📺 ☎ 🅿. ◪ 🆎 ⓘ 𝗩𝗜𝗦𝗔
closed 2 weeks at Christmas and New Year — **M** 7.70/10.90 **st.** and a la carte ♠ 3.50 — **56 rm**
⌷ 25.00/60.00 **st.** — SB 40.00/75.00 **st.** A e

Gogarth Abbey, West Shore, LL30 2QY, ℘ 76211, ≤, ◪, 🌳 — 📺 ⏢wc 🛁wc 🅿. ◪ 🆎
𝗩𝗜𝗦𝗔. ✘ A s
M (bar lunch)/dinner 10.00 **t.** and a la carte ♠ 3.00 — **41 rm** ⌷ 20.00/46.00 **t.**, **1 suite** 56.00/64.00 **t.** — SB 40.00/64.00 **st.**

St. Tudno, North Par., LL30 2LP, ℘ 74411, « Tasteful decor », ◪ — 🛗 📺 ⏢wc 🛁wc ☎. ◪
🆎 ⓘ 𝗩𝗜𝗦𝗔. ✘ A c
closed 22 December-24 January — **M** (bar lunch Monday to Saturday)/dinner 14.00 **t.** ♠ 3.25 —
21 rm ⌷ 25.00/66.00 **t.** — SB (except Bank Holidays) 50.00/82.50 **st.**

Dunoon, Gloddaeth St., LL30 2DW, ℘ 77078 — 🛗 📺 ⏢wc 🅿 A r
Mid March-October — **M** 5.50/6.50 **st.** ♠ 2.50 — **58 rm** ⌷ 10.00/38.00 **st.** — SB 30.00/50.00 **st.**

Bryn-y-Bia Lodge, Bryn-y-Bia Rd, Craigside, LL30 3AS, E : 1 ½ m. on A 546 ℘ 49644, 🌳 —
📺 ⏢wc 🛁wc 🅿 by A 546 B
closed January and December — **M** (closed lunch Saturday and Sunday) (bar lunch)/dinner
10.50 **t.** — **18 rm** ⌷ 16.50/39.00 **t.** — SB (October-May) 40.00/48.00 **st.**

Bromwell Court, Promenade, 6 Craig-y-Don Par., LL30 1BG, ℘ 78416 — 📺 ⏢wc 🛁wc. ◪
𝗩𝗜𝗦𝗔 B u
M (bar lunch)/dinner 9.00 **st.** ♠ 3.50 — **11 rm** ⌷ 16.00/37.00 **st.** — SB (October-May) (except Bank Holidays) 44.00/48.00 **st.**

Headlands, Hill Terr., LL30 2LS, ℘ 77485, ≤ Llandudno and Ormes Bay — 📺 ⏢wc 🛁wc
🅿. ◪ 𝗩𝗜𝗦𝗔 AB a
closed January and February — **M** (bar lunch)/dinner 8.50 **t.** and a la carte — **17 rm**
⌷ 14.00/36.00 **t.** — SB 45.00/51.00 **st.**

↑ **Clontarf,** 1 Great Orme's Rd, West Shore, LL30 2AS, ✆ 77621 – ▥wc **P**. ⚘   A **u**
February-October – **10 rm** ☲ 11.75/18.50 **t.**

↑ **Sunnymede,** West Par., West Shore, LL30 2BD, ✆ 77130 – ▣ ➟wc ▥wc **P**. ◪ *VISA* ⚘
April-October – **18 rm** ☲ 12.00/28.00 **t.**   A **x**

↑ **Cranleigh,** Great Orme's Rd, West Shore, LL30 2AR, ✆ 77688 – ▥wc **P**   A **u**
Easter-October – **13 rm** ☲ 10.00/28.50 **t.**

XX **Floral,** Victoria St., Craig y Don, LL30 1LJ, ✆ 75735 – ◪ ⓞ *VISA*   B **s**
closed Saturday lunch, Monday, 2 weeks April and 2 weeks September – **M** a la carte
10.00/13.60 **t.** ⓙ 2.80.

X **No. 1,** 1 Old Rd, LL30 2HA, ✆ 75424, Bistro   A **i**
closed Sunday dinner – **M** a la carte 3.80/5.90 **t.** ⓙ 2.80.

CITROEN Herkomer Rd ✆ 77607   PEUGEOT-TALBOT Conwy Rd ✆ 77461

LLANELLI Dyfed **408** H 29 – pop. 45,336 – ECD : Tuesday – ✆ 0554.
Envir. : Kidwelly (Castle★★) *AC*, NW : 9 m.
♦London 206 – Carmarthen 20 – ♦Swansea 11.

🏨 **Stradey Park** (T.H.F.), Furnace, SA15 4HA, N : ¾ m. on B 4309 ✆ 758171, Telex 48521 – ▮⬥▮
▣ ➟wc ➟ **P**. ⚟. ◪ AE ⓞ *VISA*
M 8.50 **st.** and a la carte ⓙ 2.80 – ☲ 5.50 – **77 rm** 33.00/41.00 **st.**

🏛 **Diplomat,** Felinfoel Rd, SA15 3PJ, NE : 1 m. on A 276 ✆ 756156 – ▮⬥▮ ▣ ➟wc ▥ ➘ **P**. ◪
AE ⓞ *VISA*
M *(closed Sunday dinner)* 7.95/12.60 **t.** and a la carte ⓙ 2.80 – **12 rm** ☲ 25.50/37.50 **t.** – SB
(weekends only) 48.00/68.00 **st.**

AUSTIN-ROVER Vauxhall St. ✆ 3371   FORD Sandy Rd ✆ 3285

LLANELWY = St. Asaph.

LLANFAIR-YM-MUALLT = Builth Wells.

LLANFYLLIN Powys **402 408** K 25 – pop. 1,210 – ECD : Friday – ✆ 069 184.
♦London 188 – Chester 42 – Shrewsbury 24 – Welshpool 11.

🏛 **Bodfach Hall** ⚘, SY22 5HS, NW : 1 m. on B 4391 ✆ 272, ≼, « Country house in extensive
gardens », park – ▣ ➟wc ▥wc **P**. ◪ AE ⓞ
closed January and February – **M** (bar lunch Monday to Saturday)/dinner 8.50 **t.** – **9 rm**
☲ 18.50/37.00 **t.** – SB 43.00/54.00 **st.**

LLANGAMMARCH WELLS Powys **408** J 27 – ECD : Wednesday – ✆ 059 12.
♦London 200 – Brecon 17 – Builth Wells 8.

🏨 **Lake** ⚘, LD4 4BS, E : ¾ m. ✆ 202, ≼, ⛳, ⚓, ☈, park, ⚘ – ▣ ➟wc ▥wc **P**. ◪ *VISA*
M (bar lunch)/dinner 11.50 **st.** ⓙ 2.95 – **25 rm** ☲ 24.50/48.50 **st.** – SB 57.00/65.00 **st.**

LLANGOLLEN Clwyd **402 408** K 25 – pop. 2,546 – ECD : Thursday – ✆ 0978.
See : Plas Newydd★★ (the house of the Ladies of Llangollen) *AC*.
Envir. : Horseshoe Pass★, NW : 4 ½ m. – Chirk Castle★ (gates★)*AC*, SE : 7 ½ m.
▜ Vale of Llangollen, Holyhead Rd ✆ 860040, E : 1 ½ m.
🅩 Town Hall, ✆ 860828 (summer only).
♦London 194 – Chester 23 – Holyhead 76 – Shrewsbury 30.

🏛 **Bryn Howel,** LL20 7UW, E : 2 ¾ m. on A 539 ✆ 860331, ≼, ⚓, ☈ – ▣ ➟wc ➘ **P**. ⚟. ◪
AE *VISA*
closed Christmas day – **M** 6.75/10.00 **st.** and a la carte ⓙ 3.75 – **35 rm** ☲ 30.00/44.00 **st.**

🏛 **Royal** (T.H.F.), Bridge St., LL20 8PG, ✆ 860202, ≼, ⚓ – ▣ ➟wc ➘ **P**. ⚟. ◪ AE ⓞ *VISA*
M (bar lunch Monday to Saturday)/dinner 11.50 **st.** ⓙ 2.70 – ☲ 5.50 – **33 rm** 31.50/45.00 **st.**

🏠 **Ty'n-y-Wern,** LL20 7PH, E : 1 m. on A 5 ✆ 860252, ≼, ☈ – ▣ ➟wc **P**. *VISA*
closed Christmas day – **M** (lunch by arrangement Monday to Saturday)/dinner 9.95 **st.**
and a la carte ⓙ 2.50 – **10 rm** ☲ 16.00/35.00 **st.** – SB (November-March) 32.00/37.00 **st.**

X **Caesar's,** Deeside Lane, LL20 8NT, ✆ 860133, ≼ – ◪ *VISA*
M (dinner only) 11.50 **st.** ⓙ 3.20.

FORD ✆ 860270

LLANGURIG Powys **408** J 26 – pop. 620 – ECD : Thursday – ✉ Llanidloes – ✆ 055 15.
♦London 188 – Aberystwyth 25 – Carmarthen 75 – Shrewsbury 53.

↑ **Old Vicarage,** SY18 6RN, ✆ 280, ☈ – **P**
April-September – **4 rm** ☲ 11.50/21.00 **t.**

LLANGYBI Gwent – see Usk.

LLANILLTUD FAWR = Llantwit Major.

LLANNEFYDD Clwyd 402 403 J 24 – ⊠ Denbigh – ☎ 074 579.
♦London 225 – Chester 37 – Shrewsbury 63.

  🏠 **Hawk and Buckle Inn,** LL16 5ED, ℰ 249, ≤ – TV ⇔wc ☎ Ⓟ. 🅰 AE VISA. ⅏
    M *(closed lunch Monday to Friday during winter)* (bar lunch)/dinner 9.50 t. ⅃ 2.85 – **10 rm**
    ⊡ 21.00/29.00 t. – SB 42.00/54.00 st.

AUSTIN-ROVER Denbigh Rd ℰ 227

LLANRHIDIAN West Glam. – see Swansea.

LLANRWST Gwynedd 402 403 I 24 – pop. 2,908 – ECD : Thursday – ☎ 0492.
See : Gwydir Castle★.
Envir. : Capel Garmon (Burial Chamber★) SE : 6 m.
♦London 230 – Holyhead 50 – Shrewsbury 66.

  🏛 **Maenan Abbey,** N : 2 ½ m. on A 470, LL26 0UL, ℰ 049 269 (Dolgarrog) 247, ⌇, 🚗 – TV
    ⇔wc ⋔wc 🚗 Ⓟ. 🅰 AE ① VISA
    M 5.50/8.50 t. and a la carte ⅃ 2.95 – **12 rm** ⊡ 15.00/36.00 t. – SB (except summer)
    36.00/40.00 st.

  XX **Meadowsweet** with rm, Station Rd, LL26 0DS, ℰ 640732, ≤ – TV ⋔wc ☎ Ⓟ. 🅰 AE VISA
    M (closed lunch Monday to Saturday November-February) 9.00/13.50 t. and a la carte ⅃ 2.75 –
    10 rm ⊡ 19.00/38.00 t. – SB (except Bank Holidays) 48.50/56.00 st.

AUSTIN-ROVER Kerry Garage ℰ 640381   FORD Betws Rd ℰ 640684

LLANTWIT MAJOR (LLANILLTUD FAWR) South Glam. 403 J 29 – pop. 13,375 (inc. St. Athan) –
☎ 044 65.
♦London 175 – ♦Cardiff 18 – ♦Swansea 33.

  🏠 **West House,** West St., CF6 9SP, ℰ 2406, 🚗 – TV ⇔wc Ⓟ. 🅰 AE VISA
    M 7.50 t. (lunch) and a la carte 7.55/11.70 t. ⅃ 4.00 – **19 rm** ⊡ 16.50/34.00 st. – SB (weekends
    only) 40.00 st.

  XX **Quaintways,** Colhugh St., CF6 9RE, ℰ 2321 – Ⓟ. 🅰 VISA
    closed Sunday and 26 December-6 January – **M** (dinner only) a la carte 8.00/12.65 t. ⅃ 2.90.

TOYOTA 2 Colhugh St. ℰ 3466

LLANWENARTH Gwent – see Abergavenny.

LLANWRTYD WELLS Powys 403 J 27 – pop. 528 – ECD : Wednesday – ☎ 059 13.
See : Cambrian Mountains : road★★ from Llanwrtyd to Tregaron.
Envir. : Rhandir-mwyn (≤★ of Afon Tywi Valley) SW : 12 m.
♦London 214 – Brecon 32 – Carmarthen 39.

  🏠 **Lasswade House,** Station Rd, LD5 4RW, ℰ 515, ≤, ⅃, 🚗 – TV ⇔wc ⋔wc Ⓟ
    M (lunch by arrangement) 7.00/8.00 t. and a la carte ⅃ 3.50 – **8 rm** ⊡ 17.00/36.00 st.

  at Abergwesyn NW : 5 m. – ⊠ Builth Wells – ☎ 059 13 Llanwrtyd Wells :

  🏠 **Llwynderw** ⌇, LD5 4TW, ℰ 238, ≤ countryside and hills, 🚗 – ⇔wc Ⓟ. AE. ⅏
    April-October – **M** (lunch by arrangement) 15.00/20.00 t. ⅃ 4.50 – **10 rm** ⊡ (dinner inclu-
    ded) 55.00/75.00.

LLANYCHAER Dyfed 403 F 28 – see Fishguard.

LLWYNMAWR Clwyd 402 403 K 25 – ⊠ Llangollen – ☎ 069 172 Glyn Ceiriog.
♦London 192 – Shrewsbury 28 – Wrexham 15.

  🏠 **Golden Pheasant** ⌇, LL20 7BB, ℰ 281, Telex 35664, ≤, 🚗 – TV ⇔wc ⋔wc Ⓟ. 🅰 AE VISA
    M 10.00/12.00 t. ⅃ 3.50 – **19 rm** ⊡ 30.00/53.00 t. – SB (except Bank Holidays) 71.00/81.00 st.

LODDISWELL Devon – see Kingsbridge.

LODDON Norfolk 404 Y 26 – pop. 2,508 – ECD : Wednesday – ☎ 0508.
♦London 121 – Great Yarmouth 16 – ♦Ipswich 48 – ♦Norwich 11.

  ↟ **Rackham's Stubbs House** ⌇, Stubbs Green, NR14 6EA, SW : ¾ m. ℰ 20231, 🚗 – ⋔wc
    Ⓟ. ⅏
    February-October – **9 rm** ⊡ 13.00/42.00 t.

LOFTUS Cleveland 402 R 20 – pop. 5,626 – ECD : Wednesday – ⊠ Saltburn by the Sea –
☎ 0287 Guisborough.
♦London 264 – ♦Leeds 73 – ♦Middlesbrough 17 – Scarborough 36.

  🏛 **Grinkle Park** ⌇, Easington, TS13 4UB, SE : 3 ½ m. by A 174 ℰ 40515, ≤, 🚗, park – TV
    ⇔wc Ⓟ. 🅰 AE VISA
    M 6.90/10.95 st. and a la carte ⅃ 2.60 – **20 rm** ⊡ 17.65/39.55 st. – SB (except Christmas, Easter
    and Bank Holidays) 70.90/111.00 st.

LONDON

LONDON (Greater) **404** folds ㉒ to ㊹ — **London G.** — pop. 7,566,620 — ✪ 01.

✈ Heathrow, ☎ 759 4321, Telex 934892, p. 8 AY — **Terminal**: Airbus (A1) from Victoria, Airbus (A2) from Paddington — Underground (Piccadilly line) frequent service daily — Helicopter service to Gatwick Airport.

✈ Gatwick, ☎ 0293 (Crawley) 28822 and ☎ 01 (London) 668 4211, Telex 877725, p. 9 : by A 23 EZ and M 23 — **Terminal**: Coach service from Victoria Coach Station (Flightline 777) — Railink (Gatwick Express) from Victoria (24 h service) — Helicopter service to Heathrow Airport.

✈ Stansted, at Bishop's Stortford, ☎ 0279 (Bishop's Stortford) 502380, Telex 81102, NE : 34 m. off M 11 and A 120.

BA Air Terminal : Victoria Station, ☎ 834 2323, p. 30 BX

British Caledonian Airways, Victoria Air Terminal : Victoria Station, SW1, ☎ 834 9411, p. 30 BX

🚃 Euston ☎ 387 8541 — King's Cross ☎ 837 4200 ext 4700 — Paddington ☎ 723 7000 ext 3148.

🛈 National Tourist Information Centre, Victoria Station Forecourt, SW1, ☎ 730 3488.
London Visitor and Convention Bureau Telephone Information Service ☎ 730 3485.
Teletourist ☎ 246 8041 (English), 246 8043 (French), 246 8045 (German).

Major sights in London and the outskirts .... pp. 2 and 3
Maps and lists of streets .... pp. 4 to 31
   Greater London .... pp. 4 to 11
   Central London .... pp. 12 to 25
   Detailed maps of :
   Mayfair, Soho, St. James's, Marylebone .... pp. 26 and 27
   South Kensington, Chelsea, Belgravia .... pp. 28 and 29
   Victoria, Strand, Bayswater, Kensington .... pp. 30 and 31
Hotels and Restaurants
   Alphabetical list of hotels and restaurants .... pp. 32 to 35
   Alphabetical list of areas included .... p. 35
   Starred establishments in London .... p. 36
   Restaurants classified according to type .... pp. 37 to 42
   Restaurants open on Sunday and restaurants taking last orders after
   11.30 p.m. .... pp. 43 to 46
   Hotels and Restaurants listed by boroughs .... pp. 47 to 68
Car dealers and repairers .... pp. 69 and 70

The maps in this section of the Guide are based upon the Ordnance Survey of Great Britain with the permission of the Controller of Her Majesty's Stationery Office. Crown Copyright reserved.

SIGHTS
CURIOSITÉS
LE CURIOSITÀ
SEHENSWÜRDIGKEITEN

■ HISTORIC BUILDINGS AND MONUMENTS

Palace of Westminster★★★ : House of Lords★★, Westminster Hall★★ (hammerbeam roof★★★), Robing Room★, Central Lobby★, House of Commons★, Big Ben★, Victoria Tower★ p. 19 NX — Tower of London★★★ (Crown Jewels★★★, White Tower or Keep★★★, St. John's Chapel★★, Beauchamp Tower★) p. 20 QU.

Banqueting House★★ p. 19 NV — Buckingham Palace★★ (Changing of the Guard★★, Royal Mews★★) p. 30 BV — Kensington Palace★★ p. 18 JV — Lincoln's Inn★★ p. 31 FV — London Bridge★★ p. 20 QV — Royal Hospital Chelsea★★ p. 29 FU — St. James's Palace★★ p. 27 EP — South Bank Arts Centre★★ (Royal Festival Hall★, National Theatre★, County Hall★) p. 19 NV — The Temple★★ (Middle Temple Hall★) p. 15 NU — Tower Bridge★★ p. 20 QV.

Albert Memorial★ p. 28 CQ — Apsley House★ p. 26 BP — Bloomsbury★ p. 15 NT — Burlington House★ p. 27 EM — Charterhouse★ p. 16 PT — Commonwealth Institute★ p. 17 HX — Design Centre★ p. 27 FM — George Inn★, Southwark p. 20 QV — Gray's Inn★ p. 15 NT — Guildhall★ (Lord Mayor's Show★★) p. 16 PT — Imperial College of Science and Technology★ p. 28 CR — Dr Johnson's House★ p. 16 PTU A — Lancaster House★ p. 27 EP — Leighton House★ p. 17 GX — Linley Sambourne House★ p. 17 HX — Mansion House★ (plate and insignia★★) p. 16 QU P — The Monument★ (⚹★) p. 16 QU G — Royal Opera Arcade★ (New Zealand House) p. 27 FGN — Old Admiralty★ p. 19 MV — Royal Exchange★ p. 16 QU V — Royal Opera House★ (Covent Garden) p. 31 EV — Somerset House★ p. 31 EV — Staple Inn★ p. 15 NT Y — Stock Exchange★ p. 16 QTU — Westminster Bridge★ p. 19 NX.

■ CHURCHES

The City Churches

St. Paul's Cathedral★★★ (Dome ⩽★★★) p. 16 PU.

St. Bartholomew the Great★★ (vessel★) p. 16 PT K — St. Dunstan-in-the-East★★ p. 16 QU F — St. Mary-at-Hill★★ (plan★, woodwork★★) p. 16 QU B — Temple Church★★ p. 15 NU.

All Hallows-by-the-Tower (font cover★★, brasses★) p. 16 QU Y — Christ Church★ p. 16 PT E — St. Andrew Undershaft (monuments★) p. 16 QU A — St. Bride★ (steeple★★) p. 16 PU J — St. Clement Eastcheap (panelled interior★★) p. 16 QU E — St. Edmund the King and Martyr (tower and spire★) p. 16 QU D — St. Giles Cripplegate★ p. 16 PT N — St. Helen Bishopsgate★ (monuments★★) p. 16 QTU R — St. James Garlickhythe (tower and spire★, sword rests★) p. 16 PU R — St. Katherine Cree (sword rest★) p. 16 QU J — St. Magnus the Martyr (tower★, sword rest★) p. 16 QU K — St. Margaret Lothbury★ (tower and spire★, woodwork★, screen★, font★) p. 16 QT S — St. Margaret Pattens (woodwork★) p. 16 QU N — St. Martin Ludgate (tower and spire★, door cases★) p. 16 PU B — St. Mary Abchurch★ (tower and spire★, dome★, reredos★) p. 16 QU X — St. Mary-le-Bow (tower and steeple★★) p. 16 PU G — St. Michael Paternoster Royal (tower and spire★) p. 16 PU D — St. Nicholas Cole Abbey (tower and spire★) p. 16 PU F — St. Olave★ p. 16 QU S — St. Peter upon Cornhill (screen★) p. 16 QU L — St. Stephen Walbrook★ (tower and steeple★, dome★) p. 16 QU Z — St. Vedast (tower and spire★, ceiling★) p. 16 PTU E.

Other Churches

Westminster Abbey★★★ (Chapel of Edward the Confessor★★, Henry VII Chapel★★★, Chapter House★★) p. 19 MX.

Southwark Cathedral★★ p. 20 QV.

Queen's Chapel★ p. 27 EP — St. Clement Danes★ p. 31 FV — St. James's★ p. 27 EM — St. Margaret's★ p. 19 NX A — St. Martin-in-the-Fields★ p. 31 DX — St. Paul's★ (Covent Garden) p. 31 DV — Westminster Roman Catholic Cathedral★ p. 19 MX B.

■ PARKS

Regent's Park★★★ p. 14 KS (terraces★★), Zoo★★★.

Hyde Park★★ p. 18 JU — St. James's Park★★ p. 19 MV.

Kensington Gardens★ p. 18 JV (Orangery★ A).

■ STREETS AND SQUARES

The City★★★ p. 16 PU.

Bedford Square★★ p. 15 MT — Belgrave Square★★ p. 30 AV — Burlington Arcade★★ p. 27 DM — The Mall★★ p. 27 FP — Piccadilly★★ p. 27 EM — The Thames★★ pp. 18-20 — Trafalgar Square★★ p. 31 DX — Whitehall★★ (Horse Guards★) p. 19 MV.

Barbican★ p. 16 PT — Bond Street★ pp. 26-27 CK-DM — Canonbury Square★ p. 16 PR — Carlton House Terrace★ p. 27 GN — Charing Cross★ p. 31 DX — Cheyne Walk★ p. 18 JZ — Fitzroy Square★ p. 15 LT — Jermyn Street★ p. 27 EN — Merrick Square★ p. 20 PX — Montpelier Square★ p. 29 EQ — Piccadilly Arcade★ p. 27 DEN — Portman Square★ p. 26 AJ — Queen Anne's Gate★ p. 19 MX — Regent Street★ p. 27 EM — St. James's Square★ p. 27 FN — St. James's Street★ p. 27 EN — Shepherd Market★ p. 26 CN — Strand★ p. 31 DX — Trinity Church Square★ p. 20 PX — Victoria Embankment★ p. 31 EX — Waterloo Place★ p. 27 FN.

■ MUSEUMS

British Museum★★★ p. 15 MT — National Gallery★★★ p. 27 GM — Science Museum★★★ p. 28 CR — Tate Gallery★★★ p. 19 MY — Victoria and Albert Museum★★★ p. 29 DR.

Courtauld Institute Galleries★★ p. 15 MT M — Museum of London★★ p. 16 PT M — National Portrait Gallery★★ p. 27 GM — Natural History Museum★★ p. 28 CS — Queen's Gallery★★ p. 30 BV — Wallace Collection★★ p. 26 AH.

Clock Museum★ (Guildhall) p. 16 PT — Geological Museum★ p. 28 CR — Imperial War Museum★ p. 20 PX — London Transport Museum★ p. 31 EV — Madame Tussaud's★ p. 14 KT M — Museum of Mankind★ p. 27 DM — National Army Museum★ p. 29 FU — Percival David Foundation of Chinese Art★ p. 15 MS M — Sir John Soane's Museum★ p. 15 NT M — Wellington Museum★ p. 26 BP.

■ OUTER LONDON

Hampton Court p. 8 BZ (The Palace★★★, gardens★★★) — Kew p. 9 CY Royal Botanic Gardens★★★ : Palm House★★, Temperate House★, Kew Palace or Dutch House★★, Orangery★, Pagoda★, Japanese Gateway★ — Windsor (Castle★★★) by A 4, M 4 AX.

Blackheath p. 11 GY terraces and houses★, Eltham Palace★ A — Brentford p. 8 BY Syon Park★★, gardens★ — Chiswick p. 9 CX Chiswick Mall★★, Chiswick House★ D, Hogarth's House★ E — Greenwich pp. 10 and 11 : Cutty Sark★★ FX F, National Maritime Museum★★ (Queen's House★★) FX M, Royal Naval College★★ (Painted Hall★, the Chapel★) FX G, Old Royal Observatory★ (Meridian Building : collection★★) GX K, Ranger's House★ FY N — Hampstead Kenwood House★★ (Adam Library★★, paintings★★) p. 5 EV P, Fenton House★ p. 13 GR — Hendon p. 5 CU Royal Air Force Museum★★ M — Hounslow p. 8 BX Osterley Park★★ — Lewisham p. 10 FY Horniman Museum★ M — Richmond pp. 8 and 9 : Richmond Park★★, ✵★★★ CY, Richmond Bridge★★ BY R, Richmond Green★★ BY S (Maids of Honour Row★★, Trumpeter's House★), Asgill House★ BY B, Ham House★★ BY V.

Dulwich p. 10 FY Dulwich College Picture Gallery★ X — Shoreditch p. 6 FV Geffrye Museum★ M — Tower Hamlets p. 6 FX St. Katharine Dock★ (HMS Discovery★) Y — Twickenham p. 8 BY Marble Hill House★ Z, Strawberry Hill★ A.

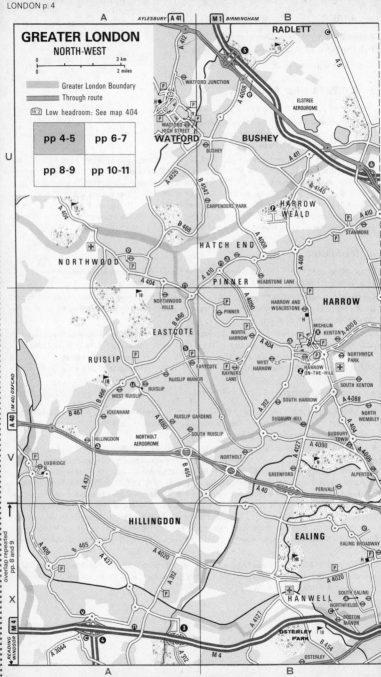

GREATER LONDON
NORTH-WEST

0   3 km
0   2 miles

Greater London Boundary
Through route

16.2 Low headroom: See map 404

pp 4-5	pp 6-7
pp 8-9	pp 10-11

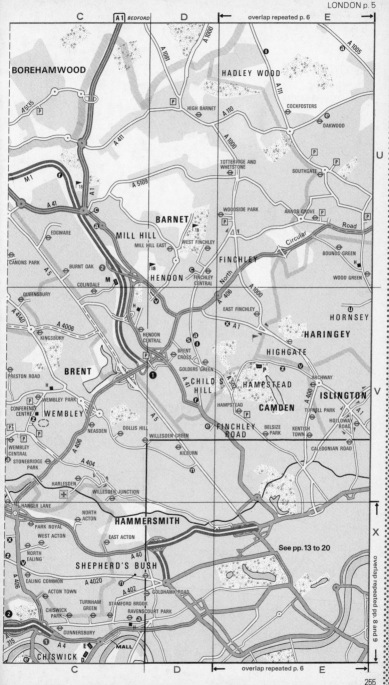

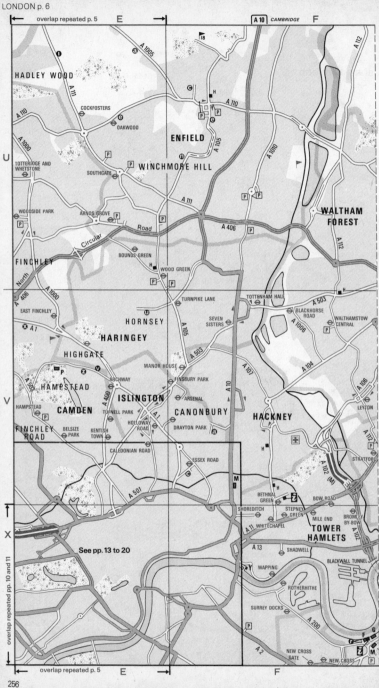

overlap repeated p. 5

A 10 CAMBRIDGE

HADLEY WOOD

COCKFOSTERS

OAKWOOD

ENFIELD

WINCHMORE HILL

TOTTERIDGE AND WHETSTONE

SOUTHGATE

WOODSIDE PARK

ARNOS GROVE

WALTHAM FOREST

Road

Circular

BOUNDS GREEN

FINCHLEY

North

WOOD GREEN

TURNPIKE LANE

TOTTENHAM HALE

EAST FINCHLEY

BLACKHORSE ROAD

WALTHAMSTOW CENTRAL

HORNSEY

SEVEN SISTERS

HARINGEY

HIGHGATE

MANOR HOUSE

FINSBURY PARK

HAMPSTEAD

ARCHWAY

ISLINGTON

ARSENAL

LEYTON

HAMPSTEAD

CANONBURY

HACKNEY

CAMDEN

TUFNELL PARK

FINCHLEY ROAD

BELSIZE PARK

KENTISH TOWN

HOLLOWAY ROAD

DRAYTON PARK

STRATFORD

CALEDONIAN ROAD

ESSEX ROAD

BETHNAL GREEN

BOW ROAD

SHOREDITCH

STEPNEY GREEN

MILE END

BROMLEY BY-BOW

See pp. 13 to 20

WHITECHAPEL

TOWER HAMLETS

A 13

SHADWELL

BLACKWALL TUNNEL

WAPPING

ROTHERHITHE

SURREY DOCKS

NEW CROSS GATE

NEW CROSS

overlap repeated pp. 10 and 11

overlap repeated p. 5

E

F

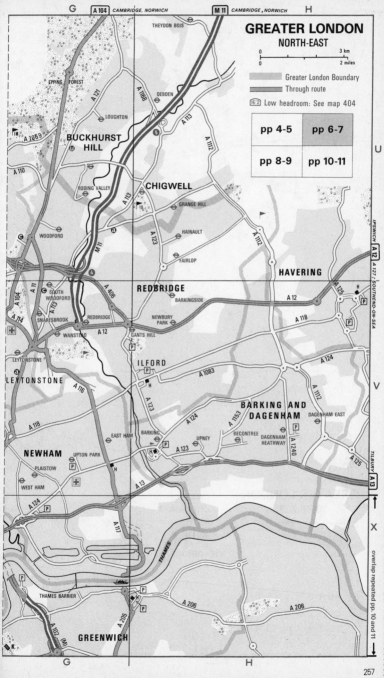

GREATER LONDON
NORTH-EAST

| 0 | | 3 km |
| 0 | | 2 miles |

Greater London Boundary
Through route

16.2 Low headroom: See map 404

| pp 4-5 | pp 6-7 |
| pp 8-9 | pp 10-11 |

THEYDON BOIS

EPPING FOREST

DEBDEN

LOUGHTON

BUCKHURST HILL

RODING VALLEY

CHIGWELL

GRANGE HILL

HAINAULT

WOODFORD

FAIRLOP

HAVERING

SOUTH WOODFORD

REDBRIDGE

BARKINGSIDE

SNARESBROOK

REDBRIDGE

NEWBURY PARK

WANSTEAD

GANTS HILL

LEYTONSTONE

LEYTONSTONE

ILFORD

BARKING AND DAGENHAM

DAGENHAM EAST

EAST HAM

BARKING

UPNEY

BECONTREE

DAGENHAM HEATHWAY

NEWHAM

UPTON PARK

PLAISTOW

WEST HAM

THAMES

THAMES BARRIER

GREENWICH

257

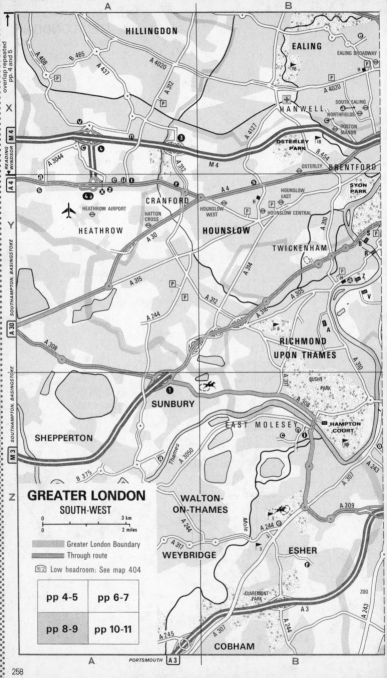

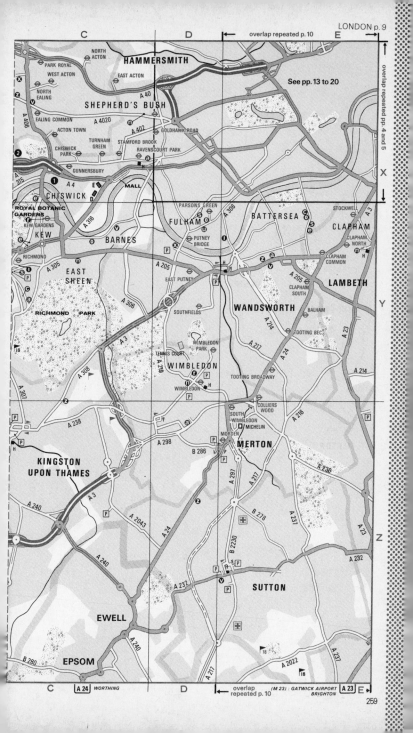

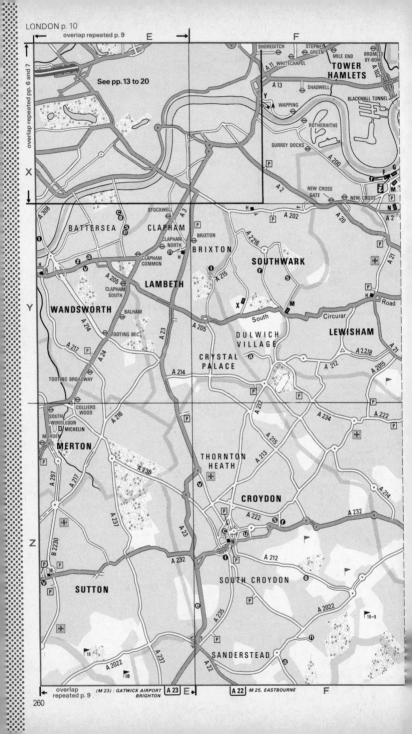

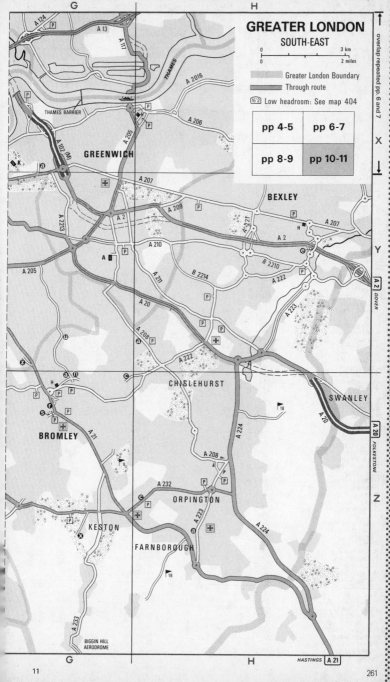

GREATER LONDON
SOUTH-EAST

0   3 km
0   2 miles

Greater London Boundary
Through route

16 2   Low headroom: See map 404

| pp 4-5 | pp 6-7 |
| pp 8-9 | pp 10-11 |

overlap repeated pp. 6 and 7

X

Y

N

A 2   DOVER

A 20   FOLKESTONE

THAMES

A 124
A 13
A 117
A 2016
A 206
A 205
THAMES BARRIER
A 102 (M)
GREENWICH
A 207
BEXLEY
A 2213
A 2
A 209
A 221
A 207
A 210
A 2
A 205
B 2214
B 2210
A 222
A 2lb
A 20
A 2213
A 208
A 222
CHISLEHURST
SWANLEY
A 20
A 224
A 208
BROMLEY
A 21
A 232
A 223
ORPINGTON
A 224
KESTON
FARNBOROUGH
A 233
BIGGIN HILL
AERODROME

G

H

HASTINGS A 21

Beauchamp Place . . . . SW3 p. 29 **ER**
Brompton Road . . . . SW1, SW3 p. 29 **DS**
Burlington Arcade . . . . W1 p. 27 **DM**
Camden Passage . . . . N1 p. 16 **PR** 70
Carnaby Street . . . . W1 p. 27 **EK**
Jermyn Street . . . . SW1 p. 27 **EN**
Kensington High Street . . . . . W8, W14 p. 17 **HX**
King's Road . . . . SW3, SW10, SW6 p. 29 **DU**
Knightsbridge . . . . SW1, SW7 p. 29 **EQ**
Middlesex Street . . . . E1 p. 16 **QT**
New Bond Street . . . . W1 p. 26 **CK**
Old Bond Street . . . . W1 p. 27 **DM**
Oxford Street . . . . W1 p. 26 **BK**
Piccadilly . . . . W1 p. 27 **EM**
Portobello Road . . . . W11, W10 p. 13 **GU**
Regent Street . . . . W1 p. 27 **EM**
Sloane Street . . . . SW1 p. 29 **FR**

Abbey Road . . . . NW8 p. 14 **JR**
Abbey Street . . . . SE1 p. 20 **QX**
Abbotsbury Road . . . . W14 p. 17 **GV**
Abercorn Place . . . . NW8 p. 14 **JS**
Abingdon Road . . . . W8 p. 17 **HX** 2
Acacia Road . . . . NW8 p. 14 **JR**
Adam Street . . . . WC2 p. 31 **EX**
Adam's Row . . . . W1 p. 26 **BM**
Addison Crescent . . . . W14 p. 17 **GX** 3
Addison Gardens . . . . W14 p. 17 **GX**
Addison Road . . . . W14 p. 17 **GX**
Adelaide Road . . . . NW3 p. 14 **JR**
Agar Grove . . . . NW1 p. 15 **LR**
Akenside Road . . . . NW3 p. 13 **GR**
Albany Street . . . . NW1 p. 15 **LS**
Albert Bridge . . . . SW3, SW11 p. 18 **KZ**
Albert Bridge Road . . . . SW11 p. 18 **KZ**
Albert Embankment . . . . SE1 p. 19 **NZ**
Albion Street . . . . W2 p. 31 **EY**
Aldersgate Street . . . . EC1 p. 16 **PT**
Alford Street . . . . W1 p. 26 **BM**
Aldgate High Street . . . . EC3 p. 16 **QU**
Aldwych . . . . WC2 p. 31 **EV**
Allitsen Road . . . . NW8 p. 14 **JR**
Allsop Place . . . . NW1 p. 14 **KT** 4
Amwell Street . . . . EC1 p. 15 **NS**
Argyll Street . . . . W1 p. 27 **DJ**
Arkwright Road . . . . NW3 p. 13 **GR**
Arlington Street . . . . SW1 p. 27 **DN** 6
Artesian Road . . . . W2 p. 30 **AY**
Artillery Row . . . . SW1 p. 30 **CV** 7
Arundel Street . . . . WC2 p. 31 **FV**
Ashburn Place . . . . SW7 p. 28 **BS**
Ashley Place . . . . SW1 p. 30 **BV**
Atterbury Street . . . . SW1 p. 19 **MY** 8
Avenue Road . . . . NW8, NW3 p. 14 **JR**
Avery Row . . . . W1 p. 26 **CL** 12
Aybrook Street . . . . W1 p. 26 **AH**
Baker Street . . . . W1, NW1 p. 26 **AH**
Bark Place . . . . W2 p. 30 **BZ**
Barkston Gardens . . . . SW5 p. 28 **AT** 14
Barlby Road . . . . W10 p. 13 **GT**
Barnsbury Road . . . . N1 p. 15 **NR**
Barnsbury Street . . . . N1 p. 16 **PR**
Baron's Court Road . . . . W14 p. 17 **GZ**
Bartholomew Road . . . . NW5 p. 15 **LR** 16
Basil Street . . . . SW3 p. 29 **ER**
Bateman Street . . . . W1 p. 27 **FK** 18
Bath Street . . . . EC1 p. 16 **PS**
Battersea Bridge . . . . SW3, SW11 p. 18 **JZ**
Battersea Bridge Road . . . . SW11 p. 18 **JZ**
Battersea Park Road . . . . . . SW8, SW11 p. 19 **LZ** 19
Baylis Road . . . . SE1 p. 19 **NX**
Bayswater Road . . . . W2 p. 30 **BZ**
Beak Street . . . . W1 p. 27 **EL**
Beauchamp Place . . . . SW3 p. 29 **ER**
Beaufort Street . . . . SW3 p. 28 **CU**
Bedfort Square . . . . WC1 p. 15 **MT**
Bedfort Square . . . . WC2 p. 31 **DV**
Beech Street . . . . EC2 p. 16 **PT**
Belgrave Place . . . . SW1 p. 30 **AV**
Belgrave Road . . . . SW1 p. 30 **BX**
Belgrave Square . . . . SW1 p. 30 **AV**
Belsize Avenue . . . . NW3 p. 13 **GR**
Belsize Crescent . . . . NW3 p. 13 **GR** 22
Belsize Lane . . . . NW3 p. 13 **GR**
Belsize Park . . . . NW3 p. 14 **JR**
Belsize Road . . . . NW6 p. 13 **HR**
Belsize Park Gardens . . . . NW3 p. 14 **JR**
Belvedere Road . . . . SE1 p. 19 **NV** 23
Berkeley Square . . . . W1 p. 26 **CM**
Berkeley Street . . . . W1 p. 27 **DN**
Bermondsey Street . . . . SE1 p. 20 **QX**
Bernard Street . . . . WC1 p. 15 **NS** 25
Berwick Street . . . . W1 p. 27 **FK** 26

Bessborough Gardens . . . . SW1 p. 19 **MZ** 27
Bessborough Street . . . . SW1 p. 19 **MZ** 30
Bethnal Green Road . . . . E1, E2 p. 16 **QS** 32
Bevis Marks . . . . EC3 p. 16 **QT** 34
Bina Gardens . . . . SW5 p. 28 **BT**
Binney Street . . . . W1 p. 26 **BL** 35
Birdcage Walk . . . . SW1 p. 30 **CV**
Bishop's Bridge Road . . . . W2 p. 14 **JT**
Bishopsgate . . . . EC2 p. 16 **QT** 36
Bishops Road . . . . N6 p. 17 **GZ**
Blackfriars Bridge . . . . EC4, SE1 p. 16 **PU** 38
Blackfriars Road . . . . SE1 p. 20 **PV**
Black Prince Road . . . . SE11, SE1 p. 19 **NY**
Blandford Street . . . . W1 p. 26 **AH**
Blomfield Road . . . . W9 p. 14 **JT**
Bloomsbury Street . . . . WC1 p. 15 **MT** 39
Bloomsbury Way . . . . WC1 p. 15 **NT**
Bly the Road . . . . W14 p. 17 **GX**
Bolton Gardens . . . . SW5 p. 28 **AT**
Bolton Street . . . . W1 p. 26 **CN**
Boltons (The) . . . . SW10 p. 28 **BU**
Borough High Street . . . . SE1 p. 20 **PX**
Borough Road . . . . SE1 p. 20 **PX**
Boundary Road . . . . NW8 p. 14 **JR**
Bourne Street . . . . W1 p. 29 **FT**
Bowling Green Lane . . . . EC1 p. 16 **PS** 43
Bow Street . . . . WC2 p. 31 **EV**
Braganza Street . . . . SE17 p. 20 **PZ**
Bramham Gardens . . . . SW5 p. 28 **AT**
Bramley Road . . . . W10 p. 13 **GU**
Bray Place . . . . SW3 p. 29 **ET** 45
Bream's Buildings . . . . EC4 p. 31 **FV** 47
Bressenden Place . . . . SW1 p. 30 **FV** 48
Brewer Street . . . . W1 p. 27 **EM**
Brewery Road . . . . N7 p. 15 **NR**
Brick Street . . . . W1 p. 26 **BP**
Bridgefoot . . . . SE1 p. 19 **NZ** 49
Brixton Road . . . . SW9 p. 19 **NZ**
Broadhurst Gardens . . . . NW6 p. 13 **HR**
Broadley Street . . . . NW8 p. 14 **JT**
Broad Sanctuary . . . . SW1 p. 19 **MX** 52
Broad Walk (The) . . . . W8 p. 30 **BZ**
Broadwick Street . . . . W1 p. 27 **EK**
Brompton Road . . . . SE6 p. 29 **DS**
Brook Drive . . . . SE11 p. 20 **PX**
Brook Green . . . . W6 p. 17 **GX**
Brook's Mews . . . . W1 p. 26 **CL**
Brook Street . . . . W1 p. 26 **BL**
Brushfield Street . . . . E1 p. 16 **QT**
Bruton Street . . . . W1 p. 26 **CM**
Bryanston Square . . . . W1 p. 14 **KT**
Bryanston Street . . . . W1 p. 26 **AK**
Buckingham Gate . . . . SW1 p. 30 **CV** 56
Buckingham Palace Road . . . . SW1 p. 30 **AX**
Bunhill Row . . . . EC1 p. 16 **QS**
Burlington Arcade . . . . W1 p. 27 **DM**
Bury Street . . . . SW1 p. 27 **EN**
Bute Street . . . . SW7 p. 28 **CS** 59
Butterwick . . . . W6 p. 17 **GY** 60
Byward Street . . . . EC3 p. 16 **QU** 62
Cadogan Gardens . . . . SW3 p. 29 **FS**
Cadogan Place . . . . SW1 p. 29 **FR**
Cadogan Square . . . . SW1 p. 29 **FS**
Cadogan Street . . . . SW3 p. 29 **ET**
Caithness Road . . . . W14 p. 17 **GX** 63
Caledonian Road . . . . N1, N7 p. 15 **NR**
Cale Street . . . . SW3 p. 29 **DT**
Calshot Street . . . . N1 p. 15 **NS**
Calthorpe Street . . . . WC1 p. 15 **NS** 65
Camberwell New Road . . . . SE5 p. 20 **PZ**
Cambridge Avenue . . . . NW6 p. 13 **HR**
Cambridge Circus . . . . WC2 p. 27 **GK**
Cambridge Square . . . . W2 p. 31 **EY** 67
Camden High Street . . . . NW1 p. 15 **LR**
Camden Passage . . . . N1 p. 16 **PR** 70
Camden Road . . . . E11 p. 15 **LR**
Camden Street . . . . NW1 p. 15 **LR**
Camomile Street . . . . EC3 p. 16 **QT** 71
Campden Hill Road . . . . W8 p. 17 **HV**
Cannon Street . . . . EC4 p. 16 **PU**
Canonbury Square . . . . N1 p. 16 **PR**
Carey Street . . . . WC2 p. 31 **FV**
Carlisle Place . . . . SW1 p. 30 **BX**
Carlos Place . . . . W1 p. 26 **BM**
Carlton Gardens . . . . SW1 p. 27 **FP** 74
Carlton Hill . . . . NW8 p. 14 **JR**
Carlton House Terrace . . . . SW1 p. 27 **FN**
Carlton Vale . . . . NW6 p. 13 **HS**
Carnaby Street . . . . W1 p. 27 **EK**
Carriage Road (the) . . . . SW7, SW11 p. 29 **EQ**
Carriage Drive East . . . . SW11 p. 18 **KZ**

Continued p. 21

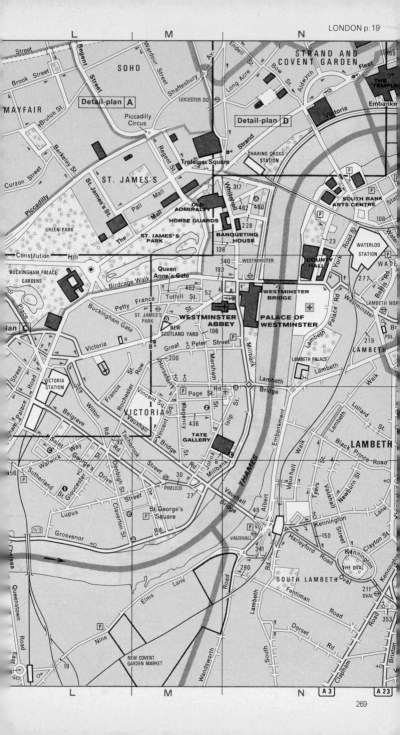

SOHO

MAYFAR

Brook Street

Bruton St.

Berkeley St.

Curzon Street

Piccadilly

Regent Street

Wardour Street

Shaftesbury

LEICESTER SQ.

Detail-plan A

Piccadilly
Circus

Long Acre

Endell St.

Bow St.

Aldwych

Fleet

STRAND AND
COVENT GARDEN

Victoria

THE
TEMPLE

Embankment

Detail-plan D

Strand

CHARING CROSS
STATION

ST. JAMES'S

St. James's St.

Pall Mall

The Mall

OLD
ADMIRALTY

HORSE GUARDS

BANQUETING
HOUSE

Whitehall

317

462 460

228

138

23

SOUTH BANK
ARTS CENTRE

108

P

Constitution Hill

BUCKINGHAM PALACE
GARDENS

lan C

Birdcage Walk

ST. JAMES'S
PARK

Queen
Anne's Gate

WESTMINSTER

340

193

COUNTY
HALL

WATERLOO
STATION

277

WATE

Buckingham Gate

Petty France

Tothill St.

402

52

NEW
SCOTLAND YARD

ST. JAMES'S PARK

B

WESTMINSTER
ABBEY

196

WESTMINSTER
BRIDGE

PALACE OF
WESTMINSTER

LAMBETH NORTH

Br

219

LAMBETH

Victoria

Francis St.

Rochester Row

VICTORIA
STATION

Vincent Sq.

Great   Peter   Street

200

Horseferry

Marsham

Millbank

LAMBETH PALACE

Lambeth

Lambeth
Bridge

Lambeth

Lambeth Walk

Lollard St.

Black Prince Road

LAMBETH

Belgrave

Wilton Road

Tachbrook

Vauxhall Bridge Rd.

VICTORIA

Page St.

Regency St.

Islip St.

436

TATE
GALLERY

John Islip St.

Millbank

Embankment

THAMES

Vauxhall
Walk

Tyers St.

Vauxhall St.

Newburn St.

Saint George's Dve.

Warwick Way

Denbigh St.

Claverton St.

Tachbrook Street

30

27

PIMLICO

St. George's
Square

Lupus Street

Grosvenor Road

149

Sutherland St.

P

56

Vauxhall
Bridge

49 Albert

Kennington

Harleyford   Road

150

Kennington Lane

Clayton St.

VAUXHALL

341

290

Elms   Lane

Road

SOUTH LAMBETH

Fentiman

Kennington
Oval

THE OVAL

211
OVAL

Dorset   Rd

353

Queenstown Road

Chelsea

Nine   Elms   Lane

NEW COVENT
GARDEN MARKET

Wandsworth   Road

Lambeth   Road

South

Clapham

Brixton Road

19

L   M   N   A 3   A 23

269

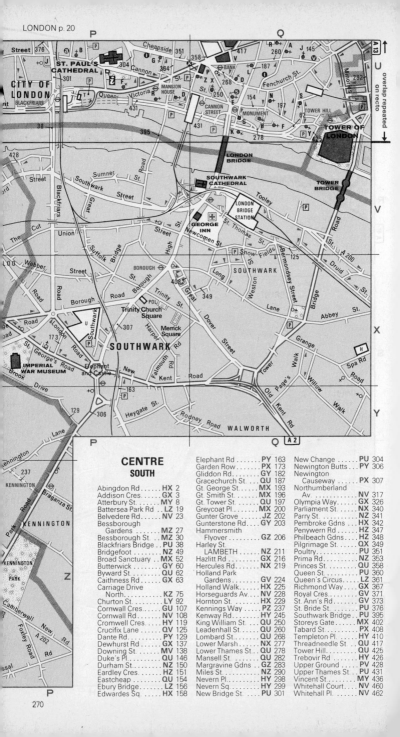

CENTRE
SOUTH

Abingdon Rd . . . . . . HX 2
Addison Cres. . . . . . GX 3
Atterbury St. . . . . . . MY 8
Battersea Park Rd . . LZ 19
Belvedere Rd. . . . . . NV 23
Bessborough
    Gardens . . . . MZ 27
Bessborough St. . . . MZ 30
Blackfriars Bridge . . PU 38
Bridgefoot . . . . NZ 49
Broad Sanctuary . . . MX 52
Butterwick . . . . GY 60
Byward St. . . . . QU 62
Caithness Rd. . . . . . GX 63
Carriage Drive
    North. . . . . KZ 75
Churton St. . . . . . . LY 92
Cornwall Cres. . . . . GU 107
Cornwall Rd. . . . . . NV 108
Cromwell Cres. . . . . HY 119
Crucifix Lane . . . . . QV 125
Dante Rd. . . . . PY 129
Dewhurst Rd . . . . . . GX 137
Downing St. . . . . . . MV 138
Duke's Pl. . . . . QU 146
Durham St. . . . . . . NZ 150
Eardley Cres. . . . . . HZ 151
Eastcheap . . . . QU 154
Ebury Bridge . . . . . LZ 156
Edwardes Sq. . . . . . HX 158

Elephant Rd . . . . PY 163
Garden Row . . . . . . PX 173
Gliddon Rd. . . . . . . GY 182
Gracechurch St. . . . . QU 187
Gt. George St. . . . . . MX 193
Gt. Smith St. . . . . . . MX 196
Gt. Tower St. . . . . . . QU 197
Greycoat Pl. . . . . . . MX 200
Gunter Grove . . . . . JZ 202
Gunterstone Rd. . . . . GY 203
Hammersmith
    Flyover . . . . GZ 206
Harley St.
    LAMBETH . . . . . NZ 211
Hazlitt Rd . . . . GX 216
Hercules Rd. . . . . . . NX 219
Holland Park
    Gardens . . . . GV 224
Holland Walk. . . . . . HX 225
Horseguards Av . . . . NV 228
Hornton St. . . . . HX 229
Kennings Way . . . . . PZ 237
Kenway Rd. . . . . . . HY 245
King William St. . . . . QU 250
Leadenhall St. . . . . . QU 260
Lombard St. . . . . . . QU 268
Lower Marsh . . . . . . NX 277
Lower Thames St. . . . QU 278
Mansell St. . . . . QU 282
Margravine Gdns . . . GZ 283
Miles St. . . . . NZ 290
Nevern Pl. . . . . HY 298
Nevern Sq. . . . . HY 299
New Bridge St. . . . . . PU 301

New Change . . . . . . PU 304
Newington Butts. . . . PY 306
Newington
    Causeway . . . . . . PX 307
Northumberland
    Av. . . . . NV 317
Olympia Way. . . . . . GX 326
Parliament St. . . . . . NX 340
Parry St. . . . . NZ 341
Pembroke Gdns . . . . HX 342
Penywern Rd . . . . . . HZ 347
Philbeach Gdns . . . . HZ 348
Pilgrimage St. . . . . . QX 349
Poultry. . . . . PU 351
Prima Rd. . . . . NZ 353
Princes St. . . . . QU 358
Queen St. . . . . PU 360
Queen's Circus. . . . . LZ 361
Richmond Way . . . . . GX 367
Royal Cres. . . . . GV 371
St. Ann's Rd. . . . . . . GV 373
St. Bride St. . . . . . . PU 376
Southwark Bridge . . . PU 395
Storeys Gate. . . . . . MX 402
Tabard St. . . . . PX 408
Templeton Pl . . . . . . HY 410
Threadneedle St. . . . QU 417
Tower Hill. . . . . QU 425
Trebovir Rd . . . . HY 426
Upper Ground . . . . . PV 428
Upper Thames St. . . . QU 431
Vincent St. . . . . MY 436
Whitehall Court. . . . . NV 460
Whitehall Pl. . . . . . . NV 462

Street	Map	Page	Grid	No.
Carriage Drive North	SW11	p. 18	KZ	75
Castle Lane	SW1	p. 30	CV	
Cavendish Square	W1	p. 26	CJ	
Central Street	EC1	p. 16	PS	
Chalk Farm Road	NW1	p. 14	KR	
Chamberlayne Road	NW10	p. 13	GS	
Chancery Lane	WC2	p. 31	FV	78
Chandos Place	WC2	p. 31	DX	
Chandos Street	W1	p. 26	CH	
Chapel Market	N1	p. 15	NS	
Chapel Street	SW1	p. 30	AV	
Charlbert Street	NW8	p. 14	KS	79
Charles II Street	SW1	p. 27	FN	
Charles Street	W1	p. 26	CN	
Charing Cross	SW1	p. 31	DX	
Charing Cross Road	WC2	p. 27	GJ	
Charterhouse Square	EC1	p. 16	PT	81
Charterhouse Street	EC1	p. 16	PT	83
Cheapside	EC2	p. 16	PU	
Chelsea Bridge	SW1, SW8	p. 19	LZ	
Chelsea Bridge Road	SW1	p. 18	KZ	
Chelsea Embankment	SW3	p. 18	KZ	
Chelsea Manor Street	SW3	p. 29	EU	
Chelsea Square	SW3	p. 29	DU	
Cheltenham Terrace	SW3	p. 29	FT	
Chepstow Crescent	W11	p. 30	AZ	84
Chepstow Place	W2	p. 30	AY	
Chepstow Road	W2	p. 30	AY	
Chesham Place	SW2	p. 29	FR	
Chesham Street	SW1	p. 29	FS	
Chester Road	NW1	p. 14	KS	
Chester Row	SW1	p. 30	AX	
Chester Square	SW1	p. 30	AX	88
Chester Street	SW1	p. 30	AV	
Chesterton Road	W10	p. 13	GT	
Cheval Place	SW7	p. 29	ER	
Cheyne Walk	SW3, SW10	p. 18	JZ	
Chilworth Street	W2	p. 30	CY	90
Chippenham Road	W9	p. 13	HS	
Chiswell Street	EC1	p. 16	PT	
Church Row	NW3	p. 13	GR	
Church Street	NW8, NW1	p. 14	JT	
Churton Street	SW1	p. 19	LY	92
Circus Road	NW8	p. 14	JS	
City Road	EC1	p. 16	PS	
Clapham Road	SW9	p. 19	NZ	
Clarendon Place	W2	p. 31	EY	93
Clarendon Road	W11	p. 13	GU	
Claverton Street	SW1	p. 19	LZ	
Clayton Street	SE11	p. 19	NZ	
Clerkenwell Road	EC1	p. 16	PT	
Cleveland Gardens	W2	p. 30	CY	94
Cleveland Square	W2	p. 30	CY	
Cleveland Street	W1	p. 15	LT	
Cleveland Terrace	W2	p. 30	CY	
Clifford Street	W1	p. 27	DM	
Cliveden Place	SW1	p. 29	FS	
Cockspur Street	SW1	p. 27	GN	
Colet Gardens	W14	p. 17	GY	
Collingham Gardens	SW5	p. 28	AT	99
Collingham Road	SW5	p. 28	AT	101
Commercial Street	E1	p. 16	QT	
Conduit Street	W1	p. 27	DL	
Connaught Square	W2	p. 31	FY	103
Connaught Street	W2	p. 31	EY	
Constantine Road	NW3	p. 13	GR	106
Constitution Hill	SW1	p. 15	NR	
Copenhagen Street	N1	p. 15	NR	
Cork Street	W1	p. 27	DM	
Cornwall Crescent	W11	p. 13	GU	107
Cornwall Gardens	SW7	p. 28	AR	
Cornwall Road	SE1	p. 19	NV	108
Corporation Row	EC1	p. 16	PS	110
Courtfield Gardens	SW5	p. 28	AT	
Courtfield Road	SW7	p. 28	BS	
Coventry Street	W1	p. 27	FM	
Cowcross Street	EC1	p. 16	PT	113
Crabtree Lane	SW6	p. 17	GZ	
Cranbourn Street	WC2	p. 31	DV	115
Cranley Gardens	SW7	p. 28	CT	
Craven Hill	W2	p. 30	CZ	
Craven Road	W2	p. 31	DY	
Craven Street	WC2	p. 31	DX	
Craven Terrace	W2	p. 31	DZ	
Crawford Place	W1	p. 14	KT	116
Crawford Street	W1	p. 14	KT	
Cromwell Crescent	SW5	p. 17	HY	119
Cromwell Place	SW7	p. 28	CS	120
Cromwell Road	SW7, SW5	p. 28	CS	
Crowndale Road	NW1	p. 15	LR	
Crucifix Lane	SE1	p. 20	QV	125
Culross Street	W1	p. 26	AM	
Curtain Road	EC2	p. 16	QS	126
Curzon Street	W1	p. 26	BN	
Cut (The)	SE1	p. 20	PV	
Dante Road	SE11	p. 20	PY	129
D'Arblay Street	W1	p. 27	EK	
Davies Street	W1	p. 26	BK	
Dawes Road	SW6	p. 17	GZ	
Dawson Place	W2	p. 30	AZ	
Deanery Street	W1	p. 26	BN	132
Dean Street	W1	p. 27	FJ	
Delancey Street	NW1	p. 15	LR	
Delaware Road	W9	p. 13	HS	
Denbigh Street	SW1	p. 19	LZ	
Denman Street	W1	p. 27	FM	133
Denmark Street	WC2	p. 27	GJ	134
De Vere Gardens	W8	p. 28	BQ	
Devonshire Street	W1	p. 14	KT	
Devonshire Terrace	W2	p. 30	CY	136
Dewhurst Road	W14	p. 17	GX	137
Dorset Road	SW8	p. 19	NZ	
Dorset Street	W1	p. 26	AH	
Dovehouse Street	SW3	p. 29	DU	
Dover Street	W1	p. 27	DM	
Downing Street	SW1	p. 19	MV	138
Downshire Hill	NW3	p. 13	GR	139
Draycott Avenue	SW3	p. 29	ET	
Draycott Place	SW3	p. 29	ET	
Drayton Gardens	SW10	p. 28	BT	
Druid Street	SE1	p. 20	QX	
Drury Lane	WC2	p. 31	EV	
Dufferin Street	EC1	p. 16	PS	141
Duke of Wellington Place	SW1	p. 30	AV	142
Duke of York Street	SW1	p. 27	EN	143
Duke's Place	EC3	p. 16	QU	145
Duke Street	W1	p. 26	BK	
Duke Street ST. JAMES	SW1	p. 27	EN	146
Duncannon Street	WC2	p. 31	DX	147
Dunraven Street	W1	p. 26	AL	149
Durham Street	SE11	p. 19	NZ	150
Eardley Crescent	SW5	p. 17	HZ	151
Earlham Street	WC2	p. 31	DV	153
Earl's Court Road	W8, SW5	p. 17	HX	
Eastbourne Terrace	W2	p. 31	DY	
Eastcastle Street	W1	p. 27	EJ	
Eastcheap	EC3	p. 16	QU	154
East Heath Road	NW3	p. 13	GR	
East Road	N1	p. 16	QS	
Eaton Place	SW1	p. 30	AV	
Eaton Square	SW1	p. 30	AV	
Ebury Bridge	SW1	p. 19	LZ	156
Ebury Street	SW1	p. 30	AX	
Ebury Bridge Road	SW1	p. 18	KZ	
Eccleston Bridge	SW1	p. 30	BX	157
Eccleston Square	SW1	p. 30	BX	
Eccleston Street	SW1	p. 30	AX	
Edgware Road	W2	p. 14	JT	
Edith Grove	SW10	p. 18	JZ	
Edith Road	W14	p. 17	GY	
Edwardes Square	W8	p. 17	HX	158
Egerton Gardens	SW3	p. 29	DS	160
Egerton Terrace	SW3	p. 29	DR	161
Egerton Gardens Mews	SW3	p. 29	ER	162
Elephant and Castle	SE11	p. 20	PX	
Elephant Road	SE17	p. 20	PY	163
Elgin Avenue	W9	p. 13	HS	
Elizabeth Street	SW1	p. 30	AX	
Elm Park Gardens	SW10	p. 28	CU	
Elm Park Road	SW3	p. 28	CU	
Elsworthy Road	NW3	p. 14	JR	
Elvaston Place	SW7	p. 28	BR	
Elystan Place	SW3	p. 29	ET	
Elystan Street	SW3	p. 29	DT	
Endell Street	WC2	p. 31	DV	
England's Lane	NW3	p. 14	KR	
Ennismore Gardens	SW7	p. 29	DQ	
Essex Street	WC2	p. 31	FV	
Estcourt Road	SW6	p. 17	GZ	
Eton Avenue	NW3	p. 14	JR	
Euston Road	NW1	p. 15	MS	
Evelyn Gardens	SW7	p. 28	CU	
Eversholt Street	NW1	p. 15	LS	
Exeter Street	WC2	p. 31	EV	
Exhibition Road	SW7	p. 28	CQ	
Fairfax Road	NW6	p. 14	JR	
Fairhazel Gardens	NW6	p. 14	JR	
Falmouth Road	SE1	p. 20	PX	
Farm Street MAYFAIR	W1	p. 26	BM	
Fann Street	W1	p. 16	PT	166
Farringdon Road	EC1	p. 15	NS	

Continued on next page

Farringdon Street	EC4 p. 16	PT	168
Fenchurch Street	EC3 p. 16	QU	
Fentiman Road	SW8 p. 19	NZ	
Ferdinand Street	NW1 p. 14	KR	
Fernhead Road	W9 p. 13	GS	
Fetter Lane	EC4 p. 15	NT	169
Fifth Avenue	W10 p. 13	GS	
Filmer Road	SW6 p. 17	GZ	
Finborough Road	SW10 p. 28	AU	
Finchley Road	NW8, NW3		
	NW2, NW11 p. 14	JR	
Fitzjohn's Avenue	NW3 p. 14	JR	
Fitzroy Square	W1 p. 15	LT	
Fleet Road	NW3 p. 13	GR	
Fleet Street	EC4 p. 15	NU	
Flood Street	SW3 p. 29	EU	
Floral Street	WC2 p. 31	DV	
Foulis Terrace	SW7 p. 28	CT	170
Foxley Road	SW9 p. 20	PZ	
Frampton Street	NW8 p. 14	JS	
Francis Street	SW1 p. 30	CX	
Franklin's Row	SW3 p. 29	FU	
Frith Street	W1 p. 27	FK	
Frognal	NW3 p. 13	GR	
Frognal Rise	NW3 p. 13	GR	171
Fulham Palace Road	W6, SW6 p. 17	GZ	
Fulham Road	SW3, SW10, SW6 p. 18	JZ	
Garden Row	SE1 p. 20	PX	173
Garrick Street	WC2 p. 31	DV	
Garway Road	W2 p. 30	BY	
Gascony Avenue	NW6 p. 13	HR	
Gayton Road	NW3 p. 13	GR	
George Street	W1 p. 26	AJ	
Gerrard Street	W1 p. 27	GL	174
Gilbert Street	W1 p. 26	BL	175
Gillingham Street	SW1 p. 30	BX	
Gilston Road	SW10 p. 28	BU	
Giltspur Street	EC1 p. 16	PT	178
Glasshouse Street	W1 p. 27	EM	179
Glendower Place	SW7 p. 28	CS	180
Gliddon Road	W14 p. 17	GY	182
Gloucester Avenue	NW1 p. 14	KR	
Gloucester Place	W1, NW1 p. 14	KS	
Gloucester Road	SW7 p. 28	BR	
Gloucester Square	W2 p. 31	EY	183
Gloucester Street	SW1 p. 19	LZ	
Gloucester Terrace	W2 p. 30	CY	
Golborne Road	W10 p. 13	GT	
Golden Square	W1 p. 27	EL	
Goodge Street	W1 p. 15	LT	184
Goswell Road	EC1 p. 16	PS	
Gower Street	WC1 p. 15	NT	
Gracechurch Street	EC3 p. 16	QU	187
Grafton Street	W1 p. 27	DM	
Grange Road	SE1 p. 20	QX	
Granville Place	W1 p. 26	AK	188
Gray's Inn Road	WC1 p. 15	NS	
Gt. Castle Street	W1 p. 27	DJ	189
Gt. Cumberland Place	W1 p. 31	FY	191
Gt. Dover Street	SE1 p. 20	QX	
Gt. Eastern Street	EC2 p. 16	QS	192
Gt. George Street	SW1 p. 19	MX	193
Gt. Marlborough Street	W1 p. 27	EK	
Gt. Peter Street	SW1 p. 19	MX	
Gt. Queen Street	WC2 p. 31	EV	
Gt. Russell Street	WC1 p. 15	NT	
Gt. Smith Street	SW1 p. 19	MX	196
Gt. Suffolk Street	SE1 p. 20	PV	
Gt. Tower Street	EC3 p. 16	QU	197
Gt. Western Road	W9, W11 p. 13	HT	
Gt. Windmill Street	W1 p. 27	FM	
Greek Street	W1 p. 27	GK	198
Greencroft Gardens	NW6 p. 14	JR	
Green Street	W1 p. 26	AL	
Grenville Place	SW7 p. 28	BS	
Gresham Street	EC2 p. 16	PT	
Greville Place	NW6 p. 13	HR	
Greycoat Place	SW1 p. 19	MX	200
Greyhound Road	W6, W14 p. 17	GZ	
Grosvenor Crescent	SW1 p. 30	AV	
Grosvenor Gardens	SW1 p. 30	BV	
Grosvenor Place	SW1 p. 30	AV	
Grosvenor Road	SW1 p. 19	LZ	
Grosvenor Square	W1 p. 26	BL	
Grosvenor Street	W1 p. 26	BL	
Grove End Road	NW8 p. 14	JS	
Guildhouse Street	SW1 p. 30	BX	201
Guilford Street	WC1 p. 15	NT	
Gunter Grove	SW10 p. 18	JZ	202
Gunterstone Road	W14 p. 17	GY	203
Hackney Road	E2 p. 16	QS	
Half Moon Street	W1 p. 26	CN	
Halford Road	SW6 p. 17	HZ	
Halkin Street	SW1 p. 31	AV	
Hall Road	NW8 p. 14	JS	
Hamilton Place	W1 p. 26	BP	205
Hamilton Terrace	NW8 p. 14	JS	
Hammersmith Flyover	W6 p. 17	GZ	206
Hammersmith Road	W14, W6 p. 17	GY	
Hampstead Grove	NW3 p. 13	GR	207
Hampstead High Street	NW3 p. 13	GR	209
Hampstead Road	NW1 p. 15	LS	
Hanover Square	W1 p. 26	CK	210
Hanover Street	W1 p. 27	DK	
Hans Crescent	SW1 p. 29	ER	
Hans Place	SW1 p. 29	ER	
Hans Road	SW3 p. 29	ER	
Harcourt Terrace	SW10 p. 28	AU	
Harley Street	SE11		
LAMBETH	p. 19	NZ	211
Harley Street	W1		
WESTMINSTER	p. 26	CH	
Harleyford Road	SE11 p. 19	NZ	
Harper Road	SE1 p. 20	PX	
Harriet Street	SW1 p. 29	FQ	214
Harrington Gardens	SW7 p. 28	BT	
Harrington Road	SW7 p. 28	CS	215
Harrow Road	W2, W9		
	W10, NW10 p. 13	JT	
Harvist Road	NW6 p. 13	GS	
Harwood Road	SW6 p. 17	HZ	
Hasker Street	SW3 p. 29	ES	
Haverstock Hill	NW3 p. 14	KR	
Haymarket	SW1 p. 27	FM	
Hay's Mews	W1 p. 26	BN	
Hazlitt Road	W14 p. 17	GX	216
Heath Street	NW3 p. 13	GR	
Hemingford Road	N1 p. 15	NR	
Henrietta Place	W1 p. 26	BJ	
Henrietta Street	WC2 p. 31	DV	217
Herbrand Street	WC1 p. 15	MS	218
Hercules Road	SE1 p. 19	NX	219
Hereford Road	W2 p. 30	AY	
Hertford Street	W1 p. 26	BP	220
Heygate Street	SE17 p. 20	PY	
High Holborn	WC1 p. 15	NT	
Hill Street	W1 p. 26	BN	
Hobart Place	SW1 p. 30	AV	
Holbein Place	SW1 p. 29	FT	
Holbein Mews	SW1 p. 29	FT	223
Holborn	EC1 p. 15	NT	
Holborn Viaduct	EC1 p. 16	PT	
Holland Park	W11 p. 17	GV	
Holland Park Avenue	W11 p. 17	GV	
Holland Park Gardens	W11 p. 17	GV	224
Holland Road	W14 p. 17	GX	
Holland Street	W8 p. 17	HX	
Holland Walk	W8 p. 17	HX	225
Holland Villas Road	W14 p. 17	GX	
Holles Street	W1 p. 26	CJ	
Holloway Road	N7, N19 p. 16	PR	
Hollybush Hill	E11 p. 13	GR	227
Hollywood Road	SW10 p. 28	BU	
Horseferry Road	SW1 p. 19	MX	
Horsequards Avenue	SW1 p. 19	NV	228
Hornton Street	W8 p. 17	HX	229
Houndsditch	EC3 p. 16	QT	
Howick Place	SW1 p. 30	CV	
Howland Street	W1 p. 15	LT	232
Hoxton Street	N1 p. 16	QS	
Hugh Street	SW1 p. 30	BX	
Hunter Street	WC1 p. 15	NS	233
Hyde Park Gardens	W2 p. 31	EZ	
Hyde Park Square	W2 p. 31	EY	234
Hyde Park Street	W2 p. 31	EY	
Ifield Road	SW10 p. 28	AU	
Inverness Terrace	W2 p. 30	BY	
Iverson Road	NW6 p. 13	HR	
Ixworth Place	SW3 p. 29	DT	
James Street	W1 p. 26	BJ	
James Street	WC2		
SOHO	p. 27	EL	
Jermyn Street	SW1 p. 27	EN	
John Adam Street	WC2 p. 31	DX	
John Islip Street	SW1 p. 19	NY	
Jubilee Place	SW3 p. 29	ET	
Judd Street	WC1 p. 15	MS	
Keat's Grove	NW3 p. 13	GR	235
Kemble Street	WC2 p. 31	EV	
Kendal Street	W2 p. 31	EY	
Kennings Way	SE11 p. 20	PZ	237
Kennington Lane	SE11 p. 19	NZ	
Kennington Oval	SE11 p. 19	NZ	
Kennington Park Road	SE11 p. 20	PZ	
Kennington Road	SE1, SE11 p. 19	NZ	
Kensal Road	W10 p. 13	GS	

Kensington Church Street	W8 p. 30	**AZ**	238	
Kensington Court	W8 p. 28	**AQ**	241	
Kensington Court Place	W8 p. 28	**AR**	242	
Kensington Gardens Square	W2 p. 30	**BY**	243	
Kensington Gore	SW7 p. 28	**CQ**		
Kensington High Street	W8, W14 p. 17	**HX**		
Kensington Palace Gardens	W8 p. 17	**HV**		
Kensington Park Road	W11 p. 13	**GU**		
Kensington Place	W8 p. 30	**AZ**		
Kensington Road	W8, SW7 p. 28	**BQ**		
Kensington Square	W8 p. 28	**AQ**		
Kentish Town Road	NW1, NW5 p. 15	**LR**		
Kenway Road	SW5 p. 17	**HY**	245	
Kilburn Lane	W10, W9 p. 13	**GS**		
Kilburn Priory	NW6 p. 13	**HR**	246	
Kilburn High Road	NW6 p. 13	**HR**		
Kilburn Park Road	NW6 p. 13	**HS**		
King Edward Street	EC1 p. 16	**PT**	247	
Kingly Street	W1 p. 27	**DK**		
King's Cross Road	WC1 p. 15	**NS**		
Kingsland Road	E2, E8 p. 16	**QS**		
King's Road	SW3, SW10, SW6 p. 29	**DU**		
King Street	SW1			
ST. JAMES'S	p. 27	**EN**		
King Street	WC2			
STRAND	p. 31	**DV**		
Kingsway	WC2 p. 31	**EV**		
King William Street	EC4 p. 16	**QU**	250	
Knaresborough Place	SW5 p. 28	**AS**		
Knightsbridge	SW1, SW7 p. 29	**EQ**		
Ladbroke Grove	W10, W11 p. 13	**GT**		
Lambeth Bridge	SW1, SE1 p. 19	**NX**		
Lambeth Palace Road	SE1 p. 19	**NX**		
Lambeth Road	SE1 p. 19	**NX**		
Lambeth Walk	SE11 p. 19	**NY**		
Lancaster Gate	W2 p. 30	**CZ**	256	
Lancaster Grove	NW3 p. 14	**JR**		
Lancaster Place	SW19 p. 31	**EV**		
Lancaster Terrace	W2 p. 31	**DZ**	258	
Lansdowne Walk	W11 p. 17	**GV**		
Lauderdale Road	W9 p. 13	**HS**		
Launceston Place	W8 p. 28	**BR**	259	
Lawn Road	NW3 p. 13	**GR**		
Leadenhall Street	EC3 p. 16	**QU**	260	
Lees Place	W1 p. 26	**AL**		
Leicester Square	WC2 p. 27	**GM**	261	
Leinster Gardens	W2 p. 30	**CY**		
Leinster Square	W2 p. 30	**AY**		
Leinster Terrace	W2 p. 30	**CZ**		
Lennox Gardens	NW10 p. 29	**ES**		
Lennox Gardens Mews	SW3 p. 29	**ES**	263	
Lever Street	EC1 p. 16	**PS**		
Lexham Gardens	W8 p. 28	**AS**		
Lexington Street	W1 p. 27	**EL**		
Lillie Road	SW6 p. 17	**GZ**		
Lincoln's Inn Fields	WC2 p. 31	**EV**		
Lisle Street	WC2 p. 27	**GL**		
Lisson Grove	NW1, NW8 p. 14	**JS**		
Little Boltons (The)	SW10 p. 28	**BU**		
Little Britain	EC1 p. 16	**PT**	264	
Liverpool Road	N1, N7 p. 16	**PR**		
Liverpool Street	EC2 p. 16	**QT**		
Lloyd Baker Street	WC1 p. 15	**NS**	265	
Lollard Street	SE11 p. 19	**NY**		
Lombard Street	EC3 p. 16	**QU**	268	
London Bridge	SE1, EC4 p. 20	**QV**		
London Road	SE1 p. 20	**PX**		
London Street	W2 p. 31	**DY**		
London Wall	EC2 p. 16	**PT**		
Long Acre	WC2 p. 31	**DV**		
Long Lane	EC1			
CITY	p. 16	**PT**	270	
Long Lane	SE1			
SOUTHWARK	p. 20	**QX**		
Lothbury	EC2 p. 16	**QT**	273	
Lots Road	SW10 p. 18	**JZ**		
Loudoun Road	NW8 p. 14	**AV**		
Lower Belgrave Street	SW1 p. 30	**AV**		
Lower Grosvenor Place	SW1 p. 30	**BV**	274	
Lower Marsh	SE1 p. 19	**NX**	277	
Lower Sloane Street	SW1 p. 29	**FT**		
Lower Terrace	NW3 p. 13	**GR**		
Lower Thames Street	EC3 p. 16	**QU**	278	
Lowndes Square	SW1 p. 29	**FQ**		
Lowndes Street	SW1 p. 29	**FR**	279	
Luke Street	EC2 p. 16	**QS**		
Lupus Street	SW1 p. 19	**LZ**		
Lyall Street	SW1 p. 29	**FR**		
Lyndhurst Road	NW3 p. 13	**GR**		
Macklin Street	WC2 p. 31	**DV**		
Maddox Street	W1 p. 27	**DK**		
Maida Avenue	W2 p. 14	**JT**		
Maida Vale	W9 p. 14	**JS**		

Maiden Lane	WC2 p. 31	**DX**		
Malden Road	E15 p. 14	**KR**		
Mall (The)	SW1 p. 27	**FP**		
Malvern Road	NW6 p. 13	**HS**		
Manchester Square	W1 p. 26	**AJ**	281	
Manchester Street	W1 p. 26	**AH**		
Manresa Road	SW3 p. 29	**DU**		
Mansell Street	E1 p. 16	**QU**	282	
Marble Arch	W1 p. 31	**FY**		
Margaret Street	W1 p. 27	**DJ**		
Margravine Gardens	W6 p. 17	**GZ**	283	
Margravine Road	W6 p. 17	**GZ**		
Market Place	W1 p. 27	**DJ**	286	
Market Road	N7 p. 15	**NR**		
Markham Street	SW3 p. 29	**ET**		
Marlborough Place	NW8 p. 14	**JS**		
Marloes Road	W8 p. 17	**HX**		
Marshall Street	W1 p. 27	**EK**		
Marsham Street	SW1 p. 30	**MX**		
Marylebone High Street	W1 p. 14	**KT**		
Marylebone Lane	W1 p. 26	**BJ**	287	
Marylebone Road	NW1 p. 14	**KT**		
Masbro Road	W14 p. 17	**GX**		
Melbury Road	W14 p. 17	**GX**		
Merrick Square	SE1 p. 20	**PX**		
Merton Rise	NW3 p. 14	**KR**		
Middlesex Street	E1 p. 16	**QT**		
Midland Road	NW1 p. 15	**MS**		
Miles Street	SW8 p. 19	**NZ**	290	
Millbank	SW1 p. 19	**NX**		
Milner Street	SW3 p. 29	**ES**		
Minford Gardens	W14 p. 17	**GX**		
Minories	EC3 p. 16	**QU**		
Monmouth Street	WC2 p. 31	**DV**		
Montagu Square	W1 p. 26	**AH**		
Montpelier Square	SW7 p. 29	**EQ**		
Montpelier Street	SW7 p. 29	**ER**		
Montpelier Walk	SW7 p. 29	**DR**		
Moore Street	SW3 p. 29	**ES**		
Moorgate	EC2 p. 16	**QT**		
Moreland Street	EC1 p. 16	**PS**	293	
Mortimer Road	NW10 p. 13	**GS**		
Mortimer Street	W1 p. 15	**LT**		
Moscow Road	W2 p. 30	**BZ**		
Mossop Street	SW3 p. 29	**ES**		
Mount Row	W1 p. 26	**BM**		
Mount Street	W1 p. 26	**BM**		
Munster Road	SW6 p. 17	**GZ**		
Musard Road	W6 p. 17	**GZ**		
Museum Street	WC1 p. 31	**DV**	294	
Myddelton Street	EC1 p. 16	**PS**	296	
Nassington Road	NW3 p. 13	**GR**	297	
Neal Street	WC2 p. 31	**DV**		
Netherhall Gardens	NW3 p. 13	**GR**		
Nevern Place	SW5 p. 17	**HY**	298	
Nevern Square	SW5 p. 17	**HY**	299	
Neville Terrace	SW7 p. 28	**CT**	300	
New Bond Street	W1 p. 26	**CK**		
New Bridge Street	EC4 p. 16	**PU**	301	
Newburn Street	SE11 p. 19	**NZ**		
New Cavendish Street	W1 p. 26	**BH**		
New Change	EC4 p. 16	**PU**	304	
Newcomen Street	SE1 p. 20	**QV**		
New End Square	NW3 p. 13	**GR**	305	
Newgate Street	EC1 p. 16	**PT**		
Newington Butts	SE1, SE11 p. 20	**PY**	306	
Newington Causeway	SE1 p. 20	**PX**		
New Kent Road	SE1 p. 20	**PX**	307	
Newman Street	W1 p. 15	**LT**		
New Oxford Street	WC1 p. 31	**DV**	308	
New Row	WC2 p. 31	**DV**		
New Square	WC2 p. 31	**FV**		
Newton Road	W2 p. 30	**BY**		
Newton Street	WC2 p. 31	**EV**	309	
Nine Elms Lane	SW8 p. 19	**MZ**		
Noel Street	W1 p. 27	**EJ**		
Norfolk Crescent	W2 p. 31	**EY**	310	
Norfolk Square	W2 p. 31	**DY**	313	
North Audley Street	W1 p. 26	**AK**	314	
North Carriage Drive	W2 p. 31	**EZ**		
North End Road	W14, SW6 p. 17	**GY**		
North Row	W1 p. 26	**AL**		
Northumberland Avenue	WC2 p. 31	**NV**	317	
Notting Hill Gate	W11 p. 30	**AZ**		
Nutley Terrace	NW3 p. 13	**GR**		
Oakley Street	SW3 p. 29	**DU**		
Offord Road	N1 p. 15	**NR**		
Old Bailey	EC4 p. 16	**PT**	318	
Old Bond Street	W1 p. 27	**DM**		
Old Broad Street	EC2 p. 16	**QT**	319	
Old Brompton Road	SW7, SW5 p. 28	**BT**		

Continued on next page

Old Burlington Street	W1 p. 27	DM	322	
Old Church Street	SW3 p. 28	CU		
Old Compton Street	W1 p. 27	GK	323	
Old Kent Road	SE1, SE15 p. 20	QY		
Old Marylebone Road	NW1 p. 14	KT	324	
Old Park Lane	W1 p. 26	BP		
Old Street	EC1 p. 16	PS		
Olympia Way	W14 p. 17	GX	326	
Onslow Gardens	SW7 p. 28	CT		
Onslow Square	SW7 p. 28	CT		
Orange Street	WC2 p. 27	GM		
Orchard Street	W1 p. 26	AK		
Ordnance Hill	NW8 p. 14	JR		
Orme Court	W2 p. 30	BZ	328	
Ormonde Gate	SW3 p. 29	FU	329	
Ornan Road	NW3 p. 13	GR	331	
Ossulton Street	NW1 p. 15	MS		
Outer Circle	NW1 p. 14	KS		
Oxford Circus	W1 p. 27	DJ		
Oxford Gardens	W10 p. 13	GT		
Oxford Square	W2 p. 31	EY	332	
Oxford Street	W1 p. 26	BK		
Paddington Street	W1 p. 14	KT	333	
Page Street	SW1 p. 19	MY		
Page's Walk	SE1 p. 20	QX		
Palace Court	W2 p. 30	BZ		
Palace Gardens Terrace	W8 p. 30	AZ	335	
Palace Gate	W8 p. 28	BQ		
Palace Street	SW1 p. 30	BV		
Pall Mall	SW1 p. 27	FN		
Palmer Street	SW1 p. 30	CV		
Pancras Road	NW1 p. 15	MR		
Panton Street	SW1 p. 27	FM	336	
Parade (The)	SW11 p. 18	KZ		
Park Crescent	W1 p. 15	LT	337	
Parker Street	WC2 p. 31	EV		
Parkgate Road	SW11 p. 18	KZ		
Park Lane	W1 p. 26	AM		
Park Road	NW1, NW8 p. 14	KS		
Park Street	W1 p. 26	AL		
Park Village East	NW1 p. 15	LS		
Park Walk	SW10 p. 28	CU		
Parkway	NW1 p. 15	LR		
Parliament Hill	NW3 p. 13	GR		
Parliament Street	SW1 p. 19	NX	340	
Parry Street	SW8 p. 19	NZ	341	
Paul Street	EC2 p. 16	QS		
Pelham Street	SW7 p. 29	DS		
Pembridge Gardens	W2 p. 30	AZ		
Pembridge Road	W11 p. 30	AZ		
Pembridge Square	W2 p. 30	AZ		
Pembridge Villas	W11 p. 30	AY		
Pembrocke Gardens	W8 p. 17	HX	342	
Pembrocke Road	W8 p. 17	HY		
Penton Rise	WC1 p. 15	NS	345	
Penton Street	N1 p. 15	NS	346	
Pentonville Road	N1 p. 15	NS		
Penywern Road	SW5 p. 17	HZ	347	
Percival Street	EC1 p. 16	PS		
Petty France	SW1 p. 30	CV		
Philbeach Gardens	SW5 p. 17	HZ	348	
Piccadilly	W1 p. 27	EM		
Piccadilly Circus	W1 p. 27	FM		
Pilgrimage Street	SE1 p. 20	QX	349	
Pimlico Road	SW1 p. 18	KZ		
Pitfield Street	N1 p. 16	QS		
Poland Street	W1 p. 27	EJ		
Pond Street	NW3 p. 13	GR		
Pont Street	SW1 p. 29	ER		
Porchester Gardens	W2 p. 30	BY		
Porchester Road	W2 p. 13	HT	350	
Porchester Terrace	W2 p. 30	CZ		
Portland Place	W1 p. 15	LT		
Portman Square	W1 p. 26	AJ		
Portman Street	W1 p. 26	AK		
Portobello Road	W11, W10 p. 13	GU		
Portugal Street	WC2 p. 31	EV		
Poultry	EC2 p. 16	PU	351	
Praed Street	W2 p. 14	JU		
Pratt Street	NW1 p. 15	LR		
Prima Road	SW9 p. 19	NZ	353	
Primrose Hill Road	NW3 p. 14	KR		
Prince Albert Road	NW1, NW8 p. 14	KR		
Prince Consort Road	SW7 p. 28	CR		
Prince of Wales Road	NW5 p. 14	KR		
Prince's Gardens	SW7 p. 28	CR	357	
Prince's Street	W1 p. 27	DK		
Princes Street	EC2 p. 16	QU	358	
Princess Road	NW1 p. 14	KR	359	
Priory Road	NW6 p. 13	HR		
Queen Anne's Gate	SW1 p. 19	MX		
Queen Anne Street	W1 p. 26	BH		
Queensberry Place	SW7 p. 28	CS	360	
Queensborough Terrace	W2 p. 30	CZ		
Queen's Circus	SW8 p. 19	LZ	361	
Queen's Gardens	W2 p. 30	CY	362	
Queen's Gate	SW7 p. 28	BQ		
Queen's Gate Gardens	SW7 p. 28	BR		
Queen's Gate Place	SW7 p. 28	BR	363	
Queen's Gate Terrace	SW7 p. 28	BR		
Queen's Grove	NW8 p. 14	JR		
Queenstown Road	SW8 p. 28	BR		
Queen Street	EC4 p. 16	PU	364	
Queen's Walk	SW1 p. 27	DN		
Queensway	W2 p. 30	BY		
Queen Victoria Street	EC4 p. 16	PU		
Quex Road	NW6 p. 13	HR		
Radnor Place	W2 p. 31	EY		
Radnor Walk	SW3 p. 29	EU		
Randolph Avenue	W9 p. 13	HS		
Randolph Street	NW1 p. 15	LR	365	
Rannoch Road	W6 p. 17	GZ		
Rawlings Street	SW3 p. 19	ES		
Redcliffe Gardens	SW10 p. 28	AU		
Redcliffe Square	SW10 p. 28	AU		
Redesdale Street	SW3 p. 29	EU	366	
Red Lion Street	WC1 p. 15	NT		
Reeves Mews	W1 p. 26	AM		
Regency Street	SW1 p. 19	MY		
Regent's Park Road	NW1 p. 14	KR		
Regent Street	SW1, W1 p. 27	EM		
Richmond Avenue	N1 p. 15	NR		
Richmond Way	W12, W14 p. 17	GX	367	
Robert Street	NW1 p. 15	LS		
Rochester Row	SW1 p. 30	CX		
Rodney Road	N1 p. 20	QY		
Roland Gardens	SW7 p. 28	BT		
Roman Way	N7 p. 15	NR		
Romilly Street	W1 p. 27	GL	368	
Rosebery Avenue	EC1 p. 15	NS		
Rosslyn Hill	NW3 p. 13	GR		
Rossmore Road	NW1 p. 14	KS	369	
Rowan Road	W6 p. 17	GY		
Royal College Street	NW1 p. 15	LR		
Royal Crescent	W11 p. 17	GV	371	
Royal Hospital Road	SW3 p. 29	FU		
Rupert Street	W1 p. 27	FL		
Russell Square	WC1 p. 15	MT		
Russell Street	WC2 p. 31	EV		
Rutland Gate	SW7 p. 29	DQ		
Rylston Road	SW6 p. 17	GZ		
Sackville Street	W1 p. 27	EM		
St. Albans Grove	W8 p. 26	AR		
St. Andrews Street	EC4 p. 16	PT	372	
St. Ann's Road	W11 p. 17	GV	373	
St. Ann's Villas	W11 p. 17	GV		
St. Bride Street	EC4 p. 16	PU	376	
St. Dunstan's Road	W6 p. 17	GZ		
St. George's Drive	SW1 p. 19	LZ		
St. George's Road	SE1 p. 20	PX		
St. George's Square	SW1 p. 19	MZ		
St. George Street	W1 p. 27	DL		
St. Giles Circus	W1, WC1, WC2 p. 27	GJ		
St. Giles High Street	WC2 p. 31	DV	377	
St. James's Place	SW1 p. 27	EN		
St. James's Square	SW1 p. 27	FN		
St. James's Street	SW1 p. 27	EN		
St. James Street	E17 p. 31	DV		
St. John Street	EC1 p. 16	PS		
St. John's Wood High Street	NW8 p. 14	JS	378	
St. John's Wood Park	NW8 p. 14	JR	379	
St. John's Wood Road	NW8 p. 14	JS		
St. Leonard's Terrace	SW3 p. 29	FU		
St. Mark's Road	W11, W10 p. 13	GT		
St. Martin's Lane	WC2 p. 31	DX		
St. Martin's-le-Grand	EC1 p. 16	PT	380	
St. Pancras Way	NW1 p. 15	LR		
St. Petersburgh Place	W2 p. 30	BZ		
St. Quintin Avenue	W10 p. 13	GT		
St. Thomas Street	SE1 p. 20	QV		
Sardinia Street	WC2 p. 31	EV	381	
Savile Row	W1 p. 27	DM		
Savoy Place	WC2 p. 31	EX		
Savoy Street	WC2 p. 31	EX		
Scarsdale Villas	W8 p. 17	HX		
Seagrave Road	SW6 p. 17	HZ		
Serle Street	WC2 p. 31	FV		
Serpentine Road	W2 p. 26	AP		
Seymour Street	W1, W2 p. 26	AK		
Shaftesbury Avenue	W1, WC2 p. 27	FL		
Sheffield Terrace	W8 p. 17	HV		
Shelton Street	WC2 p. 31	DV		
Shepherd Market	W1 p. 26	CN		
Shepherd's Bush Road	W6 p. 17	GX		
Shepherd Street	W1 p. 26	BP		
Sherriff Road	NW6 p. 13	HR		

Shirland Road .... W9 p. 13 HS
Shoreditch High Street .... E1 p. 16 QS 385
Shorts Gardens.................... WC2 p. 31 DV
Sidmouth Street................... WC1 p. 15 NS 386
Sinclair Road .... W14 p. 17 GX
Sloane Avenue .... SW3 p. 29 ET
Sloane Square .... SW1 p. 29 FT
Sloane Street .... SW1 p. 29 FR
Smith Street .... SW3 p. 29 EU
Snowfields .... SE1 p. 20 QV
Soho Square .... W1 p. 27 FJ
Southampton Row................. WC1 p. 15 NT 387
Southampton Street .... WC2 p. 31 EV 388
South Audley Street................ W1 p. 26 BM
South Eaton Place .... SW1 p. 30 AX 389
South End Road.................... NW3 p. 13 GR
South Hill .... NW3 p. 13 GR 390
South Lambeth Road.............. SW8 p. 19 NZ
South Molton Street................. W1 p. 26 BK
South Parade .... SW3 p. 28 CU
South Place........................ EC2 p. 16 QT 391
South Street .... W1 p. 26 BN
South Terrace .... SW7 p. 29 DS
Southwark Bridge............ SE1, EC4 p. 16 PU 395
Southwark Bridge Road .... SE1 p. 20 PX
Southwark Street.................. SE1 p. 20 PV
Southwick Street................... W2 p. 31 EY
Spa Road.......................... SE16 p. 20 QX
Spencer Street .... EC1 p. 16 PS 398
Spital Square........................ E1 p. 16 QT 399
Spring Street .... W2 p. 31 DY
Stamford Street .... SE1 p. 19 NV
Stanhope Gardens .... SW7 p. 28 BS
Stanhope Place .... W2 p. 31 FY 400
Stanhope Terrace .... W2 p. 31 DZ
Star Road .... W14 p. 17 GZ
Storeys Gate .... SW1 p. 19 MX 402
Strand .... WC2 p. 31 DX
Stratton Street .... W1 p. 27 DN
Sumner Place .... SW7 p. 28 CT
Sumner Street .... SE1 p. 20 PV
Surrey Street .... WC2 p. 31 EV
Sussex Gardens .... W2 p. 31 DY
Sussex Place .... W2 p. 31 EY
Sussex Square .... W2 p. 31 DZ 404
Sutherland Avenue................. W9 p. 13 HT
Sutherland Street .... SW1 p. 19 LZ
Swinton Street .... WC1 p. 15 NS
Sydney Place .... SW7 p. 29 DT 405
Sydney Street .... SW3 p. 29 DT
Symons Street .... SW3 p. 29 FT 407
Tabard Street .... SE1 p. 20 PX 408
Tachbrook Street .... SW1 p. 19 LY
Talgarth Road .... W14, W6 p. 17 GZ
Tavistock Place.................... WC1 p. 15 MS
Tavistock Square .... WC1 p. 15 MS 409
Tavistock Street .... WC2 p. 31 EV
Tedworth Square .... SW3 p. 29 EU
Temple Place .... WC2 p. 31 FV
Templeton Place .... SW5 p. 17 HY 410
Terminus Place .... SW1 p. 30 BV 412
Thayer Street .... W1 p. 26 BJ 413
Theobald's Road .... WC1 p. 15 NT
Thirleby Road .... SW1 p. 30 CV 416
Thornhill Road .... N1 p. 15 NR
Threadneedle Street .... EC2 p. 16 QU 417
Throgmorton Street............... EC2 p. 16 QT 418
Thurloe Place .... SW7 p. 28 CS 421
Thurloe Square .... SW7 p. 29 DS
Tilney Street......................... W1 p. 26 BN 422
Tite Street .... SW3 p. 29 EU
Tooley Street...................... SE1 p. 20 QV
Tothill Street .... SW1 p. 19 MX
Tottenham Court Road .... W1 p. 15 LT
Tower Bridge........................ E1 p. 20 QV
Tower Bridge Road .... SE1 p. 20 QX
Tower Hill .... EC3 p. 16 QU 425
Trafalgar Square .... WC2, SW1 p. 31 DX
Trebovir Road..................... SW5 p. 17 HY 426
Tregunter Road................... SW10 p. 28 BU
Trevor Place....................... SW7 p. 29 EQ
Trevor Square .... SW7 p. 29 ER
Trinity Church Square .... SE1 p. 20 PX
Trinity Street...................... SE1 p. 20 PX
Tyers Street...................... SE11 p. 19 NZ
Union Street...................... SE1 p. 20 PV
Upper Belgrave Street .... SW1 p. 30 AV
Upper Berkeley Street .... W1 p. 31 FY
Upper Brook Street................ W1 p. 26 AM
Upper Grosvenor Street........... W1 p. 26 AM
Upper Ground .... SE1 p. 20 PV 428
Upper St. Martin's Lane .... WC2 p. 29 DV 430
Upper Street....................... N1 p. 16 PR

Upper Thames Street .... EC4 p. 16 PU 431
Upper Woburn Place............. WC1 p. 15 MS 432
Uxbridge Road W7, W13
                W5, W3, W12 p. 17 GV
Vale (The) .... SW3 p. 28 CU
Vanston Place .... SW6 p. 17 HZ
Vassal Road .... SW9 p. 20 PZ
Vauxhall Bridge .... SW1, SE1 p. 19 NZ
Vauxhall Bridge Road .... SW1 p. 30 BX
Vauxhall Street.................. SE11 p. 19 NZ
Vauxhall Walk.................... SE11 p. 19 NZ
Vere Street .... W1 p. 26 BJ
Victoria Embankment SW1
               WC2, EC4 p. 31 EX
Victoria Grove .... W8 p. 28 BR
Victoria Road NW6
  BRENT .... p. 13 HR
Victoria Road W8
  KENSINGTON..................... p. 28 BQ
Victoria Street..................... SW1 p. 30 BV
Vigo Street .... W1 p. 27 EM
Villiers Street..................... WC2 p. 31 DX
Vincent Square .... SW1 p. 19 MY
Vincent Street .... SW1 p. 19 MY 436
Virginia Road....................... E2 p. 16 QS
Wakeman Road .... NW10 p. 13 GS
Walterton Road .... W9 p. 13 HS
Walton Street .... SW3 p. 29 ES
Wandsworth Road .... SW8 p. 19 MZ
Wardour Street .... W1 p. 27 FJ
Warrington Crescent .... W9 p. 14 JS
Warwick Avenue .... W2, W9 p. 14 JT 441
Warwick Road .... SW5, W14 p. 17 GY
Warwick Street .... W1 p. 27 EM 444
Warwick Way .... SW1 p. 19 LY
Waterloo Bridge .... WC2, SE1 p. 31 EX
Waterloo Place .... SW1 p. 27 FN
Waterloo Road .... SE1 p. 19 NV
Waverton Street .... W1 p. 26 BN
Webber Street .... SE1 p. 20 PX
Weighhouse Street .... W1 p. 26 BK
Welbeck Street .... W1 p. 26 BH
Wellington Road .... NW8 p. 14 JS
Wellington Street .... WC2 p. 31 EV
Wells Street .... W1 p. 27 EJ
Well Walk .... NW3 p. 13 GR
Westbourne Crescent .... W2 p. 31 DZ 448
Westbourne Grove .... W2, W11 p. 30 AY
Westbourne Park Road ..... W2, W11 p. 13 GT
Westbourne Park Villas .... W2 p. 13 HT 449
Westbourne Street .... W2 p. 31 DZ 450
Westbourne Terrace .... W2 p. 31 DY
Westbourne Road .... N7 p. 15 NR
Westbourne Terrace Road .... W2 p. 14 JT 452
West Cromwell Road ...... SW5, W14 p. 17 HY
West End Lane .... NW6 p. 13 HR
West Halkin Street .... SW1 p. 29 FR
Westminster Bridge .... SW1, SE1 p. 19 NX
Westminster Bridge Road .... SE1 p. 19 NX
Weston Street .... SE1 p. 20 QX
West Smithfield .... EC1 p. 16 PT 454
Westway .... N18 p. 13 HT
Wetherby Gardens .... SW5 p. 28 BT
Wharfdale Road.................... N1 p. 15 NR 455
Whitcomb Street .... WC2 p. 27 GM
Whitechapel High Street........... E1 p. 16 QT 456
Whitecross Street............. EC1, EC2 p. 16 PS
Whitehall .... SW1 p. 19 MV
Whitehall Court................... SW1 p. 19 NV 460
Whitehall Place................... SW1 p. 19 NV 462
Whitehead's Grove .... SW3 p. 29 ET 463
White Lion Street.................. N1 p. 15 NS 466
Wigmore Street.................... W1 p. 26 BJ
Wild Street .... WC2 p. 31 EV
William IV Street .... WC2 p. 31 DX 467
William Street .... SW1 p. 29 FQ 468
Willoughby Road .... NW3 p. 13 GR 470
Willow Road .... NW3 p. 13 GR
Willow Walk .... SE1 p. 20 QY
Wilson Street .... EC2 p. 16 QT
Wilton Place .... SW1 p. 29 FQ
Wilton Road .... SW1 p. 30 BX
Wilton Street .... SW1 p. 30 AV
Wimpole Street .... W1 p. 26 BH
Winslow Road .... W6 p. 17 GZ
Woburn Place..................... WC1 p. 15 MS
Woodlawn Road .... SW6 p. 17 GZ
Woods Mews .... W1 p. 26 AL
Wormwood Street................. EC2 p. 16 QT 472
Worship Street .... EC2 p. 16 QT
York Road .... SE1 p. 19 NX
York Way .... N1, N7 p. 15 MR
Young Street .... W8 p. 28 AQ

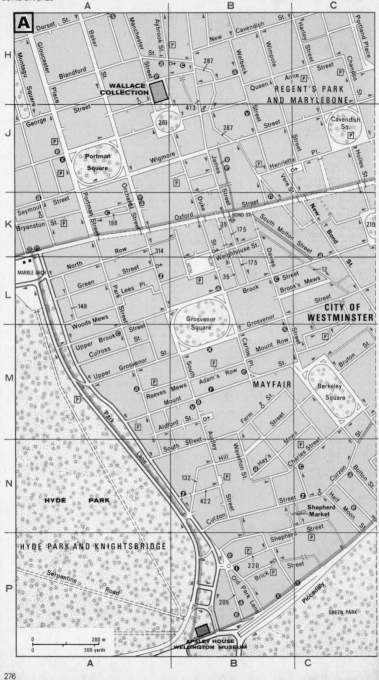

Arlington Street .... **DN** 6	Dunraven Street .... **AL** 149	Manchester Square .... **AJ** 281
Avery Row .... **CL** 12	Gerrard Street .... **GL** 174	Market Place .... **DJ** 286
Bateman Street .... **FK** 18	Gilbert Street .... **BL** 175	Marylebone Lane .... **BJ** 287
Berwick Street............ **FK** 26	Glasshouse Street .... **EM** 179	North Audley Street ...... **AK** 314
Binney Street............. **BL** 35	Granville Place .... **AK** 188	Old Burlington Street ..... **DM** 322
Carlton Gardens........... **FP** 74	Great Castle Street .... **DJ** 189	Old Compton Street....... **GK** 323
Deanery Street............ **BN** 132	Greek Street .... **GK** 198	Panton Street .... **FM** 336
Denman Street............ **FM** 133	Hamilton Place .... **BP** 205	Romilly Street .... **GL** 368
Denmark Street........... **GJ** 134	Hanover Square .... **CK** 210	Thayer Street .... **BJ** 413
Duke of York Street ...... **EN** 143	Hertford Street .... **BP** 220	Tilney Street .... **BN** 422
Duke Street ST. JAMES.... **EN** 146	Leicester Square .... **GM** 261	Warwick Street........... **EM** 444

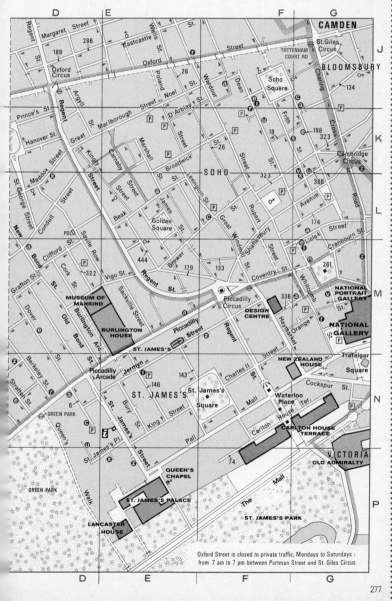

Oxford Street is closed to private traffic, Mondays to Saturdays : from 7 am to 7 pm between Portman Street and St. Giles Circus

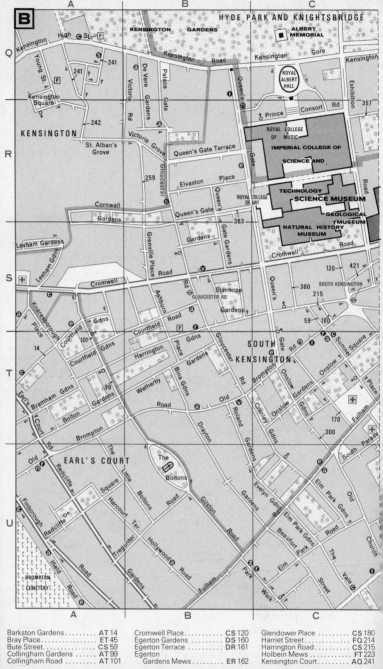

B

HYDE PARK AND KNIGHTSBRIDGE

KENSINGTON GARDENS

ALBERT MEMORIAL

Kensington High St.

Gore

Kensington

Young St.

241

241

Kensington Road

De Vere Gardens

Palace Gate

Queen's

Gate

ROYAL ALBERT HALL

Exhibition

357

Kensington Square

242

Victoria Rd

Prince Consort Rd

ROYAL COLLEGE OF MUSIC

KENSINGTON

St. Alban's Grove

Victoria Grove

IMPERIAL COLLEGE OF SCIENCE AND

Queen's Gate Terrace

Gloucester

259

Elvaston Place

ROYAL COLLEGE OF ART

TECHNOLOGY

SCIENCE MUSEUM

Cornwall Gardens

Queen's Gate

363

GEOLOGICAL MUSEUM

NATURAL HISTORY MUSEUM

Lexham Gardens

Gardens

Cromwell

120 421

Lexham Gdns

Road

Cromwell

Rd

SOUTH KENSINGTON

360

215

59 180

Knaresborough Place

Gdns

Courtfield Road

Ashburn

Stanhope

GLOUCESTER RD

Gardens

Queen's

Gate

Courtfield

101

Courtfield Gdns

P

SOUTH KENSINGTON

Onslow Square

14

Harrington

Place

Gloucester Rd

Brompton

Onslow Gardens

Onslow Gdns

Bramham Gdns

Courtfield Gardens

99

Wetherby

Bina Gdns

Gardens

170

Bolton Gardens

Road

Old

Cranley Gdns

300

Earl's Court Rd

Brompton

Drayton

Roland Gardens

South Parade

Old

EARL'S COURT

The Little Boltons

The Boltons

Gliston Road

Evelyn Gdns

Elm Park Gdns

Redcliffe Square

Harcourt Ter.

Boltons

Elm Park Gdns

Old

Finborough

Redcliffe

Treguter

Hollywood Road

Fulham

Beaufort Park

Church

BROMPTON CEMETERY

Ifield Road

Gardens

Park

Elm

Street

The Vale

Walk

Barkston Gardens	AT 14	
Bray Place	ET 45	
Bute Street	CS 59	
Collingham Gardens	AT 99	
Collingham Road	AT 101	
Cromwell Place	CS 120	
Egerton Gardens	DS 160	
Egerton Terrace	DR 161	
Egerton Gardens Mews	ER 162	
Glendower Place	CS 180	
Harriet Street	FQ 214	
Harrington Road	CS 215	
Holbein Mews	FT 223	
Kensington Court	AQ 241	

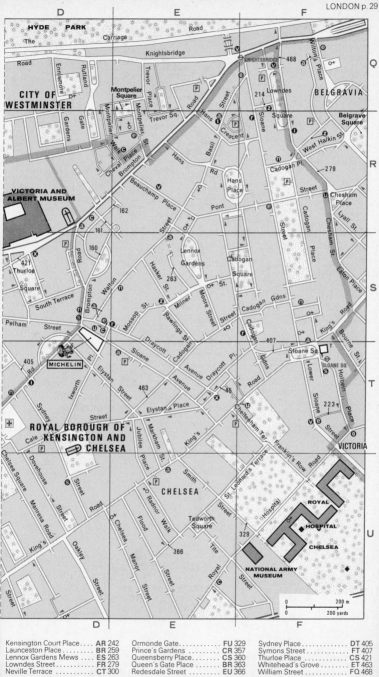

Kensington Court Place....	**AR** 242	Ormonde Gate..........	**FU** 329	Sydney Place.............	**DT** 405
Launceston Place	**BR** 259	Prince's Gardens........	**CR** 357	Symons Street...........	**FT** 407
Lennox Gardens Mews	**ES** 263	Queensberry Place.......	**CS** 360	Thurloe Place	**CS** 421
Lowndes Street...........	**FR** 279	Queen's Gate Place	**BR** 363	Whitehead's Grove	**ET** 463
Neville Terrace	**CT** 300	Redesdale Street	**EU** 366	William Street	**FQ** 468

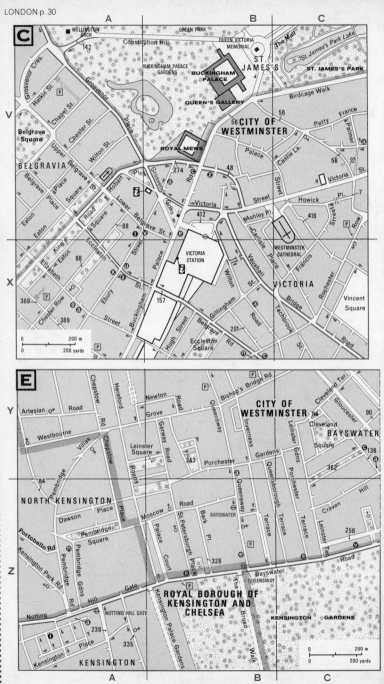

C

WELLINGTON ARCH

GREEN PARK

QUEEN VICTORIA MEMORIAL

The Mall

St. James's Park Lake

Constitution Hill

142

ST. JAMES'S

ST. JAMES'S PARK

Grosvenor Cres.

BUCKINGHAM PALACE GARDENS

BUCKINGHAM PALACE

Halkin St.

Chapel St.

Birdcage Walk

QUEEN'S GALLERY

Grosvenor Place

V

Chester St.

Wilton St.

Upper Belgrave

56

CITY OF WESTMINSTER

56

Petty France

Palmer St.

Belgrave Square

ROYAL MEWS

Palace Street

Castle La.

56

Belgrave Place

Hobart Pl.

274

48

Victoria St.

7

BELGRAVIA

Lower Belgrave St.

Grosvenor Gdns.

Rd

Street

Howick Pl.

416

Belgrave Place

Eaton Square

Victoria Street

Ashley Pl.

King's Road

Eccleston Street

88

412

Carlisle Place

WESTMINSTER CATHEDRAL

Eaton

88

Palace Street

Vauxhall

Francis St.

Rochester Row

Elizabeth

X

389

Chester Row

Ebury Street

VICTORIA STATION

Wilton St.

VICTORIA

Vincent Square

389

Buckingham

157

Hugh Street

Gillingham St.

Belgrave Rd

201

Tachbrook

Eccleston Square

Bridge Road

St.

0   200 m
0   200 yards

E

Chepstow Rd

Newton Rd

Bishop's Bridge Rd

Cleveland Terr.

Gloucester

Hereford Rd

Grove

Queensway

Inverness

CITY OF WESTMINSTER

94

90

Y

Artesian Road

Garway Road

Leinster Gdns

Cleveland Square

BAYSWATER

Westbourne

Chepstow Villas

Leinster Square

243

Porchester Gardens

Queensborough Terrace

Porchester Terrace

136

362

84

Pembridge

Chepstow Road

NORTH KENSINGTON

Dawson Place

Moscow Road

Bark Pl.

BAYSWATER

Craven

256

Portobello Rd

Pembridge Square

St. Petersburgh Place

Palace Court

Queensway

Hill

Leinster Ter.

Kensington Park Rd

Pembridge Gdns

328

Bayswater Road

Z

Pembridge

Gate

The Broad Walk

Queensway

ROYAL BOROUGH OF KENSINGTON AND CHELSEA

KENSINGTON GARDENS

Notting Hill Gate

Kensington Palace Gardens

238

335

KENSINGTON

0   200 m
0   200 yards

A   **B**   **C**

280

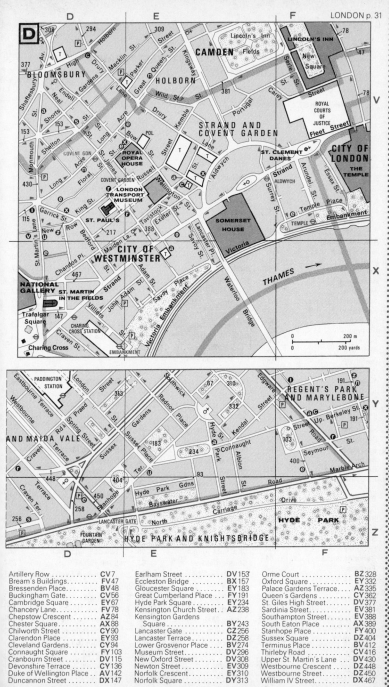

Artillery Row	CV	7
Bream's Buildings	FV	47
Bressenden Place	BV	48
Buckingham Gate	CV	56
Cambridge Square	EY	67
Chancery Lane	FV	78
Chepstow Crescent	AZ	84
Chester Square	AX	88
Chilworth Street	CY	90
Clarendon Place	EY	93
Cleveland Gardens	CY	94
Connaught Square	FY	103
Cranbourn Street	DV	115
Devonshire Terrace	CY	136
Duke of Wellington Place	AV	142
Duncannon Street	DX	147
Earlham Street	DV	153
Eccleston Bridge	BX	157
Gloucester Square	EY	183
Great Cumberland Place	FY	191
Hyde Park Square	EY	234
Kensington Church Street	AZ	238
Kensington Gardens Square	BY	243
Lancaster Gate	CZ	256
Lancaster Terrace	DZ	258
Lower Grosvenor Place	BV	274
Museum Street	DV	296
New Oxford Street	DV	308
Newton Street	EV	309
Norfolk Crescent	EY	310
Norfolk Square	DY	313
Orme Court	BZ	328
Oxford Square	EY	332
Palace Gardens Terrace	AZ	335
Queen's Gardens	CY	362
St. Giles High Street	DV	377
Sardinia Street	EV	381
Southampton Street	EV	388
South Eaton Place	AX	389
Stanhope Place	FY	400
Sussex Square	DZ	404
Terminus Place	BV	412
Thirleby Road	CV	416
Upper St. Martin's Lane	DV	430
Westbourne Crescent	DZ	448
Westbourne Street	DZ	450
William IV Street	DX	467

ALPHABETICAL LIST OF HOTELS AND RESTAURANTS
LISTE ALPHABÉTIQUE DES HOTELS ET RESTAURANTS
ELENCO ALFABETICO DEGLI ALBERGHI E RISTORANTI
ALPHABETISCHES HOTEL- UND RESTAURANTVERZEICHNIS

	page pagina Seite
A	
Aerodrome	50
Alexander	59
Allandale	61
Alonso's	61
Amoureux (Les)	59
Anna's Place	54
Ariel	54
Ark (The)	58
Arlequin (L')	61
Arlington	54
Artagnan (D')	65
Artiste Affamé (L')	57
Asuka	65
Athenaeum	62
Auberge (L')	60
Aventure (L')	65
Ayudhya	59
Azami	67
Aziz	52
B	
Bagatelle	56
Barbarella	52
Barbino (II)	58
Barbino (II)	65
Bardon Lodge	52
Barkston	57
Barn	54
Barnaby's	60
Basil Street	55
Bastille (La)	50
Beccofino	56
Bellamore (II)	60
Berkeley	62
Berkeley Arms	54
Berners	64
Bewick's	56
Biagi's	65
Bill Bentley's	50
Bois St. Jean (Au)	65
Bombay Brasserie	59
Bombay Palace	62
Bonnington	48
Bouffe (La)	61
Boulestin	67
Bourse Plate (La)	50

	page pagina Seite
Brasserie (La)	56
Briarley	50
Brinkley's	57
Brittania	63
Bromley Continental	48
Bromley Court	48
Brown's	63
Bryanston Court	65
Bubb's	50
Bumbles	68
C	
Cadogan Thistle	55
Café Pelican	67
Café St. Pierre	54
Canaletto da Leo	62
Canaletto 2	53
Capisano	48
Capital	55
Caprice (Le)	66
Carlo's Place	52
Carnarvon	51
Cavendish	66
Cézanne	60
Chanterelle	59
Chaopraya	65
Chariot Wheel	48
Charles Bernard	49
Chateaubriand	49
Chateau Napoleon	51
Chelsea Room	55
Chesa (Swiss Centre)	66
Chesham House	68
Chesterfield	63
Chez Max	59
Chez Moi	58
Chez Nico	61
Chez Solange	67
Chiang Mai	66
Churchill	64
Ciboure	68
City Tiberio	50
Claridges's	62
Clarke's	57

	page pagina Seite
Clifton Ford	64
Coach House	53
Colonnade	61
Concorde	65
Concordia	62
Concordia Notte	62
Connaught	62
Corney and Barrow	50
Crest (Bexley)	47
Crest	54
Crocodile (Le)	57
Croisette (La)	57
Crowther's	60
Cumberland	53
Cumberland	64
D	
Dan's	56
Daphne's	56
Dawson House	49
Dene	60
Don Luigi	56
Dorchester	62
Dragon Garden	52
Drury Lane Moat House	49
Dukes	66
Dunheved	51
Durrants	64
Dylan	61
E	
Eatons	68
Ebury Court	68
Ecu de France (A l')	66
Eden Plaza	59
Eleven Park Walk	56
Elio	51
Elizabeth	68
Embassy House	58
English Garden	56
English House	56
Escargot (L')	66
Etoile (L')	49
Evergreen	60
Excelsior	53

F

Fenja	55
Finezza (La)	56
Flounders	67
Fogareiro	47
Fontana (La)	68
Fortune Cookie	62
Foxes	48
Français (Le)	56
Franco Ovest	58
Frederick's	55
Frère Jacques	67
Frith's	66
Frognal Lodge	49
Fuji	66
Fung Shing	66

G

Gallery Rendezvous	66
Gamin (Le)	50
Gastronome One	52
Gavroche (Le)	63
Gavvers	56
Gay Hussar	66
Gaylord	65
Giannino's	48
Ginnan	50
Gino's	51
Giralda (La)	53
Gloucester	58
Good Earth	47
Good Earth	56
Good Earth	56
Gore	58
Goring	68
Grafton	48
Gran Paradiso	68
Great Northern	49
Green Cottage II	49
Greenhouse	64
Grianan	48
Grimes	67
Grims Dyke	53
Grosvenor	68
Grosvenor House	62

H

Hallam	65
Hamilton House	68
Happiness Garden	51
Happy Wok	67
Harewood	65
Harlingford	48
Harrow	53
Heart of the Dragon	65
Heathrow Penta	53

Hendon Hall	47
Hiders	52
Hilaire	59
Hilton International	57
Hilton International	63
Hiroko	57
Hogarth	57
Ho-Ho	59
Ho-Ho	64
Holiday Inn	50
Holiday Inn	50
Holiday Inn	54
Holiday Inn	55
Holiday Inn	63
Holiday Inn	64
Holtwhites	51
Hospitality Inn	61
Hotel (L')	55
Howard	67
Hunan	68
Hyatt Carlton Tower	55
Hyde Park	62

I

I Ching	57
Ikeda	64
Inigo Jones	67
Inn on the Park	62
Inter-Continental	63
Interlude de Tabaillau	67

J

Jardin des Gourmets (Au)	66
Jasmin	61
Jasper's Bun in the Oven	60
John Howard	58
Joy King Lau	67
Julius's	55
Junk Two	58

K

Kalamaras Taverna	62
Kaya	66
Keats	49
Kenilworth	48
Ken Lo's Memories of China	68
Kennedy	49
Kensington Close	57
Kensington Palace Thistle	57
Kenton House	51
Kew Rendezvous	60
Khyber	51
Kingsley	48
Kundan	68

L

Ladbroke	49
Ladbroke	53
Ladbroke Westmoreland	64
Laguna 50	67
Lal Qila	49
Lampwicks	61
Langans Bistro	65
Langan's Brasserie	64
Leith's	58
Leonis Quo Vadis	66
Lichfield's	60
Lockets	68
Loggia (La)	65
Londonderry	63
London Embassy	61
Londoner	64
London International	58
London Metropole	61
London Ryan	54
London Tara	57
London West	52
Lords Rendezvous	65
Lowndes Thistle	62
Luigi's	60
Luigi's " Belmont "	47

M

Ma Cuisine	56
Madrague (La)	47
Magnos Brasserie	67
Mama San	57
Mange Tout (Le)	60
Mao Tai	52
Mario	48
Mario	56
Marriott	63
Martini	54
Martin's	57
Masako	65
Master Brewer Motel	54
Master Robert Motel	54
Maxim	51
Maxim's de Paris	66
May Fair	63
Mazarin (Le)	68
Mean Time	52
Memories of India	59
Ménage à Trois	56
Meridiana	56
Mimmo d'Ischia	68
Mirabelle	63
Miyama	64
Mr Kai	49
Mr Kai	64
Mr Lui	60

Moghul Brasserie 48
Mon Plaisir 49
Monsieur Thompsons . . 58
Montcalm 64
Montpeliano 62
Montpelier 51
Mornington Lancaster . . 61
Motcombs 62
M'sieur Frog 52
M'sieur Frog 55
Muscadet (Le) 65

N

Naraine 57
Nayab 56
Neal Street 49
New Piccadilly 62
Ninety Park Lane 63
Non-Ya 59
Norfolk 51
Novotel London 52
Number Sixteen 59

O

Oakwood 50
Odins 65
Oiseau Noir (L') 51
Old Etonian 53
Olivier (L') 57
Ombrello (L') 48
One Hampstead Lane . . 52
One Two Three 64
Opera (L') 49
Oven d'Or 48

P

Paesana (La) 57
Papillon (Le) 52
Park Lane 63
Parkwood 61
Partners 23 60
Pastoria 66
Pavona (La) 65
Peking Diner 48
Peking Duck 47
Pembridge
  Court 58
Perfumed Conservatory 52
Peter's 50
Petersham 60
Pier 31 56
Poissonnerie
  de l'Avenue 56
Pollyanna's 61
Pomegranates 68
Pomme d'Amour
  (La) 57

Poons of Covent
  Garden 67
Poons (Soho) 66
Ponte Nuovo 56
Porte de la Cité 49
Portman
  Inter-Continental 64
Portman Court 65
Portobello 58
Portofino 55
Post House 49
Post House 54
Poulbot (Le)
  (basement) 50
Poule au Pot (La) 68
Pratts 50
Prince Regent 59
Princess Garden 63
Provençal (Au) 59
Pun 59

Q - R

Quai St. Pierre (Le) 58
Quincy's 84 47
Reads 59
Red Fort 66
Red Lion 60
Regent Crest 64
Regency 58
Rembrandt 58
Résidence (La) 57
Restaurant (The) 68
Richmond Gate 60
Ritz 66
Royal Chace 51
Royal Court 55
Royal Garden 57
Royal Horseguards
  Thistle 68
Royal Lancaster 61
Royal Trafalgar Thistle . . 66
Royal
  Westminster Thistle . . 68
Ruelle (La) 57
Rue St. Jacques 65
Rugantino 66
Russell 48

S

Sailing Junk 58
St. George's 64
St. Quentin 56
Saigon 67
Salloos 62
Sambuca 53
San Carlo 52
Sandringham 49
San Frediano 56

San Lorenzo Fuoriporta . . 59
San Marino 62
San Ruffillo 56
Santini 68
Savoy 67
Savoy Court 64
Scott's 63
Scratchwood
  TraveLodge 47
Selfridge 64
Selsdon Park 51
Shares 50
Sheekey's 67
Sheraton Belgravia 62
Sheraton Heathrow 54
Sheraton
  Park Tower 55
Sheraton
  Skyline 53
Sheridan's 49
Sherlock Holmes 64
Shezan 62
Shireen 52
Shogun 64
Simpson's-in-the
  Strand 67
Skyway 54
Soufflé (Le) 63
Stafford 66
Stakis St. Ermins 68
Stratford Court 65
Suntory 66
Suquet (Le) 56
Swan 53
Swiss Cottage 49

T

Taicoon 47
T'ang 56
Tante Claire (La) 55
Tate Gallery Rest. 68
Terrace (The) 63
Thierry's 56
Thirty four Surrey Street . 51
Thomas de Quincey's . . 67
Tiberio 63
Tiger Lee 57
Tonino 65
Topo d'Oro 58
Toto 56
Tourment d'Amour 67
Town House 57
Trattoo 58
Trattoria Fiori 64
Trattoria Imperia 67
Trattoria Parmigiana . . . 61
Trat West 62
Trusha 67
Twenty Trinity Gardens . 59

V

Vanderbilt	58
Varnom's	55
Venezia	66
Viceroy of India	65
Vijay	47
Villa Augusta	50
Villa Bianca	49
Villa Claudius	68
Villa Medici	68

W - Z

Waldorf	67
Waltons	55
Wembley International	48
Westbury	63
West Lodge Park	51
Wheeler's	50
Wheeler's	56

White House	50
White's	61
White Tower	49
Wilbraham	55
Willett	55
Woodford Moat House	59
Worcester House	59
Zen	55

ALPHABETICAL LIST OF AREAS INCLUDED
LISTE ALPHABÉTIQUE DES QUARTIERS CITÉS
ELENCO ALFABETICO DEI QUARTIERI CITATI
LISTE DER ERWÄHNTEN BEZIRKE

	page pagina seite		page pagina seite		page pagina seite
Barnes	60	**Fulham**	52	**Northwood**	54
Battersea	61	**Greenwich**	52	**Orpington**	48
Bayswater and Maida Vale	61	**Hadley Wood**	51	**Peckham Rye**	60
Belgravia	62	**Hammersmith**	52	**Pinner**	53
Bexley	47	**Hampstead**	49	**Regent's Park**	50
Blackheath	52	**Hanwell**	51	**Regent's Park and Marylebone**	64
Bloomsbury	48	**Harrow Weald**	53		
Brixton	59	**Hatch End**	53	**Richmond**	60
Bromley	48	**Heathrow Airport**	53	**Romford**	53
Canonbury	54	**Hendon**	47	**Ruislip**	54
Central Harrow	53	**Highgate**	52	**St. James's**	66
Chelsea	55	**Hillingdon**	54	**Sanderstead**	51
Child's Hill	47	**Holborn**	49	**Shepherd's Bush**	52
Chislehurst	48	**Hornchurch**	53	**Soho**	66
City of London	50	**Hornsey**	52	**Southgate**	51
Clapham	61	**Hounslow**	54	**South Kensington**	58
Cranford	54	**Hyde Park and Knightsbridge**	62	**South Woodford**	59
Croydon	50			**Strand and Covent Garden**	67
Dulwich Village	60	**Islington**	55		
Ealing	51	**Kensington**	57	**Surbiton**	59
Earl's Court	57	**Keston**	48	**Sutton**	60
Eastcote	53	**Kew**	60	**Swiss Cottage**	50
East Dulwich	60	**Kilburn**	47	**Thornton Heath**	51
East Sheen	60	**King's Cross**	49	**Twickenham**	60
Enfield	51	**Kingston Upon Thames**	59	**Victoria**	68
Euston	49	**Leytonstone**	61	**Wembley**	48
Farnborough	48	**Mayfair**	62	**West Kensington**	52
Finchley	47	**Merton**	59	**Wimbledon**	59
Finchley Road	49	**Mill Hill**	47	**Winchmore Hill**	52
Finsbury	54	**North Kensington**	58	**Woodford**	59

STARRED ESTABLISHMENTS IN LONDON
LES ÉTABLISSEMENTS A ÉTOILES DE LONDRES
GLI ESERCIZI CON STELLE A LONDRA
DIE STERN-RESTAURANTS LONDONS

❀❀❀

	Area	Page
XXXX **Le Gavroche**	Mayfair	63

❀❀

	Area	Page
XXXXX **The Terrace**	Mayfair	63
XXX **La Tante Claire**	Chelsea	55

❀

	Area	Page			Area	Page
🏠 **Connaught**	Mayfair	62	XX	**L'Arlequin**	Battersea	61
🏠 **Capital**	Chelsea	55	XX	**Chez Nico**	Battersea	61
XXXX **Chelsea Room**	Chelsea	55	XX	**Lichfield's**	Richmond	60
XXXX **Waltons**	Chelsea	55	XX	**Ma Cuisine**	Chelsea	56
XXXX **Le Soufflé**	Mayfair	63	XX	**Le Mazarin**	Victoria	68
XXX **Rue St. Jacques**	Regent's Park and Marylebone	65	XX	**Tiger Lee**	Earl's Court	57

FURTHER ESTABLISHMENTS WHICH MERIT YOUR ATTENTION
AUTRES TABLES QUI MÉRITENT VOTRE ATTENTION
ALTRE TAVOLE PARTICOLARMENTE INTERESSANTI
WEITERE EMPFEHLENSWERTE HÄUSER

M

		Area	Page			Area	Page
XXX	**Martins**	Earl's Court	57	XX	**Ken Lo's Memories of China**	Victoria	68
XXX	**Odins**	Regent's Park and Marylebone	65	XX	**Lampwick's**	Battersea	61
XXX	**Suntory**	St. James's	66	XX	**Le Poulbot**	City	50
XX	**Bagatelle**	Chelsea	56	X	**Bubb's**	City	50

RESTAURANTS CLASSIFIED ACCORDING TO TYPE

RESTAURANTS CLASSÉS SUIVANT LEUR GENRE

RISTORANTI CLASSIFICATI SECONDO IL LORO GENERE

RESTAURANTS NACH ART UND EINRICHTUNG GEORDNET

Borough	Area	Restaurant		Page
BISTRO				
Islington	Islington	✗	**M'sieur Frog**	55
Wandsworth	Clapham	✗	**Pollyanna's**	61
Westminster (City of)	Regent's Park & Marylebone	✗	**Langan's Bistro**	65
—	Victoria	✗	**Bumbles**	68
DANCING				
Hammersmith	Fulham	✗✗	**Barbarella**	52
Westminster (City of)	Bayswater & Maida Vale	✗✗	**Concordia Notte**	62
—	Mayfair	✗✗✗	**Tiberio**	63
—	St. James's	✗✗✗✗✗	**Maxim's de Paris**	66
SEAFOOD				
Barnet	Finchley	✗✗	**Fogareiro**	47
City of London	City of London	✗✗✗	**Wheeler's**	50
—	—	✗✗	**Bill Bentley's**	50
Croydon	Croydon	✗	**34 Surrey Street**	51
Kensington & Chelsea (Royal Borough of)	Chelsea	✗✗	**Poissonnerie de l'Avenue**	56
—	—	✗✗	**Suquet (Le)**	56
—	—	✗	**Wheelers**	56
—	Earl's Court	✗✗	**Croisette (La)**	57
—	—	✗✗	❀ **Tiger Lee**	57
—	Kensington	✗	**Quai St. Pierre (Le)**	58
Westminster (City of)	Mayfair	✗✗✗✗	**Scott's**	63
—	Strand & Covent Garden	✗✗	**Frère Jacques**	67
—	—	✗✗	**Sheekey's**	67
—	—	✗	**Flounders**	67
—	—	✗	**Grimes**	67

Borough	Area		Restaurant	Page

CHINESE

Borough	Area		Restaurant	Page
Barnet	Finchley	X	Peking Duck	47
—	Mill Hill	XX	Good Earth	47
—	—	XX	Taicoon	47
Bromley	Bromley	X	Peking Diner	48
Camden	Bloomsbury	XX	Mr Kai	49
—	Finchley Road	XX	Green Cottage II	49
Ealing	Ealing	X	Maxim	51
—	Hanwell	X	Happiness Garden	51
Enfield	Winchmore Hill	XX	Dragon Garden	52
Hammersmith	Fulham	XX	Mao Tai	52
Harrow	Hatch End	X	Swan	53
Kensington & Chelsea (Royal Borough of)	Chelsea	XXX	Zen	55
—	—	XX	Good Earth	56
—	—	XX	Good Earth	56
—	Earl's Court	XX	✿ Tiger Lee	57
—	Kensington	XX	I Ching	57
—	—	XX	Junk Two	58
—	—	XX	Mama San	57
—	—	X	Sailing Junk	58
—	South Kensington	XX	Pun	59
Redbridge	South Woodford	XX	Ho-Ho	59
Richmond-upon-Thames	Richmond	XX	Evergreen	60
—	—	XX	Kew Rendezvous	60
—	—	X	Red Lion	60
Southwark	East Dulwich	X	Mr Lui	60
Wandsworth	Clapham	X	Jasmin	61
Westminster (City of)	Bayswater & Maida Vale	XXX	Bombay Palace	62
—	—	X	Fortune Cookie	62
—	Mayfair	XXX	Princess Garden	63
—	—	XX	Ho-Ho	64
—	—	XX	Mr Kai	64
—	Regent's Park & Marylebone	XX	Lords Rendezvous	65
—	Soho	XX	Poons	66
—	—	X	Fung Shing	66
—	—	X	Gallery Rendezvous	66
—	—	X	Joy King Lau	67
—	Strand & Covent Garden	X	Happy Wok	67
—	—	X	Poons of Covent Garden	67
—	Victoria	XX	Hunan	68
—	—	XX	Ken Lo's Memories of China	68

ENGLISH

Borough	Area		Restaurant	Page
Kensington & Chelsea (Royal Borough of)	Chelsea	XX	English Garden	56
—	—	XX	English House	56
Westminster (City of)	Strand & Covent Garden	XXX	Simpson's-in-the-Strand	67
—	Victoria	XXX	Lockets	68
—	—	X	Tate Gallery Rest.	68

Borough	Area	Restaurant	Page

FRENCH

Borough	Area	Restaurant	Page
Barnet	Finchley	✗ La Madrague	47
Bromley	Orpington	✗✗✗ Oven d'Or	48
Camden	Bloomsbury	✗✗✗ Etoile (L')	49
—	—	✗✗ Porte de la Cité	49
—	—	✗ Mon Plaisir	49
—	Hampstead	✗✗✗ Keats	49
City of London	City of London	✗✗ Poulbot (Le) (basement)	50
—	—	✗ Bastille (La)	50
—	—	✗ Bourse Plate (La)	50
—	—	✗ Bubb's	50
—	—	✗ Gamin (Le)	50
Hammersmith	Fulham	✗✗ Gastronome One	52
Kensington & Chelsea (Royal Borough of)	Chelsea	✗✗✗ Français (Le)	56
—	—	✗✗✗ ✿✿ Tante Claire (La)	55
—	—	✗✗ Bagatelle	56
—	—	✗✗ Gavvers	56
—	—	✗✗ ✿ Ma Cuisine	56
—	—	✗✗ Poissonnerie de l'Avenue	56
—	—	✗✗ St. Quentin	56
—	—	✗✗ Suquet (Le)	56
—	—	✗ Brasserie (La)	56
—	—	✗ Thierry's	56
—	Earl's Court	✗✗ Croisette (La)	57
—	Kensington	✗✗✗ Ruelle (La)	57
—	—	✗✗ Crocodile (Le)	57
—	—	✗✗ Pomme d'Amour (La)	57
—	—	✗✗ Résidence (La)	57
—	—	✗ Ark (The)	58
—	—	✗ Quai St. Pierre (Le)	58
—	North Kensington	✗✗ Chez Moi	58
—	—	✗✗ Monsieur Thompsons	58
Richmond-upon-Thames	Barnes	✗ Barnaby's	60
Southwark	Peckham Rye	✗ Auberge (L')	60
Wandsworth	Battersea	✗✗ ✿ Arlequin (L')	61
—	—	✗✗ ✿ Chez Nico	61
Westminster (City of)	Mayfair	✗✗✗✗✗ ✿✿ Terrace (The)	63
—	—	✗✗✗✗ ✿✿✿ Gavroche (Le)	63
—	Regents Park & Marylebone	✗✗✗ ✿ Rue St. Jacques	65
—	—	✗✗ Artagnan (D')	65
—	—	✗ Aventure (L')	65
—	—	✗ Bois St. Jean (Au)	65
—	—	✗ Muscadet (Le)	65
—	St. James's	✗✗✗✗✗ Maxims de Paris	66
—	—	✗✗✗✗ Ecu de France (A l')	66
—	Soho	✗✗ Jardin des Gourmets (Au)	66
—	—	✗✗ Chez Solange	67
—	—	✗✗ Interlude de Tabaillau	67
—	Strand & Covent Garden	✗✗✗✗ Boulestin	67
—	—	✗✗ Tourment d'Amour	67
—	—	✗ Café Pelican	67
—	—	✗ Magnos Brasserie	67

289

Borough	Area	Restaurant	Page

FRENCH (continued)

Westminster (City of)	Victoria	XX Ciboure	68
–	–	XX ❁ Mazarin (Le)	68
–	–	XX Restaurant (The)	68
–	–	X Poule au Pot (La)	68

GREEK

Camden	Bloomsbury	XXX White Tower	49
Westminster (City of)	Bayswater & Maida Vale	X Kalamaras Taverna	62

HUNGARIAN

Westminster (City of)	Soho	XX Gay Hussar	66

INDIAN & PAKISTANI

Borough	Area	Restaurant	Page
Brent	Kilburn	X Vijay	47
–	Wembley	XX Moghul Brasserie	48
Camden	Bloomsbury	XX Lal Qila	49
Croydon	Croydon	X Khyber	51
Hammersmith	Hammersmith	X Aziz	52
–	Shepherd's Bush	XX Shireen	52
Kensington & Chelsea (Royal Borough of)	Chelsea	X Nayab	56
	South Kensington	XXX Bombay Brasserie	59
–	–	XX Memories of India	59
Westminster (City of)	Bayswater & Maida Vale	XXX Bombay Palace	62
–	Belgravia	XX Salloos	62
–	Hyde Park & Knightsbridge	XXX Shezan	62
–	Regent's Park & Marylebone	XX Gaylord	65
–	–	XX Viceroy of India	65
–	Soho	XX Red Fort	66
–	–	X Trusha	67
–	Victoria	XXX Kundan	68

ITALIAN

Borough	Area	Restaurant	Page
Barnet	Finchley	XX Luigi's " Belmont "	47
Bromley	Bromley	XX Chariot Wheel	48
–	–	X Capisano	48
–	Chislehurst	XX Mario	48
–	Farnborough	XX Ombrello (L')	48
–	Keston	XX Giannino's	48
Camden	Hampstead	X Villa Bianca	49
City of London	City of London	XXX City Tiberio	50
–	–	XX Villa Augusta	50
Croydon	Sanderstead	X Elio	51
Ealing	Ealing	XX Gino's	51
Hammersmith	Fulham	XX Barbarella	52
Haringey	Highgate	XX San Carlo	52

Borough	Area		Restaurant	Page

ITALIAN (continued)

Borough	Area		Restaurant	Page
Harrow	Hatch End	XX	Canaletto 2	53
Hillingdon	Eastcote	X	Sambuca	53
–	Northwood	XX	Martini	54
Islington	Islington	XX	Portofino	55
Kensington & Chelsea (Royal Borough of)	Chelsea	XXX	Mario	56
–	–	XX	Beccofino	56
–	–	XX	Don Luigi	56
–	–	XX	Eleven Park Walk	56
–	–	XX	Finezza (La)	56
–	–	XX	Meridiana	56
–	–	XX	Ponte Nuovo	56
–	–	XX	San Frediano	56
–	–	XX	San Ruffillo	56
–	–	XX	Toto	56
–	Kensington	XX	Franco Ovest	58
–	–	XX	Paesana (La)	57
–	–	XX	Topo d'Oro	58
–	–	XX	Trattoo	58
–	–	X	Barbino (II)	58
Merton	Wimbledon	XX	San Lorenzo Fuoriporta	59
Richmond-upon-Thames	Barnes	X	Bellamore (II)	60
Southwark	Dulwich Village	XX	Luigi's	60
Waltham Forest	Leytonstone	X	Trattoria Parmigiana	61
Westminster (City of)	Bayswater & Maida Vale	XX	Canaletto da Leo	62
–	–	XX	Concordia Notte	62
–	–	XX	San Marino	62
–	–	XX	Trat West	62
–	–	X	Concordia	62
–	Hyde Park & Knightsbridge	XX	Montpeliano	62
–	Mayfair	XXX	Tiberio	63
–	–	X	Trattoria Fiori	64
–	Regent's Park & Marylebone	XX	Loggia (La)	65
–	–	XX	Pavona (La)	65
–	–	XX	Tonino	65
–	–	X	Barbino (II)	65
–	–	X	Biagi's	65
–	Soho	XXX	Leonis Quo Vadis	66
–	–	XX	Rugantino	66
–	–	XX	Venezia	66
–	–	X	Trattoria Imperia	67
–	Strand & Covent Garden	X	Laguna 50	67
–	Victoria	XXX	Santini	68
–	–	XX	Gran Paradiso	68
–	–	XX	Villa Claudius	68
–	–	X	Fontana (La)	68
–	–	X	Mimmo d'Ischia	68
–	–	X	Villa Medici	68

Borough	Area	Restaurant	Page

JAPANESE

Borough	Area	Restaurant	Page
City of London	City of London	✕ Ginnan	50
Kensington & Chelsea (Royal Borough of)	Kensington	✕✕ Hiroko	57
Westminster (City of)	Mayfair	✕✕ Miyama	64
–	–	✕✕ One Two Three	64
–	–	✕✕ Shogun	64
–	–	✕ Ikeda	64
–	Regent's Park & Marylebone	✕✕ Asuka	65
–	–	✕✕ Masako	65
–	St. James's	✕✕✕ Suntory	66
–	Soho	✕✕ Fuji	66
–	Strand & Covent Garden	✕✕ Azami	67

KOREAN

Westminster (City of)	Soho	✕✕ Kaya	66

ORIENTAL

Kensington & Chelsea (Royal Borough of)	Chelsea	✕✕ T'ang	56
	South Kensington	✕✕ Non-Ya	59
Westminster (City of)	Regent's Park & Marylebone	✕ Heart of the Dragon	65

THAI

Kingston	Kingston	✕ Ayudhya	59
Westminster (City of)	Regent's Park & Marylebone	✕ Chaopraya	65
–	Soho	✕ Chiang Mai	66

VIETNAMESE

Westminster (City of)	Soho	✕ Saigon	67

RESTAURANTS OPEN ON SUNDAY (L : lunch - D : dinner) AND RESTAU-RANTS TAKING LAST ORDERS AFTER 11.30 p.m.

RESTAURANTS OUVERTS LE DIMANCHE (L : déjeuner - D : dîner) ET RES-TAURANTS PRENANT LES DERNIÈRES COMMANDES APRÈS 23 h 30

RISTORANTI APERTI LA DOMENICA (L : colazione - D : pranzo) E RISTO-RANTI CHE ACCETTANO ORDINAZIONI DOPO LE 23. 30

RESTAURANTS, DIE SONNTAGS GEÖFFNET SIND (L : Mittagessen - D : Abendessen), BZW. BESTELLUNGEN AUCH NACH 23. 30 UHR ANNEHMEN

Borough	Area	Restaurant		Sunday	11.30 p. m.	Page
Barnet	Child's Hill	✗	Quincy's 84	L		47
—	Finchley	✗✗	Luigi's « Belmont »	L D		47
—	—	✗✗	Fogareiro		x	47
—	Mill Hill	✗✗	Good Earth	L D		47
—	—	✗✗	Taicoon	L D	x	47
Brent	Kilburn	✗	Vijay	L D		47
—	Wembley	✗✗	Moghul Brasserie	L D		48
Camden	Bloomsbury	✗✗	Mr Kai	L D	x	49
—	Finchley Road	✗	Sheridans	L D	x	49
—	Hampstead	✗✗✗	Keats		x	49
—	—	✗	Chateaubriand (12.00)		x	49
—	Holborn	✗✗✗	Opera (L') (12.00)		x	49
—	Regents Park	✗✗	Pratts	L		50
—	Swiss Cottage	✗✗	Peter's	L	x	50
Croydon	Croydon	✗✗✗	Chateau Napoleon	L		51
—	—	✗	Khyber	L D	x	51
Ealing	Ealing	✗✗	Gino's		x	51
—	—	✗	Maxim (12.00)	D	x	51
—	Hanwell	✗	Happiness Garden	D	x	51
Enfield	Southgate	✗✗	L'Oiseau Noir	L		51
—	Winchmore Hill	✗✗	Dragon Garden	L D	x	52
Greenwich	Greenwich	✗✗	Papillon (Le)	L		52
—	—	✗	Mean Time	L D		52

Borough	Area	Restaurant	Sunday	11.30 p. m.	Page
Hammersmith	Fulham	XX Barbarella (1.00)		x	52
—	—	XX Hiders		x	52
—	—	XX Mao Tai (11.45)	L D	x	52
—	—	X Carlo's Place		x	52
—	—	X Perfumed Conservatory		x	52
—	Hammersmith	X Aziz		x	52
—	Shepherd's Bush	XX Shireen	L D	x	52
Haringey	Highgate	XX One Hampstead Lane	L	x	52
—	—	XX San Carlo	L D	x	52
Harrow	Hatch End	X Swan	L D		53
Hillingdon	Eastcote	X Sambuca		x	53
Islington	Islington	XX Frederick's		x	55
—	—	XX Portofino		x	55
—	—	XX Varnoms	L		55
—	—	X M'sieur Frog		x	55
Kensington & Chelsea (Royal Borough of)	Chelsea	🏛 ❀ Capital	L D		55
—	—	XXXX ❀ Chelsea Room	L D		55
—	—	XXXX ❀ Waltons	L D	x	55
—	—	XXX Mario	L D	x	56
—	—	XXX Zen	L D	x	55
—	—	XX Beccofino		x	56
—	—	XX Bewick's	D	x	56
—	—	XX Daphne's (12.00)		x	56
—	—	XX English Garden	L D	x	56
—	—	XX English House	L D	x	56
—	—	XX Good Earth	L D		56
—	—	XX Good Earth	L D		56
—	—	XX Ménage à Trois (12.15)		x	56
—	—	XX Meridiana (12.00)	L D	x	56
—	—	XX Pier 31	L D	x	56
—	—	XX Poissonnerie de l'Avenue		x	56
—	—	XX St. Quentin (12.00)	L D	x	56
—	—	XX Suquet (Le)	L D	x	56
—	—	XX T'ang (11.45)		x	56
—	—	XX Toto	L D	x	56
—	—	X Brasserie (La) (12.00)	L D	x	56
—	—	X Thierry's		x	56
—	—	X Wheelers	L D		56
—	Earl's Court	XXX Martin's		x	57
—	—	XX Brinkley's		x	57
—	—	XX Croisette (La)	L D	x	57
—	—	XX L'Olivier		x	57
—	—	XX ❀ Tiger Lee	D		57
—	Kensington	🏛 Royal Garden (Royal Roof)		x	57
—	—	XXX Ruelle (La)		x	57
—	—	XX Franco Ovest		x	58
—	—	XX Mama San	L D		57

Borough	Area	Restaurant	Sunday	11.30 p. m.	Page
–	–	XX Paesana (La) (11.45)		x	57
–	–	XX Residence (La)	L D		57
–	–	XX Topo d'Oro	L D	x	58
–	–	XX Trattoo (11.45)	L D	x	58
–	–	X Ark (The)	D		58
–	–	X Barbino (II) (12.00)		x	58
–	–	X Quai St. Pierre (Le)		x	58
–	–	X Sailing Junk	D		58
–	North Kensington	XXX Leith's (11.45)	D	x	58
–	–	XX Chez Moi		x	58
–	South Kensington	XXX Bombay Brasserie (12.00)	L D	x	59
–	–	XX Reads	L		59
–	–	X Chanterelle (12.00)	L D	x	59
Kingston	Kingston	X Ayudhya	L D		59
Lambeth	Brixton	X Au Provençal	L D		59
Redbridge	South Woodford	XX Ho Ho	L D		59
Richmond-upon-Thames	Barnes	X Il Bellamore	L D	x	60
–	Kew	XX Mange Tout (Le)	L		60
–	Richmond	XX Evergreen	L D	x	60
–	–	XX Kew Rendezvous	L D		60
Southwark	Peckham Rye	X L'Auberge	L		60
Waltham Forest	Leytonstone	X Trattoria Parmigiana		x	61
Wandsworth	Battersea	XX Alonso's		x	61
–	Clapham	X Bouffe (La)	D		61
–	–	X Jasmin	L D	x	61
–	–	X Pollyanna's (12.00)	L D	x	61
Westminster (City of)	Bayswater & Maida Vale	XX Concordia Notte (1.00)		x	62
		XX San Marino		x	62
–	–	X Concordia (11.45)		x	62
–	–	X Fortune Cookie	L D		62
–	Belgravia	🏨 Berkeley (Restaurant)	L D		62
–	Hyde Park & Knightsbridge	XXX Shezan		x	62
–	Mayfair	🏨 Claridges (Causerie)	L D		62
–	–	🏨 Inn on the Park (Four Seasons)	L D		62
		(Lanes 12.00)	L D	x	62
–	–	XXXX ❀ Soufflé (Le)	L D	x	63
–	–	XXXX Scott's	D		63
–	–	XXX Princess Garden	L D	x	63

Borough	Area	Restaurant	Sunday	11.30 p. m.	Page
–	–	XXX Tiberio (1.00)		x	63
–	–	XX Langan's Brasserie (11.45)		x	64
–	–	X Ikeda	D		64
–	Regent's Park & Marylebone	XXX Odins		x	65
–		XX Gaylord	L D	x	65
–	–	XX Loggia (La)		x	65
–	–	XX Lords Rendezvous	L D		65
–	–	XX Viceroy of India	L D	x	65
–	–	X Bois St. Jean (Au)	L D	x	65
–	–	X Barbino (II) (11.45)		x	65
–	–	X Biagi's	L D		65
Westminster (City of)	St. James's	XXXXX Maxim's de Paris (11.45)		x	66
–	–	XXXX Ecu de France (A l')	D	x	66
–	–	XX Caprice (Le) (12.00)	L D	x	66
–	Soho	XXX Leonis Quo Vadis	D		66
–	–	XX Chesa (Swiss Centre) (12.00)	L D	x	66
–	–	XX Kaya	D		66
–	–	XX Poons		x	66
–	–	XX Red Fort	L D		66
–	–	XX Rugantino		x	66
–	–	X Chiang Mai	L D	x	66
–	–	X Frith's		x	66
–	–	X Fung Shing (11.45)	L D	x	66
–	–	X Gallery Rendezvous	L D		66
–	–	X Joy King Lau	L D		67
–	–	X Saigon		x	67
–	–	X Trattoria Imperia		x	67
–	–	X Trusha		x	67
–	Strand & Covent Garden	Savoy (River)	L D		67
		(Grill)		x	67
–	–	XXX Inigo Jones		x	67
–	–	XX Chez Solange (12.15)		x	67
–	–	XX Frere Jacques		x	67
–	–	XX Interlude de Tabaillau		x	67
–	–	XX Tourment d'Amour		x	67
–	–	X Café Pelican (12.30)	L D	x	67
–	–	X Flounders		x	67
–	–	X Grimes		x	67
–	–	X Happy Wok		x	67
–	–	X Magnos Brasserie		x	67
–	–	X Poons of Covent Garden		x	67
–	Victoria	XXX Kundan		x	68
–	–	XX Ciboure		x	68
–	–	XX Gran Paradiso		x	68
–	–	XX ✿ Mazarin (Le)		x	68
–	–	XX Restaurant (The)		x	68
–	–	X Fontana (La)	L D		68
–	–	X Villa Medici (12.00)		x	68

BOROUGHS and AREAS

Greater London is divided, for administrative purposes, into 32 boroughs plus the City ; these sub-divide naturally into minor areas, usually grouped around former villages or quarters, which often maintain a distinctive character.

⊙ of Greater London : 01 except special cases.

BARNET pp. 4 and 5.

Child's Hill – ⊠ NW2.

✗ **Quincy's 84,** 675 Finchley Rd, NW2 2JP, 𝒫 794 8499 – 🔼   DV **r**
closed Saturday lunch, Sunday dinner, Monday and 1 to 14 January – **M** 12.75/13.50 **t.** and a la carte ⓕ 3.00.

Finchley – ⊠ N3/N12/NW11.

🛇 Nether Court, Frith Lane 𝒫 346 2436.

✗✗ **Luigi's Belmont,** 1-4 Belmont Par., Finchley Rd, NW11 6XP, at Temple Fortune 𝒫 455 0210, Italian rest. – 🔼 🖭 ① 𝘝𝘐𝘚𝘈   DV **a**
closed Monday, 28 March and 25 December – **M** a la carte 8.85/13.15 **t.** ⓕ 3.50.

✗✗ **Fogareiro,** 16-18 Hendon Lane, N3, 𝒫 346 0315, Seafood – 🔼 🖭 ① 𝘝𝘐𝘚𝘈   DU **c**
closed Saturday lunch, Sunday and Bank Holidays – **M** 7.35 **t.** (lunch) and a la carte 9.65/11.45 **t.** ⓕ 2.50.

✗ **La Madrague,** 816 Finchley Rd, NW11 6XL, at Temple Fortune 𝒫 455 8853, French rest. – 🖭   DV **i**
closed Sunday – **M** (dinner only) 24.00 **t.** and a la carte.

✗ Peking Duck, 30 Temple Fortune Par., Finchley Rd, NW11, 𝒫 458 3558, Chinese rest.   DV **s**

Hendon – ⊠ NW4/NW7.

🛇 off Sanders Lane 𝒫 346 6023.

🏨 **Hendon Hall,** Ashley Lane, NW4 1HF, 𝒫 203 3341, Telex 8956088, 🐴 – 📞 📺 🅿. 🛱. 🔼 🖭 ① 𝘝𝘐𝘚𝘈   DV **v**
M 9.75 **t.** and a la carte ⓕ 3.00 – ⊆ 5.25 – **52 rm** 44.00/56.00 **t.** – SB (weekends only) 60.00 **st.**

🏨 **Scratchwood TraveLodge** (T.H.F.) without rest., NW7 3HB, at Scratchwood Service Area on M 1 𝒫 906 0611, Telex 8814796 – 📺 🛏️wc 🕾 🕭 🅿. 🛱. 🔼 🖭 ① 𝘝𝘐𝘚𝘈   CU **r**
97 rm 34.00/46.00 **st.**

Mill Hill – ⊠ NW7.

🛇 100 Barnet Way 𝒫 959 2282.

✗✗ **Good Earth,** 143-145 The Broadway, NW7 4RN, 𝒫 959 7011, Chinese rest. – 🔼 🖭 ① 𝘝𝘐𝘚𝘈
closed 24 to 27 December – **M** 15.95 **t.** and a la carte ⓕ 2.80.   CU **a**

✗✗ **Taicoon,** 655 Watford Way, NW7 3JR, at Apex Corner 𝒫 959 5037, Chinese rest. – 🔼 🖭 ① 𝘝𝘐𝘚𝘈   CU **c**
closed 28 March and 25-26 December – **M** 16.80 **t.** and a la carte.

BEXLEY pp. 10 and 11.

Bexley – ⊠ Kent – ⊙ 0322 Crayford.

🏨 **Crest** (Crest), Black Prince Interchange, Southwold Rd, DA5 1ND, on A 2 𝒫 526900, Telex 8956539 – 📞 📺 🛏️wc 🕭 🅿. 🛱. 🔼 🖭 ① 𝘝𝘐𝘚𝘈   HY **e**
M (closed Saturday lunch) approx. 11.50 **st.** – ⊆ 5.75 – **78 rm** 46.50/56.50 **st.** – SB (weekends only) 51.00 **st.**

BRENT pp. 4 and 5.

Kilburn.

✗ **Vijay,** 49 Willesden Lane, NW6 7RF, 𝒫 328 1087, South Indian rest. – 🍽. 🔼 🖭 ① 𝘝𝘐𝘚𝘈
M a la carte 5.00/7.00 **t.** ⓕ 5.50.   DV **n**

Wembley − ✉ Middx.

🏌 Horsenden Hill, Whitton Av. ℘ 902 4555.

🏨 **Wembley International,** Empire Way, HA9 8DS, ℘ 902 8839, Telex 24837 − 📶 📺 ⚙ 🅿. 🏛
324 rm. CV **z**

XX **Moghul Brasserie,** 525 High Rd, HA0 4AG, ℘ 903 6967, Indian rest. − 🍽. 🖾 ÆE ⓞ 𝗩𝗜𝗦𝗔
closed Christmas Day − **M** a la carte 7.30/10.40 **t.** CV **a**

BROMLEY pp. 10 and 11.

Bromley − ✉ Kent.

🏌 Magpie Hall Lane ℘ 462 7014.

🏨 **Bromley Court** 🍸, Bromley Hill, BR1 4JD, ℘ 464 5011, Telex 896310, 🚗 − 📶 📺 ☎ 🅿. 🏛.
🖾 ÆE ⓞ 𝗩𝗜𝗦𝗔 GY **z**
M 7.50/8.50 **t.** and a la carte ⓜ 2.75 − **130 rm** ⊒ 40.00/54.00 **t.**

⌂ **Grianan,** 23 Orchard Rd, BR1 2PR, ℘ 460 1795 − 🏵wc 🅿. 🛇 GYZ **n**
12 rm ⊒ 11.50/23.00 **st.**

⌂ **Bromley Continental,** 56-58 Plaistow Lane, BR1 3JE, ℘ 464 2415, 🚗 − 🅿. 🖾 𝗩𝗜𝗦𝗔. 🛇
21 rm ⊒ 12.50/23.50 **t.** GZ **a**

XX **Chariot Wheel,** 21-22 Westmoreland Pl., Bromley South Shopping Centre, BR1 1DS, ℘
460 8477, Italian rest. − 🖾 ÆE ⓞ 𝗩𝗜𝗦𝗔 GZ **r**
closed Sunday, Monday and Bank Holidays − **M** 6.25 **t.** (lunch) and a la carte 10.75/19.00 **t.**
ⓜ 2.85.

X **Capisano,** 9 Simpsons Rd, BR2 9AP, ℘ 464 8036, Italian rest. − 🖾 ÆE 𝗩𝗜𝗦𝗔 GZ **s**
closed Sunday, Monday, 15 August-5 September and Bank Holidays − **M** 7.00 **t.** (lunch) and a
la carte 8.50/12.70 **t.** ⓜ 2.80.

X Peking Diner, 71 Burnt Ash Lane, ℘ 464 7911, Chinese rest. GY **u**

Chislehurst − ✉ Kent.

XX **Foxes,** 43 High St., BR7 5AF, ℘ 467 2094 − 🖾 ÆE ⓞ 𝗩𝗜𝗦𝗔 HY **a**
closed Saturday lunch, Sunday and Bank Holidays − **M** a la carte 13.00/15.50 **t.** ⓜ 2.60.

XX **Mario,** 53 Chislehurst Rd, BR7 5NP, ℘ 467 1341, Italian rest. − 🖾 ÆE ⓞ 𝗩𝗜𝗦𝗔 GZ **c**
closed Monday lunch, Sunday and Bank Holidays − **M** a la carte 9.80/13.70 **t.** ⓜ 2.50.

Farnborough − ✉ Kent − 🕿 0689 Farnborough.

🏌 High Elms, High Elms Rd ℘ 58175, off A 21 via Shire Lane.

XX **L'Ombrello,** 360 Crofton Rd, Locks Bottom, BR6 7XX, ℘ 52286, Italian rest. − 🖾 ÆE ⓞ 𝗩𝗜𝗦𝗔
closed Sunday − **M** 6.95 **t.** (lunch) and a la carte 8.25/14.10 **t.** ⓜ 2.50. HZ **c**

Keston − ✉ Kent − 🕿 0689 Farnborough.

XX **Giannino's,** 6 Commonside, BR4 2TS, ℘ 56410, Italian rest. − 🖾 ⓞ 𝗩𝗜𝗦𝗔 GZ **x**
closed Sunday and Monday − **M** 9.25 **t.** (lunch) and a la carte 13.35/16.35 **t.** ⓜ 2.75.

Orpington − ✉ Kent − 🕿 0689 Orpington.

🏌 Cray Valley, St. Paul's Cray ℘ 37909.

XXX **Oven d'Or,** 4a Crescent Way, BR2 1BY, ℘ 52170, French rest. − 🖾 ÆE ⓞ 𝗩𝗜𝗦𝗔 HZ **a**
closed 6 weeks summer and first 2 weeks January − **M** (dinner only) 9.95 **st.** ⓜ 4.50.

CAMDEN Except where otherwise stated see pp. 13-16.

Bloomsbury − ✉ NW1/W1/WC1.

🏨 **Russell** (T.H.F.), Russell Sq., WC1B 5BE, ℘ 837 6470, Telex 24615 − 📶 📺 ☎. 🏛. 🖾 ÆE ⓞ
𝗩𝗜𝗦𝗔 NT **o**
M (carving rest.) 9.25 **st.** and a la carte ⓜ 2.70 − ⊒ 6.50 − **316 rm** 49.50/61.50 **st.**

🏨 **Grafton,** 130 Tottenham Court Rd, W1P 9HP, ℘ 388 4131, Telex 297234 − 📶 🍽 rest 📺 ☎.
🏛. 🖾 ÆE ⓞ 𝗩𝗜𝗦𝗔. 🛇 LT **n**
M 10.75 **t.** and a la carte ⓜ 3.50 − ⊒ 6.50 − **171 rm** 59.90/78.90 **st.**

🏨 **Kenilworth,** 97 Great Russell St., WC1B 3LB, ℘ 637 3477 − 📶 📺 ☎. 🏛. 🖾 ÆE ⓞ 𝗩𝗜𝗦𝗔
M a la carte 10.25/14.75 **t.** ⓜ 3.00 − ⊒ 6.50 − **180 rm** 59.90/78.90 **st.**, **1 suite** 200.00/275.00 **st.** MT **a**

🏨 **Bonnington,** 92 Southampton Row, WC1B 4BH, ℘ 242 2828, Telex 261591 − 📶 📺 🛁wc 📶
🅔. 🏛. 🖾 ÆE ⓞ 𝗩𝗜𝗦𝗔 NT **s**
M (buffet lunch)/dinner 8.50 **t.** and a la carte ⓜ 2.95 − **242 rm** ⊒ 29.00/60.00 **t.** − SB (weekends
only) 53.00/64.00 **t.**

🏨 Kingsley (Mt. Charlotte), Bloomsbury Way, WC1A 2SD, ℘ 242 5881, Telex 21157 − 📶 📺
🛁wc ☎. 🏛. 🖾 𝗩𝗜𝗦𝗔. 🛇 NT **r**
M (*closed lunch Saturday and Sunday*) − **146 rm** ⊒ 65.00/73.00 **st.**, **1 suite** 160.00/195.00 **st.**

⌂ **Harlingford,** 61-63 Cartwright Gdns, WC1H 9EL, ℘ 387 1551 − 📺. 🖾 𝗩𝗜𝗦𝗔. 🛇 MS **n**
40 rm ⊒ 19.50/37.00 **st.**

XXX **White Tower,** 1 Percy St., W1P 0ET, ✆ 636 8141, Greek rest. – 🍽 🔺 AE ⑩ VISA   MT **u**
closed Saturday, Sunday, 3 weeks August, 1 week Christmas and Bank Holidays – **M** a la carte
11.10/22.75 t. ₰ 3.00.

XXX **L'Etoile,** 30 Charlotte St., W1P 1HJ, ✆ 636 7189, French rest. – 🔺 AE ⑩ VISA   LT **e**
closed Saturday, Sunday and Bank Holidays – **M** a la carte 14.85/27.35 t. ₰ 3.00.

XX **Neal Street,** 26 Neal Street, WC2 9PH, ✆ 836 8368 – 🍽 🔺 AE ⑩ VISA   p. 31   DV **s**
closed Saturday, Sunday and Christmas-New Year – **M** a la carte 16.30 t.

XX **Mr Kai,** 50 Woburn Pl., WC1 0JU, ✆ 580 1188, Chinese-Peking rest. – 🍽 🔺 AE ⑩ VISA
closed Bank Holidays – **M** 15.00 t. and a la carte.   MT **z**

XX **Porte de la Cité,** 65 Theobalds Rd, WC1 8TA, ✆ 242 1154, French rest. – 🍽 🔺 AE ⑩ VISA
closed Saturday and Bank Holidays – **M** (lunch only) 14.50 st. ₰ 3.00.   NT **c**

XX Lal Qila, 117 Tottenham Court Rd, W1P 9HL, ✆ 387 4570, Indian rest.   LT **u**

X **Mon Plaisir,** 21 Monmouth St., WC2H 9DD, ✆ 836 7243, French rest.   p. 31   DV **a**
closed Saturday lunch, Sunday and Bank Holidays – **M** 7.50 t. (lunch) and a la carte 7.30/12.50 t.
₰ 3.30.

Euston – ✉ NW1.

🏠 **Kennedy** (Mt. Charlotte), 43 Cardington St., NW1 2LP, ✆ 387 4400, Telex 28250 – 🛗 🍽 📺
⚲wc ☎ 🔺 AE ⑩ VISA   LS **r**
M 8.50 st. and a la carte ₰ 3.50 – 🍸 3.25 – **320 rm** 45.00/57.00 st. – SB (weekends only)
63.00 st.

Finchley Road – ✉ NW1/NW3.

🏠 **Charles Bernard,** 5 Frognal, NW3 6AL, ✆ 794 0101, Telex 23560 – 🛗 📺 ⚲wc ☎ 🅿. 🔺 AE
⑩ VISA   GR **s**
M (bar lunch)/dinner a la carte 5.80/9.00 st. ₰ 2.80 – **57 rm** 🍸 39.10/55.20 st. – SB (weekends
only) 41.00/61.00 st.

⌂ **Dawson House,** 72 Canfield Gdns, NW6 3ED, ✆ 624 0079, 🌳 – ⚘   HR **a**
15 rm 🍸 11.00/20.00 st.

XX Green Cottage II, 122a Finchley Rd, NW3 5HT, ✆ 794 3833, Chinese Vegetarian rest. – 🍽
JR **u**

X **Sheridan's,** 351 West End Lane, NW6 1LT, ✆ 794 3234 – 🔺 AE ⑩ VISA   pp. 4 and 5   DV **e**
closed Saturday lunch, Monday and 23 December-1 January – **M** 7.50/12.75 t. ₰ 3.00.

Hampstead – ✉ NW3.

🏨 Ladbroke (Ladbroke), Primrose Hill Rd, NW3 3NA, ✆ 586 2233, Telex 22759 – 🛗 📺 ☎ 🅿.
⚘ ⚘   KR **a**
84 rm.

🏠 **Swiss Cottage,** 4 Adamson Rd, NW3 3HP, ✆ 722 2281, Telex 297232, « Antique furniture
collection » – 🛗 📺 ⚲wc 🎬wc ☎ 🔺 AE ⑩ VISA. ⚘   JR **n**
M 6.00/8.00 t. ₰ 2.00 – 🍸 4.50 – **65 rm** 33.00/67.00 t., **4 suites** 67.00/80.00 st.

🏠 **Post House** (T.H.F.), 215 Haverstock Hill, NW3 4RB, ✆ 794 8121, Telex 262494 – 🛗 📺
⚲wc ☎ 🅿. 🔺 🔺 AE ⑩ VISA   GR **r**
M 7.95 st. and a la carte ₰ 2.70 – 🍸 5.50 – **140 rm** 46.00/54.00 st.

⌂ **Sandringham** 🌸, 3 Holford Rd, NW3 1AD, ✆ 435 1569, ≼, 🌳 – 🅿. ⚘   GR **u**
13 rm 🍸 18.00/36.00 st.

⌂ **Frognal Lodge,** 14 Frognal Gdns (off Church Row), NW3 6UX, ✆ 435 8238, Telex 8812714 –
🛗 ⚲wc ☎. 🔺 AE ⑩ VISA   GR **v**
17 rm 🍸 21.00/45.00 st.

XXX **Keats,** 3-4 Downshire Hill, NW3 1NR, ✆ 435 3544, French rest. – 🔺 AE ⑩ VISA   GR **i**
closed Sunday – **M** (dinner only) 19.00 st. and a la carte ₰ 10.00.

X Villa Bianca, 1 Perrin's Court, NW3 1QR, ✆ 435 3131, Italian rest.   GR **c**

X **Chateaubriand,** 48 Belsize Lane, NW3 5AR, ✆ 435 4882 – 🔺 AE ⑩ VISA   GR **n**
closed Sunday, 28 March and 24 to 26 December – **M** (dinner only) 12.00 t. and a la carte
₰ 2.50.

Holborn – ✉ WC2.

🏨 **Drury Lane Moat House** (Q.M.H.), 10 Drury Lane, High Holborn, WC2B 5RE, ✆ 836 6666,
Telex 8811395 – 🛗 🍽 📺 ☎. 🔺 🔺 AE ⑩ VISA. ⚘   p. 31   DV **c**
M 11.25 st. (lunch) and a la carte 12.15/16.20 st. ₰ 3.95 – 🍸 6.50 – **128 rm** 65.00/95.00 st. – SB
(weekends only) 74.00 st.

XXX **L'Opera,** 32 Great Queen St., WC2B 5AA, ✆ 405 9020 – 🔺 AE ⑩ VISA   p. 31   EV **n**
closed Saturday lunch and Sunday – **M** 11.45 t. and a la carte 12.50/15.15 t. ₰ 2.50.

King's Cross – ✉ N1.

🏠 **Great Northern,** N1 9AN, ✆ 837 5454 – 🛗 📺 ⚲wc ☎. 🔺 🔺 AE ⑩ VISA. ⚘   MNS **s**
closed Christmas – **M** (carving rest.) 8.50 st. ₰ 3.30 – **87 rm** 🍸 47.50/63.00 st.

Regent's Park – ⊠ NW1.

🏨 **White House** (Rank), Albany St., NW1 3UP, ℰ 387 1200, Telex 24111 – 🛗 🗐 rest 📺 ☎ &.
🖭. 🖸 🖭 ⓪ 𝘝𝘐𝘚𝘈
LS o
M a la carte 9.50/19.75 **t.** 🅗 2.75 – 🖵 6.00 – **580 rm** 56.00/79.00 **t.**, **18 suites** 100.00/280.00 **t.**

XX **Pratts,** Commercial Pl., Camden Lock, NW1 8AF, ℰ 485 9987, ≼, « Attractive setting at
Camden Lock » – 🖸 🖭 ⓪
LR a
closed Saturday lunch, Sunday dinner, Monday, 25-26 December and 1 January – **M** a la carte
10.55/14.35 **t.** 🅗 4.00.

Swiss Cottage – ⊠ NW3.

🏨 **Holiday Inn,** 128 King Henry's Rd, NW3 3ST, ℰ 722 7711, Telex 267396, 🔄 – 🛗 🗐 📺 ☎ &.
🅟. 🖭. 🖸 🖭 ⓪ 𝘝𝘐𝘚𝘈
JR a
M (buffet lunch) 12.50 (wine included) dinner/12.00 **t.** and a la carte – 🖵 6.60 – **291 rm**
78.00/101.20 **t.**, **4 suites** 182.00/225.00 **t.** – SB (weekends only) 87.00/95.00 **st.**

XX **Peter's,** 65 Fairfax Rd, NW6 4EE, ℰ 624 5804 – 🖸 🖭 ⓪ 𝘝𝘐𝘚𝘈
JR i
closed Saturday lunch and Sunday dinner – **M** 8.95 **t.** (lunch) and a la carte 9.10/13.35 **t.** 🅗 2.50.

CITY OF LONDON Except where otherwise stated see p. 16.

🛈 St. Paul's Churchyard, EC4, ℰ 606 3030 ext 2456.

XXX **Wheeler's,** 33 Foster Lane, EC2V 6HD, ℰ 606 8254, Seafood – 🖸 🖭 ⓪ 𝘝𝘐𝘚𝘈
PT o
closed Saturday, Sunday and Bank Holidays – **M** (lunch only) 11.25/26.75 **t.** 🅗 2.50.

XXX **City Tiberio,** 8-11 Lime St., EC3M 7AA, ℰ 623 3616, Italian rest. – 🗐. 🖸 🖭 ⓪ 𝘝𝘐𝘚𝘈
QU i
closed Saturday, Sunday and Bank Holidays – **M** (lunch only) a la carte 10.00/13.00 **t.** 🅗 2.75.

XX **Le Poulbot** (basement), 45 Cheapside, EC2V 6AR, ℰ 236 4379, French rest. – 🗐. 🖸 🖭 ⓪
𝘝𝘐𝘚𝘈
PU i
closed Saturday, Sunday and Bank Holidays – **M** (lunch only) 24.50 **st.**

XX **Corney and Barrow,** 118 Moorgate, EC2M 6UR, ℰ 628 2898 – 🗐. 🖸 🖭 ⓪ 𝘝𝘐𝘚𝘈
QT a
closed Saturday and Sunday – **M** a la carte 13.45/18.45 **t.** 🅗 3.50.

XX **Bill Bentley's,** Swedeland Court, 202-204 Bishopsgate, EC2M 4NR, ℰ 283 1763, Seafood –
🖸 🖭 ⓪ 𝘝𝘐𝘚𝘈
QT e
closed Saturday, Sunday and Bank Holidays – **M** (lunch only) a la carte 13.60/20.45 **t.** 🅗 3.00.

XX **Shares,** 12-13 Lime St., EC3M 7AA, ℰ 623 1843 – 🖸 🖭 ⓪ 𝘝𝘐𝘚𝘈
QU s
closed Saturday, Sunday and Bank Holidays – **M** (lunch only) 19.00 **t.**

XX **Villa Augusta,** Bucklersbury House, Queen Victoria St., EC4 9XX, ℰ 248 0095, Italian rest.
– 🖸 🖭 ⓪ 𝘝𝘐𝘚𝘈
PQU x
closed Saturday, Sunday and Bank Holidays – **M** (lunch only) a la carte approx. 13.50 **t.**

X **Bubb's,** 329 Central Market, Farringdon St., EC1A 9NB, ℰ 236 2435, French rest.
PT a
closed Saturday, Sunday, August and Bank Holidays – **M** (booking essential) a la carte
13.20/14.60 **t.** 🅗 3.50.

X **La Bourse Plate,** 78 Leadenhall St., EC3A 3DN, ℰ 623 5159, French rest. – 🖸 🖭 ⓪ 𝘝𝘐𝘚𝘈
QU v
closed Saturday and Sunday – **M** (lunch only) 15.00 **st.** 🅗 3.10.

X **La Bastille,** 116 Newgate St., EC1A 7AE, ℰ 600 1134, French rest. – 🖸 🖭 ⓪ 𝘝𝘐𝘚𝘈
PT z
closed dinner Monday and Friday, Saturday, Sunday, Christmas and Easter – **M** 13.95 **st.**
(lunch) and a la carte 13.70/17.65 **st.** 🅗 3.00.

X **Le Gamin,** 32 Old Bailey, EC4M 7HS, ℰ 236 7931, French rest. – 🖸 🖭 ⓪ 𝘝𝘐𝘚𝘈
PU a
closed Saturday, Sunday and Bank Holidays – **M** (lunch only) 16.75 **st.**

X **Ginnan,** 5 Cathedral Pl., St. Paul's, EC4M 7EA, ℰ 236 4120, Japanese rest.
PT e

CROYDON pp. 10 and 11.

Croydon – ⊠ Surrey.

🏌 🏌 🏌 Addington Court, Featherbed Lane ℰ 657 0281, E : 3 m. – 🏌 Coulsdon Court
Municipal ℰ 660 0468.

🛈 Central Library, Katherine St. ℰ 688 3627 ext 45/6.

🏨 Holiday Inn, 7 Altyre Rd, CR9 5AA, ℰ 680 9200, Telex 8956268, 🔄, squash – 🛗 📺 ⌷wc ☎
&. 🅟. 🖭. 🖸 🖭 ⓪ 𝘝𝘐𝘚𝘈
FZ u
214 rm.

🏨 Aerodrome (Anchor), Purley Way, CR9 4LT, ℰ 688 5185, Telex 893814, 🌣 – 📺 ⌷wc ☎ 🅟.
🖭. 🖸 🖭 ⓪ 𝘝𝘐𝘚𝘈. 🎾
FZ e
M a la carte 7.90/11.50 **st.** 🅗 3.00 – **85 rm.**

🏨 **Oakwood,** 69-71 Outram Rd, CR0 6XJ, ℰ 654 2835, 🌣 – 📺 ⌷wc 🛁wc 🅟. 🖸 🖭 ⓪ 𝘝𝘐𝘚𝘈
FZ s
closed 25 and 26 December – **M** (closed lunch Saturday and Sunday) (bar lunch)/dinner
7.00 **st.** 🅗 2.50 – **14 rm** 🖵 28.50/37.00 **st.**

🏨 **Briarley,** 8-10 Outram Rd, CR0 6XE, ℰ 654 1000, 🌣 – 📺 ⌷wc 🛁wc ☎ 🅟. 🖸 🖭 ⓪ 𝘝𝘐𝘚𝘈
M (closed Sunday dinner) (bar lunch Monday to Saturday) dinner 7.50 **t.** and a la carte –
19 rm 🖵 35.00/43.00 **t.** – SB (weekends only) 45.00/55.00 **st.**
FZ r

XXX **Chateau Napoleon,** Coombe Lane, CR0 5RE, ℰ 686 1244 – **ⓟ**. 🔌 🅰🅴 ⓞ 𝘝𝘐𝘚𝘈   FZ **o**
  closed Sunday dinner – **M** 8.95/9.95 **st.** and a la carte.

X **Thirty Four Surrey Street,** 34 Surrey St., CR0 1RJ, ℰ 686 0586, Seafood, Jazz Monday
  and Friday – 🔌 🅰🅴 ⓞ 𝘝𝘐𝘚𝘈   FZ **c**
  closed Saturday lunch and Sunday – **M** a la carte 7.75/15.20 **t.** ♦ 2.75.

X **Khyber,** 284 High St., CR0 1NG, ℰ 686 1729, Indian rest. – 🔌 🅰🅴 ⓞ 𝘝𝘐𝘚𝘈   FZ **i**
  M 5.50/6.50 **t.** and a la carte 5.90/11.55 **t.** ♦ 3.75.

  Sanderstead – ✉ Surrey.
  🛅 Selsdon Park Hotel, Addington Rd ℰ 657 4129.

🏨 **Selsdon Park** (Best Western), Addington Rd, CR2 8YA, ℰ 657 8811, Telex 945003, ≤,
  ⤳ heated, 🛅, 🎋, park, ⚻ – 🛗 🅣🅥 ⅙ **ⓟ**. 🔌 🅰🅴 ⓞ 𝘝𝘐𝘚𝘈   FZ **n**
  M 11.00/12.50 **st.** and a la carte ♦ 5.00 – **150 rm** ⋤ 55.00/98.00 **st.** – SB (weekends only)(not
  Easter) 80.00/120.00 **st.**

X **Elio,** 17 Limpsfield Rd, CR2 9LA, ℰ 657 2953, Italian rest. – ⓞ 𝘝𝘐𝘚𝘈   FZ **a**
  closed Sunday and Bank Holidays – **M** 8.75 **st.** and a la carte 11.25/13.35 **t.**

  Thornton Heath – ✉ Surrey.

⌂ **Dunheved,** 639-641 London Rd, CR4 6AZ, ℰ 684 2009, 🎋 – **ⓟ**. 🔌 𝘝𝘐𝘚𝘈. ⚻   FZ **v**
  closed 25 and 26 December – **15 rm** ⋤ 18.00/36.00 **st.**

EALING pp. 4 and 5.

  Ealing – ✉ W5.

🏨 **Carnarvon,** Ealing Common, W5 3HN, ℰ 992 5399, Telex 935114 – 🛗 🅣🅥 🛏wc **ⓟ** ☎ 🅐.
  🔌 🅰🅴 ⓞ 𝘝𝘐𝘚𝘈 🅐   CX **v**
  M a la carte 9.25/14.15 **st.** ♦ 3.35 – ⋤ 4.25 – **145 rm** 47.50/59.50 **st.**

🏨 **Kenton House,** 5 Hillcrest Rd, Hanger Hill, W5 2JL, ℰ 997 8436, Telex 8812544 – 🅣🅥 🛏wc
  🛐wc 🄰 **ⓟ**. 🔌 🅰🅴 ⓞ 𝘝𝘐𝘚𝘈 🅐   CX **x**
  M (bar lunch)/dinner a la carte 7.30/11.00 **st.** ♦ 1.90 – **51 rm** ⋤ 28.75/44.75 **st.** – SB (weekends
  only) 41.00 **st.**

🏨 **Montpelier** ⚘, 9 Montpelier Av., W5 2XP, ℰ 991 1508, 🎋 – 🅣🅥 🛏wc 🛐wc 🄰 **ⓟ**. 🅰🅴 𝘝𝘐𝘚𝘈.
  ⚻   BX **e**
  M (dinner only, residents only) 8.50 **st.** and a la carte – **9 rm** ⋤ 30.00/50.00 **st.**

XX **Gino's,** 4 The Mall, W5 2PJ, ℰ 567 3681, Italian rest. – 🔌 🅰🅴 ⓞ 𝘝𝘐𝘚𝘈   CX **z**
  closed Saturday lunch, Sunday, Christmas and Bank Holidays – **M** a la carte 8.25/17.25 **t.**

X **Maxim,** 153-155 Northfield Av., W13 9QT, ℰ 567 1719, Chinese-Peking rest. – 🔌 🅰🅴 ⓞ 𝘝𝘐𝘚𝘈
  closed Sunday lunch – **M** a la carte 9.00/19.00 **st.** ♦ 2.50.   BX **a**

  Hanwell – ✉ W7.
  🛅 Brent Valley, Church Rd, Hanwell ℰ 567 1287.

X **Happiness Garden,** 22 Boston Par., Boston Rd, W7 2DG, ℰ 567 9314, Chinese rest. – 🔌
  🅰🅴 ⓞ 𝘝𝘐𝘚𝘈   BX **c**
  closed lunch Sunday and Monday – **M** 12.00/15.00 **t.** and a la carte ♦ 2.30.

ENFIELD pp. 6 and 7.

  Enfield – ✉ Middx.
  🛅 Whitewebbs, Enfield Municipal, Whitewebbs Park ℰ 363 4454, N : 1 m.

🏨 **Royal Chace,** 162 The Ridgeway, EN2 8AR, ℰ 366 6500, Telex 266628, ≤, ⤳, 🎋 – 🅣🅥 ⅙ **ⓟ**.
  🅐 🔌 🅰🅴 ⓞ 𝘝𝘐𝘚𝘈. ⚻   EU **a**
  M 7.70/8.80 **st.** and a la carte ♦ 3.75 – ⋤ 4.00 – **92 rm** 35.00/46.00 **st.**

🏨 **Holtwhites,** 92 Chase Side, EN2 0QN, ℰ 363 0124, Telex 299670 – 🅣🅥 🛏wc 🛐wc 🄰 **ⓟ**. 🔌
  🅰🅴 ⓞ 𝘝𝘐𝘚𝘈   FU **c**
  M *(closed dinner Friday, Saturday and Sunday)* (bar lunch)/dinner a la carte 10.95/19.65 **t.**
  ♦ 2.50 – **28 rm** ⋤ 29.50/49.50 **t.**

XXX **Norfolk,** 80 London Rd, EN2 6HU, ℰ 363 0979 – 🔌 🅰🅴 ⓞ 𝘝𝘐𝘚𝘈   FU **e**
  closed Monday dinner, Sunday, first 3 weeks August and Bank Holidays – **M** a la carte
  9.90/16.80 **t.** ♦ 2.90.

  Hadley Wood – ✉ Herts.

🏨 **West Lodge Park** ⚘, off Cockfosters Rd, ✉ Barnet, EN4 0PY, ℰ 440 8311, Telex 24734, ≤,
  🎋, park – 🛗 🅣🅥 ☎ **ⓟ**. 🅐 🔌 🅰🅴 ⓞ 𝘝𝘐𝘚𝘈. ⚻   EU **i**
  M a la carte 8.40/16.50 **t.** – **52 rm** ⋤ 45.00/58.00 **st.**

  Southgate – ✉ N 14.

XX **L'Oiseau Noir,** 163 Bramley Rd, N14, ℰ 367 1100 – **ⓟ**. 🔌 🅰🅴 ⓞ 𝘝𝘐𝘚𝘈   EU **e**
  closed Sunday dinner, Monday and Bank Holidays – **M** a la carte 8.50/11.50 **t.** ♦ 2.00.

Winchmore Hill – ⊠ N21.

XX **Dragon Garden,** 869 Green Lanes, N21 2QS, ℰ 360 9125, Chinese rest. – 🔼 AE ⓪ 💌
closed 25 and 26 December – **M** 5.00 **t.** and a la carte approx. 7.55 **t.**　　　　　　FU **n**

MICHELIN Branch, Eley's Estate, Angel Rd, N18 3DQ, ℰ 803 7341/4

GREENWICH pp. 10 and 11.

Blackheath – ⊠ SE3.

🏛 **Bardon Lodge** without rest., 15-17 Stratheden Rd, SE3 7TH, ℰ 853 4051 – 📺 🏬 🅿. 🛠
28 rm ⊆ 20.00/34.00 **st.**　　　　　　　　　　　　　　　　　　　　GX **a**

Greenwich – ⊠ SE10.

🛈 Cutty Sark Gardens, near Greenwich Pier, SE10, ℰ 858 6376 (summer only).

XX **Le Papillon,** 57 Greenwich Church St., SE10 9BL, ℰ 858 2668 – 🔼 AE ⓪ 💌　　FX **r**
closed Saturday lunch, Sunday dinner, 4 days at Christmas and Bank Holidays – **M** 9.75 **t.**
(lunch) and a la carte 11.25/19.00 **t.** ₰ 3.75.

X **Mean Time,** 47-49 Greenwich Church St., SE10 9BL, ℰ 858 8705 – 🔼 AE ⓪ 💌　　FX **r**
closed Saturday lunch, 28 and 31 March – **M** a la carte 11.95/16.85 **st.** ₰ 3.50.

HAMMERSMITH Except where otherwise stated see pp. 17-20.

Fulham – ⊠ SW6.

XX **Hiders,** 755 Fulham Rd, SW6, ℰ 736 2331 – 🔼 AE 💌　　　　　　pp. 8 and 9　DY **s**
closed Saturday lunch, Sunday, 25 December-1 January and Bank Holidays – **M** a la carte
lunch/dinner 12.50 **t.**

XX Mao Tai, 58 New Kings Rd., Parsons Green, SW6, ℰ 731 2520, Chinese - Szechuan rest. –
▤　　　　　　　　　　　　　　　　　　　　　　　　　pp. 8 and 9　DY **o**

XX **Gastronome One,** 311-313 New Kings Rd, SW6 4RS, ℰ 731 6381, French rest. – 🔼 AE ⓪
💌　　　　　　　　　　　　　　　　　　　　　　　　pp. 8 and 9　DY **u**
closed Saturday lunch, Sunday, August and 25 December-1 January – **M** 11.00/13.00 **t.** and a
la carte 14.00/19.00 **t.** ₰ 4.00.

XX **Barbarella,** 428 Fulham Rd, SW6 1DU, ℰ 385 9434, Italian rest., Dancing – 🔼 AE ⓪ 💌
closed Sunday and Bank Holidays – **M** (dinner only) 15.00 **t.** and a la carte ₰ 2.85.　　HZ **x**

X **Perfumed Conservatory,** 182 Wandsworth Bridge Rd, SW6 1EX, ℰ 731 0732 – 🔼 AE 💌
closed Saturday lunch, Sunday, Monday, Christmas and Bank Holidays – **M** a la carte approx.
18.50 **t.**　　　　　　　　　　　　　　　　　　　　　pp. 8 and 9　EY **i**

X **Carlo's Place,** 855 Fulham Rd, SW6 5HJ, ℰ 736 4507 – ▤. 🔼 AE ⓪ 💌
closed Sunday, 24 to 30 December and Bank Holidays – **M** 5.75/9.75 **st.** and a la carte
9.85/13.85 **st.** ₰ 3.25.　　　　　　　　　　　　　　　pp. 8 and 9　DY **s**

Hammersmith – ⊠ W6/W12/W14.

🏨 **Novotel London,** 1 Shortlands, W6 8DR, ℰ 741 1555, Telex 934539 – 🛗 ▤ 📺 ☎ & 🅿. 🏩
🔼 AE ⓪ 💌　　　　　　　　　　　　　　　　　　　　　　　GY **a**
M 9.50 **st.** and a la carte – ⊆ 5.00 – **640 rm** 53.00/60.00 **st.**, **4 suites** 99.00 **st.**

X **Aziz,** 116 King St., W6, ℰ 748 1826, Indian rest. – AE ⓪ 💌　　pp. 8 and 9　CX **a**
closed Sunday and 25-26 December – **M** 6.00/10.00 **st.** and a la carte ₰ 3.60.

Shepherd's Bush – ⊠ W 12.

XX **Shireen,** 270 Uxbridge Rd, W12 8NR, ℰ 749 5927, Indian rest. – ▤. 🔼 AE ⓪ 💌
closed 25 and 26 December – **M** a la carte 7.90/9.05 **t.**　　　pp. 8 and 9　CX **n**

West Kensington – ⊠ SW6/W14.

🏨 **London West,** Lillie Rd, SW6 1UQ, ℰ 385 1255, Telex 917728 – 🛗 ▤ 📺 🛁wc ☎ 🅿. 🏩
🔼 AE ⓪ 💌. 🛠　　　　　　　　　　　　　　　　　　　　　HZ **e**
M (carving rest.) 10.25 **st.** and a la carte ₰ 3.50 – ⊆ 5.75 – **500 rm** 50.00/60.00 **st.**, **4 suites**
120.00 **st.**

HARINGEY pp. 6 and 7.

Highgate – ⊠ N6.

XX **San Carlo,** 2 High St., N6 5JL, ℰ 340 5823, Italian rest. – 🔼 AE ⓪ 💌　　　EV **v**
closed Monday and Bank Holidays – **M** a la carte 11.70/20.15 **st.** ₰ 3.25.

XX **One Hampstead Lane,** 1 Hampstead Lane, N6, ℰ 340 4444 – 🔼 ⓪ 💌　　　EV **z**
closed Sunday dinner – **M** 8.00 **t.** (lunch) and a la carte 14.45/20.45 **t.** ₰ 3.75.

Hornsey – ⊠ N8.

X **M'sieur Frog,** 36 The High St., N8 7NX, ℰ 340 2116 – 🔼 💌　　　　　　EV **u**
closed Sunday, Monday, 3 weeks August-September and Bank Holidays – **M** (dinner only)
10.50 **t.** and a la carte ₰ 2.50.

HARROW pp. 4 and 5.

Central Harrow – ⊠ Middx.

🏛 **Harrow**, 12-22 Pinner Rd, HA1 4HZ, ℰ 427 3435, Telex 917898 – 📺 🛏wc �🛏wc 📞 🄿 🛆 🗚 🖭 ⓪ 𝑉𝐼𝑆𝐴 ⚡
closed 26 December-6 January – **M** 10.50 **st.** and a la carte ⏺ 3.00 – **76 rm** ⊆ 43.00/61.50 **st.**　　　BV **a**

🏛 **Cumberland**, 1 St. John's Rd, HA1 2EF, ℰ 863 4111 – 📺 🛏wc ⏸wc 📞 🄿 🗚 🖭 ⓪ 𝑉𝐼𝑆𝐴 ⚡
M 7.95/8.95 **st.** and a la carte ⏺ 2.95 – **77 rm** ⊆ 30.00/49.00 **t.** – SB (weekends only) 52.90/67.90 **st.**　　　BV **x**

✗ **Old Etonian**, 38 High St., Harrow Hill, HA1 3LL, ℰ 422 8482 – 🗚 🖭 ⓪ 𝑉𝐼𝑆𝐴　　　BV **z**
closed Saturday lunch, Sunday and Bank Holidays – **M** a la carte 11.85/13.75 **t.** ⏺ 2.55.

Harrow Weald – ⊠ Middx.

🏛 **Grims Dyke** (Best Western) ⏃, Old Redding, HA3 6SH, ℰ 954 4227, 🚗, park – 📺 🛏wc 📞 🄿 🛆 🗚 🖭 ⓪ 𝑉𝐼𝑆𝐴　　　BU **r**
closed 25 to 29 December – **M** 10.25 **st.** and a la carte ⏺ 3.20 – ⊊ 5.75 – **48 rm** 44.00/55.00 **st.** – SB (weekends only) 83.00/93.00 **st.**

Hatch End – ⊠ Middx.

✗✗ **Canaletto 2**, 302 Uxbridge Rd, HA5 4HR, ℰ 428 4232, Italian rest. – 🗚 ⓪ 𝑉𝐼𝑆𝐴　　　BU **a**
closed Saturday lunch, Sunday and Bank Holidays – **M** a la carte 11.15/17.90.

✗ **Swan**, 322 Uxbridge Rd, ℰ 428 8821, Chinese-Peking rest. – 🗚 🖭 ⓪ 𝑉𝐼𝑆𝐴　　　BU **n**
M a la carte 12.00/15.00 **t.**

Pinner – ⊠ Middx.

✗ **La Giralda**, 66-68 Pinner Green, HA5 2AB, ℰ 868 3429 – 🗚 🖭 ⓪ 𝑉𝐼𝑆𝐴　　　AUV **n**
closed Sunday, Monday and August – **M** 6.00/9.50 **t.** ⏺ 2.55.

Groß-London (GREATER LONDON) besteht aus der City und 32 Verwaltungsbezirken (Borough). Diese sind wiederum in kleinere Bezirke (Area) unterteilt, deren Mittelpunkt ehemalige Dörfer oder Stadtviertel sind, die oft ihren eigenen Charakter bewahrt haben.

HAVERING pp. 6 and 7.

Hornchurch by A 12 – HU – on A 127 – ⊠ Essex – 🄯 040 23 Ingrebourne.

🏛 **Ladbroke** (Ladbroke), Southend Arterial Rd (A 127), RM11 3UJ, ℰ 46789, Telex 897315 – 📺 🛏wc 📞 🕭 🄿 🛆 🗚 🖭 ⓪ 𝑉𝐼𝑆𝐴
M (closed Saturday lunch)8.25/10.25 **t.** ⏺ 3.70 – ⊊ 5.75 – **137 rm** 44.00/63.00 **t.** – SB (weekends only) 94.00/114.00 **st.**

Romford by A 118 – HV – ⊠ Essex – 🄯 0708.

⌂ **Coach House**, 48 Main Rd, RM1 3DB, on A 118 ℰ 751901 – 📺 🄿 🗚 ⚡
14 rm ⊆ 17.50/28.50 **st.**

HILLINGDON pp. 4 and 8.

Eastcote – ⊠ Middx.

✗ **Sambuca**, 113 Field End Rd, HA5 1QG, ℰ 866 7500, Italian rest. – 🗚 🖭 ⓪ 𝑉𝐼𝑆𝐴　　　AV **s**
closed Sunday, mid August-mid September and Bank Holidays – **M** (dinner only) 13.50 **t.**

Heathrow Airport – ⊠ Middx.
🛈 Heathrow Central Station, London Airport ℰ 730 3488.

🏩 **Sheraton Skyline**, Bath Rd, Harlington, Hayes, UB3 5BP, ℰ 759 2535, Telex 934254, « Exotic indoor garden with ▧ » – 🛗 ▤ 📺 📞 🕭 🄿 🛆 🗚 🖭 ⓪ 𝑉𝐼𝑆𝐴 ⚡　　　AY **u**
M 6.50/8.25 **t.** and a la carte ⏺ 3.15 – ⊊ 6.45 – **354 rm** 60.00/82.00 **s.**, **5 suites** 150.00/420.00 **s.**

🏩 **Excelsior** (T.H.F.), Bath Rd, West Drayton, UB7 0DU, ℰ 759 6611, Telex 24525, 🛆 heated – 🛗 ▤ 📺 📞 🕭 🄿 🛆 🗚 🖭 ⓪ 𝑉𝐼𝑆𝐴　　　AY **x**
M 9.25 **st.** and a la carte ⏺ 2.70 – ⊊ 6.50 – **609 rm** 57.00/62.50 **st.**

🏩 **Heathrow Penta**, Bath Rd, Hounslow, TW6 2AQ, ℰ 897 6363, Telex 934660, <, ▧ – 🛗 ▤ 📺 🕭 🄿 🗚 🖭 ⓪ 𝑉𝐼𝑆𝐴　　　AY **z**
M 10.25/11.00 **st.** and a la carte ⏺ 4.75 – ⊊ 6.75 – **670 rm** 62.10/78.20 **st.**, **9 suites** 97.75/207.00 **st.**

13

🏨 **Holiday Inn,** Stockley Rd, West Drayton, UB7 9NA, ℰ 0895 (West Drayton) 445555, Telex 934518, 🏊, 🍽 – 🛗 🗏 📺 🕿 🕹 🅿. 🔬. 🖭 🖭 *VISA*
                   AX **v**
M 9.75 **st.** and a la carte ⏲ 3.00 – � 4.95 – **400 rm** 55.00/65.00 **st.**, **2 suites** 75.00/160.00 **st.**

🏨 **Sheraton Heathrow,** Colnbrook by-pass, West Drayton, UB7 0HJ, ℰ 759 2424, Telex 934331, 🏊 – 🛗 🗏 📺 🕿 🕹 🅿. 🔬. 🖭 🖭 *VISA*. 🍽
                   AXY **a**
M 5.90/7.50 **st.** and a la carte ⏲ 3.00 – ⊒ 5.50 – **405 rm** 49.50/58.50, **5 suites** 110.00/135.00.

🏨 **Skyway** (T.H.F.), 140 Bath Rd, Hayes, UB3 5AW, ℰ 759 6311, Telex 23935, 🏊 heated – 🛗 🗏 rest 📺 🕹 🅿. 🔬. 🖭 🖭 ⓞ *VISA*
                   AY **e**
M 8.50 **st.** and a la carte ⏲ 2.70 – ⊒ 6.50 – **411 rm** 44.00/50.50 **st.**

🏨 **Post House** (T.H.F.), Sipson Rd, West Drayton, UB7 0JU, ℰ 759 2323, Telex 934280 – 🛗 🗏 📺 🕿 🕹 🅿. 🔬. 🖭 🖭 ⓞ *VISA*
                   AX **c**
M 9.25 **st.** and a la carte ⏲ 2.80 – ⊒ 6.50 – **597 rm** 49.50/57.00 **st.**

🏨 **Crest** (Crest), Bath Rd, Longford, West Drayton, UB7 0EQ, ℰ 759 2400, Telex 934093 – 📺 🕿 🅿. 🔬. 🖭 🖭 ⓞ *VISA*
                   AY **s**
M *(closed Sunday)* approx. 11.50 **st.** – ⊒ 5.75 – **314 rm** 49.50/59.50 **st.** – SB (weekends only) 55.00 **st.**

🏨 **Ariel** (T.H.F.), Bath Rd, Hayes, UB3 5AJ, ℰ 759 2552, Telex 21777 – 🛗 📺 ⫶wc 🖼 🕹 🅿. 🔬. 🖭 ⓞ *VISA*
                   AY **i**
M 9.25 **st.** and a la carte ⏲ 2.80 – ⊒ 6.50 – **177 rm** 46.00/54.00 **st.**

🏨 **Arlington,** Shepiston Lane, Hayes, UB3 1LP, ℰ 573 6162 – 📺 ⫶wc ⫶wc 🖼 🅿. 🔬. 🖭 🖭 ⓞ *VISA*
                   AX **n**
M *(closed lunch Saturday and Sunday)* 8.00 **st.** and a la carte ⏲ 3.15 – ⊒ 4.00 – **80 rm** 32.50/45.00 **st.**

Hillingdon – ✉ Middx. – ☎ 0895 Uxbridge.
🛈 22 High St., Uxbridge ℰ 50706.

🏨 **Master Brewer Motel,** Western Av., Hillingdon Circus, UB10 9BR, ℰ 51199 – 📺 ⫶wc 🖼 🅿. 🔬. 🖭 🖭 ⓞ *VISA*
                   AV **a**
M (buffet lunch)/dinner a la carte 6.10/8.75 **t.** ⏲ 2.85 – ⊒ 4.00 – **64 rm** 40.00/48.00 **st.** – SB (weekends only) 50.00 **st.**

Northwood – ✉ Middx. – ☎ 092 74 Northwood – 🛅 Haste Hill, The Drive ℰ 22877.

✗✗ **Martini,** 27 Green Lane, ℰ 27052, Italian rest. – 🖭 🖭 ⓞ *VISA*
                   AU **e**
closed Sunday and Bank Holidays – **M** a la carte 8.90/15.60 **t.** ⏲ 3.60.

Ruislip – ✉ Middx. – ☎ 089 56 Ruislip – 🛅 Ickenham Rd ℰ 32004.

🏨 **Barn,** West End Rd, HA4 6JB, ℰ 36057, Telex 892514, 🌳 – 📺 ⫶wc 🖼 🅿. 🔬. 🖭 *VISA*
                   AV **u**
closed 24 December-2 January – **M** *(closed Saturday lunch and Sunday dinner)* 7.95 **st.** ⏲ 3.90 – ⊒ 3.50 – **56 rm** 29.50/57.25 **st.**

HOUNSLOW pp. 8 and 9.
🛅 Wyke Green, Syon Lane, Isleworth ℰ 560 8777, ½ m. from Gillettes Corner (A 4).

Cranford – ✉ Middx.

🏨 **Berkeley Arms** (Embassy), Bath Rd, TW5 9QE, ℰ 897 2121, Telex 935728, 🌳 – 🛗 📺 ⫶wc 🖼 🅿. 🔬. 🖭 🖭 ⓞ *VISA*. 🍽
                   AY **r**
M 10.00 **st.** and a la carte ⏲ 2.75 – ⊒ 5.00 – **41 rm** 43.00/52.00 **st.** – SB (weekends only) 43.00 **st.**

Hounslow – ✉ Middx.

🏨 **Master Robert Motel,** 366 Great West Rd, TW5 0BD, ℰ 570 6261 – 📺 ⫶wc ⫶wc 🖼 🅿. 🔬. 🖭 🖭 ⓞ *VISA*
                   BY **s**
M a la carte 6.10/8.75 **t.** ⏲ 2.85 – ⊒ 4.00 – **63 rm** 40.00/48.00 **st.** – SB (weekends only) 50.00 **st.**

ISLINGTON pp. 13-16.

Canonbury – ✉ N1.

✗ **Anna's Place,** 90 Mildmay Park, N1, ℰ 249 9379
                   pp. 6 and 7   FV **a**
closed Sunday, Monday, 1 week at Easter, August and 1 week at Christmas – **M** (booking essential) 12.00/16.00 **st.** and a la carte.

Finsbury – ✉ WC1/EC1.

🏨 **London Ryan** (Mt. Charlotte), Gwynne Pl., King Cross Rd, WC1X 9QN, ℰ 278 2480, Telex 27728 – 🛗 🗏 rest 📺 ⫶wc 🕿 🅿. 🔬. 🖭 🖭 ⓞ *VISA*. 🍽
                   NS **a**
M (bar lunch)/dinner 8.50 **t.** and a la carte ⏲ 3.25 – ⊒ 5.00 – **211 rm** 40.50/72.50.

✗✗ **Café St. Pierre,** 29 Clerkenwell Green (1st floor), EC1, ℰ 251 6606 – 🖭 🖭 ⓞ *VISA*
                   PT **t**
closed lunch Sunday Easter-September and Saturday, Sunday dinner, 25 December-1 January and Bank Holidays – **M** 12.50 **t.** (dinner) and a la carte 15.40/19.00 **t.** ⏲ 2.40.

Islington – ⊠ N1.

XX **Frederick's,** Camden Passage, N1 8EG, ℰ 359 2888, « Conservatory and walled garden » – ▤. ☒ ㏂ ⑩ ﷼
PR a
closed Sunday, 25 December, 1 January and Bank Holidays – **M** a la carte 12.00/15.95 **t.** ⅄ 3.10.

XX **Varnom's,** 2 Greenman St., N1 8SB, ℰ 359 6707 – ▤. ☒ ㏂ ⑩ ﷼
p. 6 FV c
closed Saturday lunch, Sunday dinner and Monday – **M** 8.95/12.95 **t.** and a la carte ⅄ 3.00.

XX **Portofino,** 39 Camden Passage, N1 8EA, ℰ 226 0884, Italian rest. – ▤ ☒ ㏂ ⑩ ﷼
PR o
closed Sunday, Easter, 25 December and Bank Holidays – **M** a la carte 11.10/13.95 **t.** ⅄ 2.85.

XX **Julius's,** 39 Upper St., N1 0PN, ℰ 226 4380 – ▤. ☒ ㏂ ⑩ ﷼
PR i
closed Saturday lunch, Sunday and Bank Holidays – **M** a la carte 12.75/16.60 **t.** ⅄ 2.40.

X **M'sieur Frog,** 31a Essex Rd, N1 2SE, ℰ 226 3495, Bistro – ☒ ﷼
PR n
closed Sunday, 3 weeks August, 1 week at Christmas and Bank Holidays – **M** (dinner only) a la carte 12.75/15.45 **t.** ⅄ 2.50.

KENSINGTON and CHELSEA (Royal Borough of).

Chelsea – ⊠ SW1/SW3/SW10 – Except where otherwise stated see pp. 28 and 29.

🏨 **Hyatt Carlton Tower,** 2 Cadogan Pl., SW1X 9PY, ℰ 235 5411, Telex 21944, ≤, ☞, ℅ – 🛗 ▤ ㏄ ☎ & ㉿ ☒ ㏂ ⑩ ﷼ ℅
FR n
M (see **Chelsea Room** below) – **Rib Room** 18.50 **t.** (lunch) and a la carte 21.50/29.50 **t.** ⅄ 5.00 – **217 rm** 126.00/166.00 **t.**, **30 suites** 220.00/1250.00 **s.**

🏨 **Sheraton Park Tower,** 101 Knightsbridge, SW1X 7RN, ℰ 235 8050, Telex 917222 – 🛗 ▤ ㏄ ☎ & ㉿ ☒ ㏂ ⑩ ﷼
FQ v
M 10.75 **st.** (lunch) and a la carte 16.85/29.00 **st.** – ⚏ 7.00 – **295 rm** 115.00/125.00 **s.**, **22 suites** 260.00/515.00 **s.**

🏨 ⍟ **Capital,** 22-24 Basil St., SW3 1AT, ℰ 589 5171, Telex 919042 – 🛗 ▤ ㏄ ☎ ☒ ㏂ ⑩ ﷼ ℅
ER a
M 14.50/16.50 **st.** and a la carte 20.50/27.50 **st.** ⅄ 5.00 – ⚏ 7.50 – **60 rm** 95.00/110.00 **st.**
Spec. Salade de pêcheurs tiède au Xérès, Suprême de canard au miel et au citron, Escalope de loup de mer viennoise.

🏨 **Basil Street,** 8 Basil St., SW3 1AH, ℰ 581 3311, Telex 28379 – 🛗 ㏄ ☎. ㉿ ☒ ㏂ ⑩ ﷼
FQ o
M 9.25 **st.** (lunch) and a la carte 12.25/17.00 **st.** ⅄ 3.50 – ⚏ 5.90 – **95 rm** 33.00/78.50 **st.**, **1 suite** 110.90 **st.**

🏨 **Holiday Inn,** 17-25 Sloane St., SW1X 9NU, ℰ 235 4377, Telex 919111, ☒ – 🛗 ▤ ㏄ ☎. ㉿ ☒ ㏂ ⑩ ﷼
FR r
M a la carte 12.00/15.50 **st.** ⅄ 4.20 – ⚏ 5.80 – **198 rm** 81.65/94.30 **st.**, **4 suites** 224.25 **st.**

🏨 **Cadogan Thistle** (Thistle), 75 Sloane St., SW3 9SG, ℰ 235 7141, Telex 267893 – 🛗 ㏄ ☎. ㉿ ☒ ㏂ ⑩ ﷼. ℅
FR e
M a la carte 10.50/15.00 **t.** ⅄ 3.65 – ⚏ 6.25 – **68 rm** 60.00/110.00 **st.**, **5 suites** 130.00 **st.**

🏨 **Royal Court** (Norfolk Cap.), Sloane Sq., SW1W 8EG, ℰ 730 9191, Telex 296818 – 🛗 ▤ rest ㏄ ☎. ㉿ ☒ ㏂ ⑩ ﷼. ℅
FST a
M a la carte 11.55/14.95 **t.** – ⚏ 6.50 – **98 rm** 65.00/80.00 **st.**, **5 suites** 98.00/120.00 **st.** – SB (weekends only)(except summer) 76.50 **st.**

🏨 **L'Hotel** without rest., 28 Basil St., SW3 1AT, ℰ 589 6286, Telex 919042 – 🛗 ㏄ ➡wc ☎. ㏂. ℅
ER i
12 rm 70.00/85.00 **st.**

🏨 **Wilbraham** without rest., 1-5 Wilbraham Pl., Sloane St., SW1X 9AE, ℰ 730 8296 – 🛗 ➡wc ⋔wc ☎. ℅
FS n
⚏ 3.50 – **56 rm** 24.00/52.00.

🏠 **Fenja** without rest., 69 Cadogan Gdns, SW3 2RB, ℰ 589 1183 – 🛗 ➡wc ☏. ℅
FS r
16 rm.

🏠 **Willett** without rest., 32 Sloane Gdns, Sloane Sq., SW1W 8DJ, ℰ 730 0634 – ㏄ ➡wc. ℅
FT s
17 rm ⚏ 25.00/38.00 **t.**

XXXX ⍟ **Chelsea Room** (at Hyatt Carlton Tower H.), 2 Cadogan Pl., SW1X 9PY, ℰ 235 5411 – ㉿. ☒ ㏂ ⑩ ﷼
FR n
M 16.50 **t.** (lunch) and a la carte 21.50/28.50 **t.** ⅄ 5.00
Spec. Pâté de crabe sauce rouille, Fricassée de turbot et homard aux concombres, Filet d'agneau à la crème d'ail et champignons.

XXXX ⍟ **Waltons,** 121 Walton St., SW3 2HP, ℰ 584 0204 – ▤. ☒ ㏂ ⑩ ﷼
DS a
closed Bank Holidays – **M** 12.65/20.15 **st.** and a la carte ⅄ 5.00
Spec. 'Moneybag' of chicken and asparagus, Pan-fried rosettes of beef with wild mushrooms, Little apple turnover.

XXX ⍟⍟ **La Tante Claire,** 68 Royal Hospital Rd, SW3 2HP, ℰ 352 6045, French rest. – ㏂ ⑩
EU c
closed Saturday, Sunday, 10 days at Easter, 3 weeks August-September, 10 days at Christmas-New Year and Bank Holidays – **M** 18.00 **st.** (lunch) and a la carte 25.60/31.00 **st.**
Spec. Galette de foie gras à la laitue et brunoise de légumes, Rougets rôtis au cumin et tomate-gateau de foie, Pied de cochon farci aux morilles-pomme mousseline.

XXX **Zen,** Chelsea Cloisters, Sloane Av., SW3 3DW, ℰ 589 1781, Chinese rest. – ▤. ☒ ㏂ ⑩ ﷼
ET a
closed 25 to 27 December – **M** a la carte 14.50/33.50 **t.**

XXX **Le Français,** 257-259 Fulham Rd, SW3 6HY, ☎ 352 4748, French rest. – 🖭 📷   CU **a**
closed Sunday and 4 days at Christmas – **M** 15.00 **st.** ⬥ 5.70.

XXX **Mario,** 260-262a Brompton Rd, SW3 2AS, ☎ 584 1724, Italian rest. – 🖭 🖭 ⓞ 📷   DS **n**
closed Bank Holidays – **M** 8.50 **t.** (lunch) and a la carte 15.00/23.60 **t.**

XX **Daphne's,** 110-112 Draycott Av., SW3 3AE, ☎ 589 4257 – 🖭 🖭 ⓞ 📷   DS **e**
closed Sunday and Bank Holidays – **M** (dinner only) a la carte 12.20/20.00 **t.** ⬥ 3.25.

XX La Finezza, 62-64 Lower Sloane St., SW1, ☎ 730 8630, Italian rest.   FT **v**

XX Eleven Park Walk, 11 Park Walk, SW10, ☎ 352 3449, Italian rest.   CU **r**

XX **English Garden,** 10 Lincoln St., SW3 2TS, ☎ 584 7272, English rest. – 🖽 🖭 🖭 📷
closed 28 March and Christmas Day – **M** a la carte 14.25/19.75 **st.** ⬥ 3.50.   ET **x**

XX **English House,** 3 Milner St., SW3 2QA, ☎ 584 3002, English rest. – 🖭 🖭 ⓞ 📷   ES **z**
closed 25 and 26 December – **M** 10.50/14.50 **st.** and a la carte ⬥ 3.50.

XX **Toto,** Walton House, Walton St., SW3 2JH, ☎ 589 0075, Italian rest. – 🖭 🖭 📷   ES **a**
closed Christmas – **M** a la carte 16.50/21.50 **t.** ⬥ 2.75.

XX Ponte Nuovo, 126 Fulham Rd, SW3, ☎ 370 6656, Italian rest.   CU **e**

XX ❀ **Ma Cuisine,** 113 Walton St., SW3 2JY, ☎ 584 7585, French rest. – 🖭 ⓞ   DS **a**
closed Saturday, Sunday, 10 days Easter, 14 July-14 August, 10 days Christmas and Bank Holidays – **M** a la carte 13.20/17.10 **t.** ⬥ 4.25
Spec. Galette de lotte et St Jacques au pistou, Filet de porc aux épices, Mousse brûlée.

XX **Gavvers,** 61-63 Lower Sloane St., SW1W 8DH, ☎ 730 5983, French rest. – ⓞ   FT **e**
closed Sunday, 24 December-2 January and Bank Holidays – **M** (dinner only) 18.25 (wine included) **st.**

XX **Poissonnerie de l'Avenue,** 82 Sloane Av., SW3 3DZ, ☎ 589 2457, French rest., Seafood –
🖭 🖭 ⓞ 📷   DS **u**
closed Sunday, 10 days at Christmas and Bank Holidays – **M** a la carte 13.50/17.50 **t.** ⬥ 3.50.

XX **Ménage à Trois,** 15 Beauchamp Pl., SW3 1NQ, ☎ 589 4252 – 🖭 🖭 ⓞ 📷   ER **v**
closed Sunday, 28 March, 25-26 December and Bank Holidays – **M** (booking essential) a la carte 10.40/26.25 **t.** ⬥ 3.00.

XX **St. Quentin,** 243 Brompton Rd, SW3 2EP, ☎ 589 8005, French rest. – 🖭 🖭 ⓞ 📷   DR **a**
M 8.50/12.90 **t.** and a la carte ⬥ 4.40.

XX **Bagatelle,** 5 Langton St., SW10 0JL, ☎ 351 4185, French rest. – 🖭 🖭 ⓞ 📷
closed Sunday and Bank Holidays – **M** 11.00 **t.** (lunch) and a la carte 13.80/17.50 **t.** ⬥ 2.90.
                                                      pp. 17-20   JZ **u**

XX **Pier 31,** 31 Cheyne Walk, SW3 5HG, ☎ 352 5006 – 🖽 🖭 🖭 ⓞ 📷   pp. 17-20   KZ **c**
M 11.00 **st.** (lunch) and a la carte 12.60/17.00 **st.** ⬥ 3.50.

XX **Bewick's,** 87-89 Walton St., SW3 3HP, ☎ 584 6711 – 🖭 🖭 ⓞ 📷   ES **n**
closed 28-30 March and 24 December-1 January – **M** (dinner only) a la carte 16.45/20.50 **t.** ⬥ 4.00.

XX **Meridiana,** 169 Fulham Rd, SW3 6SP, ☎ 589 8815, Italian rest. – 🖭 🖭 ⓞ 📷   DT **i**
closed Monday and Bank Holidays – **M** a la carte 16.80/23.20 **t.** ⬥ 2.90.

XX **Good Earth,** 233 Brompton Rd, SW3 2EP, ☎ 584 3658, Chinese rest. – 🖭 🖭 ⓞ 📷   DR **c**
M a la carte 8.50/17.20 **t.** ⬥ 2.40.

XX **Good Earth,** 91 King's Rd, SW3, ☎ 352 9231, Chinese rest. – 🖭 🖭 ⓞ 📷   EU **a**
closed 24 to 27 December – **M** a la carte 7.95/15.30 **t.**

XX Don Luigi, 316 King's Rd, SW3, ☎ 352 0025, Italian rest.   CU **i**

XX **T'ang,** 294 Fulham Rd, SW10 9EW, ☎ 351 2599, Oriental cuisine.   pp. 17-20   JZ **a**
closed Saturday lunch, Sunday and Bank Holidays – **M** a la carte 10.40/32.80 **t.** ⬥ 3.00.

XX **Le Suquet,** 104 Draycott Av., SW3 3AE, ☎ 581 1785, French rest., Seafood – 🖭   DS **c**
closed 2 weeks at Christmas – **M** a la carte 12.40/18.90 **t.**

XX **Beccofino,** 100 Draycott Av., SW3, ☎ 584 3600, Italian rest. – 🖭 🖭 📷   ES **r**
closed Sunday and Bank Holidays – **M** a la carte 7.20/13.20 **t.** ⬥ 2.50.

XX **San Frediano,** 62-64 Fulham Rd, SW3 6HH, ☎ 584 8375, Italian rest. – 🖭 🖭 ⓞ 📷   DT **n**
closed Sunday and Bank Holidays – **M** a la carte 10.50/13.00 **st.** ⬥ 2.60.

XX **San Ruffillo,** 8 Harriet St., SW1 9JW, ☎ 235 3969, Italian rest. – 🖭 🖭 ⓞ 📷   FQ **z**
closed Sunday and Bank Holidays – **M** a la carte 9.50/14.70 **st.** ⬥ 2.35.

X Dan's, 119 Sydney St., SW3 6NR, ☎ 352 2718 – 🖭 ⓞ 📷   DU **s**
closed Saturday lunch, Saturday dinner October-May, Sunday and Bank Holidays.

X **Wheeler's,** 33c King's Rd, SW3 4LX, ☎ 730 3023, Seafood – 🖭 🖭 ⓞ 📷   FT **u**
M 12.75 **st.** (lunch) and a la carte 14.50/19.75 **t.** ⬥ 2.50.

X Nayab, 9 Park Walk, SW10, ☎ 352 2137, Indian rest.   BU **z**

X **Thierry's,** 342 King's Rd, SW3, ☎ 352 3365, French rest. – 🖭 ⓞ 📷   CU **c**
closed Sunday, Easter, 18 to 31 August, Christmas and Bank Holidays – **M** 6.50 **t.** (restricted lunch) and a la carte 11.70/15.05 **t.** ⬥ 2.75.

X **La Brasserie,** 272 Brompton Rd, SW3 2AW, ☎ 584 1668, French rest. – 🖭 🖭 ⓞ 📷
closed 25 and 26 December – **M** a la carte 10.20/12.50 **t.** ⬥ 2.90.   DS **s**

Earl's Court – ⊠ SW5/SW10 – Except where otherwise stated see pp. 28 and 29.

🏠 **Barkston,** 34-44 Barkston Gdns, SW5 0EW, ℰ 373 7851, Telex 8953154 – 🛗 📺 ⊏wc ☎.
🔼. 🔼 AE ⓪ VISA
AT c
M (buffet lunch)/dinner 9.00 **st.** and a la carte – � 5.00 – **80 rm** 38.00/50.00 **st.**

🏠 **Hogarth,** 27-35 Hogarth Rd, SW5 0QQ, ℰ 370 6831, Telex 8951994 – 🛗 ▤ rest 📺 ⊏wc
📶wc ☎. 🔼 AE ⓪ VISA. ⋇
AS a
M (bar lunch)/dinner a la carte 6.00/9.00 **st.** ⱡ 3.00 – ⊆ 3.50 – **85 rm** 30.00/48.00 **st.** – SB
(weekends only) (November-February) 68.00/80.00 **st.**

🏠 **Town House,** 44-48 West Cromwell Rd, SW5 9QL, ℰ 373 4546, Telex 918554 – 📺 📶wc ☎.
🔼 AE ⓪ VISA
HY o
M 8.25 **st.** and a la carte ⱡ 2.25 – **40 rm** ⊆ 21.00/50.00 **st.**

XXX **Martin's,** 88 Ifield Rd, SW10 9AD, ℰ 352 5641 – 🔼 AE VISA
AU e
closed Sunday and 24 to 31 December – **M** (dinner only) 19.50 **t.** ⱡ 4.00.

XX ✿ **Tiger Lee,** 251 Old Brompton Rd, SW5 9HP, ℰ 370 2323, Chinese rest., Seafood – ▤. 🔼
AE ⓪ VISA
AU n
closed Christmas Day – **M** (dinner only) a la carte 19.80/24.50 **t.**
Spec. Prawn and Beancurd wafer appetiser, Shredded crispy fillet of eel, Sunflawer Pigeon.

XX **L'Olivier,** 116 Finborough Rd, SW10, ℰ 370 4183 – 🔼 AE VISA
AU c
closed Monday lunch, Sunday and 2 weeks at Christmas – **M** 18.00 **t.** and a la carte.

XX **Brinkley's,** 47 Hollywood Rd, SW10 9HY, ℰ 351 1683 – ▤. 🔼 AE ⓪ VISA
BU a
closed Sunday and Bank Holidays – **M** (dinner only) a la carte approx. 13.90 **t.**

XX **La Croisette,** 168 Ifield Rd, SW10 9AF, ℰ 373 3694, French rest., Seafood – AE
AU a
closed Tuesday lunch, Monday and 2 weeks at Christmas – **M** 18.00 **t.**

XX **L'Artiste Affamé,** 243 Old Brompton Rd, SW5 9HP, ℰ 373 1659 – 🔼 AE ⓪ VISA
AU r
closed Sunday, 24 to 26 December and Bank Holidays – **M** 9.50 **t.** and a la carte ⱡ 3.50.

Kensington – ⊠ SW7/W8/W11/W14 – Except where otherwise stated see pp. 17-20.

🏨 **Royal Garden** (Rank), Kensington High St., W8 4PT, ℰ 937 8000, Telex 263151, ⪦ – 🛗 ▤ 📺
☎ ⓟ 🔼. 🔼 AE ⓪ VISA. ⋇
pp. 28 and 29 AQ c
M Royal Roof (closed Sunday) (Dancing) 14.00/20.00 **t.** and a la carte – ⊆ 7.50 – **395 rm**
77.50/140.00 **st.**, **38 suites**.

🏨 **Kensington Palace Thistle** (Thistle), De Vere Gdns, W8 5RA, ℰ 937 8121, Telex 262422 –
🛗 ▤ rest 📺 ☎. 🔼. 🔼 AE ⓪ VISA
pp. 28 and 29 BQ a
M 9.00/10.50 **t.** and a la carte ⱡ 3.25 – ⊆ 5.25 – **298 rm** 54.00/85.00 **t.**

🏨 **Hilton International,** 179-199 Holland Park Av., W11 4UL, ℰ 603 3355, Telex 919763 – 🛗 ▤
📺 ☎ ⅋ ⓟ. 🔼. 🔼 AE ⓪ VISA. ⋇
GV s
M 16.00 **st.** and a la carte ⱡ 3.50 – ⊆ 6.75 – **606 rm** 53.95/82.65.

🏨 **London Tara** (Best Western), Scarsdale Pl., W8 5SR, ℰ 937 7211, Telex 918834 – 🛗 ▤ 📺
☎ ⅋ ⓟ. 🔼. 🔼 AE ⓪ VISA. ⋇
HX u
M 8.50/10.00 **st.** and a la carte ⱡ 3.40 – ⊆ 5.60 – **831 rm** 49.00/60.00 **st.**

🏨 **Kensington Close** (T.H.F.), Wrights Lane, W8 5SP, ℰ 937 8170, Telex 23914, 🔼, 🏊, squash
– 🛗 📺 ☎ ⓟ 🔼. 🔼 AE ⓪ VISA
HX c
M (buffet lunch)/dinner 11.50 **st.** and a la carte ⱡ 2.70 – ⊆ 5.50 – **530 rm** 44.00/54.00 **st.**

XXX **La Ruelle,** 14 Wright's Lane, W8 6TF, ℰ 937 8525, French rest. – ▤. 🔼 AE ⓪ VISA
HX i
closed Saturday, Sunday, Christmas, New Year and Bank Holidays – **M** 12.50 **st.** (lunch) and a la
carte 15.20/26.60 **st.** ⱡ 4.10.

XX **Le Crocodile,** 38c Kensington Church St., W8, ℰ 938 2501, French rest. – ▤. 🔼 AE ⓪ VISA
HV a
closed Saturday lunch, Sunday, first 2 weeks August and Bank Holidays – **M** 10.75/16.75 **t.** and
a la carte ⱡ 3.50.

XX **Clarke's,** 124 Kensington Church St., W8, ℰ 221 9225 – ▤. 🔼 VISA
HV c
closed Saturday lunch, Sunday, 2 weeks August-September and 1 week Christmas –
M 11.50/17.00 **st.**

XX **La Pomme d'Amour,** 128 Holland Park Av., W11 4UE, ℰ 229 8532, French rest. – ▤. 🔼 AE
⓪ VISA
GV e
closed Saturday lunch, Sunday and Bank Holidays – **M** 9.50 **t.** (lunch) and a la carte 9.00/15.60 **t.**
ⱡ 4.25.

XX **La Résidence,** 148 Holland Park Av., W11 4UE, ℰ 221 6090, French rest. – ▤. 🔼 AE ⓪ VISA
closed Saturday lunch, Monday and Bank Holidays – **M** 8.60 (lunch) and a la carte 10.30/18.00 **t.**
ⱡ 2.75.
GV z

XX **La Paesana,** 30 Uxbridge St., W8 7TA, ℰ 229 4332, Italian rest. – ▤. AE ⓪ VISA
pp. 30 and 31 AZ i
closed Sunday, 28 to 30 March and 25-26 December – **M** a la carte 9.15/11.55 **t.** ⱡ 2.30.

XX **Mama San,** 11 Russell Gdns, W14, ℰ 602 0312, Chinese rest. – ▤. 🔼 AE ⓪ VISA
GX 6
closed Saturday lunch, 25 to 27 December and Bank Holidays – **M** 11.75/17.50 **t.** and a la carte
ⱡ 3.00.

XX **Hiroko** (at Hilton International H.), 179-199 Holland Park Av., W11 4UL, ℰ 603 5003, Japanese
rest. – ⓟ
GV s

XX I Ching, 40 Earls Court Rd, W8 6EJ, ℰ 937 7047, Chinese rest. – ▤
HX a

XX **Trattoo,** 2 Abingdon Rd, W8 6AF, *&* 937 4448, Italian rest. – ▤. ◪ ◭ ⓪ *VISA*   HX **e**
closed Easter and Christmas – **M** 7.50 **t.** (lunch) and a la carte 10.00/14.75 **t.** ▮ 5.00.

XX **Franco Ovest,** 3 Russell Gdns, W14 8EZ, *&* 602 1242, Italian rest. – ◪ ◭ ⓪ *VISA*   GX **u**
closed Saturday lunch, Sunday and August – **M** a la carte 12.40/17.40 **t.** ▮ 3.50.

XX **Topo d'oro,** 39 Uxbridge St., W8, *&* 727 5813, Italian rest. – ▤. ◪ ◭ ⓪ *VISA*
closed 25 and 26 December – **M** 12.00/14.00 **t.** and a la carte ▮ 2.50.   pp. 30 and 31   AZ **a**

XX Junk Two, 2-4 Thackeray St., W8 5ET, *&* 937 8508, Chinese rest.   pp. 28 and 29   AR **a**

X **The Ark,** Kensington Court, 35 Kensington High St., W8 5BA, *&* 937 4294, French rest. – ▤.
◪ ⓪ *VISA*   pp. 28 and 29   AU **s**
closed lunch Sunday and Bank Holidays, 4 days at Easter and 4 days at Christmas – **M** a la
carte 9.25/13.50 **t.** ▮ 2.50.

X **Sailing Junk,** 59 Marloes Rd, W8 6LE, *&* 937 5833, Chinese rest. – ◪ ◭ ⓪ *VISA*   HX **x**
closed 25 and 26 December – **M** (dinner only) 11.90 **t.** ▮ 3.00.

X **Le Quai St. Pierre,** 7 Stratford Rd, W8, *&* 937 6388, French rest., Seafood   HX **r**
closed Monday lunch, Sunday and 2 weeks at Christmas – **M** a la carte 12.40/18.90.

X **Il Barbino,** 32 Kensington Church St., W8, *&* 937 8752, Italian rest. – ◪ ◭ ⓪ *VISA*   HV **o**
closed Saturday lunch, Sunday and Bank Holidays – **M** a la carte 8.60/12.80 **t.** ▮ 2.50.

▐ **North Kensington** ▌ – ✉ W2/W10/W11 – Except where otherwise stated see pp. 13-16.

🏛 **Portobello,** 22 Stanley Gdns, W11 2NG, *&* 727 2777, Telex 21879, « Attractive town house in
Victorian terrace » – |≡| ▥ ⇌wc �filwc ☎. ◪ ◭ ⓪ *VISA*   GU **n**
closed 24 December-2 January – **M** (residents only) a la carte 11.75/15.20 **s.** ▮ 2.95 – ⌷ 7.50 –
25 rm 39.10/75.00 **t.**

🏛 **Pembridge Court,** 34 Pembridge Gdns, W2 4DX, *&* 229 9977, Telex 298363 – ▤ rest ▥
⇌wc filwc ☎. ◪ ◭ ⓪ *VISA*   pp. 30 and 31   AZ **n**
M *(closed Sunday and Bank Holidays)* (dinner only) a la carte approx. 10.50 **t.** ▮ 3.00 – **34 rm**
⌷ 35.00/100.00 **s.**

XXX **Leith's,** 92 Kensington Park Rd, W11 2PN, *&* 229 4481 – ▤. ◪ ◭ ⓪ *VISA*   GU **e**
closed 25-26 August and 4 days at Christmas – **M** (dinner only) 28.50 **st.**

XX **Chez Moi,** 1 Addison Av., Holland Park, W11 4QS, *&* 603 8267, French rest. – ◪ ◭ ⓪ *VISA*
closed Sunday, 2 weeks August, 2 weeks at Christmas and Bank Holidays – **M** (dinner only) a
la carte 14.50/20.75 **t.** ▮ 3.50.   pp. 17-20   GV **n**

XX **Monsieur Thompsons,** 29 Kensington Park Rd, W11 2EU, *&* 727 9957, French rest. – ◪
◭ ⓪ *VISA*   GU **a**
closed Sunday, Christmas-New Year and Bank Holidays – **M** 10.00/13.00 **t.** and a la carte
▮ 3.00.

▐ **South Kensington** ▌ – ✉ SW5/SW7/W8 – pp. 28 and 29.

🏛🏛 **Gloucester** (Rank), 4-18 Harrington Gdns, SW7 4LH, *&* 373 6030, Telex 917505 – |≡| ▤ ▥ ☎
& **℗**. 🛆. ◪ ◭ ⓪ *VISA*. ⋇   BS **r**
M 12.75/18.75 **t.** and a la carte ▮ 5.25 – ⌷ 7.00 – **531 rm** 86.50/112.00 **t.**, **12 suites** 220.00/
525.00 **t.**

🏛🏛 London International (Swallow), 147c Cromwell Rd, SW5 0TH, *&* 370 4200, Telex 27260 – |≡|
▥ ☎ **℗**. 🛆   AS **c**
416 rm.

🏛 **Gore** (Best Western), 189 Queen's Gate, SW7 5EX, *&* 584 6601, Telex 296244, « Attractive
decor » – |≡| ▥ ⇌wc filwc ☎. ◪ ◭ ⓪ *VISA*. ▮ 2.75 – ⌷ 5.50 – **56 rm** 45.00/60.00 **t.**   BR **n**
M (coffee shop) a la carte 7.00/13.50 **t.**

🏛 **John Howard,** 4 Queen's Gate, SW7 5EH, *&* 581 3011, Telex 8813397 – |≡| ▤ ▥ ⇌wc
filwc ☎. ◪ ◭ ⓪ *VISA*. ⋇   BQ **i**
M 20.00/35.00 **st.** and a la carte ▮ 6.00 – ⌷ 6.50 – **44 rm** 65.00/95.00 **st.**, **1 suite** 130.00/
190.00 **st.**

🏛 **Vanderbilt,** 76-86 Cromwell Rd, SW7 5BT, *&* 589 2424, Telex 919867 – |≡| ▥ ⇌wc filwc ☎.
◪ ◭ ⓪ *VISA*   BS **v**
M 8.75/9.75 **t.** and a la carte ▮ 3.25 – ⌷ 6.50 – **230 rm** 50.90/69.90 **st.**

🏛 **Embassy House** (Embassy), 31-33 Queen's Gate, SW7 5JA, *&* 584 7222, Telex 8813387 – |≡|
▥ ⇌wc ☜. ◪ ◭ ⓪ *VISA*. ⋇   BR **e**
M *(closed lunch Saturday and Sunday)* (restricted lunch) 6.00/10.00 **st.** ▮ 2.50 – **69 rm**
⌷ 48.00/60.00 **st.**

🏛 **Rembrandt,** 11 Thurloe Pl., SW7 2RS, *&* 589 8100, Telex 295828 – |≡| ▤ rest ▥ ⇌wc ☜.
🛆. ◪ ◭ ⓪ *VISA*   DS **x**
M approx. 12.00 **st.** and a la carte ▮ 3.50 – ⌷ 7.00 – **190 rm** 60.00/80.00 **st.**, **1 suite** 80.00/
105.00 **st.**

🏛 **Regency,** 100-105 Queen's Gate, SW7 5AG, *&* 370 4595, Telex 267594 – |≡| ▥ ⇌wc filwc
☎. 🛆. ◪ ◭ ⓪ *VISA*. ⋇   CT **e**
M 8.00 **t.** and a la carte ▮ 3.15 – ⌷ 6.50 – **200 rm** 62.00/77.00 **st.**, **2 suites** 85.00 **st.**

🏠 **Number Sixteen** without rest., 15-17 Sumner Pl., SW7 3EG, ℰ 589 5232, Telex 266638, 🚗 –
🛗 🚪wc 🛠wc ☎. 🖪 🖭 ⑩ 𝑽𝑰𝑺𝑨. ⅏   CT c
32 rm 31.00/75.00 st.

🏠 **Alexander** without rest., 9 Sumner Pl., SW7 3EE, ℰ 581 1591, Telex 917133, 🚗 – 📺 🚪wc
🛠wc ☎. 🖪 🖭 ⑩ 𝑽𝑰𝑺𝑨. ⅏   CT a
40 rm ⊊ 40.00/75.00 st.

XXX **Bombay Brasserie,** Courtfield Close, 140 Gloucester Rd, SW7 4QH, ℰ 370 4040, Indian
rest. – 🖪 🖭 𝑽𝑰𝑺𝑨   BS a
M (buffet lunch) 8.95/17.50 **t.** and a la carte ⓙ 5.95.

XX **Reads,** 152 Old Brompton Rd, SW5 0BE, ℰ 373 2445 – 🖪 🖭 ⑩ 𝑽𝑰𝑺𝑨   BT a
closed Sunday dinner, 2 weeks Christmas-New Year and Bank Holidays – **M** 12.50 **t.** (lunch)
and a la carte 16.90/20.80 **t.**

XX **Hilaire,** 68 Old Brompton Rd, SW7, ℰ 584 8993 – 🖪 🖭 ⑩ 𝑽𝑰𝑺𝑨   CT n
closed Saturday lunch, Sunday and Bank Holidays – **M** (booking essential) 12.50/21.50 **t.**

XX Non-Ya, 73 Old Brompton Rd, SW7 3JS, ℰ 584 4323, Oriental cuisine – 🍽   CT i

XX Memories of India, 18 Gloucester Rd, SW7 4RB, ℰ 589 6450, Indian rest.   BR s

XX Pun, 53 Old Brompton Rd, SW7, ℰ 225 1609, Chinese rest. – 🍽   CST r

X **Chanterelle,** 119 Old Brompton Rd, SW7 3RN, ℰ 373 5522 – 🖪 🖭 ⑩ 𝑽𝑰𝑺𝑨   BT v
closed 4 days at Christmas – **M** 7.00/11.00 **t.** ⓙ 3.35.

KINGSTON UPON THAMES p. 9.

🛈 Heritage Centre, Fairfield West ℰ 546 5386.

Kingston – ✉ Surrey.

X **Ayudhya,** 14 Kingston Hill, KT2 7NH, ℰ 549 5984, Thai rest. – 🖭 ⑩ 𝑽𝑰𝑺𝑨   CYZ z
closed Tuesday lunch – **M** a la carte 8.70/12.20 **t.** ⓙ 2.45.

Surbiton – ✉ Surrey.

XX **Chez Max,** 85 Maple Rd, KT6 4AW, ℰ 399 2365 – 🖪 🖭 ⑩ 𝑽𝑰𝑺𝑨   BZ o
closed Saturday lunch, Sunday, Monday, 2 weeks August-September and 2 weeks after Christmas – **M** (booking essential) 15.00/20.00 **t.** and a la carte.

LAMBETH pp.10 and 11.

Brixton – ✉ SW9/SE24.

X **Twenty Trinity Gardens,** 20 Trinity Gdns., SW9 8DP, ℰ 733 8838 – 𝑽𝑰𝑺𝑨   EY n
closed Saturday lunch, Sunday and 25-26 December – **M** 11.50 **t.** ⓙ 2.50.

X **Au Provençal,** 295 Railton Rd, SE24 0JP, ℰ 274 9163 – 🖪 𝑽𝑰𝑺𝑨   FY i
M (dinner only and Sunday lunch)/dinner 8.95 **t.** and a la carte ⓙ 3.45.

LONDON HEATHROW AIRPORT – see Hillingdon, London p. 51.

MERTON pp. 8 and 9.

Merton – ✉ SW19.

X Les Amoureux, 156 Merton Hall Rd, SW19 3PZ, ℰ 543 0567.   DZ a

Wimbledon – ✉ SW19.

↑ **Worcester House,** 38 Alwyne Rd, SW19 7AE, ℰ 946 1300 – 📺 🛠wc. ⅏   DY r
9 rm ⊊ 21.00/38.00.

XX San Lorenzo Fuoriporta, 38 Worple Rd Mews, SW19 4DB, ℰ 946 8463, Italian rest.   DY n

MICHELIN Branch, Deer Park Rd, Merton, SW19 3UD, ℰ 540 9034/7 South London Branch (Merton)
p. 9

REDBRIDGE pp. 6 and 7.

South Woodford – ✉ Essex.

XX **Ho-Ho,** 20 High Rd, E18 2QL, ℰ 989 1041, Chinese rest. – 🖪 🖭 ⑩ 𝑽𝑰𝑺𝑨   GV c
M 6.00/16.00 **t.**

Woodford – ✉ Essex.

🏛 **Woodford Moat House** (Q.M.H.), Oak Hill, Woodford Green, IG8 9NY, ℰ 505 4511 – 🛗 📺
🚪wc 🛠wc 🏤 🅿. 🛓. 🖪 🖭 ⑩ 𝑽𝑰𝑺𝑨   GU c
M (bar lunch Saturday) 8.20 **t.** and a la carte – **99 rm** ⊊ 42.50/52.00 st. – SB (weekends only)
50.00 st.

🏛 Prince Regent, Manor Rd, Woodford Bridge, IG8 8AE, E : ¾ m. ℰ 504 7635, 🚗 – 🍽 📺
🚪wc 🛠wc 🏤 🅿. 🛓. ⅏ – **10 rm**.   GU a

RICHMOND-UPON-THAMES pp. 8 and 9.

Barnes – ⊠ SW13.

✗ **Barnaby's,** 39b High St., SW13 9LN, ✆ 878 4750, French rest. CY **v**
closed lunch Saturday and Monday, Sunday, Easter; 3 weeks September, Christmas and Bank Holidays – **M** a la carte 10.95/14.05 **st.** ₪ 2.80.

✗ **Il Bellamore,** 5 White Hart Lane, SW13 0PX, ✆ 876 3335, Italian rest. – ◪ 쬬 ⓞ 𝘝𝘐𝘚𝘈
M 7.50 **st.** and a la carte ₪ 2.10. CY **o**

East Sheen – ⊠ Surrey.

✗✗ **Crowther's,** 481 Upper Richmond Rd West, SW14 7PU, ✆ 876 6372 – ◪ 쬬 CY **n**
closed Saturday lunch, Sunday, Monday, 1 week February, 2 weeks August and 26 to 31 December – **M** (booking essential) 16.00 **t.** and a la carte ₪ 3.00.

Kew – ⊠ Surrey.

✗✗ **Le Mange Tout,** 3 Royal Par. (Station Approach), TW9 3QB, ✆ 940 9304 – ▤. ◪ 쬬 ⓞ 𝘝𝘐𝘚𝘈
closed Saturday lunch, Sunday dinner, 25 and 26 December and 1 and 2 January – **M** 9.85 **t.**
and a la carte ₪ 2.65. CY **r**

✗ **Jasper's Bun in the Oven,** 11 Kew Green, TW9 3AA, ✆ 940 3987 – ◪ 쬬 ⓞ 𝘝𝘐𝘚𝘈 CX **e**
closed Sunday and Bank Holidays – **M** 9.50 **t.** and a la carte ₪ 3.20.

Richmond – ⊠ Surrey.

🛆, 🛆 Richmond Park ✆ 876 3205 – 🛈 Central Library, Little Green ✆ 940 9125.

🏛 **Richmond Gate,** Richmond Hill, TW10 6RP, ✆ 940 0061, Telex 928556, 🌫 – 📺 ⌂wc ☎
ⓟ. 🛆. ◪ 쬬 ⓞ 𝘝𝘐𝘚𝘈. ⅏ CY **a**
M (restricted lunch)/dinner 11.25 **st.** and a la carte ₪ 3.50 – **49 rm** ⌷ 55.00/80.00 **st.** – SB (weekends only) 70.00 **st.**

🏛 **Petersham,** Nightingale Lane, Richmond Hill, TW10 6RP, ✆ 940 7471, Telex 928556, ≤ – 📶
📺 ⌂wc ☎ ⓟ. 🛆. ◪ 쬬 ⓞ 𝘝𝘐𝘚𝘈. ⅏ CY **c**
M *(closed lunch on Bank Holidays and Saturday)* 11.00 **st.** and a la carte ₪ 3.50 – **52 rm**
⌷ 55.00/65.00 **st.** – SB (weekends only) 70.00 **st.**

✗✗ ❀ **Lichfield's,** 13 Lichfield Terr., Sheen Rd, TW9 1DP, ✆ 940 5236 – ▤. ◪ 쬬 CY **i**
closed Saturday lunch, Sunday, Monday, 26 May-1 June, first 2 weeks September and 1 week at Christmas – **M** (booking essential) 14.00 **st.** (lunch) and a la carte approx. 22.25 **st.** ₪ 3.50
Spec. Hot tart of foie gras and apples, Game (in season), Salmon with confit of onions (April-October).

✗✗ **Kew Rendezvous,** 110 Kew Rd, TW9 2PQ, ✆ 948 4343, Chinese-Peking rest. – ▤. ◪ 쬬
ⓞ 𝘝𝘐𝘚𝘈 CY **e**
closed 25 and 26 December – **M** 12.00 **st.** and a la carte.

✗✗ **Evergreen,** 102-104 Kew Rd, TW9 2PQ, ✆ 940 9044, Chinese rest. – ▤. ◪ 쬬 ⓞ 𝘝𝘐𝘚𝘈
closed 25 to 27 December – **M** a la carte 5.60/8.10 **t.** ₪ 3.70. CY **e**

✗ Red Lion, 18 Red Lion St., TW9 1RW, ✆ 940 2371, Chinese-Peking rest. CY **s**

Twickenham – ⊠ Middx.

🛈 District Library, Garfield Rd ✆ 892 0032.

✗✗ **Cézanne,** 68 Richmond Rd, TW1 3BE, ✆ 892 3526 – ◪ 쬬 𝘝𝘐𝘚𝘈 BY **a**
closed Saturday lunch, Sunday and 1 week at Christmas – **M** a la carte 9.00/12.60 **t.** ₪ 2.15.

SOUTHWARK pp. 10 and 11.

Dulwich Village – ⊠ SE21.

✗✗ **Luigi's,** 129 Gipsy Hill, SE19 1QS, ✆ 670 1843, Italian rest. – ◪ 쬬 ⓞ 𝘝𝘐𝘚𝘈 FY **a**
closed Saturday lunch, Sunday, August and Bank Holidays – **M** a la carte 11.30/14.85 **t.** ₪ 3.80.

East Dulwich – ⊠ SE22.

✗ Mr Lui, 148 Lordship Lane, SE22, ✆ 693 8266, Chinese-Peking rest. – ▤ FY **r**

Peckham Rye – ⊠ SE22.

✗ **L'Auberge,** 44 Forest Hill Rd, SE22, ✆ 299 2211, French rest. FY **s**
closed Sunday dinner, Monday and 3 weeks August – **M** (dinner only and Sunday lunch)/dinner 11.95 **st.**

SUTTON pp. 8 and 9 – 🛆 Oak Sports Centre, Woodmansterne Rd, Carshalton ✆ 643 8363.

Sutton – ⊠ Surrey.

⌂ **Dene,** 39 Cheam Rd, SM1 2AT, ✆ 642 3170, 🌫 – 📺 ⌂wc ⍒wc ⓟ. 𝘝𝘐𝘚𝘈. ⅏ EZ **v**
17 rm ⌷ 13.80/39.10 **t.**

✗✗ **Partners 23,** 23 Stonecot Hill, SM3 9HB, ✆ 644 7743 – ◪ 쬬 ⓞ 𝘝𝘐𝘚𝘈 DZ **z**
closed Saturday lunch, Sunday, Monday and 25 December-2 January – **M** (booking essential) 16.50/14.50 **t.** ₪ 3.00.

WALTHAM FOREST pp. 6 and 7 – ▮₈ at Chingford, 158 Station Rd ℰ 529 5708.

    Leytonstone – ✉ E11.

✗ **Trattoria Parmigiana**, 715 High Rd, E11 4RD, ℰ 539 1700, Italian rest. – ◪ ▲ⅇ Ⓞ ⱽⁱˢᵃ
closed Sunday and Bank Holidays – **M** a la carte 9.50/13.50 **t.** ⒜ 2.90.   GV **a**

WANDSWORTH pp. 8 and 9.

    Battersea – ✉ SW8/SW11.

✗✗ ✿ **Chez Nico,** 129 Queenstown Rd, SW8 3RH, ℰ 720 6960, French rest. – ◪ Ⓞ ⱽⁱˢᵃ   EY **c**
closed Saturday , Sunday, 4 days at Easter, 3 weeks July-August, 10 days at Christmas and Bank Holidays – **M** (booking essential) 19.50 **st.** (lunch) and a la carte 25.00/31.25 **st.** ⒜ 4.75
Spec. Escalope barbue en feuilleté garni crabe et gingembre au beurre blanc, Ris de veau rôti au lard avec sa sauce truffe, Mousse légère d'oranges avec sa sauce au zeste.

✗✗ **Alonso's,** 32 Queenstown Rd, SW8 3RX, ℰ 720 5986 – ◪ ▲ⅇ Ⓞ ⱽⁱˢᵃ   EY **e**
closed Saturday lunch, Sunday and Bank Holidays – **M** 8.15/13.75 **t.** and a la carte.

✗✗ **Lampwicks,** 24 Queenstown Rd, SW8 3RX, ℰ 622 7800 – ▤ ◪ ▲ⅇ Ⓞ ⱽⁱˢᵃ   EY **s**
closed Sunday, last 2 weeks August and Christmas – **M** 10.50/17.50 **t.** ⒜ 3.50.

✗✗ ✿ **L'Arlequin,** 123 Queenstown Rd, SW8, ℰ 622 0555, French rest. – ▤ ◪ Ⓞ ⱽⁱˢᵃ   EY **o**
closed Saturday, Sunday, 3 weeks August and 2 weeks at Christmas – **M** 11.50 **st.** (lunch) and a la carte 23.20/27.50 **st.** ⒜ 6.50
Spec. Persillé de ris de veau et homard, Rable de lièvre aux betteraves (October-February), Délice au cassis.

    Clapham – ✉ SW11.

✗ **Pollyanna's,** 2 Battersea Rise, SW11 1ED, ℰ 228 0316, Bistro – ◪ ▲ⅇ Ⓞ ⱽⁱˢᵃ   EY **a**
closed 24 to 27 December and 1 January – **M** (dinner only and Sunday lunch)/dinner a la carte 11.60/14.85 **t.** ⒜ 2.80.

✗ **Jasmin,** 50 Battersea Rise, SW11 1EG, ℰ 228 0336, Chinese rest. – ◪ ▲ⅇ Ⓞ ⱽⁱˢᵃ   EY **z**
M 10.00/13.00 **st.** and a la carte ⒜ 2.00.

✗ **La Bouffe,** 13 Battersea Rise, SW11 1HG, ℰ 228 3384 – ◪ ⱽⁱˢᵃ   EY **v**
closed lunch Saturday and Sunday, Bank Holiday Sundays and 23 December-5 January – **M** 10.95 **t.** (dinner) and a la carte ⒜ 2.15.

WESTMINSTER (City of)

    Bayswater and Maida Vale – ✉ W2/W9 – Except where otherwise stated see pp. 30 and 31.

🏨 **Royal Lancaster** (Rank), Lancaster Terr., W2 2TY, ℰ 262 6737, Telex 24822, ≤ – 🛗 ▤ rest
📺 ⛛ 🄿 ⒜ ◪ ▲ⅇ ⱽⁱˢᵃ ⊰   DZ **e**
M *(closed Saturday lunch and Sunday)* 11.50/14.95 **t.** and a la carte ⒜ 4.75 – � 7.00 – **418 rm** 85.00/125.00 **st.**, **27 suites** 250.00/815.00 **st.**

🏨 **London Metropole,** Edgware Rd, W2 1JU, ℰ 402 4141, Telex 23711, ≤ – 🛗 ▤ 📺 ☎ 🄿.
⒜ ◪ ▲ⅇ Ⓞ ⱽⁱˢᵃ ⊰   pp. 13-16   JT **c**
M (dinner only) a la carte approx. 18.00 **t.** – ⊰ 7.25 – **586 rm** 58.50/75.00 **st.**, **9 suites**.

🏨 **Hospitality Inn** (Mt. Charlotte), 104 Bayswater Rd, W2 3HL, ℰ 262 4461, Telex 22667, ≤ –
🛗 📺 ☎ 🄿. ⒜ ◪ ▲ⅇ Ⓞ ⱽⁱˢᵃ   CZ **n**
M 6.50/9.50 **t.** and a la carte ⒜ 3.50 – ⊰ 6.25 – **175 rm** 52.50/85.00 **t.**, **1 suite** 140.00/180.00 **t.**

🏨 **White's** (Mt. Charlotte), Bayswater Rd, 90-92 Lancaster Gate, W2 3NR, ℰ 262 2711, Telex
24771 – 🛗 📺 ⌧wc ☎ 🄿. ⒜ ◪ ▲ⅇ Ⓞ ⱽⁱˢᵃ   CZ **v**
M 17.00/19.00 **t.** and a la carte ⒜ 4.00 – ⊰ 5.75 – **61 rm** 55.00/115.00 **st.** – SB (weekends only) 85.00/100.00 **st.**

🏨 **London Embassy** (Embassy), 150 Bayswater Rd, W2 4RT, ℰ 229 1212, Telex 27727 – 🛗 ▤
📺 ⌧wc ☎ & 🄿. ⒜ ◪ ▲ⅇ Ⓞ ⱽⁱˢᵃ ⊰   BZ **o**
M (carving rest.) 9.50 **st.** and a la carte ⒜ 2.75 – ⊰ 5.00 – **192 rm** 54.00/76.00 **st.**, **1 suite** 95.00/105.00 **st.**

🏨 **Colonnade,** 2 Warrington Cres., W9 1ER, ℰ 286 1052, Telex 298930 – 🛗 📺 ⌧wc �𝚏wc ≋.
◪ ▲ⅇ Ⓞ ⱽⁱˢᵃ ⊰   pp. 13-16   JT **e**
M (dinner only) 7.95 **t.** ⒜ 2.50 – **53 rm** ⊰ 28.50/49.50 **t.**

🏨 **Mornington Lancaster** (Best Western) without rest., 12 Lancaster Gate, W2 3LG, ℰ
262 7361, Telex 24281 – 🛗 📺 ⌧wc ☎. ◪ ▲ⅇ Ⓞ ⱽⁱˢᵃ   DZ **s**
closed Christmas – ⊰ 3.00 – **65 rm** 30.00/52.00 **st.**

⬠ **Dylan,** 14 Devonshire Terr., Lancaster Gate, W2 3DW, ℰ 723 3280 – ⌧wc 𝚏wc. ▲ⅇ Ⓞ ⱽⁱˢᵃ
⊰   CY **c**
18 rm ⊰ 18.00/36.00 **t.**

⬠ **Parkwood,** 4 Stanhope Pl., W2 2HB, ℰ 402 2241, Group Telex 8812714 – 📺 ⌧wc ☎. ≋
18 rm.   FY **e**

⬠ **Allandale,** 3 Devonshire Terr., Lancaster Gate, W2 3DN, ℰ 723 8311 – 📺 ⌧wc 𝚏wc. ◪
Ⓞ ⱽⁱˢᵃ ⊰   CY **a**
20 rm ⊰ 12.00/30.00.

XXX Bombay Palace, 50 Connaught St., Hyde Park Sq., W2, ℰ 723 8855, North Indian rest. EY **a**

XX **San Marino,** 26 Sussex Pl., W2 2TH, ℰ 723 8395, Italian rest. – ⬛ AE ⓘ VISA EY **u**
closed Sunday and Bank Holidays – **M** a la carte 12.30/15.00 **t.** ⓵ 3.80.

XX Trat West, 143 Edgware Rd, W2 2HR, ℰ 723 8203, Italian rest. pp. 13-16 KT **i**

XX **Concordia Notte,** 29-31 Craven Rd, W2 3BX, ℰ 402 4985, Italian rest., Dancing – ⬛ AE ⓘ
VISA DY **r**
closed Sunday, August, 24 December and Bank Holidays – **M** (dinner only) a la carte
16.00/27.00 **t.** ⓵ 4.50.

XX **Canaletto da Leo,** 451 Edgware Rd, W2 1TH, ℰ 262 7027, Italian rest. – ⬛ AE ⓘ VISA
closed Saturday lunch, Sunday and Bank Holidays – **M** a la carte 9.85/15.25 **t.** ⓵ 3.20.
pp. 13-16 JT **v**

X **Concordia,** 29-31 Craven Rd, W2 3BX, ℰ 723 3725, Italian rest. – **M** a la carte 10.50/13.00 **t.** ⓵ 2.40. DY **r**
closed Sunday, 24 December and Bank Holidays

X **Fortune Cookie,** 1 Queensway, W2 4QJ, ℰ 727 7260, Chinese rest. – ⬛ VISA BZ **v**
M 9.00 **t.** and a la carte ⓵ 2.25.

X Kalamaras Taverna, 76-78 Inverness Mews, W2 3JQ, ℰ 727 9122, Greek rest. BY **a**

■ **Belgravia** – ✉ SW1 – Except where otherwise stated see pp. 28 and 29.

🏨 Berkeley, Wilton Pl., SW1X 7RL, ℰ 235 6000, Telex 919252, ⬛ – 🛗 ☰ TV ☎ � ⇔. 🅰️. ⬛
AE ⓘ VISA 🕸 FQ **e**
M Restaurant (closed Saturday) a la carte approx. 21.00 **st.** – **Buttery** (closed Sunday and
August) a la carte 16.50/20.75 **st.** – **160 rm**, **26 suites**.

🏨 **Lowndes Thistle** (Thistle), 21 Lowndes St., SW1X 9ES, ℰ 235 6020, Telex 919065 – 🛗 TV
⬛ AE ⓘ VISA 🕸 FR **i**
M 13.75 **t.** and a la carte – ⊇ 6.75 – **79 rm** 78.00/120.00 **st.**, **5 suites**.

🏨 **Sheraton-Belgravia,** 20 Chesham Pl., SW1X 8HQ, ℰ 235 6040, Telex 919020 – 🛗 ☰ TV ☎.
⬛ AE ⓘ VISA 🕸 FR **u**
M (closed lunch Saturday and Bank Holidays) 15.00 **t.** (lunch) and a la carte 12.25/16.25 **t.**
⓵ 3.50 – ⊇ 7.00 – **89 rm** 97.00/112.00 **t.**, **7 suites** 170.00/200.00 **t.**

XX **Motcombs,** 26 Motcomb St., SW1X 8JU, ℰ 235 6382 – ⬛ AE ⓘ VISA FR **z**
closed Sunday, Easter, Christmas and Bank Holiday Mondays – **M** a la carte 11.25/14.50 **t.**
⓵ 2.70.

XX **Salloos,** 62-64 Kinnerton St., SW1 8ER, ℰ 235 4444, Indian and Pakistani rest. – ☰. ⬛ AE
ⓘ VISA – closed Sunday and Bank Holidays – **M** a la carte 14.80/18.80 **t.** ⓵ 2.50. FQ **a**

■ **Hyde Park and Knightsbridge** – ✉ SW1/SW7 – pp. 28 and 29.
🔳 Harrods, Knightsbridge, SW1 ℰ 730 3488.

🏨 **Hyde Park** (T.H.F.), 66 Knightsbridge, SW1Y 7LA, ℰ 235 2000, Telex 262057, ⬉ – 🛗 ☰ TV
☎. 🅰️. ⬛ AE ⓘ VISA EQ **v**
M (closed Saturday) 14.50/19.50 **st.** and a la carte ⓵ 5.50 – ⊇ 9.00 – **180 rm** 115.00/129.00 **st.**,
20 suites.

XXX **Shezan,** 16-22 Cheval Pl., Montpelier St., SW7 1ES, ℰ 589 7918, Indian and Pakistani rest. –
☰. ⬛ AE ⓘ VISA ER **c**
closed Sunday and Bank Holidays – **M** 14.00/16.00 **t.** and a la carte.

XX Montpeliano, 13 Montpelier St., SW7 1HQ, ℰ 589 0032, Italian rest. ER **e**

■ **Mayfair** – ✉ W1 – pp. 26 and 27.

🏨 **Claridge's,** Brook St., W1A 2JQ, ℰ 629 8860, Telex 21872 – 🛗 ☰ TV ☎ �. ⬛ AE ⓘ VISA. 🕸
M a la carte 21.50/24.50 **st.** ⓵ 3.30 – **Causerie** – ⊇ 11.00 – **205 rm** 100.00/175.00 **st.**, **55 suites**
275.00/550.00 **st.** BL **c**

🏨 **Dorchester,** Park Lane, W1A 2HJ, ℰ 629 8888, Telex 887704 – 🛗 ☰ TV ☎ �. ⇔. 🅰️. 🕸
M (see The Terrace below) – **Grill** 16.00 **st.** and a la carte – ⊇ 9.50 – **280 rm** 105.00/160.00 **st.**,
66 suites 250.00/500.00 **st.** BN **z**

🏨 **Grosvenor House** (T.H.F.), Park Lane, W1A 3AA, ℰ 499 6363, Telex 24871, ⬛ – 🛗 TV ☎ �.
🅿️. 🅰️. ⬛ AE ⓘ VISA. 🕸 AM **a**
M (see 90 Park Lane below) – ⊇ 6.50 – **472 rm** 102.00/118.00 **st.**, **50 suites**.

🏨 **Inn on the Park,** Hamilton Pl., Park Lane, W1A 1AZ, ℰ 499 0888, Telex 22771 – 🛗 ☰ TV ☎
�. 🅰️. ⬛ AE ⓘ VISA. 🕸 BP **a**
M Four Seasons 20.50/22.50 **st.** and a la carte ⓵ 6.50 – **Lanes** 21.00 **st.** (lunch) and a la carte
20.50/22.50 **st.** ⓵ 6.50 – ⊇ 7.50 – **228 rm** 130.00/162.00 **s.**, **19 suites** 260.00/607.00 **s.**

🏨 **New Piccadilly,** Piccadilly, W1V 0BH, ℰ 734 8000, Telex 25795, ⬛, squash – 🛗 ☰ TV ☎
�. 🅰️. ⬛ AE ⓘ VISA. 🕸 EM **a**
M 14.00/28.00 **st.** and a la carte ⓵ 5.50 – **290 rm** 105.00/130.00 **st.**, **19 suites** 150.00/350.00 **st.**

🏨 ❀ Connaught, 16 Carlos Pl., W1Y 6AL, ℰ 499 7070 – 🛗 ☰ rest TV ☎. ⬛. 🕸 BM **e**
M (booking essential) – **90 rm**, **25 suites**
Spec. Pâté de turbot froid au homard, sauce pudeur, Rendez-vous du pêcheur, sauce légère au parfum d'Armo-
rique, Salmis de canard strasbourgeoise en surprise.

🏨 **Athenaeum** (Rank), 116 Piccadilly, W1V 0BJ, ℰ 499 3464, Telex 261589 – 🛗 ☰ rest TV ☎.
🅰️. ⬛ AE ⓘ VISA. 🕸 CP **s**
M 16.50 **st.** (lunch) and a la carte 19.05/24.45 **st.** ⓵ 4.00 – ⊇ 8.00 – **112 rm** 108.00/150.00 **st.**,
22 suites 180.00/220.00 **st.** – SB (weekends only) 90.00/100.00 **st.**

🏨 **Brown's** (T.H.F.), 29-34 Albemarle St., W1A 4SW, ✆ 493 6020, Telex 28686 – 🔁 📺 🕾. 🅰.
🔄 AE 🅾 VISA
DM **e**
M 22.00/23.00 **st.** and a la carte 🍷 4.25 – ⊐ 8.00 – **125 rm** 88.00/113.00 **st.**, **5 suites**.

🏨 **May Fair** (Inter-Con.), Stratton St., W1A 2AN, ✆ 629 7777, Telex 262526 – 🔁 🔲 🕾. 🅰.
🔄 AE 🅾 VISA. 🛠
DN **z**
M 15.00/18.00 **t.** and a la carte 🍷 5.50 – ⊐ 8.10 – **327 rm** 90.00/125.00, **24 suites** 175.00/700.00.

🏨 **Marriott**, Duke St., Grosvenor Sq., W1A 4AW, ✆ 493 1232, Telex 268101 – 🔁 🔲 📺 🕾 🔄
🅿. 🅰. 🔄 AE 🅾 VISA
BL **a**
M 17.50 **t.** and a la carte 🍷 4.50 – ⊐ 8.00 – **229 rm** 115.00/140.00 **t.**, **18 suites** 230.00/805.00 **t.**

🏨 **Inter-Continental** (Inter-Con.), 1 Hamilton Pl., Hyde Park Corner, W1V 0QY, ✆ 409 3131,
Telex 25853 – 🔁 🔲 🕾 ⌫. 🅰. 🔄 AE 🅾 VISA. 🛠
BP **o**
M (see also **Le Souffle** below) 16.00/28.00 **t.** and a la carte 🍷 6.40 – ⊐ 9.00 – **491 rm** 121.00/141.00, **15 suites** 220.00/810.00.

🏨 **Britannia** (Inter-Con.), Grosvenor Sq., W1A 3AN, ✆ 629 9400, Telex 23941 – 🔁 🔲 🕾. 🅰.
🔄 AE 🅾 VISA. 🛠
BM **x**
M 15.50 **st.** and a la carte 🍷 4.50 – ⊐ 9.00 – **356 rm** 88.00/160.00 **s.**, **12 suites** 200.00/1075.00 **s.**

🏨 **Westbury** (T.H.F.), New Bond St. (entrance on Conduit St.), W1A 4UH, ✆ 629 7755, Telex
24378 – 🔁 📺 🕾 🔄 🅿. 🅰. 🔄 AE 🅾 VISA
DM **a**
M 12.25 **t.** (lunch) and a la carte 21.15/28.70 **t.** 🍷 5.50 – ⊐ 8.00 – **240 rm** 85.00/99.00 **st.**, **15 suites**.

🏨 **Londonderry**, Park Lane, W1Y 8AP, ✆ 493 7292, Telex 263292 – 🔁 🔲 📺 🕾 ⌫. 🔄 AE 🅾
VISA. 🛠
BP **i**
M a la carte 22.00/29.00 **st.** 🍷 6.50 – ⊐ 8.50 – **150 rm** 115.00/140.00 **s.**, **12 suites** 180.00/265.00 **s.**

🏨 **Hilton International**, 22 Park Lane, W1A 2HH, ✆ 493 8000, Telex 24873, ≤ London – 🔁 🔲
📺 🕾 🅿. 🅰. 🔄 AE 🅾 VISA
BP **e**
M 18.90/25.00 **st.** and a la carte 🍷 6.50 – ⊐ 8.50 – **501 rm** 125.00/145.00, **54 suites** 175.00/700.00.

🏨 **Holiday Inn**, 3 Berkeley St., W1X 6NE, ✆ 493 8282, Telex 24561 – 🔁 🔲 📺 🕾 ⌫. 🅰. 🔄
AE 🅾 VISA
DN **r**
M 11.00/12.00 **st.** and a la carte – ⊐ 7.50 – **188 rm** 83.00/95.00 **st.**, **7 suites** 175.00/345.00 **st.**

🏨 **Park Lane**, Piccadilly, W1Y 8BX, ✆ 499 6321, Telex 21533 – 🔁 📺 🕾 🅿. 🅰. 🔄 AE 🅾 VISA
🛠
BP **x**
M 13.50/15.50 **st.** and a la carte 🍷 5.50 – ⊐ 7.50 – **323 rm** 89.95/120.00 **st.**, **54 suites** 130.00/350.00 **st.**

🏨 **Chesterfield**, 35 Charles St., W1X 8LX, ✆ 491 2622, Telex 269394 – 🔁 📺 🕾. 🔄 AE 🅾 VISA
🛠
CN **c**
closed 25 and 26 December – **M** 15.00/16.00 **t.** and a la carte 🍷 4.50 – ⊐ 7.25 – **114 rm** 95.00/110.00 **st.**, **1 suite** 200.00 **st.**

XXXXX ❀❀ **The Terrace,** (at Dorchester H.), Park Lane, W1A 2HJ, ✆ 629 8888, Telex 887704, French
rest. – 🔲. 🔄 AE 🅾 VISA
BN **z**
closed Sunday – **M** (dinner only) 32.00 **st.** and a la carte 23.50/30.00 **st.**
Spec. Parfait de foies de volailles aux truffes, Sole de douvre poêlée aux poireaux et truffes, Rosette de bœuf pochée, sabayon parfumé aux grains de moutarde.

XXXXX **Mirabelle**, 56 Curzon St., W1Y 8DL, ✆ 499 4636, 🌿 – 🔲. 🔄 AE 🅾 VISA
CN **n**
closed Sunday and Bank Holidays – **M** 13.50/30.00 **st.** and a la carte 🍷 7.50.

XXXXX **90 Park Lane** (T.H.F.), (at Grosvenor House H.), Park Lane, W1A 3AA, ✆ 409 1290, Telex
24871 – 🔲. 🔄 AE 🅾 VISA
AM **a**
closed Saturday lunch, and Sunday and Bank Holidays – **M** 17.50/39.00 **st.** and a la carte 🍷 6.25.

XXXX ❀❀❀ **Le Gavroche,** 43 Upper Brook St., W1P 1PS, ✆ 408 0881, French rest. – 🔲. 🔄 AE 🅾
VISA
AM **c**
closed Saturday, Sunday, 24 December-2 January and Bank Holidays – **M** (booking essential) 19.50/30.00 **st.** and a la carte 🍷 4.90
Spec. Soufflé suissesse, Assiette du boucher, Sablé aux fraises.

XXXX ❀ **Le Soufflé** (at Inter-Continental H.), 1 Hamilton Pl., Hyde Park Corner, W1V 0QY, ✆
409 3131, Telex 25853 – 🔲 ⌫. 🔄 AE 🅾 VISA
BP **o**
M 16.00/28.00 **t.** and a la carte 🍷 6.40
Spec. Paupiettes de turbot aux langoustines, Salade de homard au foie gras, Filets d'agneau au basilic.

XXXX **Scott's**, 20 Mount St., W1Y 6HE, ✆ 629 5248, Seafood – 🔲. 🔄 AE 🅾 VISA
BM **r**
closed Sunday lunch and Bank Holidays – **M** a la carte 27.70/40.20 **t.** 🍷 3.25.

XXX **Princess Garden**, 8-10 North Audley St., W1Y 1WF, ✆ 493 3223, Chinese-Peking rest. –
🔄 AE 🅾 VISA
AL **z**
M 20.00/35.00 **t.** and a la carte 🍷 4.00.

XXX **Tiberio**, 22 Queen St., W1X 7PJ, ✆ 629 3561, Italian rest., Dancing – 🔄 AE 🅾 VISA
CN **z**
closed Saturday lunch, Sunday and Bank Holidays – **M** a la carte 17.05/28.25 **t.**

XX **Greenhouse,** 27a Hay's Mews, W1X 7RJ, ℰ 499 3331 – 🖃 AE **VISA**
closed Saturday lunch, Sunday, 24 December-5 January and Bank Holidays – **M** a la carte
12.80/16.40 t. ₰ 2.65.
BN **a**

XX **Langan's Brasserie,** Stratton St., W1X 5FD, ℰ 491 8822 – 🖃 AE ⓞ **VISA**
closed Saturday lunch, Sunday and Bank Holidays – **M** (booking essential) a la carte
13.30/20.00 t. ₰ 4.50.
DN **e**

XX **Miyama,** 38 Clarges St., W1Y 7PJ, ℰ 499 2443, Japanese rest. – 🔳 🖃 AE ⓞ **VISA**
closed Saturday lunch, Sunday, Christmas-New Year and Bank Holidays – **M** 7.00/24.00 t. and
a la carte.
CN **e**

XX Mr. Kai, 65 South Audley St., W1Y 5FD, ℰ 493 8988, Chinese-Peking rest. 🔳
BM **v**

XX Shogun (at Britannia H.), Adams Row, W1, ℰ 493 1255, Telex 8813271, Japanese rest.
BM **i**

XX **Ho-Ho,** 29 Maddox St., W1, ℰ 493 1228, Chinese rest. – 🔳 🖃 AE ⓞ **VISA**
closed Sunday and Bank Holidays – **M** 8.00/13.00 t. and a la carte.
DL **x**

XX One Two Three, 27 Davies St., W1, ℰ 409 0750, Japanese rest. – 🔳
BM **s**

X **Ikeda,** 30 Brook St., W1Y 1AG, ℰ 629 2730, Japanese rest. – 🔳 🖃 AE ⓞ **VISA**
closed Sunday lunch, Saturday and Bank Holidays – **M** 10.00/25.00 t. and a la carte.
CKL **a**

X **Trattoria Fiori,** 87-88 Mount St., W1Y 5HG, ℰ 499 1447, Italian rest. – 🖃 AE ⓞ **VISA**
closed Bank Holidays – **M** 15.80 t. and a la carte ₰ 2.80.
BM **o**

Regent's Park and Marylebone – ✉ NW1/NW6/NW8/W1 – Except where otherwise
stated see pp. 26 and 27.

🛈 Selfridges, Oxford St., W1 ℰ 730 3488.

🏨 **Churchill,** 30 Portman Sq., W1A 4ZX, ℰ 486 5800, Telex 264831 – 🛗 🖃 📺 ☎ ₺ Ⓟ. 🅐. 🖃
AE ⓞ **VISA**. 🛇
M a la carte 15.80/23.80 t. – � 7.50 – **489 rm** 95.00/107.00, **39 suites** 175.00/420.00.
AJ **x**

🏨 **Portman Inter-Continental** (Inter-Con.), 22 Portman Sq., W1H 9FL, ℰ 486 5844, Telex
261526 – 🛗 🖃 📺 ☎ ₺ Ⓟ. 🅐. 🖃 AE ⓞ **VISA**. 🛇
M 15.00 t. (lunch) and a la carte 26.00/34.00 t. ₰ 8.00 – ⊟ 8.50 – **278 rm** 94.00/121.00, **8 suites**
275.00/350.00.
AJ **o**

🏨 Montcalm, Great Cumberland Pl., W1A 2LF, ℰ 402 4288, Telex 28710 – 🛗 🖃 📺 ☎. 🅐. 🛇
116 rm.
pp. 30 and 31   FY **x**

🏨 **Holiday Inn,** 134 George St., W1H 6DN, ℰ 723 1277, Telex 27983, 🔲 – 🛗 🖃 📺 ☎ ₺ Ⓟ.
🅐. 🖃 AE ⓞ **VISA**
pp. 30 and 31   FY **i**
M 12.50 t. and a la carte ₰ 4.30 – ⊟ 6.60 – **241 rm** 94.30/100.05 st., **2 suites** 250.00/375.00 st.

🏨 **Selfridge Thistle,** 400 Orchard St., W1H 0JS, ℰ 408 2080, Telex 22361 – 🛗 🖃 📺 ☎ ₺ Ⓟ.
🅐. 🖃 AE ⓞ **VISA**. 🛇
AK **e**
M 12.50/14.50 t. and a la carte ₰ 3.95 – ⊟ 7.00 – **298 rm** 85.00/106.00 t.

🏨 **Ladbroke Westmoreland** (Ladbroke), 18 Lodge Rd, NW8 7JT, ℰ 722 7722, Telex 23101 –
🛗 🖃 📺 ☎ Ⓟ. 🅐. 🖃 AE ⓞ **VISA**
pp. 13-16   JS **v**
M (carving rest.) 12.50 t. and a la carte ₰ 4.00 – ⊟ 7.00 – **347 rm** 69.00/95.00 st. – SB (weekends
only) 73.00/80.00 st.

🏨 **Clifton Ford,** 47 Welbeck St., W1M 8DN, ℰ 486 6600, Telex 22569 – 🛗 📺 ☎. 🅐. 🖃 AE ⓞ
VISA
BH **a**
M a la carte 13.45/19.95 st. ₰ 3.95 – ⊟ 6.75 – **220 rm** 65.00/97.00 st., **2 suites**.

🏨 **St. George's** (T.H.F.), Langham Pl., W1N 8QS, ℰ 580 0111, Telex 27274, < – 🛗 📺 ☎. 🖃 AE
ⓞ **VISA**
pp. 13-16   LT **a**
M 13.50 st. and a la carte ₰ 2.75 – ⊟ 6.50 – **85 rm** 64.50/82.00 st., **3 suites**.

🏨 **Cumberland** (T.H.F.), Marble Arch, W1A 4RF, ℰ 262 1234, Telex 22215 – 🛗 📺 ☎ ₺. 🅐. 🖃
AE ⓞ **VISA**. 🛇
AK **n**
M (carving rest.) 9.65 st. and a la carte ₰ 2.70 – ⊟ 6.00 – **894 rm** 61.50/79.00 st., **9 suites**.

🏨 **Durrants,** 26-32 George St., W1H 6BJ, ℰ 935 8131, Telex 894919 – 🛗 📺 ➡wc ☎. 🅐. 🖃
AE ⓞ **VISA**. 🛇
AH **e**
M a la carte 12.90/16.80 t. ₰ 3.25 – ⊟ 5.00 – **102 rm** 29.00/60.00 st., **3 suites** 150.00 st.

🏨 **Savoy Court,** Granville Pl., W1H 0EH, ℰ 408 0130, Telex 8955515 – 🛗 📺 ➡wc ☎ ₺. 🖃 AE
ⓞ **VISA**. 🛇
AK **c**
M 10.50 t. and a la carte – ⊟ 6.00 – **97 rm** 55.90/79.90 st.

🏨 **Regent Crest** (Crest), Carburton St., W1P 8EE, ℰ 388 2300, Telex 22453 – 🛗 🖃 rest 📺
➡wc ⓐ Ⓟ. 🅐. 🖃 AE ⓞ **VISA**. 🛇
pp. 13-16
M approx. 12.50 st. – ⊟ 6.75 – **317 rm** 60.00/72.00 st., **6 suites** – SB (weekends only) 55.00 st.

🏨 Berners, 10 Berners St., W1A 3BE, ℰ 636 1629, Telex 25759 – 🛗 🖃 rest 📺 ➡wc ☎ ₺. 🅐.
🖃 AE ⓞ **VISA**. 🛇
FJ **r**
M (carving rest.) – ⊟ 6.50 – **234 rm** 69.00/97.00 st.

🏨 **Londoner,** 57-59 Welbeck St., W1M 8HS, ℰ 935 4442, Telex 894630 – 🛗 📺 ➡wc ☎. 🖃 AE
ⓞ **VISA**. 🛇
BJ **v**
M 9.50/10.00 t. – ⊟ 7.00 – **142 rm** 50.00/80.00 st.

🏨 Sherlock Holmes, Baker St., W1M 1LB, ℰ 486 6161, Telex 8954837 – 🛗 📺 ➡wc ☎. 🅐.
M (Italian rest.) – **149 rm**.
pp. 13-15   KT **a**

🏨 **Stratford Court,** 350 Oxford St., W1N 0BY, ☏ 629 7474, Telex 22270 – 🛗 📺 🚾wc ☎. 🅿️
　　🟦 🅰🅴 ⓪ 𝘝𝘐𝘚𝘈　　　　　　　　　　　　　　　　　　　　　　　　　　　　　　　　BK **n**
　　M (carving rest.) 9.50 t. 🍷 2.75 – 🍽 6.50 – **140 rm** 55.90/78.90 **st.**

🏨 **Harewood,** Harewood Row, NW1 6SE, ☏ 262 2707, Telex 297225 – 🛗 📺 🚾wc ☎. 🅿️ 🅰🅴
　　⓪ 𝘝𝘐𝘚𝘈 🍷　　　　　　　　　　　　　　　　　　　　　　　　　　　pp. 13-16　KT **x**
　　M (grill rest. only) 6.50 **st.** and a la carte 🍷 4.00 – 🍽 5.50 – **93 rm** 46.50/62.50 **st.**

🏨 **Bryanston Court,** 56-60 Great Cumberland Pl., W1H 7FD, ☏ 262 3141, Group Telex 262076
　　– 🛗 📺 🚾wc 🛁wc ☎. 🅿️ 🅰🅴 ⓪ 𝘝𝘐𝘚𝘈. 🎊　　　　　　　　　pp. 30 and 31　FY **z**
　　M (closed Saturday, Sunday and Bank Holidays) 11.50 t. 🍷 2.50 – 🍽 4.00 – **53 rm** 39.00/52.00 **st.**

🏨 **Hallam** without rest., 12 Hallam St., W1N 5LJ, ☏ 580 1166 – 🛗 📺 🚾wc 🛁wc 🅿️ 🅰🅴 𝘝𝘐𝘚𝘈. 🎊
　　23 rm 35.00/45.00 **t.**　　　　　　　　　　　　　　　　　　　pp. 13-16　LT **r**

🏨 **Concorde** without rest., 50 Great Cumberland Pl., W1H 7FD, ☏ 402 6169, Group Telex
　　262076 – 🛗 📺 🚾wc 🛁wc ☎. 🅿️ 🅰🅴 ⓪ 𝘝𝘐𝘚𝘈. 🎊　　　　　　pp. 30 and 31　FY **n**
　　🍽 3.00 – **28 rm** 35.00/45.00 **st.**

🏠 **Portman Court,** 28-30 Seymour St., W1H 5WD, ☏ 402 5401 – 📺 🚾wc 🛁 🕭. 🅿️ 🅰🅴 ⓪
　　𝘝𝘐𝘚𝘈. 🎊　　　　　　　　　　　　　　　　　　　　　　　　　　　　　　　AK **a**
　　🍽 1.50 – **30 rm** 22.00/39.00 **st.**

XXX **Odins,** 27 Devonshire St., W1N 1RS, ☏ 935 7296 – 🅰🅴　　　　　pp. 13-16　KT **n**
　　closed Saturday lunch, Sunday and Bank Holidays – **M** 13.00 t. (lunch) and a la carte
　　15.05/23.60 t. 🍷 3.25.

XXX ⌾ **Rue St. Jacques,** 5 Charlotte St., W1P 1HD, ☏ 637 0222, French rest. – 🍽. 🅿️ 🅰🅴 ⓪ 𝘝𝘐𝘚𝘈
　　closed Saturday lunch, Sunday, 25 to 28 December and Bank Holidays – **M** 15.00 t. (lunch)
　　and a la carte 21.20/31.25 t.　　　　　　　　　　　　　　　　　pp. 13-16　MT **c**
　　Spec. Warm oysters with a very light vinaigrette, Sauteed scallops garnished with mussels, Cutlets of Venison
　　and piquant blackcurrant sauce.

XX **D'Artagnan,** 19 Blandford St., W1H 3AD, ☏ 935 1023, French rest. – 🅿️ 🅰🅴 ⓪ 𝘝𝘐𝘚𝘈　AH **a**
　　closed Saturday lunch, Sunday and Bank Holidays – **M** 11.50/13.50 t. and a la carte.

XX **Gaylord,** 79-81 Mortimer St., W1N 7TB, ☏ 580 3615, Indian and Pakistani rest. – 🍽. 🅿️ 🅰🅴
　　⓪ 𝘝𝘐𝘚𝘈　　　　　　　　　　　　　　　　　　　　　　　　　　　pp. 13-16　LT **c**
　　M 8.25 t. and a la carte 🍷 3.60.

XX **La Pavona,** 5-7 Blandford St., W1H 3AF, ☏ 486 9696, Italian rest. – 🍽. 🅿️ 🅰🅴　BH **c**
　　closed Saturday lunch, Sunday and Bank Holidays – **M** 8.25 t. (lunch) and a la carte
　　13.00/19.00 t. 🍷 3.00.

XX **Lords Rendezvous,** 24 Finchley Rd, NW8 6ES, ☏ 586 4280, Chinese-Peking rest. – 🅿️ 🅰🅴
　　⓪ 𝘝𝘐𝘚𝘈　　　　　　　　　　　　　　　　　　　　　　　　　　　　pp. 13-16　JR **r**
　　closed 25-26 December and Bank Holidays – **M** a la carte 10.80/15.50 t.

XX **Masako,** 6-8 St. Christopher's Pl., W1M 5HB, ☏ 935 1579, Japanese rest. – 🍽. 🅿️ 🅰🅴 ⓪
　　𝘝𝘐𝘚𝘈　　　　　　　　　　　　　　　　　　　　　　　　　　　　　　　　　　BJ **e**
　　closed Sunday, 1 to 3 January, Easter, 25-26 December and Bank Holidays – **M** 9.50/19.00 t.
　　and a la carte.

XX **Asuka,** Berkeley Arcade, 209a Baker St., NW1 6AB, ☏ 486 5026, Japanese rest. – 🅿️ 🅰🅴 ⓪
　　𝘝𝘐𝘚𝘈　　　　　　　　　　　　　　　　　　　　　　　　　　　　pp. 13-16　KT **u**
　　closed Saturday lunch, Sunday, 24 December-4 January and Bank Holidays – **M** 6.50 **st.**
　　(lunch) and a la carte 15.80/29.00 **st.** 🍷 4.50.

XX **Tonino,** Berkeley Court, 12 Glentworth St., NW1 5PG, ☏ 935 4220, Italian rest. – 🅿️ 🅰🅴 ⓪
　　𝘝𝘐𝘚𝘈　　　　　　　　　　　　　　　　　　　　　　　　　　　pp. 13-16　KT **e**
　　closed Saturday lunch, Sunday and Bank Holidays – **M** 5.75 **st.** and a la carte 9.80/15.70 t.
　　🍷 3.00.

XX **Viceroy of India,** 3-5 Glentworth St., NW1 5PG, ☏ 486 3401, Indian rest. – 🅿️ 🅰🅴 ⓪ 𝘝𝘐𝘚𝘈
　　closed 25 December – **M** 7.50/8.75 t. and a la carte 🍷 3.00.　　pp. 13-16　KT **o**

XX **La Loggia,** 68 Edgware Rd, W2 2EG, ☏ 723 0554, Italian rest. – 🍽. 🅿️ 🅰🅴 ⓪ 𝘝𝘐𝘚𝘈
　　closed Sunday and Bank Holidays – **M** a la carte 11.00/18.50 t. 🍷 2.95.　pp. 30 and 31　FY **a**

X **Le Muscadet,** 25 Paddington St., W1M 3RF, ☏ 935 2883, French rest. – 🍽. 🅿️ 𝘝𝘐𝘚𝘈
　　closed Saturday lunch, Sunday, 3 weeks August, 2 weeks Christmas-New Year and Bank
　　Holidays – **M** a la carte 8.15/9.90 t. 🍷 2.80.　　　　　　　　　pp. 13-16　KT **s**

X **L'Aventure,** 3 Blenheim Terr., NW8 4JS, ☏ 624 6232, French rest.　　pp. 13-16　JR **s**

X **Au Bois St. Jean,** 122 St. John's Wood High St., NW8 7SG, ☏ 722 0400, French rest. – 🅿️
　　𝘝𝘐𝘚𝘈　　　　　　　　　　　　　　　　　　　　　　　　　　　pp. 13-16　JS **e**
　　closed Saturday lunch and Bank Holidays – **M** 10.50/13.00 **st.** 🍷 3.00.

X **Langan's Bistro,** 26 Devonshire St., W1N 1RS, ☏ 935 4531　　　pp. 13-16　KT **r**

X **Biagi's,** 39 Upper Berkeley St., W1H 7PG, ☏ 723 0394, Italian rest. – 🅿️ 🅰🅴 ⓪ 𝘝𝘐𝘚𝘈
　　closed Bank Holidays – **M** a la carte 8.10/16.55 t. 🍷 2.85.　　pp. 30 and 31　FY **c**

X **Heart of the Dragon,** 52 Dorset St., W1H 3FA, ☏ 4861135, Chinese, Shanghai and Szechuan
　　rest. – 🅿️ 🅰🅴 𝘝𝘐𝘚𝘈　　　　　　　　　　　　　　　　　　　　　　　　　　AH **s**
　　closed Sunday and Bank Holidays – **M** 12.50/18.00 t. and a la carte 🍷 2.90.

X **Il Barbino,** 64 Seymour St., W1H 5AF, ☏ 402 6866, Italian rest. – 🅿️ 🅰🅴 ⓪ 𝘝𝘐𝘚𝘈
　　closed Saturday lunch, Sunday and Bank Holidays – **M** a la carte 9.00/13.20 t. 🍷 2.50.
　　　　　　　　　　　　　　　　　　　　　　　　　　　　　　　pp. 30 and 31　FY **r**

X **Chaopraya,** 22 St. Christopher's Place, W1M 5DH, ☏ 486 0777, Thai rest. – 🅿️ 🅰🅴 ⓪ 𝘝𝘐𝘚𝘈
　　closed Saturday lunch, Sunday and Bank Holidays – **M** 10.00/12.00 t. and a la carte 🍷 3.50.
　　　　　　　　　　　　　　　　　　　　　　　　　　　　　　　　　　　　　BJ **o**

St. James's – ✉ W1/SW1/WC2 – pp. 26 and 27.

🏨🏨🏨🏨🏨 **Ritz,** Piccadilly, W1V 9DG, ☎ 493 8181, Telex 267200, « Elegant restaurant in Louix XV style » – ⇅ [TV] ☎. ▣ [AE] ◐ [VISA]. 🚫🐕 DN **a**
M 17.50/26.50 **st.** and a la carte 🍷 5.25 – ☕ 8.50 – **139 rm** 100.00/160.00 **st.**, **17 suites** 300.00/525.00 **st.**

🏨🏨🏨🏨 **Stafford** 🌿, 16-18 St. James's Pl., SW1A 1NJ, ☎ 493 0111, Telex 28602 – ⇅ [TV] ☎. 👥. [AE] ◐. 🚫🐕 DN **u**
M 15.00/17.50 **st.** and a la carte – ☕ 7.50 – **62 rm** 103.00/136.50 **st.**, **5 suites** 198.00/400.00 **st.**

🏨🏨🏨🏨 **Dukes** 🌿, 35 St. James's Pl., SW1A 1NY, ☎ 491 4840, Telex 28283 – ⇅ [TV] ☎. ▣ [AE] ◐ [VISA]. 🚫🐕 EP **x**
M a la carte 22.00/27.00 **st.** – ☕ 7.50 – **51 rm** 90.00/140.00 **st.**, **14 suites** 190.00/400.00 **st.**

🏨🏨🏨🏨 **Cavendish** (T.H.F.), Jermyn St., SW1Y 6JF, ☎ 930 2111, Telex 263187 – ⇅ ❄ rest [TV] ☎ ♿ [P]. 👥. ▣ [AE] ◐ [VISA] EN **i**
M (bar lunch Saturday) 12.95 **st.** (lunch) and a la carte 16.00/24.00 🍷 3.95 – ☕ 6.00 – **253 rm** 71.00/90.50 **st.**

🏨🏨🏨 **Royal Trafalgar Thistle** (Thistle), Whitcomb St., WC2H 7HG, ☎ 930 4477, Telex 298564 – ⇅ ❄ rest [TV] 🛁wc ☎. ▣ [AE] ◐ [VISA] GM **r**
M a la carte 10.50/16.00 **t.** 🍷 3.65 – ☕ 5.95 – **108 rm** 52.00/78.00 **t.**

🏨 **Pastoria,** 3-6 St. Martin's St., WC2H 7HL, ☎ 930 8641, Telex 25538 – ⇅ [TV] 🛁wc ☎. ▣ [AE] ◐ [VISA]. 🚫🐕 GM **v**
closed January and February – **M** 12.50 **t.** 🍷 3.00 – ☕ 5.00 – **52 rm** 57.00/75.00 **st.**

XXXXX **Maxim's de Paris,** 32-34 Panton St., SW1, ☎ 839 4809, French rest., Dancing – ❄. ▣ [AE] ◐ [VISA] GM **a**
closed Saturday lunch, Sunday, Christmas and Bank Holidays – **M** 18.50 **t.** (lunch) and a la carte 19.20/28.20 **t.** 🍷 4.50.

XXXX **A L'Ecu de France,** 111 Jermyn St., SW1, ☎ 930 2837, French rest. – ❄. ▣ [AE] ◐ [VISA] FM **z**
closed lunch Saturday and Sunday – **M** 15.00/22.00 **st.** and a la carte 🍷 5.50.

XXX **Suntory,** 72-73 St. James's St., SW1A 1PH, ☎ 409 0201, Japanese rest. – ❄. ▣ [AE] ◐ [VISA] EP **z**
closed Sunday and Bank Holidays – **M** 20.00 and a la carte 12.30/23.40.

XX **Le Caprice,** Arlington House, Arlington St., SW1A 1RT, ☎ 629 2239 – ❄. ▣ [AE] ◐ [VISA] DN **c**
closed lunch Saturday and Bank Holidays and 25 December-2 January – **M** a la carte 11.25/15.75 **t.**

Soho – ✉ W1/WC2 – pp. 26 and 27.

XXX **Leonis Quo Vadis,** 26-29 Dean St., W1V 6LL, ☎ 437 9585, Italian rest. – ▣ [AE] ◐ [VISA] FK **u**
closed lunch Saturday, Sunday and Bank Holidays – **M** a la carte 11.95/16.45 **t.** 🍷 2.95.

XX **Au Jardin des Gourmets,** 5 Greek St., Soho Sq., W1V 5LA, ☎ 437 1816, French rest. – ▣ [AE] ◐ [VISA] GJ **a**
closed lunch Saturday and Bank Holidays, Sunday and 4 days at Christmas – **M** 20.00 **t.** and a la carte 11.65/19.40 **t.** 🍷 2.75.

XX **L'Escargot,** 48 Greek St., W1V 5LQ, ☎ 437 2679 – ▣ [AE] ◐ [VISA] GK **e**
closed Saturday lunch, Sunday, Christmas-New Year and Bank Holidays – **M** a la carte approx. 15.50 **t.**

XX **Gay Hussar,** 2 Greek St., W1V 6NB, ☎ 437 0973, Hungarian rest. – ❄ GJ **c**
closed Sunday and Bank Holidays – **M** 10.00 **t.** (lunch) and a la carte 13.00/17.50 **t.** 🍷 3.00.

XX **Red Fort,** 77 Dean St., W1V 5HA, ☎ 437 2525, Indian rest. – ▣ [AE] ◐ [VISA] FJK **r**
M 10.00/15.00 **t.**

XX **Chesa (Swiss Centre),** 2 New Coventry St., W1V 3HG, ☎ 734 1291 – ❄. ▣ [AE] ◐ [VISA] GM **n**
closed Christmas Day – **M** 14.50 **st.** and a la carte 11.40/18.20 **st.** 🍷 2.60.

XX **Venezia,** 21 Great Chapel St., W1V 3AQ, ☎ 437 6506, Italian rest. – ▣ [AE] ◐ [VISA] FJ **a**
closed Saturday lunch, Sunday and Bank Holidays – **M** a la carte 9.75/16.45 **t.** 🍷 2.40.

XX **Kaya,** 22-25 Dean St., W1, ☎ 437 6630, Korean rest. – ❄ FJ **i**
closed lunch Saturday and Bank Holidays – **M** 6.00/17.00 **t.** and a la carte.

XX **Poons,** 4 Leicester St., WC2, ☎ 437 1528, Chinese rest. – ❄ GM **i**
closed Sunday and Christmas – **M** 8.50 **t.** 🍷 3.80.

XX **Rugantino,** 26 Romilly St., W1V 5TQ, ☎ 437 5302, Italian rest. – ▣ [AE] ◐ [VISA] GK **u**
closed Saturday lunch, Sunday and Bank Holidays – **M** 13.50 **st.** and a la carte 10.95/13.05 **t.** 🍷 2.25.

XX Fuji, 36-40 Brewer St., W1R 3HP, ☎ 734 0957, Japanese rest. FL **c**

X **Frith's,** 14 Frith St., W1, ☎ 439 3370 – ▣ [AE] ◐ [VISA] FGK **s**
closed Saturday lunch and Sunday – **M** 15.00 **t.** 🍷 3.00.

X **Chiang Mai,** 48 Frith St., W1, ☎ 437 7444, Thai rest. – ▣ [AE] ◐ [VISA] GK **v**
M a la carte approx. 12.00 **t.** 🍷 2.60.

X **Gallery Rendezvous,** 53-55 Beak St., W1R 3DH, ☎ 734 0445, Chinese-Peking rest. – ❄. ▣ [AE] ◐ [VISA] EL **a**
M 15.00/30.00 **t.** and a la carte 🍷 2.60.

X **Fung Shing,** 15 Lisle St., WC2H 7BE, ☎ 437 1539, Chinese-Cantonese rest. – ▣ [AE] ◐ [VISA] GL **a**
M 10.00/15.00 **t.** and a la carte.

✗ **Joy King Lau,** 3 Leicester St., WC2H 7BL, ☎ 437 1132, Chinese rest. – AE ⓪   GM e
    M 9.00 t. and a la carte ⓪ 2.00.

✗ **Saigon,** 45 Frith St., W1V 5TE, ☎ 437 7109, Vietnamese rest. – ⓝ AE ⓪ VISA   GL x
    closed Sunday and Bank Holidays – **M** 8.70 t. and a la carte.

✗ **Trusha,** 11-12 Dean St., W1V 5AH, ☎ 437 3559, Indian rest. – ⓝ AE ⓪ VISA   FJ e
    closed Sunday and Bank Holidays – **M** 12.50/16.00 st. and a la carte.

✗ **Trattoria Imperia,** 19 Charing Cross Rd, WC2H 0ES, ☎ 930 8364, Italian rest. – ⓝ AE ⓪
    VISA   GM z
    closed Saturday lunch, Sunday, 25-26 December and Bank Holidays – **M** 13.00/15.00 t. and a
    la carte ⓪ 2.60.

Strand and Covent Garden – ✉ WC2 – p. 31.

🏨🏨🏨 **Savoy,** Strand, WC2R 0EU, ☎ 836 4343, Telex 24234 – 🛗 📺 ☎ 🚗, 🅿️, ⓝ AE ⓪ VISA ✁
    M Grill *(closed Saturday lunch, Sunday, first 3 weeks August and Bank Holidays)* a la carte
    15.75/30.25 **st.** ⓪ 3.50 – **River** 16.50/25.00 **st.** and a la carte ⓪ 3.30 – � 8.25 – **200 rm**
    110.00/135.00 **st.**, **48 suites**.   EX a

🏨🏨 **Howard,** 12 Temple Pl., WC2R 2PR, ☎ 836 3555, Telex 268047 – 🛗 📺 ☎ 🚗, 🅿️, ⓝ AE
    ⓪ VISA ✁   FV e
    141 rm, **2 suites**.

🏨🏨 **Waldorf** (T.H.F.), Aldwych, WC2B 4DD, ☎ 836 2400, Telex 24574 – 🛗 rest 📺 ☎ 🅿️, ⓝ
    AE ⓪ VISA   EV x
    M *(closed lunch Saturday and Sunday)* 15.00/10.50 **st.** and a la carte ⓪ 4.00 – ⊃ 6.00 – **310 rm**
    63.50/81.50 **st.**

XXXX **Boulestin,** 1a Henrietta St., WC2E 8PS, ☎ 836 7061, French rest. – ⬛, ⓝ AE ⓪ VISA   EV r
    closed Saturday lunch, Sunday, last 3 weeks August and Bank Holidays – **M** 14.00 t. (lunch)
    and a la carte approx. 17.25 t. ⓪ 5.00.

XXX **Inigo Jones,** 14 Garrick St., WC2E 9BJ, ☎ 836 6456 – ⬛, ⓝ AE ⓪ VISA   DV v
    closed Saturday lunch, Sunday and Bank Holidays – **M** 14.75 t. and a la carte 24.50/33.50 t.
    ⓪ 6.10.

XXX **Simpson's-in-the-Strand,** 100 Strand, WC2R 0EW, ☎ 836 9112, English rest. – ⬛, ⓝ AE
    ⓪ VISA   EV o
    closed Sunday, Easter, 25 and 26 December, 1 January and Bank Holidays – **M** a la carte
    14.60/19.85 **st.** ⓪ 2.90.

XXX **Thomas de Quincey's,** 36 Tavistock St., WC2E 7PB, ☎ 240 3972 – ⓝ AE ⓪ VISA   EV c
    closed Saturday lunch, Sunday, last 3 weeks August and Bank Holidays – **M** 25.00/30.00 **st.**
    and a la carte ⓪ 3.50.

XX **Interlude de Tabaillau,** 7-8 Bow St., WC2, ☎ 379 6473, French rest. – ⬛, ⓝ AE ⓪ VISA
    *closed Saturday lunch, Sunday, 1 week Easter, 3 weeks August, 1 week Christmas and Bank
    Holidays* – **M** 18.50/23.00 (wine included) **st.**.   DEV x

XX **Tourment d'Amour,** 19 New Row, WC2N 4LA, ☎ 240 5348, French rest. – ⓝ AE ⓪ VISA
    closed Saturday lunch, Sunday, 1 week Christmas and Bank Holidays – **M** 18.00 t. ⓪ 4.40.
     DV z

XX **Sheekey's,** 28-32 St. Martin's Court, WC2N 4AL, ☎ 240 2565, Seafood – ⬛, ⓝ AE ⓪ VISA
    closed Sunday, 24 to 26 December, 1 January and Bank Holidays – **M** a la carte 12.95/15.65 t.
     DV v

XX **Chez Solange,** 35 Cranbourn St., WC2H 7AD, ☎ 836 5886, French rest. – ⬛, ⓝ AE ⓪ VISA
    closed Sunday – **M** 11.50 t. and a la carte 11.95/17.55 t. ⓪ 2.95.   DV i

XX **Azami,** 13-15 West St., WC2H 9BL, ☎ 240 0634, Japanese rest.   pp. 26 and 27   GK z

XX **Frère Jacques,** 38 Longacre, WC2, ☎ 836 7823, Seafood – ⬛, ⓝ AE ⓪ VISA   DV n
    closed Sunday – **M** 10.00 **st.** and a la carte 12.55/16.10 t. ⓪ 2.50.

✗ **Poons of Covent Garden,** 41 King St., WC2E 8JS, ☎ 240 1743, Chinese-Cantonese rest. –
    AE ⓪ VISA   DV r
    closed Sunday and 24 to 27 December – **M** 7.50/14.00 t. and a la carte.

✗ **Café Pelican,** 45 St. Martins Lane, WC2N 4EJ, ☎ 379 0309, French rest., « Art deco » – ⬛,
    ⓝ AE ⓪ VISA   DX e
    M 10.95 t. and a la carte ⓪ 3.45.

✗ **Magnos Brasserie,** 65A Long Acre, WC2E 9JH, ☎ 836 6077, French rest. – ⓝ AE ⓪ VISA
    closed Saturday lunch, Sunday, 24 December-2 January and Bank Holidays – **M** 7.45 **st.**
    (dinner) and a la carte 12.05/16.65 t. ⓪ 4.25.   EV e

✗ **Laguna 50,** 50 St. Martin's Lane, WC2N 4EA, ☎ 836 0960, Italian rest.   DV u

✗ **Flounders,** 19 Tavistock St., WC2, ☎ 836 3925, Seafood – ⬛, ⓝ AE ⓪ VISA   EV a
    closed Sunday and Bank Holidays – **M** a la carte 10.80/12.80 t. ⓪ 3.15.

✗ **Happy Wok,** 52 Floral St., WC2, ☎ 836 3696, Chinese rest. – ⓝ AE ⓪ VISA   DV n
    closed Sunday – **M** 18.00 t. and a la carte.

✗ **Grimes,** 6 Garrick St., WC2R 9BH, ☎ 836 7008, Seafood – ⓝ AE ⓪ VISA   DV x
    closed Saturday lunch, Sunday and 24 to 27 December – **M** 9.00 t. (lunch) and a la carte
    12.00/15.50 t. ⓪ 2.50.

Victoria – ✉ SW1 – Except otherwise stated see p. 30.

🏨🏨 **Goring,** 15 Beeston Pl., Grosvenor Gdns, SW1W 0JW, ℰ 834 8211, Telex 919166 – 🛗 🎬 📺
🕾. 🏄. 🔼 🅰🅴 ⓞ 𝑉𝐼𝑆𝐴. 🞀
                                                          BV **a**
M 12.50/14.00 t. and a la carte ▯ 3.50 – ⌧ 6.50 – **90 rm** 67.50/95.00 st., **4 suites** 140.00 st.

🏨🏨 **Royal Horseguards Thistle** (Thistle), 2 Whitehall Court, SW1A 2EX, ℰ 839 3400, Telex
917096 – 🛗 🎬 rest 📺 🕾. 🏄. 🔼 🅰🅴 ⓞ 𝑉𝐼𝑆𝐴. 🞀   pp. 17-20 NV **a**
M 12.00 t. and a la carte ▯ 6.45 – ⌧ 5.75 – **284 rm** 59.00/69.00 t., **6 suites**.

🏨🏨 **Stakis St. Ermin's** (Stakis), Caxton St., SW1H 0QW, ℰ 222 7888, Telex 917731 – 🛗 🎬 rest
📺 🕾. 🏄. 🔼 🅰🅴 ⓞ 𝑉𝐼𝑆𝐴. 🞀   CV **a**
M (carving rest.) 25.00 t. and a la carte – ⌧ 6.50 – **250 rm** 68.00/83.00 t., **6 suites** approx.
150.00 t.

🏨🏨 **Royal Westminster Thistle** (Thistle), 49 Buckingham Palace Rd, SW1W 0QT, ℰ 834 1821,
Telex 916821 – 🛗 📺 🕾. 🏄. 🔼 🅰🅴 ⓞ 𝑉𝐼𝑆𝐴   BV **z**
M 9.00/15.00 t. and a la carte ▯ 3.15 – ⌧ 5.50 – **118 rm** 53.50/95.00 t., **18 suites**.

🏨 **Grosvenor,** 101 Buckingham Palace Rd, SW1W 0SJ, ℰ 834 9494, Telex 916006 – 🛗 🎬 rest 📺
🚰wc 🕾. 🏄. – **365 rm**.   BV **e**

🏨 **Ebury Court,** 26 Ebury St., SW1W 0LU, ℰ 730 8147 – 🛗 🚰wc. 🔼 𝑉𝐼𝑆𝐴   AV **i**
M a la carte 7.10/11.90 t. ▯ 2.10 – **39 rm** ⌧ 32.00/58.00 t.

🏨 **Hamilton House,** 60-64 Warwick Way, SW1V 1SA, ℰ 821 7113 – 📺 🚰wc 🕾. 🔼 𝑉𝐼𝑆𝐴
M (grill rest. only) (dinner only) a la carte approx. 4.10 t. ▯ 2.30 – **40 rm** ⌧ 24.00/43.00 t. – SB
(November-March) 42.00 st.   BX **n**

⌂ **Chesham House,** 64-66 Ebury St., SW1, ℰ 730 8513 – 📺 – **23 rm**.   AX **x**

⌂ **Elizabeth,** 37 Eccleston Sq., SW1V 1PB, ℰ 828 6812 – 🕮. 🞀   pp. 17-20 LY **c**
24 rm ⌧ 20.00/46.00 st.

XXX **Lockets,** Marsham Court, Marsham St., SW1P 4JY, ℰ 834 9552, English rest.
                                                          pp. 17-20 MY **z**

XXX **Kundan,** 3 Horseferry Rd, SW1P 2AN, ℰ 834 3434, Indian and Pakistani rest. – 🍽. 🔼 🅰🅴 ⓞ
𝑉𝐼𝑆𝐴   pp. 17-20 NXY **a**
closed Sunday and Bank Holidays – **M** 10.00/15.00 ▯ 5.00.

XXX **Santini,** 29 Ebury St., SW1W 0NZ, ℰ 730 4094, Italian rest. – 🍽   ABV **v**

XX **Ken Lo's Memories of China,** 67-69 Ebury St., SW1W 0NZ, ℰ 730 7734, Chinese rest. –
🔼 🅰🅴 ⓞ 𝑉𝐼𝑆𝐴   AX **u**
closed Sunday and Bank Holidays – **M** 15.50/20.50 t. and a la carte.

XX ⊛ **Le Mazarin,** 30 Winchester St., SW1, ℰ 828 3366, French rest. – 🍽. 🔼 🅰🅴 ⓞ
closed Sunday – **M** (dinner only) 22.50 st. ▯ 5.70.   pp. 17-20 LZ **i**
Spec. Fricassée de poulet au basilic, Filet de sole Mazarin, Tranchettes d'onglet poêlé aux échalotes.

XX **Villa Claudius,** 10A The Broadway, SW1, ℰ 222 3338, Italian rest.   pp. 17-20 MX **a**

XX **The Restaurant,** Dolphin Square, Chichester St., SW1V 3LX, ℰ 828 3207, French rest.,
« Art deco » – 🔼 🅰🅴 ⓞ 𝑉𝐼𝑆𝐴   pp. 17-20 LZ **e**
closed Sunday and Bank Holidays – **M** 16.50 t. and a la carte ▯ 3.50.

XX **Pomegranates,** 94 Grosvenor Rd, SW1V 3LG, ℰ 828 6560 – 🔼 🅰🅴 𝑉𝐼𝑆𝐴   pp. 17-20 LMZ **a**
closed Saturday lunch, Sunday and Bank Holidays – **M** 15.90 t. (lunch) and a la carte
13.60/19.80 t. ▯ 3.50.

XX **Eatons,** 49 Elizabeth St., SW1W 9PP, ℰ 730 0074 – 🔼 🅰🅴 ⓞ 𝑉𝐼𝑆𝐴   AX **a**
closed Saturday, Sunday and Bank Holidays – **M** a la carte 10.15/14.00 s. ▯ 2.80.

XX **Ciboure,** 21 Eccleston St., SW1W 9LX, ℰ 730 2505, French rest. – 🔼 🅰🅴 ⓞ 𝑉𝐼𝑆𝐴   AX **a**
closed Saturday lunch, Sunday and Bank Holidays – **M** 17.00 t. (lunch) and a la carte
14.55/16.85 s. ▯ 2.95.

XX **Hunan,** 51 Pimlico Rd, SW1W 8WE, ℰ 730 5712, Chinese rest.   pp. 17-20 KZ **a**

XX **Gran Paradiso,** 52 Wilton Rd, SW1V 1DE, ℰ 828 5818, Italian rest. – 🔼 🅰🅴 ⓞ 𝑉𝐼𝑆𝐴   BX **a**
closed Saturday lunch and Sunday – **M** a la carte 10.20/12.70 t. ▯ 2.20.

X **La Fontana,** 101 Pimlico Rd, SW1W 8PH, ℰ 730 6630, Italian rest. – 🔼 🅰🅴 ⓞ
closed Bank Holidays – **M** a la carte 10.90/15.60 t. ▯ 3.00.   pp. 28 and 29 FT **u**

X **La Poule au Pot,** 231 Ebury St., SW1W 8UT, ℰ 730 7763, French rest.   pp. 17-20 KY **n**

X **Mimmo d'Ischia,** 61 Elizabeth St., SW1W 9PP, ℰ 730 5406, Italian rest. – 🔼 🅰🅴 ⓞ 𝑉𝐼𝑆𝐴
closed Sunday, Easter, Christmas and Bank Holidays – **M** a la carte 12.65/17.75 t. ▯ 3.75.

                                                                  AX **o**

X **Tate Gallery Rest.,** Tate Gallery, Millbank, SW1P 4RG, ℰ 834 6754, English rest., « Rex
Whistler murals » – 🍽   pp. 17-20 NY **c**
M (lunch only).

X **Bumbles,** 16 Buckingham Palace Rd, SW1W 0QP, ℰ 828 2903, Bistro – 🔼 🅰🅴 ⓞ 𝑉𝐼𝑆𝐴
closed Saturday lunch and Sunday – **M** 10.95 t. and a la carte 10.25/12.20 t. ▯ 2.15.   BV **c**

X **Villa Medici,** 35 Belgrave Rd, SW1, ℰ 828 3613, Italian rest. – 🔼 🅰🅴 ⓞ 𝑉𝐼𝑆𝐴   BX **c**
closed Saturday lunch, Sunday and Bank Holidays – **M** a la carte 9.50/15.60 t. ▯ 2.50.

Le Grand Londres (GREATER LONDON) est composé de la City et de 32 arrondisse-
ments administratifs (Borough) eux-mêmes divisés en quartiers ou villages ayant
conservé leur caractère propre (Area).

CAR REPAIRS IN LONDON

RÉPARATION DE VOITURES A LONDRES

RIPARAZIONE DI VETTURA A LONDRA

KFZ-REPARATUR IN LONDON

In the event of a breakdown in London, the location of the nearest dealer for your make of car can be obtained by calling the following numbers between 9am and 5pm.

En cas de panne à Londres, vous pouvez obtenir l'adresse du plus proche concessionnaire de votre marque d'automobile en appelant les numéros suivants entre 9 heures et 17 heures.

In caso di guasto a Londra, Vi sara' possibile ottenere l'indirizzo del concessionario della vostra marca di automobile, chiamando i seguenti numeri dalle ore 9.00 alle ore 17.00.

Im Pannenfall können sie die Adresse der nächstgelegenen Reparaturwerkstatt ihrer Automarke zwischen 9 Uhr und 17 Uhr unter folgenden Telefon-Nr. erfahren.

ALFA ROMEO	Alfa Romeo (GB) Ltd Edgware Rd London NW2 6LX (01) 450 9191	**AUSTIN ROVER**	(includes Morris, Triumph, MG, Vanden Plas) Kennings Northern The Hyde Colindale NW9 (01) 205 5402
BMW	BMW (GB) Ltd Ellesfield Av. Bracknell Berks. RG12 4TA (0344) 46565	**CITROEN**	Citroen Cars Ltd Mill St. Slough Berks. SL2 5DE (0753) 23808
COLT-MITSUBISHI	Colt Car Co. Ltd Watermore Cirencester Glos. GL7 1LS (0285) 5777 ext 204/5	**DATSUN-NISSAN**	Datsun (UK) Ltd New Rd Durrington Worthing West Sussex (0903) 68561
FIAT	Fiat Information Service PO Box 39 Windsor Berkshire SL4 3SP 0753 556307	**FORD**	Ford Motor Co. Ltd Becket House Chapel High Brentwood Essex CM14 4BY (0277) 251100
HONDA	Honda (UK) Ltd Power Rd Chiswick London W4 5YT (01) 747 1400	**JAGUAR**	H.R. Owen Ltd Lyttleton Rd Barnet London (01) 458 7111
LAND ROVER-RANGE ROVER	Land Rover Ltd Lode Lane Solihull West Midlands (021) 743 4242	**MAZDA**	Mazda Cars (UK) Ltd Mount Ephraim Tunbridge Wells Kent TN5 8BS (0892) 40123

MERCEDES BENZ

Mercedes Benz (UK) Ltd
403 Edgware Rd
Colindale
London NW9
(01) 205 1212

PORSCHE

Porsche Cars (GB) Ltd
23-30 Richfield Av.
Reading
Berks. RG1 8PH
(0734) 595411

RELIANT

Chequered Flag
(Engineering) Ltd
548/580 High Rd
Chiswick
London W4
(01) 995 0102

RENAULT

Renault Ltd
Western Av.
Acton
London W3 ORZ
(01) 992 3481

SAAB

Saab (GB) Ltd
Saab House
Fieldhouse Lane
Marlow
Bucks.
(06284) 6977

SKODA

Skoda (GB) Ltd
150 Goswell Rd
London EC1
(01) 253 7441

TALBOT-PEUGEOT

Warwick Wright Motors
Ltd
Chiswick Roundabout
North Circular Rd
Chiswick
London W4
(01) 995 1466

TOYOTA

Toyota (GB) Ltd
The Quadrangle
Redhill
Surrey RH1 1PS
(0737) 68585

VAUXHALL-OPEL

Hamilton Motors Ltd
466-490 Edgware Rd
London W2 1EL
(01) 723 0022
(01) 961 1177
(24 hr recovery)

VOLKSWAGEN-AUDI

V.A.G. (UK) Ltd
Yeomans Drive
Blakelands
Milton Keynes
Bucks. MK14 5AN
(0908) 679121

VOLVO

Volvo Concessionnaires
Ltd
Raeburn Rd South
Ipswich
Suffolk IP3 OES
(0473) 715131 ext 3460

LONGBRIDGE Warw. – see Warwick.

LONG EATON Derbs. 402 403 404 Q 25 – see Nottingham (Notts.).

LONGFORD West Midlands 403 404 P 26 – see Coventry.

LONGHORSLEY Northumb. 401 402 O 18 – see Morpeth.

LONG MELFORD Suffolk 404 W 27 – pop. 2,739 – ECD : Thursday – ✆ 0787 Sudbury.
See : Holy Trinity Church★ 15C.
♦ London 62 – ♦Cambridge 34 – Colchester 18 – ♦Ipswich 24.

🏨 **Bull** (T.H.F.), Hall St., CO10 9JG, ℰ 78494, « Part 15C coaching inn » – 📺 🛁wc 📶 🅿. 🔣
AE ⊙ VISA
M 6.95/10.80 **st.** and a la carte ⓘ 2.70 – 🖵 5.50 – **27 rm** 37.50/51.00 **st.**

LONGNOR Staffs. 402 403 404 O 24 – pop. 381 – ⊠ Buxton – ✆ 029 883.
♦ London 161 – Derby 29 – ♦Manchester 31 – ♦Stoke-on-Trent 22.

🏠 **Ye Olde Cheshire Cheese,** High St., SK17 0NS, ℰ 218 – 🅿. 🔣 AE ⊙ VISA
M *(closed Sunday dinner and Monday)*6.00/12.00 **t.** and a la carte ⓘ 3.00 – **5 rm** 🖵 14.00/23.00 **t.**

LOOE Cornwall 403 G 32 The West Country G. – pop. 4,279 – ECD : Thursday – ✆ 050 36.
See : Site★ – Monkey Sanctuary★AC.
🅂 Looe Bin Down ℰ 050 34 (Widegates) 247, E : 3 m.
🆔 The Guildhall, Fore St. ℰ 2072 (summer only).
♦ London 264 – ♦Plymouth 21 – Truro 39.

🏨 **Hannafore Point** (Best Western), Marine Drive, West Looe, PL13 2DG, ℰ 3273, ⩽ Looe Bay, ☑ heated – 📺 🛁wc 📶 🅿. 🔣 AE ⊙ VISA
closed January and February – **M** (bar lunch)/dinner 10.00 **st.** and a la carte ⓘ 3.00 – **40 rm** 🖵 28.00/66.00 **st.** – SB 53.00/73.00 **st.**

🏨 **Rock Towers,** Marine Drive, Hannafore Rd, West Looe, PL13 2DQ, ℰ 2140, ⩽ Looe Bay and harbour – 🛁wc 🅿. 🔣 VISA 🛁
M (bar lunch)/dinner 8.00 **t.** and a la carte ⓘ 3.90 – **20 rm** 🖵 15.00/30.00 **t.** – SB (October-22 May)(except Easter and Christmas) 32.00/44.00 **st.**

🏨 **Klymiarven** 🍴, Barbican Hill, East Looe, PL13 1BH, ℰ 2333, ⩽ Looe and harbour, ☑ heated, 🌿 – 📺 🛁wc 🅿
closed 23 December-February – **M** (bar lunch)/dinner 7.25 **t.** ⓘ 2.85 – **14 rm** 🖵 12.50/36.00 **t.**

🏨 **Fieldhead,** Portruan Rd, Hannafore, PL13 2DR, ℰ 2689, ⩽ Looe Bay, ☑ heated, 🌿 – 🛁wc
🍴 🅿. 🔣 AE ⊙ VISA. 🛁
closed December and January – **M** 6.75 **st.** (dinner) and a la carte ⓘ 2.95 – **13 rm** 🖵 16.00/40.00 **st.** – SB (except summer) 40.00/48.00 **st.**

XX **Trelaske Country** 🍴 with rm, Polperro Rd, Trelaske, PL13 2JS, W : 2 ¼ m. by A 387 ℰ 2159, ⩽, 🌿 – 🍴wc 🅿. VISA. 🛁
closed January – **M** (dinner only and Sunday lunch) 9.50 **t.** and a la carte ⓘ 2.95 – **4 rm** 🖵 22.50/36.00 **t.** – SB (October-April) 39.00/43.00 **st.**

at Sandplace N : 2 ¼ m. on A 387 – ⊠ ✆ 050 36 Looe :

🏨 **Polraen Country House,** PL13 1PJ, ℰ 3956, 🌿 – 🍴wc 🅿. 🔣 VISA
M (bar lunch)/dinner 8.45 **t.** ⓘ 2.85 – **5 rm** 🖵 14.50/30.00 **t.** – SB (October-April)(except Easter and Christmas) 38.00/42.00 **st.**

at Widegates NE : 3 ½ m. on B 3253 – ⊠ Looe – ✆ 050 34 Widegates :

↑ **Coombe Farm** 🍴, PL13 1QN, ℰ 223, ⩽ countryside, ☑ heated, 🌿, park – 🅿. 🛁
March-October – **8 rm** 🖵 14.80/27.30 **t.**

at Talland Bay SW : 4 m. by A 387 – ⊠ Looe – ✆ 0503 Polperro :

🏨 **Talland Bay** 🍴, PL13 2JB, ℰ 72667, ⩽, « Country house atmosphere », ☑ heated, 🌿 – 📺 🛁wc 📶 🔥 🅿. 🔣 AE ⊙ VISA. 🛁
closed mid December-mid February – **M** (bar lunch in winter)(buffet lunch in summer)/dinner 10.00 **t.** and a la carte ⓘ 2.10 – **23 rm** 🖵 (dinner included) 28.00/89.00 **t.**, **1 suite.**

🏨 **Allhays Country House** 🍴, PL13 2JB, ℰ 72434, ⩽, 🌿 – 📺 🛁wc 🍴 🅿. 🔣 VISA
M (bar lunch)/dinner 7.50 **s.** ⓘ 3.00 – **6 rm** 🖵 10.40/32.50 **s.**

LORTON Cumbria – ✆ 090 085.
♦London 307 – ♦Carlisle 29 – Keswick 14.

🏨 **Hollin House** 🍴, Church Lane, CA13 9UN, ℰ 656, ⩽, « Converted rectory », 🌿 – 🅿. 🔣
VISA 🛁
March-October – **M** (bar lunch)/dinner 10.00 **st.** ⓘ 2.50 – **6 rm** 🖵 12.00/32.00 **st.**

Ensure that you have up to date **Michelin** maps in your car.

LOSTWITHIEL Cornwall **403** G 32 The West Country G. – pop. 1,972 – ECD : Wednesday –
✆ 0208 Bodmin.

Envir. : Restormel Castle★ *AC* (❄★), N : 1 ½ m.

🛈 Community Centre, Liddicoat Rd ℰ 872207.

◆ London 273 – ◆Plymouth 30 – Truro 23.

🏨 **Carotel Motel,** 17 Castle Hill, PL22 0DD, on A 390 ℰ 872223 – 📺 ⌐wc ⑉wc ☎ 🅿. 🔊 ⚌
　 ⓪ 𝘝𝘐𝘚𝘈
　 M (bar lunch)/dinner 8.30 **st.** ⑆ 2.80 – ☐ 3.00 – **32 rm** 20.00/29.00 **t.** – SB (except Bank
　 Holidays) 40.00/48.00 **st.**

✕ **Trewithen,** 3 Fore St., PL22 0AD, ℰ 872373 – 🔊 ⓪ 𝘝𝘐𝘚𝘈
　 closed Monday in winter, Sunday . May and 1 week Christmas – **M** (dinner only) a la carte
　 9.35/11.10 **t.** ⑆ 4.00.

LOUGHBOROUGH Leics. **402 403 404** Q 25 – pop. 44,895 – ECD : Wednesday – ✆ 0509.

🛈 John Storer House, Wards End ℰ 230131.

◆ London 117 – ◆Birmingham 41 – ◆Leicester 11 – ◆Nottingham 15.

🏨 **King's Head** (Embassy), High St., LE11 2QL, ℰ 233222 – 🔆 📺 ⌐wc ⑉wc ☎ 🅿. 🔊 🔊 ⚌
　 ⓪ 𝘝𝘐𝘚𝘈. 🦅
　 M (carving rest.) 7.00/8.25 **st.** ⑆ 2.50 – ☐ 5.00 – **86 rm** 24.00/42.00 **st.** – SB 50.00 **st.**

🏨 **Cedars,** Cedar Rd, LE11 2AB, S : 1 m. off Leicester Rd ℰ 214459, ⤳ heated, �🌲 – 📺 ⌐wc
　 ⑉wc ☎ 🅿. 🔊 🔊 𝘝𝘐𝘚𝘈
　 closed 25 to 28 December – **M** *(closed Sunday dinner to non-residents)*
　 6.00/12.00 **t.** and a la carte ⑆ 2.70 – **37 rm** ☐ 16.50/38.00 **t.** – SB (weekends only) 56.00 **st.**

✕✕✕ **Roger Burdell,** The Manor House, 11-12 Sparrow Hill, LE11 1BT, ℰ 231813 – 🔊 ⚌ ⓪ 𝘝𝘐𝘚𝘈
　 M *(closed Sunday dinner and Monday lunch)* 9.00/18.50 **st.** ⑆ 3.80.

　 at Quorn SE : 3 m. on A 6 – ✉ ✆ 0509 Loughborough :

🏨 **Quorn Country,** Charnwood House, 66 Leicester Rd, LE12 8BB, ℰ 415050, �🌲 – 🔲 📺 ☎
　 🍴 🅿. ⚌ ⓪ 𝘝𝘐𝘚𝘈
　 M 7.50/9.95 **t.** and a la carte ⑆ 3.50 – **19 rm** ☐ 50.00/65.00 **st.**, **3 suites** 120.00 **st.** – SB (week-
　 ends only) (except Christmas) 50.00/60.00 **st.**

AUSTIN-ROVER-JAGUAR Woodgate ℰ 262710
COLT Southfield Rd ℰ 212330
FIAT Station Rd ℰ 05097 (Kegworth) 2523
MAZDA Clarence St. ℰ 266901
NISSAN Nottingham Rd ℰ 212949
RENAULT Nottingham Rd ℰ 267657

SUBARU Charnwood Rd ℰ 503339
TOYOTA Pinfold Gate ℰ 215731
VAUXHALL-OPEL Woodgate ℰ 213030
VOLVO Derby Rd ℰ 217777
VW, AUDI 28 Market St. ℰ 217080

LOUTH Lincs. **402 404** U 23 – pop. 13,019 – ECD : Thursday – ✆ 0507.

See : St. James' Church★ 15C – 🍴 Crowtree Lane ℰ 603681.

◆ London 155 – Boston 33 – Grimsby 17 – Lincoln 26.

🏨 **Priory,** Eastgate, LN11 9AJ, ℰ 602930, �🌲, 🦅 – 📺 ⌐wc ⑉wc 🅿. 🔊 𝘝𝘐𝘚𝘈. 🦅
　 closed 23 December-2 January – **M** (dinner only) 7.50 **t.** ⑆ 3.25 – **12 rm** ☐ 24.00/40.00 **t.**

LOWER BEEDING West Sussex **404** T 30 – see Horsham.

LOWER PEOVER Cheshire **402 403 404** M 24 – see Knutsford.

LOWER SLAUGHTER Glos. **403 404** O 28 – see Stow-on-the-Wold.

LOWER SWELL Glos. **403 404** O 28 – see Stow-on-the-Wold.

LOWESTOFT Suffolk **404** Z 26 – pop. 59,430 – ECD : Thursday – ✆ 0502.

🛈 The Esplanade ℰ 65989.

◆ London 116 – ◆Ipswich 43 – ◆Norwich 30.

🏨 **Victoria,** Kirkley Cliff, NR33 0BZ, ℰ 4433, ≤, ⤳ heated – 🔆 📺 ⌐wc ⑉wc 📶 🅿. 🔊
　 ⚌ ⓪ 𝘝𝘐𝘚𝘈
　 M (buttery lunch) dinner 7.95 **t.** and a la carte ⑆ 2.75 – **46 rm** ☐ 28.50/40.00 **t.** – SB (weekends
　 only) 40.00/45.00 **st.**

⌂ **Rockville,** 6 Pakefield Rd, NR33 0HS, ℰ 81011 – 🔊 𝘝𝘐𝘚𝘈. 🦅
　 7 rm ☐ 9.50/26.50 **st.**

　 at Oulton NW : 2 m. by B 1074 – ✉ ✆ 0502 Lowestoft :

🏨 **Parkhill** 🦅, Parkhill, NR32 5DQ, N : ½ m. on A 1117 ℰ 730322, �🌲 – 📺 ⌐wc 📶 🅿. 🔊 🔊
　 𝘝𝘐𝘚𝘈
　 M *(closed lunch Saturday and Sunday)* a la carte 9.90/15.00 **t.** ⑆ 4.00 – **12 rm** ☐ 25.00/35.00 **t.**

AUSTIN-ROVER 97/99 London Rd South ℰ 61711
FORD Whapload Rd ℰ 653553
NISSAN High St. ℰ 65301
RENAULT 50-58 Long Rd ℰ 2783
TALBOT, PEUGEOT Beccles Rd, Oulton Broad ℰ 63622

VAUXHALL-OPEL, BEDFORD London Rd South ℰ 3512
VW, AUDI Cooke Rd, South Lowestoft Industrial Estate ℰ 2583

322

LOWESWATER Cumbria **402** K 20 – pop. 231 – ECD : Thursday – ✉ Cockermouth – ☎ 090 085 Lorton.

♦ London 305 – ♦Carlisle 33 – Keswick 12.

🏠 **Scale Hill** ⌒, CA13 9UX, ℰ 232, ≼, 🚗 – 🚪wc ⅋ ℗
closed 4 January-February – **M** (bar lunch)/dinner 10.00 **st.** – **14 rm** ⌑ 20.00/45.00 **st.**

LOWICK GREEN Cumbria **402** K 21 – see Ulverston.

LOW LAITHE North Yorks. – see Pateley Bridge.

LOW ROW North Yorks. – ✉ ☎ 0748 Richmond.

♦ London 256 – ♦ Carlisle 64 – ♦ Leeds 66 – ♦ Middlesbrough 39.

🏠 **Punch Bowl Inn,** DL11 6PF, ≼ – 🚪wc 🚪wc ℗, 🔺 🖅 ⓞ 𝘝𝘐𝘚𝘈
M (bar lunch)/dinner 10.00 **t.** ⓙ 2.50 – **14 rm** ⌑ 16.00/41.00 **t.**

LUDLOW Salop **403** L 26 – pop. 7,496 – ECD : Thursday – ☎ 0584.

See : Castle* (ruins 11C-16C) *AC* – Parish Church* 13C – Feathers Hotel* early 17C – Broad Street* 17C.

Envir. : Stokesay Castle* (13C) *AC*, NW : 6 ½ m.

🏌 Bromfield ℰ 058 477 (Bromfield) 285, N : 2 m. on A 49.

🏥 Castle St. ℰ 3857 (summer only).

♦ London 162 – ♦Birmingham 39 – Hereford 24 – Shrewsbury 29.

🏨 **Feathers,** Bull Ring, SY8 1AA, ℰ 5261, Telex 35637, « Part Elizabethan house » – ▯ 📺 ☎
℗, 🔺 🖅 ⓞ 𝘝𝘐𝘚𝘈, ⅙
M 8.50/14.50 **t.** and a la carte ⓙ 3.25 – **35 rm** ⌑ 42.00/64.00 **st.** – SB (November-March) 69.00/86.00 **st.**

🏨 **Overton Grange** ⌒, Hereford Rd, SY8 4AD, S : 1 ¾ m. on old A 49 ℰ 3500, 🚗 – 📺 🚪wc
🚪wc ☏ ℗, 🔺 🖅 ⓞ 𝘝𝘐𝘚𝘈
M 7.95/8.50 **t.** and a la carte ⓙ 2.95 – **17 rm** ⌑ 15.50/40.50 **st.** – SB (except Christmas) 41.00/50.00 **st.**

🏠 **Angel,** 8 Broad St., SY8 1NG, ℰ 2581 – 📺 🚪wc ☎ ⇦ ℗, 🔺 🖅 ⓞ 𝘝𝘐𝘚𝘈
M 6.00/8.50 **t.** ⓙ 2.70 – **17 rm** ⌑ 32.00/45.00 **st.** – SB 55.00/60.00 **st.**

⌂ **Croft,** 12 Dinham, SY8 1EJ, ℰ 2076
8 rm ⌑ 9.00/22.00 **s.**

⌂ **Cecil,** Sheet Rd, SY8 1LR, ℰ 2442, 🚗 – ℗
11 rm ⌑ 10.00/20.00 **st.**

AUSTIN-ROVER Corve St. ℰ 2301   VOLVO, SUBARU Bromfield Rd ℰ 4666
FIAT St. John's Lane ℰ 4531

LUDWELL Wilts. – see Shaftesbury (Dorset).

LUGWARDINE Heref. and Worc. – see Hereford.

LUNDY (Isle of) Devon **403** FG 30 The West Country G – pop. 52.

See : Site **.

Helicopter service to Ilfracombe (Hartland Point) ℰ 062 882 (Littlewick Green) 3431.

⛴ to Bideford (Lundy Co.) 2-3 weekly (2 h 30 mn).

   Hotels see : Ilfracombe.

LUTON Beds. **404** S 28 – pop. 163,209 – ECD : Wednesday – ☎ 0582.

See : Luton Hoo* (Wernher Collection**) and park* *AC*.

🏌 Stockwood Park, London Rd ℰ 413704, S : 1 m. on A 6.

✈ Luton International Airport : ℰ 36061, Telex 826409, E : 1 ½ m. – **Terminal :** Luton Bus Station.

🏥 Central Library, St. George's Sq. ℰ 32629.

♦ London 35 – ♦Cambridge 36 – ♦Ipswich 93 – ♦Oxford 45 – Southend-on-Sea 63.

🏨 **Chiltern** (Crest), Waller Av., Dunstable Rd, LU4 9RU, NW : 2 m. on A 505 ℰ 575911, Telex 825048 – ▯ 📺 ⅋ ℗, 🔺 🔺 🖅 ⓞ 𝘝𝘐𝘚𝘈, ⅙
M approx 12.25 **st.** – ⌑ 5.50 – **99 rm** 49.00/58.00 **st.** – SB (weekends only) 59.00 **st.**

🏨 **Strathmore Thistle** (Thistle), Arndale Centre, LU1 2TR, ℰ 34199, Telex 825763 – ▯ 📺 ☎
℗, 🔺 🔺 🖅 ⓞ 𝘝𝘐𝘚𝘈, ⅙
M 9.50 **t.** and a la carte ⓙ 2.95 – ⌑ 5.25 – **151 rm** 44.00/65.00 **st.**

🏨 **Crest** (Crest), 641 Dunstable Rd, LU4 8RQ, NW : 2 ¾ m. on A 505 ℰ 575955, Telex 826283 –
▯ 📺 🚪wc ☏ ℗, 🔺 🖅 ⓞ 𝘝𝘐𝘚𝘈, ⅙
M approx 11.50 **st.** – ⌑ 5.75 – **139 rm** 45.50/54.50 **st.** – SB (weekends only) 55.00 **st.**

P.T.O. →

  🏠 **Leaside,** 72 New Bedford Rd, LU3 1BT, ℰ 417643 – 📺 🛁wc ☏ 🅿. 🅾 AE ⓪ VISA. ℀
    closed Christmas Day – **M** *(closed Saturday lunch and Sunday dinner)* 12.00 **st.** and a la carte
    ◊ 3.00 – **12 rm** 🖙 28.00/40.00 **st.** – SB (weekends only)(except Bank Holidays) 58.00 **st.**

  🏠 **Red Lion,** Castle St., LU1 3AA, ℰ 27337 – 📺 🛁wc ☏ 🅿 – **48 rm.**

  ⬆ **Humberstone,** 618 Dunstable Rd, LU4 8BT, NW : 2 ½ m. on A 505 ℰ 574399 – 📺 🛁wc 🅿.
    ℀
    closed 24 to 27 December – **13 rm** 🖙 14.95/31.90 **st.**

AUSTIN-ROVER-DAIMLER-JAGUAR Latimer Rd ℰ
411311
AUSTIN-ROVER Leagrave Rd ℰ 571221
BMW 80-88 Marsh Rd ℰ 576622
FORD 326/340 Dunstable Rd ℰ 31133

NISSAN, RENAULT 619 Hitchin Rd ℰ 35332
VAUXHALL-OPEL 15 Hitchin Rd ℰ 454666
VAUXHALL-OPEL 540/550 Dunstable Rd ℰ 575944
VAUXHALL Memorial Rd ℰ 572577
RENAULT, VW-AUDI Castle St. ℰ 417505

LYDDINGTON Leics. – see Uppingham.

LYME REGIS Dorset **408** L 31 **The West Country G.** – pop. 4,510 – ECD : Thursday – 🌣 029 74.
See : Site ★ – The Cobb ★.

🛦 Timber Hill ℰ 2043 – 🛈 The Guildhall, Bridge St. ℰ 2138.

♦London 160 – Dorchester 25 – Exeter 31 – Taunton 27.

  🏨 **Mariners,** Silver St., DT7 3HS, ℰ 2753, Telex 46491, 🐎 – 📺 🛁wc 🛁wc 🅿. 🅾 AE ⓪ VISA.
    ℀
    March-October – **M** (bar lunch)/dinner 11.25 **t.** ◊ 2.85 – **16 rm** 🖙 22.00/47.00 – SB (except
    summer) 50.00/53.50 **st.**

  🏨 **Alexandra,** Pound St., DT7 3HZ, ℰ 2010, ≤, 🐎 – 📺 🛁wc 🛁wc 🅿. 🅾 AE ⓪ VISA
    closed January-mid February – **M** 6.15/9.25 **t.** and a la carte ◊ 1.60 – **26 rm** 🖙 20.00/60.00 **t.** –
    SB (except mid June - mid October) 40.00/53.00 **st.**

  ⬆ **Kersbrook,** Pound Rd, DT7 3HX, ℰ 2596, 🐎 – 🛁wc 🛁wc 🅿. 🅾 AE VISA
    closed 10 November-January – **13 rm** 🖙 15.00/31.00 **t.**

  ✕ **Toni's,** 14-15 Monmouth St., DT7 3PX, ℰ 2079 – AE ⓪ VISA
    Easter-September – **M** *(closed Sunday and Monday)* (dinner only) a la carte 7.50/12.00 **t.**
    ◊ 3.00.

  at Rousdon (Devon) W : 3 m. on A 3052 – ✉ 🌣 029 74 Lyme Regis :

  🏨 **Dower House,** DT7 3RB, ℰ 0297 (Seaton) 21047, 🐎 – 🛁wc 🛁wc 🅿. 🅾 AE ⓪ VISA
    closed January-mid February – **M** 6.00/8.50 **t.** and a la carte ◊ 2.45 – **10 rm** 🖙 18.00/54.00 **t.** –
    SB 41.00/50.00 **st.**

  🏠 **Orchard Country,** DT7 3XW, ℰ 2972, 🐎 – 🛁wc 🛁wc 🅿. 🅾
    March-October, Christmas and New Year – **M** (bar lunch)/dinner 8.50 **st.** ◊ 2.85 – **14 rm**
    🖙 21.00/42.00 **t.** – SB 45.00/47.00 **st.**

  at Uplyme (Devon) NW : 1 ¼ m. on A 3070 – ✉ 🌣 029 74 Lyme Regis :

  🏨 **Devon** (Best Western), Lyme Rd, DT7 3TQ, ℰ 3231, ≤, 🏊 heated, 🐎, park, – 🛁wc 🅿. 🅾
    AE ⓪ VISA
    April-October and Christmas – **M** (bar lunch)/dinner 10.00 **t.** ◊ 3.00 – **21 rm** 🖙 24.00/57.00 **t.**
    – SB 52.00/56.00 **st.**

LYMINGTON Hants. **408 404** P 31 – pop. 11,614 – ECD : Wednesday – 🌣 0590.

🚢 to the Isle of Wight : Yarmouth (Sealink) 13-16 daily (30 mn).

♦London 104 – Bournemouth 18 – ♦Southampton 19 – Winchester 32.

  🏨 **Stanwell House,** 14 High St., SO4 9AA, ℰ 77123, Telex 477463, 🐎 – 📺 🛁wc ☏. 🅾 AE
    ⓪ VISA. ℀
    closed 24 to 26 December – **M** (rest. see **Railings** below) – **33 rm** 🖙 19.25/47.00 **st.** – SB
    (November-March) 52.00/57.00 **st.**

  ✕✕ **Railings,** (at Stanwell House H.) 14 High St., SO4 9AA, ℰ 77124 – 🅾 AE ⓪ VISA
    closed 24 to 26 December – **M** 9.00/12.50 **st.** and a la carte ◊ 2.50.

  ✕ **Limpets,** 9 Gosport St., SO4 9BG, ℰ 75595 – 🅾 AE
    closed Sunday and Monday October-April and December – **M** (dinner only) a la carte
    8.60/13.00 **t.** ◊ 2.45.

  at Mount Pleasant NW : 2 m. by A 337 – ✉ 🌣 0590 Lymington :

  🏨 **Passford House** 🦢, Mount Pleasant Lane, SO4 8FS, ℰ 682398, ≤, 🏊 heated, 🐎, park, 🎾
    – 📺 🅿. 🕭. 🅾 AE VISA. ℀
    M 6.00/10.50 **t.** and a la carte ◊ 3.00 – **51 rm** 🖙 36.00/60.00 **st.** – SB (except summer)
    60.00/66.00 **st.**

  at Sway NW : 4 m. by A 337 on B 3055 – ✉ 🌣 0590 Lymington :

  🏠 **White Rose,** Station Rd, SO4 0BA, ℰ 682754, 🏊, 🐎, park – 🕭 📺 🛁wc 🅿. 🅾 VISA
    M 6.00/7.00 **st.** and a la carte ◊ 2.95 – **13 rm** 🖙 21.00/60.00 **st.** – SB (except August and
    September) 45.00/55.00 **st.**

FIAT Sway ℰ 059 068 (Sway) 2212

LYMM Cheshire **402 403 404** M 23 – pop. 10,036 – ECD : Wednesday – ✆ 092 575.
🛅 Whitbarrow Rd ☎ 2177.
♦ London 193 – Chester 24 – ♦Liverpool 23 – ♦Manchester 15.

🏨 **Lymm** (De Vere), Whitbarrow Rd, WA13 9AQ, ☎ 2233, Telex 629455, ☞ – TV ⇌wc 🛄wc
🕿 ☎. 🔄. 🅰 🆎 ⓪ 𝗩𝗜𝗦𝗔
M 7.50/10.50 **st.** and a la carte 🍷 3.60 – **69 rm** ⇌ 39.50/49.00 **st.** – SB (weekends only)
50.00/55.00 **st.**

LYMPSTONE Devon **403** J 32 – see Exmouth.

LYNDHURST Hants. **403 404** P 31 – pop. 2,828 – ECD : Wednesday – ✆ 042 128.
See : New Forest★.
🛅 New Forest ☎ 2450 – 🅱 Main Car Park ☎ 2269 (summer only).
♦London 95 → Bournemouth 20 – ♦Southampton 10 – Winchester 23.

🏨 **Parkhill** ⏃, Beaulieu Rd, SO4 7FZ, SE : 1 ¼ m. by B 3056 ☎ 2944, ≼, « Tastefully furnished
country house », 🛆 heated, ☞, park – TV ⇌wc 🕿 ☎. 🔄 🅰 🆎 ⓪ 𝗩𝗜𝗦𝗔
closed 28 December-10 January – **M** 7.65/11.80 **t.** and a la carte 🍷 3.50 – **22 rm** ⇌ 30.00/60.00 **t.**
– SB 70.00/90.00 **st.**

🏨 **Crown** (Best Western), 9 High St., SO4 7NF, ☎ 2722 – 🔤🔀 TV ⇌wc 🐾 ☎. 🔄 🅰 🆎 ⓪ 𝗩𝗜𝗦𝗔
M 9.50 **t.** and a la carte 🍷 2.50 – **42 rm** ⇌ 34.00/56.00 **t.** – SB (weekends only) 62.00/65.00 **st.**

🏠 **Pikes Hill Forest Lodge,** Pikes Hill, Romsey Rd, SO4 7AS, ☎ 3677, 🛆 heated, ☞ – TV
⇌wc 🛄wc 🐾 🖑. ☎. 🅰 🆎 ⓪ 𝗩𝗜𝗦𝗔
M (bar lunch)/dinner 10.50 **t.** and a la carte 🍷 2.75 – **20 rm** ⇌ 19.00/45.00 **t.** – SB 53.00/59.00 **st.**

🏠 **Forest Point,** Romsey Rd, SO4 7AR, ☎ 2420 – ☎. 🔄 🅰 🆎 ⓪ 𝗩𝗜𝗦𝗔. 🌸
M (dinner only and bar lunch July-October) 7.75 **t.** (dinner) and a la carte 🍷 3.50 – **10 rm**
⇌ 12.00/39.00 **t.**

⌂ **Whitemoor House,** Southampton Rd, SO4 7BU, ☎ 2186 – ☎
5 rm ⇌ 15.00/25.00 **st.**

⌂ **Ormonde House,** Southampton Rd, SO4 7BT, ☎ 2806, ☞ – TV ⇌wc 🛄wc ☎. 🔄 🅰 🆎 𝗩𝗜𝗦𝗔.
🌸
closed first 2 weeks January – **14 rm** ⇌ 12.80/31.00 **st.**

at Woodlands NE : 3 ½ m. by A 35 – ✉ ✆ 042 129 Ashurst :

🏠 **Woodlands Lodge** ⏃, Bartley Rd, SO4 2GN, ☎ 2257, ☞ – TV ⇌wc ☎. 🖑. 🔄 𝗩𝗜𝗦𝗔. 🌸
M (bar lunch)/dinner 8.25 **st.** 🍷 2.80 – **11 rm** ⇌ 19.00/44.00 – SB (October-May) 44.00/50.00 **st.**

AUSTIN-ROVER 77 High St. ☎ 2861   VAUXHALL-OPEL Romsey Rd ☎ 2609

LYNMOUTH Devon **403** I 30 – see Lynton.

LYNTON Devon **403** I 30 The West Country G. – pop. 2,075 (inc. Lynmouth) – ECD : Thursday –
✆ 059 85 (4 fig.) and 0598 (5 fig.).
See : Site ★ (≼★★) – **Envir. :** Valley of the Rocks ★, W : 1 m. – Watersmeet ★, E : 1 ½ m.
🅱 Town Hall, Lee Rd ☎ 2225.
♦London 206 – Exeter 59 – Taunton 44.

🏠 **Lynton Cottage** ⏃, North Walk, EX35 6ED, ☎ 52342, ≼ bay and Countisbury hill, ☞ –
⇌wc 🛄wc ☎. 🔄 🅰 🆎 ⓪ 𝗩𝗜𝗦𝗔
closed January – **M** (bar lunch)/dinner 8.85 **t.** and a la carte 🍷 3.30 – **21 rm** ⇌ 15.00/49.00 **t.** –
SB (November-March) 40.00/50.00 **st.**

🏠 **Hewitt's** ⏃, North Walk, EX35 6HJ, ☎ 52293, ≼ bay and Countisbury hill, ☞, park – TV
⇌wc ☎. 🔄 🅰 🆎 ⓪ 𝗩𝗜𝗦𝗔. 🌸
March-October – **M** (bar lunch)/dinner 9.50 **t.** 🍷 2.00 – **12 rm** ⇌ 11.00/57.00 **t.** – SB (weekdays
only) 40.70/52.70 **st.**

🏠 **Crown,** Sinai Hill, EX35 6AG, ☎ 52253 – TV ⇌wc ☎. 🔄 🅰 🆎 ⓪ 𝗩𝗜𝗦𝗔
closed December and January – **M** (bar lunch)/dinner 9.50 **t.** and a la carte 🍷 3.00 – **16 rm**
⇌ 21.00/40.50 **t.** – SB (except Easter) 47.00/54.00 **st.**

🏠 **Rockvale,** EX35 6HW, off Lee Rd ☎ 52279 – TV ⇌wc ☎
March-October – **M** (closed Saturday lunch) (bar lunch)/dinner 7.50 **st.** 🍷 2.20 – **9 rm**
⇌ 13.00/21.00 **st.** – SB 38.00/42.00 **st.**

🕏 **Chough's Nest** ⏃, North Walk, EX35 6HJ, ☎ 53315, ≼ – ⇌wc. 🌸
Easter-mid October – **M** (dinner only) 6.50 **st.** 🍷 2.30 – **11 rm** ⇌ 12.65/28.00 **st.** – SB
40.00/44.00 **st.**

🕏 **Castle Hill House,** Castle Hill, EX35 6JA, ☎ 52291 – TV ⇌wc 🛄. 🔄 𝗩𝗜𝗦𝗔. 🌸
closed 15 December-1 February – **M** 10.50 **t.** – **9 rm** ⇌ 16.50/28.00 **t.** – SB (mid September-
June) 33.00/45.00 **st.**

⌂ **Seawood** ⏃, North Walk, EX35 6HJ, ☎ 52272, ≼ – 🛄wc ☎
Mid March-November – **12 rm** ⇌ 11.50/28.00 **t.**

⌂ **Combe Park** ⏃, Hillsford Bridge, EX35 6LE, S : 3 ½ m. by A 39 ☎ 52356, ☞ – ⇌wc 🛄wc ☎
9 rm.

P.T.O. →

Neubia House, Lydiate Lane, EX35 6AH, ☎ 52309 – wc wc Ⓟ
closed December and January – **12 rm** 14.25/30.50 **st.**

Pine Lodge, Lynway, EX35 6AX, ☎ 53230, ≤, – Ⓟ
Easter and mid May-October – **8 rm** 9.50/24.00 **st.**

at Lynmouth – ✉ Lynmouth – ☎ 059 85 Lynton :

Tors, EX35 6NA, ☎ 53236, ≤ Lynmouth and bay, heated, – | wc Ⓟ.
March-mid November – **M** 4.75/10.00 **st.** and a la carte 3.00 – **39 rm** 16.00/52.00 **st.** – SB (except summer) 44.00/48.00 **st.**

Bath, EX35 6EL, ☎ 52238 – wc Ⓟ. AE VISA
weekends only in March and April-October – **M** (bar lunch Monday to Saturday)/dinner 8.00 **st.** and a la carte 3.00 – **24 rm** 10.50/36.00 **st.** – SB (except August and September) 31.00/48.00 **st.**

Beacon, Countisbury Hill, EX35 6ND, E : ½ m. on A 39 ☎ 53268, ≤, – TV wc wc Ⓟ.
closed December and January – **M** 5.00/7.50 **st.** and a la carte 2.00 – **7 rm** 13.50/29.00 **st.** – SB (except July, August and Bank Holidays) 32.80/39.50 **st.**

Heatherville, Tors Park, EX35 6NB, ☎ 52327 – wc Ⓟ.
March-October – **8 rm** 11.00/22.00 **t.**

at Brendon E : 4 m. by A 39 – ✉ Lynton – ☎ 059 87 Brendon :

Stag Hunters, High St., EX35 1PS, ☎ 222, ≤, , – wc Ⓟ. VISA
closed January-mid March – **18 rm** 16.00/34.00 **t.** – SB 88.00 **st.**

at Woody Bay W : 3 ¼ m. via Coast Road – ✉ ☎ 059 83 Parracombe :

Woody Bay, Parracombe, EX31 4QX, ☎ 264, ≤ bay – wc Ⓟ. VISA
closed February – **M** (bar lunch)/dinner 8.50 **t.** and a la carte 3.00 – **13 rm** 16.50/44.00 **t.** – SB 43.00/56.00 **st.**

at Martinhoe W : 4 ¼ m. via Coast Road – ✉ ☎ 059 83 Parracombe :

Old Rectory, EX31 4QT, ☎ 368, – wc Ⓟ
Mid March-October – **M** (dinner only) 10.50 **t.** 2.60 – **10 rm** 10.50/36.00 **t.** – SB (except summer) 38.50/45.00 **st.**

at Heddon's Mouth W : 5 ¾ m. by B 3234 off A 39 – ✉ ☎ 059 83 Parracombe :

Heddon's Gate, Parracombe, EX31 4PZ, ☎ 313, ≤, , park – TV wc wc Ⓟ. AE
Easter-October – **M** (bar lunch)/dinner 12.50 **t.** 3.30 – **15 rm** 21.90/45.40 **t.**, **2 suites** 35.40/50.00 **t.**.

LYTHAM ST ANNE'S Lancs. 402 L 22 – pop. 39 ,599 – ECD : Wednesday – ☎ 0253 St. Anne's.
18 Fairhaven, Lytham Hall Park ☎ 736741, E : 2 m. – 18 St. Anne's Old Links, Highbury Rd ☎ 723597.
St. Anne's Sq. ☎ 725610 and 721222 ext 416.
♦London 237 – ♦Blackpool 7 – ♦Liverpool 44 – Preston 13.

Grand, 77 South Promenade, FY8 1NB, ☎ 721288, Telex 67481 – | TV wc ☎ Ⓟ. AE VISA
M 5.25/8.50 **t.** and a la carte – **40 rm** 39.50/50.00 **t.** – SB (except Christmas) 55.00 **st.**

at Lytham SE : 3 m. – ✉ ☎ 0253 Lytham :

Clifton Arms (Best Western), West Beach, FY8 5QJ, ☎ 739898, Telex 677463 – | TV Ⓟ. AE VISA
M 7.50/9.50 **t.** and a la carte – **45 rm** 42.00/60.00 **t.**, **1 suite** – SB (weekends only)(except Bank Holidays) 55.00/80.00 **st.**

AUSTIN-ROVER-DAIMLER Kings Rd ☎ 728051
CITROEN Henry St. ☎ 736670
FORD Preston Rd ☎ 733261
RENAULT Heyhouse Lane ☎ 726799
RENAULT Sefton Rd ☎ 726821
VAUXHALL Heeley Rd ☎ 726714
VOLVO St. Georges Rd ☎ 722241

MACCLESFIELD Cheshire 402 403 404 N 24 – pop. 47 ,525 – ECD : Wednesday – ☎ 0625.
Town Hall, Market Pl. ☎ 21955 ext 115.
♦London 186 – Chester 38 – ♦Manchester 18 – ♦Stoke-on-Trent 21.

Sutton Hall, Bullocks Lane, Sutton, SK11 0HE, SE : 2 m. by A 523 ☎ 3211, – TV wc ☎ Ⓟ. AE VISA
M 5.25 **st.** (lunch) and a la carte 7.90/13.85 **st.** 2.50 – **9 rm** 28.00/60.00 **st.**

Fourways Diner Motel, Cleulow Cross, Wincle, SK11 0QL, SE : 4 ½ m. on A 54 ☎ 026 07 (Wincle) 228, ≤, – TV wc wc Ⓟ. VISA
7 rm 18.00/25.00 **t.**

Olivers Bistro, 101-103 Chestergate, SK11 6DU, ☎ 32003 – VISA
M (dinner only) 8.50 **st.** and a la carte 2.95.

AUSTIN-ROVER Hobson St. ☎ 615555
FIAT London Rd ☎ 28866
FORD Hibel Rd ☎ 27766
HONDA Beech Lane ☎ 23592
PEUGEOT, TALBOT Waters Green ☎ 22226
RENAULT Davenport St. ☎ 23677
VAUXHALL, OPEL 98 Chestergate ☎ 22909
VW-AUDI Crossall St. ☎ 23036

MACHYNLLETH Powys [402] [403] I 26 – pop. 1,952 – ECD : Thursday – ☏ 0654.

Envir. : NW : Cader Idris (road ** **to Cader Idris : Cregenneu lakes) – Aberangell Clipiau (site★) NE : 10 m. – SE : Llyfnant Valley ★ via Glaspwll.**

[i] Canolfan Owain Glyndwr ☎ 2401.

♦London 220 – Shrewsbury 56 – Welshpool 37.

🏨 **Wynnstay** (T.H.F.), Maengwyn St., SY20 8AE, ☎ 2941 – [TV] 🛁wc 📞 [P]. [A] [AE] [D] [VISA]
M (buffet lunch Monday to Saturday)/dinner 9.00 **st.** and a la carte 🍷 2.70 – ☕ 5.50 – **26 rm** 33.50/41.00 **st.**

🏨 **Plas Dolguog** 🐦, SY20 8UJ, E : 1 ½ m. by A 489 ☎ 2244, <, « 17C country house », 🎣, 🌳 – 🛁wc [P]. [A] [VISA]. 🐕
M *(closed lunch to non-residents)* a la carte 7.30/11.35 **t.** – **7 rm** ☕ 22.00/42.00 **t.** – SB 43.00/53.00 **st.**

🍴 **Janie's,** 57 Maengwyn St., SY20 8EE, ☎ 2126
Easter-mid October – **M** *(closed Monday except Bank Holidays)* (dinner only and Sunday lunch) a la carte 7.75/12.75 **t.** 🍷 2.95.

at Corris (Gwynedd) N : 5 ¼ m. on A 487 – ✉ Machynlleth (Powys) – ☏ 065 473 Corris :

🏠 **Braich Goch,** SY20 9RD, on A 487 ☎ 229, <, 🌳 – 🚿wc [P]. [A]
M 5.50/5.75 **t.** and a la carte 🍷 3.10 – **6 rm** ☕ 12.00/28.00 **t.** – SB (October-April)(except Easter and Christmas) 26.00/31.00 **st.**

at Eglwysfach (Dyfed) SW : 6 m. on A 487 – ✉ Machynlleth (Powys) – ☏ 065 474 Glandyfi :

🏨 **Ynyshir Hall** 🐦, SY20 8TA, ☎ 209, <, « Country house in large gardens », park – 🛁wc [P]. [A] [AE] [D] [VISA]
M 8.50/14.95 **t.** 🍷 2.50 – **11 rm** ☕ 39.50/79.00 **t.** – SB (November-March) 68.00 **st.**

AUSTIN-ROVER Station Garage ☎ 2108
FORD ☎ 065 04 (Dinas Mawddwy) 326

MADINGLEY Cambs. [404] U 27 – see Cambridge.

MAENORBYR = Manorbier.

MAIDENCOMBE Devon [403] J 32 – see Torquay.

MAIDENHEAD Berks. [404] R 29 – pop. 59,809 – ECD : Thursday – ☏ 0628.

[i] Central Library, St. Ives Rd ☎ 781110.

London 33 – ♦Oxford 32 – Reading 13.

🏨 **Crest** (Crest), Manor Lane, SL6 2RA, ☎ 23444, Telex 847502, 🏊, 🌳, squash – [lift] [TV] 📞 ♿ [P]. 🏛 [A] [AE] [D] [VISA] 🐕
M (rest. see **Shoppenhangers Manor** below) – ☕ 6.25 – **190 rm** 54.50/64.50 **st.**, **1 suite** 71.00/115.00 **st.** – SB (weekends only) 67.00 **st.**

🏨 **Fredrick's,** Shoppenhangers Rd, SL6 2PZ, ☎ 35934, 🌳 – [TV] 🛁wc 🚿wc 📞 [P]. 🏛. [A] [AE] [D] [VISA]. 🐕
M (rest. see **Fredrick's** below) – **30 rm** ☕ 49.00/72.00 **t.**

🏨 Bear, 8-10 High St., SL6 1QJ, ☎ 25183 – [TV] 🚿 📞. [A] [VISA]
12 rm ☕ 30.00/38.00 **t.**

🍴🍴🍴 **Fredrick's** (at Fredrick's H.), Shoppenhangers Rd, SL6 2PZ, ☎ 24737, 🌳 – ❄ [P]. [A] [AE] [D] [VISA]
closed Saturday lunch – **M** 16.50/23.50 **t.** 🍷 4.25.

🍴🍴🍴 **Shoppenhangers Manor** (Crest) (at Crest H.), Manor Lane, SL6 2RA, ☎ 23444, Telex 847502, 🌳 – [P]. [A] [AE] [D] [VISA]
closed Saturday lunch, Sunday, 26 December-12 January and Bank Holidays – **M** 22.00 **st.** and a la carte 20.55/30.00 **st.** 🍷 5.00.

🍴🍴 **Franco's,** Ray Mead Rd, SL6 8NJ, ☎ 33522, Italian rest. – [P]. [A] [AE] [D] [VISA]
closed Saturday lunch and Sunday – **M** a la carte 9.80/13.60 **t.** 🍷 2.50.

🍴🍴 **Jasmine Peking,** 29 High St., SL6 1JG, ☎ 20334, Chinese rest. – [A] [AE] [D] [VISA]
M 9.25 **t.** and a la carte 6.25/9.00 **t.** 🍷 2.85.

🍴🍴 **Chez Michel et Valérie,** 7 Glynwood House, Bridge Av., SL6 1RS, ☎ 22450, French rest. – [A] [AE] [D] [VISA]
closed Saturday lunch, Sunday, Monday, first 2 weeks July and 2 weeks December - January – **M** 10.00 **t.** and a la carte 🍷 3.50.

🍴 **Maidenhead Chinese,** 45-47 Queen St., SL6 1LT, ☎ 24545, Chinese rest – [AE] [D] [VISA]
closed Sunday and Christmas – **M** a la carte 9.00/14.00 **t.** 🍷 3.50.

BMW 84 Altwood Rd ☎ 37611
FIAT Woodlands Park ☎ 062 882 (Littlewick Green) 3211
FORD Bath Rd, Taplow ☎ 29711
HONDA, MAZDA 14/20 Bath Rd ☎ 21331
ROLLS ROYCE 128 Bridge Rd ☎ 33188
VAUXHALL Braywick Rd ☎ 25321

Une voiture bien équipée, possède à son bord
des **cartes Michelin** à jour.

MAIDSTONE Kent **404** V 30 – pop. 86 ,067 – ECD : Wednesday – ✆ 0622.

See : All Saints' Church★ – Carriage Museum★ *AC* – Chillington Manor (Museum and Art Gallery★).

Envir. : Leeds Castle★ *AC*, SE : 4 ½ m. – Aylesford (The Friars carmelite priory : great courtyard★)
NW : 3 ½ m. – Coldrum Long Barrow (prehistoric stones) site★ : NE : 1 m. from Trottiscliffe plus
5 mn walk, NW : 12 m.

🛈 The Gatehouse, Old Palace Gardens, Mill St. ✆ 671361 ext 169 and 673581.

♦London 36 – ♦Brighton 64 – ♦Cambridge 84 – Colchester 72 – Croydon 36 – ♦Dover 45 – Southend-on-Sea 49.

⌂ **Grange Moor,** 4-8 St. Michael's Rd (off Tonbridge Rd), ME16 8BS, ✆ 677623 – 📺 📶wc ❷
🔼 *VISA*
M 6.00 **st.** and a la carte – **31 rm** ⌑ 14.00/34.00 **st.**

⌂ **Rock House,** 102 Tonbridge Rd, ME16 8SL, ✆ 51616 – ❷. 🔼 *VISA*. ⚶
closed 24 December-1 January – **10 rm** ⌑ 13.80/22.15 **st.**

⌂ **Carval,** 56-58 London Rd, ME16 8QL, ✆ 62100 – 📺 ❷. 🔼 *AE* ⓞ *VISA*. ⚶
8 rm ⌑ 12.00/15.00 **st.**

at Bearsted E : 3 m. by A 249 – ✉ ✆ 0622 Maidstone

XX **Sueffle,** The Green, ET14 4ND, ✆ 37065 – ❷
M (restricted lunch).

at Larkfield W : 3 ¼ m. on A 20 – ✉ Larkfield – ✆ 0732 West Malling :

🏨 **Larkfield** (Anchor), 812 London Rd, ME60 6HJ, ✆ 846858, Telex 957420 – ▤ rest 📺 ⇋wc
☎ & ❷. 🔬 🔼 *AE* ⓞ *VISA*
M *(closed lunch Saturday and Bank Holidays)* (carving rest.) a la carte 10.00/16.00 **t.** ⓗ 3.00 –
52 rm ⌑ 39.50/55.00 **t.**

XXX **Wealden Hall,** 773 London Rd, ME20 6DE, ✆ 840259 – ❷. 🔼 *AE* ⓞ *VISA*
closed Sunday dinner – **M** 7.95/9.50 **st.** and a la carte.

AUSTIN-ROVER-DAIMLER-JAGUAR Bircholt Rd ✆ 65461
BMW Broadway ✆ 686666
CITROEN Bow Rd, Wateringbury ✆ 812358
COLT Forstal Rd, Aylesford ✆ 76421
FIAT, LANCIA 29 Union St. ✆ 52439
FORD Ashford Rd ✆ 56781
HONDA Upper Stone St. ✆ 53096
LADA Loose Rd ✆ 52584

NISSAN Ashford Rd, Harrietsham ✆ 859363
PEUGEOT, TALBOT Mill St. ✆ 53333
RENAULT Ashford Rd ✆ 54744
SAAB Linton Rd, Loose ✆ 46629
VAUXHALL-OPEL, MERCEDES-BENZ Park Wood,
Sutton Rd ✆ 55531
VAUXHALL London Rd, Ditton ✆ 0732 (West Malling) 844922
VW, AUDI Upper Stone St. ✆ 50821

MALDON Essex **404** V 28 – pop. 14 ,638 – ECD : Wednesday – ✆ 0621.

🛈 2 High St. ✆ 56503.

♦London 42 – Chelmsford 9 – Colchester 17.

🏠 **Blue Boar** (T.H.F.), Silver St., CM9 7QE, ✆ 52681 – 📺 ⇋wc 🕮 ❷. 🔬 🔼 *AE* ⓞ *VISA*
M 9.40/8.00 **st.** and a la carte ⓗ 2.70 – ⌑ 5.50 – **23 rm** 32.00/43.00 **st.**

⌂ **Benbridge,** The Square, Heybridge, CM9 7LT, ✆ 57666 – 📺 ⇋wc 📶wc 🕮 ❷. 🔼 *AE* ⓞ
VISA
M 6.50 **t.** and a la carte ⓗ 3.00 – **14 rm** ⌑ 21.50/31.00 **t.** – SB (weekends only) 40.00/49.00 **st.**

X **Francine's,** 1a High St., CM9 7PB, ✆ 56605 – ❷. 🔼 *VISA*
closed Sunday, Monday, 1 week February, 2 weeks August and 1 week at Christmas – **M**
(dinner only) (booking essential) a la carte 9.90/13.00 **t.** ⓗ 3.20.

AUSTIN-ROVER Heybridge ✆ 52468
BMW Spital Rd ✆ 52131

FORD 1 Spital Rd ✆ 52345
VAUXHALL-OPEL 127/131 High St. ✆ 52424

MALHAM North Yorks. **402** N 21 – pop. 130 – ✉ Skipton – ✆ 072 93 Airton.

♦London 231 – Burnley 32 – ♦Leeds 42 – York 58.

⌂ **Buck Inn,** BD23 4DA, ✆ 317 – ❷
M (bar lunch Monday to Saturday)/dinner 5.50 **t.** and a la carte ⓗ 2.65 – **10 rm** ⌑ 12.00/34.00 **t.**
– SB (except summer) 33.00 **st.**

MALMESBURY Wilts. **403 404** N 29 – pop. 4 ,220 – ECD : Thursday – ✆ 066 62.

See : Site ★ – Market Cross ★★ – Abbey ★.

🛈 Town Hall, Cross Hayes ✆ 2143/3478.

♦London 108 – ♦Bristol 28 – Gloucester 24 – Swindon 19.

🏨 Old Bell, Abbey Row, SN16 0BW, ✆ 2344, ✍ – 📺 ⇋wc 📶wc ☎ ❷. 🔬 🔼 *AE* ⓞ *VISA*
M 8.00/12.00 **t.** and a la carte ⓗ 3.50 – **19 rm.**

at Crudwell N : 4 m. on A 429 – ✉ ✆ 066 67 Crudwell :

🏠 **Mayfield House,** SN16 9EW, ✆ 409, ✍ – ❷. 🔼 *VISA*
M (dinner only and Sunday lunch) 9.50 **t.** ⓗ 2.30 – **21 rm** ⌑ 15.00/33.00 **t.** – SB 34.00/36.00 **st.**

at Easton Grey W : 2 m. on B 4040 – ✉ ✆ 066 62 Malmesbury :

🏨 **Whatley Manor** ⚓, SN16 0RB, E : ½ m. on B 4040 ✆ 2888, Telex 449380, ≤, « 18C Manor
house », ⌇ heated, ⚓, ✍, park – 📺 ☎ ❷. 🔼 *AE* ⓞ *VISA*
M 9.00/14.95 **t.** ⓗ 3.75 – **25 rm** ⌑ 40.00/70.00 **t.** – SB (weekends only except Bank Holidays)
65.00/75.00 **st.**

PEUGEOT-TALBOT Gloucester Rd ✆ 3434

328

MALPAS Cheshire ⁴⁰²⁴⁰³ L 24 – pop. 1,522 – ✪ 0948.

♦London 77 – ♦Birmingham 60 – Chester 15 – Shrewsbury 26 – ♦Stoke-on-Trent 30.

XX **Market House,** Church St., SY14 8NU, ℰ 860400, 🐎 – 🔄 VISA
   closed Sunday dinner, Monday, 1 week January and 2 weeks August – **M** (lunch by arrangement)/dinner a la carte 7.10/12.35 **t.** ⬧ 3.25.

MALTON North Yorks. ⁴⁰² R 21 – pop. 4,033 – ECD : Thursday – ✪ 0653.

Envir. : Castle Howard** (18C) *AC*, SW : 6 m. – Flamingo Park Zoo* *AC*, N : 4 ½ m.

📁₈ Malton and Norton, Welham Park ℰ 2959.

♦London 229 – ♦Kingston-upon-Hull 36 – Scarborough 24 – York 17.

🏠 **Talbot** (T.H.F.), Yorkersgate, YO17 0AA, ℰ 4031 – 📺 ⊜wc ☎ 🅿. 🔄 AE ⓪ VISA
   M a la carte lunch/dinner 9.00 **st.** ⬧ 2.70 – ⊑ 5.50 – **23 rm** 36.50/43.00 **st.**

AUSTIN-ROVER Wintringham ℰ 09442 (Rillington)   BMW Church St., Norton ℰ 5151
242   VOLVO Horse Market Rd ℰ 3019

MALVERN Heref. and Worc. ⁴⁰³⁴⁰⁴ N 27 – see Great Malvern.

MALVERN WELLS Heref. and Worc. ⁴⁰³⁴⁰⁴ N 27 – see Great Malvern.

MANCHESTER Greater Manchester ⁴⁰²⁴⁰³⁴⁰⁴ N 23 – pop. 437,612 – ECD : Wednesday – ✪ 061.

See : Town Hall* 19C DZ **H** – City Art Gallery* DZ **M** – Whitworth Art Gallery* BY **M** – Cathedral 15C (chancel*) DZ **B** – John Ryland's Library (manuscripts*) CZ **A**.

Envir. : Heaton Hall* (18C) *AC*, N : 5 m. AX **M**.

📁₈ Heaton Park, ℰ 798 0295, N : by A 576 ABX – 📁₈ Fairfield Golf and Sailing, Booth Rd, Audenshaw, ℰ 370 1641, E : by A 635 BY.

✈ Manchester International Airport ℰ (061) 489 3717 or 489 2404 (British Airways), S : 10 m. by A 5103 AY and M 56 – Terminal : Coach service from Victoria Station.

🛈 Magnum House, Portland St., Piccadilly ℰ 247 3694 and 3712/3 – Town Hall Extension, Lloyd St. ℰ 236 1606/2035 – Manchester International Airport, Concourse and Arrivals Hall ℰ 437 5233/5262.

♦London 202 – ♦Birmingham 86 – ♦Glasgow 221 – ♦Leeds 43 – ♦Liverpool 35 – ♦Nottingham 72.

Plans on following pages

🏯 **Piccadilly** (Embassy), Piccadilly Plaza, M60 1QR, ℰ 236 8414, Telex 668765, ≤ – ⊟ 📺 ☎ 🅿.
   🅰. 🔄 AE ⓪ VISA. ⌖   DZ **s**
   M 11.00 **st.** and a la carte 10.25/16.25 **st.** ⬧ 3.50 – ⊑ 5.75 – **250 rm** 55.00/77.00 **st.**, **9 suites** 90.00/160.00 **st.**

🏨 **Portland Thistle** (Thistle), Portland St., Piccadilly Gdns., M1 6DP, ℰ 228 3400, Telex 669157
   – ⊟ 🔲 📺 ☎. 🅰. 🔄 AE ⓪ VISA   DZ **v**
   M 8.50/9.75 **t.** – ⊑ 5.50 – **219 rm** 54.00/85.00 **t.**, **1 suite** 85.00 **t.**

🏨 **Grand** (T.H.F.), Aytoun St., M1 3DR, ℰ 236 9559, Telex 667580 – ⊟ 📺. 🅰. 🔄 AE ⓪ VISA
   M (carving rest.) 9.25 **st.** and a la carte ⬧ 2.70 – **140 rm** ⊑ 48.50/59.00 **st.**, **3 suites.**   DZ **u**

🏠 **Hazeldean,** 467 Bury New Rd, M7 ONX, ℰ 792 6667 – 📺 ⊜wc ⊞wc 🅿. 🔄 AE ⓪ VISA. ⌖
   M (*closed dinner Friday to Sunday and Bank Holidays*) (bar lunch Monday to Saturday)/dinner a la carte 9.40/14.60 **t.** ⬧ 3.20 – **21 rm** ⊑ 22.80/43.00 **st.**   AX **a**

↑ **New Central,** 144/146 Heywood St., M8 7PD, ℰ 205 2169 – ⊞ 🅿. ⌖   BX **e**
   closed 23 December-1 January – **10 rm** ⊑ 15.50/28.00 **st.**

↑ **Sabre d'Or,** 392 Wilbraham Rd, Chorlton-cum-Hardy, M21 1UH, S : 5 m. by A 5103 on A
   6010 ℰ 881 5055 – 📺 🅿   AY **c**
   9 rm ⊑ 15.75/25.00 **st.**

XXX Terrazza, 14 Nicholas St., M1 4FE, ℰ 236 4033, Italian rest.   DZ **r**

XX **Isola Bella,** 6a Booth St., M2 4AW, ℰ 236 6417, Italian rest. – 🔄 VISA   DZ **e**
   closed Sunday and Bank Holidays – **M** a la carte 10.50/16.40 **t.** ⬧ 3.00.

XX **Gaylord,** Amethyst House, Marriott's Court, Spring Gardens, M2 1EA, ℰ 832 6037, Indian
   rest. – 🔄 AE ⓪ VISA   DZ **c**
   M 7.45 **t.** and a la carte ⬧ 3.50.

XX **Leen Hong,** 35 George St., M1 4HQ, ℰ 228 0926, Chinese rest. – AE ⓪   DZ **z**
   M a la carte 6.50/9.85 **st.**

XX Rajdoot, St. James' House, South King St., M2 6DW, ℰ 834 2176, Indian rest.   CZ **c**

X **Truffles,** 63 Bridge St., M3 6BQ, ℰ 832 9393 – 🔄 AE ⓪ VISA   CZ **a**
   closed Saturday lunch, Sunday, Monday first 2 weeks August and Bank Holidays – **M** 9.95 **t.** (lunch) and a la carte 11.40/17.45 **t.** ⬧ 3.50.

X **Market,** 30 Edge St., M4 1HN, ℰ 834 3743, Bistro – 🔄 AE   DZ **o**
   closed Sunday, Monday, 1 week spring, August and 1 week after Christmas – **M** (dinner only) a la carte 6.90/10.45 **t.** ⬧ 2.50.

X **Mina,** 63 George St., ℰ 228 2598, Japanese rest. – 🔄 AE ⓪ VISA   DZ **i**
   closed Sunday and 1 January – **M** 8.00/16.00 **t.** and a la carte.

X **Yang Sing,** 34 Princess St., ℰ 236 2200, Chinese rest. – 🔄 AE   DZ **a**
   M 2.30/7.75 **t.** and a la carte.

329

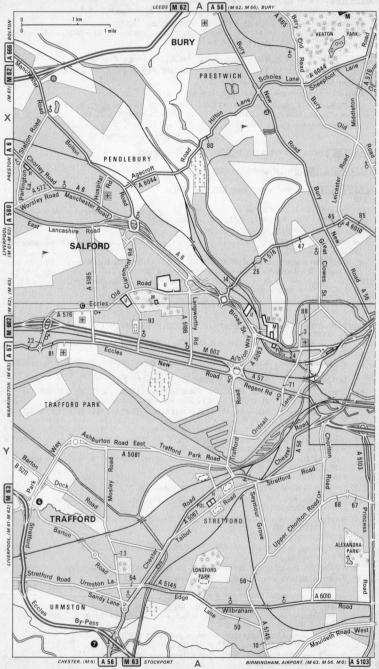

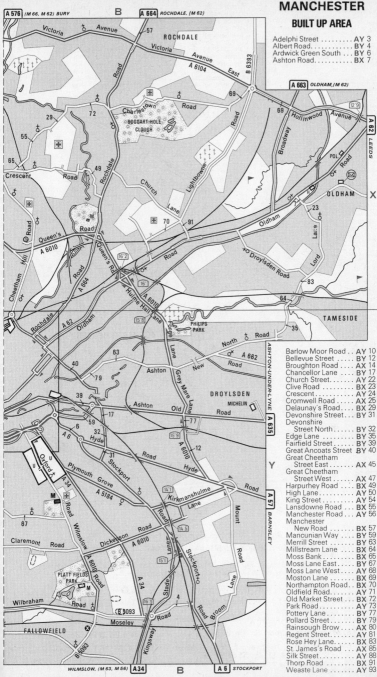

MANCHESTER
BUILT UP AREA

Adelphi Street .... AY 3
Albert Road .... BY 4
Ardwick Green South ... BY 6
Ashton Road .... BX 7

Barlow Moor Road .. AY 10
Bellevue Street ..... BY 12
Broughton Road .... AX 14
Chancellor Lane .... BY 17
Church Street ...... AY 22
Clive Road .... BX 23
Crescent .... AY 24
Cromwell Road .... AX 25
Delaunay's Road.... BX 29
Devonshire Street ... BY 31
Devonshire
     Street North ..... BY 32
Edge Lane .... BY 35
Fairfield Street ..... BY 39
Great Ancoats Street BY 40
Great Cheetham
     Street East ...... AX 45
Great Cheetham
     Street West ..... AX 47
Harpurhey Road ... BX 49
High Lane .... AY 50
King Street .... AY 54
Lansdowne Road ... BX 55
Manchester Road ... AY 56
Manchester
     New Road ..... BX 57
Mancunian Way .... BY 59
Merrill Street ...... BY 63
Millstream Lane .... BX 64
Moss Bank .... BX 65
Moss Lane East..... BY 67
Moss Lane West.... BY 68
Moston Lane .... BX 69
Northampton Road.. BX 70
Oldfield Road....... AY 71
Old Market Street ... BX 72
Park Road .... AY 73
Pottery Lane .... BY 77
Pollard Street ...... BY 79
Rainsough Brow .... AX 80
Regent Street ...... AY 81
Rose Hey Lane..... BX 83
St. James's Road ... AX 85
Silk Street.......... AY 88
Thorp Road .... BX 91
Weaste Lane .... AY 93

MANCHESTER
CENTRE

Deansgate . . . . **CZ**
Lower Mosley Street . . . . **DZ**
Market Place . . . . **DZ**
Market Street . . . . **DZ**
Mosley Street . . . . **DZ**
Princess Street . . . . **DZ**

Addington Street . . . . **DZ** 2
Albert Square . . . . **CDZ** 5

Aytoun Street . . . . **DZ** 8
Blackfriars Street . . . . **CZ** 13
Cannon Street . . . . **DZ** 15
Cateaton Street . . . . **DZ** 16
Cheetham Hill Road . . . . **DZ** 18
Chepstow Street . . . . **DZ** 19
Chorlton Street . . . . **DZ** 20
Church Street . . . . **DZ** 21
Dale Street . . . . **DZ** 27
Dawson Street . . . . **CZ** 28
Ducie Street . . . . **DZ** 33
Egerton Street . . . . **CZ** 36
Fairfield Street . . . . **DZ** 39

Great Bridgewater Street . . . . **CZ** 41
Great Ducie Street . . . . **CZ** 48
High Street . . . . **DZ** 51
John Dalton Street . . . . **CZ** 52
King Street . . . . **DZ** 53
Parker Street . . . . **CZ** 75
Peter Street . . . . **CZ** 76
St. Ann's Street . . . . **CZ** 84
St. Peter's Square . . . . **CZ** 87
Spring Gardens . . . . **DZ** 89
Viaduct Street . . . . **CZ** 92
Whitworth Street West . . . . . **CZ** 95
Withy Grove . . . . **DZ** 97

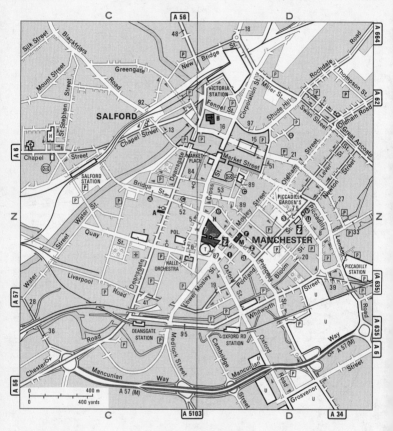

at Fallowfield S : 3 m. on B 5093 – ⊠ ✆ 061 Manchester :

🏨 **Willow Bank,** 340 Wilmslow Rd, M14 6AF, ✆ 224 0461, Telex 668222 – 📺 ⌂wc ☎ 🄿 ⚠
AE ⓪ VISA
BY **x**
M *(closed lunch Sunday and Bank Holidays)* 4.00/7.00 **st.** and a la carte ⏐ 3.00 – ⲥ 4.00 –
123 rm 20.00/35.00 **st.** – SB (weekends only) 42.00/54.00 **st.**

at Northenden S : 6 ½ m. by A 5103 – AY – and M 56 – ⊠ ✆ 061 Manchester :

🏨 **Post House** (T.H.F.), Palatine Rd, M22 4FH, ✆ 998 7090, Telex 669248 – 🛗 📺 ⌂wc ☎ ⚿
🄿 ⚠ AE ⓪ VISA
M 6.95/9.25 **st.** and a la carte – ⲥ 5.50 – **200 rm** 43.00/50.50 **st.**

at Manchester Airport S : 9 m. by A 5103 – AY – and M 56 – ⊠ ✆ 061 Manchester :

🏨 **Excelsior** (T.H.F.), Ringway Rd, Wythenshawe, M22 5NS, ✆ 437 5811, Telex 668721, ⤢ heated – 🛗 🍽 📺 ☎ ⚿ 🄿 ⚠ AE ⓪ VISA
M *(closed Saturday lunch)* 6.45/7.95 **st.** and a la carte ⏐ 2.70 – ⲥ 5.50 – **304 rm** 49.00/58.00 **st.**,
4 suites.

🍴🍴🍴 **Moss Nook,** Ringway Rd, Moss Nook, M22 5NA, ☎ 437 4778 – [P]. ▣ [AE] ⦿ [VISA]
closed lunch Saturday and Monday, Sunday, 2 weeks Christmas and Bank Holidays – **M** 18.00 **t.** and a la carte.

at Heald Green S : 10 m. by A 5103 – AY – and M 56 – ✉ ☏ 061 Manchester :

🍴🍴 **La Bonne Auberge,** 224 Finney Lane, SK8 3QA, ☎ 437 5701 – [P]. ▣ [AE] ⦿
closed Monday dinner, Sunday and Bank Holidays – **M** 8.00 **t.** (lunch) and a la carte 10.60/13.40 **t.**

MICHELIN Branch, Ferris St., off Louisa St., Openshaw, M11 1BS, ☎ **223 2010 and 3274** BY

ALFA-ROMEO 123 a/b Jersey St. ☎ 205 2213
AUSTIN-ROVER Gill St. ☎ 205 2792
AUSTIN-ROVER 208 Bury New Rd ☎ 792 4343
BMW 325/327 Deansgate ☎ 832 8781
BMW Gt Bridgewater St. ☎ 832 8781
CITROEN, FIAT, LANCIA Ashton Old Rd ☎ 273 4411
FORD 292 Bury New Rd ☎ 792 6161
FORD 391 Palatine Rd ☎ 998 3427
FORD Oxford Rd ☎ 224 7301
FORD 660 Chester Rd ☎ 872 2201
FORD 3/5 New Wakefield St. ☎ 236 4168
HONDA Liverpool St. ☎ 737 3540
LOTUS, MORGAN, RELIANT, RENAULT Ashley Rd, Hale ☎ 941 1916
MAZDA Oldham Rd, Ashton ☎ 330 8135
MAZDA 54, Sackville St. ☎ 228 6727
MERCEDES-BENZ Upper Brook St. ☎ 273 8123
NISSAN Victoria Rd ☎ 330 3840
NISSAN Regent Rd, Salford ☎ 832 6041
PEUGEOT, TALBOT Chester Rd ☎ 834 6677
PORSCHE Bury New Rd at Whitefield ☎ 796 7414
RENAULT Blackfriars Rd ☎ 832 6121 770 Chester Rd ☎ 865 1151
SAAB Water St. ☎ 832 6566
TALBOT, PEUGEOT 119 Wilmslow Rd ☎ 224 7282
TOYOTA Greenside Lane ☎ 370 2145
TOYOTA Moseley Rd ☎ 224 6265
VAUXHALL-OPEL Middleton Rd ☎ 740 2812
VAUXHALL-OPEL 141 Waterloo Rd ☎ 792 4321
VAUXHALL-OPEL Blackfriars Rd ☎ 834 8200
VAUXHALL-OPEL 80/90 Port St., Gt Ancoats St. ☎ 236 4311
VAUXHALL-OPEL 799 Chester Rd ☎ 872 2141
VOLVO Rowsley St. ☎ 223 7272
VW, AUDI Ashton Old Rd ☎ 273 4361
VW, AUDI Stamford Rd ☎ 320 5454

MANNINGTREE Essex [404] X 28 – pop. 3,909 – ☏ 0260 Colchester.

♦London 67 – Colchester 9 – ♦Ipswich 12.

🍴 **Bucks,** Cattawade, CO11 1RG, N : 1 ½ m. by B 1352 off A 137 ☎ 392571 – [P]. ▣ [AE] ⦿ [VISA]
closed Sunday – **M** 12.50 **s.** and a la carte 🍷 2.50.

MANORBIER (MAENORBYR) Dyfed [403] F 29 – pop. 1,154 – ECD : Saturday – ☏ 083 482.

See : Castle★ (13C) *AC*.

♦London 253 – Carmarthen 33 – Haverfordwest 18.

🏠 **Castle Mead** 🌿, SA70 7TA, ☎ 358, ⩽ Manorbier Bay, 🌳 – 🛁wc [P]. [AE]. 🚫🐕
Easter-October – **M** (bar lunch)/dinner 6.50 **t.** 🍷 2.40 – **11 rm** 🛏 14.00/30.00 **t.**

at Jameston W : 2 m. on A 4139 – ✉ ☏ 083 482 Manorbier :

🏠 Tudor Lodge 🌿, SA70 7SS, ☎ 320, 🌳 – [TV] 🛁wc 🚿wc [P]
10 rm.

MARAZION Cornwall [403] D 33 The West Country G. – pop. 1,366 – ECD : Wednesday – ✉ Penzance – ☏ 0736.

♦London 318 – Penzance 3 – Truro 26.

🏠 **Mount Haven,** TR17 0DQ, on A 394 ☎ 710249, ⩽ St. Michael's Mount and Mount's Bay – [TV] 🛁wc [P]. ▣ [VISA]. 🚫🐕
M (bar lunch Monday to Saturday)/dinner a la carte 9.30/12.75 **t.** 🍷 3.00 – **15 rm** 🛏 17.00/38.50 **t.** – SB 45.00/52.00 **st.**

at Perranuthnoe SE : 1 ¾ m. by A 394 – ✉ ☏ 0736 Penzance :

🏡 **Ednovean House** 🌿, TR20 9LZ, ☎ 711071, ⩽ St. Michael's Mount and Mount's Bay, 🌳 – 🚿wc [P]. 🚫🐕
8 rm 🛏 12.50/33.00 **st.**

MARKET DEEPING Lincs. [402] [404] T 25 – pop. 9,621 – ☏ 0778.

♦London 94 – ♦Cambridge 44 – ♦Leicester 41 – Lincoln 42.

🏨 **Deeping Stage,** Market Pl., PE6 8EA, ☎ 343234 – [P]. [VISA]
M *(closed Sunday dinner)* (Dancing Saturday) 4.25/5.25 **t.** and a la carte – **8 rm** 🛏 14.00/25.00 **st.**

MARKET DRAYTON Salop [402] [403] [404] M 25 – pop. 9,003 – ECD : Thursday – ☏ 0630.

♦London 161 – ♦Birmingham 44 – Chester 33 – Shrewsbury 19 – ♦Stoke-on-Trent 16.

🏨 **Corbet Arms,** 8 High St., TF9 1PY, ☎ 2037 – [TV] 🛁wc 🚿wc [P]. ▣ [AE] ⦿ [VISA]
M (bar lunch Monday to Saturday)/dinner 8.75 **t.** and a la carte 🍷 2.10 – **10 rm** 🛏 18.00/34.00 **t.** – SB (weekends only) 32.50/43.50 **st.**

PEUGEOT-TALBOT Shrewsbury Rd ☎ 2027
RENAULT Shrewsbury Rd ☎ 4257
VAUXHALL, VOLVO Cheshire St. ☎ 2444

MARKET HARBOROUGH Leics. 404 R 26 – pop. 15,852 – ECD : Wednesday – ✆ 0858.

🖪 Pen Lloyd Library, Adam and Eve St. ✆ 62649/62699.

◆London 88 – ◆Birmingham 47 – ◆Leicester 15 – Northampton 17.

🏨 **Three Swans,** 21 High St., LE16 7NJ, ✆ 66644 – 📺 ➰wc ⋔wc ☂ Ⓟ. 🅰 AE ⓪ VISA
M *(closed Sunday dinner)* 6.50/10.50 **st.** and a la carte ⚌ 5.00 – **18 rm** ⌿ 35.00/49.00 **st.**

at Marston Trussell (Northants.) W : 3 ¼ m. by A 427 – ✉ ✆ 0858 Market Harborough :

🏠 **Sun Inn** ⤳, Main St., LE16 9TY, ✆ 65531 – 📺 ➰wc ☂ Ⓟ. 🅰 VISA. ⋇
M 5.95/12.00 and a la carte ⚌ 3.00 – **10 rm** ⌿ 25.00/35.00.

ALFA-ROMEO Main St. ✆ 66984
FIAT St. Mary's Rd ✆ 32255
FORD Leicester Rd ✆ 66688

RENAULT Abbey St. ✆ 32530
VAUXHALL-OPEL Springfield St. ✆ 67177
VW-AUDI Northampton Rd ✆ 65511

MARKET RASEN Lincs. 402 404 T 23 – pop. 3,050 – ECD : Thursday – ✆ 0673.

◆London 159 – Grimsby 20 – Lincoln 16.

🏨 **Limes,** Gainsborough Rd, LN8 3JW, ✆ 842357, ㆓, squash – 📺 ➰wc ⋔wc ☂ Ⓟ. 🅰 AE
VISA. ⋇
M *(closed Saturday lunch)* a la carte 5.50/13.20 **t.** ⚌ 2.35 – **15 rm** ⌿ 30.00/35.00 **t.** – SB (week-
ends only) 42.00 **st.**

XX **Carafe,** 5 King St., LN8 3BB, ✆ 843427 – 🅰 AE ⓪
closed Sunday, Monday and 25-26 December – **M** 5.00/15.00 **t.**

MARKET WEIGHTON Humberside 402 S 22 – pop. 3,775 – ECD : Thursday – ✉ York – ✆ 0696.

◆London 208 – ◆Kingston-upon-Hull 18 – ◆Leeds 40 – York 19.

🏠 **Londesborough Arms,** High St., YO4 3AH, ✆ 72219 – 📺 ➰wc ⋔wc ☎ Ⓟ. 🅰 AE ⓪ VISA
M 5.00 **t.** and a la carte ⚌ 2.40 – **14 rm** ⌿ 18.00/28.00.

MARKINGTON North Yorks. 402 P 21 – see Harrogate.

☛ *To go a long way quickly, use Michelin maps at a scale of 1:1 000 000.*

MARKS TEY Essex 404 W 28 – see Colchester.

MARLBOROUGH Wilts. 403 404 O 29 The West Country G. – pop. 5,330 – ECD : Wednesday –
✆ 0672.

See : Site ⋆.

Envir. : Savernake Forest⋆⋆ (Grand Avenue⋆⋆⋆), SE : 2 m. off A 346 – The Ridgeway Path⋆⋆,
85 miles starting from Overton Hill near Avebury including White Horse ≼⋆ – West Kennett Long
Barrow⋆, W : 4 ½ m. – Silbury Hill⋆, W : 6 m. – Pewsey : Vale of Pewsey⋆, S : 7 m. on A 3455 – at
Avebury⋆, The Stones⋆, Church⋆, W : 7 m. – Wilton Windmill⋆ AC, S : 9 m. by A 346 on A 338 – at
Great Bedwyn, Crofton Beam Engines⋆ AC, on Kennet and Avon Canal, SE : 10 m.

🖫 The Common ✆ 52147, N : 1 m.

🖪 St. Peter's Church, High St. ✆ 53989 (summer only).

◆London 84 – ◆Bristol 47 – ◆Southampton 40 – Swindon 12.

🏠 **Castle and Ball** (T.H.F.), High St., SN8 1LZ, ✆ 55201 – 📺 ➰wc ☂ Ⓟ. 🅰 AE ⓪ VISA
M 6.25/8.50 **st.** and a la carte ⚌ 2.70 – ⌿ 5.50 – **30 rm** 37.00/45.00 **st.**

🏠 **Ivy House,** High St., SN8 1HJ, ✆ 53188 – 📺 ➰wc ☂ Ⓟ. 🅰 VISA. ⋇
M (restricted dinner, Sunday) 7.95/14.00 **t.** and a la carte ⚌ 4.50 – **12 rm** ⌿ 38.50/58.00 **t.** – SB
57.00/75.00 **st.**

AUSTIN-ROVER 80/83 High St. ✆ 52076   PORSCHE London Rd ✆ 52381

MARLOW Bucks. 404 R 29 – pop. 18,584 – ECD : Wednesday – ✆ 062 84.

◆London 35 – Aylesbury 22 – ◆Oxford 29 – Reading 14.

🏨 **Compleat Angler** (T.H.F.), Marlow Bridge, Bisham Rd, SL7 1RG, ✆ 4444, Telex 848644, ≼
River Thames, « Riverside setting and gardens », ⤳, ⋇ – 📺 ☎ Ⓟ. 🖄 🅰 AE ⓪ VISA
M 18.00 **st.** (lunch) and a la carte ⚌ 7.50 – **46 rm** 64.50/75.00 **st.** **4 suites**.

X **Hare and Hounds,** Henley Rd, SL7 2DF, SW : ¾ m. on A 4155 ✆ 3343 – Ⓟ. 🅰 AE
closed Sunday – **M** a la carte 12.00/14.00 **t.** ⚌ 2.60.

AUSTIN-ROVER Oxford Rd ✆ 6333

MARSTON TRUSSELL Northants. – see Market Harborough (Leics.).

MARTINHOE Devon – see Lynton.

MARTON Cleveland – see Middlesbrough.

MARY TAVY Devon 403 H 32 – see Tavistock.

334

MASHAM North Yorks. **402** P 21 – pop. 976 – ECD : Thursday – ✉ Ripon – ☎ 0677 Bedale.
♦London 231 – ♦Leeds 38 – ♦Middlesbrough 37 – York 32.

🏛 **Jervaulx Hall** ॐ, HG4 4PH, NW : 5 ½ m. on A 6108 ☎ 60235, ≤, « Country house atmosphere », ☛, park – 🚻wc ℗. ☒ *VISA*
closed 20 December-February – **M** (dinner only) 11.00 **t.** ⚬ 2.95 – **8 rm** ☐ (dinner included) 31.20/74.00 **t.** – SB (late October to Easter) 121.00 **st.**

↑ **Bank Villa**, HG4 4DB, on A 6108 ☎ 0765 (Ripon) 89605, ☛ – ⛪
March-October – **7 rm** ☐ 12.50/21.00 **st.**

MATLOCK Derbs. **402 403 404** P 24 – pop. 13,706 – ECD : Thursday – ☎ 0629.
See : Site✶ – Envir. : Riber Castle (ruins) ≤✶ (Fauna Reserve and Wildlife Park *AC*) SE : 2 ½ m.
🛈 The Pavilion ☎ 55082.
♦London 153 – Derby 17 – ♦Manchester 46 – ♦Nottingham 24 – ♦Sheffield 24.

🏛 **Riber Hall** ॐ, Riber, DE4 5JU, SE : 3 m. by A 615 ☎ 2795, ≤, « Elizabethan manor house », ☛ – ☑ 🚻wc ℗. ☒ ஊ ⓞ *VISA*. ℅
M 7.20 **t.** (lunch) and a la carte 15.00/18.25 **t.** – ☐ 4.00 – **11 rm** 45.00/59.00 **t.** – SB (mid October-mid April) 76.25/100.25 **st.**

at Matlock Bath S : 1 ½ m. on A 6 – ✉ ☎ 0629 Matlock :

🏛 **New Bath** (T.H.F.), New Bath Rd, DE4 3PX, ☎ 3275, ⛲ heated, ☒, ☛, ℅ – ☑ 🚻wc ☎ ℗. ⛴. ☒ ஊ ⓞ *VISA*
M 6.75/9.80 **st.** and a la carte – ☐ 5.50 – **56 rm** 35.50/47.50 **st.**

AUSTIN-ROVER Bakewell Rd ☎ 3291   FORD 41 Causeway Lane ☎ 2231

MATLOCK BATH Derbs. **402 403 404** P 24 – see Matlock.

MAWGAN Cornwall **403** E 33 – ✉ Helston – ☎ 032 622.
♦London 317 – Falmouth 18 – Penzance 19 – Truro 22.

✗ **Yard Bistro,** Trelowarren, TR12 6AF, SE : 1 ½ m. ☎ 595, « Converted coach house » – ℗
closed Sunday dinner, Monday except Bank Holidays and mid December-March – **M** (restricted lunch)/dinner a la carte 7.80/10.90 **t.** ⚬ 3.00.

MAWGAN PORTH Cornwall **403** E 32 – ECD : Wednesday – ✉ Newquay – ☎ 0637 St. Mawgan.
♦London 293 – Newquay 7 – Truro 20.

🏛 **Tredragon**, TR8 4DQ, ☎ 860213, ≤ Mawgan Porth, ☒, ☛ – 🚻wc ⛪wc ℗. ☒ *VISA*
Easter-October and Christmas – **M** (bar lunch Monday to Saturday)/dinner 6.50 **st.** ⚬ 2.70 – **30 rm** ☐ 15.00/40.00 **st.**

MAWNAN SMITH Cornwall **403** E 33 – see Falmouth.

MAYFIELD East Sussex **404** U 30 – pop. 1,784 – ECD : Wednesday – ☎ 0435.
♦London 46 – ♦Brighton 25 – Eastbourne 22 – Lewes 17 – Royal Tunbridge Wells 9.

✗ **Old Brew House,** High St., TN20 6AG, ☎ 872342 – ஊ ⓞ *VISA*
closed Sunday, Monday, 3 weeks September-October and 24 December-3 January – **M** (dinner only and Saturday lunch) 6.50/11.50 **t.** ⚬ 3.70.

MEASHAM Leics. **402 403 404** P 25 – pop. 4,184 – ECD : Wednesday – ☎ 0530.
♦London 122 – ♦Birmingham 25 – ♦Leicester 21 – ♦Nottingham 26.

🏛 **Measham Inn,** Tamworth Rd, DE12 7DY, ☎ 70095 – ☑ 🚻wc ☎ ℗. ☒ ஊ ⓞ *VISA*
M (bar lunch)/dinner 6.50 **t.** and a la carte ⚬ 3.35 – **31 rm** ☐ 26.50/35.00 **t.**

MELBOURN Cambs. **404** U 27 – pop. 3,846 – ✉ ☎ 0763 Royston (Herts.).
♦London 44 – ♦Cambridge 10.

✗✗ **Pink Geranium,** 25 Station Rd, SG8 6JP, ☎ 60215, ☛ – ℗. ☒ ஊ ⓞ *VISA*
closed Saturday lunch, Sunday, Monday, last 2 weeks August and Bank Holidays – **M** 6.95 **t.** (lunch) and a la carte 10.00/11.25 **t.**

✗✗ **Sheen Mill** with rm, Station Rd, SG8 6DH, ☎ 61393, ≤, ☛ – ☑ ⛪wc ℗. ☒ ஊ ⓞ *VISA*. ℅
closed Bank Holidays – **M** (closed Sunday dinner to non-residents) (Dancing Saturday) 7.00 **t.** (lunch) and a la carte 9.90/15.95 **t.** ⚬ 2.50 – **3 rm** ☐ 25.00/42.00 **st.**

MELKSHAM Wilts. **403 404** N 29 – pop. 13,248 – ECD : Wednesday – ☎ 0225.
🛈 Round House, Church St. ☎ 707424.
♦London 113 – ♦Bristol 25 – Salisbury 35 – Swindon 28.

✗✗✗ **Beechfield House** with rm, Beanacre, SN12 7PU, N : 1 m. on A 350 ☎ 703700, Telex 444969, ≤, « Country house and gardens », ⛲ heated, ☜, park, ℅ – ☑ 🚻wc ☎ ℗. ☒ ஊ ⓞ *VISA*. ℅
M 10.50 **st.** (lunch) and a la carte 17.15/19.40 **st.** ⚬ 3.95 – **16 rm** ☐ 45.00/90.00 **st.** – SB (November-March) 75.00 **st.**

14   335

MELKSHAM

at Shaw NW : 1 ¼ m. on A 365 – ⊠ Melksham – ✪ 0225 Shaw :

⋔ **Shaw Farm,** Bath Rd, SN12 8EF, on A 365 🖉 702836, 🔥 heated, 🦌 – 🍴wc 🅿. 🛇
 11 rm 🛏 14.50/29.50 **t.**

AUSTIN-ROVER Lancaster Rd 🖉 702256

MELTHAM West Yorks. 402 404 O 23 – pop. 7,098 – ⊠ ✪ 0484 Huddersfield.
🏌 Thick Hollins Hall 🖉 850227, E : 1 m.
◆London 192 – ◆Leeds 21 – ◆Manchester 23 – ◆Sheffield 26.

🏨 **Durker Roods,** Bishops Way, HD7 3AG, 🖉 851413, ☆ – 📺 ⬆️wc 🍴wc 🕿 🅿. 🦽. 🔼 AE
 ⓪ VISA
 closed Christmas night – **M** (closed Saturday lunch and Sunday dinner) 6.50/9.00
 st. and a la carte 🍷 3.50 – **32 rm** 🛏 28.00/38.00 **st.** – SB (weekends only) 50.00 **st.**

MELTON MOWBRAY Leics. 402 404 R 25 – pop. 23,379 – ECD : Thursday – ✪ 0664.
🏌 Thorpe Arnold 🖉 62118, NE : 2 m. – 🚩 Carnegie Museum, Thorpe End, 🖉 69946.
◆London 113 – ◆Leicester 15 – Northampton 45 – ◆Nottingham 18.

🏨 **George,** High St., LE13 0TR, 🖉 62112 – 📺 ⬆️wc 🍴wc 🕿 🅿. 🦽. 🔼 AE ⓪ VISA
 M 5.25/11.25 **t.** and a la carte 🍷 3.20 – **20 rm** 🛏 36.50/49.00 **st.** – SB (weekends only)
 48.00/53.00 **st.**

🏨 **Harboro** (Anchor), Burton St., LE13 1AF, 🖉 60121, Group Telex 858875 – 📺 ⬆️wc 🍴wc 🕿
 🅿. 🦽. 🔼 AE ⓪ VISA
 M 7.40/9.25 **t.** and a la carte 🍷 3.00 – **27 rm** 🛏 39.00/49.00 **t.** – SB (July and August)(weekends
 only September-June) 51.00 **st.**

FIAT Mill St. 🖉 60141   VOLVO 56 Scalford Rd 🖉 63241
TALBOT 26 Victoria St. 🖉 62235

MENTMORE Bucks. 404 R 28 – pop. 196 – ⊠ Leighton Buzzard – ✪ 0296 Cheddington.
◆London 46 – Aylesbury 10 – Luton 15.

✗✗ **Stag Inn,** The Green, LU7 0QF, 🖉 668423 – 🅿. 🔼 AE ⓪ VISA
 closed Monday – **M** 6.75 **t.** (lunch) and a la carte 11.20/16.40 **t.** 🍷 2.75.

MERE Wilts. 403 404 N 30 The West Country G. – pop. 2,201 – ECD : Wednesday – ✪ 0747.
Envir. : Stourhead House★★★ AC, NW : 3 m. – 🚩 The Square, Church St. 🖉 860341.
◆London 113 – Exeter 65 – Salisbury 26 – Taunton 40.

🏠 **Old Ship,** Castle St., BA12 6JE, 🖉 860258 – 📺 ⬆️wc 🅿. 🔼 ⓪
 M a la carte 7.85/12.20 **t.** 🍷 3.00 – **22 rm** 🛏 21.50/38.00 **st.** – SB 50.00 **st.**

AUSTIN-ROVER Salisbury St. 🖉 860244   CITROEN Castle St. 🖉 860404

MERE BROW Lancs. 402 L 23 – ⊠ Preston – ✪ 077 473 Hesketh Bank.
◆London 221 – ◆Liverpool 22 – Preston 11 – Southport 6.

✗ **Crab and Lobster,** behind the Leigh Arms, Tarleton, PR4 6LA, 🖉 2734, Seafood – 🅿
 closed Sunday, Monday and Christmas-late January – **M** (dinner only) a la carte 7.20/13.35 **t.**
 🍷 3.00.

MERIDEN West Midlands 403 404 P 26 – see Coventry.

MERSHAM Kent – see Ashford.

MERTHYR TYDFIL Mid Glam. 403 J 28 – pop. 38,893 – ECD : Thursday – ✪ 0685.
Envir. : Road★ from Merthyr Tydfil to Brecon – Craig-y-Nos (Dan-yr-Ogof Caves★ AC),W : 17 m.
🚩 Brecon Mountain Railway, Pant Station 🖉 71491 (summer only).
◆London 181 – Brecon 17 – ◆Cardiff 24 – ◆Swansea 30.

🏨 **Baverstock's,** Heads of the Valley Rd, CF44 0LX, W : 3 m. by A 4102 on A 465 ⊠Aberdare
 🖉 6221 – 📺 ⬆️wc 🕿 🅿. 🦽. 🔼 AE ⓪ VISA. 🛇
 M 4.00 **st.** and a la carte 🍷 4.10 – **43 rm** 🛏 24.00/38.00 – SB (weekends only) 95.00 **st.**

FORD Pentrebach Rd 🖉 74111

MEVAGISSEY Cornwall 403 F 33 The West Country G. – pop. 1,896 – ECD : Thursday – ✪ 0726.
See : Site ★★.
◆London 287 – Newquay 21 – ◆Plymouth 44 – Truro 20.

🏠 **Trevalsa Court** ♨, School Hill, Polstreath, PL26 6TH, 🖉 842468, ≼, 🦌 – ⬆️wc 🍴wc 🅿.
 🔼 AE ⓪ VISA
 closed 4 weeks December-January – **M** (bar lunch)/dinner 7.50 **t.** and a la carte 🍷 2.50 – **9 rm**
 🛏 14.50/35.00 **t.** – SB (October-April)(except Bank Holidays) 42.00 **st.**

⋔ **Spa** ♨, Polkirt Hill, Portmellon, PL26 6UY, 🖉 842244, 🦌, 🛇, ✗ – ⬆️wc 🅿. 🔼 AE ⓪ VISA. 🛇
 10 rm 🛏 14.50/38.00 **st.**

MICKLETON Glos. 408 404 O 27 – see Chipping Campden.

MIDDLEHAM North Yorks. 402 O 21 – pop. 737 – ECD : Thursday – ☎ 0969 Wensleydale.
♦London 233 – Kendal 45 – ♦Leeds 47 – York 45.

    Miller's House, Market Pl., Leyburn, DL8 4NR, ℰ 22630, ☞ – ▣ ⌂wc ℗. ⚒
    closed December and January – **M** (dinner only) a la carte 9.50/12.50 **t.** ♦ 1.90 – **6 rm**
    ⊡ 25.00/38.00 **t.** – SB (except summer) 46.00/48.00 **st.**

MIDDLESBROUGH Cleveland 402 Q 20 – pop. 158 ,516 – ECD : Wednesday – ☎ 0642.
🖪 Middlesbrough Municipal, Ladgate Lane ℰ 315533, S : by Acklam Rd AZ.
✈ Teesside Airport : ℰ 0325 (Darlington) 332811, SW : 13 m. by A 66 AZ and A 19 on A 67.
🛈 125 Albert Rd ℰ 245750/245432 ext 3580.

♦London 246 – ♦Kingston-upon-Hull 89 – ♦Leeds 66 – ♦Newcastle-upon-Tyne 41.

MIDDLESBROUGH

Cleveland Centre	**ABY**
Corporation Road	**BY** 8
Dundas Street	**ABY** 12
Grange Road	**ABY**
Hill Street Centre	**AY**
Linthorpe Road	**AY**
Newport Road	**AY**

Albert Road	**BY** 2
Ayresome Green Lane	**AZ** 3
Bridge Street West	**AY** 4
Bright Street	**BY** 5
Clairville Road	**BZ** 6
Cleveland Street	**BY** 7
Devonshire Road	**AZ** 10
Eastbourne Road	**AZ** 14
Ferry Road	**BY** 15

Finsbury Street	**AZ** 16
Gresham Road	**AZ** 18
Hartington Road	**AY** 19
Longford Street	**AZ** 22
Ormesby Road	**BZ** 24
Princes Road	**AZ** 26
St. Barnabas Road	**AZ** 27
Saltersgill Avenue	**BZ** 28

Smeaton Street	**BY** 30
South Bank Road	**BY** 31
Tees Bridge Approach Road	**AZ** 34
West Terrace	**BZ** 35
Westbourne Grove	**BZ** 36
Wilson Street	**AY** 38
Zetland Street	**ABY** 39

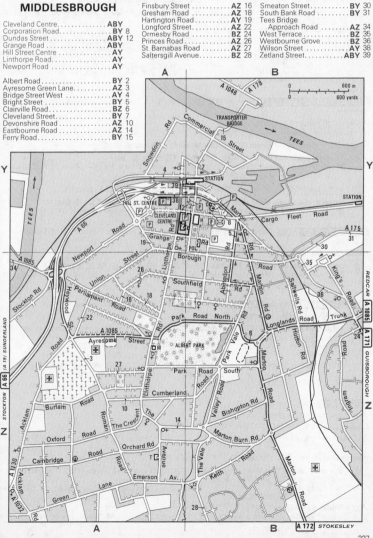

🏨 **Ladbroke Dragonara** (Ladbroke), Fry St., TS1 1JH, ℰ 248133, Telex 58266 – 🛗 🍴 rest 📺
⌷wc 🕿 🅿 🛦 🖭 ⒶⒺ ⓪ 𝘝𝘐𝘚𝘈 BY **c**
M (carving rest.) 7.00/9.75 **t.** 🍷 3.70 – 🖵 6.00 – **144 rm** 28.00/43.00 **t.**, **3 suites** 57.00 **t.** – SB
(weekends only) 47.00/57.00 **st.**

🏨 **Baltimore,** 250 Marton Rd, TS4 2EZ, ℰ 224111, Telex 58517 – 📺 ⌷wc 🕿 🅿 🛦 🖭 ⒶⒺ ⓪ 𝘝𝘐𝘚𝘈.
🍴 BZ **e**
M (closed lunch Saturday and Bank Holidays) 5.50/6.50 **st.** and a la carte 🍷 2.50 – 🖵 3.95 –
31 rm 29.50/39.50 **st.**, **1 suite**.

🏨 **Marton Way Motel,** Marton Rd, TS4 3BS, S : 2 m. on A 172 ℰ 817651, Telex 587783 – 📺
⌷wc 🅿 🛦 BZ **a**
M (carving rest.) – **53 rm**.

⌂ **Grey House,** 79 Cambridge Rd, TS5 5NL, ℰ 817485, 🏖 – ⌷wc 🅿 🛦 𝘝𝘐𝘚𝘈 AZ **n**
closed 2 weeks at Christmas – **10 rm** 🖵 13.25/28.00 **s.**

at Marton SE : 4 m. on A 172 – BZ – ✉ ☎ 0642 Middlesbrough :

🏨 **Blue Bell** (Swallow), Acklam Rd, TS5 7HL, W : 1 ¾ m. on B 1380 ℰ 593939, Group Telex 53168
– 🛗 📺 ⌷wc 🕾 🅿 🛦 🖭 𝘝𝘐𝘚𝘈
60 rm 🖵 32.50/42.00 **st.** – SB 42.00 **st.**

AUSTIN-ROVER 336 Stokesley Rd, Marton ℰ 317171
CITROEN Linthorpe Rd ℰ 822884
FORD North Ormesby Rd ℰ 242451
LADA Granville Rd ℰ 219151
RENAULT Newport Rd ℰ 249346
SKODA Eston Grange ℰ 452436

TALBOT Marton Rd ℰ 242873
TOYOTA Eastbourne Rd ℰ 816658
VAUXHALL-OPEL Marton Rd ℰ 243415
VOLVO Longlands Rd ℰ 244651
VW, AUDI Park End ℰ 317971

MIDDLETON IN TEESDALE Durham 🟦🟦 N 20 – pop. 1,132 – ECD : Wednesday – ☎ 0833
Teesdale.

Envir. : High Force★★ (waterfalls) AC, NW : 5 m.

🛈 1 Market Pl. ℰ 40806.

♦London 268 – ♦ Carlisle 40 – ♦Leeds 68 – ♦Middlesbrough 41 – ♦Newcastle-upon-Tyne 49.

🏠 **Teesdale,** Market Pl., DL12 0QG, ℰ 40264 – 📺 ⌷wc 🅿. 𝘝𝘐𝘚𝘈
M (bar lunch Monday to Saturday)/dinner 8.75 **t.** and a la carte 🍷 3.00 – **14 rm** 🖵 15.50/33.90 **t.**
– SB (6 January-4 May) 46.50/47.50 **st.**

at Romaldkirk SE : 4 m. on B 6277 – ✉ Barnard Castle – ☎ 0833 Teesdale :

🏨 **Rose and Crown,** DL12 9EB, ℰ 50213 – 📺 ⌷wc ⌷wc 🕾 🅿 🛦 🖭 ⒶⒺ ⓪ 𝘝𝘐𝘚𝘈 🍴
M 3.50/11.50 **st.** 🍷 3.25 – **15 rm** 🖵 19.50/44.00 **st.** – SB (November-June) 44.00/52.00 **st.**

MIDDLETON STONEY Oxon. 🟦🟦 Q 28 – pop. 238 – ECD : Saturday – ✉ Bicester –
☎ 086 989.

♦London 66 – Northampton 30 – ♦Oxford 12.

🏠 **Jersey Arms Inn,** Ardley Rd, OX6 8SE, ℰ 234 – 📺 ⌷wc 🅿 🛦 ⒶⒺ 𝘝𝘐𝘚𝘈 🍴
M (closed Sunday dinner to non-residents) a la carte 8.40/11.45 **t.** 🍷 2.90 – **9 rm** 🖵 29.50/39.50 **t.**
– SB (weekends only) 52.50 **st.**

MIDDLE WALLOP Hants. 🟦🟦 P 30 – ✉ Stockbridge – ☎ 0264 Andover.

♦London 80 – Salisbury 11 – ♦Southampton 21.

🏨 **Fifehead Manor,** SO20 8EG, on A 343 ℰ 781565, « 16C converted manor house », 🏖 – 📺
⌷wc ⌷wc 🕾 🅿 🛦 ⒶⒺ ⓪ 𝘝𝘐𝘚𝘈
closed 1 week at Christmas – **M** 12.00/15.00 **st.** and a la carte 🍷 3.50 – 🖵 2.50 – **12 rm**
36.00/58.00 **st.** – SB (November-March only) 60.00 **st.**

✕✕ **Old Drapery Stores** with rm, Station Rd, SO20 8HN, ℰ 781301, 🏖 – 🅿 ⒶⒺ ⓪ 𝘝𝘐𝘚𝘈 🍴
closed 26 December and 1 January – **M** (closed Saturday lunch and Sunday) a la carte
10.15/12.15 **t.** – **2 rm** 🖵 17.90/36.00 **st.**

MIDHURST West Sussex 🟦🟦 R 31 – pop. 5,991 – ECD : Wednesday – ☎ 073 081.

See : Cowdray House (Tudor ruins)★ AC.

Envir. : Uppark★ (17C-18C) AC, SW : 12 m.

🛆 Cowdray Park ℰ 2088, NE : 1 m. on A 272 – 🛆 at Petersfield ℰ 0730 (Petersfield) 67732, W :
10 m.

♦London 57 – ♦Brighton 38 – Chichester 12 – ♦Southampton 41.

🏨 **Spread Eagle** (Best Western), South St., GU29 9NH, ℰ 2211, Telex 86853, « 15C hostelry »
– 📺 ⌷wc 🕾 🅿 🛦 🖭 ⓪ 𝘝𝘐𝘚𝘈
M 9.00/13.50 **t.** and a la carte 🍷 4.25 – **27 rm** 🖵 41.00/85.00 **st.** – SB (except Easter, Christmas
and New Year) 65.00/80.00 **st.**

✕✕ **Mida,** Wool Lane, GU29 9BY, ℰ 3284
closed Sunday, Monday, 1 week spring and 1 week autumn – **M** (booking essential) a la carte
approx. 15.00 **t.**

at Bepton SW : 2 ¼ m. by A 286 – ⊠ ✪ 073 081 Midhurst :

🏠 **Park House** 🦢, GU29 0JB, ℰ 2880, 🛥 heated, 🌫, ✗ – 📺 🛁wc ℗
M (dinner only)(residents only) 9.50 **s.** 🍴 1.95 – **8 rm** ⇄ 23.50/55.00.

at Trotton W : 3 ¼ m. on A 272 – ⊠ Petersfield (Hants.) – ✪ 073 080 Rogate :

🏠 **Southdowns** 🦢, GU31 5JN, S : 1 m. ℰ 521, 🌫 – 📺 ⚟ ℗. 🔳 VISA
M 12.50 **t.** and a la carte – **8 rm** ⇄ 30.00/45.00 **t.** – SB (weekends only) 49.00 **st.**

AUSTIN-ROVER Petersfield Rd ℰ 2443   RENAULT Rumbolds Hill ℰ 2162

MILDENHALL Suffolk 🅰🅾🅰 V 26 – pop. 9,794 – ECD : Thursday – ✪ 0638.

♦London 73 – ♦Cambridge 22 – ♦Ipswich 38 – ♦Norwich 41.

🏠 **Bell** (Best Western), High St., IP28 7EA, ℰ 717272 – 📺 🛁wc ☎ ℗. 🔳 AE ① VISA
M 5.50 **t.** (lunch) and a la carte 6.35/10.95 **t.** – **18 rm** ⇄ 22.00/36.00 **t.** – SB (weekends only) 48.00/50.00 **st.**

MILFORD-ON-SEA Hants. 🅰🅾🅱 🅰🅾🅰 P 31 – pop. 3,953 – ECD : Wednesday – ⊠ Lymington – ✪ 0590.

♦London 109 – Bournemouth 15 – ♦Southampton 24 – Winchester 37.

🏨 **South Lawn,** Lymington Rd, SO4 0RF, ℰ 43911, 🌫 – 📺 🛁wc ☎ ℗. 🔳 VISA ✗
closed mid December-mid January – **M** *(closed Sunday and Monday to non-residents)* (dinner only and Sunday lunch) 9.25 **st.** 🍴 3.60 – **17 rm** ⇄ 26.00/45.00 **t.** – SB (November-April)(except Easter) 51.00/53.00 **st.**

🏨 **Westover Hall,** Park Lane, SO4 0PT, ℰ 43044, ⩽ Solent and the Needles, « Restored Victorian mansion » – 📺 🛁wc 🛁wc ℗. 🔳 AE ① VISA
M 5.50/9.50 **t.** and a la carte 🍴 3.00 – **11 rm** ⇄ 15.00/50.00 **t.** – SB 44.00/60.00 **st.**

↑ **Seaspray,** 8 Hurst Rd, SO4 0PY, ℰ 42627, ⩽ Solent and the Needles – 📺 🛁wc ℗. ✗
March-October – **6 rm** ⇄ 15.00/28.00 **st.**

AUSTIN-ROVER High St. ℰ 0590 (Lymington) 42161

MILNROW Greater Manchester 🅰🅾🅱 🅰🅾🅰 N 23 – pop. 11,647 – ⊠ Rochdale (Lancs.) – ✪ 045 77 Saddleworth.

♦London 222 – ♦Manchester 14 – Rochdale 2.

XXX **Moorcock,** Huddersfield Rd, OL16 3TJ, SE : 3 m. on A 640 ℰ 2659, ⩽ – ℗. 🔳 AE ① VISA
closed Saturday lunch, Sunday and Monday – **M** 8.75 **t.** and a la carte 10.40/16.10 **t.**

MILTON ABBAS Dorset 🅰🅾🅱 🅰🅾🅰 N 31 The West Country G. – pop. 433 – ⊠ Blandford – ✪ 0258.

See : Village★.

♦London 127 – Bournemouth 23 – Weymouth 19.

🏠 **Milton Manor** 🦢, DT11 0AZ, ℰ 880254, ⩽, « Country house atmosphere », 🌫, park – 🛁wc 🛁wc ℗. ✗
April-October – **M** (bar lunch)/dinner 7.00 **st.** 🍴 2.75 – **12 rm** ⇄ 18.00/32.00 **st.**

MILTON DAMEREL Devon 🅰🅾🅱 H 31 – pop. 454 – ⊠ Holsworthy – ✪ 040 926.

♦London 249 – Barnstaple 21 – ♦Plymouth 48.

🏨 **Woodford Bridge,** EX22 7LL, N : 1 m. on A 388 ℰ 481, « Part 15C inn », 🔳, 🦢, 🌫, ✗, squash – 📺 ☎ ℗. ⚖ ✗
M (bar lunch)/dinner 12.50 **t.** 🍴 1.50 – **22 rm** ⇄ 32.50/63.00 **t.** – SB (October-May only) 54.00/73.00 **st.**

MILTON KEYNES Bucks. 🅰🅾🅰 R 27 – pop. 93,305 – ✪ 0908.

🅱 425-427 Midsummer House, Midsummer Boulevard ℰ 678361.

♦London 56 – ♦Birmingham 72 – Bedford 16 – Northampton 18 – ♦Oxford 37.

at Woughton on the Green SE : 2 m. by A 509 off A 4146 – ⊠ ✪ 0908 Milton Keynes :

🏠 Woughton House, MK6 3LR, ℰ 661919, 🌫 – 📺 🛁wc 🛁wc ☎ – **20 rm**.

at Stony Stratford NW : 5 m. – ⊠ ✪ 0908 Milton Keynes :

XX **Stratfords,** St. Paul's Court, 118 High St., MK11 1LJ, ℰ 566577, « Converted Victorian church » – ℗. 🔳 ① VISA
closed Saturday lunch, Sunday, Monday, 20 July - 6 August and 21 December - mid January – **M** 13.50/16.50 **t.** 🍴 2.50.

MILTON ON STOUR Dorset 🅰🅾🅱 🅰🅾🅰 N 30 – ECD : Thursday – ✪ 074 76 Gillingham.

♦London 115 – Shaftesbury 6 – Taunton 42.

🏠 **Milton Lodge** 🦢, SP8 4PR, ℰ 2262, 🛥 heated, 🌫 – 📺 🛁wc ⚟ ℗. 🔳
M (bar lunch Monday to Saturday)/dinner 12.00 **t.** 🍴 3.50 – **10 rm** ⇄ 25.00/60.00 **t.** – SB 60.50/77.00 **st.**

MINEHEAD Somerset 〔403〕 J 30 The West Country G. – pop. 8 ,449 – ECD : Wednesday – ☺ 0643.
See : Site ★ – Higher Town : Church Steps ★ – St. Michael's Church ★ – West Somerset
Railway ★ – Envir. : Selworthy★ : Church★★ (≤★★★ from Church of Dunkery Beacon), W : 4½ m. –
Timberscombe Church★, S : 5 m.

🅃 Warren Rd ♟ 2057 – 🅱 Market House, The Parade ♟ 2624.

♦London 187 – ♦Bristol 64 – Exeter 43 – Taunton 25.

🏨 **Northfield** (Best Western) ⌘, Northfield Rd, TA24 5PU, ♟ 5155, Telex 42513, « ≤ gardens »
   – 🗦 ⌁wc ﬁﬂwc ⅙ 🅟. 🄰 🄰🄴 🄾 𝗩𝗜𝗦𝗔
   closed January-7 February – **M** 5.95/8.95 t. 🛈 2.85 – **27 rm** 🖙 28.90/72.50 st. – SB (November-
   March only) 56.50/60.50 st.

🏨 **Beach** (T.H.F.), The Avenue, TA24 5AP, ♟ 2193, ⅏ heated – 🆃🆅 ⌁wc 🆎 🅟. 🄰 🄰🄴 🄾 𝗩𝗜𝗦𝗔
   M (buffet lunch)/dinner 9.50 st. and a la carte 🛈 2.85 – 🖙 5.50 – **34 rm** 33.50/42.00 st.

🏠 **Benares** ⌘, Northfield Rd, TA24 5PT, ♟ 2340, ⅏ – ⌁wc 🅟. 🄰 𝗩𝗜𝗦𝗔
   closed January and February – **M** (bar lunch)/dinner 9.45 t. and a la carte 🛈 2.65 – **21 rm**
   🖙 19.50/42.00 t.

🏠 **Merton**, Western Lane, The Parks, TA24 8BZ, ♟ 2375, ⅏ – ⌁wc ﬁﬂwc ⅙ 🅟. 𝗩𝗜𝗦𝗔
   April-October – **M** (bar lunch)/dinner 7.75 st. – **12 rm** 🖙 10.40/28.60 st. – SB (except summer)
   35.60/38.80 st.

🏠 **Remuera**, Northfield Rd, TA24 5QH, ♟ 2611, ⅏ – 🆃🆅 ⌁wc 🅟. 𝗩𝗜𝗦𝗔
   closed January and February – **M** (bar lunch)/dinner 7.00 🛈 2.05 – **8 rm** 🖙 15.00/32.00 – SB
   28.00/40.00.

☝ **York**, 48 The Avenue, TA24 5AN, ♟ 5151 – ⌁wc ﬁﬂwc 🅟. 🄰 🄰🄴 🄾 𝗩𝗜𝗦𝗔. ⅍
   M 6.50 st. (dinner) and a la carte 🛈 3.00 – **20 rm** 🖙 12.00/30.00 st. – SB 30.00/42.00 st.

⌂ **Mentone**, The Parks, TA24 8BS, ♟ 5229, ⅏ – 🆃🆅 ⌁wc ﬁﬂwc 🅟. 🄰 🄰🄴 𝗩𝗜𝗦𝗔
   March-October – **9 rm** 🖙 9.50/33.00 st.

⌂ **Woodbridge,** The Parks, TA24 8BS, ♟ 4860 – ﬁﬂwc 🅟. 🄰 🄰🄴 𝗩𝗜𝗦𝗔
   10 rm 🖙 13.25/21.10 t.

   at Blue Anchor SE : 5 m. by A 39 on B 3191 – ☺ 064 382 Dunster :

⌂ **Langbury**, TA24 6LB, ♟ 821375, ⅏, ⅏ – ﬁﬂwc 🅟
   March-October – **9 rm** 🖙 11.00/28.00 st.

FIAT, VAUXHALL Townsend Rd ♟ 3379 　　　　　VW, AUDI-NSU . Mart Rd Industrial Estate ♟ 6868
RENAULT Blue Anchor ♟ 821571

MINSTER-IN-THANET Kent 〔404〕 Y 29 – see Ramsgate.

MINSTER LOVELL Oxon. 〔403〕〔404〕 P 28 – pop. 1 ,364 – ✉ ☺ 0993 Witney.
♦London 72 – Gloucester 36 – ♦Oxford 16.

🏠 **Old Swan** ⌘, Main St., OX8 5RN, ♟ 75614, ⅏ – 🆃🆅 ⌁wc ☎ 🅟. 🄰 🄰🄴 🄾 𝗩𝗜𝗦𝗔. ⅍
   M 8.75/13.00 t. and a la carte 🛈 2.95 – **10 rm** 🖙 32.00/55.00 t. – SB (October-March only)
   68.00/70.00 st.

MINSTERWORTH Glos. 〔403〕〔404〕 N 28 – see Gloucester.

MITHIAN Cornwall 〔403〕 E 33 – see St. Agnes.

MODBURY Devon 〔403〕 I 32 – pop. 1 ,259 – ECD : Wednesday – ✉ Ivybridge – ☺ 0548.
🅱 31 Church St. ♟ 830159 (summer only).
♦London 237 – Exeter 37 – ♦Plymouth 12.

🏠 **Ermewood House,** Totnes Rd, Ermington, PL21 9NS, NW : 2 ½ m. by A 379 on B 3210 ♟
   830741, ⅏ – 🆃🆅 ⌁wc ﬁﬂwc 🅟. 🄰 🄰🄴 🄾 𝗩𝗜𝗦𝗔
   closed 25 December-3 January – **M** (bar lunch Monday to Saturday)/dinner 8.00 t. and a la carte
   🛈 3.10 – **9 rm** 🖙 24.00/50.00 st. – SB 44.00/56.00 st.

MOLD (YR WYDDGRUG) Clwyd 〔402〕〔403〕 K 24 – pop. 8 ,487 – ECD : Thursday – ☺ 0352.
🅃 Pantymwyn ♟ 740318, W : 4 m. – 🅃 Old Padeswood, Station Rd ♟ 0244 (Buckley) 547401, E :
2 m. on A 5118 – 🅱 Town Hall, Earl St. ♟ 59331 (summer only).
♦ London 211 – Chester 12 – ♦ Liverpool 29 – Shrewsbury 45.

🏠 **Bryn Awel,** Denbigh Rd, CH7 1BL, on A 541 ♟ 58622 – 🆃🆅 ⌁wc 🆎 🅟. 🄰 𝗩𝗜𝗦𝗔
   M a la carte 5.30/11.55 t. 🛈 2.75 – **20 rm** 🖙 22.00/38.50 t. – SB (weekends only) 38.00/44.00 st.

MONK FRYSTON North Yorks. 〔402〕 Q 22 – pop. 737 – ✉ Lumby – ☺ 0977 South Milford.
Envir. : Selby Abbey Church★★ 12C-16C, E : 8½ m. – Carlton Towers★ (19C) AC, SE 14½ m.
♦London 190 – ♦Kingston-upon-Hull 42 – ♦Leeds 13 – York 20.

🏨 **Monk Fryston Hall,** LS25 5DU, ♟ 682369, « Italian garden », park – 🆃🆅 ⌁wc ﬁﬂwc 🅟. 🄰.
   🄰🄴 𝗩𝗜𝗦𝗔
   M 6.75/10.25 st. and a la carte 🛈 3.90 – **24 rm** 🖙 35.00/50.00 st. – SB (weekends only)
   53.00/58.00 st.

🏨 **Selby Fork** (Anchor), LS25 5LF, W : 2 ¼ m. by A 63 on A 1 ♟ 682711, Group Telex 557074,
   🖾, ⅍ – 🆃🆅 ⌁wc ﬁﬂwc ⅙ 🅟. 🄰 🄰 🄰🄴 🄾 𝗩𝗜𝗦𝗔
   M (carving rest.) 10.25 t. 🛈 3.00 – **109 rm** 🖙 40.50/50.50 t. – SB (weekends only) 55.00/59.00 st.

MONMOUTH (TREFYNWY) Gwent 🄓🄞🄑 L 28 – pop. 7,379 – ECD : Thursday – ☎ 0600.

Envir. : SE : Wye Valley★ – Raglan (castle★ 15C) SW : 7 m. – Skenfrith (castle and church★) NW : 6 m.

🚩 National Trust Visitor Centre, Church St. ℰ 3899.

♦London 147 – Gloucester 26 – Newport 24 – ♦Swansea 64.

🏨 **King's Head,** Agincourt Sq., NP5 3DY, ℰ 2177, Telex 497294 – 📺 ➡wc 🏧wc ☎ 🅿. 🏃. 🔼
🝆🔘 *VISA*
closed 25 and 26 December – **M** 8.50/12.50 **t.** and a la carte 🍴 3.50 – ☲ 5.00 – **25 rm** 36.00/44.00 **t.** – SB 52.50/62.50 **st.**

🛎 **Leasbrook** 🦢, Dixton, NP5 5JN, NE : ¾ m. on A 40 ℰ 2831, ☞ – 🝆 🅿. 🔼. ⁂
closed 1 week at Christmas – **M** *(closed Sunday lunch)* (buffet lunch)/dinner 10.50 **st.** and a la carte 🍴 2.45 – **7 rm** ☲ 18.50/32.50 **st.** – SB (except Christmas) 40.00/42.00 **st.**

at Ganarew (Heref and Worc) NE : 3 ¼ m. by A 40 – ✉ ☎ 0600 Monmouth (Gwent)

🏠 **Ganarew House** 🦢, NP5 3SS, ℰ 890442, ≼, ☞ – 📺 ➡wc 🏧wc 🅿.
M (dinner only) (booking essential) 9.50 **t.** 🍴 2.90 – **9 rm** ☲ 16.00/36.00 **t.**

at Whitebrook S : 8 ½ m. by A 466 – ✉ ☎ 0600 Monmouth :

XX **Crown at Whitebrook** 🦢 with rm, NP5 4TX, ℰ 860254, ☞ – ➡wc 🏧wc ☎ 🅿. 🔼 🝆 🔘
VISA
M 9.75 **st.** (lunch) and a la carte approx. 18.50 **st.** – **8 rm** ☲ 27.00/43.00 **st.** – SB 62.00/70.00 **st.**

AUSTIN-ROVER St. James Sq. ℰ 2773
FORD 77/79 Monnow St. ℰ 2366
MERCEDES-BENZ Dixton Rd ℰ 3118

VAUXHALL-OPEL, BEDFORD, CITROEN Wonastow
Rd ℰ 2896

MONTACUTE Somerset 🄓🄞🄑 L 31 – see Yeovil.

MONTGOMERY (TREFALDWYN) Powys 🄓🄞🄑 K 26 – pop. 1,035 – ☎ 068 681.

♦ London 194 – ♦ Birmingham 71 – Chester 53 – Shrewsbury 30.

🛎 **Dragon,** SY15 6PA, ℰ 476, 🔼 – 📺 ➡wc 🏧wc 🅿.
15 rm.

MORECAMBE Lancs. 🄓🄞🄩 L 21 – pop. 41,432 – ECD : Wednesday – ☎ 0524.

See : Marineland★ *AC.*

🏌 Clubhouse ℰ 412841, on sea front.

🚩 Marine Rd Central ℰ 414110.

♦London 248 – ♦Blackpool 29 – ♦Carlisle 66 – Lancaster 4.

🏨 **Midland,** Marine Rd, LA4 4BZ, ℰ 417180, ≼ – 📲 📺 ➡wc 🏧wc ⊛ 🅿. 🏃. 🔼 🝆 🔘 *VISA*
M 6.25/9.00 **st.** and a la carte 🍴 4.00 – **46 rm** ☲ 32.50/60.00 **st.** – SB (weekends only) 54.00/65.00 **st.**

🏨 **Strathmore,** Marine Rd East, East Promenade, LA4 5AP, ℰ 411314, Group Telex 57515 (attn. 103), ≼ – 📲 📺 ➡wc 🏧wc 🅕 🅿. 🔼 🝆 🔘 *VISA*. ⁂
closed 1 week at Christmas – **M** 5.50/6.00 **t.** and a la carte 🍴 3.00 – **55 rm** ☲ 15.00/33.00 **t.** – SB (weekends only) (except July-September) 40.00/46.00 **st.**

🏨 **Elms,** Princes Crescent, Bare, LA4 6DD, ℰ 411501, ☞ – 📲 📺 ➡wc ⊛ 🅿. 🔼 🝆 🔘 *VISA*. ⁂
M 4.75/7.50 **t.** and a la carte 🍴 3.00 – **39 rm** ☲ 18.00/38.00 **t.** – SB (weekends only) (except Easter) 42.00/45.00 **st.**

🛏 **Prospect,** 363 Marine Rd, East Promenade, LA4 5AQ, ℰ 417819 – ➡wc
April-October – **14 rm** ☲ 9.00/18.00 **s.**

AUSTIN-ROVER Marine Rd Central ℰ 410134
TOYOTA West Gate ℰ 413891
VAUXHALL Bare Lane ℰ 410205

VOLVO Marlborough Rd ℰ 417437
VW, AUDI Heysham Rd ℰ 415833

MORETONHAMPSTEAD Devon 🄓🄞🄑 I 32 **The West Country G.** – pop. 1,420 – ECD : Thursday – ✉ Newton Abbot – ☎ 0647.

🏌 Manor House Hotel ℰ 40355.

♦London 213 – Exeter 12 – ♦Plymouth 38.

🏩 **Manor House** 🦢, TQ13 8RE, SW : 2 m. on B 3212 ℰ 40355, Telex 42794, ≼, 🏌, 🐟, ☞,
park, ⁂, squash – 📲 📺 🅕 🅿. 🏃. 🔼 🝆 🔘 *VISA*
M (buffet lunch)/dinner 13.50 **st.** 🍴 3.75 – **66 rm** ☲ 47.00/89.00 **st.** – SB 80.00/90.00 **st.**

🛏 **Wray Barton Manor** 🦢, TQ13 8SE, SE : 1½ m. on A 382 ℰ 40246, ≼, ☞ – 📺 ➡wc 🅿.
⁂
closed December and January – **6 rm** ☲ 10.50/23.50 **st.**

Do not lose your way in Europe, use the Michelin
Main Road maps, scale : 1 inch : 16 miles.

341

MORETON-IN-MARSH Glos. 408 404 O 28 — pop. 2 ,545 — ECD : Wednesday — ✆ 0608.
Envir. : Chastleton House★★ (Elizabethan) *AC*, SE : 3 ½ m.

🏛 Council Offices, High St. ☎ 50881.

◆London 86 — ◆Birmingham 40 — Gloucester 31 — ◆Oxford 29.

   🏨 **Manor House,** High St., GL56 0LJ, ☎ 50501, Telex 837151, « 17C manor house, gardens »,
      ◱ — 🛏 TV ⌨ wc ⏥wc ⊛ ℗ 🅿. 🔼 AE ① VISA. ⋇
      M 8.50/12.50 t. and a la carte 🍴 3.00 — **40 rm** ⊆ 22.00/59.50 t. — SB (November-April only)
      32.50/46.00 **st.**

   🏠 **White Hart Royal** (T.H.F.), High St., GL56 0BA, ☎ 50731 — TV ⌨ wc ⊛ ℗. 🔼. 🔼 AE ①
      VISA
      M (bar lunch Monday to Saturday)/dinner a la carte 7.95/15.35 **st.** 🍴 2.70 — ⊆ 5.50 — **27 rm**
      36.50/44.50 **st.**

BMW High St. ☎ 50323   RENAULT Little Compton ☎ 74202
PEUGEOT-TALBOT London Rd ☎ 50585

MORPETH Northumb. 401 402 O 18 — pop. 14 ,301 — ECD : Thursday — ✆ 0670.
Envir. : Brinkburn Priory (site★, church★ : Gothic) *AC*, NW : 10 m.

📐 Newbiggin-by-the-Sea ☎ 817344, E : 9 m. — 📐 The Common ☎ 2065.

🏛 The Chantry, Bridge St. ☎ 511323.

◆London 301 — ◆Edinburgh 93 — ◆Newcastle-upon-Tyne 15.

   🏠 **Queen's Head,** Bridge St., NE61 1NB, ☎ 512083 — TV ⌨ wc 🍴 ⊛ ℗. 🔼 AE ① VISA. ⋇
      closed 24-26 December and 1 January — **M** (closed Sunday dinner) 6.95 **t.** and a la carte 🍴 2.75
      — **23 rm** ⊆ 17.50/31.00 **t.**

   at Longhorsley NW : 7 ½ m. by A 192 on A 697 — ✉ ✆ 0670 Morpeth :

   🏰 **Linden Hall** ⧫, NE65 8XF, N : 1 m. on A 697 ☎ 56611, Telex 538224, ≼, « Country house in
      extensive grounds », 🎋, park, ✗ — 🛏 TV ☎ ⅋ ℗. 🔼. 🔼 AE ① VISA. ⋇
      M a la carte 18.50/23.50 **st.** 🍴 3.00 — **45 rm** ⊆ 46.50/57.50 **st.** — SB (weekends only)
      69.50/89.50 **st.**

AUSTIN-ROVER Hillgate ☎ 57441   RENAULT Clifton ☎ 512538
FORD 53/55 Bridge St. ☎ 519611   VAUXHALL Bridge End ☎ 512115
PEUGEOT, TALBOT Ellington ☎ 860327   VW, AUDI Castle Sq. ☎ 519011

MORTEHOE Devon 408 H 30 — see Woolacombe.

During the season, particularly in resorts, it is wise to book in advance.

MOULSFORD Oxon. 408 404 Q 29 — pop. 494 — ✆ 0491 Cholsey.

◆London 58 — ◆Oxford 17 — Reading 13 — Swindon 37.

   🏨 **Beetle and Wedge** ⧫, Ferry Lane, OX10 9JF ☎ 651381, ≼, 🎋 — TV ⌨ wc ☎ ℗. 🔼 AE ①
      VISA
      M 9.50 **t.** and a la carte 🍴 3.25 — **15 rm** ⊆ 29.00/48.00 **st.** — SB (October-March except Christmas)
      50.00 **st.**

MOULTON Northants. 404 R 27 — see Northampton.

MOULTON North Yorks. 402 P 20 — ✉ Richmond — ✆ 032 577 Barton.

◆London 243 — ◆Leeds 53 — ◆Middlesbrough 25 — ◆Newcastle-upon-Tyne 43.

   XX **Black Bull Inn,** DL10 6QJ, ☎ 289, « Brighton Belle Pullman coach » — ℗
      closed Sunday and 23 December-1 January — **M** (restricted lunch) 6.50 **t.** and a la carte
      9.00/18.50 **t.** 🍴 3.00.

MOUNT PLEASANT Hants. 408 404 P 31 — see Lymington.

MOUSEHOLE Cornwall 408 D 33 The West Country G. — ECD : Wednesday except summer — ✉
✆ 0736 Penzance.

See : Site★.

◆London 321 — Penzance 3 — Truro 29.

   🏨 **Lobster Pot,** South Cliff, TR19 6QX, ☎ 731251, ≼ — ⌨ wc 🍴 wc
      closed mid January-February — **M** 4.50/9.50 **t.** and a la carte 🍴 3.25 — **24 rm** ⊆ 13.20/56.10 **st.**

   🏠 **Carn Du** ⧫, Raginnis Hill, TR19 6SS, ☎ 731233, ≼ Mounts Bay, — 🍴 wc ℗. 🔼 VISA. ⋇
      End March-October — **M** (dinner only) 8.00 **st.** 🍴 3.00 — **7 rm** ⊆ 17.00/36.00 **st.**

   ⌂ **Tavis Vor,** The Parade, TR19 6PR, ☎ 731306, ≼ Mounts Bay, 🎋 — 🍴 wc. ⋇
      March-September — **7 rm** ⊆ 10.50/27.00 **t.**

MUDEFORD Dorset 408 404 O 31 — see Christchurch.

MUCH BIRCH Heref. and Worc. — see Hereford.

MULLION Cornwall **403** E 33 The West Country G. − pop. 1,958 − ECD : Wednesday − ✉ Helston − ☎ 0326.

See : Mullion Cove★★★ (Church★).

♦London 323 − Falmouth 21 − Penzance 21 − Truro 26.

   🏨 **Polurrian** ⟩, TR12 7EN, SW : ½ m. ✆ 240421, ⩽ Mounts Bay, ☌ heated, 🐎, ✗, squash − 📺 ⌂wc ☎ **P**. ☒ ① **VISA**
     Mid April-October − **M** 6.50/10.00 **st.** and a la carte − **42 rm** � 15.00/60.00 **st.**

MUMBLES West Glam. **403** I 29 − ECD : Wednesday − ✉ ☎ 0792 Swansea.

See : Mumbles Head★ − **Envir.** : Cefn Bryn (⁂★★★ from the reservoir) W : 12 m. − Rhosili (site and ⩽ ★★★) W : 18 m. − W : Oxwich Bay★.

♦London 202 − ♦Swansea 6.

   🏨 **Osborne** (Embassy), Rotherslade Rd, Langland Bay, SA3 4QL, W : ¾ m. ✆ 66274, ⩽ − 🛗 📺 ⌂wc ☎ **P**. ☒ ⅍E ① **VISA**. ✗
     M *(closed Sunday to non-residents)* 5.50/8.00 **st.** and a la carte ⅃ 2.55 − **37 rm** ⊐ 26.00/47.00 **st.** − SB *(except July and August)* 49.00/53.00 **st.**

   🏨 **Langland Court** (Best Western) ⟩, 31 Langland Court Rd, Langland Bay, SA3 4TD, W : 1 m. ✆ 61545, 🐎 − 📺 ⌂wc ⋔wc ☎ ⟸ **P**. ☒ ⅍E ① **VISA**
     closed 23 to 27 December − **M** *(closed Sunday dinner)* (bar lunch Monday to Saturday)/dinner 7.50 **t.** and a la carte ⅃ 3.40 − **21 rm** ⊐ 28.00/45.00 **t.** − SB 50.00/60.00 **st.**

   🏛 **Old School House,** 37 Nottage Rd, Newton, SA3 4SU, W : 1 m. ✆ 61541 − 📺 ⋔wc ☎ **P**. ☒ ⅍E ① **VISA**. ✗
     closed 24-30 December − **M** *(closed Saturday lunch and Sunday dinner)* (bar lunch)/dinner 9.95 **t.** and a la carte ⅃ 2.60 − **8 rm** ⊐ 23.00/38.00 **t.** − SB (weekends only) 45.00/55.00 **st.**

   ↑ **Wittemberg,** 2 Rotherslade Rd, Langland, SA3 4QN, W : ¾ m. ✆ 69696 − ⋔wc **P**. ✗
     closed 1 week at Christmas − **11 rm** ⊐ 15.00/28.00 **t.**

   XXX **Norton House** with rm, 17 Norton Rd, SA3 5TQ, ✆ 404891 − 📺 ⌂wc ⋔wc ☎ **P**. ☒ **VISA**. ✗
     closed 1 week August and 2 weeks Christmas − **M** *(closed Sunday)* (dinner only) 9.50 **st.** and a la carte 8.55/13.30 **t.** ⅃ 2.90 − ⊐ 4.50 − **16 rm** 28.00/34.00 **st.**

AUSTIN-ROVER 54 Mumbles Rd, Blackpill ✆ 23451

MUNGRISDALE Cumbria **401 402** L 19 20 − pop. 336 − ✉ Penrith − ☎ 059 683 Threlkeld.

♦London 301 − ♦Carlisle 33 − Keswick 8.5 − Penrith 13.

   ☖ **Mill** ⟩, CA11 0XR, ✆ 659, 🐎 − ⌂wc **P**. ✗
     March-November − **M** (dinner only) 9.25 **st.** ⅃ 2.75 − **8 rm** ⊐ 13.00/33.00 **t.**

NAFFERTON Humberside **402** S 21 − see Great Driffield.

NANTWICH Cheshire **402 403 404** M 24 − pop. 11,867 − ECD : Wednesday − ☎ 0270.

🛈 Council Offices, Beam St. ✆ 623914.

♦London 176 − Chester 20 − ♦Liverpool 45 − ♦Stoke-on-Trent 17.

   🏯 **Rookery Hall** ⟩, Worleston, CW5 6DQ, N : 2 ½ m. by A 51 on B 5074 ✆ 626866, Telex 367169, ⩽, « 19C country house », ⅃, 🐎, park, ✗ − 📺 ☎ **P**. ☒ ⅍E ① **VISA**. ✗
     M (booking essential) 12.95/22.50 **t.** and a la carte ⅃ 6.50 − **11 rm** ⊐ 55.00/115.00 **t.**, **1 suite** 140.00 **t.** − SB (October - 16 March only) 120.00/165.00 **st.**

   XX **Churche's Mansion,** 150 Hospital St., CW5 5RY, ✆ 625933, « 16C half-timbered house », 🐎 − **P**
     closed Sunday dinner, 25 to 29 December and 1 January − **M** 6.25/11.95 **t.** ⅃ 3.50.

AUSTIN-ROVER London Rd ✆ 623151
FORD Crewe Rd ✆ 623739
HONDA Whitchurch Rd ✆ 780300
SAAB Welsh Row ✆ 627678
VAUXHALL-OPEL Station Rd ✆ 624027

NARBOROUGH Leics. **403 404** Q 26 − see Leicester.

NASSINGTON Northants. **404** S 26 − see Peterborough (Cambs.).

NATIONAL EXHIBITION CENTRE West Midlands **403 404** O 26 − see Birmingham.

NAWTON North Yorks. − see Helmsley.

NAYLAND Suffolk **404** W 28 − see Colchester (Essex).

NEASHAM Durham **402** P 20 − see Darlington.

NEATISHEAD Norfolk **404** Y 25 − pop. 524 − ☎ 0692 Horning.

♦London 122 − North Walsham 8.5 − ♦Norwich 11.

   🏛 **Barton Angler Lodge** ⟩, Irstead Rd, NR12 8XP, E : ¾ m. ✆ 630740, « Country house atmosphere », 🐎 − 📺 ⌂wc ⋔wc **P**. ☒ ⅍E ① **VISA**
     M (bar lunch Monday to Saturday)/dinner 12.00 **t.** ⅃ 2.10 − **6 rm** ⊐ 12.50/40.00 **t.** − SB 49.00/64.00 **st.**

NEEDHAM MARKET Suffolk 404 X 27 – pop. 3,420 – ECD : Tuesday – ✉ 🕾 0449.

♦ London 77 – ♦ Cambridge 47 – ♦ Ipswich 8.5 – ♦ Norwich 38.

🏠 **Limes,** 99 High St., IP6 8DQ, ✎ 720305 – 📺 ➪wc 🕾 🅿. 🔼 🅰🄴 ⓞ. ⅍
closed Christmas – **M** 7.50/8.50 **st.** and a la carte ⅄ 2.30 – **11 rm** ⌾ 30.00/48.00 **st.** – SB
(weekends only) 48.50/52.00 **st.**

NEFYN Gwynedd 402 403 G 25 – pop. 2,236 – ECD : Wednesday – 🕾 0758.

See : Site ⋆.

🛅 ✎ 720218, W : 1 ½ m.

♦London 265 – Caernarfon 20.

🏡 **Caeau Capel** ⌾, Rhodfa'r Mor, LL53 6EB, ✎ 720240, 🍴 – ➪wc 🅿. 🔼 VISA
Easter-September – **M** (bar lunch)/dinner 6.00 ⅄ 1.50 – **23 rm** ⌾ 12.65/40.25 **t.**

AUSTIN-ROVER Church St. ✎ 720206

NETTLECOMBE Dorset – see Bridport.

NEW ALRESFORD Hants. 403 404 Q 30 – pop. 4,157 – ECD : Wednesday – 🕾 096 273.

🛅 Cheriton Rd ✎ 3153, S : 1 m.

♦London 63 – ♦Southampton 19 – Winchester 8.

🏠 **Swan,** West St., SO24 9AG, ✎ 2302 – 📺 ➪wc 🅿. 🔼 VISA. ⅍
M a la carte 3.85/8.90 **t.** ⅄ 2.75 – **13 rm** ⌾ 18.00/30.00 **t.**

AUSTIN-ROVER 47 West St. ✎ 2601
FORD The Dene, Ropley ✎ 096 277 (Ropley) 2416

SAAB, SUBARU New Cheriton ✎ 096 279 (Bram-dean) 400

NEWARK-ON-TRENT Notts. 402 404 R 24 – pop. 33,143 – ECD : Thursday – 🕾 0636.

🛈 The Ossington, Beast Market Hill, Castlegate ✎ 78962.

♦London 127 – Lincoln 16 – ♦ Nottingham 20 – ♦ Sheffield 42.

🏨 **Robin Hood** (Anchor), Lombard St., NG24 1XB, ✎ 703858, Group Telex 858875 – 📺 ➪wc
🕾 🅿 🛋. 🔼 🅰🄴 VISA
M 8.35 **st.** ⅄ 3.00 – **20 rm** ⌾ 35.00/45.00 **st.** – SB (weekends only) 47.00/52.00 **st.**

🏠 **Clinton Arms,** 44 Market Pl., NG24 1EG, ✎ 72299 – 📺 ➪wc 🏮wc. 🔼 VISA. ⅍
M (closed Sunday) 4.00 **t.** (lunch) and a la carte 4.75/9.45 **t.** ⅄ 3.00 – **18 rm** ⌾ 22.50/37.50 **t.**

🏡 **Grange,** 73 London Rd, Charles St. Corner, NG24 1RZ, ✎ 703399, 🍴 – 📺 ➪wc 🅿. 🔼 VISA
⅍
closed Christmas – **M** (bar lunch)/dinner a la carte 6.20/8.25 **st.** ⅄ 2.95 – **6 rm** ⌾ 17.95/35.00 **st.**
– SB (weekends only) 36.00/40.00 **st.**

AUSTIN-ROVER 69 Northgate ✎ 703413
FIAT Sleaford Rd ✎ 703405
FORD Farndon Rd ✎ 704131
LADA London Rd ✎ 704937
NISSAN Lombard St. ✎ 77533

PEUGEOT-TALBOT 50 Albert St. ✎ 707272
RENAULT Clinton St. ✎ 704619
SKODA London Rd ✎ 705845
VAUXHALL-OPEL 116 Farndon Rd ✎ 705431
VW, AUDI Northern Rd ✎ 704484

NEWBRIDGE Cornwall – see Penzance.

NEWBURY Berks. 403 404 Q 29 – pop. 31,488 – ECD : Wednesday – 🕾 0635.

🛈 District Museum, The Wharf ✎ 30267.

♦London 67 – ♦ Bristol 66 – ♦ Oxford 28 – Reading 17 – ♦ Southampton 38.

🏨 **Elcot Park Country House** (Best Western) ⌾, RG16 8NJ, W : 5 m. by A 4 ✎ 0488 (Kint-bury) 58100, ≼, 🍴, park, ⅍ – 📺 ➪wc 🕾 🅿 🛋. 🔼 🅰🄴 ⓞ VISA
M 7.50/11.75 **t.** and a la carte ⅄ 3.60 – **20 rm** ⌾ 45.00/75.00 **t.** – SB 65.00/85.00 **st.**

🏨 **Chequers** (T.H.F.), 7-8 Oxford St., RG13 1JB, ✎ 38000, Telex 849205, 🍴 – 📺 ➪wc 🕾 🅿.
🛋. 🔼 🅰🄴 ⓞ VISA
M 8.50/8.95 **st.** and a la carte ⅄ 2.70 – ⌾ 5.50 – **59 rm** 37.50/50.50 **st.**

✗ **Sapient Pig,** 29 Oxford St., RG13 1JG, ✎ 47425 – 🔼 VISA
closed Saturday lunch and Sunday – **M** a la carte 9.65/16.00 **t.**

AUSTIN-ROVER London Rd ✎ 41100
RENAULT London Rd ✎ 41020

VW-AUDI 22 Newtown Rd ✎ 41911

NEWBY BRIDGE Cumbria 402 L 21 – ECD : Saturday – ✉ Ulverston – 🕾 0448.

♦London 270 – Kendal 16 – Lancaster 27.

🏨 **Swan,** LA12 8NB, ✎ 31681, Telex 65108, ≼, ⅀, 🍴 – 📺 ➪wc 🕾 🅿. 🛋. 🔼 🅰🄴 ⓞ VISA. ⅍
closed 2 to 10 January – **M** 6.75/10.25 **t.** and a la carte ⅄ 3.75 – **36 rm** ⌾ 30.00/52.00 **t.**, **1 suite**
60.00 **t.** – SB (winter only)(weekends only)(not Bank Holidays) 55.00/66.00 **st.**

🏨 **Whitewater,** The Lakeland Village, LA12 8PX, SW : 1 ½ m. by A 590 ✎ 31133, Telex 54173 –
🎬📺 ➪wc 🕾 🛗. 🔼 🅰🄴 ⓞ VISA. ⅍
M 6.50/9.95 **t.** and a la carte ⅄ 3.10 – **34 rm** ⌾ 42.00/52.00 **t.** – SB 60.00 **st.**

NEWBY WISKE North Yorks. – see Northallerton.

NEWCASTLE EMLYN (CASTELL NEWYDD EMLYN) Dyfed **403** G 27 – pop. 1 ,230 – ECD : Wednesday – ☎ 0239.

Envir. : Cenarth Falls★ W : 3 m.

Exc. : E : Teifi Valley★.

♦London 240 – Carmarthen 20 – Fishguard 29.

🏛 Emlyn Arms, Bridge St., SA38 9DU, ℰ 710317 – 📺 🛏wc 🐕 🅿. 🔼 🅰🅴 ⓞ 𝘝𝘐𝘚𝘈
M 6.70 t. and a la carte ⌗ 2.75 – **38 rm**.

FORD New Rd ℰ 710245

In July and August, hotels are often overcrowded and staff overworked.
You will be more satisfied if you go in other months.

NEWCASTLE-UNDER-LYME Staffs. **402 403 404** N 24 – pop. 73 ,208 – ECD : Thursday –
☎ 0782 Stoke-on-Trent.

🏌 Newcastle Municipal, Keele Rd ℰ 627596, NW : 2 m. on A 525 V.

🛈 Area Reference Library, Ironmarket ℰ 618125.

♦London 161 – ♦Birmingham 46 – ♦Liverpool 56 – ♦Manchester 43.

Plan of Built up Area : see Stoke-on-Trent

🏛🏛 **Clayton Lodge** (Embassy),
Clayton Rd, Clayton, ST5 4AF,
S : 1 ¼ m. on A 519 ℰ 613093
– 📺 🛏wc ☎ 🅿. 🔼 🔼 🅰🅴
ⓞ 𝘝𝘐𝘚𝘈 ⚘   V e
M 8.25 st. and a la carte ⌗ 2.75
– � 5.00 – **50 rm** 38.50/43.00
st. – SB 50.00/51.00 st.

🏛🏛 **Crest** (Crest), Liverpool Rd,
Cross Heath, ST5 9DX, N : 2 m.
on A 34 ℰ 612431, Telex 36681
– 🔳 rest 📺 🛏wc 🐕 👤 🅿.
🔼 ⚘   U a
74 rm.

🏛🏛 **Post House** (T.H.F.), Clayton
Rd, Clayton, ST5 4DL, S : 2 m.
on A 519 ℰ 625151, Telex 36531
– 📺 🛏wc 🐕 🅿. 🔼 🔼 🅰🅴
ⓞ 𝘝𝘐𝘚𝘈   V n
M 7.25/9.25 st. and a la carte
⌗ 2.70 – � 5.50 – **126 rm**
40.50/47.50 st.

⌂ **Grove Court**, 100 Lancaster
Rd, ST5 1DS, ℰ 614406, 🚗
– 📺 🛏wc 📶wc 🔼 𝘝𝘐𝘚𝘈
⚘   o
11 rm � 11.50/23.00 t.

AUSTIN-ROVER Brook Lane ℰ 618461
BMW Pool Dam ℰ 620811
CITROEN, PEUGEOT-TALBOT Hassell St.
ℰ 614621
COLT Brunswick St. ℰ 614791
DATSUN Talke Rd, Chesterton ℰ 563711
FIAT Higherland ℰ 622141
FORD London Rd ℰ 621199
MAZDA North St. ℰ 612274
RENAULT High St., Wolstanton ℰ 626284

**NEWCASTLE-
UNDER-LYME
CENTRE**

High Street

Blackfriars Road 2

Church Street 5
Higherland 6
Iron Market 7
Liverpool Road 9
Merrial Street 10
North Street 12
Upper Green 14
Vessey Terrace 15

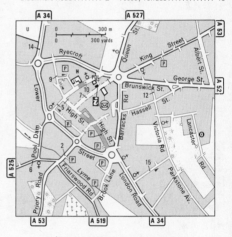

VAUXHALL-OPEL Higherland ℰ 610941
VOLVO Knutton Rd, Wolstanton ℰ 625333
VW, AUDI Brunswick St. ℰ 617321

NEWCASTLE-UPON-TYNE Tyne and Wear **401 402** O 19 – pop. 199 ,064 – ECD : Monday and
Wednesday – ☎ 0632 (6 fig.) or 091 (7 fig.).

See : Cathedral★ 14C CZ **A**.

🏌 Gosforth Park, High Gosforth Park ℰ 364867, AV – 🏌 Broadway East, Gosforth, ℰ 856710, N :
3 m. by Kenton Rd AV – 🏌 Whorlton Grange, Westerhope, ℰ 869125, W : 5 m. by B 6324 AV.

✈ Newcastle Airport : ℰ 2860966, Telex 537831 NW : 5 m. by A 696 AV – Terminal : Bus Assembly :
Central Station Forecourt.

🚃 ℰ 611234 ext 2621.

⚓ Shipping connections with the Continent : to Norway (Bergen, Stavanger) (Norway Line)
summer only – to Denmark (Esbjerg) (DFDS Seaways) summer only – to Sweden (Götenborg)
(DFDS Seaways) summer only.

🛈 Central Library, Princess Sq. ℰ 610691 – Blackfriars, Monk St. ℰ 615367.

♦London 276 – ♦Edinburgh 105 – ♦Leeds 95.

NEWCASTLE-
UPON-TYNE

Adelaide Terrace	....	**AX** 2
Askew Road	....	**AX** 3
Atkinson Road	....	**AX** 4
Bath Street	....	**BX** 6
Bensham Road	....	**AX** 7
Benton Bank	....	**BV** 8
Buddle Street	....	**BV** 13
Church Avenue	....	**AV** 17
Church Road	....	**AV** 18
Clayton Road	....	**BV** 21
Coldwell Lane	....	**BX** 26
Coldwell Street	....	**BX** 27
Condercum Road	....	**AX** 30
Fossway	....	**BV** 35
Haddrick's Mill Road	....	**BV** 41
Heathery Lane	....	**BV** 42
High Street West	....	**BV** 44
Jesmond Dene Road	....	**BV** 45
Killingworth Road	....	**BV** 46
Lobley Hill Road	....	**AX** 48
Matthew Bank	....	**BV** 53
Neptune Road	....	**BV** 60
Red Hall Drive	....	**BV** 71
Saltwell Road	....	**BX** 80
Shipdon Road	....	**AX** 82
Springfield Road	....	**AV** 85
Station Road	....	**BX** 87
Stephenson Road	....	**BV** 90
Sunderland Road	....	**BX** 93
Sutton Street	....	**BV** 95
Swalwell Bank	....	**AX** 96
Waverdale Avenue	....	**BV** 102
West Farm Avenue	....	**BV** 104
Whickham Bank	....	**AX** 105
Windy Nook Road	....	**BX** 106

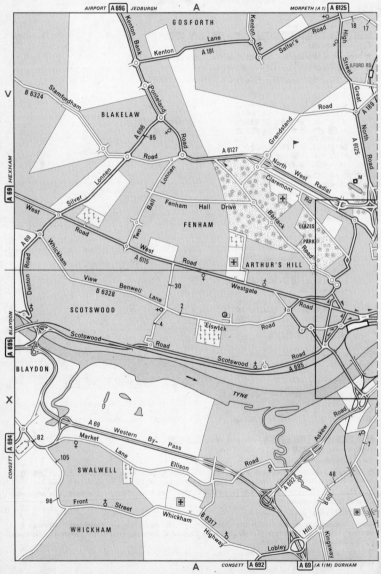

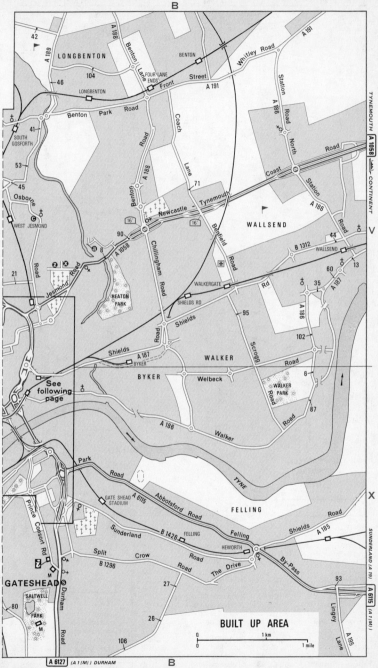

BUILT UP AREA

Scale: 0 — 1 km / 0 — 1 mile

See following page

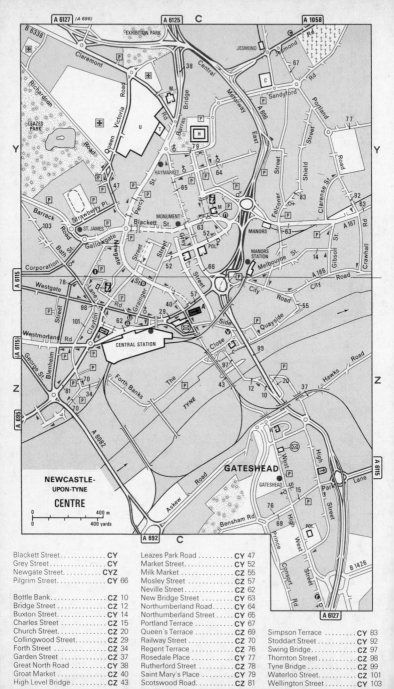

Blackett Street	**CY**	
Grey Street	**CY**	
Newgate Street	**CYZ**	
Pilgrim Street	**CY** 66	
Bottle Bank	**CZ** 10	
Bridge Street	**CZ** 12	
Buxton Street	**CY** 14	
Charles Street	**CZ** 15	
Church Street	**CZ** 20	
Collingwood Street	**CZ** 29	
Forth Street	**CZ** 34	
Garden Street	**CZ** 37	
Great North Road	**CY** 38	
Groat Market	**CZ** 40	
High Level Bridge	**CZ** 43	
Leazes Park Road	**CY** 47	
Market Street	**CY** 52	
Milk Market	**CZ** 55	
Mosley Street	**CZ** 57	
Neville Street	**CZ** 62	
New Bridge Street	**CY** 63	
Northumberland Road	**CY** 64	
Northumberland Street	**CY** 65	
Portland Terrace	**CY** 67	
Queen's Terrace	**CZ** 69	
Railway Street	**CZ** 70	
Regent Terrace	**CY** 76	
Rosedale Place	**CY** 77	
Rutherford Street	**CZ** 78	
Saint Mary's Place	**CY** 79	
Scotswood Road	**CZ** 81	
Simpson Terrace	**CY** 83	
Stoddart Street	**CY** 92	
Swing Bridge	**CZ** 97	
Thornton Street	**CZ** 98	
Tyne Bridge	**CZ** 99	
Waterloo Street	**CZ** 101	
Wellington Street	**CY** 103	

🏨 **Swallow** (Swallow), Newgate Arcade, Newgate St., NE1 5SX, ℰ 325025, Telex 538230 – 🛉
📺 🖴wc ☎ 🅿. 🅐. 🔜 🝙 ⓪ 𝘝𝘐𝘚𝘈　　　　　　　　　　　　　　　　　　　　CZ **o**
M 6.00/10.50 **st.** and a la carte 🍷 3.40 – **93 rm** ⊊ 41.50/55.00 **st.**

🏨 **Crest** (Crest), New Bridge St., NE1 8BS, ℰ 326191, Telex 53467 – 🛉 ▤ rest 📺 🖴wc ☎ ఉ
🅿. 🅐. 🔜 🝙 ⓪ 𝘝𝘐𝘚𝘈. ⁂　　　　　　　　　　　　　　　　　　　　　　　　CY **n**
M approx 11.50 – ⊊ 5.75 – **179 rm** 45.00/55.00, **1 suite** – SB (weekends only) 55.00.

🏨 **Imperial** (Swallow), Jesmond Rd, NE2 1PR, ℰ 281 5511, Telex 537972, 🔲 – 🛉 🖴wc ☎
🅿. 🅐. 🔜 🝙 ⓪ 𝘝𝘐𝘚𝘈　　　　　　　　　　　　　　　　　　　　　　　　　CY **c**
M 5.50/7.70 **st.** and a la carte 🍷 3.50 – **127 rm** ⊊ 37.50/46.50 **st.**

🏨 **County Thistle** (Thistle), Neville St., NE99 1AH, ℰ 322471, Telex 537873 – 🛉 📺 🖴wc ☎.
🅐. 🔜 🝙 ⓪ 𝘝𝘐𝘚𝘈　　　　　　　　　　　　　　　　　　　　　　　　　　CZ **a**
M 7.75 **t.** and a la carte 🍷 2.75 – ⊊ 4.75 – **115 rm** 36.00/55.00 **t.**

🏦 **New Kent**, 127 Osborne Rd, Jesmond, NE2 2TB, ℰ 281 1083 – 📺 🖴wc ☎ 🅿. 🔜 🝙 ⓪ 𝘝𝘐𝘚𝘈.
⁂　　　　　　　　　　　　　　　　　　　　　　　　　　　　　　　　　BV **c**
M *(closed Sunday dinner)* (dinner only and lunch, Saturday and Sunday) 11.90 **t.** and a la carte
🍷 3.80 – **35 rm** – SB (weekends only) 57.60 **st.**

⌂ **Avenue**, 2 Manor House Rd, Jesmond, NE2 2LU, ℰ 091 (Tyneside) 281 1396 – 🔜 🝙 ⓪. ⁂
9 rm ⊊ 14.50/23.50 **s.**　　　　　　　　　　　　　　　　　　　　　　BV **x**

⌂ **Westland**, 27 Osborne Av., Jesmond, NE2 1JR, ℰ 091 (Tyneside) 281 0412 – 🖴wc　BV **z**
closed Christmas and New Year – **16 rm** ⊊ 14.50/27.50 **t.**

⌂ **Clifton Cottage**, Dunholme Rd, NE4 6XE, ℰ 091 (Tyneside) 273 7347 – 📺 🅿　　AX **e**
6 rm ⊊ 10.50/18.00 **st.**

�XX **Fisherman's Wharf**, 15 The Side, NE1 3JE, ℰ 321057, Seafood – 🔜 🝙 ⓪ 𝘝𝘐𝘚𝘈　CZ **v**
closed Saturday lunch, Sunday, 25 December - 2 January and Bank Holidays – **M** 8.00 **t.**
(lunch) and a la carte 13.90/22.80 **t.** 🍷 3.20.

�XX **Fisherman's Lodge**, Jesmond Dene, Jesmond, NE7 7BQ, ℰ 091 (Tyneside) 281 3281,
Seafood – 🅿. 🔜 🝙 ⓪ 𝘝𝘐𝘚𝘈　　　　　　　　　　　　　　　　　　　　　BV **a**
closed Saturday lunch, Sunday, 25 December-1 January and Bank Holidays – **M** 9.50 **t.** (lunch)
and a la carte 12.50/20.50 **t.** 🍷 3.30.

�XX **Ming Dynasty**, 41 Stowell St., NE1 4YB, ℰ 615787, Chinese - Peking rest. – 🔜 🝙 ⓪ 𝘝𝘐𝘚𝘈
M 3.80/6.50 **t.** and a la carte 🍷 3.50.　　　　　　　　　　　　　　　　　CY **i**

🗙 Mario, 59 Westgate Rd, NE1 1SG, ℰ 320708, Italian rest.　　　　　　　　　　CZ **u**

at Gosforth N : 4 ¾ m. on A 6125 – AV – ✉ ✪ 0632 Newcastle-upon-Tyne :

🏨 **Gosforth Park Thistle** (Thistle), High Gosforth Park, NE3 5HN, on B 1318 ℰ 0632 (Wideopen) 364111, Telex 53655, ≤, 🔲, 🏊, park, squash – 🛉 📺 ☎ ఉ 🅿. 🔜 🝙 ⓪ 𝘝𝘐𝘚𝘈
M 7.00/8.00 **t.** and a la carte – ⊊ 5.95 – **178 rm** 52.00/80.00 **t.**, **5 suites** 95.00 **t.**

at Seaton Burn N : 8 m. on A 6125 – AV – ✉ Newcastle-upon-Tyne – ✪ 0632 Wideopen :

🏨 Holiday Inn, Great North Rd, NE13 6BP, N : ¾ m. on junction with A 1 ℰ 365432, Telex 53271,
🔲 – ▤ 📺 ☎ ఉ 🅿. 🅐
156 rm, 1 suite.

at Wallsend NE : 6 m. on A 1058 – BV – ✉ Newcastle-upon-Tyne – ✪ 091 Tyneside :

🏨 **Newcastle Moat House** (Q.M.H.), Coast Rd, NE28 9HP, at junction with A 1 ℰ 262 8989,
Telex 53583 – 🛉 📺 🖴wc ☎ 🅿. 🅐. 🔜 🝙 ⓪ 𝘝𝘐𝘚𝘈
M 7.75/8.25 **st.** and a la carte 🍷 2.75 – **158 rm** ⊊ 37.50/47.50 **st.** – SB 45.00 **st.**

at Newcastle Airport NW : 6 m. on A 696 – AV – ✉ Woolsington – ✪ 0661 Ponteland :

🏨 **Stakis Airport** (Stakis), NE13 8DJ, ℰ 24911, Telex 537121 – 🛉 📺 🖴wc ☎ ఉ 🅿. 🅐. 🔜
🝙 ⓪ 𝘝𝘐𝘚𝘈
M (buffet lunch)/dinner 11.00 **t.** – **98 rm** ⊊ 41.00/48.00 **t.**

ALFA-ROMEO, YUGO Diana St. ℰ 322314	PORSCHE Melbourne St. ℰ 612591
AUSTIN-ROVER Etherstone Av. ℰ 2663311	RENAULT Shiremoor ℰ 2532318
AUSTIN-ROVER Newburn Rd ℰ 2674449	RENAULT Scotswood Rd ℰ 2730101
AUSTIN-ROVER Westgate Rd ℰ 2737901	SAAB Whitley Rd, Longbenton ℰ 2668223
CITROEN Westgate Rd ℰ 2737821	SUBARU 87 Osborne Rd ℰ 811677
COLT Jesmond ℰ 370658	TALBOT Benton Rd ℰ 2666361
FIAT Railway St. ℰ 2732131	VAUXHALL Two Ball Lonnen ℰ 2741000
FORD Market St. ℰ 611471	VAUXHALL Great North Rd ℰ 363176
FORD Scotswood Rd ℰ 2735121	VAUXHALL Dunn St. ℰ 2735211
HONDA Sunniside ℰ 4887298	VOLVO Brunton Lane ℰ 2867111
LAND ROVER Comington ℰ 2676271	VOLVO Jesmond Rd ℰ 2815151
NISSAN Benfield Rd ℰ 2659171	VW, AUDI Fossway ℰ 2657121

▉NEW DENHAM▉ Bucks. 🔟🔟🔟 ⑫ – ✉ ✪ 0895 Uxbridge.

♦London 20 – Aylesbury 25 – ♦Oxford 40.

🗙🗙🗙 **Giovanni's**, at Denham Lodge, Oxford Rd, UB9 4AA, on A 4020 ℰ 31568, Italian rest. – 🅿.
🔜 🝙 ⓪ 𝘝𝘐𝘚𝘈
closed Saturday lunch, Sunday and Bank Holidays – **M** a la carte 10.90/14.25 **st.** 🍷 2.95.

NEWDIGATE Surrey 404 T 30 – pop. 1,444 – ✆ 030 677.

♦London 32 – ♦Brighton 32 – Guildford 18.

XX **Forge,** Parkgate Rd, RH5 5DZ, N : 1 m. ℰ 582, Italian rest. – 🅿. AE ⦿
   closed Saturday lunch, Sunday, Monday and January – **M** a la carte 10.75/13.05 **t.** ▮ 3.50.

NEWHAVEN East Sussex 404 U 31 – pop. 10,697 – ECD : Wednesday – ✆ 0273.

🏌 Peacehaven, Brighton Rd ℰ 514049.

⚓ Shipping connections with the Continent : to France (Dieppe) (Sealink).

♦London 63 – ♦Brighton 9 – Eastbourne 14 – Lewes 7.

FORD Drove Rd ℰ 515303   VAUXHALL-OPEL Avis Way ℰ 5941

NEWLYN Cornwall 403 D 33 – see Penzance.

NEWMARKET Suffolk 404 V 27 – pop. 15,861 – ECD : Wednesday – ✆ 0638.

🏌 Links, Cambridge Rd ℰ 662708, SW : 1 m.

♦London 64 – ♦Cambridge 13 – ♦Ipswich 40 – ♦Norwich 48.

🏨 **Newmarket Moat House** (Q.M.H.), Moulton Rd, CB8 8DY, ℰ 667171 – 📺 🅿. 🚗. 🔺 AE
   ⦿ VISA
   M *(closed lunch Saturday and Bank Holidays)* 8.95 **st.** and a la carte ▮ 2.70 – **44 rm**
   ⓦ 35.00/48.00 **st.** – SB (weekends only) 52.00 **st.**

🏨 **White Hart,** High St., CB8 8JP, ℰ 663051 – 📺 ⎚wc ⤬ 🅿. 🚗. 🔺 VISA
   M 6.05/7.50 **st.** – **21 rm** ⓦ 20.00/40.00 **st.**

   at Six Mile Bottom (Cambs.) SW : 6 m. on A 1304 – ✉ Newmarket – ✆ 063 870 Six Mile
   Bottom :

🏨 **Swynford Paddocks,** CB8 0UE, ℰ 234, ≼, « Country house », ⛲, park, ⚹ – 📺 ⎚wc ☎
   🅿. 🔺 AE ⦿ VISA
   M 7.50 **t.** and a la carte 13.10/19.40 **t.** ▮ 3.95 – **15 rm** ⓦ 49.50/88.00 **t.** – SB (weekends only)
   85.00 **st.**

TOYOTA Bury Rd ℰ 662130   VOLVO Dullingham ℰ 063 876 (Stetchworth) 244
VAUXHALL-OPEL All Saints Rd ℰ 663121

NEW MILTON Hants. 403 404 P 31 – ECD : Wednesday – ✆ 0425.

♦London 106 – Bournemouth 12 – ♦Southampton 21 – Winchester 34.

🏨 ⚙ **Chewton Glen** ⦿, Christchurch Rd, BH25 6QS, W : 2 m. by A 337 and Ringwood Rd on
   Chewton Farm Rd ℰ 042 52 (Highcliffe) 5341, Telex 41456, ≼, « Gardens », ⬛ heated, park,
   ⚹ – 📺 🅿. 🚗. 🔺 AE ⦿ VISA. ⛟
   M 11.50/27.00 **st.** and a la carte ▮ 3.85 – ⓦ 5.00 – **44 rm** 56.00/124.00 **st.**, **11 suites** 174.00/275.00
   st.
   Spec. Loup de mer mouginoise (April-September), Homard de pays Robert Morley, Aiguillettes de poulet péri-
   gourdine.

AUSTIN-ROVER Old Milton Rd ℰ 614665   NISSAN 25 Station Rd ℰ 610034
COLT Christchurch Rd ℰ 611198   RENAULT 53 Lymington Rd ℰ 612296
FORD Fernhill Lane ℰ 612121

NEWPORT I.O.W. 403 404 Q 31 – see Wight (Isle of).

NEWPORT (CASNEWYDD-AR-WYSG) Gwent 403 L 29 – pop. 115,896 – ECD : Thursday –
✆ 0633.

Envir. : Caerleon : Roman Amphitheatre★ AC, NE : 3 m.

🎫 Museum and Art Gallery, John Frost Sq. ℰ 842962.

♦London 145 – ♦Bristol 31 – ♦Cardiff 12 – Gloucester 48.

🏨 **Celtic Manor,** Coldra Woods, NP6 2YA, E : 3 m. by A 48 ℰ 413000, ≼ – 📺 ⎚wc ☎ 🅿. 🚗.
   🔺 AE ⦿ VISA. ⛟
   M a la carte lunch/dinner 23.00 **t.** ▮ 3.00 – **17 rm** ⓦ 56.00/72.00 **t.**

🏨 **Ladbroke** (Ladbroke), The Coldra, Chepstow Rd, NP6 2YG, E : 3 m. on A 48 ℰ 412777, Telex
   497205 – 📺 ⎚wc ☎ & 🅿. 🚗. 🔺 AE ⦿ VISA
   M (restricted lunch) 8.50/10.25 **t.** and a la carte ▮ 3.00 – **119 rm** 40.00/50.00 **st.**

🏨 **Queens** (Anchor), 19 Bridge St., NPT 4RN, ℰ 62992 – 📺 ⎚wc �📶wc ⤬. 🚗. 🔺 AE ⦿ VISA
   M *(closed Sunday dinner)* (carving rest.) 8.85 **t.** and a la carte ▮ 3.00 – **43 rm** ⓦ 35.00/42.50 **st.**
   – SB (weekends only) 47.00/49.00 **st.**

   at Langstone E : 4 ½ m. on A 48 – ✉ Newport – ✆ 0633 Llanwern :

🏨 **New Inn Motel** (Golden Oak), Chepstow Rd, NP6 2JN, ℰ 412426 – 📺 📶wc ☎ 🅿. 🚗. 🔺
   AE VISA. ⛟
   M *(closed Saturday lunch)* 5.50/5.95 **t.** and a la carte ▮ 3.75 – **34 rm** ⓦ 35.00/39.75 **st.**

AUSTIN-ROVER Shaftesbury St. ℰ 858451   FORD Lee Way Industrial Estate ℰ 278020
AUSTIN-ROVER Bassaleg Rd ℰ 63717   NISSAN ℰ 273414
AUSTIN-ROVER Bassaleg Rd ℰ 53771

NEWPORT (TREFDRAETH) Dyfed **403** F 27 – pop. 1 ,224 – ECD : Wednesday – ✆ 0239.

See : Site★ – Envir. : Pentre Ifan (burial chamber★) SE : 4 ½ m. – ┌s̄ Newport Sands ♗ 820244.

🛈 Pembrokeshire Coast National Park Centre, East St. ♗ 820912 (summer only) – ♦London 258 – Fishguard 7.

　　XX　**Pantry,** Market St., SA64 0PH, ♗ 820420 – **P**. 🅰 **VISA**
　　　March-October and Saturdays in Winter – **M** *(closed Sunday and Monday except Bank Holidays)* (dinner only) (booking essential) 11.00 **t**. ⱡ 3.00.

　　at Velindre (Felindre Farchog) E : 2 ¾ m. on A 487 – ⊠ Cardigan – ✆ 0239 Newport :

　　🛆　**Salutation Inn,** SA41 3UY, ♗ 820564, 🐎 – **TV** ⇌wc **P**. 🅰 **VISA**
　　　M (bar lunch)/dinner 7.10 **st**. and a la carte ⱡ 2.50 – **8 rm** 🖙 12.50/27.90 **st**. – SB (weekdays only) (winter only) 40.00 **st**.

NEWPORT Salop **402 403 404** M 25 – pop. 10 ,339 – ECD : Thursday – ✆ 0952.

🛈 9 St. Mary's St. ♗ 814109.

♦London 150 – ♦Birmingham 33 – Shrewsbury 18 – ♦Stoke-on-Trent 21.

　　🏛　**Royal Victoria,** St. Mary's St., TF10 7BJ, ♗ 810831 – **TV** ⇌wc ▥wc **P**. 🅰 **AE** **VISA**. 🛠
　　　M 7.50/9.50 **t**. and a la carte ⱡ 2.85 – **21 rm** 🖙 23.50/35.00 **t**.

NEWPORT PAGNELL Bucks. **404** R 27 – pop. 10 ,733 – ECD : Thursday – ✆ 0908.

♦London 57 – Bedford 13 – Luton 21 – Northampton 15.

　　🏨　**TraveLodge** (T.H.F.) without rest., M 1 Service Area 3, MK16 8DS, W : 1 ½ m. by A 422 on M 1 ♗ 610878, Telex 826186 – **TV** ⇌wc ▦ **P**. ⬚ 🅰 **AE** **①** **VISA**
　　　97 rm 28.00/38.00 **t**.

　　🏛　**Swan Revived,** High St., MK16 8AR, ♗ 610565 – ▤ **TV** ⇌wc ▥wc ☎ **P**. ⬚ 🅰 **AE** **①** **VISA**
　　　M a la carte 4.20/9.55 **t**. ⱡ 3.00 – **31 rm** 🖙 16.00/36.00 **st**. – SB 47.00/79.00 **st**.

PEUGEOT High St. ♗ 611715

NEWQUAY Cornwall **403** E 32 The West Country G. – pop. 13 ,905 – ECD : Wednesday – ✆ 063 73 (4 and 5 fig.) or 0637 (6 fig.).

Envir. : Pentire Points and Kelsey Head★ (≼★★) SW : 5 m. by A 3075 Y – Trerice Manor ★ *AC* S : 3 ½ m. by A 392 Y.

┌s̄ Perranporth ♗ 087 257 (Perranporth) 2454, SW : 6 m. by A 3075 Y – ┌s̄ Tower Rd ♗ 4354 Z.

✈ Newquay Civil Airport : ♗ 063 74 (St. Mawgan) 551, NE : 6 m. by A 3059 Y – 🛈 Cliff Rd ♗ 71345/6.

♦London 291 – Exeter 83 – Penzance 34 – ♦Plymouth 48 – Truro 14.

Plan on next page

　　🏨🏨　**Bristol,** Narrowcliff, TR7 2PQ, ♗ 875181, ≼, 🅽 – ▤ **TV** **P**. 🅰 **AE** **①** **VISA**　　　　　　Z **r**
　　　M 6.50/9.00 **st**. and a la carte ⱡ 2.50 – **97 rm** 🖙 21.00/52.00 **st**. – SB (weekends only)(except summer) 50.00 **st**.

　　🏨🏨　**Riviera** (Best Western), Lusty Glaze Rd, TR7 3AA, ♗ 874251, ≼, ⵩ heated, 🐎, squash – ▤
　　　P. 🅰 **AE** **VISA**　　　　　　　　　　　　　　　　　　　　　　　　　　　　　　　　　　　Z **o**
　　　M (buffet lunch Monday to Saturday)/dinner 8.00 **t**. and a la carte ⱡ 3.00 – **50 rm** 🖙 25.00/62.00 **t**. – SB (weekends only except Bank Holidays) 50.00/65.00 **st**.

　　🏛🏛　**Trebarwith,** Trebarwith Cres., Island Estate, TR7 1BZ, ♗ 872288, ≼ bay and coast, 🅽, 🐎 –
　　　TV ⇌wc ▥wc **P**. 🅰 **VISA**. 🛠　　　　　　　　　　　　　　　　　　　　　　　　　　　　Z **a**
　　　27 March-27 September – **M** (bar lunch)/dinner 9.00 **st**. ⱡ 3.50 – **44 rm** 🖙 12.00/50.00 **st**.

　　🏛🏛　**Windsor,** Mount Wise, TR7 2AY, ♗ 875188, ⵩ heated, 🅽, 🐎, squash – **TV** ⇌wc **P**. 🅰
　　　VISA　　Z **n**
　　　Easter-October – **M** (bar lunch)/dinner 9.00 **st**. and a la carte ⱡ 2.50 – **42 rm** 🖙 15.00/60.00 **st**.

　　🏛🏛　**Kilbirnie,** Narrowcliff, TR7 2RS, ♗ 875155, 🅽 – **TV** ⇌wc ▦ **P**. 🅰 **VISA**　　　　　Z **e**
　　　closed Christmas – **M** (bar lunch)/dinner 8.50 **st**. ⱡ 2.50 – **70 rm** 🖙 19.50/29.75 **st**. – SB (October-May only) 40.00/45.50 **st**.

　　🏛🏛　**Mordros,** 4 Pentire Av., TR7 1PA, ♗ 876700, ⵩ heated – ⇌wc **P**. 🅰 **VISA**. 🛠　　　Y **x**
　　　M *(closed Saturday lunch)* (bar lunch)/dinner 10.00 **st**. and a la carte ⱡ 3.00 – **30 rm** 🖙 21.75/57.00 **st**. – SB (mid September-mid May) 43.50/57.00 **st**.

　　🏛　**Porth Veor Manor,** 56 Porth Way, TR7 3LW, ♗ 873274, 🐎 – **TV** ⇌wc ▥wc **P**. 🅰 **AE** **VISA**
　　　closed December – **M** 7.20/11.00 **st**. and a la carte ⱡ 2.75 – **14 rm** 🖙 19.50/42.00 **t**. – SB (except summer) 36.00/40.00 **st**.　　　　　　　　　　　　　　　　　　　　　　　　　　　　　　　Y **e**

　　🏛　**Corisande Manor** 🌿, Riverside Av., Pentire, TR7 1PL, ♗ 872042, ≼ Gannel Estuary, 🐎 –
　　　⇌wc ▥wc **P**　　　　　　　　　　　　　　　　　　　　　　　　　　　　　　　　　　　　　Y **n**
　　　May-October – **M** (bar lunch)/dinner 6.00 **t**. ⱡ 2.25 – **19 rm** 🖙 10.50/33.00 **t**. – SB (except July-August) 27.00/37.00 **st**.

　　🏛　**Water's Edge,** Esplanade Rd, Pentire, TR7 1QA, ♗ 872048, ≼ Fistral Bay, 🐎 – ⇌wc ▥wc
　　　P. 🛠　　Y **u**
　　　Easter and 14 May-4 October – **M** (bar lunch)/dinner 8.25 **t**. ⱡ 2.25 – **20 rm** 🖙 (dinner included) 13.25/44.85 **t**.

　　🏛　**Bewdley,** 10 Pentire Rd, TR7 1NX, ♗ 872883, ≼, ⵩ heated – ⇌wc ▥wc **P**. 🅰 **VISA**　　Y **s**
　　　March-October – **M** 4.50/7.50 **st**. ⱡ 2.00 – **30 rm** 🖙 10.00/22.00 **t**. – SB 33.00/42.00 **st**.

　　🛆　**Porth Enodoc,** 4 Esplanade Rd, Pentire, TR7 1PY, ♗ 872372, ≼ Fistral Bay – ▥wc **P**. 🛠
　　　March-October and Christmas – **9 rm** 🖙 10.00/26.00 **t**.　　　　　　　　　　　　　　Y **i**

　　🛆　**Pasadera,** 15 Edgcumbe Av., TR7 2NJ, ♗ 873235 – ▥ **P**. 🛠　　　　　　　　　　　Z **i**
　　　March-October – **16 rm** 🖙 7.00/11.50 **s**.

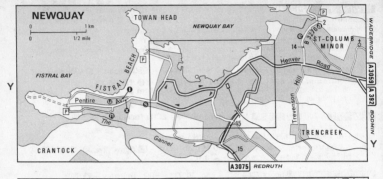

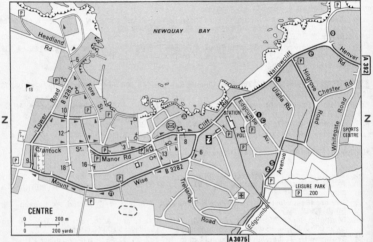

Bank Street .... Z 3	Beacon Road .... Z 5	Marcus Hill .... Z 13
East Street .... Z 8	Berry Road .... Z 6	Porth Way .... Y 14
Fore Street .... Z	Higher Tower Road .... Z 9	Trevemper Road .... Y 15
Alexander Road .... Y 2	Hope Terrace .... Z 10	St. Georges Road .... Z 16
	Jubilee Street .... Z 12	St. John's Road .... Z 18

↑ **Wheal Treasure**, 72 Edgcumbe Av., TR7 2NN, ℰ 874136 – ⬛wc 🅿. ⅏ — — — — — — — — — — — — — Z z
  26 May-September – **9 rm** ⊊ (dinner included) 11.50/28.50 **st.**

↑ **Copper Beech**, 70 Edgcumbe Av., TR7 2NN, ℰ 873376 – ⬛ 🅿. *VISA*. ⅏ — — — — — — — — — — — — — — — — Z s
  Easter-October – **15 rm** ⊊ 8.65/20.10 **st.**

↑ **Hepworth**, 27 Edgcumbe Av., TR7 2NJ, ℰ 873686, ⚘ – ⬛wc 🅿. ⅏ — — — — — — — — — — — — — — — — — — Z c
  Easter-September – **13 rm** ⊊ 8.00/30.00 **t.**

↑ **Pendeen**, 7 Alexandra Rd, Porth, TR7 3ND, ℰ 873521, ⚘ – ⬜wc ⬛wc 🅿. ⅏ — — — — — — — — — — — — — Y a
  April-October – **15 rm** ⊊ 10.50/48.00 **st.**

  at St. Columb Minor NE : 3 m. by A 3059 – Y – ⊠ ☯ 063 73 Newquay :

☂ Cross Mount, 60 Church St., TR7 3EX, ℰ 2669 – ⬜wc ⬛wc 🅿. ⅏ – **12 rm**.

  at Crantock SW : 4 m. by A 3075 – Y – ⊠ Newquay – ☯ 0637 Crantock :

🏠 **Fairbank**, West Pentire Rd, TR8 5SA, ℰ 830424, ≼, ⚘ – 📺 ⬜wc ⬛wc 🅿. 🔼 ⑩ *VISA*. ⅏
  April-October – **M** (bar lunch)/dinner 7.00 **t.** – **29 rm** ⊊ 13.00/30.00.

🏠 **Crantock Bay** ⑊, West Pentire, TR8 5SE, W : ¾ m. ℰ 830229, ≼ Crantock Bay, ⚘ –
  ⬜wc 🅿. *VISA*
  April-mid October – **M** (buffet lunch)/dinner 7.25 **t.** ≬ 2.20 – **30 rm** ⊊ 12.00/38.60 **t.**

AUSTIN-ROVER Quintrell Downs ℰ 2410
COLT, VOLVO Summercourt ℰ 087 251 (Mitchell)
386

FIAT Tower Rd ℰ 2378
VOLVO Newlyn East ℰ 087 251 (Mitchell) 347

NEW ROMNEY Kent **404** W 31 – pop. 4,547 – ECD : Wednesday – ✿ 0679.

Envir. : Lydd (All Saints' Church tower : groined vaulting★) SW : 3 ½ m. – Brookland (St. Augustine's Church : belfry★ 15C, Norman font★) W : 6 m.

♦London 71 – Folkestone 14 – Hastings 23 – Maidstone 33.

☎ **Blue Dolphins**, Dymchurch Rd, TN28 8BE, ℰ 63224 – 🍴 **ℙ**. **A** **VISA**. ✵
  M (closed Sunday) (dinner only) 11.75 **t.** ▮ 2.90 – **8 rm** ⭐ 13.25/23.50 **t.**

FORD The Avenue, Littlestone ℰ 62184   RENAULT Sussex Rd ℰ 2404

NEWTON ABBOT Devon **403** J 32 **The West Country G.** – pop. 20,567 – ECD : Thursday – ✿ 0626 – 🚗 ℰ 66490 (to Stirling) – ℰ 01 (London) 723 7000 ext. 3148 – 🛈 8 Sherborne Rd ℰ 67494.

♦London 216 – Exeter 16 – ♦ Plymouth 31 – Torquay 7.

🏠 **Queen's**, Queen St., TQ12 2EZ, ℰ 63133 – 📺 🚻wc **ℙ**. 🛁. **A** **⓪** **VISA**
  M 6.00/8.00 **st.** and a la carte ▮ 2.50 – **25 rm** ⭐ 19.00/35.00 **st.** – SB (except Bank Holidays) 42.50 **st.**

ALFA-ROMEO, VOLVO Wolborough St. ℰ 2545
AUSTIN-ROVER, LAND ROVER-RANGE ROVER 64/72 Wolborough St. ℰ 4141
CITROEN Unit a, Decoy Industrial Estate ℰ 61834
FIAT The Avenue ℰ 2526
FORD Wolborough St. ℰ 65081

PEUGEOT-TALBOT 174 Exeter Rd, Kingsteignton ℰ 3545
PEUGEOT-TALBOT, RENAULT Kingsteignton Rd ℰ 68322
TOYOTA Highweek ℰ 4702
VAUXHALL-OPEL 177/187 Queen St. ℰ 3838
VW, AUDI The Avenue ℰ 2641

NEWTON FERRERS Devon **403** H 33 **The West Country G.** – pop. 1,609 – ✿ 0752 Plymouth.

♦London 242 – Exeter 42 – ♦Plymouth 11.

🏠 **Court House** ⚓, Court Rd, PL8 1AQ, ℰ 872324, ⬕ heated, 🎾 – 🚻wc **ℙ**. **VISA**
  closed 3 January-15 February – **M** (bar lunch)/dinner 9.95 **t.** and a la carte – **11 rm** ⭐ 22.00/46.00 **t.**

at Battisborough Cross E : 3 m. – ✉ Newton Ferrers – ✿ 075 530 Holbeton :

🏠🏠 **Alston Hall** ⚓, PL8 1HN, ℰ 259, ≤, ⬕ heated, 🎾, ✵ – 📺 🚻wc ☎ **ℙ**. **A** **⓪** **VISA**. ✵
  M 12.50/15.00 **t.** ▮ 3.95 – **9 rm** ⭐ 37.50/60.00 **st.** – SB (except July-September and Bank Holidays) 65.00/75.00 **st.**

NEWTON SOLNEY Derbs. **402** **403** **404** P 25 – see Burton-upon-Trent (Staffs.).

NEWTOWN (DRENEWYDD) Powys **403** K 26 – pop. 8,906 – ECD : Thursday – ✿ 0686.

🛈 St. Davids House ℰ 25580.

♦London 196 – Aberystwyth 44 – Chester 56 – Shrewsbury 32.

🏠🏠 **The Bear**, Broad St., SY16 2LU, ℰ 26964, Telex 35205 – 📺 🚻wc 🍴wc ☎ **ℙ**. **A** **AE** **⓪** **VISA**
  M 8.25/8.50 **st.** and a la carte ▮ 2.25 – **36 rm** ⭐ 22.25/46.00 **st.** – SB (weekends only) 49.50/55.50 **st.**

🏠 **Elephant and Castle**, Broad St., SY16 2BQ, ℰ 26271 – 📺 🚻wc **ℙ**. **VISA**
  M 5.00/6.50 **st.** and a la carte – **21 rm** ⭐ 17.00/28.00 **st.**

at Abermule (Aber-Miwl) NE : 4 ½ m. on A 483 – ✉ ✿ 068 686 Abermule :

🏠 **Dolforwyn Hall** ⚓, Dolforwyn, SY15 6JG, N : ½ m. on A 483 ℰ 221 – 📺 🚻wc 🍴wc **ℙ**. **A** **VISA**
  M 3.00/11.00 **st.** and a la carte ▮ 1.60 – **7 rm** ⭐ 16.50/32.00 **st.**

AUDI, VW Abermule ℰ 068 686 (Abermule) 615
AUSTIN-ROVER Pool Rd ℰ 25942

FORD Pool Rd ℰ 25514

NORMAN CROSS Cambs. **404** T 26 – see Peterborough.

NORTHALLERTON North Yorks. **402** P 20 – pop. 13,566 – ECD : Thursday – ✿ 0609.

Envir. : Bedale, Leyburn Rd (Parish church★ 13C-14C) SW : 7 ½ m. – 🎋 at Bedale ℰ 0677 (Bedale) 22451, SW : 7 ½ m. – 🛈 207 High St. ℰ 774324 – ♦London 238 – ♦Leeds 48 – ♦Middlesbrough 24 – York 33.

🏠 **Golden Lion** (T.H.F.), High St., DL7 8PP, ℰ 2404 – 📺 🚻wc ⊕ **ℙ**. 🛁. **A** **⓪** **VISA**
  M 5.50/8.25 **st.** and a la carte ▮ 2.85 – ⭐ 5.50 – **29 rm** 36.00/43.00 **st.**

XX **McCoys at the Tontine** with rm, Staddlebridge, DL6 3JB, NE : 8 ½ m. by A 684 on A 19 ℰ 060 982 (East Harlsey) 671, « 1930's decor » – 📺 🚻wc ☎ **ℙ**. **A** **AE** **⓪** **VISA**
  closed 24-26 December and 31 December-1 January – **M** (closed Sunday) (dinner only) 25.00 **t.** and a la carte 16.00/22.70 **t.** ▮ 3.95 – **7 rm** ⭐ 37.50/50.00 **t.**

XX **Romanby Court**, 5 Romanby Court, High St., DL7 8PG, ℰ 774918 – **A** **VISA**
  closed Sunday, Monday, 25-26 December and Bank Holidays – **M** 13.95 **t.** (dinner) and a la carte ▮ 3.00.

X **McCoy's Bistro**, Staddlebridge, DL6 3JB, NE : 8 ½ m. by A 684 on A 19 ℰ 671 – **ℙ**. **A** **AE** **⓪** **VISA**
  closed 25 December and 1 January – **M** 6.00/11.00 **t.** and a la carte ▮ 3.75.

at Newby Wiske S : 2 ½ m. by A 167 – ✉ ✿ 0609 Northallerton :

🏠🏠 **Solberge Hall** (Best Western) ⚓, DL7 9ER, ℰ 779191, 🎾, park – 📺 🚻wc ⊕ **ℙ**. **A** **AE** **⓪** **VISA**
  M 5.50/10.50 **t.** and a la carte ▮ 3.00 – **15 rm** ⭐ 32.00/57.00 **st.** – SB 65.00/75.00 **st.**

AUSTIN-ROVER Brompton Rd ℰ 3891   HONDA, SAAB East Rd ℰ 3921

NORTHAMPTON

Abington Street........... **X**
Drapery Street........... **X** 18
Gold Street............. **X**
Grosvenor Centre....... **X**
Weston
  Favell Centre......... **Y**

Abington Square .... **X** 2
Ashley Way .... **X** 3
Bewick Road .... **Y** 4
Billing Road .... **X** 7
Bridge Street .... **X** 8
Campbell Street .... **X** 9
Charnwood Avenue ..... **Y** 10
Church Lane .... **X** 13
College Street .... **X** 14
Derngate .... **X** 15
Earl Street .... **X** 19
Grey Friars .... **X** 23
Guildhall Road .... **X** 24
Horse
  Shoe Street .... **X** 28
Kenmuir Avenue .... **X** 29
Kettering Road .... **X** 30
Kingsthorpe Grove ..... **X** 34
Lower Mounts .... **X** 35
Mare Fair .... **X** 37
Oaklands Drive .... **Y** 38
Overstone Road .... **X** 39
Park Avenue North ..... **Y** 40
Park Avenue South ..... **Z** 43
Rushmere Road .... **Z** 44
St. Andrew's Road ...... **Y** 45
St. Edmund's Road...... **X** 48

St. James's Road .... **X** 49
St. John's Street .... **X** 50
St. Leonard's Road .... **Z** 52
St. Michael's Road .... **X** 53
Sheep Street .... **X** 54
Silver Street .... **X** 55

Spencer Bridge Road .... **X, Z** 57
Towcester Road .... **Z** 58
Upper Mounts................. **X** 59
Waveney Way .... **Y** 60
West Bridge.................. **X** 62
Windrush Way .... **Y** 63

NORTHAMPTON Northants. **404** R 27 – pop. 154,172 – ✆ 0604.

See : Church of the Holy Sepulchre★ 12C X A – Central Museum and Art Gallery (collection of footwear★) X M – Envir. : Brixworth (All Saints Church★ 7C Saxon) N : 7 m. by A 508 Y – Earls Barton (All Saints Church : 10C Saxon tower★) NE : 5 m. by A 45 Y – Castle Ashby★ (16C-17C) AC, NE : 8 m. by A 428 Z.

🏁 Delapre, Eagle Drive ✆ 64036 Z – 🏁 Kettering Rd ✆711054 Y.

🛫 21 St. Giles St. ✆ 22677 and 34881 ext 404.

♦London 69 – ♦Cambridge 53 – ♦Coventry 34 – ♦Leicester 42 – Luton 35 – ♦Oxford 41.

Plan on preceding page

🏨 **Northampton Moat House** (Q.M.H.), Silver St., NN1 2TA, ✆ 22441, Telex 311142 – 📶 📺 ☖ 🄿 🛁 🝙 🄰🄴 ⓞ 𝐕𝐈𝐒𝐀   X n
  M 5.45/7.50 **t.** and a la carte ▯ 2.95 – 🖙 4.95 – **134 rm** 38.00/48.00 **t.**, **4 suites** 75.00/135.00 **t.** – SB (weekends only) 56.00 **st.**

XX Royal Bengal, 39-41 Bridge St., ✆ 38617, Indian rest.   X s

X **Napoleon's Bistro**, 9-11 Welford Rd, Kingsthorpe, NN2 8AE, N : 1 ¾ m. by A 508 on A 50 ✆ 713899 – 🝙 🄰🄴 ⓞ 𝐕𝐈𝐒𝐀   Y c
  closed Saturday lunch, Sunday, Monday and 25 December-2 January – **M** 5.70 **t.** (lunch) and a la carte 7.25/11.35 **t.** ▯ 2.80.

X **Ca d'Oro**, 334 Wellingborough Rd, NN1 4ES, ✆ 32660, Italian rest. – 🝙 🄰🄴 ⓞ 𝐕𝐈𝐒𝐀   Z e
  closed Saturday lunch, Sunday and Bank Holidays – **M** a la carte 7.80/14.60 **t.**

  at Weston Favell NE : 3 ½ m. by A 4500 – ✉ ✆ 0604 Northampton :

🏨 Westone Moat House (Q.M.H.), Ashley Way, NN3 3EA, ✆ 406262, Telex 312587, ⛫ – 📶 ▤ rest 📺 ≝wc 🐾 🄿 🛁   Y a
  64 rm, **1 suite**.

  at Moulton NE : 4 ½ m. by A 43 – Y – ✉ ✆ 0604 Northampton :

⋔ **Poplars**, 33 Cross St., NN3 1RZ, ✆ 43983, ⛫ – ≝wc 🝙wc 🄿 🝙
  21 rm 🖙 16.50/32.00 **t.**

AUSTIN-ROVER Weedon Rd ✆ 54041
AUSTIN-ROVER 46/50 Sheep St. ✆ 35471
AUSTIN-ROVER-DAIMLER-JAGUAR, LAND ROVER-
RANGE ROVER 592 Wellingborough Rd ✆ 401141
CITROEN 194/200 Kingsthorpe Grove ✆ 713202

FIAT, LANCIA 74 Kingsthorpe Rd ✆ 714555
MERCEDEZ-BENZ 42/50 Harborough Rd ✆ 716716
RENAULT Bedford Rd ✆ 39645
TOYOTA 348 Wellingborough Rd ✆ 31086
VOLVO Bedford Rd ✆ 21363

NORTH BOVEY Devon **403** I 32 – pop. 368 – ✉ Newton Abbot – ✆ 0647 Moretonhampstead.

♦London 214 – Exeter 13 – ♦Plymouth 31 – Torquay 21.

🏠 **Glebe House** 🝙, TQ13 8RA, ✆ 40544, ≤, ⛫, park – ≝wc 🝙wc 🄿 🝙 🄰🄴 𝐕𝐈𝐒𝐀
  closed 24 December-14 February – **M** (bar lunch residents only)/dinner 12.50 **t.** ▯ 2.50 – **9 rm** 🖙 15.50/25.50 **t.**

🏠 **Blackaller House** 🝙, TQ13 8QY, ✆ 40322, ≤, ⛫ – ≝wc 🄿 🝙 🄰🄴 𝐕𝐈𝐒𝐀
  Mid March-November – **M** (dinner only) 12.00 **t.** ▯ 2.85 – **6 rm** 🖙 17.10/39.20 **t.** – SB 54.45/59.20 **st.**

NORTH CAVE Humberside **402** S 22 – pop. 1,728 – ✆ 043 02.

♦London 206 – ♦Kingston upon Hull 17 – ♦Leeds 46 – York 28.

XX **Sundial**, 18 Westgate, HU15 2NJ, ✆ 2537, English rest. – 🝙 🄰🄴 𝐕𝐈𝐒𝐀
  closed Sunday, Monday, 2 weeks January and 2 weeks August – **M** (dinner only) a la carte 9.10/13.00 **t.** ▯ 2.40.

NORTHENDEN Greater Manchester **402** ㉝ **403** ③ **404** ⑩ – see Manchester.

NORTH FERRIBY Humberside **402** S 22 – see Kingston upon-Hull.

NORTHFIELD West Midlands **403** ㉘ **404** ⑳ – see Birmingham.

NORTHIAM East Sussex **404** V 31 – pop. 1,657 – ECD : Wednesday – ✉ Rye – ✆ 079 74.

♦London 55 – Folkestone 36 – Hastings 12 – Maidstone 27.

🏨 **Hayes Arms**, Village Green, TN31 6NN, ✆ 3142, « Part Tudor and Georgian country house », ⛫ – 📺 ≝wc 🄿 🝙 🄰🄴 ⓞ 𝐕𝐈𝐒𝐀
  closed 24 January-10 February – **M** (bar lunch)/dinner 10.50 **t.** ▯ 2.50 – **7 rm** 🖙 24.00/48.00 **t.** – SB (except Easter, Christmas and Bank Holidays) 45.00/60.00 **st.**

NORTH PETHERTON Somerset **403** K 30 – pop. 3,177 – ECD : Thursday and Saturday – ✆ 0278.

♦London 161 – ♦Bristol 43 – Taunton 8.

🏠 **Walnut Tree Inn**, TA6 6QA, ✆ 662255 – 📺 ≝wc 🄿 🛁 🝙 🄰🄴 ⓞ 𝐕𝐈𝐒𝐀 🍴
  M a la carte approx 8.50 **t.** ▯ 2.50 – 🖙 3.25 – **11 rm** 28.00/40.00 **t.** – SB (weekends only) 24.00 **st.**

NORTHREPPS Norfolk 404 Y 25 – pop. 643 – ⊠ Cromer – ✪ 026 378 Overstrand.
♦London 131 – ♦Norwich 22.

  XX **Church Barn,** Church St., NR27 0LG, ✆ 588, « Converted barn » – ℗. VISA
      closed Sunday and Monday in winter and 3 weeks January-February – **M** (dinner only and
      Sunday lunch in summer) (booking essential) a la carte 10.95/15.55 **t.**

NORTH STIFFORD Essex 404 ⓐ – ⊠ Grays – ✪ 0375 Grays Thurrock.
♦London 22 – Chelmsford 24 – Southend-on-Sea 20.

  🏨 **Stifford Moat House** (Q.M.H.), High Rd, RM16 1UE, ✆ 71451, �, ⅗ – 📺 ⊟wc ☎ ℗.
      🔼 AE ⓞ VISA
      closed 27 to 30 December – **M** *(closed Saturday lunch)* 9.25 **st.** and a la carte ▯ 2.85 – ⚌ 4.50
      – **64 rm** 36.50/45.00 **st.** – SB (weekends only) 50.00 **st.**

NORTH STOKE Oxon. – see Wallingford.

NORTH WALSHAM Norfolk 403 404 Y 25 – pop. 7,929 – ECD : Wednesday – ✪ 0692.
♦London 125 – ♦Norwich 16.

  ⌂ **Beechwood House,** 20 Cromer Rd, NR28 0HD, ✆ 403231, � – ⊟wc 🕯wc ℗
      closed 24 December-6 January – **11 rm** ⚌ 11.50/27.00 **t.**

    at Knapton NE : 3 ½ m. on B 1145 – ⊠ North Walsham – ✪ 0263 Mundesley :

  🏠 **Knapton Hall,** NR28 0SB, ✆ 720405, ⬜ heated, � – 📺 ⊟wc ☎ ℗. 🔼 AE VISA. ⅗
      M a la carte 10.20/14.20 **t.** ▯ 3.00 – **8 rm** ⚌ 25.00/50.00 **st.** – SB (October-May) (except Easter,
      Christmas and Bank Holidays) 54.00 **st.**

NORWICH Norfolk 404 Y 26 – pop. 169,814 – ✪ 0603.

See : Cathedral** 11C-12C (bosses** of nave vaulting) Y – Castle (museum**) *AC* Z M – St.
Peter Mancroft's Church* (Perpendicular) Z B – Sainsbury Centre for Visual Arts* (University of
East Anglia) *AC*, by B 1108 X – Envir. : Norfolk Wildlife Park* *AC*, NW : 12 m. by A 1067 V.

🏌 Barnham Broom ✆ 060 545 (Barnham Broom) 393, W : 7 m. off A 47 V.

✈ 411923, Telex 97209, N : 3 ½ m. by A 140 V – 🅱 Augustine Steward House, 14 Tombland ✆
666071/2.

♦London 109 – ♦Kingston-upon-Hull 148 – ♦Leicester 117 – ♦Nottingham 120.

Plan opposite

  🏛🏛 **Maid's Head** (Q.M.H.), Tombland, NR3 1LB, ✆ 628821, Telex 975080 – ▯ 📺 ℗. 🔼 AE
      ⓞ VISA   Y u
      M 6.00/9.50 **t.** and a la carte ▯ 3.45 – ⚌ 4.25 – **80 rm** 33.00/63.50 **st.** – SB (weekends only)(except
      Easter) 53.00/61.00 **st.**

  🏨 **Nelson** (Best Western), Prince of Wales Rd, NR1 1DX, ✆ 628612, Telex 975203, ≼ – ▯
      ▯ rest 📺 ⊟wc ☎ 🔥 ℗. 🔼 🔼 AE VISA. ⅗   Z a
      M 8.50 **st.** and a la carte ▯ 3.05 – **122 rm** ⚌ 39.50/54.00 **st.**, **3 suites** 60.00 **st.** – SB
      58.00/63.00 **st.**

  🏨 **Post House** (T.H.F.), Ipswich Rd, NR4 6EP, S : 2 ¼ m. on A 140 ✆ 56431, Telex 975106,
      ⬜ heated – 📺 ⊟wc ☎ 🔥 ℗. 🔼 🔼 AE ⓞ VISA   on A 140   X
      M 8.75/25.00 **st.** and a la carte ▯ 2.75 – ⚌ 5.50 – **120 rm** 39.00/47.00 **st.**

  🏨 **Norwich** (Best Western), 121-131 Boundary Rd, NR3 2BA, on A 47 ✆ 410431, Telex 975337 –
      📺 ⊟wc ☎ 🔥 ℗. 🔼 🔼 AE ⓞ VISA. ⅗   V r
      M (carving lunch) 8.50 **st.** and a la carte ▯ 3.05 – **102 rm** ⚌ 37.80/48.30 **st.**, **3 suites** 52.50 **st.** –
      SB 50.00 **st.**

  🏠 **Lansdowne** (Embassy), 116 Thorpe Rd, NR1 1RU, ✆ 620302 – ▯ 📺 ⊟wc ☎ ℗. 🔼 🔼 AE
      ⓞ VISA. ⅗   X i
      M 7.50 **st.** and a la carte ▯ 2.50 – ⚌ 5.00 – **39 rm** 24.00/42.00 **st.** – SB 50.00 **st.**

  ⌂ **Riverside,** 11-12 Riverside Rd, NR1 1SQ, ✆ 623978 – 📺   Z s
      10 rm ⚌ 10.00/28.00 **st.**

  ⌂ **Conway,** 2 Aspland Rd, NR1 1SH, ✆ 624761 – 📺. 🔼 VISA. ⅗   Z v
      9 rm ⚌ 13.00/32.00 **st.**

  XX **Marco's,** 17 Pottergate, NR2 1DS, ✆ 624044, Italian rest – 🔼 AE ⓞ VISA   YZ e
      closed Sunday, Monday and August – **M** 8.50 **st.** (lunch) and a la carte 9.60/16.50.

  X **Bombay,** 9 Magdalen St., NR3 1LE, ✆ 666618, Indian rest. – 🔼 AE ⓞ VISA   Y x
      closed Christmas Day – **M** a la carte 4.85/5.95 **t.** ▯ 3.00.

    at Horsham St. Faith N : 4 ½ m. by A 140 – V – ⊠ ✪ 0603 Norwich :

  ⌂ **Elm Farm Chalet,** 55 Norwich Rd, NR10 3HH, ✆ 898366, � – 📺 🕯wc ℗. 🔼 VISA. ⅗
      15 rm ⚌ 16.00/30.00 **st.**

    at Thorpe St. Andrew E : 2 ½ m. on A 47 – X – ⊠ ✪ 0603 Norwich :

  🏠 **Oaklands,** 89 Yarmouth Rd, NR7 0HH, ✆ 34471, � – 📺 ⊟wc ℗. 🔼 VISA
      closed 24 and 25 December – **M** 4.25/6.25 **st.** and a la carte ▯ 3.00 – **42 rm** ⚌ 18.75/26.75 **st.**
      – SB (weekends only)(except Bank Holidays) 39.50/45.00 **st.**

    at Blofield E : 7 ½ m. by A 47 – X – ⊠ ✪ 0603 Norwich :

  XX **La Locanda,** Fox Lane, NR13 4LW, ✆ 713787, Italian rest. – ℗. 🔼 AE ⓞ VISA
      closed Sunday – **M** 5.60/12.00 **t.** and a la carte ▯ 3.10.

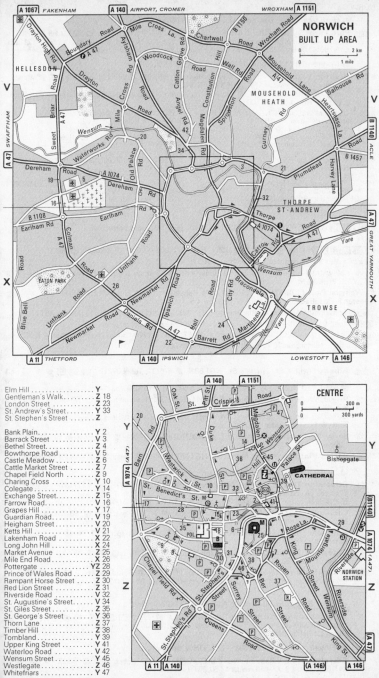

NORWICH

BUILT UP AREA

Elm Hill .... Y
Gentleman's Walk .... Z 18
London Street .... Z 23
St. Andrew's Street .... Y 33
St. Stephen's Street ...... Z

Bank Plain .... Y 2
Barrack Street .... Y 3
Bethel Street .... Z 4
Bowthorpe Road .... V 5
Castle Meadow .... Z 6
Cattle Market Street ..... Z 7
Chapel Field North .... Z 9
Charing Cross .... Z 10
Colegate .... Y 14
Exchange Street .... Z 15
Farrow Road .... V 16
Grapes Hill .... Z 17
Guardian Road .... V 19
Heigham Street .... V 20
Ketts Hill .... V 21
Lakenham Road .... X 22
Long John Hill .... X 24
Market Avenue .... Z 25
Mile End Road .... X 26
Pottergate .... YZ 28
Prince of Wales Road ..... Z 29
Rampant Horse Street ..... Z 30
Red Lion Street .... Z 31
Riverside Road .... Z 32
St. Augustine's Street ... V 34
St. Giles Street .... Z 35
St. George's Street ...... Y 36
Thorn Lane .... Z 37
Timber Hill .... Z 38
Tombland .... Y 39
Upper King Street .... Y 41
Waterloo Road .... V 42
Wensum Street .... Y 45
Westlegate .... Z 46
Whitefriars .... Y 47

CENTRE

at Hethersett SW : 6 m. on A 11 – X – ✉ ☎ 0603 Norwich :

🏨 **Park Farm** 🌳, NR9 3DL, ☎ 810264, 🏊, 🌲, 🎾 – [TV] 🛁wc 🚿wc ☎ [P]. [S] [AE] [O] [VISA]. 🚫
M *(closed Sunday dinner to non-residents)* 5.25/8.00 **t.** and a la carte 🍷 2.50 – **21 rm** ☕ 30.00/44.00 **st.** – SB (weekends only) (except Bank Holidays) 50.00/55.00 **st.**

at Drayton NW : 5 m. on A 1067 – V – ✉ ☎ 0603 Norwich :

🍴🍴🍴 **Drayton Wood** 🌳 with rm, Drayton High Rd, NR8 6BL, SW : 1 ½ m. on A 1067 ☎ 409451, 🌲, park – [TV] 🛁wc ☎ [P]. 🏛. [S] [AE] [O] [VISA]. 🚫
closed 25 to 30 December – **M** *(closed Sunday dinner)* 7.50 **t.** (lunch) and a la carte 9.60/14.85 **t.** 🍷 3.50 – **4 rm** ☕ 32.00/40.00 **t.**

ALFA-ROMEO, MERCEDES-BENZ, VW, AUDI Heigham Causeway, Heigham St. ☎ 612111
ASTON-MARTIN, AUSTIN-ROVER Ipswich Rd, Long Stratton ☎ 0508 (Long Stratton) 30491
AUSTIN-ROVER 162 Cromer Rd ☎ 46946
AUSTIN-ROVER Norwich Rd, Stoke Holy Cross ☎ 05086 (Framingham Earl) 2218
AUSTIN-ROVER Mile Cross Lane ☎ 483001
AUSTIN-ROVER, DAIMLER-JAGUAR, ROLLS ROYCE 5 Prince of Wales Rd ☎ 628383
BMW 26/29 Cattlemarket St. ☎ 621471
CITROEN Earlham Rd ☎ 621393
FIAT, LANCIA Aylsham Rd ☎ 45345
FORD 39 Palace St. ☎ 624144
HONDA 36 Duke St. ☎ 629825
NISSAN Constitution Hill ☎ 43944
NISSAN 79 Mile Cross Lane ☎ 410661
PORSCHE Vulcan Rd South ☎ 401814
RENAULT 22 Heigham St. ☎ 628911
TALBOT, VW, AUDI, PEUGEOT 116 Prince of Wales Rd ☎ 628811
TOYOTA Rouen Rd ☎ 629655
VAUXHALL-OPEL Aylsham Rd, Mile Cross ☎ 414321
VAUXHALL-OPEL Mountergate ☎ 623111
VOLVO Westwick St. ☎ 626192

NOTTAGE (DRENEWYDD YN NOTAIS) Mid Glam. [403] I 29 – see Porthcawl.

NOTTINGHAM Notts. [402] [403] [404] Q 25 – pop. 273 ,300 – ECD : Thursday – ☎ 0602.

See : Castle★ (Renaissance) and museum★ *AC* CZ **M.**

Envir. : Newstead Abbey★★ 16C and gardens★★*AC*, N : 9 m. by B 683 AY – Wollaton Hall★ (16C) *AC*, W : 3 ½ m. AZ **M.**

⛳18 Wollaton Park ☎ 787574, W : 2 m. AZ – ⛳18 Bulwell Hall Park Links ☎ 278021, N : 5 m. AY – ⛳18 Beeston Fields, Beeston ☎ 257062, S : 4 m. by A 52 AZ.

✈ East Midlands Airport : Castle Donington ☎ 0332 (Derby) 810621, SW : 15 m. by A 453 AZ.

[i] 18 Milton St. ☎ 470661 – Castle Gatehouse, Castle Rd ☎ 470661 (summer only).

[i] at Long Eaton : Central Library, Tamworth Rd ☎ 0602 735426 – at West Bridgford : County Hall ☎ 823823.

♦London 135 – ♦Birmingham 50 – ♦Leeds 74 – ♦Manchester 72.

Plans on following pages

🏨 **Albany** (T.H.F.), St. James's St., NG1 6BN, ☎ 470131, Telex 37211 – [lift] ▤ [TV] ☎ ♿. 🏛. [S] [AE] [O] [VISA] CYZ **a**
M 6.95/14.50 **st.** and a la carte 🍷 2.90 – ☕ 5.50 – **152 rm** 42.00/53.50 **st.**

🏨 **Royal,** Wollaton St., NG1 5RH, ☎ 414444, Telex 37101, squash – [lift] ▤ [TV] ☎. 🏛. [S] [AE] [O] [VISA]. 🚫 CY **e**
closed 25 and 26 December – **M** 6.95/11.00 **st.** and a la carte 🍷 2.00 – ☕ 3.95 – **201 rm** 35.00/43.00 **st.**, **1 suite** 120.00 **st.**.

🏨 Savoy, 296 Mansfield Rd, NG5 2BT, ☎ 602621, Telex 377429 – [lift] [TV] 🛁wc ☎ [P]. 🚫 BY **u**
125 rm.

🏨 **Stakis Victoria** (Stakis), Milton St., NG1 3PZ, ☎ 419561, Telex 37401 – [lift] [TV] 🛁wc ☎. 🏛. [S] [AE] [O] [VISA] DY **a**
M (buffet lunch)/dinner 9.00 **t.** – **167 rm** ☕ 38.00/43.00 **t.**

🏨 **Strathdon Thistle** (Thistle), 44 Derby Rd, NG1 5FT, ☎ 418501, Telex 377185 – [lift] [TV] 🛁wc 🚿wc ☎. 🏛. [S] [AE] [O] [VISA] CY **c**
M 6.25/9.50 **t.** and a la carte 🍷 2.25 – ☕ 5.25 – **64 rm** 37.00/50.00 **t.**

🏨 **Lucieville,** 349 Derby Rd, NG7 2DZ, ☎ 787389, 🌲 – [TV] 🛁wc 🚿wc [P]. [S] [VISA]. 🚫 AZ **c**
M (residents only) 7.50/9.00 **t.** 🍷 3.50 – **9 rm** ☕ 27.50/46.00 **t.**

🏠 **Royston,** 326 Mansfield Rd, NG5 2EF, ☎ 622947 – [TV] 🚿wc [P]. [S] [AE] [O]. 🚫 BY **e**
15 rm ☕ 15.75/29.00 **st.**

🏠 **Cotswold,** 332 Mansfield Rd, NG5 2EF, ☎ 623547 – [TV] 🚿wc [P]. [S] [AE] [O] [VISA] BY **c**
18 rm ☕ 13.95/30.00 **st.**

🍴🍴 **Trattoria Conti,** 14-16 Wheeler Gate, NG1 2NB, ☎ 474056, Italian rest. – [S] [AE] [O] [VISA]
closed Sunday, 29 July-27 August and Bank Holidays – **M** 4.35/12.00 **t.** and a la carte 🍷 2.50. CY **n**

at West Bridgford SE : 2 m. on A 52 – ✉ ☎ 0602 Nottingham :

🏨 **Windsor Lodge,** 116 Radcliffe Rd, NG2 5HG, ☎ 813773 – [TV] 🚿wc [P]. [S] [VISA]. 🚫 BZ **x**
closed 25 and 26 Decemer – **M** *(closed Friday to Sunday)* (bar lunch)/dinner 6.00 🍷 2.50 – **43 rm** ☕ 15.00/28.00.

at Edwalton S : 3 m. on A 606 – ✉ ☎ 0602 Nottingham :

🏨 **Edwalton Hall,** Village St., NG12 4AE, ☎ 231116, 🌲 – 🛁wc 🚿 ☎ [P]. [S] [AE] [O] [VISA]. 🚫
M 5.50/8.50 **t.** 🍷 3.00 – **12 rm** ☕ 14.50/35.00. BZ **r**

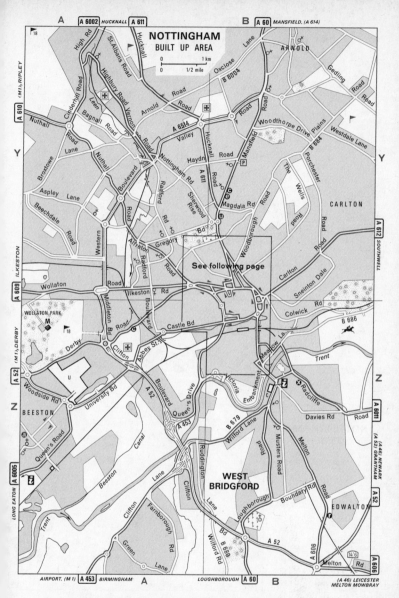

<u>at Beeston</u> SW : 4 ¼ m. by A 52 on B 6006 – ⊠ ☺ 0602 Nottingham :

✗ **Les Artistes Gourmands,** 61 Wollaton Rd, NG9 2NG, ℰ 228288, French rest. – ⚎ ᴀᴇ 𝘝𝘐𝘚𝘈
closed Sunday, Monday, 1 to 8 January and 18 to 31 August – **M** 7.20/13.80 **st.** ⑂ 3.00.
AZ **a**

<u>at Toton</u> SW : 6 ½ m. on A 6005 – AZ – ⊠ Nottingham – ☺ 0602 Long Eaton :

⋔ **Manor,** Nottingham Rd, NG9 6EF, junction with B 6003 ℰ 733487 – ⊟wc ℗. ⚎ 𝘝𝘐𝘚𝘈
closed Christmas – **17 rm** ⊐ 15.50/30.00.

P.T.O. →

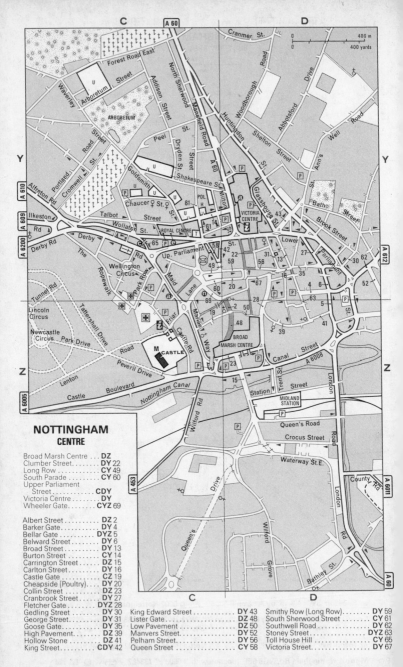

NOTTINGHAM
CENTRE

Broad Marsh Centre	DZ
Clumber Street	DY 22
Long Row	CY 49
South Parade	CY 60
Upper Parliament Street	CDY
Victoria Centre	DY
Wheeler Gate	CYZ 69

Albert Street	DZ 2
Barker Gate	DY 4
Bellar Gate	DYZ 5
Belward Street	DY 6
Broad Street	DY 13
Burton Street	CY 14
Carrington Street	DZ 15
Carlton Street	DY 16
Castle Gate	CZ 19
Cheapside (Poultry)	DY 20
Collin Street	DZ 23
Cranbrook Street	DY 27
Fletcher Gate	DYZ 28
Gedling Street	DY 30
George Street	DY 31
Goose Gate	DY 35
High Pavement	DZ 39
Hollow Stone	DZ 41
King Street	CDY 42

King Edward Street	DY 43
Lister Gate	DZ 48
Low Pavement	DZ 50
Manvers Street	DY 52
Pelham Street	DY 56
Queen Street	CY 58

Smithy Row (Long Row)	DY 59
South Sherwood Street	CY 61
Southwell Road	DY 62
Stoney Street	DYZ 63
Toll House Hill	CY 65
Victoria Street	DY 67

*If you find you cannot take up a hotel booking you have made,
please let the hotel know immediately.*

360

at Long Eaton (Derbs.) SW : 8 m. by A 52 on B 6002 – AZ – ✉ Nottingham – ☺ 0602 Long Eaton :

🏨 **Novotel Nottingham,** Bostock Lane, NG10 4EP, ℰ 720106, Telex 377585, ⤵ heated, ⋙ –
▤ ▤ ⛔ ⌂wc ☎ ⅋ 🄿. ⤤ ⚠ ℻ ⓪ 𝘝𝘐𝘚𝘈
M 8.50 **st.** and a la carte ⅋ 3.75 – ⥵ 4.50 – **112 rm** 39.00/46.00 **st.** – SB (weekends only) 55.00 **st.**

at Sandiacre (Derbs.) SW : 8 m. on A 52 – AZ – ✉ ☺ 0602 Nottingham :

🏨 **Post House** (T.H.F.), Bostocks Lane, NG10 5NJ, ℰ 397800, Telex 377378 – ⚏ ⌂wc ☜ 🄿.
⤤ ⚠ ℻ ⓪ 𝘝𝘐𝘚𝘈
M 4.45/8.95 **st.** and a la carte ⅋ 2.70 – ⥵ 5.50 – **107 rm** 42.50/50.50 **st.**

ALFA-ROMEO 499-509 Woodborough Rd ℰ 606674
AUSTIN-ROVER 136 Burton Rd, Carlton ℰ 617111
AUSTIN-ROVER, DAIMLER, ROLLS ROYCE-BENTLEY Derby Rd ℰ 787701
AUSTIN-ROVER 199 Mansfield Rd, Arnold ℰ 204141
CITROEN, FIAT, LANCIA 333 Mansfield Rd ℰ 621000
COLT 61a Mansfield Rd ℰ 475635
DATSUN Woodborough Rd ℰ 623324
DATSUN Greasley St., Bulwell ℰ 272228
FIAT Wilford Rd, Ruddington ℰ 844114
FORD Derby Rd ℰ 476111
FORD Nottingham Rd, Stapleford ℰ 395000
FORD London Rd ℰ 506282
MAZDA Station Rd, Plumtree ℰ Plumtree (060 77) 5111
PEUGEOT-TALBOT Pasture Rd, Stapleford ℰ 394444

PEUGEOT-TALBOT 134/138 Loughborough Rd ℰ 814320
RENAULT Ilkestone Rd ℰ 781938
RENAULT Sawley, Long Eaton ℰ 0602 (Long Eaton) 733124
RENAULT Clifton Lane, Clifton ℰ 211228
SAAB Beechdale Rd ℰ 293023
SKODA 81 Bramcote Ave., Chilwell ℰ 256117
TOYOTA North Sherwood St. ℰ 474568
VAUXHALL-OPEL 5 Haywood Rd, Mapperley ℰ 603231
VAUXHALL-OPEL Main St., Bulwell ℰ 277031
VOLVO 50 Plains Rd ℰ 266336
VOLVO 131 Alfreton Rd ℰ 708181
VW, AUDI 180 Loughborough Rd ℰ 813813

NUNEATON Warw. 🄰🄳🄴 🄰🄳🄴 P 26 – pop. 60 ,377 – ECD : Thursday – ☺ 0203.
Envir. : Arbury Hall★ (Gothic house 18C) *AC*, SW : 4 m.
🛈 Public Library, Church St. ℰ 384027.
♦London 107 – ♦Birmingham 25 – ♦Coventry 10 – ♦Leicester 18.

🏨 **Longshoot Motel,** Watling St., CV11 6JH, NE : 2 ½ m. on A 47 at junction with A 5
ℰ 329711, Telex 311100 – ⚏ ⌂wc ☎ ⅋ 🄿. ⤤ ⚠ ℻ ⓪ 𝘝𝘐𝘚𝘈. ⋙
M (carving rest.) 4.95 – **47 rm** ⥵ 18.50/33.50 **t.**

🏠 **Chase** (Golden Oak), Higham Lane, CV11 6AG, NE : 1 m. by A 47 ℰ 341013, ⋙ – ⚏ ⌂wc
☜ 🄿. ⤤ ⚠ ℻ 𝘝𝘐𝘚𝘈. ⋙
M 5.50 **t.** and a la carte 6.95/11.05 **t.** ⅋ 2.60 – **28 rm** ⥵ 28.00/35.50 **st.** – SB (weekends only except Bank Holidays) 35.50/40.00 **st.**

AUSTIN-ROVER Weddington Rd ℰ 383471
FIAT Haunchwood Rd ℰ 382807
RENAULT Nuneaton Rd, Bulkington ℰ 383344

PEUGEOT-TALBOT 208/214 Edward St. ℰ 383339
TOYOTA 45 Attleborough Rd ℰ 382241

NUNNINGTON North Yorks. 🄰🄾🄲 R 21 – see Helmsley.

OADBY Leics. 🄰🄾🄴 🄰🄾🄴 🄰🄾🄴 Q 26 – see Leicester.

OAKFORDBRIDE Devon – see Tiverton.

OAKHAM Leics. 🄰🄾🄴 🄰🄾🄴 R 25 – pop. 7 ,914 – ECD : Thursday – ☺ 0572.
🛈 Public Library, Catmos St. ℰ 2918.
♦London 103 – ♦Leicester 26 – Northampton 35 – ♦Nottingham 28.

🏨 **Crown** (Best Western), 16 High St., LE15 6AP, ℰ 3631 – ⚏ ⌂wc ☜ 🄿. ⤤ ⚠ ℻ ⓪ 𝘝𝘐𝘚𝘈
closed 24 to 26 December – **M** 7.50/10.00 **t.** and a la carte ⅋ 3.00 – **27 rm** ⥵ 24.00/45.00 **t.** –
SB (weekends only) 45.00/50.00 **st.**

🏠 **Boultons,** 4 Catmos St., LE15 6HW, ℰ 2844, ⋙ – ⌂wc ⃒wc 🄿. ⤤ ⚠ ℻ ⓪ 𝘝𝘐𝘚𝘈. ⋙
M *(closed Sunday dinner)* 4.75/6.50 **st.** and a la carte ⅋ 2.50 – **14 rm** ⥵ 22.50/29.50 **st.** – SB
(except weekdays in summer) 40.00/53.00 **st.**

at Hambleton E : 3 m. by A 606 – ✉ ☺ 0572 Oakham :

🏛 ❀ **Hambleton Hall** ⌃⌂, LE15 8TH, ℰ 56991, Telex 342888, ≼ Rutland water, ⤳, ⋙, park, ⤨
– ▤ ⚏ ⍢ 🄿. ⤤ ⚠ ℻ 𝘝𝘐𝘚𝘈. ⋙
M 26.00 **st.** and a la carte ⅋ 5.00 – **15 rm** 60.00/110.00 **st.**
Spec. Charcoal grilled quail salad and foie gras, Hot pot of the sea in a buttery mussel broth flavoured with saffron, Basket of berries with a grand marnier mousse.

AUSTIN-ROVER, LAND ROVER-RANGE ROVER Burley Rd ℰ 2657

OAKHILL Somerset 🄰🄾🄴 🄰🄾🄴 M 30 – see Shepton Mallet.

OAKLEY Hants. 🄰🄾🄴 🄰🄾🄴 Q 30 – see Basingstoke.

OBORNE Dorset 🄰🄾🄴 🄰🄾🄴 M 31 – see Sherborne.

OCKHAM Surrey **404** @ – ⊠ Ripley – ✪ 0483 Guildford.
♦London 29 – Guildford 8.

XXX **Hautboy Inn,** Alms Heath, GU23 6NP, ℰ 225355, Dancing (Friday and Saturday) – **❶**. ⚑ ⚑ Ⓞ *VISA*
closed Sunday dinner, Monday and Bank Holidays – **M** a la carte 10.15/13.25 **t.** ⚬ 3.00.

ODIHAM Hants. **404** R 30 – pop. 3,002 – ECD : Wednesday – ✪ 025 671.
♦London 51 – Reading 16 – Winchester 25.

XX **Mill House,** North Warnborough, RG25 1ET, NW : 1 m. by A 287 on A 32 ℰ 2953, ≼, « Riverside terrace and gardens » – **❶**

MERCEDES-BENZ The Square ℰ 2294

ODSTOCK Wilts. **403** **404** O 30 – see Salisbury.

OLDHAM Greater Manchester **402** **404** N 23 – pop. 107,095 – ECD : Tuesday – ✪ 061 Manchester.
🛇 Lees New Rd ℰ 624 4986 – 🛇 Crompton and Royton, High Barn ℰ 624 2154 – 🛇 Saddleworth, Uppermill ℰ 045 77 (Saddleworth) 2059, E : 5 m.
🛈 Local Studies Library, 84 Union St. ℰ 678 4654.
♦London 212 – ♦ Leeds 36 – ♦Manchester 7 – ♦Sheffield 38.

🏨 **Bower** (De Vere), Hollingwood Av., Chadderton, OL9 8DE, SW : 3 ¼ m. by A 62 on A 6104 ℰ 682 7254, Telex 666883, ⚘ – 📺 ⌁wc 🛏wc ☎ ⅋ ❶. ⚑ ⚑ Ⓞ *VISA*
closed 23 to 31 December – **M** (closed Saturday lunch) 6.95/7.95 **st.** and a la carte ⚬ 3.30 –
66 rm ⊒ 17.50/55.00 **st.** – SB (weekends only) 49.00 **st.**

MAZDA Oldham Rd, Springhead ℰ 624 3620   RENAULT Manchester Rd, Hollinwood ℰ 624 1979
NISSAN Huddersfield Rd ℰ 624 6042

OLLERTON Notts. **402** **403** **404** Q 24 – pop. 11,303 (inc. Boughton) – ECD : Thursday – ⊠ Newark – ✪ 0623 Mansfield.
🛇 Woodhouse ℰ 0623 (Mansfield) 23521 SW : 7 m.
♦London 151 – ♦Leeds 53 – Lincoln 25 – ♦Nottingham 19 – ♦Sheffield 27.

🏛 **Hop Pole,** Main St., NG22 9AD, ℰ 822573 – 🛏 ❶. ⚑ *VISA*
M (carving rest.) 8.00 **t.** and a la carte ⚬ 2.70 – **12 rm** ⊒ 19.00/36.50.

at Kirton NE : 3 m. on A 6075 – ⊠ Newark – ✪ 0623 Mansfield :

↑ **Old Rectory** ⌂, NG22 9LP, ℰ 861540, ⚘ – ❶. ⚘
closed December – **10 rm** ⊒ 12.50/29.50 **st.**

ORFORD Suffolk **404** Y 27 – pop. 665 – ECD : Wednesday – ⊠ Woodbridge – ✪ 039 45.
♦London 93 – ♦Ipswich 20 – ♦Norwich 48.

🏛 **Crown and Castle** (T.H.F.), Market Hill, IP12 2LJ, ℰ 205, ⚘ – 📺 ⌁wc ☎ ❶. ⚑ ⚑ Ⓞ *VISA*
M (bar lunch Monday to Saturday)/dinner 8.95 **st.** ⚬ 2.70 – ⊒ 5.50 – **19 rm** 33.50/43.00 **st.**

OSWESTRY Salop **402** **403** K 25 – pop. 13,200 – ECD : Thursday – ✪ 0691.
🛇 at Llanymynech ℰ 0691 (Llanymynech) 830542, S : 5 m.
🛈 Little Chef rest., A 5, Babbinswood Whittington ℰ 662488 (summer only) – Library, Arthur St. ℰ 662753.
♦London 182 – Chester 28 – Shrewsbury 18.

🏨 **Wynnstay** (T.H.F.), 43 Church St., SY11 2SZ, ℰ 655261 – 📺 ⌁wc ☎ ❶. ⚑ ⚑ Ⓞ *VISA*
M (bar lunch)/dinner 8.50 **st.** and a la carte ⚬ 2.70 – ⊒ 5.50 – **31 rm** 33.50/41.50 **st.**

🏛 **Ashfield,** Llwyn-y-Maen, Trefonen Rd, SY10 9DD, SW : 1 ½ m. ℰ 655200, ≼, ⚘ – 📺 ⌁wc 🛏wc ❶. ⚘
M (dinner only) 7.00 **t.** and a la carte ⚬ 3.50 – **14 rm** ⊒ 22.00/36.00 **st.** – SB 36.00 **st.**

at Rhydycroesau W : 3 ½ m. on B 4580 – ⊠ ✪ 0691 Oswestry :

🏛 **Pen-y-Dyffryn Hall** ⌂, SY10 7DT, ℰ 653700, ≼, ⚘ – ❶. ⚘
M 7.50/9.00 **st.** ⚬ 3.00 – **6 rm** ⊒ 13.50/24.00 **st.** – SB (weekends only) 35.00 **st.**

ALFA-ROMEO Gobowen ℰ 61233
AUSTIN-ROVER Lower Brook St. ℰ 652285
BMW Victoria Rd ℰ 652413
FORD Salop Rd ℰ 654141
HONDA ℰ 653491
LANCIA Gobowen ℰ 661233

PEUGEOT-TALBOT Llansantffraid-Ym-Mechain ℰ 069 181 (Llansantffraid) 283
PEUGEOT-TALBOT Willow St. ℰ 652301
SKODA Gobowen ℰ 661233
VAUXHALL-OPEL Smithfield St. ℰ 652235
VOLVO West Felton ℰ 069 188 (Queens Head) 451

OTLEY West Yorks. **402** O 22 – pop. 14,136 – ✪ 0943.
♦London 216 – Harrogate 14 – ♦Leeds 12 – York 28.

🏨 **Chevin Lodge** ⌂, Yorkgate, LS21 3NU, S : 2 m. by East Chevin Rd ℰ 467818, Telex 51538, « Pine log cabin », ⚘, park – ▤ rest 📺 ⌁wc ☎ ⅋ ❶. ⚑ ⚑ Ⓞ *VISA*
M 8.95/9.95 **t.** and a la carte ⚬ 3.10 – **18 rm** ⊒ 45.50/55.50 **t.** – SB (weekends only) 56.50 **st.**

OTTERBURN Northumb. **401 402** N 18 – pop. 1,506 – ECD : Thursday – ✆ 0830.

♦London 314 – ♦Carlisle 54 – ♦Edinburgh 74 – ♦Newcastle-upon-Tyne 31.

🏨 **Percy Arms,** NE19 1NR, ℰ 20261, ᎒, ⚘ – ▥ ➟wc ᐧ �‖wc ☎ 🅿 🏂 ☒ 🆎 ⓪ *VISA*
M (bar lunch)/dinner 11.50 **t.** and a la carte ◊ 2.00 – **30 rm** ⌸ 25.50/46.00 **t.** – SB 56.00/60.00 **st.**

🏠 **Otterburn Tower,** NE19 1NB, ℰ 20620, « Crenellated Victorian house », park – ➟wc 🅿
☒ 🆎 ⓪ *VISA*
M (bar lunch Sunday) 7.50/8.50 **t.** and a la carte ◊ 2.75 – **15 rm** ⌸ 20.00/40.00 **st.** – SB (except Christmas-New Year) 41.00/51.00 **st.**

OTTERY ST MARY Devon **403** K 31 The West Country G. – pop. 3,957 – ECD : Wednesday – ✆ 040 481.

See : Site ✶ – St. Mary's Church ✶✶ – 🖪 Silver St. ℰ 3964.

♦London 167 – Exeter 12 – Bournemouth 71 – ♦Plymouth 53 – Taunton 23.

✕✕ **The Lodge,** 17 Silver St., EX11 1DB, ℰ 2356 – 🆎 ⓪ *VISA*
closed Sunday dinner – **M** 16.00 **t.** ◊ 3.00.

OULTON West Yorks. **402** ⑩ – see Leeds.

OULTON Suffolk – see Lowestoft.

OUNDLE Northants. **404** S 26 – pop. 3,225 – ECD : Wednesday – ✉ Peterborough – ✆ 0832.

♦London 89 – ♦Leicester 37 – Northampton 30.

🏨 **Talbot** (Anchor), New St., PE8 4EA, ℰ 73621, Group Telex 32364, ⚘ – ▥ ➟wc ☞ 🅿 🏂
☒ 🆎 ⓪ *VISA*
M (buffet lunch)/dinner a la carte 9.65/14.20 **t.** ◊ 3.00 – **38 rm** ⌸ 39.50/55.50 **t.** – SB (weekends only) 55.00/58.00 **st.**

✕ **Tyrrells,** 6-8 New St., PE8 4EA, ℰ 72347 – ☒ *VISA*
closed Sunday dinner, Monday lunch and Bank Holidays – **M** a la carte approx. 10.90.

AUSTIN-ROVER 1 Station Rd ℰ 73542   AUSTIN-ROVER 1 Benefield Rd ℰ 73519

OUTLANE West Yorks. – see Huddersfield.

OWERMOIGNE Dorset **403 404** N 32 – see Dorchester.

OWLSWICK Bucks. **404** R 28 – ✉ Aylesbury – ✆ 084 44 Princes Risborough.

♦London 47 – ♦Oxford 20.

🏠 Shoulder of Mutton ⌂, HP17 9RH, ℰ 4304, Telex 837002, ⚘ – ▥ ➟wc ☞ 🅿 ⌖ – **20 rm**.

OXFORD Oxon. **403 404** Q 28 – pop. 113,847 – ECD : Thursday – ✆ 0865.

See : Colleges Quarter✶✶✶ : Merton College✶, (Old Library✶✶✶, hall✶, quadrangle✶, chapel windows and glass✶)BZ – Christchurch College✶ (hall✶✶, cathedral✶, quadrangle✶, tower✶) BZ – Bodleian Old Library✶✶ (painted ceiling✶✶) BZ M2 – Divinity School (carved vaulting✶✶) BZ M2 – Magdalen College✶✶ (cloister✶✶, chapel✶) BZ – New College (cloister✶, chapel✶) BZ Y – All Souls College (chapel✶) BZ A – University College (gateway✶) BZ V – Corpus Christi College (quadrangle and sundial✶) BZ E – Radcliffe Camera✶ BZ O – Sheldonian Theatre✶ BZ M3 – High Street✶ BZ – Ashmolean Museum✶✶ BY M1.

🛆 Banbury Rd ℰ 54415, N : by A 423 AY – 🛆 Southfield, Hill Top Rd ℰ 242158 AZ.

🖪 St. Aldates Chambers, St. Aldates ℰ 726871.

♦London 59 – ♦Birmingham 63 – ♦Brighton 105 – ♦Cardiff 107 – ♦Coventry 54 – ♦Southampton 64.

Plans on following pages

🏨 **Randolph** (T.H.F.), Beaumont St., OX1 2LN, ℰ 247481, Telex 83446 – 🛗 ▥ ⟵➟ 🏂 ☒ 🆎
⓪ *VISA*   BZ n
M 5.65/12.40 **st.** and a la carte ◊ 2.70 – ⌸ 6.00 – **109 rm** 46.00/57.00 **st.**

🏨 **Cotswold Lodge,** 66a Banbury Rd, OX2 6JP, ℰ 512121 – ▥ ➟wc ☞ 🅿 🏂 ☒ 🆎 ⓪
VISA ⌖   BY i
closed Christmas Night-1 January – **M** 8.50/12.50 **t.** and a la carte ◊ 2.75 – **52 rm**
⌸ 38.50/53.50 **t.** – SB (weekends only) 52.50/59.25 **t.**

🏨 **Eastgate** (Anchor), Merton St., The High, OX1 4BE, ℰ 248244, Group Telex 83302 – 🛗 ▥
➟wc ☎ 🅿 ☒ 🆎 ⓪ *VISA*   BZ z
M (carving lunch)/dinner 7.35 **t.** and a la carte ◊ 3.65 – **42 rm** ⌸ 49.50/90.00 **t.** – SB (weekends only) 69.00/75.00 **st.**

🏨 **Ladbroke Linton Lodge** (Ladbroke), 9-13 Linton Rd, off Banbury Rd, OX2 6UJ, ℰ 53461,
Telex 837093, ⚘ – 🛗 ▥ ➟wc ☞ 🅖 🅿 🏂 ☒ 🆎 ⓪ *VISA* ⌖   AY e
M 8.50/9.50 **st.** – ⌸ 6.00 – **72 rm** 41.00/63.00 **st.** – SB (weekends only) 62.50 **st.**

🏨 **Oxford Moat House** (Q.M.H.), Wolvercote Roundabout, OX2 8AL, N : 2 ½ m. at junction A
40 and A 4144 ℰ 59933, Telex 837926 – ▥ ➟wc ☎ 🅿 🏂 ☒ 🆎 ⓪ *VISA*   AY s
M 6.25/8.25 **st.** and a la carte ◊ 2.95 – **155 rm** ⌸ 42.00/52.00 **st.** – SB (weekends only) 55.00 **st.**

🏨 TraveLodge (T.H.F.) without rest., Pear Tree Roundabout, Woodstock Rd, OX2 8JU, N : 3 m.
at junction of A 34 and A 43 ℰ 54301, Telex 83202, ⤳ heated – ▥ ➟wc ☞ 🅖 🅿 🏂 AY n
100 rm.

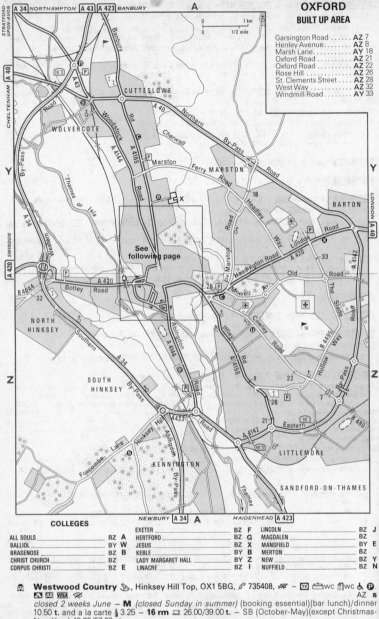

See following page

OXFORD
BUILT UP AREA

Garsington Road	**AZ** 7
Henley Avenue	**AZ** 8
Marsh Lane	**AY** 18
Oxford Road	**AZ** 21
Oxford Road	**AZ** 22
Rose Hill	**AZ** 26
St. Clements Street	**AZ** 28
West Way	**AZ** 32
Windmill Road	**AY** 33

COLLEGES

ALL SOULS	**BZ A**	EXETER	**BZ F**	LINCOLN	**BZ J**
BALLIOL	**BY W**	HERTFORD	**BZ G**	MAGDALEN	**BZ**
BRASENOSE	**BZ B**	JESUS	**BZ X**	MANSFIELD	**BY E**
CHRIST CHURCH	**BZ**	KEBLE	**BY B**	MERTON	**BZ**
CORPUS CHRISTI	**BZ E**	LADY MARGARET HALL	**BY Z**	NEW	**BZ Y**
		LINACRE	**BZ I**	NUFFIELD	**BZ N**

🏨 **Westwood Country** ⌕, Hinksey Hill Top, OX1 5BG, ℰ 735408, 🐎 – 📺 ⌂wc 🛁wc ᕦ 🅿.   **AZ s**
▩ 🆎 𝘝𝘐𝘚𝘈 🛰
closed 2 weeks June – **M** *(closed Sunday in summer)* (booking essential)(bar lunch)/dinner
10.50 **t.** and a la carte ᕯ 3.25 – **16 rm** ⇌ 26.00/39.00 **t.** – SB (October-May)(except Christmas-New Year) 48.00/57.00 **st.**

🏨 **Old Parsonage,** 1-3 Banbury Rd, OX2 6NN, ℰ 54843, 🐎 – 🅿. ▩ ① 𝘝𝘐𝘚𝘈   **BY u**
M (dinner only and Sunday lunch) a la carte 5.70/10.50 **t.** ᕯ 3.80 – **34 rm** ⇌ 17.50/31.00 **t.**

🏨 **Old Black Horse,** 102 St. Clements, OX4 1AR, ℰ 244691 – 📺 ⌂wc 🛁wc 🅿. ▩ 𝘝𝘐𝘚𝘈   – **8 rm**
closed Christmas and New Year – **M** *(closed Sunday dinner)* (dinner only) 10.00 **t.**   **AZ c**
⇌ 28.50/47.00 **t.**

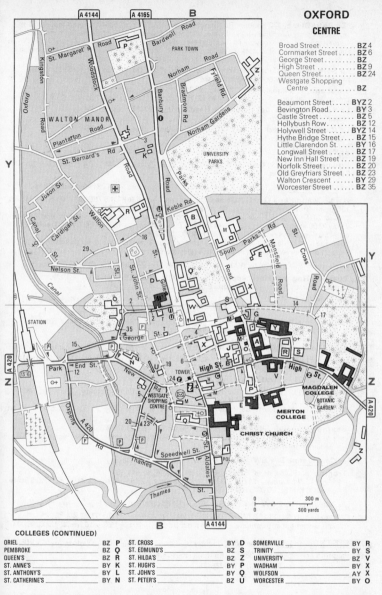

OXFORD

CENTRE

Broad Street . . . . **BZ** 4
Cornmarket Street . . . . . **BZ** 6
George Street . . . . **BZ**
High Street . . . . **BZ** 9
Queen Street . . . . **BZ** 24
Westgate Shopping
Centre . . . . **BZ**

Beaumont Street . . . . . **BYZ** 2
Bevington Road . . . . . . **BY** 3
Castle Street . . . . **BZ** 5
Hollybush Row . . . . **BZ** 12
Holywell Street . . . . . . **BYZ** 14
Hythe Bridge Street . . . **BZ** 15
Little Clarendon St. . . . . **BY** 16
Longwall Street . . . . . . **BZ** 17
New Inn Hall Street . . . . **BZ** 19
Norfolk Street . . . . **BZ** 20
Old Greyfriars Street . . . **BZ** 23
Walton Crescent . . . . . **BY** 29
Worcester Street . . . . . **BZ** 35

COLLEGES (CONTINUED)

ORIEL	BZ	**P**	ST. CROSS	BY	**D**	SOMERVILLE	BY **R**
PEMBROKE	BZ	**Q**	ST. EDMUND'S	BZ	**S**	TRINITY	BY **S**
QUEEN'S	BZ	**R**	ST. HILDA'S	BZ	**Z**	UNIVERSITY	BZ **V**
ST. ANNE'S	BY	**K**	ST. HUGH'S	BY	**P**	WADHAM	BY **X**
ST. ANTHONY'S	BY	**L**	ST. JOHN'S	BY	**Q**	WOLFSON	AY **X**
ST. CATHERINE'S	BY	**N**	ST. PETER'S	BZ	**U**	WORCESTER	BY **O**

⌂ **Earlmont,** 322-324 Cowley Rd, OX4 2AF, ✆ 240236 – 📺 ⌂ 🅿 ⌖   AZ **u**
11 rm � 11.00/24.00 **st.**

⌂ **Willow Reaches,** 1 Wytham St., via Norrey's Av., OX1 4SU, ✆ 721545 – 📺 ⌂wc. 🅰🅴 ⓪
🆅🅸🆂🅰 ⌖   AZ **e**
8 rm � 13.50/31.00 **st.**

XXX **Elizabeth,** 84 St. Aldates, OX1 1RA, ✆ 242230 – 🔲 🅰🅴 ⓪ 🆅🅸🆂🅰   BZ **s**
closed Monday, 28 March and 24 to 31 December – **M** 10.00 **st.** (lunch) and a la carte
17.00/21.25 **st.** ⌂ 4.75.

P.T.O. →
365

XX ⊛ **Le Petit Blanc,** 272 Banbury Rd, Summertown, OX2 7DY, ℰ 53540, French rest. – 🔄 VISA
closed Monday lunch, Sunday, 4 days at Easter, 2 weeks August-September, first 2 weeks
January and Bank Holidays – **M** (booking essential) 14.50/19.50 **t.** ⌕ 2.25   AY **c**
Spec. Paté de Coquilles St Jacques aux huitres et citron vert (September-March), Filet d'agneau farci de son Ris
en enveloppe d'épinard, sauce porto, Gratin de poire au chocolat et noix.

XX **La Sorbonne,** 1st floor, 130a High St., OX1 4DH, ℰ 241320, French rest. – 🔄 AE ⓪ VISA
M 13.00 **st.** and a la carte 13.40/19.50 **st.** ⌕ 3.50.   BZ **c**

XX **Saraceno,** 15 Magdalen St., OX1 3AE, ℰ 249171, Italian rest. – AE ⓪ VISA   BZ **u**
closed Sunday and Bank Holidays – **M** 12.00/16.00 **t.** and a la carte 2.95.

XX **La Salle à Manger,** 146 London Rd, Headington, ℰ 62587 – ▤. 🔄 VISA   AY **x**
closed Sunday and 26-30 December – **M** 11.95 **t.** and a la carte 7.40/18.40 **t** ⌕ 3.30.

X **La Cantina,** 34 Queen St., OX1 1ED, ℰ 247760, Italian rest. – 🔄 ⓪ VISA   BZ **r**
closed Monday – **M** a la carte 7.50/14.30 **t.** ⌕ 2.80.

at Kidlington N : 4 ½ m. on A 4237 – AY – ⊠ Oxford – ☎ 086 75 Kidlington :

⌂ **Bowood House,** 238 Oxford Rd, OX5 1EB, ℰ 2839, ⊐ heated, ☛ – ▥ ⌁wc ⋔wc ℗. ⁑
9 rm ⊑ 12.50/29.50 **st.**

at Great Milton SE : 12 m. by A 40 and A 329 Y – ⊠ Oxford – ☎ 084 46 Great Milton :

XXXX ⊛⊛ **Le Manoir aux Quat' Saisons** ⌁ with rm, Church Rd, OX9 7PD, ℰ 230, ≤, « 15C and
16C manor house », ⊐ heated, ☛, park, ⁑ – ▥ ⌁wc ℗. 🔄 VISA. ⁑
closed 24 December-21 January – **M** *(closed Tuesday lunch, Sunday dinner and Monday)*
21.50/40.00 **st.** and a la carte 34.00/41.00 **st.** ⌕ 7.05 – **10 rm** ⊑ 100.00/180.00 **st.**, **1 suite** 210.00
st. – SB (weekdays only)(October-April) 140.00/180.00 **st.**
Spec. Sole soufflée à la brunoise de petits légumes et coquilles St Jacques, Assiette aux saveurs de mon terroir à
l'essence de cèpes, Feuilleté tiède de poire rôtie au gingembre et citron vert.

at Cumnor SW : 4 ½ m. by A 420 – AY – off B 4017 – ⊠ Oxford – ☎ 0865 Cumnor :

XX **Bear and Ragged Staff,** Appleton Rd, OX2 9QH, ℰ 862329 – ℗. 🔄 AE ⓪ VISA
closed Saturday lunch – **M** a la carte 9.50/14.65 **t.** ⌕ 2.40.

AUDI, VW Abingdon Rd ℰ 242241
AUSTIN-ROVER Oxford Rd, Kidlington ℰ 086 75
(Kidlington) 4363
CITROEN 281 Banbury Rd ℰ 512277
DATSUN 72 Rose Hill ℰ 774696

MERCEDES-BENZ Banbury Rd, Shipton-on-Cher-
well ℰ 086 75 (Kidlington) 71011
SAAB 75 Woodstock Rd ℰ 57028
VAUXHALL-OPEL Woodstock Rd ℰ 59955

PADSTOW Cornwall 📖 F 32 The West Country G. – pop. 2 ,256 – ECD : Wednesday – ☎ 0841.
See : Site ★ – Envir. : Bedruthan Steps★★AC, SW : 8 m. to Trevone (Cornwall Coast Path★★), W :
3 m. – Trevose Head★ (≤★★), W : 6 m.
♦London 288 – Exeter 78 – ♦Plymouth 45 – Truro 23.

🏨 **Metropole** (T.H.F.), Station Rd, PL28 8DB, ℰ 532486, ≤ Camel Estuary, ⊐ heated, ☛ – 📶
▥ ⌁wc ⌁ & ℗. 🔄 AE ⓪ VISA
M (bar lunch Monday to Saturday)/dinner 8.25 **st.** and a la carte ⌕ 2.70 – ⊑ 5.50 – **43 rm**
31.00/49.50 **st.**

XX **Seafood,** Riverside, PL28 8BY, ℰ 532485, Seafood – 🔄 AE ⓪ VISA
closed Sunday, 1 May, Monday to Wednesday November-December and 21 December-7 March
– **M** (dinner only) 10.80 **t.** and a la carte ⌕ 3.20.

at Constantine Bay SW : 4 m. by B 3276 – ⊠ ☎ 0841 Padstow :

🏨 **Treglos** ⌁, PL28 8JH, ℰ 520727, ≤, 🔲, ☛ – 📶 ▥ ☎ ⇔ ℗
14 March-5 November – **M** 6.95/10.50 **t.** and a la carte ⌕ 2.45 – **43 rm** ⊑ 24.00/72.00 **t.**, **3 suites**
64.00/96.00 **t.** – SB 60.00/84.00 **t.**

at Treyarnon Bay SW : 4 ¾ m. by A 3276 – ⊠ ☎ 0841 Padstow :

🏠 **Waterbeach** ⌁, PL28 8JW, ℰ 520292, ≤, ☛, ⁑ – ⌁wc ⋔ ℗. 🔄 AE VISA. ⁑
closed December and January – **M** (bar lunch)/dinner 9.00 **t.** ⌕ 1.50 – **16 rm** ⊑ 15.00/46.00 **t.**

PAIGNTON Devon 📖 J 32 The West Country G. – pop. 39 ,565 – ECD : Wednesday – ☎ 0803.
See : Paignton Zoo★★AC, by A 385 Z – Kirkham House★AC Y B.
🛈 Festival Hall, Esplanade Rd ℰ 558383 and 555447.
♦London 226 – Exeter 26 – ♦Plymouth 29.

Plan of Built up Area : see Torbay

🏨 **Palace** (T.H.F.), Esplanade Rd, TQ4 6BJ, ℰ 555121, ⊐ heated, ☛, ⁑, squash – 📶 ▥ ℗.
🔄 AE ⓪ VISA   Y **e**
M (buffet lunch Monday to Saturday)/dinner 9.00 **st.** and a la carte ⌕ 2.70 – ⊑ 5.50 – **54 rm**
33.50/51.50 **st.**

🏨 **Redcliffe,** 4 Marine Drive, TQ3 2NL, ℰ 526397, ≤ Torbay, ⊐ heated, ☛ – 📶 ℗. 🏋 🔄 AE
VISA   Y **n**
M 5.25/8.75 **t.** and a la carte ⌕ 2.80 – **57 rm** ⊑ 22.00/56.00 **t.** – SB 48.00/64.00 **st.**

🏠 **St. Ann's,** 6 Alta Vista Rd, TQ4 6BZ, ℰ 557360, ≤, ⊐ heated, ☛ – ⌁wc ⋔wc & ℗. 🔄
March-October – **M** (bar lunch)/dinner 9.00 **st.** ⌕ 2.00 – **26 rm** ⊑ 14.50/47.25 **st.**   Z **o**

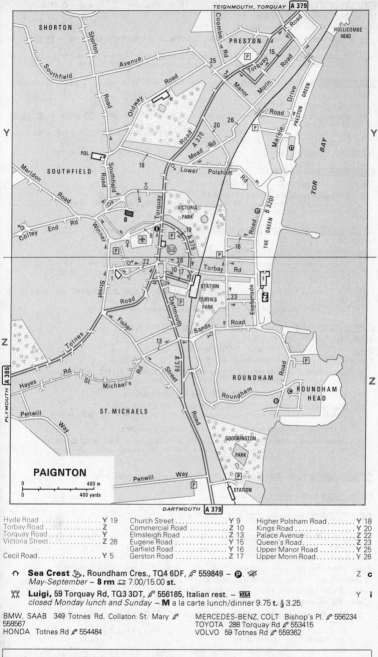

Hyde Road	Y 19	Church Street	Y 9
Torbay Road	Z	Commercial Road	Z 10
Torquay Road	Y	Elmsleigh Road	Z 13
Victoria Street	Z 28	Eugene Road	Y 15
		Garfield Road	Y 16
Cecil Road	Y 5	Gerston Road	Z 17

Higher Polsham Road	Y 18
Kings Road	Y 20
Palace Avenue	Z 22
Queen's Road	Z 23
Upper Manor Road	Y 25
Upper Morin Road	Y 26

↑ **Sea Crest** , Roundham Cres., TQ4 6DF, ℘ 559849 – ℗. 　　　　Z **c**
　　May-September – **8 rm** ⊆ 7.00/15.00 **st.**

XX **Luigi,** 59 Torquay Rd, TQ3 3DT, ℘ 556185, Italian rest. – VISA　　　　Y **i**
　　closed Monday lunch and Sunday – **M** a la carte lunch/dinner 9.75 **t.** ₰ 3.25.

BMW, SAAB 349 Totnes Rd, Collaton St. Mary ℘ 558567　　MERCEDES-BENZ, COLT Bishop's Pl. ℘ 556234
HONDA Totnes Rd ℘ 554484　　　　　　　　　　　　　　TOYOTA 288 Torquay Rd ℘ 553415
　　　　　　　　　　　　　　　　　　　　　　　　　　VOLVO 59 Totnes Rd ℘ 559362

Reisen Sie nicht heute mit einer Karte von gestern.

15　　　　　　　　　　　　　　　　　　　　　　　　　　　　　　　　　367

PAINSWICK Glos. 🔲🔲 N 28 – pop. 1,757 – ECD : Saturday – ✉ Stroud – ☎ 0452.

🛈 The Library, Stroud Rd ✆ 812569.

♦London 107 – ♦Bristol 35 – Cheltenham 10 – Gloucester 7.

🏨 **Painswick** ⬕, Kemps Lane, Tibiwell, GL6 6YB, ✆ 812160, Telex 43605, ☞ – 📺 🛏wc ⊛ ⓟ 🅰 🅰🅴 ⓪ 𝑽𝑰𝑺𝑨
M *(closed Sunday dinner to non-residents)* (buffet lunch Monday to Saturday) 7.25/13.00 **t.**
🍸 2.50 – **15 rm** ☷ 30.00/58.00 **t.** – SB (except Bank Holidays) 45.00/69.00 **st.**

PANGBOURNE Berks. 🔲🔲 Q 29 – pop. 3,445 (inc. Whitchurch) – ECD : Thursday –
☎ 073 57.

♦London 56 – ♦Oxford 22 – Reading 6.

🏨 **Copper Inn** (Best Western), 2 Church Rd, RG8 4AR, ✆ 2244, ☞ – 📺 🛏wc ☎ ⓟ 🎿 🅰
🅰🅴 ⓪ 𝑽𝑰𝑺𝑨 ❀
closed 24 to 26 December – **M** 9.75 **t.** (lunch) and a la carte 13.80/18.50 **t.** 🍸 3.00 – ☷ 4.50 –
21 rm 39.00/47.50 **st.** – SB (weekends only) 52.00 **st.**

AUSTIN-ROVER Reading Rd ✆ 2376   MERCEDES-BENZ Station Rd ✆ 3322

PANT MAWR Powys 🔲 I 26 – ✉ ☎ 055 15 Llangurig.

♦London 219 – Aberystwyth 21 – Shrewsbury 55.

🏨 **Glansevern Arms,** SY18 6SY, on A 44 ✆ 240, ≼, ⬔ – 📺 🛏wc ⓟ. ❀
closed 1 week at Christmas – **M** (booking essential) 9.00/12.00 **t.** 🍸 2.50 – **7 rm** ☷ 18.00/30.00 **t.**
– SB (November-March only) 46.00 **st.**

PARKGATE Cheshire 🔲🔲 K 24 – pop. 3,480 – ECD : Wednesday – ✉ Wirral – ☎ 051
Liverpool.

♦London 206 – Birkenhead 10 – Chester 11 – ♦Liverpool 12.

🏨 **Ship** (Anchor), The Parade, L64 6SA, ✆ 336 3931 – 📺 🛏wc ⊛ ⓟ. 🅰 🅰🅴 ⓪ 𝑽𝑰𝑺𝑨. ❀
closed Christmas – **M** 5.50/8.00 **t.** and a la carte 🍸 3.00 – **26 rm** ☷ 37.00/50.00 **t.** – SB
(weekends only) 56.00 **st.**

XX **Mr Chow's Eating House,** The Parade, L64 6RW, ✆ 336 2385, Chinese rest. – 🅰 🅰🅴 ⓪
𝑽𝑰𝑺𝑨
closed 25-26 December – **M** (booking essential)(dinner only) 8.00 **t.** and a la carte.

PATELEY BRIDGE North Yorks. 🔲🔲 O 21 – ✉ ☎ 0423 Harrogate.

Envir. : Brimham Rocks★ E : 4 ½ m.

🛈 Southlands Car Park, off High St. ✆ 71147 (summer only).

♦London 225 – ♦Leeds 28 – ♦Middlesbrough 46 – York 32.

🏨 **Grassfield Country House** ⬕, Ramsgill Rd, HG3 5HL, ✆ 711412, ☞ – 🛏wc 🛏wc ⓟ
March-October – **M** (dinner only) 7.50 **st.** 🍸 3.20 – **9 rm** ☷ 17.50/33.00 **st.** – SB 45.00/47.00 **st.**

at Low Laithe SE : 2 ¾ m. on B 6165 – ✉ ☎ 0423 Harrogate :

XX **Dusty Miller,** Main Rd, HG3 4BU, ✆ 780837 – ⓟ. 🅰 𝑽𝑰𝑺𝑨
closed Sunday, Monday and first 2 weeks August – **M** (dinner only) a la carte 10.90/15.90 **t.**

at Wath-in-Nidderdale NW : 2 ¼ m. – ✉ ☎ 0423 Harrogate :

XX **Sportsman's Arms** ⬕ with rm, HG3 5PP, ✆ 711306, ☞ – 🛏wc ⓟ. 🅰 🅰🅴 ⓪ 𝑽𝑰𝑺𝑨
M *(closed Sunday dinner)* (bar lunch Monday to Saturday)/dinner a la carte 11.70/16.70 **t.**
🍸 3.60 – **7 rm** ☷ 22.00/38.00 **t.** – SB 55.00/60.00 **st.**

PATTINGHAM Staffs. 🔲🔲🔲 N 26 – see Wolverhampton (W. Midlands).

PEASLAKE Surrey 🔲 S 30 – see Dorking.

PEASMARSH East Sussex 🔲 W 31 – see Rye.

PEMBROKE (PENFRO) Dyfed 🔲 F 28 – pop. 15,284 – ECD : Wednesday – ☎ 064 63 (4 fig.).
0646 (6 fig.).

See : Site★ – Castle★★.

Envir. : Lamphey (Bishop's palace★) *AC*, E : 2 m. – Carew (castle★ 13C) *AC*, NE : 4 ½ m.

🛡 Defensible Barracks, Pembroke Dock ✆ 3817.

⚓ to Ireland (Rosslare) (B & I Line) 1-2 daily (4 h 15 mn).

♦London 252 – Carmarthen 32 – Fishguard 26.

🏨 **Underdown Country House** ⬕, Grove Hill, SA71 5PR, ✆ 683350, « Antiques and gardens » – 📺 🛏wc 🛏wc ⓟ. 🅰 𝑽𝑰𝑺𝑨
M *(closed Sunday to non-residents)* (booking essential) a la carte 9.35/14.25 **t.** 🍸 2.10 – **6 rm**
☷ 72.50/45.00 **t.** – SB 50.00 **st.**

🏨 **Old Kings Arms,** 13 Main St., SA72 4UQ, ✆ 683611 – 📺 🛏wc ⊛ ⓟ. 🅰 🅰🅴 𝑽𝑰𝑺𝑨
closed 25-26 December and 1 January – **M** a la carte 6.40/14.50 **t.** 🍸 1.95 – **21 rm**
☷ 19.50/34.00 **t.**

368

at Lamphey E : 1 ¾ m. on A 4139 – ⊠ Pembroke – ☎ 0646 Lamphey :

🏛 **Court** (Best Western) 🦢, SA71 5NT, 𝒫 672273, 🍴, 🔲, 🛋 – 📺 ➘wc ☎ 🅿. 🔼 🎫 ⑩ 𝓥𝓘𝓢𝓐 ⚘
M (bar lunch)/dinner 8.50 **st.** and a la carte ⅄ 3.25 – **21 rm** ⊐ 29.50/47.00 **st.** – SB 44.00/64.00 **st.**

at Pembroke Dock NW : 2 m. on A 4139 – ⊠ ☎ 0646 Pembroke :

🏛 **Cleddau Bridge,** Essex Rd, SA72 6UT, NE : 1 m. by A 4139 on A 477 (at Toll Bridge) 𝒫 685961, 🍛 heated – ➘wc ☎ 🅿. 🔼 🔼 🎫 ⑩ 𝓥𝓘𝓢𝓐
M (bar lunch Saturday) a la carte 8.90/12.05 **st.** ⅄ 2.30 – **24 rm** ⊐ 35.00/45.00 **st.** – SB (weekends only) 45.50 **st.**

PEMBROKESHIRE (Coast) ** Dyfed 𝟒𝟎𝟑 E 27 28.

See : From Cemaes Head to Strumble Head** : Newport (site*) – Bryn Henllan (site*) – Goodwick ⇐** – Strumble Head (⇐** from the lighthouse). From Strumble Head to Solva** : Trevine ⇐** – Porthgain (cliffs ✳***) – Abereiddy (site*) – St. David's Head** – Whitesand Bay** – Solva (site*). From Solva to Dale** : Newgale ⇐** – Martin's Haven ✳** – St. Ann's Head ⇐** – Dale ⇐*. From Dale to Freshwater West* : Freshwater West (site*). From Freshwater West to Pendine Sands** (Stack Rocks**) – St. Govan's Chapel (site*) – Freshwater East (site*) – Manorbier (castle*) – Tenby (site**) – Amroth (site*) – Pendine Sands*.

PENARTH South Glam. 𝟒𝟎𝟑 K 29 – pop. 22,467 – ECD : Wednesday – ☎ 0222.
🄸 West House 𝒫 707201 – Piermaster's Office, The Pier 𝒫 706555 (summer only).
♦London 161 – ♦Cardiff 4.

XXX **Caprice,** 1st floor, 1 Beach Cliff, The Esplanade, CF6 2AS, 𝒫 702424, ⇐ – 🔼 🎫 ⑩ 𝓥𝓘𝓢𝓐
closed Sunday and Bank Holidays – **M** 7.25/11.55 **t.** and a la carte ⅄ 2.45.

X **Le Gourmand,** 6a Andrew Buildings, Stanwell Rd, CF6 2AA, 𝒫 708742.

at Swanbridge S : 2 ½ m. by B 4267 – ⊠ Penarth – ☎ 0222 Sully :

XXX **Sully House** 🦢 with rm, Lavernock Beach Rd, St. Mary's Well Bay, CF6 2XR, 𝒫 530448, ⇐, 🛋 – 📺 ➘wc 🅿. ⑩ 𝓥𝓘𝓢𝓐 ⚘
closed Sunday, 25-26 December and Bank Holiday Mondays – **M** (closed Saturday lunch) 13.50 **t.** – **4 rm** ⊐ 26.00/36.00 **t.**

AUSTIN-ROVER Windsor Rd 𝒫 703024

PENCRAIG Heref and Worc – see Ross-on-Wye.

PENDOGGETT Cornwall 𝟒𝟎𝟑 F 32 – ⊠ – ☎ 0208 Bodmin.
♦London 264 – Newquay 22 – Truro 30.

🏠 **Cornish Arms,** PL30 3HH, on B 3314 𝒫 880263, 🛋 – ➘wc 🅿. 🔼 🎫 ⑩ 𝓥𝓘𝓢𝓐 ⚘
closed 24 to 26 December – **M** (buffet lunch Monday to Saturday)/dinner a la carte 6.45/12.85 **t.** – **7 rm** ⊐ 19.00/38.00 **st.** – SB (November-April) 49.00 **st.**

PENFRO = Pembroke.

PENGETHLEY Heref. and Worc. 𝟒𝟎𝟑 𝟒𝟎𝟒 M 28 – see Ross-on-Wye.

PENMAENHEAD Clwyd – see Colwyn Bay.

PENMAENPOOL Gwynedd 𝟒𝟎𝟐 𝟒𝟎𝟑 I 25 – see Dolgellau.

PENMORFA Gwynedd – see Porthmadog.

PENRITH Cumbria 𝟒𝟎𝟏 𝟒𝟎𝟐 L 19 – pop. 12,086 – ECD : Wednesday – ☎ 0768.
🄸 Robinson's School, Middlegate 𝒫 67466 (summer only).
♦London 290 – ♦Carlisle 24 – Kendal 31 – Lancaster 48.

🏛 **George,** Devonshire St., CA11 7SU, 𝒫 62696 – ➘wc 🍴wc 🅿. 🔼 🔼
closed 25-26 December and 1 January – **M** 5.10/10.00 **st.** ⅄ 2.80 – **32 rm** ⊐ 25.00/40.00 **st.** – SB (November-May) (weekends only) (not Bank Holidays) 72.50/80.00 **st.**

🏠 **Abbotsford,** Wordsworth St., CA11 7QY, 𝒫 63940, 🛋 – 📺 ➘wc 🍴wc 🅿. 🔼 🎫 ⑩ 𝓥𝓘𝓢𝓐
M 5.00/7.50 **st.** and a la carte ⅄ 3.00 – **11 rm** ⊐ 16.50/45.65 **st.** – SB (weekends only)(October-May) 45.00/52.00 **st.**

↑ **Limes Country** 🦢, Redhills, Stainton, CA11 0DT, Access off A 592 𝒫 63343, ⇐, 🛋 – 🅿. ⚘
April-October – **8 rm** ⊐ 10.00/20.00.

X **Passepartout,** 51 Castlegate, CA11 7HY, 𝒫 65852 – 🔼 𝓥𝓘𝓢𝓐
closed Sunday except Bank Holiday weekends, July and August – **M** (dinner only) a la carte 12.25/14.40 **t.** ⅄ 3.00.

AUDI, CITROEN, TALBOT Ullswater Rd 𝒫 64545
AUSTIN-ROVER Victoria Rd 𝒫 63666
FIAT King St. 𝒫 64691
FORD Old London Rd 𝒫 64571

RENAULT 11 King St. 𝒫 62371
TOYOTA 15 Victoria Rd 𝒫 64555
VAUXHALL-OPEL Scotland Rd 𝒫 63756

PENSHURST Kent **404** U 30 – pop. 1,749 – ✪ 0892.

See : Penshurst Place★ (and Tudor gardens★★ 14C) AC.

Envir. : Chiddingstone (castle : Egyptian and Japanese collections★ AC) NW : 5 m. – Hever Castle★ (13C) AC, W : 6 m.

♦London 38 – Maidstone 19 – Royal Tunbridge Wells 6.

🏠 **Leicester Arms,** High St., TN11 8BT, ℰ 870551 – 📺 🚿wc 🅿. 🔄 🆎 ⑩ 𝘝𝘐𝘚𝘈
   M 6.50/8.75 t. and a la carte ⬧ 2.40 – **7 rm** ⊑ 24.50/34.00 t. – SB (October-March) 49.50 st.

  at Chiddingstone NW : 5 m. by B 2176 and B 2027 – ✉ Edenbridge – ✪ 0892 Penshurst :

🟥🟥 **Castle Inn,** TN8 7AH, ℰ 870247, 🚗 – 🔄 🆎 ⑩ 𝘝𝘐𝘚𝘈
   closed Wednesday lunch and Tuesday – **M** 8.25/17.00 st. ⬧ 2.50.

PEN-Y-BONT = Bridgend.

PENZANCE Cornwall **403** D 33 The West Country G. – pop. 18,501 – ECD : Wednesday – ✪ 0736.

See : Site★ – Outlook★★★ – Western Promenade (≤★★★) YZ – Chapel St. ★ Y – Museum of Nautical Art★ AC Y M1.

Envir. : St. Michael's Mount★★★, (≤★★) E : 5 m. by A 30 Y – Sancreed Church★★, Celtic Crosses★★, W : 4 m. by A 30 Z – St. Buryan★★ (Church Tower★★), SW : 4 ½ m. by A 30 Z – Chysauster★★ AC, N : 4 ½ m. by B 3311 Y – Morvah, North Cornwall Coast Path (≤★★), NW : 6 ½ m. by B 3312 Y – Trengwainton Garden★★ AC, NW : 2 m. by B 3312 Y – Prussia Cove★, SE : 9 m. by A 30 and A 394 Y – Land's End★ (cliff scenery★★★), SW : 10 m. by A 30 Z.

Access to the Isles of Scilly by helicopter ℰ 3871.

🚗 ℰ 5831.

⛴ to the Isles of Scilly : Hugh Town, St. Mary's (Isles of Scilly Steamship Co.) summer Monday to Saturday 1-2 daily ; winter 3 weekly (2 h 30 mn).

🖪 Alverton St. ℰ 62207 and 62341 ext 292.

♦London 319 – Exeter 113 – ♦Plymouth 77 – Taunton 155.

Plan opposite

🏨 **Queens,** Promenade, TR18 4HG, ≤ – 🖓 📺 🚿wc 🅿. 🔄 🆎 ⑩ 𝘝𝘐𝘚𝘈   Z u
   M (lunch by arrangement) 5.50/5.90 t. ⬧ 2.50 – **71 rm** ⊑ 22.50/49.50 t. – SB (weekends only) (October-March) 42.50/45.00 st.

🏨 **Mount Prospect,** Britons Hill, TR18 3AE, ≤, 🔄 heated, 🚗 – 📺 🚿wc ⋔wc ☎ 🅿. 🔄 🆎 ⑩ 𝘝𝘐𝘚𝘈   Y e
   M (bar lunch)/dinner 8.50 **s.** and a la carte ⬧ 2.95 – **26 rm** ⊑ 26.00/42.00 **s.** – SB (November-April) 48.30/63.30 st.

🏠 **Abbey,** Abbey St., TR18 4AR, ℰ 66906, « Attractively furnished 17C house », 🚗 – 📺 🚿wc ⋔wc 🅿   Y u
   M (dinner only) 10.50 **st.** – **6 rm** ⊑ 35.00/60.00 **st.** – SB (November-March) 45.00/55.00 st.

🏠 **Sea and Horses,** 6 Alexandra Terr., TR18 4NX, ℰ 61961 – ⋔wc 🅿. 𝘝𝘐𝘚𝘈. 🍽   Z s
   M (bar lunch)/dinner 6.50 **st.** ⬧ 2.20 – **11 rm** ⊑ 11.50/25.00 **st.**

🏠 **Alexandra,** Alexandra Terr., TR18 4NX, ℰ 62644, ≤ – 📺 🚿wc ⋔wc 🄫 🅿. 🔄 🆎 𝘝𝘐𝘚𝘈
   M (bar lunch)/dinner 6.50 **st.** ⬧ 2.80 – **21 rm** ⊑ 10.50/30.00 **st.** – SB (October-May) 30.00/34.00 st.   Z a

↥ **Tarbert,** 11 Clarence St., TR18 2NU, ℰ 63758, 🚗 – ⋔wc. 🔄 🆎 ⑩ 𝘝𝘐𝘚𝘈   Y i
   closed Christmas – **12 rm** ⊑ 10.50/30.00 **st.**

↥ **Dunedin,** Alexandra Rd, TR18 4LZ, ℰ 62652 – 📺   Y r
   9 rm ⊑ 7.50/15.00 t.

↥ **Kimberley House,** 10 Morrab Rd, TR18 4EZ, ℰ 62727 – 🔄 𝘝𝘐𝘚𝘈. 🍽   Y s
   closed November – **9 rm** ⊑ 9.00/20.00 **st.**

↥ **Carnson House,** 2 East Terr., Market Jew St., TR18 2TD, ℰ 65589 – 🔄 🆎 ⑩ 𝘝𝘐𝘚𝘈. 🍽   Y c
   closed November and Christmas – **6 rm** ⊑ 9.00/20.00 **st.**

🟥🟥 **Harris's,** 46 New St., TR18 2LZ, ℰ 64408 – 🆎 ⑩ 𝘝𝘐𝘚𝘈   Y a
   closed Monday in winter, Sunday, 25-26 December and 1 January – **M** a la carte 10.20/14.95 t. ⬧ 2.65.

  at Newbridge NW : 3 m. on A 3071 – Y – ✉ ✪ 0736 Penzance :

🟥🟥 **Enzo,** TR20 8QH, ℰ 63777, Italian rest. – 🅿. 🔄 🆎 ⑩
   closed Sunday and 25-26 December – **M** (dinner only) (booking essential) a la carte 5.25/11.90 t. ⬧ 2.95.

  at Newlyn SW : 1 ½ m. on B 3315 – Z – ✉ ✪ 0736 Penzance :

🏨 **Higher Faugan** 🍃, TR18 5NS, SW : ¾ m. on B 3315 ℰ 62076, « Country house atmosphere », 🔄 heated, 🚗, park, 🍽 – 📺 🚿wc ⋔wc 🅿. 🔄 🆎 ⑩. 🍽
   March-September – **M** *(closed Sunday lunch)* (bar lunch)/dinner 10.35 t. ⬧ 2.80 – **12 rm** ⊑ 23.00/53.00 t.

🟥🟥 **Tolcarne,** Tolcarne Terr., TR18 5QH, ℰ 66966 – 🔄 ⑩ 𝘝𝘐𝘚𝘈   Z v
   closed Sunday and last 2 weeks October – **M** (dinner only) a la carte 8.70/13.90 t. ⬧ 2.95.

PEUGEOT, TALBOT Hayle Terr. ℰ 753143   PEUGEOT, TALBOT Newlyn ℰ 62038

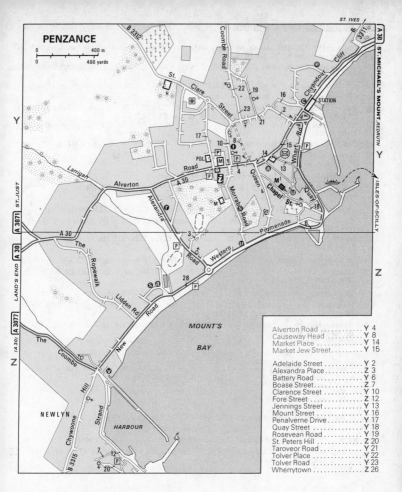

PENZANCE

0 — 400 m
0 — 400 yards

Alverton Road	Y	4
Causeway Head	Y	8
Market Place	Y	14
Market Jew Street	Y	15

Adelaide Street	Y	2
Alexandra Place	Z	3
Battery Road	Y	6
Boase Street	Z	7
Clarence Street	Z	12
Fore Street	Z	13
Jennings Street	Y	16
Mount Street	Y	17
Penalverne Drive	Y	18
Quay Street	Y	19
Rosevean Road	Y	20
St. Peters Hill	Z	20
Taroveor Road	Y	21
Tolver Place	Y	22
Tolver Road	Y	23
Wherrytown	Z	26

In alta stagione, e soprattutto nelle stazioni turistiche,
è prudente prenotare con un certo anticipo.
Avvertite immediatamente l'albergatore se non potete più
occupare la camera prenotata.
Se scrivete ad un albergo all'estero, allegate alla vostra
lettera un tagliando - risposta internazionale (disponibile presso gli uffici postali)

PERRANUTHNOE Cornwall **403** D 33 – see Marazion.

PERSHORE Heref. and Worc. **403** **404** N 27 – pop. 6,850 – ECD : Thursday – ☎ 038 65 (4 fig.)
0386 (6 fig.).
🛈 Council Offices, 37 High St. ℘ 554711.
♦London 106 – ♦Birmingham 32 – Cheltenham 22 – Stratford-on-Avon 21 – Worcester 9.

※ **Zhivago's,** 22 Bridge St., WR10 1AT, ℘ 553828 – 🔄 AE ⓞ VISA
  closed Sunday dinner, Monday, 25-26 December, 1 January and first 2 weeks August – **M**
  5.80/12.50 **t.** and a la carte 🍷 3.00.

  at Wyre Piddle NE : 2 m. by B 4082 and B 4083 on B 4084 – ⊠ Pershore – ☎ 0386 Pershore :

🏠 **Avonside,** Main Rd, WR10 2JB, ℘ 552654, ≤, ⊐ heated, ⊐, ⇔ – TV ⇔wc ℗
  closed December and January – **M** (bar lunch)/dinner 10.90 **t.** 🍷 4.50 – **7 rm** ⊐ 32.00/50.00 **t.**
  – SB (September-May) 50.00/60.00 **st.**

371

PETERBOROUGH Cambs. 402 404 T 26 – pop. 113,404 – ECD : Monday and Thursday – ✪ 0733.

See : Cathedral** 12C-13C (nave : painted roof***) – **Envir.** : Crowland : Abbey Church* (8C ruins), Triangular Bridge* 13C, NE : 8 m.

🛝 Thorpe Wood, Nene Parkway ✆ 267701, W : 3 m. on A 47 – 🛝 Ramsey ✆ 0487 (Ramsey) 813573, SE : 12 m.

🛈 Central Library, Broadway ✆ 48343 – Town Hall, Bridge St. ✆ 63141 or 63396 (Saturday only in summer).

◆London 85 – ◆Cambridge 35 – ◆Leicester 41 – Lincoln 51.

🏨 **Peterborough Moat House,** Thorpe Wood, PE3 6SG, SW : 2 ¼ m. at Roundabout 33 ✆ 260000, Telex 32708 – 🛗 📺 ⌷wc ☏ & 🅿 🍴 🔼 🗚 ⓪ 𝘝𝘐𝘚𝘈
M 8.00/9.00 t. and a la carte ♨ 3.50 – ⌷ 4.95 – **98 rm** 32.00/59.90 t. – SB (weekends only) 49.00 st.

🏨 **Bull** (Mt. Charlotte), Westgate, PE1 1RB, ✆ 61364 – 📺 ⌷wc ☏ 🅿 🔼 – **112 rm**.

🏠 **Newark,** 239 Eastfield Rd, PE1 4BH, ✆ 69811 – ⌷wc 🚿wc ☏ 🅿
M 6.50 s. – **38 rm** ⌷ 13.00/26.00 t.

at Whittlesey SE : 7 m. on A 605 – ⌷ ✪ 0733 Peterborough :

🏠 **Falcon,** Paradise Lane, PE7 1BH, ✆ 203247 – 📺 ⌷wc 🅿 🔼 🗚 ⓪ 𝘝𝘐𝘚𝘈 🎿
M a la carte 8.55/12.20 t. ♨ 2.80 – **8 rm** ⌷ 20.00/38.00 st.

at Norman Cross S : 5 ¾ m. on A 15 at junction with A 1 – ⌷ ✪ 0733 Peterborough :

🏨 **Crest** (Crest), Great North Rd, PE7 3TB, ✆ 240209, Telex 32576 – 📺 📺 ⌷wc ☏ & 🅿 🍴 🔼 🗚 ⓪ 𝘝𝘐𝘚𝘈
M (carving lunch) approx. 11.50 st. – ⌷ 5.75 – **97 rm** 42.50/52.50 st. – SB (weekends only) 51.00 st.

at Nassington (Northants.) SW : 10 ¾ m. by A 47 – ⌷ Peterborough – ✪ 0780 Stamford :

XX **Black Horse Inn,** 2 Fotheringhay Rd, PE8 6QU, ✆ 782324, 🍴 – 🅿 🔼 🗚 ⓪ 𝘝𝘐𝘚𝘈
M a la carte 6.35/11.45 st. ♨ 3.50.

at Wansford W : 8 ½ m. by A 47 – ⌷ Peterborough – ✪ 0780 Stamford :

🏨 **Haycock,** Great North Rd, PE8 6JA, ✆ 782223, 🍴 – 📺 ⌷wc ☏ 🅿 🍴 🔼 🗚 ⓪ 𝘝𝘐𝘚𝘈
M a la carte 14.00/16.50 st. ♨ 3.00 – **28 rm** ⌷ 28.00/55.00 st.

🏠 **Sibson House,** Great North Rd, PE8 6ND, SE : 1 ¾ m. on A 1 ✆ 782227, 🍴 – 📺 ⌷wc ☏
🅿 🔼 🗚 ⓪ 𝘝𝘐𝘚𝘈 🎿
M 6.50/9.00 t. and a la carte – **11 rm** ⌷ 27.00/55.00 t. – SB (weekends only) 45.00/60.00 st.

ALFA-ROMEO, SUZUKI 659 Lincoln Rd ✆ 52141
AUSTIN-ROVER, JAGUAR 7 Oundle Rd ✆ 66011
BMW Helpston Rd, Glinton ✆ 253333
FIAT, LANCIA Midland Rd ✆ 314431
FORD 27/53 New Rd ✆ 40104
MAZDA, YUGO 50/64 Burghley Rd ✆ 65787
MERCEDES-BENZ High St., Eye ✆ 222363

NISSAN Oxney Rd ✆ 49336
PEUGEOT, TALBOT 343 Eastfield Rd ✆ 310900
RENAULT, VAUXHALL Bretton Way ✆ 264981
VAUXHALL-OPEL, BEDFORD, RENAULT Sturrock Way ✆ 264981
VW, AUDI Oxney Rd ✆ 312213

PETERSFIELD Hants. 404 R 30 – pop. 10,078 – ECD : Thursday – ✪ 0730.

🛝 The Heath ✆ 67732, E : ½ m. – 🛈 Library, 27 The Square ✆ 63451.

◆ London 59 – ◆ Brighton 45 – Guildford 25 – ◆ Portsmouth 19 – ◆ Southampton 32 – Winchester 19.

🏨 **Langrish House** 🦌, Langrish, GU32 1RN, W : 3 ½ m. on A 272 ✆ 66941, ≤, 🍴, park – 📺
⌷wc ☏ 🅿 🔼 🗚 ⓪ 🎿
M (closed Sunday) (dinner only) a la carte 10.00/12.00 t. ♨ 2.25 – ⌷ 2.00 – **12 rm** 25.00/40.00 t.
– SB (weekends only) (October-April) 48.00 st.

AUSTIN-ROVER 38 Collace St. ✆ 62206
CITROEN Alton Rd, Froxfield ✆ 073 084 (Hawkley) 200
FORD Station Rd ✆ 62992

NISSAN Alton Rd, Steep ✆ 66341
RENAULT Winchester Rd ✆ 66241
VOLVO 23 London Rd ✆ 64541

PETWORTH West Sussex 404 S 31 – pop. 2,003 – ECD : Wednesday – ✪ 0798.

See : Petworth House*** 17C (paintings*** and carved room***) AC.

◆London 54 – ◆Brighton 31 – ◆Portsmouth 33.

XX **Paddington's Table,** East St., GU28 0AB, ✆ 43149 – 🔼 🗚 ⓪ 𝘝𝘐𝘚𝘈
closed Sunday dinner and 25-27 December – **M** a la carte 10.45/16.00 t. ♨ 2.95.

PEVENSEY East Sussex 404 V 31 – see Eastbourne.

PICKERING North Yorks. 402 R 21 – pop. 5,316 – ECD : Wednesday – ✪ 0751.

See : SS. Peter and Paul's Church (wall paintings* 15C) – Norman castle* (ruins) : ≤* AC.

🛈 The Station, Park St. ✆ 73791 (summer only).

◆London 237 – ◆Middlesbrough 43 – Scarborough 19 – York 25.

🏠 **Forest and Vale,** Malton Rd, YO18 7DL, ✆ 72722, 🍴 – 📺 📺 ⌷wc 🚿wc 🅿 🔼 🗚 ⓪ 𝘝𝘐𝘚𝘈
M 5.75/9.00 t. and a la carte ♨ 2.70 – **23 rm** ⌷ 18.00/40.00 t. – SB 45.00/51.00 t.

🏠 **White Swan,** Market Place, YO18 7AA, ✆ 72288 – 📺 ⌷wc 🅿 𝘝𝘐𝘚𝘈
M (lunch by arrangement) 5.75/8.75 t. – **13 rm** ⌷ 25.00/52.50 t., **1 suite** 62.50 t. – SB (winter only) 46.50/50.00 st.

at Wrelton NW : 2 ½ m. on A 170 – ⊠ ۞ 0751 Pickering :

✗ **Huntsman** with rm, Main St., YO18 8PG, ℰ 72530 – ⊟wc ℗
closed 2 weeks January and 1 week November – **M** *(closed Sunday dinner and Monday)* (bar lunch) a la carte 8.95/10.95 **t.** – **3 rm** ⊒ 11.50/25.00 **st.** – SB 36.50 **st.**

FORD, MERCEDES-BENZ Eastgate ℰ 72251　　　　　FORD Middleton ℰ 72331

PICKHILL North Yorks. ⓸⓿⓶ P 21 – pop. 300 (inc. Roxby) – ⊠ ۞ 0845 Thirsk.
♦London 229 – ♦Leeds 41 – ♦Middlesbrough 30 – York 34.

🛏 **Nags Head**, YO7 4JG, ℰ 567391 – 📺 ⊟wc 🚿wc ℗ ◪ 𝗩𝗜𝗦𝗔 . ❄
M (lunch by arrangement) 7.50/13.50 **st.** – **8 rm** ⊒ 14.00/28.00 **st.**

PIDDLETRENTHIDE Dorset ⓸⓿⓷ ⓸⓿⓸ M 31 – pop. 610 – ⊠ Dorchester – ۞ 030 04.
♦London 141 – ♦Bristol 54 – Exeter 62 – ♦Southampton 53.

🏠 **Old Bakehouse**, DT2 7QR, S : 1 m. on B 3143 ℰ 305, ⚓ heated, ⟨⟩ – 📺 ⊟wc ℗ ◪ 𝗩𝗜𝗦𝗔
closed first 3 weeks January – **M** (dinner only and Sunday lunch) 7.50 **t.** and a la carte – **10 rm**
⊒ 14.50/35.00 **t.** – SB (October-April) 40.00/44.00 **st.**

PILLATON Cornwall ⓸⓿⓷ H 32 – pop. 464 – ⊠ Saltash – ۞ 0579 St. Dominick.
♦London 254 – ♦Plymouth 11.

🏠 **Weary Friar**, PL12 6QS, ℰ 50238, « Part 12C inn » – 📺 ⊟wc ℗ ◪ 𝖠𝖤 ⓪ 𝗩𝗜𝗦𝗔
M 6.00/15.00 **t.** – **12 rm** ⊒ 26.00/38.00 **t.**

PIMPERNE Dorset ⓸⓿⓷ ⓸⓿⓸ N 31 – see Blandford Forum.

PINHOE Devon ⓸⓿⓷ J 31 – see Exeter.

PLAYDEN East Sussex – see Rye.

PLUCKLEY Kent ⓸⓿⓸ W 30 – pop. 1 ,109 – ۞ 023 384.
♦London 53 – Folkestone 25 – Maidstone 18.

🛏 **Elvey Farm**, TN27 0SU, W : 3 m. by B 2077 off Mundy Boys Road ℰ 442 – 📺 ⊟wc 🚿wc
℗ ❄
10 rm ⊒ 19.75/28.00 **st.**

PLYMOUTH Devon ⓸⓿⓷ H 32 **The West Country** G. – pop. 238 ,583 – ECD : Wednesday – ۞ 0752.
See : Site ✶✶ – Smeaton's Tower (⩽✶✶) *AC* BZ – Royal Citadel✶ *AC* (The Ramparts ⩽✶✶) BZ –
City Museum and Art Gallery✶*AC* BZ **M.**
Envir. : Buckland Abbey✶✶*AC*, N : 7 m. by A 386 ABY – Antony House✶✶*AC*, W : 5 m. by A 374 AY
– Saltram House ✶✶ *AC* E : 3 ½ m. BY A – Yelverton Paperweight Centre✶*AC*, N : 9 m. on a 386
ABY – Mount Edgcumbe (⩽✶) *AC*, W : 9 m. by car ferry from Cremyll or passenger ferry from
Stonehouse.
🅖 Whitsand Bay Hotel, Portwrinkle, Torpoint ℰ 0503 (St. Germans) 30276 W : 6 m. by A 374 AY – 🅖
Elfordleigh, Plympton, ℰ 336428, E : 6 m. by A 374 BY.
✈ Roborough Airport : ℰ 772752, N : 3 ½ m. by A 386 ABY.
⛴ Shipping connections with the Continent : to France (Roscoff) (Brittany Ferries) – to Spain
(Santander) (Brittany Ferries).
🅲 Civic Centre, Royal Parade ℰ 264851 and 264849 – 12 The Barbican ℰ 23806 (summer only).
♦London 242 – ♦Bristol 124 – ♦Southampton 161.

Plans on following pages

🏨 Holiday Inn, Armada Way, PL1 2HJ, ℰ 662866, Telex 45637, ⩽ city and Sound, 🔲 – 🛗 📺 📺
⬧ ℗ ◪ 𝖠𝖤 ⓪ 𝗩𝗜𝗦𝗔　　　　　　　　　　　　　　　　　　　　　　　　　　　　　BZ **e**
M 9.45/8.95 **st.** and a la carte 🍷 4.75 – ⊒ 5.75 – **217 rm**.

🏨 **Mayflower Post House** (T.H.F.), Cliff Rd, The Hoe, PL1 3DL, ℰ 662828, Telex 45442, ⩽
Plymouth Sound, ⚓ heated – 🛗 📺 ⊟wc ☞ ℗ ⬧ ◪ 𝖠𝖤 ⓪ 𝗩𝗜𝗦𝗔　　　　　　　　　AZ **c**
M 7.25/11.25 **st.** and a la carte 🍷 2.70 – ⊒ 5.50 – **104 rm** 43.00/51.50 **st.**

🏨 **Novotel Plymouth**, Marsh Mills Roundabout, PL6 8NH, ℰ 21422, Telex 45711, ⚓ heated –
🛗 📺 ⊟wc ☞ ⬧ ℗ ◪ 𝖠𝖤 ⓪ 𝗩𝗜𝗦𝗔　　　　　　　　　　　　　　　　　　　　　　　BY **i**
M 7.00/9.00 **st.** and a la carte 🍷 2.85 – ⊒ 4.50 – **100 rm** 38.00/45.00 **st.** – SB (weekends only)
57.00 **st.**

🏨 **Astor**, 14-22 Elliott St., The Hoe, PL1 2PS, ℰ 25511 – 🛗 📺 ⊟wc ☞ ◪ ❄　　　　　　BZ **c**
58 rm

🏨 **Duke of Cornwall** (Best Western), Millbay Rd, PL1 3LG, ℰ 266256, Telex 45424 – 🛗 📺
⊟wc 🚿wc ☞ ℗ ◪ 𝖠𝖤 ⓪ 𝗩𝗜𝗦𝗔　　　　　　　　　　　　　　　　　　　　　　　　AZ **a**
closed 24 to 27 December – **M** 6.50/8.50 **st.** and a la carte 🍷 3.00 – **67 rm** ⊒ 30.00/42.00 **t.** –
SB (weekends only) 48.00/54.00 **st.**

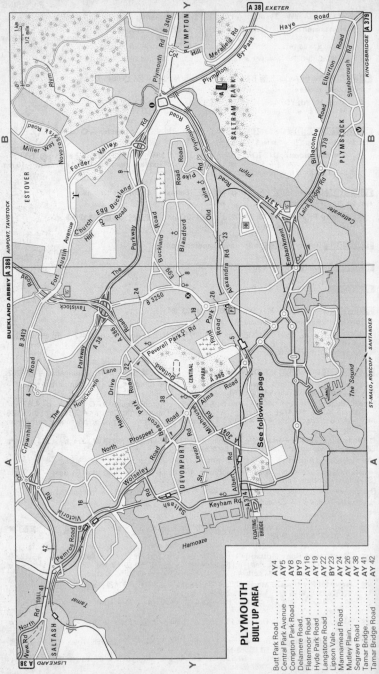

PLYMOUTH
BUILT UP AREA

Butt Park Road AY4
Central Park Avenue AY5
Compton Park Road AY8
Delamere Road BY9
Fletemoor Road AY16
Hyde Park Road AY19
Langstone Road AY22
Lipson Vale BY23
Mannamead Road AY24
Mutley Plain AY26
Segrave Road AY38
Tamar Bridge AY41
Tamar Bridge Road AY42

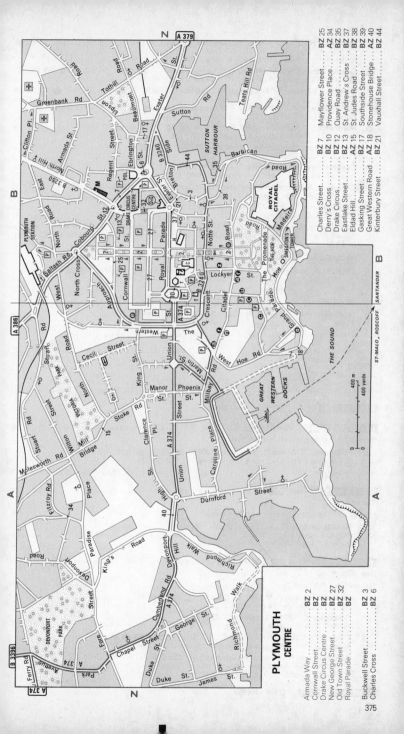

PLYMOUTH
CENTRE

Armada Way .... BZ 2
Cornwall Street .... BZ
Drake Circus Centre .... BZ
New George Street .... BZ 27
Old Town Street .... BZ 32
Royal Parade .... BZ

Buckwell Street .... BZ 3
Charles Cross .... BZ 6

Charles Street .... BZ 7
Derry's Cross .... BZ 10
Drake Circus .... BZ 12
Eastlake Street .... BZ 13
Eldad Hill .... AZ 15
Gasking Street .... BZ 17
Great Western Road .... AZ 18
Kinterbury Street .... BZ 21

Mayflower Street .... BZ 25
Providence Place .... AZ 34
Quay Road .... BZ 35
St Andrew's Cross .... BZ 37
St Judes Road .... BZ 38
Southside Street .... BZ 39
Stonehouse Bridge .... AZ 40
Vauxhall Street .... BZ 44

🏠 **Georgian House,** 51 Citadel Rd, The Hoe, PL1 3AU, ☎ 663237 – 📺 📞wc 🚿wc. 🔼 🅰🇪 ⓞ **VISA**   AZ **r**
M (bar lunch)/dinner 7.50 **t.** and a la carte ⅄ 2.25 – **10 rm** 🚪 19.00/27.50 **t.**

🏠 **Grosvenor,** 9 Elliott St., The Hoe, PL1 2PP, ☎ 260411 – 📺 📞wc 🚿wc 📠. 🔼 🅰🇪 ⓞ **VISA**. 🛇
M 5.00/12.00 **st.** and a la carte ⅄ 2.60 – **14 rm** 🚪 21.35/33.70 **st.**   BZ **u**

🏠 **Merlin,** 2 Windsor Villas, Lockyer St., The Hoe, PL1 2QD, ☎ 28133 – 📺 🚿wc ⓟ. 🔼 🅰🇪 ⓞ
VISA   BZ **z**
closed Christmas and New Year – **M** *(closed Sunday)* 6.50 **st.** (dinner) and a la carte ⅄ 2.85 –
24 rm 🚪 14.95/31.00 **st.**

⌂ **Mooreton,** 71 Mannamead Rd, PL4 5ST, ☎ 266566 – 📺 🚿wc ⓟ. 🔼 **VISA**. 🛇   AY **x**
closed 22 to 29 December – **8 rm** 🚪 21.70/35.50 **st.**

⌂ **Sea Breezes,** 28 Grand Par., West Hoe, PL1 3DJ, ☎ 667205   AZ **o**
7 rm 🚪 8.00/16.00 **st.**

⌂ **Cranbourne,** 282 Citadel Rd, The Hoe, PL1 2PZ, ☎ 263858 – 🚿. 🛇   BZ **r**
closed 2 weeks at Christmas – **10 rm** 🚪 16.00/20.00 **st.**

⌂ **Carnegie,** 172 Citadel Rd, The Hoe, PL1 3BD, ☎ 25158 – 🚿. 🔼 🅰🇪 ⓞ **VISA**. 🛇   AZ **n**
closed 23 December-3 January – **9 rm** 🚪 11.00/24.00 **t.**

⌂ **Chichester,** 280 Citadel Rd, The Hoe, PL1 2PZ, ☎ 662746 – **VISA**   BZ **a**
10 rm 🚪 8.00/16.00 **t.**

✕ **Chez Nous,** 13 Frankfort Gate, PL1 1QA, ☎ 266793, French rest. – 🔼 🅰🇪 ⓞ **VISA**   AZ **e**
closed Sunday, Monday, 1 to 10 February, 1 to 10 September and Bank Holidays – **M** 14.00 **st.**
and a la carte ⅄ 3.50.

at Colebrook E : 6 ½ m. by A 374 – BY – ✉ 🌝 0752 Plymouth :

🏠 Elfordleigh, Shaugh Prior Rd, PL7 5EB, N : 1 ½ m. by Borrington Hill ☎ 336428, ≼, 🛆 heated,
🛏9, 🐎, park, ✕, squash – 📞wc 🚿wc ⓟ
12 rm.

at Plymstock SE : 3 m. on A 379 – ✉ 🌝 0752 Plymouth :

🏠 Highlands, Dean Cross Rd, PL9 7AZ, ☎ 43643, 🛆 – 📺 📞wc 🚿wc ⓟ   BY **v**
15 rm.

ALFA-ROMEO Weston Park Rd ☎ 266099	LANCIA Budshead Rd ☎ 771123
AUSTIN-ROVER Union St. ☎ 263355	MAZDA Elm Rd, Mannamead ☎ 21594
BMW Union St. ☎ 669202	MERCEDES-BENZ Crown Hill ☎ 785611
CITROEN Colebrook Rd ☎ 336606	NISSAN The Crescent ☎ 668332
CITROEN 87 Crownhill Rd ☎ 772345	VAUXHALL-OPEL Normandy Way ☎ 361251
COLT Colebrook, Plympton ☎ 336462	VAUXHALL-OPEL Bretonside ☎ 667111
FORD Millbay ☎ 668040	VAUXHALL-OPEL Cobourg St. ☎ 668886
HONDA, SAAB Albert Rd ☎ 51810	VOLVO Valley Rd, Plympton ☎ 338306

PLYMSTOCK Devon **403** H 32 – see Plymouth.

POCKLINGTON Humberside **402** R 22 – pop. 5,051 – ECD : Wednesday – ✉ York – 🌝 075 92.
◆London 213 – ◆Kingston-upon-Hull 25 – York 13.

🏠 **Feathers,** 56 Market Pl., YO4 2UN, ☎ 3155 – 📺 📞wc ⓟ. 🔼 🅰🇪 **VISA**. 🛇
M 5.00/9.00 **t.** and a la carte ⅄ 3.00 – **12 rm** 🚪 20.00/34.00 **t.**

FORD Hallgate ☎ 2768   RENAULT Kilnwick Rd ☎ 3221

POLKERRIS Cornwall **403** F 32 The West Country G. – ✉ Fowey – 🌝 072 681 Par.
See : Site★.

◆London 277 – Newquay 22 – ◆Plymouth 34 – Truro 20.

✕ **Rashleigh Inn,** PL24 2TL, ☎ 3991, ≼ – ⓟ
closed Sunday dinner April-October and weekdays October-April – **M** (buffet lunch) a la carte
8.25/13.25 **t.** ⅄ 2.10.

POLPERRO Cornwall **403** G 33 The West Country G. – pop. 1,192 – ✉ Looe – 🌝 0503.
See : Site ★.

◆London 271 – ◆Plymouth 28.

⌂ **Lanhael House,** PL13 2PW, ☎ 72428, ≼, 🛆, 🐎 – ⓟ. 🛇
March-September – **6 rm** 🚪 16.00/25.00.

⌂ **Claremont,** PL13 2RG, ☎ 72241 – 🚿wc ⓟ
Easter-October – **9 rm** 🚪 12.50/25.00 **t.**

✕ **Captain's Cabin,** Lansallos St., PL13 2QU, ☎ 72292 – 🔼 ⓞ **VISA**
March-October – **M** *(closed Sunday)* 11.50 **t.** and a la carte ⅄ 2.95.

✕ **Kitchen,** Fish Na Bridge, The Coombes, PL13 2RQ, ☎ 72780 – 🔼 🅰🇪 ⓞ **VISA**
closed Monday, Sunday except summer and Tuesday to Thursday in winter – **M** (dinner only)
(booking essential) 10.50 **t.** ⅄ 3.75.

PONTARFYNACH = Devil's Bridge.

♦London 218 – Carmarthen 6 – ♦Swansea 25.

☆ **Cothi Bridge,** SA32 7NG, ℰ 251, ≼, ☜ – ⌷wc ℗. ☒ ஊ ⊚ ☑
M 7.50/10.00 **st.** and a la carte ⧊ 3.20 – **16 rm** ⊑ 21.00/32.00 **st.** – SB (weekends only) 36.00 **st.**

PONT-Y-PANT Gwynedd – see Betws-y-Coed.

POOLE Dorset **403** **404** O 31 The West Country G. – pop. 122,815 – ECD : Wednesday – ☻ 0202.

See : Site⋆ – The Three Museums⋆AC by A 35 AX – Envir. : Compton Acres Gardens⋆⋆, (≼⋆⋆⋆) AC, SE : 3 m. AX – Brownsea Island⋆, Baden Powell Stone (≼⋆⋆) AC, by boat from Poole Quay or Sandbanks AC.

i Poole Quay ℰ 673322 – Arndale Centre.
♦London 116 – Bournemouth 4 – Dorchester 23 – Weymouth 28.

Plan : see Bournemouth

🏛 **Mansion House,** 11 Thames St., BH15 1JN, ℰ 685666, Telex 41495, « 18C town house, staircase » – ▤ rest ⓉⓋ ⌷wc ☎ ℗. ⚘. ☒ ஊ ⊚ ☑. ❀   by A 35 AX
  closed 26 December-6 January – **M** (closed Saturday lunch) (residents and club members only) 8.50/12.50 **t.** and a la carte ⧊ 3.60 – **19 rm** ⊑ 44.00/66.00 **st.** – SB (weekends only) 80.00 **st.**

🏛 Hospitality Inn (Mt. Charlotte), The Quay, BH15 1HD, ℰ 671200, Telex 418374, ≼ – ▯ ⓉⓋ ⌷wc ℗. ⚘. ☒ ஊ ⊚ ☑   by A 35 AX
  68 rm ⊑ 45.50/55.00 **st.** – SB (weekends only) 58.00 **st.**

🏛 **Dolphin,** 180 High St., BH15 1DU, ℰ 673612 – ▯ ⓉⓋ ⌷wc ⌷wc ⊛ ℗. ⚘. ☒ ஊ ⊚ ☑
  M 5.35/8.80 **t.** ⧊ 4.50 – **71 rm** ⊑ 21.00/40.00 **t.** – SB (weekends only) 45.00/90.00 **st.**
          by A 35 AX

↑ **Redcroft** ❀, 20 Pinewood Rd, Branksome Park, BH13 6JS, ℰ 763959 – ⌷wc ℗. ❀
  10 rm ⊑ 14.00/31.00 **t.**   BX **e**

↑ Dene ❀, 16 Pinewood Rd, Branksome Park, BH13 6JS, ℰ 761143 – ⓉⓋ ⌷wc ℗. ❀   BX **c**
  16 rm.

✗ **Ca D'Oro Due,** 129 Parkstone Rd, Park Gates, BH15 2PB, ℰ 740223, Italian rest. – ☒ ஊ ⊚ ☑   by A 35 AX
  closed Sunday – **M** (dinner only) a la carte 14.75/18.75 **t.** ⧊ 3.90.

✗ **John B's,** 20 High St., BH15 1BP, ℰ 672440 – ☒ ஊ ⊚ ☑   by A 35 AX
  closed Sunday – **M** (dinner only) 9.95 **t.** ⧊ 2.60.

✗ **Isabel's,** 32 Station Rd, Lower Parkstone, BH14 8UD, ℰ 747885 – ஊ ⊚ ☑   AX **a**
  closed Sunday, first week June, 2 weeks October-November and 25-26 December – **M** (dinner only) a la carte 9.90/15.70 **t.**

✗ **Edelweiss,** 232 Ashley Rd, Upper Parkstone, BH14 9BZ, ℰ 747703, Austrian rest. – ☒ ஊ ⊚ ☑   AX **e**
  closed Tuesday dinner – **M** (lunch by arrangement)/dinner 8.75 **t.** and a la carte 7.95/15.65 **t.** ⧊ 2.70.

  at Lilliput SE : 2 ½ m. on B 3369 – ⊠ Poole – ☻ 0202 Canford Cliffs :

✗ **Gullivers,** 292 Sandbanks Rd, BH14 8HX, ℰ 708810 – ☒ ☑   AX **i**
  closed Sunday and January – **M** (dinner only) a la carte 8.40/10.80 **t.** ⧊ 4.50.

AUDI, VW Cabot Lane ℰ 745000
AUSTIN-ROVER The Quay ℰ 674187
CITROEN Broadstone ℰ 693501

CITROEN, PEUGEOT, TALBOT Blandford Rd ℰ 623636
VAUXHALL-OPEL Poole Rd, Branksome ℰ 763361

POOLEY BRIDGE Cumbria **401** **402** L 20 – see Ullswater.

POOL IN WHARFEDALE West Yorks. **402** P 22 – pop. 1,706 – ⊠ Otley – ☻ 0532 Arthington.
♦London 204 – Bradford 10 – Harrogate 8 – ♦Leeds 10.

✗✗✗ **Pool Court** with rm, Pool Bank, LS21 1EH, ℰ 842288, ☞ – ▤ rest ⓉⓋ ⌷wc ☎ ℗. ☒ ஊ ⊚ ☑. ❀
  closed Sunday, Monday, 2 weeks July-August and 2 weeks Christmas – **M** (dinner only) (booking essential) 10.00 **t.** and a la carte ⧊ 5.20 – ⊑ 4.95 – **4 rm** 42.00/67.00 **t.**

PORLOCK Somerset **403** J 30 The West Country G. – pop. 1,453 (inc. Oare) – ECD : Wednesday – ☻ 0643.

See : Site⋆ – St. Dubricius Church⋆.
Envir. : St. Culbone⋆, NW : 5 m. including 3 m. return on foot.

🏛 **Oaks,** TA24 8ES, ℰ 862265, ☞ – ⓉⓋ ⌷wc ⌷wc ℗. ஊ
  closed December and January – **M** (dinner only) 8.75 **t.** ⧊ 3.75 – **11 rm** ⊑ 22.50/37.50 **t.** – SB (spring and autumn only) 46.00/52.00 **t.**

  at Porlock Weir NW : 1 ½ m. – ⊠ Minehead – ☻ 0643 Porlock :

🏛 **Anchor and Ship,** TA24 8PB, ℰ 862753, ≼ – ⓉⓋ ⌷wc ☎ ℗. ☒ ஊ ⊚ ☑
  closed first 3 weeks January – **M** (bar lunch)/dinner 9.75 **t.** and a la carte ⧊ 3.30 – **23 rm** ⊑ 19.50/57.00 **st.** – SB (except Christmas and Bank Holidays) 50.00/72.00 **st.**

PORT DINORWIC (FELINHELI) Gwynedd **402 403** H 24 – ⚙ 0248.

✦London 249 – Caernarfon 4 – Holyhead 23.

※ **Seahorse,** 20 Snowdon St., LL56 4HQ, ℰ 670546 – 🅂 VISA
closed Sunday, 1 week mid February, 1 weekend May, 2 weeks October, 24-26 December and 1 January – **M** (dinner only) a la carte 8.55/10.90 ⌈ 2.40.

at Seion E : 2 ½ m. by A 487 and off B 4547 – ✉ Caernarfon – ⚙ 0248 Port Dinorwic

⌂ **Ty'n Rhos Farm** ⟨⟩, Llanddeiniolen, LL55 3AE, ℰ 670489, ≤, ✿ – ⌷wc 🅿. ⚘
closed Christmas and New Year – **9 rm** ⟐ 11.00/26.00 **st.**

PORTHCAWL Mid Glam. **403** I 29 – pop. 15,162 – ECD : Wednesday – ⚙ 065 671.
🛈 The Old Police Station, John St. ℰ 6639 (summer only).

✦London 183 – ✦Cardiff 28 – ✦Swansea 18.

🏛 **Seabank,** The Promenade, CF36 3LU, ℰ 2261, ≤, ⚒ heated – 🛗 📺 🅿. 🅰 🅂 🆎 ⓪ VISA. ⚘
M 6.00/7.50 **t.** and a la carte ⌈ 2.45 – **64 rm** ⟐ 29.00/52.00 **t.** – SB (weekends only) 53.00/55.00 **st.**

🏛 **Atlantic,** West Drive, Sea Front, CF36 3LT, ℰ 5011, ≤ – 🛗 📺 ⌷wc ☎ 🅿. 🅂 🆎 ⓪ VISA
M (closed Sunday dinner to non-residents) 5.75/7.75 **t.** and a la carte ⌈ 3.20 – **18 rm** ⟐ 30.00/40.00 **st.** – SB (weekends only) 42.00 **st.**

🏛 **Seaways,** 26-30 Mary St., CF36 3YA, ℰ 3510 – 📺 ⌷wc ⋔wc. 🅂 🆎 ⓪ VISA
M (bar lunch Monday to Saturday)/dinner 9.50 **t.** and a la carte ⌈ 2.50 – **16 rm** ⟐ 15.00/32.50 **t.** – SB (weekends only) 31.50/41.00 **st.**

at Nottage (Drenewydd yn Notais) N : ¾ m. by A 4229 – ✉ ⚙ 065 671 Porthcawl :

🏛 **Maid of Sker,** West Rd, CF36 3RT, ℰ 2172 – 📺 ⌷wc 🅿. 🅂 🆎 VISA
M (bar lunch)/dinner 10.90 **t.** and a la carte ⌈ 3.25 – **10 rm** ⟐ 29.00/39.00 **t.** – SB (weekends only) (except summer) 42.00 **st.**

🏛 **Rose and Crown,** Heol-y-Capel, CF36 3ST, ℰ 4850 – 📺 ⌷wc 🅿. 🅂 🆎 ⓪ VISA. ⚘
M 5.95 **st.** ⌈ 3.30 – **7 rm** ⟐ 19.50/29.50 **t.**

PORTHMADOG Gwynedd **402 403** H 25 – pop. 2,865 – ECD : Wednesday – ⚙ 0766.
🛫 Morfa Bychan ℰ 2037, W : 2 m.

🛈 High St. ℰ 2981 (summer only).

✦ London 245 – Caernarfon 20 – Chester 70 – Shrewsbury 81.

🏛 **Royal Sportsman** (T.H.F.), High St., LL49 9HA, ℰ 2015 – 📺 ⌷wc ⊜ 🅿. 🅂 🆎 ⓪ VISA
M (bar lunch Monday to Saturday)/dinner 9.00 **st.** ⌈ 2.60 – ⟐ 5.00 – **16 rm** 34.50/42.50 **st.**

at Penmorfa NW : 2 m. on A 487 – ✉ ⚙ 0766 Porthmadog :

🏛 **Bwlch-y-Fedwen Country House,** LL49 9RY, ℰ 2975, « Tastefully renovated 17C inn » – ⌷wc 🅿. ⚘
April-October – **M** (residents only) (bar lunch) – **5 rm** ⟐ (dinner included) 30.00/48.00 **t.**

PORT ISAAC Cornwall **403** F 32 The West Country G. – ECD : Wednesday – ⚙ 0208 Bodmin.

✦London 266 – Newquay 24 – Tintagel 14 – Truro 32.

🏛 **Port Gaverne,** Port Gaverne, PL29 3SQ, S : ½ m. ℰ 880244 – ⌷wc 🅿. 🅂 🆎 ⓪ VISA
closed 15 January-22 February – **M** (buffet lunch)/dinner 9.50 **st.** and a la carte ⌈ 2.45 – **18 rm** ⟐ 19.50/47.00 **st.** – SB (except Bank Holidays) 50.00/70.00 **st.**

⌂ **Archer Farm** ⟨⟩, Trewetha, PL29 3RU, SE : ½ m. by B 3276 ℰ 880522, ≤, ✿ – ⋔wc 🅿
March-November – **8 rm** ⟐ 11.50/30.00 **t.**

PORTLAND Dorset **403 404** M 32 The West Country G. – pop. 12,405 – ECD : Wednesday – ⚙ 0305.

See : Site ✶ (vantage point ✶✶).

🛈 St. George's Centre, Reforne ℰ 823406.

✦London 149 – Dorchester 14 – Weymouth 6.

🏛 **Portland Heights** (Best Western), Yeates Corner, Wakeham, DT5 2EN, ℰ 821361, Telex 418493, ≤, ⚒ heated, squash – 🛗 📺 ⌷wc ☎ 🅿. 🅰 🅂 🆎 ⓪ VISA
M a la carte 7.20/10.90 **t.** ⌈ 3.00 – **68 rm** ⟐ 35.00/55.00 **t.** – SB (weekends only) 45.00/58.00 **st.**

🏛 **Pennsylvania Castle,** Pennsylvania Rd, Wakeham, DT5 1HT, ℰ 820561, ≤, ✿ – 📺 ⌷wc ⋔wc ⊜ 🅿. 🅂 🆎 ⓪ VISA
M 7.50 **t.** and a la carte ⌈ 2.60 – **12 rm** ⟐ 27.00/40.00 **t.** – SB (weekends only) (September-June) 36.00/44.00 **st.**

FORD   Easton Lane ℰ 820483

Pour parcourir l'Europe,
utilisez les cartes Michelin **Grandes Routes** à 1/1 000 000.

PORTLOE Cornwall 🗺️ F 33 – ✉ ⊛ 0872 Truro.

♦London 296 – St. Austell 15 – Truro 15.

🏠 **Lugger,** TR2 5RD, ℰ 501322, ≤ – 📺 🚼wc ☰ 🅿 📶 AE ⓞ VISA. ⊛
March-mid November – **M** (bar lunch Monday to Saturday)/dinner 10.25 **t.** and a la carte
🍴 1.75 – **20 rm** ☲ (dinner included) 29.50/70.00 **t.** – SB 56.00/70.00 **st.**

PORTSCATHO Cornwall 🗺️ F 33 – ECD : Wednesday and Saturday – ✉ Truro – ⊛ 087 258.

♦London 298 – ♦ Plymouth 55 – Truro 16.

🏠 **Rosevine** ⊛, Porthcurnick Beach, TR2 5EW, N : 2 m. by A 3078 ℰ 206, ≤, ⌖ – 🚼wc ☰
🅿 📶 AE ⓞ – **M** (bar lunch)/dinner 10.00 **t.** 🍴 3.25 – **16 rm** ☲ 25.00/65.00 **t.**

🏠 **Gerrans Bay,** Tregassick Rd, TR2 5ED, ℰ 338, ⌖ – 🚼wc 🅿 📶 AE VISA
April-October and Christmas – **M** (bar lunch)/dinner 9.00 **t.** 🍴 2.40 – **15 rm** ☲ 13.50/36.00 **st.**

🏠 **Roseland House** ⊛, Rosevine, TR2 5EW, N : 2 m. by A 3078 ℰ 644, ≤ Gerrans Bay, ⌖ –
🚼wc ☰
closed January – **M** (bar lunch)/dinner 8.50 **st.** – **19 rm** ☲ 18.00/52.00 **st.** – SB (except
summer) 38.00/46.00 **st.**

PORTSMOUTH and SOUTHSEA Hants. 🗺️ 🗺️ Q 31 – pop. 174 ,218 – ECD : Monday, Wednesday and Thursday – ⊛ 0705.

See : H.M.S. Victory★★★ BY and Victory Museum★ M1 AC – Royal Marines' Museum★, at Eastney
AZ **M2** – 🔟 Great Salterns ℰ 664549. AY.

🚢 Shipping connections with the Continent : to France (Cherbourg) (Townsend Thoresen) (Sealink) – to France (Le Havre) (Townsend Thoresen) – to France (Saint-Malo) (Brittany Ferries) – to
the Isle of Wight : Fishbourne (Sealink) 15-18 daily (45 mn) – to St. Helier, Jersey (Sealink) summer :
1 daily, winter : 6 weekly (8 h 45 mn) – to St. Helier, Jersey (Channel Island Ferries) 1 daily (7 h
45 mn) – to St. Peter Port, Guernsey (Sealink) summer : 1 daily, winter : 6 weekly (11 h 30 mn).

🚢 to the Isle of Wight : Ryde (Sealink from Portsmouth Harbour) 15-24 daily (25 to 30 mn) – from
Southsea to the Isle of Wight : Ryde (Hovertravel from Southsea Clarence Pier) summer frequent
services daily; winter 8-12 daily (restricted Sundays) (9 mn).

🅱 Civic Offices, Guildhall Sq. ℰ 834092/3 – Castle Buildings, Clarence Esplanade, Southsea ℰ 826722 –
Continental Ferry Terminal, Mile End ℰ 698111 (summer only).

♦London 78 – ♦Southampton 21.

Plans on following pages

🏨 **Crest** (Crest), Pembroke Rd, PO1 2TA, ℰ 827651, Telex 86397 – 📳 📺 🚼wc ☎ 🅿 🏋️ 📶 AE
ⓞ VISA   BZ **o**
M approx 11.50 **st.** – ☲ 5.75 – **165 rm** 49.50/59.50 **st.** – SB (weekends only) 59.00 **st.**

🏨 **Pendragon** (T.H.F.), Clarence Par., Southsea, PO5 2HY, ℰ 823201, Telex 86376 – 📳 📺
🚼wc ☎ 🅿 🏋️ 📶 AE ⓞ VISA   BZ **c**
M 5.00/8.50 **st.** and a la carte 🍴 2.70 – ☲ 5.50 – **58 rm** 33.50/45.00 **st.**

🏨 **Hospitality Inn** (Mt. Charlotte), South Parade, Southsea, PO4 0RN, ℰ 731281, Telex 86719,
≤ – 📳 📺 🚼wc 🍽 🅿 🏋️ 📶 AE ⓞ VISA   BZ **r**
M 7.00/8.50 **t.** and a la carte 🍴 2.95 – **108 rm** ☲ 39.50/50.00 **t.** – SB (weekends only)
50.00/55.00 **st.**

🏠 **Keppel's Head** (Anchor), 24-26 The Hard, PO1 3DT, ℰ 833231, Group Telex 858875 – 📳 📺
🚼wc ☰wc 🍽 🅿 📶 AE ⓞ VISA   BY **a**
M (carving rest.) 10.00 **t.** – **24 rm** ☲ 41.00/54.00 **t.** – SB (weekends only) 52.00 **st.**

🏠 **Goodwood House,** 1 Taswell Rd, Southsea, PO5 2RG, ℰ 824734 – ☰. ⊛   BZ **e**
closed 24 December-1 January – **8 rm** ☲ 11.00/22.50 **st.**

✕ **Le Talisman,** 123 High St., Old Portsmouth, PO1 2HW, ℰ 811303 – 📶 ⓞ VISA   BZ **v**
closed Saturday lunch, Sunday, Monday and 25-26 December – **M** a la carte 11.00/16.00 **t.**

✕ **Bistro Montparnasse,** 103 Palmerston Rd, Southsea, PO5 3PS, ℰ 816754 – 📶 AE ⓞ VISA
closed Sunday, 25-26 December, first week January and Bank Holidays – **M** (dinner only) a la
carte 9.75/14.80 **t.** 🍴 4.60.   BZ **a**

at Cosham N : 3 ¾ m. by A 3, M 275, M27 and A 27 – ✉ Portsmouth – ⊛ 0705 Cosham :

🏨 Holiday Inn, North Harbour, PO6 4SH, ℰ 383151, Telex 86611, ≤, 🏊 – 📳 📺 ♨ ⅙ 🅿 🏋️
170 rm.   AY **a**

AUSTIN-ROVER-DAIMLER-JAGUAR   Granada Rd,
Southsea ℰ 735311
AUSTIN-ROVER   Hambledon Rd ℰ 070 14 (Water-
looville) 2641
FIAT   117 Copnor Rd ℰ 691621
FORD   Southampton Rd ℰ 370944

NISSAN   135/153 Fratton Rd ℰ 827551
RENAULT   128 Milton Rd ℰ 815151
TALBOT   Grove Rd South, Southsea ℰ 823261
TOYOTA   Gamble Rd ℰ 660734
VAUXHALL-OPEL   London Rd, Hilsea ℰ 661321
VW, AUDI   41/53 Highland Rd ℰ 815111

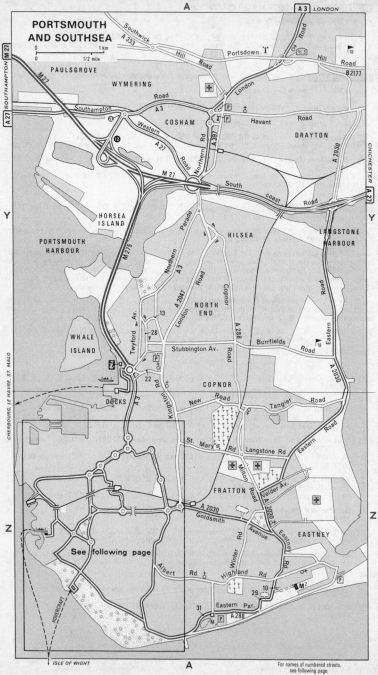

PORTSMOUTH AND SOUTHSEA

0 ____ 1 km
0 ____ 1/2 mile

For names of numbered streets,
see following page.

PORTSMOUTH AND SOUTHSEA

Arundel Street . . . . **BY**
Charlotte Street . . . . **BY** 9
Commercial Road . . . . **BY**
Palmerston Road . . . . **BZ**
Tricorn Centre . . . . **BY**

Alec Rose Lane . . . . **BY** 2
Alfred Road . . . . **BY** 5

Anglesea Road . . . . **BY** 6
Bellevue Terrace . . . . **BZ** 7
Bradford Road . . . . **BY** 8
Cromwell Road . . . . **AZ** 10
Edinburgh Road . . . . **BY** 12
Gladys Avenue . . . . **AY** 13
Gordon Road . . . . **BZ** 14
Grove Road South . . . . **BZ** 15
Guildhall Walk . . . . **BY** 16
Gunwharf Road . . . . **BY** 17
Hampshire Terrace . . . . **BY** 18
Hard (The) . . . . **BY** 19

Isambard Brunel Road . . . . . **BY** 20
King's Terrace . . . . **BZ** 21
Kingston Crescent . . . . **AY** 22
Landport Terrace . . . . **BZ** 23
Lennox Road South . . . . **BZ** 24
Ordnance Row . . . . **BY** 26
Stamshaw Road . . . . **AY** 28
St. George's Road . . . . **AZ** 29
St. Helen's Parade . . . . **AZ** 31
St. Michael's Road . . . . **BY** 33
Southsea Terrace . . . . **BZ** 36
Stanhope Road . . . . **BY** 37

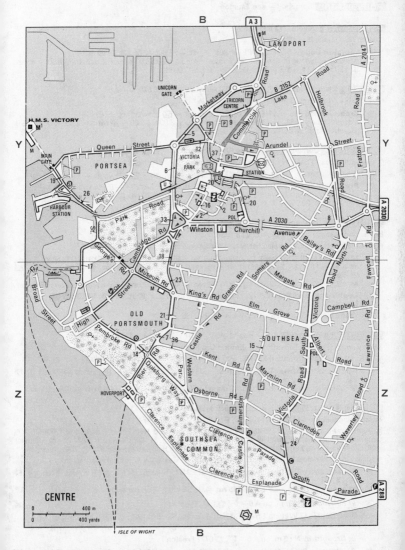

Town plans: roads most used by traffic and those on which guide listed hotels and restaurants stand are fully drawn ; the beginning only of lesser roads is indicated.

PORT TALBOT West.Glam. 408 I 29 – pop. 40 ,078 – ECD : Thursday – ☎ 0639.

♦London 187 – ♦Cardiff 32 – ♦Swansea 9.

  🏨 **Twelve Knights** (Ladbroke), Margam Rd, SA13 1DB, SE : 2 m. on A 48 ♟ 882381 – 📺
    ⌷wc 📶 🅿. 🖭 AE ⓪ *VISA*
    closed 24 to 27 December – **M** a la carte 4.65/8.75 **t.** ▮ 2.00 – **11 rm** � 26.00/42.00 **t.** – SB
    (weekends only) 36.20/50.90 **t.**

POUND HILL West Sussex – see Crawley.

POUNDISFORD Somerset – see Taunton.

POUNDSGATE Devon – ☎ 036 43.

♦London 225 – Exeter 29 – ♦Plymouth 29.

  🏯 **Leusdon Lodge** ⤸, TQ13 7PE, ♟ 304, ≤, 🐎 – ⌷wc ₺ 🅿. 🖭 AE ⓪ *VISA*
    booking essential in winter – **M** *(closed Monday)* 5.00/8.50 **t.** and a la carte ▮ 3.00 – **8 rm**
    ⊡ 11.75/30.40 **t.** – SB (Easter-October) 33.50/41.00 **st.**

POWBURN Northumb. 401 402 O 17 – ✉ Alnwick – ☎ 066 578.

♦London 312 – ♦Edinburgh 73 – ♦Newcastle-upon-Tyne 36.

  🏨 **Breamish House** ⤸, NE66 4LL, ♟ 266, ≤, 🐎 – 📺 ⌷wc 📶wc 📶 🅿. 🛥
    closed January – **M** (lunch by arrangement) 8.00/13.00 **t.** ▮ 3.00 – **10 rm** ⊡ 22.00/45.00 **t.** – SB
    (October-April) 58.00/62.00 **st.**

PRAA SANDS Cornwall 408 D 33 The West Country G. – ✉ ☎ 0736 Penzance.

🏮 Germoe Cross ♟ 3445, N : 1 m. on A 394 – ♦London 321 – Penzance 8 – Truro 24.

  🏨 Lesceave Cliff ⤸, TR20 9TX, ♟ 2325, ≤ Mounts Bay, 🐎 – 📺 ⌷wc 🅿 – **26 rm**.

  🏠 **Prah Sands**, Chy-an-Dour Rd, TR20 9SY, ♟ 762438, ≤, 🐎, 🎾 – 📺 ⌷wc 🅿. 🖭
    closed December and January – **M** 5.50/7.75 **t.** ▮ 2.50 – **20 rm** ⊡ 10.00/19.50 **t.** – SB (except
    July-August) 30.00/49.00 **st.**

PRESTBURY Cheshire 402 403 404 N 24 – pop. 2 ,970 – ☎ 0625.

Envir. : Adlington Hall★ (15 C) *AC*, N : 3 ½ m.

♦London 184 – ♦Liverpool 43 – ♦Manchester 17 – ♦Stoke-on-Trent 25.

  🏰 **Mottram Hall** (De Vere) ⤸, Wilmslow Rd, Mottram St. Andrew, SK10 4QT, NW : 2 ¼ m.
    on A 538 ♟ 828135, Telex 668181, ≤, « Part 18C mansion in park », 🐎, 🎾 – 📺 🕿 🅿. ⛾. 🖭
    AE ⓪ *VISA*
    M 7.50/12.50 **st.** and a la carte ▮ 3.50 – **72 rm** ⊡ 48.50/60.00 **st.** – SB (weekends only) 65.00 **st.**

  XXX **Legh Arms and Black Boy**, The Village, SK10 4DG, ♟ 829130 – 🅿. 🖭 AE ⓪ *VISA*
    M 6.50/10.50 **t.** and a la carte ▮ 3.50.

  XX White House, The Village, SK10 4DG, ♟ 829376.

PRESTEIGNE Powys 408 K 27 – pop. 1 ,490 – ECD : Thursday – ☎ 0544.

See : Church (Flemish Tapestry★) – **Envir. :** Old Radnor (church★) SW : 7 ½ m.

🏮 at Kington ♟ 0544 (Kington) 230340, S : 7 m. – ♦London 159 – Llandrindod Wells 20 – Shrewsbury 39.

  🏨 **Radnorshire Arms** (T.H.F.), High St., LD8 2BE, ♟ 267406, 🐎 – 📺 ⌷wc 📶 🅿. 🖭 AE ⓪
    VISA
    M (bar lunch Monday to Saturday)/dinner 8.50 **st.** ▮ 2.70 – ⊡ 5.00 – **16 rm** 34.50/43.00 **st.**

PRESTON Lancs. 402 L 22 – pop. 166 ,675 – ECD : Thursday – ☎ 0772.

Envir. : Samlesbury Old Hall★ (14C) *AC*, E : 2 ½ m.

🏮 Ashton and Lea, Lea ♟ 726480, W : 3 m. – 🏮 Fulwood Hall Lane, Fulwood ♟ 700011 – 🏮
Longridge, Fell Barn, Jeffrey Hill ♟ 077 478 (Longridge) 3291, NE : 8 m. off B 6243 – 🏮 Fishwick
Hall, Glenluce Drive, Farrington Park ♟ 798300 – 🖼 Town Hall, Lancaster Rd ♟ 53731/54881 ext 6103.

♦London 226 – ♦Blackpool 18 – Burnley 22 – ♦Liverpool 30 – ♦Manchester 34 – ♦Stoke-on-Trent 65.

  🏨 **Crest** (Crest), The Ring Way, PR1 3AU, ♟ 59411, Telex 677147 – 🔊 📺 ⌷wc 📶 🅿. ⛾. 🖭
    AE ⓪ *VISA*
    M approx 11.50 **st.** – ⊡ 5.75 – **126 rm** 44.00/54.00 **st.** – SB (weekends only) 51.00 **st.**

  at Fulwood N : 1½ m. on A 6 – ✉ ☎ 0772 Preston :

  ↑ **Briarfield**, 147 Watling Street Rd., off Garstang Rd, PR2 4AE, ♟ 700917 – 📶wc 🅿. 🛥
    closed 24 December-1 January – **9 rm** ⊡ 12.65/30.55 **t.**

  at Broughton N : 3 m. on A 6 – ✉ ☎ 0772 Preston :

  🏨 **Broughton Park**, 418 Garstang Rd, PR3 5JB, ♟ 864087, Group Telex 67180, 🔲, 🐎 – 📺
    ⌷wc 📶wc 🕿 ₺ 🅿. ⛾. 🖭 AE ⓪ *VISA*
    M *(closed Saturday lunch)* 5.60/9.85 **t.** and a la carte ▮ 3.25 – **63 rm** ⊡ 33.00/43.00 **t.** – SB
    (weekends only) 49.50 **st.**

at Samlesbury E : 2 ½ m. at junction M 6 and A 59 – ⊠ Preston – ✪ 077 477 Samlesbury :

🏨 **Trafalgar,** Preston New Rd, PR5 0UL, E : 1 m. at junction A 59 and A 677 ✆ 351, Telex 677362, 🔲, squash – 🛎 📺 🚻wc 🛁wc 🍴 ⓟ 🎿 🔼 AE ⓞ VISA ✀
M a la carte 5.80/9.75 t. 🍷 2.85 – 🍽 4.00 – **80 rm** 36.00/48.00 t. – SB (weekends only) 45.00/60.00 st.

🏨 **Tickled Trout,** Preston New Rd, PR5 0UJ, ✆ 671, Telex 677625, ≼, 🔲, – 📺 🚻wc ☎ ⓟ. 🎿 🔼 AE VISA
M *(closed Christmas Night)* a la carte approx. 10.50 **st.** 🍷 3.95 – **66 rm** 🍽 39.00/48.00 **st.** – SB (weekends only) 60.00 **st.**

at Bamber Bridge S : 5 m. on A 6 – ⊠ ✪ 0772 Preston

🏨 **Novotel,** Reedfield Place, Walton Summit, PR5 6AB, SE : ¾ m. by A6 at junction with M6 ✆ 313331, Telex 677164, 🔲 heated, 🎿 – 🛎 📺 🚻wc ☎ & ⓟ. 🎿 🔼 AE ⓞ VISA
M 8.50 **st.** and a la carte 🍷 3.30 – 🍽 4.50 – **100 rm** 40.00/94.00 **st.**

MICHELIN Branch, Unit 20, Roman Way, Longridge Rd, Ribbleton, PR2 5BB, ✆ 651411

BMW Blackpool Rd, Ashton ✆ 724391
CITROEN Garstang Rd ✆ 718852
COLT Grimsargh Rd ✆ 652323
FIAT 306/310 Ribbleton Lane ✆ 792823
FORD Penwortham ✆ 744471
FORD Marsh Lane ✆ 54083
HONDA Corporation St. ✆ 58862
LADA Watling Street Rd ✆ 717262
NISSAN Manchester Rd ✆ 704704

NISSAN Chorley Rd ✆ 53911
RELIANT Blackpool Rd ✆ 726066
SKODA New Hall Lane ✆ 794491
TALBOT Blackpool Rd ✆ 735811
TOYOTA 350 Blackpool Rd ✆ 719841
VAUXHALL Blackpool Rd ✆ 793054
VOLVO Strand Rd ✆ 50501
VW, AUDI ✆ 702288

PRIORS HARDWICK Warw. 403 404 Q 27 – pop. 167 – ⊠ Rugby – ✪ 0327 Byfield.
♦London 94 – ♦Coventry 17 – Northampton 26 – Warwick 15.

XXX **Butchers Arms,** CV23 8SN, ✆ 60504, English rest., 🎿 – ⓟ
closed Saturday lunch, Sunday dinner and New Year – **M** 7.50 t. (lunch) and a la carte 10.25/14.00 **s.** 🍷 2.60.

PUDDINGTON Cheshire 402 403 K 24 – pop. 318 – ⊠ South Wirral – ✪ 051 Liverpool.
♦London 204 – Birkenhead 12 – Chester 8.

XXX **Craxton Wood** 🦌 with rm, Parkgate Rd, L66 9PB, on A 540 ✆ 339 4717, « ≼ picturesque grounds and gardens », park – 📺 🚻wc ☎ & ⓟ. 🔼 AE ⓞ VISA ✀
closed last 2 weeks August – **M** *(closed Sunday and Bank Holidays)* 14.15 **s.** and a la carte 🍷 4.00 – **14 rm** 🍽 20.50/45.00 **s.**, **1 suite** 47.50/59.50 **s.**.

PULBOROUGH West Sussex 404 S 31 – pop. 3,197 – ECD : Wednesday – ✪ 079 82.
Envir. : Hardham (church : wall paintings* 12C) S : 1 m.
♦London 49 – ♦Brighton 25 – Guildford 25 – ♦Portsmouth 35.

🏨 **Chequers,** Church Pl., RH20 1AD, NE : ¼ m. on A 29 ✆ 2486, 🎿 – 🚻wc ⓟ. 🔼 AE ⓞ VISA
M (bar lunch Monday to Saturday)/dinner 8.50 **st.** 🍷 2.50 – **9 rm** 🍽 22.50/35.00 **st.** – SB (except Christmas) 44.00/46.50 **st.**

XX **Stane Street Hollow,** Codmore Hill, RH20 1BG, NE : 1 m. on A 29 ✆ 2819 – ⓟ
closed Tuesday and Saturday lunch, Sunday, Monday, 2 weeks May, 3 weeks October and 24 December-5 January – **M** (booking essential) 4.55 t. (lunch) and a la carte 10.45/12.75 t. 🍷 3.50.

AUSTIN-ROVER London Rd ✆ 2407   HONDA London Rd ✆ 079 881 (Bury) 691

PUTSBOROUGH Devon 403 H 30 – ⊠ Braunton – ✪ 0271 Croyde.
♦London 233 – Barnstaple 14 – Exeter 51 – Ilfracombe 9.

🏨 **Putsborough Sands,** EX33 1LB, ✆ 890555, ≼, 🔲, squash – 🚻wc ⓟ. 🔼 AE VISA
April-September – **M** (bar lunch)/dinner 9.50 t. 🍷 2.80 – **54 rm** 🍽 14.00/52.00 t. – SB (April-mid July and September) 42.00/60.00 **st.**

QUORN Leics. – see Loughborough.

RADLETT Herts. 404 T 28 – pop. 7,749 – ECD : Wednesday – ✪ 092 76.
🏌 at Aldenham, Radlett Rd ✆ 7775, SW : 3 m. BU – ♦London 21 – Luton 15.

Plan : see Greater London (North-West)

🏨 Red Lion, Watling St., WD7 7NP, ✆ 5341 – 📺 🚻wc 📞 ⓟ – **17 rm**.   BU **c**

AUSTIN-ROVER 411 Watling St. ✆ 5681   FORD 203/205 Watling St. ✆ 4851
BMW 74/76 Watling St. ✆ 4802

RAMSBOTTOM Greater Manchester 402 N 23 – pop. 16,334 – ✪ 070 682.
♦London 223 – ♦Blackpool 39 – Burnley 12 – ♦Leeds 46 – ♦Manchester 13 – ♦Liverpool 39.

🏨 **Old Mill,** Springwood St., off Carr St., BL0 9DS, ✆ 2991 – 📺 🚻wc ☎ ⓟ. 🎿. 🔼 AE ⓞ VISA ✀
M 5.50/12.50 t. and a la carte 🍷 3.30 – **17 rm** 🍽 31.50/47.50 **st.** – SB (weekends only) 68.00 **st.**

RAMSBURY Wilts. 408 404 P 29 – pop. 1,557 – ECD : Wednesday and Saturday – ⊠ ✆ 0672 Marlborough.

♦London 79 – ♦Southampton 51 – Swindon 13.

⁂⁂ **Bell,** The Square, SN8 2PE, ✆ 20230, 🍽 – ℗. 🔲 AE ⓪ VISA
M 11.50 t. ⓘ 2.25.

RAMSGATE Kent 404 Y 30 – pop. 36,678 – ECD : Thursday – ✆ 0843 Thanet.

See : St. Augustine's Abbey Church (interior★).

Envir. : Minster-in-Thanet (abbey : remains★ 7C-12C) W : 4 ½ m. – Birchington-on-Sea : in Quex Park (Powell-Cotton Museum★ of African and Asian natural history and ethnology, *AC*), NW : 9 m.

🚢 Shipping connections with the Continent : to France (Dunkerque) (Sally Line).

🖥 Argyle Centre, Queen St. ✆ 591086.

♦London 77 – ♦Dover 19 – Maidstone 45 – Margate 4.5.

🏨 **Savoy,** 43 Grange Rd, CT11 9NO, ✆ 592637 – 📺 ⌷wc ▥wc ☎ ℗. 🔲 AE ⓪ VISA
closed February – **M** (closed Sunday in winter) 6.00 **st.** (lunch) and a la carte 4.70/13.00 **st.** ⓘ 2.60 – **25 rm** ⊊ 14.00/30.00 **st.**

🏠 **Abbeygail,** 17 Penshurst Rd, East Cliff, CT11 8EG, ✆ 594154 – 🍽
closed Christmas – **11 rm** ⊊ 8.50/17.00 **st.**

at Minster-in-Thanet W : 5 ½ m. by A 253 on B 2048 – ⊠ ✆ 0843 Thanet :

⁂⁂ **Old Oak Cottage,** 53 High St., CT12 4BT, ✆ 821229 – ℗. 🔲 AE ⓪ VISA
closed Sunday – **M** (dinner only) a la carte 12.00/15.75 **st.**

AUSTIN-ROVER Grange Rd ✆ 583541
FORD Boundary Rd ✆ 53784
RENAULT Margate Rd ✆ 52629

VAUXHALL West Cliff Rd ✆ 53877
VW, AUDI St. Lawrence ✆ 52333

RANGEWORTHY Avon 408 M 29 – pop. 325 – ⊠ Bristol – ✆ 045 422 Rangeworthy.

♦London 122 – ♦Bristol 13 – Gloucester 30 – Swindon 39.

🏨 **Rangeworthy Court** 🍸, BS17 5ND, ✆ 347, « Part 15C manor house », ⬛ heated, 🍽 – ▥wc ℗. VISA
closed 23 December-7 January – **M** (closed Sunday) (lunch by arrangement residents only) 10.25 **t.** dinner and a la carte ⓘ 1.35 – **15 rm** ⊊ 19.70/33.00 **t.** – SB (weekends only) 38.00/42.00 **st.**

AUSTIN-ROVER Hatters Lane, Chipping Sodbury ✆ 313181

BEDFORD, VAUXHALL-OPEL West End Garage, Chipping Sodbury ✆ 318311

RASKELF North Yorks. – pop. 338 – ⊠ York – ✆ 0347 Easingwold.

♦London 199 – ♦Middlesbrough 36 – York 15.

🏨 **Old Farmhouse,** YO6 3LF, ✆ 21971 – ⌷wc ▥wc ℗
closed 15 December-January – **M** (dinner only residents only) 7.00 **st.** ⓘ 2.00 – **10 rm** ⊊ 17.00/28.00 **st.** – SB (February-March and November-mid December) 34.00/42.00 **st.**

RAVENSTONEDALE Cumbria 402 M 20 – pop. 501 – ECD : Thursday – ⊠ Kirkby Stephen – ✆ 058 73 Newbiggin-on-Lune.

♦London 280 – ♦Carlisle 43 – Kendal 19 – Kirkby Stephen 5.

🏨 **Black Swan** 🍸, CA17 4NG, ✆ 204, 🍽 – ⌷wc ℗. AE VISA
closed January and February – **M** (closed Sunday dinner) (bar lunch Monday to Saturday)/dinner 11.25 **st.** and a la carte ⓘ 2.85 – **6 rm** ⊊ 20.00/36.00 **st.** – SB (weekends only) (October-May) 42.00 **st.**

🍴 **Fat Lamb,** Fell End, CA17 4LL, SE : 1 ¾ m. on A 683 ✆ 242 – ⌷wc ♿ ℗
M 8.00 **t.** and a la carte ⓘ 2.10 – **9 rm** ⊊ 16.00/33.00 **t.** – SB 43.00/46.00 **st.**

READING Berks. 408 404 Q 29 – pop. 194,727 – ✆ 0734.

Envir. : Stratfield Saye Park★ *AC*, S : 7 m. by A 33 X – Mapledurham House★ *AC*, NW : 3 ½ m. by A 329 X.

🟩 Kidmore End Rd, Emmer Green ✆ 472909 NE : 4 ½ m. by Peppard Road X – 🟩 Bearwood, Mole Rd, Sindlesham ✆ 760060 by A329 X.

🖥 Civic Offices, Civic Centre ✆ 55911 and 592388.

♦London 43 – ♦Brighton 79 – ♦Bristol 78 – Croydon 47 – Luton 62 – ♦Oxford 28 – ♦Portsmouth 67 – ♦Southampton 46.

Plans opposite

🏨 **Ramada,** Oxford Rd, RG1 7RH, ✆ 586222, Telex 847785, 🔲 – 🛗 🍽 📺 ☎ ♿ ℗. 🔲 AE ⓪ VISA
Z i
M 8.25 **st.** (lunch) and a la carte ⓘ 3.25 – ⊊ 5.25 – **200 rm** 59.50/66.50 **st.**, **1 suite** 130.00 **st.** – SB (weekends only) 56.00/60.00 **st.**

🏨 **Post House** (T.H.F.), Basingstoke Rd, RG2 0SL, S : 2 ½ m. on A 33 ✆ 875485, Telex 849160, 🔲 – 📺 ⌷wc ☎ ♿ ℗. 🔲 AE ⓪ VISA
X a
M 8.50 **st.** and a la carte ⓘ 2.70 – ⊊ 5.50 – **143 rm** 47.50/55.00 **st.**

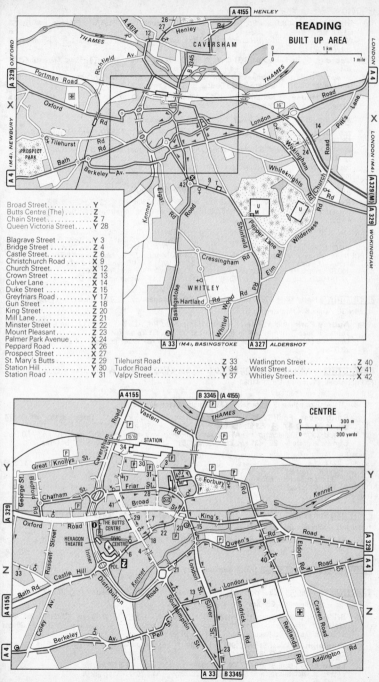

Broad Street............ Y
Butts Centre (The)...... Z
Chain Street........... Z 7
Queen Victoria Street.. Y 28

Blagrave Street .... Y 3
Bridge Street .... Z 4
Castle Street .... Z 6
Christchurch Road .... X 9
Church Street .... X 12
Crown Street .... Z 13
Culver Lane .... X 14
Duke Street .... Z 15
Greyfriars Road .... Y 17
Gun Street .... Z 18
King Street .... Z 20
Mill Lane .... Z 21
Minster Street .... Z 22
Mount Pleasant .... Z 23
Palmer Park Avenue ..... X 24
Peppard Road .... X 26
Prospect Street .... X 27
St. Mary's Butts .... Z 29
Station Hill .... Y 30
Station Road .... Y 31

Tilehurst Road .... Z 33
Tudor Road .... Y 34
Valpy Street................. Y 37

Watlington Street .... Z 40
West Street .... Y 41
Whitley Street................. X 42

🏨 **Ship** (Anchor), 4-8 Duke St., RG1 4RY, ✆ 583455, Group Telex 858875 – 📺 🚿wc ☎ 🅿 🖨
🔼 🖂 ⑩ 💳 Z e
M *(closed Saturday lunch)* (carving rest.) 8.85 t. 🍷 3.00 – **32 rm** 🛏 27.00/51.00 t. – SB (weekends only) 52.00 **st.**

🏨 **Upcross,** 68 Berkeley Av., RG1 6HY, ✆ 590796, Telex 849021, 🌳 – 📺 🚿wc 🛎wc 🅿 🔼 🖂
💳 Z c
closed 10 days at Christmas and New Year – **M** *(closed Friday, Saturday and Sunday dinner)* (bar lunch)/dinner a la carte 6.35/9.00 **st.** 🍷 2.75 – **29 rm** 🛏 20.00/40.00 **st.**

🔼 **Private House,** 98 Kendrick Rd, RG1 5DW, ✆ 874142 – 🅿. 🚫 X x
closed Christmas – **7 rm** 🛏 13.00/20.50 **st.**

at Shinfield S : 4 ¼ m. on A 327 – X – 🖂 ✪ 0734 Reading :

XXX ✪✪ **Chez Nico** The Old Vicarage, Church Lane, RG2 9BY, ✆ 883783, French rest., 🌳 – 🅿.
🔼 🖂 ⑩ 💳
closed Monday lunch, Sunday Easter, 3 weeks July-August and 10 days at Christmas – **M**
19.50/24.50 **st.** and a la carte
Spec. Foie gras frais au gelée sauternes et sa petite salade, Tourte de cailles au fumet de Truffes, Gratin de fruits rouges à la crème vanille.

at Burghfield SW : 5 m. by A 4 – X – 🖂 ✪ 0734 Reading :

XX **Knight's Farm,** Berrys Lane, RG3 3XE, NE : 2 m. ✆ 52366, 🌳 – 🅿. 🔼 🖂 ⑩ 💳
closed Sunday, 3 weeks August-September and 1 week at Christmas – **M** (booking essential)
14.50/17.50 **t.** 🍷 3.25.

AUSTIN-ROVER-DAIMLER-JAGUAR 38 Portman Rd
✆ 585011
BMW 209/211 Shinfield Rd ✆ 871620
CITROEN 44 George St. ✆ 586425
FIAT Eaton Pl., Chatham St. ✆ 582521
FORD 160 Basingstoke Rd ✆ 875333
PEUGEOT-TALBOT Christchurch Rd ✆ 875242

RENAULT Chatham St. ✆ 583322
RENAULT Wokingham Rd ✆ 669456
TOYOTA 569/575 Basingstoke Rd ✆ 871278
VAUXHALL-OPEL Vastern Rd ✆ 55501
VOLVO 406/412 London Rd ✆ 67321
VW, AUDI Erleigh Rd ✆ 666111
VW, AUDI Oxford Rd ✆ 418181

REDBOURN Herts. 404 S 28 – pop. 5 ,114 – ECD : Wednesday – 🖂 St. Albans – ✪ 058 285.
♦London 31 – Luton 6 – Northampton 42.

🏨 **Aubrey Park** (Best Western), Hemel Hempstead Rd, AL3 7AF, SW : 1 m. on B 487 ✆ 2105,
Telex 825562, 🔺 heated, 🌳 – 📺 🚿wc 🕿 🅿 🍴 🔼 🖂 ⑩ 💳
M 6.50/9.50 **st.** and a la carte 🍷 2.75 – 🛏 5.00 – **80 rm** 39.50/55.00 **st.** – SB (weekends only)
70.00 **st.**

REDDITCH Heref. and Worc. 403 404 O 27 – pop. 61 ,639 – ECD : Wednesday – ✪ 0527.
🏬 Pitcheroak, Plymouth Rd ✆ 41054.
🇮 9-11 Royal Square ✆ 60806.
♦London 111 – ♦Birmingham 15 – Cheltenham 33 – Stratford-upon-Avon 15.

🏨 **Southcrest,** Pool Bank, Southcrest District, B97 4JG, ✆ 41511, Telex 338455, 🌳 – 📺
🚿wc 🛎wc ☎ 🅿 🍴 🔼 🖂 ⑩ 💳
closed 25 to 30 December – **M** *(closed Sunday dinner and Bank Holiday Mondays)* 7.50/9.00
t. and a la carte 🍷 3.25 – **31 rm** 🛏 35.00/45.00 **t.** – SB (weekends only) 50.00/54.00 **st.**

AUSTIN-ROVER Alcester Rd, Studley ✆ 052 785
(Studley) 2297
AUSTIN-ROVER Washford Drive ✆ 25055
CITROEN Birmingham Rd ✆ 63636
PEUGEOT-TALBOT Alcester Rd, Beoley ✆ 056 44
(Tamworth) 2553

FORD Battens Drive ✆ 21212
SKODA 1124 Evesham Rd ✆ 052 789 (Astwood Bank)
2433
VW, AUDI Clive Rd ✆ 69111
VW, AUDI 530 Evesham Rd, Crabe Cross ✆ 44554

REDHILL Surrey 404 T 30 – pop. 48 ,241 (inc. Reigate) – ECD : Wednesday – ✪ 0737.
♦London 22 – ♦Brighton 31 – Guildford 20 – Maidstone 34.

🔼 **Ashleigh House,** 39 Redstone Hill, RH1 4BG, ✆ 64763, 🔺 heated, 🌳 – 🕌 🅿. 🚫
closed Christmas – **9 rm** 🛏 15.50/28.30 **st.**

REDLYNCH Wilts. 403 404 O 31 – see Salisbury.

REIGATE Surrey 404 T 30 – pop. 48 ,241 (inc. Redhill) – ECD : Wednesday – ✪ 073 72.
♦London 26 – ♦Brighton 33 – Guildford 20 – Maidstone 38.

🏨 **Bridge House,** Reigate Hill, RH2 9RP, ✆ 46801, ≤ – 📺 🚿wc ☎ 🅿. 🍴 🔼 🖂 ⑩ 💳 🚫
closed 25-26 December and 1 January – **M** 8.85/14.50 **t.** and a la carte – 🛏 3.75 – **30 rm**
38.50/49.50 **st.** – SB (weekends only) 65.40/97.90 **st.**

🔼 **Cranleigh,** 41 West St., RH2 9BL, ✆ 40600, 🔺 heated, 🌳 – 📺 🚿wc 🅿. 🔼 🖂 ⑩ 💳 🚫
🛏 2.00 – **10 rm** 19.00/38.00 **st.**

X **La Barbe,** 71 Bell St., RH2 7AN, ✆ 41966, French Bistro – 🔼 🖂 ⑩ 💳
closed lunch Monday and Saturday and Sunday – **M** 9.50/17.00 **st.** 🍷 2.95.

RENISHAW Derbs. 402 403 404 P 24 – pop. 1,809 – ✉ Sheffield (South Yorks.) – ✿ 0246 Eckington.

♦London 157 – Derby 33 – ♦Nottingham 31 – ♦Sheffield 8.

🏛 **Sitwell**, Station Rd, S31 9WE, ℰ 435226, Telex 547303 – 📺 ☎ 🅿. 🏧. 🔼 AE ⓞ 𝘝𝘐𝘚𝘈
closed Christmas Night – **M** (bar lunch Saturday)/dinner 9.50 **t.** and a la carte ≬ 3.50 – 🍷 3.95
– **31 rm** 25.50/45.00 **t.**, **1 suite** 45.00/55.00 **t.** – SB (weekends only) (April-September) 49.00/86.80 **st.**

RHAEADR = Rhayader.

RHAYADER (RHAEADR) Powys 403 J 27 – pop. 1,672 – ECD : Thursday – ✿ 0597.
🇮 The Old Swan, West St. ℰ 810591 (summer only).

♦London 179 – Aberystwyth 34 – Carmarthen 75 – Shrewsbury 62.

🏠 **Elan Valley** ⅏, LD6 5HN, SW : 2 ½ m. on B 4518 ℰ 810448, ≤, ➷ – ➘wc 🅿. AE
closed Christmas – **M** 6.00/7.00 **t.** – **11 rm** 🍷 18.00/32.00 **t.** – SB (winter only) 35.00/43.00 **st.**

RHOSMAEN Dyfed 403 I 28 – see Llandeilo.

RHOS-ON-SEA (LLANDRILLO-YN-RHOS) Clwyd 402 403 I 24 – see Colwyn Bay.

RHUTHUN = Ruthin.

RHYDAMAN = Ammanford.

RHYDGALED (CHANCERY) Clwyd 403 H 26 – see Aberystwyth (Dyfed).

RHYDYCROESAU Salop – see Oswestry.

RICHMOND North Yorks. 402 O 20 – pop. 7,596 – ECD : Wednesday – ✿ 0748.
See : Castle★ (Norman ruins) *AC*.

Envir. : Bolton Castle★ (15C) *AC*, ≤★, SW : 13 m.

🛇 Bend Hagg ℰ 2457 – 🛇 Catterick Garrison, Leyburn Rd ℰ 0748 (Richmond) 833268, S : 3 m.
🇮 Friary Gardens, Queens Rd ℰ 3525 (summer only).

♦London 243 – ♦Leeds 53 – ♦Middlesbrough 26 – ♦Newcastle-upon-Tyne 44.

🏠 **Frenchgate**, 59-61 Frenchgate, DL10 7AE, ℰ 2087, 🌫 – 📺 ➘wc 🏱wc 🕾 🅿. 🔼 AE 𝘝𝘐𝘚𝘈
closed mid December-mid February – **M** (bar lunch)/dinner 8.00 **st.** and a la carte ≬ 2.40 –
12 rm 🍷 19.50/36.50 **t.** – SB (October-May) 42.00/44.00 **t.**

AUSTIN-ROVER Victoria Rd ℰ 2539   CITROEN Darlington Rd ℰ 3014

RINGWOOD Hants. 403 404 O 31 – pop. 10,941 – ECD : Monday and Thursday – ✿ 042 54.
🛇 Ringwood ℰ 042 53 (Burley) 2431, NE : 4 m.

♦London 102 – Bournemouth 11 – Salisbury 17 – ♦Southampton 20.

🏩 **Little Moortown House,** 244 Christchurch Rd, BH24 3AS, ℰ 3325 – 📺 🏱wc 🅿. 🔼 𝘝𝘐𝘚𝘈
M (dinner only) 48.50 **t.** ≬ 2.80 – **6 rm** 🍷 18.00/36.00 **st.**

at Ibsley N : 2 ½ m. on A 338 – ✉ ✿ 042 54 Ringwood :

✗ **Old Beams,** Salisbury Rd, BH24 1AS, ℰ 3387, « 14C thatched cottage » – 🅿. 🔼 AE 𝘝𝘐𝘚𝘈
M 5.95 **st.** (lunch)and a la carte 7.50/11.45 **st.** ≬ 2.00.

at Avon S : 4 m. on B 3347 – ✉ Christchurch – ✿ 0425 Bransgore :

🏠 **Tyrrells Ford** ⅏, BH23 7BH, ℰ 72646, 🌫, park – ≋🚽 📺 ➘wc 🏱wc 🅿. 🔼 AE ⓞ 𝘝𝘐𝘚𝘈. ❄
M (bar lunch Monday to Saturday)/dinner 10.95 **t.** and a la carte ≬ 2.70 – **13 rm** 🍷 25.00/55.00 **t.**
– SB (except Bank Holidays) 60.00/70.00 **st.**

FIAT Salisbury Rd ℰ 6111

RIPLEY Surrey 404 S 30 – pop. 1,903 – ECD : Wednesday – ✿ 0483 Guildford.
♦London 28 – Guildford 6.

✗✗✗ **Clock House,** 13 Portsmouth Rd, GU23 6AQ, ℰ 224777, 🌫 – 🔼 AE ⓞ 𝘝𝘐𝘚𝘈
closed Sunday dinner and Monday – **M** 7.50/19.60 **t.** and a la carte ≬ 2.90.

RIPON North Yorks. 402 P 21 – pop. 13,036 – ECD : Wednesday – ✿ 0765.
See : Cathedral★ 12C-15C.

Envir. : Fountains Abbey★★★ (ruins 12C-13C, floodlit in summer) – Studley Royal Gardens★★ and Fountains Hall★ (17C) *AC*, SW : 3 m. – Newby Hall★ (18C) *AC* (the tapestry room★★ and gardens★ *AC*) SE : 3 ½ m.

🛇 Palace Rd ℰ 3640, N : 1 m. on A 6108.
🇮 Wakemans House, Market Pl. ℰ 4625 (summer only).

♦London 222 – ♦Leeds 26 – ♦Middlesbrough 35 – York 23.

🏨 **Ripon Spa** (Best Western), Park St., HG4 2BU, ℰ 2172, Telex 57780, ≼, 🚗 – 🛊 TV ⌷wc
🍴wc ☎ & 🅿 🔄 AE ① VISA
M 8.50/12.00 t. 🛆 2.90 – **41 rm** ⌕ 33.00/58.00 t. – SB (except Christmas and New Year) 50.00/64.00 **st.**

✗ **New Hornblower,** Duck Hill, HG4 1BL, ℰ 4841 – 🔄 VISA
closed Sunday in winter, Monday and February – **M** (dinner only) a la carte 7.60/10.70 **t.** 🛆 3.10.

FIAT, MERCEDES-BENZ, VAUXHALL Kirkby Rd ℰ 4491
FORD North St. ℰ 2324

RENAULT Water Skellgate ℰ 2083
TALBOT Blossom Gate ℰ 4268
VOLVO Palace Rd ℰ 2461

RIPPONDEN West Yorks. 🄌🄍🄋 O 22 – pop. 3,464 – ⊠ 🕲 0422 Halifax.
♦London 210 – Halifax 5 – Huddersfield 9 – ♦Leeds 21.

✗✗ **Over the Bridge,** Millfold, HX6 4LD, at junction of A 58 and B 6113 ℰ 823722 – 🅿 AE VISA
closed Sunday and Bank Holidays – **M** (dinner only)(booking essential) 14.50 **t.**

ROCHDALE Greater Manchester 🄌🄍🄋 🄌🄍🄌 N 23 – pop. 97,292 – ECD : Tuesday – 🕲 0706.
♦London 212 – ♦Blackpool 53 – ♦Leeds 37 – ♦Liverpool 46 – ♦Manchester 13.

🏨 **Broadfield** 📎, Sparrow Hill, OL16 1AF, ℰ 44085 – TV ⌷wc 🍴wc 🅿 🔄 AE VISA
M 5.00/6.60 **t.** and a la carte 🛆 2.80 – **18 rm** ⌕ 30.00/40.00 **t.** – SB (weekends only) 40.00/60.00 **st.**

ROCHESTER Kent 🄌🄍🄌 V 29 – pop. 23,840 – ECD : Wednesday – ⊠ Chatham – 🕲 0634 Medway.

See : Castle*, ⚒** (142 steps) *AC* – Cathedral* (interior**) – Eastgate House* 1590 – Fort Pitt Hill ≼* – Envir. : Cobham Hall (Gilt Hall*) *AC*, W : 4 m.

🔖 Park Pale ℰ 047 482 (Gravesend) 3411, W : on A 2 – 🔃 Eastgate Cottage, Eastgate High St. ℰ 43666.
♦London 30 – ♦Dover 45 – Maidstone 8 – Margate 46.

🏨 **Crest** (Crest), Maidstone Rd, ME5 9SE, SE : 2 ½ m. by A 2 on A 229 ℰ 687111, Telex 965933
– 🛊 🍴 rest TV ⌷wc ☎ & 🅿 🔥 🔄 AE ① VISA
M approx 11.50 **st.** – ⌕ 5.25 – **105 rm** 46.50/56.50 **st.** – SB (weekends only) 59.00 **st.**

AUSTIN-ROVER-JAGUAR 16 Medway St., Chatham ℰ 41122
AUSTIN-ROVER Commercial Rd, Strood ℰ 408451
FIAT, LANCIA Pier Rd, Gillingham ℰ 52333
NISSAN 100 Watling St. ℰ 576741
PEUGEOT, TALBOT High St. ℰ 42231

RELIANT Gundulph Rd, Chatham ℰ 41857
RENAULT Hoath Lane, Wigmore ℰ 31688
TOYOTA High St. ℰ 407788
VAUXHALL Station Rd, Strood ℰ 721021
VOLVO Wood St., Gillingham ℰ 402777
VW, AUDI 1 Ferndale Rd, Gillingham ℰ 572327

ROCHFORD Essex 🄌🄍🄌 W 29 – pop. 13,426 – ECD : Wednesday – ⊠ 🕲 0702 Southend-on-Sea.
♦London 43 – Southend-on-Sea 4.

✗✗ **Renouf's,** 1 South St., SS4 1BL, ℰ 544393 – 🔄 AE ① VISA
closed Saturday lunch, Sunday, Monday, first 3 weeks January and 8 to 22 June – **M** 8.50 **t.** and a la carte 🛆 3.25.

ROCK Cornwall 🄌🄍🄉 F 32 – ECD : Wednesday – ⊠ Wadebridge – 🕲 020 886 Trebetherick.
♦London 288 – Newquay 22 – ♦Plymouth 45 – Truro 30.

🏨 **St. Enodoc** 📎, PL27 6LA, ℰ 2311, ≼, 🚗, squash – TV ⌷wc 🍴wc 🅿 🔄 AE VISA
M (bar lunch Monday to Saturday)/dinner 7.95 **st.** and a la carte 🛆 3.15 – **14 rm** ⌕ 18.50/57.00 **st.** – SB (except summer) 43.00/46.00 **st.**

🏠 **Gleneglos,** Trewint Lane, PL27 6LU, ℰ 2369, 🚗 – ⌷wc 🅿 🔄 VISA. 🍴
closed mid December-mid February – **M** (closed Sunday dinner) (bar lunch Monday to Saturday)/dinner 8.50 **t.** and a la carte 🛆 2.50 – **8 rm** ⌕ 14.00/32.00 **t.** – SB 39.60/44.00 **st.**

RODBOROUGH Glos. – see Stroud.

ROEWEN Gwynedd – see Conwy.

ROLLESTON ON DOVE Staffs. 🄌🄍🄋 🄌🄍🄌 🄌🄍🄌 P 25 – see Burton-upon-Trent.

ROMALDKIRK Durham 🄌🄍🄋 N 20 – see Middleton-in-Teesdale.

ROMSEY Hants. 🄌🄍🄌 🄌🄍🄌 P 31 – pop. 14,818 – ECD : Wednesday – 🕲 0794.
See : Abbey Church* 12C-13C (interior**).

🔖 Dunwood Manor, Shootash Hill ℰ 0794 (Lockerley) 40549, SE : 4 m. on A 27 – 🔖 Ampfield Par
Three ℰ 68480, NE : on A 31 – 🔖 Romsey Rd ℰ 0703 (Southampton) 6673, S : on A 3057.
🔃 Bus Station car park, Broadwater Rd ℰ 512987 (summer only).
♦London 82 – Bournemouth 28 – Salisbury 16 – ♦Southampton 8 – Winchester 10.

🏨 **White Horse** (T.H.F.), Market Pl., SO5 8ZJ, ℰ 512431 – TV ⌷wc 🍴wc ☎ & 🅿 🔄 AE ① VISA
M 5.95/9.35 **st.** and a la carte 🛆 2.70 – ⌕ 5.50 – **33 rm** 38.50/49.50 **st.**

XX **Old Manor House,** 21 Palmerston St., SO5 8HJ, ℰ 517353 – **⊕**. ⟵ AE ⓞ VISA
closed Sunday dinner, Monday and 24 to 30 December – **M** 6.95 **t.** and a la carte ⋀ 2.75.

AUSTIN-ROVER Winchester Rd ℰ 512850 VAUXHALL-OPEL 24 Middlebridge St. ℰ 513806
MAZDA, PEUGEOT 45/55 Winchester Hill ℰ 513185

ROSEDALE ABBEY North Yorks. 四〇二 R 20 – ⊠ Pickering – ✪ 075 15 Lastingham.
♦London 247 – ♦Middlesbrough 27 – Scarborough 25 – York 36.

🏠 **White Horse Farm,** YO18 8SE, ℰ 239, ⪡ – 📺 ⊟wc ⋔wc **⊕**. AE ⓞ
M (bar lunch Monday to Saturday)/dinner 12.00 **st.** and a la carte ⋀ 3.40 – **15 rm**
⊠ 24.50/39.00 **st.** – SB 48.00/50.00 **st.**

🏠 **Milburn Arms,** YO18 8RA, ℰ 312 – 📺 ⊟wc ⋔wc **⊕**. ⟵ AE ⓞ VISA
M (bar lunch)/dinner a la carte 8.55/11.30 **t.** ⋀ 2.00 – **7 rm** ⊠ 23.50/37.50 **t.** – SB (October-Easter) 36.00/43.00 **st.**

ROSSINGTON South Yorks. 四〇二 四〇三 四〇四 Q 23 – see Doncaster.

ROSS-ON-WYE Heref. and Worc. 四〇三 四〇四 M 28 – pop. 8,281 – ECD : Wednesday – ✪ 0989.
Envir. : Goodrich (Castle★ : ruins 12C-14C) *AC*, SW : 3 ½ m. – 🄸 20 Broad St. ℰ 62768.
♦London 118 – Gloucester 15 – Hereford 15 – Newport 35.

🏨 **Chase** (Q.M.H.), Gloucester Rd, HR9 5LH, on A 40 ℰ 63161, ⛲ – 📺 ⊟wc ⋔wc ⊛ **⊕**. ⚒
40 rm.

🏨 **Royal** (T.H.F.), Palace Pound, Royal Par., HR9 5HZ, ℰ 65105, ⪡, ⛲ – 📺 ⊟wc ⊛ **⊕**. ⚒
⟵ AE ⓞ VISA
M 6.25/10.50 **st.** and a la carte – ⊠ 5.50 – **30 rm** 38.50/48.50 **st.**

🏠 **Chasedale,** Walford Rd, HR9 5PQ, ℰ 62423, ⛲ – ⊟wc **⊕**. ⟵ VISA
M a la carte 8.00/10.50 **st.** ⋀ 2.50 – **12 rm** ⊠ 17.00/36.00 **st.** – SB 38.00/49.00 **st.**

at Weston-Under-Penyard E : 2 m. on A 40 – ⊠ ✪ 0989 Ross-on-Wye :

🏠 **Hunsdon Manor,** HR9 7PE, ℰ 62748, ⛲ – 📺 ⊟wc ⋔wc **⊕**. ⟵ AE ⓞ VISA
M (bar lunch Monday to Saturday)/dinner 7.50 **t.** and a la carte – **12 rm** ⊠ 19.00/33.00 **st.** – SB (except Christmas and New Year) 36.00/42.00 **st.**

at Walford S : 2 m. on B 4228 – ⊠ ✪ 0989 Ross-on-Wye :

XX **Walford House** with rm, HR9 5RY, ℰ 63829, ⛲ – 📺 ⊟wc ☎ ⅙ **⊕**. ⟵ AE ⓞ VISA
M 12.50 **st.** (dinner) and a la carte ⋀ 3.50 – **10 rm** ⊠ 30.00/40.00 **st.** – SB 50.00/60.00 **st.**

at Pencraig SW : 3 ¾ m. on A40 – ⊠ Ross-on-Wye – ✪ 098 984 Llangarron

🏠 **Pencraig Court,** HR9 6HR, ℰ 306, ⛲ – ⊟wc **⊕**. ⟵ AE VISA. ⛬
March-October – **M** (bar lunch)/dinner 9.00 **st.** ⋀ 2.60 – **11 rm** ⊠ 18.00/36.00 **st.**

at Goodrich SW : 5 m. by A 40 on B 4229 – ⊠ Ross-on-Wye – ✪ 0600 Symonds Yat :

🏠 **Ye Hostelrie,** HR9 6HX, ℰ 890241, ⛲ – ⋔wc **⊕**
M (bar lunch)/dinner 8.50 **t.** and a la carte ⋀ 2.50 – **7 rm** ⊠ 20.00/36.00 **t.**

at Pengethley NW : 4 m. on A 49 – ⊠ Ross-on-Wye – ✪ 098 987 Harewood End :

🏨 Pengethley (Best Western) ⛬, HR9 6LL, ℰ 211, ⪡, ⟰ heated, ⛲, park – 📺 ⊟wc ⋔wc ⊛
⅙ **⊕** – **20 rm**.

AUSTIN-ROVER Cantilupe Rd ℰ 62400 RENAULT Overross St. ℰ 63666
FORD ℰ 62637 VW, AUDI Whitchurch ℰ 0600 (Monmouth) 890235
PEUGEOT-TALBOT High St. ℰ 62447

ROSTHWAITE Cumbria 四〇二 K 20 – see Keswick.

ROSUDGEON Cornwall – ⊠ ✪ 0736 Penzance.
♦London 321 – Penzance 6 – Truro 24.

X **Trevarrack Cottage,** Helston Rd, TR20 9PA, ℰ 762257 – **⊕**. ⟵ AE ⓞ VISA
closed 2 weeks in February – **M** 5.25 **t.** (lunch) and a la carte 7.00/14.05 **t.** ⋀ 3.15.

ROTHAY BRIDGE Cumbria – see Ambleside.

ROTHBURY Northumb. 四〇一 四〇二 O 18 – pop. 1,694 – ECD : Wednesday – ⊠ Morpeth – ✪ 0669.
♦London 311 – ♦Edinburgh 84 – ♦Newcastle-upon-Tyne 29.

🏠 **Orchard,** High St., NE65 7TL, ℰ 20684, ⛲ – ⛬
6 rm ⊠ 12.50/21.00 **st.**

ROTHERHAM South Yorks. 四〇二 四〇三 四〇四 P 23 – pop. 122,374 – ECD : Thursday – ✪ 0709.
🄸 Thrybergh Park ℰ 850480, E : 3 m. – 🄸 Sitwell Park, Shrogs Wood Rd ℰ 0709 (Wickersley)
541046, E : 2 ½ m. – ♦London 166 – ♦Kingston-upon-Hull 61 – ♦Leeds 36 – ♦Sheffield 6.

🏨 **Rotherham Moat House** (Q.M.H.), 102-104 Moorgate Rd, S60 2BG, ℰ 364902, Telex 547810
– 🄸 📺 ☎ ⊛ **⊕**. ⟵ AE ⓞ VISA
M 5.95/9.95 **t.** and a la carte ⋀ 2.65 – ⊠ 4.25 – **62 rm** 36.50/42.00 **t.**

ROTHERWICK Hants – see Hook.

ROTHLEY Leics. **402 403 404** Q 25 – see Leicester.

ROTTINGDEAN East Sussex **404** T 31 – pop. 10,888 (inc. Saltdean) – ECD : Wednesday – ✉
⚙ 0273 Brighton – ◆London 58 – ◆Brighton 4 – Lewes 9 – Newhaven 5.

  🏠 **Olde Place,** High St., BN2 7HE, ℰ 31051 – 📺 ⌷wc ☎ 🅿 🔼 AE *VISA*
    M *(closed Sunday dinner)* (dinner only and Sunday lunch) a la carte 5.40/8.40 t. ▮ 3.25 – **21 rm**
    ⌿ 20.00/38.50 st. – SB 30.00/44.00 st.

ROUSDON Devon **403** L 31 – see Lyme Regis.

ROWLEY REGIS West Midlands **403 404** N 26 – pop. 12,926 – ECD : Thursday – ✉ ⚙ 021
Birmingham.

◆London 132 – ◆Birmingham 9 – Wolverhampton 10.

                Plan : see Birmingham p. 2

  ↰ **Highfield House,** Waterfall Lane, off Holly Rd, B65 0BH, ℰ 559 1066 – 🅿 ⅏   BU **a**
    12 rm ⌿ 12.00/24.00 st.

ROWSLEY Derbs. **402 403 404** P 24 – pop. 200 – ECD : Thursday – ✉ Matlock – ⚙ 0629
Darley Dale.

◆London 157 – Derby 23 – ◆Manchester 40 – ◆Nottingham 30.

  🏨 **Peacock** (Embassy), Bakewell Rd, DE4 2EB, ℰ 733518, « 17C stone house with antiques »,
    🍃, 🐎 – 📺 ⌷wc ⌷wc ☎ 🅿 🔼 AE ⓪ *VISA* ⅏
    M (restricted lunch) 10.75/15.75 st. ▮ 2.50 – ⌿ 5.00 – **20 rm** 25.00/49.50 st.

ROYAL LEAMINGTON SPA Warw. **403 404** P 27 – pop. 56,552 – ECD : Monday and Thursday
– ⚙ 0926.

🏌 Newbold-Comyn, Newbold
Terrace East ℰ 21157, off Willes
Rd.

🎫 Jephson Lodge, The Parade ℰ
311470.

◆London 99 – ◆Birmingham 23 –
◆Coventry 9 – Warwick 3.

  🏨 **Manor House** (Anchor),
    Avenue Rd, CV31 3NJ, ℰ
    23251, Telex 311653 – 📳
    📺 ⌷wc ⌷wc ☎ 🅿 🔼.
    🔼 AE ⓪ *VISA*   **i**
    M (carving rest.) 6.95 **st.**
    and a la carte ▮ 3.00 –
    53 rm ⌿ 42.00/52.50 **st.** –
    SB (weekends only)
    65.00 **st.**

  🏨 **Regent** (Best Western),
    77 The Parade, CV32 4AX,
    ℰ 27231, Telex 311715 –
    📳 📺 ⌷wc ☎ 🅿 🔼 🔼
    AE ⓪ *VISA*   **r**
    M 7.50/9.75 **st.** and a la
    carte ▮ 5.50 – **80 rm**
    ⌿ 30.00/57.00 t. – SB
    (weekends only)
    46.00/47.00 **st.**

  🏨 **Blackdown** 🍃, Sandy
    Lane off Stoneleigh Rd,
    CV32 6RD, N : 2 ¼ m. by A
    452 ℰ 24761, 🐎 – 📺
    ⌷wc ☎ 🅿 🔼 🔼 🔼 ⓪
    VISA   by A 452
    M 9.95/12.95 t. and a la
    carte ▮ 3.00 – **11 rm**
    ⌿ 33.00/55.00 **st.**

  🏨 **Falstaff,** 16-20 Warwick
    New Rd, CV32 5JQ, ℰ
    312044 – 📳 📺 ⌷wc ⌷wc
    ☎ 🅿 🔼 🔼 AE ⓪ *VISA*
    M 8.00/14.00 **st.** and a la
    carte ▮ 2.75 – **54 rm**
    ⌿ 25.00/40.00 **st.** – SB
    (weekends only) 40.00 **st.**
    plan of Warwick   **Z u**

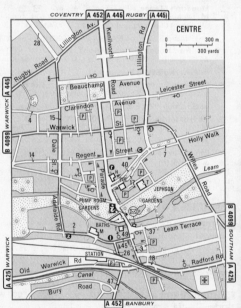

COVENTRY **A 452** **A 445** RUGBY **(A 445)**

CENTRE
0   300 m
0   300 yards

A 452 BANBURY

ROYAL
LEAMINGTON SPA

Parade
Regent Street
Warwick Street

Avenue Road 2
Bath Street 3
Beauchamp Hill 4
Binswood Street 5

Brandon Parade 7
Church Hill 14
Clarendon Place 15
Hamilton Terrace 17
High Street 18
Lower Avenue 26
Northumberland Road 28
Priory Terrace 37
Regent Grove 40
Spencer Street 45
Tachbrook Road 47
Victoria Terrace 49

🏚 **Lansdowne,** 87 Clarendon St., CV32 4PF, 🖉 21313, Telex 337556 – 🛏wc 🅿. 🔼. 🛠 **a**
M *(closed 26 December-10 January)* (dinner only) 9.75 **t.** 🍴 2.65 – **10 rm** 🛏 17.50/32.00 **st.** –
SB 42.90/47.90 **st.**

🏚 **Abbacourt,** 40 Kenilworth Rd, CV32 6JF, 🖉 311188, 🚗 – 📺 🛏wc 🛏wc 🅿. 🔼 AE ① VISA
M a la carte 7.50/10.70 **s.** 🍴 2.65 – **21 rm** 🛏 16.00/36.00 **s.** – SB (weekends only) 33.10/50.70 **st.**
plan of Warwick   Z **r**

🏚 **Beech Lodge,** 28 Warwick New Rd, CV32 5JJ, 🖉 22227 – 🛏wc 🅿. 🔼
M *(closed Sunday dinner)* (dinner only, residents only) 8.50 **t.** 🍴 3.50 – **12 rm** 🛏 18.00/32.50 **st.**
– SB (except Christmas and Bank Holidays) 45.00/48.50 **t.**   plan of Warwick   Z **s**

🏚 **Angel,** 143 Regent St., CV32 4NZ, 🖉 881296 – 📺 🛏wc 🕾 🅿. 🔼 AE VISA   **c**
M 5.95/8.95 **st.** and a la carte 🍴 2.75 – **16 rm** 🛏 27.50/34.00 **st.** – SB (weekends only)
39.50/50.00 **st.**

↑ **Buckland Lodge,** 35 Avenue Rd, CV31 3PG, 🖉 23843 – 🛏wc 🅿   **z**
closed Christmas and New Year – **11 rm** 🛏 10.50/25.00 **st.**

XXX ❀ **Mallory Court** 🦢 with rm, Harbury Lane, Bishop's Tachbrook, CV33 9QB, S : 2 m. by A
452 🖉 30214, Telex 317294, ≼, 🔼, 🚗, park, squash – 📺 🛏wc 🕾 🗢 🅿. 🔼 AE VISA. 🛠
closed 24 December-2 January – **M** (restricted lunch) (booking essential) 16.00/30.00 **st.** – 🛏
6.95 – **9 rm** 60.00/110.00 **st.**, **1 suite** 195.00 **st.**   see plan of Warwick   Z **a**
Spec. Terrine de homard sauce verte, Filet d'agneau au romarin (April-October), Gratin de poires.

AUDI, VW   Dormer Pl. 🖉 36511
AUSTIN-ROVER   Station Approach 🖉 27156
COLT   Wood St. 🖉 24681
FORD   Sydenham Drive 🖉 29411
PEUGEOT-TALBOT   Spencer St. 🖉 30115

RENAULT   Russell St. 🖉 21171
SAAB, DAIHATSU   Lime Av. 🖉 23221
VAUXHALL-OPEL   Old Warwick Rd 🖉 20861
VOLVO   Tachbrook Rd 🖉 882111

☛   *Michelin puts no plaque or sign*
   on the hotels and restaurants mentioned in this Guide.

ROYAL TUNBRIDGE WELLS   Kent 🗺🗺🗺 U 30 – pop. 57,699 – ECD : Wednesday – ☎ 0892.

See : The Pantiles✶ (promenade 18C) B – Town Hall Museum (wood-mosaic articles✶) B **M**.
Envir. : Scotney Castle Gardens (trees ✶, Bastion view ✶) *AC*, SE : 8 m. by B 2169 A.
🛈 Town Hall 🖉 26121.
✦London 36 – ✦Brighton 33 – Folkestone 46 – Hastings 27 – Maidstone 18.

ROYAL TUNBRIDGE WELLS

Calverley Road . . . . B
High Street . . . . B 14
Mount Pleasant Road . . . . B 25
Pantiles (The) . . . . B 26

Benhall Mill Road . . . . A 3
Bishop's Down . . . . A 4
Calverley Park Gardens . . . . B 7

Clarence Road . . . . B 8
Crescent Road . . . . B 9
Fir Tree Road . . . . A 10
Grosvenor Road . . . . B 12
Hall's Hole Road . . . . A 13
High Rocks Lane . . . . A 16
Hungershall Park Road . . . . . A 17
Lansdowne Road . . . . B 18
Lower Green Road . . . . A 20
Major York's Road . . . . A 22

Mount Ephraim . . . . A 23
Mount Ephraim Road . . . . . . B 24
Prospect Road . . . . A 27
Rusthall Road . . . . A 28
St. John's Road . . . . B 29
Tea Garden Lane . . . . A 30
Upper Grosvenor Road . . . . . B 31
Vale Road . . . . B 33
Victoria Road . . . . B 34
Warwick Park . . . . B 35

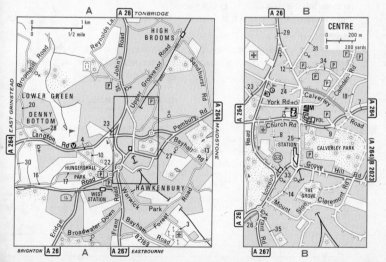

🏠 **Spa**, Mount Ephraim, TN4 8XJ, ℰ 20331, Telex 957188, ≤, ≈, park, ℅ – 📶 📺 ☎ 🅿 🛴 🔼
AE ① VISA   A   v
M a la carte 11.15/18.45 **t.** – �/ 5.50 – **69 rm** 40.00/60.00 **st.**, **3 suites** – SB (weekends only)
65.00/75.00 **st.**

🏛 **Russell**, 80 London Rd, TN1 1DZ, ℰ 44833, Telex 95177 – 📺 ➿wc 🛁wc ☎ 🅿 🔼 AE ①
VISA ⚗   B   a
M (bar lunch)/dinner 9.50 **t.** and a la carte ▮ 3.00 – **20 rm** ⊐ 33.00/44.00 **st.** – SB (except
Christmas and New Year) 52.00/57.00 **st.**

XX **Thackeray's House**, 85 London Rd, TN21 1EA, ℰ 37558, ≈ – 🔼 VISA   B   e
closed Sunday, Monday, 1 week Easter, 2 weeks summer, 1 week Christmas and Bank Holidays
*– **M** 13.50/14.85 **t.** ▮ 2.95.*

at Southborough N : 2 m. on A 26 – A – ✉ ✆ 0892 Royal Tunbridge Wells :

XX **Weavers**, London Rd, TN4 0PU, ℰ 29896 – 🅿 🔼 ① VISA
closed Sunday dinner, Monday, 29 July-12 August, 25 to 30 December and Bank Holidays – **M**
7.50/8.75 **t.** and a la carte ▮ 3.30.

at Speldhurst NW : 3 ½ m. by A 26 – A – ✉ Royal Tunbridge Wells – ✆ 089 286 Langton :

XX **George and Dragon Inn**, Barden Rd, TN3 0NN, ℰ 3125, « 13C inn » – 🅿 🔼 AE ① VISA
closed Saturday lunch and Sunday dinner – **M** 8.50/16.75 **t.** and a la carte.

AUSTIN-ROVER Crescent Rd ℰ 25266	FORD Commercial Rd, Paddock Wood ℰ (089 283)
AUSTIN-ROVER-DAIMLER-JAGUAR Mount Sion ℰ	Paddock Wood 6388
26463	NISSAN 13/17 London Rd ℰ 29292
BMW St. John's Rd ℰ 39355	RENAULT Langton Rd ℰ 39466
CITROEN, FIAT, LANCIA 321 St. Johns Rd ℰ 35111	PEUGEOT-TALBOT, ALFA-ROMEO 49 Mount Pleasant
COLT, RELIANT Grosvenor Rd ℰ 27174	sant ℰ 27202
FORD Mount Ephraim ℰ 20323	VW, AUDI Currie Rd ℰ 44733

▬ **RUAN-HIGH-LANES** Cornwall 403 F 33 – see Veryan.

▬ **RUGBY** Warw. 403 404 Q 26 – pop. 59,039 – ECD : Wednesday – ✆ 0788.

Envir. : Stanford-on-Avon (castle 17C : park★ *AC*) NE : 5 m.

🄱 Public Library, St. Matthew's St. ℰ 2687 and 71813.

♦London 88 – ♦Birmingham 33 – ♦Leicester 21 – Northampton 20 – Warwick 17.

🏛 Three Horse Shoes (Best Western), Sheep St., CV21 3BX, ℰ 4585 – 📺 ➿wc 🛁wc ☜. 🛴
32 rm, **1 suite**.

🏠 **Carlton**, 130 Railway Terr., CV21 3HE, ℰ 3076 – 📺 ➿wc 🛁wc ☜ 🅿 🔼 VISA
closed Saturday lunch, Sunday dinner, 26 December and Bank Holidays – **M** 5.10/6.00
t. and a la carte – **12 rm** ⊐ 16.00/31.00 **t.**

at Kilsby SE : 6 ¼ m. by A 428 on A 5 – ✉ Rugby – ✆ 0788 Crick :

XX **Hunt House**, Main St., CV23 8XR, ℰ 823282, ≈ – 🅿 🔼 AE ① VISA
closed Sunday and Monday – **M** (dinner only) 12.50 **t.** ▮ 2.85.

at Crick SE : 6 m. on A 428 – ✉ ✆ 0788 Rugby :

🏠 **Post House** (T.H.F.), NN6 7XR, W : ½ m. on A 428 ℰ 822101, Telex 311107 – 📺 🅿 🛴 🔼
AE ① VISA
M 6.95/9.25 **st.** and a la carte ▮ 2.70 – ⊐ 5.50 – **96 rm** 41.00/49.50 **st.**

at Stretton Under Fosse NW : 7 ½ m. by A 426 and B 4112 on A 427 – ✉ ✆ 0788 Rugby :

🏠 **Ashton Lodge** ⚗, CV23 0PJ, N : 1 m. by A 427 on B 4112 ℰ 832278, ≈ – 📺 ➿wc 🛁wc
🅿 🔼 AE ① ⚗
M (bar lunch)/dinner 18.65 **t.** and a la carte ▮ 2.55 – **10 rm** ⊐ 19.50/35.00 **t.** – SB (weekends
only) 37.75/69.65 **st.**

AUSTIN-ROVER Railway Terrace ℰ 3477	NISSAN Temple St. ℰ 3094
CITROEN 339 Hillmorton Rd ℰ 73671	RENAULT 100 Railway Terr. ℰ 2660

▬ **RUGELEY** Staffs. 402 403 404 O 25 – pop. 23,751 – ECD : Wednesday – ✆ 088 94.

Envir. : Blithfield Hall★ (Elizabethan) *AC*, N : 5 m.

♦London 135 – ♦Birmingham 23 – Stafford 9 – ♦Stoke-on-Trent 23.

🏠 **Eaton Lodge**, 118 Wolsley Rd, WS15 2ET, ℰ 3454, ≈ – 📺 🛁 🅿 🔼 AE VISA.
M a la carte 6.00/8.95 **t.** ▮ 2.85 – **11 rm** ⊐ 16.50/28.50 **st.**

at Armitage SE : 3 m. on A 513 – ✉ Rugeley – ✆ 0543 Armitage :

XX **Old Farmhouse**, Armitage Rd, WS15 4AT, ℰ 490353 – 🅿 🔼 AE ① VISA
*closed Sunday, Monday, 25 to 31 May, last 2 weeks July, 24 December-3 January and Bank
Holidays* – **M** 8.95/12.45 **t.** ▮ 2.50.

Do not use yesterday's maps for today's journey.

RUNCORN Cheshire 402 403 L 23 – pop. 63 ,995 – ECD : Wednesday – ✪ 092 85 (5 fig.) or 0928 (6 fig.).

🔟 Highfield Rd, Widnes ✆ 051 (Liverpool) 424 2995, N : 4 m.

🛈 57-61 Church St. ✆ 76776 and 69656.

♦London 202 – ♦Liverpool 14 – ♦Manchester 29.

🏛 **Crest** (Crest), Wood Lane, Beechwood, WA7 3HA, SE : ½ m. off junction 12 of M 56 ✆ 714000, Telex 627426 – 📳 📺 ⌷wc ☎ 🅿 ♨ 🆘 🖭 🅰🅴 🆅🆂🅰
M (carving lunch) approx 11.50 **st.** – ⌷ 5.75 – **128 rm** 46.50/56.50 **st.** – SB (weekends only) 55.00 **st.**

AUSTIN-ROVER Balfour St. ✆ 72271   MAZDA Picow Farm Rd ✆ 63099
FORD Victoria Rd ✆ 74333

RUSHDEN Northants. 404 S 27 – pop. 22 ,394 – ECD : Thursday – ✪ 0933.
See : Higham Ferrers (St. Mary's Church★ 13C-14C).

♦ London 72 – Bedford 13 – ♦ Cambridge 36 – ♦ Leicester 38 – Northampton 15.

↟ **Westward,** Shirley Rd, NN10 9BY, ✆ 312376, 🛏 heated – 📺 🎞 🅿. 🛇
closed 23 December-3 January – **26 rm** ⌷ 16.00/32.00 **t.**

AUSTIN-ROVER High St. South ✆ 59111

RUSHLAKE GREEN East Sussex 404 U 31 – ✉ Heathfield – ✪ 0435.

♦London 57 – Eastbourne 14 – Hastings 15 – Royal Tunbridge Wells 21.

🏛 **Priory Country House** 🦢, TN21 9RG, N : 1 m. by Dallington Rd. ✆ 830553, Telex 957210, ≼, « 15C priory with country house atmosphere », 🐾, 🌳, park – 📺 ⌷wc ☎ 🅿
closed 24 December-10 January – **M** 11.45/17.20 **t.** 🍷 3.75 – **15 rm** ⌷ 36.80/94.30 **t.**

RUSPER West Sussex 404 T 30 – pop. 2 ,678 – ✪ 029 384.

♦London 30 – ♦Brighton 35 – Horsham 6.

XXX **Ghyll Manor** with rm, High St., RH12 4PX, ✆ 571, ≼, 🛏 heated, 🌳, park, 🛇 – 📺 ⌷wc ☎ 🅿 ♨
11 rm.

RUTHIN (RHUTHUN) Clwyd 402 403 K 24 – pop. 4 ,417 – ECD : Thursday – ✪ 082 42.
See : Church★.

🔟 at Pantymwyn ✆ 0352 (Mold) 740318, NE : 8 m. – 🔟 Pwllglas ✆ 2296, S : 2 ½ m.

🛈 Ruthin Craft Centre ✆ 3992.

♦London 210 – Birkenhead 31 – Chester 23 – Shrewsbury 46.

🏛 **Ruthin Castle** (Best Western) 🦢, Corwen Rd, LL15 2NU, ✆ 2664, Telex 61169, ≼, « Reconstructed medieval castle », 🐾, 🌳, park – 📳 ⌷wc ☎ 🅿 🆘 🅰🅴 🆅🆂🅰
M (buffet lunch)/dinner 7.95 **st.** and a la carte – **58 rm** ⌷ 29.50/57.00 **st.** – SB 48.00/60.00 **st.**

🏛 **Castle (and Myddleton Arms),** St. Peter's Sq., LL15 1AA, ✆ 2479, Telex 617074 – 📺 ⌷wc ☎ 🅿 ♨ 🆘 🅰🅴 ⓞ 🆅🆂🅰
M 4.00/6.95 **t.** and a la carte 🍷 3.75 – **25 rm** ⌷ 24.00/37.00 **t.** – SB (weekends only) 35.50/37.50 **st.**

AUSTIN-ROVER High St. ✆ 074 578 (Llanynys) 227   VAUXHALL-OPEL Well St. ✆ 2645

RYDAL Cumbria 402 L 20 – see Ambleside.

RYDE I.O.W. 403 404 Q 31 – see Wight (Isle of).

RYE East Sussex 404 W 31 – pop. 4 ,127 – ECD : Tuesday – ✪ 0797.
See : Old Town★ (chiefly : Mermaid Street) – Ypres Tower ≼★.
Envir. : Winchelsea (Church of St. Thomas the Martyr★ 1283 : Tombs★★ 12C) SW : 3 m. – Small Hythe (Ellen Terry's House★ *AC*) N : 7 ½ m.

🛈 48 Cinque Ports St., Ferry Rd ✆ 222293.

♦London 61 – ♦Brighton 49 – Folkestone 27 – Maidstone 33.

🏛 **George** (T.H.F.), High St., TN31 7JP, ✆ 222114 – 📺 ⌷wc 🎞wc 🅿 ♨ 🆘 🅰🅴 ⓞ 🆅🆂🅰
M 9.00 **st.** and a la carte 🍷 2.70 – ⌷ 5.50 – **17 rm** 35.50/48.50 **st.**

🏛 **Mermaid,** Mermaid St., TN31 7EY, ✆ 223065, Group Telex 957141, « 15C inn » – ⌷wc 🎞wc 🅿 🅰🅴 ⓞ 🆅🆂🅰 🛇
closed midweek January-February – **M** 7.50/9.00 **t.** and a la carte – **28 rm** ⌷ 24.00/48.00 **t.** – SB (except Bank Holidays) 64.00/70.00 **st.**

🏠 **Hope Anchor,** Watchbell St., TN31 7HA, ✆ 222216, ≼ – ⌷wc 🅿 🆘 🅰🅴 ⓞ 🆅🆂🅰
M (bar lunch Monday-Saturday)/dinner 8.10 **t.** and a la carte – **15 rm** ⌷ 18.00/34.00 **t.**

XXX **Old Vicarage** with rm, 15 East St., TN31 7JY, ✆ 225131, ≼ – 📺 ⌷wc. 🆘 🆅🆂🅰 🛇
closed first 2 weeks August and 1 to 14 January – **M** *(closed Sunday and Monday)* (dinner only) a la carte approx. 13.00 **t.** 🍷 3.50 – **4 rm** ⌷ 25.00/34.00 **t.**

393

XX **Flushing Inn,** Market St., TN31 7LA, ✆ 223292, Seafood, « 15C inn with 16C mural » – [VISA] AE [DC] VISA
closed Monday dinner, Tuesday and 31 December-20 January – **M** 9.00/13.50 **t.** and a la carte 🍾 3.40.

XX **Simmons,** 68 The Mint, TN31 7EW, ✆ 222026 – [VISA] AE [DC] VISA
closed Sunday dinner, Monday, 3 weeks February, 26 December and 1 January – **M** (dinner only and Sunday lunch) 6.95/9.50 **t.** and a la carte 🍾 3.00.

at Playden N : 1 m. on A 268 – ✉ ☎ 0797 Rye :

🏨 **Playden Oasts,** TN31 7UL, on A 268 ✆ 223502, 🌳 – [TV] 🛁wc 🚿wc ☎ [P]. [VISA] AE VISA
M a la carte 8.60/10.75 **t.** 🍾 2.30 – **8 rm** ☕ 20.00/40.00 **t.** – SB (winter only) (except Bank Holidays) 40.00/48.00 **st.**

at Peasmarsh NW : 4 m. on A 268 – ✉ Rye – ☎ 079 721 Peasmarsh :

🏨 **Flackley Ash** (Best Western), London Rd, TN31 6YH, ✆ 381, 🌳 – [TV] 🛁wc 🚿wc [P]. [VISA] AE [DC] VISA
M (bar lunch)/dinner 11.00 **t.** and a la carte 🍾 2.95 – **20 rm** ☕ 29.00/46.00 **t.** – SB 50.00/66.00 **st.**

ALFA-ROMEO, CITROEN Cinque Ports St. ✆ 3196
AUSTIN-ROVER-JAGUAR, LAND ROVER-RANGE ROVER Fishmarket Rd ✆ 223334
RENAULT Rye Harbour Rd ✆ 4888

SAFFRON WALDEN Essex [404] U 27 – pop. 11,879 – ECD : Thursday – ☎ 0799.

See : Parish Church★ (Perpendicular) – Audley End House★ (Jacobean : interior★★) *AC.*

[i] Corn Exchange, Market Sq. ✆ 24282.

♦London 46 – ♦Cambridge 15 – Chelmsford 25.

🏨 **Saffron,** 10-18 High St., CB10 1AY, ✆ 22676 – [TV] 🛁wc 🚿 📞 [P]. [VISA] VISA. 🐕
M *(closed Sunday and Bank Holidays to non-residents)* 12.95 **st.** and a la carte 🍾 2.45 – ☕ 2.50 – **18 rm** 14.50/38.00 **st.**

X **Staircase,** 21 High St., CB10 1AT, ✆ 22226 – [VISA] AE [DC] VISA
closed January – **M** 9.95 **st.** and a la carte 10.75/16.15 **st.**

AUSTIN-ROVER High St. ✆ 27909
AUSTIN-ROVER 66 High St. ✆ 23597
VAUXHALL-OPEL 13/15 Station St. ✆ 23238

ST. AGNES Cornwall [403] E 33 **The West Country G.** – pop. 2,421 – ECD : Wednesday – ☎ 087 255.

See : St. Agnes Beacon★★ (✻★★).

♦London 302 – Newquay 12 – Penzance 26 – Truro 9.

🏨 **Trevaunance Point** 🐴, Quay Rd, Trevaunance Cove, TR5 0RZ, ✆ 3235, ≤ bay and cliffs, 🌳 – 🛁wc [P]. [VISA] AE [DC] VISA
M 5.50/9.25 **t.** and a la carte 🍾 3.25 – **11 rm** ☕ 18.50/49.00 **t.** – SB (weekends only) (October-May) 47.00/50.00 **st.**

🏠 **Sunholme** 🐴, Goonvrea Rd, Goonvrea, TR5 0NW, SW : 1 m. by B 3277 ✆ 2318, 🌳 – [P]. [VISA] VISA
April-October – **11 rm** ☕ 10.50/30.00 **t.**

🏠 **Rosevean,** Rosemundy Rd, TR5 0UD, ✆ 2277, 🌳 – 🚿wc [P]
closed October and Christmas – **9 rm** ☕ 8.00/21.00 **s.**

at Mithian E : 2 m. by B 3285 – ✉ ☎ 087 255 St. Agnes :

🏨 **Rose-in-Vale** 🐴, TR5 0QD, ✆ 2202, ≤, 🏊 heated, 🌳 – 🛁wc 🚿wc [P]. [VISA] [DC]
M (bar lunch)/dinner 6.95 **st.** and a la carte 🍾 2.55 – **14 rm** ☕ 19.35/43.15 **st.** – SB (October-May) 34.75 **st.**

FORD Trevellas Garage, Trevellas ✆ 2372

ST. ALBANS Herts. [404] T 28 – pop. 76,709 – ECD : Thursday – ☎ 0727.

See : Site★★ – Cathedral and Abbey Church★ (Norman Tower★).

Envir. : Hatfield House★★★ *AC* **(gardens★ and Old Palace★)** E : 6 m. – **Verulamium (Roman remains★ and museum)** *AC*, W : 2 m.

⛳18 Batchwood Hall ✆ 52101.

[i] 37 Chequer St. ✆ 64511.

♦London 27 – ♦Cambridge 41 – Luton 10.

🏨 **St. Michael's Manor** 🐴, Fishpool St., AL3 4RY, ✆ 64444, « Manor house, lake, ≤ garden », park – [TV] 🛁wc 🚿wc ☎ [P]. 🎭. [VISA] AE [DC] VISA. 🐕
closed Christmas night – **M** 8.50/10.75 **t.** and a la carte 🍾 3.10 – **26 rm** ☕ 40.00/58.00 **st.**

🏨 **Noke Thistle** (Thistle) Watford Rd, AL2 3DS, SW : 2 ½ m. at junction A 405 and B 4630 ✆ 54252, Telex 893834 – [TV] 🛁wc 📞 [P]. 🎭. [VISA] AE [DC] VISA
M 12.95 **t.** and a la carte 🍾 3.25 – ☕ 5.75 – **57 rm** 48.00/65.00 **t.**

🏨 **Sopwell House** 🐴, Cottonmill Lane, AL1 2HQ, SE : 1 ½ m. by A 1081 and Mile House Lane ✆ 64477, 🌳, park – [TV] 🛁wc ☎ [P]. 🎭. [VISA] AE [DC] VISA. 🐕
M *(closed Sunday dinner)* 8.80/11.80 **t.** and a la carte – ☕ 5.40 – **30 rm** 24.75/49.50 **st.** – SB (weekends only) 68.10/84.05 **st.**

↟ **Melford House,** 24 Woodstock Rd North, AL1 4QQ, ☎ 53642 – 📶wc 🅿
12 rm ⌷ 17.25/34.50 **st.**

↟ **Ardmore House,** 54 Lemsford Rd, AL1 3PR, ☎ 59313 – 📺 📶wc 🅿. 🎇
15 rm ⌷ 16.00/32.00 **s.**

✗ **La Province,** 13 George St., AL3 4ER, ☎ 52142, French rest. – 🔃 AE ⓪ VISA
closed Sunday, Monday, 1 week after Easter, last 2 weeks August and 1 week at Christmas –
M 8.00/15.00 **t.** and a la carte ⵉ 2.25.

✗ **Langtry's,** London Rd, AL1 1SP, ☎ 61848, Seafood – 🔃 AE ⓪ VISA
closed Saturday lunch and Sunday – **M** 6.50 **t.** (lunch) and a la carte 10.70/13.75 **t.** ⵉ 2.50.

AUSTIN-ROVER-DAIMLER-JAGUAR, ROLLS ROYCE-BENTLEY Acrewood Way, Hatfield Rd ☎ 66522
AUSTIN-ROVER Park St., Frogmore ☎ 72626
CITROEN, VAUXHALL-OPEL 66-70 High St., Potters Bar ☎ 0707 (Potters Bar) 42391
CITROEN, OPEL, SCIMITAR, VAUXHALL 101 Holy-well Hill ☎ 65756

FIAT Beech Rd ☎ 50871
FORD London Rd ☎ 59155
HONDA, PEUGEOT Catherine St. ☎ 54342
PEUGEOT-TALBOT 220 London Rd ☎ 63377
RENAULT 99/111 London Rd ☎ 52345
VAUXHALL-OPEL 100 London Rd ☎ 50601
VW, AUDI Valley Rd ☎ 36236
VW, AUDI 229/233 Hatfield Rd ☎ 36366

ST. ASAPH (LLANELWY) Clwyd 402 403 J 24 – pop. 3,156 – ECD : Thursday – ☏ 0745.
Envir. : Rhuddlan (castle★ 13C) *AC*, NW : 3 m.

🏌 ☎ 074 571 (Denbigh) 4159, S : 6 m.

♦London 225 – Chester 29 – Shrewsbury 59.

🏨 **Oriel House,** Upper Denbigh Rd, LL17 0LW, S : ¾ m. on A 525 ☎ 582716, 🐎 – 📺 📶wc
📶wc ☎ 🅿 🏛 🔃 AE ⓪ VISA
M *(closed Christmas Night and 26 December)* 5.00/12.95 **t.** and a la carte ⵉ 2.15 – **18 rm** ⌷ 24.00/39.00 **t.** – SB (weekends only) 45.00/50.00 **st.**

ALFA-ROMEO High St. ☎ 583475
AUSTIN-ROVER Bod Ewr Corner ☎ 582345

RENAULT The Roe ☎ 582233

ST. AUSTELL Cornwall 403 F 32 The West Country G. – pop. 20,267 – ECD : Thursday – ☏ 0726.
See : Holy Trinity★★.
Envir. : St. Austell Bay★★ (Gribbin Head ★★), E : 3 m. by A 3601 – Wheal Martyn Museum★★*AC*,
N : 2 m. on A 391 – Polkerris★, E : 9 m. by A 3082.

🏌 Carlyon Bay ☎ 072 681 (Par) 4250, E : 2 m.

🚗 ☎ 01 (London) 723 7000 ext. 3148.

♦London 281 – Newquay 16 – ♦Plymouth 38 – Truro 14.

🏨 **White Hart,** Church St., PL25 4AT, ☎ 72100 – 📺 📶wc 📶. 🔃 AE ⓪ VISA
closed 25-26 December – **M** 5.40/8.25 **st.** ⵉ 2.50 – **20 rm** ⌷ 17.50/35.00 **st.** – SB (weekends only) (except summer) 35.00 **st.**

at Tregrehan E : 2 ½ m. by A 390 – ✉ St. Austell – ☏ 072 681 Par :

✗✗ **Boscundle Manor** 🍴 with rm, PL25 3RL, ☎ 3557, « Tastefully converted 18C manor »,
🍴 heated, 🐎, park – 📶wc 📶wc ☎ 🅿. 🔃 AE VISA. 🎇
closed 23 December-7 February – **M** *(closed Sunday)* (restricted lunch residents only)/dinner 15.00 **st.** ⵉ 3.00 – **9 rm** ⌷ 33.00/60.00 **st.**

at Carlyon Bay E : 2 ½ m. by A 3601 – ✉ St. Austell – ☏ 072 681 Par :

🏨 **Carlyon Bay** 🍴, PL25 3RD, ☎ 2304, ≤ Carlyon Bay, « Extensive gardens », 🍴 heated, 🔃,
🏌, park, 🎇 – 🕴 📺 🅿. 🔃 AE ⓪ VISA. 🎇
M 7.75/10.50 **st.** and a la carte – **72 rm** ⌷ 35.00/44.25 **t.** – SB (except Easter, late May, summer and Christmas – New Year) 60.00/78.50 **st.**

🏨 **Porth Avallen** 🍴, Sea Rd, PL25 3SG, ☎ 2802, ≤ Carlyon Bay, 🐎 – 📺 📶wc ☎ 🅿. 🏛. 🔃
AE ⓪ VISA. 🎇
M 4.00/9.75 **st.** ⵉ 1.95 – ⌷ 3.50 – **24 rm** 21.50/34.50 **t.** – SB (except summer) 58.00/72.00 **st.**

at Charlestown SE : 2 m. by A 390 on A 391 – ✉ ☏ 0726 St. Austell :

🏠 **Pier House,** Harbour Front, PL25 3NJ, ☎ 75272, ≤ – 📶wc 🅿
M (bar lunch)/dinner 6.00 **t.** and a la carte ⵉ 2.10 – **12 rm** ⌷ 13.00/31.00, **t.**.

AUSTIN-ROVER Carlyon Bay ☎ 072 681 (Par) 2451
CITROEN 77 Fore St. ☎ 850 241
FIAT East Hill ☎ 5624

FORD Slades Rd ☎ 2333
PEUGEOT-TALBOT Gwendra, St. Stephen ☎ 822566

ST. COLUMB MINOR Cornwall – see Newquay.

Per i 🏨🏨🏨 , 🏨🏨 , 🏨 , non diamo il dettaglio
delle installazioni, poichè questi alberghi
dispongono ognuno di ogni confort.

📶wc 📶wc

☎

395

ST. DAVIDS (TYDDEWI) Dyfed 403 E 28 – pop. 1,428 – ECD : Wednesday – ☎ 0437.

See : Cathedral★★ 12C (site★) – Bishops Palace★ *AC*.

Envir. : Porthgain (cliffs ★★★) NE : 7 m. – Whitesand Bay★★ and St. David's Head★★ NW : 2 m. – Newgale (≤★★) by Solva (site★) E : 7 m. – Abereiddy (site★) NE : 5 m.

Pembrokeshire Coast National Park Centre, City Hall ☎ 720747 (summer only).

♦London 266 – Carmarthen 46 – Fishguard 16.

Warpool Court, SA62 6BN, ☎ 720300, ≤ sea and countryside, – wc wc P. AE VISA
closed January-mid February – **M** 8.50/14.50 **st.** and a la carte 2.75 – **25 rm** 28.00/60.00 **st.** – SB 54.00/86.00 **st.**

St. Non's, Catherine St., SA62 6RJ, ☎ 720239, – TV wc P. AE VISA
M (bar lunch)/dinner 4.25 **t.** and a la carte 2.40 – **20 rm** 17.00/42.00 **t.** – SB (except 20 July-31 August) 45.70/49.50 **t.**

Old Cross, Cross Sq., SA62 6SP, ☎ 720387, – wc P
March-October – **M** (bar lunch)/dinner 8.00 **t.** and a la carte – **17 rm** 17.00/42.00 **t.** – SB (except summer) 36.00 **st.**

Belmont, Cross Sq., SA62 6SE, ☎ 720264, no smoking – P.
8 rm.

ST. HELENS Merseyside 402 403 L 23 – pop. 114,397 – ECD : Thursday – ☎ 0744.

Sherdley Park ☎ 813149, E : 2 m. on A 570.

♦London 204 – ♦Liverpool 14 – ♦Manchester 21 – Preston 25.

Fleece (Greenall Whitley), 15 Church St., WA10 1BA, ☎ 26546, Telex 629811 – TV wc P.
73 rm.

AUSTIN ROVER Prescott Rd ☎ 34441
AUSTIN ROVER Elephant Lane ☎ 811565
FIAT Gaskell St. ☎ 21961
FORD City Rd ☎ 26381
LADA, NISSAN Jackson St. ☎ 26681
MAZDA, FSO Dentons Green Lane ☎ 24748
NISSAN, VOLVO Mill Lane, Newton-Le-Willows ☎ 092 52 (Newton-Le-Willows) 4411
PEUGEOT-TALBOT, CITROEN Knowsley Rd ☎ 32411
RENAULT East Lancashire Rd ☎ 27373
SAAB Aspinal Pl. ☎ 55333
VAUXHALL-OPEL Knowlsey Rd ☎ 35221

Red Lion — If the name of the hotel is not in bold type, on arrival ask the hotelier his prices.

ST. IVES Cornwall 403 D 33 The West Country G. – pop. 9,439 – ECD : Thursday – ☎ 0736 Penzance.

See : Site ★★ – Barbara Hepworth Museum★★ *AC* Y **M1** – St. Ia Church★ Y **A** – Barnes Museum of Cinematography★ *AC* Y **M2**.

The Guildhall, Street-an-Pol ☎ 797600.

♦London 319 – Penzance 10 – Truro 25.

Plan opposite

Garrack, Burthallan Lane, Higher Ayr, TR26 3AA, ☎ 796199, ≤, – wc wc P. AE VISA — Y **a**
M *(closed November-March)* 9.50 **t.** dinner and a la carte 3.00 – **18 rm** 15.50/40.00 **t.** – SB (April, May and October only) 46.00 **st.**

Porthminster (Best Western), The Terrace, TR26 2BN, ☎ 795221, ≤, heated, – TV wc wc P. AE VISA — Y **s**
closed mid December-mid January – **M** 9.00 **t.** (dinner) and a la carte 3.00 – **50 rm** 24.00/68.00 **t.** – SB (October-May) 44.00 **st.**

Pedn-Olva, Porthminster Beach, TR26 2EA, ☎ 796222, ≤ coastline – wc wc P.
March-October – **M** (bar lunch)/dinner 8.50 **t.** 3.20 – **33 rm** 18.00/48.00 **t.** — Y **n**

Dean Court, Trelyon Av., TR26 2AD, ☎ 796023, ≤ St. Ives and bay – TV wc wc P.
Mid April-mid October – **M** (dinner only) 6.00 **st.** 2.30 – **12 rm** 19.00/46.00 **st.** – SB (except summer) 42.00/46.00 **st.** — Y **e**

Old Vicarage, Parc-an-Creet, TR26 2ET, ☎ 796124, – wc P. VISA — Y **i**
closed Christmas – **8 rm** 10.00/24.00 **t.**

Pondarosa, 10 Porthminster Terr., TR26 2DQ, ☎ 795875 – P. — Y **r**
May-September – **9 rm** 8.00/24.00 **st.**

at Carbis Bay S : 1 ½ m. on A 3074 – ✉ St. Ives – ☎ 0736 Penzance :

Boskerris, Boskerris Rd, TR26 2NQ, ☎ 795295, ≤, heated, – wc P. — Z **x**
Easter-mid October – **M** (bar lunch)/dinner 9.00 **t.** 2.20 – **20 rm** 15.00/38.00 **t.** – SB (September-May) 42.00 **st.**

St. Uny, Boskerris Rd, TR26 2NQ, ☎ 795011, ≤, – wc P. VISA — Z **z**
April-mid October – **M** (bar lunch)/dinner 8.10 **t.** 2.50 – **32 rm** 16.00/48.00 **st.**

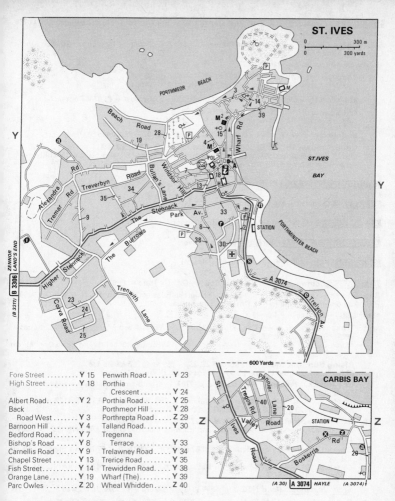

ST. IVES

Fore Street	Y 15	Penwith Road	Y 23	
High Street	Y 18	Porthia		
		Crescent	Y 24	
Albert Road	Y 2	Porthia Road	Y 25	
Back		Porthmeor Hill	Y 28	
Road West	Y 3	Porthrepta Road	Y 29	
Barnoon Hill	Y 4	Talland Road	Y 30	
Bedford Road	Y 7	Tregenna		
Bishop's Road	Y 8	Terrace	Y 33	
Carnellis Road	Y 9	Trelawney Road	Y 34	
Chapel Street	Y 13	Trerice Road	Y 35	
Fish Street	Y 14	Trewidden Road	Y 38	
Orange Lane	Y 19	Wharf (The)	Y 39	
Parc Owles	Z 20	Wheal Whidden	Z 40	

CARBIS BAY

During the season, particularly in resorts, it is wise to book in advance.
However, if you find you cannot take up a hotel booking you have made,
please let the hotel know immediately.

If you are writing to a hotel abroad enclose an International Reply Coupon
(available from Post Offices.)

ST. IVES Cambs. **404** T 27 – pop. 13 ,431 – ECD : Thursday – ☎ 0480.

See : Bridge★ 15C.

♦London 75 – ♦Cambridge 14 – Huntingdon 6.

🏨 **Slepe Hall,** Ramsey Rd, PE17 4RB, ℰ 63172, Telex 32339 – 📺 ⇋wc ☎ 🅿 🛦 ⟳ 🆎 ⓪ **VISA**

closed 25 and 26 December – **M** 10.50 **t.** and a la carte 👖 3.15 – **14 rm** ⇆ 28.00/40.00 **t.** – SB (weekends only) 43.00/81.00 **st.**

🏩 **St. Ives Motel,** London Rd, PE17 4EX, S : ¾ m. on A 1096 ℰ 63857 – 📺 ⇋wc ☎ 🅿 🛦 ⟳ 🆎 ⓪ **VISA**

closed 25 and 26 December – **M** a la carte 8.05/13.20 **t.** 👖 3.15 – ⇆ 4.35 – **16 rm** 22.50/30.50 **t.** – SB (weekends only) 40.00/45.00 **t.**

AUSTIN-ROVER The Quadrant ℰ 62871   FORD Ramsey Rd ℰ 63184
FIAT, LANCIA Station Rd ℰ 62641

ST. JUST Cornwall **403** C 33 The West Country G. — pop. 1,903 — ECD : Thursday — ☎ 0736 Penzance.

See : Site★ — Church★ — Envir. : Cape Cornwall★ (≤★★), W : 1 ½ m. — Carn Euny★ *AC*, SE : 3 m. — Geevor Tin Mine★ *AC*, N : 3 m.

♦London 325 — Penzance 7.5 — Truro 35.

  🏠 **Boscean** ⌖, TR19 7QP, ℰ 788748, ≤, ╦ — ⌂wc **P**. ⛾
     March-October — **M** (bar lunch) 7.00 **t**. — **10 rm** ⊃⊂ 9.75/37.00 **t**.

    at Little Kelynack S : 1 ½ m. by A 3071 on B 3306 — ⊠ St. Just — ☎ 0736 Penzance :

  XX **Old School**, TR19 7RH, ℰ 788911, ╦ — **P**. **ꗩ** **AE** **①**
     closed Sunday — **M** (dinner only) a la carte 8.95/12.00 **t**. ⓪ 3.50.

    at Botallack NW : 2 ¼ m. by B 3306 — ⊠ St. Just — ☎ 0736 Penzance :

  XX **Count House**, TR19 7QQ, ℰ 788588, ≤ coastline — **P**. **ꗩ** **AE** **①** **VISA**
     closed Sunday dinner, Monday and Tuesday — **M** (dinner only and Sunday lunch)(booking essential) a la carte 10.65/14.50 **t**. ⓪ 2.95.

ST JUST IN ROSELAND Cornwall — see St. Mawes.

ST. KEYNE Cornwall — see Liskeard.

ST LAWRENCE I.O.W. — see Wight (Isle of) : Ventnor.

ST. MARGARET'S BAY Kent **404** Y 30 — see Dover.

ST. MARY'S Cornwall **403** ㉚ — see Scilly (Isles of).

ST. MAWES Cornwall **403** E 33 The West Country G. — ⊠ Truro — ☎ 0326.

See : Site ★★ — Castle★ *AC* (≤★) — Envir. : St. Just-in-Roseland Church★★★, N : 2 ½ m. by A 3078 — St. Anthony-in-Roseland (≤★★), 8 m. round peninsula.

♦London 299 — ♦Plymouth 56 — Truro 18.

  🏨 **Tresanton** ⌖, 27 Lower Castle Rd, TR2 5DR, ℰ 270544, ≤ estuary, « Converted cottages », ╦ — ⌂wc **P**. **ꗩ** **AE** **①** **VISA**
     March-October and 23 December-1 January — **M** (buffet lunch)/dinner 13.75 **t**. — **21 rm** ⊃⊂ 35.50/69.40 **t**.

  🏨 **Rising Sun**, The Square, TR2 5DJ, ℰ 270233 — ⌂wc **P**. **ꗩ** **AE** **①** **VISA**
     M (bar lunch)/dinner 12.00 **t**. ⓪ 2.00 — **16 rm** ⊃⊂ 20.00/55.00 **t**.

  🏨 **Idle Rocks**, Tredenham Rd, TR2 5AN, ℰ 270771, ≤ harbour and estuary — ⌂wc ▥wc. **ꗩ** **AE** **①** **VISA**
     15 March-4 November — **M** (bar lunch)/dinner 10.25 **t**. and a la carte ⓪ 1.75 — **22 rm** ⊃⊂ (dinner included) 29.50/72.00 **t**. — SB 56.00/70.00 **st**.

  🏠 **St. Mawes**, The Seafront, TR2 5DW, ℰ 270266, ≤ — ⌂wc. **ꗩ** **VISA**
     closed December and January — **M** (bar lunch)/dinner 8.00 **t**. and a la carte ⓪ 2.70 — **8 rm** ⊃⊂ 15.00/34.00 **t**.

  XX **Green Lantern** with rm, Marine Par., TR2 5DW, ℰ 270502, ≤ — **TV** ⌂wc ▥wc. **ꗩ** **AE** **①** **VISA**. ⛾
     closed mid December-mid February — **M** (bar lunch Monday to Saturday)/dinner 12.50 **t**. ⓪ 2.50 — **10 rm** ⊃⊂ 15.00/35.00.

    at St. Just in Roseland N : 2 ½ m. on A 3078 — ⊠ Truro — ☎ 0326 St. Mawes :

  🏠 **Rose da Mar** ⌖, TR2 5JB, N : ¼ m. on B 3289 ℰ 270450, ≤, ╦ — ⌂wc **P**. ⛾
     April-October — **M** (dinner only) 9.00 **t**. ⓪ 2.75 — **9 rm** ⊃⊂ 15.50/34.80 **t**.

ST. NEOTS Cambs. **404** T 27 — pop. 12,468 — ☎ 0480 Huntingdon.

See : St. Mary's Church★ 15C — ▮ₐ Cross Hall Rd ℰ 72363, W : 1 m. — ▮ₐ Eynesbury Hardwicke, St. Neots Leisure Centre ℰ 215153, SE : 2 m.

♦London 60 — Bedford 11 — ♦Cambridge 17 — Huntingdon 9.

  XX **Chequers Inn**, St. Mary's St., Eynesbury, PE19 2TA, S : ½ m. on B 1043 ℰ 72116 — **P**. **ꗩ** **AE** **①** **VISA**
     closed Christmas Night — **M** 6.95/9.95 **t**. and a la carte ⓪ 3.00.

  XX **Raj Douth**, 12 High St. ⊠ Huntingdon, ℰ 219626, Indian rest. — **ꗩ** **AE** **①** **VISA**
     M 2.95/4.50 **st**. and a la carte.

AUSTIN-ROVER 42 Huntingdon St. ℰ 73237   FORD Cambridge St. ℰ 73321

SALCOMBE Devon **403** I 33 The West Country G. — pop. 1,968 — ECD : Thursday — ☎ 054 884.

Envir. : Kingsbridge ★, N : 5 m. by A 381 Y — Prawle Point (≤★★★), E : 16 m. around coast by A 381 Y — Sharpitor Overbecks Museum and Garden (≤★★) *AC*, SW : 2 m. by South Sands Z.

🛈 Main Rd ℰ 2736 (summer only).

♦London 243 — Exeter 43 — ♦Plymouth 27 — Torquay 28.

SALCOMBE

Fore Street . . . . Y

Allenhayes Road . . . . Y 2
Bonaventure Road . . . . . . Y 3
Buckley Street . . . . Y 4
Camperdown Road . . . . . Y 7
Church Street . . . . Y 8
Coronation Road . . . . Y 9
Devon Road . . . . Y 13
Fortescue Road . . . . Z 14
Grenville Road . . . . Y 15
Herbert Road . . . . Z 18
Knowle Road . . . . Y 19
Moult Road . . . . Z 20
Newton Road . . . . Y 23
Sandhills Road . . . . Z 24
Shadycombe Road . . . . . . Y 25

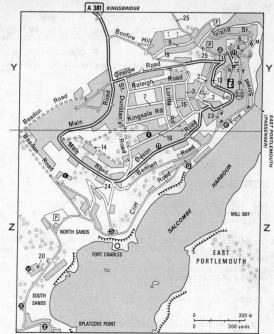

Town plans
roads most used
by traffic and those
on which guide listed
hotels and restaurants
stand are fully drawn ;
the beginning only
of lesser roads
is indicated.

🏨 **Marine,** Cliff Rd, TQ8 8JH, ℰ 2251, Telex 45185, ≼ estuary, ⌁ heated, ⌁ – ⌹ 📺 ☎ 🅿. ⌁
AE ① VISA ⌖   Y e
  closed January and February – **M** (buffet lunch)/dinner 19.50 t. ⏦ 3.50 – **51 rm**
  ⌕ 35.00/108.00 st., **1 suite** 108.00/158.00 st. – SB (27 October-9 April) 72.00 st.

🏨 **Tides Reach,** South Sands, TQ8 8LJ, ℰ 3466, ≼, ⌁, ⌖, squash – ⌹ 📺 ⌁wc ⊛ 🅿. ⌁
AE ① VISA
  March-October – **M** (buffet lunch)/dinner 14.00 t. and a la carte ⏦ 3.50 – **40 rm** ⌕ (din-
  ner included) 36.00/96.00 t. – SB (October-May) (except Bank Holidays) 73.00/79.00 st.

🏨 **Bolt Head** (Best Western) ⌖, South Sands, TQ8 8LL, ℰ 2780, ≼ estuary, ⌁ heated – 📺
⌁wc 🅿. ⌁ AE ① VISA   Z z
  20 March-15 November – **M** (buffet lunch)/dinner 14.50 t. ⏦ 3.00 – **28 rm** ⌕ 27.00/77.00 t. –
  SB (15 September-22 May) 54.00/60.00 st.

🏨 **St. Elmo** ⌖, Sandhills Rd, TQ8 8JR, ℰ 2233, ≼, ⌖ – 📺 ⌁wc ⋔wc 🅿. ⌁ VISA. ⌖   Z r
  Easter-October – **M** (bar lunch)/dinner 16.00 t. – SB (except
  23 May-19 September) 47.50/54.00 st.

🏨 **Grafton Towers** ⌖, Moult Rd, TQ8 8LG, ℰ 2882, ≼, ⌖ – 📺 ⌁wc ⋔wc 🅿. ⌁ VISA
  Easter-5 October – **M** (bar lunch)/dinner 8.50 t. ⏦ 3.00 – **15 rm** ⌕ 12.00/43.00 t. – SB (April,
  May and late September) 35.00/42.00 st.   Z v

🏨 **Castle Point** ⌖, Sandhills Rd, TQ8 8JP, ℰ 2167, ≼ estuary, ⌖ – 📺 ⌁wc ⋔wc 🅿. ⌁ ①
VISA. ⌖   Z s
  Easter-mid October – **M** (bar lunch)/dinner 9.50 t. ⏦ 2.50 – **20 rm** ⌕ 14.00/49.00 t. – SB
  (April-10 June) (except Bank Holidays) 25.00/45.00 st.

🏨 **Knowle,** Onslow Rd, TQ8 8HY, ℰ 2846, ⌖ – 📺 ⌁wc ⋔wc 🅿. ⌁ VISA   Y a
  March-October – **M** (bar lunch)/dinner 5.75 st. ⏦ 2.30 – **14 rm** ⌕ 12.50/34.00 st. – SB (March-
  June and October) (except Bank Holidays) 39.00 st.

↑ **Bay View,** Bennett Rd, TQ8 8JJ, ℰ 2238, ≼ estuary – 🅿. VISA. ⌖   Z o
  March-October – **11 rm** ⌕ 15.00/36.00 t.

↑ **Woodgrange,** Devon Rd, TQ8 8HJ, ℰ 2439, ⌖ – 📺 ⌁wc 🅿. ⌁ AE VISA   Z n
  April-October – **11 rm** ⌕ 11.00/28.00 st.

↑ **Penn Torr,** Herbert Rd, TQ8 8HN, ℰ 2234 – ⌁wc ⋔wc 🅿. ⌖   Z i
  April-October – **9 rm** ⌕ 11.00/27.00 st.

✕ **Wellingtons,** 84-86 Fore St., TQ8 8BY, ℰ 3385 – ⌁ AE ① VISA   Y n
  February-October – **M** (closed Sunday and Monday during February, March and October)
  (dinner only) 6.95 t. and a la carte ⏦ 3.50.

at Soar Mill Cove SW : 3 m. via Cliff Rd – Y – ⊠ Malborough – ✪ 0548 Kingsbridge :

🏠 **Soar Mill Cove** ⬧, TQ7 3DS, ℰ 561566, ≤, 🔁 heated, 🏖 – 📺 ⌷wc ⅋ 🅿 ⏚ 𝗩𝗜𝗦𝗔 ❀
Mid March-mid October – **M** (bar lunch)/dinner 16.00 **t.** ⏶ 3.00 – **14 rm** ⌷ 31.00/70.00 **t.**

at Hope Cove W : 4 m. by A 381 – Y – ⊠ ✪ 0548 Kingsbridge :

🏠 **Cottage** ⬧, TQ7 3HJ, ℰ 561555, ≤ Bolt Tail and Bigbury Bay, 🏖 – ⌷wc ⅏wc 🅿
closed January – **M** (bar lunch Monday to Saturday)/dinner 10.60 **st.** and a la carte ⏶ 3.00 –
35 rm ⌷ 23.90/55.30 **st.** – SB (November-Easter) 35.35/40.30 **st.**

🏠 **Lantern Lodge** ⬧, TQ7 3HE, ℰ 561280, ≤, 🔁, 🏖 – ⌷wc ⅏wc 🅿 ⏚ 𝗩𝗜𝗦𝗔 ❀
March-November and Christmas – **M** (bar lunch)/dinner 10.00 **t.** ⏶ 3.75 – **14 rm**
⌷ 18.50/54.00 **t.** – SB (October-April) 39.00/54.00 **st.**

⚓ **Port Light** ⬧, Bolberry Down, TQ7 3DY, SE : 1 ¾ m. ℰ 561384, ≤, 🏖 – ⅏wc 🅿 ⏚ 𝗩𝗜𝗦𝗔
23 March-October – **M** (bar lunch)/dinner 10.30 **t.** and a la carte ⏶ 2.90 – **6 rm** ⌷ 14.75/43.00 **t.**
– SB (April, May and October) 39.00/45.00 **st.**

🖝 *Pour aller loin rapidement, utilisez les **cartes Michelin** à 1/1 000 000.*

SALISBURY Wilts. **四0三 四0四** O 30 **The West Country G.** – pop. 36 ,890 – ECD : Wednesday –
✪ 0722.

See : Site *** – Cathedral***AC Z – The Close* Z : Mompesson House**AC Z A, **Military**
MuseumAC Z M1 – Salisbury and South Wiltshire Museum**AC Z M2 – Sarum St. Thomas
Church* Y B.

Envir. : Stonehenge***AC, NW : 10 m. by A 345 Y – Wilton House***AC, W : 2 ½ m. by A 30 Y –
Old Sarum*AC N : 2 m. by A 345 Y – at Wilton Village, Royal Wilton Carpet Factory*AC, W :
2 ½ m. by A 30 Y – Heale House*AC N : 7 m. by Stratford Road Y – Wardour Castle*AC, W : 10 m.
by A 30. Y.

🛆, 🛆 Salisbury and South Wilts., Netherhampton ℰ 742645, by A 3094 Z – 🛆 High Post, Great
Durnford ℰ 072 273 (Middle Woodford) 231, N : 4 m. by A 345. Y.

🛈 10 Endless St. ℰ 334956.

◆London 91 – Bournemouth 28 – ◆Bristol 53 – ◆Southampton 23.

Plan opposite

🏨 **White Hart** (T.H.F.), 1 St. John St., SP1 2SD, ℰ 27476 – 📺 ⌷wc ☎ 🅿 ⏛ ⏚ 𝗔𝗘 ⓪ 𝗩𝗜𝗦𝗔
M 6.25/9.45 **st.** and a la carte ⏶ 2.95 – ⌷ 5.50 – **70 rm** 35.50/46.00 **st.**   Z s

🏨 **Old Bell Inn,** 2 St. Ann St., SP1 2DN, ℰ 27958, « Converted 14C inn » – ⅏wc. ⏚ 𝗔𝗘 ⓪ 𝗩𝗜𝗦𝗔
❀   Z v
closed Christmas – **M** *(closed Sunday dinner)* 5.00/15.00 **t.** and a la carte ⏶ 3.00 – ⌷ 3.50 –
7 rm 35.00/40.00 **st.**

🏨 **Cathedral,** 7 Milford St., SP1 2AJ, ℰ 20144 – ⍰ 📺 ⌷wc ⅏. ⏚ 𝗩𝗜𝗦𝗔. ❀   Y a
M (buffet lunch)/dinner 6.75 **t.** and a la carte ⏶ 3.15 – **30 rm** ⌷ 21.50/44.50 **t.** – SB (October-
April except Christmas and Easter) 38.50/46.50 **st.**

🏨 **Kings Arms,** 9 St. John's St., SP1 2SB, ℰ 27629, « Part 13C and part 15C inn » – 📺 ⌷wc
⅏. ⏚ 𝗔𝗘 ⓪ 𝗩𝗜𝗦𝗔. ❀   Z r
M 8.00 **t.** and a la carte ⏶ 2.00 – **16 rm** ⌷ 20.20/36.50 **t.** – SB (October-May) 40.00/50.00 **st.**

⌂ **Stratford Lodge,** 4 Park Lane, Castle Rd, SP1 3NP, ℰ 25177, 🏖 – 📺 ⌷wc 🅿 ❀
closed December and January – **5 rm** ⌷ 20.00/30.00 **s.**

⌂ **Byways House,** 31 Fowlers Rd, off Milford Hill, SP1 2QP, 🏖 – ⅏wc 🅿 ❀   Z e
17 rm ⌷ 11.00/25.00 **st.**

✗✗ **Dutch Mill,** 58a Fisherton St., SP2 7RB, ℰ 23447 – ⏚ 𝗔𝗘 ⓪ 𝗩𝗜𝗦𝗔   Y i
M (lunch by arrangement) a la carte 8.75/11.25 **t.** ⏶ 2.50.

✗ **Eugene's,** 127 South Western Rd, SP1 1DF, ℰ 331270   Y e

at Redlynch SE : 8 ½ m. by A 338 – Z – off B 3080 – ⊠ Salisbury – ✪ 0794 Romsey :

✗✗ **Langley Wood** ⬧ with rm, Hamptworth Rd, SP5 2PB, SE : 1 ½ m. ℰ 390348, 🏖 – 🅿 ⏚
𝗔𝗘 ⓪ 𝗩𝗜𝗦𝗔
M *(closed Sunday dinner to non-residents)* (lunch by arrangement) a la carte 9.50/12.00 **t.**
⏶ 2.25 – **3 rm** ⌷ 11.00/22.00 **t.**

at Odstock S : 2 ½ m. by A 338 – Z – ⊠ ✪ 0722 Salisbury :

✗ **Yew Tree Inn,** SP5 4JE, ℰ 29786, 🏖 – 🅿 ⏚ 𝗔𝗘 ⓪ 𝗩𝗜𝗦𝗔
closed Sunday dinner, Monday and Christmas Day – **M** a la carte 6.35/11.65 **t.**

at Downton S : 6 m. by A 338 – Z – ⊠ ✪ 0725 Downton :

⌂ **Warren,** 15 High St., SP5 3PG, ℰ 20263, 🏖 – 🅿
closed mid December-mid January – **7 rm** ⌷ 11.00/24.00 **s.**

at Harnham SW : 1 ½ m. by A 3094 – ⊠ ✪ 0722 Salisbury :

🏨 **Rose and Crown** (Q.M.H.), Harnham Rd, SP2 8JQ, ℰ 27908, Telex 47224, ≤, « Riverside
location », 🏖 – 📺 ⌷wc ☎ ⏛ 🅿 ⏚ 𝗔𝗘 ⓪ 𝗩𝗜𝗦𝗔. ❀   Z u
M 6.50/9.50 **st.** and a la carte ⏶ 2.95 – ⌷ 4.95 – **27 rm** 45.45/49.45 **st.** – SB (weekends only)
70.00/79.00 **st.**

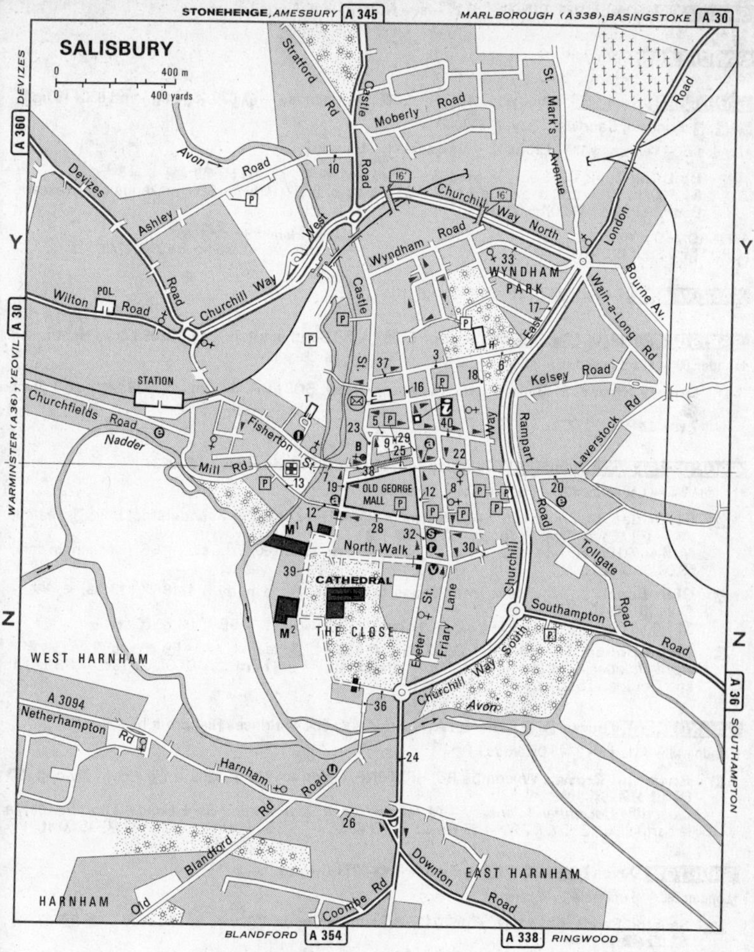

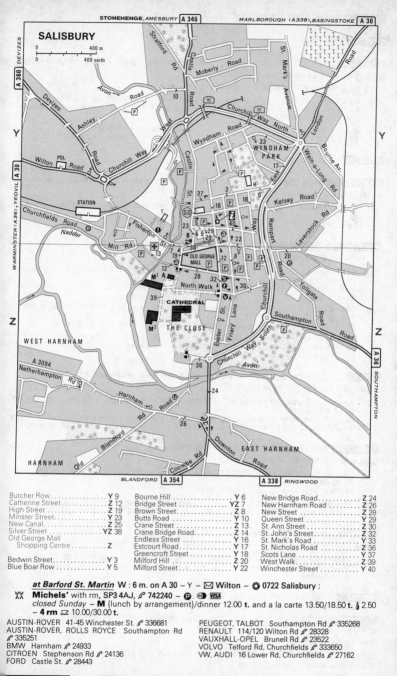

Butcher Row	Y 9	Bourne Hill	Y 6	New Bridge Road	Z 24
Catherine Street	Z 12	Bridge Street	YZ 7	New Harnham Road	Z 26
High Street	Z 19	Brown Street	Z 8	New Street	Z 28
Minster Street	Y 23	Butts Road	Y 10	Queen Street	Y 29
New Canal	Z 25	Crane Street	Z 13	St. Ann Street	Z 30
Silver Street	YZ 38	Crane Bridge Road	Z 14	St. John's Street	Z 32
Old George Mall Shopping Centre	Z	Endless Street	Y 16	St. Mark's Road	Y 33
		Estcourt Road	Y 17	St. Nicholas Road	Z 36
		Greencroft Street	Y 18	Scots Lane	Y 37
Bedwin Street	Y 3	Milford Hill	Z 20	West Walk	Z 39
Blue Boar Row	Y 5	Milford Street	Y 22	Winchester Street	Y 40

at Barford St. Martin W : 6 m. on A 30 – Y – ✉ **Wilton** – ☎ **0722 Salisbury :**

XX **Michels'** with rm, SP3 4AJ, ☎ 742240 – Ⓟ. ◑ VISA
closed Sunday – **M** (lunch by arrangement)/dinner 12.00 **t.** and a la carte 13.50/18.50 **t.** 🍷 2.50 – **4 rm** ☕ 10.00/30.00 **t.**

AUSTIN-ROVER 41-45 Winchester St. ☎ 336681
AUSTIN-ROVER, ROLLS ROYCE Southampton Rd ☎ 335251
BMW Harnham ☎ 24933
CITROEN Stephenson Rd ☎ 24136
FORD Castle St. ☎ 28443
PEUGEOT, TALBOT Southampton Rd ☎ 335268
RENAULT 114/120 Wilton Rd ☎ 28328
VAUXHALL-OPEL Brunell Rd ☎ 23522
VOLVO Telford Rd, Churchfields ☎ 333650
VW, AUDI 16 Lower Rd, Churchfields ☎ 27162

SAMLESBURY Lancs. **402** M 22 – see Preston.

SANDIACRE Derbs. 402 403 404 Q 25 – see Nottingham (Notts.).

SANDPLACE Cornwall – see Looe.

SANDWICH Kent 404 Y 30 – pop. 4,184 – ECD : Wednesday – ✆ 030 46 (4 fig.) and 0304 (6 fig.).
🏌, 🏌, 🏌 Prince's, Sandwich Bay 🖉 612000.
♦London 72 – Canterbury 13 – ♦Dover 12 – Maidstone 41 – Margate 9.

🏨 **Bell,** The Quay, CT13 9EF, 🖉 613388 – 📺 ➭wc ☎ 🅿 🔥 🔊 AE ⓪ VISA
M 7.00/10.50 **st.** and a la carte 🅙 4.25 – **33 rm** ➭ 30.00/50.00 **st.** – SB (weekends only) (except Bank Holidays) 48.00/56.00 **st.**

ALFA-ROMEO 🖉 611654
FORD New St. 🖉 612308

LANCIA Harnet St. 🖉 613685
RENAULT Woodnesborough 🖉 812349

SANDYPARK Devon 403 I 31 – see Chagford.

SARISBURY Hants. 403 404 Q 31 – pop. 5,682 – ✉ Southampton – ✆ 048 95 Locks Heath.
♦London 90 – ♦Portsmouth 16 – ♦Southampton 6.

🏠 **Dormy House,** 21 Barnes Lane, Sarisbury Green, SO3 6DA, S : 1 m. 🖉 2626, 🌲 – 📺 🔊wc
🅿 ❄
7 rm ➭ 9.00/22.00 **st.**

SAUNDERSFOOT Dyfed 403 F 28 – pop. 2,196 – ECD : Wednesday – ✆ 0834.
♦London 245 – Carmarthen 25 – Fishguard 34 – Tenby 3.

🏨 **St. Brides,** St. Brides Hill, SA69 9NH, 🖉 812304, Telex 48350, ⩽ Saundersfoot Bay, 🔊 heated, 🌲 – 📺 ➭wc 🔊wc 🅿 🔥 🔊 AE ⓪ VISA
M 6.45/10.95 **st.** and a la carte 🅙 3.50 – **49 rm** ➭ 30.00/55.00 **st.** – SB (weekends only) 58.00/63.00 **st.**

🏠 **Glen Beach** ❄, Swallow Tree Woods, SA69 9DE, S : ½ m. by B 4316 🖉 813430, ⩽, 🌲 –
🔊wc 🅿 🔊 AE VISA
M 7.00/9.50 **t.** and a la carte 🅙 3.00 – **12 rm** ➭ 19.00/46.00 **t.** – SB 40.00/50.00 **st.**

🏠 **Malin House,** St. Brides Hill, SA69 9NP, 🖉 812344, 🔊 heated, 🌲 – 📺 ➭wc 🔊wc 🅿 ❄
April-October – **M** (bar lunch)/dinner 5.00 **st.** 🅙 1.70 – **11 rm** ➭ 10.00/30.00 **st.** – SB (April and October) 25.00 **st.**

SAUNDERTON Bucks. 404 R 28 – ✉ Aylesbury – ✆ 084 44 Princes Risborough.
♦London 42 – Aylesbury 9 – ♦Oxford 20.

🏠 **Rose and Crown,** Wycombe Rd, HP17 9NP, N : on A 4010 🖉 5299 – 📺 ➭wc 🔊wc 🅿 🔊
AE ⓪ VISA ❄
closed 24 December-1 January – **M** (closed lunch Saturday and Bank Holidays and Sunday) a la carte 9.30/12.55 **t.** 🅙 2.90 – **15 rm** ➭ 21.50/49.50 **st.** – SB (weekends only) 41.00/45.00 **st.**

SAUNTON Devon 403 H 30 – ✉ Braunton – ✆ 0271 Croyde.
♦London 230 – Barnstaple 8 – Exeter 48.

🏨 Saunton Sands, EX33 1LQ, 🖉 890212, ⩽ Saunton Sands, 🔊, 🌲, ✖, squash – 📺 🅿 🔥
🔊 AE ⓪ VISA ❄
M 6.50/9.50 **st.** and a la carte 🅙 3.75 – **90 rm.**

🏠 **Preston House,** EX33 1LG, 🖉 890472, ⩽ Saunton Sands, 🌲 – ➭wc 🔊wc 🅿 ❄
March-October – **M** (bar lunch residents only)/dinner 9.35 **t.** 🅙 3.40 – **12 rm** ➭ 17.50/42.00 **t.**

SAWLEY Lancs. 402 M 22 – pop. 179 – ✉ ✆ 0200 Clitheroe.
♦ London 242 – ♦ Blackpool 39 – ♦ Leeds 44 – ♦ Liverpool 54.

🏨 **Spread Eagle** ❄, BB7 4NH, 🖉 41202, 🔊 – 📺 ➭wc 🔊wc ☎ ♿ 🅿 🔊 AE ⓪ VISA ❄
M 7.50/11.50 **st.** and a la carte 🅙 2.50 – **9 rm** ➭ 22.50/50.00 **st.** – SB (weekends only) 60.00/70.00 **st.**

SCALBY North Yorks. 402 S 21 – see Scarborough.

SCARBOROUGH North Yorks. 402 S 21 – pop. 36,665 – ECD : Monday and Wednesday –
✆ 0723.
See : Castle 12C (⩽★) AC Y.
🏌 North Cliff, North Cliff Av. 🖉 360786, NW : 2 m. by A 165 Y.
🛈 St. Nicholas Cliff 🖉 372261 and 373333.
♦London 253 – ♦Kingston-upon-Hull 47 – ♦Leeds 67 – ♦Middlesbrough 52.

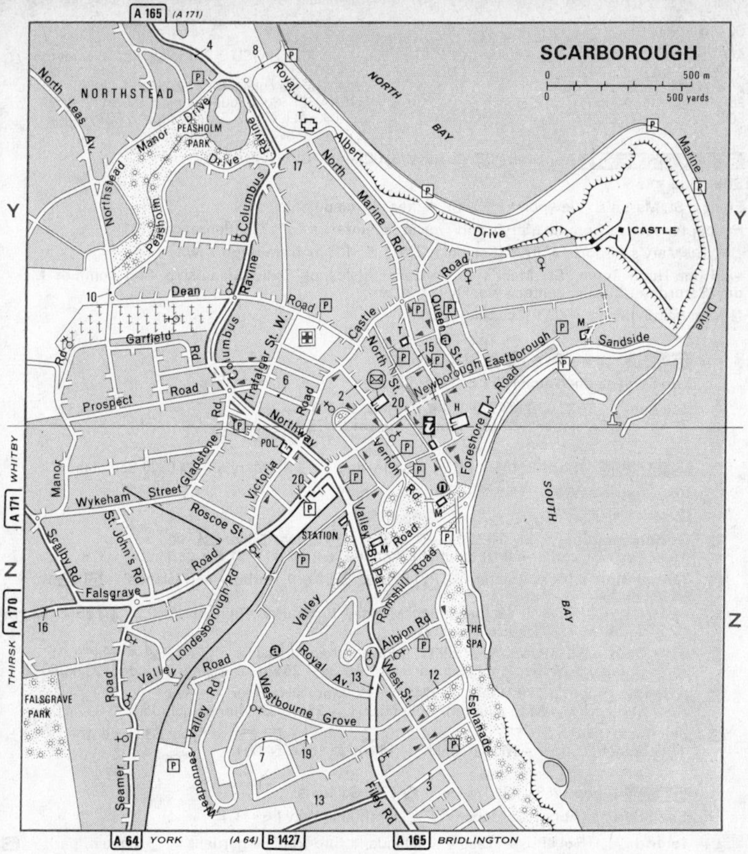

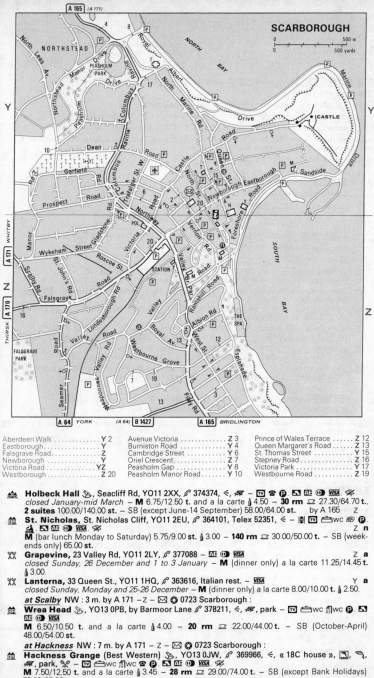

Aberdeen Walk . . . . Y 2
Eastborough . . . . Y
Falsgrave Road . . . . Z
Newborough . . . . Y
Victoria Road . . . . YZ
Westborough . . . . Z 20

Avenue Victoria . . . . Z 3
Burniston Road . . . . Y 4
Cambridge Street . . . . Y 6
Oriel Crescent . . . . Z 7
Peasholm Gap . . . . Y 8
Peasholm Manor Road . . . . . . Y 10

Prince of Wales Terrace . . . . . . Z 12
Queen Margaret's Road . . . . . . Z 13
St. Thomas Street . . . . Y 15
Stepney Road . . . . Z 16
Victoria Park . . . . Y 17
Westbourne Road . . . . Z 19

🏨 **Holbeck Hall** 🐎, Seacliff Rd, YO11 2XX, ✆ 374374, ⩽, 🌳 – [TV] ☎ [P]. 💳 [AE] [D] [VISA]. 🚫🐕
closed January-mid March – **M** 6.75/12.50 **t.** and a la carte 🍷 4.50 – **30 rm** ☕ 27.30/64.70 **t.**, **2 suites** 100.00/140.00 **st.** – SB (except June-14 September) 58.00/64.00 **st.** by A 165 Z

🏨 **St. Nicholas,** St. Nicholas Cliff, YO11 2EU, ✆ 364101, Telex 52351, ⩽ – ⇕ [TV] 🛁wc 📞 [P]. 👥. 💳 [AE] [D] [VISA]. 🚫🐕 Z **n**
M (bar lunch Monday to Saturday) 5.75/9.00 **st.** 🍷 3.00 – **140 rm** ☕ 30.00/50.00 **t.** – SB (weekends only) 65.00 **st.**

🍴🍴 **Grapevine,** 23 Valley Rd, YO11 2LY, ✆ 377088 – [AE] [D] [VISA] Z **a**
closed Sunday, 26 December and 1 to 3 January – **M** (dinner only) a la carte 11.25/14.45 **t.** 🍷 3.00.

🍴🍴 **Lanterna,** 33 Queen St., YO11 1HQ, ✆ 363616, Italian rest. – [VISA] Y **a**
closed Sunday, Monday and 25-26 December – **M** (dinner only) a la carte 8.00/10.00 **t.** 🍷 2.50.

at Scalby NW : 3 m. by A 171 – Z – ✉ ⊛ 0723 Scarborough :

🏨 **Wrea Head** 🐎, YO13 0PB, by Barmoor Lane ✆ 378211, ⩽, 🌳, park – [TV] 🛁wc 🚿wc [P]. 💳 [AE] [D] [VISA]
M 6.50/10.50 **t.** and a la carte 🍷 4.00 – **20 rm** ☕ 22.00/44.00 **t.** – SB (October-April) 48.00/54.00 **st.**

at Hackness NW : 7 m. by A 171 – Z – ✉ ⊛ 0723 Scarborough :

🏨 **Hackness Grange** (Best Western) 🐎, YO13 0JW, ✆ 369966, ⩽, « 18C house », 🏊, 🎣, 🌳, park, 🎾 – [TV] 🛁wc 🚿wc ☎ [P]. 💳 [AE] [D] [VISA]. 🚫🐕
M 7.50/12.50 **t.** and a la carte 🍷 3.45 – **28 rm** ☕ 29.00/74.00 **t.** – SB (except Bank Holidays) 59.00/83.00 **st.**

SCARBOROUGH

AUSTIN-ROVER Valley Bridge Rd ℘ 360221
CITROEN, DATSUN, PEUGEOT, TALBOT Northway
℘ 363533
FIAT Manor Rd ℘ 364111
FORD Vine St. ℘ 375581

LADA, DAIHATSU Pickering Rd, Westayton ℘
862880
MAZDA Falconers Rd ℘ 360322
RENAULT Columbus Ravine ℘ 360791
VAUXHALL-OPEL Seamer Rd ℘ 360335

SCILLY (ISLES OF) Cornwall **403** ㉚ The West Country G. – pop. 2 ,653.

See : Site ★★.

Envir. : St. Martin's : Viewpoint ★★ – St. Agnes : Horsepoint ★.

Helicopter service from St. Mary's and Tresco to Penzance : ℘ 0736 (Penzance) 3871.

✈ St. Mary's Airport : ℘ 0720 (Scillonia) 22677, E : 1 ½ m. from Hugh Town.

⛴ from Hugh Town, St. Mary's to Penzance (Isles of Scilly Steamship Co.) summer Monday/Saturday 1-2 daily; winter 3 weekly (2 h 30 mn).

🛈 Town Hall, St. Mary's ℘ 0720 (Scillonia) 22536.

Bryher – pop. 66 – ⊠ ✿ 0720 Scillonia.
See : Village on Watch Hill (≤★) – Hell Bay★.

🏨 Hell Bay ⬎, TR23 0PR, ℘ 22947, ⟵, ≈ – ▥wc. ⚠ **VISA**. ✠
20 March-10 October – **M** (bar lunch) – **10 rm** ⊑ 27.00/36.00 t.

St. Mary's – pop. 2 ,106 – ECD : Wednesday – ⊠ St. Mary's – ✿ 0720 Scillonia.
See : Garrison Walk★ (≤★★) – Peninnis Head ★.
🛈 Town Hall, ℘ 22536.

🏨 **Godolphin,** Church St., TR21 0JR, ℘ 22316 – ▥ ⟵wc. ⚠ Ⓐ **VISA**. ✠
Mid March-9 October – **M** (bar lunch)/dinner 9.00 t. ᐧ 2.80 – **31 rm** ⊑ 14.00/56.00 t.

🏨 **Tregarthen's** (Best Western), TR21 0PP, ℘ 22540, ≤ Harbour and islands – ▥ ⟵wc ⊜.
⚠ Ⓐ Ⓞ **VISA**. ✠
Mid March-October – **M** (bar lunch Monday to Saturday)/dinner 10.50 **st.** ᐧ 3.25 – **33 rm**
⊑ 21.00/56.00 st. – SB 38.00/73.00 st.

🏨 **Star Castle** ⬎, TR21 0JA, ℘ 22317, « Elizabethan fortress », ◪, ⟵, ✠ – ▥ ⟵wc
April-October – **M** (bar lunch)/dinner 9.00 t. ᐧ 2.00 – **24 rm** ⊑ (dinner included) 23.50/60.00.

🏨 **Atlantic,** Hugh St., TR21 0PL, ℘ 22417, ≤ St. Mary's Harbour – ⟵wc
April-September – **M** (bar lunch)/dinner 8.95 t. – **25 rm** ⊑ (dinner included) 23.00/44.00 t.

🏨 Bell Rock, Church St., TR21 0JS, ℘ 22575, ◪ heated – ▥ ⟵wc ▥wc. ⚠ Ⓐ Ⓞ **VISA**
11 February-October – **M** (bar lunch) – **18 rm** ⊑ 15.00/54.00 t.

Tresco – pop. 285 – ⊠ Tresco – ✿ 0720 Scillonia.
See : Site★ – Abbey Gardens★*AC* – Lighthouse Way (≤★★).

🏨🏨 **Island** ⬎, TR24 0PU, ℘ 22883, ≤ Islands, « Sub-tropical gardens », ◪ heated, park – ▥
⊜. ☜.
Mid March-mid October – **M** 16.00 **st.** (dinner) and a la carte ᐧ 3.50 – **32 rm** ⊑ 38.00/64.00 **st.**,
1 suite 65.00/76.00 **st.**

🏨 **New Inn** ⬎, TR24 0QQ, ℘ 22844, ≤, ⟵ – ⟵wc. ✠
March-October – **M** (bar lunch)/dinner 12.00 t. ᐧ 2.60 – **12 rm** ⊑ 12.50/40.00 **st.**

SCOLE Norfolk **404** X 26 – see Diss.

SCUNTHORPE Humberside **402** S 23 – pop. 79 ,043 – ECD : Wednesday – ✿ 0724.

Envir. : Normanby Hall★ (Regency) : Wildlife park★ *AC*, N : 4 m. – Barton-upon-Humber (St. Mary's Church★ 12C, Old St. Peter's Church★ 10C-11C) NE : 13 ½ m.

🏌 Ashby Decoy, Burringham Rd ℘ 842913 – 🏌 Kingsway ℘ 840945.

✈ Humberside Airport : ℘ 0652 (Barnetby) 688456, E : 15 m. by A 18.

🛈 Central Library, Carlton St. ℘ 860161.

♦London 167 – ♦Leeds 54 – Lincoln 30 – ♦Sheffield 45.

🏨 Wortley House, Rowland Rd, DN16 1ST, ℘ 842223 – ▥ ⟵wc ⊜ 🅿. ᐧᐧ
28 rm.

🏨 **Royal** (Anchor), Doncaster Rd, DN15 7DE, ℘ 868181, Telex 527479 – ▥ ⟵wc ⊜ 🅿. ᐧᐧ. ⚠
Ⓐ Ⓞ **VISA**
M *(closed Saturday lunch)* (carving rest) 8.35 **st.** ᐧ 3.00 – **33 rm** ⊑ 37.50/47.00 **st.** – SB (weekends only) 44.00 **st.**

BMW Normanby Rd ℘ 864251
COLT Doncaster Rd ℘ 860212
FIAT Normanby Rd ℘ 861191
LADA Grange Lane North ℘ 851548
RENAULT 136/144 Ashby High St. ℘ 867474

TALBOT Smith St. ℘ 869323
TOYOTA Brigg Rd ℘ 842011
VAUXHALL-OPEL Moorwell Rd Industrial Estate ℘
843284
VAUXHALL-OPEL Winterton Rd ℘ 861083

SEACROFT West Yorks. 402 ⑩ – see Leeds.

SEAFORD East Sussex 404 U 31 – pop. 16 ,367 – ECD : Wednesday – ✆ 0323.
🛱 The Downs, Sutton Rd. ✆ 897426.
♦London 65 – ♦Brighton 14 – Folkestone 64.

　　XX　Bentley's, 30A High St., BN25 1PL, ✆ 892220.

SEAHOUSES Northumb. 401 402 P 17 – pop. 1 ,709 (inc. North Sunderland) – ECD : Wednesday – ✆ 0665.
🛱 Beadnell Rd ✆ 720794.
🛿 16 Main St. ✆ 720424 (summer only).
♦London 328 – ♦Edinburgh 80 – ♦Newcastle-upon-Tyne 46.

　　🏠　**Beach House,** 12a St. Aidans, Seafront, NE68 7SR, ✆ 720337, ≤, ㎡ – 📺 ⇔wc ﬔwc ⅙ 🅿. ☒ 𝘝𝘐𝘚𝘈
　　　　April-October – **M** (bar lunch residents only)/dinner 8.50 **t.** ⅟ 3.00 – **14 rm** ⇌ 17.00/39.00 **t.** – SB (April, May and October) 43.00 **st.**
　　🏠　**St. Aidans,** Seafront, ✆ 720355, ≤ – 📺 ⇔wc ﬔwc 🅿. ☒ ⓞ 𝘝𝘐𝘚𝘈
　　　　March-October – **M** (bar lunch)/dinner 7.50 **st.** and a la carte ⅟ 3.50 – **10 rm** ⇌ 12.00/46.00 **st.** – SB (except summer) 42.00/44.00 **st.**
　　🛎　**Olde Ship,** 9 Main St., NE68 7RD, ✆ 720200, ㎡ – 📺 ⇔wc ﬔwc 🅿. ☒
　　　　Easter-October – **M** (bar lunch)/dinner 7.00 **t.** ⅟ 2.20 – **10 rm** ⇌ 13.50/30.00 **t.**

SEALE Surrey 404 R 30 – see Farnham.

SEATOLLER Cumbria – see Keswick.

SEATON Devon 403 K 31 – pop. 6 ,157 – ECD : Thursday – ✆ 0297.
♦London 167 – Bournemouth 61 – Exeter 26 – Taunton 29.

　　⌂　**Thornfield,** 87 Scalwell Lane, EX12 2ST, ✆ 20039, ⅃ heated, ㎡ – 📺 ﬔwc 🅿
　　　　closed 20 October-4 November – **9 rm** ⇌ 11.00/31.00 **st.**

SEATON BURN Tyne and Wear 402 P 18 – see Newcastle-upon-Tyne.

SEAVIEW I.O.W. 403 404 Q 31 – see Wight (Isle of).

SEAVINGTON ST. MARY Somerset 403 L 31 – pop. 321 – ✉ Ilminster – ✆ 0460 South Petherton.
♦London 142 – Taunton 14 – Yeovil 11.

　　XX　**Pheasant** ⌂ with rm, Water St., TA19 0QH, ✆ 40502, ㎡ – 📺 ⇔wc ☎ 🅿. ☒ ⒶⒺ ⓞ 𝘝𝘐𝘚𝘈. ✖
　　　　closed 26 December-3 January – **M** (dinner only) 8.50 **t.** and a la carte 10.00/14.50 **t.** ⅟ 3.00 – **7 rm** ⇌ 35.00/50.00 **t.** – SB 55.00 **st.**

SEDBERGH Cumbria 402 M 21 – pop. 1 ,644 – ECD : Thursday – ✆ 0587.
🛱 The Riggs, ✆ 20993 S : 1 m.
🛿 National Park Centre, 72 Main St. ✆ 20125 (summer only).
♦London 284 – ♦Carlisle 49 – Kendal 10 – Lancaster 27 – Penrith 30.

　　🏠　**Oakdene Country,** Garsdale Rd, LA10 5JN, NE : 1 ½ m. on A 684 ✆ 20280, ≤, ㎡ – 🅿. ☒ ⒶⒺ ⓞ 𝘝𝘐𝘚𝘈
　　　　closed mid January-February – **M** (bar lunch)/dinner 12.00 **t.** and a la carte ⅟ 2.10 – **6 rm** ⇌ 12.00/30.00 **t.**

SEDGEFIELD Durham 401 402 P 20 – pop. 4 ,749 – ✉ Stockton-on-Tees (Cleveland) – ✆ 0740.
♦London 261 – Hartlepool 14 – ♦Middlesbrough 13 – ♦Newcastle-upon-Tyne 28.

　　🏨　**Hardwick Hall** ⌂, TS21 9EH, W : 1 ½ m. on A 177 ✆ 20253, ≤, ㎡, park – 📺 ⇔wc ☎ 🅿. ✖ **17 rm.**
　　🛎　**Dun Cow Inn,** 43 Front St., TS21 3AT, ✆ 20894 – 📺 ⊛ 🅿. ☒ ⒶⒺ ⓞ 𝘝𝘐𝘚𝘈
　　　　M a la carte 4.35/10.90 **t.** ⅟ 3.00 – **6 rm** ⇌ 24.00/29.50 **t.**

SEDLESCOMBE East Sussex 404 V 31 – pop. 1 ,315 – ✉ Battle – ✆ 042 487.
♦London 56 – Hastings 7 – Lewes 26 – Maidstone 27.

　　🏨　**Brickwall,** The Green, TN33 0QA, ✆ 253, ⅃ heated, ㎡ – 📺 ⇔wc 🅿. ☒ ⒶⒺ ⓞ 𝘝𝘐𝘚𝘈
　　　　M 6.75/9.50 **t.** ⅟ 2.80 – **19 rm** ⇌ 22.00/58.00 **t.** – SB 45.00/55.00 **st.**
　　XX　**Holmes House,** The Green, TN33 0QA, ✆ 450, ⅃ heated – ☒ ⒶⒺ ⓞ 𝘝𝘐𝘚𝘈
　　　　closed Saturday lunch, Sunday dinner and Monday – **M** 7.50/9.00 **st.** and a la carte ⅟ 2.50.

SEION Gwynedd – see Port Dinorwic.

SELMESTON East Sussex 404 U 31 – pop. 187 – ✉ Polegate – ✆ 032 183 Ripe.
♦London 62 – ♦Brighton 14 – Hastings 23 – Lewes 7.5 – Maidstone 57.

  XX **Corin's,** Church Farm, BN26 6TZ, ✆ 343, « 17C farmhouse », 🌴 – **ℙ**, **ऴ** **AE** **VISA**
    closed Sunday dinner and Monday – **M** (dinner only and Sunday lunch) 6.75/11.95 **t.** ⒜ 3.00.

SELSEY West Sussex 404 R 31 – pop. 7,540 – ECD : Wednesday – ✆ 024 361 (4 fig.) and 0243 (6 fig.).
♦London 78 – ♦Brighton 40 – Chichester 9.

  🏠 **Thatched House,** 23 Warner Rd, off Clayton Rd, PO20 9DD, ✆ 602207, 🌴 – 🛏wc **ℙ**, **ऴ**
    AE **VISA**
    M 5.75 **t.** (lunch) and a la carte 8.35/12.65 **t.** ⒜ 2.50 – ⊡ 3.50 – **6 rm** 10.00/25.00.

SEMINGTON Wilts. 403 404 N 29 – pop. 780 – ✆ 0380 Keevil.
♦London 112 – ♦Bristol 30 – ♦Southampton 57 – Swindon 28.

  XX Highfield House, with rm, BA14 6JN, ✆ 870554 – **ℙ** – **2 rm**.

SENNEN Cornwall 403 C 33 The West Country G. – pop. 772 – ✉ Penzance – ✆ 073 687.
See : Wayside Cross★ – Sennen Cove★ (≼★).
Envir. : Porthcurno★, SE : 4 m.
♦London 328 – Penzance 10 – Truro 36.

  🏠 **Tregiffian** ॐ, TR19 7BE, NE : 2 ¼ m. by A 30 ✆ 408, ≼, 🌴 – 🛏wc 🛏wc **ℙ**, **ऴ** **①** **VISA**
    March-October – **M** (bar lunch)/dinner 8.00 **t.** and a la carte ⒜ 3.30 – **7 rm** ⊡ 14.00/36.80 **t.** –
    SB (except July and August) 42.00 **st.**

SETTLE North Yorks. 402 N 21 – pop. 3,153 – ECD : Wednesday – ✆ 072 92.
🏌 Giggleswick ✆ 3580, off A 65.
🛈 Town Hall, Cheapside ✆ 3617 (summer only).
♦London 238 – Bradford 34 – Kendal 30 – ♦Leeds 41.

  🏨 **Falcon Manor,** Skipton Rd, BD24 9BD, ✆ 3814, ≼, 🌴 – 📺 🛏wc 🛏wc **ℙ**, **ऴ** **①** **VISA**
    M 3.95/8.75 **st.** and a la carte ⒜ 3.00 – **21 rm** ⊡ 27.00/44.00 **st.** – SB 47.00/59.00 **st.**
  🏠 **Royal Oak,** Market Pl., BD24 9ED, ✆ 2561 – 📺 🛏wc ☎ ⇦ **ℙ**, ⌘
    M a la carte 5.85/9.35 **t.** ⒜ 2.75 – **6 rm** ⊡ 22.00/38.50 **t.**

  at Giggleswick NW : ¾ m. on A 65 – ✉ ✆ 072 92 Settle :

  ⌂ **Woodlands** ॐ, The Mains, BD24 0AX, ✆ 2576, ≼, 🌴 – **ℙ**, ⌘
    closed Christmas and New Year – **10 rm** ⊡ 15.75/31.50 **t.**

AUSTIN-ROVER Station Rd ✆ 2323

SEVENOAKS Kent 404 U 30 – pop. 24,493 – ECD : Wednesday – ✆ 0732.
See : Knole★★ (15C-17C) *AC.*
Envir. : Lullingstone (Roman Villa : mosaic panels★) *AC,* N : 6 m.
🏌 Shoreham, Darenth Valley ✆ 095 92 (Otford) 2922, N : 3 m.
🛈 Bligh's car park ✆ 450305.
♦London 26 – Guildford 40 – Maidstone 17.

  ⌂ **Moorings,** 97 Hitchen Hatch Lane, TN13 3BE, ✆ 452589, 🌴 – 📺 🛏wc **ℙ**, **ऴ** **VISA**, ⌘
    11 rm ⊡ 18.40/29.90 **st.**
  XX **Le Chantecler,** 43 High St., TN13 1JF, ✆ 454662 – **ऴ** **AE** **①** **VISA**
    closed Sunday, Monday and 2 weeks July-August – **M** 7.50/10.50 **t.** and a la carte ⒜ 3.00.
  XX **Royal Oak** with rm, Upper High St., TN14 5PG, ✆ 451109 – 📺 🛏wc ☎ **ℙ**, **ऴ** **①** **VISA**
    M *(closed Saturday lunch and Sunday dinner)* 9.00/13.00 **t.** ⒜ 3.20 – **21 rm** ⊡ 30.00/40.00 **st.**

  at Ide Hill SW : 4 ¾ m. by A 2028 and A 25 on B 2042 – ✉ Sevenoaks – ✆ 073 275 Ide Hill :

  XX **Churchill,** ✆ 596, 🌴 – **ℙ**, **ऴ** **①** **VISA**
    closed Sunday dinner – **M** 11.50 **t.** and a la carte 13.50/20.00 **t.** ⒜ 3.50.

AUSTIN-ROVER, ROLLS ROYCE-BENTLEY London
Rd ✆ 458177
BMW London Rd ✆ 450035
CITROEN Tonbridge Rd ✆ 453328
FORD The Vines ✆ 459911
NISSAN London Rd, Dunton Green ✆ 073 273
(Dunton Green) 292

RENAULT 71 St. Johns Hill ✆ 455174
SAAB Borough Green ✆ 883044
SKODA Seal Rd ✆ 454283
TOYOTA Badgers Mount ✆ 095 97 (Badgers Mount)
218
VAUXHALL-OPEL 128 Seal Rd ✆ 451337

Ne voyagez pas aujourd'hui avec une carte d'hier.

SHAFTESBURY Dorset **403 404** N 30 The West Country G. – pop. 4 ,831 – ECD : Wednesday and Saturday – ✪ 0747.

See : ≼★ – Gold Hill★ – Local History Museum★*AC*.

Envir. : Wardour Castle★*AC*, NE : 5 m.

🚹 County Library, Bell St. ✆ 2256.

◆London 115 – Bournemouth 31 – ◆Bristol 47 – Dorchester 29 – Salisbury 20.

🏨 **Grosvenor** (T.H.F.), The Commons, SP7 8JA, ✆ 2282 – 📺 ⌂wc 🅰. 🔼 🔼 ⒶⒺ ⓄⒹ *VISA*
M 6.95/13.00 **st.** – ⌇ 5.50 – **47 rm** 31.50/44.00 **st.**

🏨 **Royal Chase** (Best Western), Royal Chase Roundabout, SP7 8DB, junction of A 30 and A 350 ✆ 3355, 🔲, 🚗 – 📺 ⌂wc ☎ Ⓟ. 🔼 ⒶⒺ ⓄⒹ *VISA*
M a la carte 7.55/10.50 **st.** – **32 rm** ⌇ 31.50/56.00 **st.** – SB (except Christmas and New Year) 48.00/69.50 **st.**

at Donhead St. Andrew (Wilts.) E : 3 ½ m. on A 30 – ✉ Shaftesbury – ✪ 074 788 Donhead :

✗ **Le Radier**, SP8 9LG, ✆ 324, French rest. – Ⓟ
closed Sunday and Monday – **M** (dinner only) (booking essential) 11.50 **st.**

at Ludwell (Wilts.) E : 5 m. on A 30 – ✉ Shaftesbury (Dorset) – ✪ 074 788 Donhead :

🏠 **Grove House,** SP7 9ND, on A 30 ✆ 365, ≼, 🚗 – 🍴wc Ⓟ. 🔼 *VISA*
closed December and January – **M** (dinner only) 7.35 **st.** – **12 rm** ⌇ 17.00/34.75 **st.** – SB (except Easter) 36.00/46.00 **st.**

at Fontmell Magna S : 5 ¼ m. on A 350 – ✉ Shaftesbury – ✪ 0747 Fontmell Magna :

🏠 **Estyard House,** SP7 0PB, ✆ 811460, 🚗 – Ⓟ
closed November and Christmas – **6 rm** ⌇ 10.25/20.50 **st.**

AUSTIN-ROVER Salisbury Rd ✆ 2295

SHALDON Devon **403** J 32 – see Teignmouth.

SHANKLIN I.O.W. **403 404** Q 32 – see Wight (Isle of).

SHAW Wilts. **403 404** N 29 – see Melksham.

SHEDFIELD Hants. **403 404** Q 31 – pop. 3 ,291 – ✉ Southampton – ✪ 0329 Wickham.

◆London 75 – ◆Portsmouth 13 – ◆Southampton 10.

🏨 **Meon Valley Golf and Country Club** (Best Western), Sandy Lane, SO3 2HQ, off A 334 ✆ 833455, Telex 86272, ≼, 🔲, 🔓, 🚗, park, ✽, squash – 📺 ⌂wc ☎ Ⓟ. 🔼 🔼 ⒶⒺ ⓄⒹ *VISA*. ✾
M 7.50/10.50 **st.** and a la carte 🍴 3.75 – **54 rm** ⌇ 42.00/50.00 **st.** – SB (weekends only) 55.00/70.00 **st.**

SHEEPWASH Devon **403** H 31 – see Hatherleigh.

SHEERNESS Kent **404** W 29 – pop. 11 ,087 – ECD : Wednesday – ✪ 0795.

See : ≼★ from the pier.

Envir. : Minster (abbey : brasses★, effigied tombs★) SE : 2 ½ m.

🚢 Shipping connections with the Continent : to the Netherlands (Vlissingen) (Olau).

🚹 Bridge Rd Car Park ✆ 665324.

◆London 52 – Canterbury 24 – Maidstone 20.

🏠 **Royal,** The Broadway, ME12 1AB, ✆ 662626 – 📺 ⌂wc. 🔼 *VISA*
closed 24 to 26 December – **M** a la carte 8.80/12.75 **t.** – **12 rm** ⌇ 18.70/31.90 **st.**

AUSTIN-ROVER New Road ✆ 64329   SKODA High St. ✆ 662730

SHEFFIELD South Yorks. **402 403 404** P 23 – pop. 470 ,685 – ECD : Thursday – ✪ 0742.

See : Abbeydale Industrial Hamlet★ (steel and scythe works) *AC*, SW : by A 621 AZ.

🏌 Lees Hall, Hemsworth Rd ✆ 54402, S : 3 ½ m. AZ – 🏌 Beauchief, Abbey Lane ✆ 360648, SW : by B 6068 AZ – 🏌 Tinsley Park ✆ 442237, E : by A 57 BZ.

🚹 Town Hall Extension, Union St. ✆ 734671/2.

◆London 174 – ◆Leeds 36 – ◆Liverpool 80 – ◆Manchester 41 – ◆Nottingham 44.

Plans on following pages

🏨 **Hallam Tower Post House** (T.H.F.), Manchester Rd (A 57), S10 5DX, ✆ 686031, Telex 547293, ≼ – 🕮 📺 ☎ Ⓟ. 🅰. 🔼 ⒶⒺ ⓄⒹ *VISA*   AZ ○
M 6.50/8.75 **st.** and a la carte 🍴 2.85 – ⌇ 5.50 – **135 rm** 41.00/48.50 **st.**, **2 suites**.

🏨 **Grosvenor House** (T.H.F.), Charter Sq., S1 3EH, ✆ 20041, Telex 54312 – 🕮 🍴 rest 📺 ☎ Ⓟ. 🅰. 🔼 ⒶⒺ ⓄⒹ *VISA*   CZ **a**
M 8.25 **st.** and a la carte 🍴 2.70 – ⌇ 5.50 – **103 rm** 43.00/49.50 **st.**

SHEFFIELD
BUILT UP AREA

Barrow Road . . . . BY 4
Bawtry Road . . . . BY 5
Bradfield Road . . . . AY 7
Brocco Bank . . . . AZ 8
Broughton Lane . . . . BY 10
Burngreave Road . . . . AY 12
Handsworth Road . . . . BZ 24
Hemsworth Road . . . . AZ 27
Hollinsend Road . . . . BZ 28
Holywell Road . . . . BY 29
Main Road . . . . BZ 32
Meadow Hall Road . . . . BY 33
Middlewood Road . . . . AY 34
Newhall Road . . . . BY 36
Rustlings Road . . . . AZ 39
Westbourne Road . . . . AZ 47
Western Bank . . . . AZ 48
Whitham Road . . . . AZ 49
Woodhouse Road . . . . BZ 50

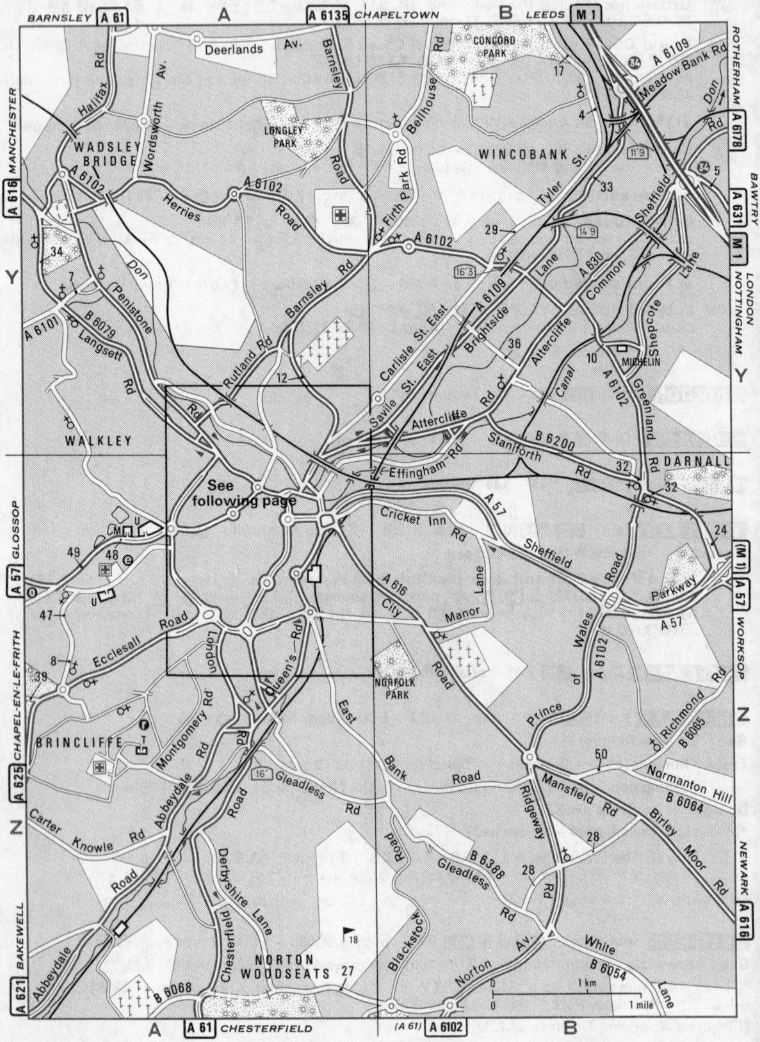

🏨 **St. George** (Swallow), Kenwood Rd, S7 1NQ, ✆ 583811, Telex 547030, ⌂, park – 🛗 TV 🛁wc ☎ ♿ **P**. 🏊. 🅂 AE ⊕ VISA AZ **r**
M 6.75/8.50 **st.** and a la carte 🍷3.40 – **118 rm** ☕ 36.00/60.00 **st.** – SB (weekends only)(except July and August) 48.00/52.00 **st.**

🏨 **Rutland,** 452 Glossop Rd, S10 2PY, ✆ 664411, Telex 547500 – 🛗 TV 🛁wc ☎ **P**. 🏊. 🅂 AE ⊕ VISA AZ **e**
M 3.95/6.75 **st.** and a la carte 🍷2.55 – **90 rm** ☕ 19.00/40.00 **st.** – SB (weekends only) 41.00/42.00 **st.**

SHEFFIELD
CENTRE

Angel Street .... **DY** 3
Commercial Street .... **DZ** 15
Fargate .... **CZ**
High Street .... **DZ**
Leopold Street .... **CZ** 31

West Street .... **CZ**
Blonk Street .... **DY** 6
Castle Gate .... **DY** 13
Charter Row .... **CZ** 14
Cumberland Street .... **CZ** 16
Fitzwilliam Gate .... **CZ** 19
Flat Street .... **DZ** 20
Furnival Gate .... **CZ** 21
Furnival Street .... **CZ** 22

Gibraltar Street .... **CY** 23
Haymarket .... **DY** 25
Moorfields .... **CY** 35
Pinstone Street .... **CZ** 37
Queen Street .... **CY** 38
St. Mary's Gate .... **CZ** 40
Shalesmoor .... **CY** 41
Snig Hill .... **DY** 42
Waingate .... **DY** 44
West Bar Green .... **CY** 45

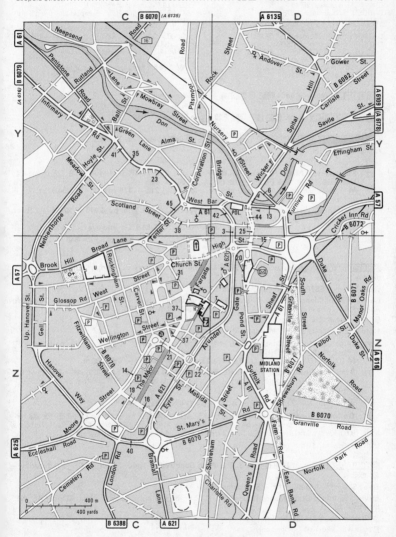

**at Worrall** NW : 4 ½ m. by A 61 off A 616 – AY – ⊠ Sheffield – ✆ 074 286 Oughtibridge :

🏛 **Middlewood Hall** ⤻, Mowson Lane, S30 3AJ, ✆ 3919, ≼, 🐎, park – 📺 🛏wc 🛁wc ☎
🅿 🛃 🅰 🆎 ⓞ ⅏ ❀
closed Bank Holidays – **M** _(closed Saturday lunch and Sunday dinner)_ 7.50/7.75 **t.** and a la
carte ♦ 2.40 – ⊊ 3.00 – **17 rm** 20.00/35.00 **st.**, **1 suite** 25.00/40.00 **st.** – SB (weekends only)
61.50/85.00 **st.**

409

MICHELIN Branch, 12 Tinsley Park Close, S9 5LX, ✆ **433264** BY

ALFA-ROMEO Scotland St. ✆ 760567 Sidney St. ✆ 77651
AUSTIN-ROVER Penistone Rd ✆ 348801
AUSTIN-ROVER Tenter St. ✆ 71141
AUSTIN-ROVER 286 Sandygate Rd ✆ 302021
AUSTIN-ROVER Broadfield Rd ✆ 588121
BMW Broad Lane ✆ 25048
CITROEN Suffolk Rd ✆ 21378
DAF, VOLVO Ecclesall Rd ✆ 753151
DATSUN 252 Crookes ✆ 669202
DATSUN 1/7 Meersbrook Rd ✆ 57315
DATSUN Shalesmoor ✆ 750000
FIAT, LANCIA 30/46 Suffolk Rd ✆ 21378
FORD 53/67 London Rd ✆ 751515
FORD 196 Gibraltar St. ✆ 29631
FORD Ecclehall Rd ✆ 686986
HONDA 918 Chesterfield Rd ✆ 748029
LADA 178-184 London Rd ✆ 557394
MAZDA 885 Chesterfield Rd ✆ 748643
MERCEDES-BENZ Hanover Way ✆ 753391
PEUGEOT-TALBOT Fitzwilliam St. ✆ 756324
RENAULT Abbeydale Rd Sth. ✆ 369041
RENAULT Crookes ✆ 669202
ROLLS ROYCE-BENTLEY Tempter St., Bromhill ✆ 71141
SAAB 115 Ecclesall Rd South ✆ 369946
TOYOTA Ellin St. ✆ 78717
VAUXHALL Saville St. ✆ 751565
VAUXHALL Eccleshall Rd ✆ 685922
VOLVO Eccleshall Rd ✆ 78739
VW, AUDI 1 Ecclesall Rd South ✆ 668441

SHELDON West Midlands **403** ㉒ **404** ⑳ – see Birmingham.

SHELTON LOCK Derbs. **402** **403** **404** P 25 – see Derby.

SHEPPERTON Surrey **404** S 29 – pop. 9 ,643 – ✆ 0932 Walton-on-Thames.
♦London 25.

Plan : see Greater London (South-West)

Shepperton Moat House (Q.M.H.), Felix Lane, TW17 8NP, E : 1 ¼ m. on B 375 ✆ 241404, Telex 928170, – TV wc ☎ P. AE VISA AZ **a**
M *(closed Saturday lunch)* 9.00 **st.** and a la carte 2.65 – **179 rm** 42.95/54.95 **st.** – SB (weekends only) 45.90 **st.**

XX **Thames Court,** Tow Path, Ferry Lane, TW17 9LJ, W : 1 ¼ m. by B 375 ✆ 221957, ≤ River Thames, – P. AE VISA by B 375 AZ
closed Sunday dinner, Monday and last week January – **M** 8.50 **t.** and a la carte 2.65.

FORD Station Approach ✆ 24811
HONDA High St. ✆ 40121
NISSAN Walton Bridge Rd ✆ 47848

SHEPTON MALLET Somerset **403** **404** M 30 The West Country G. – pop. 6 ,197 – ECD : Wednesday – ✆ 0749.

See : Site ★ – SS. Peter and Paul's Church ★.

Envir. : Oakhill Manor★*AC*, N : 4 m. off A 37 – Evercreech Church Tower★, SE : 4 m. – Downside Abbey★*AC*, N : 5 m. off A 37 and A 367 – Nunney★, W : 9 m. on A 361.

The Centre ✆ 5258 (summer only).

♦London 127 – ♦Bristol 20 – ♦Southampton 63 – Taunton 31.

Charlton House, Charlton Rd, BA4 4PR, E : 1 m. on A 361 ✆ 2008, ≤, , , park, – TV wc ☎ P. AE VISA.
M 10.50/13.50 **st.** – **16 rm** 29.00/43.00 **st.**, **1 suite** 56.00 **st.** – SB 62.00 **st.**

XX **Bowlish House** with rm, Wells Rd, BA4 5JD, W : ½ m. on A 371 ✆ 2022, – TV wc P
closed 24 to 27 December – **M** (dinner only) (booking essential) 13.00 **t.** 2.50 – 3.00 – **4 rm** 31.00 **t.**

at Oakhill NE : 3 m. by A 37 on A 367 – ✉ ✆ 0749 Shepton Mallet :

XX **Oakhill House** with rm, Bath Rd, BA3 5AQ, ✆ 840180, – wc P. AE VISA.
closed 1 to 12 January – **M** *(closed Saturday lunch, Sunday dinner and Bank Holidays)* 9.50/13.50 **t.** and a la carte 2.70 – **3 rm** 17.50/34.00 **t.** – SB 50.00/55.00 **st.**

HONDA Townsend Rd ✆ 2864
VW, AUDI High St. ✆ 4091

SHERBORNE Dorset **403** **404** M 31 The West Country G. – pop. 7 ,405 – ECD : Wednesday – ✆ 0935.

See : Site ★★★ – Abbey ★★★ – Sherborne Castle ★★*AC*.

Envir. : Sandford Orcas Manor House★*AC*, N : 4 m. by B 3148 – Purse Caundle Manor★*AC*, NE : 5 m. by A 30.

18 Clatcombe ✆ 814431, N : 1 m.

Hound St. ✆ 815341 (summer only).

♦London 128 – Bournemouth 39 – Dorchester 19 – Salisbury 36 – Taunton 31.

Post House (T.H.F.), Horsecastles Lane, DT9 6BB, W : 1 m. on A 30 ✆ 813191, Telex 46522, – TV wc ☎ P. AE VISA
M 6.95/8.95 **st.** and a la carte 2.70 – 5.50 – **60 rm** 37.50/45.00 **st.**

Eastbury, Long St., DT9 3BY, ✆ 813387, – wc P
M (bar lunch)/dinner 7.50 **st.** and a la carte 2.60 – **15 rm** 16.00/35.00 **st.** – SB (except Easter, summer and Christmas) 33.00/35.00 **st.**

at Oborne NE : 2 m. by A 30 – ⊠ ◉ 0935 Sherborne :

XX **Grange,** DT9 4LA, ℰ 813463, ≤, ⌖ – ⓟ. ◪ **VISA**
closed Sunday dinner, Monday, 1 to 7 January and 1 to 5 September – **M** (dinner only and Sunday lunch) a la carte 8.20/11.25 **t.** ⓙ 2.75.

ALFA-ROMEO, LANCIA Long St. ℰ 3262   MERCEDES-BENZ Yeovil Rd ℰ 3350
AUSTIN-ROVER Digby Rd ℰ 2436

SHERE Surrey **404** S 30 – see Dorking.

SHERINGHAM Norfolk **404** X 25 – pop. 6,861 – ECD : Wednesday – ◉ 0263 Cromer.
Envir. : Cromer : SS. Peter and Paul's Church (tower ≤★).
🛈 Station Approach ℰ 824329 (summer only).
♦London 128 – Cromer 4 – ♦Norwich 27.

⌂ **Beacon,** 1 Nelson Rd, NR26 8BT, ℰ 822019, ⌖ – ⓟ. ◪ **VISA**. ⚘
April-October – **8 rm** ⊊ 12.50/25.00 **st.**

SHIFNAL Salop **402 403 404** M 25 – pop. 6,094 – ECD : Thursday – ⊠ ◉ 0952 Telford.
See : St. Andrew's Church★ 12C-16C.
Envir. : Weston Park★ 17C (paintings★★) *AC*, NE : 5 m.
♦London 150 – ♦Birmingham 28 – Shrewsbury 16.

🏨 **Park House,** Park St., TF11 9BA, ℰ 460128, ⅃ heated, ⌖ – 📺 ☎ ⓟ. 🏛 ◪ AE ⓞ **VISA**. ⚘
M 9.00/19.50 **t.** and a la carte ⓙ 3.00 – **19 rm** ⊊ 35.00/70.00 **t.**, **1 suite** 60.00/85.00 **t.** – SB (weekends only) 58.50/68.50 **st.**

AUSTIN-ROVER Chepside ℰ 460412   FORD Park St. ℰ 460631

SHINFIELD Berks. **404** R 29 – see Reading.

SHIPDHAM Norfolk **404** W 26 – pop. 1,974 – ⊠ Thetford – ◉ 0362 Dereham.
♦London 102 – East Dereham 5 – ♦Norwich 21 – Watton 6.

XX **Shipdham Place** ⌿ with rm, Church Close, IP25 7LX, on A 1075 ℰ 820303, ⌖ – ⌷wc ⊛ ⓟ. ⚘
closed Tuesday dinner to non-residents, weekdays January and February – **M** (lunch by arrangement to residents only) (booking essential)/dinner 18.00 **t.** ⓙ 5.50 – **9 rm** ⊊ 30.00/55.00 **t.**

SHIPLEY West Yorks. **402** O 22 – pop. 28,815 – ECD : Wednesday – ◉ 0274 Bradford.
♦London 216 – Bradford 4 – ♦Leeds 12.

X **Aagrah,** 27 Westgate, BD18 3QX, ℰ 594660, Indian rest. – ◪ AE ⓞ **VISA**
M (lunch by arrangement)/dinner 8.50 **t.** and a la carte ⓙ 2.35.

SHIPSTON-ON-STOUR Warw. **403 404** P 27 – pop. 3,072 – ◉ 0608.
♦London 85 – ♦Birmingham 34 – ♦Oxford 29.

XX **Old Mill** with rm, Mill St., CV36 4AW, on B 4035 ℰ 61880, ⌖ – ⌷wc ♒wc ⓟ. ◪ AE ⓞ **VISA**
M (*closed Sunday dinner*) 4.75/14.50 **t.** and a la carte ⓙ 3.00 – **5 rm** ⊊ 19.50/33.50 **t.** – SB (October-Easter except Christmas and New Year) 45.00/48.00 **st.**

X **White Bear** with rm, High St., CV36 4AJ, ℰ 61558 – ⌷wc ⓟ. ◪ AE ⓞ **VISA**
M (*closed Sunday dinner and Bank Holidays*) (bar lunch)/dinner a la carte 7.60/12.10 **t.** ⓙ 2.50 – **9 rm** ⊊ 20.00/40.00 **t.** – SB 50.00 **st.**

AUSTIN-ROVER Church St. ℰ 092 684 (Claverdon)   FORD Church St. ℰ 61425
2208

SHIPTON GORGE Dorset – see Bridport.

SHIPTON-UNDER-WYCHWOOD Oxon. **403 404** P 28 – pop. 2,558 – ECD : Wednesday – ◉ 0993.
♦London 81 – ♦Birmingham 50 – Gloucester 37 – ♦Oxford 25.

🏠 **Shaven Crown,** OX7 6BA, ℰ 830330, « 14C hospice » – 📺 ⌷wc ⓟ. ◪ **VISA**. ⚘
M (bar lunch Monday to Saturday)/dinner a la carte 7.45/14.75 **t.** – **8 rm** ⊊ 18.00/44.00 **t.** – SB (except weekends) 50.00/56.00 **st.**

X **Lamb Inn** with rm, High St., OX7 6DQ, ℰ 830465, ⌖ – ⌷wc ⓟ. ◪ AE ⓞ **VISA**. ⚘
M (bar lunch)/dinner 14.00 **t.** ⓙ 2.50 – ⊊ 2.50 – **5 rm** 20.00/30.00 **t.** – SB (except weekends) (November-March) 50.00 **st.**

SHORNE Kent **404** V 29 – pop. 2,565 – ⊠ Gravesend – ◉ 047 482.
♦London 27 – Gravesend 4 – Maidstone 12 – Rochester 4.

🏨 **Inn on the Lake,** DA12 3HB, on A 2 ℰ 3333, Telex 966356, ≤, ⌿, ⌖, park – 📺 ⌷wc ⊛ ⓟ. 🏛 ◪ AE ⓞ **VISA**. ⚘
M a la carte 11.40/18.30 **t.** ⓙ 3.70 – **78 rm** ⊊ 36.00/52.00 **st.**

411

See : Abbey Church★ 11C-14C D – St. Mary's Church★ (Jesse Tree window★) A – Grope Lane★ 15C – **Envir. :** Wroxeter★ (Roman city and baths) AC, SE : 6 m. by A 458 and A 5 – Condover Hall★ (15C) AC, S : 5 m. by A 49.

🏌 Meole Brace 🕿 64050, S : by A 49 – 🛈 The Square 🕿 52019.

◆London 164 – ◆Birmingham 48 – ◆Cardiff 110 – Chester 43 – Derby 67 – Gloucester 93 – ◆Manchester 68 – ◆Stoke-on-Trent 39 – ◆Swansea 124.

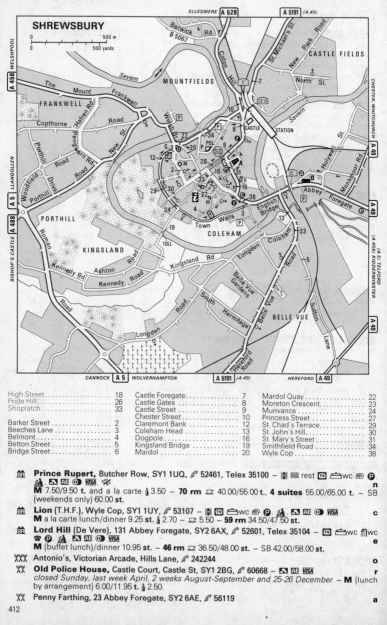

High Street	18	Castle Foregate	7	Mardol Quay	22
Pride Hill	26	Castle Gates	8	Moreton Crescent	23
Shoplatch	33	Castle Street	9	Murivance	24
		Chester Street	10	Princess Street	27
Barker Street	2	Claremont Bank	12	St. Chad's Terrace	29
Beeches Lane	3	Coleham Head	13	St. John's Hill	30
Belmont	4	Dogpole	16	St. Mary's Street	31
Betton Street	5	Kingsland Bridge	19	Smithfield Road	34
Bridge Street	6	Mardol	20	Wyle Cop	38

🏨 **Prince Rupert,** Butcher Row, SY1 1UQ, 🕿 52461, Telex 35100 – 🛗 🗏 rest 📺 ⏚wc 🕿 🅿. 🛎 🔃 AE ① VISA ⚶
  M 7.50/9.50 t. and a la carte 🛉 3.50 – **70 rm** 🖙 40.00/55.00 t., **4 suites** 55.00/65.00 t. – SB (weekends only) 60.00 st.   **n**

🏨 **Lion** (T.H.F.), Wyle Cop, SY1 1UY, 🕿 53107 – 🛗 📺 ⏚wc 🕿 🅿. 🛎 🔃 AE ① VISA   **c**
  M a la carte lunch/dinner 9.25 st. 🛉 2.70 – 🖙 5.50 – **59 rm** 34.50/47.50 st.

🏨 **Lord Hill** (De Vere), 131 Abbey Foregate, SY2 6AX, 🕿 52601, Telex 35104 – 📺 ⏚wc 🛗wc
  🕿 🅿. 🛎 🔃 AE ① VISA   **e**
  M (buffet lunch)/dinner 10.95 st. – **46 rm** 🖙 36.50/48.00 st. – SB 42.00/58.00 st.

XXX **Antonio's,** Victorian Arcade, Hills Lane, 🕿 242244   **o**

XX **Old Police House,** Castle Court, Castle St, SY1 2BG, 🕿 60668 – 🔃 AE VISA   **r**
  closed Sunday, last week April, 2 weeks August-September and 25-26 December – **M** (lunch by arrangement) 6.00/11.95 st. 🛉 2.50.

XX Penny Farthing, 23 Abbey Foregate, SY2 6AE, 🕿 56119   **a**

※ **Belmont,** Barracks Passage, Wyle Cop, SY1 1AX, ☎ 246333 – ⊠ AE ⓪ VISA   i
closed Sunday, 2 weeks September, 26 December-12 January and Bank Holidays – **M** 3.50 **t.**
(lunch) and a la carte.

at Albrighton N : 3 m. on A 528 – ⊠ Shrewsbury – ✪ 0939 Bomere Heath :

※※ **Albright Hussey,** SY4 3AF, ☎ 290523, « 16C timbered manor house and gardens » – **P.**
⊠ AE ⓪ VISA
closed Sunday dinner, Monday, August and Bank Holidays – **M** 7.50 **t.** (lunch) and a la carte
11.00/15.00 **t.** ⅄ 2.00.

ALFA-ROMEO, CITROEN 159 Abbey Foregate ☎ 57711	MERCEDES-BENZ Harlescoff ☎ 241191
	PEUGEOT-TALBOT 170 Abbey Foregate ☎ 56326
AUSTIN-ROVER Harlescott ☎ 52288	RENAULT Featherbed Lane ☎ 69611
DAIHATSU Featherbed Lane ☎ 241445	SAAB Westbury Garage ☎ 241 445
FIAT Featherbed Lane ☎ 6495	VAUXHALL-OPEL Greyfriars ☎ 52321
FORD Coton Hill ☎ 3631	VOLVO Featherbed Lane ☎ 51251
LADA Featherbed Lane ☎ 60303	VW, AUDI English Bridge ☎ 52471

■ **SHURDINGTON** Glos. 408 404 N 28 – see Cheltenham.

■ **SIDFORD** Devon 408 K 31 – see Sidmouth.

■ **SIDMOUTH** Devon 408 K 31 The West Country G. – pop. 10 ,808 – ECD : Thursday – ✪ 039 55.
Envir. : Seaton, headlands (≼★★), E : 9 m. – Branscombe★, E : 9 m. – Colyton★, E : 10 m.
⌖ Cotmaton Rd ☎ 3023.
🛈 The Esplanade ☎ 6441 (summer only).
◆London 170 – Exeter 14 – Taunton 27 – Weymouth 45.

🏨 **Victoria,** Peak Hill, EX10 8RY, ☎ 2651, ≼, ⊼ heated, ⊠, ☞, ※ – 🕸 TV **P.** ❄
62 rm.

🏨 **Riviera,** Esplanade, EX10 8AY, ☎ 5201, ≼ – 🕸 TV ⌂wc ☜ ⟵. AE ⓪
M 7.00/10.00 **s.** and a la carte ⅄ 2.60 – **34 rm** ⊊ 21.00/64.00 **s.** – SB (weekends only)
(November-April) 54.05/58.65 **st.**

🏨 **Fortfield,** Station Rd, EX10 8NU, ☎ 2403, ⊠, ☞ – 🕸 TV ⌂wc ὅ **P.** ⊠ ⓪ VISA
M (bar lunch)/dinner 8.00 **t.** and a la carte ⅄ 2.00 – **54 rm** ⊊ 21.00/64.00 **t.** – SB (October-mid
May) 42.00/50.00 **st.**

🏨 **Salcombe Hill House** ♨, Beatlands Rd, EX10 8JQ, ☎ 4697, ⊼ heated, ☞, ※ – 🕸 TV
⌂wc **P.** ⊠ ⓪ VISA
March-October – **M** 5.50/7.50 **t.** ⅄ 2.35 – **33 rm** ⊊ 17.00/63.00 **t.**

🏨 **Royal Glen,** Glen Rd, EX10 8RW, ☎ 3221, « 17C house furnished with many antiques », ☞
– TV ⌂wc 🎜wc **P.** AE VISA
M 4.75/5.00 **t.** and a la carte – **37 rm** ⊊ 12.75/46.15 **t.** – SB (November-April) 28.95/62.35 **st.**

🏨 **Littlecourt,** Seafield Rd, EX10 8HF, ☎ 5279, ⊼ heated, ☞ – ⌂wc 🎜wc **P.**
March-October and Christmas – **M** (bar lunch Monday to Saturday)/dinner 8.00 **t.** – **20 rm**
⊊ 21.00/28.00 **t.** – SB 39.00/43.00 **st.**

🏨 **Abbeydale,** Manor Rd, EX10 8RP, ☎ 2060, ☞ – TV ⌂wc **P.** ❄
21 March-5 November – **M** (bar lunch)/dinner 7.50 **t.** ⅄ 2.20 – **17 rm** ⊊ 17.00/44.00 **t.**

🏨 **Mount Pleasant,** Salcombe Rd, EX10 8JA, ☎ 4694, ☞ – ⌂wc 🎜wc **P.** ❄
April-October – **M** (dinner only) 6.00 **t.** ⅄ 3.25 – **15 rm** ⊊ 12.50/31.00 **t.**

🏨 **Woodlands,** Cotmaton Cross, EX10 8HG, ☎ 3120, ☞ – ⌂wc ὅ **P.**
M 3.00/4.00 **t.** ⅄ 2.75 – **30 rm** ⊊ 14.50/33.00 – SB (October-May) 31.05/41.50 **st.**

🏨 **Torbay,** Station Rd, EX10 8NW, ☎ 3456 – 🕸 TV ⌂wc 🎜wc **P.** VISA
M 4.00/5.50 **t.** and a la carte ⅄ 2.00 – **17 rm** ⊊ 9.60/38.00 **t.** – SB (14 October-April)
26.00/32.00 **st.**

↑ **Barrington Villa,** Salcombe Rd, EX10 8PU, ☎ 4252, ☞ – ❄
closed mid October-mid November – **9 rm** ⊊ 13.25/36.35 **st.**

at Sidford N : 2 m. – ⊠ ✪ 039 55 Sidmouth :

✿ **Applegarth,** Church St., EX10 9QP, E : on A 3052 ☎ 3174, « Garden » – **P.** ⊠ AE VISA
M (closed Sunday and Monday to non-residents) (bar lunch)/dinner 5.55 **t.** and a la carte
⅄ 2.40 – **8 rm** ⊊ 14.00/28.00 **t.**

AUSTIN-ROVER Salcombe Rd ☎ 2522	PEUGEOT-TALBOT Vicarage Rd ☎ 2433
FIAT Crossways, Sidford ☎ 3595	VOLVO Mill St. ☎ 3433
NISSAN Sidford ☎ 3334	

■ **SILCHESTER** Hants. 408 404 Q 29 – pop. 1 ,072 – ⊠ Reading (Berks.) – ✪ 0734.
◆London 62 – Basingstoke 8 – Reading 14 – Winchester 26.

🏨 **Romans** ♨, Little London Rd, RG7 2PN, ☎ 700421, ⊼ heated, ☞, ※ – TV ⌂wc ☜ **P.**
♨. ⊠ AE ⓪ VISA
closed last 2 weeks August, Christmas and New Year – **M** (closed Saturday lunch and Sunday
dinner) 13.00/16.00 **st.** ⅄ 3.50 – **25 rm** ⊊ 36.00/50.00 **st.** – SB (weekends only) 50.00/55.00 **st.**

SIMONSBATH Somerset 403 I 30 The West Country G. – ✉ Minehead – ☎ 064 383 Exford.
♦London 200 – Exeter 40 – Minehead 19 – Taunton 38.

🏨 Simonsbath House, TA24 7SH, ℰ 259, ≼, « Tastefully converted 17C country house », 🐎, squash – 📺 ➪wc ℗. ✦
8 rm.

SITTINGBOURNE Kent 404 W 29 – pop. 35 ,893 – ECD : Wednesday – ☎ 0795.
♦London 44 – Canterbury 16 – Maidstone 13.

🏨 **Coniston,** 70 London Rd, ME10 1NT, ℰ 23927 – 📺 ➪wc ℗. 🏃. 🔼 AE ⓪ VISA
M 5.50 t. and a la carte ≬ 4.40 – **50 rm** ☷ 22.50/42.00 t.

AUSTIN-ROVER Bapchild ℰ 23085
FORD Canterbury Rd ℰ 70711
MAZDA Newington ℰ 842307
NISSAN St. Michaels Rd ℰ 23422

RENAULT Chalkwell Rd ℰ 76361
TALBOT Teynham ℰ 521286
VAUXHALL-OPEL London Rd, Bapchild ℰ 76222

SIX MILE BOTTOM Cambs. – see Newmarket (Suffolk).

SKEGNESS Lincs. 402 404 V 24 – pop. 12 ,645 – ECD : Thursday – ☎ 0754.
🏌 North Shore ℰ 3298.
🛈 Embassy Centre, Grand Parade ℰ 4821 and 68333.
♦London 145 – Lincoln 41.

🏨 **County,** North Par., PE25 2UB, ℰ 2461, ≼ – 🛗 📺 ➪wc ⋔wc ☎ ℗. 🏃. 🔼 ⓪ VISA
M 7.00 st. and a la carte ≬ 3.50 – **44 rm** ☷ 27.00/44.00 st. – SB 40.00/50.00 st.

🏨 **Vine,** Vine Rd, Seacroft, PE25 3DB, S : 1 ½ m. ℰ 3018, 🐎 – 📺 ➪wc ℗. 🔼 AE ⓪ VISA
closed Christmas – **M** 9.00/10.00 t. and a la carte ≬ 3.00 – **20 rm** ☷ 18.00/34.00 t.

AUSTIN-ROVER Roman Bank ℰ 3671
DAIHATSU Burgh Rd ℰ 2244
FIAT, ALFA-ROMEO Beresford Av. ℰ 67131

FORD Wainfleet Rd ℰ 66019
YUGO Clifton Grove ℰ 3589

SKELTON North Yorks. 402 Q 22 – see York.

SKELWITH BRIDGE Cumbria 402 K 20 – see Ambleside.

SKIPTON North Yorks. 402 N 22 – pop. 13 ,009 – ECD : Tuesday – ☎ 0756.
See : Castle★ (14C) AC.
🏌 Short Lee Lane, off Grassington Rd ℰ 3257, NW : 1 m.
🛈 High St. Car Park Approach ℰ 2809 (summer only).
♦London 217 – Kendal 45 – ♦Leeds 26 – Preston 36 – York 43.

🏨 **Unicorn** without rest., Devonshire Place, Keighley Rd, BD23 2LP, ℰ 4146 – 📺 ➪wc. VISA.
✦
10 rm 22.00/31.50 st.

XX **Oats** with rm, Chapel Hill, BD23 1NL, ℰ 68118 – 📺 ➪wc ⋔wc ☎ ℗. 🔼 AE ⓪ VISA. ✦
closed Sunday and Monday – **M** a la carte 12.00/15.00 t. ≬ 3.75 – **5 rm** ☷ 42.00/68.00 t.

SLAIDBURN Lancs. 402 M 22 – pop. 332 – ☎ 020 06.
♦London 249 – Burnley 21 – Lancaster 19 – ♦Leeds 48 – Preston 27.

🏨 **Parrock Head Farm** ≫, Near Clitheroe, BB7 3AH, NW : 1 m. ℰ 614, ≼ Bowland Fells, 🐎
– 📺 ➪wc ℗. AE
closed mid December-mid February – **M** (closed Saturday and Sunday to non-residents) a la
carte 6.35/9.95 st. ≬ 2.80 – **8 rm** ☷ 25.00/39.00 st.

SLEAFORD Lincs. 402 404 S 25 – pop. 8 ,247 – ECD : Thursday – ☎ 0529.
See : St. Denis' Church★ 12C-15C.
🏌 South Rauceby ℰ 052 98 (South Rauceby) 273, W : 1 m. on A 153.
♦London 119 – ♦Leicester 45 – Lincoln 17 – ♦Nottingham 39.

🏩 **Tally Ho Inn,** Aswarby, NG34 8SA, S : 4 ½ m. on A 15 ℰ 205, ≼, 🐎 – 📺 ➪wc ⋔wc ℗.
✦
M a la carte 3.75/7.85 t. – **6 rm** ☷ 15.00/26.00 t.

AUSTIN-ROVER Carre St. ℰ 303034
COLT Holdingham ℰ 302545
FORD London Rd ℰ 302921

MAZDA Grantham Rd ℰ 052 98 (Sth. Rauceby) 674
PEUGEOT-TALBOT Boston Rd ℰ 302518
RENAULT 50 Westgate ℰ 305305

Pour les 🏨🏨🏨, 🏨🏨, 🏨, nous ne donnons pas
le détail de l'installation,
ces hôtels possédant, en général, tout le confort.

➪wc ⋔wc
🕿

SLOUGH Berks. 404 S 29 – pop. 106 ,341 – ECD : Wednesday – ✆ 0753.

Envir. : Eton (college★★) S : 2 m.

☖ Farnham Park, Park Rd, Stoke Poges ✆ 028 14 (Farnham Common) 3332, N : 2 m. – ☖ Wexham Park, Wexham St. ✆ 028 16 (Fulmer) 3271, N : 2 m.

◆London 29 – ◆Oxford 39 – Reading 19.

▲▲ **Holiday Inn,** Ditton Rd, Langley, SL3 8PT, SE : 2 ½ m. on A 4 ✆ 44244, Telex 848646, 🏊, ❨ – ▮▮ ☎ & 🅿. 🔬. 🔊 AE ⓪ VISA
　M (buffet lunch)/dinner 11.50 **st.** and a la carte – ⌷ 6.00 – **224 rm** 48.00/65.00 **s.**

SAAB　Beaconsfield Rd ✆ 028 14 (Farnham Common) 5111
VOLVO　Petersfield Av. ✆ 23031

VW, AUDI　57 Farnham Rd ✆ 33917
VW, AUDI-NSU　Colnbrook By-Pass ✆ 028 12 (Colnbrook) 2708

SMETHWICK West Midlands 403 404 O 26 – see Birmingham.

SNAINTON North Yorks. 402 S 21 – pop. 760 – ECD : Wednesday – ✉ ✆ 0723 Scarborough.

◆London 240 – Scarborough 10 – York 29.

☖ **Coachman Inn,** YO13 9PL, ✆ 85231 – 📺 ⌷wc ⌷wc 🅿. 🔊 AE ⓪ VISA
　M (bar lunch Monday to Saturday)/dinner 9.50 ▮ 2.75 – **12 rm** ⌷ 18.00/40.00 **t.** – SB (November-April) 46.00 **st.**

SNEATON North Yorks. 402 S 20 – see Whitby.

SNOWDON (YR WYDDFA) Gwynedd 402 403 H 24.

See : Ascent and ✳★★★ (1 h 15 mn from Llanberis (Pass★★) by Snowdon Mountain Railway AC).

　　Hotels and restaurant see : **Beddgelert** S : 4 m., **Caernarfon** NW : 9 m.

　　'' Short Breaks ''
　　Many hotels now offer a special rate for a stay of 2 nights
　　which includes dinner, bed and breakfast.

SOAR MILL COVE Devon – see Salcombe.

SOLIHULL West Midlands 403 404 O 26 – pop. 93 ,940 – ECD : Wednesday – ✆ 021 Birmingham.

☖ Shirley, Stratford Rd ✆ 744 6001.

🛈 Central Library, Homer Rd ✆ 705 6789 ext 505.

◆London 109 – ◆Birmingham 7 – ◆Coventry 13 – Warwick 13.

▲▲ **St. John's Swallow** (Swallow), 651 Warwick Rd, B91 1AT, ✆ 705 6777, Telex 339352 – ▮▮
　📺 ⌷wc ☎ 🅿. 🔬. 🔊 AE ⓪ VISA
　M 7.25/9.75 **st.** and a la carte – **211 rm** ⌷ 38.00/49.50 **st.**, **6 suites** – SB (weekends only) 60.00 **st.**

▲▲ **George** (Embassy), The Square, B91 3RF, ✆ 704 1241 – 📺 ⌷wc ☎ 🅿. 🔬. 🔊 AE ⓪ VISA. ❨
　closed Christmas – **M** 8.00/8.50 **st.** and a la carte ▮ 2.75 – ⌷ 5.00 – **46 rm** 25.00/44.00 **st.** – SB (weekends only) 52.00 **st.**

XX **Liaison,** 761 Old Lode Lane, B92 8JE, ✆ 743 3993, French rest. – 🔊 AE ⓪ VISA
　closed Sunday, Monday, 1 week at Easter, August and 2 weeks at Christmas – **M** (booking essential)(dinner only) a la carte 14.40/18.35 **t.** ▮ 4.25.

AUSTIN-ROVER-DAIMLER-JAGUAR　Stratford Rd, Shirley ✆ 745 5855
AUSTIN-ROVER　707 Warwick Rd ✆ 705 3028
BMW　824 Stratford Rd ✆ 744 4488
FIAT　The Green ✆ 056 44 (Tanworth) 2218
FORD　361/369 Stratford Rd ✆ 744 4456
HONDA　Station Lane ✆ 056 43 (Lapworth) 2933

RENAULT　Stratford Rd, Hockley Heath ✆ 056 43 (Lapworth) 2244
RENAULT　270 Stratford Rd, Shirley ✆ 744 1033
TALBOT　386 Warwick Rd ✆ 704 1427
TOYOTA　301 Warwick Rd ✆ 706 2801
VW, AUDI　Stratford Rd, Shirley ✆ 745 5811

SONNING-ON-THAMES Berks. 404 R 29 – pop. 1 ,469 – ECD : Wednesday – ✆ 0734 Reading.

◆London 48 – Reading 4.

▲▲ **White Hart,** Thames St., RG4 0UT, ✆ 692277, ≼, « Rose gardens on river bank » – 📺 ⌷wc 🅿. 🔊 AE ⓪ VISA ❨
　M 16.95 **t.** and a la carte – **25 rm** ⌷ 49.00/63.00 **t.** – SB (weekends only) 69.50 **st.**

XXX **French Horn** with rm, Thames St., RG4 0TN, ✆ 692204, ≼ River Thames and gardens – 📺 ⌷wc 🅿. 🔊 AE ⓪ VISA ❨
　closed 26 December, 1 January and 28 March – **M** 10.50 **st.** (lunch) and a la carte 16.50/26.00 **st.** ▮ 3.50 – **8 rm** ⌷ 45.00/65.00 **st.**

SOUTHAM Glos. 403 404 N 28 – see Cheltenham.

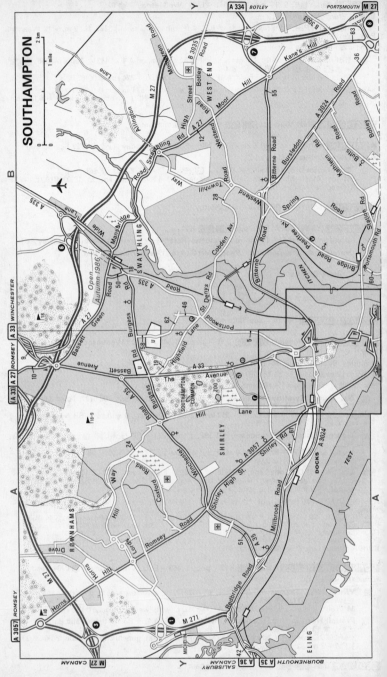

A 334 BOTLEY

PORTSMOUTH M 27

B 3035

Kane's Hill

WEST END

M 27

Allington Lane

Swaythling Road

Wide Lane

Mansbridge

SWAYTHLING

A 335

Open Autumn 1986

Bassett Green Road

A 27

WINCHESTER A 33

ROMSEY A 27 A 33

Bassett Avenue

Burgess Road

Burgess Road

Highfield Lane

St. Denys Rd.

Portswood Road

Bitterne Road

Townhill Way

Westend Road

Cobden Av.

Spring Road

Peartree Av.

ITCHEN

Bridge Road

Portsmouth Rd

Bursledon

A 3024

Kathleen Rd

Butts Road

Botley Road

BOURNEMOUTH A 35 A 36 CADNAM

SALISBURY A 36 CADNAM

M 271

M 27 CADNAM

A 3057 ROMSEY

ROWNHAMS

M 27

Horns Hill

Horns Drove

Romsey Road

Lords Hill

Corford Road

Winchester Road

Way

SOUTHAMPTON COMMON

The Avenue

Hill Lane

SHIRLEY

Shirley High St.

A 3057

Shirley Road

Millbrook Road

Redbridge Road

A 35

A 3024 DOCKS

TEST

ELING

MICHELMERSH

A 33

2 km

1 mile

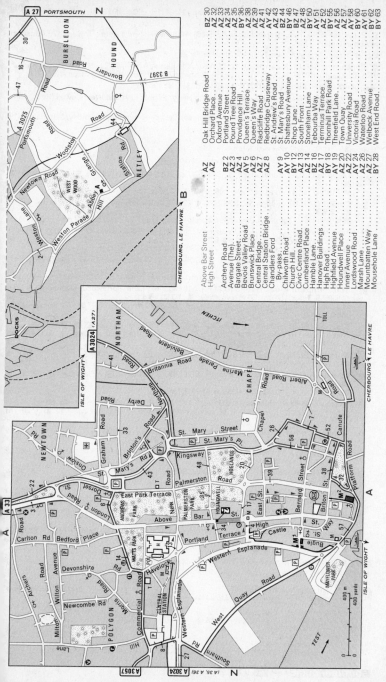

Above Bar Street	AZ
High Street	AZ
Archery Road	AZ 2
Avenue (The)	AZ 3
Bargate Street	AY 4
Bevois Valley Road	AY 5
Brunswick Place	AZ 7
Central Bridge	AZ 7
Central Station Bridge	AZ 8
Chandlers Ford	AY 9
By-pass	AY 10
Chilworth Hill	AZ 12
Church Hill	AZ 13
Civic Centre Road	AZ 14
Cumberland Place	BZ 16
Hamble Lane	AZ 17
Hanover Buildings	BY 18
High Road	AY 19
Highfield Avenue	AZ 20
Houndwell Place	AY 22
Inner Avenue	AY 24
Lordswood Road	AZ 26
Marsh Lane	AZ 27
Mountbatten Way	BY 28
Mousehole Lane		
Oak Hill Bridge Road	BZ 30
Orchard Place	AZ 32
Oxford Avenue	AZ 33
Portland Street	AZ 34
Pound Tree Road	BY 35
Providence Hill	AZ 36
Queen's Terrace	AZ 38
Queen's Way	AZ 39
Radcliffe Road	AZ 41
Redbridge Causeway	AZ 42
St. Andrew's Road	AZ 43
St. Mary's Road	AZ 44
Shaftesbury Avenue	BY 46
Shop Lane	BZ 47
South Front	AZ 48
Stoneham Lane	AY 50
Tebourba Way	AY 51
Terminus Terrace	AZ 52
Thornhill Park Road	BY 55
Threefield Lane	AZ 56
Town Quay	AZ 57
University Road	AY 58
Victoria Road	BY 60
Waterloo Road	AY 61
Welbeck Avenue	AZ 62
West End Road	BY 63

SOUTHAMPTON Hants. 403 404 P 31 – pop. 211,321 – ECD : Monday and Wednesday – ☎ 0703.

See : Docks★ AY – Tudor House Museum★ (16C) *AC* AZ **M1** – God's House Tower★ 12C (Museum of Archaelogia) AZ **M2.**

Envir. : Netley (abbey★ ruins 13C) *AC*, SE : 3 m. BZ **A.**

18 Stoneham ✆ 768151, N : 2 m. BY – 18, 9 West Side Basset Av. ✆ 768732 AY – 18 Fleming Park ✆ 0703 (Eastleigh) 612797, N : 6 m. by A 33 AY – 18 Romsey Rd ✆ 6673, NW : 4 ½ m. on A 3057 AY.

Southampton Airport : ✆ 0703 (Eastleigh) 612341, N : 4 m. BY.

– to America (New York) (Cunard) – to the Isle of Wight : East and West Cowes (Red Funnel Services) 8-18 daily (55 mn to 1 h 10 mn).

to the Isle of Wight : West Cowes (Red Funnel Services : hydrofoil) Monday/Saturday 14-19 daily ; Sunday 10 daily (20 mn).

Above Bar Precinct ✆ 221106 and 832615.

♦London 87 – ♦Bristol 79 – ♦Plymouth 161.

Plans on preceding pages

Polygon (T.H.F.), Cumberland Pl., SO9 4GD, ✆ 226401, Telex 47175 – TV P. AE VISA AZ **n**
M 7.50/9.50 **st.** 2.70 – 6.00 – **109 rm** 45.00/53.50 **st.**

Dolphin (T.H.F.), 35 High St., SO9 2DS, ✆ 226178, Telex 477735 – TV wc P. AE VISA AZ **i**
M (buffet lunch Saturday)/dinner 8.70 **st.** and a la carte 2.70 – 5.50 – **72 rm** 35.50/44.00 **st.**

Post House (T.H.F.), Herbert Walker Av., SO1 0HJ, ✆ 228081, Telex 477368, ≤, heated – TV wc P. AE VISA AZ **o**
M 6.95/9.50 **st.** and a la carte 2.70 – 5.50 – **132 rm** 42.00/50.50 **st.**

Southampton Park, Cumberland Pl., SO9 4NY, ✆ 223467, Telex 47439 – TV wc. AE VISA AZ **u**
M 6.85/9.35 **st.** and a la carte 2.15 – **77 rm** 36.50/46.50 **st.** – SB (weekends only) 44.00 **st.**

Southampton Moat House (Q.M.H.), 119 Highfield Lane, Portswood Junction, SO9 1YQ, ✆ 559555, Telex 47186 – TV wc P. AE VISA BY **e**
M *(closed Saturday lunch)* a la carte 10.45/16.45 **t.** – **70 rm** 38.00/47.00 **t.** – SB (weekends only) 37.50 **st.**

Star, 26 High St., SO9 4ZA, ✆ 226199 – TV wc wc P. AE VISA.
closed 25 and 31 December – **M** 5.50/7.00 **st.** and a la carte 3.80 – **31 rm** 28.00/44.50 **st.** – SB (weekends only) 40.00/50.00 **st.** AZ **z**

Northlands, Northlands Rd, SO9 3ZW, ✆ 333871 – TV wc P. VISA AY **a**
M *(closed lunch Saturday and Sunday)* a la carte approx. 8.80 **t.** 2.70 – **18 rm** 17.25/35.65 **t.**

Elizabeth House, 43-44 The Avenue, SO1 2SX, ✆ 224327 – TV wc wc P. AE VISA AY **e**
M (dinner only) 6.50 **t.** 2.50 – **25 rm** 17.60/35.20 **t.**

Wessex, 66-68 Northlands Rd, SO1 2LH, ✆ 31744, – TV wc wc P. VISA
closed 1 week at Christmas – **M** (bar lunch)/dinner 5.00 and a la carte 2.30 – **31 rm** 26.50/36.50 **t.** AY **r**

Hunters Lodge, 25 Landguard Rd, SO1 5DL, ✆ 227919 – P. VISA AZ **v**
closed 16 December-8 January – **17 rm** 14.40/28.00 **t.**

St. Regulus, 5 Archers Rd, SO1 2LQ, ✆ 224243, – wc P. AZ **x**
27 rm 14.75/29.00 **st.**

Earley House, 46 Pear Tree Av., Bitterne, SO2 7JP, ✆ 448117 – P BY **v**
9 rm 15.00/32.00 **t.**

Eaton Court, 32 Hill Lane, SO1 5AY, ✆ 223081 – wc P. VISA. AZ **r**
closed 2 weeks at Christmas – **12 rm** 10.75/22.50 **st.**

La Brasserie, 33-34 Oxford St., SO1 1DS, ✆ 221046, French rest. – AE VISA AZ **c**
closed Saturday lunch and Sunday – **M** 7.20 **t.** and a la carte 2.85.

Golden Palace, 1st Floor, 17 Above Bar St., SO1 0DQ, ✆ 226636, Chinese rest. – AE VISA AZ **e**
M 8.00/10.00 **t.** and a la carte.

MICHELIN Branch, Test Lane, SO1 9JX, ✆ **872344** AY

AUSTIN-ROVER-DAIMLER-JAGUAR Marsh Lane ✆ 30911
AUSTIN-ROVER The Causeway ✆ 865201
AUSTIN-ROVER High St., West End ✆ 042 18 (West End) 3773
AUSTIN-ROVER 102 High Rd ✆ 554346
AUSTIN-ROVER-DAIMLER-JAGUAR, ROLLS ROYCE The Avenue ✆ 228811
BMW Dorset St. ✆ 229003
COLT 170 Portsmouth Rd ✆ 447761
FIAT 115/125 Lodge Rd ✆ 225518
FORD 362/364 Shirley Rd ✆ 775331
FORD Palmerston Rd ✆ 228331
MAZDA Arundel Towers, Western Esplanade ✆ 38488
NISSAN 21/23 St. Denys Rd ✆ 559533
NISSAN 234 Winchester Rd ✆ 778511
PEUGEOT, TALBOT The Avenue ✆ 228801
RENAULT Portswood Rd ✆ 559902
TALBOT Southampton Rd ✆ 812250
VAUXHALL Portsmouth Rd, Sholing ✆ 449232
VOLVO Millbrook Roundabout ✆ 777616

SOUTHBOROUGH Kent 404 U 30 – see Royal Tunbridge Wells.

SOUTH BRENT Devon 403 I 32 – pop. 2,147 – ECD : Wednesday – ☎ 036 47.

♦London 228 – Exeter 28 – ♦Plymouth 16 – Torquay 17.

- **Brookdale** ⛰, North Huish, TQ10 9NR, S : 3 m. ☎ 054 882 (Gara Bridge) 402, 🌳 – TV 🛁wc P. VISA
  closed January – **M** (bar lunch)/dinner 8.50 **t.** 🍷 2.40 – **6 rm** 19.00/34.00 **t.** – SB (February-May and October-November) 41.00/43.00 **st.**
- **Glazebrook House,** Glazebrook, TQ10 9JE, SW : 1 m. ☎ 3322, 🏊, 🎾, 🌳, park – 🛁wc P. AE VISA. 🚫
  M 6.00/8.00 **t.** and a la carte 🍷 3.25 – **10 rm** 22.50/35.00 **st.** – SB (November-March) 45.00 **st.**

SOUTHEND-ON-SEA Essex 404 W 29 – pop. 155,720 – ECD : Wednesday – ☎ 0702.

Envir. : Hadleigh Castle (ruins) ≤★ of Thames *AC*, W : 3 m. – Southend Airport (Historic Aircraft museum) N : 2 m. – 🏌18 Belfairs Park, Eastwood Rd, Leigh-on-Sea ☎ 525345.

✈ ☎ 340201/6, N : 2 m. – ℹ High St. Precinct ☎ 355120 – Civic Centre, Victoria Av. ☎ 355122.

♦London 39 – ♦Cambridge 69 – Croydon 46 – ♦Dover 85.

- **Balmoral,** 34-36 Valkyrie Rd, Westcliff-on-Sea, SS0 8BU, ☎ 342947, 🌳 – TV 🛁wc 🚿wc ☎ P. VISA. 🚫
  closed 25 and 26 December – **M** *(closed Sunday dinner)* (bar lunch)/dinner 6.00 **st.** and a la carte 🍷 2.50 – **19 rm** 23.00/37.00 **st.** – SB (weekends only) 37.00/45.00 **st.**
- **West Park,** 11 Park Rd, Westcliff-on-Sea, SS0 7PQ, ☎ 330729 – TV 🛁wc 🚿wc ☎ P. VISA
  closed 22 December-1 January – **M** (bar lunch)/dinner 6.25 **t.** – **21 rm** 19.00/38.00 **t.** – SB (weekends only) 40.00/46.00 **t.**
- **Regency,** 18 Royal Terr., SS1 1DU, ☎ 340747, ≤ – TV. 🚫
  11 rm 14.00/25.00 **t.**
- **Norman,** 191 Eastern Esplanade, Thorpe Bay, SS1 3AA, ☎ 585212, 🌳 – TV. AE VISA
  9 rm 12.00/20.00 **st.**
- **Strand,** 165 Eastern Esplanade, SS1 2YB, ☎ 586611 – TV 🚿wc. 🚫
  closed January-mid February – **7 rm** 10.00/30.00 **s.**

AUSTIN-ROVER Priory Crescent ☎ 67766
FIAT 22 Belle Vue Pl. ☎ 610482
LANCIA Station Rd, Thorpe Bay ☎ 588200
NISSAN 661 London Rd, at Westcliff-on-Sea ☎ 351471
PEUGEOT, TALBOT 139/155 West Rd ☎ 347861
RENAULT 536 London Rd, Westcliff-on-Sea ☎ 344940
ROLLS ROYCE-BENTLEY, MERCEDES-BENZ Station Rd, Thorpe Bay ☎ 582233
TOYOTA 57 West Rd ☎ 346288
VW, AUDI 2 Comet Way ☎ 526411

SOUTH MIMMS Herts. 404 T 28 – ECD : Thursday – ✉ ☎ 0707 Potters Bar.

♦London 21 – Luton 17.

- **Crest** (Crest), Bignalls Corner, Potters Bar, EN6 3NH, South Mimms Services, junction of A 1 (M), A 6, M 25 on B 197 ☎ 43311, Telex 299162 – TV 🛁wc ☎ P. 🏢. AE ⓓ VISA
  M approx. 11.50 **st.** – 5.25 – **120 rm** 51.50/61.50 **st.** – SB (weekends only) 55.00 **st.**

SOUTH MOLTON Devon 403 I 30 The West Country G. – pop. 3,552 – ECD : Wednesday – ✉ ☎ 076 95.

ℹ 1 East St. ☎ 4122 (summer only).

♦London 210 – Exeter 35 – Taunton 39.

- **Marsh Hall Country House** ⛰, EX36 3HQ, N : 1 ¼ m. by North Molton rd ☎ 2666, ≤, 🌳 – TV 🛁wc 🚿wc ☎ P. AE ⓓ VISA. 🚫
  M 7.50/13.00 **t.** 🍷 2.75 – **5 rm** 19.85/28.00 **t.**
- XX **Stumbles** with rm, 131-134 East St., EX36 3BU, ☎ 3683 – TV 🛁wc P. AE ⓓ VISA. 🚫
  M a la carte 5.25/9.75 **t.** 🍷 2.95 – **7 rm** 15.00/30.00 **t.**

at East Buckland NW : 6 ¼ m. by A 361 – ✉ Barnstaple – ☎ 059 86 Filleigh :

- X **Lower Pitt** ⛰ with rm, EX32 0TD, ☎ 243, 🌳 – 🚿wc P. AE VISA. 🚫
  closed Sunday, Monday, 25-26 December and 1 January – **M** (dinner only) (booking essential) a la carte 7.30/12.35 **st.** 🍷 3.00 – **3 rm** 20.00/30.00 **st.** – SB 60.00 **st.**

FORD East St. ☎ 2137

SOUTH NORMANTON Derbs. 402 403 404 Q 24 – pop. 11,607 (inc. Pinxton) – ECD : Wednesday – ☎ 0773 Ripley.

♦ London 130 – Derby 17 – ♦ Nottingham 15 – ♦ Sheffield 31.

- **Swallow** (Swallow), Carter Lane East, DE55 2EH, on A 38 ☎ 812000, Telex 377264 – TV ☎ ♿ P. 🏢. AE ⓓ VISA
  M 8.00/10.00 **st.** and a la carte 🍷 3.40 – **123 rm** 48.00/60.00 **st.** – SB (weekends only) 58.00 **st.**

SOUTH PETHERTON Somerset 403 L 31 – pop. 2,235 – ☎ 0460.

♦London 138 – ♦Bristol 41 – Exeter 41 – Taunton 19 – Yeovil 7.5.

- XX **Le Tire-Bouchon,** 8 Palmer St., TA13 5DB, ☎ 40272, French rest., 🌳 – P. VISA
  closed Sunday dinner, Monday to Wednesday, 25-26 December and January – **M** 5.75/12.00 **t.** and a la carte 🍷 2.50.

SOUTHPORT Merseyside 402 K 23 — pop. 88 ,596 — ECD : Tuesday — 🕾 0704.

Envir. : Rufford Old Hall★ 15C (the Great Hall★★) *AC*, E : 9 m.

🏌 Park Rd ✆ 35286 — 🏌 Hesketh, Cockle Dick's Lane off Cambridge Rd ✆ 36897, N : 1 m. — 🏌 Bradshaws Lane, Ainsdale ✆ 78000, S : 3 m.

🛈 Cambridge Arcade ✆ 33133 and 40404.

◆London 221 — ◆Liverpool 20 — ◆Manchester 38 — Preston 19.

🏨 **Prince of Wales,** Lord St., PR8 1JS, ✆ 36688, Telex 67415, 🛥 — 📺 ⌂wc 🏧wc 🕾 ℗. 🛄
100 m.

🏨 **Carlton,** 86-88 Lord St., PR8 1JT, ✆ 35111 — 🛗 📺 ⌂wc 🏧wc 🕾 ℗. 🔺 🅰🅴 𝘝𝘐𝘚𝘈
M 5.50/8.25 **t.** and a la carte 👄 1.90 — **25 rm** � 20.00/42.00 **t.** — SB (weekends only) 38.00/45.00 **st.**

🏨 **Shelbourne,** 1 Lord St., PR8 2BH, ✆ 30278, 🛥 — 📺 ⌂wc 🏧wc 🕾. 🔺 🅰🅴 ⓞ 𝘝𝘐𝘚𝘈. 🍽
M (bar lunch)/dinner 5.75 **st.** and a la carte 👄 2.95 — **15 rm** ⊆ 19.00/32.00 — SB (weekends only) 78.00/88.00 **st.**

🏨 **Bold,** Lord St., PR9 0BE, ✆ 32578 — 📺 ⌂wc 🐾. 🔺 🅰🅴 ⓞ 𝘝𝘐𝘚𝘈
M 4.90/6.90 **st.** and a la carte 👄 2.50 — **25 rm** ⊆ 22.00/38.00 **st.**

🏨 **Club House,** 15 Leicester St., PR9 0ER, ✆ 33745 — ⌂wc 🏧wc 🕾 ℗. 🔺 𝘝𝘐𝘚𝘈
M (bar lunch)/dinner 6.95 **t.** 👄 1.95 — **13 rm** ⊆ 17.50/30.00 **t.** — SB 40.00/45.00 **st.**

🏠 **Crimond,** 28 Knowsley Rd, PR9 0HN, ✆ 36456, 🔲 — 📺 🏧wc 🕾 ℗. 🔺 𝘝𝘐𝘚𝘈
12 rm ⊆ 19.00/36.00 **t.**

🍴🍴 **Squires,** 78-80 King St., PR8 1LG, ✆ 30046 — 🔺 🅰🅴 ⓞ 𝘝𝘐𝘚𝘈
closed Sunday and Bank Holidays — **M** (dinner only) a la carte 9.20/12.45 **t.**

🍴🍴 **La Terrasse,** 1st. floor, 180 Lord St., PR9 0QG, ✆ 30995 — 🔺 🅰🅴 ⓞ 𝘝𝘐𝘚𝘈
closed Sunday dinner, Monday, Tuesday and first 2 weeks September — **M** (dinner only and Sunday lunch)/dinner 8.65 **t.** and a la carte 👄 2.85.

CITROEN Liverpool Rd ✆ 74127
DAIHATSU, LOTUS, SAAB 609 Liverpool Rd ✆ 74114
COLT Aughton Rd ✆ 67904
FORD Virginia St. ✆ 31550
LADA Liverpool Rd ✆ 77161
RENAULT 205 Liverpool Rd ✆ 68515
TOYOTA Tulketh St. ✆ 30909
VAUXHALL-OPEL 89/91 Bath St. North ✆ 35535
VOLVO 51 Weld Rd ✆ 66613
VW, AUDI Zetland St. ✆ 31091

SOUTHSEA Hants. 403 404 Q 31 — see Portsmouth and Southsea.

SOUTH SHIELDS Tyne and Wear 401 402 P 19 — pop. 86 ,488 — ECD : Wednesday — 🕾 0632.

🏌 Cleadon Hill ✆ 568942, SE : 3 m.

🛈 South Foreshore, Sea Rd ✆ 557411 (summer only).

◆London 284 — ◆Newcastle-upon-Tyne 9.5 — Sunderland 6.

🏨 **Sea,** Sea Rd, NE33 2LD, ✆ 566227 — 📺 ⌂wc 🐾 ℗. 🔺 🅰🅴 ⓞ 𝘝𝘐𝘚𝘈
closed 26 December — **M** 4.80/6.00 **t.** and a la carte 👄 2.70 — **28 rm** ⊆ 27.50/37.50.

SOUTH WALSHAM Norfolk 404 Y 26 — pop. 543 — ✉ Norwich — 🕾 060 549.

◆London 120 — Great Yarmouth 11 — ◆Norwich 9.

🏨 **South Walsham Hall H. and Country Club** 🛁, South Walsham Rd, NR13 6DQ, ✆ 378, Telex 97394, ≤, 🔲 heated, 🎣, 🛥, park, 🍽, squash — 📺 ⌂wc 🏧wc ℗ ℗. 🔺 🅰🅴 ⓞ 𝘝𝘐𝘚𝘈.
🍽
M 6.50/9.50 **t.** and a la carte 👄 2.50 — **19 rm** ⊆ 20.00/50.00 **st.** — SB (weekends only) 45.00/60.00 **st.**

SOUTHWELL Notts. 402 403 404 R 24 — pop. 6 ,283 — ECD : Thursday — 🕾 0636.

See : Minster★ 12C-13C (Chapter house : foliage carving★★ 13C).

◆London 135 — Lincoln 24 — ◆Nottingham 14 — ◆Sheffield 34.

🏨 **Saracen's Head** (Anchor), Market Pl., NG25 0HE, ✆ 812701, Group Telex 377201 — 📺 ⌂wc 🐾 ℗. 🛄. 🔺 🅰🅴 ⓞ 𝘝𝘐𝘚𝘈
M *(closed Saturday lunch)* 5.00/10.00 **t.** and a la carte 👄 3.00 — **23 rm** ⊆ 39.50/49.50 **t.** — SB (weekends only) 62.00 **st.**

🍴 **Leo's,** 12 King St., NG24 0EN, ✆ 812119 — 🔺 🅰🅴 ⓞ 𝘝𝘐𝘚𝘈
closed Sunday, Monday and Bank Holidays — **M** (dinner only) 15.50 **t.** 👄 2.80.

FORD Westgate ✆ 813741

SOUTHWOLD Suffolk 404 Z 27 — pop. 3 ,756 — ECD : Wednesday — 🕾 0502.

🛈 Town Hall, Market Place ✆ 722366 (summer only).

◆London 108 — Great Yarmouth 24 — ◆Ipswich 35 — ◆Norwich 34.

🏨 **Swan,** Market Pl., IP18 6EG, ✆ 722186, 🛥 — 🛗 📺 ⌂wc 🐾 ℗. 🛄. 🔺 🅰🅴 ⓞ 𝘝𝘐𝘚𝘈
M 7.85/8.85 **t.** and a la carte — **52 rm** ⊆ 28.00/50.00 **t.** — SB (November-March) 45.00/48.00 **st.**

🏨 **Crown,** High St., IP18 6DP, ✆ 722275 — 📺 ⌂wc 🏧wc ℗. 🔺 🅰🅴 𝘝𝘐𝘚𝘈
M 9.00/10.00 **st.** and a la carte — ⊆ 1.20 — **10 rm** 22.00/34.00 **st.**

🏨 **Pier Avenue,** Station Rd, IP18 6AY, ✆ 722632 — 📺 ⌂wc 🏧wc. 🔺 🅰🅴 𝘝𝘐𝘚𝘈
M 5.25/8.00 **st.** and a la carte 👄 3.00 — **13 rm** ⊆ 16.50/37.00 **st.** — SB (October-June) 35.00/42.50 **st.**

SOUTH WOODHAM FERRERS Essex 404 V 29 – pop. 6,975 – ✉ ✪ 0245 Chelmsford.
♦London 36 – Chelmsford 12 – Colchester 34 – Southend-on-Sea 13.

🏠 Oakland, Merchant St., CM3 5XE, ✆ 322811 – 📺 ⎔wc ☎ – **27 rm**.

SOUTH ZEAL Devon 403 I 31 The West Country G. – ECD : Thursday – ✉ ✪ 0837 Okehampton.
♦London 218 – Exeter 17 – ♦Plymouth 36 – Torquay 27.

🏠 **Oxenham Arms,** EX20 2JT, ✆ 840244, « 12C inn », 🐴 – 📺 ⎔wc **P**. 🔺 � AE Ⓞ VISA
M 7.50/12.00 t. 🍷 2.45 – **8 rm** ⇄ 28.00/40.00 t. – SB (November-March) 40.00/46.00 **st.**

⋔ **Poltimore,** EX20 2PD, S : 1 m. by A 30 ✆ 840209, 🐴 – ⎔wc **P**
7 rm ⇄ 11.00/27.00 **st.**

SOWERBY North Yorks. – see Thirsk.

SPALDING Lincs. 402 404 T 25 – pop. 18,182 – ECD : Thursday – ✪ 0775.
See : Parish church★ 13C – Ayscoughfee Hall★ 15C.
🛈 Ayscoughfee Hall, Churchgate ✆ 5468.
♦London 106 – ♦Leicester 51 – Lincoln 44 – ♦Nottingham 54.

🏠 **White Hart** (T.H.F.), Market Pl., PE11 1SU, ✆ 5668 – 📺 ⎔wc ☎ **P**. 🔺 🔲 AE Ⓞ VISA
M a la carte lunch/dinner 7.80 **st.** 🍷 2.70 – ⇄ 5.50 – **28 rm** 33.50/41.50 **st.**

ALFA-ROMEO Bourne Rd ✆ 5459
AUSTIN-ROVER Pinchbeck Rd ✆ 3651
FORD St. Johns Rd ✆ 67651
PEUGEOT-TALBOT High St. ✆ 820219
PEUGEOT Pinchbeck ✆ 3033

RENAULT Swan St. ✆ 66666
VAUXHALL Pinchbeck Rd ✆ 3391
VW-AUDI Winsover Rd ✆ 2315
VOLVO High Rd ✆ 0406 (Holbeach) 370307

SPARK BRIDGE Cumbria – see Ulverston.

SPELDHURST Kent 404 U 30 – see Royal Tunbridge Wells.

SPRIGG'S ALLEY Oxon. – see Chinnor.

SPROTBROUGH South Yorks. 402 403 404 Q 23 – see Doncaster.

STAFFORD Staffs. 402 403 404 N 25 – pop. 60,915 – ECD : Wednesday – ✪ 0785.
See : High House★ 16C – St. Mary's Church (Norman font★).
🛈 Civic Offices, Riverside ✆ 3181 ext. 216.
♦London 142 – ♦Birmingham 26 – Derby 32 – Shrewsbury 31 – ♦Stoke-on-Trent 17.

🏨 **Tillington Hall** (De Vere), Eccleshall Rd, ST16 1JJ, NW : 1 ½ m. on A 5013 ✆ 53531, Telex
36566 – 🛗 📺 ⎔wc ☎ 🔺 **P**. 🔺 🔲 AE Ⓞ VISA
closed 1 week at Christmas – **M** (closed Saturday lunch) 7.25 **st.** and a la carte – **93 rm**
⇄ 27.00/50.00 **st.** – SB (weekends only) 54.00/57.00 **st.**

🏠 Garth, Moss Pit, ST17 9JD, S : 2 m. on A 449 ✆ 56124 – 📺 ⎔wc ☎ **P**. 🔺 – **32 rm**.

🏠 Swan, 46 Greengate St., ST16 2JA, ✆ 58142 – 📺 ⎔wc ☎ **P**. 🏂 – **31 rm**.

🏡 Vine, Salter St., ST16 2JU, ✆ 51071 – 📺 ⎔wc – **26 rm**.

AUSTIN-ROVER-DAIMLER-JAGUAR Lichfield Rd ✆ 51366
AUSTIN-ROVER Silkmore Lane ✆ 56111
BMW Lichfield Rd ✆ 46999
CITROEN Astonfields Rd ✆ 3336
DATSUN Lichfield Rd ✆ 59313
FIAT Milford ✆ 661226
FORD Stone Rd ✆ 51331

LADA Sandon Rd ✆ 45299
MAZDA Derby St. ✆ 55486
PEUGEOT-TALBOT Newport Rd ✆ 51084
RENAULT Wolverhampton Rd ✆ 52118
SAAB Yarlet Bank ✆ 088 97 (Sandon) 248
VAUXHALL-OPEL Walton ✆ 661293
VOLVO Lichfield Rd ✆ 47221

STAINES Surrey 404 S 29 – pop. 51,949 – ECD : Thursday – ✪ 0784.
♦London 26 – Reading 25.

🏨 **Thames Lodge** (Anchor), Thames St., TW18 4SF, ✆ 64433, Group Telex 8812552, ≤ – 📺
⎔wc **P**. 🔺 🔲 AE Ⓞ VISA
M (closed Saturday lunch) a la carte 7.95/13.50 **t.** 🍷 3.25 – **47 rm** ⇄ 46.00/52.00 **st.** – SB
(weekends only) 58.00/62.00 **st.**

AUSTIN-ROVER 236 Central Trading Estate ✆ 51698   TALBOT Staines Bridge ✆ 55301
PEUGEOT-TALBOT 186 High St., Egham ✆ 38787

STAMFORD Lincs. 402 404 S 26 – pop. 16,127 – ECD : Thursday – ✪ 0780.
See : Burghley House★★ 16C (paintings : Heaven Room★★★) AC.
🛈 Luffenham ✆ 720205, W : 5 m.
🛈 6 St. Mary's Hill ✆ 64444.
♦London 92 – ♦Leicester 31 – Lincoln 50 – ♦Nottingham 45.

🏨 **The George of Stamford,** 71 St, Martin's, PE9 2LB, ✆ 55171, Telex 32578, « 17C coaching
inn with walled monastic garden » – 📺 ☎ **P**. 🔺 🔲 AE Ⓞ VISA
M a la carte 15.15/21.05 **st.** – **44 rm** ⇄ 46.00/74.00 **st.**

🏨 **Lady Anne's,** 36-38 High St., St. Martin's, ℰ 53175, 🚗 – 📺 ➬wc 🏛wc ☎ 🅿. 🛦. 🔼 ᴁᴇ 🔵 𝘝𝘐𝘚𝘈
M 6.50/7.50 **t.** and a la carte 🍴 3.20 – **27 rm** ⟐ 27.50/45.00 t. – SB (weekends only) (November-March) 40.00/60.00 **st.**

🏨 **Garden House,** St. Martin's, PE9 2LP, ℰ 63359, 🚗 – 📺 ➬wc ☎ 🅿. 🔼 𝘝𝘐𝘚𝘈
M (bar lunch)/dinner 10.50 **st.** – **21 rm** ⟐ 20.00/50.00 **st.** – SB (weekends only) (November-March) 55.00/70.00 **st.**

XX **Candlesticks** with rm, 1 Church Lane, PE9 2JU, ℰ 64033 – 📺 ➬wc 🅿. 🔼 𝘝𝘐𝘚𝘈. ⅏
M *(closed Monday)* 4.95/7.50 and a la carte 🍴 3.00 – **4 rm** 17.50/20.00 t.

XX **The Courtyard,** 18a Maiden Lane, PE9 2AZ, ℰ 51505 – 🔼 ᴁᴇ 🔵 𝘝𝘐𝘚𝘈
closed Monday lunch, Sunday dinner, 26 December, 1 January and Bank Holiday Mondays –
M 10.50 **t.** (dinner) and a la carte 9.40/12.50 t.

at Collyweston (Northants.) SW : 3 ¾ m. on A 43 – ⊠ Stamford – ✆ 078 083 Duddington :

🏤 **Cavalier,** Main St., PE9 3PQ, ℰ 288 – 📺 ➬wc 🅿. 🔼
M 10.00/14.00 **t.** and a la carte 🍴 2.75 – **5 rm** ⟐ 12.50/29.00 t. – SB (weekends only) 30.00/55.00 **st.**

AUSTIN-ROVER St. Paul's St. ℰ 52741
FORD Wharf Rd ℰ 55151
NISSAN West St. ℰ 62571
PEUGEOT-TALBOT Scotgate ℰ 4003

RENAULT Water St. ℰ 63532
TOYOTA Collyweston ℰ 078 083 (Duddington) 271
VAUXHALL Rock House, Scotgate ℰ 51826

STANDISH Greater Manchester 🟦🟦🟦 🟦🟦🟦 M 23 – pop. 11,504 – ECD : Wednesday – ⊠ Wigan – ✆ 0257.

♦London 210 – ♦Liverpool 22 – ♦Manchester 21 – Preston 15.

XX **The Beeches** with rm., School Lane, WN6 0TD, on B 5239 ℰ 426432 – 📺 ➬wc 🏛wc 🅿. 🔼 ᴁᴇ 🔵 𝘝𝘐𝘚𝘈. ⅏
M 6.00 **st.** and a la carte 🍴 3.20 – ⟐ 2.95 – **7 rm** 19.00/28.00 **st.**

STANSTEAD ABBOTS Herts. 🟦🟦🟦 U 28 – pop. 1,906 – ⊠ Ware – ✆ 027 979 Roydon.

♦London 22 – ♦Cambridge 37 – Luton 32 – ♦Ipswich 66.

🏯 **Briggens House,** SG12 8LD, E : 2 m. on A 414 ℰ 2416, Telex 817906, ≼, « Arboretum », 🔼 heated, 🎣, 🚗, park, ⚒ – ♻ 📺 🅿. 🛦. 🔼 ᴁᴇ 🔵 𝘝𝘐𝘚𝘈. ⅏
M 8.50/10.00 **t.** and a la carte 🍴 3.50 – **47 rm** ⟐ 29.00/70.00 t. – SB (weekends only) 54.00/70.00 **st.**

STANTON HARCOURT Oxon 🟦🟦🟦 🟦🟦🟦 P 28 – pop. 774 – ⊠ ✆ 0865 Oxford.

♦London 71 – Gloucester 45 – ♦Oxford 13 – Swindon 27.

🏨 Harcourt Arms, OX8 1RJ, ℰ 882192 – 📺 ➬wc 🅿 – **16 rm**.

STAPLETON Durham 🟦🟦🟦 P 20 – see Darlington.

STAVERTON Devon 🟦🟦🟦 I 32 – pop. 643 – ⊠ Totnes – ✆ 080 426.

♦London 226 – Exeter 26 – ♦Plymouth 24 – Torquay 13.

🏤 **Sea Trout Inn,** TQ9 6PA, ℰ 274 – 🅿. 🔼 ᴁᴇ 🔵 𝘝𝘐𝘚𝘈
M (bar lunch Monday to Saturday)/dinner 6.00 **t.** and a la carte 🍴 2.20 – **6 rm** ⟐ 14.00/27.00 t.

STEVENAGE Herts. 🟦🟦🟦 T 28 – pop. 74,757 – ECD : Monday and Wednesday – ✆ 0438.

Envir. : Knebworth House (furniture★) S : 3 m. – ▣ Aston Lane ℰ 043 888 (Shephall) 424.

🅉 Central Library, Southgate ℰ 69441 – ♦London 36 – Bedford 25 – ♦Cambridge 27.

🏨 **Stevenage Moat House** (Q.M.H.), High St., Old Town, SG1 3AL, ℰ 359111, 🚗 – 📺 ➬wc 🏛wc 🅿. 🛦. 🔼 ᴁᴇ 🔵 𝘝𝘐𝘚𝘈
M 7.65 **st.** and a la carte 🍴 3.75 – **60 rm** ⟐ 36.95/44.95 **st.** – SB (weekends only) 62.30/64.30 **st.**

🏠 **Northfield,** 15 Hitchin Rd, Old Town, SG1 3BJ, ℰ 314537 – ➬wc 🏛wc 🅿. ⅏
closed Christmas-New Year – **10 rm** ⟐ 15.00/29.00 **st.**

at Broadwater S : 1 ¾ m. by A 602 on B 197 – ⊠ ✆ 0438 Stevenage :

🏨 **Roebuck Inn** (T.H.F.), Old London Rd, SG2 8DS, ℰ 65444, Telex 825505, 🚗 – 📺 ➬wc ➬ 🅿. 🛦. 🔼 ᴁᴇ 🔵 𝘝𝘐𝘚𝘈
M 6.00/8.25 **st.** and a la carte 🍴 2.90 – ⟐ 5.50 – **54 rm** 37.50/46.00 **st.**

AUDI, VW Lyton Way ℰ 354691
BMW Hertford Rd, Broadwater ℰ 351565

NISSAN Broadwater Crescent ℰ 315555
VAUXHALL-OPEL 124/6 High St. ℰ 51113

STEYNING West Sussex 🟦🟦🟦 T 31 – pop. 8,318 (inc. Upper Beeding) – ECD : Thursday – ✆ 0903.

See : St. Andrew's Church (the nave★ 12C) – ♦London 52 – ♦Brighton 12 – Worthing 10.

🏨 **Springwells** without rest., 9 High St., BN4 3GG, ℰ 812446, 🔼 heated, 🚗 – 📺 ➬wc ➬ 🅿. 🔼 ᴁᴇ 🔵 𝘝𝘐𝘚𝘈
11 rm ⟐ 20.00/45.00 **st.**

at Bramber S : 1 m. by A 283 – ⊠ ✪ 0903 Steyning :

XX **Maharajah,** The Street, BN4 3WE, ✆ 814746, Indian rest. – 🔼 AE ⓪ VISA
M 4.00/8.00 t. and a la carte.

STOBOROUGH Dorset – see Wareham.

STOCKBRIDGE Hants. 408 404 P 30 – pop. 524 – ECD : Wednesday – ✪ 0264 Andover.
♦London 75 – Salisbury 14 – Winchester 9.

🏠 **Grosvenor,** High St., SO20 6EU, ✆ 810606, ☞ – TV P. 🔼 AE ⓪ VISA
M 6.50/10.50 st. and a la carte – **14 rm** ☲ 38.00/46.00 st. – SB (weekends only) 70.00 st.

🏠 **Old Three Cups,** High St., SO20 6HB, ✆ 810527, « 15C inn », ☞ – ⇔wc. 🔼 VISA ⋇
closed January and Christmas – **M** (closed Monday lunch and dinner Sunday and Monday to
non-residents) 4.95/6.75 t. and a la carte ▯ 2.95 – **8 rm** ☲ 12.00/28.00.

🏠 **Carbery,** Salisbury Hill, SO20 6EZ, on A 30 ✆ 810771, ⬎, ☞ – P. ⋇
closed 2 weeks at Christmas – **11 rm** ☲ 11.50/23.00 st.

AUSTIN-ROVER High St. ✆ 711

SAAB Middle Wallop ✆ 026 478 (Middle Wallop)
460

STOCKLAND Devon – see Honiton.

STOCKPORT Greater Manchester 402 403 404 N 23 – pop. 135,489 – ECD : Thursday – ✪ 061
Manchester.

Envir. : Lyme Park★ (16C-18C) *AC*, SE : 4 ½ m.

🏌 Heaton Moor, Heaton Mersey ✆ 432 2134 – 🏌 Offerton Rd ✆ 427 2001 – 🏌 Goosehouse Green,
Romiley ✆ 430 2392, NE : 2 m. – 🚊 9 Princes St. ✆ 480 0315.

♦London 201 – ♦Liverpool 42 – ♦Manchester 6 – ♦Sheffield 37 – ♦Stoke-on-Trent 34.

🏨 **Alma Lodge** (Embassy), 149 Buxton Rd, SK2 6EL, on A 6 ✆ 483 4431 – TV ⇔wc P. 🏄.
🔼 AE ⓪ VISA ⋇
M 8.25 st. and a la carte ▯ 2.75 – ☲ 5.00 – **70 rm** 24.00/43.50 st. – SB 49.00 st.

🏠 **Wycliffe Villa,** 74 Edgeley Rd, Edgeley (via Greek St.), SK3 9NQ, ✆ 477 5395 – TV ⇔wc
🏌wc 🕿 P. 🔼 AE ⓪ VISA ⋇
M (closed Saturday lunch, Sunday and Bank Holidays) 4.00/10.00 st. and a la carte ▯ 2.60 –
12 rm ☲ 25.00/34.00 st.

AUSTIN-ROVER 35 Buxton Rd ✆ 480 4244
AUSTIN-ROVER Town Hall Sq. ✆ 480 7966
AUSTIN-ROVER Wellington Rd North ✆ 432 6201
BMW, HONDA, SAAB 31/33 Buxton Rd ✆ 483 6271
CITROEN Waterloo Rd ✆ 480 4118
COLT School Lane, Heaton Chapel ✆ 432 4790
FIAT Heaton Lane ✆ 480 6661
FORD Oak St., Hazel Grove ✆ 483 9431
FORD Adswood Rd ✆ 480 0211
MAZDA Wellington Rd North ✆ 442 6466

NISSAN 596 Didsbury Rd, Heaton Mersey ✆
442 6050
NISSAN 91 Heaton Moor Rd ✆ 432 9416
PEUGEOT-TALBOT 110 Buxton Rd ✆ 480 0831
RENAULT 79 Lancashire Hill ✆ 480 7476
SAAB 31/33 Buxton Rd ✆ 483 6271
VAUXHALL-OPEL Wellington Rd South ✆ 480 6146
VAUXHALL-OPEL 398 Wellington Rd North ✆
432 3232
VOLVO Wellington Rd South ✆ 429 7099
VW-AUDI Gt. Portwood St. ✆ 480 1131

STOCKTON-ON-TEES Cleveland 402 P 20 – pop. 86,699 – ECD : Thursday – ✪ 0642.
✈ Tees-side Airport : ✆ 0325 (Darlington) 332811, SW : 6 m.
♦London 251 – ♦ Leeds 61 – ♦ Middlesbrough 4.

🏨 **Swallow** (Swallow), 10 John Walker Sq., TS18 1AQ, ✆ 679721, Telex 587895 – ▮ TV 🕿 ⅙
P. 🏄. 🔼 AE ⓪ VISA
M 6.50/15.00 st. and a la carte ▯ 3.40 – **126 rm** ☲ 43.00/55.00 st. – SB 44.00 st.

at Eaglescliffe S : 3 ½ m. on A 135 – ⊠ ✪ 0642 Stockton-on-Tees :

🏨 **Parkmore** (Best Western), 636 Yarm Rd, TS16 0DH, ✆ 786815, ☞ – TV ⇔wc 🏌wc 🕿 P.
🔼 AE ⓪ VISA
M (bar lunch)/dinner 8.95 t. and a la carte ▯ 2.95 – **40 rm** ☲ 26.00/35.00 t., **1 suite** 34.00/44.00
t. – SB (weekends only) 42.00/48.00 st.

ALFA-ROMEO Norton Av. ✆ 531127
BMW 45 Norton Rd ✆ 675361
CITROEN Yarm Rd ✆ 780095
FORD Yarm Rd ✆ 675471
LANCIA Billingham Rd ✆ 551542

NISSAN Middleway Mandale Industrial Estate ✆
672671
SAAB, SUBARU Chapel St. ✆ 679781
TOYOTA 336 Norton Rd ✆ 553003
VAUXHALL-OPEL Boathouse Lane ✆ 607804
VOLVO Prince Regent St. ✆ 673251

STOKE BRUERNE Northants. 404 R 27 – pop. 345 – ⊠ Towcester – ✪ 0604 Roade.
♦London 70 – ♦Coventry 38 – ♦Leicester 46 – Northampton 7.

X **Butty,** 5 Canalside, ✆ 863654, Italian rest., « Picturesque setting on Grand Union Canal » –
P. 🔼 VISA
closed Saturday lunch, Sunday, Monday, 1 week spring, 1 week summer and 1 week autumn –
M 8.50/14.50 st. and a la carte ▯ 4.00.

STOKE GABRIEL Devon 🔲403🔲 J 32 – see Totnes.

STOKE MANDEVILLE Bucks. 🔲404🔲 R 28 – see Aylesbury.

STOKE-ON-TRENT Staffs. 🔲402🔲 🔲403🔲 🔲404🔲 N 24 – pop. 272 ,446 – ECD : Thursday – ✪ 0782.
See : City Museum and Art Gallery★ Y – Gladstone Pottery Museum★ *AC* V – National Garden Festival U – Envir. : Little Moreton Hall★★ (16C) *AC*, NW : 8 m. on A 34 U – 🖪 Central Library, Bethesda St., Hanley 🖉 281242 and 23122.

♦London 162 – ♦Birmingham 46 – ♦Leicester 59 – ♦Liverpool 58 – ♦Manchester 41 – ♦Sheffield 53.

STOKE-ON-TRENT
NEWCASTLE-UNDER-LYME
BUILT UP AREA

Alexandra Road	U 3	Cobridge Road	U 15
Bedford Road	U 5	Davenport Street	U 16
Brownhills Road	U 7	Elder Road	U 18
Church Lane	U 12	Etruria Vale Road	U 21
		Grove Road	V 23
		Hanley Road	U 24
		Heron Street	V 27
		High Street	U 28
		Higherland	V 29
		Manor Street	V 34

Mayne Street	V 35
Moorland Road	U 36
Newcastle Street	U 37
Park Hall Road	U 40
Porthill Road	U 44
Snow Hill	U 48
Stoke Road	U 51
Strand (The)	V 52
Victoria Park Road	V 56
Watlands View	U 57

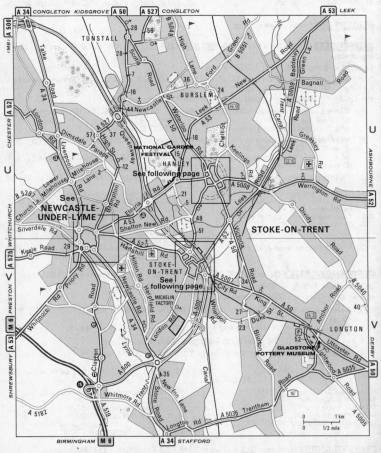

NATIONAL GARDEN FESTIVAL
1st MAY – 26th OCTOBER 1986 – *Open daily from 10.00am till dusk*
See street plan for location.

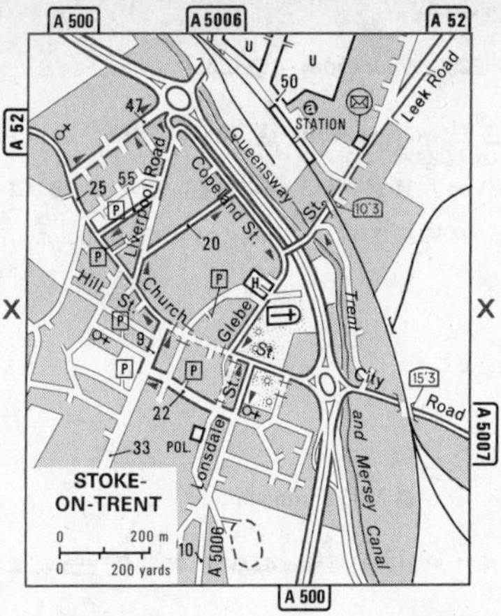

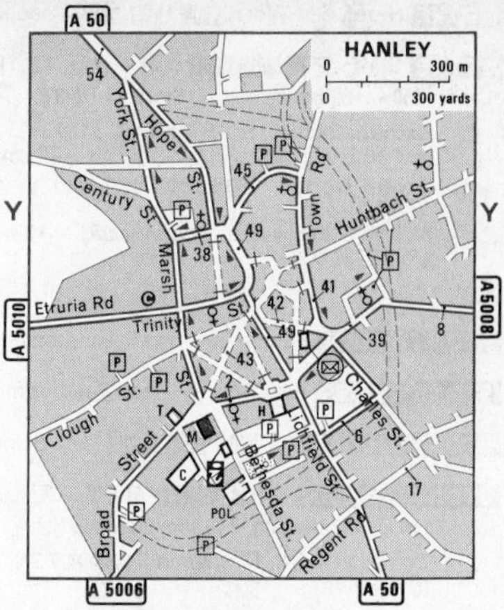

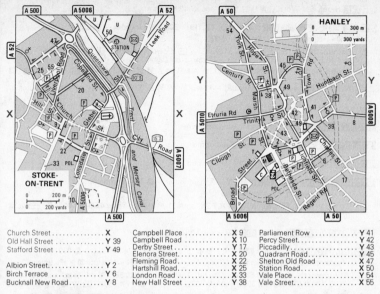

Church Street X
Old Hall Street . . . . Y 39
Stafford Street . . . . Y 49

Albion Street. . . . . Y 2
Birch Terrace . . . . Y 6
Bucknall New Road. . . . . Y 8

Campbell Place . . . . X 9
Campbell Road . . . . X 10
Derby Street . . . . Y 17
Elenora Street. . . . . X 20
Fleming Road. . . . . X 22
Hartshill Road. . . . . X 25
London Road . . . . X 33
New Hall Street . . . . Y 38

Parliament Row . . . . Y 41
Percy Street. . . . . Y 42
Piccadilly. . . . . Y 43
Quadrant Road. . . . . Y 45
Shelton Old Road . . . . X 47
Station Road. . . . . X 50
Vale Place . . . . Y 54
Vale Street. . . . . X 55

North Stafford (T.H.F.), Station Rd, ST4 2AE, ✆ 48501, Telex 36287 – 🛗 TV ⛀wc ⛆wc ☎ Ⓟ. 🏃. AE ◑ VISA X a
M (bar lunch Saturday) 6.95/8.95 **st.** and a la carte 🍷2.70 – ☕ 5.50 – **69 rm** 41.50/50.50 **st.**, **2 suites**.

White House, 94 Stone Rd, Trent Vale, ST4 6SP, S : 2 ¼ m. on A 34 ✆ 642460 – Ⓟ. ✻
closed 1 to 14 January – **8 rm** ☕ 16.00/35.00 **t.** V e

at Hanley NW : 2 m. by A 5006 – ✉ ☏ 0782 Stoke-on-Trent :

Stakis Grand (Stakis), 66 Trinity St., ST1 5NB, ✆ 22361 – 🛗 TV ⛀wc ☎ Ⓟ. 🏃. AE ◑ VISA Y c
M (grill rest. only) (bar lunch Saturday) 4.95 **t.** (lunch) and a la carte 5.55/10.60 **st.** 🍷3.50 – **93 rm**.

at Basford NW : 1 ¾ m. by A 500 off A 53 – ✉ ☏ 0782 Stoke-on-Trent :

Haydon House, 5-9 Haydon St., ST4 6JD, ✆ 629311 – TV ⛀wc ⛆wc ☎ Ⓟ. 🏃. AE ◑ VISA. ✻ U a
M (bar lunch Sunday and Monday) 8.75/10.75 **t.** and a la carte 🍷3.50 – **24 rm** ☕ 21.00/42.00 **st.**, **4 suites** 55.00/75.00 **st.** – SB (weekends only) 60.00/120.00 **st.**

MICHELIN Branch, Jamage Road Industrial Estate, Talke Pits, ST7 1QF, ✆ 078 16 (Kidsgrove) 71211/2/3/4 by A 34 U

ALFA ROMEO High St., Tunstall ✆ 89226
AUDI, TOYOTA, VW Leek Rd, Hanley ✆ 264888
AUSTIN-ROVER Leek Rd, Endon ✆ 503160
AUSTIN-ROVER Station Rd, Barlaston ✆ 2014
AUSTIN-ROVER Broad St. ✆ 29500
AUSTIN-ROVER King St., Longton ✆ 335533
BMW ✆ 620811
CITROEN Uttoxeter Rd ✆ 312235
DAIHATSU Ashbank ✆ 2426
FIAT Lightwood Rd, Longton ✆ 319212
FIAT Leek Rd, Hanley ✆ 20244
FORD Clough St. ✆ 29591
FORD King St. ✆ 317381
HONDA Sneyd St., Cobridge ✆ 261593
LADA 292 Waterloo Rd, Cobridge ✆ 22265
LADA Congleton Rd, Biddulph ✆ 512250
LANCIA Leek Rd, Hanley ✆ 20244
MAZDA Moorland Rd ✆ 84215
MERCEDES-BENZ Clough St. ✆ 267872
PEUGEOT-TALBOT Leek Rd ✆ 24371
PEUGEOT-TALBOT Bullocks House Rd ✆ 513952
RENAULT Werrington Rd, Bucknall ✆ 25406
RENAULT Blue Gates, Biddulph ✆ 514444
SAAB Victoria Rd, Fenton ✆ 416666
SKODA Leek Rd ✆ 261784
SKODA Shelton New Rd ✆ 615106
SUBARU High St., Tunstall ✆ 88997
TOYOTA Leek Rd ✆ 264888
VAUXHALL-OPEL Victoria Rd, Hanley ✆ 271872
VAUXHALL-OPEL Lightwood Rd ✆ 310237
VOLVO Duke St. ✆ 334204

STOKE PRIOR Heref. and Worc. – see Leominster.

STONE Glos. 403 404 M 29 – pop. 667 (inc. Ham) – ✉ Berkeley – ☏ 0454 Falfield.
♦London 130 – ♦Bristol 17 – Gloucester 18.

Elms, GL13 9JX, on A 38 ✆ 260279 – Ⓟ
10 rm ☕ 11.00/21.00 **st.**

STONE Heref. and Worc. **403** **404** N 26 – see Kidderminster.

STONE Staffs. **402** **403** **404** N 25 – pop. 12 ,119 – ECD : Wednesday – ✆ 0785.
♦London 150 – ♦Birmingham 36 – ♦Stoke-on-Trent 9.

🏨 **Crown,** 38 High St., ST15 8AS, ✆ 813535 – 📺 ⬛wc ⬛wc ☎ Ⓟ. 🅰. 🆎 ⓞ 𝘝𝘐𝘚𝘈
M 4.50/6.00 **t.** and a la carte ⏹ 2.65 – **29 rm** ⌁ 26.50/36.00 **t.**

🏨 **Stone House,** ST15 0BQ, S : 1 ¼ m. by A 520 on A 34 ✆ 815531, ☞ – 📺 ⬛wc ☎ Ⓟ. 🅰
🆎 𝘝𝘐𝘚𝘈
M 5.95/9.25 **t.** and a la carte ⏹ 2.50 – **17 rm** ⌁ 19.50/39.00 **t.** – SB (weekends only) (October-March) 39.00 **st.**

FORD Darlaston Rd ✆ 813332

STON EASTON Somerset – see Farrington Gurney.

STONE CROSS East Sussex – see Eastbourne.

STONEHOUSE Glos. **403** **404** N 28 – see Stroud.

STONEY CROSS Hants. **403** **404** P 31 – ✉ Lyndhurst – ✆ 0703 Southampton.
♦London 94 – Bournemouth 19 – ♦Southampton 12.

🏨 **Compton Arms,** Ringwood Rd, SO4 7GN, on A 31 ✆ 812134, Telex 477945, ☞ – 📺 ⬛wc ☎
Ⓟ – **18 rm**.

STONY STRATFORD Bucks. **404** R 27 – see Milton Keynes.

STORRINGTON West Sussex **404** S 31 – pop. 6 ,915 – ECD : Wednesday – ✆ 090 66.
Envir. : Parham House★ (Elizabethan) *AC*, W : 1 ½ m. – ♦London 54 – ♦Brighton 20 – ♦Portsmouth 36.

🏨 **Abingworth Hall** 🦢, Storrington Rd, Thakeham, RH20 3EF, N : 1 ¾ m. on B 2139 ✆
07983 (West Chiltington) 3636, Telex 877835, ≼, ⌇ heated, ☞, ℅ – 📺 ☎ Ⓟ. 🅰. 🆎 ⓞ
𝘝𝘐𝘚𝘈. ℅
M 10.00/12.50 **t.** and a la carte ⏹ 3.00 – **23 rm** ⌁ 38.00/70.00 **t.**, **1 suite** 75.00/100.00 **t.** – SB 70.00/90.00 **st.**

🏨 **Little Thakeham** 🦢, Merrywood Lane, Thakeham, RH20 3HE, N : 1 ¾ m. by B 2139 ✆ 4416,
≼, « Lutyens house, gardens by Gertrude Jekyll, country house atmosphere », ⌇ heated, ℅
– 📺 ⬛wc ☎ Ⓟ. 🅰 🆎 ⓞ 𝘝𝘐𝘚𝘈. ℅
closed 2 weeks Christmas and New Year – **M** (closed Monday lunch and Sunday dinner)
(booking essential) 15.00/19.50 **s.** ⏹ 3.50 – **9 rm** ⌁ 50.00/80.00 **s.**

✕✕✕ **Manley's,** Manleys Hill, RH20 4BT, ✆ 2331 – Ⓟ. 🅰 🆎 ⓞ 𝘝𝘐𝘚𝘈
closed Sunday dinner, Monday, 3 weeks August-September and first week January – **M** a la carte 12.60/19.90 **s.** ⏹ 3.40.

AUSTIN-ROVER The Square ✆ 3282

STOURBRIDGE West Midlands **403** **404** N 26 – pop. 55 ,136 – ECD : Thursday – ✆ 0384.
♦London 147 – ♦Birmingham 14 – Wolverhampton 10 – Worcester 21.

Plan : see Birmingham p.2

🏨 Talbot, High St., DY8 1DW, ✆ 394350 – 📺 ⬛wc ⬛wc Ⓟ
22 rm.   see plan of Birmingham p.2   AU   **a**

↑ **Limes,** 260 Hagley Rd, Pedmore, DY9 0RW, SE : 1 ½ m. on A 491 ✆ 0562 (Hagley) 882689,
☞ – Ⓟ   AU   **z**
10 rm ⌁ 12.50/20.00 **st.**

at Belbroughton SE : 7 ½ m. by A 491 on B 4188 – AU – ✉ Stourbridge – ✆ 0562 Bel-broughton :

✕✕✕ **Bell Inn,** Bromsgrove Rd, Bell End, DY9 9XU, E : 1 ½ m. on A 491 ✆ 730232 – Ⓟ. 🅰 🆎 ⓞ
𝘝𝘐𝘚𝘈
closed Saturday lunch, Sunday dinner, Monday , 1 to 8 January and Bank Holidays – **M**
17.50 **t.** ⏹ 3.25.

at Kinver (Staffs.) W : 5 m. by A 458 – AU – ✉ Stourbridge (West Midlands) – ✆ 0384
Kinver :

✕✕ **Berkley's (Piano Room),** High St., DY7 1BR, ✆ 873679 – 🅰 🆎 ⓞ 𝘝𝘐𝘚𝘈
closed Saturday lunch and Sunday – **M** (dinner only) 15.00 **t.** ⏹ 2.40.

ALFA-ROMEO Hagley Rd ✆ 393031
AUSTIN-ROVER Stourbridge Rd, Lye ✆ 038 482 (Lye)
2788
AUSTIN-ROVER Hagley Rd ✆ 393022
AUSTIN-ROVER Bridgnorth Rd ✆ 4757
CITROEN Enville St. ✆ 370914
FIAT Clent ✆ 0562 (Belbroughton) 730557
FORD Hagley Rd ✆ 392131
MERCEDES-BENZ, PORSCHE Grange Lane, Lye ✆
038 482 (Lye) 5575

NISSAN High St ✆ 393231
RENAULT Norton Rd ✆ 396655
TOYOTA 181/183 Bromsgrove Rd, Halesowen ✆ 0562
(Romsley) 710243
VAUXHALL-OPEL The Hayes, Lye ✆ 038 482 (Lye)
3001
VAUXHALL-OPEL Bridgnorth Rd ✆ 394757
VAUXHALL 131-135 Hagley Rd, Oldswinford ✆
393034
VW-AUDI Birmingham St. ✆ 392626

STOURPORT-ON-SEVERN Heref. and Worc. 403 404 N 26 – pop. 17,880 – ECD : Wednesday – 🅰 029 93.

🄸 Public Library, County Buildings, Worcester St. 🖉 2866.

♦London 137 – ♦Birmingham 21 – Worcester 12.

🏛 **Mount Olympus,** 35 Hartlebury Rd, DY13 9LT, E : 1 ¼ m. on B 4193 🖉 77333, ⌁ heated, ⚘, park, ✕, squash – 📺 ➾wc ⋔wc ☎ 🅿 ⛭ ▣ 🄰🄴 ⓪ 𝘷𝘪𝘴𝘢
M 5.50/7.95 t. and a la carte ⌁ 3.75 – **42 rm** 🖃 33.50/44.50 **st.** – SB (weekends only) 50.00 **st.**

🏠 **Swan** (Golden Oak), 56 High St., DY13 8BX, 🖉 71661 – 📺 ➾wc ⋔wc ⚙ 🅿. ✕
33 rm.

⌂ **Oakleigh,** 17 York St., DY13 9EE, 🖉 77568, ⚘ – 📺 ⋔wc 🅿. ✕
6 rm 🖃 10.00/25.00 **st.**

✕✕ **Severn Tandoori,** 11 Bridge St., DY13 8UX, 🖉 3090, Indian rest. – ▣ 🄰🄴 ⓪ 𝘷𝘪𝘴𝘢
M a la carte 5.65/11.80 t. ⌁ 2.75.

COLT Dunley 🖉 3357   VAUXHALL-OPEL Vale Rd 🖉 2760

STOWMARKET Suffolk 404 W 27 – pop. 10,913 – ECD : Tuesday – 🅰 0449.

♦London 86 – ♦Cambridge 43 – ♦Ipswich 12 – ♦Norwich 40.

✕✕ **Les Jardins** with rm, The Grove, 33 Ipswich Rd, IP14 1BY, 🖉 613002, ⚘ – ➾wc 🅿. ▣ 🄰🄴 𝘷𝘪𝘴𝘢
M (closed Sunday) 7.95/13.50 t. ⌁ 2.75 – **4 rm** 🖃 18.00/40.00 t. – SB (weekends only) (except Easter) 62.70/72.70 **st.**

STOW-ON-THE-WOLD Glos. 403 404 O 28 – pop. 1,596 – ECD : Wednesday – 🅰 0451 Cotswold.

🄸 Public Library, St. Edwards Hall 🖉 30352 (summer only).

♦London 86 – ♦Birmingham 44 – Gloucester 27 – ♦Oxford 30.

🏛 **Unicorn Crest** (Crest), Sheep St., GL54 1HQ, 🖉 30257 – 📺 ➾wc ⚙ 🅿. ▣ 🄰🄴 ⓪ 𝘷𝘪𝘴𝘢
M approx. 10.85 **st.** – ⌁ 5.25 – **20 rm** 38.50/48.50 **st.** – SB (weekends only) 31.50 **st.**

🏛 **Stow Lodge,** The Square, GL54 1AB, 🖉 30485, ⚘ – 📺 ➾wc 🅿. 🄰🄴 ⓪. ✕
closed 20 December-mid January – **M** (bar lunch Monday to Saturday)/dinner 8.75 t. and a la carte ⌁ 3.20 – **20 rm** 🖃 54.00 t. – SB (November-Easter) 44.00/55.00 **st.**

🏠 **Fosse Manor,** Fosse Way, GL54 1JX, S : 1 ¼ m. on A 429 🖉 30354, ⚘ – 📺 ➾wc ⋔wc 🅿. ▣ 🄰🄴 ⓪ 𝘷𝘪𝘴𝘢
closed 1 week at Christmas – **M** 8.75 **st.** (dinner) and a la carte ⌁ 2.65 – **22 rm** 🖃 23.00/55.00 **st.** – SB (except summer) 39.00/48.00 **st.**

🏠 **Old Stocks,** The Square, GL54 1AF, 🖉 30666 – ➾wc ⋔wc. ▣ 🄰🄴 𝘷𝘪𝘴𝘢
closed 25 to 30 December – **M** (bar lunch)/dinner 7.45 t. ⌁ 2.75 – **19 rm** 🖃 17.50/35.00 t. – SB (November-June) 37.00/45.00 **st.**

🏤 **King's Arms,** The Square, GL54 1AF, 🖉 30364 – 📺 🅿. ▣ 🄰🄴 ⓪ 𝘷𝘪𝘴𝘢. ✕
closed Christmas – **M** 10.00 **st.** and a la carte ⌁ 2.50 – **8 rm** 🖃 12.00/24.00 **st.**

⌂ **Limes,** Evesham Rd, GL54 1EJ, 🖉 30034, ⚘ – 🅿
5 rm 🖃 9.00/24.00 s.

✕ **Rafters,** Park St., GL54 1AG, 🖉 30200 – ▣ 🄰🄴 ⓪ 𝘷𝘪𝘴𝘢
closed Sunday dinner, Monday and mid January-mid February – **M** 7.00 t. (lunch) and a la carte approx. 11.50 t. ⌁ 6.00.

at Upper Oddington E : 2 ½ m. by A 436 – ✉ Moreton-in-Marsh – 🅰 0451 Cotswold :

🏤 **Horse and Groom,** GL56 0XH, 🖉 30584 – ⋔wc 🅿. ✕
M (bar lunch)/dinner 7.50 t. – **5 rm** 🖃 16.50/32.00 **st.** – SB (November-March) 37.00/40.00 **st.**

at Lower Slaughter SW : 3 m. by A 429 – ✉ Bourton-on-the-Water – 🅰 0451 Cotswold :

🏛 **Manor** (Best Western) ⌖, GL54 2HP, 🖉 20456, ⛰, ⌖, ⚘, ✕ – 📺 ➾wc ☎ 🅿. ▣ 🄰🄴 ⓪ 𝘷𝘪𝘴𝘢
M (buffet lunch Monday to Saturday) 9.50/12.00 t. and a la carte ⌁ 4.25 – **20 rm** 🖃 46.00/68.00 t. – SB 73.00/81.00 **st.**

at Upper Slaughter SW : 3 ¼ m. by B 4068 – ✉ Bourton-on-the-Water – 🅰 0451 Cotswold :

🏛 **Lords of the Manor** ⌖, GL54 2JD, 🖉 20243, « 17C manor house », ⌖, ⚘, park – ➾wc ⚙ 🅿. ▣ 🄰🄴 ⓪ 𝘷𝘪𝘴𝘢. ✕
closed 6 to 19 January – **M** 10.50 **st.** (lunch) and a la carte 11.50/16.25 **st.** ⌁ 2.95 – 🖃 3.75 – **14 rm** 38.00/80.00 **st.** – SB (November-March) 60.00/65.00 **st.**

at Lower Swell W : 1 ¼ m. on B 4068 – ✉ Stow-on-the-Wold – 🅰 0451 Cotswold :

✕ **Old Farmhouse** with rm, GL54 1LF, 🖉 30232, ⚘ – 📺 ➾wc 🅿. ✕
closed 6 to 31 January – **M** (bar lunch Monday to Saturday)/dinner 8.90 t. and a la carte ⌁ 2.50 – **13 rm** 🖃 25.00/42.00 t. – SB (except Christmas, New Year and Bank Holidays) 42.50/57.00 **st.**

SUBARU Stow Rd, near Andoversford 🖉 045 15   VW Oddington, Moreton-in-Marsh 🖉 30422
(Guiting Power) 274

See : Shakespeare's birthplace★ (16C) *AC*, AB – Hall's Croft★ (16C) *AC*, A B – Anne Hathaway's cottage★ *AC*, W : by Shottery Rd A – Holy Trinity Church★ 14C-15C A – **Envir. :** Charlecote Park (castle 16C : intérior★) *AC*, NE : 5 m. by B 4086 B – Wilmcote (Mary Arden's House★) (16C) *AC*, NW : 5 m. by A 34 A – 🔲 Tiddington Rd ☏ 205677, E : by B 4086 B – 🔢 Judith Shakespeare's House, 1 High St. ☏ 293127 – ◆London 96 – ◆Birmingham 23 – ◆Coventry 18 – ◆Oxford 40.

STRATFORD-UPON-AVON

Bridge Street . . . . **B** 8
Henley Street . . . . **A** 29
High Street . . . . **A** 31
Sheep Street . . . . **AB** 35
Wood Street . . . . **A** 47

Banbury Road . . . . **B** 2
Benson Road . . . . **B** 3
Bridge Foot . . . . **B** 6
Chapel Lane . . . . **A** 13
Chapel Street . . . . **A** 14
Church Street . . . . **A** 16
Clopton Bridge . . . . **A** 18
College Lane . . . . **A** 19
Ely Street . . . . **A** 22
Evesham Place . . . . **A** 24
Great William Street . . . . **A** 25
Greenhill Street . . . . **A** 27
Guild Street . . . . **A** 28
Scholars Lane . . . . **A** 33
Tiddington Road . . . . **B** 38
Trinity Street . . . . **A** 40
Warwick Road . . . . **B** 42
Waterside . . . . **A** 43
Windsor Street . . . . **A** 45

Town plans : the names of main shopping streets are indicated in red at the beginning of the list of streets.

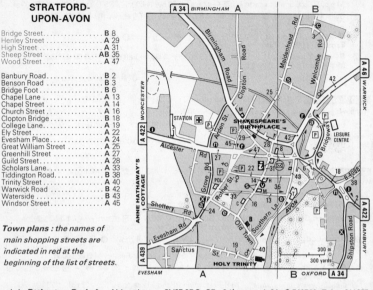

🏨 **Ettington Park** ﹩, Alderminster, CV37 8DS, SE : 6 ¼ m. on A 34 ☏ 740740, Telex 311825, ≼, « Victorian Gothic mansion », 🔲, 🔧, 🐎, park, ✗ – 📳 📺 ☎ 🅿 . 🏊 . 🔼 🄰🄴 ⓞ 𝗩𝗜𝗦𝗔 . ✗
M 12.50/21.50 **st.** and a la carte $ 2.85 – ⬚ 6.50 – **49 rm** 95.00/120.00 **s.**, **5 suites** 95.00/120.00
s. – SB (weekends only) 116.00 **st.**   on A 34   B

🏨 **Moat House International** (Q.M.H.), Bridgefoot, CV37 6YR, ☏ 67511, Telex 311127, 🐎 –
📳 📺 ☎ ⅙ 🅿 . 🏊 . 🔼 🄰🄴 ⓞ 𝗩𝗜𝗦𝗔   B e
M 7.50/9.00 **t.** and a la carte $ 3.60 – ⬚ 5.50 – **249 rm** 44.00/62.50 **t.**, **2 suites** 82.00/105.00 **t.** –
SB (weekends only) 66.00 **st.**

🏨 **Welcombe** ﹩, Warwick Rd, CV37 0NR, NE : 1 ½ m. on A 46 ☏ 295252, Telex 31347, ≼, « 19C mansion in grounds », 🏌, 🐎, park – 📺 ☎ 🅿 . 🏊 . 🔼 🄰🄴 ⓞ 𝗩𝗜𝗦𝗔   on A 46   B
closed 29 December-3 January – **M** 11.00/16.50 **st.** and a la carte – **84 rm** ⬚ 44.50/75.50 **st.** –
SB 64.50/80.00 **st.**

🏨 **Shakespeare** (T.H.F.), Chapel St., CV37 6ER, ☏ 294771, Telex 311181, « 16C timbered inn »
– 📳 📺 🅿 . 🏊 . 🔼 𝗩𝗜𝗦𝗔   A v
M 7.50/11.25 **st.** and a la carte $ 3.75 – ⬚ 5.50 – **66 rm** 45.50/62.00 **st.**, **1 suite**

🏨 **Alveston Manor** (T.H.F.), Clopton Bridge, CV37 7HP, ☏ 204581, Telex 31324 – 📺 ☎ 🅿 . 🏊 .
🔼 𝗩𝗜𝗦𝗔   B i
M a la carte lunch/dinner 10.25 **st.** $ 2.70 – ⬚ 5.50 – **108 rm** 38.50/50.50 **st.**, **3 suites**

🏨 **White Swan** (T.H.F.), Rother St., CV37 6NH, ☏ 297022 – 📺 ➧wc ☏ . 🏊 . 🔼 🄰🄴 ⓞ 𝗩𝗜𝗦𝗔
M (buffet lunch)/dinner a la carte 10.50/13.00 **st.** $ 2.70 – ⬚ 5.50 – **42 rm** 33.50/45.00 **st.**
                                              A r

🏨 **Falcon** (Q.M.H.), Chapel St., CV37 6HH, ☏ 205777, Telex 312522 – 📳 📺 ➧wc ☏ 🅿 . 🏊 . 🔼
🄰🄴 ⓞ 𝗩𝗜𝗦𝗔   A s
M 7.50/9.25 **st.** and a la carte $ 3.00 – **73 rm** ⬚ 40.00/58.00 **st.**

🏨 **Arden**, 44 Waterside, CV37 6BA, ☏ 294949, Telex 311726, 🐎 – 📺 ➧wc 🎞wc ☏ 🅿 . 🏊 .
🔼 🄰🄴 ⓞ 𝗩𝗜𝗦𝗔   B o
M (carving lunch) 6.75 **st.** /dinner 12.50 **st.** $ 3.35 – **59 rm** ⬚ 25.00/53.00 **t.** – SB (except Christmas and New Year) 52.00/65.00 **st.**

🏨 **Grosvenor House** (Best Western), 12-14 Warwick Rd, CV37 6YT, ☏ 69213, Telex 311699,
📺 ➧wc 🎞wc ☏ 🅿 . 🏊 . 🔼 🄰🄴 ⓞ 𝗩𝗜𝗦𝗔 . ✗   B r
closed 24 to 28 December – **M** 7.00/8.50 **t.** and a la carte $ 3.00 – **57 rm** ⬚ 20.00/41.00 **st.** –
SB 41.00/50.50 **st.**

🏨 **Swan's Nest** (T.H.F.), Bridgefoot, CV37 7LT, ☏ 66761, 🐎 – 📺 ➧wc ☏ ⅙ 🅿 . 🏊 . 🔼 🄰🄴
ⓞ 𝗩𝗜𝗦𝗔   B n
M (buffet lunch)/dinner 8.95 **st.** and a la carte $ 2.70 – ⬚ 5.50 – **60 rm** 38.50/50.50 **st.**

🏠 **Haytor** 🦢, Avenue Rd, CV37 6UX, ℰ 297799, 🍴 – 📺 🛏wc 🛏wc Ⓟ   B **c**
M 6.50/10.00 t. 🍴 4.00 – **15 rm** ⌿ 24.00/48.00 t.

🏠 **Hylands** without rest., Warwick Rd, CV37 6YW, ℰ 297962 – 📺 🛏wc Ⓟ. 🖪 𝗩𝗜𝗦𝗔. 🛇   B **a**
closed Christmas and New Year – **16 rm** ⌿ 20.00/50.00 st.

↟ **Moonraker House,** 40 Alcester Rd, CV37 9DB, ℰ 67115 – 📺 🛏wc 🛏wc Ⓟ   A **i**
18 rm ⌿ 18.00/24.00 st.

↟ **Hardwick House,** 1 Avenue Rd, CV37 6UY, ℰ 204307 – 📺 Ⓟ. 🛇   B **s**
closed Christmas – **12 rm** ⌿ 9.50/30.00 st.

↟ **Marlyn,** 3 Chestnut Walk, CV37 6HG, ℰ 293752 – 🛇   A **e**
closed Christmas – **8 rm** ⌿ 10.95/21.90 st.

↟ **Melita,** 37 Shipston Rd, CV37 7LN, ℰ 292432, 🍴 – 📺 🛏wc Ⓟ. 🛇   B **x**
closed Christmas-New Year – **13 rm** ⌿ 14.00/30.00 st.

↟ **Stratheden,** 5 Chapel St., CV37 6EP, ℰ 297119 – 📺 🛏wc 🛏wc. 🛇   A **s**
closed February, last 2 weeks November and 24 December-2 January – **10 rm** ⌿ 11.50/31.00 st.

↟ **Grosvenor Villa,** 9 Evesham Pl., CV37 6HT, ℰ 66192 – Ⓟ. 🛇   A **a**
8 rm ⌿ 8.00/20.00 st.

↟ **Virginia Lodge,** 12 Evesham Pl., CV37 6HT, ℰ 292157 – Ⓟ. 🛇   A **x**
8 rm ⌿ 7.50/20.00 st.

    at Wellesbourne E : 6 m. by B 4086 – B – on A 429 – ✉ Wellesbourne – ☏ 0789 Stratford-upon-Avon :

☝ King's Head, CV35 9LT, on A 429 ℰ 840206 – 🛏wc 🛏wc Ⓟ
11 rm.

    at Ettington SE : 6 ½ m. on A 422 – B – ✉ ☏ 0789 Stratford-upon-Avon :

XXX **The Chase Country House** 🦢 with rm, Banbury Rd, CV37 7NZ, ℰ 740000, ≤, 🍴, park –
📺 🛏wc Ⓟ. 🖪 🅰🅴 ⓪ 𝗩𝗜𝗦𝗔. 🛇
closed 24 to 31 December and 1 to 21 January – **M** *(closed Saturday lunch and Sunday dinner to non-residents)* 10.00/16.00 t. 🍴 3.20 – **11 rm** ⌿ 27.50/49.50 t.

    at Clifford Chambers SW : 2 m. by A 34 – B – on A 46 – ✉ ☏ 0789 Stratford-upon-Avon :

🏛 **Clifford Manor** 🦢, CV37 8HU, ℰ 292616, « Queen Anne house and walled gardens », 🦢,
🛇 – 🛏wc Ⓟ. 🅰🅴 🛇
closed January – **M** 20.00/25.00 st. 🍴 2.75 – **8 rm** ⌿ 50.00/80.00 st.

    at Billesley NW : 4 m. by A 422 – B – ✉ ☏ 0789 Stratford-upon-Avon :

🏰 **Billesley Manor** 🦢, B49 6NF, ℰ 763737, Telex 312599, ≤, 🔲, 🍴, park, 🛇 – 📺 ☎ Ⓟ. 🔥.
🖪 🅰🅴 ⓪ 𝗩𝗜𝗦𝗔. 🛇
M 20.00 t. (dinner) and a la carte 🍴 3.95 – **28 rm** ⌿ 41.00/95.00 st. – SB (weekends only) 85.00/100.00 st.

    at Wilmcote NW : 4 m. by A 34 – A – ✉ ☏ 0789 Stratford-upon-Avon :

🏠 **Swan House,** The Green, CV37 9XJ, ℰ 67030, 🍴 – 📺 🛏wc Ⓟ. 🖪 🅰🅴 𝗩𝗜𝗦𝗔. 🛇
M (bar lunch)/dinner 8.00 t. 🍴 2.90 – **11 rm** ⌿ 22.00/34.00 st. – SB (except Christmas) 46.00/50.00 st.

AUDI, VW Western Rd ℰ 294477
AUSTIN-ROVER-DAIMLER-JAGUAR Birmingham Rd ℰ 67555
BEDFORD, VAUXHALL-OPEL Rother St. ℰ 66254
CITROEN 23 Weston Rd ℰ 293577

FIAT, LANCIA Western Rd ℰ 68913
PEUGEOT, TALBOT Alderminster ℰ 078 987 (Alderminster) 331
RENAULT Western Rd ℰ 67911
VOLVO Western Rd ℰ 292468

STRATTON Glos. 🟨🟨🟨 🟨🟨🟨 O 28 – see Cirencester.

STRATTON ST. MARGARET Wilts. 🟨🟨🟨 🟨🟨🟨 O 29 – see Swindon.

STREATLEY Berks. 🟨🟨🟨 🟨🟨🟨 Q 29 – pop. 1 ,055 – ✉ ☏ 0491 Goring.
♦ London 56 – ♦ Oxford 16 – Reading 11.

🏛 **Swan,** High St., RG8 9HR, ℰ 873737, Telex 848259, « ≤ Thameside setting », 🍴 – 📺
🛏wc ☎ Ⓟ. 🖪 🅰🅴 ⓪ 𝗩𝗜𝗦𝗔. 🛇
M 13.50/19.50 st. 🍴 4.00 – **25 rm** ⌿ 45.00/80.00 st., **1 suite** 90.00/125.00 st.

STREET Somerset 🟨🟨🟨 L 30 **The West Country G.** – pop. 9 ,454 – ECD : Wednesday – ☏ 0458.
See : The Shoe Museum★*AC*.
Envir. : at Somerton★, Market Place★, St. Michaels Church★, S : 6 m. – at High Ham (St. Andrews Church★), SW : 8 m.
♦London 138 – ♦Bristol 28 – Taunton 20.

🏠 **Bear,** 53 High St., BA16 0EF, ℰ 42021 – 📺 🛏wc 🛏wc Ⓟ. 🖪 🅰🅴 𝗩𝗜𝗦𝗔
M 6.75/8.95 t. and a la carte 🍴 3.25 – **16 rm** ⌿ 29.00/45.00 t. – SB 50.00/56.00 st.

AUSTIN-ROVER Creeches Lane, Walton ℰ 42735   FORD 189 High St. ℰ 47147

STREETLY West Midlands **403 404** O 26 – see Birmingham.

STRETE Devon – see Dartmouth.

STRETTON Cheshire **402 403 404** M 23 – see Warrington.

STRETTON UNDER FOSSE Warw. **403 404** Q 26 – see Rugby.

STROUD Glos. **403 404** N 28 – pop. 37 ,791 – ECD : Thursday – ● 045 36.
Envir. : Severn Wildfowl Trust★ *AC*, W : 11 m.
☞ Minchinhampton ♟ 045 383 (Nailsworth) 2642 (Old Course) E : 3 m.
🛈 Council Offices, High St. ♟ 4252 – ♦London 113 – ♦Bristol 30 – Gloucester 9.

- 🏛 **London**, 30-31 London Rd, GL5 2AJ, ♟ 79992 – 📺 ⊟wc ⋔wc 🅿. 🆇 ⓞ *VISA*. ✳
  M *(closed Sunday to non-residents)* 6.00/8.00 **t.** and a la carte 🍴 2.50 – **10 rm** ⊑ 20.00/36.00 **t.**
  – SB (except Easter, Christmas and Bank Holidays) 85.00/95.00 **st.**

- ⌂ **Downfield**, 134 Cainscross Rd, GL5 4HN, ♟ 4496 – ⊟wc ⋔wc 🅿
  closed 20 December- 3 January – **21 rm** ⊑ 12.50/27.00 **st.**

- ✕✕ **Mr Baillie's**, 56 Westward Rd, Cainscross, GL5 4JA, W : 1 ½ m. on A 419 ♟ 79111 – 🆇 ⓞ
  closed Sunday and Monday – **M** (dinner only)(booking essential) 10.15 **st.** 🍴 3.75.

  at Brimscombe SE : 2 ¼ m. on A 419 – ✉ Stroud – ● 0453 Brimscombe :

- 🏛 **Burleigh Court** ⧈, Burleigh Hill, GL5 2PF, SW : ½ m. off Burleigh Rd ♟ 883804, ≼, ⌇ heated, ☞ – 📺 ⊟wc ⋔wc 🅿. ⚿. 🆇 🅰🅴 *VISA*. ✳
  closed 24 December-1 January – **M** 8.50/12.50 **t.** 🍴 2.50 – **11 rm** ⊑ 35.00/58.00 **t.** – SB (except
  Bank Holidays) 57.00/68.00 **st.**

  at Rodborough S : ¾ m. by A 46 – ✉ Stroud – ● 045 387 Amberley :

- 🏛 **Bear of Rodborough** (Anchor), Rodborough Common, GL5 5DE, E : 1 ½ m. ♟ 3522, Telex
  437130, ☞ – 📺 ⊟wc ⊛ 🅿. ⚿. 🆇 🅰🅴 ⓞ *VISA*
  M *(closed Saturday lunch)* 11.50 **t.** and a la carte – **48 rm** ⊑ 38.50/48.50 **t.** – SB (except
  Christmas) 56.00/62.00 **st.**

  at Stonehouse W : 2 m. on A 419 – ✉ Stroud – ● 045 382 Stonehouse :

- 🏛 **Stonehouse Court**, Bristol Rd, GL10 3RA, ♟ 5155, Telex 437244, ☞, park – 📺 ⊟wc
  ⋔wc ⊛ 🅿. ⚿. 🆇 🅰🅴 ⓞ *VISA*. ✳
  closed 2 weeks after Christmas – **M** 8.95/10.50 **t.** and a la carte 🍴 2.75 – **23 rm** ⊑ 38.00/51.00 **t.**
  – SB (weekends only) 62.00 **st.**

ALFA ROMEO Lansdown Rd ♟ 4845
AUSTIN-ROVER Caincross Rd ♟ 3671
CITROEN London Rd ♟ 2861
FIAT Stratford Rd ♟ 4007
FORD London Rd ♟ 71341
NISSAN Westward Rd, Ebley ♟ 2000

PEUGEOT-TALBOT Rodborough Common ♟
045 387 (Amberley) 3559
RENAULT London Rd ♟ 4203
TALBOT Stonehouse ♟ 045 382 (Stonehouse) 2139
VAUXHALL-OPEL Westward Rd ♟ 5522

STUBBINGTON Hants. **403 404** Q 31 – pop. 11 ,531 – ● 0329.
♦London 89 – ♦Portsmouth 15 – ♦Southampton 12.

- ✿ **Crofton Manor,** off Titchfield Rd, PO14 3NA, ♟ 662014, ☞ – ⋔wc 🅿. 🆇 🅰🅴 ⓞ *VISA*
  M *(closed Sunday)* (bar lunch)/dinner a la carte 6.15/10.50 **st.** 🍴 3.90 – **7 rm** ⊑ 24.50/36.50 **st.**

STUCKTON Hants. – see Fordingbridge.

STUDLAND Dorset **403 404** O 32 The West Country G. – pop. 559 – ECD : Thursday – ✉ Swa-
nage – ● 092 944.
☞ Isle of Purbeck ♟ 361.
♦London 130 – Bournemouth 22 – Dorchester 26.

- 🏛 **Knoll House**, BH19 3AH, ♟ 251, ⌇ heated, ☞, ☞, park, ✽ – ⊟wc ⊛ 🅿
  April-October – **M** 7.50 **t.** 🍴 3.50 – **111 rm** ⊑ 26.00/80.00 **st.**

- 🏛 **Manor House** ⧈, Beach Rd, Studland Bay, BH19 3AU, ♟ 288, ≼ Old Harry rocks and Poole
  Bay, ☞, park – ⊟wc ⋔wc 🅿
  Easter-October – **M** (bar lunch)/dinner 10.00 **t.** – **18 rm** ⊑ (dinner included) 22.00/56.00 – SB
  (weekends only in summer) 44.00/60.00 **st.**

STURMINSTER NEWTON Dorset **403 404** N 31 – pop. 1 ,781 – ● 0258.
♦London 123 – Bournemouth 30 – ♦Bristol 49 – Salisbury 28 – Taunton 41.

- ✕✕✕ **Plumber Manor** ⧈ with rm, Hazelbury Bryan Rd, DT10 2AF, SW : 1 ¾ m. ♟ 72507, ≼,
  « 18C manor house », ☞, park, ✽ – 📺 ⊟wc ⊛ 🅿. ✳
  M *(closed Sunday and Monday November-March and Monday April-October to non-residents)*
  (dinner only) 16.00 **t.** 🍴 3.00 – **12 rm** ⊑ 35.00/60.00 **st.**

LADA, MAZDA Station Rd ♟ 72155

SUDBURY Derbs. and **SUDBURY** Suffolk – Follow the town plan of Sunderland.

430

The
best tyres
in the
world

The story of Michelin
is the history of the
motor vehicle. Most of
the important developments in tyre technology
have been originated by Michelin: this started with
the first detachable cycle tyre in 1892. In 1948 the
introduction of the first radial, Michelin X, heralded a
concept that inside two decades was to change
the standards of tyre performance for ever.

In earlier days the introduction of new types was
uncommon. Today, with more rigorous demands
from both manufacturer and driver, there is something new from Michelin nearly every year. Family
cars, fast cars, exotic cars, ordinary roads, motorways, off-the-road, winter roads: there is a Michelin
for every driver in every condition.

The MX Range

The car tyre range today is bigger than ever before. In 1983 a whole new range was launched: MX for family cars, MXL low profile for the sport derivatives, MXV for performance cars.

MX

MX was introduced as a replacement for the world famous XZX and is made in 80 series. The multi-siped tread pattern ensures rapid water dispersal, providing excellent grip, particularly in wet conditions. No compromises have been made in the design so the long mileage associated with Michelin radials is maintained. With MX the advantages of previous Michelin radials have been maintained, including the retention of low rolling resistance providing excellent fuel economy.

MXL

MXL was developed as a tyre for the sportier saloon. Many top of the range cars and sports derivatives are fitted with low profile tyres as original equipment. MXL will out perform other tyres of this type. Sizes are available in 60, 65 and 70 Series and either S rated (180 km/h: 113 mph) or T rated (190 km/h: 120 mph).

MXL give superb grip in all conditions; broad grooves lead from the tread centre to the shoulders, ensuring efficient water clearance for good wet road grip. The tyre has the usual Michelin attributes of long life, coupled with excellent fuel economy.

MXV

MXV tyres have been designed specifically for many of the truly fast sports cars that require low profile, high performance tyres. After a short period the MXV has already gained an enviable reputation with manufacturers, tyre dealers and motorists.

To give positive grip at high speeds great attention has been paid to tread design: broad, deep circumferential grooves ensure excellent water dispersal and transverse grooves link the crown to the shoulder to give extra clearance. As with all Michelin radials, MXV tyres have a low rolling resistance and therefore save fuel.

MXV will progressively replace most XAS and XVS sizes and are available in 60, 65, 70 and 80 series.

TRX AND TDX TYRES

A further development in radial tyre technology came in the mid '70s with the launch of Michelin TRX. Because there are certain inherent disadvantages with the conventional design of tyre and rim, Michelin returned to basics and redesigned the tyre/wheel assembly as a unit. With standard profile rims the near vertical flange imposes stresses to the sidewall which results in a reversal of the direction in sidewall movement above the top edge of the flange. This results in an awkward 'S' shaped distortion of the sidewall. The TR rim has a gently sloping flange that allows the casing to adopt a natural 'C' curve. With the TR concept, stresses

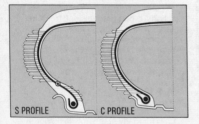

S PROFILE   C PROFILE

within the tyre are equalised; performance is enhanced, mileage increased due to more even wear and fuel

economy improved. And even though TRX tyres are all low profile tyres there is no reduction in comfort compared with more conventional tyres because there is a longer sidewall flexing area.

In 1983 an additional development to the TR principle was announced; this is called TDX. This new tyre takes the TRX concept further with changes to the bead area. The bead has an extended toe which locates in a channel in the rim base. With this development of the TR design a limited run-on capability is added to the already considerable advantages of the TRX tyre: the tyre

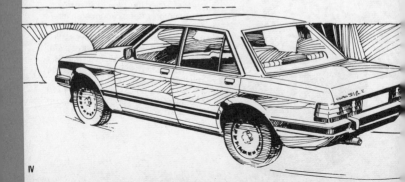

cannot leave the rim after a sudden deflation because the bead toe cannot be dislodged, so the car can always be brought to a safe stop. TDX is the great new tyre for the future and means total safety, security and peace of mind.

OTHER TYRES IN THE RANGE

The comparatively new MX Series, plus TRX and TDX, represent the great bulk of Michelin car tyres sold today. Nevertheless there are of course many other types of tyre for every possible type of application in the total Michelin car tyre range.

Although the great mass of drivers seldom use their cars on anything other than tarmac roads, wet or dry, there are still those people that need extra traction. Service engineers for water, gas, electricity and land line authorities, rally enthusiasts, drivers operating in areas of heavy snowfalls, including mountain rescue teams and even certain types of farm representative, all these need something extra that conventional tread patterns cannot give. Then there are the out and out racing cars on which Michelin has been so successful in recent years.

The list is endless, and all are catered for by Michelin. The Michelin car tyre range taken in its entirety must offer the widest choice in the world today.

Conventional tyre on rim

MICHELIN MAPS & GUIDES

At the end of the last century motor cars were still a rarity, horse power still meant a flying mane, steel-bound wheels and a hard ride. But if motor cars were rare, route maps were almost unheard of and guide books with hotels and restaurants just didn't exist.

The development of the pneumatic tyre was the one factor without which the motor car would have remained a noisy, slow and cumbersome toy with little future. The tyre gave life to the motor car and provided fast long-distance travel to the masses in a relatively short space of time. André Michelin, one of the Company's founders, sensed the need for accurate information and in 1900 published the first Hotel and Restaurant Guide for France. The whole vast Michelin range of maps and guides available today stems from this first publication.

HOTEL & RESTAURANT GUIDES

This Hotel and Restaurant Guide to Great Britain and Ireland is one of a world famous range of similar publications. The complete list is: Benelux, France, Germany, Great Britain and Ireland, Italy, Main Cities Europe and Spain and Portugal.

The guides are all prepared to the same standards and updated annually. Easy to understand (and to remember) symbols give details of the size and grade of the hotel or restaurant and the varying facilities available (see the reference pages at the front of this guide).

There is also another special guide for the visitor to France who prefers the open air life, also revised annually – this is Camping and Caravaning in France.

GREEN TOURIST GUIDES

The first touring guides appeared before the First World War. In those days they did not have a standard format; the shape and binding varied from guide to guide. Some of the earliest guides were of places that even today a visit is still an adventure. The guide of the Sunny Countries featured parts of North Africa as well as Southern Europe.

Within a year of Armistice Day a special series of tourist books was published that today are collector's pieces; these are the Guides to the Battlefields. In words and pictures the horror and destruction at Amiens and Arras, Lille, the Marne Campaigns and Rheims, Soissons, the Somme, Verdun, Ypres and Yser helped a multitude of visitors to fully appreciate what had happened.

Today there are guides to important cities: Paris, London, Rome, New York; to countries: Canada, Portugal, Spain, Austria, Germany, Greece, Italy, Belgium-Luxembourg, and Switzerland, the regions of France, Great Britain, The West Country and our latest Scotland and New England. And of course all the Guides are to the same standard and with the familiar green covers.

All Green Tourist Guides are revised and updated regularly (but not necessarily annually).

MAPS

The Michelin archives contain many maps produced by the Company shortly after the first Michelin red guide, in other words some 80 years ago. Like the Guide, the early maps were of France. However as the coverage of the guides spread to cover the Mediterranean area and the British Isles so did the maps. Indeed in those areas that have never been blessed with motorways an old Michelin map is still quite usable (if you ignore the size of the towns and villages) because they were produced to such accuracy.

The range and scope of Michelin maps increases all the time and today covers the whole of Europe and Africa. Indeed the Michelin Africa maps are the only truly motoring maps of that vast continent.

Setting aside the rather special maps; of specific areas, geologic regions of France, city environs, historic events etc., the map range divides into three categories: main roads, regional maps and detailed maps. A one sheet map covers Europe from east to west and as far north as Bergen. There are main road maps of the whole of western Europe. The biggest expansion in new Michelin maps at this time is of the regional maps. The British Isles are covered completely by five maps; there is a regional map for each significant part of France so that the whole country is covered. Spain and Portugal, the Benelux countries, Switzerland and Austria are already in the series and the next countries to be tackled will be Italy and West Germany. The detailed maps are primarily of France and the country is in 37 sheets.

We have said that the Michelin maps are for motorists; we believe that they are the only maps designed and produced with the driver in mind. They are famous not only for what they include but also for what is omitted. There is none of the clutter so often associated with some other maps which can make reference so difficult. On regional maps there is a handsome overlap from sheet to sheet so that no town or place is on the join.

Motorist does of course mean every type of driver from tourist to business-man and we are all both at some time or another. And truck drivers need good maps too. Because Michelin maps set out to cater for all drivers, the extra references are for all sorts of people. You will find a cross reference against any place where we recommend a hotel or restaurant in our appropriate hotel guide, and equally detail a place of natural beauty or other tourist attraction.

We could go on, but it is sufficient to say that we believe that, like our tyres, our maps and guides are the best too. Changes are never made for cosmetic reasons but rather because our con-stant reviews, our research and the help we get from our customers keep us up to date and on our toes.

EUROPE
GREAT BRITAIN

AUSTRIA
BENELUX
FRANCE
GERMANY
GREECE
IRELAND
ITALY
PORTUGAL
SPAIN
SWITZERLAND
YUGOSLAVIA

AFRICA

The Rally Scene

Let us look back just 100 years to 1884. Karl Benz was just about to patent his first motor vehicle. The age of the motor car was about to begin. In just two decades from this date the advances were enormous. From a slow, cumbersome, eratic and unreliable alternative to the horse drawn carriage came the monsters and the landaulets, the sport and the elegance, that were Edwardian motoring. It is hard to believe that so much could have happened so quickly, from nothing to 10 litres of thundering Delage or 12 litres of Itala and many many more.

Without the pneumatic tyre none of this could have happened. Cars would have remained slow and heavy to withstand the shocks transmitted from the road.

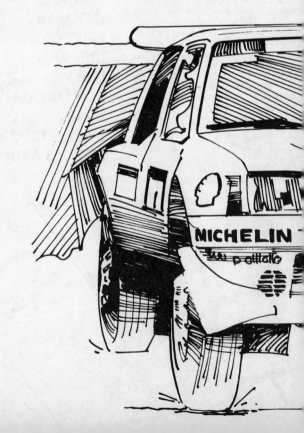

But something was needed to get through to ordinary people. Sport was the answer and motor sport was to capture the imagination in a couple of years. Artists like Montaut saw the thrills and recorded them on canvas, and today we can see the fear on the face of the mechanic. Gordon Bennett of other adventures and sporting fame presented a cup for his own race and all the long distance events of those early years, culminating in the Paris-Madrid, were organised. You can see many of those races recorded on the tile frieze that graces the walls of Michelin House in London's Chelsea, the Michelin commercial offices in the U.K. from 1910 to 1985.

In those early days, like today, Michelin was the world's leading tyre manufacturer. So we were into racing in a very serious way. In fact we remained involved until the 1920s, by which time it was decided that at least for the present competition involvement was no longer appropriate.

However, 40 years on, a decision was made to re-enter competitive sport. The time was ripe to show the world that Michelin radials would more than hold their own in the toughest rallies and the most severe test of all, the Formula 1 race circuits. And so it was proved.

MICHELIN'S seven seasons in Formula One saw 59 victories, three Constructors and three Drivers Championship plus establishing radial tyre technology in the pinnacle of motor racing.

Rallying is now receiving Michelin's full attention. The 1985 season has seen Michelin equipped teams dominating the World Rally Championship, British Open Series and the British National Series.

On two wheels Michelin radial technology has assisted America's Freddie Spencer to the first ever double World Championship 250 cc and 500 cc; and established radial tyres at the pinnacle of motorcycling racing.

Michelin's record speaks for itself.

SUNDERLAND

Central Area .... B
Fawcett Street .... B 15
High Street West .... B 15
Holmeside .... B 16
John Street .... B 16

Albion Place .... B 2
Barnes Park Road .... A 3
Bedford Street .... B 4
Borough Road .... B 5
Bridge Street .... B 6
Charlton Road .... A 8
Chester Road .... B 10
Derwent Street .... B 12
Green Terrace .... B 13
Harbour View .... A 14
Kayll Road .... A 17
Livingstone Road .... B 18
New Durham Road .... B 19
Northern Way .... A 20
Ormonde Street .... A 21
Pallion Road .... A 22
Park Lane .... B 23
Roker Terrace .... A 24
St. Luke's Terrace ...... A 26
St. Mary's Way .... B 27
Shields Road .... A 29
Southwick Road .... B 30
Station Road .... A 32
Sunderland Road .... A 33
Trimdon Street .... A 35
Vine Place .... B 36
Wessington Way .... A 38

17

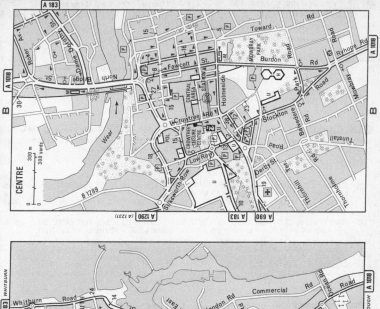

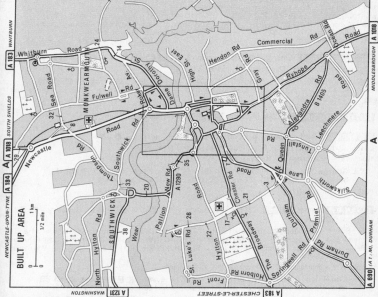

Plans de villes :
Dans la liste des rues
des plans de ville
les noms en rouge
indiquent les principales
voies commerçantes.

SUDBURY Derbs. 402 403 404 O 25 – pop. 839 – ✉ Derby – ☎ 028 372 Marchington.
See : Sudbury Hall★★ (17C) *AC*.

♦London 138 – ♦Birmingham 33 – Derby 13 – ♦Stoke-on-Trent 23.

Hotel and restaurant see : Tutbury SE : 6 m., *Uttoxeter* W : 4 ½ m.

SUDBURY Suffolk 404 W 27 – pop. 17,723 – ECD : Wednesday – ☎ 0787.
🛈 Public Library, Market Hill ☎ 72092 – ♦London 59 – ♦Cambridge 37 – Colchester 15 – ♦Ipswich 21.

🏛 Mill, Walnut Tree Lane, CO10 0BD, ☎ 75544, ≼, ⌐ – 📺 ⌷wc ☎ ℗. 🏊 – **45 rm**.

↟ Hill Lodge, 8 Newton Rd, CO10 6RG, ☎ 77568 – 📺 🕯wc ℗. ⌖
  closed 1 week at Christmas – **16 rm** ⌷ 11.00/26.00 **s**.

VAUXHALL-OPEL Cornard Rd ☎ 72301

SUNDERLAND Tyne and Wear 401 402 P 19 – pop. 195,064 – ECD : Wednesday – ☎ 0783.
🛈 Wearside, Coxgreen ☎ 344269, W : 2 m. by A 183 A – 🛈 Whitburn, Lizard Lane ☎ 0783 (Whitburn)
292144, N : 2 m. by A 183 A – 🛈 Crowtree Leisure Centre, Crowtree Rd ☎ 650960 and 650990.

♦London 272 – ♦Leeds 92 – ♦Middlesbrough 29 – ♦Newcastle-upon-Tyne 12.

Plan on preceding page

🏛 Seaburn (Swallow), Queen's Par., SR6 8DB, N : 2 ½ m. on A 183 ☎ 292041, Group Telex
  53168, ≼ – 🛗 📺 ⌷wc ☎ ℗. 🏊 🔃 AE ⓪ VISA   A c
  M 6.20/7.75 **st.** and a la carte ⸙ 3.40 – **82 rm** ⌷ 38.00/52.00 **st.** – SB (weekends only)
  48.00/52.00 **st**.

🏠 Gelt House, 23 St. Bedes Terrace, SR2 8HS, ☎ 672990 – 📺 ⌷wc 🕯wc ℗. 🔃 VISA   B a
  M (residents only) (lunch by arrangement) 5.50/6.90 t. ⸙ 2.90 – **23 rm** ⌷ 16.00/30.00 **t**.

ALFA-ROMEO, HYUNDAI, RELIANT ☎ 650281
AUSTIN-ROVER 190 Roker Av. ☎ 656221
AUSTIN-ROVER Allison Rd, West Boldon ☎ 362726
AUSTIN-ROVER Warwick ☎ 210838
BMW Ryhope Rd ☎ 657631
COLT Nth. Bridge St. ☎ 659252
FIAT Durham Rd ☎ 657191

FORD Trimdon St. ☎ 40311
HONDA Toward Rd, Doker ☎ 77588
LADA High St. West ☎ 40337
RENAULT High St. West ☎ 43441
TALBOT Newcastle Rd ☎ 488811
VAUXHALL Paley St. ☎ 42841
VOLVO Nth. Hylton Rd ☎ 491277

SUTTON BENGER Wilts. 403 404 N 29 – pop. 839 – ✉ Chippenham – ☎ 0249 Seagry.
♦London 92 – ♦Bristol 26 – Chippenham 4.5 – Swindon 16.

🏛 Bell House, High St., SN15 4RH, ☎ 720401, ⇗ – 📺 ⌷wc ⊛ ℗. 🏊 🔃 AE ⓪ VISA
  M a la carte 6.80/13.40 t. ⸙ 3.50 – ⌷ 4.95 – **14 rm** 24.50/44.50 t. – SB (weekends only)
  73.50/109.80 **st**.

SUTTON COLDFIELD West Midlands 403 404 O 26 – see Birmingham.

SWAFFHAM Norfolk 404 W 26 – pop. 4,742 – ECD : Thursday – ☎ 0760.
Envir. : Oxburgh Hall (15C) : Gate house★ *AC*, SW : 7 ½ m.

♦London 97 – ♦Cambridge 46 – King's Lynn 16 – ♦Norwich 27.

🏠 George, Station St., PE37 7LJ, ☎ 21238 – 📺 ⌷wc ⊛ ℗. 🏊 🔃 AE ⓪ VISA. ⌖
  M a la carte 7.50/9.75 t. – **32 rm** ⌷ 22.00/38.50 t. – SB 49.00/58.00 **st**.

FORD London St. ☎ 21239

SWANAGE Dorset 403 404 O 32 The West Country G. – pop. 8,411 – ECD : Thursday – ☎ 092 92
(4 fig.) or 0929 (6 fig.).
See : Site ★ – Durlston Country Park (≼★★) – The Great Globe★ – **Envir. : St. Aldhelm's Head★★**
(≼★★★), SW : 4 m. by B 3069 – Corfe Castle★★ (≼★★)*AC*, NW : 6 m. – Old Harry Rocks★★ (Studland
Village - St. Nicholas Church★) N : 4 ½ m. – Studland Beach (≼★), N : 5 m. – 🛈 The White House,
Shore Rd ☎ 422885.

♦London 130 – Bournemouth 22 – Dorchester 26 – ♦Southampton 52.

🏛 The Pines, Burlington Rd, BH19 1LT, ☎ 425211, ≼, ⇗ – 🛗 📺 ⌷wc ☎ ℗. 🔃 VISA
  M 5.75/8.25 and a la carte ⸙ 2.10 – ⌷ 19.00/44.00 – SB 54.05/65.55 **st**.

🏛 Grand, 12 Burlington Rd, BH19 1LU, ☎ 423353, ≼, ⇗ – 🛗 ⌷wc 🕯wc ☎ ℗. 🔃 AE ⓪ VISA
  M a la carte lunch/dinner 8.05 t. ⸙ 2.50 – **28 rm** ⌷ 22.70/45.40 t. – SB (October-April)
  50.00/55.00 **st**.

🏠 Ship Inn, 23 High St., BH19 2LR, ☎ 422078 – ⊛ ℗ – **18 rm**.

↟ Suncliffe, 1 Burlington Rd, BH19 1LR, ☎ 423299, ⇗ – 🕯wc ℗. ⌖
  Easter-September – **13 rm** ⌷ 14.80/29.70 t.

↟ Eversden, 5 Victoria Rd, BH19 1LY, ☎ 423276 – ⌷wc 🕯wc ℗. ⌖
  12 rm ⌷ 9.00/23.00 t.

↟ Havenhurst, 3 Cranborne Rd, BH19 1EA, ☎ 424224 – 🕯wc ℗. ⌖
  March-October – **16 rm** ⌷ 11.50/38.00 t.

FORD 281 High St. ☎ 422877   MAZDA Victoria Av. ☎ 422888

SWANBRIDGE South Glam. 403 K 29 – see Penarth.

SWANSEA

College Street .... B 13
Kingsway (The) .... B
Oxford Street .... B
Princess Way .... B
Quadrant Centre .... B
St. David's Square .... B

Alexandra Road .... B 2
Belle Vue Way .... B 4
Carmarthen Road .... B 7
Christina Street .... B 9
Clarence Terrace .... B 10
Clase Road .... A 12
De La Beche Street .... B 14
Dillwyn Street .... B 15
Fabian Way .... B 16
Grove Place .... B 18
Martin Street .... A 20
Nelson Street .... A 21
Pen-y-Graig Road .... A 22
Plasmarl By-Pass .... A 23
Ravenhill Road .... A 24
Station Road .... A 25
St. Helen's Road .... B 27
St. Mary's Square .... B 28
Terrace Road .... A 29
Thomas Street .... B 31
Union Street .... B 32
Uplands Crescent .... A 34
Vivian Road .... A 35
Walter Road .... A 36
Wellington Street .... B 37
West Way .... B 38
William Street .... B 39
Woodfield Street .... A 40
York Street .... B 42

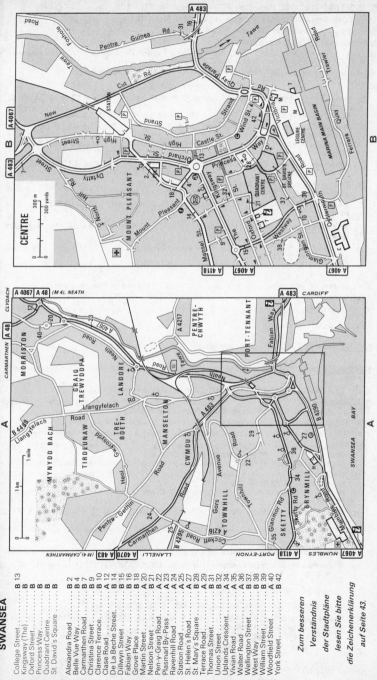

*Zum besseren
Verständnis
der Stadtpläne
lesen Sie bitte
die Zeichenerklärung
auf Seite 43.*

SWANSEA (ABERTAWE) West Glam. 🔢 l 29 – pop. 172 ,433 – ECD : Thursday – 📞 0792.

Envir. : Cefn Bryn (❋*** from the reservoir) W : 12 m. by A 4118 A.

Exc. : Rhosili (site and ⟨***) W : 18 m. by A 4118 A.

🏌 Morriston 🗲 71079, N : 4 m. by A 48 A.

🛈 Crymlin Burrows, Jersey Marine 🗲 462403 (summer only) – Singleton St. 🗲 468321 – Ty Croeso, Gloucester Pl. 🗲 465204 – Oystermouth Sq., The Mumbles 🗲 61302 (summer only).

◆London 191 – ◆Birmingham 136 – ◆Bristol 82 – ◆Cardiff 40 – ◆Liverpool 187 – ◆Stoke-on-Trent 175.

Plan on preceding page

🏨 **Dragon** (T.H.F.), 39 The Kingsway, SA1 5LS, 🗲 51074, Telex 48309 – 🅿️ 📺 ☎ 🅿️. 🏊. 🔼 🆎   B a
   ⓪ 𝗩𝗜𝗦𝗔
   M 6.50/9.50 **st.** and a la carte 🍴 2.70 – ⚏ 5.50 – **118 rm** 41.00/51.50 **st., 1 suite.**

🏨 **Windsor Lodge,** 15 Mount Pleasant, SA1 6EG, 🗲 42158, « Contemporary decor » – 📺   B r
   ⇌wc ▥wc 🅿️. 🔼 🆎 𝗩𝗜𝗦𝗔
   closed 25 December – **M** (booking essential) 12.00/15.00 **t.** 🍴 2.60 – **18 rm** ⚏ 24.75/42.50 **t.** –
   SB (weekends only) 50.50/60.50 **st.**

♨ **Alexander,** 3 Sketty Rd, Uplands, SA2 0EU, 🗲 470045 – 📺 ⇌wc ▥wc. 🔼 🆎 ⓪ 𝗩𝗜𝗦𝗔. ❄   A c
   closed Christmas – **M** (dinner only) 7.00 **st.** – **7 rm** ⚏ 14.00/32.00 **st.**

🍴🍴 **Drangway,** 66 Wind St., SA9 1AH, 🗲 461397 – 🔼 🆎 ⓪ 𝗩𝗜𝗦𝗔   B c
   closed Sunday and Monday – **M** 14.95 **t.** and a la carte 11.85/17.85 **t.** 🍴 3.25.

🍴 **Jasmine,** 326 Oystermouth Rd, SA1 3UL, 🗲 52912, Chinese rest. – 🔼 🆎 ⓪ 𝗩𝗜𝗦𝗔   A e
   M approx. 12.00 **t.**

   at Llanrhidian W : 10 ½ m. by A 4118 – A – and B 4271 – ✉ Reynoldston – 📞 0792
   Gower :

🏨 **Fairyhill** 🦋, SA3 1BS, W : 2 ½ m. off B 4295 (Llangennith rd) 🗲 390139, park – 📺 ⇌wc
   ▥wc 🅿️ ☎. 🔼 🆎 ⓪ 𝗩𝗜𝗦𝗔
   M (closed Sunday dinner) (dinner only and Sunday lunch)/dinner 14.95 **t.** 🍴 2.00 – **11 rm**
   ⚏ 35.00/50.00.

AUSTIN-ROVER-DAIMLER-JAGUAR 511 Carmarthen Rd 🗲 588141
FORD Garngoch 🗲 893041
HONDA, SAAB Llangyfelach 🗲 71960
NISSAN Sway Rd 🗲 75271
PEUGEOT, TALBOT Neath Rd 🗲 73391

RENAULT Eaton Rd, Manselton 🗲 53125
VAUXHALL William St. 🗲 41311
VAUXHALL Neath Rd, Morriston 🗲 75101
VW, AUDI-NSU Gorseinon Rd 🗲 0792 (Gorseinon) 894951

SWAY Hants. 🔢 🔢 P 31 – see Lymington.

SWINDON Wilts. 🔢 🔢 O 29 The West Country G. – pop. 127 ,348 – ECD : Wednesday – 📞 0793.

See : Great Western Railway Museum★*AC* – **Railway Village Museum**★*AC*.

🏌 Bremhill Park, 🗲 782946, E : 4 m. – 🏌 Ogbourne St. George 🗲 067 284 (Ogbourne St. George) 327, S : 7 m. on A 345 – 🏌, 🏌 Broome Manor, Pipers Way 🗲 32403, 2 m. from centre.

🛈 32 The Arcade, David Murray John Building, Brunel Centre 🗲 30328 and 26161 ext. 3056.

◆London 83 – Bournemouth 69 – ◆Bristol 40 – ◆Coventry 66 – ◆Oxford 29 – Reading 40 – ◆Southampton 65.

🏨 **Post House** (T.H.F.), Marlborough Rd, SN3 6AQ, SE : 2 ¾ m. on A 345 🗲 24601, Telex
   444464, ⬭ heated – 📺 ⇌wc ☎ 🅿️. 🔼 🆎 ⓪ 𝗩𝗜𝗦𝗔
   M (bar lunch Saturday) 8.50 **st.** and a la carte 🍴 2.80 – ⚏ 5.50 – **103 rm** 43.00/50.00 **st.**

🏨 **Goddard Arms** (Anchor), 1 High St., Old Town, SN1 3EW, 🗲 692313, Telex 444764 – 📺
   ⇌wc ☎ 🅿️. 🏊. 🔼 🆎 ⓪ 𝗩𝗜𝗦𝗔
   M (closed Saturday lunch and Sunday dinner) – **65 rm** ⚏ 49.50/54.00 **t.** – SB (weekends only)
   56.00 **st.**

🏨 **Wiltshire,** Fleming Way, SN1 1TN, 🗲 28282, Telex 444250 – 🅿️ 📺 ⇌wc ☎ 🅿️. 🔼 🆎
   ⓪ 𝗩𝗜𝗦𝗔
   M 9.90 **t.** and a la carte 🍴 3.00 – **85 rm** ⚏ 46.00/56.00 **st.** – SB (weekends only) (except Easter)
   46.00 **st.**

   at Blunsdon N : 4 ½ m. on A 419 – ✉ 📞 0793 Swindon :

🏨 **Blunsdon House** (Best Western), The Ridge, SN2 4AD, 🗲 721701, Telex 444491, 🎣 – 🅿️
   📺 ☎ 🅑 🅿️. 🏊. 🔼 🆎 ⓪ 𝗩𝗜𝗦𝗔. ❄
   M 6.50/8.00 **st.** and a la carte 🍴 3.00 – **92 rm** ⚏ 40.00/80.00 **st.** – SB (weekends only) (except
   Easter) 59.00/64.00 **st.**

   at Stratton St. Margaret NE : 2 m. on A 420 – ✉ 📞 0793 Swindon :

🏨 **Crest** (Crest), Oxford Rd, SN3 4TL, NE : 1 ½ m. on A 420 🗲 822921, Telex 444456 – ▦ rest 📺
   ⇌wc ☎ 🅑 🅿️. 🏊. 🔼 🆎 ⓪ 𝗩𝗜𝗦𝗔
   M approx. 11.50 **st.** – ⚏ 5.75 – **98 rm** 45.50/55.50 **st.** – SB (weekends only) 55.00 **st.**

AUSTIN-ROVER, DAIMLER, JAGUAR Dorkan Way 🗲 612091
BEDFORD, FIAT, VAUXHALL Drove Rd 🗲 20971
BMW High St. at Wroughton 🗲 812387

FORD 30 Marlborough Rd 🗲 20002
RENAULT Elgin Drive 🗲 693841
VAUXHALL 13/21 The Street, Moredon 🗲 23457
VW, AUDI-NSU Eldene Drive 🗲 31333

SYMONDS YAT Heref. and Worc. 403 404 M 28 – ✉ Ross-on-Wye – ✆ 0600.
See : Symond's Yat Rock ≤★★.
♦London 126 – Gloucester 23 – Hereford 17 – Newport 31.

at Symonds Yat (West) – ✉ Ross-on-Wye – ✆ 0600 Symonds Yat :

↑ **Woodlea** ⚘, HR9 6BL, ✆ 890206, ⚒, ⇗ – ⬛wc ℗
 10 rm ⊊ 12.25/27.00 st.

XX **Gallery,** Wayside, Whitchurch, HR9 6DJ, ✆ 890408, ⇗ – ℗. ◼ AE VISA
 closed Sunday and 2 weeks mid November – **M** a la carte 14.50/19.50 st.

TADCASTER North Yorks. 402 Q 22 – pop. 5 ,877 – ECD : Wednesday – ✆ 0937.
♦London 176 – Harrogate 16 – ♦Kingston-upon-Hull 47 – ♦Leeds 16 – York 10.

🏠 **Shann House** without rest., 47 Kirkgate, LS24 9AQ, ✆ 833931 – TV ⇔wc ⬛wc ℗. ◼ VISA
 8 rm ⊊ 15.50/26.00 st.

TALLAND BAY Cornwall 403 G 32 – see Looe.

TAL-Y-BONT Gwynedd 402 403 I 24 – see Conwy.

TAL-Y-LLYN Gwynedd 402 403 I 25 – pop. 623 (inc. Corris) – ✉ Tywyn – ✆ 065 477 Abergynol-wyn.
♦London 224 – Dolgellau 9 – Shrewsbury 60.

🏠 **Minffordd,** LL36 9AJ, NE : 2 ¾ m. by B 4405 on A 487 ✆ 065 473 (Corris) 665, ≤, « Converted
 18C farmhouse and inn », ⇗ – ⇔wc ⬛wc ℗. ◼ ⓞ VISA. ⁂
 closed January and February – **M** *(closed Sunday and Monday to non-residents)* (buffet lunch
 residents only)/dinner 10.50 **st.** – **7 rm** ⊊ 27.50/49.00 **st.** – SB (spring and autumn) 44.00 **st.**

🏠 **Tynycornel,** LL35 9AJ, on B 4405 ✆ 282, ≤ lake and mountains, ⚒, ⇗ – TV ⇔wc ☎ ℗.
 ◼ ⓞ VISA
 closed January – **M** 5.00/9.50 **t.** and a la carte ▮ 1.75 – **16 rm** ⊊ (dinner included) 30.00/66.00 **t.**

Si vous écrivez à un hôtel à l'étranger,
joignez à votre lettre un coupon-réponse international.
(disponible dans les bureaux de poste).

TAMWORTH Staffs. 402 403 404 O 26 – pop. 63 ,260 – ✆ 0827.
🛈 Marmion House, Lichfield St. ✆ 64222.
♦London 118 – ♦Birmingham 12 – ♦Leicester 32 – ♦Nottingham 35 – ♦Stoke on Trent 37.

XX **Kealey's,** 36, Market St., B79 7LR, ✆ 55444 – ◼ VISA
 closed Sunday, Monday and 1 week Christmas – **M** (lunch by arrangement)/dinner 10.95 **t.**
 ▮ 2.50.

AUSTIN-ROVER Bolebridge St. ✆ 63535
FORD Upper Gungate ✆ 68411
PEUGEOT-TALBOT Lichfield St. ✆ 61317

RENAULT Watling St. ✆ 892428
VAUXHALL-OPEL Watling St. ✆ 282052
VW-AUDI Coleshill Rd ✆ 288282

TARRANT MONKTON Dorset – see Blandford Forum.

TAUNTON Somerset 403 K 30 The West Country G. – pop. 47 ,793 – ECD : Thursday – ✆ 0823.
See : Site★★ – St. Mary Magdalene's Church★★ – Museum★ *AC* – St. James Church★ – Hammett
St.★ – The Crescent★ – Bath Alley★.
Envir. : Muchelney★★ (Parish Church★★), E : 14 ½ m. – Wellington Monument (≤★★), W : 10 m. –
Trull : Church★, S: 2 m. – Bishops Lydeard★ (Church★), NW : 5 m. – Combe Florey★, NW: 7 m. –
Wellington Church★, W : 8 m. – Gaulden Manor★*AC*, NW : 9 m. – Midelney Manor★*AC* E : 12 m.
🛈 Public Library, Corporation St. ✆ 74785 and 70479.
♦London 168 – Bournemouth 69 – ♦Bristol 50 – Exeter 37 – ♦Plymouth 78 – ♦Southampton 93 – Weymouth 50.

🏰 ✿ **Castle,** Castle Green, TA1 1NF, ✆ 72671, Telex 46488, « Part 12C castle with Norman
 garden » – ▮ TV ☎ ᪲ ⇔ ℗. ◼ AE ⓞ VISA
 M 9.25/16.90 **t.** and a la carte ▮ 3.20 – ⊊ 6.25 – **35 rm** 41.50/115.00 **t.**, **1 suite** 185.00 **t.** – SB
 89.00 **t.**
 Spec. Local scallops served with spinach and mushrooms with a Champagne sauce, Cutlet of veal, two sauces of
 leek ; port and mustard, Parma ham garnish, Fig and Armagnac ice cream with hazelnut biscuits.

🏨 **County** (T.H.F.), East St., TA1 3LT, ✆ 87651, Telex 46484 – ▮ TV ⇔wc ᪲ ℗. ⚗. ◼ AE ⓞ
 VISA
 M 5.95/8.75 **st.** and a la carte ▮ 1.85 – ⊊ 5.50 – **68 rm** 34.50/46.00 **st.**

🏠 **Corner House,** Park St., TA1 4DQ, ✆ 84683 – TV ⇔wc ℗. ⁂
 22 rm.

at Henlade E : 3 ½ m. on A 358 – ✉ Taunton – ✆ 0823 Henlade :

🏠 **Falcon,** TA3 5DH, on A 358 ✆ 442502, ⇗ – TV ⇔wc ⬛wc ℗. ◼ VISA. ⁂
 closed 1 to 14 January – **M** *(closed Sunday to non-residents)* (bar lunch)/dinner a la carte
 7.50/10.50 **st.** ▮ 2.50 – **9 rm** ⊊ 27.25/46.50 **st.** – SB (weekends only) (except Bank Holidays)
 50.50/55.50 **st.**

at Hatch Beauchamp SE : 6 m. on A 358 – ⊠ Taunton – ✆ 0823 Hatch Beauchamp :

XXX **Farthings Country House** with rm, TA3 6SG, ✆ 480664, « Tastefully decorated country house », ♨ – ▥ ➪wc ☏ ℗. ⚠ ᵛⁱˢᵃ.
M (lunch residents only)/dinner 15.00 t. ♦ 3.60 – **6 rm** ⊡ 38.00/70.00 t. – SB (weekends only) (November-March) 68.00/80.00 t.

at Poundisford S : 3 ¾ m. by B 3170 – ⊠ Taunton – ✆ 082 342 Blagdon Hill :

XX **Well House,** Poundisford Park, TA3 7AF, ✆ 566, ♨ – ℗. ⚠ ᴀᴇ ⓪ ᵛⁱˢᵃ
closed Sunday dinner and Monday – **M** 5.25/8.95 t. ♦ 2.25.

at Bradford-on-Tone W : 4 m. on A 38 – ⊠ Taunton – ✆ 082 346 Bradford-on-Tone :

🏨 **Heatherton Grange,** Wellington Rd, TA4 1ET, on A 38 ✆ 777 – ▥ ➪wc 🏧wc ℗. ⚠ ᴀᴇ
⓪ ᵛⁱˢᵃ
M 7.50 t. and a la carte ♦ 2.50 – **18 rm** ⊡ 20.00/32.00 t.

AUDI, MERCEDES-BENZ, VW Silver St. ✆ 88371
AUSTIN-ROVER, DAIMLER-JAGUAR South St. ✆ 88991
FIAT Priory Av. ✆ 87611

FORD 151/6 East Reach ✆ 85481
LADA, YUGO 16 Kingston Rd ✆ 88288
RENAULT 138 Bridgwater Rd, Bathpool ✆ 412559
SAAB 60 East Reach ✆ 88351

TAVISTOCK Devon ❹❿❸ H 32 The West Country G. – pop. 8 ,508 – ECD : Wednesday – ✆ 0822.
Envir. : Dartmoor National Park★★ – Lydford★★, Lydford Gorge★★ *AC*, N : 9 m. – Morwellham★*AC*, W : 4 m. – at Launceston★, Castle★ *AC* (≤★), St. Mary Magdalene Church★ South Gate★ *AC*, NW : 14 m. – 🏮 Down Rd ✆ 2049, SW : 1 m. – 🅰 Guildhall, Bedford Sq. ✆ 2938 (summer only).
♦London 239 – Exeter 38 – ♦Plymouth 15.

🏨 **Bedford** (T.H.F.), 1 Plymouth Rd, PL19 8BB, ✆ 3221 – ▥ ➪wc ☎ ⇦. 🔥. ⚠ ᴀᴇ ⓪ ᵛⁱˢᵃ
M (buffet lunch)/dinner 8.95 st. and a la carte ♦ 2.70 – ⊡ 5.50 – **31 rm** 34.50/45.50 st.

at Gulworthy W : 3 m. on A 390 – ⊠ Tavistock – ✆ 0822 Gunnislake :

XX **Horn of Plenty** ⟡ with rm, PL19 8JD, ✆ 832528, ≤ Tamar Valley and Bodmin Moor, 🍴 –
▥ ➪wc 🏧wc ☎ ℗. ⚠ ᵛⁱˢᵃ. ⟡
closed Christmas Day – **M** *(closed Friday lunch and Thursday)* 12.50/26.00 t. (wine included) and a la carte ♦ 3.65 – ⊡ 6.50 – **6 rm** 42.00/62.00 t.

at Mary Tavy N : 4 ½ m. by A 386 – ⊠ Tavistock – ✆ 082 281 Mary Tavy :

🏨 **Moorland Hall** ⟡, Brentor Rd, PL19 9PY, ✆ 466, « Country house atmosphere », 🍴 –
➪wc 🏧wc ℗. ⚠ ᵛⁱˢᵃ
closed Christmas and New Year – **M** (bar lunch to residents only)/dinner 9.50 st. ♦ 3.75 –
10 rm ⊡ 18.00/33.00 st. – SB 45.00/60.00 st.

AUSTIN-ROVER Plymouth Rd ✆ 2301

FORD 122 Plymouth Rd ✆ 3735

TEBAY Cumbria ❹❿❷ M 20 – pop. 594 – ⊠ Penrith – ✆ 05874 Orton.
♦London 281 – ♦Carlisle 38 – Kendal 13.

🏨 **Tebay Mountain Lodge,** at Tebay West service area, CA10 3SB, ✆ 351 – ▥ ➪wc ☎ ℗.
⚠ ᴀᴇ ⓪ ᵛⁱˢᵃ
M (dinner only) 6.50 st. and a la carte ♦ 2.80 – ⊡ 4.25 – **30 rm** 27.50/40.70 st. – SB (October-April) 35.00/42.00 st.

TEDBURN ST. MARY Devon ❹❿❸ I 31 – pop. 755 – ECD : Thursday – ⊠ Exeter – ✆ 064 76.
♦London 209 – Exeter 8.5 – ♦Plymouth 51.

⌂ **King's Arms Inn,** EX6 6EG, ✆ 224, 🍴 – ▥ ℗. ⚠ ᵛⁱˢᵃ
M *(closed Sunday dinner)* 4.85/9.00 t. and a la carte ♦ 2.50 – **10 rm** ⊡ 12.00/24.00 t.

TEESSIDE AIRPORT Durham ❹❿❷ P 20 – see Darlington.

TEIGNMOUTH Devon ❹❿❸ J 32 The West Country G. – pop. 11 ,995 – ECD : Thursday – ✆ 062 67.
🅱 The Den, Sea Front ✆ 6271 ext 207/258 – ♦London 216 – Exeter 16 – Torquay 8.

🏨 **London,** 24 Bank St., TQ14 8AW, ✆ 6336, ⬙ heated – 🛗 ▥ ➪wc 🏧wc ℗. ⚠ ᴀᴇ ⓪ ᵛⁱˢᵃ
M 4.75/8.00 t. and a la carte ♦ 2.90 – **26 rm** ⊡ 18.00/45.00 t. – SB (October-May except Bank Holidays) 40.00 st.

🏨 **Venn Farm Country House** (Best Western) ⟡, Higher Exeter Rd, TQ14 9PB, ✆ 2196, ≤,
🍴 – ▥ ➪wc 🏧wc ℗. ⚠ ᴀᴇ ⓪ ᵛⁱˢᵃ. ⟡
closed Christmas and New Year – **M** *(closed Sunday dinner)* (bar lunch)/dinner a la carte 8.50/14.45 t. ♦ 3.50 – **10 rm** ⊡ 25.00/48.00 t. – SB (weekends only)(November-mid May) 43.00/46.00 st.

⌂ **Belvedere,** 19 Barnpark Rd, TQ14 8PJ, ✆ 4561 – 🏧wc ℗. ⚠. ⟡
13 rm ⊡ 9.00/26.00 st.

at Shaldon S : 1 m. on A 379 – ⊠ Teignmouth – ✆ 062 687 Shaldon :

⌂ **Glenside,** Ringmore Rd, TQ14 0EP, W : ½ m. on B 3195 ✆ 2448 – ▥ 🏧wc ℗. ⚠ ᵛⁱˢᵃ
10 rm ⊡ 9.00/29.50 st.

NISSAN 106 Bitton Park Rd ✆ 2501

436

TELFORD Salop 402 403 404 M 25 – pop. 76,330 – ✪ 0952.

Envir. : Ironbridge Gorge Museum★ (Iron Bridge★★) *AC*, S : 5 m. – Buildwas Abbey★ (ruins 12C) S : 7 m.

✦London 152 – ✦Birmingham 33 – Shrewsbury 12 – ✦Stoke-on-Trent 29.

🏨 **Telford Hotel, Golf and Country Club** (Q.M.H.), Great Hay, Sutton Hill, TF7 4DT, S : 4 ½ m. by M 54 and A 442 ♧ 585642, Telex 35481, ≤, 🖾, ⅛, squash – 📺 ⌂wc ☎ ₺ 🅿. 🛦. ◪ 📧 🆎 ⓸ *VISA*. ⅍
M 6.90/10.00 st. ₰ 3.00 – **58 rm** ⌷ 40.00/56.00 st. – SB (weekends only) 50.00/60.00 st.

🏨 **Buckatree Hall** (Best Western) ⅏, Ercall Lane, The Wrekin, Wellington, TF6 5AL, S : 1 m. off M 54 junction 7 ♧ 51821, ㎡, park – 📺 ⌂wc ☎ ₺ 🅿. 🛦
25 rm, 1 suite.

🏦 **Charlton Arms,** Church St., Wellington, TF1 1DG, ♧ 51351 – 📺 ⌂wc ☜ 🅿. 🛦. ◪ 🆎 ⓸ *VISA*
closed 25 to 31 December – **M** *(closed Sunday dinner)* 6.50/8.00 **st.** and a la carte ₰ 3.75 – **27 rm** ⌷ 33.00/48.00 **st.** – SB (weekends only) 52.50/56.50 **st.**

AUSTIN-ROVER-VANDEN PLAS   Market St., Wellington ♧ 44896
CITROEN   Holyhead Rd ♧ 617273
FIAT   Trench Rd ♧ 605301
FORD   Haygate Rd ♧ 42433

PEUGEOT-TALBOT   Holyhead Rd ♧ 617272
RENAULT   Watling St. ♧ 53221
TOYOTA   Wellington Rd ♧ 605616
TOYOTA   Ironbridge Rd ♧ 882100
VAUXHALL-OPEL   Holyhead Rd ♧ 618081

TEMPLE SOWERBY Cumbria 401 402 M 20 – pop. 341 – ECD : Thursday – ✉ Penrith – ✪ 0930 Kirkby Thore.

✦London 297 – ✦Carlisle 31 – Kendal 38.

🏨 **Temple Sowerby House,** CA10 1RZ, ♧ 61578, ㎡ – 📺 ⌂wc ☎ ₺ 🅿. ◪ 🆎 *VISA*. ⅍
closed 24 December-2 January – **M** *(closed Sunday dinner to non-residents)* (dinner only) 10.50 t. ₰ 2.25 – **12 rm** ⌷ 26.00/38.00 t. – SB 50.00/55.00 st.

TENBY (DINBYCH-Y-PYSGOD) Dyfed 403 F 28 – pop. 5,226 – ECD : Wednesday – ✪ 0834.

See : Site★★.

⅛ ♧ 2978.

🄱 Guildhall, The Norton ♧ 2402 and 3510.

✦London 247 – Carmarthen 27 – Fishguard 36.

🏨 **Imperial** (Best Western), The Paragon, SA70 7HR, ♧ 3737, ≤ sea and bay – ⧮ 📺 ⌂wc ⬚wc ☜ ⟵. ◪ 🆎 ⓸ *VISA*
M (bar lunch Monday to Saturday)/dinner 9.75 t. and a la carte – **46 rm** ⌷ 20.00/76.00 t. – SB (except Christmas and Bank Holidays) 36.00/68.00 st.

🏦 **Fourcroft,** Croft Terr., SA70 8AP, ♧ 2516, ≤, 🝔 heated, ㎡ – ⧮ 📺 ⬚wc. ◪ *VISA*. ⅍
25 April-mid October – **M** (bar lunch)/dinner 8.50 st. ₰ 2.50 – **38 rm** ⌷ 18.00/38.00 st. – SB 42.00/50.00 st.

🏦 **Royal Lion,** 1 High St., SA70 7ES, ♧ 2127 – ⧮ 📺 ⌂wc. ◪ *VISA*
March-mid November – **M** (bar lunch Monday to Saturday)/dinner 8.00 t. and a la carte ₰ 3.00 – **36 rm** ⌷ 13.00/44.00 t. – SB 46.00/55.00 st.

🏦 **Harbour Heights,** 11 Croft Terrace, SA70 8AP, ♧ 2132, ≤ – 📺 ⬚wc. ◪ 🆎 ⓸ *VISA*. ⅍
March-October – **M** (bar lunch)/dinner 7.00 **st.** ₰ 2.25 – **10 rm** ⌷ 15.00/30.00 **st.** – SB (except July and August) 38.00/42.00 **st.**

🏦 **Buckingham,** Esplanade, SA70 7DU, ♧ 2622, ≤ – ⌂wc ⅀wc. ◪ 🆎 ⓸ *VISA*
March-October – **M** (bar lunch)/dinner 7.50 t. ₰ 2.00 – **22 rm** ⌷ 12.50/33.00 t.

🛏 **Heywood Lodge,** Heywood Lane, SA70 8BN, ♧ 2684, ㎡ – ⬚wc 🅿
April-September – **13 rm** ⌷ 9.50/23.00 st.

AUSTIN-ROVER   Greenhill Rd ♧ 2459

TENTERDEN Kent 404 W 30 – pop. 5,698 – ECD : Wednesday – ✪ 058 06.

🄱 Town Hall, High St. ♧ 3572 (summer only).

✦ London 57 – Folkestone 26 – Hastings 21 – Maidstone 19.

🏦 **White Lion,** High St., TN30 6BD, ♧ 2921 – ⌂wc 🅿. ◪ 🆎 ⓸ *VISA*
M 7.95/12.95 t. and a la carte ₰ 4.95 – **12 rm** ⌷ 25.50/38.50 t. – SB 42.00/52.00 st.

🛏 **West Cross House,** 2 West Cross, TN30 6JL, ♧ 2224 – 🅿
March-October – **7 rm** ⌷ 9.00/22.00 st.

AUSTIN-ROVER   High St. ♧ 4444   NISSAN   St. Michaels ♧ 3413

TERN HILL Salop 402 403 404 M 25 – ✉ Market Drayton – ✪ 063 083.

✦London 161 – ✦Birmingham 44 – Chester 30 – Shrewsbury 16 – ✦Stoke-on-Trent 19.

🏦 Tern Hill Hall ⅏, TF9 3PU, SW : ¼ m. on A 53 ♧ 310, ≤, ㎡ – 📺 ⌂wc ⅀ 🅿. ⅍
11 rm.

Non viaggiate oggi con una carta stradale di ieri.

TETBURY Glos. **403 404** N 29 – pop. 4 ,467 – ECD : Thursday – ✆ 0666.

Envir. : Westonbirt Arboretum★ *AC*, SW : 3 ½ m.

🏌 Westonbirt 066 66 (Westonbirt) 242, S : 3 m.

🎫 The Old Court House, Long St. ✆ 53552 (summer only).

♦London 113 – ♦Bristol 27 – Gloucester 19 – Swindon 24.

🏨 **Snooty Fox** (Best Western), Market Pl., GL8 8DD, ✆ 52436, Telex 449848 – 📺 ☎. 🔲 AE ⓪
VISA. ❄
M 20.00 t. § 2.80 – ⊊ 4.00 – **12 rm** 41.00/77.00 t. – SB (except Christmas, New Year and Bank
Holidays) 60.00/88.00 **st.**

XXX **The Close** with rm, 8 Long St., GL8 8AQ, ✆ 52272, Group Telex 43232, ☞ – 📺 ➪wc ♒wc
☎ ℗. 🔲 AE ⓪ **VISA**. ❄
M 11.00/14.00 t. and a la carte § 2.70 – ⊊ 3.75 – **12 rm** 32.50/76.00 **st.**

at Avening N : 3 m. on B 4014 – ✉ Tetbury – ✆ 045 383 Nailsworth :

XX **Gibbons,** High St., GL8 8NF, ✆ 3070 – 🔲 AE ⓪ **VISA**
closed Sunday dinner and first 2 weeks February – **M** (booking essential)(lunch by arrangement)/dinner 14.00 **t.** and a la carte 13.50/20.00 **t.**

at Westonbirt SW : 2 ½ m. on A 433 – ✉ Tetbury – ✆ 066 688 Westonbirt :

🏨 **Hare and Hounds** (Best Western), GL8 8QL, ✆ 233, ☞, park, ❀, squash – 📺 ➪wc ♒
⟹ ℗. 🏌. 🔲 AE ⓪
M 7.00/11.00 **st.** and a la carte § 3.20 – **27 rm** ⊊ 32.00/52.00 **st.** – SB (except 22 August-
November) 45.00/60.00 **st.**

at Calcot W : 3 ½ m. on A 4135 – ✉ Tetbury – ✆ 066 689 Leighterton :

🏨 **Calcot Manor** ≫, GL8 8YJ, ✆ 355, 🅹 heated, ☞ – 📺 ➪wc ☎ ℗. 🔲 AE ⓪ **VISA**. ❄
M (closed Sunday dinner to non-residents) 12.50/18.50 **st.** § 2.50 – **10 rm** ⊊ 40.00/95.00 **st.** –
SB (November-March except Christmas) 75.00/120.00 **st.**

VW, AUDI London Rd ✆ 52473

TEWKESBURY Glos. **403 404** N 28 – pop. 9 ,454 – ECD : Thursday – ✆ 0684.

See : Abbey Church★ 12C-14C.

🎫 Tewkesbury Museum, 64 Barton St. ✆ 295027 (summer only).

♦London 108 – ♦Birmingham 39 – Gloucester 11.

🏨 **Royal Hop Pole** (Crest), Church St., GL20 5RT, ✆ 293236, Telex 437176, ☞ – 📺 ➪wc ♒
℗. 🏌. 🔲 AE ⓪ **VISA**. ❄
M approx. 11.50 **st.** – ⊊ 5.75 – **29 rm** 43.50/57.00 **st.** – SB (weekends only) 63.00 **st.**

🏨 Tewkesbury Park Hotel, Golf and Country Club ≫, Lincoln Green Lane, GL20 7DN, S : 1 ¼ m.
by A 38 ✆ 295405, Telex 43563, ≼, 🔲, 🏌, park – 📺 ➪wc ☎ ℗. 🏌
52 rm.

🏨 **Tudor House,** 51 High St., GL20 5BH, ✆ 297755, ☞ – 📺 ➪wc ♒wc ☎. 🔲 AE ⓪ **VISA**. ❄
M (bar lunch Monday to Saturday)/dinner 8.25 **t.** and a la carte – **16 rm** ⊊ 25.00/40.00 **st.**

at Corse Lawn SW : 6 m. by A 38 and A 438 on B 4211 – ✉ Gloucester – ✆ 045 278 Tirley :

XXX **Corse Lawn House** with rm, GL19 4LZ, ✆ 479, ☞ – 📺 ➪wc ☎ ℗. 🔲 AE ⓪ **VISA**
M (closed Sunday dinner and Monday) 9.50/12.75 **st.** and a la carte § 2.50 – **4 rm**
⊊ 22.50/36.50 **st.**

ALFA-ROMEO Shuthonger ✆ 293448
AUSTIN-ROVER Gloucester Rd ✆ 293122
FORD Ashchurch Rd ✆ 292398
NISSAN Bredon ✆ 72333
PEUGEOT-TALBOT Bredon Rd ✆ 297575
TALBOT Bredon Rd ✆ 293071

THAME Oxon. **404** R 28 – pop. 8 ,300 – ECD : Wednesday – ✆ 084 421.

See : St. Mary's Church★ 13C – **Envir. :** Rycote Chapel★ (15C) *AC*, W : 3 ½ m.

🎫 Town Hall ✆ 2834.

♦London 48 – Aylesbury 9 – ♦Oxford 13.

🏨 **Spread Eagle** (Best Western), 16 Cornmarket, OX9 2BR, ✆ 3661 – 📺 ➪wc ♒ ℗. 🏌. 🔲
AE ⓪ **VISA**. ❄
M (closed lunch Saturday and Sunday) 8.25/9.75 **st.** and a la carte § 2.45 – ⊊ 3.75 – **26 rm**
39.85/48.45 **st.** – SB (weekends only) 59.00/65.00 **st.**

🏧 Jolly Sailor, 14 Wellington St., OX9 3BN, ✆ 2682 – 📺 ℗. ❄
16 rm.

X **Thatchers** with rm, 29-30 Lower High St., OX9 2AA, ✆ 2146 – ➪wc ♒wc. 🔲 **VISA**
closed Monday lunch and Sunday – **M** 10.50 **t.** and a la carte § 3.00 – **6 rm** ⊊ 32.50/47.50 **t.**

VAUXHALL-OPEL Park St. ✆ 2505

THAXTED Essex **404** V 28 – pop. 2 ,177 – ✆ 0371.

♦London 44 – ♦Cambridge 24 – Colchester 31 – Chelmsford 20.

🏧 **Fox and Hounds,** Walden Rd, CM6 2RE, NW : ½ m. on B 184 ✆ 830129 – 📺 ♒wc ℗. AE
VISA
M 5.95 **st.** and a la carte – **10 rm** ⊊ 26.00/29.50 **st.** – SB (weekends only) 49.50 **st.**

at Broxted SW : 3 ¾ m. on B 1051 – ⊠ Great Dunmow – ✪ 0279 Bishop's Stortford :

XX **Whitehall** with rm, Church End, CM6 2BZ, 𝒫 850603, ≤, « Country house and gardens », ⌷ heated, 𝔸 – 📺 ⌷wc ☎ 🅿. 🅰 AE VISA ✼
closed 2 to 23 January – **M** *(closed Sunday dinner and Monday to non-residents)* 14.00/22.50 t. and a la carte ⌀ 5.00 – **4 rm** ⊊ 60.00/85.00 t.

THETFORD Norfolk 404 W 26 – pop. 19,591 – ECD : Wednesday – ✪ 0842.
🇮 Ancient House Museum, 21 White Hart St. 𝒫 2599.
♦London 83 – ♦Cambridge 32 – ♦Ipswich 33 – King's Lynn 30 – ♦Norwich 29.

🏨 **Bell** (T.H.F.), King St., IP24 2AZ, 𝒫 4455, Telex 818868 – 📺 🅿. 🅰 AE ⓞ VISA
M 6.95/9.50 st. and a la carte ⌀ 2.70 – ⊊ 5.50 – **42 rm** 36.50/47.50 st.

🏠 **The Historical Thomas Paine** (Best Western), White Hart St., IP24 1AA, 𝒫 5631 – 📺 ⌷wc ⋒ ☎ 🅿. 🅰 AE ⓞ VISA
M 6.00/8.50 t. and a la carte – **14 rm** ⊊ 26.95/38.95 t. – SB (weekends only) 48.00 st.

AUSTIN-ROVER, LAND-ROVER Guildhall St. 𝒫 4427

THIRSK North Yorks. 402 P 21 – pop. 7,174 – ECD : Wednesday – ✪ 0845.
See : St. Mary's Church★ (Gothic) – Envir. : Sutton Bank (≤★★) E : 6 m. on A 170.
🇮 Thirsk Museum, 16 Kirkgate 𝒫 22755 (summer only).
♦London 227 – ♦Leeds 37 – ♦Middlesbrough 24 – York 24.

🏠 **Golden Fleece** (T.H.F.), Market Pl., YO7 1LL, 𝒫 23108 – 📺 ⌷wc ⋒ 🅿. 🅰 AE ⓞ VISA
M 5.80/9.00 st. and a la carte ⌀ 2.70 – ⊊ 5.50 – **22 rm** 36.50/45.00 st.

at Sowerby S : ½ m. – ⊠ ✪ 0845 Thirsk :

🏠 **Sheppard's**, Church Farm, Front St., YO7 1JF, 𝒫 23655 – 📺 ⌷wc 🅿. 🅰 AE ⓞ VISA ✼
closed 1 to 13 January – **M** *(closed Sunday dinner to non-residents)* (dinner only and Sunday lunch) 7.50 t. and a la carte ⌀ 3.50 – **7 rm** ⊊ 12.00/35.00 t.

AUSTIN-ROVER Long St. 𝒫 23152   PEUGEOT Station Rd 𝒫 22370

THORNABY-ON-TEES Cleveland 402 Q 20 – pop. 26,319 – ⊠ ✪ 0642 Middlesbrough.
♦London 250 – ♦Leeds 62 – ♦Middlesbrough 3 – York 49.

🏨 **Post House** (T.H.F.), Low Lane, Stainton Village, TS17 9LW, SE : 3 ½ m. by A 1045 on A 1044 𝒫 0642 (Middlesbrough) 591213, Telex 58426 – 📺 ⌷wc ⋒ 🅿. 🅰 🅰 AE ⓞ VISA
M 6.25/11.50 st. and a la carte ⌀ 2.70 – ⊊ 5.50 – **136 rm** 35.00/42.50 st.

VAUXHALL Acklam Rd 𝒫 593333

THORNAGE Norfolk – see Holt.

THORNBURY Avon 403 404 M 29 The West Country G. – pop. 11,948 – ECD : Thursday – ⊠ Bristol – ✪ 0454.
♦London 128 – ♦Bristol 12 – Gloucester 23 – Swindon 43.

🏨 **Thornbury Castle** ⟅, Castle St., BS12 1HH, 𝒫 418511, Telex 449986, « 16C castle », 𝔸, park – 📺 ☎ 🅿. 🅰 AE ⓞ VISA ✼
closed 1 week at Christmas – **M** 13.50/dinner a la carte 22.25/24.50 st. ⌀ 3.00 – ⊊ a la carte approx. 5.00 – **12 rm** 48.00/130.00 st., **1 suite** 158.00 st.

THORNTHWAITE Cumbria 402 K 20 – see Keswick.

THORNTON West Yorks. 402 O 22 – see Bradford.

THORNTON HOUGH Merseyside 402 403 K 24 – ⊠ Wirral – ✪ 051 Liverpool.
♦London 208 – Chester 12 – ♦Liverpool 13.

🏨 **Thornton Hall**, Neston Rd, Wirral, L63 1JF, 𝒫 336 3938, Telex 628678, 𝔸 – 📺 ⌷wc ☎ 🅿. 🅰 AE ⓞ VISA ✼
M (dinner only and Sunday lunch) 7.90 t. and a la carte – **38 rm** ⊊ 21.50/49.00 t., **1 suite** 49.00/60.00 t..

THORPE Derbs. 402 403 404 O 24 – pop. 227 – ⊠ Ashbourne – ✪ 033 529 Thorpe Cloud.
Envir. : N : Dovedale (valley)★★ – Ashbourne (St. Oswald's Church★ 13C) SE : 3 m.
🇮₅ at Ashbourne 𝒫 0335 (Ashbourne) 42078, SE : 5 m.
♦London 151 – Derby 16 – ♦Sheffield 33 – ♦Stoke-on-Trent 26.

🏨 **Izaak Walton** ⟅, Dovedale, DE6 2AY, W : 1 m. 𝒫 261, ≤ Dovedale, ⟍, 𝔸 – 📺 ⌷wc ⋒ 🅿. 🅰 🅰 AE ⓞ VISA
M 5.00 t. and a la carte ⌀ 3.00 – **27 rm** ⊊ 32.55/49.35 st.

🏨 **Peveril of the Peak** (T.H.F.) ⟅, Dovedale, DE6 2AW, 𝒫 333, ≤, 𝔸, ⟋ – 📺 ⌷wc ⋒ 🅿. 🅰 🅰 AE ⓞ VISA
M 7.25/9.75 st. and a la carte ⌀ 2.55 – ⊊ 5.50 – **41 rm** 36.00/47.50 st.

THORPE LE SOKEN Essex 404 X 28 – pop. 1 ,680 – ⊠ ❀ 0255 Clacton-on-Sea.

♦London 68 – Colchester 13 – ♦Ipswich 28.

✗ **Loblollies,** High St., CO16 0DY, ℰ 861616 – ℗. ◪ ▨
closed Sunday dinner, Monday and 25-26 December – **M** (dinner only and Sunday lunch) a la
carte 8.85/12.20 t. ▮ 2.50.

THORPE MARKET Norfolk 404 X 25 – pop. 221 – ⊠ North Walsham – ❀ 026 379 Southrepps.

♦London 130 – ♦Norwich 21.

🏛 **Elderton Lodge** ⚘, NR11 8TZ, S : 1 m. on A 149 ℰ 547, ඤ – ▭ ♨wc ℗. ◪ ▨
M 9.50 t. and a la carte ▮ 3.50 – **7 rm** ⊊ 15.00/36.00 t. – SB (October-March)(except Bank
Holidays) 40.00/55.00 st.

THORPE ST. ANDREW Norfolk 404 Y 26 – see Norwich.

THORVERTON Devon 403 J 31 – ECD : Wednesday – ⊠ ❀ 0392 Exeter.

♦London 200 – Exeter 9 – Taunton 33.

🏠 **Berribridge** ⚘, EX5 5JR, S : ½ m. ℰ 860259, ඤ – ♨wc ℗. ◪
M (lunch by arrangement) 8.50 t. and a la carte ▮ 3.90 – **6 rm** ⊊ 22.00/38.00 t. – SB
44.00/50.00 st.

THREE COCKS (ABERLLYNFI) Powys 403 K 27 – ⊠ Brecon – ❀ 049 74 Glasbury.

♦London 184 – Brecon 11 – Hereford 25 – ♦Swansea 55.

✗✗ **Three Cocks** with rm, LD3 0SL, on A 438 ℰ 215, ඤ – ℗. ◪ ▨. ✼
closed January – **M** (closed Tuesday except summer) 14.00 st. and a la carte ▮ 2.25 – **7 rm**
⊊ 16.00/32.00 st. – SB (except July, August and Bank Holidays) 51.00 st.

THURLESTONE Devon 403 I 33 – see Kingsbridge.

TICKTON Humberside – see Beverley.

TILBURY Essex 404 V 29 – pop. 11 ,430 – ❀ 037 52.

🚢 Shipping connections with the Continent : to USSR (Leningrad) via Norway (Oslo) and
Denmark (Copenhagen) (Baltic Shipping Co.).

🚢 to Gravesend (Sealink) frequent services daily (5 mn).

♦London 24 – Southend-on-Sea 20.

Hotels and restaurants see : London W : 24 m.

TIMPERLEY Greater Manchester 402 ② 403 ③ 404 ⑨ – see Altrincham.

TINTAGEL Cornwall 403 F 32 **The West Country G.** – pop. 1 ,566 – ECD : Wednesday except
summer – ❀ 0840 Camelford.

See : Arthur's Castle : site★★★AC – Tintagel Church★ – Old Post Office★AC.

Envir. : Delabole Quarry★AC, SE : 4 m. by B 3263 – Camelford★, SE : 6 m. by B 3263 and B 3266.

♦London 264 – Exeter 63 – ♦Plymouth 49 – Truro 41.

🏛 **Atlantic View,** Treknow, PL34 0EJ, S : 1 m. by B 3263 ℰ 770221, ≼, ◪, ඤ – ♨wc ♨wc
℗. ◪ 䅟 ◐ ▨
March-October – **M** (bar lunch)/dinner 8.50 t. ▮ 3.00 – **10 rm** ⊊ 19.50/49.00 t. – SB (except
July and August) 44.00/48.00 st.

🏛 **Bossiney House,** Bossiney, PL34 0AX, NE : ½ m. on B 3263 ℰ 770240, ◪, ඤ – ♨wc
♨wc ℗. 䅟 ◐
Easter-October – **M** (bar lunch)/dinner 8.00 st. ▮ 2.90 – **20 rm** ⊊ 15.00/36.00 st. – SB (except
mid July-August) 41.00/47.00 st.

🏠 **Trewarmett Lodge,** Trewarmett, PL34 0ET, SW : 1 ½ m. on B 3263 ℰ 770460, ≼, ඤ – ℗.
◪ ◐ ▨
M 5.50/7.00 t. and a la carte ▮ 1.85 – **6 rm** ⊊ 11.50/24.00 t. – SB 30.00/34.00 st.

✗ **Mill House Inn** with rm, Trebarwith, PL34 0HD, S : 1 ¼ m. by B 3263 via Treknow ℰ 770200,
« Former corn mill » – ▭ ♨wc ♨wc ℗. ◪ ▨
closed 24 to 28 December – **M** (bar lunch)/dinner a la carte 8.00/13.80 t. ▮ 2.45 – **9 rm**
⊊ 14.50/39.00 t. – SB (November-March) 40.00 st.

TINTERN (TYNDYRN) Gwent 403 404 L 28 – pop. 816 – ECD : Wednesday – ⊠ Chepstow –
❀ 029 18.

See : Abbey★★ (ruins) AC – 🏛 Tintern Abbey ℰ 431 (summer only).

♦London 137 – ♦Bristol 23 – Gloucester 40 – Newport 22.

🏛 **Beaufort** (Embassy), NP6 6SF, ℰ 777, ඤ – ▭ ♨wc ♨wc ☎ ℗. ◪ 䅟 ◐ ▨. ✼
M 7.75/19.50 st. and a la carte ▮ 2.50 – **25 rm** ⊊ 32.50/48.00 st. – SB 52.00 st.

🏠 **Parva Farmhouse,** NP6 6SQ, on A 466 ℰ 411 – ℗
6 rm ⊊ 15.00/24.00 st.

TITCHWELL Norfolk 404 V 25 – pop. 96 – ⊠ King's Lynn – ☎ 0485 Brancaster.

◆London 124 – ◆Cambridge 66 – ◆Norwich 41.

🏛 **Titchwell Manor** (Best Western), PE31 8BB, on A 149 ℰ 210221, ☞ – 🛏wc 🅿. 🖭 AE ⓞ VISA
   closed 24 to 30 December – **M** (booking essential) (bar lunch)/dinner 10.25 **t.** and a la carte
   🍴 3.00 – **10 rm** 🛏 21.00/40.00 **t.** – SB 44.00/54.00 **st.**

TIVERTON Devon 403 J 31 The West Country G. – pop. 14,745 – ECD : Thursday – ☎ 0884.

See : Museum ★ AC.

Envir. : at Bickleigh ★★, Mill Craft Centre and farms ★★ AC, Castle ★ AC, S : 4 ½ m. – Knightshayes
Court ★ AC, N : 2 m. on A 396 – Coldharbour Mill, Uffculme ★ AC, E : 11 m. by A 373.

🛈 Pheonix Lane ℰ 255827 (summer only).

◆London 190 – Exeter 14 – Taunton 23.

🏛 **Tiverton,** Blundells Rd, EX16 4DB, E : ½ m. on A 373 ℰ 256120 – 🍽 rest 🖭 🛏wc 🐾 🕹 🅿.
   🖭. 🖭 AE ⓞ VISA
   M 6.00/8.95 **st.** and a la carte 🍴 2.50 – **29 rm** 🛏 18.00/32.95 **st.** – SB 38.00/50.00 **st.**

✗ **Hendersons,** 18 Newport St., EX16 6NL, ℰ 254256 – 🖭 AE VISA
   closed Sunday, Monday and 4 days at Christmas – **M** 11.00 **t.** (dinner) and a la carte 🍴 2.80.

   at Oakfordbridge NW : 9 m. on A 396 – ⊠ Tiverton – ☎ 039 85 Oakford :

🏠 **Bark House,** EX16 9HZ, ℰ 236 – 🛏wc 🅿. 🖭 AE ⓞ VISA
   closed January and February – **M** (bar lunch)/dinner 9.00 **st.** 🍴 2.95 – 🛏 2.50 – **6 rm**
   12.00/28.00 **st.**

CITROEN 31 Leat St. ℰ 252170

TONBRIDGE Kent 404 U 30 – pop. 34,407 – ECD : Wednesday – ☎ 0732.

See : Tonbridge School ★ (1553).

Envir. : Ightham Mote ★ (Manor House 14C-15C) AC, site ★ N : 7 m.

🗑 Poult Wood, Higham Lane ℰ 364039, N : 2 m. by A 227.

◆London 33 – ◆Brighton 37 – Hastings 31 – Maidstone 14.

🏛 **Rose and Crown** (T.H.F.), 125 High St., TN9 1DD, ℰ 357966, ☞ – 🖭 🛏wc 🐾 🅿. 🖭. 🖭
   AE ⓞ VISA
   M 7.00/8.50 **st.** and a la carte – 🛏 5.50 – **52 rm** 35.50/48.50 **st.**, **1 suite**.

✗✗ **Winch,** 160 High St., TN9 1BB, ℰ 366755, Italian rest. – 🖭 AE ⓞ
   closed Sunday, last 2 weeks August and Bank Holidays – **M** a la carte 10.50/16.75 **t.** 🍴 3.40.

ALFA-ROMEO, PEUGEOT-TALBOT   Sovereign Way
ℰ 350288
AUSTIN-ROVER, DAIMLER-JAGUAR   Cannon Lane
ℰ 364444
FORD   Avebury Av. ℰ 356301

RENAULT   London Rd, Hildenborough ℰ 832022
VAUXHALL   Waterloo Rd ℰ 354035
VOLVO   Hildenborough ℰ 832424
VW, AUDI-NSU, MERCEDES-BENZ   Vale Rd ℰ
355822

TORQUAY Devon 403 J 32 The West Country G. – pop. 54,430 – ECD : Wednesday and Saturday
– ☎ 0803.

See : Kent's Cavern ★ AC CX A.

Envir. : Cockington ★, W : 1 m. AX.

⛴ to Channel Islands : Alderney (Torbay Seaways: Hydrofoil) summer only 1 weekly (2 h 30 mn) –
to Channel Islands : St Peter Port, Guernsey (Torbay Seaways: Hydrofoil) summer only 2 weekly
(2 h 30 mn) – to Channel Islands : St. Helier, Jersey (Torbay Seaways: Hydrofoil) summer only 2
weekly (3 h 30 mn).

🛈 Vaughan Parade ℰ 27428.

◆London 223 – Exeter 23 – ◆Plymouth 32.

Plan on next page

🏨 **Imperial** (T.H.F.), Park Hill Rd, TQ1 2DG, ℰ 24301, Telex 42849, ≤ Torbay, 🏊 heated, 🔲, ☞,
   ✗ – 🛗 🖭 🐾 🕹 🚗 🅿. 🖭. 🖭 AE ⓞ VISA   CZ **a**
   M 10.00/16.00 **st.** and a la carte 🍴 3.75 – **164 rm** 🛏 61.50/109.50 **st.**

🏨 **Palace,** Babbacombe Rd, TQ1 3TG, ℰ 22271, Telex 42606, 🏊 heated, 🔲, 🗗, ☞, ✗, squash
   – 🛗 🖭 🚗 🅿. 🖭. 🖭 AE ⓞ VISA   CX **u**
   M 6.00/12.00 **t.** and a la carte 🍴 3.00 – **138 rm** 🛏 33.00/74.00 **st.** – SB (except July, August and
   Bank Holidays) 56.00/58.00 **st.**

🏨 **Livermead House** (Best Western), Sea Front, TQ2 6QJ, ℰ 24361, Telex 42918, ≤, 🏊 heated,
   ☞, ✗, squash – 🛗 🖭 🅿. 🖭. 🖭 AE ⓞ VISA 🕹   BZ **e**
   M 5.50/8.75 **st.** and a la carte 🍴 3.10 – **69 rm** 🛏 17.50/56.00 **st.** – SB (except Christmas)
   47.00/66.50 **st.**

🏨 **Livermead Cliff** (Best Western), Sea Front, TQ2 6RQ, ℰ 22881, Telex 42918, ≤, 🏊 heated,
   ✗, ✗, squash – 🛗 🖭 🅿. 🖭. 🖭 AE ⓞ VISA 🕹   BX **r**
   M 5.50/8.75 **st.** and a la carte 🍴 3.10 – **64 rm** 🛏 17.50/58.00 **st.** – SB (except Christmas)
   47.00/66.50 **st.**

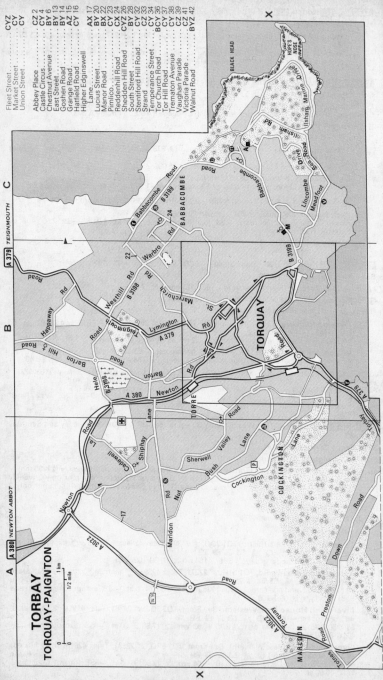

Fleet Street	CYZ
Market Street	CY
Union Street	CY
Abbey Place	CZ 2
Castle Circus	CY 4
Chestnut Avenue	BY 6
East Street	BY 13
Goshen Road	BY 14
Grange Road	AZ 15
Hatfield Road	CY 16
Higher Edginswell	
Lane	AX 17
Lucius Street	BY 20
Manor Road	BX 22
Pimlico	CY 23
Reddenhill Road	CX 24
Shedden Hill Road	CYZ 26
South Street	BY 28
Steniford Hill Road	CY 32
Strand	CZ 33
Temperance Street	CY 34
Tor Church Road	BCY 36
Tor Hill Road	CY 37
Trematon Avenue	CY 38
Vaughan Parade	CZ 39
Victoria Parade	CZ 41
Walnut Road	BYZ 42

TORBAY
TORQUAY-PAIGNTON

BLACK HEAD

442

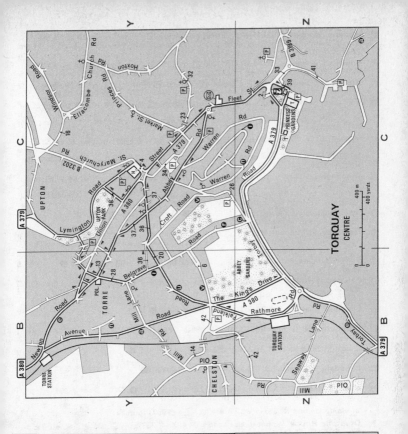

TORQUAY CENTRE

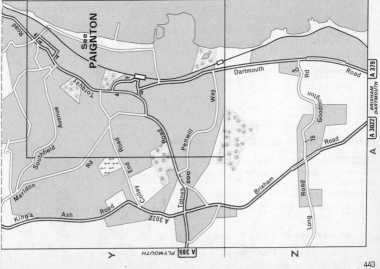

See PAIGNTON

🏨 **Homers,** Warren Rd, TQ2 5TN, ℰ 213456, ≼ Torbay – 📺 ⌿wc ⌿wc ☎. ⊠ AE ⓪ VISA
closed 5 January-15 February – **M** (lunch by arrangement) 6.95/12.50 t. ⓵ 3.85 – **14 rm**
⌷ 31.00/72.00 t. – SB (weekdays only) 52.00/76.00 st.
CZ **n**

🏨 **Toorak,** Chestnut Av., TQ2 5JS, ℰ 211866, ⤒ heated, ⋞, ⋇ – 📺 ⌿wc ℗ ⚲. ⊠ VISA
M 5.30/8.95 t. ⓵ 1.95 – **41 rm** ⌷ 19.00/75.00 t. – SB (October-May) 38.00/51.00 st.
BY **v**

🏨 **Kistor,** Belgrave Rd, TQ2 5HF, ℰ 23219, ⊠, ⋞ – ⮹ 📺 ⌿wc ℗. ⊠ AE ⓪ VISA
M (buffet lunch)/dinner 8.50 st. ⓵ 2.40 – **52 rm** ⌷ 19.00/51.00 st. – SB 44.00/60.00 st.
CY **r**

🏨 **Belgrave,** Seafront, Belgrave Rd, TQ2 5HE, ℰ 28566, ⤒ heated, ⋞ – ⮹ ⌿ rest 📺 ⌿wc
⚄ ℗. ⚲. ⊠ AE ⓪ VISA
CZ **c**
M (bar lunch)/dinner 7.50 t. – **54 rm** ⌷ 20.00/54.00 t. – SB (weekends only) (October-May)
44.00/50.00 st.

🏨 **Nepaul,** 27 Croft Rd, TQ2 5UD, ℰ 28457, ≼, ⊠, ⋞, ⋇ – ⮹ 📺 ⌿wc ⌿wc ⚄ ℗. ⊠ AE ⓪
VISA
CY **v**
M 5.50/9.50 st. and a la carte ⓵ 3.50 – **41 rm** ⌷ 17.50/58.00 st. – SB (October-May)
42.00/48.00 st.

🏨 **Gleneagles,** Asheldon Rd, Wellswood, TQ1 2QS, ℰ 23637, ≼, ⤒ heated, ⋞ – ⌿wc ℗.
AE ⓪ VISA
CX **n**
Easter-October – **M** (bar lunch)/dinner 8.50 t. ⓵ 2.90 – **40 rm** ⌷ 19.00/48.00 t. – SB
(November-Easter) 44.00/50.00 st.

🏨 Glenorleigh, 26 Cleveland Rd, TQ2 5BE, ℰ 22135, ⤒ heated, ⋞ – ⌿wc ℗. ⋇
closed Christmas – **16 rm** ⌷ 11.50/30.00 st.
BY **n**

🏨 **Nethway,** Falkland Rd, TQ2 5JR, ℰ 27630, ⤒ heated, ⋞ – ⌿wc ⌿wc ℗. VISA
BY **u**
Easter-Christmas – **M** (bar lunch)/dinner 6.75 t. and a la carte ⓵ 2.25 – **26 rm** ⌷ 13.50/35.10 t.
– SB (except summer) 35.00 st.

☎ Brigantine Motor, 56 Marldon Rd, Shiphay, ℰ 631162, ⤒, ⋞ – 📺 ⌿wc ⌿wc ℗
16 rm.
AX **s**

⌂ **Fairmount House** ⋟, Herbert Rd, Chelston, TQ2 6RW, ℰ 605446, ⋞ – ⌿wc ⌿wc ℗. AE
VISA
AX **a**
March-October – **7 rm** ⌷ 10.50/27.00 t.

⌂ Clevedon, Meadfoot Sea Rd, TQ1 2LQ, ℰ 24260, ⋞ – ℗. ⋇
16 rm.
CX **v**

⌂ **Cranborne,** 58 Belgrave Rd, TQ2 5HY, ℰ 28046 – ⌿wc ⌿. ⊠ VISA. ⋇
closed Christmas-New Year – **15 rm** ⌷ 7.50/25.00 st.
BY **i**

⌂ Concorde, 26 Newton Rd, TQ2 5BZ, ℰ 22330, ⤒ heated – ⌿ ℗
16 rm.
BY **e**

⌂ **Elmsdale,** 70 Avenue Rd, TQ2 5LF, ℰ 25929 – ⌿wc ℗. VISA
7 rm ⌷ 7.00/16.00 s.
BY **a**

⌂ **Mount Nessing,** St. Lukes Rd North, TQ2 5PD, ℰ 22970 – ℗. ⋇
Easter-October and Christmas – **13 rm** ⌷ 7.25/22.00 t.
CZ **i**

at Maidencombe N : 3 ½ m. on A 379 – BX – ✉ ✆ 0803 Torquay :

🏨 **Orestone House** ⋟, Rockhouse Lane, TQ1 4SX, ℰ 38099, ≼, ⤒ heated, ⋞ – 📺 ⌿wc
⌿wc ℗. ⊠ AE ⓪. ⋇
closed January and February – **M** (bar lunch)/dinner 9.25 t. and a la carte ⓵ 3.00 – **20 rm**
⌷ 19.00/43.00 t. – SB (October-June) 49.50/53.00 st.

at Babbacombe NE : 1 ½ m. – ✉ ✆ 0803 Torquay :

🏨 **Norcliffe,** 7 Babbacombe Downs Rd, TQ1 3LF, ℰ 38456, ≼, ⋞ – 📺 ⌿wc ⌿ ℗. ⊠ VISA
March-October – **M** (bar lunch)/dinner 6.50 t. ⓵ 1.70 – **22 rm** ⌷ 11.00/44.00 t. – SB
23.60/44.00 st.
CX **r**

XX **Green Mantle,** 135 Babbacombe Rd, TQ1 3SR, ℰ 34292 – AE ⓪ VISA
CX **a**
closed Monday in winter, Sunday and first 2 weeks November – **M** (dinner only) 11.75 t. and a
la carte ⓵ 2.40.

AUDI, VW Torwood St. ℰ 28635
AUSTIN-ROVER, JAGUAR Lawes Bridge ℰ 62781
CITROEN Walnut Rd ℰ 605858
FORD Lawes Bridge, Newton Rd ℰ 62021

PEUGEOT-TALBOT 141 Newton Rd ℰ 63626
ROLLS ROYCE-BENTLEY, FERRARI, LOTUS, SAAB
Lisburne Sq. ℰ 24321
VAUXHALL Brunswick Sq., Torre ℰ 22287

TOTLAND BAY I.O.W. 403 404 P 31 – see Wight (Isle of).

TOTNES Devon 403 I 32 The West Country G. – pop. 6,133 – ECD : Thursday – ✆ 0803.
See : Site★★ – St. Mary's Church★ – Butterwalk★ – Castle (≼★★★) AC.
🛈 The Plains ℰ 863168 (summer only).
◆London 224 – Exeter 24 – ◆Plymouth 23 – Torquay 9.

🏨 **Royal Seven Stars,** The Plains, TQ9 5DD, ℰ 862125 – 📺 ⌿wc ℗. ⊠ ⓪ VISA
M 6.00 t. (lunch) and a la carte 6.40/11.75 t. – **18 rm** ⌷ 22.50/40.00 t. – SB (weekends only)
45.00/65.00 st.

XX **Elbow Room,** 6 North St., TQ9 5NZ, ℰ 863480 – AE VISA
closed Saturday lunch, dinner Monday and Tuesday, Sunday, 2 weeks February, 2 weeks
November and 26-30 December – **M** 8.20/9.50 t. and a la carte ⓵ 2.60.

at Stoke Gabriel SE : 4 m. by A 385 – ✉ Totnes – ✆ 080 428 Stoke Gabriel :

🏨 **Gabriel Court** ॐ, TQ9 6SF, ✆ 206, ⅃ heated, 🐎, ✕ – ⇔wc �𝄢wc **Ⓟ**. 🔼 AE ⓪ VISA
closed February – **M** 7.50/12.00 st. ⋀ 3.30 – **24 rm** ⚊ 22.00/44.00 st.

at Dartington NW : 2 m. by A 385 – ✉ ✆ 0803 Totnes :

🛏 Cott Inn, TQ9 6HE, ✆ 863777 – **Ⓟ**. 🔼 AE ⓪ VISA
6 rm ⚊ 17.50/35.00 t. – SB 47.00 st.

AUSTIN-ROVER Station Rd ✆ 862404   VAUXHALL-OPEL The Plains ✆ 862247
FORD   North St. ✆ 862196

TOTON Notts. 402 403 404 Q 25 – see Nottingham.

TOWCESTER Northants. 403 404 R 27 – pop. 5 ,010 – ✆ 0327.
🏌 Woodlands, Farthingstone ✆ 36291, W : 6 m. M 1 junction 16.
♦London 70 – ♦Birmingham 50 – Northampton 9 – ♦Oxford 36.

🛏 **Brave Old Oak,** Watling St. East, NN12 7BT, ✆ 50533 – 📺 ⟦⟧ ☏ **Ⓟ**. 🔼 AE ⓪ VISA
M 5.00/9.95 t. – **12 rm** ⚊ 19.00/42.40 t.

🛏 Saracen's Head, 219 Watling St. West, NN12 7BX, ✆ 50414 – **Ⓟ** – **12 rm**.

AUSTIN-ROVER Quinbury End ✆ 0327 (Blakesley) 860208

TRALLWNG = Welshpool.

TREBETHERICK Cornwall 403 F 32 – ECD : Wednesday – ✉ Wadebridge – ✆ 020 886.
♦London 286 – Newquay 22 – ♦Plymouth 46 – Truro 32.

🏨 **Bodare** ॐ, Daymer Lane, PL27 6SA, ✆ 3210, 🐎 – ⇔wc ⟦⟧wc **Ⓟ**. 🔼 VISA
April-October – **M** (buffet lunch)/dinner 8.00 st. – **19 rm** ⚊ 13.00/32.00 s. – SB (April-June)
(except Bank Holidays) 34.00 **st.**

TREDETHY Cornwall – see Bodmin.

TREFALDWYN = Montgomery.

TREFDRAETH = Newport (Dyfed).

TREFFYNNON = Holywell.

TREFYNWY = Monmouth.

TREGREHAN Cornwall 403 F 32 – see St. Austell.

TRESCO Cornwall 403 ㉚ – see Scilly (Isles of).

TREYARNON BAY Cornwall 403 E 32 – see Padstow.

TRING Herts. 404 S 28 – pop. 10 ,610 – ECD : Wednesday – ✆ 044 282.
See : Church of St. Peter and St. Paul (interior : stone corbels★).
♦London 38 – Aylesbury 7 – Luton 14.

🏨 **Rose and Crown,** High St., HP23 5AH, ✆ 4071 – 📺 ⇔wc ☏ **Ⓟ**. 🏌 🔼 AE ⓪ VISA
M a la carte 5.55/11.50 t. – **28 rm** ⚊ 37.00/45.00 t. – SB (weekends only) 50.00/80.00 st.

HONDA, RELIANT 110 Western Rd ✆ 4144

TROTTON West Sussex – see Midhurst.

TROUTBECK Cumbria 402 L 20 – see Windermere.

TROUTBECK Cumbria – ✉ Penrith – ✆ 059 683 Threlkeld.
♦London 306 – ♦Carlisle 30 – Kendal 28 – Keswick 9.

🛏 **Lane Head Farm,** NW : 1 m. on A 66, CA11 0SY, ✆ 220, 🐎 – ⟦⟧wc **Ⓟ**. ✕
March-October – **9 rm** ⚊ 12.00/26.00 **st.**

TROWBRIDGE Wilts. 403 404 N 30 The West Country G. – pop. 27 ,299 – ECD : Wednesday –
✆ 022 14 – Envir. : Norton St. Philip (The George Inn★★), W : 6 m. – Steeple Ashton★, The
Green★, E : 7 m. – Edington (St. Mary, St. Catherine and All Saints Church★), SE : 8 m.
♦London 115 – ♦Bristol 27 – ♦Southampton 55 – Swindon 32.

🏨 **Hilbury Court,** Hilperton Rd, BA14 7JW, ✆ 2949, 🐎 – 📺 ⇔wc **Ⓟ**. 🔼 VISA. ✕
closed 24 December-1 January – **M** *(closed dinner Friday, Saturday, Sunday and Bank Holidays)*
(bar lunch)/dinner 7.50 t. ⋀ 2.80 – **12 rm** ⚊ 20.00/24.00 t.

TRURO Cornwall **403** E 33 The West Country G. – pop. 17,852 – ECD : Thursday – ☎ 0872.

See : Cornwall County Museum★ *AC* – Envir. : Trewithen★★★, NE : 7 ½ m. by A 390 – Trelissick garden★★, (<★★) *AC*, S : 8 m. by A 39 and B 3289 – at Probus★ Church Tower★ County Demonstration Garden★, NE : 8 m. – Feock (Church★), S: 8 ½ m.

🏳️ Treliske ℘ 72640, W : 2 m. on A 390 – 🅱 Municipal Building, Boscawen St. ℘ 74555.

♦London 295 – Exeter 87 – Penzance 26 – ♦Plymouth 52.

🏨 **Royal,** Lemon St., TR1 2QB, ℘ 70345 – 📺 ⇌wc ⇔ 🅿 ♨ 🔼 *VISA*
closed Christmas – **M** (closed Sunday lunch) (grill rest. only) 5.25 **st.** and a la carte 👗 2.80 – **34 rm** ⊑ 23.75/39.50 **st.** – SB (weekends only) 43.50 **st.**

🏨 **Brookdale,** Tregolls Rd, TR1 1JZ, ℘ 73513 – 📺 ⇌wc 🎬wc ⇔ 🅿 🔼 🅰🅴 *VISA*
closed 1 week at Christmas – **M** (bar lunch)/dinner 9.45 **st.** – **39 rm** ⊑ 28.75/43.70 **st.** – SB (weekends only) 58.20 **st.**

🏨 **Carlton,** 49 Falmouth Rd, TR1 2HL, ℘ 72450 – 📺 ⇌wc 🎬wc 🅿 🔼 *VISA*
closed 20 December to 6 January – **M** (dinner only) 5.35 **t.** and a la carte 👗 2.60 – **25 rm** ⊑ 18.50/29.60 **t.** – SB (weekends only)(October-May) 35.70/40.70 **st.**

at Deveron SW : 4 ½ m. by A 39 – ✉ ☎ 0872 Truro :

🏠 **Driffold** ⍰, 8 Deveron Lane, TR3 6PA, ℘ 863314, 🌳 – 🎬wc 🅿 ❊
7 rm ⊑ 10.50/34.00.

FORD Lemon Quay ℘ 73933
RENAULT Lemon Quay ℘ 74321
PEUGEOT-TALBOT Point Mills, Bissoe ℘ 0872 (Devoran) 863073

VAUXHALL Fairmantle St. ℘ 76231
VW, AUDI Three Milestone ℘ 79301

TUDWEILIOG Gwynedd **402 403** G 25 – pop. 882 – ✉ Pwllheli – ☎ 075 887.

♦London 267 – Caernarfon 25.

✕ **Dive Inn,** LL53 8PB, W : 2 m. by B 4417 ℘ 246, Seafood – 🅿
closed Sunday and Monday to Friday from November to Easter – **M** (bar lunch)/dinner 15.50 **t.** 👗 2.95.

TUNBRIDGE WELLS Kent **404** U 30 – see Royal Tunbridge Wells.

TURVEY Beds. **404** S 27 – see Bedford.

TUTBURY Staffs. **402 403 404** O 25 – pop. 5,099 (inc. Hatton) – ECD : Wednesday – ✉ ☎ 0283 Burton-upon-Trent.

♦London 132 – ♦Birmingham 33 – Derby 11 – ♦Stoke-on-Trent 27.

🏨 **Ye Olde Dog and Partridge Inn,** High St., DE13 9LS, ℘ 813030, « Part 15C timbered inn », 🌳 – 📺 ⇌wc 🎬wc ☎ 🅿 🔼 🅰🅴 *VISA*
closed 25-26 December and 1 January – **M** a la carte 9.00/15.25 **t.** 👗 3.50 – **18 rm** ⊑ 40.00/48.00 **t.**

TUXFORD Notts. **402 404** R 24 – pop. 2,547 – ECD : Wednesday – ✉ Newark – ☎ 0777.

♦London 141 – ♦Leeds 53 – Lincoln 18 – ♦Nottingham 26 – ♦Sheffield 29.

🏨 **Newcastle Arms,** Market Place, NG22 0LA, ℘ 870208 – 📺 ⇌wc 🎬wc ⇔ 🅿 ♨ 🔼 🅰🅴 ⓪ *VISA*
M 10.00/20.00 **t.** and a la carte 👗 3.50 – **12 rm** ⊑ 25.00/40.00 **t.** – SB (weekends only) 45.00/50.00 **st.**

TWEMLOW GREEN Cheshire **402 403 404** N 24 – see Holmes Chapel.

TWO BRIDGES Devon **403** I 32 The West Country G. – ✉ Yelverton – ☎ 0822 Tavistock.

♦London 226 – Exeter 25 – ♦Plymouth 17.

🏠 **Cherrybrook** ⍰, PL20 6SP, NE : 1 m. on B 3212 ℘ 88260, ≤, 🌳 – 🎬wc 🅿
closed Christmas and New Year – **7 rm** ⊑ 14.00/28.00 **st.**

TYDDEWI = St. David's.

TYNDYRN = Tintern.

TYNEMOUTH Tyne and Wear **401 402** P 18 – pop. 17,877 – ECD : Wednesday – ☎ 0632 North Shields.

See : Priory and castle : ruins★ (11C) *AC*.

♦London 290 – ♦Newcastle-upon-Tyne 8 – Sunderland 7.

🏨 **Park,** Grand Par., NE30 4JQ, ℘ 571406, ≤ – 📺 ⇌wc ⇔ 🅿 ♨ 🔼 🅰🅴 ⓪ *VISA*
closed 25, 26 and 31 December-1 January – **M** (closed Bank Holidays) 7.50/8.50 **st.** and a la carte – **27 rm** ⊑ 23.00/42.00 **st.** – SB (weekends only) 52.00 **st.**

VAUXHALL Tynemouth Rd ℘ 570346

UCKFIELD East Sussex **404** U 31 – pop. 10,938 – ECD : Wednesday – ✆ 0825.

Envir. : Sheffield Park Gardens★★ *AC*, W : 6 m.

◆London 45 – ◆Brighton 17 – Eastbourne 20 – Maidstone 34.

at Framfield SE : 1 ¾ m. on B 2102 – ✉ Uckfield – ✆ 082 582 Framfield :

✗ **Coach House,** The Street, TN22 5NL, ℰ 636, ♨ heated – **ℙ**. **AE** **⑩** **VISA**
closed Sunday dinner in winter and Monday – **M** 6.25/7.25 **t.** and a la carte § 3.95.

AUSTIN-ROVER 84/86 High St. ℰ 4255
FORD 143/145 High St. ℰ 4722
PEUGEOT-TALBOT Five Ash Down ℰ 082 581 (Buxted) 3220

RENAULT Blackboys ℰ 082 582 (Framfield) 317
VAUXHALL-OPEL Maresfield ℰ 2477

ULLSWATER Cumbria **402** L 20 – ✉ Penrith – ✆ 085 36 Pooley Bridge.

See : Lake★.

🛈 Main Car Park, Glenridding ℰ 085 32 (Glenridding) 414 (summer only) – at Pooley Bridge, Eusemere Car Park ℰ 530 (summer only).

◆London 296 – ◆Carlisle 25 – Kendal 31 – Penrith 6.

at Howtown SW : 4 m. of Pooley Bridge – ✉ Penrith – ✆ 085 36 Pooley Bridge :

🏠 **Howtown** ≫, CA10 2ND, ℰ 514, ≤, « Tastefully furnished inn », ⚟ – **ℙ**. ✾
March-October – **M** (buffet lunch Monday to Saturday)/dinner 7.25 **t.** § 2.50 – **16 rm** ⊆ (dinner included) 19.25/38.50 **t.**

at Pooley Bridge on B 5320 – ✉ Penrith – ✆ 085 36 Pooley Bridge :

🏠 **Sharrow Bay Country House** ≫, CA10 2LZ, S : 2 m. on Howtown Rd ℰ 301, ≤ lake and hills, « Lake-side setting, gardens and tasteful decor » – **TV** ➖wc ☎ **ℙ**. ✾
7 March-November – **M** 19.50/25.00 **st.** and a la carte lunch – **29 rm** ⊆ (dinner included) 60.00/160.00 **st.**, **4 suites** 130.00/160.00 **st.**

at Watermillock on A 592 – ✉ Penrith – ✆ 085 36 Pooley Bridge :

🏠🏠 **Leeming on Ullswater Country House** ≫, CA11 0JJ, on A 592 ℰ 622, Telex 64111, ≤ lake, hills and gardens, « Elegant installation and gardens », park – ☎ 🔥 **ℙ**. **AE** **⑩** **VISA**. ✾
Mid March-November – **M** (buffet lunch Monday to Saturday)/dinner 19.50 **t.** § 3.60 – ⊆ 4.50 – **25 rm** 32.00/74.00 **t.** – SB (March and November only) 92.00/103.50 **st.**

🏠 **Old Church** ≫, CA11 0JN, ℰ 204, ≤ lake and hills, « Lakeside setting », ⋙, ⚟ – ➖wc **ℙ**
21 March-2 November – **M** (bar lunch residents only)/dinner 12.00 **st.** § 4.00 – **11 rm** ⊆ 20.00/50.00 **st.**

ULVERSTON Cumbria **402** K 21 – pop. 11,976 – ECD : Wednesday – ✆ 0229.

Envir. : Furness Abbey★ (ruins 13C-15C) *AC*, SW : 6 ½ m.

🛈 Barrow, Rakesmoor, Hawcoat ℰ 0229 (Barrow-in-Furness) 25444, SW : 7 m. – 🛈 Furness, Walney Island ℰ 0229 (Barrow-in-Furness) 41232 – 🛈 Dunnerholme, Askam-in-Furness ℰ 0229 (Barrow-in-Furness) 62675.

🛈 Renaissance Centre, 17 Fountain St. ℰ 52299.

◆London 278 – Kendal 25 – Lancaster 36.

🏠 **Lonsdale House,** 11 Daltongate, LA12 7BD, ℰ 52598, ⚟ – **TV** ➖wc 🚿wc ☎. **AE** **VISA**
closed 1 week at Christmas – **M** *(closed Sunday)* (bar lunch)/dinner 10.00 **st.** § 2.50 – **23 rm** ⊆ 23.00/39.10 **st.**

at Spark Bridge N : 5 ½ m. by A 590 off A 5092 – ✉ Ulverston – ✆ 0229 85 Lowick Bridge :

🏠 **Bridgefield House** ≫, LA12 8DA, NW : 1 m. on Nibthwaite Rd ℰ 239, ⚟ – ➖wc **ℙ**. **AE** **⑩**
M (dinner only)(booking essential) 15.00 **t.** – **5 rm** ⊆ 15.00/43.00 **t.**

at Lowick Green NE : 5 m. by A 590 on A 5092 – ✉ Ulverston – ✆ 022 986 Greenodd :

🏠 **Farmers Arms,** LA12 8DT, ℰ 376 – **TV** ➖wc 🚿wc **ℙ**. **AE** **VISA**
M *(closed Saturday lunch)* a la carte 6.55/10.25 **t.** § 2.90 – **11 rm** ⊆ 14.00/32.00 **t.**

at Baycliff S : 5 m. on A 5087 – ✉ Ulverston – ✆ 022 988 Bardsea :

🏠 **Fisherman's Arms,** Coast Rd, LA12 9RJ, ℰ 387 – **TV** ➖wc **ℙ**. **AE** **⑩** **VISA**
M a la carte 9.05/12.25 **st.** § 2.75 – **12 rm** ⊆ 18.50/37.00 **st.** – SB (weekends only) 40.00/46.00 **st.**

FORD Argyle St. ℰ 53209

UMBERLEIGH Devon **403** I 31 – ✆ 0769 High Bickington.

◆London 215 – Exeter 33 – ◆Plymouth 59 – Taunton 47.

🏠 **Rising Sun,** EX37 9DU, ℰ 60447, ⋙ – ➖wc **ℙ**. **AE** **⑩** **VISA**
March-September – **M** (bar lunch Monday to Saturday)/dinner 9.00 **t.** § 2.60 – **8 rm** ⊆ 17.00/36.00 **t.**

UNDERBARROW Cumbria **402** L 21 – see Kendal.

UPLYME Devon 408 L 31 – see Lyme Regis.

UPPER ODDINGTON Glos. – see Stow-on-the-Wold.

UPPER SLAUGHTER Glos. 408 404 O 28 – see Stow-on-the-Wold.

UPPINGHAM Leics. 404 R 26 – pop. 2 ,761 – ECD : Thursday – ❸ 0572.
Envir. : Kirkby Hall★ (ruins 16 C), SE : 8 m.
♦London 101 – ♦Leicester 19 – Northampton 28 – ♦Nottingham 35.

 ☏ Central, 16 High St. West, LE15 9QD, ℰ 822352, ☞ – 📺 ⇔wc
    15 rm.

 ✗ **Lake Isle** with rm, 16 High St. East, LE15 9PZ, ℰ 822951, ☞ – 📺 ⇔wc �𝄫wc ⇐, ▩ 𝔸𝔼
    ⓞ 𝑉𝐼𝑆𝐴
    closed Sunday dinner and Monday – **M** 6.95/13.50 **t.** ▮ 2.90 – **5 rm** ⊆ 18.00/30.00 **st.** – SB
    46.00/51.00 **st.**

   at Lyddington SE : 2 m. by A 6003 – ✉ Oakham – ❸ 0572 Uppingham :

 🏛 **Marquess of Exeter** ⏧, 52 Main St., LE17 9PT, ℰ 822477 – 📺 ⇔wc �𝄫wc ☎ ⓟ. ▩ 𝔸𝔼
    ⓞ 𝑉𝐼𝑆𝐴. ⌘
    M (closed Sunday dinner to non-residents) 5.50 **st.** (lunch) and a la carte 9.55/15.70 **st.** ▮ 3.00
    – **15 rm** ⊆ 31.00/39.00 **t.**

UPTON ST. LEONARDS Glos. – see Gloucester.

UPTON UPON SEVERN Heref. and Worc. 408 404 N 27 – pop. 1 ,537 – ECD : Thursday –
❸ 068 46.
🗿 The Pepperpot, Church St. ℰ 068 45 (Malvern) 4200.
♦London 116 – Hereford 25 – Stratford-upon-Avon 29 – Worcester 11.

 🏛 **White Lion,** High St., WR8 0HJ, ℰ 2551 – 📺 ⇔wc 🕾 ⓟ. ▩ 𝑉𝐼𝑆𝐴
    M (closed Christmas Day) 9.30 **t.** and a la carte ▮ 3.10 – **10 rm** ⊆ 31.00/45.00 **t.** – SB 52.50 **st.**

 ⌂ **Pool House,** Hanley Rd, WR8 0PA, NW : ½ m. on B 4211 ℰ 2151, ≤, ⌘, ☞ – ⇔wc ⓟ. ▩
    𝔸𝔼. ⌘
    closed December and January – **9 rm** ⊆ 14.00/32.00 **st.**

USK (BRYNBUGA) Gwent 408 L 28 – pop. 1 ,783 – ECD : Wednesday – ❸ 029 13.
See : Valley★.
🛇 at Pontypool ℰ 049 55 (Pontypool) 3655, W : 7 m.
♦London 144 – ♦Bristol 30 – Gloucester 39 – Newport 10.

 🏛 **Glen-yr-Afon House,** Pontypool Rd, NP5 1SY, ℰ 2302, ☞ – �𝄫wc ⓟ
    M 7.50/8.50 **st.** and a la carte ▮ 3.50 – **15 rm** ⊆ 19.00/28.00 **t.** – SB (weekends only) (mid
    September-May) 43.00/45.00 **st.**

   at Llangybi S : 2 ½ m. on Llangybi rd – ✉ Usk – ❸ 063 349 Tredunnock :

 🏛 **Cwrt Bleddyn,** NP5 1PG, S : 1 m. ℰ 521, ☞ – 📺 ⇔wc ☎ ⓟ. ⚘. ▩ 𝔸𝔼 ⓞ 𝑉𝐼𝑆𝐴. ⌘
    M (closed Saturday lunch and Sunday dinner) a la carte 15.45/22.70 **t.** ▮ 4.95 – **8 rm**
    ⊆ 45.00/59.50 **t.**

AUSTIN-ROVER ℰ 2136   AUSTIN-ROVER ℰ 2014

UTTOXETER Staffs. 402 408 404 O 25 – pop. 10 ,008 – ECD : Thursday – ❸ 088 93.
Envir. : Alton Towers (gardens★★) AC NW : 7 ½ m.
🛇 Wood Lane ℰ 4884.
♦London 145 – ♦Birmingham 33 – Derby 19 – Stafford 13 – ♦Stoke-on-Trent 16.

 🏛 **White Hart,** Carter St., ST14 8EU, ℰ 2437 – ⇔wc ⟦𝄫⟧wc 🕾 ⓟ. ▩ 𝔸𝔼 ⓞ 𝑉𝐼𝑆𝐴. ⌘
    M a la carte 5.90/8.75 **t.** ▮ 2.75 – **24 rm** ⊆ 24.85/37.30 **st.** – SB (weekends only) 30.00/35.00 **st.**

FIAT Smithfield Rd ℰ 3838   PEUGEOT-TALBOT Market St. ℰ 2858
FORD, VAUXHALL Derby Rd ℰ 2301

VELINDRE (FELINDRE FARCHOG) Dyfed 408 F 27 – see Newport (Dyfed).

VENN OTTERY Devon 408 K 31 – ✉ ❸ 040 481 Ottery St. Mary.
♦London 209 – Exeter 11 – Sidmouth 5.

 ⌂ **Venn Ottery Barton** ⏧, EX11 1RZ, ℰ 2733, ⌘, ☞ – ⇔wc ⟦𝄫⟧wc ⓟ. ▩ 𝑉𝐼𝑆𝐴
    13 rm ⊆ 14.00/36.00 **t.**

VENTNOR I.O.W. 408 404 Q 32 – see Wight (Isle of).

448

VERYAN Cornwall 🔲🔲🔲 F 33 The West Country G. – pop. 880 – ⊠ 🔮 0872 Truro.
See : Site★★.
♦London 291 – St. Austell 13 – Truro 13.

🏛 **Nare** ⤸, Carne Beach, TR2 5PF, SW : 1 ¼ m. ℰ 501279, ≤ Carne Bay, ⌇ heated, ✿, ℁ –
　　🖵wc 🚿wc 🅿. 🛁. 🖭 🆎 🆅🆂🅰. ✄
　　M (bar lunch)/dinner 11.00 **st.** ⌗ 2.20 – **37 rm** ⌂ 16.50/58.00 **st.**

🏛 **Elerkey House,** TR2 5QA, ℰ 501261, ✿ – 🖵wc 🚿 🖭 🆅🆂🅰. ✄
　　March-October – **M** (bar lunch)/dinner 9.50 **st.** and a la carte ⌗ 2.80 – **9 rm** ⌂ 12.00/22.00 **st.**
　　– SB 40.15/49.70 **st.**

✕ **Treverbyn House,** with rm, Pendower Rd, TR2 5QL, ℰ 501201 – 🅿. ✄
　　March-October – **M** (dinner only) 10.00 ⌗ 2.80 – **4 rm** ⌂ (dinner included) 22.00/44.00.

　　at Ruan High Lanes W : 1 ¼ m. on A 3078 – ⊠ 🔮 0872 Truro :

🏛 **Polsue Manor** ⤸, TR2 5LU, ℰ 501270, ≤, ✿ – 🖵wc 🅿. 🖭 🆅🆂🅰.
　　M (bar lunch)/dinner 8.50 **st.** ⌗ 2.40 – **13 rm** ⌂ 18.95/39.90 **st.** – SB (except July and August)
　　43.00/49.00 **st.**

🏛 **Hundred House,** TR2 5JR, ℰ 501336, ✿ – 🖵 🖵wc 🚿wc 🅿. 🖭 🆎 🆅🆂🅰.
　　closed 1 to 20 December and 3 to 31 January – **M** (bar lunch)/dinner 9.50 **st.** ⌗ 2.30 – **10 rm**
　　⌂ 13.50/37.00 **st.** – SB (except Christmas-New Year) 37.00/54.00 **st.**

WADDESDON Bucks. 🔲🔲🔲 R 28 – pop. 1,644 – ECD : Thursday – 🔮 029 665.
See : Waddesdon Manor (Rothschild Collection★★★) *AC*.
♦London 52 – Aylesbury 6 – ♦Birmingham 66 – ♦Oxford 25.

　　Hotels see : **Aylesbury** E : 5 m.

WADHURST East Sussex 🔲🔲🔲 U 30 – pop. 3,643 – ECD : Wednesday – 🔮 0580 Ticehurst.
♦ London 44 – Hastings 21 – Maidstone 24 – Royal Tunbridge Wells 6.

🏛 **Spindlewood** ⤸, Wallcrouch, TN5 7JG, SE : 2 ¼ m. on B 2099 ℰ 200430, ≤, « Country
　　house atmosphere », ✿, ℁ – 🖭 🖵wc 🕿 🅿. 🖭 🆎 🆅🆂🅰. ✄
　　closed Christmas – **M** 10.00 **t.** and a la carte ⌗ 2.75 – **9 rm** ⌂ 29.00/60.00 **t.** – SB (October-June)
　　60.00/75.00 **st.**

WAKEFIELD West Yorks. 🔲🔲🔲 P 22 – pop. 74,764 – ECD : Wednesday – 🔮 0924.
Envir. : Pontefract (castle★ : ruins 12C-13C) *AC*, E : 9 m.
🏌 Woodthorpe ℰ 255104, S : 3 m. – 🏌 Painthorpe House, Painthorpe Lane ℰ 255083, near junction
39 on M 1.
🛈 Town Hall, Wood St. ℰ 370211 ext 7021/2 and 370700 (evenings and weekends).
♦London 188 – ♦Leeds 9 – ♦Manchester 38 – ♦Sheffield 23.

🏛🏛 **Cedar Court,** Denby Dale Rd., Calder Grove, WF4 3QZ, SW : 3 m. on A 636 ℰ 276310, Telex
　　557647 – 🛗 ▤ rest 🖭 🕿 🅿. 🛁. 🖭 🆎 🅾 🆅🆂🅰. ✄
　　restricted Christmas-New Year – **M** 8.95/9.95 **t.** and a la carte ⌗ 5.00 – **100 rm**
　　⌂ 49.50/59.50 **st.**, **5 suites** 65.00/90.00 **st.** – SB (weekends only) 100.00 **st.**

🏛 **Post House** (T.H.F.), Queen's Drive, Ossett, WF5 9BE, W : 2 ½ m. on A 638 ℰ 276388, Telex
　　55407 – 🛗 🖭 🖵wc 🚿 🅿. 🛁. 🖭 🆎 🆅🆂🅰.
　　M 4.60/8.75 **st.** and a la carte ⌗ 2.70 – ⌂ 5.50 – **96 rm** 43.00/50.50 **st.**

🏛 **Swallow** (Swallow), Queen St., WF1 1JU, ℰ 372111 – 🛗 🖭 🖵wc 🚿wc ⊚ 🅿. 🛁. 🖭 🆎
　　🅾 🆅🆂🅰.
　　M 6.50/8.75 **st.** and a la carte ⌗ 3.75 – **64 rm** ⌂ 38.00/52.00 **st.** – SB 45.00 **st.**

AUSTIN-ROVER　Ings Rd ℰ 370100
AUSTIN-ROVER　509　Leeds　Rd　ℰ　0532　(Leeds)
822254
BMW　Ings Rd ℰ 363796
FIAT,　CITROEN,　PEUGEOT-TALBOT　Ings　Rd　ℰ
376771

FORD　Barnsley Rd ℰ 370551
NISSAN　Barnsley Rd ℰ 255904
TOYOTA　Stanley Rd ℰ 373493
VAUXHALL-OPEL　Westgate ℰ 366261
VW-AUDI　Ings Rd ℰ 375588

WALBERSWICK Suffolk 🔲🔲🔲 Y 27 – pop. 435 – ECD : Wednesday – ⊠ 🔮 0502 Southwold.
♦London 106 – Great Yarmouth 28 – ♦Ipswich 33 – ♦Norwich 32.

🏛 **Anchor,** Main St., IP18 6UA, ℰ 722112, ✿ – 🖭 🖵wc 🅿. 🖭 🆎 🅾 🆅🆂🅰.
　　M (bar lunch)/dinner 8.00 **t.** ⌗ 3.00 – **14 rm** ⌂ 18.20/39.00 **t.** – SB (November-May)(except
　　Bank Holidays) 34.00/40.00 **st.**

WALBERTON West Sussex – see Arundel.

WALFORD Heref. and Worc. – see Ross-on-Wye.

WALL Northumb. 🔲🔲🔲 🔲🔲🔲 N 18 – see Hexham.

WALLASEY Merseyside 🔲🔲🔲 🔲🔲🔲 K 23 – pop. 62,465 – 🔮 051 Liverpool.
🏌 Warren, Grove Rd ℰ 639 5730.
⛴ to Liverpool (Merseyside Transport) frequent services daily (7-8 mn).
♦ London 226 – Birkenhead 3.5 – ♦ Liverpool 4.

WALLINGFORD Oxon. 🆔🆔🆔 Q 29 – pop. 9,041 – ECD : Wednesday – ✪ 0491.
🅱 9 St. Martin's St. ✆ 35351 ext. 3810.
♦London 54 – ♦Oxford 12 – Reading 16.

🏠 **George**, 66 High St., OX10 0BS, ✆ 36665 – 📺 🛏wc 🚿wc 🅿. 🔺 🆔 ⓪ 𝑽𝑺𝑨
   M 7.25/8.95 t. and a la carte ⌂ 3.00 – **18 rm** ⌷ 30.50/48.50 t. – SB (weekends only) 48.00 **st.**

🏠 **Shillingford Bridge**, OX10 8LZ, N : 2 m. on A 329 ✆ 086 732 (Warborough) 8567, Telex
   837763, 🛏 heated, 🔌, 🚗 – 📺 🛏wc 🚿wc 🅿. 🔺 🆔 ⓪ 𝑽𝑺𝑨 ✂
   closed 25 and 26 December – **M** 8.50 t. and a la carte – **31 rm** ⌷ 35.00/50.00 t.

✕ **Brown and Boswell**, 28 High St., OX10 0BU, ✆ 34078 – 🆔 🆔 ⓪ 𝑽𝑺𝑨
   closed Tuesday lunch, Monday, last 2 weeks March, 1 week October and Bank Holidays – **M**
   14.00 t. and a la carte 11.45/15.15 t.

   at North Stoke S : 2 ¾ m. by A 4130 and A 4074 on B 4009 – ✉ ✪ 0491 Wallingford :

🏠 **Springs** ⚲, Wallingford Rd, OX9 6BE, ✆ 36687, Telex 849794, ≼, 🛏 heated, 🚗, ✕ – 📺 ☎
   🅿. 🔺 🆔 🆔 ⓪ 𝑽𝑺𝑨
   M 12.00/16.00 t. and a la carte ⌂ 4.00 – **28 rm** ⌷ 52.00/95.00 t. – SB (weekends only) (except
   June) 95.00/120.00 **st.**

WALLSEND Tyne and Wear 🆔🆔 P 18 – see Newcastle-upon-Tyne.

WALMLEY West Midlands 🆔🆔 O 26 – see Birmingham.

WALSALL West Midlands 🆔🆔 O 26 – pop. 177,923 – ECD : Thursday – ✪ 0922.
🅱 Calderfields, Aldridge Rd ✆ 32243, N : 1 m. CT.
♦London 126 – ♦Birmingham 9 – ♦Coventry 29 – Shrewsbury 36.

Plan of enlarged area : see Birmingham pp. 2 and 3

🏠 **Crest** (Crest), Birmingham Rd, WS5 3AB, SE : 1 ½ m. on A 34 ✆ 33555, Telex 335479 – 🚿
   ▤ rest 📺 🛏wc 🚿 ⚘ 🅿. 🔺 🆔 🆔 ⓪ 𝑽𝑺𝑨   CT e
   M approx 11.50 **st.** – ⌷ 5.75 – **101 rm** 43.50/53.50 – SB (weekends only) 51.00 **st.**

   at Walsall Wood NE : 3 ½ m. on A 461 – CT – ✉ Walsall – ✪ 0543 Brownhills :

🏠 **Barons Court** (Best Western), Lichfield Rd, WS9 9AH, ✆ 376543, Telex 333061 – 🚿 📺
   🛏wc 🚿 🅿. 🔺 🆔 🆔 ⓪ 𝑽𝑺𝑨 ✂
   M (closed Saturday lunch) 8.95/9.95 t. and a la carte ⌂ 3.00 – **76 rm** ⌷ 32.00/44.00 t. – SB
   (weekends only) 42.00/46.00 **st.**

CITROEN Ward St. ✆ 32911
FORD Wolverhampton St. ✆ 21212
LADA 152 Green Lane ✆ 645347
RENAULT Day St. ✆ 613232
SAAB West Bromwich Rd ✆ 22695

TALBOT, RELIANT Charlotte St. ✆ 21723
TOYOTA Lichfield Rd, Willenhall ✆ 0922 (Bloxwich)
76484
VAUXHALL-OPEL Broadway ✆ 614336

WALSGRAVE ON SOWE West Midlands – see Coventry.

WANSFORD Cambs. 🆔 S 26 – see Peterborough.

WANTAGE Oxon. 🆔🆔 P 29 – pop. 9,708 – ECD : Thursday – ✪ 023 57.
Envir. : White Horse ≼★.
♦London 75 – ♦Bristol 58 – ♦Oxford 15 – Reading 25.

🏠 **Bear**, Market Pl., OX12 8AB, ✆ 66366, Telex 41363 – 📺 🛏wc 🚿wc 🚗. 🔺 🆔 ⓪ 𝑽𝑺𝑨
   M 6.85 **st.** (lunch) and a la carte 7.25/13.55 **st.** ⌂ 3.25 – **25 rm** ⌷ 31.50/53.00 **st.** – SB (weekends
   only) 46.00/49.95 **st.**

AUSTIN-ROVER Wallingford St. ✆ 3355
PEUGEOT-TALBOT, SAAB East Hanney ✆ 023 587
(West Hanney) 257

VW, AUDI Grove Rd ✆ 65511

WARE Herts. 🆔 T 28 – pop. 15,344 – ECD : Thursday – ✪ 0920.
♦London 24 – ♦Cambridge 30 – Luton 22.

🏠 **Ware Moat House** (Q.M.H.), Baldock St., SG12 9DR, N : ½ m. on A 1170 ✆ 5011 – 🚿 📺
   🛏wc 🚿wc 🅿. 🔺 🆔 🆔 ⓪ 𝑽𝑺𝑨
   M 8.00/8.50 **st.** and a la carte – **50 rm** ⌷ 37.50/49.00 **st.**

WAREHAM Dorset 🆔🆔 N 31 The West Country G. – pop. 2,771 – ECD : Wednesday –
✪ 092 95.
See : Site★ – St. Martin's Church★★.
Envir. : Blue Pool★AC, S : 3 m. on A 351 – Smedmore★AC, S : 7 m. by A 351 – Bovington : Tank
Museum★AC, W : 7 m. on A 352 – Lulworth Cove★, SW : 11 m. by A 352.
♦London 123 – Bournemouth 13 – Weymouth 19.

🏛 **Priory** ⚓, Church Green, BH20 4ND, ℰ 2772, « Tastefully renovated part 16C priory with gardens », ⬇ – 📺 ⬛wc ⎰wc 🕿 🅿. 🔊 🗚 ⓞ 𝘝𝘐𝘚𝘈 🕏
M 6.95/12.50 **t.** and a la carte ⓘ 2.75 – **15 rm** ⪢ 28.00/100.00 **t.**

🏛 **Kemps Country House,** East Stoke, BH20 6AL, W : 2 ¾ m. on A 352 ℰ 0929 (Bindon Abbey) 462563, 🌇 – 📺 ⬛wc ⎰wc 🅿. 🔊 🗚 ⓞ 𝘝𝘐𝘚𝘈. 🕏
closed 14 December-2 January – **M** 5.00/10.00 **t.** and a la carte – **9 rm** ⪢ 22.00/40.00 **t.** – SB 52.00/55.00 **st.**

🏛 **Worgret Manor,** Worgret Rd, BH20 6AB, W : 1 m. on A 352 ℰ 2957, 🌇 – 📺 ⎰wc 🅿. 🔊 🗚 ⓞ
closed 25 to 27 December – **M** 4.95/7.50 **t.** and a la carte ⓘ 2.95 – **9 rm** ⪢ 20.00/40.00 **t.** – SB (October-June) 42.00/50.00 **st.**

at Stoborough S : ½ m. on A 351 – ✉ ✪ 092 95 Wareham :

🏛 **Springfield Country,** Grange Rd, BH20 5AL, ℰ 2177, ⩣ heated, 🌇, 🕏 – 📺 ⬛wc 🅿. 🔊 🗚 𝘝𝘐𝘚𝘈
M (bar lunch)/dinner 8.50 **t.** and a la carte ⓘ 2.55 – **30 rm** ⪢ 26.50/61.00 **t.**

WARMINSTER Wilts. **403 404** N 30 The West Country G. – pop. 14,826 – ECD : Wednesday – ✪ 0985.

Envir. : Westbury Hill (White Horse★, ≼★) N : 6 m. – Bratton Castle (≼★★), NE : 6 m.

🖪 Library, Three Horseshoes Mall ℰ 216047.

♦London 111 – ♦Bristol 29 – Exeter 74 – ♦Southampton 47.

🏛 **Bishopstrow House** ⚓, Boreham Rd, BA12 9HH, SE : 1 ½ m. on A 36 ℰ 212312, ≼, « Tastefully furnished country house », ⩣ heated, 🔲, ⚓, 🌇, park, 🕏 – 📺 🕿 🅿. 🔊 🗚 ⓞ 𝘝𝘐𝘚𝘈. 🕏
M 15.50/19.50 **st.** ⓘ 4.00 – ⪢ 5.00 – **25 rm** 50.00/125.00 **st.**, **6 suites** 125.00/240.00 **st.**

🏛 **Old Bell,** 42 Market Pl., BA12 9AN, ℰ 216611 – 📺 ⬛wc 🅿. 🔊 🗚 ⓞ 𝘝𝘐𝘚𝘈
M (grill rest. only) a la carte 5.50/9.80 ⓘ 2.75 – **16 rm** ⪢ 24.00/35.00 **t.**

✗ **La Petite Cuisine Belge at Vincents,** 60-62 East St., BA12 9BW, ℰ 215052 – 🔊 🗚 ⓞ 𝘝𝘐𝘚𝘈
closed Monday lunch, Good Friday dinner, Sunday and 2 weeks at Christmas – **M** 5.40/12.50 **st.** and a la carte ⓘ 3.45.

at Corton SE : 5 ¼ m. by A 36 and B 3095 – ✉ ✪ 0985 Warminster :

✗ **Dove at Corton,** BA12 0SZ, ℰ 50378, 🌇 – 🔊 𝘝𝘐𝘚𝘈
closed Sunday dinner, Monday except Bank Holidays and 5 to 19 January – **M** a la carte 8.60/11.55 **t.** ⓘ 2.25.

AUSTIN-ROVER George St. ℰ 212808

WARREN ROW Berks – see Knowl Hill.

WARRINGTON Cheshire **402 403 404** M 23 – pop. 81,366 – ECD : Thursday – ✪ 0925.

See : St. Elphin's Church (chancel★ 14C).

🖪 Hill Warren ℰ 61775, S : 3 m. – 🖪 Walton Hall, Warrington Rd ℰ 630619, S : 2 m. – 🖪 Kelvin Close, Birchwood ℰ 0925 (Padgate) 818819.

🖪 80 Sankey St. ℰ 36501 and 35961 ext.90/91.

♦London 195 – Chester 20 – ♦Liverpool 18 – ♦Manchester 21 – Preston 28.

🏛 **Patten Arms,** Parker St. (Bank Quay Station), WA1 1LS, ℰ 36602 – 📺 ⬛wc ⎰wc 🕿 🅿. 🔊 🗚 ⓞ 𝘝𝘐𝘚𝘈
closed 24 to 26 December – **M** (closed Bank Holiday lunch and Sunday) 5.00/6.00 **st.** and a la carte ⓘ 3.10 – **43 rm** ⪢ 30.00/40.00 **st.**

🏛 **Birchdale** ⚓, Birchdale Rd, Stockton Heath, WA4 5AW, S : 1 ¾ m. by A 49 ℰ 63662, 🌇 – 🅿
closed 24 December-2 January – **M** (closed Saturday, Sunday and Bank Holidays) (dinner only) 7.00 **st.** ⓘ 2.50 – **21 rm** ⪢ 17.00/26.00 **st.**

at Grappenhall SE : 2 m. by A 50 – ✉ ✪ 0925 Warrington :

🏛 **Fir Grove,** Knutsford Old Rd, WA4 2LD, ℰ 67471, Telex 628117 – 📺 ⬛wc 🕿 🅿. 🔊 🗚 ⓞ 𝘝𝘐𝘚𝘈. 🕏
M 8.00 **st.** and a la carte ⓘ 2.60 – **38 rm** ⪢ 30.00/36.00 **st.** – SB (weekends only) 50.00 **st.**

at Stretton S : 3 ½ m. by A 49 on B 5356 – ✉ Warrington – ✪ 092 573 Norcott Brook :

🏛 **Old Vicarage,** Stretton Rd, WA4 4NS, ℰ 238, 🌇, 🕏 – 📺 ⬛wc ⎰wc 🅿. 🔊 𝘝𝘐𝘚𝘈
closed Bank Holidays – **M** 7.00/8.50 **st.** ⓘ 3.35 – **36 rm** ⪢ 18.50/40.00 **st.** – SB (weekends only) 60.20/65.60 **st.**

AUSTIN-ROVER Winwick St. ℰ 50011
BMW Farrell St. ℰ 35987
CITROEN 194/196 Knutsford Rd ℰ 68444

FORD Winwick Rd ℰ 51111
RENAULT Farrell St. ℰ 30448
VW, AUDI 101 Knutsford Rd ℰ 65265

See : Castle★★ (14C) *AC* Y – St. Mary's Church★ 12C-18C Y **A** – Lord Leycester's Hospital★ Y **B**.

🛐 The Racecourse 🖉 494316 Y.

🚩 The Court House, Jury St. 🖉 492212.

♦London 96 – ♦Birmingham 20 – ♦Coventry 11 – ♦Oxford 43.

WARWICK
ROYAL
LEAMINGTON SPA

High Street .... Y 19
Jury Street .... Y
Market Place .... Y 27
Smith Street .... Y
Swan Street .... Y 46

Birmingham Road .... Z 6
Bowling Green Street .... Y 7
Brook Street .... Y 9
Butts (The) .... Y 12
Castle Hill .... Y 13
Church Street .... Y 15
Lakin Road .... Y 23
Linen Street .... Y 25
North Rock .... Y 33
Old Square .... Y 34
Old Warwick Road .... Z 36
Radford Road .... Z 38
St. John's Road .... Y 42
St. Nicholas Church Street . Y 44
Theatre Street .... Y 48
West Street .... Y 50

*Les plans de villes
sont disposés le Nord en haut.*

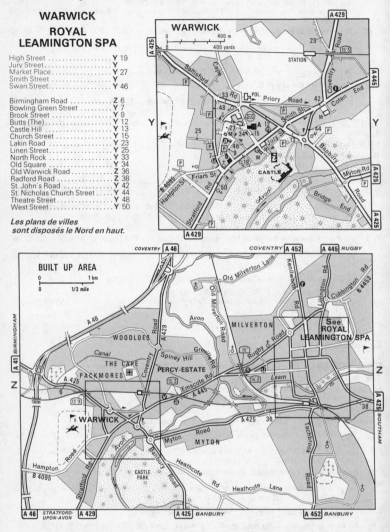

🏛 **Lord Leycester**, 17-19 Jury St., CV34 4EJ, 🖉 491481 – 📺 🛏wc 🚻wc ☎ 🅿 ⚐ 🔺 AE ⓞ
   VISA
   M 5.75/9.00 t. and a la carte – **47 rm** ⛒ 30.00/45.00 t. – SB 46.00 st.   Y n

🏨 **Woolpack**, Market Pl., CV34 4SD, 🖉 496191 – 📺 🛏wc 🚻wc ☎ 🔺 AE ⓞ VISA   Y a
   M (carving rest.) 4.95 t. 🍷 2.45 – **29 rm** ⛒ 17.00/36.00 t.

🏠 **Cambridge Villa**, 20a Emscote Rd, CV34 4PL, 🖉 491169 – 📺 🅿 🛇   Z a
   closed Christmas – **12 rm** ⛒ 10.00/40.00.

🏠 **Avon**, 7 Emscote Rd, CV34 4PH, 🖉 491367, 🌿 – 🅿 🛇   Z v
   7 rm ⛒ 9.00/18.00 t.

XXX **Westgate Arms** with rm, 3 Old Bowling Green St., CV34 4DD, ℰ 492362, English rest., ⌱
– 📺 ⌱wc ☎ 🅿. 🔼 AE ⓄI VISA. ⌱   Y u
closed Sunday and Bank Holiday Mondays – **M** 8.75/13.95 **st.** and a la carte – ⌱ 6.50 – **10 rm**
37.50/47.50.

XX **Randolph's,** 19-21 Coten End, CV34 4NT, ℰ 491292 – 🔼 VISA   Y i
closed Sunday and 1 week at Christmas – **M** (dinner only) (booking essential) a la carte
approx. 16.40 **t.** ⌱ 2.75.

XX **Aylesford,** 1 High St., CV34 4AP, ℰ 492799, Italian rest. – 🔼 AE ⓄI VISA   Y e
closed Monday dinner, Sunday, last 3 weeks in July, 1 week at Christmas and Bank Holidays –
M 7.00 **st.** (lunch) and a la carte 9.80/20.45 **st.** ⌱ 4.00.

at Barford S : 4 ½ m. on A 429 – Z – ✉ 🕸 0926 Warwick :

🏠 **Glebe** ⌱, Church St., CV35 8BS, on B 4462 ℰ 624218, ⌱ – 📺 ⌱wc ⌱wc ☎ 🅿. 🔼 AE ⓄI
VISA.
closed 2 to 11 January – **M** 8.50/9.75 **t.** and a la carte ⌱ 2.50 – **12 rm** ⌱ 26.00/50.00 **t.** – SB
(weekends only)(except Easter) 52.50/62.50 **st.**

at Longbridge SW : 2 m. on A 429 – Z – ✉ 🕸 0926 Warwick :

🏛 Ladbroke Mercury (Ladbroke), CV34 6RE, junction of A 429, A 46 and A 41 ℰ 499555, 🔼 – ⌱
📺 ⌱wc ☎ 🅿. ⌱. ⌱ – **127 rm. 1 suite**.

FIAT Wharf St. ℰ 496231   VOLVO Millers Rd ℰ 491377
PORSCHE Birmingham Rd ℰ 491731

WASDALE HEAD Cumbria 🔢 K 20 – see Gosforth.

WASHINGTON Tyne and Wear 🔢 🔢 P 19 – pop. 48,856 – ECD : Wednesday – ✉ 🕸 091
Tyneside.
♦London 278 – Durham 13 – ♦Middlesbrough 32 – ♦Newcastle-upon-Tyne 7.

🏛 **George Washington** (Best Western), Stone Cellar Rd, District 12, NE37 1PH, ℰ 417 2626,
Telex 537143, 🔼, ⌱, squash – 📺 ⌱wc ☎ 🅿. ⌱. 🔼 AE ⓄI VISA
M (buffet lunch)/dinner 10.95 **st.** and a la carte ⌱ 2.75 – ⌱ 5.75 – **70 rm** 39.50/46.00 **st.**

🏛 **Post House** (T.H.F.), Emerson, District 5, NE37 1LB, Junction A 1 (M) and A 195 ℰ 416 2264,
Telex 537574 – ⌱ 📺 ⌱wc ☎ 🅿. ⌱. 🔼 AE ⓄI VISA
M 6.95/9.95 **st.** and a la carte ⌱ 2.70 – ⌱ 5.50 – **138 rm** 37.00/45.00 **st.**

FORD Parsons Rd ℰ 4167700

WATCHET Somerset 🔢 J 30 The West Country G. – pop. 3,055 – ECD : Wednesday – 🕸 0984.
Envir. : Cleeve Abbey★★*AC*, SW : 2 m. – ♦London 180 – ♦Bristol 57 – Taunton 18.

🏠 **Downfield,** 16 St. Decumans Rd, TA23 0HR, ℰ 31267, ⌱ – 📺 ⌱wc ⌱wc 🔼 AE ⓄI
VISA
M 10.00 **st.** (dinner) and a la carte 10.00/13.00 **st.** ⌱ 2.75 – **6 rm** ⌱ 31.00/42.00 **st.** – SB
44.00/46.00 **st.**

WATERGATE BAY Cornwall 🔢 E 32 – ✉ Newquay – 🕸 0637 St. Mawgan.
♦London 293 – Newquay 2 – Padstow 8.

🏠 **Tregurrian,** TR8 4AB, ℰ 860280, ⌱ heated – ⌱wc 🅿
May-September – **M** (bar lunch)/dinner 5.25 **st.** ⌱ 2.25 – **28 rm** ⌱ 10.50/36.00 **st.** – SB
25.00/42.00 **st.**

WATERHEAD Cumbria 🔢 L 20 – see Ambleside.

WATERHOUSES Staffs. 🔢 🔢 🔢 O 24 – pop. 1,018 – ✉ Stoke-on-Trent – 🕸 053 86.
♦London 115 – ♦Birmingham 63 – Derby 23 – ♦Manchester 39 – ♦Stoke-on-Trent 17.

XX **Old Beams,** Leek Rd, ST10 3HW, ℰ 254, ⌱ – 🅿. 🔼 AE ⓄI VISA
closed Sunday, Monday and first 2 weeks in January – **M** 8.50 **t.** (lunch) and a la carte
13.10/16.95 **t.** ⌱ 3.60.

WATERMILLOCK Cumbria 🔢 L 20 – see Ullswater.

WATFORD Herts. 🔢 S 29 – pop. 109,503 – ECD : Wednesday – 🕸 0923.
♦London 21 – Aylesbury 23.

Plan : see Greater London (North-West)

🏛 Ladbroke (Ladbroke), Elton Way, WD2 8HA, Watford By-Pass E : 3 ½ m. on A 41 at junction A
4008 ℰ 35881, Telex 923422 – ⌱ 📺 ☎ 🅿. ⌱. ⌱ – **155 rm**.   BU e

AUSTIN-ROVER Pinner Rd ℰ 28680   PEUGEOT-TALBOT Aldenham ℰ 092 76 (Radlett)
HONDA, MERCEDES-BENZ High Rd at Bushey   2177
Heath ℰ 01 (London) 950 3311   VAUXHALL-OPEL 6/10 High Rd at Bushey Heath ℰ
OPEL 6/10 High Rd at Bushey Heath ℰ 01 (London) 01 (London) 950 6146
950 6146   VAUXHALL-OPEL 329 St. Albans Rd ℰ 31716

453

WATH-IN-NIDDERDALE North Yorks. – see Pateley Bridge.

WDIG (GOODWICK) Dyfed – see Fishguard.

WEEDON BEC Northants. **403 404** Q 27 – pop. 2 ,361 – ECD : Wednesday – ✉ Northampton – ✆ 0327.

♦London 74 – ♦Birmingham 54 – ♦Leicester 39 – ♦Oxford 40 – Northampton 8.5.

   🏨 **Crossroads** (Best Western), High St., NN7 4PX, at junction A 5 and A 45 ℰ 40354, Telex 312311 – 📺 🚿wc 🅿 🅰 🔼 AE ⑩ VISA ⋘
   closed 25 and 26 December – **M** a la carte 9.50/12.40 **st.** ▯ 2.95 – **28 rm** ⊊ 36.00/52.00 **st.** – SB (weekends only) 44.50 **st.**

WELLAND Heref. and Worc. **403 404** N 27 – see Great Malvern.

WELLESBOURNE Warw. **403 404** P 27 – see Statford-upon-Avon.

WELLINGBOROUGH Northants. **404** R 27 – pop. 38 ,598 – ECD : Thursday – ✆ 0933.

♦London 73 – ♦Cambridge 43 – ♦Leicester 34 – Northampton 10.

   🏨 **Hind** (Q.M.H.), Sheep St., NN8 1BY, ℰ 222827 – 📺 🚿wc 🅿 🅰 🔼 AE ⑩ VISA
   M 5.95/8.25 **st.** and a la carte ▯ 2.70 – **32 rm** ⊊ 34.50/43.70 **st.** – SB (weekends only) 50.00/52.00 **st.**

   ↑ **High View,** 156 Midland Rd, NN8 1NG, ℰ 78733 – 📺 🚿wc 🅿 🔼 AE ⑩ VISA
   16 rm ⊊ 15.00/29.00 **t.**

AUSTIN-ROVER Finedon Rd ℰ 76651   VAUXHALL-OPEL Oxford St. ℰ 223252
SKODA Talbot Rd ℰ 223924

WELLINGTON HEATH Heref. and Worc. – see Ledbury.

WELLS Somerset **403 404** M 30 **The West Country G.** – pop. 9 ,252 – ECD : Wednesday – ✆ 0749.

See : Site★★★ – Cathedral★★★ – Vicar's Close★ – Bishop's Palace★AC (≼★★ of east end of cathedral).

Envir. : Wookey Hole★★AC (Cáves ★, Papermill★, Fairground collection ★), NW : 2 m.

🔟 East Horrington Rd ℰ 72868.

🛈 Town Hall, Market Sq. ℰ 72552.

♦London 132 – ♦Bristol 20 – ♦Southampton 68 – Taunton 28.

   🏨 **Swan** (Best Western), Sadler St., BA5 2RX, ℰ 78877, Telex 449658 – 📺 🚿wc ⚏wc ☎ 🅿 🅰 🔼 AE ⑩ VISA
   M 6.95/11.50 **st.** ▯ 2.75 – **26 rm** ⊊ 30.00/45.00 **st.** – SB (weekends only) 49.50/65.00 **st.**

   🏨 **Crown,** Market Pl., BA5 2RP, ℰ 73457 – 📺 🚿wc ⚏wc 🅰 🔼 AE ⑩ VISA
   M 7.50/11.50 **t.** and a la carte ▯ 3.25 – **15 rm** ⊊ 28.00/45.00 **t.** – SB (except Christmas and Bank Holidays) 56.00 **st.**

   🏨 **Star,** The High St., BA5 2SQ, ℰ 73055 – 📺 🚿wc. 🔼 AE ⑩ VISA
   M (bar lunch)/dinner 6.95 **t.** and a la carte ▯ 2.00 – **16 rm** ⊊ 20.70/34.50 **t.**

   at Worth W : 2 ¾ m. by A 371 on B 3139 – ✉ ✆ 0749 Wells :

   🏤 **Worth House,** BA5 1LW, ℰ 72041, 🐴 – 🚿wc 🅿 ⋘
   March-November – **M** (lunch by arrangement)/dinner 6.00 **t.** and a la carte ▯ 2.50 – **8 rm** ⊊ 19.00/30.00 **t.** – SB (except May-September) 40.00/48.00 **st.**

AUSTIN-ROVER-DAIMLER-JAGUAR, LAND ROVER-   VAUXHALL-OPEL Priory Rd ℰ 73834
RANGE ROVER Glastonbury Rd ℰ 72626

WELLS-NEXT-THE-SEA Norfolk **404** V 25 – pop. 2 ,337 – ECD : Thursday – ✆ 0328 Fakenham.

Envir. : Holkam Hall★★ (18C) AC, W : 3 m.

♦London 121 – King's Lynn 31 – ♦Norwich 36.

   ↑ **Mill House,** Northfield Lane, NR23 1JZ, ℰ 710739, 🐴 – 🅿 ⋘
   closed December – **7 rm** ⊊ 10.00/18.00.

WELSHPOOL (TRALLWNG) Powys **402 403** K 26 – pop. 4 ,869 – ECD : Thursday – ✆ 0938.

🔟 Golfa Hill ℰ 093 883 (Castle Caereinion) 249.

🛈 Vicarage Garden Car Park ℰ 2043.

♦London 182 – ♦Birmingham 64 – Chester 45 – Shrewsbury 19.

   🏤 **Royal Oak,** The Cross, SY21 7RF, ℰ 2217 – 📺 🚿wc ⚏wc 🅿 🔼 AE VISA ⋘
   M 5.75/8.50 **st.** and a la carte ▯ 2.75 – **25 rm** ⊊ 18.50/37.00 **st.** – SB (weekends only except Bank Holidays) (October-April) 40.00 **st.**

AUSTIN-ROVER Union St. ℰ 3152   PEUGEOT-TALBOT ℰ 069 181 (Llansantffraid) 283
FORD Salop Rd ℰ 2391   PEUGEOT-TALBOT Forden ℰ 093 876 (Forden) 203
HONDA ℰ 3503   VAUXHALL-OPEL Newtown Rd ℰ 4444

WELWYN Herts. 404 T 28 – pop. 9,961 (inc. Codicote) – ECD : Wednesday – ✆ 043 871.
♦London 30 – Bedford 31 – ♦Cambridge 32.

   🏠 **Heath Lodge,** Danesbury Park Rd, AL6 9SL, NE : 1 ¼ m. by B 197 ✆ 7064, Telex 827618, 🐎, park – 📺 🚻wc ☎ 🅿, 🔊 🆎 ⓪ 𝗩𝗜𝗦𝗔
      M *(closed Saturday lunch)* 15.00 **t.** and a la carte 🍷 4.50 – ⧉ 2.95 – **28 rm** 34.50/43.70 **t.**

COLT 54 Great North Rd ✆ 5911   FORD By Pass Rd ✆ 6123

WELWYN GARDEN CITY Herts. 404 T 28 – pop. 40,665 – ECD : Wednesday – ✆ 070 73 Welwyn Garden.

🛦 Panshanger ✆ 33350.
🛈 The Campus ✆ 31212.
♦London 28 – Bedford 34 – ♦Cambridge 34.

   🏠 **Crest** (Crest), Homestead Lane, AL7 4LX, ✆ 24336, Telex 261523, 🐎 – 🛗 📺 🚻wc ☎ 🅿.
     🔊, 🆎 ⓪ 𝗩𝗜𝗦𝗔 ❀
      M *(carving lunch)* approx 11.50 **st.** – ⧉ 5.75 – **58 rm** 45.00/54.50 **st.** – SB (weekends only) 51.00 **st.**

AUSTIN-ROVER Stanborough Rd ✆ 35131   RENAULT Great North Rd ✆ 070 72 (Hatfield) 64567

WENTBRIDGE West Yorks. 402 404 Q 23 – ✉ ✆ 0977 Pontefract.
♦London 183 – ♦Leeds 19 – ♦Nottingham 55 – ♦Sheffield 28.

   🏠 **Wentbridge House,** Great North Rd, WF8 3JJ, ✆ 620444, 🐎 – 📺 🚻wc 🚻wc ☎ 🅿. 🔊.
     🔊 🆎 ⓪ 𝗩𝗜𝗦𝗔 ❀
     closed Christmas Day – **M** 9.00 **st.** (lunch) and a la carte 13.95/18.60 **st.** 🍷 4.25 – ⧉ 3.25 – **20 rm** 22.00/53.00 **st.**

   at Barnsdale Bar S : 2 m. on A 1 – ✉ ✆ 0977 Pontefract :

   🏚 Doncaster Travelodge (T.H.F.) without rest., Trunk Rd, WF8 3JB, on A 1 ✆ 620711, Telex 557457 – 📺 🚻wc 🅿
     70 rm.

WEOBLEY Heref. and Worc. 403 L 27 – pop. 1,080 – ECD : Wednesday – ✉ Hereford – ✆ 054 45.
♦London 145 – Brecon 30 – Hereford 12 – Leominster 9.

   🏚 Red Lion, Broad St., HR4 8SE, ✆ 220 – 📺 🚻wc 🚻wc ☎ 🅿
     7 rm.

WEST BAY Dorset 403 L 31 – see Bridport.

WEST BEXINGTON Dorset – see Bridport.

WEST BRIDGFORD Notts. 403 404 Q 25 – see Nottingham.

WEST BROMWICH West Midlands 403 404 O 26 – see Birmingham.

WEST CHILTINGTON West Sussex 404 S 31 – pop. 2,044 – ECD : Wednesday and Thursday – ✉ Pulborough – ✆ 079 83.
♦London 50 – ♦Brighton 22 – Worthing 12.

   🏠 **Roundabout** (Best Western), Monkmead Lane, RH20 2PF, S : 1 ¼ m. ✆ 3838, 🐎 – 📺 🚻wc 🚻wc ☎ 🅿. 🔊. 🔊 🆎 ⓪ 𝗩𝗜𝗦𝗔
     M 7.90/9.95 **st.** and a la carte 🍷 3.10 – **20 rm** ⧉ 30.75/49.75 **st.** – SB 54.00/79.00 **st.**

WEST CLANDON Surrey – see Guildford.

WEST COKER Somerset 403 404 M 31 – see Yeovil.

WESTERHAM Kent 404 U 30 – pop. 3,392 – ECD : Wednesday – ✆ 0959.
Envir. : Chartwell★ (Sir Winston Churchill's country home, Museum) *AC*, S : 2 m.
♦London 24 – ♦Brighton 45 – Maidstone 22.

   🏠 Kings Arms, Market Sq., TN16 1AH, ✆ 62990 – 📺 🚻wc ☎ 🅿. 🔊 🆎 ⓪ 𝗩𝗜𝗦𝗔 ❀
     M 8.90 **t.** and a la carte – **12 rm.**

   XXX **Montmorency,** Quebec Sq., TN16 1AN, on A 25 ✆ 62139, 🐎 – 🅿. 🔊 🆎 ⓪ 𝗩𝗜𝗦𝗔
     closed Sunday dinner – **M** 8.50/9.50 **st.** and a la carte.

ALFA-ROMEO London Rd ✆ 64333   RENAULT London Rd ✆ 64001
AUSTIN-ROVER High St. ✆ 62212   VW, AUDI London Rd ✆ 64333

WEST HUNTSPILL Somerset 403 L 30 – see Bridgwater.

WEST LULWORTH Dorset 403 404 N 32 – pop. 910 – ECD : Wednesday – ✉ Wareham – ✆ 092 941.

See : Lulworth Cove★.

♦London 129 – Bournemouth 21 – Dorchester 17 – Weymouth 19.

　🏠　**Mill House,** BH20 5RQ, ✆ 404, 🚗 – 🖐wc 🖐wc. 🔼 AE ⓞ VISA
　　M 3.95/6.95 t. and a la carte ⓘ 2.85 – **10 rm** ⏲ 15.00/26.00 t. – SB (October-June except Bank Holidays) 34.00/38.00 st.

　🏠　**Cromwell House,** Main Rd, BH20 5RJ, ✆ 253, ≼, 🔼, 🚗 – 🖭 ➚wc 🖐wc ⓟ
　　closed December – **7 rm** ⏲ 12.00/29.00 st.

　🏠　Lulworth, Main Rd, BH20 5RJ, ✆ 230 – 🖭 ⓟ. 🍽 – **8 rm**.

　🏠　**Gatton House,** Main Rd, BH20 5RU, ✆ 252, 🚗 – ➚wc 🖐wc ⓟ
　　closed January and February – **9 rm** ⏲ 10.00/30.00 st.

WEST MALVERN Heref. and Worc. 403 404 M 27 – see Great Malvern.

WEST MERSEA Essex 404 W 28 – pop. 5 ,245 – ✉ Colchester – ✆ 0206.
♦ London 58 – Chelmsford 27 – Colchester 9.5.

　💥💥　**Blackwater** with rm, 20-22 Church Rd, CO5 8QH, ✆ 383338 – 🖭 🖐wc ⓟ. 🔼 AE
　　closed 7 to 21 January – **M** (closed Tuesday lunch and Sunday dinner) 7.75/14.65 t. and a la carte – **7 rm** ⏲ 16.00/35.00 t. – SB (except Christmas and Bank Holidays) 39.50/42.50 st.

WESTONBIRT Glos. 403 404 N 29 – see Tetbury.

WESTON FAVELL Northants. 404 R 27 – see Northampton.

WESTON-ON-THE-GREEN Oxon. 403 404 Q 28 – pop. 479 – ✉ ✆ 0869 Bletchington.
♦London 65 – ♦Birmingham 61 – Northampton 33 – ♦Oxford 8.

　🏨　Weston Manor (Best Western) ⑤, on A 43, OX6 8QL, ✆ 50621, Telex 83409, 🔼 heated, 🚗, park, squash – 🖭 ➚wc ☎ ⓟ. 🔼 AE ⓞ VISA. 🍽
　　M (bar lunch) – **23 rm** ⏲ 42.50/80.00 s. – SB 59.50/69.50 st.

Pleasant hotels and restaurants
are shown in the Guide by a red sign.　　　🏰🏰🏰 ... 🏠
Please send us the names
of any where you have enjoyed your stay.　　🎄🎄🎄🎄🎄 ... 💥
Your Michelin Guide will be even better.

WESTON-SUPER-MARE Avon 403 K 29 The West Country G. – pop. 60 ,821 – ECD : Thursday – ✆ 0934.

See : Sea front ≼★★.

🏌 Worlebury ✆ 23214, 2 m. from station BY – 🏌 Uphill Rd North ✆ 21360 AZ.
🚩 Beach Lawns ✆ 26838.

♦London 147 – ♦Bristol 24 – Taunton 32.

Plan opposite

　🏨🏨　**Grand Atlantic** (T.H.F.), Beach Rd, BS23 1BA, ✆ 26543, ≼, 🔼 heated, 🚗, 🍽 – 📶 🖭 ⓟ.
　　🏛. 🔼 AE ⓞ VISA　　　　　　　　　　　　　　　　　　　　　　　BZ **e**
　　M 6.50/9.25 st. and a la carte ⓘ 2.70 – ⏲ 5.50 – **79 rm** 34.50/51.50 st.

　🏨　**Royal Pier,** 55-57 Birnbeck Rd, BS23 2EJ, ✆ 26644, ≼ – 📶 🖭 ➚wc ☎ ⓟ. 🏛 🔼 AE ⓞ
　　VISA. 🍽　　　　　　　　　　　　　　　　　　　　　　　　　　　　　AY **a**
　　M 4.50/9.75 t. and a la carte ⓘ 2.95 – **41 rm** ⏲ 23.50/55.00 t., **2 suites** 65.00 t. – SB (weekends only) (November-April) 49.50 st.

　🏨　**Berni Royal,** South Par., BS23 1JU, ✆ 23601, 🚗 – 📶 🖭 ➚wc ☎ ⓟ. 🏛. 🔼 AE ⓞ VISA
　　M 7.50/8.50 t. and a la carte – **36 rm** ⏲ 24.00/43.00 t. – SB (weekends only) 47.00/59.00 st.
　　　　　　　　　　　　　　　　　　　　　　　　　　　　　　　　　　BZ **a**

　🏠　**Queenswood,** Victoria Park, BS23 2HZ, ✆ 21759, ≼ – ➚wc 🖐wc. 🔼 AE ⓞ VISA　BZ **s**
　　M 6.00/8.00 t. ⓘ 2.50 – **19 rm** ⏲ 13.30/33.00 t. – SB (except Bank Holidays) 30.90/35.10 st.

　🏠　**Beachlands,** 17 Uphill Rd North, BS23 4NG, ✆ 21401, 🚗 – ➚wc 🖐wc ⓖ. 🔼 AE ⓞ VISA
　　closed January, February and Christmas – **M** (bar lunch)/dinner 6.25 t. ⓘ 2.50 – **18 rm**
　　⏲ 12.00/34.00 t. – SB (October-May) 35.00/39.00 st.　　　　　　　AZ **c**

AUSTIN-ROVER Alfred St. ✆ 21451
AUSTIN-ROVER 264 Milton Rd ✆ 25707
CITROEN Baker St. ✆ 23995
DAIHATSU, SAAB Bridgwater Rd ✆ 813012
DAIHATSU, SAAB Main Rd ✆ 0934 (Bleadon) 812546
FORD Locking Rd ✆ 28291

HONDA Bridgwater Rd ✆ 812244
PEUGEOT-TALBOT Broadway ✆ 0934 (Bleadon) 812479
RENAULT Locking Rd ✆ 414007
VAUXHALL-OPEL, BEDFORD Winterstoke Rd ✆ 417886

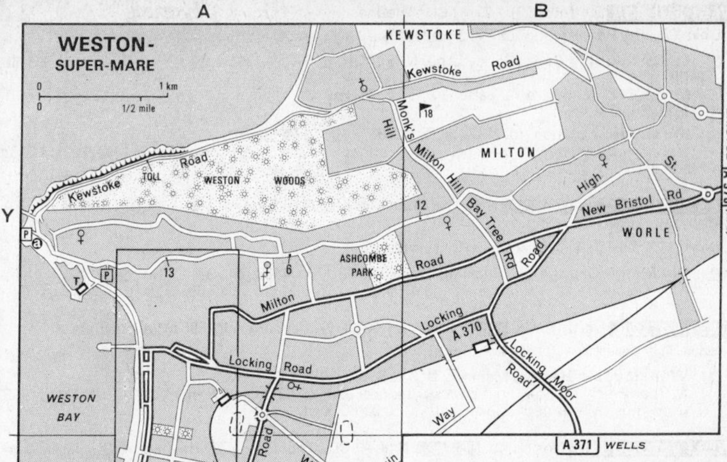
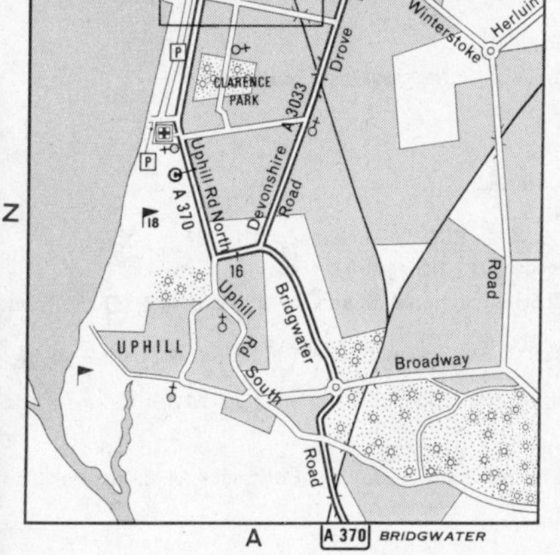

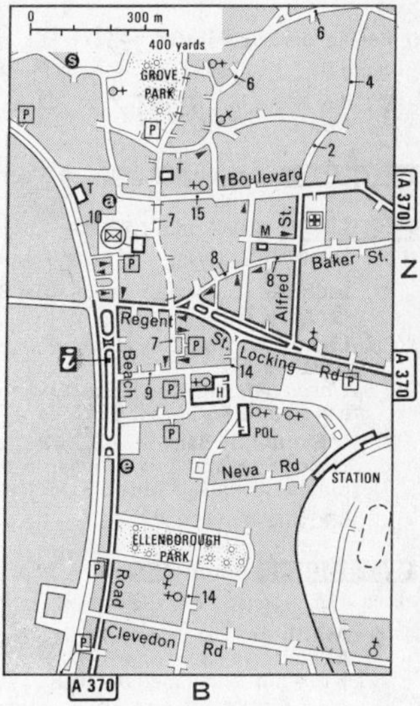

High Street	**BZ** 7	Bristol Rd Lower	**AY, BZ** 6
Oxford Street	**BZ** 9	Meadow Street	**BZ** 8
Regent Street	**BZ**	Upper Bristol Road	**BY** 12
Royal Parade	**BZ** 10	Upper Church Road	**AY** 13
		Walliscote Road	**BZ** 14
Albert Quadrant	**BZ** 2	Waterloo Street	**BZ** 15
Arundell Road	**BZ** 4	Windwhistle Road	**AZ** 16

Town plans : *roads most used by traffic and those on which guide listed hotels and restaurants stand are fully drawn ; the beginning only of lesser roads is indicated.*

WESTON TURVILLE Bucks. [404] R 28 – see Aylesbury.

WESTON-UNDER-PENYARD Heref. and Worc. [403] [404] M 28 – see Ross-on-Wye.

WESTON-UNDER-REDCASTLE Salop [402] [403] [404] M 25 – pop. 256 – ✉ Shrewsbury – ☎ 093 924 Lee Brockhurst.

⛳, ⛳ Hawkstone Park ☎ 611.

♦London 165 – Chester 31 – ♦Birmingham 48 – Shrewsbury 12 – ♦Stoke-on-Trent 25.

🏨 **Hawkstone Park** (Best Western) 🐎, SY4 5UY, ☎ 611, ≤, 🏊, ⛳, 🏌, 🌳, park, 🎾 – [TV] 🛁wc ☎ ♿ [P]. 🏋. [AE] [VISA]
M 5.50/7.75 **st.** – **59 rm** ☕ 28.00/49.50 **st.**, **1 suite** 66.00/75.00 **st.** – SB (January-March) 39.95/42.50 **st.**

WEST RUNTON Norfolk ⑭⑭ X 25 – ECD : Wednesday – ✉ Cromer – ☻ 026 375.

🔓 Links Country Park Hotel ♟ 691 – ♦London 135 – King's Lynn 42 – ♦Norwich 24.

  🏨 **Links Country Park,** Sandy Lane, NR27 9QH, ♟ 691, 🔓, 🚗 – 📺 🛏wc 🛏wc 🕿 **P.** 🔅 **AE**
    VISA
    M 6.50/9.25 **t.** and a la carte 🍷 2.95 – **34 rm** ⊏⊐ (dinner included) 24.50/69.00 **t.** – SB
    46.00/66.00 **st.**

  XX **Mirabelle,** 7 Station Rd, NR27 9QD, ♟ 396 – **P.** 🔅 **AE** ⓞ **VISA**
    closed Sunday dinner November-May, Monday and first 2 weeks November – **M** 8.00/12.00 **t.**
    and a la carte 🍷 2.60.

WESTWARD HO Devon ⑭⓪③ H 30 The West Country G. – pop. 1 ,315 – ECD : Tuesday – ✉
☻ 023 72 Bideford.

♦London 235 – Bideford 4 – Exeter 47 – ♦Plymouth 62.

  🏠 **Buckleigh Grange** 🦌, Buckleigh Rd, EX39 3PU, ♟ 74468, 🚗, ℀ – 🛏wc **P.**
    May-October – **M** (bar lunch)/dinner 6.95 **st.** 🍷 2.25 – **11 rm** ⊏⊐ 11.55/42.20 **st.**

WEST WITTON North Yorks. ⑭⓪② O 21 – pop. 338 – ✉ Leyburn – ☻ 0969 Wensleydale.

♦London 241 – Kendal 39 – ♦Leeds 60 – York 53.

  🏠 **Wensleydale Heifer,** Main St., DL8 4LS, ♟ 22322 – 📺 🛏wc 🛏wc **P.** 🔅 **AE** **VISA**
    M (bar lunch Monday to Saturday)/dinner 10.95 **t.** 🍷 3.25 – **17 rm** ⊏⊐ 20.00/40.00 **t.** – SB
    (November-May except Bank Holidays) 50.00/60.00 **st.**

WEST WOODBURN Northumb. ⑭⓪① ⑭⓪② N 18 – ECD : Thursday – ✉ Hexham – ☻ 0660 Bellingham.

🔓 Bellingham ♟ 20446, SW : 4 ½ m.

♦ London 316 – ♦ Carlisle 49 – ♦ Edinburgh 78 – Hawick 35 – ♦ Newcastle-upon-Tyne 35.

  🏠 Bay Horse Inn, NE48 2RX, ♟ 70218, 🚗 – **P.**
    4 rm ⊏⊐ 13.00/23.00 **st.**

WETHERAL Cumbria ⑭⓪① ⑭⓪② L 19 – see Carlisle.

WETHERBY West Yorks. ⑭⓪② P 22 – pop. 9 ,467 – ECD : Wednesday – ☻ 0937.

🖸 Council Offices, 24 Westgate ♟ 62706/7 – ♦London 208 – Harrogate 8 – ♦Leeds 13 – York 14.

  🏨 Ladbroke (Ladbroke), Leeds Rd, LS22 5HE, junction A 58 and A 1 ♟ 63881 – 🕻 📺 🛏wc 🕿
    P. 🏊 – **72 rm.**

  XXX **Linton Spring,** Sicklinghall Rd, LS22 9XX, W : 1 ¾ m. by A 661 ♟ 65353, 🚗, park – **P.** 🏊
    🔅 **AE** ⓞ **VISA**
    closed Saturday lunch, Sunday dinner, Monday and first week January – **M** 8.95 **t.** (lunch) and
    a la carte 12.45/16.25 **t.** 🍷 3.00.

  XX **L'Escale,** 16 Bank St., LS22 4NQ, ♟ 63613 – **P.** 🔅 **AE** ⓞ **VISA**
    closed Sunday dinner, Monday, first 2 weeks January and Bank Holidays – **M** (dinner only and
    Sunday lunch) a la carte 8.95/20.15 **t.** 🍷 3.50.

AUSTIN-ROVER North St. ♟ 62623

WEYBOURNE Norfolk ⑭⑭ X 25 – pop. 553 – ✉ Holt – ☻ 026 370.

♦London 128 – Cromer 7.5 – ♦Norwich 26.

  🏨 **Maltings,** The Street, NR25 6SY, on A 149 ♟ 275, 🚗 – 📺 🛏wc **P.** 🔅 **AE** ⓞ **VISA**
    M (buffet lunch)/dinner 12.00 **st.** and a la carte 🍷 3.00 – **21 rm** ⊏⊐ 21.00/42.00 **st.** – SB (except
    weekends in summer) 50.00/58.00 **st.**

  XX **Gasché's Swiss,** The Street, NR25 7SY, on A 149 ♟ 220 – **P.** 🔅 **AE** ⓞ **VISA**
    closed Sunday dinner and Monday – **M** approx. 6.95/14.95 **t.** and a la carte 🍷 1.70.

WEYBRIDGE Surrey ⑭⑭ S 29 – pop. 50 ,031 (inc. Walton-on-Thames) – ECD : Wednesday –
☻ 0932 – ♦London 23.

Plan : see Greater London (South-West)

  🏨 **Ship Thistle** (Thistle), Monument Green, High St., KT13 8BQ, ♟ 48364, Telex 894271 – 📺
    🛏wc 🕿 **P.** 🏊 🔅 **AE** ⓞ **VISA**   by A 3050 AZ
    M 9.25 **t.** and a la carte 🍷 3.00 – ⊏⊐ 5.25 – **39 rm** 55.00/75.00 **t.**

  XXX **Casa Romana,** 2 Temple Hall, Monument Hill, KT13 8RH, ♟ 43470, Italian rest. – **P.** 🔅 **AE**
    VISA   by A 3050 AZ
    closed Saturday lunch and Monday – **M** 8.45 **t.** (lunch) and a la carte 11.30/16.45 **t.**

  XX Gaylord, 73 Queens Rd, ♟ 42895, Indian rest.   by A 317 AZ

AUSTIN-ROVER Woodham Lane, New Haw ♟
093 23 (Byfleet) 42870
AUSTIN-ROVER 30 Queens Rd ♟ 42233
FIAT, LANCIA Brooklands Rd ♟ 093 23 (Byfleet)
52941
FORD Monument Hill ♟ 46231

RENAULT 51/59 Baker St. ♟ 48247
SAAB Spinney Hill, Addlestone ♟ 093 287 (Ottershaw) 3726
VAUXHALL-OPEL New Haw Rd ♟ 53101
VOLVO 168 Oatlands Drive ♟ 54422

WEYMOUTH Dorset **403** **404** M 32 The West Country G. – pop. 38 ,384 – ECD : Wednesday – ✆ 030 57 (5 fig.) or 0305 (6 fig.).

See : Boat Trip★ (Weymouth Bay and Portland Harbour).

Envir. : Chesil Beach★★ (from Portland★ (S : 1 ½ m.) to Abbotsbury) – at Abbotsbury★★, NW : 9 m. by B 3157 Swannery Gardens★AC, Sub Tropical Gardens★AC, St. Catherines Chapel★AC.

⚓ Shipping connections with the Continent : to France (Cherbourg) (Sealink) – to Channel Islands : St Peter Port, Guernsey (Sealink) 5-7 weekly (4 h 30 mn day 10 h night) – to Channel Islands : St. Helier, Jersey (Sealink) 5-7 weekly (5 h 45 mn-7 h 30 mn).

🛈 Pavilion Complex, The Esplanade ℘ 72444 – King's Statue, The Esplanade ℘ 785747 (summer only).

◆London 142 – Bournemouth 35 – ◆Bristol 68 – Exeter 59 – Swindon 94.

🏨 **Streamside,** 29 Preston Rd, Overcombe, DT3 6PX, NE : 2 m. on A 353 ℘ 833121, ⇲ – 📺 ⌂wc 🏧 **P.** ⚠ AE ⓞ VISA ⚘
M 5.00/8.50 **t.** and a la carte 🍷 2.50 – **15 rm** ⛭ 18.00/40.00 **t.** – SB (weekends only)(except summer) 48.00/50.00 **t.**

🏨 **Glenburn,** 42 Preston Rd, Overcombe, DT3 6PZ, NE : 2 m. on A 353 ℘ 832353 – 📺 ⌂wc 🏧wc **P.** ⚠ VISA ⚘
M 6.50/7.50 **t.** and a la carte – **13 rm** ⛭ 18.75/37.00 **t.** – SB (except summer) 46.50 **st.**

🏨 **Rex,** 29 The Esplanade, DT4 8DN, ℘ 773485 – 🛗 📺 ⌂wc 🏧wc ⚠ VISA
closed 25 and 26 December – **M** (closed lunch to non-residents) 5.00/6.00 **t.** and a la carte 🍷 3.00 – **21 rm** ⛭ 18.40/41.85 **t.** – SB 41.40/46.75 **st.**

↖ **Ellendale,** 88 Rodwell Av., DT4 8SQ, ℘ 786650 – **P.** ⚘ – **18 rm**.

FORD Dorchester Rd ℘ 782222   PEUGEOT-TALBOT 172 Dorchester Rd ℘ 786311

WHALLEY Lancs. **402** M 22 – pop. 4 ,745 – ✉ Blackburn – ✆ 025 482.

◆London 233 – ◆Blackpool 32 – Burnley 12 – ◆Manchester 28 – Preston 15.

🏨 **Mytton Fold Farm,** Whalley Rd., Langho, BB6 8AB, SW : 1 ¾ m. on A 59 ℘ 48255, ⇲ – 📺 ⌂wc 🏧wc ⚑ & **P.** ⚠ VISA ⚘
closed 24 to 31 December – **M** a la carte 7.30/13.10 **t.** 🍷 3.25 – **12 rm** ⛭ 22.00/28.00 **t.** – SB (weekends only) 40.00/50.00 **st.**

XXX **Foxfields,** Whalley Rd, Billington, BB6 9HY, SW : 1 ½ m. on A 59 ℘ 2556 – **P.** ⚠ AE ⓞ VISA
closed Saturday lunch, Monday and Bank Holidays – **M** 8.50 **t.** (lunch) and a la carte 12.25/16.50 **t.** 🍷 3.50.

WHEPSTEAD Suffolk **404** W 27 – see Bury St. Edmunds.

WHETSTONE Leics. – see Leicester.

WHIMPLE Devon **403** J 31 – see Exeter.

WHIPPINGHAM I.O.W. **403** **404** Q 31 – see Wight (Isle of).

WHITBY North Yorks. **402** S 20 – pop. 12 ,982 – ECD : Wednesday – ✆ 0947.

See : Abbey ruins★ (13C) AC, Old St. Mary's Church★ 12C, East Terrace ⩤★.

🏌 Low Straggleton ℘ 602768.

🛈 New Quay Rd ℘ 602674.

◆London 257 – ◆Middlesbrough 31 – Scarborough 21 – York 45.

🏨 **Stakesby Manor,** High Stakesby, YO21 1HL, ℘ 602773, ⇲ – 📺 ⌂wc 🏧wc **P.** ⚘
closed 2 weeks February – **M** (dinner only) 6.50 **t.** and a la carte – **8 rm** ⛭ 19.00/38.00 **t.** – SB (October-March except Christmas and New Year) 40.00 **st.**

↖ **Hudsons,** 24 Hudson St., YO21 3EP, ℘ 605277 – 📺 🏧
6 rm ⛭ 12.00/18.00 **st.**

at Sneaton S : 3 m. by A 171 on B 1416 – ✉ ✆ 0947 Whitby :

🏨 **Sneaton Hall,** YO22 5HP, ℘ 605929, ⇲ – 📺 ⌂wc 🏧wc **P.** ⓞ
Easter-November – **M** (dinner only and Sunday lunch) 10.00 **t.** 🍷 3.00 – **9 rm** ⛭ 17.00/34.00 **t.**

AUSTIN-ROVER 6 Upgang Lane ℘ 603321   RENAULT 18 Silver St. ℘ 602093
FORD Silver St. ℘ 602237   VAUXHALL Argyle Rd ℘ 602898
NISSAN Castle Park ℘ 602841

WHITCHURCH Salop **402** **403** **404** L 25 – pop. 7 ,246 – ECD : Wednesday – ✆ 0948.

🏌 Hill Valley, Terrick Rd ℘ 3584, N : 1 m.

🛈 Civic Centre, High St. ℘ 4577.

◆London 171 – ◆Birmingham 54 – Chester 22 – ◆Manchester 43 – Shrewsbury 20.

🏨 **Redbrook Hunting Lodge,** Wrexham Rd, SY13 3ET, W : 2 ½ m. on A 525 ℘ 094 873 (Red-brook Maelor) 204, ⇲ – ⌂wc 🏧wc **P.** ⚠ AE ⓞ VISA
M 7.00 **t.** and a la carte 🍷 2.00 – **11 rm** ⛭ 20.75/31.75 **t.** – SB (except Christmas and New Year) 52.25/56.55 **st.**

AUSTIN-ROVER Brownlow St. ℘ 2826   FORD Dodington ℘ 4471
AUSTIN-ROVER, LAND ROVER-RANGE ROVER   RENAULT Wrexham Rd ℘ 2257
Newport Rd ℘ 3333

WHITEBROOK Gwent – see Monmouth.

WHITFIELD Kent 404 X 30 – see Dover.

WHITLAND (HENDY-GWYN) Dyfed 403 G 28 – pop. 1,342 – ECD : Wednesday – ✆ 0994.
🛈 Canolfan Hywel Dda ℘ 240867.
♦London 235 – Carmarthen 15 – Haverfordwest 17.

  🏠 **Waungron Farm** ॐ, SA34 0QX, SW : 1 m. ℘ 240682, « Converted farm buildings », park –
      📺 ⇌wc ⚿ ⓟ. ℅
      M (booking essential) 6.95/7.50 **t.** and a la carte – **13 rm** ⊆ 18.00/35.00 **t.** – SB (spring and
      autumn) 48.00 **st.**

  ⌂ **Cilpost Farm** ॐ, SA34 4RP, N : 1 ¼ m. by North Rd ℘ 240280, ≼, ☞ – ⇌wc ⓟ. ℅
      closed winter – **7 rm** ⊆ 12.00/30.00.

WHITLEY BAY Tyne and Wear 401 402 P 18 – pop. 36,040 – ECD : Wednesday – ✆ 091 Tyne-
side.
Envir. : Seaton Delaval Hall★ (18C) *AC*, NW : 6 m.
🛈 Central Promenade, ℘ 252 4494 (summer only).
♦London 293 – ♦Newcastle-upon-Tyne 10 – Sunderland 10.

  🏠 **Ambassador,** 38-42 South Par., NE26 2RQ, ℘ 253 1218 – 📺 ⇌wc ☎ ⓟ. 🔼 ⓪ 𝘝𝘐𝘚𝘈
      closed 25 and 26 December – **M** 5.45/7.90 **t.** and a la carte ▮ 2.75 – **28 rm** ⊆ 23.00/37.00 **t.**

ALFA-ROMEO ℘ 2521848
AUSTIN-ROVER Cauldwell Lane ℘ 2522231
CITROEN Claremont Rd ℘ 2525909
FIAT Claremont Rd ℘ 2523347
FORD Whitley Rd ℘ 2531221

LADA Fox Hunters Rd ℘ 2528282
VAUXHALL Earsdon Rd, West Monkseaton ℘ 2523355
VW, AUDI Hillheads Rd ℘ 2528225

WHITSTABLE Kent 404 X 29 – pop. 26,227 – ECD : Wednesday – ✆ 0227.
Envir. : Herne Bay : Reculver (church twin towers★ *AC*), E : 8 ½ m.
🛈 1 Tankerton Rd ℘ 272233.
♦London 59 – ♦Dover 22 – Maidstone 28 – Margate 19.

  XXX **Giovanni's,** 49-55 Canterbury Rd, CT5 4HH, ℘ 273034, Italian rest. – ⓟ. 🔼 🄰🄴 ⓪ 𝘝𝘐𝘚𝘈
       closed Monday – **M** 5.50/7.50 **t.** and a la carte ▮ 2.65.

AUSTIN-ROVER Tankerton Rd ℘ 264614
COLT Swale Cliffe ℘ 0246 (Chesterfield) 2396

FORD Tankerton Rd ℘ 265613
RENAULT Tower Parade ℘ 261477

WHITTLE-LE-WOODS Lancs. 402 M 23 – see Chorley.

WHITTLESEY Cambs. 404 T 26 – see Peterborough.

WHITWELL-ON-THE-HILL North Yorks. 402 R 21 – pop. 131 – ⊠ York – ✆ 065 381.
♦London 223 – Malton 5 – York 12.

  🏨 **Whitwell Hall Country House** ॐ, YO6 7JJ, ℘ 551, Telex 57697, ≼, 🔲, ☞, park, ℁ –
      ⇌wc ⚿ ☎ ⓟ. 🔼 🔼 🄰🄴 ⓪ 𝘝𝘐𝘚𝘈
      M (lunch by arrangement) 8.00/15.00 **st.** ▮ 3.00 – **20 rm** ⊆ 30.00/66.00 **st.** – SB (November-
      April) 40.00/60.00 **st.**

WICKHAM Hants. 403 404 Q 31 – pop. 3,485 – ECD : Wednesday – ✆ 0329.
♦London 74 – ♦Portsmouth 12 – ♦Southampton 11 – Winchester 16.

  🏨 **Old House,** The Square, PO17 5JG, ℘ 833049, « Tastefully renovated Queen Anne
      house », ☞ – 📺 ⇌wc ☎ ⓟ. 🔼 🄰🄴 ⓪ 𝘝𝘐𝘚𝘈. ℅
      closed 2 weeks Easter, 17 days July-August and 2 weeks at Christmas – **M** *(closed lunch
      Saturday and Monday and Sunday)* a la carte 13.80/17.05 **st.** ▮ 3.55 – **10 rm** ⊆ 42.00/55.00 **st.**

WIDEGATES Cornwall – see Looe.

WIGAN Greater Manchester 402 404 M 23 – pop. 88,725 – ECD : Wednesday – ✆ 0942.
🏌 Haigh Hall Park ℘ 831107, NW : 3 m. – 🏌 Arley Hall, Haigh ℘ 0257 (Standish) 421360, N : 4 m. –
🏌 Pennington Recreation Area, ℘ 672823.
♦London 206 – ♦Liverpool 19 – ♦Manchester 18 – Preston 18.

  🏨 **Brocket Arms, Mesnes Rd, WN1 2DD, on A 49 ℘ 46283 – 📺 ⇌wc ☎ ⓟ. 🔼 ℅
      27 rm**

FIAT Miry Lane ℘ 39107
FORD Wallgate ℘ 41393
LADA Chapel St., Pemberton ℘ 214028
NISSAN Crompton St. ℘ 42281

RELIANT Cerrell Post ℘ 214437
VAUXHALL-OPEL Warrington Rd ℘ 494848
VOLVO Platt Bridge ℘ 866594

🚢 from East to West Cowes to Southampton (Red Funnel Services) 8-18 daily (55 mn to 1 h 10 mn) – from Yarmouth to Lymington (Sealink) 13-16 daily (30 mn) – from Fishbourne to Portsmouth (Sealink) 15-18 daily (45 mn).

🚢 From West Cowes to Southampton (Red Funnel Services : hydrofoil) Monday to Saturday 14-19 daily ; Sunday 10 daily (20 mn) – from Ryde to Southsea (Hovertravel to Southsea Clarence Pier) summer frequent services daily ; winter 8-12 daily (restricted Sundays) (9 mn) – from Ryde to Portsmouth (Sealink to Portsmouth Harbour) 15-24 daily (25-30 mn).

Bembridge – pop. 3 ,470 – ✉ ✿ 0983 Isle of Wight.
Newport 14.

🏨 **Highbury,** Lane End Rd, PO35 5SU, ✆ 872838, ⌆ heated, ☞ – 📺 ⇱wc ⋔wc ☜ 🅿 ⩗ Æ ⓪ 𝘝𝘐𝘚𝘈
closed 24 to 27 December – **M** 5.50/10.00 **st.** and a la carte ⓘ 2.85 – **9 rm** ⊠ 17.50/40.50 **st.** – SB (November-April) 44.00/49.50 **st.**

🏠 **Elms Country** ⌂, Swaines Rd, PO35 5XS, ✆ 872248, ☞ – 📺 ⇱wc ⋔wc 🅿
March-mid October – **M** (buffet lunch) – **12 rm** ⊠ 24.00/32.00 **st.**

PEUGEOT Church Rd ✆ 2121

Chale – pop. 561 – ECD : Thursday – ✉ Ventnor – ✿ 0983 Isle of Wight.
Newport 9.

🏠 **Clarendon,** Newport Rd, PO38 2HA, ✆ 730431, <, ☞ – ⇱wc ⋔wc 🅿
M 6.50 **st.** (dinner) and a la carte 4.50/6.50 **st.** ⓘ 1.65 – **13 rm** ⊠ (dinner included) 12.00/40.00 – SB (except summer) 36.00/40.00 **st.**

Cowes – pop. 16 ,371 – ECD : Wednesday – ✉ ✿ 0983 Isle of Wight.
Envir. : Osborne House★ (19C) *AC*, E : 1 m.
🏌₉ Crossfield Av. ✆ 293529.
🛈 1 Bath Rd ✆ 291914 (summer only).
Newport 4.

🏨 **Holmwood,** Egypt Point, 65 Queens Rd, PO30 8BW, ✆ 292508, < – 📺 ⇱wc ⋔wc ☜ 🅿. ⩗ Æ ⓪ 𝘝𝘐𝘚𝘈
closed November-mid January – **M** 8.50/10.25 **t.** and a la carte ⓘ 2.25 – **18 rm** ⊠ 19.50/50.00 **t.**

🏠 **Cowes,** 260 Artic Rd, PO31 7PJ, ✆ 291541, ⌆ – 📺 ⇱wc ☜ 🅿. ⩗ Æ ⓪ 𝘝𝘐𝘚𝘈
closed Christmas – **M** 8.00 and a la carte ⓘ 1.95 – **13 rm** ⊠ 21.00/31.00.

✗ **G's,** 10 Bath Rd, PO31 7QN, ✆ 297021 – ⩗ Æ ⓪ 𝘝𝘐𝘚𝘈
closed Sundays except Bank Holidays, 25 to 27 December, 1 to 3 January and February – **M** (lunch by arrangement) a la carte 7.85/15.35 **t.** ⓘ 4.20.

Freshwater Bay – pop. 5 ,073 – ECD : Thursday – ✉ ✿ 0983 Isle of Wight.
🏌₁₈ ✆ 752955.
Newport 13.

🏨 **Albion,** PO40 9RA, ✆ 753631, <, ☞ – 📺 ⇱wc ☜ 🅿. ⩗ 𝘝𝘐𝘚𝘈
April-October – **M** (bar lunch only November-March) 5.50/9.00 **st.** ⓘ 2.30 – **43 rm** ⊠ 15.00/38.00 **st.**

⌂ **Blenheim House,** Gate Lane, PO40 9QD, ✆ 752858, ⌆ heated – ⋔wc 🅿. ✗✗
May-October – **8 rm** ⊠ 13.00/26.00 **st.**

Newport – pop. 19 ,758 – ECD : Thursday – ✉ ✿ 0983 Isle of Wight.
Envir. : Shorwell (St. Peter's Church★ 15C) SW : 5 m. – Carisbrooke Castle★★ 12C-16C (keep <★) *AC* SW : 1 ½ m.
🏌₉ St. George's Down, Shide ✆ 525076, SE : 1 m.
🛈 21 High St. ✆ 524343.

🏨 **Bugle,** 117 High St., PO30 1TP, ✆ 522800 – 📺 ⇱wc ☜ 🅿. ⩙. ⩗ Æ ⓪ 𝘝𝘐𝘚𝘈
M a la carte 7.00/12.55 **st.** – **26 rm** ⊠ 34.00/45.00 **st.** – SB (weekends only) 54.00 **st.**

AUDI, MERCEDES-BENZ, VW Medina Avenue ✆ BMW Blackwater ✆ 523684
523232

Ryde – pop. 19 ,384 – ECD : Thursday – ✉ ✿ 0983 Isle of Wight.
🏌₉ Ryde House Park ✆ 62088.
🛈 Western Gardens, Esplanade ✆ 62905 (summer only).
Newport 7.5.

🏨 **Yelf's** (T.H.F.), Union St., PO33 2LG, ✆ 64062 – 📺 ⇱wc ☜. ⩙. ⩗ Æ ⓪ 𝘝𝘐𝘚𝘈
M 7.00/8.50 **st.** and a la carte ⓘ 3.00 – ⊠ 5.50 – **21 rm** 32.00/43.00 **st.**

AUSTIN-ROVER Elmfield ✆ 62717
FORD Gorfield Rd ✆ 62281
HONDA Brading Rd ✆ 64166
LANCIA Victoria St. ✆ 63661

SKODA Havenstreet ✆ 0983 (Wootton Bridge) 882455
VW, AUDI-NSU Fishbourne Lane ✆ 0983 (Wootton Bridge) 882465

Seaview – ✉ 🕙 098 371 Seaview.

🏠 **Seaview,** High St., PO34 5EX, ✆ 2711 – 🛏wc 🅿. 🗚 🖭 𝗩𝗜𝗦𝗔
M 7.50/8.50 **st.** and a la carte ≬ 2.95 – **14 rm** ☲ 18.00/38.00 **t.** – SB (except August and Bank Holidays) 40.00/50.00 **st.**

Shanklin – pop. 8 ,109 – ECD : Wednesday – ✉ 🕙 0983 Isle of Wight.
See : Old Village (thatched cottages)★ – The Chine★ *AC.*
Envir. : Brading (Roman Villa : mosaics★ *AC*) N : 3 ½ m.
🛈 67 High St. ✆ 862942.
Newport 9.

🏨 **Cliff Tops,** 1-5 Park Rd, PO37 6BB, ✆ 863262, ≤, 🏊 heated, �── – 🛗 🖭 ☎ 🅿. 🛎. 🗚 🖭 ⓞ
𝗩𝗜𝗦𝗔
closed Christmas and New Year – **M** 5.40/7.80 **st.** and a la carte ≬ 2.25 – **98 rm** ☲ 20.00/55.00 **st.**
– SB (October-May) 50.00 **st.**

🏨 **Hartland,** 41 Victoria Av., PO37 6LT, ✆ 863123, 🗚, �── – 🖭 🛏wc 🛁wc 🅿. 🛇
24 rm.

🏠 **Carlton** 🍴, Eastcliff Promenade, PO37 6AY, ✆ 862517, ≤, �── – 🛏wc 🅿. 🛇
April-October – **11 rm** ☲ 13.00/38.00 **st.** – SB (September-May) 32.00/36.00 **st.**

🏠 **Bourne Hall Country** 🍴, Luccombe Rd, PO37 6RR, ✆ 862820, 🏊 heated, 🗚, �──, 🍴 – 🖭
🛏wc 🅿. 🗚 🖭 ⓞ 𝗩𝗜𝗦𝗔. 🛇
closed January and December – **M** (bar lunch)/dinner 8.00 **t.** ≬ 2.00 – **22 rm** ☲ 17.40/46.50 **t.**
– SB 38.60/54.45 **st.**

🏠 **Queensmead,** 12 Queens Rd, PO37 6AN, ✆ 862342, 🏊 heated, �── – 🛏wc 🛁wc. 🛇
March-October – **M** (bar lunch) – **26 rm.**

🏠 **Delphi Cliff,** 7 St. Boniface Cliff Rd, PO37 6ET, ✆ 862179, ≤, �── – 🛏wc 🅿. 🛇
Easter-October – **11 rm** ☲ 10.00/27.00 **st.**

🏠 **Overstrand,** Howard Rd, PO37 6HD, ✆ 862100, ≤, 🌚, 🍴 – 🛏wc 🛁wc 🅿. 🗚. 🛇
April-September – **15 rm** ☲ 12.00/32.20 **t.**

✕ **Cottage,** 8 Eastcliff Rd, PO37 6AA, ✆ 862504 – 🗚 𝗩𝗜𝗦𝗔
closed dinner Sunday, Monday except dinner in summer, mid February-mid March and October
– **M** (restricted lunch)(booking essential) 5.50 **st.** (lunch) and a la carte 10.00/12.60 **t.**

'' Short Breaks '' (SB)
De nombreux hôtels proposent des conditions avantageuses
pour un séjour de deux nuits
comprenant la chambre, le dîner et le petit déjeuner.

Totland Bay – pop. 2 ,316 – ECD : Wednesday – ✉ 🕙 0983 Isle of Wight.
Envir. : Alum Bay (coloured sands★) and the Needles★ SW : 1 m.
Newport 13.

🏨 **Country Garden,** Church Hill, PO39 0ET, on B 3322 ✆ 754521, ≤, 🌚 – 🖭 🛏wc 🖼 🅿. 🗚
🖭 ⓞ 𝗩𝗜𝗦𝗔
closed 25 and 26 December – **M** 5.50/8.00 **st.** and a la carte ≬ 2.90 – **16 rm** ☲ 27.00/58.00 **st.**
– SB 46.00/50.00 **st.**

🏠 **Sentry Mead,** Madeira Rd, PO39 0BJ, ✆ 753212, 🌚 – 🛏wc 🅿. 🛇 – **13 rm.**

🏠 **Nodes Country** 🍴, Alum Bay, Old Road, PO39 0HZ, SW : 1 ½ m. by B 3322 ✆ 752859, 🌚 –
🛏wc 🛁wc 🅿. 🛇
March-October – **11 rm** ☲ 12.00/30.00 **t.**

Ventnor – pop. 7 ,956 – ECD : Wednesday – ✉ 🕙 0983 Isle of Wight.
Envir. : St. Catherine's Point (≤★ from the car-park) W : 5 m.
🇬 Steephill Drive Rd ✆ 853326.
🛈 34 High St. ✆ 853625 (summer only).
Newport 10.

🏨 **Ventnor Towers,** 54 Madeira Rd, PO38 1QT, ✆ 852277, ≤, 🏊 heated, 🌚, 🍴 – 🖭 🛏wc
🖼 🅿. 🗚 🖭 ⓞ 𝗩𝗜𝗦𝗔
M 6.00/9.00 **st.** and a la carte ≬ 4.50 – ☲ 5.00 – **30 rm** 19.50/29.50 **st.** – SB 49.00/53.00 **st.**

🏨 **Royal** (T.H.F.), Belgrave Rd, PO38 1JJ, ✆ 852186, 🏊 heated, 🌚 – 🛗 🖭 🛏wc 🖼 🅿. 🗚 🖭
ⓞ 𝗩𝗜𝗦𝗔
M (buffet lunch)/dinner 7.50 **st.** and a la carte ≬ 2.70 – ☲ 5.50 – **54 rm** 30.00/45.00 **st.**

🏠 **Madeira Hall** 🍴, Trinity Rd, PO38 1NS, ✆ 852624, 🏊 heated, 🌚 – 🛏wc 🅿. 🗚 🖭 𝗩𝗜𝗦𝗔
Mid March-October – **12 rm** ☲ 18.00/46.00 **st.**

🏠 **Channel View,** Hambrough Rd, PO38 1SQ, ✆ 852230, ≤ – 🍴. 🖭 ⓞ 𝗩𝗜𝗦𝗔. 🛇
April-October – **14 rm** ☲ 10.00/32.00 **st.**

at Bonchurch – ⊠ ✪ 0983 Isle of Wight :

🏛 **Winterbourne** ⤸, PO38 1RG, ♨ 852535, ⩽ gardens and sea, « Country house and gardens », ⌸ heated – 📺 ⇔wc �🍴wc 🅿. 🔼 🄰🄴 *VISA*
February-November – **M** (bar lunch)/dinner 15.00 **t**. ♦ 2.50 – **19 rm** ⌑ 31.35/75.90 **st**.

🏚 **Bonchurch Manor** ⤸, Bonchurch Shute, PO38 1NU, ♨ 852868, ⩽, 🔼, 🎠 – 📺 ⇔wc
🍴wc 🅿
closed January – **M** (dinner only and Sunday lunch) 5.75/8.95 **t**. and a la carte ♦ 2.50 – **11 rm**
⌑ 20.00/40.00 **st**. – SB (October-April) 50.00/56.00 **st**.

🏚 **Highfield,** Leeson Rd, Upper Bonchurch, PO38 1PU, on A 3055 ♨ 852800, ⩽, 🎠 – 📺 ⇔wc
🅿 🔼 *VISA*
M (bar lunch)/dinner 7.25 and a la carte – **8 rm** ⌑ 14.95/38.60 **st**. – SB (except Christmas)
40.00/46.00 **st**.

🏨 **Lake** ⤸, Shore Rd, PO38 1RF, ♨ 852613, 🎠 – 🍴wc 🅿
March-October – **M** (bar lunch)/dinner 4.50 **t**. ♦ 2.25 – **23 rm** ⌑ 9.00/25.00 **t**. – SB
25.50/33.00 **st**.

↑ **Under Rock** ⤸, Shore Rd, PO38 1RF, ♨ 852714, « Gardens » – 📺 🅿. 🍃
March-October – **7 rm** ⌑ 15.00/30.00 **t**.

↑ **Horseshoe Bay** ⤸, Shore Rd, PO38 1RN, ♨ 852487, ⩽ – ⇔wc 🅿. 🔼
April-October – **7 rm** ⌑ 8.50/26.00.

🆇🆇 **Peacock Vane** ⤸ with rm, Bonchurch Village Rd, PO38 1RJ, ♨ 852019, ⩽, « Country house
atmosphere », 🔼, 🎠 – 📺 ⇔wc 🅿. 🔼 🄰🄴 ⓞ *VISA*
March-3 November and Christmas – **M** *(closed lunch Monday and Tuesday)* (lunch by arrangement) 10.00/16.00 **st**. ♦ 2.50 – **9 rm** ⌑ (dinner included) 40.00/70.00 **st**.

at St. Lawrence – ⊠ ✪ 0983 Ventnor :

↑ **Woody Bank,** Undercliff Drive, PO38 1XF, ♨ 852610, ⩽, 🎠 – 🍴wc 🅿
March-October – **9 rm** ⌑ 13.00/28.00 **t**.

AUSTIN-ROVER Victoria St. ♨ 852650

Whippingham – ⊠ ✪ 0983 Isle of Wight.
Newport 3.5.

🏛 **Padmore House** ⤸, Beatrice Av., PO32 6LP, ♨ 293210, 🎠 – 📺 ⇔wc 🍴 ☎ 🅿. 🔼 🄰🄴 ⓞ
VISA
M *(closed Saturday lunch)* 7.25/9.50 **t**. ♦ 2.50 – **11 rm** ⌑ 19.75/49.80 **t**. – SB 43.00/49.00 **st**.

Yarmouth – pop. 1,003 – ECD : Wednesday – ⊠ ✪ 0983 Isle of Wight.
🅱 Quay Rd ♨ 760015 (summer only).
Newport 10.

🏚 **Bugle,** St. James Sq., PO41 0NS, ♨ 760272 – ⇔wc 🅿. 🔼 🄰🄴 ⓞ *VISA*. 🍃
M (bar lunch)/dinner 15.00 **st**. – **10 rm** ⌑ 16.50/23.00 **t**.

AUSTIN-ROVER Mill Rd ♨ 760436

WILLENHALL West Midlands 🄓🄓🄓 🄓🄓🄓 N 26 – see Coventry.

WILLERBY Humberside 🄓🄓🄓 S 22 – see Kingston-upon-Hull.

WILLERSEY Heref. and Worc. 🄓🄓🄓 🄓🄓🄓 O 27 – see Broadway.

WILLERSEY HILL Glos. 🄓🄓🄓 🄓🄓🄓 O 27 – see Broadway (Heref. and Worc.).

WILLINGDON East Sussex 🄓🄓🄓 U 31 – see Eastbourne.

WILLITON Somerset 🄓🄓🄓 K 30 The West Country G. – pop. 2,410 – ECD : Saturday – ✪ 0984.
♦London 177 – Minehead 8 – Taunton 16.

🏚 **White House,** 11 Long St., TA4 4QW, ♨ 32306 – ⇔wc 🅿
May-October – **M** (dinner only) 14.50 **t**. ♦ 1.90 – **13 rm** ⌑ 21.00/42.00 **t**. – SB 53.00/59.00 **st**.

🏨 **Fairfield House,** 51 Long St., TA4 4QY, ♨ 32636 – 🅿. 🔼 🄰🄴 *VISA*
closed January and February – **M** (dinner only) 6.00 **t**. ♦ 2.50 – **5 rm** ⌑ 12.00/20.00 **t**. – SB
30.00/34.00 **st**.

AUSTIN-ROVER West Quantoxhead ♨ 32437   PEUGEOT, TALBOT High St. ♨ 32761

WILMCOTE Warw. 🄓🄓🄓 🄓🄓🄓 O 27 – see Stratford-upon-Avon.

WILMINGTON Devon 🄓🄓🄓 K 31 – see Honiton.

WILMINGTON East Sussex 🄓🄓🄓 U 31 – see Eastbourne.

♦London 189 – ♦Liverpool 38 – ♦Manchester 12 – ♦Stoke-on-Trent 27.

🏨 **Stanneylands** ॐ, Stanneylands Rd, SK9 4EY, N : 1 m. by A 34 ℰ 525225, Telex 666358, « Gardens » – 🖼 rest 🆅 ☎ & 🅿. 🚇. 🔼 🖭 🛇
closed 28 March and 1 January – **M** *(closed Sunday dinner)* 6.50/15.00 **st.** and a la carte ⑂ 2.50 – ⌼ 5.00 – **33 rm** 38.00/50.00 **st.** – SB (weekends only) 68.00/93.00 **st.**

🏨 **Valley Lodge,** Oversley Ford, Altrincham Rd, SK9 4LR, NW : 2 ¾ m. on A 538 ℰ 529201, Telex 666401 – 🕸 🆅 ⌻wc ⋔wc ☎ 🅿 🚇. 🔼 🖭 ⓪ 🎬 🛇
M 6.45/7.45 **st.** and a la carte ⑂ 2.75 – ⌼ 4.40 – **105 rm** 33.50/41.00 **st.**

at Handforth N : 3 m. on A 34 – ✉ Wilmslow :

🏨 **Belfry,** Stanley Rd, SK9 3LD, ℰ 061 (Manchester) 437 0511, Telex 666358, ⚓ – 🕸 🆅 & 🅿.
🔼 🖭 ⓪ 🎬 🛇
M 8.20/9.35 **t.** and a la carte ⑂ 3.50 – ⌼ 5.00 – **92 rm** 39.50/49.50 **t.**, **3 suites** 47.50/65.00 **t.**

🏨 **Pinewood,** 180 Wilmslow Rd, SK9 3LG, ℰ 0625 (Wilmslow) 529211, ⚓ – 🕸 🆅 ⌻wc ☎
🅿. 🔼 🖭 ⓪ 🎬
M 6.50/9.00 **st.** – ⌼ 4.00 – **64 rm** 33.00/40.00 **st.**

BMW Manchester Rd ℰ 523542
NISSAN Station Rd, Styal ℰ 524145
PORSCHE Green Lane ℰ 526392

RENAULT Station Rd ℰ 527356
RENAULT Knutsford Rd ℰ 523669
VAUXHALL-OPEL Water Lane ℰ 527311

See : Site★ – ॑ Ashley Wood ℰ 0258 (Blandford) 52253, NW : 8 m.
🛈 The Quarter Jack, 6 Cook Row, ℰ 886116.
♦London 112 – Bournemouth 10 – Dorchester 23 – Salisbury 27 – ♦Southampton 30.

🏨 **King's Head** (T.H.F.), The Square, BH21 1JA, ℰ 880101 – 🕸 🆅 ⌻wc ☏ 🅿. 🚇. 🔼 🖭 ⓪
🎬
M 5.95/9.50 **st.** and a la carte ⑂ 2.70 – ⌼ 5.50 – **28 rm** 37.00/48.50 **st.**

XX **Old Town House,** 9 Church St., BH21 1JH, ℰ 888227 – 🎬
closed Sunday, Monday and 2 weeks at Easter – **M** (dinner only) a la carte 10.70/13.55 **t.**
⑂ 3.00.

at Horton N : 6 m. on B 3078 – ✉ Wimborne Minster – ☺ 0258 Witchampton :

🏨 **Horton Inn,** Cranborne Rd, BH21 5AD, ℰ 840252 – 🆅 ⌻wc 🅿. 🔼 🖭 ⓪ 🎬 🛇
M *(closed Sunday dinner, Monday and Christmas night)* a la carte 9.55/11.30 **t.** – ⌼ 2.50 –
5 rm 18.00/29.00 **st.**

at Broadstone S : 3 ¼ m. by A 349 on B 3074 – ✉ Poole – ☺ 0202 Broadstone :

⌂ **Fairlight** ॐ, 1 Golf Links Rd, BH18 8BE, ℰ 694316, ⚓ – ⌻wc 🅿. 🔼 🎬
10 rm ⌼ 15.00/28.00 **st.**

AUSTIN-ROVER West St. ℰ 882261
FORD Poole Rd ℰ 886211

OPEL Walford Bridge ℰ 884211
VOLVO 41 Leigh Rd ℰ 887163

🛈 Public Library, 7 Carrington Way ℰ 32173.
♦London 119 – ♦Bristol 37 – Taunton 34 – Yeovil 16.

🏨 **Holbrook House** ॐ, Holbrook, BA9 8BS, W : 1 ½ m. on A 371, ℰ 32377, ≼, « Country mansion », 🛆 heated, ⚓, park, 🛇 – ⌻wc ⋔wc 🅿. 🔼 🖭 🎬
M 6.50/8.00 **t.** and a la carte ⑂ 2.60 – **20 rm** ⌼ 18.00/42.00 **t.** – SB (except Christmas) 40.00/45.00 **st.**

AUSTIN-ROVER Station Rd ℰ 32021

See : Cathedral★★★ 11C-13C B – Winchester College★★ 14C B B – Pilgrim's Hall★ 14C B E – St. Cross Hospital★ 12C-15C A.
Envir. : Marwell Zoological Park★★ *AC*, SE : 5 m. on A 333 A.
🛈 The Guildhall, The Broadway ℰ 68166 and 65406 (weekends).
♦London 72 – ♦Bristol 76 – ♦Oxford 52 – ♦Southampton 12.

Plan opposite

🏨 **Wessex** (T.H.F.), Paternoster Row, SO23 9LQ, ℰ 61611, Telex 47419, ≼ – 🕸 🆅 🅿. 🚇. 🔼
🖭 ⓪ 🎬
                             B **c**
M 9.50/13.00 **st.** and a la carte ⑂ 2.70 – ⌼ 5.50 – **94 rm** 45.50/56.00 **st.**

🏨 **Lainston House** ॐ, Sparsholt, SO21 2LT, NW : 3 ½ m. by A 272 ℰ 63588, Telex 477375, ≼, « 17C manor house », ⚓, park, 🛇 – 🆅 ☎ & 🅿. 🔼 🖭 ⓪ 🎬 by A 272 A
M 13.50/22.50 **t.** and a la carte ⑂ 3.50 – ⌼ 6.00 – **32 rm** 45.00/85.00 **t.**, **4 suites** 85.00/125.00 **st.**

🏨 **Royal,** St. Peter St., SO23 8BS, ℰ 53468, Telex 477071, ⚓ – 🆅 ⌻wc ☎ 🅿. 🚇. 🔼 🖭 ⓪
🎬
                            B **n**
M (buttery lunch)/dinner 9.50 **t.** ⑂ 3.25 – ⌼ 4.85 – **59 rm** 38.50/47.50 **t.** – SB (weekends only) 48.00 **st.**

WINCHESTER

High Street . . . . B

Alresford Road. . . . . A 2
Andover Road . . . . B 3
Bereweeke Road. . . . . A 5
Bridge Street . . . . B 6
Broadway (The) . . . . B 8
Chilbolton Avenue. . . . . A 9
City Road. . . . . B 10
Clifton Terrace . . . . B 12
East Hill . . . . B 15
Eastgate Street. . . . . B 16
Easton Lane . . . . A 18
Friarsgate . . . . B 19
Garnier Road . . . . A 20
Kingsgate Road . . . . A 22
Magdalen Hill. . . . . B 23
Middle Brook Street . . . . B 24
Morestead Road . . . . A 25
Park Road . . . . A 26
Quarry Road . . . . A 29
St. George's Street. . . . . B 32
St. Paul's Hill. . . . . B 33
St. Peter's Street. . . . . B 34
Southgate Street . . . . B 35
Stoney Lane . . . . A 36
Stockbridge Road . . . . B 37
Sussex Street . . . . B 38
Union Street . . . . B 39
Upper High Street . . . . B 40

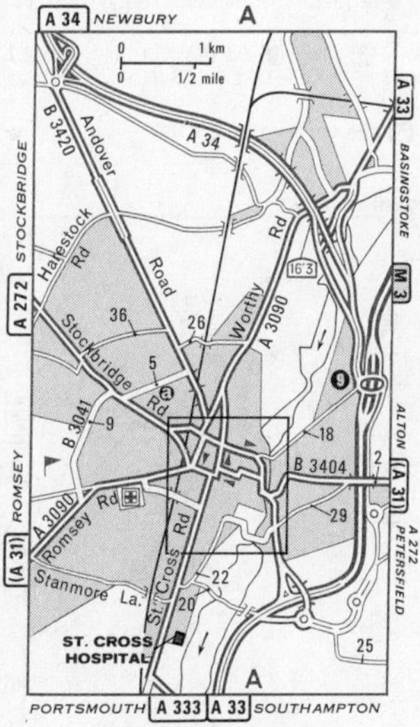

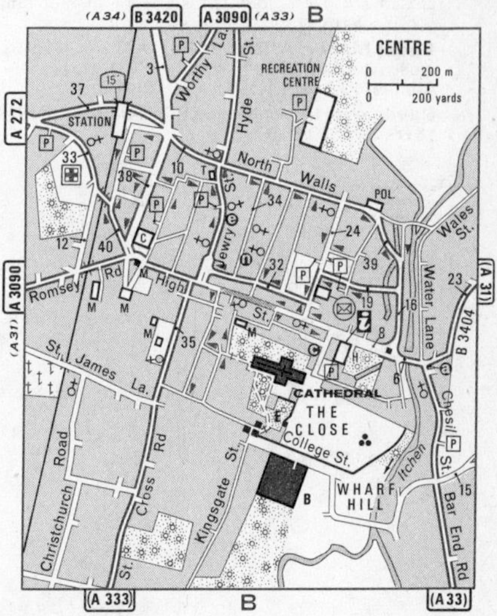

🏠 **Chantry Mead**, 22 Bereweeke Rd, SO22 6AJ, ✆ 52767, 🌳 – 📺 🛁wc ☎ 🅟 — A **a**
17 rm.

XX **Old Chesil Rectory,** Chesil St., SO23 8HU, ✆ 53177, French rest., « 14C restored rectory » – AE ① VISA — B **a**
closed Sunday and 23 December-23 January – **M** (booking essential)(dinner only) 13.95 **t.** 🍷 3.00.

XX **Cellar Peking,** 32-33 Jewry St., SO23 8RY, ✆ 64178, Chinese-Peking and Szechuan – AE ① VISA — B **e**
closed 30 March and 24 to 26 December – **M** 3.50/10.50 **t.** and a la carte 🍷 2.50.

ASTON-MARTIN Hursley ✆ 75218, Breakdown, 04892 (Botley) 6
AUSTIN-ROVER St. Swithin St. ✆ 68461
AUSTIN-ROVER Easton Lane, The By-pass ✆ 69182
FORD Bar-End Rd ✆ 62211
NISSAN Gordon Rd ✆ 69544
RENAULT Stockbridge Rd ✆ 63344
TALBOT, CITROEN 2/4 St. Cross Rd ✆ 61855
VOLVO Kingsworthy ✆ 881414
VW, AUDI St. Cross Rd ✆ 66331

WINDERMERE Cumbria 402 L 20 – pop. 6,835 – ECD : Thursday – ☎ 096 62.

See : Lake★ – Envir. : Kirkstone Pass (on Windermere ≤★) N : 7 m. by A 592 Y.

18 Cleabarrow ✆ **3123 by A 5074** Z **and B 5284** – ℹ Victoria St. ✆ 4561.

ℹ at Bowness : The Glebe ✆ 2895 (summer only).

♦London 274 – ♦Blackpool 55 – ♦Carlisle 46 – Kendal 10.

Plan on next page

🏨 **Langdale Chase** 🐎, LA23 1LW, NW : 3 m. on A 591 ✆ 0966 (Ambleside) 32201, ≤ Lake Windermere and mountains, « Extensive grounds with lake frontage », 🌳, park, 🎾 – ▤ rest 📺 ♿ 🅟. AE ① VISA — on A 591 Y
M 7.95/15.00 **st.** 🍷 3.50 – ☕ 4.50 – **35 rm** 29.00/70.00 **st.** – SB (October-April) 60.00/64.00 **st.**

🏨 **Wild Boar** (Best Western), Crook Rd, LA23 3NF, SE : 4 m. by A 5074 on B 5284 ✆ 5225, 🌳 – 📺 🛁wc 🚿wc ☎ 🅟. 🏔. AE ① VISA — by A 5074 Z
M 7.75/13.25 **st.** and a la carte 🍷 3.25 – **38 rm** ☕ 31.50/65.75 **st.** – SB 72.00/82.75 **st.**

🏨 **Priory Country House,** Rayrigg Rd, LA23 1EX, NW : ¾ m. by A 591 on A 592 ✆ 4377, ≤ Lake Windermere and mountains, 🌳, park – 📺 🛁wc ☎ 🅟. AE ① VISA. 🐕
M (bar lunch Monday to Saturday)/dinner 15.00 **t.** 🍷 3.50 – **15 rm** ☕ 40.00/70.00 **t.** – SB (weekends only)(October-March) 85.00 **st.** — by A592 Y

- **Holbeck Ghyll Country House** ⌖, Holbeck Lane, LA23 1LU, NW : 3 ½ m. by A 591 ℰ 0966 (Ambleside) 32375, ≤, « Country house atmosphere », ⚞ – ➛wc **P**. ⚐.
  Easter-November – **M** (dinner only) 9.00 **t**. ⚑ 2.50 – **11 rm** ⪪ 25.00/42.00 **t**. – SB (spring and November) 42.00/50.00 **st**.
  by A 591   Y

- **Quarry Garth** ⌖, Ambleside Rd, LA23 1LF, NW : 2 m. on A 591 ℰ 3761, ⚞, park – **P**
  M (dinner only and Sunday lunch) 6.00/11.00 **t**. ⚑ 3.00 – **7 rm** ⪪ 17.50/36.00 **t**. – SB (weekdays only in winter) 30.00/56.00 **st**.
  by A 591   Y

- **Glencree**, Lake Rd, LA23 2EQ, ℰ 5822 – **tv** ➛wc ⋔wc **P**. ⚒   Z **s**
  closed mid December-January – **M** (dinner only by arrangement)(residents only) 14.00 **st**.
  ⚑ 2.75 – **5 rm** ⪪ 34.00/39.00 **st**.

- **Cedar Manor,** Ambleside Rd, LA23 1AX, ℰ 3192, ⚞ – **tv** ⋔wc **P**. ⚐ VISA. ⚒   Y **i**
  closed January – **M** (dinner only) 10.00 **st**. ⚑ 2.90 – **6 rm** ⪪ 18.00/36.00 **t**. – SB (November-mid April)(except Bank Holidays) 40.00/44.00 **st**.

- **Ravensworth,** Ambleside Rd, LA23 1BA, ℰ 3747 – **tv** ➛wc ⋔wc **P**. ⚐ VISA   Y **e**
  13 rm ⪪ 15.00/36.00 **st**.

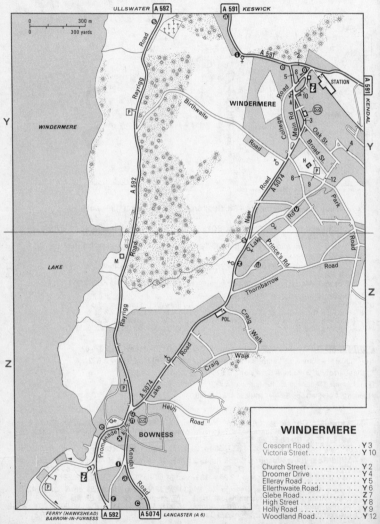

WINDERMERE

Crescent Road . . . . Y 3
Victoria Street . . . . Y 10

Church Street . . . . Y 2
Droomer Drive . . . . Y 4
Elleray Road . . . . Y 5
Ellerthwaite Road . . . . Y 6
Glebe Road . . . . Z 7
High Street . . . . Y 8
Holly Road . . . . Y 9
Woodland Road . . . . Y 12

⋔ **Braemount House** ॐ, Sunny Bank Rd, LA23 2EN, ℰ 5967 – 🖵 ⌂wc ☎ 🅿. 🔼 AE VISA
March-October – **4 rm** ⌂ 17.50/30.00 **t.**   Z u

⋔ **Willowsmere**, Ambleside Rd, LA23 1ES, ℰ 3575, ☞ – ⌂wc ⋔wc 🅿. 🔼 AE ⓪ VISA
March-mid November – **14 rm** ⌂ 14.50/29.00 **st.**   Y a

⋔ **Rosemount**, Lake Rd, LA23 2EQ, ℰ 3739 – ⋔wc 🅿. 🔼 VISA. ৯
closed December and January – **8 rm** ⌂ 9.50/24.00 **t.**   Z z

⋔ **Mylne Bridge**, Lake Rd, LA23 2BY, ℰ 3314 – ⋔wc 🅿. ৯
March-October – **12 rm** ⌂ 9.25/22.00 **st.**   Y v

XX **Miller Howe** with rm, Rayrigg Rd, LA23 1EY, ℰ 2536, ≤ Lake Windermere and mountains,
☞ – ▬ rest ⌂wc ⋔wc 🅿. 🔼 AE ⓪   Y s
March-December – **M** (dinner only) 20.00 **t.** – **13 rm** ⌂ (dinner included) 75.00/160.00 **t.**

XX **Roger's**, 4 High St., LA23 1AF, ℰ 4954 – 🔼 AE ⓪ VISA   Y o
closed Monday lunch, Sunday and 5 to 21 January – **M** (booking essential) a la carte
9.70/14.20 **st.** ⱷ 2.95.

at Bowness-on-Windermere S : 1 m. – ✉ ☏ 096 62 Windermere :

🏨 **Old England** (T.H.F.), LA23 3DF, ℰ 2444, Telex 65194, ≤ Lake Windermere and mountains,
⌶ heated, ☞ – ⌸ 🖵 🅿. 🔏 🔼 AE ⓪ VISA   Z e
M (buffet lunch Monday to Saturday)/dinner 11.50 **st.** and a la carte ⱷ 2.70 – ⌂ 5.50 – **82 rm**
36.50/57.00 **st.**

🏨 **Belsfield** (T.H.F.), Kendal Rd, LA23 3EL, ℰ 2448, Telex 65238, ≤ Lake Windermere and
mountains, 🔼, ☞ – ⌸ 🖵 ৳ 🅿. 🔏 🔼 AE ⓪ VISA   Z i
M (buffet lunch Monday to Saturday)/dinner 8.50 **st.** and a la carte ⱷ 2.70 – ⌂ 5.50 – **64 rm**
35.00/51.00 **st.**

🏨 **Linthwaite** ॐ, Crook Rd, LA23 3JA, S : ¾ m. by A 5074 on B 5284 ℰ 3688, ≤ Belle Isle,
Lake Windermere and mountains, « Extensive grounds and private lake », �‚ ☞, park – 🖵
⌂wc 🅿. ৯   by A 5074
Easter-November – **M** (dinner only) 9.50 **st.** ⱷ 3.00 – **11 rm** ⌂ (dinner included) 33.00/61.00 **st.**

🏨 **Burnside**, Kendal Rd, LA23 3EP, ℰ 2211, ≤, ☞ – ⌸ 🖵 ⌂wc ⋔wc ☎ 🅿. 🔏. 🔼 AE ⓪
VISA   Z c
M (bar lunch Monday to Saturday)/dinner 8.50 **t.** and a la carte ⱷ 2.75 – **46 rm** ⌂ 26.00/60.00 **t.**
– SB (November-March) 50.00/54.00 **st.**

🏨 **Burn How Motel**, Back Belsfield Rd, LA23 3HH, ℰ 6226, ☞ – 🖵 ⌂wc 🅿. 🔼 AE ⓪ VISA.
৯   Z r
closed January – **M** (bar lunch)/dinner 16.00 **st.** and a la carte ⱷ 3.00 – ⌂ 4.50 – **25 rm**
25.00/50.00 **st.** – SB (except summer) 49.00/54.00 **st.**

🏨 **Lindeth Fell Country House** ॐ, Kendal Rd, LA23 3JP, S : 1 m. on A 5074 ℰ 3286, ≤ Lake
Windermere and mountains, ➚, ☞, park, ୫ – 🖵 ⌂wc ⋔wc 🅿. 🔼 AE ⓪ VISA. ৯
Easter-mid November – **M** (bar lunch)/dinner 12.00 **t.** ⱷ 1.80 – **13 rm** ⌂ 25.00/55.00 **t.**
                                                                                                                                      by A 5074   Z

🏨 **Cranleigh**, Kendal Rd, LA23 3EW, ℰ 3293 – 🖵 ⌂wc 🅿. ৯   Z a
M (dinner only) 8.50 **st.** ⱷ 2.80 – **9 rm** ⌂ 21.00/38.00 **st.** – SB 31.00/49.00 **st.**

🏨 **St. Martin's**, Lake Rd, LA23 3DE, ℰ 3731 – ⌂wc ⋔wc 🅿   Z x
17 rm

⋔ **Brooklands**, Ferry View, LA23 3JB, ℰ 2344 – ⋔wc 🅿. ৯   on A 5074   Z
14 February-11 November – **6 rm** ⌂ (dinner included) 19.55/43.00 **t.**

XXX **Gilpin Lodge Country House** ॐ with rm, Crook Rd, LA23 3NE, SE : 2 ½ m. by A 5074 on B
5284 ℰ 2295, ≤, ☞, ୫ – 🖵 ⌂wc 🅿. 🔼 AE ⓪ VISA. ৯   by A 5074   Z n
closed 3 weeks January – **M** (lunch by arrangement) 10.50/16.50 **st.** ⱷ 3.25 – **6 rm** ⌂ (dinner included) 48.00/80.00 **st.**

XX **Porthole Eating House**, 3 Ash St., LA23 3EB, ℰ 2793 – 🔼 AE ⓪ VISA   Z n
closed Tuesday and mid December-mid February – **M** (dinner only) a la carte 9.85/14.85 **t.**
ⱷ 3.30.

at Troutbeck N : 4 m. by A 592 – Y – ✉ Windermere – ☏ 096 63 Ambleside :

🏨 **Mortal Man** ॐ, LA23 1PL, ℰ 3193, ≤, ☞ – ⌂wc 🅿   Z
Mid February-mid November – **M** (bar lunch Monday to Saturday)/dinner 11.00 **st.** ⱷ 3.10 –
12 rm ⌂ 28.00/33.00 **st.** – SB (weekends only)(spring and autumn) 55.00/60.00 **st.**

AUSTIN-ROVER College Rd ℰ 2451   PEUGEOT-TALBOT Main Rd ℰ 2441
HONDA Kendal Rd ℰ 2000

When travelling for business or pleasure
in England, Wales, Scotland and Ireland :

– use the series of five maps
  (nos **401**, **402**, **403**, **404** *and* **405**) *at a scale of 1:400 000*
– they are the perfect complement to this Guide
  as towns underlined in red on the maps will be found in this Guide.

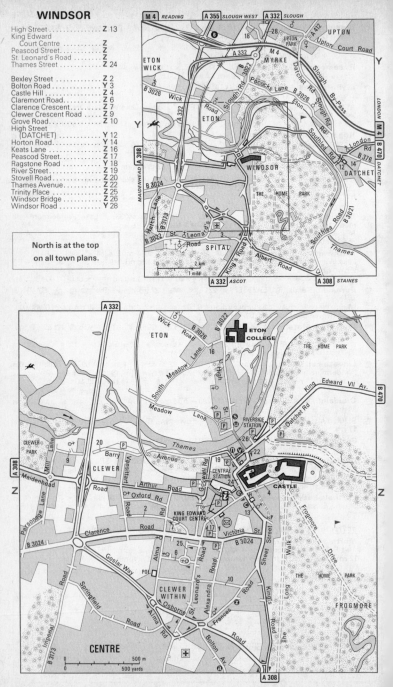

WINDSOR

High Street . . . . Z 13
King Edward
 Court Centre . . . . Z
Peascod Street . . . . Z
St. Leonard's Road . . . . Z
Thames Street . . . . Z 24

Bexley Street . . . . Z 2
Bolton Road . . . . Y 3
Castle Hill . . . . Z 4
Claremont Road . . . . Z 6
Clarence Crescent . . . . Z 7
Clewer Crescent Road . . . . . Z 9
Grove Road . . . . Z 10
High Street
 (DATCHET) . . . . Y 12
Horton Road . . . . Y 14
Keats Lane . . . . Z 16
Peascod Street . . . . Z 17
Ragstone Road . . . . Y 18
River Street . . . . Z 19
Stovell Road . . . . Z 20
Thames Avenue . . . . Z 22
Trinity Place . . . . Z 25
Windsor Bridge . . . . Z 26
Windsor Road . . . . Y 28

**North is at the top
on all town plans.**

CENTRE

WINDSOR Berks. 🄼🄸🄳 S 29 – pop. 30 ,832 (inc. Eton) – ECD : Wednesday – ☻ 075 35.

See : Castle★★★ (St. George's Chapel★★★) Z – **Envir. :** Eton (College★★) N : 1 m. Z – Runnymede (signing of the Magna Carta, 1215, museum) *AC*, SE : 4 m. by A 308 Y.

🛈 Central Station, Thames St. ℰ 52010.

◆London 28 – Reading 19 – ◆Southampton 59.

Plan opposite

🏨🏨 **Oakley Court** ⌘, Windsor Rd, Water Oakley, SL4 5UR, W : 3 m. on A 308 ℰ 0628 (Maidenhead) 74141, Telex 849958, ≼, « Part Gothic mansion on banks of River Thames », 雨, park –
📺 ☎ 🄿. 🏖. 🄰🄴 🄾 🆅🆂🅰. ⌘   by A 308   Y
M 12.00/18.00 **st.** and a la carte 🍷 4.95 – **92 rm** ⅏ 58.00/139.00 **st.** – SB (weekends only) 94.00 **st.**

🏨🏨 **Castle** (T.H.F.), High St., SL4 1LJ, ℰ 51011, Telex 849220 – 🛗 📺 🄿. 🏖. 🄰🄴 🄾 🆅🆂🅰
M 8.50/11.50 **st.** and a la carte 🍷 2.80 – ⅏ 5.50 – **85 rm** 48.50/59.00 **st.**   Z c

🏨 **Wren's Old House,** Thames St., SL4 1PX, ℰ 61354, Telex 847938, ≼, « Former residence of Sir Christopher Wren », 雨 – 📺 ⇋wc 🄿. 🄰🄴 🄾 🆅🆂🅰   Z v
M *(closed Saturday lunch)* 10.00/12.00 **t.** and a la carte 🍷 3.20 – **39 rm** ⅏ 49.00/75.00 **st.** – SB (weekends only) (October-March) 73.00 **st.**

🏠 **Aurora Garden,** 14 Bolton Av., SL4 3JF, ℰ 58838, 雨 – 📺 ⇋wc 雷 🄿. 🏖. 🄰🄴 🄾 🆅🆂🅰
M *(closed Sunday dinner)* (bar lunch)/dinner 8.50 **st.** 🍷 4.00 – ⅏ 3.50 – **13 rm** 27.50/42.50 **st.** – SB (weekends only) (October-March) 45.00/55.00 **st.**   Z a

🏠 Ye Harte and Garter, 21 High St., SL4 1LR, ℰ 63426 – 🛗 📺 ⇋wc ⇋wc 雷 🄿. 🄰🄴 🄾 🆅🆂🅰. ⌘   Z e
closed 25 and 26 December – **M** (grill rest. only) – **48 rm**.

↟ **Fairlight Lodge,** 41 Frances Rd, SL4 3AQ, ℰ 61207 – ⌘   Z z
8 rm ⅏ 13.50/25.00 **s.**

✕ **La Taverna,** 2 River St., SL4 1QT, ℰ 63020, Italian rest. – 🄰🄴 🄾 🆅🆂🅰   Z n
closed Sunday and 25-26 December – **M** a la carte 8.00/12.80 **t.** 🍷 2.80.

at Eton – ✉ ☻ 075 35 Windsor :

🏠 **Christopher,** 110 High St., SL4 6AN, ℰ 52359 – 📺 ⇋wc ☎ 🄿. 🄰🄴 🄾 🆅🆂🅰   Z u
M *(closed Saturday lunch and Christmas)* a la carte 10.00/13.00 **st.** 🍷 3.00 – ⅏ 3.55 – **21 rm** 28.00/36.00 **s.**

✕✕ **Antico,** 42 High St., SL4 6BD, ℰ 63977, Italian rest. – 🄰🄴 🄾 🆅🆂🅰   Z s
closed Saturday lunch, Sunday and Bank Holidays – **M** a la carte 12.10/16.80 **st.** 🍷 2.50.

VAUXHALL-OPEL 72-74 Arthur Rd ℰ 60131

WINKLEIGH Devon 🄼🄾🄳 I 31 – pop. 1 ,431 – ☻ 083 783.

◆London 214 – Barnstaple 20 – Exeter 22 – ◆Plymouth 41.

✕✕ **Kings Arms,** The Square, EX19 8HQ, ℰ 384 – 🄴. 🄰🄴 🄾 🆅🆂🅰
closed Sunday and Monday, last 2 weeks February and last 3 weeks November – **M** (dinner only)(booking essential) 16.50 **st.** 🍷 2.40.

WINSFORD Somerset 🄼🄾🄳 J 30 The West Country G. – pop. 340 – ECD : Thursday – ✉ Minehead – ☻ 064 385.

◆London 194 – Exeter 31 – Minehead 10 – Taunton 32.

🏠 Royal Oak Inn, TA24 7JE, ℰ 232 – 📺 ⇋wc 🄿 – **11 rm**.

🏡 **Karslake House,** TA24 7JE, ℰ 242, 雨 – 🍴 🄿
M 6.00/7.25 **t.** 🍷 2.60 – **11 rm** ⅏ 13.50/26.00 **t.** – SB (weekends only) (November-March) 38.00 **st.**

WINTERBOURNE Avon 🄼🄾🄳 🄼🄾🄴 M 29 – see Bristol.

WISBECH Cambs. 🄼🄾🄼 🄼🄾🄴 U 25 – pop. 22 ,932 – ECD : Wednesday – ☻ 0945.

Envir. : March (St. Wendreda's Church 15C : the Angel roof★) SW : 10 m. – Long Sutton (St. Mary's Church★ : Gothic) NW : 10 m.

🛈 District Library, Ely Pl. ℰ 583263 and 64009.

◆London 106 – ◆Cambridge 47 – ◆Leicester 62 – ◆Norwich 57.

🏠 **White Lion,** 5 South Brink, PE13 1JD, ℰ 584813 – 📺 ⇋wc ⇋wc ☎ 🄿. 🏖. 🄰🄴 🄾 🆅🆂🅰
M *(closed Sunday dinner)* 7.50 **t.** and a la carte 🍷 4.15 – **18 rm** ⅏ 22.00/37.25 **st.**

AUSTIN-ROVER 46 Norwich Rd ℰ 584342   VAUXHALL-OPEL Elm High Rd ℰ 582471
FORD Elm Rd ℰ 582681   VOLVO Sutton Rd ℰ 583082

In questa guida
uno stesso simbolo, uno stesso carattere
stampati in rosso o in nero, in magro o in **grassetto**
hanno un significato diverso.
Leggete attentamente le pagine esplicative (p. 28 a 35).

WITHAM Essex 404 V 28 – pop. 21,875 – ECD : Wednesday – ✪ 0376.
♦London 42 – ♦Cambridge 46 – Chelmsford 9 – Colchester 13.

  ⋒ **White Hart,** 39 Newland St., CM8 2AF, ✆ 512245 – 📺 🚪wc 🅿. 🔼 🆎 ⓞ 𝘝𝘐𝘚𝘈
    M (carving rest.) 5.95 t. 🍴 2.90 – **13 rm** 🛏 21.00/33.00 **st.** – SB (weekends only) 53.90 **st.**

  ⋒ Batsford Court, 100 Newland St., CM8 1AH, ✆ 517777 – 📺 🚿wc 🕾 🅿
    22 rm.

AUSTIN-ROVER   Newland St. ✆ 513272
FORD   Colchester Rd ✆ 513496

                                             NISSAN   London Rd ✆ 515575

WITHERSLACK Cumbria – see Grange-over-Sands.

WITHYPOOL Somerset 403 J 30 The West Country G. – pop. 231 – ECD : Thursday – ✉
✪ 064 383 Exford.
♦London 204 – Exeter 34 – Taunton 36.

  ⋒ **Royal Oak Inn,** TA24 7QP, ✆ 236, ↘ – 📺 🚪wc 🚿wc 🅿. 🔼 🆎 ⓞ 𝘝𝘐𝘚𝘈
    M (bar lunch)/dinner 12.50 t. 🍴 2.75 – **8 rm** 🛏 18.00/38.00 **t.** – SB 27.50/34.00 **st.**

  ⋒ **Westerclose Country House** ⌕, TA24 7QR, NW : ¼ m. ✆ 302, 🐎 – 🚪wc 🔼 🆎 𝘝𝘐𝘚𝘈
    closed 22 December-14 February – **M** (bar lunch)/dinner 12.00 t. 🍴 2.30 – **8 rm** 🛏 15.00/52.00 **t.**

WITNEY Oxon. 403 404 P 28 – pop. 14,215 – ECD : Tuesday – ✪ 0993.
🛈 Town Hall, Market Sq. ✆ 4379 – Cogges Farm Museum, Chuch Lane ✆ 72602.
♦London 69 – ♦Birmingham 63 – ♦Oxford 12 – Swindon 24.

  ⋔ **Greystones Lodge,** 34 Tower Hill, OX8 5ES, ✆ 71898, 🔼 heated, 🐎 – 🅿. 🌿
    10 rm 🛏 15.00/36.00 **s.**

    '' Short Breaks '' (SB)
    Molti alberghi propongono delle condizioni vantaggiose
    per un soggiorno di due notti
    comprendente la camera, la cena e la prima colazione.

WIVELISCOMBE Somerset 403 K 30 The West Country G. – pop. 1,457 – ECD : Thursday –
✪ 0984.
♦ London 185 – Barnstaple 38 – Exeter 37 – Taunton 14.

  ⋒ **Langley House** ⌕, Langley Marsh, TA4 2UF, NW : ½ m. ✆ 23318, « Country house atmos-
    phere », 🐎 – 📺 🚪wc 🚿wc 🅿
    M (dinner only) (booking essential) 14.00 **st.** – **6 rm** 🛏 24.75/45.65 **st.**

WOBURN Beds. 404 S 28 – pop. 824 – ECD : Wednesday – ✉ Milton Keynes – ✪ 052 525.
See : Woburn Abbey★★★ (18C) *AC*, Wild Animal Kingdom★★ *AC*.
♦London 49 – Bedford 13 – Luton 13 – Northampton 24.

  🏛 **Bedford Arms,** 1 George St., MK17 9BX, ✆ 441, Telex 825205 – 📺 🚪wc 🕾 🅿. 🛆. 🔼 🆎
    ⓞ 𝘝𝘐𝘚𝘈
    M 9.50/10.50 **t.** and a la carte 🍴 3.00 – 🛏 5.75 – **55 rm** 44.00/85.00 **t.** – SB (weekends only)
    60.00/68.00 **st.**

  XXX 🕸 **Paris House,** Woburn Park, MK17 9QP, SE : 2 ¼ m. on B 528 ✆ 692, « Reproduction
    timbered house in Park », 🐎 – 🅿. 🔼 🆎 ⓞ 𝘝𝘐𝘚𝘈
    closed Sunday dinner, Monday and February – **M** 12.50/15.00 **st.** and a la carte 🍴 2.70
    Spec. Feuilleté de langues d'agneau et champignons, Filet de barbue au Champagne, Soufflé aux framboises.

WOLF'S CASTLE (CAS-BLAIDD) Dyfed 403 F 28 – ✉ Haverfordwest – ✪ 043 787 Treffgarne.
♦London 258 – Fishguard 7 – Haverfordwest 8.

  XX **Wolfscastle Country** with rm, SA62 5LZ, on A 40 ✆ 225, 🐎, ✂, squash – 📺 🚪wc 🅿.
    🔼 🆎 𝘝𝘐𝘚𝘈
    closed 5 days at Christmas – **M** (bar lunch)/dinner a la carte 8.65/14.10 t. 🍴 2.75 – **12 rm**
    🛏 18.00/34.00 **t.** – SB (weekdays only) (except July, August and Bank Holidays) 45.00 **st.**

WOLVERHAMPTON West Midlands 402 403 404 N 26 – pop. 263,501 – ECD : Thursday –
✪ 0902.
See : St. Peter's Church★ 15C B A.
🏌 Oxley Park, Bushbury ✆ 20506, N : 1 ½ m. A – 🏌 Blackhill Wood, Bridgnorth Rd ✆ 892279, S :
5 m. by A 449 A.
♦London 132 – ♦Birmingham 15 – ♦Liverpool 89 – Shrewsbury 30.

                      Plan of Enlarged Area : see Birmingham pp. 2 and 3

  🏛 **Goldthorn,** 126 Penn Rd, WV3 0ER, ✆ 29216, Telex 339516 – 📺 🚪wc 🕾 🅿. 🛆. 🔼 🆎 ⓞ
    𝘝𝘐𝘚𝘈   B i
    closed 25 and 26 December – **M** 7.85/8.40 **t.** and a la carte 🍴 2.20 – **86 rm** 🛏 22.00/49.50 **t.**

WOLVERHAMPTON

Darlington Street .... B
Mander Centre .... B
Victoria Street .... B 24
Wulfrun Centre .... B

Alfred Squire Road .... A 2
Birmingham New Road .... A 3
Bridgnorth Road .... A 6
Cleveland Street............. B 7
Garrick Street .... B 8
Lichfield Road .... A 10
Lichfield Street .... B 12

Market Street .... B 14
Princess Street.............. B 15
Queen Square .... B 17
Railway Drive .... B 20
Salop Street .... B 22
Thompson Avenue .... A 23
Wolverhampton Road .... A 26

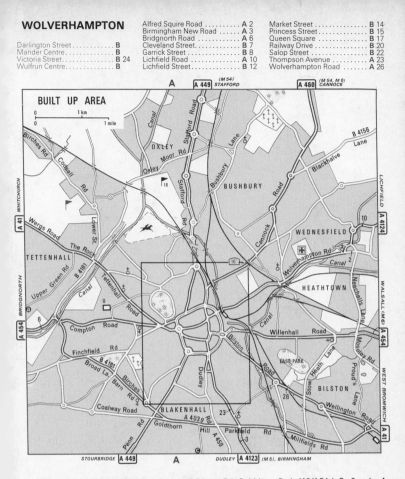

🏨 **Park Hall** (Embassy) ॐ Park Drive, off Ednam Rd, Goldthorn Park, WV4 5AJ, S : 2 m. by A 449 ℰ 331121, 🐎 – 📺 ⌷wc ☎ 🅿 🛬 🛐 🆎 ⓞ 𝘝𝘐𝘚𝘈 ❀   A c
M *(closed Saturday lunch and Sunday dinner to non-residents)* 7.50 **st.** and a la carte � 2.75 –
� 5.00 – **57 rm** 22.50/43.50 **st.** – SB (weekends only) 47.00 **st.**

🏨 **Mount** (Embassy) ॐ, Mount Rd, Tettenhall Wood, WV6 8HL, W : 2 ½ m. by A 454 ℰ 752055, 🐎 – 📺 ⌷wc ☎ 🅿 🛬 🛐 🆎 ⓞ 𝘝𝘐𝘚𝘈 ❀   A a
M *(bar lunch Saturday)/dinner* 9.50 **st.** and a la carte � 2.50 – � 5.00 – **58 rm** 36.00/49.50 **st.** – SB 50.00 **st.**

at Pattingham (Staffs.) W : 6 ¼ m. by A 454 – A – ✉ ☎ 0902 Pattingham :

🏨 **Lakeside Lodge** ॐ, Patshull Park, WV6 7HR, W : 1 ¾ m. by Patshull Rd ℰ 700100, ≤, 🖼, ॐ, park – 📺 ⌷wc ☎ 🅿 🛬 🛐 🆎 ⓞ 𝘝𝘐𝘚𝘈
M *(bar lunch)/dinner* 7.50 **t.** and a la carte � 3.00 – � 4.25 – **28 rm** 27.50/36.50 **t.** – SB (weekends only) 58.50/72.50 **t.**

ALFA-ROMEO, CITROEN Merridale Lane ℰ 23295
AUSTIN ROVER-DAIMLER-JAGUAR Stafford St. ℰ 29122
AUSTIN-ROVER Chapel Ash ℰ 26781
AUSTIN-ROVER Wolverhampton Rd, Wednesfield ℰ 731372
BMW, VW, AUDI Rabey St. ℰ 54602
COLT Lichfield Rd ℰ 731689
FIAT Warstones Rd ℰ 339104
FORD Bilston Rd ℰ 51515

LADA 372 Penn Rd, Penn ℰ 335570
MERCEDES-BENZ Penn Rd ℰ 27897
RENAULT Bilston Rd ℰ 53111
SKODA Vulcan Rd, Bilston ℰ 402222
TOYOTA Wolverhampton Rd East ℰ 333131
VAUXHALL-OPEL Dudley Rd ℰ 58000
VAUXHALL-OPEL 67/71 Bilston Rd ℰ 52611
VOLVO Parkfield Rd ℰ 333211
VW-AUDI Raby St. ℰ 54602

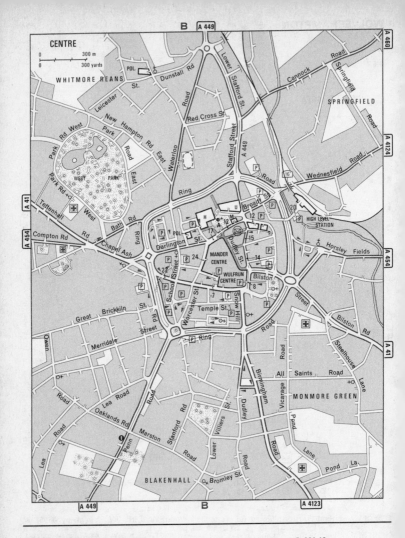

WOODBRIDGE Suffolk 🅔🅞🅐 X 27 – pop. 9,697 – ECD : Wednesday – ☎ 039 43.

🏌, 🏌 Bromeswell Heath ℰ 2038, E : 2 m.

♦London 81 – Great Yarmouth 45 – ♦Ipswich 8 – ♦Norwich 47.

🏛 **Seckford Hall** 🐾, IP13 6NU, SW : 1 ¼ m. by A 12 ℰ 5678, Telex 987446, ≼, « Part Tudor country house », 🐾, 🐾, park – 📺 🕾wc ☎ 🅿. 🕾 🄰🄴 ⓪ 🆅🅸🆂🅰
closed Christmas Day – **M** 6.95 st. (lunch) and a la carte 10.20/14.40 st. ≬ 2.50 – **24 rm** ⚌ 34.00/52.00 st. – SB (summer and weekends only in winter) 70.00/79.50 st.

🏛 **Crown** (T.H.F.), Thoroughfare, IP12 1AD, ℰ 4242 – 📺 🕾wc ☎ 🅿. 🄰🄴 ⓪ 🆅🅸🆂🅰
M 4.95/8.75 st. and a la carte ≬ 2.70 – ⚌ 5.50 – **24 rm** 36.50/47.50 st.

AUSTIN-ROVER Melton Rd ℰ 3456   FORD Bawdsey ℰ 039 441 (Shottisham) 1368
FORD 96 Thorough Fare ℰ 3333

WOODHALL SPA Lincs. 🅔🅞🅑 🅔🅞🅐 T 24 – pop. 2,526 – ECD : Wednesday – ☎ 0526.

Envir. : Tattershall Castle★ (15C Keep) *AC*, SE : 3 ½ m. – 🏌 ℰ 52511.

🗓 Jubilee Park, Stixwould Rd ℰ 52448 and 52461 (summer only).

♦London 138 – Lincoln 18.

🏛 **Golf,** The Broadway, LN10 6SG, ℰ 53535, 🛏 – 📺 ⏢wc 🏛wc 🅿️ 🍴. 🔼 AE ⓪ 𝘝𝘐𝘚𝘈
M (bar lunch)/dinner 8.00 **t.** and a la carte 🍷 2.50 – **51 rm** ☲ 33.00/43.00 **t.** – SB 53.00/58.00 **st.**

🏛 **Petwood** ⌁, Stixwould Rd, LN10 6QF, ℰ 52411, 🛏, park – 🎿 📺 ⏢wc ☎ 🅿️. 🍴
30 rm, **2 suites.**

🏛 **Dower House** ⌁, Manor Estate, off Spa Rd, LN10 6PY, ℰ 52588, « Country house atmosphere », 🛏 – ⏢wc 🅿️. 🔼 AE 𝘝𝘐𝘚𝘈
M (closed Sunday November-February) (bar lunch)/dinner 8.00 **t.** and a la carte 🍷 2.80 – **7 rm** ☲ 20.00/37.00 **t.**

⌂ **Dunns,** The Broadway, LN10 6SQ, ℰ 52969 – 🅿️. ⌖
6 rm ☲ 8.50/16.00 **t.**

WOODLANDS Hants. – see Lyndhurst.

WOODSTOCK Oxon. 🐾 🐾 P 28 – pop. 3,057 – ECD : Wednesday – ✿ 0993.
See : Blenheim Palace★★★ 18C (park and gardens★★★) AC – Envir. : Rousham (Manor House gardens : statues★) NE : 5 m. – Ditchley Park★ (Renaissance) AC, NW : 6 m. – 🅱 Library, Hensington Rd ℰ 811038 and 812231 (summer only) – ◆London 65 – Gloucester 47 – ◆Oxford 8.

🏛 **Bear,** Park St., OX7 1SZ, ℰ 811511, Telex 837921, « Part 16C inn » – 📺 ☎ 🅿️. 🍴
41 rm, **2 suites.**

🏛 **Feathers,** Market St., OX7 1SX, ℰ 812291, Telex 83138, « Tastefully furnished » – 📺 ⏢wc 🏛wc ☎. 🍴. 🔼 AE ⓪ 𝘝𝘐𝘚𝘈
M 11.50/14.50 **st.** and a la carte 🍷 3.25 – **15 rm** ☲ 35.00/88.00 **st.** – SB (November-April except Christmas) 78.00/88.00 **st.**

🏛 **Kings Arms,** Market St., OX7 1ST, ℰ 811412 – 📺 ⏢wc 🏛wc 🔼. 🔼 AE ⓪ 𝘝𝘐𝘚𝘈
closed 24 to 28 December – **M** (Seafood rest.) a la carte 14.50/26.50 **t.** – **10 rm** ☲ 35.00/56.00 **st.** – SB 48.00/65.00 **st.**

🏛 **Marlborough Arms,** Oxford St., OX7 1TS, ℰ 811227 – 📺 ⏢wc 🏛wc 📠 🅿️
closed 24 to 28 December – **M** 6.50/8.95 **t.** 🍷 2.95 – **15 rm** ☲ 22.00/56.00 **st.**

AUSTIN-ROVER 2 Oxford St. ℰ 811286

WOODY BAY Devon 🐾 I 30 – see Lynton.

WOOLACOMBE Devon 🐾 H 30 The West Country G. – pop. 1,171 – ECD : Wednesday – ✿ 0271 – Envir. : Mortehoe★★ – Morte Point (vantage point ★) – Mortehoe Church ★.
🅱 Hall 70, Beach Rd ℰ 870553 (summer only) – ◆London 237 – Barnstaple 15 – Exeter 55.

🏛 **Little Beach,** The Esplanade, EX34 7DJ, ℰ 870398, ≤ – ⏢wc 🏛wc 🅿️. 🔼 𝘝𝘐𝘚𝘈
February-October – **M** (bar lunch)/dinner 9.75 **st.** 🍷 2.25 – **10 rm** ☲ (dinner included) 24.00/62.00 **st.** – SB 42.80/58.00 **st.**

🏛 **Water's Fall,** Beach Rd, EX34 7AD, ℰ 870365, ≤ Woolacombe Bay, 🛏 – ⏢wc 🅿️
closed November, January and February – **M** (dinner only and Sunday lunch)/dinner 7.50 **t.** 🍷 2.95 – **17 rm** ☲ 13.50/37.00 **t.** – SB (spring and October) 38.00/40.00 **st.**

at Mortehoe N : ½ m. – ✉ ✿ 0271 Woolacombe :

🏛 **Watersmeet,** The Esplanade, EX34 7EB, ℰ 870333, ≤, ⤒ heated, ⌖ – ⏢wc 🅿️. 🔼 AE ⓪. ⌖
Easter-October – **M** 6.75/8.25 **st.** 🍷 3.15 – **34 rm** ☲ (dinner included) 28.00/65.00 **st.**

🏛 **Sunnycliffe,** Chapel Hill, EX34 7EB, ℰ 870597, ≤ – 📺 ⏢wc 🏛wc 🅿️. ⌖
closed December and January – **M** (residents only) (bar lunch)/dinner 7.00 **st.** – **8 rm** ☲ 15.00/34.00 **st.** – SB (September-mid July) 38.00/40.00 **st.**

⌂ **Lundy House,** EX34 7DZ, ℰ 870372, ≤, 🛏 – 🏛wc 🅿️
closed November-27 December – **11 rm** ☲ 8.00/25.00 **st.**

WOOLER Northumb. 🐾 🐾 N 17 – pop. 1,925 – ECD : Thursday – ✿ 0668.
🅱 Bus Station Car Park, High St. ℰ 81602 (summer only).
◆London 332 – ◆Edinburgh 62 – ◆Newcastle-upon-Tyne 46.

🍴 **Ryecroft,** 28 Ryecroft Way, NE71 6AB, ℰ 81459 – 🅿️. 🔼 𝘝𝘐𝘚𝘈
closed 2 to 13 November and 23 to 27 December – **M** (bar lunch Monday to Saturday)/dinner 10.00 **t.** 🍷 2.50 – **11 rm** ☲ 15.00/29.00 **st.** – SB 34.50/48.00 **st.**

🍴 **Tankerville Arms,** 22 Cottage Rd, NE71 6AD, on A 697 ℰ 81581, 🛏 – ⏢wc 🏛wc 🅿️
M (bar lunch)/dinner 8.50 **st.** and a la carte 🍷 2.60 – **16 rm** ☲ 17.85/38.60 **st.** – SB (except July and August) 33.00/35.00 **st.**

FORD Haughead ℰ 81316   RENAULT South Rd ℰ 81472

WOOLVERTON Somerset – see Bath.

WORCESTER Heref. and Worc. 🐾 🐾 N 27 – pop. 75,466 – ECD : Thursday – ✿ 0905.
See : Cathedral★★ 13C-15C (crypt★★ 11C) – The Commandery★ (15C) AC B – Envir. : Great Witley : Witley Court (ruins) and the Parish Church of St. Michael and All Saints (Baroque interior★★) NW : 12 m. by A 443 – 🅱 Guildhall, High St. ℰ 23471.
◆London 124 – ◆Birmingham 26 – ◆Bristol 61 – ◆Cardiff 74.

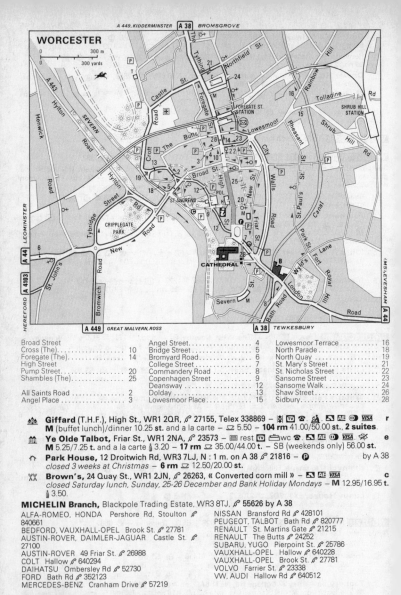

WORCESTER

Broad Street	
Cross (The)	10
Foregate (The)	14
High Street	
Pump Street	20
Shambles (The)	25
All Saints Road	2
Angel Place	3

Angel Street	4
Bridge Street	5
Bromyard Road	6
College Street	7
Commandery Road	8
Copenhagen Street	9
Deansway	12
Dolday	13
Lowesmoor Place	15

Lowesmoor Terrace	16
North Parade	18
North Quay	19
St. Mary's Street	21
St. Nicholas Street	22
Sansome Street	23
Sansome Walk	24
Shaw Street	26
Sidbury	28

Giffard (T.H.F.), High St., WR1 2QR, ℰ 27155, Telex 338869 – 劇 📺 ☎. 🔥. 🔼 🖭 ① 𝘝𝘐𝘚𝘈 r
M (buffet lunch)/dinner 10.25 **st.** and a la carte – ☲ 5.50 – **104 rm** 41.00/50.00 **st.**, **2 suites.**

Ye Olde Talbot, Friar St., WR1 2NA, ℰ 23573 – 🍽 rest 📺 ⌂wc ☎. 🔼 🖭 ① 𝘝𝘐𝘚𝘈 ⁓ e
M 5.25/7.25 **t.** and a la carte 🛢 3.20 – **17 rm** ☲ 35.00/44.00 **t.** – SB (weekends only) 56.00 **st.**

Park House, 12 Droitwich Rd, WR3 7LJ, N : 1 m. on A 38 ℰ 21816 – 🅿 by A 38
closed 3 weeks at Christmas – **6 rm** ☲ 12.50/20.00 **st.**

Brown's, 24 Quay St., WR1 2JN, ℰ 26263, « Converted corn mill » – 🔼 🖭 𝘝𝘐𝘚𝘈 c
closed Saturday lunch, Sunday, 25-26 December and Bank Holiday Mondays – **M** 12.95/16.95 **t.**
🛢 3.50.

MICHELIN Branch, Blackpole Trading Estate, WR3 8TJ, ℰ 55626 by A 38

ALFA-ROMEO, HONDA Pershore Rd, Stoulton ℰ 840661
BEDFORD, VAUXHALL-OPEL Brook St. ℰ 27781
AUSTIN-ROVER, DAIMLER-JAGUAR Castle St. ℰ 27100
AUSTIN-ROVER 49 Friar St. ℰ 26988
COLT Hallow ℰ 640294
DAIHATSU Ombersley Rd ℰ 52730
FORD Bath Rd ℰ 352123
MERCEDES-BENZ Cranham Drive ℰ 57219

NISSAN Bransford Rd ℰ 428101
PEUGEOT, TALBOT Bath Rd ℰ 820777
RENAULT St. Martins Gate ℰ 21215
RENAULT The Butts ℰ 24252
SUBARU, YUGO Pierpoint St. ℰ 25786
VAUXHALL-OPEL Hallow ℰ 640228
VAUXHALL-OPEL Brook St. ℰ 27781
VOLVO Farrier St. ℰ 23338
VW, AUDI Hallow Rd ℰ 640512

WORFIELD Salop – see Bridgnorth.

WORKINGTON Cumbria 🏴🏴 J 20 – pop. 25,978 – ECD : Thursday – 🕙 0900.
🏌 Branthwaite Rd ℰ 3460 – 🏌 Bankend, Maryport ℰ 090 081 (Maryport) 2605, N : 7 m. on A 596.
♦London 314 – ♦Carlisle 33 – Keswick 21.

Westland, Branthwaite Rd, CA14 4SS, SE : 2 m. by A 596 ℰ 4544 – 📺 ⌂wc 🗋wc ☎ 🅿. 🔥.
48 rm.

AUSTIN-ROVER Central Sq. ℰ 2113
COLT, HYUNDAI Guard St. ℰ 64455
FORD Washington St. ℰ 67101

PEUGEOT-TALBOT Finkle St. ℰ (0946) 830247
RENAULT Clay Flatts Estate ℰ 4542
TOYOTA ℰ (0946) 830247

474

WORRALL South Yorks. – see Sheffield.

WORTH Somerset – see Wells.

WORTHING West Sussex **404** S 31 – pop. 90,687 – ECD : Wednesday – ✪ 0903.

Envir. : Shoreham-by-Sea (St. Mary of Haura's Church★ 12C-13C – St. Nichola's Church carved arches★ 12C) E : 5 m. by A 259 BY.

🏌 Worthing Hill Barn, Hill Barn Lane ✆ 37301 BY.

✈ Shoreham Airport : ✆ 079 17 (Shoreham-by-Sea) 2304, E : 4 m. by A 27 BY.

🛈 Town Hall, Chapel Rd ✆ 39999 ext 132/3 – Marine Parade ✆ 210022 (summer only).

♦London 59 – ♦Brighton 11 – ♦Southampton 50.

Plan on next page

🏨 **Beach,** Marine Par., BN11 3QJ, ✆ 34001, ≤ – 🛗 📺 🅿. 🏧 🔼 AE ⓞ VISA ⁓. %%   AZ **e**
M 7.25/9.25 **st.** and a la carte – **90 rm** ⊑ 26.75/49.50 **st.** – SB (weekends only)(October-April) 47.75/55.50 **st.**

🏨 **Chatsworth,** Steyne Gdns, BN11 3DU, ✆ 36103, Telex 877046 – 🛗 📺 ⊟wc 📾. 🏧. 🔼 VISA
M 7.50/8.50 **st.** and a la carte ⎮ 2.20 – **90 rm** ⊑ 29.00/49.00 **st.** – SB (weekends only) (winter only) 50.00/55.00 **st.**   BZ **x**

🏨 **Eardley,** 3-10 Marine Par., BN11 3PW, ✆ 34444, Group Telex 877046, ≤ – 🛗 📺 ⊟wc 📾 🅿.
🏧. 🔼 VISA   BZ **u**
M (carving lunch) 6.25/7.00 **t.** and a la carte ⎮ 2.70 – **83 rm** ⊑ 21.00/50.00 **t.** – SB (weekends only) (October-April) 45.00/55.00 **st.**

🏠 **Beechwood Hall,** Wykeham Rd, BN11 4AH, ✆ 32872, 🌫 – 📺 ⊟wc 🅿. 🔼 AE VISA   AZ **a**
M a la carte 4.50/8.00 **t.** ⎮ 2.80 – **14 rm** ⊑ 23.50/35.00 **t.** – SB (weekends only) 40.00/50.00 **st.**

🏠 **Ardington,** Steyne Gdns, BN11 3DZ, ✆ 30451 – 📺 ⊟wc ⎮wc. 🔼   BZ **s**
closed Christmas – **M** (dinner only and Sunday lunch)/dinner 7.00 **t.** and a la carte ⎮ 3.00 –
51 rm ⊑ 20.00/42.00 **t.**

⋔ **Wansfell,** 49 Chesswood Rd, BN11 2AA, ✆ 30612, 🌫 – 📺 ⊟wc ⎮wc 🅿. 🔼. %%   BY **a**
closed Christmas – **12 rm** ⊑ 12.00/34.00 **t.**

⋔ **Ainslea Court,** Abbey Rd, BN11 3RW, ✆ 30442   AZ **r**
8 rm ⊑ 10.35/20.70 **st**

%% **Paragon,** 9-10 Brunswick Rd, BN11 3NG, ✆ 33367 – 🔼 AE ⓞ VISA   AZ **c**
closed Sunday, 2 weeks Christmas and Bank Holidays – **M** 7.50/9.85 **st.** and a la carte ⎮ 2.75.

% **La Gondola,** 121 Rectory Rd, BN14 7PH, ✆ 66384, Italian rest. – 🔼 AE ⓞ VISA   AY **e**
closed Sunday and Monday – **M** (booking essential) a la carte 7.00/12.75 **t.** ⎮ 3.00.

at Findon N : 4 m. by A 24 – AY – ✉ Worthing – ✪ 090 671 Findon :

🏨 **Findon Manor** ﹩, High St., BN14 0TA, ✆ 2733, 🌫 – 📺 ⊟wc ☎ 🅿. 🏧. 🔼 AE ⓞ VISA
closed 24 to 31 December – **M** (closed lunch Saturday and Monday and Sunday dinner) a la carte 10.25/14.75 **t.** ⎮ 2.75 – **9 rm** ⊑ 32.00/52.00 **t.** – SB (weekends only) 57.00/67.00 **st.**

♨ **Village House,** The Square, BN14 0TE, ✆ 3350, 🌫 – 🅿
9 rm.

at East Preston W : 6 ½ m. by A 259 – AY – off B 2225 – ✉ Littlehampton – ✪ 0903
Rustington :

%% **Old Forge,** The Street, BN16 1JJ, ✆ 782040, « 17C cottage » – 🅿. 🔼 AE ⓞ VISA
closed Sunday dinner and Monday – **M** 5.95 **t.** (lunch) and a la carte 7.00/18.50 **t.** ⎮ 2.50.

ALFA-ROMEO Lancing ✆ 766981	SAAB, PEUGEOT-TALBOT St. Lawrence Av. ✆
AUSTIN-ROVER 55 Broadwater Rd ✆ 31111	207703
BMW Angermering ✆ 090 62 (Rushington) 4147	SKODA Tarring ✆ 34363
CITROEN 28 Broadwater Rd ✆ 39573	TALBOT Broadwater Rd ✆ 262338
FIAT 123 Upper Brighton Rd ✆ 36065	TOYOTA 93 Rowlands Rd ✆ 32571
NISSAN Broadwater Rd ✆ 206091	VAUXHALL-OPEL Goring Rd ✆ 42389
RENAULT Portland Rd ✆ 200820	VOLVO 187 Findon Rd ✆ 090 671 (Findon) 3022

WOUGHTON ON THE GREEN Bucks. – see Milton Keynes.

WRAFTON Devon **403** H 30 – ✉ ✪ 0271 Braunton.

♦London 227 – Barnstaple 5 – Exeter 45 – Ilfracombe 9.

🏠 **Poyers,** EX33 2DN, ✆ 812149, 🌫 – 📺 ⊟wc ⎮wc 🅿. 🔼 AE ⓞ VISA
closed 24 December-15 January – **M** (closed Sunday) (dinner only) 9.00 **t.** and a la carte –
10 rm ⊑ 21.50/38.00 **t.** – SB 48.60/65.00 **st.**

WRELTON North Yorks. **402** R 21 – see Pickering.

WRENTHAM Suffolk **404** Z 26 – pop. 898 – ECD : Wednesday – ✉ Beccles – ✪ 050 275.

♦London 110 – Great Yarmouth 17 – ♦Ipswich 37 – ♦Norwich 26.

%% **Quiggins,** 2 High St., NR34 7HB, ✆ 397, « Tasteful decor » – 🅿. 🔼 AE VISA
closed Sunday dinner and Monday – **M** (booking essential) 5.50/14.50 **t.** ⎮ 3.00.

WORTHING

Chapel Road .... **BZ**
Guildbourne Centre .... **BZ**
Montague Street .... **BZ**
Liverpool Road .... **BZ** 22
South Street (WORTHING) .. **BZ**

Broadwater Road .... **BZ** 3
Broadwater Street West ... **BY** 5
Broadway (The) .... **BZ** 6
Brougham Road .... **BY** 7
Brunswick Road .... **AZ** 8
Christchurch Road .... **BZ** 10

Church Road .... **AY** 12
Cowper Road .... **AZ** 13
Crockhurst Hill .... **AY** 14
Durrington Hill .... **AY** 15
Eriswell Road .... **ABZ** 16
Goring Street .... **AY** 17
Goring Way .... **AY** 18
Grafton Road .... **BZ** 20
High Street .... **BZ** 21
Montague Place .... **BZ** 23
Mulberry Lane .... **AY** 24
Portland Road .... **BZ** 25
Rectory Road .... **AY** 26
Reigate Road .... **AY** 27
Sompting Avenue .... **BY** 28

Sompting Road .... **BY** 29
South Street
  (WEST TARRING) .... **AY, AZ** 30
Southfarm Road .... **ABZ** 31
Steyne (The) .... **BZ** 32
Steyne Garden .... **BZ** 33
Stoke Abbot Road .... **BZ** 34
Tennyson Road .... **AZ** 36
Thorn Road .... **AZ** 37
Union Place .... **BZ** 38
Warwick Road .... **BZ** 40
Warwick Street .... **BZ** 41
West Street .... **BZ** 42
Western Place .... **BZ** 44
Wykeham Road .... **AZ** 45

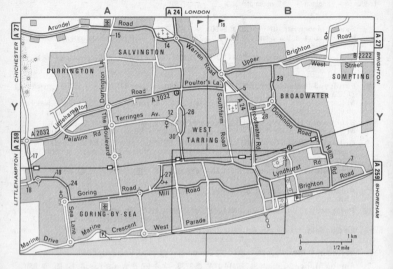

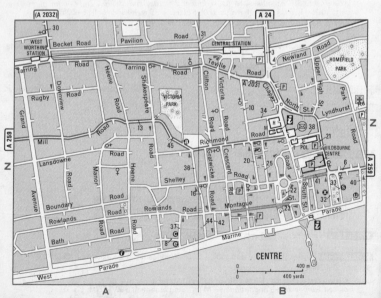

CENTRE

WREXHAM (WRECSAM) Clwyd [402] [403] L 24 – pop. 39,929 – ECD : Wednesday – ☎ 0978.
See : St. Giles' Church (tower★) – **Envir.** : Erddig★ (17C-18C) *AC*, SW : 2 m. – [i] Guildhall Car Park, Town Centre ☎ 357845 (summer only) – ♦London 192 – Chester 12 – Shrewsbury 28.

🏨 **Cross Lanes,** Marchwiel, LL13 0TF, SE : 3 ½ m. on A 525 ☎ 780555, 🏊, 🧖, 🌳, park – [TV] 🛁wc 🚿wc ☎ [P]. [S] [AE] [O] [VISA]
M 7.00 **st.** and a la carte 🍷 3.00 – ☕ 3.50 – **20 rm** 21.00/35.00 **st.** – SB (weekends only) 38.00 **st.**

AUSTIN-ROVER Hightown Rd ☎ 364151
CITROEN Holt Rd ☎ 356707
FORD Holt Rd ☎ 351001
NISSAN ☎ 757838
RENAULT, NISSAN Regent St. ☎ 356822
SKODA Wrexham Rd ☎ 263438
TOYOTA Wrexham Rd ☎ 840578
VAUXHALL-OPEL Mold Rd ☎ 263777
VOLVO Hill St. ☎ 262685
VW-AUDI Wrexham Rd ☎ 355777

WRIGHTINGTON BAR Lancs. [402] [404] L 23 – pop. 3,160 – ✉ Wigan – ☎ 025 75 Appley Bridge.
♦London 210 – ♦Liverpool 24 – ♦Manchester 30 – Preston 15.

🍴🍴 **Highmoor,** Highmoor Lane, by Robin Hood Lane, ☎ 2364, « 17C inn » – [P]. [S] [AE] [O] [VISA]
closed Sunday dinner, Monday, first week January and last 2 weeks August – **M** a la carte 11.40/15.00 **t.** 🍷 3.95.

WROTHAM HEATH Kent – pop. 1,669 – ✉ ☎ 0732 Sevenoaks – ♦London 35 – Maidstone 10.

🏨 **Post House** (T.H.F.), London Rd, TN15 7RS, ☎ 883311, Telex 957309, 🏊, 🌳 – [TV] ☎ [P]. 🏋. [S] [AE] [O] [VISA]
M a la carte lunch/dinner 13.40 **st.** 🍷 2.70 – ☕ 5.50 – **119 rm** 43.00/51.50 **st.**, **2 suites**.

at Ightham W : 2 ½ m. by A 25 on A 227 – ✉ Sevenoaks – ☎ 0732 Borough Green :

🍴🍴🍴 **Town House,** The Street, TN15 9HH, ☎ 884578, « 15C hall », 🌳 – [P]. [S] [AE] [O] [VISA]
closed Sunday, Monday, 2 weeks Easter, 2 weeks August-September and 2 weeks Christmas – **M** (booking essential) 14.50/22.50 **st.** 🍷 3.90.

WROXHAM Norfolk [404] Y 25 – pop. 2,954 (inc. Hoveton) – ECD : Wednesday – ✉ Norwich – ☎ 060 53 – ♦London 118 – Great Yarmouth 21 – ♦Norwich 7.

🏨 **Wroxham,** Broads Centre, NR12 8AJ, ☎ 2061, ≤ – [TV] 🛁wc ☎ [P]. [S] [AE] [O] [VISA]
M 5.50/6.00 **t.** and a la carte 🍷 2.95 – **18 rm** ☕ 20.50/41.00 **t.**

WROXTON Oxon. [403] [404] P 27 – see Banbury.

WYCH CROSS East Sussex [404] U 30 – see Forest Row.

WYE Kent [404] W 30 – pop. 1,396 – ECD : Wednesday – ✉ Ashford – ☎ 0233.
♦London 61 – Folkestone 21 – Maidstone 24 – Margate 28.

🍴🍴 **Wife of Bath,** 4 Upper Bridge St., TN25 5EU, ☎ 812540 – [P]. [S] [AE]
closed Sunday, Monday and 1 week Christmas – **M** a la carte 11.60/13.00 **t.** 🍷 3.60.

AUSTIN-ROVER Bridge St. ☎ 812331
RENAULT Bramble Lane ☎ 812270

WYMONDHAM Norfolk [404] X 26 – pop. 9,088 – ECD : Wednesday – ☎ 0953.
♦London 110 – ♦Cambridge 53 – ♦Norwich 9.

🍴 **Adlards,** 16 Damgate St., NR18 0BQ, ☎ 603533 – [S] [VISA]
closed Sunday and Monday – **M** (dinner only) (booking essential) 15.50 **st.**

WYNDS POINT Heref. and Worc. [403] [404] M 27 – see Great Malvern.

WYRE PIDDLE Heref. and Worc. – see Pershore.

YARCOMBE Devon [403] K 31 – pop. 418 – ☎ 040 486 Upottery.
♦London 157 – Exeter 25 – Taunton 12 – Weymouth 42.

🍺 Yarcombe Inn, ☎ 218 – [P] – **7 rm**.

YARM Cleveland [402] P 20 – pop. 6,360 – ☎ 0642 Middlesbrough.
♦ London 242 – Middlesbrough 8.

🏨 **Crathorne Hall** 🐌, Crathorne, TS15 0AR, S : 3 ½ m. by A 67 ☎ 700398, Telex 587426, « Converted Edwardian mansion house », 🌳, park – [TV] ☎ [P]. 🏋. [S] [AE] [O] [VISA]. 🚫
M 7.95/10.95 **t.** and a la carte – **31 rm** ☕ 36.50/55.00 **t.**, **1 suite** 75.00 **t.** – SB (weekends only) 65.50/71.00 **st.**

YARMOUTH I.O.W. [403] [404] P 31 – see Wight (Isle of).

YATTENDON Berks. [403] [404] Q 29 – pop. 568 – ECD : Saturday – ✉ Newbury – ☎ 0635 Hermitage – ♦London 62 – Newbury 8 – Reading 12.

🍴🍴 **Royal Oak** with rm, The Square, RG16 0UF, ☎ 201325, 🌳 – [TV] 🛁wc ☎ [P]. [S] [AE] [VISA]. 🚫
M (booking essential) a la carte 7.95/20.25 **t.** 🍷 3.75 – **5 rm** ☕ 37.50/55.00 **t.** – SB (weekends only)(November-March) 70.00 **st.**

♦London 234 – Exeter 33 – ♦Plymouth 9.

🏨 **Moorland Links** ⤴, PL20 6DA, S : 2 m. on A 386 ℰ 852245, ≼, 🍴, park, 🎾 – 📺 🛏wc ☎
🅟 🅰 🔼 🆎 ⑩ **VISA**
closed 24 to 31 December – **M** 8.00/9.95 st. – **23 rm** 🖙 34.00/42.00 st. – SB (weekends only)
56.00 st.

⌂ **Overcombe** ⤴, Horrabridge, PL20 7RN, N : 1 ¼ m. on A 386 ℰ 853501, ≼, 🍴 – 🛏wc 🅟 🔼
🆎 ⑩ **VISA**
7 rm 🖙 12.90/28.80 st.

See : St. John the Baptist Church★.

Envir. : Montacute House★★★ *AC*, W : 4 m. on A 3088 – Fleet Air Arm Museum★★ *AC*, NW : 8 m. by
A 37 – Long Sutton★ (Church★★), NW : 10 m. – Huish Episcopi : Church Tower★★, NW : 13 m. –
Martock : All Saints Church★★, W : 7 m. – Cadbury Castle (≼★★), NE : 11 m. by A 359 – Ham Hill
(≼★★) W : 4 m. – Tintinhull House★ *AC*, NW : 5 m.

🛅 Sherborne Rd ℰ 75949.

🎫 Johnson Hall, Hendford ℰ 22884.

♦London 136 – Exeter 48 – ♦Southampton 72 – Taunton 26.

🏨 **Manor Crest** (Crest), Hendford Rd, BA20 1TG, ℰ 353431, Telex 23116, 🍴 – 🍽 rest 📺
🛏wc ☎ 🅟 🅰 🔼 🆎 ⑩ **VISA** 🎿
M approx 11.50 st. – 🖙 5.75 – **42 rm** 43.50/53.50 st. – SB (weekends only) 59.00 st.

⌂ **Preston**, 64 Preston Rd, BA20 2DL, ℰ 74400 – 📺 🛏wc 🅟 🔼 **VISA**
11 rm 🖙 11.00/27.00 t.

at Barwick S : 2 m. by A 30 off A 37 – ✉ ✪ 0935 Yeovil :

🍴🍴 **Little Barwick House** ⤴ with rm, BA22 9TD, ℰ 23902, ≼, 🍴 – 📺 🛏wc 🅟 🔼 🆎 ⑩
VISA
M (closed Sunday to non-residents) (dinner only) 14.00 st. 🍷 3.00 – **3 rm** 🖙 22.00/37.00 st. –
SB (October-March) 46.50 st.

at West Coker SW : 3 ½ m. on A 30 – ✉ Yeovil – ✪ 093 586 West Coker :

🏨 **Four Acres**, High St., BA22 9AJ, ℰ 2555, Telex 46666, 🍴 – 📺 🛏wc 🛏wc ☎ 🅟 🔼 🆎 ⑩
VISA
M (restricted Sunday dinner) 8.50 t. and a la carte – **24 rm** 🖙 30.00/38.50 t. – SB (weekends
only) 43.00/57.00 st.

at East Chinnock SW : 5 m. on A 30 – ✉ Yeovil – ✪ 093 586 West Coker :

⌂ **Barrows Country House** ⤴, Weston St., BA22 9EJ, ℰ 2390, 🍴 – 🅟 🎿
closed 24 December-1 January – **6 rm** 🖙 9.00/24.00.

at Montacute W : 4 m. on A 3088 – ✉ Yeovil – ✪ 0935 Martock :

🏠 **Kings Arms**, Bishopston, TA15 6UU, ℰ 822513, 🍴 – 📺 🛏wc ☎ 🅟 🔼 🆎 ⑩ **VISA** 🎿
M (closed Sunday dinner to non-residents) a la carte 9.00/13.00 t. – **10 rm** 🖙 33.00/49.50 t.

🍴🍴 **Milk House**, 17 The Borough, TA15 6XB, ℰ 823823 – 🔼 🆎 ⑩ **VISA**
closed Sunday lunch and Monday except Bank Holidays – **M** a la carte 5.65/13.05 t. 🍷 2.40.

AUSTIN-ROVER, DAIMLER-JAGUAR Market St. ℰ   SAAB 12 Oxford Rd ℰ 26701
75242   VAUXHALL-OPEL Addlewell Lane ℰ 74842
FORD West Henford ℰ 27421

Y-FENNI = Abergavenny.

See : Minster★★★ 13C-15C (Chapter House★★★, 🌟★★ from tower, *AC*, 275 steps) CDY – National
Railway Museum★★★ CY – Castle Museum★★ *AC* DZ **M2** – Clifford's Tower★ (13C) *AC* DYZ **B** – Art
Gallery★ CX **M3** – Treasurer's House★ (14C) *AC* DX **E** – City Walls★ 14C – The Shambles★ DY.

🛅 Lords Moor Lane, Strensall ℰ 490304, NE : 6 m. by Huntington Rd BY.

🎫 De Grey Rooms, Exhibition Sq. ℰ 21756/7.

♦London 303 – ♦Kingston-upon-Hull 38 – ♦Leeds 26 – ♦Middlesbrough 51 – ♦Nottingham 88 – ♦Sheffield 62.

Plan opposite

🏨🏨 **Royal York**, Station Rd, YO2 2AA, ℰ 53681, Telex 57912, ≼, 🍴 – 🛗 📺 🅟 🅰 🔼 🆎 ⑩
VISA   CY **e**
M (bar lunch)/dinner 10.50 st. and a la carte – **129 rm** 🖙 26.50/66.00 st. – SB 76.00/86.00 st.

Annex : 🏨 Friars Garden, Station Rd, YO2 2AA, ℰ 53681, Telex 57912, 🍴 – 📺 🛏wc ☎
🅟 – **M** (see Royal York H.) – **22 rm**   CY **e**

🏨🏨 **Middlethorpe Hall** ⤴, Bishopthorpe Rd, YO2 1QP, S : 1 m. ℰ 641241, Telex 57802, ≼,
« Tastefully decorated Queen Anne house », 🍴, park – 🛗 📺 ☎ 🅟 🅰 🔼 🆎 ⑩ **VISA** 🎿
M 12.00/17.50 st. and a la carte 🍷 3.50 – 🖙 4.50 – **31 rm** 60.00/80.00 st., **3 suites** 150.00 st. –
SB (November-April)(except Bank Holidays) 90.00/110.00 st.   by A 19 BZ

YORK

Blake Street	CY	5
Coney Street	CY	13
Davygate	CY	16
Lendal	CY	32
Parliament Street	DY	42
Shambles (The)	DY	54
Stonegate	CY	58

Bishopgate Street	CZ	3
Bishophill Senior	CZ	4
Campleshon Road	AZ	7
Church Street	DY	8

Clarence Street	CX	9
Clifford Street	DY	12
Colliergate	DY	12
Cromwell Road	CZ	15
Deangate	DY	18
Duncombe Place	CY	20
Fawcett Street	DZ	21
Fetter Lane	CY	22
Fossgate	DY	23
Goodramgate	DY	25
High Petergate	CY	26
Knavesmire Re	AZ	28
Leeman Road	AY, CY	29
Lord Mayor's Walk	DX	30

Low Petergate	DY	35
Melrosegate	BY	36
Museum Street	CY	39
Pavement	DY	43
Peasholme Green	DX	45
Penley's Grove Street	DX	46
Queen Street	CZ	49
St. Helen's Road	AZ	50
St. Leonard's Place	CY	52
St. Maurice's Road	DXY	53
Station Road	CY	55
Stonebow (The)	DY	56
Tower Street	DY	59
University Road	BZ	60
Wetherby Road	AZ	62

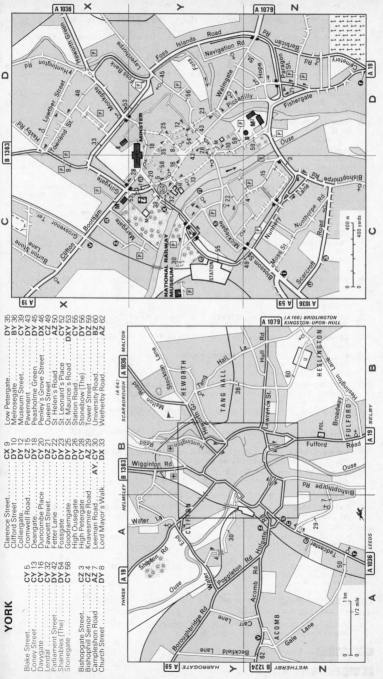

479

🏨 **Viking** (Q.M.H.), North St., YO1 1JF, ℰ 59822, Telex 57937, ⬿ – 📳 🍽 rest 📺 ☎ 🅿 🏧 ⚞
AE ⓞ VISA
CY n
M (carving lunch)/dinner a la carte approx. 8.00 **st.** – **187 rm** ⏛ 49.50/68.75 **st.** – SB (weekends only) 62.00/68.00 **st.**

🏨 **Judges' Lodging,** 9 Lendal, YO1 2AQ, ℰ 38733, « Tastefully restored 18C Judges' lodgings » – 📺 ☎ 🅿 AE ⓞ VISA
CY x
M (bar lunch)/dinner 16.50 and a la carte ⓖ 3.75 – **14 rm** ⏛ 35.00/90.00 – SB (November-March) 86.25/120.75 **st.**

🏨 **Post House** (T.H.F.), Tadcaster Rd, YO2 2QF, SW : 1 ¾ m. on A 64 ℰ 707921, Telex 57798, ⌦ – 📳 📺 ⇔wc ⊛ 🅿 🏧 🔽 AE ⓞ VISA
AZ r
M 8.05/9.75 **st.** and a la carte ⓖ 2.70 – ⏛ 5.50 – **147 rm** 43.00/56.00 **st.**

🏨 **Mount Royale,** 119 The Mount, YO2 2DA, ℰ 28856, Telex 57414, 🔟 heated, 🌳 – 📺 ⇔wc ☎ 🅿 🔽 AE ⓞ VISA. 🎐
AZ s
closed 23 December-6 January – **M** (dinner only) 15.00 **t.** ⓖ 3.00 – **19 rm** ⏛ 42.50/60.00 **t.**

🏨 **Ambassador,** 123-125 The Mount, YO2 2DA, ℰ 64136, 🌳 – 📺 ⇔wc 🍴wc ☎ 🅿 🔽 AE ⓞ VISA. 🎐
AZ c
M (bar lunch Monday to Saturday)/dinner 9.50 **st.** and a la carte ⓖ 2.90 – **19 rm** ⏛ 28.00/38.00 **st.** – SB (October-April) 50.00 **st.**

🏨 **Hudsons,** 58-60 Bootham, YO3 7BZ, ℰ 21267 – 📺 ⇔wc 🍴wc ☎ 🅿 🔽 AE ⓞ VISA. 🎐
CX a
closed 24 to 26 December – **M** 7.00/12.00 **t.** ⓖ 3.00 – **28 rm** ⏛ 32.00/48.00 **t.** – SB (November-May) 47.00 **st.**

🏨 **Dean Court** (Best Western), Duncombe Pl., YO1 2EF, ℰ 25082 – 📳 📺 ⇔wc ☎ 🔽 AE ⓞ VISA. 🎐
CY a
M 8.50/12.50 **st.** ⓖ 3.45 – **36 rm** ⏛ 39.00/72.00 **st.** – SB 76.00/82.00 **st.**

🏠 **Town House,** 98-104 Holgate Rd, YO2 4BB, ℰ 36171, 🌳 – 📺 ⇔wc 🍴wc ☎ 🅿 🔽 AE ⓞ VISA
AZ z
closed 24 December-1 January – **M** (bar lunch)/dinner 7.75 **t.** and a la carte ⓖ 2.60 – **23 rm** ⏛ 12.00/38.00 **t.** – SB (October-April) 44.00 **st.**

🏠 **Hill,** 60 York Rd, Acomb, YO2 5LW, W : 2 m. by A 59 on B 1224 ℰ 790777, 🌳 – 📺 ⇔wc ☎ 🅿 🔽 AE ⓞ VISA. 🎐
AZ v
closed 14 December-21 January – **M** (bar lunch)/dinner 9.50 **t.** ⓖ 3.25 – **10 rm** ⏛ 22.50/42.00 **t.** – SB 46.00/52.00 **st.**

🏠 **Sheppard,** 63 Blossom St., YO2 2BD, ℰ 20500 – 📺 ⇔wc 🍴 ⊛ 🅿 🔽 VISA
CZ i
M 5.00/7.50 **t.** and a la carte ⓖ 2.10 – **19 rm** ⏛ 27.00/40.00 **st.** – SB 38.00/48.00 **st.**

🏠 **Grasmead House** without rest., 1 Scarcroft Hill, YO2 1DF, ℰ 29996 – 📺 ⇔wc. VISA. 🎐
CZ a
6 rm ⏛ 25.00/38.00 **st.**

🏠 **Mayfield,** 75 Scarcroft Rd, YO2 1DB, ℰ 54834 – 📺 ⇔wc 🍴wc. 🔽 AE VISA. 🎐
CZ u
M (dinner only) a la carte approx. 13.20 **st.** ⓖ 2.95 – **7 rm** ⏛ 17.00/35.00 **st.** – SB (except Christmas and Bank Holidays) 42.00/50.00 **st.**

🏠 **Field House,** 2 St. Georges Pl., YO2 2DR, ℰ 39572, 🌳 – 📺 🍴wc ☎ 🅿 🔽 AE VISA. 🎐
AZ e
closed 3 days at Christmas – **M** (dinner only) 8.00 **st.** ⓖ 3.25 – **17 rm** ⏛ 23.00/44.00 **st.** – SB (November-May) 44.00/54.00 **st.**

⌂ **Crook Lodge,** 26 St. Mary's, Bootham, YO3 7DD, ℰ 55614 – 📺 ⇔wc 🅿
CX z
7 rm ⏛ 18.00/26.00 **st.**

⌂ **Hedley House,** 3 Bootham Terr., YO3 7DH, ℰ 37404 – 📺 ⇔wc ♿ 🅿 VISA
CX v
15 rm ⏛ 15.00/34.00 **t.**

⌂ **Priory,** 126 Fulford Rd, YO1 4BE, ℰ 25280, 🌳 – 📺 🍴wc 🅿 🔽 AE ⓞ VISA. 🎐
DZ r
closed 1 week at Christmas – **20 rm** ⏛ 16.40/28.75 **st.**

✕ **Tony's,** 39 Tanner Row, YO1 1JP, ℰ 59622 – 🔽 AE VISA
CY s
closed Saturday lunch and Sunday – **M** 5.25 **t.** (lunch) and a la carte 6.55/10.70 **t.**

at Skelton NW : 3 m. on A 19 – AY – ✉ ☻ 0904 York :

🏨 **Fairfield Manor,** Shipton Rd, YO3 6XW, ℰ 25621, 🌳 – 📺 ☎ 🅿 🔽 AE ⓞ VISA. 🎐
M 6.25/8.25 **t.** ⓖ 3.50 – **25 rm** ⏛ 40.00/52.00 **t.** – SB (except Bank Holidays) 58.00/64.00 **st.**

ALFA-ROMEO Leeman Rd ℰ 22772
AUSTIN-ROVER, FORD, VAUXHALL-OPEL 117 Long St. ℰ 0347 (Easingwold) 21694
CITROEN Lowther St. ℰ 22064
COLT Fulford ℰ 33139
FORD Piccadilly ℰ 25371
JAGUAR-DAIMLER Layerthorpe ℰ 58252
LADA Leeman Rd ℰ 59241

LANCIA Piccadilly ℰ 34321
NISSAN 21-27 Layerthorpe ℰ 58809
PEUGEOT, TALBOT The Stonebow ℰ 55118
RENAULT Clifton ℰ 58647
TOYOTA 172 Fulford Rd ℰ 52947
VAUXHALL-OPEL Rougier St. ℰ 25444
VAUXHALL-OPEL 100 Layerthorpe ℰ 56671
VOLVO 88/96 Walmgate ℰ 53798

YOXFORD Suffolk **404** Y 27 – pop. 690 – ✉ Saxmundham – ☻ 072 877.
♦London 95 – ♦Ipswich 25 – ♦Norwich 55.

✕ **Jacey's,** Blythburgh House, High St., IP17 3EU, ℰ 298 – 🔽 VISA
closed Sunday lunch – **M** a la carte 5.00/10.55 **t.** ⓖ 2.25.

YR WYDDFA = Snowdon.

YR WYDDGRUG = Mold.

Scotland

Place with at least :

one hotel or restaurant	● Tongue
one pleasant hotel	🏠 , ✗ with rm
one quiet, secluded hotel	⌖
one restaurant with	❀, ❀❀, ❀❀❀, M
See this town for establishments located in its vicinity	ABERDEEN

Località offrant au moins :

une ressource hôtelière	● Tongue
un hôtel agréable	🏠 , ✗ with rm
un hôtel très tranquille, isolé	⌖
une bonne table à	❀, ❀❀, ❀❀❀, M
Localité groupant dans le texte les ressources de ses environs	ABERDEEN

La località possiede come minimo :

una risorsa alberghiera	● Tongue
un albergo ameno	🏠 , ✗ with rm
un albergo molto tranquillo, isolato	⌖
un'ottima tavola con	❀, ❀❀, ❀❀❀, M
La località raggruppa nel suo testo le risorse dei dintorni	ABERDEEN

Ort mit mindestens :

einem Hotel oder Restaurant	● Tongue
einem angenehmen Hotel	🏠 , ✗ with rm
einem sehr ruhigen und abgelegenen Hotel	⌖
einem Restaurant mit	❀, ❀❀, ❀❀❀, M
Ort mit Angaben über Hotels und Restaurants in seiner Umgebung	ABERDEEN

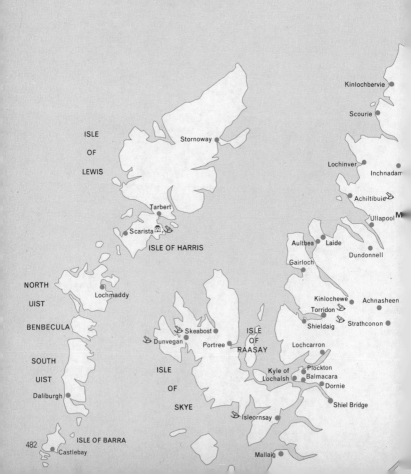

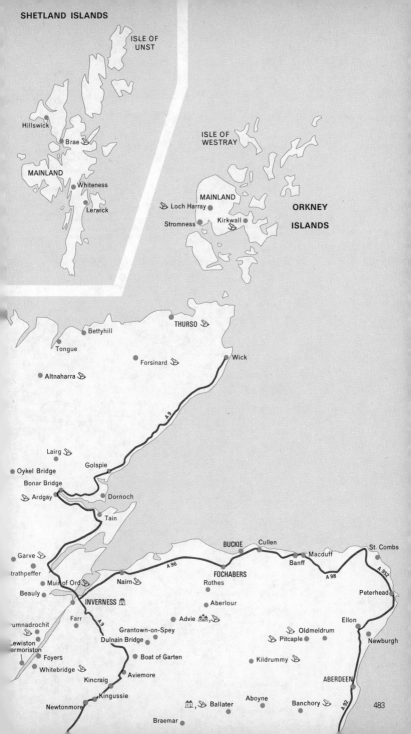

SHETLAND ISLANDS

ISLE OF UNST

Hillswick

Brae

MAINLAND

Whiteness

Lerwick

ISLE OF WESTRAY

MAINLAND

Loch Harray

ORKNEY

Stromness   Kirkwall

ISLANDS

THURSO

Bettyhill

Tongue   Forsinard   Wick

Altnaharra

A 9

Lairg

Oykel Bridge   Golspie

Bonar Bridge

Ardgay   Dornoch

Tain

BUCKIE   Cullen   St. Combs

Garve   A 96   Macduff   A 952

trathpeffer   FOCHABERS   Banff   A 98

Muir of Ord   Nairn   Rothes   Peterhead

Beauly   Aberlour

INVERNESS

Advie   Ellon

rumnadrochit   Farr   A 9   Oldmeldrum

ewiston   Grantown-on-Spey   Pitcaple   Newburgh

ermoriston   Dulnain Bridge

Foyers   Boat of Garten   Kildrummy

Whitebridge   ABERDEEN

Kincraig   Aviemore

Kingussie

Newtonmore   Ballater   Aboyne   Banchory   A 92

Braemar   483

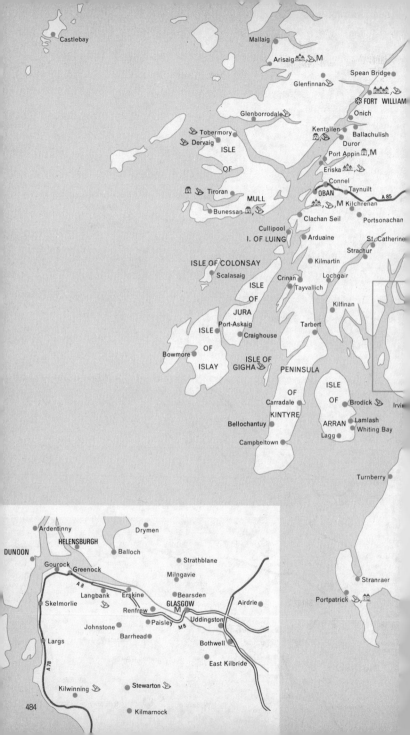

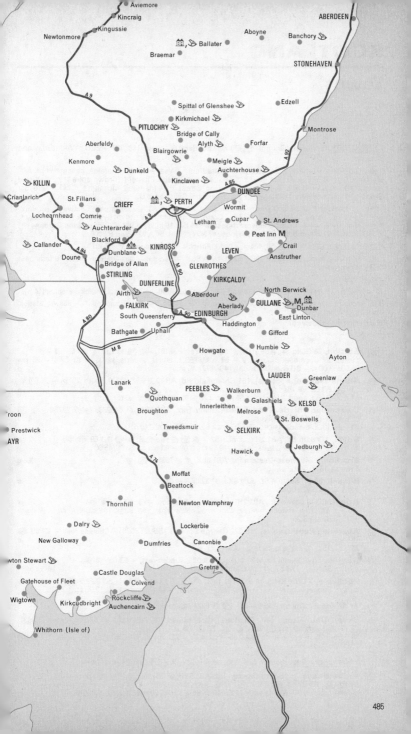

Aviemore
Kincraig
Kingussie
Newtonmore

ABERDEEN

Aboyne
Banchory
STONEHAVEN

Ballater
Braemar

Edzell

Spittal of Glenshee
Kirkmichael
PITLOCHRY
Bridge of Cally
Blairgowrie
Aberfeldy
Kenmore
Dunkeld
Kinclaven

Montrose

Forfar
Alyth
Meigle
Auchterhouse

KILLIN
Crianlarich
St. Fillans
Lochearnhead
Comrie
Auchterarder
Blackford
Callander
Doune
Dunblane
Bridge of Allan
STIRLING
Airth
FALKIRK
South Queensferry
Bathgate
Uphall

CRIEFF
PERTH
DUNDEE
Wormit
Letham
Cupar
St. Andrews
Peat Inn M
Crail
Anstruther
LEVEN
GLENROTHES
KIRKCALDY
Aberdour
Aberlady
GULLANE
North Berwick
Dunbar
East Linton
KINROSS
DUNFERLINE
EDINBURGH
Haddington
Gifford
Humbie
Ayton

M 8
Lanark
Howgate

LAUDER
Greenlaw

PEEBLES
Quothquan
Broughton
Walkerburn
Innerleithen
Galashiels
Melrose
St. Boswells
KELSO

Tweedsmuir
SELKIRK
Hawick
Jedburgh

Moffat
Beattock
Thornhill
Newton Wamphray

Dalry
New Galloway
Lockerbie
Dumfries
Canonbie

wton Stewart
Castle Douglas
Gatehouse of Fleet
Colvend
Wigtown
Kirkcudbright
Rockcliffe
Auchencairn
Gretna

Whithorn (Isle of)

roon
Prestwick
AYR

SCOTLAND

Towns

ABERDEEN Aberdeen. (Grampian) **401** N 12 **Scotland** G – pop. 186 ,757 – ECD : Wednesday and Saturday – ✪ 0224.

See : Old Aberdeen★★ X – St. Machar's Cathedral★★ (West front★★★, heraldic ceiling★★★) X **A** – Mercat Cross★★ Y **B** – Art Gallery★★ Y **M** – King's College Chapel★ (Crown spire★★★, medieval fittings★★★) X **D** – Brig o'Balgownie★ by Don Street X – Maritime Museum★ Z **M1** – Provost Skene's House★ (Painted ceiling★★) Y **E** – Marischal College★ Y **U**.

Envir. : Deeside★★ and Lin O'Dee★ Tour of 64 m., W : by A 93 X – Grampian Castles★★ (Craigievar★★★) W : 27 m. by A 944 X and B 9119 – Crathes Castle★★, SW : 14 m. by A 93 X – Kildrummy★, NW : 36 m. by A 944 X – Castle Fraser★ (exterior★★) W : 16 m. by A 944 X – Pitmedden Gardens★★, N : 16 m. by A 92 X and B 999 – Haddo House★, NW : 26 m. by A 92 X and B 9005.

🏌 King's Links, 19 Golf Rd 𝒫 581464 X – 🏌 St. Fittick's Rd, Balnagask 𝒫 876407 X.

✈ Aberdeen Airport 𝒫 722331 NW : 7 m. by A 96 X – **Terminal :** Bus Station, Guild St. (adjacent to Railway Station).

🚗 𝒫 582005.

⚓ by P & O Ferries : Orkney & Shetland Services : to Shetland Islands : Lerwick 3 weekly (14 h).

🛈 St. Nicholas House, Broad St. 𝒫 632727 – Stonehaven Rd 𝒫 873030 (summer only) – Railway Station, Guild St. (summer only).

♦Edinburgh 130 – ♦Dundee 67.

Plans on following pages

🏨 **Station**, 78 Guild St., AB9 2DN, 𝒫 587214, Telex 73161 – 📶 📺 ☎ 📭 🖾. 🔳 🖽 ⓞ 𝗩𝗜𝗦𝗔   Z **o**
   closed 24 December-3 January – **M** 6.00/9.50 **t.** and a la carte ⏷ 3.00 – ⊑ 5.25 – **59 rm** 25.00/53.00 **t.** – SB (weekends only) 48.75/71.40 **st.**

🏨 **Stakis Tree Tops** (Stakis), 161 Springfield Rd, AB9 2QH, 𝒫 33377, Telex 73794 – 📶 📺 ☎   X **s**
   📭 🖾. 🔳 🖽 ⓞ 𝗩𝗜𝗦𝗔
   M 6.50/9.95 **t.** and a la carte ⏷ 3.50 – ⊑ 3.75 – **92 rm** 47.50/58.00 **t.**

🏛 **Caledonian Thistle** (Thistle), 10-14 Union Terr., AB9 1HE, 𝒫 640233, Telex 73758 – 📶 📺   Z **i**
   🖾wc 📶 📭. 🔳 🖽 ⓞ 𝗩𝗜𝗦𝗔
   M 7.25/10.25 **t.** and a la carte ⏷ 3.10 – ⊑ 5.50 – **75 rm** 45.00/70.00 **t.**

🏩 **Royal**, 1-3 Bath St., AB1 2HY, 𝒫 585152 – 📶 📺 🖾wc 📶wc 📶 📭. 🔳 🖽 ⓞ 𝗩𝗜𝗦𝗔   Z **a**
   M (bar lunch)/dinner a la carte 6.50/10.40 **t.** ⏷ 3.00 – **43 rm** ⊑ 36.00/45.00 **t.**

🏠 **Bracklinn**, 348 Great Western Rd, AB1 6LX, 𝒫 317060 – 📺. 🛇   X **c**
   6 rm ⊑ 16.00/25.50 **st.**

🏠 **Russell**, 50 St. Swithin St., AB1 6XJ, 𝒫 323555 – 📭. 🛇   Z **c**
   9 rm ⊑ 14.00/26.00 **st.**

🍴🍴 **Atlantis**, 145 Crown St., AB1 2HR, 𝒫 591403, Seafood – 📭. 🔳 🖽 ⓞ 𝗩𝗜𝗦𝗔   Z **r**
   closed Saturday lunch, Sunday, Christmas, New Year and Bank Holidays – **M** a la carte 9.10/19.80 **t.** ⏷ 3.25.

🍴🍴 **Aberdeen Rendezvous**, 218-222 George St., AB1 1BS, 𝒫 633610, Chinese rest. – 🔳 🖽 ⓞ   Y **c**
   𝗩𝗜𝗦𝗔
   M 5.50/15.50 **t.** and a la carte ⏷ 3.80.

🍴🍴 **Nargile**, 77-79 Skene St., AB1 1QD, 𝒫 636093, Turkish rest. – 🔳 🖽 ⓞ 𝗩𝗜𝗦𝗔   Y **a**
   closed Sunday – **M** 3.95/12.50 **t.** and a la carte.

🍴 **Poldino's**, 7 Little Belmont St., AB1 1JG, 𝒫 647777, Italian rest. – 🔳 🖽 ⓞ 𝗩𝗜𝗦𝗔   YZ **u**
   closed Sunday, Christmas Day and New Years Day – **M** a la carte 8.80/12.30 **st.** ⏷ 3.20.

   at Altens S : 3 m. on A 956 – X – ⊠ ✪ 0224 Aberdeen :

🏨 **Skean Dhu Altens** (Mt. Charlotte), Souterhead Rd, AB1 4LF, 𝒫 877000, Telex 739631,
   📶, heated – 📶 🍴 rest 📺 ☎ & 📭. 🖾. 🔳 🖽 ⓞ 𝗩𝗜𝗦𝗔
   M 7.95/9.25 **st.** and a la carte ⏷ 2.85 – ⊑ 4.25 – **221 rm** 48.50/56.50 **st.** – SB (weekends only) 45.00/55.00 **st.**

   at Banchory-Devenick SW : 4 ½ m. on B 9077 – X – ⊠ ✪ 0224 Aberdeen :

🏛 **Ardoe House** 🛪, South Deeside Rd, AB1 5YP, 𝒫 867355, ≤, ❧, 🖾, park – 📺 🖾wc 📶
   📶 📭. 🖾. 🔳 🖽 ⓞ 𝗩𝗜𝗦𝗔
   closed 1 January – **M** a la carte 11.65/19.45 **st.** ⏷ 3.50 – **20 rm** ⊑ 28.00/60.00 **st.**

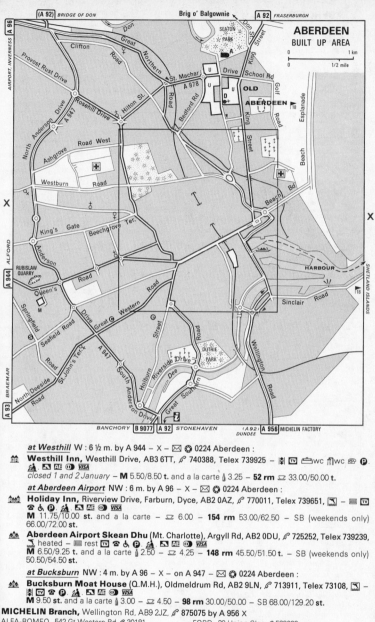

0   1 km
0   1/2 mile

at Westhill W : 6 ½ m. by A 944 – X – ⊠ ✪ 0224 Aberdeen :

🏠 **Westhill Inn,** Westhill Drive, AB3 6TT, ℰ 740388, Telex 739925 – 🕸 📺 ➡wc 🏮wc ☎ 🅿.
🍴 ᴧ AE ⓪ *VISA*
closed 1 and 2 January – **M** 5.50/8.50 **t.** and a la carte ᐧ 3.25 – **52 rm** ⇌ 33.00/50.00 **t.**

at Aberdeen Airport NW : 6 m. by A 96 – X – ⊠ ✪ 0224 Aberdeen :

🏨 **Holiday Inn,** Riverview Drive, Farburn, Dyce, AB2 0AZ, ℰ 770011, Telex 739651, 🔲 – 📼 📺
📺 ☎ 🕭 🅿. 🍴 ᴧ AE ⓪ *VISA*
M 11.75/10.00 **st.** and a la carte – ⇌ 6.00 – **154 rm** 53.00/62.50 – SB (weekends only)
66.00/72.00 **st.**

🏛 **Aberdeen Airport Skean Dhu** (Mt. Charlotte), Argyll Rd, AB2 0DU, ℰ 725252, Telex 739239,
🔲 heated – 📼 rest 📺 ☎ 🕭 🅿. 🍴 ᴧ AE ⓪ *VISA*
M 6.50/9.25 **t.** and a la carte ᐧ 2.50 – ⇌ 4.25 – **148 rm** 45.50/51.50 **t.** – SB (weekends only)
50.50/54.50 **st.**

at Bucksburn NW : 4 m. by A 96 – X – on A 947 – ⊠ ✪ 0224 Aberdeen :

🏛 **Bucksburn Moat House** (Q.M.H.), Oldmeldrum Rd, AB2 9LN, ℰ 713911, Telex 73108, 🔲 –
🕸 📺 ☎ 🕭 🅿. 🍴 ᴧ AE ⓪ *VISA*
M 9.50 **st.** and a la carte ᐧ 3.00 – ⇌ 4.50 – **98 rm** 30.00/50.00 – SB 68.00/129.20 **st.**

MICHELIN Branch, Wellington Rd, AB9 2JZ, ℰ 875075 by A 956 X

ALFA-ROMEO 542 Gt Western Rd ℰ 30181
AUSTIN-ROVER 92 Crown St. ℰ 590381
AUSTIN-ROVER, ROLLS ROYCE 19 Justice Mill Lane
ℰ 596151
BMW Grey St. ℰ 33355
NISSAN 78 Powis Terr. ℰ 41313
FIAT 870 Gt Northern Rd ℰ 695573
FORD Menzies Rd ℰ 879024

FORD 29 Union Glen ℰ 589022
LANCIA 3 Whitehall Rd ℰ 641349
MERCEDES-BENZ, OPEL 366 King St. ℰ 634211
RENAULT Lang Stracht ℰ 683181
SUBARU 16/22 Mid Stocket Rd ℰ 631950
VAUXHALL-OPEL 16 Dee St. ℰ 589216
VW, AUDI 94 Hilton Drive ℰ 43327

ABERDEEN

George Street .... **Y**
St. Nicolas Street .... **Y** 30
Union Street .... **Z**

Broad Street .... **Y** 6
Castle Street .... **Y** 7
College Street .... **Z** 9
Craigie Loanings .... **Y** 12
East North Street .... **Y** 16

Great Southern Road .... **Z** 18
Guild Street .... **Z** 19
Justice Street .... **Y** 21
Loch Street .... **Y** 22
Millburn Street .... **Z** 23
Regent Quay .... **Z** 24
Rosemount
  Terrace .... **Y** 25
Rosemount Viaduct .... **Y** 26
St. Andrew Street .... **Y** 28
St. Swithin Street .... **Z** 31
School Hill .... **YZ** 32

South Esplanade West ...... **Z** 33
South Mount Street .... **Z** 34
Springbank Terrace .... **Z** 35
Spring Garden .... **Y** 36
Trinity Quay .... **Z** 37
Union Terrace .... **Z** 39
Upperkirkgate .... **Y** 40
Victoria Street .... **Z** 42
Waverley Place .... **Z** 43
Wellington Place .... **Z** 45
Wellington Road .... **Z** 47
Woolmanhill .... **Y** 48

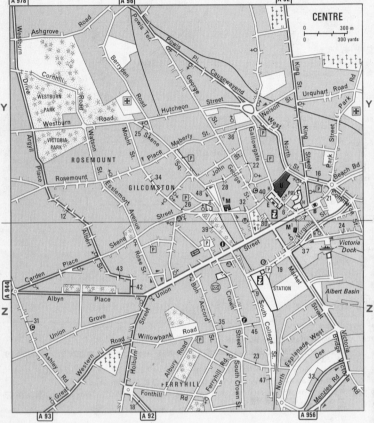

When visiting the West Country,
*use the Michelin Green Guide '' **England-The West Country** ''.*

– Detailed descriptions of places of interest
– Touring programmes by county
– Maps and street plans
– The history of the region
– Photographs and drawings of monuments, beauty spots, houses...

ABERDOUR Fife. (Fife) **401** K 15 Scotland G – pop. 1 ,460 – ECD : Wednesday – ✆ 0383.
See : Site★ – Castle★.
🏌 Dodhead, Burntisland ⌀ 0592 (Burntisland) 873247, E : 5 m. on A 92.
◆Edinburgh 17 – Dunfermline 7.

🏠 Woodside, Main St., KY3 9SW, ⌀ 860328 – 📺 🛏wc 🚿wc 🅿 🔄 ⒶⒺ ① 𝑽𝑰𝑺𝑨
12 rm ⌧ 19.00/48.00 t.

488

ABERFELDY Perth. (Tayside) **401** I 14 Scotland G – pop. 1,477 – ECD : Wednesday – ☎ 0887.
See : Site★.
Envir. : St. Mary's Church (Painted ceiling★) NE : 2 m. by A 827 – Loch Tay★★, SW : 6 m. by A827.
🛈 District Tourist Association, 8 Dunkeld St. ℰ 20276 (summer only).
◆Edinburgh 76 – ◆Glasgow 73 – ◆Oban 77 – Perth 32.

🏠 **Guinach House** ⬩, Urlar Rd, PH15 2ET, ℰ 20251, 🐴 – 📺
   March-October – **M** 6.00/9.50 **st.** ⬩ 3.30 – **7 rm** ⌖ 16.00/32.00. **st.**

♨ **Cruachan,** Kenmore St., PH15 2BL, ℰ 20545, 🐴 – 📺 🛁wc 🅿. ⓞ
   M (bar lunch)/dinner 9.50 **t.** and a la carte – **9 rm** ⌖ 15.00/34.00 **t.** – SB (October-March)
   40.00/45.00 **st.**

⌂ **Balnearn,** Crieff Rd, PH15 2BJ, ℰ 20431, 🐴 – 🅿
   13 rm ⌖ 11.50/23.00 **t.**

AUSTIN-ROVER, FORD Dunkeld St. ℰ 20254

ABERFOYLE Perth. (Central) **401** G 15 – pop. 546 – ECD : Wednesday – ✉ Stirling – ☎ 087 72.
🏌 Braeval ℰ 493.
🛈 Main St. ℰ 352 (summer only).
◆Edinburgh 56 – ◆Glasgow 27.

   Hotels see : Callander NE : 10 ½ m., Drymen SW : 11 ½ m.

ABERLADY E. Lothian (Lothian) **401** L 15 – pop. 884 – ECD : Wednesday – ☎ 087 57.
🏌 Kilspindie, ℰ 216.
◆Edinburgh 16 – Haddington 5 – North Berwick 7.5.

♨ **Kilspindie House,** Main St., EH32 0RE, ℰ 319 – 🛁wc 🚿wc 🅿. 🔼 VISA
   M (bar lunch)/dinner 8.00 **t.** and a la carte ⬩ 2.90 – **12 rm** ⌖ 18.50/35.00 **st.** – SB (weekends
   only) (October-March) 39.00 **st.**

✕ **Green Craig House** ⬩ with rm, SW : ¾ m. on A 198, EH32 0PY, ℰ 301, ≤, 🐴 – 📺 🛁wc
   🅿. 🔼 VISA
   M 13.50 **t.** ⬩ 3.00 – **8 rm** ⌖ 35.00/55.00 **t.**

ABERLOUR Banff. (Grampian) **401** K 11 – pop. 879 – ECD : Wednesday – ☎ 034 05.
Envir. : Dufftown (Glenfiddich Distillery★) SE : 4 m. by A 941 – Huntly Castle (Heraldic carvings★★★)
E : 1 ½ m. by A 941 and A 920.
◆Edinburgh 189 – ◆Aberdeen 59 – ◆Inverness 54.

🏠 **Dowans,** AB3 9LS, SW : ¾ m. by A 95 ℰ 488, ≤, 🐎, 🐴 – 🛁wc 🅿. 🔼 VISA
   closed mid December-mid February – **M** 4.00/7.00 ⬩ 2.60 – **13 rm** ⌖ 12.00/32.00.

AUSTIN-ROVER, LAND ROVER-RANGE ROVER 15-19 High St. ℰ 505

ABOYNE Aberdeen. (Grampian) **401** L 12 – pop. 1,477 – ECD : Thursday – ☎ 0339.
Envir. : Craigievar Castle★★★ (17C) *AC*, NE : 12 m.
🏌 Formaston Park ℰ 2328, E : end of Village – 🏌 Tarland ℰ 033 981 (Tarland) 413, NW : 5 m.
◆Edinburgh 131 – ◆Aberdeen 30 – ◆Dundee 68.

🏠 **Birse Lodge** ⬩, Charleston Rd, AB3 5EL, ℰ 2253, 🐴 – 🛁wc 🅿. 🔼 ⓞ
   Mid March-mid October – **M** (bar lunch)/dinner 10.50 **t.** ⬩ 3.30 – **16 rm** ⌖ 20.00/40.00 **t.**

AUSTIN-ROVER Main Rd ℰ 2440

ACHILTIBUIE Ross and Cromarty (Highland) **401** D 9 – ☎ 085 482.
◆Edinburgh 243 – ◆Inverness 84 – Ullapool 25.

🏠 **Summer Isles** ⬩, IV26 2YG, ℰ 282, « ≤ Picturesque setting overlooking Summer Isles »,
   🐎 – 🛁wc 🅿
   April-October – **M** (dinner only) 18.00 **st.** ⬩ 3.50 – **13 rm** ⌖ 16.00/60.00 **st.**

ACHNASHEEN Ross and Cromarty (Highland) **401** E 11 – ECD : Wednesday – ☎ 044 588.
◆Edinburgh 202 – ◆Inverness 43.

🏨 **Ledgowan Lodge** (Best Western) ⬩, IV22 2EJ, on A 890 ℰ 252, ≤, 🐎, 🐴 – 🛁wc 🅿. 🔼
   🔼 ⓞ VISA
   Easter-mid October – **M** 6.00/12.50 **t.** and a la carte ⬩ 2.50 – **17 rm** ⌖ 19.75/45.00 **t.** – SB
   52.00/70.00 **st.**

ADVIE Moray. (Highland) **401** J 11 – ✉ Grantown-on-Spey – ☎ 080 75.
◆Edinburgh 153 – ◆Inverness 46.

🏯 **Tulchan Lodge** ⬩, PH26 3PW, on B 9102 ℰ 200, Telex 75405, ≤ Spey Valley, « Tasteful
   decor », 🐎, 🐴, park – ☎ 🅿 🖂
   closed February and March – **M** 10.00/25.00 **t.** ⬩ 5.00 – **11 rm** ⌖ 85.00/130.00 **t.**

AIRDRIE Lanark. (Strathclyde) 🗺️ 401 402 I 16 – pop. 45 ,320 – ECD : Wednesday – ☎ 023 64.
♦Edinburgh 32 – ♦Glasgow 14 – Motherwell 6.5 – Perth 53.

🏨 **Staging Post,** 8-10 Anderson St., ML6 0BZ, ☎ 67525 – 📺 ➡️wc ⊛ 🅿 🔲 AE ⓞ VISA 🍴
closed 1 and 2 January – **M** 3.75/5.50 **t.** and a la carte 🍴 3.05 – **8 rm** ⇌ 27.00/39.00 **st., 1 suite** 39.00 **st.**

FORD South Biggar Rd ☎ 64702

AIRTH Stirling. (Central) 401 I 15 – pop. 972 – ✉️ Falkirk – ☎ 032 483.
♦Edinburgh 30 – Dunfermline 14 – Falkirk 7 – Stirling 8.

🏰 **Airth Castle** ⟨⟩, FK2 8JF, ☎ 411, Telex 777975, ≼, « Former castle in extensive grounds »,
🔲, 🌳, park – 📺 ☎ 🅿 🔲 AE ⓞ VISA 🍴
M 8.95 **st.** 🍴 3.20 – **23 rm** ⇌ 45.00/71.00 **st.** – SB (weekends only)(October-April) 50.00/70.00 **st.**

ALLOWAY Ayr (Strathclyde) 401 402 G 17 – see Ayr.

ALTENS Aberdeen. (Grampian) – see Aberdeen.

ALTNAHARRA Sutherland (Highland) 401 G 9 – ✉️ Lairg – ☎ 054 981.
♦Edinburgh 39 – ♦Inverness 83 – Thurso 61.

🏨 Altnaharra ⟨⟩, IV27 4UE, ☎ 222, ≼, ≈, 🌳 – ➡️wc 🅿
21 rm. **3 suites**.

ALYTH Perth. (Tayside) 401 K 14 – pop. 2 ,258 – ECD : Wednesday – ☎ 082 83.
🏌️ Pitcrocknie ☎ 2268, E : 1 ½ m.
♦Edinburgh 63 – ♦Aberdeen 69 – ♦Dundee 16 – Perth 21.

🏰 **Lands of Loyal** ⟨⟩, Loyal Rd, PH11 8JQ, N : ½ m. by B 954 ☎ 3151, ≼, « Victorian country
house », 🌳, park – ➡️wc ☎ 🅿 AE
M 8.50/12.00 **t.** and a la carte 🍴 3.50 – **14 rm** ⇌ 22.50/48.00 **t.** – SB 60.00/69.00 **st.**

ANSTRUTHER Fife. (Fife) 401 L 15 – pop. 2 ,865 – ECD : Wednesday – ☎ 0333 - 🏌️.
See : Scottish Fisheries Museum★★.
Envir. : The East Neuk★★ (coastline from Crail to St. Monance by A 917) – Kellie Castle★, NW :
7 m. by A 959.
🏌️ Marsfield ☎ 310387.
🛈 Scottish Fisheries Museum, St. Ayles ☎ 310628.
♦Edinburgh 46 – ♦Dundee 23 – Dunfermline 34.

🏰 **Craw's Nest,** Bankwell Rd, KY10 3DR, ☎ 310691, 🌳 – 📺 ➡️wc 🛁wc ☎ 🅿 🔲, 🔲 AE ⓞ
VISA 🍴
M 6.25/10.50 **t.** and a la carte 🍴 3.50 – **50 rm** ⇌ 25.00/44.00 **t.** – SB 56.00/59.50 **st.**

✗ **Cellar,** 24 East Green, KY10 3AA, ☎ 310378, Seafood – 🔲 VISA
closed Sunday dinner, 1 week May, first 2 weeks November and 24-26 December – **M** a la
carte 10.00/15.00.

ARBROATH Angus (Tayside) 401 M 14 Scotland G – pop. 23 ,934 – ECD : Wednesday – ☎ 0241.
See : Site★ – Abbey★ AC.
Envir. : St. Vigeans Museum★ by A 92.
🏌️ Elliot ☎ 72272, S : 1 m.
🛈 Market Pl., ☎ 72609 and 76680.
♦Edinburgh 72 – ♦Aberdeen 51 – ♦Dundee 16.

Hotel see : Montrose NE : 13 ½ m.

BMW Montrose Rd ☎ 72919   FORD Millgate ☎ 73051

ARDENTINNY Argyll. (Strathclyde) 401 F 15 – ECD : Wednesday – ✉️ Dunoon – ☎ 036 981.
♦Edinburgh 107 – Dunoon 13 – ♦Glasgow 64 – Oban 71.

🏨 **Ardentinny** ⟨⟩, PA23 8TR, ☎ 209, ≼ Loch Long, 🌳 – ➡️wc 🛁wc 🅿 🔲 AE ⓞ VISA
Mid March-October – **M** (bar lunch)/dinner 13.50 **t.** 🍴 2.95 – **11 rm** ⇌ 19.00/39.50 **t.**

ARDEONAIG Perth. (Central) – see Killin.

ARDGAY Ross and Cromarty (Highland) 401 G 10 – ☎ 086 32.
♦Edinburgh 205 – ♦Inverness 49 – Wick 77.

↥ **Croit Mairi** ⟨⟩, Kincardine Hill, IV24 3DJ, S : 1 ¼ m. off A 9 ☎ 504, ≼ Dornoch Firth an⟨⟩
hills, 🌳 – 🅿 🔲 AE ⓞ VISA 🍴
closed 2 weeks October-November – **5 rm** ⇌ 12.00/20.00 **st.**

490

ARDROSSAN Ayr. (Strathclyde) **401 402** F 17 – pop. 11 ,386 – ECD : Wednesday – ✆ 0294.
🚢 by Isle of Man Steam Packet Co. : to the Isle of Man : Douglas July-August 1 weekly (6 h) –
by Caledonian MacBrayne : to the Isle of Arran : Brodick 3-10 daily (1 h).
♦Edinburgh 75 – ♦Ayr 18 – ♦Glasgow 32.

    Hotels see : Kilmarnock SE : 11 ½ m., *Largs* N : 11 ½ m.

ARDUAINE Argyll. (Strathclyde) **401** D 15 – ECD : Wednesday – ✉ Oban – ✆ 085 22 Kilmelford.
♦Edinburgh 142 – ♦Oban 20.

🏨 **Loch Melfort** 🌳, PA34 4XG, ☞ 233, ≤ Sound of Jura, ☛ – 🚻wc **P**. ☒
    Easter-mid October – **M** (buffet lunch)/dinner 13.50 **t**. and a la carte – 🍽 2.50 – **26 rm**
    25.00/70.00 **t**.

ARISAIG Inverness. (Highland) **401** C 13 – ECD : Thursday – ✆ 068 75.
See : Site★ – ≤★ of Sound of Arisaig.
Envir. : Silver Sands of Morar★, N : 6 m. by A 830.
♦Edinburgh 172 – ♦Inverness 102 – ♦Oban 88.

🏰 **Arisaig House** 🌳, Beasdale, PH39 4NR, SE : 3 ¼ m. on A 830 ☞ 622, ≤ Loch Nan Uamh
    and Roshven Mountains, ☛, park – **TV** ☎ **P**. **VISA** ☒
    April-October – **M** (booking essential) (restricted lunch residents only)/dinner 19.00 **st**. ⧉ 4.50
    – **16 rm** 🍽 28.50/80.50 **st**.

🏠 **Arisaig,** PH39 4NH, ☞ 210, ≤ – 🚻wc **P**
    March-October – **M** (bar lunch)/dinner 12.00 **st**. ⧉ 2.50 – **13 rm** 🍽 33.00/34.50 **st**.

ARMADALE Inverness. (Highland) **401** C 12 – Shipping Services : see Skye (Isle of).

ARRAN (Isle of) Bute. (Strathclyde) **401 402** DE 16 17 **Scotland G** – pop. 4 ,726.
See : Site★★ – Brodick Castle★★.
🚢 by Caledonian MacBrayne : from Brodick to Ardrossan 3-10 daily (1 h) – from Lochranza to
Claonaig (Kintyre Peninsula) summer only : 6-8 daily (30 mn).

    Brodick – pop. 884 – ECD : Wednesday – ✉ ✆ 0770 Brodick.
    🏌 ☞ 2349, ½ m. from Pier.
    🛈 The Pier ☞ 2401/2140.

ʌ **Auchrannie** 🌳, KA27 8BZ, ☞ 2234, ☛ – 🚻wc **P**
    April-September – **16 rm** 🍽 10.00/24.00 **st**.

ʌ **Altanna,** KA27 8DW, ☞ 2232 – 🚻wc 🚻wc **P**
    April-September – **13 rm** 🍽 12.00/30.00 **st**.

    Lagg – ✉ Kilmory – ✆ 077 087 Sliddery.

🏠 **Lagg,** KA27 8PQ, ☞ 255, ☛ – 🚻wc **P**
    7 March-28 October – **M** 6.50/12.50 **t**. and a la carte ⧉ 2.60 – **17 rm** 🍽 19.00/42.00 **t**.

    Lamlash – pop. 908 – ECD : Wednesday except summer – ✉ Brodick – ✆ 077 06 Lam-
    lash.
    🏌 ☞ 296.

ʌ **Glenisle,** Shore Rd, KA27 8LY, ☞ 258, ≤, ☛ – 🚻wc **P**
    April-October – **16 rm** 🍽 8.35/24.50 **t**.

    Whiting Bay – ECD : Wednesday except summer – ✉ Brodick – ✆ 077 07 Whiting Bay.
    🏌·

🏠 **Whiting Bay,** Shore Rd, KA27 8QJ, ☞ 247, ≤, ☛, ☜ – **TV** 🚻wc 🚻wc **P**. ☒ **VISA**
    Mid March-October and Christmas-New Year – **M** (closed lunch to non-residents)/dinner
    9.50 **t**. and a la carte ⧉ 3.00 – **18 rm** 🍽 15.00/38.00 **t**.

🏠 **Cameronia,** Shore Rd, ☞ 254 – **P**. ☜
    M (bar lunch)/dinner 15.00 **t**. and a la carte ⧉ 2.50 – **6 rm** 🍽 14.00/28.00 **t**.

AUCHENCAIRN Kirkcudbright. (Dumfries and Galloway) **401 402** I 19 – ✉ Castle Douglas –
✆ 055 664.
♦Edinburgh 98 – ♦Dumfries 21 – Stranraer 62.

🏨 **Balcary Bay** 🌳, Balcary, DG7 1QZ, SE : 2 m. by A 711 ☞ 217, ≤ Auchencairn bay, hills and
    countryside, ☛ – 🚻wc ☎ **P**. ☜
    March-November and Christmas – **M** 8.50 and a la carte ⧉ 2.75 – **9 rm** 23.00/50.00.

Do not lose your way in Europe, use the Michelin
Main Road maps, scale : 1 inch : 16 miles.

AUCHTERARDER Perth. (Tayside) **401** I 15 – pop. 2 ,838 – ECD : Wednesday – ✆ 076 46.

🏌 Orchil Rd ✆ 2804, SW : 1 m. – 🏌, 🏌, 🏌, 🏌 Gleneagles ✆ 3543.

🛈 Crown Wynd, High St., ✆ 3450 (summer only).

◆Edinburgh 55 – ◆Glasgow 45 – Perth 14.

🏨🏨🏨 **Gleneagles,** PH3 1NF, SW : 1 ½ m. by A 9 ✆ 2231, Telex 76105, ≤, « Championship golf courses and extensive leisure facilities », 🏊, 🏌, 🏖, 🎾, park, ✗, squash – 💲 🆃🆅 🔲 ⚄ 🅿.
🅰. 🕭 🅰🅴 ⓪ 🆅🅸🆂🅰.
M (see also Eagle's Nest rest.) 15.25/18.75 **st.** and a la carte 🅟 4.25 – 🆎 7.95 – **254 rm** 50.00/110.00 t., **20 suites** 155.00/195.00 t. – SB 110.00/129.00 **st.**

🏨🏨 **Auchterarder House** 🦢, PH3 1DZ, N : 1 ½ m. on B 8062 ✆ 2939, « Scottish Jacobean house », 🎗, park – 🆃🆅 🗄wc ☎ 🅿. 🔲 🅰🅴 🆅🅸🆂🅰.
M (booking essential) 15.00/25.00 st. 🅟 3.50 – **11 rm** 🆎 40.25/80.00 t.

🏨 Cairn Lodge 🦢, Orchill Rd, PH3 1LX, ✆ 2634, 🎗 – 🆃🆅 🗄wc ☎ 🅿 – **5 rm**.

🏠 **Coll Earn House,** PH3 1DF, ✆ 3553, 🎗 – 🆃🆅 🗄wc ☎ 🅿. 🔲 🅰🅴 ⓪ 🆅🅸🆂🅰
M 9.00 t. and a la carte 🅟 3.00 – **6 rm** 🆎 25.00/40.00 t. – SB 54.00 **st.**

✕✕✕ Eagle's Nest (at Gleneagles H.), PH3 1NF, SW : 1 ½ m. by A 9 ✆ 2231, Telex 76105 – 🅿.

AUCHTERHOUSE Angus. (Tayside) **401** K 14 – ✉ Dundee – ✆ 082 626.

◆Edinburgh 69 – ◆Dundee 7 – Perth 24.

✕✕✕ **Old Mansion House** 🦢 with rm, DD3 0QN, ✆ 366, ≤, « 15-17C country house », 🏊 heated, 🎗, park, ✗ – 🆃🆅 🗄wc ☎ 🅿. 🔲 🅰🅴 🆅🅸🆂🅰
closed 25 to 26 December and 31 December-7 January – **M** 8.95 t. (lunch) and a la carte 12.25/17.95 t. – **6 rm** 🆎 40.00/65.00 t.

AULTBEA Ross and Cromarty (Highland) **401** D 10 – ECD : Wednesday – ✆ 044 582.

◆Edinburgh 234 – ◆Inverness 79 – Kyle of Lochalsh 80.

🏠 **Aultbea,** IV22 2HX, ✆ 201, ≤ – 🗄wc 🅿. 🔲 🆅🅸🆂🅰
April-October – **M** (bar lunch)/dinner 10.50 t. 🅟 2.00 – **8 rm** 🆎 15.00/35.00 t.

For maximum information from town plans : consult the conventional signs key, p. 19.

AVIEMORE Inverness. (Highland) **401** I 12 **Scotland G** – pop. 1 ,510 – ECD : Wednesday – Winter Sports – ✆ 0479.

See : Site★ – Envir. : ❄★★★ from Cairn Gorm (alt. 4,084 ft.) SE : 8 ½ m. by B 970 (chair lift *AC*) – Highland Wildlife Park★, S : by A 9.

🛈 Grampian Rd ✆ 810363.

◆Edinburgh 129 – ◆Inverness 29 – Perth 85.

🏨🏨 Stakis Coylumbridge (Stakis), PH22 1QH, SE : 1 ¾ m. by B 970 ✆ 810661, Telex 75272, ≤, 🏊,
🎗, 🎗, ✗ – 🆃🆅 🔲 ⚄ 🅿. 🅰
153 rm

🏨🏨 **Strathspey Thistle** (Thistle), Aviemore Centre, PH22 1PF, ✆ 810681, Telex 75213, ≤ Cairngorms – 💲 🆃🆅 🅿. 🔲 🅰🅴 ⓪ 🆅🅸🆂🅰
M 4.50/8.50 t. 🅟 3.00 – **88 rm** 🆎 47.50/54.00 t.

🏨 **Post House** (T.H.F.), Aviemore Centre, PH22 1PJ, ✆ 810771, Telex 75597, ≤ – 💲 🆃🆅 🗄wc
🌐 ⚄ 🅿. 🅰. 🔲 🅰🅴 ⓪ 🆅🅸🆂🅰
M (dinner only) 8.50 st. and a la carte 🅟 2.70 – 🆎 5.50 – **103 rm** 34.50/47.50 **st.**

🏨 **Badenoch** (Osprey), Aviemore Centre, PH22 1PH, ✆ 810261, ≤ – 💲 🆃🆅 🗄wc 🌐 🅿. 🔲 🅰🅴
⓪ 🆅🅸🆂🅰
M (bar lunch)/dinner 9.00 st. and a la carte 🅟 3.00 – **77 rm** 🆎 14.70/35.80 **st.** – SB (except Easter, Christmas and New Year) 32.00/44.00 **st.**

🏠 **Lynwilg,** PH22 1QB, S : 2 ¼ m. on A 9 ✉ Loch Alvie ✆ 810207, ≤, 🎗 – 🗄wc 🅿. 🔲 🅰🅴
🆅🅸🆂🅰. ✗
M (bar lunch)/dinner 8.45 t. and a la carte 🅟 2.50 – **12 rm** 🆎 13.75/27.00 t.

AUSTIN-ROVER Main Rd ✆ 810492   FORD 115 Grampian Rd ✆ 810232

AYR Ayr. (Strathclyde) **401 402** G 17 **Scotland G** – pop. 48 ,493 – ECD : Wednesday – ✆ 0292.

Envir. : Alloway★ (Burns' Cottage and Museum★) S : 3 m. by B 7024 BZ – Culzean Castle★ (Setting★★★, Oval staircase★★) SW : 14 m. by A 719 BZ.

🏌 Belleisle ✆ 0292 (Alloway) 41258 BZ – 🏌 Dalmilling, Westwood Av., Whitletts ✆ 263893 BZ.

🛈 39 Sandgate ✆ 284196.

◆Edinburgh 81 – ◆Glasgow 35.

Plan opposite

🏨 Marine Court, 12 Fairfield Rd, KA7 2AR, ✆ 267461, 🏊, – 🆃🆅 🗄wc 🗄wc ☎ 🅿. 🅰   AY **a**
29 rm.

🏨 **Belleisle House** 🦢, Doonfoot Rd, Belleisle Park, KA7 4DU, S : 1 ½ m. on A 719 ✆ 42331, ≤
– 🆃🆅 🗄wc 🗄wc 🌐 🅿. 🅰. 🔲 🅰🅴 ⓪ 🆅🅸🆂🅰   BZ **u**
M 5.50/9.95 t. and a la carte 🅟 2.95 – **17 rm** 🆎 29.50/39.50 t.

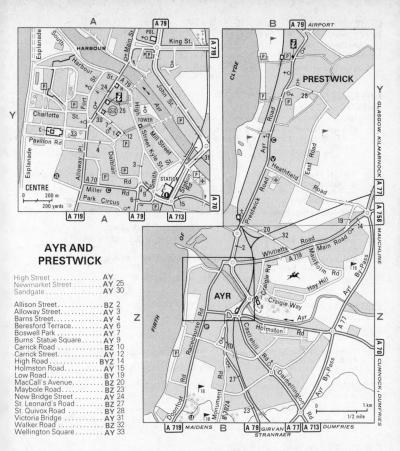

AYR AND PRESTWICK

High Street . . . . AY
Newmarket Street . . . . AY 25
Sandgate . . . . AY 30

Allison Street . . . . BZ 2
Alloway Street . . . . AY 3
Barns Street . . . . AY 4
Beresford Terrace . . . . AY 6
Boswell Park . . . . AY 7
Burns' Statue Square . . . . . . AY 9
Carrick Road . . . . BZ 10
Carrick Street . . . . AY 12
High Road . . . . BYZ 14
Holmston Road . . . . AY 15
Low Road . . . . BY 19
MacCall's Avenue . . . . BZ 20
Maybole Road . . . . BZ 23
New Bridge Street . . . . AY 24
St. Leonard's Road . . . . BZ 27
St. Quivox Road . . . . BY 28
Victoria Bridge . . . . AY 31
Walker Road . . . . BZ 32
Wellington Square . . . . AY 33

🏨 **Pickwick**, 19 Racecourse Rd, KA7 2TD, ℰ 260111, 🌳 – 📺 🛁wc 🚿wc ☎ 🅿 VISA 🐾
M 7.00/11.00 t. and a la carte 🍷 1.70 – **15 rm** ⬚ 30.00/45.00 t. BZ **e**

🏨 **Stakis Station (Stakis)**, Burns Statue Sq., KA7 3AT, ℰ 263268 – 🛗 📺 🛁wc 🚿wc ☎ 🅿 🏋
73 rm, **2 suites**. AY **i**

↑ **Clifton**, 19 Miller Rd, KA7 2AX, ℰ 264521 – 🚿wc 🅿 🔼 🆎 VISA 🐾
11 rm ⬚ 15.00/27.00 t. AY **c**

at Alloway S : 3 m. on A 719 – BZ – ✉ ☎ 0292 Ayr :

🏨 **Balgarth**, Dunure Rd, KA7 4HR, on A 719 ℰ 42441, 🌳 – 📺 🛁wc 🚿wc ☎ 🅿 – **15 rm**.

ALFA-ROMEO, FIAT Galloway Av. ℰ 260416
AUSTIN-ROVER, DAIMLER-JAGUAR 18 Holmston Rd ℰ 266944
MERCEDES-BENZ Heathfield Industrial Estate ℰ 282727
NISSAN Alloway Pl. ℰ 263140

SAAB Cambuslea Rd ℰ 266146
TOYOTA 65 Peebles St. ℰ 267606
VAUXHALL 196 Prestwick Rd ℰ 261631
VOLVO Burn's Statue Sq. ℰ 282711
VW, AUDI 24 Dalblair Rd ℰ 269522
YUGO 49 New Rd ℰ 266261

AYTON Berwick. (Borders) 401 402 N 16 – ECD : Thursday – ☎ 039 02.

Envir. : Manderston★, SW : 10 m. by B 6355 and A 6105 – Foulden★ S : 4 m. – Eyemouth (Museum★) N : 2 m. by B 6255 – St. Abb's Head★★, N : 5 m. – Fast Castle (Site★★) NW : 7 m. off A 1107.

🏌 at Eyemouth, Gunsgreen House ℰ 0390 (Eyemouth) 50551, N : 3 m. by A 6355.

◆ Edinburgh 48 – Berwick-upon-Tweed 8.

🏰 **Red Lion**, High St., TD14 5QP, ℰ 400 – 🅿 🔼 🆎 ⓪ VISA
M a la carte 7.75/9.55 – **9 rm** ⬚ 11.50/21.00 st.

493

BALLACHULISH Argyll. (Highland) 401 E 13 – ECD : Wednesday – ✪ 085 52.
Envir. : Glen Coe★★, E : 6 m. by A 82.
🏠 ⌖ 296 (summer only).
◆Edinburgh 117 – ◆ Inverness 80 – Kyle of Lochalsh 90 – ◆ Oban 38.

　⌂ **Lyn Leven,** White St., PA39 4JW, ⌖ 392, ≤ – 🏧wc 🅿
　　closed 23 to 28 December – **8 rm** 🍽 9.50/24.00.

BALLATER Aberdeen. (Grampian) 401 K 12 – pop. 1 ,051 – ECD : Thursday – ✪ 0338.
🏌18 ⌖ 55567 – 🚉 Station Sq. ⌖ 55306 (summer only).
◆Edinburgh 111 – ◆Aberdeen 41 – ◆Inverness 70 – Perth 67.

　🏨 **Craigendarroch Hotel and Country Club** 🦌, Braemar Rd, AB3 5XA, on A 93 ⌖ 55858,
　　Telex 739952, ≤Dee valley and Grampians, 🏊, 🎾, squash – 📺 🏧wc ☎ 🅿. 🏊. 🔼 AE
　　VISA
　　(dinner only) 17.25 **st.** – **23 rm** 🍽 61.00/90.00 **st.** – SB (except Christmas and Bank Holidays)
　　80.00/99.00 **st.**
　🏨 **Tullich Lodge** 🦌, AB3 5SB, E : 1 ½ m. on A 93 ⌖ 55406, ≤ Dee valley and Grampians,
　　« Country house atmosphere », 🎾 – 🏧wc 🏧wc 🅿. AE
　　April-November – **M** (bar lunch) (booking essential)/dinner 15.00 **st.** ⅄ 3.60 – **10 rm** 🍽 (din-
　　ner included) 50.00/100.00 **st.**
　🏨 **Darroch Learg,** Braemar Rd, AB3 5UX, ⌖ 55443, ≤ Dee Valley and Grampians, 🎾 – 🏧wc
　　🏧wc 🅿
　　February-October – **M** 5.00/9.00 **st.** ⅄ 2.00 – **23 rm** 🍽 17.50/40.00 **st.**
　🏠 **Alexandra,** 12 Bridge Sq., AB3 6QJ, ⌖ 55376 – 📺 🏧wc 🅿. 🔼 AE ① VISA
　　M (bar lunch)/dinner 15.00 **st.** and a la carte ⅄ 2.20 – **6 rm** 🍽 16.00/30.00 **st.** – SB 42.00/56.00 **st.**
　⌂ **Moorside House,** 26 Braemar Rd, AB3 5RL, ⌖ 55492, 🎾 – 🏧wc 🅿
　　May-October – **8 rm** 🍽 13.00/20.00.
　⌂ **Morvada,** Braemar Rd, AB3 5RL, ⌖ 55501, 🎾 – 🏧wc 🅿. 🍴
　　May-September – **6 rm** 🍽 13.00/22.00 **s.**

BALLOCH Dunbarton (Strathclyde) 401 G 15 – ✪ 038 985 Arden.
Envir. : Loch Lomond★★ – Ben Lomond★★ – Luss N : 9 m. by A 82.
🚉 ⌖ 0389 (Alexandria) 53533 (summer only).
◆Edinburgh 62 – ◆Glasgow 18 – Helensburgh 7.

　🏨 **Lomond Castle** 🦌, G83 8RB, N : 2 m. on A 82 ⌖ 681, ≤, 🏊, 🦌, 🎾, park – 📺 ☎ 🅿. 🏊.
　　🔼 AE VISA 🍴
　　M 8.00/10.00 **t.** and a la carte – **21 rm** 🍽 30.00/55.00 **t.** – SB 60.00/75.00 **st.**

BALMACARA Ross and Cromarty (Highland) 401 D 12 – ECD : Wednesday – ✉ Kyle of Lochalsh
– ✪ 059 986.
◆Edinburgh 197 – Kyle of Lochalsh 4.5.

　🏨 **Balmacara,** IV40 8DH, ⌖ 283, ≤ coast and mountains – 🏧wc 🏧wc 🅿. 🔼 VISA
　　April-October – **M** (bar lunch)/dinner 9.75 **t.** and a la carte ⅄ 3.50 – **29 rm** 🍽 22.50/39.00 **t.**

BALNAKEIL Sutherland (Highland) 401 F 8.
◆Edinburgh 294 – Durness 2 – ◆Inverness 135 – Thurso 83.

BANAVIE Inverness. (Highland) 401 E 13 – see Fort William.

BANCHORY Kincardine. (Grampian) 401 M 12 – pop. 4 ,683 – ECD : Thursday – ✪ 033 02.
Envir. : Crathes Castle★★, E : 2 m. by A 93 – Craigievar Castle★★★, N : 17 m. by A 980 – Castle
Fraser★ (exterior★★) N : 14 m. by A 980 and B 977.
🏌18 Kinneskie ⌖ 2365 – 🏌 Torphins ⌖ 033 982 (Torphins) 493, NW : 6 m.
🚉 Dee St. Car Park ⌖ 2000 (summer only).
◆Edinburgh 118 – ◆Aberdeen 17 – ◆Dundee 55 – ◆Inverness 94.

　🏨 **Banchory Lodge** 🦌, Dee St., AB3 3HS, ⌖ 2625, ≤, « Part 18C house on River Dee », 🦌,
　　🎾 – 📺 🏧wc 🅿. 🔼 AE VISA
　　closed December-January – **M** 7.50/15.50 **st.** and a la carte – **25 rm** 🍽 25.00/50.00 **s.**
　🏨 **Raemoir House** 🦌, AB3 4ED, N : 2 ½ m. on A 980 ⌖ 4884, ≤, « 18C mansion in extensive
　　grounds », 🎾, park – 📺 🏧wc 🅿. 🔼 AE ① VISA
　　M (bar lunch Monday to Saturday)/dinner 15.50 **t.** ⅄ 3.60 – **23 rm** 🍽 32.00/60.00 **t.** – SB
　　(except Christmas and New Year) 66.00 **st.**
　🏨 **Tor-Na-Coille** 🦌, Inchmarlo Rd, AB3 4AB, ⌖ 2242, 🎾, park – 🛗 📺 🏧wc 🏧wc ☎ 🅿.
　　🏊. 🔼 AE VISA
　　M (bar lunch)/dinner 12.00 **st.** and a la carte ⅄ 3.25 – **25 rm** 🍽 20.00/40.00 **st.** – SB (weekends
　　only) 56.00/64.00 **st.**

AUSTIN-ROVER North Deeside Rd ⌖ 2255　　　　　RENAULT North Deeside Rd ⌖ 2847

BANCHORY-DEVENICK Aberdeen. (Grampian) – see Aberdeen.

BANFF Banff. (Grampian) **401** M 10 Scotland G − pop. 3 ,843 − ECD : Wednesday − ✪ 026 12.
See : Site★ − Duff House★ − Mercat Cross★.
🏌 Royal Tarlair, Macduff ✆ 0261 (Macduff) 32897.
🎫 Collie Lodge ✆ 2419 (summer only).
◆Edinburgh 177 − ◆Aberdeen 47 − Fraserburgh 26 − ◆Inverness 74.

🏦 **Banff Springs,** Golden Knowes Rd, AB4 2JE, W : ¾ m. on A 98 ✆ 2881, ≤ − 📺 ➚wc 🛁wc
⊛ **Ⓟ**. 🅰. 🔼 🆎 ⑩ 𝘝𝘐𝘚𝘈. ⅏
M (bar lunch)/dinner 10.00 **t.** and a la carte ⓪ 2.85 − **30 rm** ⊑ 27.60/34.00 **t.** − SB (weekends only) 40.00 **st.**

🏦 **County,** 32 High St., AB4 1AE, ✆ 5353, ≤, 🍴 − 📺 ➚wc ⊛ **Ⓟ**. 🆎 ⑩
M 4.25/11.50 **t.** ⓪ 3.50 − **7 rm** ⊑ 16.50/44.00 **t.** − SB (weekends only) 45.00/60.00 **st.**

⌂ **Carmelite House,** 40 Low St., AB4 1AY, ✆ 2152 − **Ⓟ**
8 rm ⊑ 9.50/19.00 **st.**

AUSTIN-ROVER Castle St. ✆ 2473   FORD Bridge Rd ✆ 2673

BANNISKIRK Caithness (Highland) − see Thurso.

BARRA (Isle of) Inverness. (Outer Hebrides) (Western Isles) **401** X 12 13 − pop. 1 ,232.
✈ at North Bay ✆ 041 889 1311.
🚢 by Caledonian MacBrayne : from Castlebay to Oban 1-2 weekly (5-8 h) − to Lochboisdale (South Uist) 1-4 weekly(2 h).
🚢 by Western Isles Council : to Vatersay Monday/Saturday 4 daily (5 mn).

Castlebay − ✉ ✪ 087 14 Castlebay.
🎫 ✆ 336 (summer only).
🏦 **Isle of Barra** ☙, Tangusdale Beach, PA80 5XW, NW : 2 m. on A 888 ✆ 383, ≤ sea and mountains − ➚wc **Ⓟ**. 🔼 🆎 ⑩ 𝘝𝘐𝘚𝘈
March-October − **M** (bar lunch)/dinner 10.50 **t.** ⓪ 2.75 − **14 rm** ⊑ 18.50/43.00 **st.** − SB 55.00 **st.**

BARRHEAD Renfrew. (Strathclyde) **401** **402** G 16 − pop. 18 ,419 − ECD : Tuesday − ✉ ✪ 041 Glasgow.
◆Edinburgh 56 − ◆Ayr 32 − ◆Glasgow 10.

🏦 **Dalmeny Park,** Lochlibo Rd, G78 1LG, SW : ½ m. on A 736 ✆ 881 9211, « Gardens » − 📺
🛁wc ⊛ **Ⓟ**. 🅰. 🔼 🆎 ⑩ 𝘝𝘐𝘚𝘈. ⅏
closed 26 December and 1-2 January − **M** *(closed Sunday dinner to non-residents)* 6.95/9.50 **t.** and a la carte ⓪ 3.75 − **18 rm** ⊑ 28.00/42.00 **t.**

BATHGATE W. Lothian (Lothian) **401** J 16 − pop. 14 ,429 − ECD : Wednesday − ✪ 0506.
Envir. : Cairnpapple Hill★ (burial cairn★) N : 3 m.
🏌 Edinburgh Rd ✆ 52232.
◆Edinburgh 20 − ◆Glasgow 28.

🏦 **Golden Circle** (Swallow), Blackburn Rd, EH48 2EL, S : 1 ¾ m. on B 792 ✆ 53771, Telex 72606 − ⬚ 📺 ➚wc 🛁wc ⊛ **Ⓟ**. 🅰. 🔼 🆎 ⑩ 𝘝𝘐𝘚𝘈
M 5.50/9.00 **st.** and a la carte ⓪ 1.90 − **74 rm** ⊑ 33.00/44.00 **st.** − SB (weekends only) 42.00 **st.**

FORD Linlithgow Rd ✆ 56685   VW, AUDI Blackburn Rd ✆ 52948

BEARSDEN Dunbarton. (Strathclyde) **401** G 16 − pop. 27 ,146 − ECD : Tuesday and Saturday − ✉ ✪ 041 Glasgow.
◆Edinburgh 51 − ◆Glasgow 5.

🏦 **Stakis Burnbrae** (Stakis), Milngavie Rd, G61 3TA, NE : 1 m. on A 81 ✆ 942 5951 − 📺 ➚wc ⊛ **Ⓟ**. 🅰. 🔼 🆎 ⑩ 𝘝𝘐𝘚𝘈
M a la carte 6.60/11.50 **t.** ⓪ 3.25 − **18 rm** ⊑ 40.00/50.00 **t.**

✗ **La Bavarde,** 19 New Kirk Rd, G61 9JS, ✆ 942 2202 − 🔼 🆎 ⑩ 𝘝𝘐𝘚𝘈
closed Sunday, Monday, last 3 weeks July and 24 December-8 January − **M** 3.90 **t.** (lunch) and a la carte 8.10/11.00 **t.** ⓪ 2.50.

✗ **Amritsar Tandoori,** 9 Kirk Rd, G61 3RG, ✆ 942 7710, Indian rest. − 🔼 🆎 ⑩ 𝘝𝘐𝘚𝘈
closed Sunday lunch − **M** a la carte 8.00/11.75 **t.**

PEUGEOT-TALBOT, VOLVO Bearsden Cross ✆   PORSCHE Maxwell Av. ✆ 943 1155
942 2225

Dieser Führer ist kein vollständiges Hotel- und Restaurantverzeichnis.

Um den Ansprüchen aller Touristen gerecht zu werden, haben wir uns auf eine Auswahl in jeder Kategorie beschränkt.

BEATTOCK Dumfries. (Dumfries and Galloway) [401] [402] J 18 – ✉ Moffat – ✆ 068 33.

♦Edinburgh 60 – ♦Carlisle 41 – ♦Dumfries 20 – ♦Glasgow 59.

🏨 **Auchen Castle** 🪑, DG10 9SH, N : 2 m. by A 74 ✆ 407, ⩽, 🎣, 🌳, park – [TV] 🛁wc 🚿wc ☎ [P]. [S] [AE] [O] [VISA]
closed January – **M** (bar lunch)/dinner 11.00 **st.** 🍾 3.00 – **25 rm** ☕ 28.00/42.00 **st.** – SB 43.00/57.00 **st.**

🏨 **Beattock House,** DG10 9QB, ✆ 403, 🌳 – 🚿wc [P]. [AE] [VISA]
M 5.95/9.95 **t.** 🍾 3.10 – **7 rm** ☕ 15.50/36.00 **t.**

BEAULY Inverness. (Highland) [401] G 11 – pop. 1,135 – ECD : Thursday – ✆ 0463.

♦Edinburgh 69 – ♦Inverness 13 – ♦Wick 25.

🏨 **Priory,** The Square, IV4 7BX, ✆ 782309 – [TV] 🛁wc 🚿wc ☎. [S] [AE] [O] [VISA]
M (bar lunch)/dinner 12.50 **t.** and a la carte 🍾 2.25 – **12 rm** ☕ 19.75/36.00 **t.** – SB 70.00/97.00 **st.**

SUBARU High St. ✆ 782266

BELLOCHANTUY Argyll. (Strathclyde) [401] C 17 – see Kintyre (Peninsula).

BENBECULA Inverness. (Western Isles) [401] X 11 – see Uist (Isles of).

BETTYHILL Sutherland (Highland) [401] H 8 – ✉ Thurso – ✆ 064 12.

[i] ✆ 342 (summer only).

♦Edinburgh 225 – ♦Inverness 113 – Thurso 31.

🏨 **Bettyhill,** KW14 7SP, ✆ 202, ⩽, 🎣 – 🛁wc [P]. [S] [AE] [VISA]
M (bar lunch)/dinner 8.50 **t.** – **22 rm** ☕ 12.65/23.60 **st.**

BIRSAY Orkney (Orkney Islands) [401] K 6 – see Orkney Islands (Mainland).

BLACKFORD Perth. (Tayside) [401] I 15 – pop. 551 – ECD : Wednesday – ✉ Auchterarder – ✆ 076 482.

♦Edinburgh 53 – ♦Glasgow 44 – Perth 18.

🏨 **Blackford,** Moray St., PH4 1QF, ✆ 246 – 🛁wc 🚿wc [P]
M (bar lunch)/dinner a la carte 3.40/8.00 **t.** 🍾 3.00 – **4 rm** ☕ 17.00/30.00 **t.**

BLAIRGOWRIE Perth (Tayside) [401] J 14 – pop. 7,028 – ✆ 0250.

[i] Wellmeadow ✆ 2960 (2258 when closed)(summer only).

♦Edinburgh 60 – ♦Dundee 19 – Perth 16.

🏨 **Kinloch House** 🪑, PH10 6SG, W : 3 m. on A 923 ✆ 025 084 (Essendy) 237, ⩽, « Country house atmosphere », 🌳, park – 🛁wc 🚿wc [P]. [S] [AE] [O]
closed last week January and first 2 weeks February – **M** (bar lunch)/dinner 11.75 **st.** 🍾 2.40 – **12 rm** ☕ 25.00/42.00 **st.**

🏨 **Altamount House** 🪑, Coupar Angus Rd, PH10 6JN, ✆ 3512, 🌳 – [TV] 🛁wc 🚿wc [P]. [S] [O] [VISA]. 🚫🐕
closed Monday from mid October-Easter, 4 January-15 February, 1 week October and 25-26 December – **M** *(closed Sunday dinner in winter)* (bar lunch Monday to Saturday)/dinner 10.95 **t.** – **7 rm** ☕ 25.00/50.00 **t.**

🏨 **Rosemount Golf,** Golf Course Rd, PH10 6LJ, SE : 1 ¾ m. off A 923 ✆ 2604, 🌳 – [TV] 🛁wc 🚿wc [P]
M a la carte 2.40/7.75 **t.** 🍾 3.20 – **12 rm** ☕ 15.00/25.00 **t.**

BLAIRLOGIE Stirling. (Central) – see Stirling.

BOAT OF GARTEN Inverness. (Highland) [401] I 12 – ECD : Thursday – ✆ 047 983.

⛳18 ✆ 282 – [i] Boat Hotel Car park ✆ 307 (summer only).

♦Edinburgh 133 – ♦Inverness 28 – ♦Perth 89.

🏨 **The Boat,** PH24 3BH, ✆ 258, 🌳 – [TV] 🛁wc 🚿wc [P]. [S] [AE] [O] [VISA]
closed 15 November-20 December – **M** a la carte lunch/dinner 12.50 **t.** 🍾 2.95 – **34 rm** ☕ 21.00/46.00 **t.** – SB (weekdays only) 50.00/55.00 **st.**

⌂ **Moorfield House,** Deshar Rd, PH24 3BN, ✆ 646, 🌳 – [P]
closed November-20 December – **6 rm** ☕ 13.50/39.50 **t.**

BONAR BRIDGE Sutherland (Highland) [401] G 10 – pop. 533 – ECD : Wednesday – ✆ 086 32 Ardgay.

⛳9 ✆ 577 – [i] ✆ 333 (summer only).

♦Edinburgh 206 – ♦Inverness 50 – ♦Wick 76.

🏨 **Bridge,** Dornoch Rd, IV24 3EB, ✆ 204, ⩽ – [TV] 🛁wc 🚿wc ☎ [P]. [S] [AE] [O] [VISA]
M (bar lunch)/dinner a la carte 7.00/15.10 **t.** 🍾 2.40 – **16 rm** ☕ 16.50/38.00 **t.** – SB 36.00 **st.**

BONNYRIGG Midlothian (Lothian) [401] [402] K 16 – see Edinburgh.

BOTHWELL Lanark. (Strathclyde) **401 402** H 16 Scotland G – ✪ 0698.
See : Castle★.
Envir. : Blantyre : David Livingstone Centre (Museum★) off A 724.
♦Edinburgh 39 – ♦Glasgow 8.5.

   🏰 **Silvertrees**, 27 Silverwells Crescent, G71 8DP, ⌂ 852311, ☞ – 🔳 ⌷wc ☎ 🅿 🅰 ⬛ 🅰🅴 ⓪ *VISA*
     closed 1 to 3 January – **M** *(closed Sunday dinner)* 6.50/8.00 **t.** and a la carte ₪ 3.60 – **26 rm**
     ⊡ 35.00/40.00 **t.**, **2 suites** 42.00/45.00 **t.**

BOWMORE Argyll. (Strathclyde) **401** B 16 – see Islay (Isle of).

BRAE Shetland (Shetland Islands) **401** P 2 – see Shetland Islands (Mainland).

BRAEMAR Aberdeen. (Grampian) **401** J 12 – ECD : Thursday except summer – ✪ 033 83.
Envir. : Lin O' Dee★, W : 7 m.
🛈 Kindrochit Castle ⌂ 600 (summer only).
♦Edinburgh 85 – ♦Aberdeen 58 – ♦Dundee 51 – Perth 51.

   ⌂ **Callater Lodge**, 9 Glenshee Rd, AB5 5YQ, ⌂ 275, ☞ – 🅿
     closed mid October-26 December – **9 rm** ⊡ 11.10/22.20 **st.**

AUSTIN-ROVER Ballater Rd ⌂ 301

BRESSAY (Isle of) Shetland (Shetland Islands) **401** Q 3 – Shipping services : see Shetland Islands.

BRIDGE OF ALLAN Stirling. (Central) **401** I 15 – pop. 4,551 – ECD : Wednesday – ✪ 0786.
Envir. : Dollar (Castle Campbell★ (site★★★) E : 12 m. by a 91 – Wallace Monument (⁂★★) S : 2 m. by A 9 – Doune★ (Castle★, Motor Museum★) NW : 7 m. by A 9 and B 824.
♦Edinburgh 21 – ♦Dundee 54 – ♦Glasgow 33.

   🏰 **Royal** (Best Western), 55 Henderson St., FK9 4HG, ⌂ 832284, Group Telex 778982, ☞ – 🛗
     🔳 ⌷wc ☎ 🅿 🅰 ⬛ 🅰🅴 ⓪ *VISA*
     M (bar lunch Monday to Saturday)/dinner 9.00 **st.** and a la carte ₪ 3.75 – **32 rm**
     ⊡ 27.00/52.00 **st.** – SB (September-May) 50.95 **st.**

BRIDGE OF CALLY Perth. (Tayside) **401** J 14 – ⊠ Blairgowrie – ✪ 025 086.
♦Edinburgh 66 – ♦Dundee 25 – Perth 22.

   🏠 **Bridge of Cally**, PH10 7JJ, on A 93 ⌂ 231, ⌦, ☞ – ⌷wc ⌽wc 🅿 ⬛ ⓪ *VISA* ⌾
     closed November, 25-26 December and 1-2 January – **M** (bar lunch)/dinner 10.40 **t.** ₪ 2.35 –
     9 rm ⊡ 16.50/25.50 **t.**

BROADFORD Inverness. (Highland) **401** C 12 – see Skye (Isle of).

BRODICK Bute. (Strathclyde) **401 402** E 17 – see Arran (Isle of).

BROUGHTON Peebles. (Borders) **401 402** J 17 – ECD : Wednesday – ⊠ Biggar (Lanark) –
✪ 089 94.
🛈ₛ Broughton Rd, Biggar ⌂ 0899 (Biggar) 20618, W : 6 m.
♦Edinburgh 30 – Moffat 24 – Peebles 12.

   🏠 **Greenmantle,** Main St., ML12 6HQ, ⌂ 302, ☞ – 🔳 ⌷wc 🅿 ⬛ ⓪ *VISA*
     March-November – **M** 7.50/12.50 **st.** and a la carte ₪ 3.00 – **9 rm** ⊡ 25.00/42.00 **st.** – SB
     35.00/50.00 **st.**

BROUGHTY FERRY Angus (Tayside) **401** L 14 – see Dundee.

BUCKIE Banff. (Grampian) **401** L 10 – pop. 7,869 – ECD : Wednesday – ✪ 0542.
🛈ₛ Buckpool, Barrhill Rd ⌂ 32236 – 🛈ₛ Strathlene ⌂ 31798, E : ½ m.
♦Edinburgh 195 – ♦Aberdeen 66 – ♦Inverness 56.

   🏠 **Cluny,** 2 High St., AB5 1AL, ⌂ 32922 – ⌷wc 🅿 ⬛ 🅰🅴 ⓪ *VISA*
     closed 1 and 2 January – **M** 4.00 **t.** (lunch) and a la carte 6.20/10.45 **t.** ₪ 3.00 – **16 rm**
     ⊡ 14.50/33.00 **t.** – SB (weekends only) 46.00/56.00 **st.**

   at Drybridge S : 2 m. by A 942 – ⊠ Drybridge – ✪ 0542 Buckie :

   XX **Old Monastery**, AB5 2JB, SW : 2 m. ⌂ 32660 – 🅿
     closed Sunday, Monday, 3 weeks January, 2 weeks October and 3 days at Christmas – **M** 5.00
     t. (lunch) and a la carte 8.60/11.35 **t.** ₪ 2.50.

BUCKSBURN Aberdeen. (Grampian) **401** N 12 – see Aberdeen.

BUNESSAN Argyll. (Strathclyde) **401** B 15 – see Mull (Isle of).

BUSBY Lanark. (Strathclyde) **401** **402** H 16 – see Glasgow.

BUTE (Isle of) Bute. (Strathclyde) **401** **402** E 16 – pop. 7 ,733.

⏴ by Caledonian MacBrayne : from Rothesay to Wemyss Bay 4-13 daily (30 mn) – from Rhubodach to Colintraive frequent services daily (5 mn).

🛈 Rothesay : The Pier ✆ 0700 (Rothesay) 2151.

CAIRNGORM (Mountains) Inverness. (Highland) **401** J 12 Scotland G.

See : ❄ ★★★ from Cairn Gorm (alt. 4,048 ft.) (chairlift *AC*).

   Hotels see : Aviemore NW, *Braemar* SE.

CAIRNRYAN Wigtown. (Dumfries and Galloway) **401** **402** E 19.

⏴ by Townsend Thoresen : to Larne 2-7 daily (2 to 2 h 30 mn).

◆ Edinburgh 126 – ◆ Ayr 45 – Stranraer 6,5.

   Hotel see : Stranraer S : 6 ½ m.

CALLANDER Perth. (Central) **401** H 15 Scotland G – pop. 2 ,286 – ECD : Wednesday except
summer – ✆ 0877.

See : Site★ – Envir. : The Trossachs★★★: Loch Katrine★★ – Hilltop Viewpoint (❄★★★) W : 10 m.
by A 821 – Inchmahone Priory (Monument★) S : 6 m. by A 81 and B 8034.

🛅 ✆ 30090 – 🛈 Leny Rd ✆ 30342 (summer only).

◆Edinburgh 52 – ◆Glasgow 43 – ◆Oban 71 – Perth 41.

🏛 **Roman Camp** 🦢, Main St., FK17 8BG, ✆ 30003, ≼, « 17C hunting lodge in extensive
    gardens », 🐟, park – 📺 🚻wc 🛗wc 🅿
    closed December-mid February – **M** (bar lunch Monday-Friday residents only)/dinner 18.00 **st.**
    🍴 3.60 – **11 rm** 🍽 32.00/62.00 **st.**, **3 suites** – SB (mid October-May) 65.00/79.00 **st.**

🏠 **Lubnaig**, Leny Feus, FK17 8AS, ✆ 30376, 🌳 – 🛗wc 🛀
    closed November – **M** (dinner only) 9.00 **st.** 🍴 2.00 – **10 rm** 🍽 18.50/28.50 **st.**

🏠 **Bridgend**, Bridgend, FK17 8AA, ✆ 30130, 🌳 – 📺 🚻wc 🛗wc 🐾 🅿 🅰 🆎 **VISA**
    closed November – **M** (bar lunch)/dinner a la carte 6.80/13.15 **t.** 🍴 2.20 – **7 rm** 🍽 26.00/40.00 **t.**

🏠 **Highland House**, 8 South Church St, FK17 8BN, ✆ 30269 – 🛗wc
    April-October – **10 rm** 🍽 10.00/25.00 **t.**

🏠 **Glenorchy**, Leny Rd, FK17 8AL, ✆ 30329 – 🚻wc 🛗wc 🅿 **VISA** 🦢
    11 rm 🍽 11.50/28.00 **t.**

CAMPBELTOWN Argyll (Strathclyde) **401** D 17 – see Kintyre (Peninsula).

CANNA (Isle of) Inverness. (Highland) **401** A 12 – Shipping Services : see Mallaig.

CANONBIE Dumfries (Dumfries and Galloway) **401** **402** L 18 – ✆ 054 15 Canonbie.

◆Edinburgh 80 – ◆Carlisle 15 – ◆Dumfries 34.

XX **Riverside Inn** with rm, DG14 0UX, ✆ 295 – 🚻wc 🅿 🅰 **VISA** 🦢
    closed last 2 weeks January – **M** *(closed Sunday lunch)* (booking essential)(bar lunch)/dinner
    12.00 **t.** 🍴 2.45 – **6 rm** 🍽 28.00/38.00 **t.** – SB (November-April) 48.00 **st.**

CARFRAEMILL Berwick (Borders) **401** **402** L 16 – see Lauder.

CARRADALE Argyll. (Strathclyde) **401** D 17 – see Kintyre (Peninsula).

CASTLEBAY Inverness. (Outer Hebrides) (Western Isles) **401** X 13 – see Barra (Isle of).

CASTLE DOUGLAS Kirkcudbright. (Dumfries and Galloway) **401** **402** I 19 Scotland G –
pop. 3 ,546 – ECD : Thursday – ✆ 0556.

Envir. : Threave Garden★★ and Castle★, SW : 3 m. by A 75.

🛅 ✆ 2801 – 🛈 Markethill ✆ 2611 (summer only).

◆Edinburgh 98 – ◆Ayr 49 – ◆Dumfries 18 – Stranraer 57.

🏠 **King's Arms**, St. Andrew St., DG7 1EL, ✆ 2626 – 🚻wc 🛗wc 🅿 🅰 🆎 ① **VISA**
    closed 1 January – **M** (bar lunch)/dinner 11.50 **st.** 🍴 3.50 – **15 rm** 🍽 16.00/42.00 – SB
    44.00/48.00 **st.**

AUSTIN-ROVER Morris House ✆ 2560   VAUXHALL-OPEL King St. ✆ 2038
FORD, LADA Oakwell Rd ✆ 2805

CATTERLINE Kincardine (Grampian) **401** N 13 – see Stonehaven.

CLACHAN SEIL Argyll. (Strathclyde) **401** D 15 – ECD : Wednesday – ⊠ Oban – ✆ 085 23 Balvicar – ✦Edinburgh 137 – ✦Oban 14.

⌂ **Willowburn** ⌂, Isle of Seil, PA34 4TJ, ✆ 276, ≼ – 🛏wc **P**. **⚑** **AE** **⓪** **VISA**
   closed 7 January-10 February – **M** (bar lunch)/dinner a la carte 7.50/10.75 **t**. 🍷 3.20 – **6 rm**
   ⊡ 11.00/33.00 **t**.

CLAONAIG (Cap) Argyll. (Strathclyde) **401** **402** D 16 – Shipping Services : see Kintyre (Peninsula).

CLEISH Fife. (Tayside) **401** J 15 – see Kinross.

CLOCHAN Banff. (Grampian) – see Fochabers.

COLINTRAIVE Argyll. (Strathclyde) **401** **402** E 16 – ✆ 070 084.
🚢 by Caledonian MacBrayne : to Rhubodach (Isle of Bute) frequent services daily (5 mn).
✦Edinburgh 127 – ✦Glasgow 81 – ✦Oban 81.

COLL (Isle of) Argyll. (Strathclyde) **401** A 14 – pop. 153.
🚢 by Caledonian MacBrayne : from Arinagour to Oban 3-4 weekly (3 h 30 mn) – from Arinagour to Isle of Tiree 3-4 weekly (1 h).
🚢 by Caledonian MacBrayne : from Arinagour to Tobermory (Isle of Mull) 3 weekly (1 h 30 mn) – from Arinagour to Lochaline May to September 2 weekly (2 h 30 mn).

COLONSAY (Isle of) Argyll. (Strathclyde) **401** B 15 – pop. 132 – ✆ 095 12 Colonsay.
🛏₈ ✆ 316 – 🚢 by Caledonian MacBrayne : from Scalasaig to Oban 3 weekly (2 h 30 mn).

   Scalasaig – ECD : Wednesday – ⊠ ✆ 095 12 Colonsay.

🏛 **Isle of Colonsay** ⌂, PA61 7YP, ✆ 316, ≼, « 18C inn », 🌿 – 🛏wc **P**. **⚑** **AE** **⓪** **VISA**
   M (bar lunch)/dinner 10.75 **st**. 🍷 2.35 – **11 rm** ⊡ 21.50/43.50 **st**. – SB (except summer) 40.00/44.00 **st**.

COLVEND Kircudbright. (Dumfries and Galloway) – ⊠ Dalbeattie – ✆ 055 663 Rockcliffe.
✦ Edinburgh 99 – ✦Dumfries 19.

⌂ **Clonyard House,** DG5 4QW, NW : 1 m. on A 710 ✆ 372, 🌿 – **TV** 🛏wc 🛏wc 👍 **P**. **⚑** **VISA**
   M (bar lunch)/dinner 8.00 **st**. and a la carte 🍷 3.00 – **11 rm** ⊡ 12.00/34.50 **st**. – SB (November-March) 35.00 **st**.

COMRIE Perth. (Tayside) **401** I 14 – pop. 1 ,406 – ECD : Wednesday – ✆ 0764 – 🛏₉.
✦Edinburgh 61 – ✦Glasgow 51 – ✦Oban 70 – Perth 24.

🏛 **Royal,** Melville Sq., PH6 2DN, ✆ 70200, 🌿 – **TV** 🛏wc ☎ **P**. **⚑** **AE** **VISA**
   M 7.50/10.50 **t**. and a la carte 🍷 2.80 – **14 rm** ⊡ 20.00/40.00 **t**. – SB (except Christmas and New Year) 60.00/64.00 **st**.

🏛 **Comrie,** Drummond St., PH6 2DY, ✆ 70239, – 🛏wc 🛏wc **P**
   Easter-October – **M** 6.00/9.00 **st**. and a la carte 🍷 2.50 – **12 rm** ⊡ 13.00/35.00 **st**.

CONNEL Argyll. (Strathclyde) **401** D 14 – ECD : Wednesday – ✆ 063 171.
✦Edinburgh 118 – ✦Glasgow 88 – ✦Inverness 113 – ✦Oban 5.

🏛 **Lochnell Arms,** North Connel, PA37 1RF, ✆ 408, ≼, 🌿 – 🛏wc **P**. **⚑** **AE** **⓪** **VISA**
   M 5.00/10.00 **st**. 🍷 2.50 – **11 rm** ⊡ 15.00/28.00 **st**. – SB (October-April) 40.00/45.00 **st**.

🏛 **Ossian's** ⌂, Bonawe Rd, North Connel, PA37 1RB, ✆ 322, ≼, 🌿 – 🛏wc **P**. **AE** **VISA**
   First week April-first week October – **M** (bar lunch)/dinner 9.50 **t**. 🍷 2.95 – **14 rm** ⊡ 15.20/32.40 **t**.

CRAIGHOUSE Argyll. (Strathclyde) **401** C 16 – see Jura (Isle of).

CRAIL Fife. (Fife) **401** M 15 – pop. 1 ,106 – ECD : Wednesday – ✆ 033 35.
See : Site★★ – Old Town★★ – Upper Crail★.
Envir. : The East Neuk★★ (coastline from Crail SW by A 917 to St. Monande).
🛏₈ Balcomie Clubhouse ✆ 50278.
✦Edinburgh 54 – ✦Dundee 25 – Dunfermline 41.

⌂ **Marine,** 54 Nethergate South, KY10 3TZ, ✆ 50207, ≼, 🌿 – 🛏. **⚑** **VISA**
   M (bar lunch)/dinner 8.50 **t**. 🍷 3.50 – **12 rm** ⊡ 9.50/19.00 **t**. – SB (October-March) 31.00/36.00 **st**.

CRIANLARICH Perth (Central) **401** G 16 – ✆ 083 83.
✦Edinburgh 82 – ✦Glasgow 52 – Perth 53.

⌂ **Allt-Chaorain House** ⌂, FK20 8RU, NW : 1 m. on A 82 ✆ 283, ≼, 🌿 – 🛏wc **P**
   restricted opening November-March – **9 rm** ⊡ 12.00/28.00 **t**.

CRIEFF Perth. (Tayside) **401** I 14 Scotland G – pop. 5 ,101 – ECD : Wednesday – ✪ 0764.
See : Site★.

Envir. : Drummond Castle Gardens★ *AC*, S : 2 m. by A 822 – Tullibardine Chapel★, S : 6 m. by A 822 and A 823 – Strathallan Aero Park★, SE : 6 m. by B 8062 – Upper Strathearn★ (Loch Earn★★) NW : 12 m. by A 85.

🛅 Perth Rd ✎ 2909 – 🛅 Peat Rd, Muthill ✎ 3319, S : 3 m. on A 822.

🖸 James Sq. ✎ 2578 (summer only).

♦Edinburgh 60 – ♦Glasgow 50 – ♦Oban 76 – Perth 18.

🏠 **Murraypark** ⤶, Connaught Terr., PH7 3DJ, ✎ 3731, ☞ – ⌂wc ® ℗. ⓪ 𝓥𝓘𝓢𝓐
M 9.00/13.00 **t.** and a la carte ⒜ 3.00 – **15 rm** ⌸ 19.00/45.00 **t.**

🏨 **Gwydyr House,** Comrie Rd, PH7 4BP, on A 85 ✎ 3277, ≼, ☞ – ⓣⓥ ℗
April-October – **M** (bar lunch)/dinner 6.95 **t.** and a la carte ⒜ 2.70 – **10 rm** ⌸ 11.00/22.00 **t.**

↟ **Leven House,** Comrie Rd, PH7 4BA, on A 85 ✎ 2529, ≼
9 rm ⌸ 9.50/19.00 **st.**

   at Sma'Glen NE : 4 m. by A 85 on A 822 – ✉ ✪ 0764 Crieff :

🏨 **Foulford Inn** ⤶, PH7 3LN, ✎ 2407 – ℗
closed February – **M** *(closed Sunday dinner)* (bar lunch)/dinner 7.50 **t.** and a la carte ⒜ 2.90 – **11 rm** ⌸ 11.00/28.00 **t.** – SB 36.00/42.00 **st.**

AUSTIN-ROVER Comrie Rd ✎ 2125   VAUXHALL-OPEL ✎ 2147

CRINAN Argyll. (Strathclyde) **401** D 15 – ✉ Lochgilphead – ✪ 054 683.
See : Site★.

Envir. : Kilmory Knap (Macmillan's Cross★) SW : 14 m.

♦Edinburgh 137 – ♦Glasgow 91 – ♦Oban 36.

🏨 **Crinan,** PA31 8SR, ✎ 235, « ≼ imposing setting, overlooking Loch Crinan and Sound of Jura », ☞ – ⒧ ⌂wc ® ℗ 𝓝 𝓥𝓘𝓢𝓐
April-October – **M** (buffet lunch)/dinner 17.00 **t.** ⒜ 3.95 (rest. see also **Lock 16** below) – **22 rm** ⌸ 32.00/67.00 **t.**

XX **Lock 16** (at Crinan H.), PA31 8SR, ✎ 235, Seafood, « ≼ imposing setting, overlooking Loch Crinan and Sound of Jura » – ℗ 𝓝 𝓥𝓘𝓢𝓐
April-October – **M** (booking essential) 22.50 **t.** (dinner) and a la carte ⒜ 3.95.

CROSSFORD Fife. (Fife) – see Dunfermline.

CULLEN Banff. (Grampian) **401** L 10 Scotland G – pop. 1 ,378 – ECD : Wednesday – ✪ 0542.
See : Auld Kirk★ (Sacrament house★, carved panels★).

Envir. : Deskford Church (Sacrament house★) S : 4 m. by B 9018 – Portsoy★ E : 5 ½ m. by A 98.

🛅 The Links ✎ 40685.

🖸 20 Seafield St. ✎ 40757 (summer only).

♦Edinburgh 189 – ♦Aberdeen 59 – Banff 12 – ♦Inverness 61.

🏨 **Seafield Arms,** Seafield St., AB5 2SG, ✎ 40791 – ⓣⓥ ⌂wc ® ℗ 𝓝 𝓐𝓔 ⓪ 𝓥𝓘𝓢𝓐
M 5.50/9.00 **t.** and a la carte ⒜ 3.35 – **24 rm** ⌸ 21.80/40.50 **t.** – SB 52.00/56.00 **st.**

CULLIPOOL Argyll. (Strathclyde) **401** D 15 – see Luing (Isle of).

CULLODEN MOOR Inverness. (Highland) **401** H 11 – see Inverness.

CUPAR Fife. (Fife) **401** K 15 – pop. 6 ,662 – ECD : Thursday – ✪ 0334.
🖸 Fluthers car park ✎ 53722 (summer only).

♦Edinburgh 45 – ♦Dundee 15 – Perth 23.

X **Ostler's Close,** 25 Bonnygate, KY15 4BU, ✎ 55574 – 𝓝 𝓥𝓘𝓢𝓐
closed Monday lunch, Sunday and 2 weeks February – **M** a la carte 11.95/14.75 **t.**

DALIBURGH Inverness. (Outer Hebrides) (Western Isles) **401** X 12 – see Uist (South) (Isles of).

DALRY (ST. JOHN'S TOWN OF) Kirkcudbright. (Dumfries and Galloway) **401** **402** H 18 – ✉ Castle Douglas – ✪ 064 43.

♦Edinburgh 82 – ♦Dumfries 27 – ♦Glasgow 66 – Stranraer 47.

🏨 **Milton Park** ⤶, DG7 3SR, N : 1 m. by A 713 ✎ 286, ≼, ⤷, ☞, ℁ – ⌂wc ℗
March-October – **M** (bar lunch)/dinner 10.00 **t.** ⒜ 3.00 – **17 rm** ⌸ 15.00/36.00 **t.**

DERVAIG Argyll. (Strathclyde) **401** B 14 – see Mull (Isle of).

DIRLETON E. Lothian (Lothian) **401** **402** L 15 – see Gullane.

500

DORNIE Ross and Cromarty (Highland) 𝟒𝟎𝟏 D 12 – ⊠ Kyle of Lochalsh – ☎ 059 985.
♦Edinburgh 212 – ♦Inverness 74 – Kyle of Lochalsh 8.

🏠 **Loch Duich**, IV40 8DY, 𝒫 213, ≼ Eilean Donan Castle and hills, 🍴 – 🅿
Mid March-October – **M** (bar lunch)/dinner 10.00 **t.** 🍷 2.35 – **18 rm** ⇌ 16.50/33.00 **t.** – SB 44.00/49.00 **st.**

DORNOCH Sutherland. (Highland) 𝟒𝟎𝟏 H 10 Scotland G – pop. 1 ,006 – ECD : Thursday – ☎ 0862.
See : Site★.

🛆, 🏌 Royal Dornoch, Golf Rd 𝒫 810219.

🛈 The Square, 𝒫 810400.

♦Edinburgh 219 – ♦Inverness 63 – ♦Wick 65.

🏨 **Royal Golf** ⟡, Grange Rd, IV25 3LG, 𝒫 810283, Group Telex 779713, ≼Dornoch Firth, 🍴 – 📺 ➡wc ☎ 🅿 🄰 🄰🄴 🆅🆂🄰
March-October – **M** (bar lunch)/dinner 15.00 **st.** 🍷 4.50 – **35 rm** ⇌ 20.00/70.00 **st.**, **2 suites** 90.00/150.00 **st.**

🏨 **Dornoch Castle,** Castle St., IV25 3SD, 𝒫 810216, « Former bishop's palace, part 16C », 🍴 – 🅸 ➡wc 🏧wc 🅿 🄰 🄰🄴 🆅🆂🄰
April-October – **M** 7.50/12.00 **t.** – **20 rm** ⇌ 16.00/53.00 **t.** – SB 48.00/72.00 **st.**

TALBOT St. Gilbert St. 𝒫 810255

DOUNE Perth. (Central) 𝟒𝟎𝟏 H 15 Scotland G – pop. 1 ,020 – ECD : Wednesday – ☎ 0786.
See : Site★ – Castle★.
Envir. : Doune Motor Museum★, NW : 1 m. by A 84.
♦Edinburgh 45 – ♦Glasgow 35 – Perth 33 – Stirling 8.

🏠 **Woodside,** Stirling Rd, FK16 6AB, on A 84 𝒫 841237, 🍴 – ➡wc 🅿 🄰
M *(closed Sunday dinner to non-residents)* (bar lunch)/dinner a la carte 7.25/13.75 **t.** 🍷 3.50 – **14 rm** ⇌ 18.00/34.00 **t.**

✗ **Broughton's,** Blair Drummond, FK9 4XE, SE : 3 m. by A 84 on A 873 𝒫 841897 – 🅿 🄰
closed Sunday, Monday and 1 month in spring – **M** (booking essential)(lunch by arrangement)/dinner 12.50 **t.** 🍷 2.95.

DRUMNADROCHIT Inverness. (Highland) 𝟒𝟎𝟏 G 11 – pop. 542 – ⊠ Milton – ☎ 045 62.
Envir. : Loch Ness★★ – Loch Ness Monster Exhibition★.
♦Edinburgh 172 – ♦Inverness 16 – Kyle of Lochalsh 67.

🏨 **Polmaily House** ⟡, IV3 6XT, W : 2 m. on A 831 𝒫 343, « Country house atmosphere », 🏊, 🍴, park, 🎾 – ➡wc 🅿 🄰 🄰🄴 🄾 🆅🆂🄰 🎇
Easter-mid October – **M** (bar lunch, residents only)/dinner a la carte 8.45/11.10 **t.** 🍷 3.50 – **9 rm** ⇌ 22.00/48.00 **t.**

DRYBRIDGE Banff. (Grampian) – see Buckie.

DRYMEN Stirling. (Central) 𝟒𝟎𝟏 G 15 – pop. 771 – ECD : Wednesday – ☎ 0360.
Envir. : Loch Lomond★★, W : 3 m.
♦Edinburgh 64 – ♦Glasgow 18 – Stirling 22.

🏨 **Buchanan Arms,** Main St., G63 0BQ, 𝒫 60588, 🍴 – 📺 ➡wc 🅿 ⅙ 🅿 🄰 🄰 🄰🄴 🄾 🆅🆂🄰
M 8.35/11.25 **st.** 🍷 5.00 – **35 rm** ⇌ 24.00/52.00 **st.** – SB (November-March except Christmas) 52.00 **st.**

DULNAIN BRIDGE Inverness. (Highland) 𝟒𝟎𝟏 J 12 – ECD : Wednesday – ⊠ Grantown-on-Spey – ☎ 047 985.
♦Edinburgh 140 – ♦Inverness 31 – Perth 96.

🏠 **Muckrach Lodge,** PH26 3LY, W : ½ m. on A 938 𝒫 257, ≼, 🍴 – 🅿 🎇
closed mid January-February – **M** (booking essential)(bar lunch)/dinner 14.00 **t.** 🍷 3.20 – **9 rm** ⇌ 18.00/40.00 **st.**

🏠 **Skye of Curr,** Skye of Curr Rd, PH26 3PA, 𝒫 345, ≼, 🍴 – 🅿 🄰 🄰🄴 🄾 🆅🆂🄰
M (bar lunch)/dinner 9.75 **t.** – **8 rm** ⇌ 13.50/27.00 **st.**

DUMFRIES Dumfries. (Dumfries and Galloway) 𝟒𝟎𝟏 𝟒𝟎𝟐 J 18 Scotland G – pop. 31 ,307 – ECD : Thursday – ☎ 0387.
See : Site★ – Midsteeple★ A A – Lincluden College (Tomb★) by College Street A.
Envir. : Sweetheart Abbey★, S : 8 ¼ m. by A 710 A – Caerlaverock Castle★, SE : 9 m. by B 725 B – Ruthwell Cross★, SE : 16 m. by B 725 B – Glenkiln (Sculptures★) E : 10 m. by A 75 B – Kippford★, SW : 18 m. by A 710 A and A 711 A – Drumlanrig Castle★★, NW : 18 m. by A 76 A.
🛆 Lauriston Av. 𝒫 3582 A – 🏌 Lochmaben 𝒫 552, NE : 8 m. by A 709 B.
🛈 Whitesands 𝒫 53862 (summer only).
♦Edinburgh 80 – ♦Ayr 59 – ♦Carlisle 34 – ♦Glasgow 79 – ♦Manchester 155 – ♦Newcastle-upon-Tyne 91.

DUMFRIES

High Street . . . . A 18
Shopping Centre . . . . B

Aldermanhill Road . . . . B 2
Bank Street . . . . A 3
Buccleuch Street . . . . A 4
Cardoness Street . . . . B 5
Cassalands . . . . A 6
Castle Street . . . . A 7
Castle Douglas Road . . . . . . A 8
Catherine Street . . . . B 9

Corberry Avenue . . . . A 10
Friars Vennel . . . . A 13
Galloway Street . . . . A 14
Glebe Street . . . . B 15
Great King Street . . . . A 16
Hermitage Drive . . . . A 17
Laurieknowe . . . . A 20
Loreburn Street . . . . A 21
Nith Street . . . . AB 22
Queen Street . . . . B 23
Queensberry Street . . . . A 24
Rae Street . . . . B 26
St. Mary's Street . . . . B 27
St. Michael Street . . . . B 28

St. Michael's Bridge Road . . . . A 30
Shakespeare Street . . . . B 31
Union Street . . . . A 32
Whitesands . . . . A 34

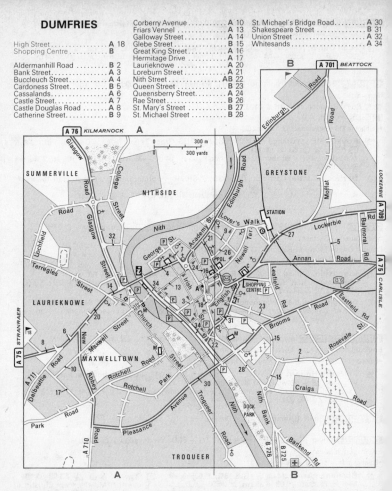

🏨 **Station,** 49 Lovers Walk, DG1 1LT, 𝒫 54316 – 📶 📺 🛏️wc 🚿wc ☎ 🅿. 🔼 🅰🄴 ⓪ *VISA*   B e
M 4.00/9.50 **t.** and a la carte ⓵ 3.00 – **30 rm** ⌯ 30.00/45.00 **t.** – SB (weekends only) 48.00 **st.**

FIAT 123 Whitesands 𝒫 64875
FORD Main Rd 𝒫 038771 (Amisfield) 710491
LANCIA, COLT St. Michaels St. 𝒫 63733

PEUGEOT-TALBOT St. Mary's Industrial Estate 𝒫 63076
VOLVO Annan Rd 𝒫 61437

☛ *There is no paid publicity in this Guide.*

DUNAIN PARK Inverness. (Highland) – see Inverness.

DUNBAR E. Lothian (Lothian) **401** M 15 Scotland G – pop. 5 ,795 – ECD : Wednesday – ✪ 0368.
See : Tolbooth★ – John Muir's Birthplace★.

Envir. : Museum of Flight★, W : 5 m. by A 1087 and A 1 – Preston Mill★, W : 6 m. by A 1087, A 1 and B 1407 – Tyninghame★, NW : 6 m. by A 1 and A 198 – Tantallon Castle★★, NW : 10 m. by A 1087, A 1 and A 198.

📙 Winterfield, North Rd 𝒫 62280 – 📙 East Links 𝒫 62317, S : ½ m.
🎫 Town House, High St. 𝒫 63353.
♦Edinburgh 28 – ♦Newcastle-upon-Tyne 90.

⌂ **Marine,** 7 Marine Rd, EH42 1AR, 𝒫 63315
9 rm ⌯ 8.50/17.00 **s.**

502

[DUNBLANE] Perth. (Central) [401] I 15 **Scotland G** – pop. 6,783 – ECD : Wednesday – ☎ 0786.
See : Site★ – Cathedral★★.
[i] Stirling Rd ☎ 824428 (summer only).
◆Edinburgh 42 – ◆Glasgow 33 – Perth 29.

Cromlix House ≫, FK15 9JT, N : 3 ¼ m. by A 9 on B 8033 ☎ 822125, ≤, « Antique furnishings », 🐟, ⛟, park, 🎾 – [TV] [P]. [AE] [VISA]
closed February and 24 to 27 December – **M** (booking essential)(lunch by arrangement) 13.00/25.00 **st.** 🍷 3.75 – **14 rm** 55.00/97.50 **st.**, **5 suites** 110.00/125.00 **st.**

AUSTIN-ROVER Stirling Rd ☎ 823271

[DUNDEE] Angus (Tayside) [401] L 14 **Scotland G** – pop. 172,294 – ECD : Wednesday – ☎ 0382.
See : The Frigate Unicorn★ Y **A**.
⛳18, ⛳9 Caird Park ☎ 453606 off Kingsway Bypass at Mains Loan Z – ⛳18 Camperdown Park ☎ 645450, NW : 2 m. by A 923 Z.
✈ Dundee Airport : ☎ 643242, SW : 1 ½ m. Z.
[i] Nethergate Centre ☎ 27723 – ◆Edinburgh 63 – ◆Aberdeen 67 – ◆Glasgow 83.

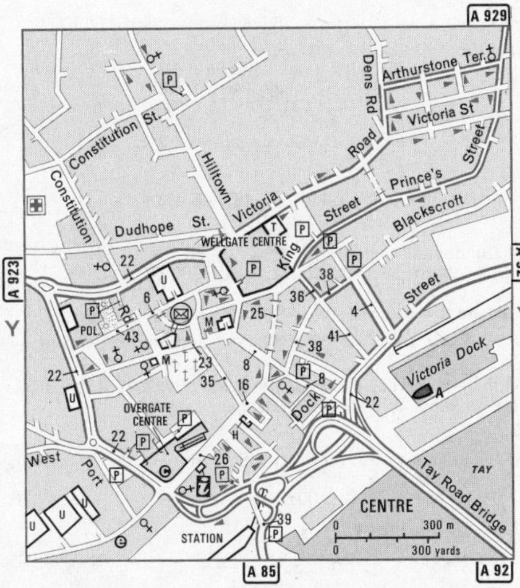

DUNDEE

Commercial Street	Y 8
High Street	Y 16
Murraygate	Y 25
Nethergate	Y 26
Overgate Centre	Y
Reform Street	Y 35
Wellgate Centre	Y
Albert Street	Z 2
Allan Street	Y 4
Ancrum Road	Z 5
Bell Street	Y 6
Coupar Angus Road	Z 9
Douglas Road	Z 10
Drumgeith Road	Z 12
Dudhope Terrace	Z 13
East Dock Street	Z 14
Greendykes Road	Z 15
Logie Street	Z 18
Longtown Road	Z 20
Mains Road	Z 21
Marketgait	Y 22
Meadowside	Y 23
Moncur Crescent	Z 24
Old Glamis Road	Z 32
Provost Road	Z 34
St. Andrews Street	Y 36
Seagate	Y 38
South Union Street	Y 39
Strathmartine Road	Z 40
Trades Lane	Y 41
Ward Road	Y 42
West Bell Street	Y 43

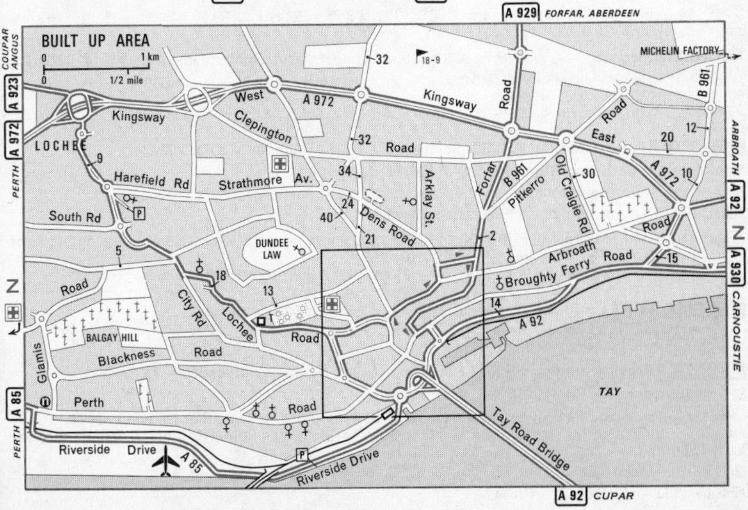

Angus Thistle (Thistle), 101 Marketgait, DD1 1QU, ℰ 26874, Telex 76456 – 🛗 📺 ➾wc ☎
🄿 🚗 AE ⓞ VISA
Y c
M 6.00/10.00 t. and a la carte – ➩ 5.25 – **58 rm** 38.00/52.00 t., **5 suites** 65.00 t.

Invercarse, 371 Perth Rd, DD2 1PG, W : 2 m. on B 911 ℰ 69231, Telex 76608, 🚗 – 📺 ➾wc
🍴wc ☎ 🄿 🚗 AE ⓞ VISA
Z n
M (bar lunch Saturday) 5.90/9.50 t. and a la carte ⅙ 2.80 – ➩ 4.50 – **41 rm** 34.00/42.00 t.,
1 suite 55.00 t. – SB (weekends only) 47.00 st.

Queen's, 160 Nethergate, DD1 4DU, ℰ 22515 – 🛗 📺 ➾wc ☎ 🄿 🚗 AE ⓞ VISA ❄
M (bar lunch)/dinner 9.50 t. and a la carte ⅙ 2.90 – ➩ 4.50 – **56 rm** 24.00/40.00 st. – SB
40.00/64.00 st.
Y e

at Broughty Ferry E : 4 ½ m. by A 930 – Z – (Dundee Road) – ✉ ✪ 0382 Dundee :

Tayview without rest., 71-73 St. Vincent St., DD5 2EZ, ℰ 79438 – ➾wc. ❄
11 rm ➩ 25.00/45.00 t.

at Invergowrie W : 4 ¾ m. by A 85 on A 872 – Z – ✉ ✪ 0382 Dundee :

Swallow (Swallow), Kingsway West (Dundee Ring Road), DD2 5JT, ℰ 641122, Telex 76694,
🔲, 🚗 – 🛗 📺 ➾wc 🍴 ☎ 🄿 🚗 AE ⓞ VISA ❄
M 6.00/10.00 st. and a la carte – **69 rm** ➩ 47.50/55.00 st. – SB (weekends only) 53.50/57.50 st.

ALFA-ROMEO, HONDA   Queen St., Broughty Ferry
ℰ 77257
AUSTIN-ROVER   64 Ward Rd ℰ 24013
CITROEN   3 Roseangle ℰ 28483
DAIHATSU, RELIANT   25 Rosebank St. ℰ 25406
FIAT, LADA, LANCIA   MacAlpine Rd ℰ 818004
FORD   Balfield Rd ℰ 60191

MAZDA   166 Seagate ℰ 25007
RENAULT   Riverside Drive ℰ 644401
TOYOTA   East Kingsway ℰ 41715
VAUXHALL   East Dock St. ℰ 26521
VOLVO   Riverside Drive ℰ 643295
VW, AUDI   45/53 Gellatly St. ℰ 24251

DUNDONNELL Ross and Cromarty (Highland) 401 E 10 – ✉ Garve – ✪ 085 483.
♦Edinburgh 215 – ♦Inverness 59.

Dundonnell, IV23 2QS, ℰ 204, ≼ Dundonnell Valley – 📺 ➾wc 🄿 🔲 VISA
April-October – **M** 5.50/11.25 t. ⅙ 2.75 – **24 rm** ➩ 19.50/42.00 t. – SB 50.00/60.00 st.

DUNFERMLINE Fife. (Fife) 401 J 15 Scotland G – pop. 52,105 – ECD : Wednesday – ✪ 0383.
See : Site★ – Abbey★ (Norman nave★★) – **Envir.** : Culross★★★ (Palace★★ and Study★) E : 7 m. by
A 994.
🅁 Canmore, Venturefair ℰ 724969, N : 1 m. – 🅁 Pitreavie, Queensferry Rd ℰ 722591 – 🅁 Saline,
Kinneddar Hill ℰ, 852591, NW : 5 m. – 🄳 Glen Bridge Car Park ℰ 20999 (summer only).
♦Edinburgh 16 – ♦ Dundee 48 – Motherwell 39.

King Malcolm Thistle (Thistle), Queensferry Rd, KY11 5DS, S : 1 m. on A 823 ℰ 722611,
Telex 727721 – 📺 ➾wc ☎ 🄿 🚗 AE ⓞ VISA
M 9.50 t. and a la carte ⅙ 3.00 – ➩ 5.25 – **48 rm** 38.00/65.00 t.

at Crossford SW : 1 ¾ m. on A 994 – ✉ ✪ 0383 :

Keavil House ⚶, KY12 8NY, ℰ 736258, Telex 728227, 🚗, ❄ – 📺 ➾wc 🍴wc ☎ 🄿 🔲
AE VISA ❄
M dinner 14.00 t. and a la carte 6.70/10.30 t. ⅙ 2.85 – **32 rm** ➩ 29.00/44.00 t. – SB (weekends
only) 60.00/72.00 st.

MICHELIN Branch, Taxi Way, Hillend Industrial Estate, Hillend, Dunfermline, KY11 5JT, ℰ 822961

AUSTIN-ROVER   18 Halbeath Rd ℰ 731041
FIAT   128/138 Pittencrieff St. ℰ 722565
PEUGEOT-TALBOT   206 Rumbingwell ℰ 731791

RENAULT   Headwell Av. ℰ 721914
TOYOTA   Bruce St. ℰ 723675
VAUXHALL   3 Carnock Rd ℰ 721511

DUNKELD Perth. (Tayside) 401 J 14 Scotland G – ECD : Thursday – ✪ 035 02.
See : Site★ – Cathedral Street★ – 🅁 ℰ 524, N : 1 m. on A 923.
🄳 The Cross ℰ 688 (summer only).
♦Edinburgh 58 – ♦ Aberdeen 88 – ♦ Inverness 98 – Perth 14.

Dunkeld House ⚶, PH8 0HX, ℰ 771, ≼, « Country house in extensive grounds on banks of
river Tay », 🚗, 🚗, park, ❄ – 📺 🔲 🄿 VISA
M 8.50/12.00 st. and a la carte ⅙ 3.20 – **31 rm** ➩ 21.75/87.50 st., **1 suite** 88.50/96.50 st.

DUNNET HEAD Caithness. (Highland) 401 J 7 – ♦Edinburgh 303 – ♦Wick 23.
Hotel see : Wick SE : 23 m.

DUNOON Argyll. (Strathclyde) 401 F 16 – pop. 8,797 – ECD : Wednesday – ✪ 0369.
🅁 Cowal, Ardenslate Rd ℰ 2216, NE : boundary.
🚢 by Caledonian MacBrayne : from Dunoon Pier to Gourock Railway Pier frequent services daily
(20 mn) – by Western Ferries : from Hunters Quay to McInroy's Point, Gourock frequent services
daily (20 mn).
🄳 Pier Esplanade ℰ 3785.
♦Edinburgh 73 – ♦Glasgow 27 – ♦Oban 77.

at Kirn N : 1 m. on A 815 – ✉ ☏ 0369 Dunoon :

Enmore, Marine Par., PA23 8HH, ☎ 2230, ⋞ Firth of Clyde, 🌳, squash – ⇔wc ⋔wc **P**. ⓓ VISA
March-October – **M** (bar lunch)/dinner 12.50 **t.** 🍷 3.50 – **17 rm** SB ⊏ (dinner included) 28.00/42.50 **t.** – SB 75.00 **st.**

at Sandbank N : 2 ½ m. on A 815 – ✉ ☏ 0369 Dunoon :

Firpark, Shore Rd, PA23 8QG, ☎ 6506, ⋞ Holy Loch, 🌳 – TV ⇔wc **P**. VISA
M (bar lunch)/dinner a la carte 6.00/9.45 **t.** 🍷 2.35 – **6 rm** ⊏ 15.00/35.00 **t.**

AUSTIN-ROVER East Boy Promenade ☎ 3094
FORD George St. ☎ 3234
RENAULT Shore St., Inverary ☎ 0499 (Inverary) 2271

DUNVEGAN Inverness. (Highland) **401** A 11 – see Skye (Isle of).

DUROR Argyll. (Strathclyde) **401** E 14 – ✉ Appin – ☏ 063 174.
♦Edinburgh 125 – Fort William 19 – ♦Oban 31.

Stewart (Best Western) 🐎, Glen Duror, PA38 4BW, ☎ 268, ⋞, 🌳, park – TV ⇔wc **P**. AE ⓓ VISA
Easter-October – **M** (bar lunch)/dinner 13.00 **t.** 🍷 3.50 – **26 rm** ⊏ 28.00/55.00 **t.** – SB 58.00/62.00 **st.**

EAST KILBRIDE Lanark. (Strathclyde) **401** **402** H 16 – pop. 70 ,454 – ECD : Wednesday – ☏ 035 52.
⛳18 Torrance House, Strathaven Rd ☎ 48638.
♦Edinburgh 46 – ♦Ayr 35 – ♦Glasgow 10.

Bruce (Swallow), Cornwall St., G74 1AF, ☎ 29771, Telex 778428 – ⬍ TV **P**. 🏛. AE ⓓ VISA
M *(closed Sunday lunch)* 6.00/9.50 **st.** and a la carte 🍷 3.80 – **84 rm** ⊏ 40.50/50.00 **st.** – SB (weekends only) 42.00 **st.**

Stuart (Thistle), 2 Cornwall Way, G74 1JR, ☎ 21161, Telex 778504 – ⬍ TV ⇔wc ⋔wc ☎ ♿. 🏛. AE ⓓ VISA
M 5.25 **t.** (lunch) and a la carte 6.65/10.75 **t.** 🍷 3.00 – **30 rm** ⊏ 30.00/37.00 **t.** – SB (weekends only) 43.60/63.00 **st.**

Crutherland Country House 🐎, Strathaven Rd, G75 0QZ, SE : 2 m. on A 726 ☎ 37633, 🎣, 🌳, park – TV ⇔wc ⋔wc ☎ **P**. AE VISA. 🚫
closed 1 and 2 January – **M** *(closed lunch Saturday and Sunday)* 4.25/6.50 **st.** and a la carte 🍷 2.95 – **21 rm** ⊏ 33.00/38.00 **st.**

Torrance, 67 Main St., G74 4LN, ☎ 25241 – TV ⇔wc ⋔wc ☎ **P**. AE ⓓ VISA
M (bar lunch)/dinner 7.50 **st.** and a la carte 🍷 1.75 – **26 rm** ⊏ 22.00/36.00 **st.** – SB (weekends only) 39.00 **st.**

AUSTIN-ROVER Telford Rd ☎ 23455

EAST LINTON E. Lothian (Lothian) **401** M 16 – pop. 1 ,190 – ECD : Wednesday – ☏ 0620.
♦Edinburgh 22 – ♦Newcastle-upon-Tyne 96.

Harvesters (Best Western), Station Rd, EH40 3DP, ☎ 860395, 🌳 – TV ⇔wc **P**. AE ⓓ VISA
closed 1 to 15 January – **M** (bar lunch)/dinner a la carte 8.20/13.55 **t.** 🍷 4.00 – **10 rm** ⊏ 20.00/50.00 **t.**

EDAY (Isle of) Orkney (Orkney Islands) **401** L 6 – Shipping Services : see Orkney Islands (Mainland : Kirkwall).

EDDLESTON Peebles. (Borders) **401** **402** K 16 – see Peebles.

EDINBURGH Midlothian (Lothian) **401** K 16 **Scotland G** – pop. 408 ,822 – ☏ 031.

See : Site★★★ – International Festival★★★ (August) – Castle★★ (Site★★★, ⋞★★ ✳★★★, Great Hall: hammerbeam roof★★, Palace block: Honours of Scotland★★★) DZ – Abbey and Palace of Holyrood house★★ (Plasterwork ceilings★★★) BV – Royal Mile★★ : Gladstone's Land★ EYZ **A**, St. Giles' Cathedral★★ (Crown Spire★★★) EZ, Wax Museum★ EZ **M1** – Canongate Tolbooth★ EY **B** Victoria Street★ EZ **84** – Royal Scottish Museum★★, EZ **M2** – New Town★★ : Charlotte Square★★★ CZ 14, National Museum of Antiquities★★ EY **M3**, The Georgian House★ CY **D** – National Portrait Museum★ Princes Street and Gardens : National Gallery of Scotland★★ DY **M4** – Scott Monument★ EY **F** Calton Hill EY : ✳ from Nelson Monument★★★ – Royal Botanic Gardens★★★ AV – Edinburgh Zoo★★ AV – Scottish Agricultural Museum★ by A 90 AV – Craigmillar Castle★ BX.

Envir. : Rosslyn Chapel★★, Apprentice Pillar★★★, S : 7 m. by A 101 BX.

⛳18 Silverknowes, Parkway, ☎ 336 3843 W : 4 m. AV – ⛳18 Craigmillar Park, Observatory Rd ☎ 667 2837 BX – ⛳18 Carrick Knowe, Glendevon Park ☎ 337 1096, W : 5 m. AX.

✈ ☎ 333 1000, Telex 727615, W : 6 m. by A 8 AV – **Terminal :** Waverley Bridge.

🚗 ☎ 556 1100.

ℹ Waverley Market, 3 Princes St., ☎ 557 2727 – Edinburgh Airport ☎ 333 2167.

♦Glasgow 46 – ♦Newcastle-upon-Tyne 105.

EDINBURGH

0   1 km
0   1 mile

FIRTH

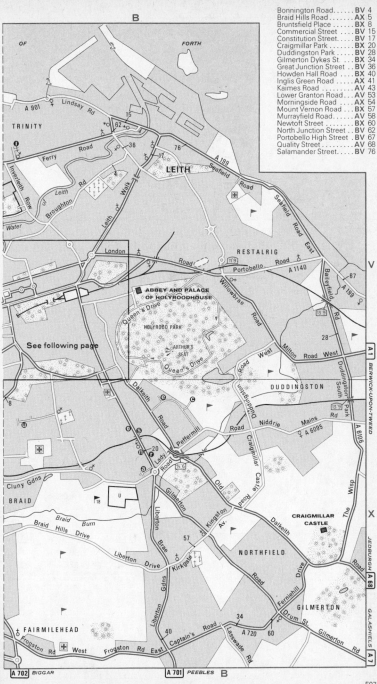

Bonnington Road . . . . . . **BV** 4
Braid Hills Road . . . . **AX** 5
Bruntsfield Place . . . . . . **BX** 8
Commercial Street . . . . **BV** 15
Constitution Street . . . . . **BV** 17
Craigmillar Park . . . . . . **BX** 20
Duddingston Park . . . . . **BV** 28
Gilmerton Dykes St. . . . **BX** 34
Great Junction Street . . **BV** 36
Howden Hall Road . . . . **BX** 40
Inglis Green Road . . . . . **AX** 41
Kaimes Road . . . . **BX** 43
Lower Granton Road . . . **AV** 53
Morningside Road . . . . . **AX** 54
Mount Vernon Road . . **BX** 57
Murrayfield Road . . . . . . **AV** 58
Newtoft Street . . . . **BX** 60
North Junction Street . . **BV** 62
Portobello High Street . **BV** 67
Quality Street . . . . **AV** 68
Salamander Street . . . . . **BV** 76

EDINBURGH
CENTRE

Castle Street .... DY
Frederick Street .... DY
George Street .... DY
Hanover Street .... DY
High Street .... EYZ 37
Lawnmarket .... EYZ
Princes Street .... DY
St James Centre .... EY
Waverley Market .... EY

Bernard Terrace .... EZ 3
Bread Street .... DZ 6
Bristo Place .... EZ 7
Candlemaker Row .... EZ 9
Castlehill .... DZ 10
Chambers Street .... EZ 12
Chapel Street .... EZ 13
Charlotte Square .... CY 14
Deanhaugh Street .... CY 23
Douglas Gardens .... CY 25
Drummond Street .... EZ 27
Forrest Road .... EZ 31
Gardner's Crescent .... CZ 32
George IV Bridge .... EZ 33
Grassmarket .... DZ 35
Home Street .... DZ 38
Hope Street .... CY 39
Johnston Terrace .... DZ 42
King's Bridge .... DZ 44
King's Stables Road .... DZ 45
Lawnmarket .... EZ 46
Leith Street .... EY 47
Leven Street .... DZ 48
Lothian Street .... EZ 51
Mound (The) .... DY 55
North Bridge .... EY 61
North St. Andrew Street ...... EY 66
Raeburn Place .... CY 69
Randolph Crescent .... CY 71
St. Mary's Street .... EY 73
St. Mary's Square .... EY 75
Shandwick Place .... CYZ 77
South Charlotte Street .... DY 78
South St. David Street .... DY 79
Spittal Street .... DZ 83
Victoria Street .... EZ 84
Waterloo Place .... EY 87
Waverley Bridge .... EY 89
West Maitland Street .... CZ 92

Caledonian, Princes St., EH1 2AB, ℰ 225 2433, Telex 72179 – 📶 📺 ☎ 🅿 🖭 🔜 🎖 ⑩ 𝘝𝘐𝘚𝘈
💸
CY **n**
M (rest. see **Pompadour** below) – ⬭ 6.80 – **254 rm** 45.00/95.00 st., **15 suites** – SB (weekends only) (October-April) 75.00 st.

Sheraton, 1 Festival Square, EH3 9SR, ℰ 229 9131, Telex 72398, 🔄 – 📶 ☰ 📺 ☎ 🔓 🅿 🖭
263 rm, 16 suites.
CDZ **v**

George (Forum), 19-21 George St., EH2 2PB, ℰ 225 1251, Telex 72570 – 📶 ☰ rest 📺 ☎ 🔓
🅿 🖭 🔜 🎖 ⑩ 𝘝𝘐𝘚𝘈 💸
DY **z**
M 9.75/12.00 st. and a la carte 🍷 3.75 – ⬭ 7.40 – **195 rm** 55.00/99.00 st., **2 suites** 132.00/242.00 st.

Carlton Highland, 1 North Bridge, EH5 1SD, ℰ 556 7277, Telex 727001, 🔄, squash – 📶
☰ rest 📺 ☎ 🔓. 🎖 – **110 rm, 4 suites**
EY **s**

Roxburghe (Best Western), 38 Charlotte Sq., EH2 4HG, ℰ 225 3921, Telex 727054 – 📶 📺 🔓.
🎖 – **76 rm, 2 suites**.
DY **o**

Ladbroke Dragonara (Ladbroke), Bells Mills, 69 Belford Rd, EH4 3DG, ℰ 332 2545, Telex
727979 – 📶 📺 ☎ 🔓 🅿 🖭 🔜 🎖 ⑩ 𝘝𝘐𝘚𝘈 💸
CY **i**
M 9.50/11.50 t. and a la carte 🍷 3.40 – ⬭ 6.25 – **146 rm** 60.00/95.00 t., **3 suites** – SB (weekends only) 67.50 st.

Royal Scot (Swallow), 111 Glasgow Rd, EH12 8NF, W : 4 ½ m. on A 8 ℰ 334 9191, Telex
727197 – 📶 📺 ☎ 🔓 🅿 🖭 🔜 🎖 ⑩ 𝘝𝘐𝘚𝘈
by A 8 AV
M (carving lunch)/dinner 10.25 st. and a la carte 🍷 3.40 – **251 rm** 50.00/62.00 st. – SB (weekends only) 55.00/60.00 st.

King James Thistle (Thistle), 1 Leith St., EH1 3SW, ℰ 556 0111, Telex 727200 – 📶 📺
⌂wc 🔓 🅿. 🎖 🔜 🖭 ⑩ 𝘝𝘐𝘚𝘈
EY **u**
M 8.50/9.50 t. and a la carte 🍷 3.00 – ⬭ 4.75 – **147 rm** 42.00/80.00 t., **5 suites** 95.00 t.

Crest (Crest), Queensferry Rd, EH4 3HL, NW : 2 m. on A 90 ℰ 332 2442, Telex 72541 – 📶
☰ rest 📺 ⌂wc ☎ 🅿 🔓 🖭 ⑩ 𝘝𝘐𝘚𝘈 💸
AV **x**
M approx. 12.25 st. – ⬭ 5.75 – **118 rm** 50.00/65.00 st. **1 suite** – SB (weekends only) 67.00 st.

Post House (T.H.F.), Corstorphine Rd, EH12 6UA, W : 3 m. on A 8 ℰ 334 8221, Telex 727103,
⬳ – 📶 📺 ⌂wc 🔓 🅿. 🎖 🔜 🖭 ⑩ 𝘝𝘐𝘚𝘈
AV **u**
M 7.50/10.45 st. and a la carte 🍷 2.70 – ⬭ 5.50 – **207 rm** 46.00/56.00 st., **1 suite**.

Howard, 32-36 Gt. King St., EH3 6QH, ℰ 557 3500, Telex 727887 – 📶 📺 ⌂wc 🕯wc ☎ 🅿.
🔜 ⑩ 𝘝𝘐𝘚𝘈
DY **s**
M (bar lunch)/dinner 15.00 t. 🍷 3.75 – **25 rm** ⬭ 40.00/70.00 t. – SB (weekends only) (November-March) 66.00 st.

Stakis Grosvenor (Stakis), Grosvenor St., EH12 5EF, ℰ 226 6001, Telex 72445 – 📶 📺
⌂wc 🕯wc ☎ 🔓. 🎖 🔜 🖭 ⑩
CZ **a**
M 5.95/7.95 t. and a la carte 🍷 3.25 – **130 rm** ⬭ 51.00/70.00.

Albany, 39-43 Albany St., EH1 3QY, ℰ 556 0397, Telex 727079 – 📺 ⌂wc 🕯wc ⬳. 🔜 🖭
⑩ 𝘝𝘐𝘚𝘈
EY **v**
M *(closed lunch Saturday and Sunday)* a la carte 8.30/13.40 t. 🍷 2.95 – ⬭ 4.95 – **21 rm** 28.00/60.00 t. – SB (weekends only) (October-April) 50.00 st.

Ellersly House, 4 Ellersly Rd, EH12 6HZ, W : 2 ½ m. by A 8 ℰ 337 6888, Telex 76357, ⬳ –
📶 📺 ⌂wc ⬳ 🅿. 🔜 🖭 ⑩ 𝘝𝘐𝘚𝘈 💸
AV **v**
M 3.50/9.00 t. and a la carte 🍷 3.00 – **55 rm** ⬭ 42.00/85.00 t.

Norton House, Ingliston, EH28 8LX, W : 9 ¼ m. on A 8 ℰ 333 1275, ⬳, park – 📺 ⌂wc ☎
🅿. 🎖 🔜 🖭 ⑩ 𝘝𝘐𝘚𝘈
on A 8 AV
M 7.25/12.95 st. and a la carte 🍷 4.00 – **19 rm** ⬭ 47.75/64.00 st. – SB (weekends only) 85.00 st.

Bruntsfield (Best Western), 69-74 Bruntsfield Pl., EH10 4HH, ℰ 229 1393, Telex 727897 – 📶
📺 ⌂wc ⬳ 🅿. 🎖 🔜 🖭 ⑩ 𝘝𝘐𝘚𝘈
DZ **e**
closed 24 to 26 December – **M** (buffet lunch)/dinner 10.50 st. and a la carte 🍷 2.95 – **54 rm**
⬭ 24.00/65.00 st. – SB 49.00/75.00 st.

Barnton Thistle (Thistle), 562 Queensferry Rd, EH4 6AS, NW : 4 ¾ m. on A 90 ℰ 339 1144,
Telex 727928 – 📶 📺 ⌂wc 🕯wc ☎ 🅿. 🎖 🔜 🖭 ⑩ 𝘝𝘐𝘚𝘈
AV **o**
M 8.50/10.50 t. and a la carte 🍷 2.75 – ⬭ 5.00 – **50 rm** 41.00/60.00 t., **3 suites** 75.00 t

Old Waverley, 43 Princes St., EH2 2BY, ℰ 556 4648, Group Telex 778215 – 📶 📺 ⌂wc 🕯wc
⬳. 💸 – **66 rm**
EY **r**

Murrayfield, 18 Corstorphine Rd, EH12 6HN, W : 2 ½ m. on A 8 ℰ 337 1844 – 📺 ⌂wc ⬳ 🅿
M (grill rest. only) – **36 rm**.
AV **z**

Kildonan Lodge, 27 Craigmillar Park, EH16 5PE, ℰ 667 2793 – 📺 🅿. 🖭
BX **r**
M (bar lunch residents only)/dinner 5.25 t. and a la carte 🍷 3.30 – **9 rm** ⬭ 12.50/25.00 t.

Iona, 17 Strathearn Pl., EH9 2AL, ℰ 447 6264 – 🕯 🅿. 🔜 𝘝𝘐𝘚𝘈
BX **u**
M 5.00/10.00 t. 🍷 3.50 – **21 rm** ⬭ 21.00/42.00 t. – SB (weekends only) (October-April) 47.00/53.00 st.

Quinton Lodge, 24 Polwarth Terr., EH11 1NA, ℰ 229 4100, ⬳ – 📺 🅿
AX **a**
6 rm ⬭ 12.00/19.00 st.

International, 37 Mayfield Gdns, EH9 2BX, ℰ 667 2511 – 📺 ⌂wc 🕯wc
BX **s**
7 rm ⬭ 11.00/25.00 st.

P.T.O. →

⌂ **Dorstan,** 7 Priestfield Rd, EH16 5HJ, ℰ 667 6721 – ⌂wc 🅟   BX **e**
   14 rm ⊆ 11.00/30.00 **st.**

⌂ **Glenisla,** 12 Lygon Rd, EH16 5QB, ℰ 667 4098 – 🅟   BX **a**
   8 rm ⊆ 12.00/27.00 **t.**

⌂ Southdown, 20 Craigmillar Park, EH16 5PS, ℰ 667 2410 – 📺 ⌂wc 🅟 – **8 rm**   BX **n**

⌂ **Lomond House,** 9 Zetland Pl., EH5 3HU, ℰ 552 3901 – 🗄wc   BV **i**
   7 rm ⊆ 10.00/30.00 **st.**

⌂ **Parklands,** 20 Mayfield Gdns., EH9 2BZ, ℰ 667 7184   BX **o**
   6 rm ⊆ 15.00/21.00 **st.**

⌂ **Galloway,** 22 Dean Park Cres., EH4 1PH, ℰ 332 3672   CY **a**
   10 rm ⊆ 11.00/30.00 **t.**

XXXX **Pompadour** (at Caledonian H.), Princes St., EH1 2AB, ℰ 225 2433, Telex 72179 – 🅟. ◨ AE
   ◨ *VISA*   CY **n**
   closed lunch Saturday and Sunday – **M** 12.50/27.00 **st.** and a la carte ◊ 3.95.

XXX **Aye,** 80 Queen St., EH2 4NF, ℰ 226 5467, Japanese rest. – ▤. ◨ AE ◓ *VISA*   CDY **e**
   closed Sunday lunch and Monday – **M** 10.00/50.00 **t.** and a la carte.

XXX **Prestonfield House** ⌂ with rm, Priestfield Rd, EH16 5UT, SE : 2 ½ m. off A 68 ℰ 667 3346,
   Telex 727396, ≼, « Elegant 17C mansion », 🐎, park – 🗄 🅟. ◨ AE ◓ *VISA*   BX **c**
   M 10.00/14.00 **t.** and dinner a la carte ◊ 2.75 – **5 rm** ⊆ 44.00/57.50 **t.**

XXX **Howtowdie,** 27a Stafford St., EH3 7BJ, ℰ 225 6291 – ◨ AE ◓ *VISA*   CY **u**
   closed Sunday, 25-26 December and 1-2 January – **M** 8.95/20.00 **st.** and a la carte ◊ 4.60.

XX **Cosmo,** 58a North Castle St., EH2 3LU, ℰ 226 6743, Italian rest. – ◨ AE   DY **r**
   closed Saturday lunch, Sunday and Monday – **M** a la carte 9.70/15.80 **t.** ◊ 2.75.

XX **Raffaelli,** 10-11 Randolph Pl., EH3 7TA, ℰ 225 6060, Italian rest. – ◨ AE ◓ *VISA*   CY **c**
   closed Saturday, Sunday, Christmas Day and New Years Day – **M** a la carte 10.35/12.80 **t.**
   ◊ 2.30.

XX **Shamiana,** 14 Brougham St., Tollcross, EH3 9JH, ℰ 228 2265, Indian rest. – ◨ AE ◓ *VISA*
   closed Sunday, Christmas Day and New Years Day – **M** (dinner only) a la carte 9.45/10.70 **t.**
   ◊ 2.60.   DZ **a**

XX **L'Auberge,** 56 St. Mary's St., EH1 1SX, ℰ 556 5888, French rest. – ◨ AE *VISA*   EYZ **c**
   closed 25-26 December and 1 January – **M** 7.50 **t.** (lunch) and a la carte 10.55/15.45 **t.** ◊ 3.50.

X **Martins,** 70 Rose St., North Lane, EH2 3DX, behind pedestrian precinct ℰ 225 3106 – ◨ AE
   ◓ *VISA*   DY **n**
   closed Saturday lunch, Sunday, Monday, 2 weeks June and 25 December-6 January – **M**
   8.50/16.50 **t.** ◊ 3.50.

X **Alp-Horn,** 167 Rose St., EH2 4LS, ℰ 225 4787, Swiss rest. – ◨   DY **x**
   closed Sunday, Monday, first 3 weeks July and 2 weeks at Christmas – **M** 5.00/13.00 **t.** and a la
   carte ◊ 3.40.

X **Verandah,** 17 Dalry Rd, EH11 2BQ, ℰ 337 5828, Indian rest. – ◨ AE ◓ *VISA*   CZ **z**
   M 7.55/9.95 **t.** and a la carte ◊ 2.95.

X Lune Town, 38 William St., ℰ 225 9388, Cantonese rest.   CZ **s**

X **Bungalow,** 23 Brougham Pl., EH3 9JV, ℰ 229 1537, Indian rest. – ◨ AE ◓ *VISA*   DZ **i**
   M 9.50 **t.** (dinner) and a la carte ◊ 3.25.

X **Vito's,** 55a Frederick St., EH2 1LH, ℰ 225 5052, Italian rest. – ◨ AE ◓ *VISA*   DY **i**
   closed Sunday – **M** 6.50 **t.** (lunch) and a la carte ◊ 2.80.

X **L'Alliance,** 7 Merchant St., ℰ 225 2002, Brasserie   EZ **a**
   closed Sunday, last 2 weeks July and 2 weeks at Christmas – **M** a la carte 5.75/9.50 **t.** ◊ 2.55.

   at Bonnyrigg S : 8 m. by A 7 – BX – on A 6094 – ✉ Bonnyrigg – ☉ 0875 Gorebridge.

🏰 **Dalhousie Castle** ⌂, EH19 3JB, SE : 1 ¼ m. on B 704 ℰ 20153, Telex 72380, ≼, « Converted
   12C castle », 🐟, park – 📺 🅟. 🛁. ◨ AE ◓ *VISA*. 🍴
   M a la carte 12.75/21.45 **t.** ◊ 3.25 – **24 rm** ⊆ 38.00/98.00 **t.**

ALFA-ROMEO 22 Canning St. ℰ 229 5561
AUSTIN-ROVER-DAIMLER-JAGUAR Westfield Av.
ℰ 337 3222
AUSTIN-ROVER Goldenacre Terr. ℰ 552 4695
AUSTIN-ROVER Lanark Rd ℰ 443 2936
AUSTIN-ROVER Falcon Rd West ℰ 447 6161
AUSTIN-ROVER 70 Slateford Rd ℰ 337 1252
CITROEN 13 Lauriston Gardens ℰ 229 4207
FIAT, LANCIA 8 Glenogle Rd ℰ 556 6404
FORD Baileyfield Rd ℰ 669 6261
FORD Fountainbridge ℰ 229 3331
FORD 12 West Mayfield ℰ 667 1900

FORD Craighall Rd ℰ 552 5524
FORD Queensferry Rd ℰ 336 2683
HONDA Westfield Rd ℰ 337 7204
PORSCHE 141 George St. ℰ 225 9266
RENAULT 553 Gorgie Rd ℰ 444 1673
RENAULT Portobello Rd ℰ 669 3201
TALBOT Lochrin Tollcross ℰ 229 8911
VOLVO 38 Seafield Rd East ℰ 669 8301
VOLVO Bankhead ℰ 442 3333
VW, AUDI-NSU 454 Gorgie Rd ℰ 346 1661
VW, AUDI-NSU Marionville Rd ℰ 652 1691

EDZELL Angus (Tayside) **401** M 13 Scotland G – pop. 751 – ECD : Thursday – ☉ 035 64.
Envir. : Castle⋆ (The Pleasance⋆⋆⋆) W : 1¼ m.

🏌 ℰ 235 – 🏌 at Brechin ℰ 035 62 (Brechin) 2383, S : 5 ½ m.
♦Edinburgh 94 – ♦Aberdeen 36 – ♦Dundee 31.

🏠 Glenesk, High St., DD9 7TF, ℰ 319, 🐟, 🐎 – 📺 ⌂wc 🗄wc ☎ 🅟. 🛁
   25 rm ⊆ 23.00/48.00 **t.**

EGILSAY (Isle of) Orkney (Orkney Islands) **401** L 6 – Shipping Services : see Orkney Islands (Mainland : Kirkwall).

EIGG (Isle of) Inverness. (Highland) **401** B 13 – Shipping Services : see Mallaig.

ELGIN Moray. (Grampian) **401** K 11 Scotland G – pop. 18 ,702 – ECD : Wednesday – ✪ 0343.
See : Site★ – Cathedral★ (Chapter House★★).
Envir. : Forres (Sueno's Stone★★) W : 12 ½ m. by A 96.
⛳ Hardhillock, Birnie Rd ℰ 2338, S : 1 m. – ⛳ Hopeman ℰ 830578, N : 7 m.
🛈 17 High St. ℰ 3388 and 2666.
◆Edinburgh 198 – ◆Aberdeen 68 – Fraserburgh 61 – ◆Inverness 39.

> *Hotels see : Fochabers* E : 9 ½ m.

AUSTIN ROVER-DAIMLER-JAGUAR Station Rd ℰ 48444
CITROEN 27 Greyfriars St. ℰ 7416
FORD East Rd ℰ 2176
FORD East Rd ℰ 7121

NISSAN Borough Briggs Rd ℰ 7473
RENAULT Edgar Rd ℰ 7688
VAUXHALL-OPEL, VOLVO South College St. ℰ 7561
VW, AUDI Blackfriars Rd ℰ 44977

ELLON Aberdeen. (Grampian) **401** N 11 – pop. 6 ,304 – ECD : Wednesday – ✪ 0358.
Envir. : Pitmedden Gardens★★, SW : 5 m. by A 920 – Haddo House★, NW : 8 m. by 9005.
⛳ McDonald ℰ 20576.
🛈 Market St. Car Park ℰ 20730 (summer only).
◆Edinburgh 147 – ◆Aberdeen 17 – Fraserburgh 27.

🏨 **Ladbroke Mercury** (Ladbroke), AB4 9NP, ℰ 20666, Telex 739200 – 📺 ⇱wc 🕿 ℗ 🛄 🔊 🅰🅴 ⓞ 𝐕𝐈𝐒𝐀
M (bar lunch)/dinner 11.50 **t.** and a la carte 🍷 3.70 – ⬜ 6.00 – **40 rm** 25.00/44.00 **t.** – SB 47.50/57.50 **st.**

ERIBOLL (Loch) Sutherland (Highland) **401** F 8.
◆Edinburgh 276 – Tongue 21.

> *Hotel see : Tongue* E : 21 m.

ERISKA (Isle of) Argyll. (Strathclyde) **401** D 14 – ✉ Oban – ✪ 063 172 Ledaig.

🏨 **Isle of Eriska** ⏃, PA37 1SD, ℰ 371, ≤ Lismore and mountains, « Country house atmosphere », 🐎, park, 🎾 – ⇱wc 🕿 ℔ ℗ 🔊 🐾
Mid February-November – **M** (buffet lunch Monday to Saturday)/dinner 20.00 🍷 3.05 – **17 rm** ⬜ (dinner included) 62.00/135.00 – SB (Mid February, March and November) 104.00 **t.**

ERSKINE Renfrew. (Strathclyde) **401 402** G 16 – ✪ 041 Glasgow.
◆Edinburgh 55 – ◆Glasgow 9.

🏨 **Crest** (Crest) ⏃, Erskine Bridge, PA8 6AN, on A 726 ℰ 812 0123, Telex 777713, ≤, 🐎 – 🛗 ▤ rest 📺 ℔ ℗ 🛄 🔊 🅰🅴 ⓞ 𝐕𝐈𝐒𝐀
M approx. 11.50 **st.** – ⬜ 5.75 – **186 rm** 46.00/55.00 **st.** – SB (weekends only) 59.00 **st.**

ETTRICKBRIDGE Selkirk. (Borders) **401 402** L 17 – see Selkirk.

FALKIRK Stirling. (Central) **401** I 16 – pop. 36 ,372 – ECD : Wednesday – ✪ 0324.
Envir. : Linlithgow★★ (Palace★★: Gateway★, Fountain★★, Great Hall: fireplace★★-Old town★, St. Michael's Church★) E : 8 m. by A 803.
⛳ Grangemouth ℰ 0324 (Polmont) 711500, E : 3 m.
◆Edinburgh 26 – Dunfermline 18 – ◆Glasgow 25 – Motherwell 27 – Perth 43.

🏨 **Stakis Park** (Stakis), Camelon Rd, Arnothill, FK1 5RY, ℰ 28331, Telex 776502 – 🛗 📺 ⇱wc ☎ ℗ 🛄 🔊 🅰🅴 ⓞ 𝐕𝐈𝐒𝐀
M 4.50 **t.** (lunch) and a la carte 8.35/12.35 **t.** 🍷 3.40 – **55 rm** ⬜ 42.00/53.00 **t.**

✕ **Pierre's,** 140 Grahams Rd, FK2 7BZ, ℰ 35843, French rest. – ℗ 🔊 🅰🅴 ⓞ 𝐕𝐈𝐒𝐀
closed Saturday lunch, Sunday, Monday, first 2 weeks January and first 2 weeks July – **M** (restricted lunch) 4.50/9.85 **t.** and a la carte 🍷 2.95.

> *at Polmont* SE : 3 m. on A 803 – ✉ ✪ 0324 Polmont :

🏨 **Inchyra Grange,** Grange Rd, FK2 0YB, ℰ 711911, Telex 777693, 🐎 – 📺 ⇱wc ☎ ℔ ℗ 🔊 🅰🅴 ⓞ 𝐕𝐈𝐒𝐀
M 7.00/9.50 **t.** and a la carte 🍷 3.55 – **30 rm** ⬜ 35.00/48.00 **st.** – SB (weekends only) 42.00/46.00 **st.**

FIAT Callendar Rd ℰ 24204
FORD Callendar Rd ℰ 21511
HYUNDAI High Station Rd ℰ 24221
MAZDA Main St., Bainsford ℰ 37921
MAZDA Main St. ℰ 22584

TOYOTA Lady'smill ℰ 35935
TOYOTA Winchester Ave., Denny ℰ 824387
VAUXHALL-OPEL 76/86 Grahams Rd ℰ 21234
VOLVO West End ℰ 23042

FARR Inverness. (Highland) **401** H 11 – ✪ 080 83.
♦Edinburgh 155 – ♦Inverness 10.

XX Grouse and Trout, Flichity, IV1 2XE, S : 4 m. by B 851 ℘ 314, ≤, 🚗 – **P**.

FEOLIN Argyll. (Strathclyde) **401** B 16 – Shipping Services : see Jura (Isle of).

FETLAR (Isle of) Shetland (Shetland Islands) **401** R 2 – Shipping Services : see Shetland Islands.

FIONNPHORT Argyll. (Strathclyde) **401** A 15 – Shipping Services : see Mull (Isle of).

FISHNISH Argyll. (Strathclyde) **401** C 14 – Shipping Services : see Mull (Isle of).

FLOTTA (Isle of) Orkney (Orkney Islands) **401** K 7 – Shipping Services : see Orkney Islands.

FOCHABERS Moray. (Grampian) **401** K 11 **Scotland G** – pop. 1,419 – ECD : Wednesday – ✪ 0343.
🏌 Spey Bay ℘ 820424, N : 5 m. – 🏌 Garmouth ℘ 034 387 (Spey Bay) 388.
♦Edinburgh 188 – ♦Aberdeen 58 – Fraserburgh 52 – ♦Inverness 48.

🏠 **Gordon Arms,** 87 High St., IV32 7DH, ℘ 820508 – 📺 ⌷wc ☎ **P**. 🔼 AE ⓄVISA
M 4.00/9.50 t. 🍷 2.50 – **12 rm** 🛏 28.00/38.00 t. – SB 40.00/60.00 st.

at Clochan NE : 3 ½ m. on A 98 – ⊠ Fochabers – ✪ 054 27 Clochan :

🏠 **Mill,** Tynet, AB5 2HJ, on A 98 ℘ 233 – 📺 ⌷wc ⌷wc **P**. 🔼 AE ⓄVISA
closed 1 and 2 January – **M** (closed Sunday dinner) 4.00/10.50 t. – **15 rm** 🛏 18.00/32.00 t.

FORFAR Angus (Tayside) **401** L 14 – pop. 12,652 – ECD : Thursday – ✪ 0307.
Envir. : Glamis★ (Castle★★, Angus Folk Museum★) SW : 5 ½ m. by A 94 – Meigle Museum★★ (Early Christian Monuments★★) SW : 12 ½ m. by A 94.
♦Edinburgh 75 – ♦Aberdeen 55 – ♦Dundee 12 – Perth 31.

🏨 **Benholm** 🌿, 78 Glamis Rd, DD8 1DS, SW : ½ m. on A 94 ℘ 64281, 🚗 – 📺 ⌷wc ⌷wc ☎
P. 🔼 AE ⓄVISA
M 5.75/10.35 t. and a la carte – 🛏 3.40 – **7 rm** 34.00/43.00 t. – SB (weekends only) (October-April) 60.00/100.00 st.

🏠 Royal, 31-33 Castle St., DD8 3AE, ℘ 62691 – 📺 ⌷wc ☎ **P**
21 rm.

AUSTIN-ROVER 128 Castle St. ℘ 62542   TALBOT Lochside Rd ℘ 62676
FORD Kirriemuir Rd ℘ 62347

FORSINARD Sutherland (Highland) – ✪ 064 17 Halladale.
♦Edinburgh 271 – Thurso 30 – ♦Wick 51.

🏠 **Forsinard** 🌿, KW13 6YT, ℘ 221, ≤, 🌿 – ⌷wc ⌷wc 🦆 **P**. 🔼 VISA
Easter-October – **M** (booking essential)(bar lunch)/dinner 10.00 t. 🍷 2.25 – **10 rm**
🛏 18.50/35.00 t.

FORT WILLIAM Inverness. (Highland) **401** E 13 **Scotland G** – pop. 10,805 – ECD : Wednesday except summer – ✪ 0397.
See : Site★.
Envir. : Ben Nevis★★, SE : 4 m. – Road to the Isles★★ (Glenfinnan★, Arisaig★ (≤★ of Sound of Arisaig), Silver Sands of Morar★, Mallaig★) NW : 46 m. by A 830 – Glen Nevis★, SE.
🏌 Torlundy ℘ 4464, N : 3 m. on A 82.
🅱 ℘ 3781.
♦Edinburgh 133 – ♦Glasgow 104 – ♦Inverness 68 – ♦Oban 50.

🏰 ✿ **Inverlochy Castle** 🌿, Inverlochy, PH33 6SN, NE : 3 m. on A 82 ℘ 2177, Telex 776229, ≤ garden, loch and mountains, « Victorian castle in extensive grounds », 🌿, 🚗, park, ✗ –
📺 ☎ **P**. 🔼 Ⓞ. ✗
Mid March-mid November – **M** (booking essential) 23.00/28.00 t. 🍷 4.00 – **16 rm**
🛏 88.00/120.00 t., **2 suites** 160.00 t.
Spec. Grilled Loch Linnhe prawns with pernod butter, Scottish Game (20 August-mid November), Fig Cassis served with cinnamon ice cream.

🏠 **Nevis Bank,** Belford Rd, PH33 6BY, ℘ 5721 – 📺 ⌷wc ⌷wc ☎ **P**. 🔼 VISA
M 3.95/10.00 t. and a la carte 🍷 2.95 – **32 rm** 🛏 17.50/45.00 t., **2 suites** 60.00/75.00 t. – SB (weekends only)(except July and August) 50.00/70.00 st.

↑ Guisachan, Alma Rd, PH33 6HA, ℘ 3797, ≤ – ⌷wc **P**. ✗
closed 22 December-5 January – **15 rm** 🛏 9.00/30.00 t.

at Banavie N : 3 m. by A 82 and A 830 on B 8004 – ⊠ Fort William – ✪ 039 77 Corpach :

🏠 **Moorings,** PH33 7LY, ℘ 550, ≤, 🚗 – ⌷wc ⌷wc **P**. Ⓞ VISA ✗
(March-November) – **M** (bar lunch)/dinner 13.80 t. and a la carte 🍷 2.50 – **17 rm**
🛏 22.00/40.00 t.

AUSTIN-ROVER Gordon Sq. ℘ 2345   PEUGEOT-TALBOT Canaghael ℘ 4141

512

FOYERS Inverness. (Highland) **401** G 12 – ✪ 045 63 Gorthleck.

See : Loch Ness★★.

♦Edinburgh 176 – ♦Inverness 18.

  🏠 **Foyers,** IV1 2XT, N : ½ m. on B 852 ♪ 216, ≤ Loch Ness and mountains, ⌇, 🐎 – 🎬 ✪
     M (bar lunch)/dinner 5.00 **st.** ▌2.30 – **9 rm** ⊑ 11.00/22.00 **st.**

GAIRLOCH Ross and Cromarty (Highland) **401** C 10 – ECD : Wednesday except summer –
✪ 0445.

Envir. : Inverewe Gardens★★★, NE : 8 m. by A 832 – Wester Ross★★★ (Gairloch to Ullapool★ via
Loch Maree★★★, Inverewe Gardens★★★, Falls of Measach★ and Loch Broom★★) NE : 56 m. by A
832 and A 835 – Wester Ross★★★ (Gairloch to Kyle of Lochalsh via Victoria Falls★ Loch Maree★★★,
and Plockton★) S : 102 m. by A 832, A 896 and A 890.

🏌 Achtercairn ♪ 2130.

♦Edinburgh 228 – ♦Inverness 72 – Kyle of Lochalsh 68.

  🏨 **Gairloch,** IV21 2BL, ♪ 2001, ≤ Gair Loch and Isle of Skye, ⌇, ※ – ▤ ⌂wc 🎬wc ✪. 🅰 🅰🅴
     ① **VISA**
     April-October – **M** (bar lunch)/dinner 9.50 **t.** ▌2.60 – **51 rm** ⊑ 23.00/46.00 **t.** – SB 58.00 **st.**

  🏠 **Shieldaig Lodge** ⌇, IV21 2AW, S : 4 m. by A 832 on B 8056 ♪ 044 583 (Badachro) 250,
     ≤ Gair Loch, « Former hunting lodge on lochside », ⌇, 🐎, ※ – ⌂wc ✪. 🅰 **VISA**
     M (bar lunch)/dinner 9.25 **t.** – **14 rm** ⊑ 25.00/36.00 **t.**

  🏡 **Creag Mor,** Charlestown, IV21 2AH, S : 2 m. on A 832 ♪ 2068, ⌇ – ⌂wc ✪. ※
     M (bar lunch)/dinner 8.50 **st.** – **9 rm** ⊑ 14.50/30.00 **st.**

GALASHIELS Selkirk. (Borders) **401 402** L 17 – pop. 12 ,206 – ECD : Wednesday – ✪ 0896.

🏌 Ladhope, ♪ 3724, NE : ¼ m. – 🏌 Torwoodlee, ♪ 2260, N : 1 m. on A 7.

🏤 Bank St. ♪ 55551 (summer only).

♦Edinburgh 34 – ♦Carlisle 61 – ♦Glasgow 71 – ♦Newcastle-upon-Tyne 74.

  🏨 **Woodlands House,** Windyknowe Rd, TD1 1RQ, NW : ¾ m. by A 72 and Hall St. ♪ 4722,
     🐎 – ⌂wc ☎ ✪. 🅰 🅰🅴 ① **VISA**
     M (buffet lunch)/dinner 9.75 **t.** ▌3.50 – **9 rm** ⊑ 28.50/48.00 **t.** – SB (weekends only)
     52.00/55.00 **st.**

  🏨 **Kingsknowes,** Selkirk Rd, TD1 3HY, ♪ 3478, ≤, 🐎, ※ – 📺 ⌂wc ✪. 🅰 🅰🅴 ① **VISA**
     M 8.50 **t.** and a la carte ▌3.50 – **10 rm** ⊑ 29.00/44.00 **t.** – SB (weekends only) (October-May)
     48.00/52.00 **st.**

GARVE Ross and Cromarty (Highland) **401** F 11 – ECD : Thursday – ✪ 099 74.

♦Edinburgh 184 – ♦Inverness 28 – ♦Wick 130.

  🏨 **Strathgarve Lodge** ⌇, IV23 2PU, N : 2 ¾ m. by A 832 off A 835 ♪ 204, ≤, ⌇, 🐎, park –
     📺 ⌂wc ✪. 🅰 ① **VISA**
     M (bar lunch)/dinner 9.50 **st.** and a la carte ▌2.00 – **14 rm** ⊑ 20.00/40.00 **s.**, **1 suite** 40.00/
     45.00 **s.**

GATEHOUSE OF FLEET Kirkcudbright. (Dumfries and Galloway) **401 402** H 19 – pop. 894 –
ECD : Thursday – ✪ 055 74 – 🏌.

🏤 Car Park ♪ 212 (summer only).

♦Edinburgh 113 – ♦Dumfries 33 – Stranraer 42.

  🏨 **Cally Palace** ⌇, DG7 2DL, S : 1 ½ m. by A 75 ♪ 341, ≤, ⌇ heated, ⌇, 🐎, park, ※ – ▤
     📺 ⌂wc ☎ & ✪
     M 5.00/10.00 **st.** ▌2.00 – **48 rm** ⊑ 30.00/60.00 **st.**, **1 suite** 70.00 **st.** – SB (November-March)
     55.00/65.00 **st.**

  🏨 **Murray Arms** (Best Western), High St., DG7 2HY, ♪ 207, ⌇, 🐎, ※ – 📺 ⌂wc ☎ ✪. 🅰
     🅰🅴 ① **VISA**
     M (buffet lunch)/dinner 11.00 **st.** ▌3.20 – **20 rm** ⊑ 23.00/50.00 **st.**, **1 suite** 50.00/60.00 **st.** –
     SB (weekends only) 54.00/64.00 **st.**

GIFFNOCK Renfrew. (Strathclyde) **401** ④ **402** ⑨ – see Glasgow.

GIFFORD E. Lothian (Lothian) **401** L 16 – pop. 665 – ECD : Monday and Wednesday – ✉ Haddington – ✪ 062 081.

♦Edinburgh 20 – Hawick 50.

  🏠 **Tweeddale Arms,** High St., EH41 4PR, ♪ 240 – 📺 ⌂wc 🎬wc. 🅰🅴 **VISA**
     M 7.00/10.75 **t.** and a la carte ▌2.50 – **10 rm** ⊑ 22.00/40.00 **t.** – SB 38.00/45.00 **st.**

GIGHA (Isle of) Argyll. (Strathclyde) **401** C 16 – pop. 176 – ✪ 058 35.

🚢 by Caledonian MacBrayne : from Ardminish to Tayinloan Monday/Saturday 4-6 daily; Sunday
2 May-30 September only 4 daily (20 mn).

  🏠 **Gigha** ⌇, PA41 7AD, ♪ 254, ≤ Sound of Gigha and Kintyre Peninsula, « Tastefully renovated
     inn and farmhouse », ⌇, 🐎 – ⌂wc ✪. 🅰 **VISA**
     April-October – **M** 6.00/10.00 **t.** – **9 rm** ⊑ 17.50/40.00 **t.**

GLASGOW Lanark. (Strathclyde) 401 402 H 16 Scotland G – pop. 754 ,586 – ✪ 041.

See : Site★★★ – Burrell Collection★★★ AX **M1** – Cathedral★★★ DYZ – Tolbooth Steeple★ DZ **A** – Hunterian Art Gallery★★ (Whistler Collection★★★, Mackintosh wing★★★) CY **M2** Art Gallery and Museum Kelvingrove★★ CY – City Chambers★ DZ **C** – Glasgow School of Art★ CY **B** – Museum of Transport★★ (Scottish cars★★★, Clyde Room of Ship Models★★★) BX **M3** – Pollok House★ (Spanish paintings★★) AX **D**.

Envir. : Trossachs★★★ N : by A 739 AV and A 81 – Loch Lomond★★, NW : by A 82 AV – Clyde Estuary★ (Dumbarton Castle Site★, Hill House, Helensburgh★) by A 82, AV – Bothwell Castle★ and David Livingstone Centre (Museum★) SE : 9 m. by A 724 BX.

🇷 Linn Park, Simshill Rd ℰ 637 5871, S : 4 m. BX – 🇷 Lethamhill, Cumbernauld Rd ℰ 770 6220 BV – 🇷 Knightswood, Lincoln Av. ℰ 959 2131, W : 4 m. AV – 🇷 Ruchill, Brassey St. ℰ 946 9728 BV.

Access to Oban by helicopter.

✈ Glasgow Airport : ℰ 887 1111, Telex 778219, W : 8 m. by M 8 AV – **Terminal** : Coach service from Glasgow Central and Queen Street main line Railway Stations and from Anderston Cross and Buchanan Bus Stations.

✈ see also Prestwick.

🔲 35 St. Vincent Pl. ℰ 227 4880.

♦Edinburgh 46 – ♦Manchester 221.

Plans on following pages

🏨 **Holiday Inn,** Argyle St., Anderston, G3 8RR, ℰ 226 5577, Telex 776355, 🔲 – 📶 🔲 🔲 ☎ ᕕ
🅿 ♨ 🔼 🔤 ⓪ **VISA**   CZ **a**
M 12.95 **t.** and a la carte – 🖵 6.00 – **296 rm** 52.00/62.00 **s.**, **3 suites** 147.00 **s.** – SB (weekends only) 71.90/109.90 **st.**

🏨 **Albany** (T.H.F.), Bothwell St., G2 7EN, ℰ 248 2656, Telex 77440 – 📶 🔲 🔲 ☎ 🅿 ♨ 🔼 🔤
⓪ **VISA**   CZ **z**
M 5.95/8.25 **st.** and a la carte ᣘ 2.70 – 🖵 5.50 – **251 rm** 45.50/59.00 **st.**, **3 suites**.

🏨 **Hospitality Inn** (Mt. Charlotte), 36 Cambridge St., G2 3HN, ℰ 332 3311, Telex 777334 – 📶
🔲 ☎ ᕕ 🅿 ♨ 🔼 🔤 ⓪ **VISA**   DY **x**
M 10.50/11.50 **st.** and a la carte ᣘ 3.00 – 🖵 4.75 – **316 rm** 42.50/55.00 **st.**, **2 suites** 100.00 **st.** – SB (weekends only) 48.00/60.00 **st.**

🏨 **Stakis Grosvenor** (Stakis), Grosvenor Terr., Great Western Rd, G12 0TA, ℰ 339 8811, Telex 776247 – 📶 🔲 🔲 ☎ 🅿 ♨ 🔼 🔤 **VISA**   CY **r**
M 8.50/15.00 **t.** and a la carte ᣘ 3.75 – 🖵 4.75 – **96 rm** 55.00/80.00 **t.**, **2 suites**.

🏨 **White House** ﹗ without rest., 11-13 Cleveden Cres., G12 0PA, ℰ 339 9375 – 🔲 ♨ 🔼 🔤
⓪ **VISA** ﹗   AV **r**
M (room service only) 11.60/13.60 **t.** – 🖵 5.60 – **32 rm** 45.45/65.55 **t.**, **13 suites** 84.55/92.00 **t.** – SB (weekends only) 49.65/60.30 **st.**

🏨 **Stakis Pond** (Stakis), 2-4 Shelley Rd, Great Western Rd, G12 0XP, ℰ 334 8161, Telex 776573,
🔲 – 📶 🔲 ⇔wc ☎ 🅿 ♨ 🔤 ⓪ **VISA** ﹗   AV **i**
M 7.00/9.00 **t.** and a la carte ᣘ 3.50 – **133 rm** 🖵 42.00/52.00 **t.**

🏨 **Tinto Firs Thistle** (Thistle), 470 Kilmarnock Rd, G43 2BB, ℰ 637 2353, Telex 778329 – 🔲
⇔wc ☎ 🅿 ♨ 🔼 🔤 ⓪ **VISA** ﹗   AX **c**
M (bar lunch Saturday) 6.00/11.00 **t.** and a la carte ᣘ 3.60 – 🖵 5.25 – **25 rm** 42.00/54.00 **t.**, **2 suites** 60.00 **t.**

🏨 **Stakis Ingram** (Stakis), 201 Ingram St., G1 1DQ, ℰ 248 4401 – 📶 🔲 ⇔wc ☎ 🅿 ♨ 🔼 🔤
⓪ **VISA**   DZ **c**
M (bar lunch)/dinner 9.95 **t.** and a la carte ᣘ 3.25 – **90 rm** 🖵 35.00/60.00 **t.**

🏨 **Bellahouston Swallow** (Swallow), 517 Paisley Rd West, G51 1RW, ℰ 427 3146, Telex 778795
– 📶 🔲 ⇔wc 🏵wc ☎ 🅿 ♨   AX **a**
122 rm.

🏨 **Crest** (Crest), Argyle St., G2 8LL, ℰ 248 2355, Telex 779652 – 📶 🔲 ⇔wc ☎. ♨ 🔼 🔤 ⓪
VISA. ﹗   CZ **x**
M approx. 11.50 **st.** – 🖵 5.75 – **123 rm** 42.50/51.50 **st.** – SB (weekends only) 55.00 **st.**

🏨 **Kelvin Park Lorne,** 923 Sauchiehall St., G3 7TE, ℰ 334 4891, Telex 778935 – 📶 🔲 rest 🔲
⇔wc ☎ 🅿 ♨ 🔼 🔤 ⓪ **VISA**   CY **a**
M 9.45/8.95 **t.** and a la carte – **80 rm** 🖵 39.95/49.95 **t.** – SB 49.00/70.85 **st.**

🏠 Kings Park, Mill St., Rutherglen, G73 2LX, ℰ 647 5491 – 🔲 ⇔wc ☟ 🅿   BX **e**
24 rm.

🏠 Newlands, 290 Kilmarnock Rd, G43 2XS, ℰ 632 9171 – 🔲 ⇔wc ☟   AX **n**
17 rm.

🏠 **Dalmeny,** 62 St. Andrews Drive, Nithsdale Cross, Pollokshields, G41 5EZ, ℰ 427 1106 – 🔲
⇔wc 🏵wc 🅿   AX **o**
12 rm 🖵 19.50/38.00 **st.**

🏠 **Kirklee,** 11 Kensington Gate, G12 9LG, ℰ 334 5555 – ⇔wc. ﹗   AV **c**
9 rm 🖵 20.00/30.00 **st.**

Argyle St. . . . . p. 4 **CZ**
Buchanan St. . . . . p. 5 **DZ**
Gordon St. . . . . p. 5 **DZ** 65
Jamaica St. . . . . p. 5 **DZ** 77
Oswald St. . . . . p. 5 **DZ**
Renfield St. . . . . p. 5 **DZ**
St. Vincent St. . . . . p. 5 **DZ**
Sauchiehall St. . . . . . . p. 5 **DY**
Trongate . . . . p. 5 **DZ**
Union St. . . . . p. 5 **DZ**

Admiral St. . . . . p. 4 **CZ**
Aikenhead Rd. . . . . p. 3 **BX** 2
Alexandra Par. . . . . p. 3 **BV** 3
Anderston Quay. . . . . . p. 4 **CZ**
Anniesland Rd . . . . p. 2 **AV**
Argyle St. . . . . p. 4 **CZ**
Bain St. . . . . p. 5 **DZ**
Baird St. . . . . p. 5 **DY**
Balgrayhill. . . . . p. 3 **BV** 4
Ballater St. . . . . p. 3 **BX** 6
Balmore Rd. . . . . p. 3 **BV**
Balornock Rd . . . . p. 3 **BV** 8
Balshagray Av. . . . . p. 2 **AV** 9
Bank St. . . . . p. 4 **CY**
Barrack St. . . . . p. 5 **DZ**
Barrhead Rd . . . . p. 2 **AX**
Bath St. . . . . p. 4 **CY**
Battlefield Rd . . . . p. 3 **BX** 12
Bell St. . . . . p. 5 **DZ**
Belmont St. . . . . p. 4 **CY**
Berkeley St. . . . . p. 4 **CY**
Berryknowes Rd . . . . . . p. 2 **AX** 15
Bilsland Drive . . . . p. 3 **BV** 16
Blairbeth Rd . . . . p. 3 **BX** 18
Borron St. . . . . p. 5 **DY**
Boydstone Rd . . . . p. 2 **AX**
Braidcraft Rd . . . . p. 2 **AX** 20
Brand St. . . . . p. 4 **CZ** 22
Brassey St. . . . . p. 3 **BV** 23
Bridegate . . . . p. 5 **DZ** 24
Bridge St. . . . . p. 5 **DZ** 25
Brockburn Rd . . . . p. 2 **AX**
Broomfield Rd . . . . p. 3 **BV**
Broomielaw . . . . p. 4 **CZ**
Broomloan Rd . . . . p. 2 **AV** 26
Brownside Rd . . . . p. 3 **BX**
Buchanan St. . . . . p. 5 **DZ**
Burnhill Chapel St. . . . . p. 3 **BX** 28
Byres Rd . . . . p. 2 **AV** 29
Caldarvan St. . . . . p. 5 **DY**
Caledonia Rd . . . . p. 3 **BX** 30
Cambridge St. . . . . p. 5 **DY** 32
Cambuslang Rd . . . . . . p. 3 **BX**
Cardowan Rd . . . . p. 3 **BV**
Carmunnock Rd. . . . . . . p. 3 **BX** 33
Carntyne Rd . . . . p. 3 **BV**
Carntynehall Rd . . . . . . p. 3 **BV**
Castle St. . . . . p. 5 **DY**
Cathcart Rd. . . . . p. 3 **BX**
Cathedral St . . . . p. 5 **DY**
Claremont Gardens . . . . p. 4 **CY** 34
Claremont Ter. . . . . p. 4 **CY** 35
Clarkston Rd . . . . p. 3 **BX**
Clyde Place . . . . p. 4 **CZ** 36
Clyde St. . . . . p. 5 **DZ**
Clyde Tunnel . . . . p. 2 **AV**
Clydeside
  Expressway . . . . p. 2 **AV**
Commerce St. . . . . p. 5 **DZ** 37
Cook St. . . . . p. 3 **BV** 38
Corkerhill Rd. . . . . p. 2 **AX**
Cornwald St. . . . . p. 4 **CZ** 39
Cowcaddens St. . . . . . . p. 5 **DY**
Craighall Rd . . . . p. 5 **DY**
Croftfoot Rd . . . . p. 3 **BX**
Crookston Rd . . . . p. 2 **AX**
Crow Rd . . . . p. 2 **AV**
Cumbernauld Rd . . . . . . p. 3 **BV** 40
Dalmarnock Rd . . . . p. 3 **BX**
Derby St. . . . . p. 4 **CY** 42
Dobbie's Loan . . . . p. 5 **DY**
Douglas St. . . . . p. 4 **CZ**
Doune Gdns . . . . p. 4 **CY** 43
Doune Quadrant . . . . . . p. 4 **CY** 45
Duke's Rd . . . . p. 3 **BX**
Duke St. . . . . p. 5 **DZ**
Dumbarton Rd . . . . p. 4 **CY** 47
Dumbreck Rd. . . . . p. 2 **AX**
East Kilbride Rd . . . . . . p. 3 **BX**
Edinburgh Rd. . . . . p. 3 **BV**
Edmiston Drive . . . . p. 2 **AV** 48
Eglinton Rd. . . . . p. 3 **BX**

Eglinton St. . . . . p. 3 **BX**
Elderslie St. . . . . p. 4 **CY**
Eldon St. . . . . p. 4 **CY** 50
Ellesmere St. . . . . p. 5 **DY** 52
Elmbank St. . . . . p. 4 **CY**
Farmeloan Rd . . . . p. 3 **BX** 53
Fenwick Rd . . . . p. 2 **AX** 55
Finnieston St. . . . . p. 4 **CZ**
Gallowgate. . . . . p. 5 **DZ**
Garscube Rd . . . . p. 5 **DY**
General Terminus
  Quay . . . . p. 4 **CZ**
George St. . . . . p. 5 **DZ**
Gibson St. . . . . p. 4 **CY**
Glasgow Bridge . . . . . . p. 5 **DZ** 60
Glasgow Rd
  (PAISLEY) . . . . p. 2 **AX** 62
Glasgow Rd
  (RENFREW) . . . . p. 2 **AV**
Glasgow Rd
  (RUTHERGLEN) . . . p. 3 **BX**
Glassford St. . . . . p. 5 **DZ**
Gorbals St. . . . . p. 3 **BX** 63
Gordon St. . . . . p. 5 **DZ** 65
Govan Rd . . . . p. 4 **CZ**
Grange Rd . . . . p. 3 **BX** 67
Great Western Rd . . . . . p. 4 **CY**
Greendyke St. . . . . p. 5 **DZ**
Haggs Rd . . . . p. 2 **AX** 68
Hamiltonhill Rd . . . . p. 5 **DY**
Hardgate Rd. . . . . p. 2 **AV**
Harriet St. . . . . p. 2 **AX** 70
Helen St. . . . . p. 2 **AV** 72
High St. . . . . p. 5 **DZ**
Hillington Rd . . . . p. 2 **AV**
Holmfauld Rd. . . . . p. 2 **AX** 73
Hope St. . . . . p. 5 **DZ**
Hopehill Rd . . . . p. 4 **CY**
Hospital St. . . . . p. 3 **BX** 74
Howard St. . . . . p. 5 **DZ**
Hydepark St. . . . . p. 4 **CZ**
Ingram St. . . . . p. 5 **DZ**
Inner Ring Rd . . . . p. 5 **DY**
Jamaica St. . . . . p. 5 **DZ** 77
James St. . . . . p. 3 **BX** 79
John Knox St. . . . . p. 5 **DZ** 80
Kelvin Way . . . . p. 4 **CY**
Kelvinhaugh St. . . . . . . p. 4 **CY**
Kennedy St. . . . . p. 5 **DY**
Kennishead Rd . . . . p. 2 **AX**
Kent Rd . . . . p. 4 **CY**
Kent St. . . . . p. 5 **DZ**
Keppoch Hill Rd. . . . . . . p. 5 **DY**
Killermont St. . . . . p. 5 **DY**
Kilmarnock Rd . . . . p. 2 **AX**
King's Drive . . . . p. 3 **BX** 83
King's Park Av. . . . . p. 3 **BX**
King's Park Rd . . . . p. 3 **BX** 84
Kingston St. . . . . p. 4 **CZ**
Kingsway . . . . p. 2 **AV**
Kyle St. . . . . p. 5 **DY** 86
Lamont Rd . . . . p. 3 **BV** 88
Lancefield Quay . . . . . . p. 4 **CZ**
Lancefield St. . . . . p. 4 **CZ**
Langlands Rd. . . . . p. 2 **AV**
Langside Av. . . . . p. 2 **AX** 89
Langside Drive. . . . . p. 2 **AX**
Langside Rd . . . . p. 3 **BX** 90
Langside Rd. . . . . p. 2 **AV** 91
Lincoln Av. . . . . p. 2 **AV**
Linthaugh Rd . . . . p. 2 **AX**
London Rd . . . . p. 3 **BX**
Lorne St. . . . . p. 4 **CZ** 93
Lymburn St. . . . . p. 4 **CY** 95
Lyoncross Rd . . . . p. 2 **AX** 97
McAlpine St. . . . . p. 4 **CZ**
Main St. . . . . p. 3 **BX**
Maryhill Rd . . . . p. 4 **CY**
Mavisbank Quay . . . . . . p. 4 **CZ**
Meiklerig Crescent . . . . p. 2 **AX** 98
Menock Rd . . . . p. 3 **BX** 99
Merrylee Rd . . . . p. 2 **AX**
Middlesex St. . . . . p. 4 **CZ** 100
Milnpark St. . . . . p. 4 **CZ**
Milton St. . . . . p. 5 **DY**
Mill St. . . . . p. 3 **BX**
Miller St. . . . . p. 5 **DZ**
Minard Rd. . . . . p. 2 **AX** 101
Moir St. . . . . p. 5 **DZ** 102
Morrison St. . . . . p. 4 **CZ**
Moss Rd . . . . p. 2 **AX** 103
Mosspark Boulevard . p. 2 **AX**
Mosspark Drive . . . . . . p. 2 **AX**
Napiershall St. . . . . p. 4 **CY**

Nelson St. . . . . p. 4 **CZ**
Nether Auldhouse Rd. p. 2 **AX** 104
Newlands Rd . . . . p. 2 **AX**
Nitshill Rd . . . . p. 2 **AX**
Norfolk St. . . . . p. 5 **DZ**
North St. . . . . p. 4 **CY**
North Canalbank St. . . p. 5 **DY**
North Hanover St. . . . . p. 5 **DY**
North Woodside Rd . . p. 4 **CY**
Oswald St. . . . . p. 5 **DZ**
Oxford St. . . . . p. 5 **DZ** 105
Paisley Rd. . . . . p. 2 **AV**
Paisley Rd West. . . . . . . p. 2 **AX**
Park Gdns . . . . p. 4 **CY** 106
Park Quadrant . . . . p. 4 **CY**
Park Ter. . . . . p. 4 **CY** 108
Peat Rd . . . . p. 2 **AX**
Petershill Rd. . . . . p. 3 **BV**
Pinkston Rd . . . . p. 5 **DY**
Pitt St. . . . . p. 4 **CZ**
Pollokshaws Rd . . . . . . p. 2 **AX**
Possil Rd . . . . p. 5 **DY**
Prospecthill Rd . . . . p. 3 **BX** 112
Provan Rd . . . . p. 3 **BV** 114
Queen St. . . . . p. 5 **DZ**
Queen Margaret
  Drive . . . . p. 4 **CY** 116
Raeberry St. . . . . p. 4 **CY**
Red Rd . . . . p. 3 **BV** 118
Renfield St. . . . . p. 5 **DZ**
Renfrew Rd. . . . . p. 2 **AV**
Renfrew St. . . . . p. 5 **DY**
Ring Rd . . . . p. 3 **BV**
Riverford. . . . . p. 2 **AX** 119
Robertson St. . . . . p. 4 **CZ** 120
Robroyston Rd. . . . . p. 3 **BV**
Rotten Row. . . . . p. 5 **DZ**
Royal Ter. . . . . p. 4 **CY** 122
Royston Rd. . . . . p. 3 **BV**
Rutherglen Rd . . . . p. 3 **BX**
St. Andrew's Drive . . . . p. 2 **AX**
St. George's Rd . . . . . . p. 4 **CY**
St. James Rd . . . . p. 5 **DY**
St. Mungo Av. . . . . p. 5 **DY**
St. Vincent St. . . . . p. 5 **DZ**
Saltmarket . . . . p. 5 **DZ**
Sandwood Rd . . . . p. 2 **AV** 123
Saracen St. . . . . p. 5 **DY**
Sauchiehall St. . . . . p. 5 **DY**
Scott St. . . . . p. 4 **CY**
Seaward St. . . . . p. 4 **CZ**
Shettleston Rd . . . . p. 3 **BX**
Shieldhall Rd . . . . p. 2 **AV**
Shields Rd . . . . p. 2 **AX** 124
Southbrae Drive . . . . . . p. 2 **AV**
Springburn Rd . . . . p. 3 **BV**
Springfield Rd . . . . p. 3 **BX**
Stirling Rd . . . . p. 5 **DY** 126
Stockwell St. . . . . p. 5 **DZ** 127
Stonelaw Rd. . . . . p. 3 **BX**
Striven Gdns. . . . . p. 4 **CY** 128
Suspension Bridge . . p. 5 **DZ** 130
Thornliebank Rd . . . . . . p. 2 **AX**
Titwood Rd. . . . . p. 2 **AX**
Todd St. . . . . p. 3 **BV** 131
Tollcross Rd . . . . p. 3 **BX**
Trongate . . . . p. 5 **DZ**
Union St. . . . . p. 5 **DZ**
University Av. . . . . p. 4 **CY**
Victoria Bridge . . . . p. 5 **DZ** 132
Victoria Rd . . . . p. 3 **BX**
Wallacewell Rd . . . . . . p. 3 **BV**
Waterloo St. . . . . p. 4 **CZ**
West St. . . . . p. 4 **CZ**
West Campbell St. . . . . p. 4 **CZ**
West George St. . . . . . . p. 5 **DZ**
West Graham St . . . . . . p. 4 **CY** 135
Westmuir Place . . . . . . p. 3 **BX** 136
Westmuir St. . . . . p. 3 **BX** 138
West Paisley Rd. . . . . . . p. 4 **CZ**
West Prince's St. . . . . . p. 4 **CY**
West Regent St. . . . . . . p. 5 **DY**
Wilson St. . . . . p. 5 **DZ**
Wilton St. . . . . p. 4 **CY**
Windmillcroft Quay. . . . p. 4 **CZ** 139
Wishart St. . . . . p. 5 **DZ**
Woodlands Drive . . . . . p. 4 **CY** 140
Woodlands Rd. . . . . p. 4 **CY**
Woodside Crescent . . . . p. 4 **CY** 141
Woodside Place . . . . . . p. 4 **CY**
Woodside Ter. . . . . p. 4 **CY** 143
York St. . . . . p. 4 **CZ**

GLASGOW
BUILT UP AREA

Aikenhead Road .... **BX** 2
Alexandra Parade .... **BV** 3
Balgrayhill Road .... **BV** 4
Ballater Street .... **BX** 6
Balornock Road............... **BV** 8

Balshagray Avenue .... **AV** 9
Battlefield Road .... **BX** 12
Berryknowes Road .... **AX** 15
Bilsland Drive .... **BV** 16
Blairbeth Road .... **BX** 18
Braidcraft Road............ **AX** 20
Brassey Street .... **BV** 23
Broomloan Road........... **AV** 26
Burnhill Chapel Street ... **BX** 28
Byres Road .... **AV** 29

Caledonia Road .... **BX** 30
Carmunnock Road .... **BX** 33
Cook Street .... **BV** 38
Cumbernauld Road .... **BV** 40
Edmiston Drive .... **AV** 48
Farmeloan Road .... **BX** 53
Fenwick Road .... **BX** 55
Glasgow Road (PAISLEY) .. **AX** 62
Gorbals Street .... **BX** 63
Grange Road .... **BX** 67

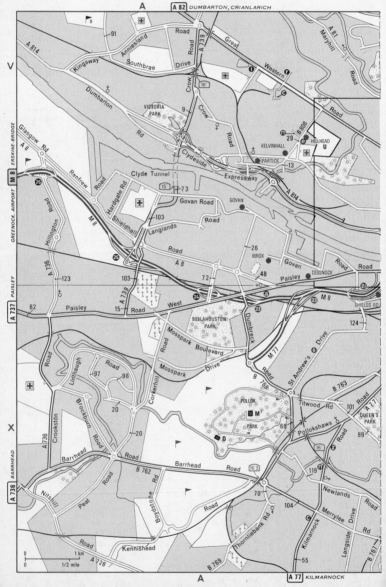

516

Haggs Road . . . . **AX** 68
Harriet Street . . . . **AX** 70
Helen Street . . . . **AV** 72
Holmfauld Road . . . . **AV** 73
Hospital Street . . . . **BX** 74
James Street . . . . **BX** 79
King's Drive . . . . **BX** 83
King's Park Road . . . . **BX** 84
Lamont Road . . . . **BV** 88

Langside Av . . . . **AX** 89
Langside Road . . . . **BX** 90
Lincoln Avenue . . . . **AV** 91
Lyoncross Road . . . . **AX** 97
Meiklerig Crescent . . . . **AX** 98
Menock Rd . . . . **BX** 99
Minard Rd . . . . **AX** 101
Moss Road . . . . **AV** 103
Nether Auldhouse Road . . . **AX** 104

Prospecthill Road . . . . **BX** 112
Provan Road . . . . **BV** 114
Red Road . . . . **BV** 118
Riverford Road . . . . **AX** 119
Sandwood Road . . . . **AV** 123
Shields Road . . . . **AX** 124
Todd Street . . . . **BV** 131
Westmuir Place . . . . **BX** 136
Westmuir Street . . . . **BX** 138

For Street Index see Glasgow p. 1b.

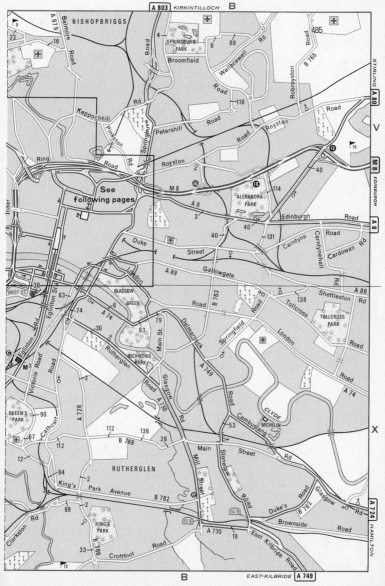

517

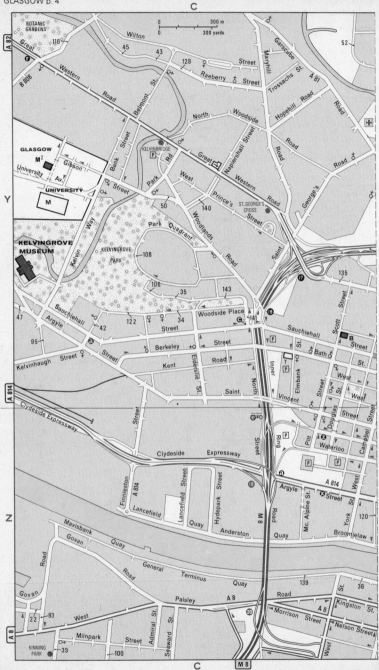

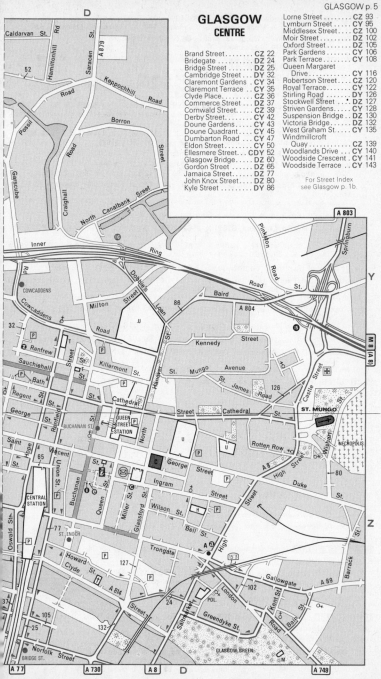

GLASGOW
CENTRE

Brand Street . . . . **CZ** 22
Bridgegate . . . . **DZ** 24
Bridge Street . . . . **DZ** 25
Cambridge Street . . . **DY** 32
Claremont Gardens . **CY** 34
Claremont Terrace . . **CY** 35
Clyde Place . . . . **CZ** 36
Commerce Street . . **DZ** 37
Cornwald Street . . . . **CZ** 39
Derby Street . . . . **CY** 42
Doune Gardens . . . . **CY** 43
Doune Quadrant . . . **CY** 45
Dumbarton Road . . . **CY** 47
Eldon Street . . . . **CY** 50
Ellesmere Street . . **CDY** 52
Glasgow Bridge . . . . **DZ** 60
Gordon Street . . . . . . **DZ** 65
Jamaica Street . . . . . **DZ** 77
John Knox Street . . . **DZ** 80
Kyle Street . . . . **DY** 86

Lorne Street . . . . **CZ** 93
Lymburn Street . . . . . **CY** 95
Middlesex Street . . . . **CZ** 100
Moir Street . . . . **DZ** 102
Oxford Street . . . . **DZ** 105
Park Gardens . . . . . . **CY** 106
Park Terrace . . . . **CY** 108
Queen Margaret
   Drive . . . . **CY** 116
Robertson Street . . . **CZ** 120
Royal Terrace . . . . . . **CY** 122
Stirling Road . . . . **DY** 126
Stockwell Street . . **DZ** 127
Striven Gardens . . . . **CY** 128
Suspension Bridge . . **DZ** 130
Victoria Bridge . . . . . . **DZ** 132
West Graham St . . . **CY** 135
Windmillcroft
   Quay . . . . **CZ** 139
Woodlands Drive . . . **CY** 140
Woodside Crescent . **CY** 141
Woodside Terrace . . **CY** 143

For Street Index
see Glasgow p. 1b.

519

XXX **Fountain,** 2 Woodside Cres., G3 7UL, 🕿 332 6396 – 🔼 AE ⓞ 𝘝𝘐𝘚𝘈 CY **c**
 closed Saturday lunch, Monday dinner and Sunday – **M** 8.00/13.50 **t.** and a la carte ⌕ 4.95.

XX **Buttery,** 652 Argyle St., G3, 🕿 221 8188 – ⓟ 🔼 AE ⓞ 𝘝𝘐𝘚𝘈 CZ **e**
 closed Saturday lunch and Sunday – **M** a la carte 12.90/17.75 **t.**

XX **Rogano,** 11 Exchange Pl., G1 3AN, 🕿 248 4055, Seafood, « Art deco » – ▤. 🔼 AE 𝘝𝘐𝘚𝘈
 closed Sunday – **M** a la carte 11.90/15.30 **t.** DZ **i**

XX **Colonial,** 25 High St., G1 1LX, 🕿 552 1923 – 🔼 AE ⓞ 𝘝𝘐𝘚𝘈 DZ **a**
 *closed Saturday lunch, Monday dinner, Sunday, 20 July-3 August, Christmas, New Year and
 Bank Holidays* – **M** 4.50/16.00 **st.** and a la carte ⌕ 3.20.

X **Poacher's,** Ruthven Lane, off Byres Rd, G12 9BG, 🕿 339 0932 – ⓟ. 🔼 AE ⓞ 𝘝𝘐𝘚𝘈 AV **n**
 closed Sunday, 31 March, 25 December and 1-2 January – **M** *(closed Bank Holiday lunch)*
 (buffet lunch Saturday)/a la carte 12.00/15.50 **t.** ⌕ 3.00.

X **Le Provençal,** 21 Royal Exchange Sq., G1 3AJ, 🕿 221 0798, French rest. – 🔼 AE ⓞ 𝘝𝘐𝘚𝘈
 closed Sunday – **M** 11.50 **t.** (dinner) and a la carte 11.75/15.65 **t.** ⌕ 3.25. DZ **r**

X Trattoria Sorrento, 87 Kilmarnock Rd, Shawlands, G41 3YR, 🕿 649 3002, Italian rest. AX **z**

X **Kensingtons,** 164 Darnley St., G41 2LL, 🕿 424 3662 – 🔼 AE ⓞ 𝘝𝘐𝘚𝘈 BX **c**
 closed Saturday lunch, Sunday and Monday – **M** 6.00/13.50 **t.** and a la carte ⌕ 2.65.

X **Ubiquitous Chip,** 12 Ashton Lane, off Byres Rd, G12 8SJ, 🕿 334 5007, Bistro – 🔼 AE ⓞ
 𝘝𝘐𝘚𝘈 AV **e**
 closed Sunday, Christmas Day and 1-2 January – **M** a la carte 5.90/16.95 **t.**

 at Busby S : 5 ½ m. by A 727 – AX – on A 726 – ✉ ✆ 041 Glasgow :

🏠 **Busby,** 1 Field Rd, Clarkston, G76 8RX, 🕿 644 2661 – 📺 ➡wc 🗂wc 🕿 ⓟ. 🔼 AE ⓞ 𝘝𝘐𝘚𝘈.
 ⌂
 closed 25 December and 1 January – **M** 5.50/7.25 **t.** and a la carte ⌕ 3.15 – **14 rm**
 �より 27.50/36.50 **t.** – SB (weekends only) 58.50/71.60 **st.**

 at Giffnock (Renfrew.) (Strathclyde) S : 5 ¼ m. by A 77 – AX – ✆ 041 Glasgow :

🏨 **MacDonald Thistle** (Thistle), Eastwood Toll, G46 6RA, at intersection of A 77 and A 726
 🕿 638 2225, Telex 779138 – 📺 ➡wc 🗂wc ✆ ⓟ. 🔼 AE ⓞ 𝘝𝘐𝘚𝘈
 M 7.00/11.00 **t.** and a la carte ⌕ 2.90 – ⊥ 5.25 – **52 rm** 42.00/54.00 **t.**, **4 suites** 60.00 **t.**

🏠 **Stakis Redhurst** (Stakis), 77 Eastwoodmains Rd, G46 6QE, 🕿 638 6465 – 📺 ➡wc 🗂 ⓟ.
 ⌂. 🔼 AE ⓞ 𝘝𝘐𝘚𝘈
 M (grill rest. only) 11.00 **t.** and a la carte ⌕ 3.30 – **19 rm** ⊥ 43.00/52.00 **t.**

 at Glasgow Airport Renfrew. (Strathclyde) W : 8 m. by M 8 – AV – ✉ ✆ 041 Glasgow :

🏨 **Excelsior** (T.H.F.), Abbotsinch, PA3 2TR, 🕿 887 1212, Telex 777733 – 📺 🕿 ⌖ ⓟ. ⌂. 🔼.
 ⓞ 𝘝𝘐𝘚𝘈
 M 8.95 **st.** and a la carte ⌕ 3.00 – ⊥ 6.00 – **290 rm** 46.00/58.00 **st.**, **7 suites**.

MICHELIN Branch, 60 Cunningham Rd, Rutherglen, G73 1PP, 🕿 647 9516 p. 3 BX

AUSTIN-ROVER 55 Hamilton Rd 🕿 778 8383
AUSTIN-ROVER 215 Queensborough Gardens 🕿 357 1234
AUSTIN-ROVER, MAZDA, TOYOTA 470 Royston Rd 🕿 552 4718
AUSTIN-ROVER Vineycombe St. 🕿 334 4761
BMW 10 Abbey Drive 🕿 959 1272
CITROEN 208 Great Western Rd 🕿 332 5955
FORD 1009 Gallowgate 🕿 554 4321
FORD Temple Industrial Estate, Anniesland 🕿 954 1500
FORD 34 Fenwick Rd 🕿 637 7161
FORD Kilbirnie St. 🕿 423 6644
HONDA Maxwell Rd 🕿 429 4298

NISSAN 77/81 Dumbarton Rd 🕿 334 1241
OPEL-VAUXHALL 10 Holmbank Av. 🕿 649 9321
OPEL-VAUXHALL 712 Edinburgh Rd 🕿 774 2791
PEUGEOT-TALBOT 100 Minerva St. 🕿 248 2345
PORSCHE Maxwell Ave., Bearsden 🕿 943 1155
RENAULT 64 Kirkintilloch Rd 🕿 772 6481
SAAB 162 Crow Rd 🕿 334 4661
VAUXHALL-OPEL 640 Pollokshaws Rd 🕿 423 3074
VAUXHALL-OPEL Grand St. 🕿 332 2626
VOLVO 2413/2493 London Rd 🕿 778 8501
VOLVO Bothwell Rd, Hamilton 🕿 728 4100
VW-AUDI Barrhead Rd 🕿 882 4601
VW, AUDI 512 Kilmarnock Rd 🕿 637 2241

☞ *Michelin puts no plaque or sign
 on the hotels and restaurants mentioned in this Guide.*

GLENBORRODALE Argyll. (Highland) 🆁🆁🆁 C 13 – ✉ Acharacle – ✆ 097 24.
♦Edinburgh 151 – ♦Inverness 108 – ♦Oban 72.

🏨 **Glenborrodale Castle** (T.H.F.) ⌂, Ardnamurchan, PH36 4JP, 🕿 266, ≤ Loch Sunart and
 gardens, « Victorian castle in extensive gardens », park – 📺 ➡wc 🗂 ⓟ. 🔼 AE ⓞ 𝘝𝘐𝘚𝘈
 closed January and February – **M** (bar lunch)/dinner 11.50 **st.** ⌕ 3.00 – **20 rm** ⊥ (dinner included) 38.50/77.00 **st.**, **1 suite**

GLENFINNAN Inverness. (Highland) 🆁🆁🆁 D 13 – ✉ Fort William – ✆ 039 783 Kinlocheil.
See : Site* – Monument.
♦Edinburgh 150 – ♦Inverness 81 – Kyle of Lochalsh 88 – ♦Oban 67.

🏠 **Glenfinnan House** ⌂, PH37 4LT, 🕿 235, ≤ Loch Shiel and Ben Nevis, 🎣, 🅿, park – 🗂wc
 April-October – **M** (bar lunch)/dinner 9.50 **st.** – **19 rm** ⊥ 18.50/40.00 **st.**

GLENROTHES Fife. (Fife) **401** K 15 – pop. 33,639 – ECD : Tuesday – ✪ 0592.

ⓖ Thornton ☎ 771111, S : 3 m. – ⓖ Leslie ☎ 41016, W : 3 m. on A 911.

🅩 Information Kiosk ☎ 754 954.

♦Edinburgh 33 – ♦Dundee 25 – Stirling 36.

🏨 **Balgeddie House** ⟨⟩, Leslie Rd, KY6 3ET, W : 2 m. by A 911, B 969, Formonthills Rd and
Balgeddie Way ☎ 742511, ≼, 🥘 – 🆅 ⌂wc ☎ 🅿 🅰 🆑 💳 ⍉
closed 1 and 2 January – **M** a la carte 10.80/14.35 **t.** ⬧ 4.00 – ⍉ 5.00 – **18 rm** 40.00/55.00 **st.** –
SB (weekends only) 45.00/55.00 **st.**

🏨 **Stakis Albany** (Stakis), North St., KY7 5NA, ☎ 752292 – 🕮 🆅 ⌂wc 🛁wc ☎ 🅿 🅰 🆑 🆎
⍉ 💳
M (grill rest. only) 6.50/12.50 **t.** ⬧ 3.25 – **29 rm** ⍉ 20.00/50.00.

at Leslie W : 3 m. by A 911 – ✉ Leslie – ✪ 0592 Glenrothes :

🏠 **Rescobie** ⟨⟩, Valley Drive, KY6 3BQ, ☎ 742143, 🥘 – 🆅 🛁wc 🅿 🅰 ⍉ 💳
M *(closed lunch Saturday and Sunday)* 5.50/9.00 **t.** and a la carte ⬧ 2.50 – **8 rm** ⍉ 22.00/45.00 **t.**

VW, AUDI North St. ☎ 752262

GLENSHEE Perth. (Tayside) **401** J 13 – see Spittal of Glenshee.

GOLSPIE Sutherland (Highland) **401** I 10 – pop. 1,385 – ECD : Wednesday – ✉ ✪ 040 83.

ⓖ ☎ 3266 – ♦Edinburgh 228 – ♦Inverness 72 – ♦Wick 54.

🏠 **Golf Links,** Church St., KW10 6TT, ☎ 3408, ≼, 🥘 – ⌂wc 🛁wc 🅿 🅰 🆎 ⍉ 💳
M (booking essential) (bar lunch)/dinner 10.00 **t.** ⬧ 3.00 – **10 rm** ⍉ 15.00/37.00 **t.**

AUSTIN-ROVER Station Rd ☎ 3205   RENAULT Old Bank Rd ☎ 3411

GOUROCK Renfrew. (Strathclyde) **401** F 16 – pop. 11,087 – ECD : Wednesday – ✪ 0475.

⛴ by Caledonian MacBrayne : from Railway Pier to Dunoon Pier frequent services daily (20 mn)
– by Western Ferries : from McInroy's Point to Hunters Quay, Dunoon frequent services daily
(20 mn).

⛴ by Caledonian MacBrayne : to Kilcreggan Monday/Saturday 4-8 daily (10 mn) – to Helensburgh
summer only Monday/Saturday 4-5 daily (40 mn).

🅩 Information Centre, Municipal Buildings, Shore St., ☎ 31126 (summer only).

♦Edinburgh 71 – ♦Ayr 47 – ♦Glasgow 27.

🏨 **Stakis Gantock** (Stakis), Cloch Rd, PA15 1AR, SW : 2 m. on A 78 ☎ 34671, ≼ Firth of Clyde –
🆅 ⌂wc ☎ 🅿 🅰
63 rm ⍉ 39.00/53.00 **t.**

🏠 **Claremont,** 34 Victoria Rd, PA19 1DF, ☎ 31687, ≼ Firth of Clyde – 🆅 🅿
6 rm ⍉ 10.00/20.00 **st.**

CITROEN Manor Crescent ☎ 32356

GRAEMSAY (Isle of) Orkney (Orkney Islands) **401** K 7 – Shipping Services : see Orkney Islands.

GRANTOWN-ON-SPEY Moray. (Highland) **401** J 12 – pop. 1,800 – ECD : Thursday – ✪ 0479.

ⓖ ☎ 2079, East town boundary – 🅩 54 High St. ☎ 2773 (summer only).

♦Edinburgh 143 – ♦Inverness 34 – Perth 99.

🏠 **Garth,** The Square, PH26 3HN, ☎ 2836, 🥘 – ⌂wc 🛁wc 🅿 ⍉ 💳
M (bar lunch)/dinner 8.50 **t.** and a la carte ⬧ 2.85 – **17 rm** ⍉ 14.70/29.60 **t.**

🏠 **Dunachton,** Coppice Close, off Grant Rd, PH26 3LD, ☎ 2098, 🥘 – 🅿 ⍉
closed November – **7 rm** ⍉ 8.50/19.00 **s.**

AUSTIN-ROVER Chapel Rd ☎ 2037   FORD Woodland Service Centre ☎ 2289

GREAT CUMBRAE ISLAND Bute (Strathclyde) **401** **402** F 16 – pop. 1,611 – ✪ 047 553 Millport.

⛴ by Caledonian MacBrayne : from Cumbrae Slip to Largs frequent services daily (10 mn).
⛴ by Caledonian MacBrayne : from Millport to Largs summer only 2-10 daily (30 mn).

GREENLAW Berwick. (Borders) **401** **402** M 16 – pop. 608 – ✪ 089 084 Leitholm.

♦ Edinburgh 39 – ♦ Newcastle-upon-Tyne 70.

🏠 Purves Hall ⟨⟩, TD10 6UJ, SE : 4 m. by A 697 ☎ 558, ⌇ heated, 🥘, park, ⍉ – ⌂wc 🛁wc
🅿 – **7 rm**.

GREENOCK Renfrew. (Strathclyde) **401** F 16 – pop. 58,436 – ECD : Wednesday – ✪ 0475.

ⓖ Whinhill, Beith Rd ☎ 210641, S : 2 m. – 🅩 Municipal Buildings, 23 Clyde St. ☎ 24400.

♦Edinburgh 70 – ♦Ayr 47 – ♦Glasgow 24 – ♦Oban 98.

🏨 **Tontine** (Best Western), 6 Ardgowan Sq., PA16 8NG, ☎ 23316 – 🆅 ⌂wc ☎ 🅿 🅰 🆑 🆎
⍉ 💳
M 5.50/8.00 **st.** and a la carte ⬧ 2.95 – ⍉ 2.75 – **32 rm** 27.50/40.00 **st.** – SB (weekends only)
46.00 **st.**

VAUXHALL-OPEL Port Glasgow Rd ☎ 42511   VW, AUDI 60 East Hamilton St. ☎ 83535
VOLVO 46 Campbell St. ☎ 21610 and 23107

GRETNA Dumfries. (Dumfries and Galloway) **401** K 19 – pop. 2,737 – ECD : Wednesday – ✪ 046 13 (3 fig.) or 0461 (5 fig.).
🗓 Annan Rd ☎ 37834 (summer only).
♦Edinburgh 91 – ♦Carlisle 10 – ♦Dumfries 24.

🏛 **Gretna Chase**, CA6 5JB, S : ¼ m. on B 721 ⊠ Carlisle (Cumbria) ☎ 37517, ⇗ – 🏛wc **P**.
🔁 AE ⓞ VISA ⚘
M a la carte 6.90/10.75 **t.** ⅙ 1.80 – **9 rm** ⊑ 18.00/40.00 **t.** – SB (weekends only) (November-Easter, not Bank Holidays) 47.00/69.50 **st.**

GRUINARD BAY Ross and Cromarty (Highland) **401** D 10.

GULLANE E. Lothian (Lothian) **401** L 15 – pop. 2,124 – ECD : Wednesday – ✪ 0620.
Envir. : Dirleton★ (Castle★) E : 2 m. by A 198.
🗓₈, 🗓₈, 🗓₈ ☎ 843115.
♦Edinburgh 19 – North Berwick 5.

🏛 **Greywalls** ⚘, Muirfield,Duncur Rd, EH31 2EG, ☎ 842144, ≼ gardens and golf course, « Edwardian country house with fine walled gardens », ⚘ – 🔲 🏛wc ☎ **P**. 🔁 AE ⓞ VISA
Mid April-mid December – **M** 19.50 **t.** (dinner) and a la carte ⅙ 4.00 – **23 rm** ⊑ 38.00/86.00 **t.**

✗ **La Potinière**, Main St., EH31 2AA, ☎ 843214 – **P**
closed Wednesday and Saturday lunch, 1 week June and October – **M** (lunch only and Saturday dinner) (booking essential) 10.50/15.00 **t.** ⅙ 3.00.

at Dirleton NE : 2 m. by A 198 – ⊠ ✪ 062 085 Dirleton :

✗✗ **Open Arms** with rm, EH39 5EG, ☎ 241, ⇗ – 🔲 🏛wc ☎ **P**. 🔁 AE ⓞ VISA
M (restricted lunch) 7.50/14.50 **t.** ⅙ 3.50 – **7 rm** ⊑ 42.50/60.00 **t.** – SB (November-mid May) 55.00/80.00 **st.**

HADDINGTON E. Lothian (Lothian) **401** L 16 Scotland G – pop. 7,988 – ECD : Thursday – ✪ 062 082.
See : Site★ – High Street★.
Envir. : Gifford★, S : 4 m. by B 8369 – Stenton★, E : 7 m. – Lennoxlove★, S : 1 m.
🗓₈ Amisfield Park, ☎ 3627.
♦ Edinburgh 17 – Hawick 53 – ♦ Newcastle-upon-Tyne 101.

✗✗ **Brown's** with rm, 1 West Rd, EH41 3RD, ☎ 2254, ⇗ – 🔲 🏛wc **P**. ⚘
closed 2 weeks October – **M** *(closed Sunday dinner)* (dinner only) (booking essential) 14.90 **t.** ⅙ 3.35 – **6 rm** ⊑ 26.00/40.00 **t.**

HARRIS (Isle of) Inverness. (Outer Hebrides) (Western Isles) **401** Z 10 – pop. 2,137.
See : St. Clement's Church, Rodel (tomb★).
⛴ by Caledonian MacBrayne : from Kyles Scalpay to the Isle of Scalpay : Monday/Saturday 5-10 daily (restricted in winter) (10 mn) – from Tarbert to Uig (Isle of Skye) Monday/Saturday 5-9 weekly (2 h) – from Tarbert to Lochmaddy (Isle of Uist) Monday/Saturday 2 weekly (2 h).

Scarista – ⊠ ✪ 085 985 Scarista.

🏛 **Scarista House** ⚘, PA85 3HX, ☎ 238, ≼ beach and mountains, ⇗ – 🏛wc **P**
Easter-October – **M** *(closed lunch and Sunday to non-residents)* (booking essential) (buffet lunch)/dinner 13.50 **t.** ⅙ 2.00 – **7 rm** ⊑ 33.00/50.00 **t.**

Tarbert – pop. 479 – ECD : Thursday – ⊠ ✪ 0859 Harris – 🗓 ☎ 2011 (summer only).

🏛 **Harris**, PA85 3DJ, ☎ 2154, ≼, ⇗ – 🏛wc 🏛wc **P**
closed January and February – **M** (bar lunch Monday to Saturday)/dinner 9.50 **t.** ⅙ 2.95 – **25 rm** ⊑ 15.50/34.00 **t.** – SB (weekends only) 27.50/30.60 **st.**

HAWICK Roxburgh. (Borders) **401** **402** L 17 Scotland G – pop. 16,213 – ECD : Tuesday – ✪ 0450.
Envir. : Jedburgh★ (Abbey★★-Mary Queen of Scots House★-Canongate Bridge★) NE : 11 m : by A 698 and B 6358 – Waterloo Monument (⚘★★) NE : 12 m. by A 698, A 68 and B 6400 – Hermitage Castle★, S : 16 m. by B 6399.
🗓₈ Vertish Hill ☎ 2293, S : 1 ½ m. – 🗓 Common Haugh, Car Park ☎ 72547 (summer only).
♦Edinburgh 51 – ♦Ayr 122 – ♦Carlisle 44 – ♦Dumfries 63 – Motherwell 76 – ♦Newcastle-upon-Tyne 62.

🏛 **Mansfield House**, Weensland Rd, TD9 9EL, NE : 1 m. on A 698 ☎ 73988, ⇗, park – 🔲 🏛wc 🏛wc ☎ **P**. 🔁 AE ⓞ VISA
M *(closed Saturday lunch and Sunday to non-residents)* (bar lunch)/dinner a la carte 7.25/13.15 **t.** ⅙ 3.00 – **10 rm** 19.00/28.00 **t.** – SB (weekends only) 30.00/38.00 **st.**

🏛 **Kirklands**, West Stewart Pl., TD9 8BH, ☎ 72263 – 🔲 🏛wc ☎ **P**
M *(closed Sunday to non-residents)* 6.50/10.50 **t.** and a la carte ⅙ 3.00 – **6 rm** ⊑ 25.00/40.00 **t.** – SB (weekends only)(October-June) 40.00/45.00 **st.**

CITROEN, PEUGEOT, TALBOT 61 High St. ☎ 72287   VW, AUDI Commercial Rd ☎ 73211
FORD Earl St. ☎ 73316

522

HEITON Roxburgh. (Borders) – see Kelso.

HELENSBURGH Dunbarton. (Strathclyde) **401** F 15 – pop. 16,432 – ECD : Wednesday – ✆ 0436.
See : Hill House★.
Envir. : Dumbarton Castle site★, E : 11 m. by A 814 – Loch Lomond★★, NE : 5 m. by B 832.
⛴ to Gourock summer only Monday/Saturday 4-5 daily (40 mn).
🛈 Pier Head Car Park, ✆ 2642 (summer only).
♦Edinburgh 68 – ♦Glasgow 22.

🏨 Commodore (Osprey), 112 West Clyde St., G84 8ER, ✆ 6924, ≤ – 🗘 🆅 🖵wc ☎ 🅿 🏛
45 rm, **1 suite**.

at Rhu NW : 2 m. on A 814 – ⊠ ✆ 0436 Rhu :

🏨 **Rosslea Hall** 🦢, Ferry Rd, G84 8NF, ✆ 820684, ≤, 🚗 – 🆅 🖵wc �🖵wc ☎ 🅿 🏛 🔺 🗚
🅥🅢🅐
M 5.75/22.50 **t.** and a la carte ⅄ 3.00 – **16 rm** ⇌ 35.00/50.00 **t** – SB (weekdays only)
62.70/70.00 **st.**

AUSTIN-ROVER 135 East Clyde St. ✆ 3344   TOYOTA 145 East Clyde St. ✆ 2779
RENAULT 103 East Clyde St. ✆ 6021

HILLSWICK Shetland (Shetland Islands) **401** P 2 – see Shetland Islands (Mainland).

HOWGATE Midlothian (Lothian) **401 402** K 16 – ⊠ ✆ 0968 Penicuik.
♦Edinburgh 11 – Peebles 11.

✗ **Old Howgate Inn,** 7 Wester Howgate, EH26 8QB, ✆ 74244, Smörrebrod – 🅿 🔺 🗚 🅞
🅥🅢🅐
closed Christmas Day and New Years Day – **M** a la carte 5.95/13.05 **t.** ⅄ 2.85.

HOY (Isle of) Orkney (Orkney Islands) **401** K 7 – see Orkney Islands.

HUMBIE E. Lothian (Lothian) **401 402** L 16 – ✆ 087 533.
♦Edinburgh 17 – ♦Carlisle 83.

🏰 **Johnstounburn House** (Mt. Charlotte) 🦢, EH36 5PL, S : ¾ m. on A 6137 ✆ 696, ≤, « Part
17C country house », 🚗, park – 🆅 ☎ 🅿 🔺 🗚 🅞 🅥🅢🅐
M 8.95/18.00 **t.** and a la carte ⅄ 3.50 – **11 rm** ⇌ 45.00/85.00 **t.** – SB (November-March)
70.00/100.00 **st.**

INCHNADAMPH Sutherland. (Highland) **401** F 9 – ⊠ Lairg – ✆ 057 12 Assynt.
♦Edinburgh 239 – ♦Inverness 83.

🏛 **Inchnadamph** 🦢, IV27 4HL, ✆ 202, ≤ Loch Assynt and mountains, 🎣 – 🖵wc 🅿 🔺 🅞
🅥🅢🅐
Mid March-October – **M** 5.00/6.75 **t.** ⅄ 2.30 – **28 rm** ⇌ 14.75/36.50 **t.**

INNERLEITHEN Peebles. (Borders) **401 402** K 17 – pop. 2,463 – ✆ 0896.
Envir. : Traquair House★★, S : 1 m. by A 709.
🛈⅄ ✆ 830951.
♦Edinburgh 30 – Galashiels 12 – ♦Glasgow 59 – Hawick 25.

↑ **Tighnuilt House,** Peebles Rd, EH44 6RD, W : ½ m. on A 72 ✆ 830491, ≤, 🎣 – 🅿
March-November – **5 rm** ⇌ 12.00/24.00.

INVERGOWRIE Perth. (Tayside) **401** K 14 – see Dundee.

INVERMORISTON Inverness. (Highland) **401** G 12 – ✆ 0320 Glenmoriston.
See : Loch Ness★★.
♦Edinburgh 168 – ♦Inverness 29 – Kyle of Lochalsh 56.

🏛 **Glenmoriston Arms,** IV3 6YA, ✆ 51206, 🎣 – 🆅 🖵wc 🅿 🔺 🗚 🅞 🅥🅢🅐
May-November – **M** (bar lunch)/dinner 17.00 **t.** and a la carte ⅄ 2.85 – **8 rm** ⇌ 30.00/42.00 **t.**

INVERNESS Inverness. (Highland) **401** H 11 Scotland G – pop. 38,204 – ECD : Wednesday –
✆ 0463.
See : Site★ – Museum and Art Gallery★★ M.
Envir. : Loch Ness★★ by A 82 – Loch Ness Monster Exhibition★ – Cawdor Castle★, E : 14 m. by A
82, A 96 and B 9090 – Clava Cairns★, E : 10 m. by B 9006 – Culloden Moor, E : 6 m. by B 9006 –
Fortrose (Cathedral Site★) N : 16 m. by B 865, A 9 and A 832.
🛈⅄ ✆ 231989, S : 1 m. by Culcabock Rd.
✈ Dalcross Airport : ✆ 232471, NE : 8 m. by A 96 – 🚌 ✆ 242124.
🛈 23 Church St. ✆ 234353.
♦Edinburgh 156 – ♦Aberdeen 107 – ♦Dundee 134.

21

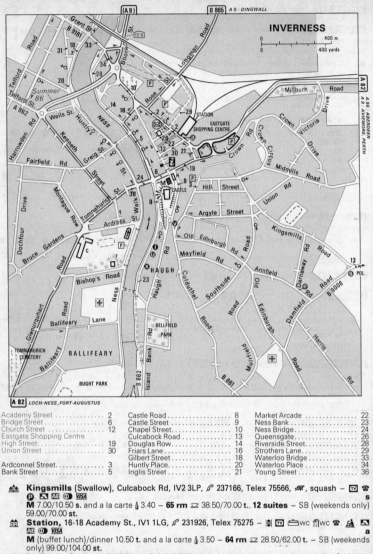

INVERNESS

A 82 LOCH-NESS, FORT-AUGUSTUS

Academy Street 2	Castle Road 8	Market Arcade 22
Bridge Street 6	Castle Street 9	Ness Bank 23
Church Street 12	Chapel Street 10	Ness Bridge 24
Eastgate Shopping Centre	Culcabock Road 13	Queensgate 26
High Street 19	Douglas Row 14	Riverside Street 28
Union Street 30	Friars Lane 16	Strothers Lane 29
	Gilbert Street 18	Waterloo Bridge 33
Ardconnel Street. 3	Huntly Place. 20	Waterloo Place 34
Bank Street 5	Inglis Street 21	Young Street 36

Kingsmills (Swallow), Culcabock Rd, IV2 3LP, ℰ 237166, Telex 75566, ☛, squash – ☑ ☎ **s**
⒫ ⌧ 匠 ① 💳
M 7.00/10.50 **s.** and a la carte ▯ 3.40 – **65 rm** ⌑ 38.50/70.00 **t.**, **12 suites** – SB (weekends only)
59.00/70.00 **st.**

Station, 16-18 Academy St., IV1 1LG, ℰ 231926, Telex 75275 – ▯ ☑ ⌷wc 魚wc ☎. ⚘. 匠 **a**
匠 ① 💳
M (buffet lunch)/dinner 10.50 **t.** and a la carte ▯ 3.50 – **64 rm** ⌑ 28.50/62.00 **t.** – SB (weekends
only) 99.00/104.00 **st.**

Ladbroke (Ladbroke), Millburn Rd, IV2 3TR, E : by A 96 at junction A 9 and A 96 ℰ 239666,
Telex 75377 – ▯ ☑ ⌷wc ☜ ⚘ ① 💳
M 4.50/9.50 **t.** and a la carte ▯ 3.70 – ⌑ 6.00 – **108 rm** 42.00/58.00 **st.**

Craigmonie, 9 Annfield Rd, IV2 3HX, ℰ 231649 – ▯ ☑ ⌷wc ☎ ⒫. ⚘. 匠 匠 ① 💳 **e**
M 6.00/11.00 **t.** and a la carte ▯ 4.05 – **30 rm** ⌑ 30.50/54.00 **t.** – SB 58.00/63.00 **st.**

Glen Mhor, 9-10 Ness Bank, IV2 4SG, ℰ 234308 – ☑ ⌷wc 魚wc ☎ ⒫. 匠 匠 ① 💳 **i**
closed 31 December-4 January – **M** 13.50 **t.** (dinner) and a la carte ▯ 3.50 – **22 rm**
⌑ 15.00/60.00 **t.** – SB (weekends only) (mid September-April) 54.00/84.00 **st.**

Glenmoriston, 20 Ness Bank, IV3 6YB, ℰ 223777, ☛ – ☑ ⌷wc 魚wc ⒫ 匠 💳 ✄ **x**
M (closed Sunday lunch) (bar lunch)/dinner 11.50 **t.** ▯ 2.95 – **20 rm** ⌑ 21.00/45.00 **t.**

Felstead, 18 Ness Bank, IV2 4SF, ℰ 231634 – ⒫ **u**
May-September – **7 rm** ⌑ 10.00/20.00 **st.**

Craigside House, 4 Gordon Terr., IV2 3HD, ℰ 231576, ⬳ – ☑ 魚wc. ✄ **v**
Mid March-mid November – **6 rm** ⌑ 10.00/26.00 **s.**

524

at Culloden Moor E : 3 m. by A 96 – ✉ ☎ 0463 Inverness :

Culloden House ⛺, IV1 2NZ, ✆ 790461, Telex 75402, ≤, 🌳, park – [TV] ☎ [P]. [S] [AE] [O] [VISA]. ⛔
M a la carte lunch/dinner 25.00 **t.** 🍾 4.45 – **20 rm** ☕ 60.00/120.00 **t.**

at Dunain Park SW : 2 ½ m. on A 82 – ✉ ☎ 0463 Inverness :

Dunain Park ⛺, IV3 6JN, ✆ 230512, ≤, « Country house and gardens », park – 🛁wc [P]
April-October – **M** (bar lunch)/dinner 19.00 **t.** 🍾 3.75 – **8 rm** ☕ 73.00 **t.**

AUSTIN-ROVER-DAIMLER-JAGUAR, LAND ROVER-RANGE ROVER, ROLLS ROYCE 66 Harbour Rd ✆ 220011
BMW Harbour Rd ✆ 236566
FIAT, LANCIA 8 Tomnahurich St. ✆ 235777
FORD Harbour Rd ✆ 238001
LADA Harbour Rd ✆ 222841
MAZDA Harbour Rd ✆ 230777
PEUGEOT, TALBOT Harbour Rd ✆ 231536
RENAULT 16 Telford St. ✆ 222848
VAUXHALL-OPEL 112 Academy St. ✆ 234311
VOLVO Harbour Rd ✆ 230885
VW, AUDI Harbour Rd ✆ 231313

IONA (Isle of) Argyll. (Strathclyde) [401] A 15 **Scotland G** – pop. 268 – ☎ 068 17.
See : Site★ – Maclean's Cross★ – St. Oran's Chapel★ – St. Martin's Cross★ – Infirmary Museum★.
⛴ by Caledonian MacBrayne : to Fionnphort (Isle of Mull) frequent services daily in summer, restricted service in winter (5 mn).

IRVINE Ayr (Strathclyde) [401] [402] F 17 – pop. 32 ,507 – ☎ 0294.
♦Edinburgh 75 – Ayr 14 – ♦Glasgow 29.

Hospitality Inn (Mt. Charlotte), Roseholm, Annick Water, E : ¾ m. on A 71 ✆ 74272, Telex 777097, 🏊 – ▤ rest [TV] ☎ ♿ [P]. 🏌. [S] [AE] [O] [VISA]
M (rest. see **Mirage** below) – ☕ 5.25 – **128 rm** 42.50/52.95 **t.**

XXX **Mirage** (Mt. Charlotte) (at Hospitality Inn), Roseholm, Annick Water, KA11 4LD, E : ¾ m. on A 71 ✆ 74272, Telex 777097 – ▤ [P]. [S] [AE] [O] [VISA]
M 8.95/14.95 **t.** and a la carte 12.80/19.95 **t.** 🍾 4.30.

ISLAY (Isle of) Argyll. (Strathclyde) [401] B 16 – pop. 3 ,997.
✈ Glenegedale Airport : ✆ 0496 (Port Ellen) 2361.
⛴ by Western Ferries : from Port Askaig to Feolin (Isle of Jura) Monday/Saturday 10-12 daily : Sunday 3-4 daily (5 mn) – by Caledonian MacBrayne : from Port Ellen to Kennacriag (Kintyre Peninsula) 1-2 daily (2 h) – from Port Askaig to Kennacraig (Kintyre Peninsula) Monday/Saturday 1 daily (1 h 45 mn).
[i] at Bowmore ✆ 049 681 (Bowmore) 254 (summer only).

Bowmore – ✉ ☎ 049 681 Bowmore.

Lochside, Shore St., PA43 7LB, ✆ 244, ≤, 🎣 – [TV] 🛁wc 🚿 ☎. [S] [AE] [VISA]
M 6.00/10.00 **t.** and a la carte 🍾 2.50 – **7 rm** ☕ 19.00/42.00 **st.**

Port Askaig – ECD : Tuesday – ✉ ☎ 049 684 Port Askaig.

Port Askaig, PA46 7RD, ✆ 245, ≤ Sound of Islay and Jura, 🌳 – [TV] 🛁wc 🚿wc [P]
M 6.50/9.50 **st.** 🍾 3.75 – ☕ 4.75 – **9 rm** 15.00/56.00 – SB 50.00/56.00 **st.**

ISLEORNSAY Inverness. (Highland) [401] C 12 – see Skye (Isle of).

JEDBURGH Roxburgh. (Borders) [401] [402] M 17 **Scotland G** – pop. 4 ,053 – ECD : Thursday – ☎ 0835.
See : Site★ – Abbey★★ – Mary Queen of Scots House★ – Canongate Bridge★.
Envir. : Waterloo Monument (✻★★) N : 3 m. by A 68 and B 6400.
♦Edinburgh 48 – ♦Carlisle 54 – ♦Newcastle upon Tyne 57.

Ferniehirst Mill Lodge ⛺, TD8 6PQ, S : 2 m. on A 68 ✆ 63279, park – 🛁wc 🚿wc [P]. ⛔
April-October – **11 rm** ☕ 18.00/36.00 **t.**

JOHN O'GROATS Caithness. (Highland) [401] K 8 – Shipping Services : see Orkney Islands.

JOHNSTONE Renfrew. (Strathclyde) [401] [402] G16 – pop. 42 ,707 – ✉ Glasgow – ☎ 0505.
♦Edinburgh 58 – ♦Ayr 35 – Greenock 15 – ♦Glasgow 12.

Lynnhurst, Park Rd, PA5 8LS, ✆ 24331, 🌳 – [TV] 🛁wc ☎ [P]. [S] [O] [VISA]
M 3.75/7.50 **st.** and a la carte 🍾 2.85 – **31 rm** ☕ 13.80/33.15 **st.**

JURA (Isle of) Argyll. (Strathclyde) [401] C 15 – pop. 239.
⛴ by Western Ferries : from Feolin to Port Askaig (Isle of Islay) Monday/Saturday 8-10 daily ; Sunday 2-4 daily (5 mn).

Craighouse – ECD : Tuesday – ✉ ☎ 049 682 Jura.

Jura ⛺, PA60 7XU, ✆ 243, ≤ Small Isles Bay, 🎣, 🌳 – 🛁wc [P]. [S] [AE] [O] [VISA]
M (bar lunch)/dinner 8.50 **st.** and a la carte 🍾 2.50 – **18 rm** ☕ 16.50/36.00 **st.**, **1 suite** 40.00 **st.**

KELSO Roxburgh. (Borders) **401 402** M 17 **Scotland** G – pop. 5 ,547 – ECD : Wednesday – ☎ 0573.

See : Site★ – Market Square★★ – ≼★ from Kelso Bridge. **Envir. :** Mellerstain★★★ (ceilings★★★-Library★★★) NW : 6 m. by A 6089 – Floors Castle★, NW : 2 m. by A 6089 – Smailholm Tower★ (❄★★) NW : 6 m. by A 6089 and B 6397 – Ladykirk (Kirk O'Steil★) NE : 16 m. by A 698, A 697, A 6112 and B 6437 – Flodden Field, NE : 11 m. by A 698 and A 697.

🛇 ✆ 23009.

🅱 66 Woodmarket ✆ 23464 (summer only).

◆Edinburgh 44 – Hawick 21 – ◆Newcastle-upon-Tyne 68.

🏨 **Cross Keys,** 36-37 The Square, TD5 7HL, ✆ 23303 – 🛗 📺 ⇌wc 🎬wc ☎ & 🅿. 🚗. ◫ 🖭
M (bar lunch)/dinner 11.00 **st.** and a la carte ♨ 2.50 – **24 rm** ⚏ 21.00/37.00 **st.** – SB (weekends only) 42.00/54.00 **st.**

🏨 **Ednam House,** Bridge St., TD5 7HT, ✆ 24168, ≼, 🌭 – ⇌wc 🎬wc ☜ 🅿. 🚗. 🖭
closed 24 December-10 January – **M** (bar lunch Monday to Saturday)/dinner 10.00 **t.** ♨ 2.30 – **33 rm** ⚏ 22.60/45.20 **t.** – SB 25.50/30.00 **st.**

at Heiton SW : 3 m. by A 698 – ⊠ Kelso – ☎ 057 35 Roxburgh.

🏨 **Sunlaws House** 🌭, TD5 8JZ, ✆ 331, Telex 728147, ≼, « Victorian country house », 🦢, 🌭, park, ❀ – 📺 ⇌wc & 🅿. 🚗 ◫ ⊙ 🖭
M a la carte 10.25/13.55 **t.** ♨ 3.50 – **15 rm** ⚏ 35.00/65.00 **t.** – SB (December-March)(except Christmas and New Year) 60.00/75.00 **st.**

AUSTIN-ROVER-JAGUAR Bridge St. ✆ 24345   TALBOT Sheddon Par. Rd ✆ 24488
RENAULT Golf Course Rd ✆ 24720

KENMORE Perth. (Tayside) **401** I 14 – ECD : Thursday except summer – ⊠ Aberfeldy – ☎ 088 73.

See : Site★.

Envir. : Loch Tay★★ – Ben Lawers★★, SW : 8 m. by A 827.

🛇 Taymouth Castle ✆ 228.

◆Edinburgh 82 – ◆Dundee 60 – ◆Oban 71 – Perth 38.

🏨 Kenmore, PH15 2NU, ✆ 205, 🛇, 🦢, 🌭 – 🛗 📺 ⇌wc ☎ 🅿. ❀ – **38 rm**.

KENNACRAIG Argyll. (Strathclyde) **401** D 16 – Shipping Services : see Kintyre (Peninsula).

KENTALLEN Argyll. (Highland) **401** E 14 – ⊠ Kentallen – ☎ 063 174 Duror.

◆Edinburgh 123 – Fort William 17 – ◆Oban 33.

🏠 **Ardsheal House** 🌭, PA38 4BX, SW : ¾ m. by A 828 ✆ 227, ≼, « Country house in lochside setting », 🌭, park, ❀ – ⇌wc 🎬wc 🅿
Easter-October – **M** (restricted lunch)/dinner 18.00 **t.** ♨ 3.50 – **13 rm** ⚏ (dinner included) 56.00/108.00 **t.**

✗ **Holly Tree,** Kentallen Pier, PA38 4BY, ✆ 292, ≼ Loch Linnhe and mountains – 🅿. 🚗 ⊙ 🖭
closed Wednesday in April May and October and January – **M** (closed lunch Monday to Saturday and dinner Monday to Wednesday in winter) 9.50 **t.** (dinner) and a la carte 10.20/15.35 **t.**

KILCHOAN Argyll. (Highland) **401** B 13 – ⊠ Acharacle – ☎ 097 23.

🚢 by Caledonian MacBrayne : to Tobermory (Isle of Mull) summer only Monday/Saturday 3-5 daily (35 mn).

◆Edinburgh 163 – ◆Inverness 120 – ◆Oban 92.

KILCHRENAN Argyll. (Strathclyde) **401** E 14 – ⊠ Taynuilt – ☎ 086 63.

◆Edinburgh 117 – ◆Glasgow 87 – ◆Oban 18.

🏨 **Ardanaiseig** 🌭, PA35 5JS, NE : 4 m. by B 845 ✆ 333, ≼ gardens and Loch Awe, « Country house in extensive informal gardens on Loch Awe », 🦢, park, ❀ – 📺 ☎ 🅿. 🚗 ◫ ⊙ 🖭
Easter-mid October – **M** a la carte lunch 10.60/12.00 **st.** /dinner 23.00 **st.** ♨ 3.75 – **14 rm** ⚏ (dinner included) 70.00/144.00 **st.**

🏨 **Taychreggan** 🌭, Lochaweside, PA35 1HQ, SE : 1 ¼ m. ✆ 211, ≼ Loch Awe, « Lochside setting », 🦢, 🌭, park – ⇌wc 🅿. 🚗 ◫ ⊙ 🖭
25 March-12 October – **M** (buffet lunch)/dinner 12.50 **t.** ♨ 3.00 – **17 rm** ⚏ 28.50/59.00 **t.**

KILCREGGAN Dunbarton. (Strathclyde) **401** F 16 – Shipping Services : see Gourock.

During the season, particularly in resorts, it is wise to book in advance.
However, if you find you cannot take up a hotel booking you have made, please let the hotel know immediately.
If you are writing to a hotel abroad enclose an International Reply Coupon (available from Post Offices.)

526

KILDRUMMY Aberdeen. (Grampian) **401** L 12 Scotland G – ✉ Alford – ✆ 033 65.

See : Castle★.

Envir. : Craigievar Castle★★★, SE : 13 m. by A 944 and A 980 – Huntly Castle (Heraldic carvings★★) N : 15 m. by A 97.

◆Edinburgh 137 – ◆Aberdeen 35.

🏨 **Kildrummy Castle** (Best Western) ⌖, AB3 8RA, S : 1 ¼ m. on A 97 ℰ 288, ≤ gardens and Kildrummy Castle, « 19C mansion in extensive park », ⌕ – 📺 ⌷wc ☎ 🅿. 🔄 🆊 ⑩ 𝕍𝕀𝕊𝔸
closed 4 January-15 March – **M** 8.50/13.50 **t.** and a la carte ⌕ 3.00 – **15 rm** ⊏ 28.00/55.00 **t.** – SB (14 March-21 May and October-21 December) 64.00 **st.**

KILFINAN Argyll. (Strathclyde) **401** E 16 – ✆ 070 082.

◆Edinburgh 124 – ◆Glasgow 78 – ◆Oban 78.

🏠 **Kilfinan** ⌖, Tighnabruaich, PA21 2AP, ℰ 201 – 📺 ⌷wc ☎. 🔄 🆊 ⑩ 𝕍𝕀𝕊𝔸. ✼
M (bar lunch)/dinner 13.00 **t.** and a la carte ⌕ 3.50 – ⊏ 4.50 – **11 rm** 20.00/33.50 **t.**

KILLIECRANKIE Perth. (Tayside) **401** I 13 – see Pitlochry.

KILLIN Perth. (Central) **401** H 14 – pop. 545 – ECD : Wednesday – ✆ 056 72.

Envir. : Loch Tay★★, Ben Lawers★★, NE : 8 m. by A 827 – Kenmore★, NE : 17 m. by A 827.

🛆 ℰ 312.

🅿 Main St. ℰ 254 (summer only).

◆Edinburgh 72 – ◆Dundee 65 – Perth 43 – ◆Oban 54.

🛖 **Morenish Lodge**, FK21 8TX, NE : 2 ½ m. on A 827 ℰ 258, ≤ Loch Tay and hills, ⌕, ✼ – ⌷wc ⌷wc 🅿. 🔄 𝕍𝕀𝕊𝔸. ✼
Mid April-mid October – **M** (bar lunch)/dinner 10.50 **t.** ⌕ 2.00 – **12 rm** ⊏ 18.00/36.00 **t.**

🛖 **Bridge of Lochay**, FK21 8TS, N : ½ m. on A 827 ℰ 272 – ⌷wc ⌷wc 🅿
March-November – **M** 5.25/7.75 **t.** ⌕ 2.30 – **17 rm** ⊏ 13.00/31.00 **t.**

🛏 **Dall Lodge**, Main St., FK21 8TN, N : ¼ m. on A 827 ℰ 217, ⌕ – ⌷wc 🅿
April-October – **9 rm** ⊏ 12.00/27.00 **t.**

at Ardeonaig NE : 7 ¼ m. – ✉ ✆ 056 72 Killin :

🏠 **Ardeonaig** ⌖, South Loch Tayside, FK21 8SU, ℰ 400, Telex 76163, ⌕, 🌳, park – ⌷wc ⌷wc 🅿
Mid March-October – **M** (bar lunch)/dinner 14.00 **st.** and a la carte ⌕ 2.60 – **14 rm** ⊏ 18.50/39.00 **st.**

KILMARNOCK Ayr. (Strathclyde) **401 402** G 17 Scotland G – pop. 51 ,799 – ECD : Wednesday – ✆ 0563.

See : Dean Castle (Arms and armour collection★-musical instruments★).

🛆 Annanhill, Irvine Rd ℰ 21644, W : 1 m. – 🛆 Caprington, Ayr Rd ℰ 23702.

🅿 62 Bank St., ℰ 39090.

◆Edinburgh 62 – ◆Ayr 13 – ◆Dumfries 58 – ◆Glasgow 22.

🏨 **Howard Park** (Swallow), 136 Glasgow Rd, KA3 1UT, N : 2 m. on B 7038 ℰ 31211, Group Telex 53168 – ⌷ 📺 ⌷wc ☎ 🅿. 🔄. 🔄 🆊 ⑩ 𝕍𝕀𝕊𝔸
M (bar lunch Saturday and Sunday) 5.00/8.75 **st.** and a la carte ⌕ 3.40 – **46 rm** ⊏ 35.00/47.75 **st.** – SB (weekends only) 42.00 **st.**

KILMARTIN Argyll. (Strathclyde) **401** D 15 – ✉ Lochgilphead – ✆ 054 65.

◆Edinburgh 138 – ◆Glasgow 92 – ◆Oban 30.

✕ **Cairn**, PA31 8RQ, ℰ 254 – 🅿. 🆊 ⑩ 𝕍𝕀𝕊𝔸
closed Monday to Wednesday November-March and Sunday – **M** (booking essential) a la carte 7.65/9.65 **t.** ⌕ 3.95.

KILNINVER Argyll. (Strathclyde) **401** D 14 – see Oban.

KILWINNING Ayr. (Strathclyde) **401 402** F 17 – pop. 16 ,196 – ✆ 0294.

◆Edinburgh 77 – ◆Ayr 16 – ◆Glasgow 31.

🏨 **Montgreenan Mansion House** ⌖, Montgreenan Estate, KA13 7QZ, NE : 3 ½ m. by B 785 (Fergushill Rd) ℰ 57733, ≤, « Georgian house in extensive grounds », 🌳, park, ✼ – 📺 ☎ 🅿. 🔄 🆊 ⑩ 𝕍𝕀𝕊𝔸
closed mid January-mid February – **M** 15.50/25.00 **t.** and a la carte ⌕ 3.95 – **11 rm** ⊏ 30.00/85.00 **t.**

KINCLAVEN Perth. (Tayside) **401** J 14 – ✉ Stanley – ✆ 025 083 Meikleour.

◆Edinburgh 56 – Perth 12.

🏨 **Ballathie House** ⌖, PH1 4QN, ℰ 268, ≤, « Country house in extensive grounds on banks of river Tay », ⌕, 🌳, park, ✼ – 📺 ⌷wc ☎ 🅿. 🔄 🆊 ⑩ 𝕍𝕀𝕊𝔸
M (bar lunch Monday to Saturday)/dinner 12.75 **t.** and a la carte ⌕ 3.40 – **21 rm** ⊏ 24.50/66.00 **t.**

527

KINCRAIG Inverness. (Highland) 🗍🄪🄪 I 12 – ECD : Wednesday – ✉ Kingussie – ☎ 054 04.

◆Edinburgh 119 – ◆Inverness 37 – Perth 75.

　🏯　**Ossian,** PH21 1NA, by A 9 ✆ 242, ≤, ⌘, 🚗 – 🅿. 🔼 ⓞ 𝗩𝗜𝗦𝗔
　　　closed 2 January-1 February and 11 November-9 December – **M** *(closed Monday to non-residents)* (dinner only and Sunday lunch) 9.00 **st.** and a la carte ⌄ 3.00 – **6 rm** ⇌ 15.00/30.00 **st.**

KINGUSSIE Inverness. (Highland) 🗍🄪🄪 H 12 – pop. 1 ,140 – ECD : Wednesday – ☎ 054 02.

🏌 ✆ 374, ½ m. from town shops off A 9.

🛈 Caledonia Buildings, King St. ✆ 297 (summer only).

◆Edinburgh 117 – ◆Inverness 41 – Perth 73.

　🏯　**Osprey,** Ruthven Rd, PH21 1EN, ✆ 510 – 🔼 🄰🄴 ⓞ 𝗩𝗜𝗦𝗔
　　　closed November and December – **M** (dinner only) 11.00 **t.** ⌄ 2.80 – **8 rm** ⇌ 12.00/21.00 **t.** – SB (5 January-30 April) 40.00/58.00 **st.**

　↑　**Columba House,** Manse Rd, PH21 1JF, ✆ 402, 🚗 – 🛁wc 🅿
　　　closed 31 October-27 December – **7 rm** ⇌ 12.00/29.00 **t.**

　✕　**The Cross,** 25-27 High St., PH21 1HX, ✆ 762
　　　closed Monday, 2 weeks May and 2 weeks October – **M** *(dinner only)* 12.50 **t.** and a la carte ⌄ 2.00.

KINLOCHBERVIE Sutherland (Highland) 🗍🄪🄪 E 8 – ECD : Wednesday – ✉ Lairg – ☎ 097 182.

Envir. : Cape Wrath★★★ (🌲★★), SE : 28 ½ m. by B 801 and A 838.

◆Edinburgh 276 – Thurso 93 – Ullapool 61.

　🏛　**Kinlochbervie** ♨, IV27 4RP, ✆ 275, ≤ Loch Inchard and sea – 📺 🛁wc ☎ 🅿. 🔼 🄰🄴 ⓞ
　　　𝗩𝗜𝗦𝗔
　　　restricted service November-Easter – **M** (booking essential) (bar lunch)/dinner 15.95 **t.** ⌄ 3.30 – **10 rm** ⇌ 30.00/66.00 **t.** – SB 55.00/92.00 **st.**

KINLOCHEWE Ross and Cromarty (Highland) 🗍🄪🄪 E 11 – ✉ Achnasheen – ☎ 044 584.

Envir. : Loch Maree★★★ and Victoria Falls★, NW : 10 m. by A 832.

◆Edinburgh 208 – ◆Inverness 52.

　🏯　**Kinlochewe,** IV22 2PA, ✆ 253, ≤, ⌘, 🚗 – 🅿. 🔼 𝗩𝗜𝗦𝗔
　　　April-November – **M** (bar lunch)/dinner 10.50 **st.** ⌄ 2.70 – **10 rm** ⇌ 18.00/36.00 **st.**

　✈　*Keine bezahlte Reklame im Michelin-Führer.*

KINROSS Kinross. (Tayside) 🗍🄪🄪 J 15 – pop. 3 ,493 – ECD : Thursday – ☎ 0577.

🏌 Green Hotel, Beeches Park ✆ 63467 – 🏌 Milnathort ✆ 64069, N : 2 m.

🛈 Turfhills Service Area (off junction 6, M 90) ✆ 63680 (summer only).

◆Edinburgh 28 – Dunfermline 13 – Perth 18 – Stirling 25.

　🏨　**Green** (Best Western), 2 The Muirs, KY13 7AS, ✆ 63467, Telex 76684, « Gardens », 🔼, 🏌,
　　　♨, squash – 📺 🛁wc ☎ 🅿. ⌄̲. 🔼 🄰🄴 ⓞ 𝗩𝗜𝗦𝗔. 🌼
　　　M (restricted lunch)/dinner 11.00 **t.** and a la carte ⌄ 3.95 – **45 rm** ⇌ 33.00/48.00 **t.** – SB (except Christmas and New Year) 56.00/80.00 **st.**

　🏨　**Windlestrae,** The Muirs, KY13 7AS, ✆ 63217, 🚗 – 📺 🛁wc ☎ 🅿. 🔼 🄰🄴 ⓞ 𝗩𝗜𝗦𝗔. 🌼
　　　M 9.00/13.00 **t.** and a la carte ⌄ 2.80 – **18 rm** ⇌ 33.00/45.00 **t.**

　🏯　**Croft Bank,** 30 Station Rd, KY13 7TG, ✆ 63819 – 📺 🛁wc 🛁wc ☎ 🅿. 🄰🄴 𝗩𝗜𝗦𝗔
　　　M a la carte lunch/dinner 10.50 **st.** ⌄ 2.85 – **6 rm** ⇌ 16.00/32.00 **st.**

　　　at Cleish SW : 4 ½ m. by B 996 and B 9097 – ✉ Kinross – ☎ 057 75 Cleish Hills :

　✕✕　**Nivingston House** ♨ with rm, KY13 7LS, ✆ 216, ≤, 🚗 – 📺 🛁wc 🛁wc ☎ 🅿. 🔼 🄰🄴 ⓞ
　　　𝗩𝗜𝗦𝗔
　　　M 10.00/14.50 **t.** ⌄ 3.90 – **7 rm** ⇌ 35.00/50.00 **t.** – SB (weekends only) 65.00 **st.**

FORD　High St. ✆ 62424

KINTYRE (Peninsula) Argyll. (Strathclyde) 🗍🄪🄪 D 16 17 Scotland G.

See : Carradale★ – Saddell (grave stones★).

🛩 at Campbeltown (Machrihanish Airport) : ✆ 0586 (Campbeltown) 53021.

🚢 by Caledonian MacBrayne : from Claonaig to Lochranza (Isle of Arran) summer only 6-8 daily (30 mn) – from Kennacraig to Port Ellen (Isle of Islay) 1-2 daily (2 h) – from Kennacraig to Port Askaig (Isle of Islay) Monday/Saturday 1 daily (1 h 45 mn).

　　　Bellochantuy – ✉ Campbeltown – ☎ 058 32 Glenbarr.

　🏛　Putechan Lodge, PA28 6QE, on A 83 ✆ 266, ≤ – 📺 🛁wc 🅿. 🔼 ⓞ 𝗩𝗜𝗦𝗔
　　　closed 6 January-February – **12 rm** ⇌ 18.00/32.00 **t.**

[Campbeltown] – ECD : Wednesday – ✉ ☎ 0586 Campbeltown.
♦Edinburgh 176.

↑ **Seafield,** Kilkerran Rd, PA28 6JL, ℰ 54385, ⇆ – ⊡ ℗
6 rm ⇌ 17.50/30.00 **st.**

[Carradale] – ECD : Wednesday – ✉ ☎ 058 33 Carradale – 🛉 ℰ 624.
♦Edinburgh 164 – ♦Glasgow 121 – ♦Oban 74.

🏠 **Carradale,** PA28 6RY, ℰ 223, ≼, ⇆, squash – 🗐wc ℗, 🖭 𝘝𝘐𝘚𝘈
M 5.00/10.50 **st.** 🍴 2.50 – **22 rm** ⇌ 16.00/36.00 **st.** – SB 80.00/108.00 **st.**

[Tarbert] – pop. 1 ,429 – ECD : Wednesday – ✉ ☎ 088 02 Tarbert.
🛉 ℰ 565, W : 1 m. – 🛈 ℰ 429 (summer only).
♦Edinburgh 139 – ♦Glasgow 96 – ♦Oban 49.

✗ **West Loch** with rm, West Tarbert, PA29 6YF, SW : 1 m. on A 83 ℰ 283, ≼ – ℗, 🖭
closed November – **M** a la carte lunch 5.65/10.50 **t.** /dinner 13.50 **t.** 🍴 3.50 – **6 rm**
⇌ 19.00/29.00 **t.** – SB (weekends only) (December-Easter) 44.00 **st.**

[KIRKCALDY] Fife. (Fife) 𝟰𝟬𝟭 K 15 Scotland G – pop. 46 ,356 – ECD : Wednesday – ☎ 0592.
🛅 Balwearie ℰ 260370 – 🛅 Dunnikier Park, Dunnikier Way ℰ 261599, North boundary.
🛈 Esplanade ℰ 267775 (summer only).
♦Edinburgh 27 – ♦Dundee 32 – ♦Glasgow 54.

at West Wemyss NE : 4 ½ m. by A 955 – ✉ ☎ 0592 Kirkcaldy :

🏠 **Belvedere,** Coxstool, KY1 4SN, ℰ 54167, ≼ – ⊡ ⌷wc ☜ ℗, 🖭 𝘈𝘌 ⓘ 𝘝𝘐𝘚𝘈
M *(closed Sunday to non-residents)* 7.50/9.00 **st.** 🍴 2.50 – **20 rm** ⇌ 25.30/40.00 **st.** – SB (weekends only) 50.00/75.00 **st.**

AUSTIN-ROVER 39 Rosslyn St. ℰ 51997	PEUGEOT, TALBOT Bennochy Rd ℰ 262191
CITROEN, VAUXHALL-OPEL 24 Victoria Rd ℰ 264755	RENAULT 15 Esplanade ℰ 263123
FORD Forth Av. ℰ 261199	SAAB 180/186 St. Clair St. ℰ 52291
HYUNDAI Meldrum Rd ℰ 200354	VOLVO Wemyssfield ℰ 262141

[KIRKCUDBRIGHT] Kirkcudbright. (Dumfries and Galloway) 𝟰𝟬𝟭 𝟰𝟬𝟮 H 19 Scotland G –
pop. 3 ,352 – ECD : Thursday – ☎ 0557.
See : Site★ – Envir. : Dundrennan Abbey★, SE : 5 m. by A 711 – 🛅 Stirling Cres.
🛈 Harbour Sq. ℰ 30494 (summer only).
♦Edinburgh 108 – ♦ Dumfries 28 – Stranraer 50.

🏩 **Selkirk Arms,** Old High St., DG6 4JG, ℰ 30402, ⇆ – ⌷wc ℗, 🖭 𝘈𝘌 ⓘ 𝘝𝘐𝘚𝘈, ✄
M (buffet lunch)/dinner 8.50 **t.** and a la carte – **26 rm** ⇌ 14.75/41.00 **t.** – SB (October-March) (except Christmas and New Year) 45.00/50.00 **t.**

AUSTIN-ROVER Mews Lane ℰ 30412

[KIRKMICHAEL] Perth. (Tayside) 𝟰𝟬𝟭 J 13 – ✉ Blairgowrie – ☎ 025 081 Strathardle.
♦Edinburgh 74 – Perth 30 – Pitlochry 12.

🏠 **Log Cabin** ⅏, Blairgowrie, PH10 7NB, W : 1 m. ℰ 288, ≼, « Scandinavian pine chalet », ⅏
– ⌷wc 🗐wc ₺, 🖭 𝘈𝘌 ⓘ 𝘝𝘐𝘚𝘈
closed mid November-mid December – **M** (bar lunch)/dinner 13.00 **st.** and a la carte 🍴 3.00 –
13 rm ⇌ 30.00/50.00 **st.** – SB (weekends only) (October-May) 66.00 **st.**

[KIRKWALL] Orkney (Orkney Islands) 𝟰𝟬𝟭 L 7 – see Orkney Islands (Mainland).

[KIRN] Argyll. (Strathclyde) 𝟰𝟬𝟭 𝟰𝟬𝟮 F 16 – see Dunoon.

[KYLEAKIN] Inverness. (Highland) 𝟰𝟬𝟭 C 12 – Shipping Services : see Skye (Isle of).

[KYLE OF LOCHALSH] Ross and Cromarty (Highland) 𝟰𝟬𝟭 C 12 Scotland G – pop. 803 – ECD :
Thursday – ☎ 0599.
Envir. : Eilean Donan Castle★ (Site★★) E : 8 m. by A 87 – Plockton★, N : 6 m.
⚓ by Caledonian MacBrayne : to Kyleakin (Isle of Skye) frequent services daily (5 mn).
⚓ by Caledonian MacBrayne : to Mallaig summer only 3 weekly (2 h).
🛈 ℰ 4276 (summer only).
♦Edinburgh 204 – ♦ Dundee 182 – ♦Inverness 82 – ♦Oban 125.

🏨 **Lochalsh,** Ferry Rd, IV40 8AF, ℰ 4202, Telex 75318, ≼ Skye Ferry and hills – 🛗 ⊡ ☎ ℗, 🖭
𝘈𝘌 ⓘ 𝘝𝘐𝘚𝘈
closed Christmas – **M** (bar lunch)/dinner 12.65 **st.** and a la carte 🍴 3.95 – **42 rm**
⇌ 35.00/85.00 **st.** – SB (November-March) (except Christmas and New Year) 65.00 **st.**

AUSTIN-ROVER The Garage ℰ 4210   FORD Main Rd ℰ 4329

KYLES SCALPAY Inverness. (Western Isles) (Highland) **401** Z 10 – Shipping Services : see Harris (Isle of).

LAGG Bute. (Strathclyde) – see Arran (Isle of).

LAIDE Ross and Cromarty (Highland) **401** D 10 – ✉ Achnasheen – ☎ 044 582 Aultbea.
Envir. : Inverewe Gardens★★★, S : 8 m. by A 832.
♦Edinburgh 232 – ♦Inverness 76.

  ↑ **Ocean View,** Sand Passage Rd, Sand, IV22 2ND, ℰ 385, ≤ sea and Summer Isles – ℗
    8 rm 😋 12.00/30.00 st.

LAIRG Sutherland (Highland) **401** G 9 – pop. 628 – ECD : Wednesday – ☎ 0549.
🛈 ℰ 2160 (summer only).
♦Edinburgh 218 – ♦Inverness 61 – ♦Wick 72.

  🏨 **Sutherland Arms,** IV27 4AT, ℰ 2291, ≤, ⌂, 🐎 – ⌷wc ℗. 🔼 AE ⓪ VISA
    April-October – **M** (bar lunch)/dinner 10.00 t. 🍷 3.00 – **24 rm** 😋 27.00/50.00 t.

  🏠 **Achany House** ⚲, IV27 4EB, S : 4 m. on B 864 ℰ 2433, « Georgian mansion with country
    house atmosphere », 🐎 – ⌷wc ℗
    April-October – **M** (bar lunch)/dinner 10.00 t. 🍷 2.10 – **6 rm** 😋 18.00/44.00 t. – SB
    54.00/62.00 st.

LAMLASH Bute. (Strathclyde) **401** E 17 – see Arran (Isle of).

LANARK Lanark. (Strathclyde) **401 402** I 16 Scotland G – pop. 9,673 – ECD : Thursday – ☎ 0555.
See : New Lanark★.
🛆 The Moor ℰ 3219.
🛈 Horsemarket, Ladyacre Rd ℰ 61661.
♦Edinburgh 34 – ♦Carlisle 78 – ♦ Glasgow 28.

  🏨 **Cartland Bridge,** ML11 9UF, NW : ¾ m. on A 73 ℰ 4426, 🐎 – ☜ ℗. 🔼. 🔼 AE ⓪ VISA
    M 6.50/9.00 st. and a la carte 🍷 3.35 – **15 rm** 😋 17.00/34.00 st.

  ✗ **Ristorante La Vigna,** 40 Wellgate, ML11 9DT, ℰ 4320, Italian rest. – 🔼 AE ⓪ VISA
    closed Sunday lunch and 16 to 29 October – **M** a la carte 7.75/13.00 st. 🍷 3.00.

AUSTIN-ROVER 17/19 Bloomgate ℰ 2371   VAUXHALL St. Leonard St. ℰ 2185
CITROEN 30 West Port ℰ 2581

LANGBANK Renfrew. (Strathclyde) **401** G 16 – ECD : Saturday – ☎ 047 554.
♦Edinburgh 63 – ♦ Glasgow 17 – Greenock 7.

  🏨 **Gleddoch House** ⚲, PA14 6YE, SE : 1 m. by B 789 ℰ 711, Telex 779801, ≤ Clyde and
    countryside, 🛆, 🐎, park, squash – 📺 ⌷wc 🍴wc ☎ ℗. 🔼 AE ⓪ VISA
    closed 26 to 27 December and 1-3 January – **M** (bar lunch Saturday) 8.00/18.50 t. and a la
    carte 🍷 3.50 – **20 rm** 😋 40.00/85.00 t., **1 suite** 95.00 t. – SB (weekends only) 40.00 st.

LARGS Ayr. (Strathclyde) **401 402** F 16 Scotland G – pop. 9,619 – ECD : Wednesday – ☎ 0475.
See : Skelmorlie Aisle★ (Monument★ and ceiling★).
🛆 Irvine Rd ℰ 673594 S : 1 m. – 🛆 Routenburn, ℰ 673230.
🚢 by Caledonian MacBrayne : to Cumbrae Slip (Great Cumbrae Island) frequent services daily
(10 mn).
🚢 by Caledonian MacBrayne : to Millport (Great Cumbrae Island) summer only 2-10 daily (30 mn).
🛈 Pierhead ℰ 673765.
♦Edinburgh 76 – ♦Ayr 32 – ♦Glasgow 30.

  🍴 **Glen Eldon,** 2 Barr Cres., KA30 8PX, ℰ 673381 – ⌷wc 🍴wc ℗. ✀
    closed mid January-mid March – **M** (dinner only) 8.00 t. 🍷 2.80 – **9 rm** 😋 20.00/40.00 t.

  ↑ **Haylie,** 108 Irvine Rd, KA30 8EY, ℰ 673207, ≤ Firth of Clyde and Islands, 🐎 – ⌷wc ℗. 🔼
    AE ⓪ VISA
    April-December – **8 rm** 😋 14.00/32.00 st.

LAUDER Berwick. (Borders) **401 402** L 16 Scotland G – pop. 799 – ECD : Thursday – ☎ 057 82.
See : Thirlestane Castle (Plasterwork ceilings★★).
🛆 ℰ 381, W : ½ m.
♦Edinburgh 27 – Hawick 31 – ♦Newcastle-upon-Tyne 78.

  🏠 **Black Bull,** Market Pl., ℰ 208 – ⌷wc ℗
    M (bar lunch in winter) 5.00/8.50 st. and a la carte 🍷 3.00 – **13 rm** 😋 16.00/20.00 st.

  at Carfraemill N : 4 m. on A 68 – ✉ Lauder – ☎ 057 85 Oxton :

  🏠 **Carfraemill,** TD2 6RA, ℰ 200 – 📺 ⌷wc ☜ ℗. VISA
    M (bar lunch)/dinner 12.00 t. 🍷 3.00 – **10 rm** 😋 30.00/40.00 t. – SB 38.00/48.00 st.

LERAGS Argyll. (Strathclyde) – see Oban.

LERWICK Shetland (Shetland Islands) **401** Q 3 – see Shetland Islands (Mainland).

LESLIE Fife. (Fife) **401** K 15 – see Glenrothes.

LETHAM Fife. (Fife) **401** K 15 – ✉ Ladybank – 🕿 033 781.
◆Edinburgh 43 – ◆Dundee 16 – Perth 18.

🏰 **Fernie Castle** (Best Western) 🦢, KY7 7RU, NE : ½ m. on A 914 🖉 381, 🐾, park – 📺 ⌂wc ｜wc 🅿 🖎 Æ ◑ 𝘝𝘐𝘚𝘈 🛳
M (booking essential for lunch) 7.50/18.50 **st.** and a la carte 🍴 3.25 – **15 rm** � 28.50/75.00 **t.** – SB (weekends only) 60.00 **st.**

LEVEN Fife. (Fife) **401** K 15 – pop. 8 ,596 – ECD : Thursday – 🕿 0333.
🛝 Leven Links 🖉 26381.
🛈 South St. 🖉 29464.
◆Edinburgh 36 – ◆Dundee 23 – ◆Glasgow 65.

at Lundin Links E : 2 m. on A 915 – ✉ 🕿 0333 Lundin Links :

🏰 **Old Manor**, Leven Rd, KY8 6AJ, 🖉 320368, ≤, 🐾 – 📺 ⌂wc 🅿 🖎 Æ ◑ 𝘝𝘐𝘚𝘈 🛳
M 7.00/12.00 **t.** and a la carte 🍴 3.00 – **19 rm** ⊒ 35.00/45.00 **t.** – SB (weekends only) (11 October-5 April) 98.00/115.00 **st.**

🏠 **Lundin Links**, Emsdorf St., KY8 6AP, 🖉 320207, 🐾 – 📺 ⌂wc ｜wc 🅿 🖎 Æ ◑ 𝘝𝘐𝘚𝘈
M 5.75/8.45 **t.** and a la carte 🍴 2.65 – **18 rm** ⊒ 23.50/36.50 **t.** – SB 47.00/53.00 **st.**

AUSTIN-ROVER The Promenade 🖉 23449   FIAT Scoonie Rd 🖉 27003

LEWIS (Isle of) Ross and Cromarty (Outer Hebrides) (Western Isles) **401** Z 8 **Scotland G.**
See : Callanish Standing Stones★★ – Carloway Broch★.
🚢 by Caledonian MacBrayne : from Stornoway to Ullapool Monday/Saturday 1-2 daily (3 h 30 mn).

Stornoway – pop. 8 ,660 – ECD : Wednesday – ✉ 🕿 0851 Stornoway.
✈ Stornoway Airport : 🖉 2256, Telex 75495, E : 2 ½ m. – **Terminal : British Airways**, Cromwell St.
🛈 Area Tourist Officer, 4 South Beach St. 🖉 3088.
🏠 **Royal**, Cromwell St., PA87 2DG, 🖉 2109 – 🖎 𝘝𝘐𝘚𝘈 🛳
M 2.10/8.00 **t.** and a la carte 🍴 3.00 – **22 rm** ⊒ 14.00/28.00 **st.**

AUSTIN-ROVER 11-16 Bayhead St. 🖉 3246   VAUXHALL-OPEL Bayhead St. 🖉 2888
FORD 80 Keith St. 🖉 3225   VW, AUDI Sandwick Rd 🖉 2956

LEWISTON Inverness. (Highland) **401** G 12 – 🕿 045 62 Drumnadrochit.
See : Loch Ness★★.
◆Edinburgh 173 – ◆Inverness 17.
🏠 **Lewiston Arms**, IV3 6UN, 🖉 225, 🐾 – 🅿 𝘝𝘐𝘚𝘈
M (bar lunch)/dinner a la carte approx 9.25 **t.** 🍴 3.00 – **8 rm** ⊒ 16.00/24.00 **t.**

LISMORE (Isle of) Argyll. (Strathclyde) **401** D 14 – pop. 156.
🚢 by Caledonian MacBrayne : from Achnacroish to Oban Monday/Saturday 2-3 daily (1 h).
🚤 to Port Appin Monday-Saturday 7 daily ; Sunday 2 daily (10 mn).
Hotels see : Oban.

LOCHALINE Argyll. (Highland) **401** C 14.
🚢 by Caledonian MacBrayne : to Fishnish (Isle of Mull) May-October Monday/Saturday 13-17 daily (15 mn).
🚤 by Caledonian MacBrayne : to Tobermory (Isle of Mull) May-September 2 weekly (1 h) – to Arinagour (Isle of Coll) May-September 2 weekly (2 h 30 mn) – to Isle of Tiree (via Coll and Tobermory) May-September 2 weekly (3 h 55 mn) – to Oban May-September 2 weekly (1 h 10 mn).
◆Edinburgh 129 – ◆Inverness 109 – Kyle of Lochalsh 116 – ◆Oban 6.
Hotels see : Mull (Isle of).

LOCHBOISDALE Inverness. (Western Isles) **401** Y 12 – Shipping Services : see Uist (South) (Isles of).

LOCHCARRON Ross and Cromarty (Highland) **401** D 11 **Scotland G** – ECD : Thursday – 🕿 052 02.
Envir. : Plockton★ S : 17 m. by A 896 and A 890.
◆Edinburgh 221 – ◆Inverness 65 – Kyle of Lochalsh 23.
🏠 **Lochcarron**, IV54 8YS, 🖉 226, ≤ Loch Carron – ⌂wc 🅿 🖎 𝘝𝘐𝘚𝘈
M (closed Sunday lunch) (bar lunch)/dinner 9.50 **t.** and a la carte 🍴 1.85 – **7 rm** ⊒ 15.00/34.00 **t.** – SB 44.00/50.00 **st.**

LOCHEARNHEAD Perth. (Central) 🗺 H 14 – ECD : Wednesday – ✆ 056 73.
♦Edinburgh 65 – ♦Glasgow 56 – ♦Oban 57 – Perth 36.

⌂ **Mansewood Country House,** FK19 8NS, S : ½ m. on A 84 ℰ 213, 🚗 – ➰wc 🅿
March-October – **6 rm** ⌸ 23.00/27.00 **st.**

LOCHGAIR Argyll. (Strathclyde) 🗺 D 15 – ✆ 0546 Minard.
♦Edinburgh 122 – ♦Glasgow 76 – ♦Oban 46.

🏛 **Lochgair,** PA31 8SA, on A 83 ℰ 86333, 🎣, 🚗 – ➰wc 🅿. 🌳
M 11.00 **t.** and a la carte ⌸ 2.70 – **10 rm** ⌸ 13.00/34.10 **t.**

LOCHGILPHEAD Argyll. (Strathclyde) 🗺 D 15 – pop. 2 ,391 – ECD : Tuesday – ✆ 0546.
🛈 Lochnell St. ℰ 2344 (summer only).
♦Edinburgh 130 – ♦Glasgow 84 – ♦Oban 38.

🏛 **Stag,** Argyll St., PA31 8NE, ℰ 2496 – 📺 ➰wc ➰wc ☎. 💳
M (bar lunch)/dinner a la carte 5.60/8.50 **t.** – **21 rm** ⌸ 17.50/35.00 **t.**

LOCH HARRAY Orkney (Orkney Islands) 🗺 K 6 – see Orkney Islands (Mainland).

LOCHINVER Sutherland (Highland) 🗺 E 9 – ECD : Tuesday – ✉ Lairg – ✆ 057 14.
🛈 ℰ 330 (summer only).
♦Edinburgh 251 – ♦Inverness 95 – ♦Wick 105.

🏨 **Culag** (Best Western), IV27 4LF, ℰ 209, ≼, 🎣, 🚗 – 🛗 ➰wc 🅿. 🔼 🅰🅴 ⓞ 💳
May-mid October – **M** (bar lunch Monday to Saturday)/dinner 11.50 **t.** and a la carte ⌸ 3.50 –
43 rm ⌸ 21.50/50.00 **t.**

⌂ **Ardglas** 🦌, IV27 4LI, ℰ 257, ≼ Loch Inver – 🅿
closed December – **8 rm** ⌸ 13.00/18.00 **st.**

LOCHMADDY Inverness. (Outer Hebrides) (Western Isles) 🗺 Y 11 – see Uist (North) (Isles of).

LOCHRANZA Bute. (Strathclyde) 🗺 🗺 E 16 – Shipping Services : see Arran (Isle of).

LOCKERBIE Dumfries. (Dumfries and Galloway) 🗺 🗺 J 18 – pop. 3 ,545 – ECD : Tuesday –
✆ 057 62.
🛈 Corrie Rd ℰ 2463.
♦Edinburgh 74 – ♦Carlisle 27 – ♦Dumfries 13 – ♦Glasgow 73.

🏛 **Dryfesdale** 🦌, Dryfe Rd, DG11 2JF, NW : 1 m. off A 74 ℰ 2427, ≼, 🚗 – 📺 ➰wc 🚬 🅿.
🔼 🅰🅴 ⓞ 💳
closed 25 December-first week January – **M** a la carte 9.00/11.60 **st.** ⌸ 2.95 – **11 rm**
⌸ 16.50/38.00 **st.** – SB (weekends only)(October-April) 44.00/52.00 **st.**

FORD Carlisle Rd ℰ 3240

LOSSIEMOUTH Moray. (Grampian) 🗺 K 10 – pop. 6 ,650 – ECD : Thursday – ✆ 034 381.
🛈₈, 🛈₈ Stotfield Rd, Moray ℰ 2018.
♦Edinburgh 203 – ♦Aberdeen 73 – Fraserburgh 66 – ♦Inverness 44.

Hotels see : Fochabers SE : 14 ½ m.

LUING (Isle of) Argyll. (Strathclyde) 🗺 D 15 – pop. 183.
🚢 to Isle of Seil (Strathclyde Regional Council) frequent sailings daily (5 mn).

Cullipool – ✉ Oban – ✆ 085 24 Luing :
✕ **Longhouse Buttery,** PA34 4TX, ℰ 209, ≼ – 🅿
Mid May-mid October – **M** (closed Sunday) a la carte 3.20/8.20 **t.** ⌸ 3.45.

LUNDIN LINKS Fife. (Fife) 🗺 L 15 – see Leven.

MACDUFF Banff. (Grampian) 🗺 M 10 – pop. 3 ,893 – ECD : Wednesday – ✆ 0261.
🛈₈ Royal Tarlair ℰ 32897.
♦ Edinburgh 176 – ♦ Aberdeen 46 – Fraserburgh 24 – ♦ Inverness 76.

🏠 **Deveron House,** 27-29 Union Rd, AB4 1UD, ℰ 32309 – 📺 ➰wc ➰wc 🅿. 🎿. 🔼 🅰🅴 ⓞ 💳
M (bar lunch Monday to Saturday)/dinner 9.50 **t.** and a la carte ⌸ 3.50 – **17 rm** ⌸ 16.00/39.00 **t.**
– SB 39.00/46.00 **st.**

MAINLAND Orkney (Orkney Islands) 🗺 KL 6 – see Orkney Islands.

MAINLAND Shetland (Shetland Islands) 🗺 PQ 3 – see Shetland Islands.

532

MALLAIG Inverness. (Highland) **401** C 12 – pop. 998 – ECD : Wednesday – ✆ 0687.

See : Site★.

Envir. : Silver Sands of Morar★, S : by A 830 – Arisaig, S : 9 m. by A 830.

🚢 by Caledonian MacBrayne : to Armadale (Isle of Skye) summer only Monday/Saturday 3-6 daily (30 mn).

🚢 by Caledonian MacBrayne : to Isles of Eigg, Muck, Rhum, Canna, return Mallaig Monday/Saturday 2-3 weekly (7 h) – to Kyle of Lochalsh summer only 3 weekly (2 h) – to Armadale (Isle of Skye) summer only 2 weekly (30 mn).

🚺 Station Buildings ✆ 2170 (summer only).

◆Edinburgh 179 – ◆ Inverness 110 – ◆Oban 96.

> 🏨 **Marine,** 10 Station Rd, PH41 4PY, ✆ 2217 – 🛁wc. 🗚
> **M** (bar lunch)/dinner 8.00 **st.** – **21 rm** ⤶ 18.00/36.00 **st.**

MEIGLE Perth. (Tayside) **401** K 14 – ✆ 082 84.

◆Edinburgh 62 – ◆Dundee 13 – Perth 18.

> 🏨 **Kings of Kinloch** ⤏, Coupar Angus Rd, PH12 8QX, W : 1 m. on A 94 ✆ 273, ≼, 🛋 – 🅿.
> 🔼. 🛇
> closed January – **M** (closed Sunday dinner) 12.50/16.60 **t.** and a la carte ⬩ 3.40 – **7 rm**
> ⤶ 22.00/42.00 **t.**

MELROSE Roxburgh. (Borders) **401** **402** L 17 **Scotland G** – pop. 2 ,143 – ECD : Thursday – ✆ 089 682.

See : Site★ – Abbey★★ (Decorative sculpture★★★).

Envir. : Eildon Hill North (🛆★★★) – Scott's View★★ – Abbotsford★★, W : 4 m. by A 6091 – Dryburgh Abbey★★★ (setting★★★) SE : 4 m. by A 6091.

🛇 Dingleton ✆ 2855, South boundary.

🚺 Priorwood Gdns, near Abbey ✆ 2555 (summer only).

◆Edinburgh 38 – Hawick 19 – ◆Newcastle-upon-Tyne 70.

> 🏨 **Burts,** Market Sq., TD6 9PN, ✆ 2285, 🛋 – 📺 🛁wc 🕸wc 🅿. 🔼 🗚 ⓞ 🆅🆂🅰
> **M** 9.00 **t.** (lunch) and a la carte 9.25/14.75 **t.** ⬩ 2.80 – **22 rm** ⤶ 17.00/38.00 **t.** – SB (November-May) 46.00/50.00 **st.**

AUSTIN-ROVER Palma Pl. ✆ 2048

MILLPORT Bute. (Strathclyde) **401** **402** F 16 – Shipping Services : see Great Cumbrae Island.

MILNGAVIE Dunbarton. (Strathclyde) **401** H 16 – pop. 12 ,030 – ECD : Tuesday and Saturday – ✉ ✆ 041 Glasgow.

🛇 Dougalston ✆ 956 5750.

◆Edinburgh 53 – ◆Glasgow 7.

> 🏨 **Black Bull Thistle** (Thistle), Main St., G62 6BH, ✆ 956 2291, Telex 778323 – 📺 🛁wc 🕸wc
> 🍽 🅿. ⬛. 🔼 🗚 ⓞ 🆅🆂🅰
> **M** 11.00 **t.** and a la carte ⬩ 3.25 – ⤶ 4.25 – **27 rm** 38.00/50.00 **t.**

AUSTIN-ROVER Main St. ✆ 956 2255   VAUXHALL-OPEL Glasgow Rd ✆ 956 1126

MOFFAT Dumfries. (Dumfries and Galloway) **401** **402** J 17 **Scotland G** – pop. 1 ,990 – ECD : Wednesday – ✆ 0683.

Envir. : Grey Mare's Tail★★.

🚺 Church Gate ✆ 20620 (summer only).

◆Edinburgh 61 – ◆Dumfries 22 – ◆Carlisle 43 – ◆Glasgow 60.

> 🏨 **Ladbroke Mercury Motor Inn** (Ladbroke), Church St., DG10 9EL, ✆ 20464 – 📺 🛁wc 🅿
> **51 rm**

> 🏨 **Beechwood Country House** ⤏, up Harthope Pl., off Academy Rd, DG10 9RS, ✆ 20210,
> 🛋 – 🛁wc 🕸wc 🍽 🅿. 🔼 🗚 ⓞ 🆅🆂🅰. 🛇
> closed January – **M** (bar lunch)/dinner 11.50 **t.** ⬩ 2.50 – **8 rm** ⤶ 19.00/45.00 **t.** – SB
> 53.00/61.00 **st.**

> 🏨 **Moffat House,** High St., DG10 9HL, ✆ 20039, 🛋 – 🛁wc 🕸wc 🅿. 🔼 🗚 ⓞ 🆅🆂🅰
> Mid March-mid November – **M** 5.65/9.50 **t.** ⬩ 3.40 – **14 rm** ⤶ 22.00/39.00 **t.**

> 🏠 **Hartfell House,** Hartfell Cres., DG10 9AL, ✆ 20153, 🛋 – 🅿
> March-October – **9 rm** ⤶ 9.50/23.80 **t.**

> 🏠 **Arden House,** High St., DG10 9HG, ✆ 20220 – 🕸wc 🅿
> March-October – **8 rm** ⤶ 8.50/19.00 **st.**

L'EUROPE en une seule feuille
Carte Michelin n° 920

MONTROSE Angus (Tayside) **401** M 13 Scotland G – pop. 12 ,127 – ECD : Wednesday – ✆ 0674.
Envir. : Brechin (Round Tower★) W : 7 m. by A 935 – Aberlemno Stones★ (summer only) W : 13 m.
by A 935 and B 9134 – Glen Esk★ (via Brechin and Edzell) 29 m. by A 935, B 9667, B 966, B 974 and A
937 – Cairn O'Mount Road★ (≤★★) N : 20 m. by A 937 and B 974.

🛆 Medal and Broomfield, East Links Rd ℰ 72634, E : 1 m. off A 92.

🛈 212 High St ℰ 72000.

♦Edinburgh 92 – ♦Aberdeen 39 – ♦Dundee 29.

🏛 **Park,** John St., DD10 8RJ, ℰ 73415, Telex 76367, 🌳 – 📺 ⊟wc 🛗wc 📶 📭 🕿 ⚕. 🔄 🔤 ⓞ
VISA
M 5.50/7.40 **t.** and a la carte 🍸 2.90 – **59 rm** ⊠ 22.00/44.00 **st.**, **1 suite** 33.00/66.00 **st.** – SB
(weekends only) 38.50/48.00 **st.**

AUSTIN-ROVER, FORD Craigo ℰ 067 483 (Hillside)   NISSAN New Wynd ℰ 3606
374/5

MUCK (Isle of) Inverness. (Highland) **401** B 13 – Shipping Services : see Mallaig.

MUIR OF ORD Ross and Cromarty (Highland) **401** G 11 – pop. 1 ,707 – ECD : Thursday – ✆ 0463.
🛆 ℰ 870825.

🛈 ℰ 870433 and 870525.

♦Edinburgh 169 – ♦Inverness 13 – ♦Wick 123.

🏛 **Ord House** 🦢, IV6 7UH, off A 832 ℰ 870492, ≤, « Country house atmosphere », 🔦, 🌳,
park – ⊟wc 📭
April-October – **M** (bar lunch)/dinner 10.00 **t.** 🍸 2.00 – **14 rm** ⊠ 16.00/36.00 **t.**

MULL (Isle of) Argyll. (Strathclyde) **401** C 14 Scotland G – pop. 2 ,605.
See : Site★ – Calgary Bay★★ – Isle of Iona★ – Torosay Castle (Gardens★-≤★).

🚢 by Caledonian MacBrayne : from Craignure to Oban summer 4-6 daily, winter Monday/Satur-
day 1 daily (45 mn) – from Fishnish to Lochaline May-October Monday-Saturday 13-17 daily (15 mn).

🚢 by Caledonian MacBrayne : from Fionnphort to Isle of Iona frequent services daily in summer,
restricted service in winter (5 mn) – from Tobermory to Kilchoan summer only Monday/Saturday
3-5 daily (35 mn) – from Tobermory to Arinagour (Isle of Coll) 3 weekly (1 h 30 mn) – from Tobermory
to Isle of Tiree 3 weekly (2 h 45 mn) – from Tobermory to Lochaline May-September 2 weekly (1 h)
– from Tobermory to Oban 3 weekly (2 h direct).

🛈 48 Main St. at Tobermory ℰ 0688 (Tobermory) 2182.

Bunessan – ECD : Wednesday – ✉ Bunessan – ✆ 068 17 Fionnphort :

🏛 **Ardfenaig House** 🦢, PA67 6DX, W : 3 m. by A 849 ℰ 210, ≤, « Country house atmosphere », 🌳, park – 📭
May-September – **M** *(closed Sunday dinner to non-residents)* (dinner only) (booking essential)
14.00 **st.** 🍸 2.00 – **5 rm** ⊠ (dinner included) 40.00/80.00 **st.**

Dervaig – ✉ Tobermory – ✆ 068 84 Dervaig.

🏛 **Druimnacroish** 🦢, PA75 6QW, SE : 2 m. by B 8073 ℰ 274, ≤ Bellart Glen, « Converted
steading », 🌳 – 📺 ⊟wc 🍴 📭 🔄 🔤 ⓞ **VISA**
May-October – **M** (dinner only) (booking essential) 15.00 **st.** 🍸 4.50 – **7 rm** ⊠ 32.00/64.00 **st.**

Tiroran – ✉ ✆ 068 15 Tiroran.

🏛 **Tiroran House** 🦢, PA69 6ES, ℰ 232, ≤, « Country house atmosphere », 🌳, park – ⊟wc
📭
May-6 October – **M** (booking essential)(lunch, residents only) 6.60/17.00 **st.** 🍸 2.50 – **9 rm**
⊠ 33.00/84.00 **st.**

Tobermory – pop. 843 – ECD : Wednesday – ✉ ✆ 0688 Tobermory.
🛆 Western Isles ℰ 2381.

🛈 48 Main St. ℰ 2182 (summer only).

🏛 **Tobermory,** 53 Main St., PA75 6NT, ℰ 2091, ≤
April-October – **M** *(closed Sunday lunch)* (buffet lunch)/dinner 7.00 **t.** (booking essential) –
15 rm ⊠ 13.75/47.00 **st.**

⌂ Linndhu House 🦢, PA75 6QB, SE : 1 ½ m. on A 848 ℰ 2425, ≤, 🌳, park – 📭 – **6 rm**.

⌂ **Suidhe,** 59 Main St., PA75 6NT, ℰ 2209, ≤ – 🍴
Mid March-October – **9 rm** ⊠ 12.00/31.00 **t.**

NAIRN Nairn. (Highland) **401** I 11 Scotland G – pop. 7 ,366 – ECD : Wednesday – ✆ 0667.
Envir. : Cawdor Castle★, S : 7 m. by A 9090 – Brodie Castle★, E : 2 m. – Forres (Sueno's Stone★★)
E : 11 m. by A 96 and B 9011.

🛆.🛆 Seabank Rd ℰ 52103 – 🛆 Nairn Dunbar, Lochloy Rd ℰ 52741.

🛈 62 King St. ℰ 52753 (summer only).

♦Edinburgh 172 – ♦Aberdeen 91 – ♦Inverness 16.

🏨 **Newton** ⤵, Inverness Rd, IV12 4RX, off A 96 ℰ 53144, ≼, « Country house in extensive grounds », 🐴, park, ✗ – 🛊 📺 🅿. 🛆. 🔼 🆎 ⓞ 𝓥𝓘𝓢𝓐
M 7.00/13.50 t. 🍴 3.80 – **44 rm** ⤭ 35.50/62.00 t. – SB 50.00/70.00 st.

🏨 **Golf View,** Seabank Rd, IV12 4HD, ℰ 52301, ≼, 🌊 heated, 🐴, ✗ – 🛊 📺 🅿. 🛆. 🔼 🆎 ⓞ 𝓥𝓘𝓢𝓐
M 6.00/14.00 t. and a la carte 🍴 2.95 – **55 rm** ⤭ 32.00/64.00 t. – SB (except Bank Holidays) 58.00/74.00 st.

🏠 **Clifton** ⤵, Viewfield St., IV12 4HW, ℰ 53119, ≼, « Tasteful decor », 🐴 – 🚪wc 🅿. 🔼 🆎 ⓞ 𝓥𝓘𝓢𝓐
April-October – **M** (booking essential) a la carte 9.05/13.25 t. – **16 rm** ⤭ 28.00/56.00 t.

🏠 **Carnach Country House** ⤵, Inverness Rd, IV12 5NT, W : 2 m. on A 96 ℰ 52094, ≼, 🐴 – 🚪wc 🅿. 🔼 𝓥𝓘𝓢𝓐. ✗
M (bar lunch, residents only)/dinner 8.50 t. 🍴 1.80 – **8 rm** ⤭ 22.00/40.00 t. – SB 40.00/50.00 st.

AUSTIN-ROVER King St. ℰ 52304.   TALBOT Inverness Rd ℰ 52335

NETHERLEY Kincardine (Grampian) 🗺 N 12 – see Stonehaven.

NEWBURGH Aberdeen. (Grampian) 🗺 N 12 – ✆ 035 86.

◆Edinburgh 144 – ◆Aberdeen 14 – Fraserburgh 33.

🏠 **Udny Arms,** Main St., AB4 0BL, ℰ 444 – 📺 🚪wc 🝠wc ☎ 🅿. 🔼 𝓥𝓘𝓢𝓐
M a la carte lunch/dinner 14.50 t. – ⤭ 4.00 – **25 rm** 30.00/40.00 t. – SB (weekends only) 63.00/67.00 st.

NEW GALLOWAY Kirkcudbright (Dumfries and Galloway) 🗺 🗺 H 18 – pop. 290 – ✆ 064 42.

◆Edinburgh 88 – ◆Ayr 36 – Dumfries 25.

🏠 **Leamington,** High St., DG7 3RN, ℰ 327 – ✗
Easter-mid October – **9 rm** ⤭ 11.00/25.00 t.

NEW SCONE Perth. (Tayside) 🗺 J 14 – see Perth.

NEWTONMORE Inverness. (Highland) 🗺 H 12 – pop. 1,010 – ECD : Wednesday – ✆ 054 03.
🔢 Golf Course Rd ℰ 328.
🛈 ℰ 274 (summer only).
◆Edinburgh 113 – ◆Inverness 43 – Perth 69.

🏠 **Ard-na-Coille,** Kingussie Rd, PH20 1AY, ℰ 214, ≼, 🐴 – 🝠wc 🅿
closed November and December – **M** (dinner only) 9.75 st. 🍴 2.25 – **10 rm** ⤭ 12.00/35.00 t.

🏠 **Coig-na-Shee,** Fort William Rd, PH20 1DG, ℰ 216, – 🅿
closed December and January – **6 rm** ⤭ 10.00/23.00 st.

✗ **Gables** with rm, Main St., ℰ 231 – **3 rm**.

NEWTON STEWART Wigtown. (Dumfries and Galloway) 🗺 🗺 G 19 – pop. 3,212 – ECD : Wednesday – ✆ 0671.

Envir. : Galloway Forest Park ✶, N – Queen's Way✶ (Newton Stewart to New Galloway) 19 m. by A 712.

🛈 Dashwood Sq. ℰ 2431 (summer only).

◆Edinburgh 131 – ◆Dumfries 51 – ◆Glasgow 87 – Stranraer 24.

🏨 **Kirroughtree** ⤵, DG8 6AN, NE : 1 ½ m. on A 712 ℰ 2141, ≼ woodland and river Cree, « Country house and gardens », park – 📺 ☎ 🅿. ✗
March-mid November – **M** (lunch by arrangement)/dinner 18.00 st. 🍴 3.50 – **22 rm** ⤭ 30.00/60.00 t. – SB (spring and autumn) 76.00/88.00 st.

🏛 **Creebridge House** ⤵, Minnigaff, DG8 6NP, ℰ 2121, 🐴 – 📺 🚪wc 🅿. 🔼 ⓞ 𝓥𝓘𝓢𝓐
accomodation closed 20 December-6 January – **M** (bar lunch)/dinner 11.50 t. and a la carte 🍴 2.65 – **17 rm** ⤭ 15.50/48.00 st. – SB (weekends only)(October-early June) 48.60/58.00 st.

🏠 **Bruce,** 88 Queen St., DG8 6JL, ℰ 2294 – 📺 🚪wc 🍸 🅿. 🔼 🆎 ⓞ 𝓥𝓘𝓢𝓐
closed December and January – **M** 5.00/11.00 st. 🍴 2.60 – **17 rm** ⤭ 22.50/41.00 – SB (October-May) 56.00 st.

🏠 **Crown,** 101 Queen St., DG8 6GW, ℰ 2727 – 🚪wc 🅿. 🔼 𝓥𝓘𝓢𝓐. ✗
M (bar lunch)/dinner 9.00 st. – **10 rm** ⤭ 14.00/32.00 st. – SB 41.00/49.80 st.

FORD Queen St. ℰ 2112   VOLVO Minnigaff ℰ 3101
RENAULT Duncan Park, Wigtown ℰ 098 84 (Wigtown) 3287

NEWTON WAMPHRAY Dumfries. (Dumfries and Galloway) 🗺 🗺 J 18 – ECD : Wednesday – ✉ Moffat – ✆ 057 64 Johnstone Bridge.

◆Edinburgh 64 – ◆Carlisle 36 – ◆Dumfries 22 – ◆Glasgow 63.

🏠 **Red House,** DG10 9NF, off A 74 ℰ 214, ≼, 🐴 – 🅿. ⓞ
Easter-15 November – **M** (residents only)(bar lunch)/dinner 7.00 t. – **6 rm** ⤭ 14.10/28.20 t.

NORTH BERWICK E. Lothian (Lothian) **401** L 15 **Scotland** G – pop. 4 ,861 – ECD : Thursday –
🕾 0620.

Envir. : Tantallon Castle★★ (Site★★★) E : 3 m. by A 198 – Tyninghame★, S : 6 m. by A 198 – Preston
Mill★, S : 8 m. by A 198 and B 1407 – Museum of Flight★, S : 10 m. by A 198 and B 1407.

🏌 New Clubhouse, Beach Rd ✆ 2135 – 🛈 Quality St. ✆ 2197.

♦Edinburgh 24 – ♦Newcastle-upon-Tyne 102.

🏨 **Marine** (T.H.F.), Cromwell Rd, EH39 4LZ, ✆ 2406, ≼, 🛴 heated, 🐾, ✵, squash – 🛗 📺 ⓟ.
🔺 🗚 🖭 ⓞ 𝚅𝙸𝚂𝙰
M (buffet lunch)/dinner 12.50 **st.** ⒜ 2.70 – ☲ 5.50 – **86 rm** 32.00/49.50 st., **1 suite**.

🏠 **Nether Abbey,** 20 Dirleton Av., EH39 4BQ, ✆ 2802, 🐾 – ⇌wc 🕽wc ⓟ. 🗚 𝚅𝙸𝚂𝙰
April-October – **M** (bar lunch)/dinner 10.50 **t.** ⒜ 3.50 – **16 rm** ☲ 14.00/31.50 t.

🏠 **Blenheim House,** 14 Westgate, EH39 4AF, ✆ 2385, ≼ – 📺 ⇌wc ⓟ
M 5.50/9.00 t. and a la carte ⒜ 3.50 – **11 rm** ☲ 15.00/36.00 t.

🏠 **Point Garry,** 20 West Bay Rd, EH39 4AW, ✆ 2380 – ⇌wc 🕽wc ⓟ
April-October – **M** (bar lunch)/dinner 7.50 **t.** and a la carte ⒜ 2.50 – **15 rm** ☲ 18.75/38.00 t.

FORD 52 Dunbar Rd ✆ 2232

NORTH RONALDSAY (Isle of) Orkney (Orkney Islands) **401** M 5 – Shipping Services : see
Orkney Islands (Mainland : Kirkwall).

OBAN Argyll. (Strathclyde) **401** D 14 **Scotland** G – pop. 7 ,476 – ECD : Thursday – 🕾 0631.

See : Site★ – **Envir. :** Loch Awe★★ – Inveraray★★(Castle★★-Interior★★★) – Loch Fyne★★ – Bonawe
Furnace★ – Cruachan Power Station★ – Auchindrain★ – Crinan★, 83 m. by A 85, A 819, A 83 and
A 816 – Sea Life Centre★, N : 11 m. off A 828 – 🏌 Glencruitten ✆ 62868, E : 1 m.

Access to Glasgow bv helicopter.

🚢 by Caledonian MacBrayne : to Craignure (Isle of Mull) summer 4-6 daily ; winter Mon-
day/Saturday 1 daily (45 mn) – to Castlebay (Isle of Barra) 1-2 weekly (5 h to 8 h) – to Lochboisdale
(South Uist) 3-6 weekly (6 h direct ; 8 h via Castlebay) – to Arinagour (Isle of Coll) 3-4 weekly (3 h
15 mn to 5 h 45 mn) – to Isle of Tiree 3-4 weekly (4 to 5 h) – to Scalasaig (Isle of Colonsay) 3 weekly
(2 h 30 mn) – to Achnacroish (Isle of Lismore) Monday/Saturday 2-3 daily (1 h).

🚢 to Tobermory (Isle of Mull) 3 weekly (1 h 45 mn to 2 h 15 mn) – to Lochaline May to September
2 weekly (1 h 10 mn).

🛈 Argyll Sq. ✆ 63122.

♦Edinburgh 123 – ♦Dundee 116 – ♦Glasgow 93 – ♦Inverness 118.

🏨 **Alexandra,** Corran Esplanade, PA34 5AA, ✆ 62381, Telex 778215, ≼ – 🛗 📺 ⇌wc ⓟ. 🗚 🖭
ⓞ 𝚅𝙸𝚂𝙰
April-October – **M** (bar lunch)/dinner 10.00 **t.** ⒜ 3.00 – **56 rm** ☲ 32.00/54.00 st.

🏨 **Great Western,** Corran Esplanade, PA34 5PP, ✆ 63101, Group Telex 778215, ≼ – 🛗 📺
⇌wc ⓟ. 🔓 🔺 🗚 🖭 ⓞ 𝚅𝙸𝚂𝙰
M (bar lunch)/dinner 10.00 **t.** ⒜ 2.90 – **76 rm** ☲ 32.00/54.00 t.

🏠 **Soroba House,** Soroba Rd, PA34 4SB, S : 1 ¼ m. on A 816 ✆ 62628, 🐾, ✵ – 📺 ⇌wc ⓟ.
🔺 ⓞ 𝚅𝙸𝚂𝙰
M 5.20/8.10 t. and a la carte ⒜ 3.00 – ☲ 3.50 – **16 rm** 18.00/36.00, **14 suites** 30.00/38.00.

🏠 **Manor House,** Gallanach Rd, PA34 4LS, ✆ 62087, ≼ – ⇌wc 🕽wc ⓟ. 🔺 ⓞ 𝚅𝙸𝚂𝙰
closed 1 and 2 January – **M** (bar lunch)/dinner 10.30 **t.** and a la carte ⒜ 2.75 – **11 rm**
☲ 35.00/44.00 t.

🏠 **Rowan Tree,** George St., PA34 5NX, ✆ 62954 – 📺 ⇌wc ⓟ. 🔺 🗚 ⓞ 𝚅𝙸𝚂𝙰
M 3.50/9.50 st. ⒜ 2.60 – **24 rm** ☲ 24.50/43.00 st.

↑ **Corriemar,** PA34 5AQ, ✆ 62476, ≼ – ⇌wc 🕽wc ⓟ
Easter-mid October – **16 rm** ☲ 13.50/33.00 t.

at Lerags S : 3 m. by A 816 – ✉ 🕾 0631 Oban :

↑ **Foxholes** 🦢, PA34 4SE, ✆ 64982, ≼, 🐾 – 📺 ⇌wc ⓟ
April-October – **7 rm** ☲ (dinner included) 32.50/50.00 t.

at Kilninver SW : 8 m. on A 816 – ✉ Oban – 🕾 085 26 Kilninver :

🏨 **Knipoch,** PA34 4QT, NE : 1 ½ m. on A 816 ✆ 251, ≼, « Tastefully furnished », 🐾 – 📺
⇌wc 🅿 🔺 🗚 ⓞ 𝚅𝙸𝚂𝙰. ✵
closed January – **M** (bar lunch)/dinner 22.50 **t.** ⒜ 3.00 – **19 rm** ☲ 42.00/84.00 t.

AUSTIN-ROVER Airds Pl. ✆ 63173   SUBARU Stevenson St. ✆ 66566
FORD Soroba Rd ✆ 63061   VOLVO, OPEL, BEDFORD Breadalbane Pl. ✆ 63066

OLDMELDRUM Aberdeen. (Grampian) **401** N 11 – pop. 1 ,343 – ECD : Wednesday – 🕾 065 12.
Envir. : Pitmedden Gardens★★, E : 5 m. by A 920 – Haddo House★, N : 9 m. by B 9170 and B 9005 –
Fyvie Castle, N : 8 m. by A 947 – 🏌.

♦Edinburgh 148 – ♦Aberdeen 18 – Fraserburgh 30 – ♦Inverness 89.

✵ **Meldrum House** 🦢 with rm, AB5 0AE, N : 1 ½ m. on A 947 ✆ 2294, ≼, 🏌, 🐾, park – 📺
⇌wc 🅿 🕽wc 🗚 ⓞ 𝚅𝙸𝚂𝙰
Mid March-mid December – **M** (closed Sunday dinner to non-residents) (bar lunch)/dinner
14.00 – **9 rm** ☲ 30.00/55.00 – SB (weekends only) 69.50/82.25 **st.**

536

ONICH Inverness. (Highland) **401** E 13 – ECD : Saturday except summer – ⊠ Fort William – 🕲 085 53.

◆Edinburgh 123 – ◆Glasgow 93 – ◆Inverness 79 – ◆Oban 39.

🏨 **The Lodge on the Loch**, Creag Dhu, PH33 6RY, on A 82 𝒫 238, ≼ Loch Linnhe and mountains, 🚗 – ⇌wc 🚽wc 🅿. 🔄 🆎 ⓪ 𝑽𝑰𝑺𝑨
23 March-October – **M** (bar lunch)/dinner 10.00 **t.** and a la carte 🍷 3.50 – **20 rm** ⊐ 19.00/45.00 **st.**

🏨 **Onich,** PH33 6RY, on A 82 𝒫 214, ≼ Loch Linnhe and mountains, 🚗 – ⇌wc 🅿. 🔄 🆎 ⓪ 𝑽𝑰𝑺𝑨
M (bar lunch)/dinner 9.00 **t.** 🍷 3.00 – **24 rm** ⊐ 15.00/42.00 **t.** – SB (October-April)(except Easter and Christmas) 50.00/56.00 **st.**

⌂ **Cuilcheanna House** 🌮, PH33 6SD, 𝒫 226, ≼, 🚗 – 🅿
Easter-September – **8 rm** ⊐ 10.00/20.00 **t.**

*Wenn Sie an ein Hotel im Ausland schreiben,
fügen Sie Ihrem Brief einen internationalen Antwortschein bei
(im Postamt erhältlich).*

ORKNEY ISLANDS Orkney (Orkney Islands) **401** KL 6 and 7 **Scotland G** – pop. 19 ,040.

🛬 see Mainland : Kirkwall.

🚢 see Mainland : Kirkwall and Stromness – by Orkney Islands Shipping Co. : service between Longhope (Isle of Hoy), Lyness (Isle of Hoy), Flotta (Isle of), Houton, Graemsay (Isle of), Stromness and return, daily itinerary varies consult operator.

🚢 by Thomas & Bews : from Burwick (South Ronaldsay) to John O'Groats summer only 2-4 daily (45 mn).

HOY

Old Man of Hoy Scotland G.
See : Old Man of Hoy★★★ (sandstone stack).

MAINLAND

Birsay Scotland G – ⊠ 🕲 085 672 Birsay.
See : Brough of Birsay (site★★).

Kirkwall Scotland G – pop. 5 ,947 – ECD : Wednesday – ⊠ 🕲 0856 Kirkwall.
See : Site★★ – St. Magnus Cathedral★★★ – Earl's Palace★ – Tankerness House Museum★.
Envir. : Italian Chapel★ – Unston Cairn★ – Ring of Brodgar★ – Corrigall Farm Museum★.
🌐 Grainbank 𝒫 2457, W : 1 m.
🛬 Kirkwall Airport : 𝒫 2421, Telex 75473, S : 3 ½ m.
🚢 to Scalloway (Shetland Islands) via Westray summer 2 weekly; winter 1 fortnightly (9 h 30 mn).
🚢 by Orkney Islands Shipping Co. : to Westray via Eday, Stronsay, Sanday and Papa Westray 3 weekly (2 to 6 h) – to North Ronaldsay 1 weekly (2 h 30 mn) – to Wyre via Rousay and Egilsay 1 weekly (1 to 4 h) – to Shapinsay 9 weekly (25 mn).
🅿 Broad St. 𝒫 2856.

🏨 **Kirkwall,** Harbour St., KW15 1LF, 𝒫 2232, ≼ – 🛗 📺 ⇌wc 🚽wc ☎. 🔄 🆎 ⓪ 𝑽𝑰𝑺𝑨
M (bar lunch)/dinner 18.00 **st.** and a la carte 🍷 2.85 – **42 rm** ⊐ 20.00/38.00 **st.**

🏨 Ayre, Ayre Rd, KW15 1QX, 𝒫 2197 – ⇌wc 🚽 🅿. 🔄 𝑽𝑰𝑺𝑨
⊐ 2.90 – **31 rm** 14.50/33.00 **st.**

🏨 **Lynnfield** 🌮, Holm Rd, KW15 1BX, S : 1 ¼ m. on A 961 𝒫 2505, 🚗 – 📺 🚽 🅿. 🔄 𝑽𝑰𝑺𝑨
M (bar lunch)/dinner 12.00 **t.** and a la carte 🍷 3.00 – **7 rm** ⊐ 20.00/44.00 **t.** – SB (weekends only) 50.00/56.00 **st.**

⌂ **Bellavista,** Carness Rd, KW15 1TB, N : 1 m. via Cromwell Rd 𝒫 2306 – 🅿. ⚘
closed October – **8 rm** ⊐ 9.00/18.00 **s.**

XX **Foveran** 🌮 with rm, St. Ola, KW15 1SF, SW : 3 m. on A 964 𝒫 2389, ≼ Sea, « Tranquil setting on the banks of Scapa Flow » – ⇌wc 🚽wc 🅿. 🔄 𝑽𝑰𝑺𝑨
closed October – **M** (closed to non-residents Sunday and Monday) (bar lunch)/dinner a la carte 8.50/14.25 **t.** 🍷 2.90 – **8 rm** ⊐ 18.50/31.00 **t.**

AUSTIN-ROVER 25 Broad St. 𝒫 2785
COLT, TALBOT Gt Western Rd 𝒫 2805
FIAT Junction Rd 𝒫 2158

FORD Castle St. 𝒫 3212
RENAULT Gt Western Rd 𝒫 2601
VAUXHALL Burnmouth Rd 𝒫 2950

Loch Harray – ⊠ Loch Harray – 🕲 085 677 Harray.

🏨 **Merkister** 🌮, KW17 2LF, 𝒫 366, ≼, 🐟, 🚗 – 🚽wc 🅿
Mid April-mid October – **M** (bar lunch)/dinner 12.00 **t.** 🍷 2.50 – **16 rm** ⊐ 17.00/36.00 **t.**

Stromness Scotland G – pop. 1 ,816 – ECD : Thursday – ✉ ☻ 0856 Stromness.

See : Site★ – Pier Arts Centre (Collection of abstract art★).

Envir. : Old Man of Hoy★★★.

🏔 Ness ✆ 850593.

⛴ by P & O Ferries : Orkney and Shetland Services : to Scrabster Monday/Saturday 1-3 daily (2 h).

⛴ to Moaness (Isle of Hoy) 2-3 daily (25 mn).

🛈 Ferry Terminal Building, Pierhead ✆ 850716 (summer only).

🏨 Stromness, 108 Victoria St., KW16 3AA, ✆ 850298, 🚗 – 🛁 ⏢wc ⋔wc
39 rm.

OUT SKERRIES Shetland (Shetland Islands) 📖 R 2 – Shipping Services : see Shetland Islands (Mainland : Lerwick).

OYKEL BRIDGE Sutherland. (Highland) 📖 F 10 – ✉ Lairg – ☻ 054 984 Rosehall.

♦Edinburgh 222 – ♦Inverness 66 – Lochinver 33.

🏨 **Oykel Bridge** ♨, IV27 4HE, ✆ 218, ≼, ⤚, 🚗 – ⏢wc ℗
March-September – **M** (bar lunch)/dinner 13.00 **st.** ⫤ 3.80 – **16 rm** ⊑ 23.00/46.00 **st.**

PAISLEY Renfrew. (Strathclyde) 📖 📖 G 16 Scotland G – pop. 84 ,330 – ECD : Tuesday – ☻ 041 Glasgow.

See : Museum and Art gallery (Paisley Shawl Section★).

🏔 Barshaw Park ✆ 889 2908, E : 1 m. of Paisley Cross off A 737.

🛈 Town Hall, Abbey Close, ✆ 889 0711.

♦Edinburgh 53 – ♦Ayr 35 – ♦Glasgow 7.5 – Greenock 17.

🏨 **Stakis Watermill** (Stakis), Lonend, PA1 1SR, ✆ 889 3201 – 🛁 📺 ⏢wc ☏ ℗. 🔺 🆎 ⓪
VISA
M a la carte 6.80/12.35 **t.** ⫤ 2.90 – **51 rm** ⊑ 38.00/50.00 **t.**

🏨 **Rockfield,** 125 Renfrew Rd, PA3 4BL, ✆ 889 6182 – 📺 ⏢wc ⋔wc ☏ ℗. 🔺 ⓪ *VISA*
closed Christmas and New Year – **M** (bar lunch)/dinner 9.00 **t.** – **20 rm** ⊑ 27.75/33.25 **st.**

AUSTIN-ROVER 46 New Sneddon St. ✆ 889 7882
AUSTIN-ROVER 92 Glasgow Rd ✆ 889 8526
FIAT 4/8 Lochfield Rd ✆ 884 2281
FORD 37/41 Lonend ✆ 887 0191

HYUNDAI, SUBARU 11/17 Weir St. ✆ 889 6866
PEUGEOT, TALBOT 7 West St. ✆ 889 0011
VAUXHALL-OPEL 69 Espedair St. ✆ 889 5254

'' Short Breaks ''

Many hotels now offer a special rate for a stay of 2 nights which includes dinner, bed and breakfast.

PAPA WESTRAY (Isle of) Orkney (Orkney Islands) 📖 L 5 – Shipping Services : see Orkney Islands (Mainland : Kirkwall).

PEAT INN Fife. (Fife) 📖 L 15 – ✉ Cupar – ☻ 033 484.

♦Edinburgh 45 – Dundee 21 – Perth 28.

✗✗ **The Peat Inn,** KY15 5LH, ✆ 206 – ℗. 🆎 ⓪ *VISA*
closed Sunday, Monday, 1 week January, 1 week April and 1 week October – **M** (booking essential) 10.00/21.50 **st.** and a la carte ⫤ 4.00.

PEEBLES Peebles. (Borders) 📖 📖 K 17 – pop. 6 ,404 – ECD : Wednesday – ☻ 0721.

🏔 Kirkland St. ✆ 20197 – 🏔 West Linton ✆ 0968 (West Linton) 60589.

🛈 Chambers Institute, High St. ✆ 20138 (summer only).

♦Edinburgh 24 – Hawick 31 – ♦Glasgow 53.

🏨 **Peebles Hydro,** Innerleithen Rd, EH45 8LX, ✆ 20602, Telex 72568, ≼, 🔲, 🚗, park, ✗✗, squash – 🛁 📺 ☏ ℗. 🏛 🔺 🆎 ⓪ *VISA*. ✗
M 7.00/11.00 **st.** ⫤ 3.25 – **139 rm** ⊑ 33.00/73.00 **st.** – SB 60.00/89.00 **st.**

🏨 **Cringletie House** ♨, EH45 8PL, N : 3 m. on A 703 ✆ 072 13 (Eddleston) 233, ≼, « Country house in extensive grounds », 🚗, park, ✗ – 🛁 ⏢wc ℗
8 March-26 December – **M** (restricted lunch Monday to Saturday)/dinner 14.50 **t.** ⫤ 3.00 –
16 rm ⊑ 21.00/48.00 **t.** – SB (except summer) 64.00/70.00 **st.**

🏨 **Tontine** (T.H.F.), 39 High St., EH45 8AJ, ✆ 20892 – 📺 ⏢wc ☏ ℗. 🔺 🆎 ⓪ *VISA*
M (bar lunch Monday to Saturday)/dinner 9.00 **st.** and a la carte ⫤ 2.70 – ⊑ 5.50 – **37 rm** 32.00/43.00 **st.**

🏨 **Park** (Swallow), Innerleithen Rd, EH45 8BA, ✆ 20451, Group Telex 53168, 🚗 – 📺 ⏢wc ☏
℗. 🔺 🆎 ⓪ *VISA*
M (buffet lunch) dinner 9.75 **st.** and a la carte ⫤ 3.40 – **26 rm** ⊑ 28.00/45.00 **st.** – SB 55.00/60.00 **st.**

at Eddleston N : 4 ½ m. on A 703 – ⊠ Peebles – ✆ 072 13 Eddleston :

XX **Horse Shoe Inn,** EH45 8QP, ✆ 225 – **P**. 🄰 AE ⓪ VISA
closed 25 December and 1 January – **M** 12.45/9.75 **t.** and a la carte ⌕ 2.95.

AUSTIN-ROVER Innerleithen Rd ✆ 20627
LANCIA, SUZUKI George St. ✆ 20545

VAUXHALL-OPEL 104 Old Town ✆ 20886

En saison, *surtout dans les stations fréquentées, il est prudent de retenir à l'avance.*
Cependant, si vous ne pouvez pas occuper la chambre que vous avez retenue,
prévenez immédiatement l'hôtelier.
Si vous écrivez à un hôtel à l'étranger, joignez à votre lettre
un coupon-réponse international (disponible dans les bureaux de poste).

PERTH Perth. (Tayside) 𝟒𝟎𝟏 J 14 Scotland G – pop. 41 ,916 – ECD : Wednesday – ✆ 0738.

See : Black Watch Regimental Museum★ Y **M1** – Georgian terraces★ Y – Museum and Art Gallery★
Y **M2** – Branklyn Garden★ by A 85 Z – Kinnoull Hill (≤★) by Bowerswell Road Y.

Envir. : Scone Palace★★, N : 2 m. by A 93 Y – Huntingtower Castle★, NW : 3 m. by A 9 Y – Elcho
Castle★, SE : by A 912 Z – Abernethy Round Tower★, SE : 8 m. by A 912 Z and A 913 – Cairnwell
(❅★★) N : 40 m. by A 93 Y.

🖪 Craigie Hill, Cherrybank ✆ 24377, West boundary, by A 9 Z.

🛈 The Round House, Marshall Pl. ✆ 22900 and 27108.

♦Edinburgh 44 – ♦Aberdeen 86 – ♦Dundee 22 – Dunfermline 29 – ♦Glasgow 64 – ♦Inverness 112 – ♦Oban 94.

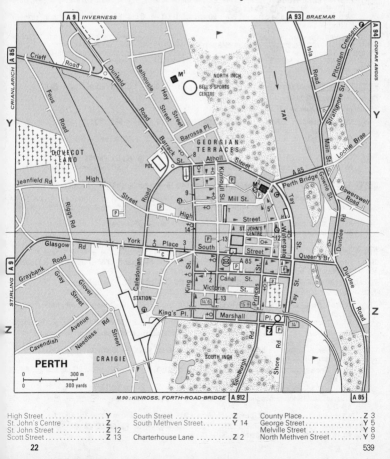

High Street	Y	South Street	Z	County Place	Z 3
St. John's Centre	Z	South Methven Street	Y 14	George Street	Y 5
St. John Street	Z 12			Melville Street	Y 8
Scott Street	Z 13	Charterhouse Lane	Z 2	North Methven Street	Y 9

🏨 **Royal George** (T.H.F.), Tay St., PH1 5LD, ℰ 24455 – 📺 ⇋wc 🏤 🅿 👶 🔼 AE ⓞ VISA
M (bar lunch)/dinner 10.00 st. and a la carte ᵢ 3.10 – ⇌ 5.50 – **43 rm** 32.00/48.00 st.　Y c

🏨 **Station**, Leonard St., PH2 8HE, ℰ 24141, Telex 76481, ℰ – 🛗 📺 ⇋wc ☎ 🅿 👶 🔼 AE ⓞ VISA
M 7.20 st. and a la carte – **70 rm** ⇌ 19.50/50.00 st., **2 suites**　Z n

🏨 **Stakis City Mills** (Stakis), West Mill St., PH1 5QP, ℰ 28281 – 📺 ⇋wc 🏤 🅿 👶 🔼 AE ⓞ VISA
M 4.50/7.50 t. ᵢ 1.50 – **78 rm** ⇌ 36.00/52.00 t., **1 suite**.　Y a

↑ **Pitcullen**, 17 Pitcullen Cresent, PH2 7HT, NE : ¾ m. on A 94 ℰ 26506 – 🅿
February-October – **6 rm** ⇌ 8.50/18.00 st.　Y r

XXX **Huntingtower** ⌂ with rm, Crieff Rd, PH1 3JT, W : 3 ½ m. on A 85 ℰ
073 883 (Almond Bank) 771, Telex 76204, ℰ, ℰ – 📺 ⇋wc ☎ 🅿 🔼 AE ⓞ VISA
closed January – **M** 8.00/12.00 t. and a la carte ᵢ 2.80 – **7 rm** ⇌ 30.00/45.00 t.　on A 85　Y

XX **Coach House,** 8 North Port, PH1 5LU, ℰ 27950 – 🔼 VISA　Y s
closed Sunday, Monday, and first 2 weeks January and first 2 weeks July – **M** 8.50/15.50 t.

X **Timothy's,** 24 St. John St., PH1 5SP, ℰ 26641, Smörrebrod – 🔼　Y e
closed Sunday, Monday and Bank Holidays – **M** a la carte 3.85/7.75 t.

at New Scone NE : 2 ½ m. on A 94 – Y – ✉ ✆ 0738 Perth :

🏨 **Balcraig House** ⌂, E : 1 ½ m. by A 94 ℰ 51123, ℰ, ℰ, park, ℅ – 📺 ⇋wc 🏤 🅿 🔼 AE
VISA
M (lunch by arrangement)/dinner 19.50 st. ᵢ 3.25 – **10 rm** ⇌ 42.50/85.00 st. – SB (weekends only) (November-March) 99.50 st.

🏨 **Murrayshall House** ⌂, PH2 7PH, E : 1 ½ m. by A 94 ℰ 51171, Telex 76197, ℰ, ℞, ℰ, park
– 📺 ⇋wc ▥wc ☎ 🅿 🔼 AE ⓞ VISA
M 5.55/8.50 t. and a la carte ᵢ 1.60 – **20 rm** ⇌ 31.00/44.00 t. – SB (November-March) (except Easter) 96.00 st.

AUSTIN-ROVER Glenearn Rd ℰ 20811
BMW, ROLLS ROYCE 50/56 Leonard St. ℰ 25481
CITROEN 60 South St. ℰ 23335
DATSUN, FIAT, LOTUS, MERCEDES-BENZ, SAAB
172 Dunkeld Rd ℰ 28211

FORD Riggs Rd ℰ 25121
VAUXHALL Dunkeld Rd ℰ 26241
VOLVO Arran Rd, North Muirton ℰ 22156
VW, AUDI Dunkeld Rd ℰ 25252

PETERHEAD Aberdeen. (Grampian) 401 O 11 – pop. 16,804 – ECD : Wednesday – ✆ 0779.
℞, ℞ Craigewan ℰ 2149.
♦Edinburgh 165 – ♦Aberdeen 35 – Fraserburgh 18.

🏨 **Waterside Inn,** 1 Fraserburgh Rd, AB4 7BN, NW : 2 m. on A 952 ℰ 71121, Telex 739413, ℰ
– 📺 🅿 👶 🔼 AE ⓞ VISA
M 5.00/12.00 st. and a la carte ᵢ 3.15 – **114 rm** ⇌ 21.00/45.00 st. – SB (weekends only) 45.00/55.00 st.

🏨 **Palace,** Prince St., AB4 6PL, ℰ 74821 – 🛗 📺 ⇋wc 🏤 🅿 🔼 AE ⓞ VISA
M 5.25/7.50 t. and a la carte ᵢ 3.20 – **93 rm** ⇌ 27.00/39.00 st. – SB (weekends only) 31.40 st.

PITCAPLE Aberdeen. (Grampian) 401 M 12 – ✆ 046 76 – ♦Edinburgh 151 – ♦Aberdeen 21.

🏨 **Pittodrie House** ⌂, AB5 9HS, SW : 1 ¾ m. off A 96 by Chapel of Gariock rd ℰ 202, Telex
739935, ℰ, « Country house with many antiques », park, ℅, squash – 📺 ⇋wc 🏤 ⇌
🅿 🔼 AE ⓞ VISA
M 12.00/20.00 st. ᵢ 3.00 – **12 rm** ⇌ 36.00/60.00 st. – SB (weekends only) (October-April) 80.00/120.00 st.

PITLOCHRY Perth. (Tayside) 401 I 13 Scotland G – pop. 2,194 – ECD : Thursday – ✆ 0796.
See : Site★ – Envir. : Blair Castle★★ and Blair Atholl (Falls of Bruar★) NW : 7 m. by A 9 – Queen's
View★★, NW : 6 m. by A 9 and B 8019.
℞ Estates Office ℰ 2117 – ℞ Blair Atholl ℰ 079 681 (Blair Atholl) 407.
🄱 22 Atholl Rd ℰ 2215 and 2751 – ♦Edinburgh 71 – ♦Inverness 85 – Perth 27.

🏨 **Atholl Palace** (T.H.F.) ⌂, PH16 5LY, ℰ 2400, Telex 76406, ℰ, ⏊ heated, ℰ, park, ℅ – 🛗
📺 🅿 👶 🔼 AE ⓞ VISA
M (bar lunch)/dinner 10.00 st. and a la carte ᵢ 2.70 – ⇌ 5.50 – **84 rm** 31.00/49.50 st., **10 suites**.

🏨 **Green Park** ⌂, Clunie Bridge Rd, PH16 5JY, ℰ 2537, ℰ Loch Faskally and mountains, ℰ –
📺 ⇋wc ▥wc 🅿 ℅
Mid March-October – **M** (bar lunch)/dinner 10.00 st. ᵢ 2.80 – **39 rm** ⇌ 19.50/49.00 st. – SB
(spring only) 52.00/66.00 st.

🏨 **Pine Trees** ⌂, Strathview Terr., PH16 5QR, ℰ 2121, ℰ, ℰ – 📺 ⇋wc ▥wc ⇌ 🅿 🔼 AE
ⓞ VISA
April-December – **M** 10.00/9.50 t. and a la carte ᵢ 2.20 – **27 rm** ⇌ 13.50/42.00 t.

🏨 **Burnside,** 19 West Moulin Rd, PH16 5EA, on A 924 ℰ 2203, ℰ – 📺 ⇋wc ▥wc ♿ 🅿 🔼
ⓞ VISA
Late March-October – **M** (bar lunch)/dinner 9.00 t. ᵢ 2.75 – **23 rm** ⇌ 18.35/38.00 t.

🏨 **Fisher's,** 75-79 Atholl Rd, PH16 5BN, ℰ 2000, ℰ – 🛗 ⇋wc 🅿 🔼 AE ⓞ VISA ℅
M 10.50/14.50 t. and a la carte ᵢ 2.50 – **75 rm**.

🏠 **Port-an-Eilean** ⟲, Strathtummel, PH16 5RU, NW : 10 m. by A 9 on B 8019 𝒫 088 24 (Tummel Bridge) 233, ≼ Loch Tummel and mountains, « Victorian shooting lodge on banks of Loch Tummel », ⟲, ⋙, park – ⌂wc 🅿
May-October – **M** (bar lunch)/dinner 8.50 **t**. 🅰 2.50 – **11 rm** ⊊ 15.50/36.00 **t**.

🏠 **Castlebeigh** ⟲, 10 Knockard Rd, PH16 5HJ, off A 924 𝒫 2925, ⋙ – ⌂wc 🅿
April-October – **M** (bar lunch)/dinner 9.50 **st**. 🅰 4.50 – **18 rm** ⊊ 14.50/33.00 **st**.

🏠 **Craigard** ⟲, Strathview Terr., PH16 5AZ, 𝒫 2592, ≼, ⋙ – 📺 ⌂wc ⋔wc 🅿. 𝘝𝘐𝘚𝘈
April-October – **M** (bar lunch)/dinner 9.50 **st**. 🅰 3.35 – **10 rm** ⊊ 13.75/36.00 **st**.

🏠 **Queen's View** ⟲, Strathtummel, PH16 5NR, NW : 6 ½ m. by A 9 on B 8019 𝒫 3291, ≼ Loch Tummel and mountains, ⟲, ⋙ – ⌂wc 🅿. 🔼 AE ⓪ 𝘝𝘐𝘚𝘈
March-November – **M** 7.65/9.20 **t**. and a la carte 🅰 3.50 – **12 rm** ⊊ 14.95/34.80 **t**.

🏠 **Acarsaid**, 8 Atholl Rd, PH16 5BX, 𝒫 2389 – ⌂wc ⋔wc 🅿. 🔼 𝘝𝘐𝘚𝘈. ⚡
Mid April-mid October – **M** (bar lunch)/dinner 10.00 **t**. and a la carte 🅰 3.00 – **19 rm** ⊊ 17.50/35.00 **t**.

🏠 **Airdaniar**, 160 Atholl Rd, PH16 5AR, 𝒫 2266, ⋙ – 📺 ⋔wc 🅿
April-October – **M** (bar lunch)/dinner 9.50 **st**. 🅰 2.20 – **10 rm** ⊊ 14.85/52.20 **st**.

🏠 **Claymore**, 162 Atholl Rd, PH16 5AR, 𝒫 2888, ⋙ – 📺 ⌂wc ⋔wc 🅿. 🔼 𝘝𝘐𝘚𝘈
April-October – **M** (bar lunch)/dinner 13.00 **st**. 🅰 2.50 – **12 rm** ⊊ 16.00/39.00 **st**.

🏠 **Moulin**, 11-13 Kirkmichael Rd, PH16 5EW, N : 1 m. on A 924 𝒫 2196, ⋙ – ⌂wc 🅿. 🔼 AE ⓪
closed January and February – **M** (bar lunch)/dinner 9.50 **t**. 🅰 2.50 – **18 rm** ⊊ 20.50/45.00 **t**. – SB (except Easter, Christmas and New Year) 24.75/28.50 **st**.

↑ **Balrobin**, Higher Oakfield, PH16 5HT, 𝒫 2901, ⋙ – ⋔wc 🅿
April-October – **8 rm** ⊊ 10.00/26.00 **t**.

↑ **Craig Urrard**, 10 Atholl Rd, PH16 5BX, 𝒫 2346, ⋙ – 📺 ⋔wc 🅿. 🔼 𝘝𝘐𝘚𝘈
12 rm ⊊ 12.70/28.40 **t**.

at Killiecrankie NW : 3 ¾ m. by A 9 on B 8079 – ✉ Pitlochry – ☎ 079 684 Killiecrankie :

🏛 **Killiecrankie** ⟲, PH16 5LG, 𝒫 3220, ≼, ⋙ – ⌂wc ⋔wc 🅿
March-October – **M** (bar lunch Monday to Saturday) 16.00 **t**. 🅰 2.30 – **12 rm** ⊊ 17.60/48.00 **t**.

FORD Pitlochry Garage, Perth Rd 𝒫 2316

PLOCKTON Ross and Cromarty (Highland) 𝟺𝟶𝟷 D 11 – pop. 425 – ☎ 059 984.
♦Edinburgh 210 – ♦Inverness 88.

🏠 **Haven**, Innes St., IV52 8TW, 𝒫 223, ≼, ⋙ – 📺 ⌂wc 🅿
M (bar lunch)/dinner 10.00 **t**. 🅰 2.35 – **12 rm** ⊊ 17.50/36.00 **t**.

POLMONT Stirling. (Central) 𝟺𝟶𝟷 𝟺𝟶𝟸 I 16 – see Falkirk.

PORT APPIN Argyll. (Strathclyde) 𝟺𝟶𝟷 D 14 – ECD : Thursday – ☎ 063 173 Appin.
⛴ to Lismore (Isle of) Monday-Saturday 7 daily ; Sunday 2 daily (10 mn).
♦Edinburgh 136 – Ballachulish 20 – ♦Oban 24.

🏠 **Airds** ⟲, PA38 4DF, 𝒫 236, ≼ Loch Linnhe and hills of Kingairloch, « Former ferry inn on lochside », ⋙ – ⌂wc ⋔wc 🅿
Mid March-mid November – **M** (bar lunch)/dinner 18.00 **t**. 🅰 4.00 – **17 rm** ⊊ (dinner included) 44.50/95.00 **t**.

PORT ASKAIG Argyll. (Strathclyde) 𝟺𝟶𝟷 B 16 – see Islay (Isle of).

PORTPATRICK Wigtown. (Dumfries and Galloway) 𝟺𝟶𝟷 𝟺𝟶𝟸 E 19 – pop. 595 – ECD : Thursday – ✉ Stranraer – ☎ 077 681.
🏌, 🏌 Dunskey 𝒫 81725.
♦Edinburgh 141 – ♦Ayr 60 – ♦Dumfries 80 – Stranraer 9.

🏛 **Knockinaam Lodge** ⟲, DG9 9AD, SE : 3 ¼ m. off A 77 𝒫 471, ≼ garden and sea, « Country house atmosphere », ⟲, park – ⌂wc 🅿. AE ⓪ 𝘝𝘐𝘚𝘈
Easter-October – **M** (bar lunch)/dinner 16.25 **t**. 🅰 3.35 – **10 rm** ⊊ (dinner included) 55.00/120.00 – SB (April and October) 80.00 **st**.

🏠 **Fernhill**, Heugh Rd, DG9 8TD, 𝒫 220, ≼, ⋙ – 📺 ⌂wc ⋔wc 🅿. 🔼 ⓪ 𝘝𝘐𝘚𝘈
restricted service mid January-February – **M** a la carte lunch/dinner 10.00 **t**. 🅰 2.75 – **15 rm** ⊊ 18.00/42.00 **t**.

↑ **South Cliff House**, DG9 8LE, 𝒫 411, ≼ – 🅿
April-September – **5 rm** ⊊ 11.00/27.00 **st**.

PORTREE Inverness. (Highland) 𝟺𝟶𝟷 B 11 – see Skye (Isle of).

Do not use yesterday's maps for today's journey.

PORTSONACHAN Argyll. (Strathclyde) **401** E 14 – ⊠ Dalmally – ❀ 086 63 Kilchrenan.

♦ Edinburgh 109 – ♦ Glasgow 72 – ♦ Oban 31 – Perth 80.

  XX **Portsonachan** ⬮ with rm, Lochaweside, PA33 1BL, ℰ 224, ≼ Loch Awe and Ben Cruachan, ⬛, ⟜ – ⊟wc. ⬛ ᴠɪꜱᴀ
    Mid February-mid November and Christmas-New Year – **M** (buffet lunch)/dinner 10.50 **t**.
    ⬧ 2.50 – **19 rm** ⊑ 15.00/59.00 **t**. – SB (except summer and Easter) 39.00/44.00 **st**.

PRESTWICK Ayr. (Strathclyde) **401 402** G 17 – pop. 13,355 – ECD : Wednesday – ❀ 0292.

⛴ ℰ 79822, Telex 77209 – Terminal : Buchanan Bus Station.

⛴ see also Glasgow.

🛈 2 The Cross, Station Rd ℰ 79234 – Prestwick Airport ℰ 77309.

♦Edinburgh 78 – ♦Ayr 2 – ♦Glasgow 32.

         Plan of Built up Area : see Ayr

  🏨 **Carlton** (Osprey), 187 Ayr Rd, KA9 1TP, ℰ 76811 – �📺 ⊟wc ☎ 🅿. ⬛ 🄰🄴 ⓪ ᴠɪꜱᴀ   BY **v**
    M (bar lunch)/dinner 9.25 **t**. and a la carte ⬧ 2.40 – **34 rm** ⊑ 27.00/42.00 **t**. – SB (weekends only) 44.00 **st**.

  ⌒ **Kincraig**, 39 Ayr Rd, KA9 1SY, ℰ 79480 – 🅿. 🍽   BY **c**
    6 rm ⊑ 9.00/18.00 **st**.

AUSTIN-ROVER 1 Monkton Rd ℰ 77415   VAUXHALL-OPEL 97/99 Main St. ℰ 70545

QUOTHQUAN Lanark. (Strathclyde) **401 402** J 17 – ⊠ ❀ 0899 Biggar.

Envir. : Biggar (Site*-Gladstone Court Museum*-Greenhill Covenanting Museum*) SW : 5 m.

♦Edinburgh 30 – ♦Carlisle 72 – ♦Glasgow 37.

  🏨 **Shieldhill House** ⬮, ML12 6NA, NE : 1 m. ℰ 20035, ≼, 🐎, ⊟wc ▥wc 🅿. ⬛ 🄰🄴 ⓪
    April-September – **M** (bar lunch)/dinner 6.00 **st**. and a la carte ⬧ 2.50 – **20 rm** ⊑ 14.00/30.00 **st**.

RAASAY (Isle of) Inverness. (Highland) **401** B 11 – pop. 182 – see Skye (Isle of).

RENFREW Renfrew. (Strathclyde) **401** G 16 – pop. 21,456 – ECD : Wednesday – ❀ 041 Glasgow.

♦Edinburgh 53 – ♦Glasgow 7.

  🏨 **Stakis Normandy** (Stakis), Inchinnan Rd, PA4 9EJ, ℰ 886 4100 – 🛗 📺 ⊟wc ☎ 🅵 🅿. 🅖.
    ⬛ 🄰🄴 ⓪ ᴠɪꜱᴀ
    M 8.50/10.50 **t**. ⬧ 3.40 – **142 rm** ⊑ 45.00/58.00 **t**.

PEUGEOT, TALBOT 18/20 Fulbar St. ℰ 886 3354   VAUXHALL-OPEL Porterfield Rd ℰ 886 2777

RHU Dunbarton. (Strathclyde) **401 402** F 15 – see Helensburgh.

RHUBODACH Bute. (Strathclyde) **401 402** E 16 – Shipping Services : see Bute (Isle of).

RHUM (Isle of) Inverness. (Highland) **401** B 13 – Shipping Services : see Mallaig.

ROCKCLIFFE Kirkcudbright. (Dumfries and Galloway) **401 402** I 19 – ⊠ Dalbeattie – ❀ 055 663.

📷 Colvend, Sand Hills ℰ 398.

♦Edinburgh 100 – ♦Dumfries 20 – Stranraer 69.

  🏨 **Baron's Craig** ⬮, DG5 4QF, ℰ 225, ≼, 🐎, park – 📺 ⊟wc 🅿
    Easter-mid October – **M** (bar lunch)/dinner 14.50 **t**. ⬧ 3.00 – **26 rm** ⊑ 24.00/68.00 **t**.

ROTHES Moray. (Grampian) **401** K 11 – pop. 1,414 – ECD : Wednesday – ❀ 034 03.

♦Edinburgh 192 – ♦Aberdeen 62 – Fraserburgh 58 – ♦Inverness 49.

  🏨 **Rothes Glen** ⬮, IV33 7AH, N : 3 m. on A 941 ℰ 254, ≼, « Country house atmosphere », 🐎,
    park – ⊟wc ☎ 🅿. ⬛ 🄰🄴 ⓪ ᴠɪꜱᴀ
    closed January – **M** 7.25/15.00 **t**. and a la carte ⬧ 5.00 – **16 rm** ⊑ 39.00/55.00 **t**. – SB (weekends only) 71.50 **st**.

ROUSAY (Isle of) Orkney (Orkney Islands) **401** K 6 – Shipping Services : see Orkney Islands (Mainland : Kirkwall).

ST. ANDREWS Fife. (Fife) **401** L 14 Scotland G – pop. 10,525 – ECD : Thursday – ❀ 0334.

See : Site** – Cathedral* – West Port*.

Envir. : The East Neuk** (coastline from Crail to St. Monance) SE : 16 m. by A 917 – Leuchars Parish Church*, NW : 6 m. by A 91 and A 919 – Ceres* (Fife Folk Museum) W : 9 m. by B 939 – Kellie Castle*, S : 9 m. by B 9131 and B 9171.

📷 Eden Course, 📷 Jubilee Course, 📷 New Course, St. Andrews Links ℰ 73393 – 📷 St. Michaels ℰ 033 483 (Leuchars) 365, N : 5 m.

🛈 South St. ℰ 72021.

♦Edinburgh 51 – ♦Dundee 14 – Stirling 51.

🏠 **Old Course Golf and Country Club,** Old Station Rd, KY16 9SP, 🏌 74371, Telex 76280, ≼ golf courses and sea, 🗐 – 🕴 TV ☎ & 🅿 🔼 🔄 AE ① VISA
   M rest see Eden below – **145 rm** ⊊ 35.00/99.50 t., **5 suites** 80.00/129.50 t.

🏠 **Rusacks Marine,** 16 Pilmour Links, KY16 9JQ, 🏌 74321, ≼ – 🕴 TV 🅿 🔼 AE ① VISA
   closed 4 to 18 January – **M** 8.00/13.50 t. and a la carte ⅄ 3.50 – **50 rm** ⊊ 35.00/76.00 t. – SB (October-April) 64.00/76.00 **st.**

🏠 **Rufflets** ⅖, Strathkinness Low Rd, KY16 9TX, W : 1 ½ m. on B 939 🏌 72594, ≼, « Country house, gardens » – TV ➜wc ☎ 🅿 🔼 AE ① VISA 🕴
   closed 6 January-2 February – **M** 6.50/14.00 t. and a la carte ⅄ 4.50 – **21 rm** ⊊ 33.50/59.00 t. – SB (November-April) (except Christmas-New Year) 64.00/70.00 **st.**

🏠 **St. Andrews Golf,** 40 The Scores, KY16 9AS, 🏌 72611, ≼ – 🕴 TV ➜wc ☎ 🔼 🔼 AE ① VISA
   M (bar lunch Monday to Saturday)/dinner 12.50 **t** and a la carte ⅄ 3.25 – **23 rm** ⊊ 38.00/60.00 t. – SB (weekends only) (November-March) 58.00/85.00 **st.**

XXX **Eden** (at Old Course Golf and C. C.), Old Station Rd, KY16 9SP, 🏌 74371 – 🅿 🔼 AE ① VISA
   M 12.50/18.50 t. and a la carte ⅄ 3.75.

AUSTIN-ROVER West Port 🏌 72101

ST. BOSWELLS Roxburgh. (Borders) 401 402 L 17 – pop. 1 ,086 – ✪ 0835.

Envir. : Dryburgh Abbey★★ (Setting★★★) – 🔼 🏌 22359, off A 68 at St. Boswells Green.

♦Edinburgh 39 – ♦ Glasgow 79 – Hawick 17 – ♦Newcastle-upon-Tyne 66.

🏠 **Dryburgh Abbey** ⅖, TD6 0RQ, N : 3 ½ m. by B 6404 on B 6356 🏌 22261, ≼, ⅄, 🚤, park – ➜wc 🅿 🔼 🔄 🔼 VISA
   M (buffet lunch)/dinner 11.00 t. ⅄ 3.10 – **28 rm** ⊊ 20.00/58.00 t. – SB (weekends only) (November-May) 60.00/66.00 **st.**

ST. CATHERINES Argyll. (Strathclyde) 401 E 15 – ✉ Cairndow – ✪ 0499 Inveraray.

Envir. : Inveraray★★ (Castle★★-interior★★★) NW : 12 m. by A 815 and A 83 – Auchindrain★, NE : 18 m. by A 815 and A 83 SW.

♦Edinburgh 99 – ♦Glasgow 53 – ♦Oban 53.

⌂ **Thistle House,** PA25 8AZ, on A 815 🏌 2209, ≼, 🚤 – 🅿 🕴
   May-September – **6 rm** ⊊ 12.00/24.00.

ST. COMBS Aberdeen. (Grampian) 401 O 11 – pop. 817 – ECD : Wednesday – ✉ Fraserburgh – ✪ 034 65 Inverallochy.

♦Edinburgh 173 – ♦Aberdeen 43 – Fraserburgh 6.

🏠 **Tufted Duck** ⅖, AB4 5YR, 🏌 2481, ≼, 🚤 – TV ➜wc 🗐wc ☎ 🅿 🔼 AE ① VISA
   M (lunch by arrangement)/dinner 12.00 t. and a la carte ⅄ 3.25 – **17 rm** ⊊ 20.95/34.95 t. – SB (weekends only) 65.00/98.60 **st.**

ST. FILLANS Perth. (Tayside) 401 H 14 – ECD : Wednesday – ✪ 076 485 – 🔼 🏌 312.

♦Edinburgh 67 – ♦Glasgow 57 – ♦Oban 64 – Perth 30.

🏠 **Four Seasons,** PH6 2NF, 🏌 333, ≼ Loch Earn and mountains, 🚤 – TV ➜wc 🗐wc ☎ 🅿 🔼 AE VISA
   April-October – **M** 8.25/12.50 t. ⅄ 3.30 – **18 rm** ⊊ 33.50/60.00 **st.**

SANDAY (Isle of) Orkney (Orkney Islands) 401 M 6 – Shipping Services : see Orkney Islands (Mainland : Kirkwall).

SANDBANK Argyll. (Strathclyde) 401 402 F 16 – see Dunoon.

SCALASAIG Argyll. (Strathclyde) 401 B 15 – see Colonsay (Isle of).

SCALLOWAY Shetland (Shetland Islands) 401 Q 3 – see Shetland Islands (Mainland).

SCALPAY (Isle of) Inverness. (Highland) 401 A 10 – Shipping Services : see Harris (Isle of).

SCARISTA Inverness. (Outer Hebrides) (Western Isles) – see Harris (Isle of).

SCOURIE Sutherland (Highland) 401 E 8 – ✉ Lairg – ✪ 0971.

♦Edinburgh 263 – ♦Inverness 107.

🏠 **Scourie** ⅖, IV27 4SX, 🏌 2396, ≼, ⅄ – ➜wc 🅿 🔼 ① VISA
   Mid March-mid October – **M** (bar lunch Monday to Saturday)/dinner 8.50 **t.** – **20 rm** ⊊ 16.00/40.00 t.

🏠 **Eddrachilles** ⅖, Badcall Bay, IV27 4TH, S : 2½ m. on A 894 🏌 2080, ≼ Badcall Bay and islands, 🚤 – ➜wc 🗐wc 🅿
   March-October – **M** (bar lunch)/dinner 6.25 **t.** and a la carte ⅄ 2.20 – **11 rm** ⊊ 21.25/37.70 t.

SCRABSTER Caithness. (Highland) **401** J 8 – Shipping Services : see Thurso.

SELKIRK Selkirk. (Borders) **401** **402** L 17 Scotland G – pop. 5 ,469 – ✆ 0750.

Envir. : Bowhill★★, W : 3 m. by A 708.

🛆 ✆ 20621, S : 1 m.

🛈 Halliwell's House ✆ 20054 (summer only).

◆Edinburgh 40 – ◆Glasgow 73 – Hawick 11 – ◆Newcastle-upon-Tyne 73.

🏛 **Philipburn House** 🦢, TD7 5LS, W : 1 m. at junction A 707 and A 708 ✆ 20747, ⌁ heated,
🍴 – 📺 ➦wc 🕾 🅿. 🖭 🖭 ⑩ 𝘝𝘐𝘚𝘈 . 🌿
closed January – **M** 8.50/14.50 **st.** and a la carte 🛈 3.15 – **16 rm** ヱ 20.00/70.00 **st.** – SB (weekends only) (November-June except Easter) 55.00/70.00 **st.**

at Ettrickbridge SW : 7 m. on B 7009 – ⊠ ✆ 075 05 Ettrickbridge :

🏛 **Ettrickshaws** 🦢, TD7 5HW, SW : 1 m. by B 7009 ✆ 52229, ≼, « Attractive setting overlooking Ettrick Water », 🦢, 🍴, park – 📺 ➦wc 🅿. 🖭 🖭 ⑩ 𝘝𝘐𝘚𝘈 . 🌿
closed January-mid February – **M** (bar lunch)/dinner 13.00 t. 🛈 4.00 – **6 rm** ヱ (dinner included) 29.00/72.00 **t.** – SB 44.00/68.00 **st.**

SHAPINSAY (Isle of) Orkney (Orkney Islands) **401** L 6 – Shipping Services : see Orkney Islands
(Mainland : Kirkwall).

If you find you cannot take up a hotel booking you have made,
please let the hotel know immediately.

SHETLAND ISLANDS Shetland (Shetland Islands) **401** PQ 3 Scotland G – pop. 27 ,271.

See : Site★ – Up Helly Aa★★ (last Tuesday in January).

🛫 see Mainland : Lerwick and Sumburgh.

🛫 Unst Airport : at Baltasound ✆ 095 781 (Baltasound) 404/7.

🚢 Shipping connections with the Continent : from Lerwick to Faroe Islands (Thorshavn) (Smyril
Line) – to Norway (Bergen) (Smyril Line) – to Iceland (Seydisfjordur via Thorshavn) (Smyril Line)
– by P & O Ferries : Orkney and Shetland Services : from Lerwick to Aberdeen 3 weekly (14 h) – by
Shetland Islands Council : from Lerwick (Mainland) to Bressay 11-13 daily (10 mn) – from Laxo
(Mainland) to Symbister (Isle of Whalsay) 5-7 daily (25 mn) – from Toft (Mainland) to Ulsta (Isle of
Yell) 16-20 daily (22 mn) – from Gutcher (Isle of Yell) to Belmont (Isle of Unst) 13-17 daily (restricted
on Sunday) (10 mn) – from Gutcher (Isle of Yell) to Oddsta (Isle of Fetlar) 2-3 daily (25 mn) – from
Scalloway to Kirkwall (Orkney Islands) via Westray (Orkney Islands) summer 2 weekly; winter 1
fortnightly (9 h 30 mn).

🚢 by J.W. Stout : from Fair Isle to Sumburgh (Gruntness) 2 weekly (2 h 45 mn) – by Shetland
Islands Council : from Lerwick (Mainland) to Skerries 2 weekly (3 h).

MAINLAND

Brae – ⊠ ✆ 080 622 Brae.

🏛 **Busta House** 🦢, ZE2 9QN, SW : 1½ m. ✆ 506, ≼, « Part 16C and 18C country house », 🍴
– 📺 ➦wc 🝙wc 🕾 🅿
closed mid December-mid January – **M** (bar lunch)/dinner 14.00 **st.** 🛈 2.90 – **21 rm**
ヱ 20.00/60.00 **st.** – SB (weekends only) 50.00/70.00 **st.**

Hillswick – ⊠ ✆ 080 623 Hillswick.

🏛 **St. Magnus Bay** 🦢, ZE2 9RW, ✆ 372, ≼, 🍴 – 📺 🝙wc 🅿. 🖭
M 5.50/12.00 **t.** and a la carte 🛈 4.25 – **26 rm** ヱ 15.40/34.00 **t.**

Lerwick Scotland G – pop. 7 ,223 – ECD : Wednesday – ⊠ ✆ 0595 Lerwick.

See : Clickhimin Broch★ – Shetland Croft House Museum★ – Mousa Broch★★★ (island site)
S : 13 m.

🛫 Tingwall Airport : ✆ 3535/2024, NW : 6 ½ m. by A 971.

🛈 Market Cross ✆ 3434.

🏛 **Shetland,** Holmsgarth Rd, ZE1 0PW, ✆ 5515, Telex 75432, ≼, 🖾 – 📶 📺 ➦wc 🕾 🕭 🅿. 🛆
🖭 🖭 ⑩ 𝘝𝘐𝘚𝘈
M 6.00/9.50 **t.** and a la carte – **64 rm** ヱ 47.00/55.00 **t.**

🏛 **Lerwick Thistle** (Thistle), 15 South Rd, ZE1 0RB, ✆ 2166, Telex 75128, ≼ – 📺 ➦wc 🕮 🅿.
🖭 🖭 ⑩ 𝘝𝘐𝘚𝘈
M 4.95/8.75 **t.** and a la carte 🛈 2.95 – ヱ 4.75 – **55 rm** 35.00/49.00 **t.**

🏛 **Kveldsro House,** Greenfield Pl., ZE1 0AN, ✆ 2195 – 📺 ➦wc 🅿. 🌿
closed 24 December-3 January – **M** 7.50/12.00 – **14 rm** ヱ 22.50/39.50.

AUSTIN-ROVER, LAND ROVER-RANGE ROVER   PEUGEOT-TALBOT, RENAULT North Rd ✆ 3315
Commercial Rd ✆ 3313
MAZDA, PEUGEOT-TALBOT 20 Commercial Rd ✆
2896

Scalloway – pop. 1,018 – ECD : Thursday – ⊠ ☎ 059 588 Scalloway.
🐂 Berry Farm ✆ 219.

Sumburgh – ⊠ ☎ 0950 Sumburgh.
See : Jarlshof★★ (prehistoric village).
✈ ✆ 60654, Telex 75451.

Voe – ⊠ ☎ 080 68 Voe.

Whiteness – ⊠ Whiteness – ☎ 059 584 Gott.
🏛 Westings, Wormadale, ZE2 9LJ, ✆ 242, ≤ The Deeps and Islands – 📺 📶wc 🅿. ⚡ – **9 rm**.

SHIEL BRIDGE Ross and Cromarty (Highland) 🗺 D 12 – ⊠ ☎ 059 981 Glenshiel.
🛈 ✆ 0599 (Glenshiel) 81264 (summer only).
◆Edinburgh 204 – ◆Inverness 66 – Kyle of Lochalsh 16.

🏛 **Kintail Lodge**, IV40 8HL, ✆ 275, ≤ Loch Duich and mountains, ⚔ – 📶wc 🅿. 🅽 𝘝𝘐𝘚𝘈
M (bar lunch)/dinner 15.00 **t.** ₫ 3.00 – **11 rm** ⊑ 20.00/50.00 **st.**

SHIELDAIG Ross and Cromarty (Highland) 🗺 D 11 – ⊠ Strachcarron – ☎ 052 05.
◆Edinburgh 226 – ◆Inverness 70 – Kyle of Lochalsh 36.

🏛 **Tigh-An Eilean**, Main St., IV54 8XN, ✆ 251, ≤ Shieldaig Islands and Loch – 📶wc 🅿. ⚡
April-October – **M** (buffet lunch)/dinner 8.50 **t.** ₫ 2.25 – **13 rm** ⊑ 17.00/34.00 **t.**

SKEABOST Inverness. (Highland) 🗺 B 11 – see Skye (Isle of).

SKELMORLIE Ayr. (Strathclyde) 🗺 F 16 – pop. 1,606 – ECD : Wednesday – ☎ 0475 Wemyss Bay.
◆Edinburgh 78 – ◆Ayr 39 – ◆Glasgow 32.

🏛 **Manor Park** 🦌, PA17 5HE, S : 2 ¾ m. on A 78 ✆ 520832, ≤ gardens and Firth of Clyde,
« Extensive gardens », park – 📺 📶wc 📶wc ☎ 🅿. ⚡
closed 3 January-4 March – **M** 11.25 **t.** (dinner) and a la carte ₫ 2.75 – **23 rm** ⊑ 30.00/60.00 **t.**
– SB 44.00/62.00 **st.**

🏛 **Redcliffe**, 25 Shore Rd, PA17 5EH, on A 78 ✆ 521036, ≤, ⚔ – 📺 📶wc 📶wc ☎ 🅿. 🅽 🅰🅴
🅞. ⚡
M 10.00/20.00 **t.** and a la carte ₫ 3.50 – **9 rm** ⊑ 27.50/42.00 **t.** – SB (weekends only)
55.00/62.00 **st.**

SKYE (Isle of) Inverness. (Highland) 🗺 B 11 and 12 **Scotland G** – pop. 8,139.
See : Site★★ – Cuillin Hills★★★.
✈ at Broadford : ✆ 047 12 (Broadford) 202.
🚢 by Caledonian MacBrayne : from Kyleakin to Kyle of Lochalsh : frequent services daily (5 mn)
– from Armadale to Mallaig summer only 2 weekly (30 mn) – from Uig to Tarbert (Isle of Harris)
Monday/Saturday 5-9 weekly (2 h 30 mn direct - 4 h 45 mn via Lochmaddy) – from Uig to Lochmaddy
(North Uist) Monday/Saturday 5-9 weekly (2 h - 2 h 30 mn direct - 4 h 45 mn via Tarbert) – from
Sconser to Isle of Raasay ; Monday/Saturday 3-5 daily (15 mn).
🚢 by Caledonian MacBrayne : from Armadale to Mallaig summer only 2 weekly (30 mn).

Broadford – pop. 839 – ECD : Wednesday – ⊠ ☎ 047 12 Broadford.
🛈 ✆ 361 and 463 (summer only).

VW, AUDI ✆ 225

Dunvegan **Scotland G** – ⊠ ☎ 047 022 Dunvegan.
See : Dunvegan Castle★.

🏛 **Harlosh** 🦌, IV51 5AB, S : 3 m. by A 863 ✆ 367, ≤ Loch Bracadale and Islands, 🌿 – 🅿
April-October – **M** (dinner only) 8.50 **t.** and a la carte ₫ 2.80 – **7 rm** ⊑ 12.00/27.00 **t.**

✗ **Three Chimneys**, Colbost, IV51 9SY, ✆ 258 – 🅿. 🅽 𝘝𝘐𝘚𝘈. ⚡
April-October – **M** (closed Sunday lunch) (booking essential) (restricted lunch)/dinner a la
carte 6.75/12.00 **t.** ₫ 2.75.

Isleornsay – ⊠ ☎ 047 13 Isleornsay.

🏛 **Kinloch Lodge** 🦌, IV43 8QY, ⊠ Sleat N : 3 ½ m. by A 851 ✆ 333, ≤ Loch Na Dal, « Country
house atmosphere », 🌿, ⚔ – 📶wc 🅿. 🅽 𝘝𝘐𝘚𝘈
closed February and Christmas – **M** (lunch by arrangement)/dinner 17.50 **t.** ₫ 3.20 – **9 rm**
⊑ 30.00/84.00 **t.** – SB (November-March) 100.00/110.00 **st.**

🏛 **Toravaig House** 🦌, IV44 8RJ, ⊠ Sleat, SW : 3 m. on A 851 ✆ 231, ⚔ – 📶wc 📶wc 🅿.
🅰🅴 🅞 𝘝𝘐𝘚𝘈
March-October – **M** (bar lunch)/dinner 10.00 **st.** and a la carte ₫ 2.75 – **10 rm** ⊑ 24.00/36.00 **st.**

SKYE (Isle of)

Portree Scotland G – pop. 1,533 – ECD : Wednesday – ✉ 🕓 0478 Portree.
See : Site★★ – Skye Croft Museum★, N : 18 m. by A 850 and A 856 – Trotternish Peninsula★★,
N : 40 m. by A 850, A 856 and A 855.
🛈 Meall House ℰ 2137.

🏠 **Rosedale**, Beaumont Cres., IV51 9DB, ℰ 2531, ≤ harbour – 🛏wc ▥wc 🅿
June-September – **M** (bar lunch)/dinner 9.50 t. 🍷 3.95 – **21 rm** ⚏ 18.00/44.00 t.

🏠 **Kings Haven** with rm, 11 Bosville Terr., IV51 9DJ, ℰ 2290 – ▥wc. ✀
April-October – **M** (bar lunch, residents only)/dinner 12.50 t. 🍷 3.20 – **7 rm** ⚏ 17.50/35.00 t.

AUSTIN-ROVER, FORD Dunvegan Rd ℰ 2554   RENAULT Dunvegan Rd ℰ 2002

Raasay Isle of – ✉ Kyle of Lochalsh – 🕓 047 862 Raasay.

🏠 Isle of Raasay ≋, IV40 8PB, ℰ 222, ≤ Narrows of Raasay and Skye, 🚗 – 📺 🛏wc ⅙ 🅿
✀ – **12 rm**.

Skeabost – ECD : Wednesday – ✉ 🕓 047 032 Skeabost Bridge.

🏛 **Skeabost House** ≋, IV51 9NP, ℰ 202, ≤ Loch Snizort Beag, « Country house in grounds
bordering loch », ⌜ѕ, ⚲, 🚗, park – 🛏wc 🅿
May-19 October – **M** (buffet lunch)/dinner 10.00 t. 🍷 3.00 – **26 rm** ⚏ 17.50/49.00 st.

Uig – ECD : Wednesday – ✉ 🕓 047 042 Uig.

SMA'GLEN Perth. (Tayside) 401 I 14 – see Crieff.

SOUTH QUEENSFERRY W. Lothian (Lothian) 401 J 16 Scotland G – pop. 7,485 – ECD : Wed-
nesday – 🕓 031 Edinburgh.
See : Forth Bridges★★.
Envir. : Dalmeny (St. Cuthbert's Church★ – Dalmeny House★) E : 2 m. by B 924 – Hopetoun
House★★, W : 2 m. by A 904 – Abercorn Parish Church (Hopetoun Loft★) W : 3 m. by A 904.
♦Edinburgh 9 – Dunfermline 7 – ♦Glasgow 41.

🏛 **Forth Bridges Moat House** (Q.M.H.), EH30 9SF, junction A 90 and Forth Bridge ℰ 331 1199,
Telex 727430, ≤ Firth of Forth and Bridges, 🏊, squash – 📺 🛏wc ➾ 🅿 🚗. 🔼 ⚠ ⓪ 𝚅𝚄𝚂𝙰
M *(closed lunch Saturday and Sunday)* 7.25/8.25 **st.** and a la carte 🍷 2.50 – ⚏ 4.85 – **108 rm**
39.50/49.75 **st.** – SB (weekends only) 56.00 **st.**

SPEAN BRIDGE Inverness. (Highland) 401 F 13 – ECD : Thursday – 🕓 039 781.
♦Edinburgh 139 – ♦Inverness 58 – Kyle of Lochalsh 65 – ♦Oban 60 – Perth 95.

🏠 **Letterfinlay Lodge**, PH34 4DZ, N : 7 ½ m. on A 82 ℰ 039 784 (Invergloy) 222, ≤ Loch Lochy
and mountains, ⚲, 🚗 – 🛏wc ▥wc 🅿. 🔼 ⚠ ⓪ 𝚅𝚄𝚂𝙰
M (bar lunch)/dinner 9.50 **st.** 🍷 2.95 – **15 rm** ⚏ 12.50/36.00 **st.**

🏠 **Spean Bridge**, PH34 4ES, ℰ 250, ⚲ – 🛏wc 🅿. 🔼 ⚠ ⓪ 𝚅𝚄𝚂𝙰
M (bar lunch)/dinner 9.00 t. 🍷 2.75 – **28 rm** ⚏ 15.50/37.00 t.

SPITTAL OF GLENSHEE Perth. (Tayside) 401 J 13 – Winter Sports – ✉ Blairgowrie – 🕓 025 085
Glenshee.
🛈 Newton Terrace, Blairgowrie ℰ 0250 (Blairgowrie) 2785.
♦Edinburgh 78 – ♦Dundee 37 – Perth 34.

🏛 **Dalmunzie House** ≋, PH10 7QG, NW : 1 ½ m. ℰ 224, ≤, ⌜ѕ, ⚲, 🚗, park, ✀ – ▤ 🛏wc
🅿 🔼 ⓪
January-19 October – **M** (bar lunch)/dinner 13.50 **st.** 🍷 3.50 – **16 rm** ⚏ 22.00/48.00 **st.**

STEWARTON Ayr. (Strathclyde) 401 402 G 16 – pop. 6,319 – ECD : Wednesday and Saturday –
🕓 0560.
♦Edinburgh 68 – ♦Ayr 21 – ♦Glasgow 22.

XXX **Chapeltoun House** ≋ with rm, KA3 3ED, SW : 2 ½ m. by B 769 ℰ 82696, ≤, « Country
house in extensive grounds », ⚲, 🚗, park – 📺 🛏wc ▥wc ➾ 🅿. 🔼 ⚠ ⓪ 𝚅𝚄𝚂𝙰. ✀
closed first 2 weeks January, last 2 weeks July and 25-26 December – **M** (booking essential)
10.50/18.50 **t.** and a la carte 🍷 3.50 – **6 rm** ⚏ 45.00/80.00 **t.**

STIRLING Stirling. (Central) 401 I 15 Scotland G – pop. 36,640 – ECD : Wednesday – 🕓 0786.
See : Site★★ – Castle★★ (Site★★★-external elevations★★★-Stirling Heads★★★) B – Argyll and
Sutherland Highlanders Regimental Museum★ B M – Argyll's Lodging★ (Renaissance decoration★)
B A – Church of the Holy Rude★ B B.
Envir. : Wallace Monument (❄★★) N : 2 ½ m. by A 9 A and B 998 – Dunblane★ (Cathedral★★)
N : 6 ½ m. by A 9 A – Doune★ (Castle★-Motor Museum★) NW : 8 m. by A 84 A, – A 9 and
B 824 – Bannockburn, S : 2 m. by A 9 A.
⌜ѕ Queens Rd ℰ 64098 B – ⌜ѕ Alva Rd, Tillicoultry ℰ 0259 (Tillicoultry) 50741, E : 9 m. by A 9 A.
🚗 ℰ 73085.
🛈 Dumbarton Rd ℰ 75019 – Bannockburn ℰ 815663 (summer only).
♦Edinburgh 37 – Dunfermline 23 – Falkirk 14 – ♦Glasgow 28 – Greenock 52 – Motherwell 30 – ♦Oban 87
– Perth 35.

STIRLING

Dumbarton Road............ B 10
Murray Place................ B 15
Port Street.................. B
Thistle Centre .... B
Upper Craigs .... B 29

Barnton Street .... B 2

Borestone Crescent .... A 3
Causewayhead Road...... A, B 4
Corn Exchange Road........ B 5
Cornton Road............... A 7
Coxithill Road............... A 8
Drummond Place............ B 9
Goosecroft Road............ B 12
King Street................. B 13
Newhouse.................. A 16
Park Place................. A 18

Queen Street .... B 20
Randolph Terrace .... A 22
St. John Street .... B 23
St. Mary's Wynd........... B 24
Seaforth Place .... B 25
Shirra's Brae Road......... A 26
Spittal Street............... B 27
Union Street .... B 28
Victoria Square............. B 30
Weaver Row................ A 31

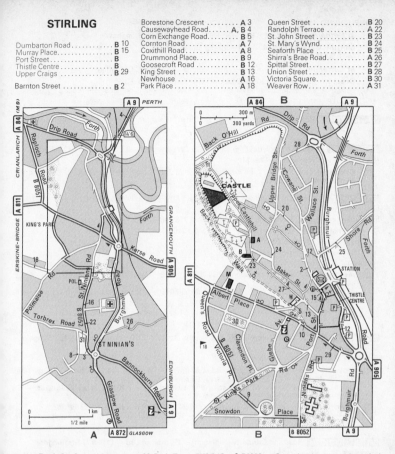

🏠 **Park Lodge** without rest., 32 Park Terr., FK8 2JS, ℰ 74862, « Georgian house with period decor », �̄ – 📺 ⇌wc 🅿. 🔊 ⓞ 𝘝𝘐𝘚𝘈. 🎫
closed Christmas and New Year – **9 rm** ⊇ 30.00/39.00.
B a

🏠 **Stakis Station** (Stakis), 56 Murray Pl., FK8 2BX, ℰ 72017 – 📺 ⇌wc 🛁wc ⊛ 🅿. 🔊. 🔊 ᴁ ⓞ 𝘝𝘐𝘚𝘈
B n
M 4.50/8.90 t. 🍴 2.30 – **25 rm** ⊇ 30.00/40.00 t. – SB 29.00/43.00 st.

🏠 King Robert, Glasgow Rd, FK7 0LJ, ℰ 811666 – 📺 ⇌wc ⊛ 🅿. 🔊 ᴁ ⓞ 𝘝𝘐𝘚𝘈. 🎫
A c
M (bar lunch)/dinner 10.00 st. and a la carte – **20 rm**.

XX **Heritage** with rm, 16 Allan Park, FK8 2QG, ℰ 73660, French rest. – 📺 ⇌wc 🅿. 🔊 ⓞ 𝘝𝘐𝘚𝘈
closed Christmas and New Year – **M** 6.60/11.00 🍴 3.00 – **4 rm** ⊇ 24.00/33.00.
B e

at Blairlogie NE : 4 ½ m. by A 9 and A 91 – A – ✉ Stirling – ✆ 0259 Alva :

🏠 **Blairlogie House**, FK9 5QE, ℰ 61441, 🌄 – ⇌wc 🛁wc 🅿. 𝘝𝘐𝘚𝘈
closed dinner Sunday and Bank Holidays to non-residents – **M** a la carte lunch/dinner 11.00 t.
🍴 3.20 – **7 rm** ⊇ 24.00/39.00 t.

CITROEN, VAUXHALL-OPEL 119/139 Glasgow Rd ℰ
0786 (Bannockburn) 811234

FIAT 44 Causeway Head Rd ℰ 62426
FORD Drip Rd ℰ 70519

STONEHAVEN Kincardine. (Grampian) 𝟰𝟬𝟭 N 13 Scotland G – pop. 7,834 – ECD : Wednesday – ✆ 0569.

Envir. : Dunnottar Castle★★ (site★★★) S : 2 m. by A 92 – Muchalls Castle (plasterwork ceilings★★) N : 5 m. by A 92.

🛈 Cowie ℰ 62124, N : 1 m. on Aberdeen Rd – 🛈 The Square ℰ 62806 (summer only).

♦Edinburgh 114 – ♦Aberdeen 16 – ♦Dundee 51.

at Netherley N : 6 m. on B 979 – ⊠ Netherley – 🕿 0569 Stonehaven :

✗ **Lairhillock,** AB3 2QS, ✆ 30001 – 🅿. 🔄 🖭 ⓘ 𝑉𝐼𝑆𝐴
 M 10.00/14.50 t. 🍷 3.50.

at Catterline S : 6 m. by A 92 – ⊠ Stonehaven – 🕿 056 95 Catterline :

✗ **Creel Inn,** S : 6 m. by A 92, AB3 2UL, ✆ 254, Seafood – 🅿. 🔄 🖭
 closed Sunday dinner, Monday and January – **M** (bar lunch)/dinner 9.85/18.75 t. 🍷 2.70.

AUSTIN-ROVER 64/74 Barclay St. ✆ 62077   FORD 110 Barclay St. ✆ 63666

STORNOWAY Ross and Cromarty (Outer Hebrides) (Western Isles) 🔢 A 9 – see Lewis (Isle of).

STRACHUR Argyll. (Strathclyde) 🔢 E 15 – ECD : Wednesday – ⊠ Cairndow – 🕿 036 986.
♦Edinburgh 104 – ♦Glasgow 58 – ♦Oban 58.

🏨 **Creggans Inn,** PA27 8BX, on A 815 ✆ 279, ≤ Loch Fyne, 🍴 – 🛏wc 🕿 🕹 🅿. 🔄 🖭 ⓘ 𝑉𝐼𝑆𝐴
 M a la carte 6.00/15.00 t. 🍷 3.20 – **22 rm** ⊐ 29.50/58.00 t.

STRANRAER Wigtown. (Dumfries and Galloway) 🔢 🔢 E 19 Scotland G – pop. 10,766 – ECD : Wednesday – 🕿 0776.
Envir. : Logan Botanic Garden★ S : 13 m. by A 77, A 716 and B 7065.
🔢 Creachmore by Stranraer, Leswalt ✆ 87245, SW : 2 m.
⚓ by Sealink : to Larne 2-9 daily (2 h 30 mn).
🚢 Port Rodie ✆ 2595 (summer only).
♦Edinburgh 132 – ♦Ayr 51 – ♦Dumfries 75.

🏨 **North West Castle,** Portroddie, DG9 8EH, ✆ 4413, Telex 777088, 🔄 – 🔋 📺 🛏wc 🕿 🅿.
 ✂
 M 5.00/12.00 t. and a la carte – **77 rm** ⊐ 26.50/54.00 t. – SB (weekends only) (October-June) 52.00/56.00 st.

AUSTIN-ROVER Leswalt Rd ✆ 3636   VOLVO Hanover Sq. ✆ 3939
COLT ✆ 87634

STRATHBLANE Stirling. (Central) 🔢 H 16 – pop. 1,933 – ECD : Wednesday – ⊠ Glasgow – 🕿 0360 Blanefield.
♦Edinburgh 52 – ♦Glasgow 11 – Stirling 26.

🏨 **Country Club** 🦢, 41 Milngavie Rd, G63 9AH, S : ¾ m. on A 81 ✆ 70491, Group Telex 777205, 🍴, park – 📺 🛏wc 🛅wc 🕿 🅿. 🔄 🖭 ⓘ 𝑉𝐼𝑆𝐴
 closed 1 to 3 January – **M** 12.50 st. and a la carte 🍷 3.60 – **10 rm** ⊐ 35.00/45.00 st. – SB (weekends only) 60.00 st.

🏨 **Kirkhouse Inn,** Glasgow Rd, G63 9AA, ✆ 70621 – 📺 🛏wc 🕿 🅿. 🔄 🖭 ⓘ 𝑉𝐼𝑆𝐴
 closed 1 January – **M** 5.75/10.25 t. 🍷 3.00 – **17 rm** ⊐ 25.00/36.00 t. – SB (weekends only) 45.00 st.

STRATHCONON Ross and Cromarty (Highland) – ⊠ Muir of Ord – 🕿 099 77 Strathconon.
♦Edinburgh 184 – ♦Inverness 28.

🏨 **East Lodge** 🦢, IV6 7QQ, W : 11 m. off A 832 ✆ 222, ≤, 🦆, 🍴 – 📺 🛏wc 🛅wc 🅿. 🔄 ⓘ 𝑉𝐼𝑆𝐴
 M (bar lunch)/dinner 9.50 t. – **10 rm** ⊐ 28.00/50.00 t.

STRATHPEFFER Ross and Cromarty (Highland) 🔢 G 11 – pop. 1,244 – ECD : Thursday – 🕿 0997.
♦ Edinburgh 174 – ♦ Inverness 18.

🏨 **Holly Lodge,** Golf Course Rd, IV14 9AR, ✆ 21254, 🍴 – 📺 🛏wc 🛅wc 🅿
 April-September – **M** (dinner only) 11.50 t. 🍷 3.00 – **7 rm** ⊐ 24.00/50.00 t.

STRATHY Sutherland (Highland) 🔢 I 8 – 🕿 064 14.
♦Edinburgh 289 – ♦Inverness 133 – Thurso 21 – Tongue 22.
 Hotel see : Bettyhill SW : 12 m.

STROMNESS Orkney (Orkney Islands) 🔢 K 7 – see Orkney Islands (Mainland).

STRONSAY (Isle of) Orkney (Orkney Islands) 🔢 M 6 – Shipping Services : see Orkney Islands (Mainland : Kirkwall).

SUMBURGH Shetland (Shetland Islands) 🔢 Q 4 – see Shetland Islands (Mainland).

Michelin road map of GREECE (scale 1:700 000), no 🔢🔢🔢.

TAIN Ross and Cromarty (Highland) **401** H 10 – pop. 3,428 – ECD : Thursday – ✆ 0862.
🛆 The Clubhouse ℰ 2314.
♦Edinburgh 191 – ♦Inverness 35 – ♦Wick 91.

  🏨 **Royal,** High St., IV19 1AB, ℰ 2013 – 📺 ➾wc ⋔wc ☎ 🅟 🅰 🌫 ⴼ 🆎 ⓞ 𝘝𝘐𝘚𝘈
  M 9.65 **t.** (dinner) and a la carte 9.55/15.25 **t.** ⌁ 3.10 – **25 rm** ⚏ 20.00/37.40 **t.**

TOYOTA Knockbreck Rd ℰ 2175

TARBERT Argyll. (Strathclyde) **401** D 16 – see Kintyre (Peninsula).

TARBERT Inverness. (Outer Hebrides) (Western Isles) **401** Z 10 – see Harris (Isle of).

TAYINLOAN Argyll. (Strathclyde) **401** D 16 – Shipping Services : see Gigha (Isle of).

TAYNUILT Argyll. (Strathclyde) **401** E 14 – ECD : Wednesday – ✆ 086 62.
♦Edinburgh 111 – ♦Glasgow 81 – ♦Oban 12.

  🏤 **Polfearn** ⤚, PA35 1JQ, N : 1 m. ℰ 251, ≼, 🚿 – ➾wc ⋔wc 🅟
  March-October – **M** (bar lunch)/dinner 9.50 **t.** ⌁ 2.75 – **16 rm** ⚏ 14.00/32.00 **t.**

TAYVALLICH Argyll. (Strathclyde) **401** D 15 – ✉ Lochgilphead – ✆ 054 67.
♦Edinburgh 141 – ♦Glasgow 95 – ♦Oban 40.

  ✗ **Tayvallich Inn,** by Lochgilphead, PA31 8PR, ℰ 282, ≼ – 🅟 🌫 𝘝𝘐𝘚𝘈
  April-October and Friday and Saturday in winter – **M** (bar lunch)/dinner a la carte 8.00/11.00 **t.**
  ⌁ 3.00.

THORNHILL Dumfries. (Dumfries and Galloway) **401 402** I 18 Scotland G – pop. 1,449 – ECD :
Thursday – ✆ 0848.
Envir. : Drumlanrig Castle★★, NW : 4 m. by A 76 – 🛆 ℰ 30546.
♦Edinburgh 64 – ♦Ayr 44 – ♦Dumfries 15 – ♦Glasgow 63.

  🏛 **Buccleuch and Queensberry,** 112 Drumlanrig St., DG3 5LU, ℰ 30215 – ➾wc 🅟 🌫 𝘝𝘐𝘚𝘈
  M (bar lunch)/dinner 11.50 **t.** and a la carte ⌁ 3.00 – **11 rm** ⚏ 15.00/35.00 **t.**

THURSO Caithness. (Highland) **401** J 8 Scotland G – pop. 8,828 – ECD : Thursday – ✆ 0847.
Envir. : Coast road to Durness via Strathy Point★ (≼★★★) – Torrisdale Bay★ – Ben Loyal★★ –
Coldbackie (≼★★) – Ben Hope★ – Loch Eriboll (≼★★★) W : 74 m. by A 836 and A 838.
🛆 ℰ 63807, 2 m. from railway station.
⛴ by P & O Ferries : Orkney and Shetland Services : from Scrabster to Stromness (Orkney
Islands) Monday/Saturday 1-3 daily (2 h).
🅱 Car Park, Riverside ℰ 2371 (summer only).
♦Edinburgh 289 – ♦Inverness 133 – ♦Wick 21.

  at Banniskirk SE : 8 m. by A 882 on A 895 – ✉ ✆ 084 783 Halkirk :

  ↑ **Banniskirk House** ⤚, KW12 6XA, ℰ 609, 🚿, park – 🅟
  May-September (booking essential in winter) – **8 rm** ⚏ 8.00/12.00 **st.**

CITROEN Couper Sq. Riverside ℰ 62778   RENAULT Bridgend ℰ 4622
FORD Mansons Lane ℰ 63101

TIREE (Isle of) Argyll. (Strathclyde) **401** Z 14 – pop. 780.
✈ ℰ 087 92 (Scarinish) 456.
⛴ by Caledonian MacBrayne : to Arinagour (Isle of Coll) 3-4 weekly (1 h) – to Oban 3-4 weekly
(4 h 30 mn-5 h).
⛴ to Tobermory (Isle of Mull) 3 weekly (2 h 45 mn) – to Lochaline (via Coll and Tobermory)
May-September 2 weekly (3 h 55 mn).

TIRORAN Argyll. (Strathclyde) **401** B 14 – see Mull (Isle of).

TOBERMORY Argyll. (Strathclyde) **401** B 14 – see Mull (Isle of).

TONGUE Sutherland (Highland) **401** G 8 – ECD : Saturday – ✉ Lairg – ✆ 080 05.
Envir. : Coast road east via Coldbackie (≼★★) – Ben Loyal★★ – Torrisdale Bay★ – Strathy Point★
(≼★★★) E : 24 m. by A 836 – Coast road west via Ben Hope★ – Loch Eriboll (≼★★★) – Cape
Wrath★★★ (≼★★) W : 44 m. by A 838.
♦Edinburgh 257 – ♦Inverness 101 – Thurso 43.

  🏛 **Ben Loyal,** Main St., IV27 4XE, ℰ 216, ≼ – ➾wc 🅟 🌫 𝘝𝘐𝘚𝘈
  closed Christmas Day – **M** (bar lunch)/dinner 8.00 **st.** ⌁ 3.50 – **18 rm** ⚏ 12.50/35.00 **t.**

TORRIDON Ross and Cromarty (Highland) **401** D 11 – ✆ 044 587.
♦Edinburgh 218 – ♦Inverness 62 – Kyle of Lochalsh 41.

  🏨 **Loch Torridon** ⤚, IV22 2EY, ℰ 242, ≼ Loch Torridon and mountains, 🟢, 🚿, park – ➾wc
  ☎ 🅟 🅰 🆎 ⓞ 𝘝𝘐𝘚𝘈
  May-September – **M** (bar lunch Monday to Saturday)/dinner 9.75 **t.** ⌁ 1.55 – **23 rm**
  ⚏ 17.40/41.40 **t.**

TROON Ayr. (Strathclyde) **401 402** G 17 – pop. 14,035 – ECD : Wednesday – ✆ 0292.
ᴦₐ ℰ 311555.

🅱 Municipal Buildings, South Beach ℰ 315131.

♦Edinburgh 77 – ♦Ayr 7 – ♦Glasgow 31.

🏛 **Marine,** 8 Crosbie Rd, KA10 6HE, ℰ 314444, Telex 777595, ≼, 🏖 – 🎧 📺 🅿. 🅰️. 🔼 🄰🄴 ⓪ VISA
M (restricted lunch in winter) 6.95/10.50 **t.** and a la carte ▮ 2.65 – **68 rm** ⇌ 44.00/64.00 **t.**, **5 suites** 73.00/93.00 **t.**

🏠 **Piersland House,** 17 Craigend Rd, KA10 6HD, ℰ 314747, 🏖 – 📺 ⇌wc 🛁wc ☎ 🅿. 🔼 🄰🄴 ⓪ VISA
M (bar lunch)/dinner 14.00 **t.** and a la carte ▮ 3.00 – **15 rm** ⇌ 30.00/58.00 **t.**

🏠 **Sun Court,** 19 Crosbie Rd, KA10 6HF, ℰ 312727, ≼, 🏖, 🏌 – 📺 ⇌wc 🛁 🅿. 🅰️. 🔼 🄰🄴 ⓪
M 7.50/11.50 **st.** and a la carte ▮ 2.00 – **20 rm** ⇌ 31.00/55.00 **st.** – SB (weekends only) 68.00 **st.**

🏡 **Ardneil,** 51 St. Meddans St., KA10 6NU, ℰ 311611 – 📺 ⇌wc 🅿. 🏌 – **8 rm.**

✗ **Campbell's Kitchen,** 3 South Beach, KA10 6EF, ℰ 314421, Bistro – 🔼
closed Sunday and Monday – **M** (dinner only) 14.85 **t.** and a la carte 10.50/14.85 **t.** ▮ 3.10.

AUSTIN-ROVER Dundonald Rd ℰ 314141   FORD 72-76 Portland St. ℰ 312312
DAIHATSU St. Meddans St. ℰ 312099

TURNBERRY Ayr. (Strathclyde) **401 402** F 18 – ECD : Wednesday – ✉ Girvan – ✆ 065 53.
ᴦ₁₈, ᴦ₁₈ Turnberry Hotel ℰ 202.

♦Edinburgh 97 – ♦Ayr 15 – ♦Glasgow 51 – Stranraer 36.

🏰 **Turnberry** ⤵, Maidens Rd, KA26 9LT, on A 719 ℰ 202, Telex 777779, ≼ golf course and bay,
🔼, ᴦ₁₈, 🏖, 🏌 – 🎧 📺 ♿ 🅿. 🅰️. 🔼 🄰🄴 ⓪ VISA
closed 1 January-6 March – **M** 12.50/21.00 **st.** and a la carte ▮ 5.60 – **120 rm** ⇌ 52.50/135.00 **st.**, **6 suites** 225.00 **st.** – SB (November-March) 167.00/182.00 **st.**

TWEEDSMUIR Lanark. (Strathclyde) **401 402** J 17 – ✉ Biggar – ✆ 089 97.

♦Edinburgh 38 – ♦Carlisle 58 – ♦Dumfries 57 – ♦Glasgow 37.

✗✗ **Crook Inn** with rm, ML12 6QN, N : 1 m. on A 701 ℰ 272, ⤿, 🏖 – ⇌wc 🅿
closed 25 and 26 December – **M** (bar lunch)/dinner 13.50 **t.** and a la carte ▮ 2.75 – **8 rm** ⇌ 24.00/48.00 **t.** – SB 50.00/64.00 **st.**

UDDINGSTON Lanark. (Strathclyde) **401 402** H 16 – pop. 10,681 – ECD : Wednesday – ✉ Glasgow – ✆ 0698.

♦Edinburgh 41 – ♦Glasgow 10.

🏠 **Redstones,** 8-10 Glasgow Rd, G71 7AS, ℰ 813774 – 📺 ⇌wc 🛁wc ☎ 🅿. 🔼 🄰🄴 ⓪ VISA
🏌
closed New Years Day – **M** (closed Sunday dinner to non-residents) 4.95/7.50 **t.** and a la carte ▮ 3.70 – **13 rm** ⇌ 31.50/42.00 **t.** – SB (weekends only) 45.00/55.00 **st.**

UIG Inverness. (Highland) **401** A 11 – see Skye (Isle of).

UIST (Isles of) Inverness. (Western Isles) **401** XY 11 and 12 – pop. 3,677.

🚢 see Benbecula.

🛳 by Caledonian MacBrayne from Lochboisdale : to Oban 3-6 weekly (5 h 30 mn direct ; 7 h 30 mn via Castle Bay) – to Castlebay (Isle of Barra) 2-4 weekly (1 h 30 mn-2 h) – from Lochmaddy to Uig (Isle of Skye) Monday/Saturday 5-9 weekly (2 h direct - 4 h 45 mn via Tarbert) – from Lochmaddy to Tarbert (Isle of Harris) Monday/Saturday 5-9 weekly 2 h direct - 4 h 45 mn via Uig.

Benbecula – ✉ Liniclate – ✆ 0870 Benbecula.
🚢 Benbecula Airport : ℰ 2051.

🏠 **Dark Island,** PA88 5PJ, ℰ 2414, ≼ – ⇌wc 🛁wc 🅿. 🔼 VISA
M 5.00/25.00 **t.** and a la carte ▮ 2.50 – **27 rm** ⇌ 17.00/50.00 **t.**

Daliburgh (South Uist) – ✉ ✆ 087 84 Lochboisdale.

🏠 **Borrodale,** PA81 5SS, ℰ 444, ≼, ⤿ – ⇌wc 🛁wc 🅿. 🔼 VISA
M 4.75/8.75 **t.** ▮ 5.00 – **13 rm** ⇌ 14.55/34.15 **st.** – SB 40.00 **st.**

Lochboisdale (South Uist) – ECD : Thursday – ✉ ✆ 087 84 Lochboisdale.
🅱 ℰ 286 (summer only).

🏠 Lochboisdale, PA81 5TH, ℰ 332, ≼ Lochboisdale and harbour, ⤿ – ⇌wc 🛁 🅿 – **20 rm.**

Lochmaddy (North Uist) – ECD : Thursday – ✉ ✆ 087 63 Lochmaddy.
🅱 ℰ 321 (summer only).

🏠 Lochmaddy, PA28 5AA, ℰ 331, ≼ Lochmaddy and islands, ⤿ – 🅿 – **15 rm.**

ULLAPOOL Ross and Cromarty (Highland) **401** E 10 **Scotland G** – pop. 1,006 – ECD : Tuesday except summer – ✆ 0854.

See : Site★.

Envir. : Falls of Measach★★ in the Corrieshalloch Gorge★, S : 11 m. by A 835 – Loch Broom★★, Loch Assynt★★ and Lochinver, N : 37 m. by A 835 and A 837.

🚢 by Caledonian MacBrayne : to Stornoway (Isle of Lewis) Monday/Saturday 1-2 daily (3 h 30 mn).

🏛 ✆ 2135 (summer only).

◆Edinburgh 215 – ◆Inverness 59.

🏨 **Royal** (Best Western), Garve Rd, IV26 2SY, ✆ 2181, ≤ Loch Broom, 🖛, 🚗, park – 🛏wc
🗱wc ☎ **P**. 🔼 **AE** ⓞ **VISA**
closed 24 December-28 February – **M** (bar lunch)/dinner 10.75 **t**. and a la carte 🖟 3.75 – **57 rm**
⌷ 18.50/54.00 **t**., **1 suite** 80.00 **t**. – SB (24 October-22 May) 56.00 **st**.

🏨 **Ladbroke Mercury Motor Inn** (Ladbroke), North Rd, IV26 2UD, ✆ 2314, ≤ – 📺 🛏wc
P. 🔼 **AE** ⓞ **VISA**
April-October – **M** (bar lunch)/dinner 10.00 **st**. and a la carte 🖟 3.70 – ⌷ 6.25 – **60 rm**
30.00/42.00 **st**.

🏠 **Ceilidh Place,** 14 West Argyle St., IV26 2TY, ✆ 2103, « Tasteful decor » – 🛏wc **P**. ⓞ
April-September – **M** (buffet lunch)/dinner a la carte 7.10/12.00 **st**. 🖟 3.00 – **15 rm**
⌷ 21.00/45.00 **st**.

🏠 Harbour Lights Motel, Garve Rd, ✆ 2222, ≤ Loch Broom, 🚗 – 🛏wc 🗱wc **P** – **22 rm**.

🏠 **Ferry Boat Inn,** Shore St., ✆ 2366, ≤ – 🔼 ⓞ
M (bar lunch)/dinner 9.50 **st**. 🖟 3.00 – **12 rm** ⌷ 15.00/26.00 **st**.

✗ **Altnaharrie Inn** 🖏 with rm, IV26 2SS, SW : ½ m. via private ferry ✆ 085 483 (Dundonnell) 230, ≤ Loch Broom and Ullapool, 🖛, 🚗 – 🛏wc
April-mid October – **M** (booking essential) (restricted lunch, residents only)/dinner 17.50 **t**.
🖟 2.50 – **4 rm** ⌷ 25.00/60.00 **t**.

UNST Shetland (Shetland Islands) **401** R 1 – Shipping Services : see Shetland Islands.

UPHALL W. Lothian (Lothian) **401** J 16 – ECD : Wednesday – ✆ 0506 Broxburn.
🏛 ✆ 856404.
◆Edinburgh 13 – ◆Glasgow 32.

🏨 **Houstoun House,** EH52 6JS, ✆ 853831, Telex 727148, ≤, « Gardens », park – 📺 🛏wc
🗱wc ☎ **P**. 🔼 **AE** ⓞ
closed 1 to 3 January – **M** 11.00/16.00 **st**. 🖟 2.50 – ⌷ 2.50 – **30 rm** 44.00/76.00 **st**. – SB
(weekends only) (November-March) 66.00/108.00 **st**.

VATERSAY Inverness (Western Isles) **401** X 13 – Shipping Services : see Barra (Isle of).

VOE Shetland (Shetland Islands) **401** Q 2 – see Shetland Islands (Mainland).

WALKERBURN Peebles. (Borders) **401** **402** K 17 – pop. 713 – ✆ 089 687.
◆Edinburgh 32 – Galashiels 10 – Peebles 8.

🏠 **Tweed Valley** 🖏, Galashiels Rd, EH43 6AA, ✆ 220, ≤, 🖛, 🚗 – 📺 🛏wc 🗱wc **P**. 🔼
ⓞ **VISA**
M 4.75/10.00 **t**. and a la carte 🖟 3.75 – **15 rm** ⌷ 24.00/48.00 **t**. – SB (except October and
November) 54.00/56.00 **st**.

WEMYSS BAY Renfrew. (Strathclyde) **401** **402** F 16 – ECD : Wednesday – ✆ 0475.
🚢 by Caledonian MacBrayne : to Rothesay (Isle of Bute) 4-13 daily (30 mn).
Hotels see : Largs S : 4 ½ m., *Skelmorlie* S : 1 ½ m.

WESTHILL Aberdeen. (Grampian) **401** N 12 – see Aberdeen.

WESTRAY (Isle of) Orkney (Orkney Islands) **401** KL 6 – Shipping Services : see Orkney Islands (Mainland : Kirkwall).

WEST WEMYSS Fife. (Fife) – see Kirkcaldy.

WHALSAY (Isle of) Shetland (Shetland Islands) **401** R 2 – Shipping Services : see Shetland Islands.

WHITEBRIDGE Inverness (Highland) **401** G 12 – ✆ 045 63 Gorthleck.
◆Edinburgh 171 – ◆Inverness 23 – Kyle of Lochalsh 67 – ◆Oban 92.

🏠 **Knockie Lodge** 🖏, IV1 2UP, SW : 3 ½ m. by B 862 ✆ 276, ≤ Loch Nanlann and mountains,
« Tastefully converted hunting lodge », 🖛, park – 🛏wc **P**. 🔼 **AE** ⓞ **VISA**
May-November – **M** (bar lunch)/dinner 15.00 **t**. – **10 rm** ⌷ 33.00/70.00 **t**.

🏠 **Whitebridge,** IV1 2UN, ✆ 226, ≤, 🖛, 🚗 – 📺 🛏wc 🗱wc **P**. 🔼 **AE** ⓞ **VISA**
28 March-October – **M** (bar lunch)/dinner 8.50 **t**. – **12 rm** ⌷ 24.50/35.00 **t**.

WHITENESS Shetland (Shetland Islands) **401** Q 3 – see Shetland Islands (Mainland).

WHITING BAY Bute (Strathclyde) **401 402** E 17 – see Arran (Isle of).

WHITHORN (Isle of) Wigtown. (Dumfries and Galloway) **401 402** G 19 **Scotland G** – pop. 989 – ECD : Wednesday – ✪ 098 85.

Envir. : Priory Museum (Early Christian Crosses★★) NW : 4 m. by A 750.

✦Edinburgh 152 – ✦Ayr 72 – ✦Dumfries 72 – Stranraer 34.

  🏠   **Steam Packet,** Harbour Rd, DG8 8LL, ☞ 334 – 📺 ➿wc
      M (bar lunch)/dinner 12.50 **t.** ᵭ 2.80 – **4 rm** � 12.50/25.00 **t.**

  🏠   **Queens Arms,** 22 Main St., DG8 8LF, ☞ 369 – 📺 ➿wc **🅿. 🔼 ᴀᴇ ⓞ** 𝘝𝘐𝘚𝘈
      M (bar lunch)/dinner 9.50 **st.** and a la carte ᵭ 2.50 – **10 rm** ⊸ 12.50/31.00 **st.** – SB (October-May) 35.00/38.00 **st.**

WICK Caithness. (Highland) **401** K 8 **Scotland G** – pop. 7 ,770 – ECD : Wednesday – ✪ 0955.

Envir. : the Hill O'Many Stanes★, S by A 9 – Grey Cairns of Camster★, S by A 9 – Duncansby Head★ and the stacks of Duncansby★★, N : 17 m. by A 9.

🏌 Reiss ☞ 2726, N : 3 m.

✈ ☞ 2215, N : 1 m.

🅱 Caithness Tourist Organisation, Whitechapel Rd off High St. ☞ 2596.

✦Edinburgh 282 – ✦Inverness 126.

  🏨   **Ladbroke Mercury Motor Inn** (Ladbroke), Riverside, KW1 4NL, ☞ 3344 – 📺 ➿wc 🅰
      🅿. 🏛. 🔼 ᴀᴇ ⓞ 𝘝𝘐𝘚𝘈
      M (closed Sunday lunch) (bar lunch)/dinner 9.50 **t.** and a la carte ᵭ 3.70 – ⊸ 6.00 – **48 rm** 35.00/48.00 **t.** – SB (weekends only) (winter only) 57.50 **st.**

AUSTIN-ROVER Bridge St. ☞ 2195
DATSUN, VAUXHALL Francis St. ☞ 4123

FORD Francis St. ☞ 2103
TALBOT George St. ☞ 2321

WIGTOWN Wigtown. (Dumfries and Galloway) **401** G 19 – pop. 1 ,040 – ECD : Wednesday – ✉ Newton Stewart – ✪ 098 886 Mochrum.

✦Edinburgh 137 – ✦Ayr 61 – ✦Dumfries 61 – Stranraer 26.

  🏨   **Corsemalzie House** 🦢, DG8 9RL, SW : 6 ½ m. by A 714 on B 7005 ☞ 254, « Country house
      atmosphere », 🎣, 🛥, park – 📺 ➿wc **🅿. 🔼 ᴀᴇ ⓞ** 𝘝𝘐𝘚𝘈
      closed 20 January-7 March – **M** 6.75/10.25 **t.** and a la carte ᵭ 2.80 – **15 rm** ⊸ 28.50/48.00 **t.** – SB (except New Year) 49.00/63.00 **st.**

WORMIT Fife. (Fife) **401** L 14 – ECD : Wednesday – ✉ ✪ 0382 Newport-on-Tay.

✦Edinburgh 53 – ✦Dundee 6 – St. Andrews 12.

  🏨   **Sandford Hill** 🦢, DD6 8RG, S : 2 m. at junction of A 914 and B 946 ☞ 541802, ≤, 🛥 – 📺
      ➿wc 🏛 **🅿. 🔼 ᴀᴇ ⓞ** 𝘝𝘐𝘚𝘈
      closed 1 and 2 January – **M** 7.00/10.90 **t.** and a la carte ᵭ 2.50 – **15 rm** ⊸ 25.00/46.00 **t.** – SB (weekends only) 47.00/52.00 **st.**

WYRE (Isle of) Orkney (Orkney Islands) **401** L 6 – Shipping Services : see Orkney Islands (Mainland : Kirkwall).

YELL (Isle of) Shetland (Shetland Islands) **401** Q 2 – Shipping Services : see Shetland Islands.

Northern
Ireland

Place with at least :

one hotel or restaurant _____ ● Londonderry
one pleasant hotel _____ 🏠 , ✕ with rm
one quiet, secluded hotel _____ 🐾
one restaurant with _____ ✿,✿✿,✿✿✿, M
See this town for establishments
located in its vicinity _____ BELFAST

La località possiede come minimo :

una risorsa alberghiera _____ ● Londonderry
un albergo ameno _____ 🏠 , ✕ with rm
un albergo molto tranquillo, isolato ___ 🐾
un'ottima tavola con _____ ✿,✿✿,✿✿✿, M
La località raggruppa nel suo testo
le risorse dei dintorni _____ BELFAST

Localité offrant au moins :

une ressource hôtelière _____ ● Londonderry
un hôtel agréable _____ 🏠 , ✕ with rm
un hôtel très tranquille, isolé _____ 🐾
une bonne table à _____ ✿,✿✿,✿✿✿, M
Localité groupant dans le texte
les ressources de ses environs _____ BELFAST

Ort mit mindestens :

einem Hotel oder Restaurant _____ ● Londonderry
einem angenehmen Hotel _____ 🏠 , ✕ with rm
einem sehr ruhigen und abgelegenen Hotel _____ 🐾
einem Restaurant mit _____ ✿,✿✿,✿✿✿, M
Ort mit Angaben über Hotels und Restaurants
in seiner Umgebung _____ BELFAST

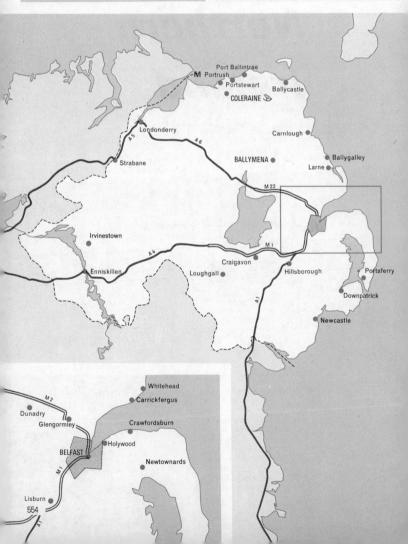

NORTHERN IRELAND

Towns

ANTRIM (Coast Road) Antrim **405** O 3.
See : Road★★★ (A 2) from Larne to Portrush.

BALLYCASTLE Antrim **405** N 2 – pop. 3 ,284 – ✆ 026 57.
See : Site★★.
Envir. : Giant's Causeway★★★ (Chaussée des Géants) basalt formation (from the car-park *AC*, ½ h Rtn on foot) NW : 12 m. – White Park Bay★★ NW : 8 ½ m. – Carrick-a-Rede (≤★★ of Rathlin Island) NW : 5 ½ m.
🏌 ✆ 62536.
🛈 Sheskburn House, 7 Mary St. ✆ 62024.
◆Belfast 60 – Ballymena 28 – Larne 40.

- ⚐ **Antrim Arms,** 75 Castle St., BT54 6AS, ✆ 62284 – 🄿
  M (bar lunch)/dinner 10.00 t. ⋀ 3.00 – **16 rm** ⌷ 12.50/29.00 t. – SB 28.00/32.00 **st.**
- ⌂ **Mount Pleasant,** 30 Quay Rd, BT54 6BH, ✆ 62118 – ♨wc 🄿. ✻
  7 rm ⌷ 7.00/9.00 **st.**

BALLYGALLEY Antrim **405** O 3 – pop. 424 – ⊠ Larne – ✆ 057 483.
◆Belfast 27 – Ballymena 24 – Larne 4.

- 🏰 Ballygally Castle, 274 Coast Rd, BT40 2QX, ✆ 212, ≤, 🐎, ✻ – 📺 ⌷wc ☎ 🄿
  30 rm.

BALLYMENA Antrim **405** N 3 – pop. 28 ,166 – ✆ 0266.
Envir. : Glen of Glenariff★★★ – Glenariff (or Waterfoot) site★ NE : 19 m.
🏌 Broughshane ✆ 861207, E : 2 m. on A 42.
🛈 2 Ballymoney Rd ✆ 46043.
◆Belfast 28 – ◆Dundalk 78 – Larne 21 – ◆Londonderry 51 – ◆Omagh 53.

- 🏰 **Adair Arms,** 1-5 Ballymoney Rd, BT43 5BS, ✆ 3674 – 📺 ⌷wc ☎ 🄿. 🏋. 🔼 🄰🄴 ⓞ 🆅🆂🄰
  M 5.75/15.00 t. and a la carte ⋀ 2.80 – **40 rm** ⌷ 28.50/44.00 t. – SB (weekends only) 32.50/35.00 **st.**

  at Kells SE : 6 m. by A 26 on B 98 – ⊠ ✆ 0266 Ballymena :

- 🏰 **Country House** ⏱, 20 Doagh Rd, BT42 3LZ, ✆ 891663, 🐎 – 📺 ⌷wc ♨wc ☎ 🄿. 🏋. 🔼 🄰🄴 ⓞ 🆅🆂🄰. ✻
  closed 25 and 26 December – **M** 7.95 t. (lunch) and a la carte 9.65/13.65 t. ⋀ 3.25 – **13 rm** ⌷ 29.50/39.50 t.

ALFA-ROMEO, TALBOT, LOTUS Broadway Av. ✆ 2161
AUSTIN-ROVER Waveney Av. ✆ 3557
RENAULT 120 Antrim Rd ✆ 2650
VW, AUDI 1/5 Railway St. ✆ 46014

BELFAST Antrim **405** O 4 – pop. 329 ,958 – ✆ 0232.
See : City Hall★★ 1906 BZ – Queen's University★★ 1906 AZ **U** – Ulster Museum★ AZ **M** – Church House★ 1905 BZ **B** – Botanic Gardens (hot houses★) AZ – Bellevue Zoological Gardens (site★, ≤★) *AC*, by A 6 AY.
Envir. : Stormont (Parliament House★ 1932, terrace : vista★★) E : 4 m. by Belmont Rd AZ – The Giant's Ring★ (prehistoric area) S : 5 m. by Malone Rd AZ – Lisburn (Castle gardens ≤★) SW : 8 m. by A 1 AZ.
🏌 Balmoral, Lisburn Rd ✆ 668540 AZ – 🏌 Fortwilliam, Downview Av. ✆ 771770, N : 2 m. AY – 🏌, 🏌 240 Upper Malone Rd, Dunmurry ✆ 612695 by A 55 AZ – 🏌 Shandon Park ✆ 793730, E : 3 m. by A 55 AZ.
✈ Belfast Airport : ✆ 229271, NW : 12 m. by M 2 Motorway AY – **Terminal :** Coach service (Ulsterbus Ltd.) from Great Victoria Street Station (40 mn).
🚢 to Liverpool (Belfast Car Ferries) 1 daily (9 h) – to Isle of Man : Douglas (Isle of Man Steam Packet Co.) July-September 1-2 weekly (4 h 30 mn).
🛈 River House, 48-52 High St. BT1 2DS ✆ 246609 – Belfast Airport, Aldergrove ✆ 084 94 (Crumlin) 52103.
◆Dublin 103 – ◆Londonderry 70.

23

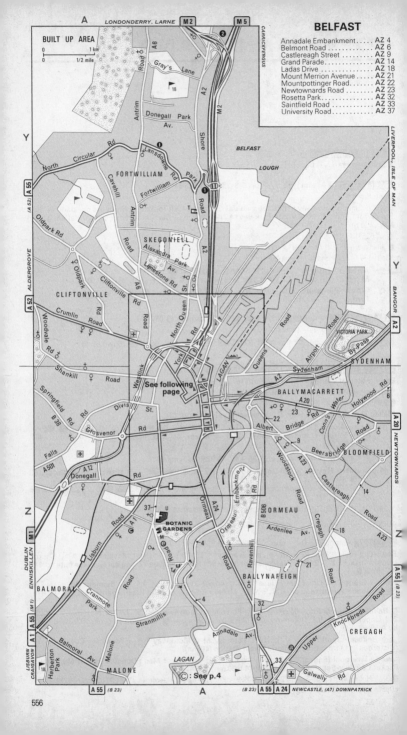

BELFAST

Annadale Embankment...... AZ 4
Belmont Road .... AZ 6
Castlereagh Street .... AZ 9
Grand Parade............. AZ 14
Ladas Drive .... AZ 18
Mount Merrion Avenue .... AZ 21
Mountpottinger Road ...... AZ 22
Newtownards Road .... AZ 23
Rosetta Park.............. AZ 32
Saintfield Road .... AZ 33
University Road........... AZ 37

Castle Place .... **BZ**
Donegal Place .... **BZ**
Royal Avenue .... **BYZ**

Albert Bridge Road .... **BZ** 2
Albert Square.............. **BY** 3
Ann Street .... **BZ** 5

Bradbury Place .... **BZ** 7
Bridge Street .... **BZ** 8
Clifton Street .... **BY** 10
Corporation Square .... **BY** 11
Donegall Quay .... **BYZ** 12
Donegall Square .... **BZ** 13
High Street .... **BYZ** 16
Howard Street .... **BZ** 17
Limestone Road .... **BY** 19
Mountpottinger
    Road .... **BZ** 22

Newtownards Road .... **BZ** 23
Queen Elizabeth
    Bridge............... **BZ** 25
Queen's Quay Road .... **BY** 26
Queen's Bridge .... **BZ** 27
Queen's Square .... **BY** 29
Rosemary Street .... **BZ** 30
Station Street............. **BY** 35
University Road........... **BZ** 37
Waring Street .... **BY** 38
Wellington Place........... **BZ** 39

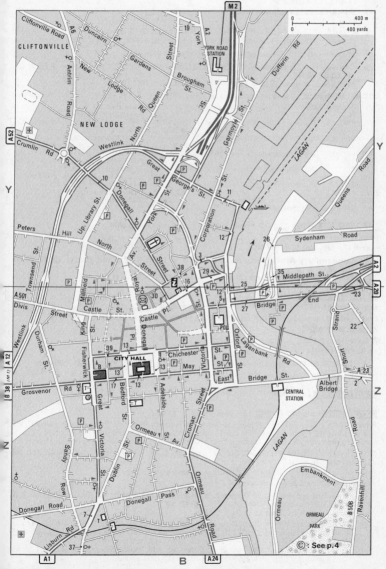

🏨 **Forum** (Forum), Great Victoria St., BT2 7AP, ℰ 245161, Telex 74491, ≼ – 🛗 📺 ☎ 🅿. 🛗. 🔼
AE ① VISA. ⁄⁄⁄
BZ **e**
M (carving rest.) 8.50/13.50 **st.** and a la carte ⅃ 3.95 – 🖙 4.75 – **200 rm** 49.50/69.50 **st.**

🏨 **Stormont**, 587 Upper Newtownards Rd, BT4 3LP, E : 4 ½ m. by A 2 on A 20 ℰ 658621 – 🛗 📺
🛏🛁 ☎ 🅿. 🛗
on A 20   AZ
67 rm.

🏨 **Drumkeen**, Upper Galwally, off Upper Knockbreda Rd, BT8 4TL, SE : 3 m. by A 24 off A 55
ℰ 645321 – 📺 🛏🛁wc ☎ 🅿. 🛗. 🔼 VISA. ⁄⁄⁄
AZ **a**
M 5.75/9.25 **st.** ⅃ 2.50 – **28 rm** 🖙 35.00/50.00 **st.**

⌂ **Camera House**, 44 Wellington Park, BT9 6DP, ℰ 660026 – 🛏🛁wc. VISA
AZ **c**
11 rm 🖙 14.40/23.00 **st.**

⌂ **Somerton**, 22 Lansdowne Rd, BT15 4DB, ℰ 778717 – 📺
AY **i**
8 rm 🖙 12.50/23.00.

✗ **Strand**, 12 Stranmillis Rd, BT9 5AA, ℰ 682266, Bistro – AE ① VISA
AZ **e**
closed Sunday and 12 to 26 July – **M** (booking essential) a la carte 3.85/10.95 **t.** ⅃ 2.45.

at Dunmurry SW : 5 ½ m. on A 1 – AZ – ✉ ☎ 0232 Belfast :

🏨 **Conway** (T.H.F.), Kingsway, BT17 9ES, ℰ 612101, Telex 74281, 🔼 heated, ⚿ – 🛗 📺 ☎ 🅿.
🛗. 🔼 AE ① VISA
M 6.00/7.50 **st.** and a la carte ⅃ 2.65 – 🖙 5.00 – **75 rm** 42.00/50.50 **st.**

MICHELIN Branch, 40 Mallusk Road, Newtonabbey, BT38 8PX, ℰ 42616 by N7 AZ

AUSTIN-ROVER-DAIMLER-JAGUAR   Saintfield Rd ℰ 649774
AUSTIN-ROVER   3 Diamond St., Shankil Rd ℰ 242456
AUSTIN-ROVER-DAIMLER-JAGUAR   10/18 Adelaide St. ℰ 230566
AUSTIN-ROVER   Upper Newtownards Rd, Dundonald ℰ 2651
BEDFORD, OPEL-VAUXHALL   17/29 Ravenhill Rd ℰ 51422
BEDFORD, OPEL-VAUXHALL   101 Kingsway, Dunmurry ℰ 614211
CITROEN   118/124 Donegall Pass ℰ 223441
FIAT   45/47 Rosetta Rd ℰ 648049

FORD   Lislea Drive ℰ 662231
FORD   58/82 Antrim Rd ℰ 744744
HYUNDAI   27, Pakenham St., Donegal Pass ℰ 232111
NISSAN   226 York St. ℰ 747133
NISSAN   397 Upper Newtownards Rd ℰ 654687
RENAULT   Boucher Rd ℰ 681721
SAAB, FIAT   250/252 Donegall St. ℰ 221019
TOYOTA   269/285 Upper Newtownards Rd ℰ 655208
TOYOTA   39/49 Adelaide St. ℰ 228225
VAUXHALL-OPEL   46 Florenceville Av. ℰ 641350
VAUXHALL-OPEL   83/87 York Rd ℰ 744869
VOLVO   59/75 Ladas Drive ℰ 703666
VW, AUDI   318a Sandown Rd ℰ 653082

CARNLOUGH Antrim 405 0 3 – pop. 1 ,462 – ✉ Ballymena – ☎ 0574.
🖪 Post Office, Harbour Rd ℰ 85210.
♦Belfast 37 – Ballymena 16 – Larne 14.

🏨 **Londonderry Arms,** Harbour Rd, BT44 0EU, ℰ 85255 – 📺 🛏🛁wc 🛁wc 🕾 🅿. 🔼 AE ①
VISA. ⁄⁄⁄
M 6.50/9.50 **t.** ⅃ 2.50 – **12 rm** 🖙 18.00/32.00 **st.** – SB 46.50/49.00 **st.**

CARRICKFERGUS Antrim 405 0 3 – pop. 17 ,633 – ☎ 096 03.
See : Castle⋆⋆ (13C) AC – Sea Front⋆ – St. Nicholas' Church⋆ 12C-18C.
Envir. : Island Magee Peninsula (Port Muck⋆, Isle of Muck⋆, Power Station ≼⋆) NE : 9 m.
🖈 North Rd ℰ 62203.
🖪 Castle Green ℰ 63604 (summer only).
♦Belfast 10 – Larne 14.

🏨 Coast Road, 28 Scotch Quarter, BT38 7DP, ℰ 61021 – 📺 🛏🛁wc 🛁wc 🕾. ⁄⁄⁄ – **20 rm**.
PEUGEOT, TALBOT   72 Belfast Rd ℰ 62299
RENAULT   Larne Rd ℰ 63516

CASTLEROCK Londonderry – see Coleraine.

COLERAINE Londonderry 405 L 2 – pop. 15 ,967 – ☎ 0265.
Envir. : Giant's Causeway⋆⋆⋆ (Chaussée des Géants) basalt formation (from the car-park AC, ½ h Rtn on foot) NE : 9 m. – Downhill Castle (Mussenden Temple⋆ 18C : ≼⋆⋆⋆ AC) NW : 7 m. – Portrush (site⋆, ≼⋆) N : 6 m. – Dunluce Castle (site⋆, ≼⋆) NE : 8 m. – W : Benevenagh Mountain⋆.
🖈 Castlerock ℰ 026 584 (Castlerock) 314, W : 5 m. – 🖈, 🖈, 🖈 Royal Portrush, Dunluce Rd, Portrush ℰ 0265 (Portrush) 822311.
🖪 Swimming Pool, Main St., Castlerock ℰ 848258 (summer only).
♦Belfast 53 – Ballymena 25 – ♦Londonderry 31 – ♦Omagh 65.

⌂ **Greenhill House** ⌇, 24 Greenhill Rd, Aghadowey, BT51 4EU, S : 9 m. by A 29 on B 66
ℰ 026 585 (Aghadowey) 241, ⚿ – 🛏🛁wc 🅿. 🔼. ⁄⁄⁄
March-October – **7 rm** 🖙 11.00/22.00 **st.**

✗✗ **MacDuffs** ⌇ with rm, Blackheath House, 112 Killeague Rd, Blackhill, BT51 4HH, S : 8 m. by
A 29 on Macosquin rd ℰ 026 585 (Aghadowey) 433, « 18C former manse », 🔼, ⚿ – 📺
🛏🛁wc 🛁wc 🅿. ①
closed last 2 weeks October and 25-26 December – **M** (closed Sunday and Monday) (dinner only) a la carte 9.30/12.10 **t.** ⅃ 2.75 – **6 rm** 🖙 20.00/35.00 **t.**

at Castlerock NW : 6 m. by A 2 off B 119 – ⊠ ✆ 0265 Castlerock :

↑ **Maritima,** 43 Main St., BT51 4RA, ✆ 848388, ≤ – ⋔wc ℗
6 rm ⊊ 10.50/21.00 t.

FORD 30-32 Church St. ✆ 2361

VAUXHALL-OPEL Hanover Pl. ✆ 2386

CRAIGAVON Armagh 405 M 4 – pop. 10 ,195 – ⊠ ✆ 0762 Portadown.

Envir. : Ardress House★ 17C (site★, drawing-room plasterwork★★) *AC*, W : 11 m. – Rich Hill (site★, church : scenery★) SW : 9 ½ m.

⛳ The Demesne, Lurgan ✆ 076 22 (Lurgan) 22087, NE : 3 m.

♦Belfast 28 – Armagh 13.

⌂ Seagoe, Upper Church Lane, BT53 5QS, ✆ 333076, ⇌ – TV ⊖wc ☎ ℗. ♨. ✻
38 rm.

CRAWFORDSBURN Down 405 O 4 – pop. 140 – ✆ 0247 Helen's Bay.

⛳ Carnalea ✆ 0247 (Bangor) 65004 – ⛳, ⛳ Clandeboye, Conlig ✆ 0247 (Bangor) 65767.

♦Belfast 10 – Bangor 3.

⌂ **Old Inn,** 15 Main St., BT19 1JH, ✆ 853255, ⇌ – TV ⊖wc ☜ ℗. ◨ AE ① VISA. ✻
closed 25 December and 1 January – **M** 4.90/9.00 t. and a la carte ⌗ 3.00 – ⊊ 3.50 – **21 rm**
28.00/45.00 t. – SB (weekends only) 58.00 st.

DOWNPATRICK Down 405 O 5 – pop. 8 ,245 – ✆ 0396.

Envir. : Saul (St. Patrick's Memorial Church : site★, ≤★) NE : 3 m. – Castle Ward 1765 (great hall★) NE : 6 m. – Portaferry : Strangford (site★, Audley's Castle : top ✻★★, 44 steps) NE : 8 m.

⛳ Saul Rd ✆ 2152 – ⛳ Castle Pl., Ardglass ✆ 0396 (Ardglass) 841219, SE : 7 m.

⚓ to Portaferry, frequent services daily (5 mn).

♦Belfast 22 – Bangor 27.

⌂ Abbey Lodge, 38 Belfast Rd, BT30 9AV, NW : 1 m. on A 7 ✆ 4511 – TV ⊖wc ☜ ℗. ♨. ✻
21 rm.

AUSTIN-ROVER St. Patrick's Av. ✆ 2215

FIAT, FORD Church St. ✆ 2777

DUNADRY Antrim 405 N 3 – ✆ 084 94 Templepatrick.

Envir. : Antrim (round tower★ 10C) NW : 5 m. – Shane's Castle★ (16C ruins) *AC*, NW : 5 ½ m. (access by miniature railway).

♦Belfast 15 – Larne 18 – ♦Londonderry 56.

🏨 **Dunadry Inn,** 2 Islandreagh Drive, BT41 2HA, ✆ 32474, Telex 747245, ⇌ – TV ☎ ℗. ♨. ◨
AE ① VISA. ✻
closed 25 to 28 December – **M** *(closed Saturday lunch and Sunday dinner)* 6.75 st. (lunch) and
a la carte 13.50/17.50 st. ⌗ 3.25 – **64 rm** ⊊ 44.00/55.00 st. – SB (weekends only) 52.00 st.

DUNMURRY Antrim 405 N 4 – see Belfast.

ENNISKILLEN Fermanagh 405 J 4 – pop. 10 ,429 – ✆ 0365.

See : Lough Erne★★★ (Upper and Lower) – On Lower Lough Erne, by boat *AC* : Devenish Island (site★★, monastic ruins : scenery★) and White Island★.

Envir. : Castle Coole★ 18C (site★) E : 1 m. – Florence Court (site★, park★) *AC*, SW : 8 m.

⛳ Castlecoole ✆ 22900.

🛈 Lakeland Visitor Centre, Shore Rd ✆ 23110 and 25050.

♦Belfast 87 – ♦Londonderry 59.

⌂ **Killyhevlin,** Dublin Rd, BT74 6HH, SE : 1 ¾ m. on A 4 ✆ 23481, ≤, ⇌, park – TV ⊖wc
⋔wc ☎ ℗. ♨. ◨ AE ① VISA. ✻
M a la carte 7.70/12.15 t. ⌗ 3.50 – **23 rm** ⊊ 19.00/50.00 t. – SB (weekends only)(except Easter)
45.00/55.00 st.

🏠 **Royal,** 4 East Bridge St., ✆ 22399 – TV ⋔wc. ◨ VISA. ✻
M 6.50/11.00 t. and a la carte ⌗ 2.30 – **9 rm** ⊊ 25.00/35.00 st. – SB (weekends only)
35.00/45.00 st.

🏠 Fort Lodge, Forthill St., ✆ 23275 – ⊖wc ⋔wc ☜ ℗
12 rm.

↑ **Willoughby,** 24 Willoughby Pl., BT74 7EX, ✆ 25275 – ℗. ✻
13 rm ⊊ 9.00/22.00 st.

AUSTIN-ROVER Dublin Rd ✆ 3475

VAUXHALL-OPEL Tempo Rd ✆ 4366

Do not lose your way in Europe, use the Michelin
Main Road maps, scale : 1 inch : 16 miles.

♦Belfast 6 – Larne 15.

🏠 **Chimney Corner,** 630 Antrim Rd, BT36 8RH, NW : 2 m. on A 6 ✆ 44925, Telex 748158, 🐾,
%% – 🔟 ⛱️wc ☎ 🅿. ▦. ⚠️ 🆎 ⓪ 𝗩𝗜𝗦𝗔. ❄️
closed 11 to 16 July and 10 days at Christmas – **M** *(closed Sunday lunch)* 6.00/10.00
st. and a la carte ▯ 3.50 – **63 rm** ⊑ 34.00/47.00 st.

XX **Sleepy Hollow,** 15 Kiln Rd, BT36 8SU, N : 2 m. by B 56 ✆ 44042 – 🅿
closed Sunday to Tuesday – **M** (dinner only) 14.75 st. ▯ 2.90.

HILLSBOROUGH Down **405** N 4 – ✪ 0849.
See : Government House★ 18C – the Fort★ 17C.
Envir. : Legananny Dolmen ≼★ S : 16 m.
🏌 Eglantine Rd, Lisburn ✆ 023 82 (Lisburn) 2186, N : 5 m.
♦Belfast 13.

🏠 **White Gables,** 14 Dromore Rd, BT26 6PE, ✆ 682755 – 🔟 ⛱️wc ☎ 🅿. ▦. ⚠️ 🆎 ⓪ 𝗩𝗜𝗦𝗔. ❄️
M 6.00/7.95 st. and a la carte ▯ 3.00 – **25 rm** ⊑ 22.00/35.00 t.

TOYOTA 23 Lisburn Rd ✆ 682188

HOLYWOOD Down **405** O 4 – pop. 9,462 – ✪ 023 17.
Envir. : Craigavad : Ulster Folk and Transport Museum★ (Cultra Manor) *AC*, NE : 3 m.
🏌 Nuns Walk, Demesne Rd ✆ 2138.
♦Belfast 5 – Bangor 6.

🏰 **Culloden** ⌂, 142 Bangor Rd, BT18 0EX, E : 1 ½ m. on A 2 ✆ 5223, Telex 74617, ≼, 🐾, park,
%%, squash – 🛗 🔟 ☎ ₫ 🅿 ▦. ⚠️ 🆎 ⓪ 𝗩𝗜𝗦𝗔
M 10.00 t. and a la carte – **74 rm** ⊑ 55.00/75.00 t. – SB (weekends only) 57.00 st.

FIAT 36/38 Shore Rd ✆ 5636

IRVINESTOWN Fermanagh **405** J 4 – pop. 1,827 – ✪ 036 56.
♦Belfast 78 – ♦Dublin 132 – Donegal 27.

☎ Mahon's, Mill St., BT74 9XX, ✆ 21656 – ⛱️wc ☜ 🅿 – **18 rm**.

KELLS Antrim **405** N 3 – see Ballymena.

LARNE Antrim **405** O 3 – pop. 18,224 – ✪ 0574.
Exc. : Antrim Coast Road★★★ (A 2) from Larne to Portrush.
🏌 Cairndhu, 192 Coast Rd ✆ 057 483 (Ballygally) 248, N : 4 m.
⚓ to Stranraer (Sealink) 2-9 daily (2 h 30 mn) – to Cairnryan (Townsend Thoresen) 2-7 daily (2 h
to 2 h 30 mn).
🅱 Council Offices, Victoria Rd ✆ 72313 – Car Park, Murrayfield Shopping Centre, Broadway ✆ 2313 (summer
only).
♦Belfast 23 – Ballymena 20.

⌂ **Derrin House,** 2 Prince's Gdns, BT40 1RQ, off Glenarm Rd (A 2) ✆ 73269 – 🅿
7 rm ⊑ 9.50/19.00 st.

AUSTIN-ROVER Point St. ✆ 2071   FORD 39 Glynn Rd ✆ 5411

LISBURN Antrim **405** N 4 – ✪ 08462.
♦Belfast 11 – ♦Dundalk 41.

XX **Hansom Cab,** 35 Railway St., BT28 1XP, ✆ 74652 – ⚠️ 🆎 ⓪ 𝗩𝗜𝗦𝗔
M (dinner only Wednesday to Saturday and Sunday lunch) 8.00/12.95 t. and a la carte ▯ 2.75.

LONDONDERRY Londonderry **405** K 2-3 – pop. 62,697 – ✪ 0504.
See : City Walls★★ 17C – Guildhall★ 1908 – Memorial Hall★.
Envir. : Grianan of Aileach★ (Republic of Ireland) (stone fort) ✳️★★★ NW : 5 m. – Dungiven (priory :
site★) SE : 18 m.
🏌 City of Derry, Victoria Rd, Prehen ✆ 42610.
✈ Eglinton Airport : ✆ 810784, E : 6 m.
🅱 Foyle St. ✆ 269501.
♦Belfast 70 – ♦Dublin 146.

🏰 **Everglades,** Prehen Rd, BT47 2PA, S : 1 ½ m. on A 5 ✆ 46722, Telex 748005 – 🔟 ☎ ₫ 🅿.
▦. ⚠️ 🆎 ⓪ 𝗩𝗜𝗦𝗔. ❄️
M 6.75/9.95 st. and a la carte ▯ 2.95 – ⊑ 4.25 – **38 rm** 25.00/35.00 st.

🏠 **White Horse Inn,** 68 Clooney Rd, BT47 3PA, NE : 5 ¼ m. on A 2 ✆ 0504 (Campsie) 860606 –
🔟 ⛱️wc ☎ 🅿. ⚠️ 🆎 ⓪ 𝗩𝗜𝗦𝗔.
M *(closed Sunday lunch)* a la carte 6.90/13.00 t. ▯ 2.50 – ⊑ 2.75 – **44 rm** 20.00/50.00 t.

BEDFORD, VAUXHALL-OPEL Maydown ✆ 860601   PEUGEOT, TALBOT Campsie ✆ 860588
FORD 173 Strand Rd ✆ 67613   VW, AUDI 24 Buncrana Rd ✆ 65985

LOUGHGALL Armagh 405 M 4 – pop. 267 – ☺ 076 289.
♦Belfast 38 – Armagh 5 – ♦Dublin 89.

   XX Bramley Apple, Old Cope School, 1 Main St., ☎ 318 – ℗.

NEWCASTLE Down 405 0 5 – pop. 6,246 – ☺ 039 67.
Envir. : Tollymore Forest Park★ *AC*, NW : 2 m. by B 180 – Dundrum (castle★ 13C ruins : top ☼★★, 70 steps) NE : 3 m. – Loughinisland (the 3 churches★ : 1000-1547-1636) NE : 8 m.
Exc. : SW : Mourne Mountains★★ (Slieve Donard★, Silent Valley★, Lough Shannagh★ : reservoir 1948).
🛈 61 Central Promenade ☎ 22222.
♦Belfast 30 – ♦Londonderry 101.

  🏠 **Enniskeen** 🦢, 98 Bryansford Rd, BT33 0LF, NW : 1 m. ☎ 22392, ≼, 🐎, park – 📺 ⌂wc 🕾
     ℗. 🔌 *VISA*.
     Mid March-October – **M** 6.50/8.00 **st.** and a la carte ¼ 2.75 – **12 rm** ⊈ 15.50/34.00 **st.** – SB
     (except Bank Holidays) 40.00/47.50 **st.**

  🏠 **Burrendale**, Castlewellan Rd, BT33 0JZ, N : 1 m. on A 50 ☎ 22599, 🐎 – 📺 ⌂wc 🕾 ℗.
     🛝. 🔌 ⓞ *VISA*
     M *(closed Sunday dinner)* (bar lunch Monday to Saturday)/dinner 8.50 **t.** and a la carte ¼ 2.75
     – **30 rm** ⊈ 19.50/30.00 **t.** – SB (weekends only)(except Easter, July and August) 35.00 **st.**

NEWRY Down 405 M N 5 – pop. 19,026 – ☺ 0693.
Envir. : Slieve Gullion★★, Ring of Gullion : Ballitemple viewpoint★★, Bernish Rock viewpoint★★, –
Cam Lough★, Killevy Churches (site★) SW : 5 m. – Derrymore House (site★) *AC*, NW : 2 ½ m. –
Rostrevor (Fairy Glen★) SE : 8 ¾ m. – Carlingford Lough★ SE : 10 m.
🚢 Warrenpoint ☎ 069 372 (Warrenpoint) 2219, S : 5 m.
🛈 Arts Centre, Bank Parade ☎ 66232.
♦Belfast 39 – Armagh 20 – ♦Dundalk 13.

AUSTIN-ROVER Railway Av. ☎ 2201   RENAULT 49/53 Merchants Quay ☎ 3626
PEUGEOT, TALBOT 18 Edward St. ☎ 2877

NEWTOWNARDS Down 405 0 4 – pop. 20,531 – ☺ 0247.
Envir. : Scrabo Tower (≼) SW : 1 m. – Mount Stewart Gardens★ *AC* – Temple of the Winds ≼
★ *AC*, SE : 5 ½ m. – Grey Abbey★ (Cistercian ruins 12C) *AC*, SW : 7 m.
🚢 Kirkstown Castle, Cloughey ☎ 024 77 (Portavogie) 71233.
♦Belfast 10 – Bangor 5.

  🏨 **Strangford Arms,** 92 Church St., BT23 4AL, ☎ 814141 – 📺 ⌂wc ☎ ℗. 🛝. 🔌 ⒶⒺ ⓞ *VISA*.
     🍴
     closed 31 March, 1 April and Christmas Day – **M** 7.50/10.50 **t.** and a la carte ¼ 4.00 – ⊈ 5.00 –
     36 rm 35.00/50.00 **t.**

FORD Regent St. ☎ 812626   VW, AUDI Portaferry Rd ☎ 815505
VAUXHALL-OPEL Portaferry Rd ☎ 813376

OMAGH Tyrone 405 K 4 – pop. 14,627 – ☺ 0662.
Envir. : Gortin Glen Forest Park★, Gortin Gap★ (on B 48) NE : 9 m. – Glenelly Valley★ NE : 17 m. by
Plumbridge.
🚢 Dublin Rd ☎ 3160 – 🚢 Fintona ☎ 0662 (Fintona) 841480, S : 5 ½ m.
🛈 1 Market St., ☎ 47831.
♦Belfast 68 – ♦Dublin 112 – ♦Dundalk 64 – ♦Londonderry 34 – ♦Sligo 69.

FORD Derry Rd ☎ 2788   VW-AUDI, VAUXHALL-OPEL 60 Dublin Rd ☎ 3116
RENAULT Cookstown Rd ☎ 3451

PORTAFERRY Down 405 P 4 – pop. 2,148 – ☺ 024 77.
🚢 to Downpatrick, frequent services daily (5 mn).
♦ Belfast 29 – Bangor 24.

  🏠 **Portaferry,** 10 The Strand, BT22 1PE, ☎ 28231, ≼ – ⌂wc 🍴wc. 🔌 ⒶⒺ ⓞ *VISA*. 🍴
     closed Christmas Day – **M** *(closed Sunday dinner to non-residents)* a la carte 9.15/12.55 **t.**
     ¼ 3.00 – **6 rm** ⊈ 16.00/30.00 **t.** – SB (except July and August) 49.00 **st.**

PORT BALLINTRAE Antrim 405 M 2 – pop. 586 – ✉ ☺ 026 57 Bushmills.
🛈 Bushmills ☎ 31672 (summer only).
♦Belfast 68 – Coleraine 15.

  🏠 **Bayview,** 2 Bayhead Rd, BT57 8RZ, ☎ 31453, ≼ – 📺 ⌂wc ☎ ℗. 🔌 *VISA*. 🍴
     M *(closed Sunday dinner)* 6.00/12.00 **st.** and a la carte ¼ 2.00 – **16 rm** ⊈ 22.00/34.00 **t.** – SB
     (weekends only)(except Easter, July and August) 50.00 **st.**

PORTRUSH Antrim 405 L 2 – pop. 5,114 – ☺ 0265.

  XX **Ramore,** The Harbour, BT56 8BN, ☎ 824313 – ℗
     closed Sunday, Monday and last 2 weeks January –   (booking essential)(dinner only) a la
     carte 8.85/12.30 **t.** ¼ 2.45.

☖₈, ☖₈ Strand Head ✆ 2015, West boundary.

🛈 Town Hall, The Crescent ✆ 2286.

♦Belfast 67 – Coleraine 6.

🏨 **Edgewater,** 88 Strand Rd, BT55 7LZ, ✆ 3314, ← – 📺 ⇌wc ⋔wc ☎ 🅿. 🔆 ⓪ 𝘝𝘐𝘚𝘈. ⚞
M 6.25/7.25 **st.** and a la carte ▯ 2.95 – **30 rm** ⇌ 18.50/35.00 **t.** – SB (weekends only)(October-June) 29.00/36.00 **st.**

↰ **The Links,** 103 Strand Rd, BT55 7LZ, ✆ 2580 – 🅿
May-October – **14 rm** ⇌ 10.00/20.00 **st.**

STRABANE Tyrone **405** J 3 – pop. 10,340 – ✪ 0504.

☖ Bally Colman ✆ 882271.

🛈 Lifford Rd ✆ 883204 (summer only).

♦Belfast 87 – Donegal 34 – ♦Dundalk 98 – ♦Londonderry 14.

🏨 **Fir Trees Lodge,** Melmont Rd, BT82 9JT, ✆ 883003 – 📺 ⇌wc ☎ 🅿. 🔆 🅰🅴 ⓪ 𝘝𝘐𝘚𝘈
M 5.95/9.50 **st.** and a la carte ▯ 2.20 – **26 rm** ⇌ 25.00/37.00 **st.**

WHITEHEAD Antrim **405** O 3 – ✉ Carrickfergus – ✪ 096 03.

♦Belfast 16 – Larne 8.5.

🏨 **Dolphin,** 16 Marine Par., BT38 9QD, ✆ 72481, ← – ⇌wc 🅿
closed 24 December-10 January – **M** 4.00/7.00 **st.** and a la carte ▯ 2.60 – **19 rm** ⇌ 14.50/25.00 **st.**

Channel

Islands

Place with at least :

one hotel or restaurant................................. ● Herm

one pleasant hotel.............................. 🏠 , 🗙 with rm

one quiet, secluded hotel .... 🐃

one restaurant with................................. ✿,✿✿,✿✿✿, M

See this town for establishments
located in its vicinity............................... GOREY

Localité offrant au moins :

une ressource hôtelière............................... ● Herm

un hôtel agréable.............................. 🏠 , 🗙 with rm

un hôtel très tranquille, isolé........................ 🐃

une bonne table à................................. ✿,✿✿,✿✿✿, M

Localité groupant dans le texte
les ressources de ses environs .... GOREY

La località possiede come minimo :

una risorsa alberghiera .... ● Herm

un albergo ameno.............................. 🏠 , 🗙 with rm

un albergo molto tranquillo, isolato .... 🐃

un'ottima tavola con .... ✿,✿✿,✿✿✿, M

La località raggruppa nel suo testo
le risorse dei dintorni .... GOREY

Ort mit mindestens :

einem Hotel oder Restaurant.......................... ● Herm

einem angenehmen Hotel.............................. 🏠 , 🗙 with rm

einem sehr ruhigen und abgelegenen Hotel ..... 🐃

einem Restaurant mit................................. ✿,✿✿,✿✿✿, M

Ort mit Angaben über Hotels und Restaurants
in seiner Umgebung................................. GOREY

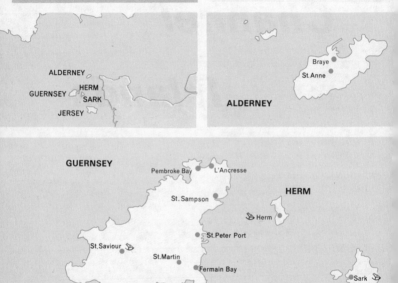

564

CHANNEL ISLANDS

Towns

ALDERNEY **408** Q 33 and **280** ⑨ – pop. 2 ,068 – ECD : Wednesday – ☻ 048 182.

See : Telegraph Bay★ (cliffs★) – Clonque Bay★ – Braye Bay★.

✈ ℰ 2711 - Booking Office : Aurigny Air Services ℰ 2889 Air Ferries ℰ 2993.

🚢 Shipping connections with the Continent : to France (Saint-Malo) (via Guernsey, Sark and Jersey)(Condor : Hydrofoil) summer only – to Torquay (Torbay Seaways : Hydrofoil) summer only 1 weekly (2 h 30 mn) – to Jersey (St. Helier) (Condor : hydrofoil) 3 weekly summer only (2 h 30 mn) – to Guernsey (St. Peter Port) (Condor : hydrofoil) summer only 3 weekly (45 mn) – to Sark (Condor : hydrofoil) summer only 2 weekly (1 h 30 mn).

🛈 States Office ℰ 2994.

St. Anne. – ⊠ St. Anne – ☻ 048 182 Alderney.

📞₉ ℰ 2835, E : 1 m.

🏛 **Chez André,** Victoria St., ℰ 2777 – ➱wc. ⚊ ⓞ 𝗩𝗜𝗦𝗔. ℅
April-October – **M** (bar lunch)/dinner 6.50 and a la carte ▯ 1.75 – **14 rm** ⊇ 16.00/22.00.

🏛 **Inchalla** ❦, Le Val, ℰ 3220, ♨ – 🆃🆅 ➱wc ℗. 𝗩𝗜𝗦𝗔. ℅
M (closed Sunday dinner) (dinner only and Sunday lunch)/dinner 8.50 **s.** and a la carte ▯ 1.60 – ⊇ 2.25 – **12 rm** 13.00/34.00 **s.** – SB (October-April) 38.00/42.00 **s.**

↰ **Town House,** 10 High St., ℰ 2330 – ℅
11 rm ⊇ 11.00/22.00 **s.**

XX **Nellie Gray's,** Victoria St., ℰ 3333 – ⚊ ᴀᴇ ⓞ 𝗩𝗜𝗦𝗔
April-October – **M** (closed Sunday lunch) (buffet lunch)/dinner a la carte 9.20/14.20 ▯ 2.40.

X **Georgian House** with rm, Victoria St., ℰ 2471 – 🆃🆅 ➱wc. ⚊ ⓞ 𝗩𝗜𝗦𝗔. ℅
M (closed Sunday dinner November-March) a la carte 4.25/11.50 ▯ 1.90 – **4 rm** ⊇ 16.50/40.00 – SB (November-March) 52.00/60.00.

Braye – ⊠ Braye – ☻ 048 182 Alderney.

X **First and Last,** ℰ 3162, ≼ Harbour – ⚊ ᴀᴇ ⓞ 𝗩𝗜𝗦𝗔
closed Monday – **M** a la carte 9.50/12.00 ▯ 2.00.

GUERNSEY **408** OP 33 and **280** ⑨ ⑩ – pop. 53 ,637 – ☻ 0481.

See : Icart Point ≼★★★ – Cobo Bay★★ – Fort Pézéries ≼★★ – Fort Doyle ≼★ – Fort Saumarez ≼★ – Moulin Huet Bay★ – Rocquaine Bay★ – Moye Point (Le Gouffre★).

✈ La Villiaze, Forest ℰ 37766.

🚢 Shipping connections with the Continent : to France (Saint-Malo) (Commodore Shipping Co.) cars only (passengers travel by hydrofoil) summer only – to France (Saint-Malo) (Emeraude Ferries) - to France (Cherbourg)(Sealink) – to Portsmouth (via Jersey)(Sealink) 6-7 weekly (12 h 30 mn) – to Weymouth (Sealink) summer 1-3 daily : winter 6 weekly (4 h 30 mn and 9 h via Jersey) – to Jersey (St. Helier) (Sealink) 1-2 daily (2 h) – to Portsmouth (Channel Island Ferries) 6-7 weekly (10 h).

🚢 Shipping connections with the Continent : to France (Saint-Malo) (Condor : hydrofoil) summer only – to France (Carteret and Cherbourg) (Service Maritime) summer only – to Jersey (St. Helier) (Condor : hydrofoil) 1-4 daily in summer (1 h) – to Alderney (Condor : hydrofoil) summer only 3 weekly (45 mn) – to Herm (Herm Seaway) 7 daily (25 mn) – to Sark (Isle of Sark Shipping Co.) 1-6 daily (40 mn) – to Torquay (Torbay Seaways : Hydrofoil) summer only 2 weekly (2 h 30 mn).

🛈 Crown Pier, St. Peter Port ℰ 23552 – The Airport, La Villiaze ℰ 37267.

L'Ancresse – ☻ 0481 Guernsey.

📞₁₈ ℰ45070.

↰ **Lynton** ❦, Hacse Lane, ℰ 45418, ♨ – ➱wc 🗲wc ℗. ℅
May-September – **14 rm** ⊇ 15.00/36.00.

Fermain Bay – ⊠ St. Peter Port – ☻ 0481 Guernsey.

🏛 **La Favorita** ❦, Fermain Lane, ℰ 35666, ♨ – 🆃🆅 ➱wc ☎ ℗. 𝗩𝗜𝗦𝗔. ℅
March-November – **M** (bar lunch)/dinner 5.10 **s.** ▯ 1.50 – **30 rm** ⊇ 14.00/43.00 **s.**

🏛 **Le Chalet** ❦, Fermain Lane, ⊠ St. Martin, ℰ 35716, ≼ – 🆃🆅 ➱wc 🗲wc ☏ ℗. ⚊ ᴀᴇ ⓞ 𝗩𝗜𝗦𝗔. ℅
21 April-14 October – **M** 5.00/7.00 **s.** and a la carte ▯ 1.50 – **50 rm** ⊇ 17.20/38.00 **s.**

565

Pembroke Bay – ⊠ Vale – ☎ 0481 Guernsey.
St. Peter Port 5.

🏛 **Pembroke** ⑤, ℰ 47573 – 📺 🏔wc ☎ ℗ 🔄 ᴀᴇ 𝑽𝑰𝑺𝑨 ⌘
M 5.50/6.50 – 🖭 3.00 – **14 rm** 26.50/49.00 – SB 50.00/65.00 **s.**

St. Martin – pop. 5,842 – ECD : Thursday – ⊠ St. Martin – ☎ 0481 Guernsey.
See : Church★ 11C.
St. Peter Port 2.

🏛 **Green Acres** ⑤, Les Hubits, ℰ 35711, ⅃ heated, 🌫 – 📺 ⌷wc ☜ ℗ 🔄 𝑽𝑰𝑺𝑨 ⌘
M (bar lunch)/dinner 6.00 and a la carte ⅃ 1.80 – **48 rm**.

🏛 **Bella Luce**, La Fosse, Moulin Huet, ℰ 38764, ⅃ heated, 🌫 – 📺 ⌷wc 🏔wc ℗
closed 3 weeks January – **M** (bar lunch Monday to Saturday)/dinner 8.45 and a la carte ⅃ 1.95
– **31 rm** 🖭 15.50/53.00.

🏛 **St. Margaret's Lodge,** Forest Rd, ℰ 35757, ⅃ heated, 🌫 – 📺 ⌷wc ☜ ℗ 🔄 ① 𝑽𝑰𝑺𝑨
M 5.25/7.50 and a la carte ⅃ 2.25 – **43 rm** 🖭 15.00/50.00 **s.** – SB (May-September) 30.00/37.50.

🏛 **La Trelade,** Forest Rd, ℰ 35454, ⅃ heated – 🛗 📺 ⌷wc ☎ ℗ 🔄 𝑽𝑰𝑺𝑨
M (bar lunch)/dinner 6.50 and a la carte ⅃ 2.00 – **45 rm** 🖭 14.50/45.00 – SB (October-March)
48.00.

🏠 **La Cloche** ⑤, Les Traudes, ℰ 35421, ⅃ heated, 🌫 – 📺 ⌷wc 🏔wc ☎ ℗ ⌘
March-October – **10 rm** 🖭 19.00/44.00.

🏠 **Windmill,** Rue Poudreuse, ℰ 37402, ⅃ heated, 🌫 – 📺 ⌷wc 🏔wc ℗ ⌘
April-October – **M** (residents only)(bar lunch)/dinner 7.00 ⅃ 1.70 – **19 rm** 🖭 18.00/38.00.

⌂ **Wellesley,** Sausmarez Rd, ℰ 38028, 🌫 – ⌷wc 🏔wc ℗
April-October – **9 rm** 🖭 14.00/28.00 **s.**

ALFA ROMEO, FERRARI, FIAT, MAZDA Forest Rd   AUSTIN-ROVER Ville au Roi ℰ 37661
ℰ 35753

In July and August, hotels are often overcrowded and staff overworked.
You will be more satisfied if you go in other months.

St. Peter Port – pop. 15,587 – ECD : Thursday – ⊠ St. Peter Port – ☎ 0481 Guernsey.
See : St. Peter's Church★ 14C Z – Castle Cornet★ (❄★) *AC* Z – Hauteville House (Victor
Hugo Museum★ : 5 pearl-embroidered tapestries★★) *AC* Z – Victoria Tower : top ❄★★, 100
steps Y – **Envir. :** Les Vauxbelets (Little Chapel★) SW : 2 ½ m. by Mount Durand Z –
Saumarez Park★ W : 2 ½ m. by Grange Rd Z – Vale (castle ≼ ★) NW : 4 ½ m. by St. Georges
Esplanade Y.
🛈 Crown Pier ℰ 23552.

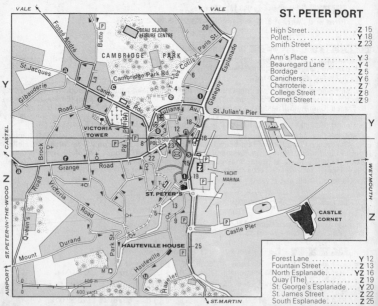

ST. PETER PORT

High Street . . . . **Z** 15
Pollet . . . . **Y** 18
Smith Street . . . . **Z** 23

Ann's Place . . . . **Y** 3
Beauregard Lane . . . . **Y** 4
Bordage . . . . **Z** 5
Canichers . . . . **Y** 6
Charroterie . . . . **Z** 7
College Street . . . . **Z** 8
Cornet Street . . . . **Z** 9

Forest Lane . . . . **Y** 12
Fountain Street . . . . **Z** 13
North Esplanade . . . . **YZ** 16
Quay (The) . . . . **Z** 19
St. George's Esplanade . . . **Y** 20
St. James Street . . . . **Z** 22
South Esplanade . . . . **Z** 25

🏨 **St. Pierre Park,** Rohais, by Grange Rd, ℰ 28282, Telex 4191662, ≤, 🔲, 🛏, 🚗, park, 🍴 –
🛗 📺 ☎ 👤 👤. 🔥 🔺 🅰🅴 ⓪ VISA. 🛂 Z
M a la carte lunch/dinner 5.50 🍷 2.10 (see also rest. **Victor Hugo**) – **131 rm** 🛏 35.75/75.50 **s.**

🏨 **Old Government House,** St. Ann's Pl., ℰ 24921, Telex 4191144, 🔥 heated, 🚗 – 🛗 📺 🔥
👤. 🔺 🅰🅴 ⓪ VISA Y o
M 5.00/7.50 and a la carte 🍷 2.00 – **73 rm** 🛏 23.00/70.00.

🏨 **Duke of Richmond,** Cambridge Park, ℰ 26221, Telex 4191462, 🔥 heated – 🛗 🍽 rest 📺
☎. 🔺 🅰🅴 ⓪ VISA Y c
M 5.50/8.50 🍷 2.00 – **74 rm** 🛏 25.00/65.00 – SB (weekends only) 50.00/60.00 **s.**

🏨 **Royal,** Glategny Esplanade, ℰ 23921, Telex 4191221, ≤, 🔥 heated, 🚗 – 🛗 📺 👤. 🔥 🔺 🅰🅴
⓪ VISA Y i
M a la carte 7.00/10.00 🍷 3.85 – **79 rm** 🛏 18.50/74.00 **s.**

🏨 **La Collinette,** St. Jacques, ℰ 22585, 🔥 heated, 🚗 – 📺 🚻wc 🚗 👤. 🔺 🅰🅴 ⓪ VISA. 🛂
M 4.50/6.00 🍷 2.80 – **22 rm** 🛏 15.00/46.00. Y a

🏨 Dunchoille, Guelles Rd, ℰ 22912, 🔥 heated, 🚗 – 🚻wc 🚻wc 👤. 🛂 N : by la Butte Y
24 rm.

🏨 **Grange Lodge,** The Grange, ℰ 25161, 🔥 heated, 🚗 – 📺 🚻wc 👤. 🔺 VISA Z r
March-November – **M** (bar lunch) 🍷 1.50 – **33 rm** 🛏 (dinner included) 14.00/36.00.

🏨 **Moore's Central,** Le Pollet, ℰ 24452 – 🛗 📺 🚻wc 🚗. 🔺 🅰🅴 ⓪ VISA Y n
M 4.50/6.50 **s.** and a la carte 🍷 1.50 – **40 rm** 🛏 12.00/39.50 **s.** – SB (November-March)
35.00/38.00 **s.**

↑ **Midhurst House,** Candie Rd, ℰ 24391, 🚗 – 📺 🚻wc 🛂 Y r
closed January, February and November – **7 rm** 🛏 15.00/30.00 **s.**

↑ **Baltimore House,** Les Gravées, ℰ 23641, 🚗 – 🚻wc. 🔺 🅰🅴 ⓪ VISA Z a
March-October – **12 rm** 🛏 11.75/31.00 **s.**

↑ **Havelet Court** without rest., Havelet, ℰ 26410, ≤ Havelet Bay, 🚗 – 🚻wc. 🛂 Z u
Mid April-October – 🛏 1.50 – **12 rm** 15.50/29.00.

XXXX **Victor Hugo** (at St. Pierre Park H.), Rohais, by Grange Rd, ℰ 28282, Telex 4191662 – 👤. 🔺
🅰🅴 ⓪ VISA Z
closed Saturday lunch and Sunday dinner – **M** 7.50 (lunch)/dinner a la carte 10.50/14.75
🍷 2.10.

XXX **La Frégate** 🌳 with rm, Les Côtils, ℰ 24624, ≤ town and harbour, « Country house atmosphere », 🚗 – 🍽 rest 🚻wc 🚗 👤. 🔺 🅰🅴 ⓪ VISA. 🛂 Y e
M (booking essential) 7.00/10.00 **s.** and a la carte 🍷 2.00 – 🛏 5.00 – **13 rm** 18.50/55.00 **s.**

XX **Le Nautique,** Quay Steps, ℰ 21714, ≤ – 🔺 🅰🅴 ⓪ VISA Z s
closed Sunday and 1 to 20 January – **M** (booking essential) a la carte 7.00/11.70 🍷 2.00.

XX **Steak and Stilton,** The Quay, ℰ 23080 – 🔺 🅰🅴 ⓪ VISA Z i
closed 22 December-24 January – **M** a la carte 7.20/11.30 🍷 2.20.

ASTON-MARTIN, LANCIA, NISSAN, PEUGEOT-TAL-   FORD   Les Banques ℰ 24774
BOT, ROLLS ROYCE   Rue du Pré ℰ 24261   HONDA   Doyle Rd ℰ 24025
BMW, MERCEDES-BENZ   16 Glategny Esplanade ℰ   RENAULT   Upland Rd ℰ 26846
23916

St. Sampson – pop. 6 ,947 – ✉ St. Sampson's – ☎ 0481 Guernsey.
St. Peter Port 3.5.

↑ **Pinetops** 🌳, Pointues Rocques, Delancey, off Vale Rd, ℰ 44020 – 📺 🚻wc 👤. 🛂
15 rm 🛏 12.50/37.00 **s.**

St. Saviour – pop. 2 ,432 – ✉ St. Saviour – ☎ 0481 Guernsey.
St. Peter Port 4.

🏨 **L'Atlantique,** Perelle Bay, ℰ 64056, ≤, 🔥 heated, 🚗 – 📺 🚻wc 🚗 👤. 🔺 🅰🅴 ⓪ VISA. 🛂
M (bar lunch)/dinner 7.25 **s.** and a la carte 🍷 1.75 – **21 rm** 🛏 13.00/40.00 **s.**

🏨 **La Hougue Fouque Farm,** Route-des-Bas-Courtil, ℰ 64181, 🔥 heated – 📺 🚻wc ☎ 👤.
🔺 VISA. 🛂
M 5.50/7.50 and a la carte 🍷 1.90 – **16 rm** 🛏 25.00/60.00.

🏨 **La Girouette Country House** 🌳, ℰ 63269, 🚗 – 📺 🚻wc 🚻wc 👤. 🔺 🅰🅴 VISA. 🛂
closed November and December – **M** (dinner only and Sunday lunch) 5.50 **s.** 🍷 2.00 – **14 rm**
🛏 11.00/21.25 **s.**

HERM ISLAND 40🔢 P 33 and 23🔢 ⑩ – pop. 37 – ☎ 0481 Guernsey.
🚢 to Guernsey (Herm Seaway) 7 daily (25 mn).
🄱 Administrative Office ℰ 22377.

Herm – ✉ Herm – ☎ 0481 Guernsey.

🏨 **White House** 🌳, ℰ 22159, ≤, 🔥, 🚗, park, 🍴 – 🚻wc. VISA. 🛂
April-October – **M** 5.50/7.50 and a la carte 🍷 2.00 – **30 rm** 🛏 (dinner included) 25.00/68.00.

See : Devil's Hole★ (site★★) *AC* private access, ¾ h Rtn on foot by a steep road – Grosnez Castle
≤★ – La Hougue Bie Tumulus★ (prehistoric tomb) *AC* – St. Catherine's Bay★ – Fliquet Bay (St.
Catherine's Breakwater ≤★★) – Sorel Point ≤★ – Noirmont Point ≤★ – Jersey zoo (site★) *AC*.

✈ States of Jersey Airport ℘ 46111, Telex 4192332.

⟋ Shipping connections with the Continent : to France (Saint-Malo) (Emeraude Ferries) - to
France (Cherbourg)(Sealink) – to France (Saint-Malo) (Commodore Shipping Co.) cars only (passengers travel by hydrofoil) summer only – to Portsmouth (Sealink) 6-7 weekly (9 h 30 mn) – to
Weymouth (Sealink) summer only 1 daily (6 h 15 mn) – to Guernsey (St. Peter Port) (Sealink) 6-7
weekly (2 h 45 mn) – to Portsmouth (Channel Island Ferries) 6-7 weekly (7 h 45 mn).

⟋ Shipping connections with the Continent : to France (Saint-Malo) (Condor : hydrofoil) (Vedettes
Blanches, summer only) (Vedettes Armoricaines) – to France (Granville) (Vedettes Armoricaines
and Vedettes Vertes Granvillaises) - from Gorey to France (Carteret) (Service Maritime Carteret
and Vedettes Blanches et Verts) – from Gorey to France (Portbail) (Service Maritime Carteret) – to
Sark (Condor : hydrofoil) summer only Monday/Saturday 1-2 daily (45 mn-1 h 30 mn) – to Guernsey
(St. Peter Port) (Condor : hydrofoil) 1-4 daily in summer (1 h) – to Alderney (Condor : hydrofoil)
summer 3 weekly (2 h 5 mn) – to Torquay (Torbay Seaways : Hydrofoil) summer only 2 weekly (3 h
30 mn).

🛈 Weighbridge. St. Helier ℘ 78000 and 24779.

Archirondel – ⊠ Gorey – ✪ 0534 Jersey.
St. Helier 5.

🏨 **Les Arches,** ℘ 53839, Telex 4192085, ≤, ⚓ heated, ⚓ – ⊖wc 🛉wc 🅿 🚗 📶 *VISA*
M 10.50/15.00 **s.** 🍷 2.00 – **54 rm** ⚏ 16.00/47.00 **s.** – SB (weekends only)(November-March)
36.00 **s.**

Bonne Nuit Bay – ⊠ St. John – ✪ 0534 Jersey.
St. Helier 6.

🏨 **Cheval Roc** ◈, ℘ 62865, ≤ Bonne Nuit Bay, ⚓ heated – ⊖wc 🛉wc 🅿 *VISA*
May-September – **M** 4.00/7.50 **s.** 🍷 2.00 – **45 rm** ⚏ 16.00/55.00 **s.**

🏨 **Bonne Nuit,** ℘ 61644, ≤ Bonne Nuit Bay, ⚓ – ⊖wc 🛉wc 🚗 🅿 📶 AE ⓿ *VISA* ⚘
closed 1 to 3 January – **M** (seafood) 7.00 and a la carte 🍷 1.95 – **30 rm** ⚏ 11.50/49.00 **s.**

Bouley Bay – ⊠ Trinity – ✪ 0534 Jersey.
St. Helier 5.

🏨 **Water's Edge** ◈, ℘ 62777, Group Telex 4191462, ≤ Bouley Bay, ⚓ heated, ⚓ – 🛗 📺 🅿
📶 AE ⓿ *VISA*
Mid April-mid October – **M** 9.00/13.00 **s.** and a la carte 🍷 2.50 – **56 rm** ⚏ 29.50/80.00.

Corbiere – ⊠ St. Brelade – ✪ 0534 Jersey.
St. Helier 8.

✕✕ **Sea Crest,** with rm, Petit Port, ℘ 42687, ≤, ⚓, ⚓ – 📺 ⊖wc 🚗 🅿 📶 AE *VISA* ⚘
accomodation closed 5 November-February – **M** a la carte 8.50/17.00 🍷 2.00 – **7 rm** ⚏ 50.00.

L'Etacq – ⊠ St. Ouens – ✪ 0534.
St. Helier 15.

🏛 **Lobster Pot,** Mont du Vallet, ℘ 82888 – 📺 ⊖wc ☎ 🅿 📶 AE ⓿ *VISA* ⚘
M 6.00/9.00 and a la carte 🍷 1.75 – **13 rm** ⚏ 37.00/72.00 **s.**

Gorey – ⊠ St. Martin – ✪ 0534 Jersey.
See : Mont Orgueil Castle★ (≤★★, paintings★) *AC*.
St. Helier 4.

🏨 Old Court House, Gorey Village, ℘ 54444, Telex 4192032, ⚓ heated, ⚓ – 🛗 📺 ⊖wc 🚗 🅿
📶 AE ⓿ *VISA* ⚘
April-October – **M** 4.50/7.00 **s.** and a la carte 🍷 1.50 – **58 rm**.

🏛 **Trafalgar Bay,** Gorey Village, ℘ 53216, Telex 4192349, ⚓ heated, ⚓ – ⊖wc 🅿 📶 *VISA*.
⚘
June-September – **M** (bar lunch)/dinner 6.00 **s.** and a la carte 🍷 1.85 – **37 rm** ⚏ 11.75/38.50 **s.**

at Gorey Pier – ⊠ St. Martin – ✪ 0534 Jersey :

🏛 **Moorings,** ℘ 53633, Telex 4192371 – 🍽 rest 📺 ⊖wc 🚗 🅿 📶 *VISA*
M 7.00 (lunch) and a la carte 10.30/13.80 🍷 2.20 – **16 rm** ⚏ 18.00/50.00 **s.**

🏕 Seascale, ℘ 54395 – ⊖wc 🛉wc – **10 rm**.

🏕 **Dolphin,** ℘ 53370, Group Telex 4192085 – 🛉wc 🚗 📶 *VISA* ⚘
M 6.00/9.00 **st.** and a la carte 🍷 2.00 – **17 rm** ⚏ 15.00/40.00 **st.**

La Haule – ⊠ St. Brelade – ✪ 0534 Jersey.

🏨 La Place ◈, Route du Coin, by B 25 on B 43 ℘ 44261, Telex 4191462, ⚓ heated – 📺 🅿 📶
AE ⓿ *VISA*
M 7.00/10.00 and a la carte – **40 rm**.

Portelet Bay – ⊠ St. Brelade – ☎ 0534 Jersey.
St. Helier 5.

🏨 **Portelet** ⤴, ℰ 41204, Telex 4192039, ≤, ⤴ heated, 🏖, ℀ – 📺 🅟, 🔌 🅰🅴 ⓄⓄ *VISA*. ❄
May-mid October – **M** 6.00/8.50 and a la carte – **86 rm** � 28.00/72.00.

La Pulente – ⊠ St. Brelade – ☎ 0534 Jersey.
St. Helier 7.

🏨 **Atlantic** ⤴, La Moye, ℰ 44101, Telex 4192405, ≤, ⤴ heated, 🏖, ℀ – 🛗 📺 ☎ 🅟, 🧖 🔌 🅰🅴 Ⓞ *VISA*. ❄
closed January-8 March – **M** 7.50/12.00 and a la carte 🍷 2.75 – **46 rm** ⊆ 35.00/90.00.

Rozel Bay – ⊠ St. Martin – ☎ 0534 Jersey.
St. Helier 6.

🏨 **Le Couperon de Rozel,** ℰ 62190, ⤴ heated – 🚾 🅟, 🔌 🅰🅴 Ⓞ *VISA*. ❄
closed 22 December-1 March – **M** 8.00/10.00 and a la carte 🍷 1.90 – **24 rm** ⊆ 15.50/67.00 s.

St. Aubin – ⊠ St. Aubin – ☎ 0534 Jersey.
St. Helier 4.

🏵🏵 **Portofino,** High St., ℰ 42100, Italian rest. – 🔌 *VISA*
closed Wednesday and Christmas Day – **M** 4.95/7.65 and a la carte 🍷 2.10.

🏵 **Old Court House Inn** with rm, St. Aubin's Harbour, ℰ 41156 – 📺 🚾 ☎. ❄
M 7.00 s. (lunch) and a la carte 6.20/14.00 s. 🍷 2.00 – **8 rm** ⊆ 16.50/30.00 s.

St. Brelade's Bay – pop. 8,566 – ⊠ St. Brelade – ☎ 0534 Jersey.
See : Site★.
St. Helier 6.

🏨 **L'Horizon,** ℰ 43101, Telex 4192281, ≤ St. Brelades Bay, ⤴ – 🛗 📺 ☎ & 🅟, 🧖 🔌 🅰🅴 Ⓞ
VISA. ❄
M dinner 15.00 s. and a la carte approx. 13.80 s. 🍷 2.05 (see also rest. **Star Grill** below) –
104 rm.

🏨 **St. Brelade's Bay,** ℰ 43281, ≤, ⤴ heated, 🏖, ℀ – 🛗 📺 ☎ 🅟. ❄
79 rm.

🏨 **Château Valeuse,** rue de la Valeuse, ℰ 43476, ⤴ heated, 🏖 – 🚾 🍴🚾 🅟. 🔌 🅰🅴 *VISA*
March-October – **M** 6.00/8.00 and a la carte 🍷 1.80 – **26 rm** ⊆ 20.00/50.00.

🏵🏵🏵 **Star Grill,** (at L'Horizon H.), ℰ 43101, Telex 4192281, ≤ St. Brelades Bay – 🅟, 🔌 🅰🅴 Ⓞ *VISA*
M *(closed Monday)* (booking essential) a la carte approx 15.80 s. 🍷 2.05.

FORD Airport Rd ℰ 43222   HONDA Route de Noirmont ℰ 41911

St. Clement – pop. 6,541 – ⊠ St. Clement – ☎ 0534 Jersey.
St. Helier 2.

🏨 **Ambassadeur,** St. Clement's Coast Rd, ℰ 24455, Group Telex 4192296, ≤, ⤴ heated – 🛗
📺 🚾 ☜ 🅟, 🔌 🅰🅴 *VISA*
April-December – **M** 10.00 and a la carte 🍷 1.90 – **41 rm** ⊆ 14.00/69.50 s.

🏨 **Shakespeare,** Samares, St. Clement's Coast Rd, ℰ 51915 – 📺 🚾 ☜ 🅟, 🔌 🅰🅴 Ⓞ *VISA*
closed 2 January-1 March – **M** 8.00/10.00 s. and a la carte 🍷 2.00 – **26 rm** ⊆ 20.00/50.00 s.

St. Helier – pop. 29,941 – ECD : Thursday and Saturday – ⊠ St. Helier – ☎ 0534 Jersey.
See : Fort Regent ❄★★★ (Militia Museum) *AC* Z – Elizabeth Castle ❄★ *AC* Z – Rocher des
Proscrits (au Havre des Pas) Z.
🛈 Weighbridge ℰ 78000 and 24779.

Plan on next page

🏨 **De la Plage,** Havre des Pas, ℰ 23474, Telex 4192328, ≤ – 🛗 📺 🅟, 🔌 🅰🅴 Ⓞ *VISA*. ❄   Z s
16 April-25 October – **M** 6.50/8.25 and a la carte 🍷 2.00 – **96 rm** ⊆ 22.50/65.00 s.

🏨 **Beaufort,** Green St., ℰ 32471, Telex 4192160 – 🛗 📺 🅟, 🔌 🅰🅴 Ⓞ *VISA*. ❄   Z r
M (dinner only) 7.50 🍷 1.90 – **54 rm** ⊆ 27.00/50.00 s.

🏨 **Pomme d'Or,** The Esplanade, ℰ 78644, Telex 4192309 – 🛗 ▤ rest 📺 🚾 ☎. 🧖 🔌 🅰🅴
Ⓞ *VISA*. ❄   Z u
M (carving lunch)/dinner 8.00 s. 🍷 1.80 – **151 rm** ⊆ 29.00/61.00 s.

🏨 **Savoy,** Rouge Bouillon, ℰ 30012, ⤴ heated – 🛗 📺 🚾 🍴🚾 🅟. ❄   Y i
Easter-October – **M** 5.00/7.00 s. and a la carte 🍷 2.00 – **61 rm** ⊆ 15.50/48.00 s.

🏨 **Apollo,** 9 St. Saviour's Rd, ℰ 25441, Telex 4192086 – 🛗 📺 🚾 ☜ 🅟, 🔌 🅰🅴 *VISA*. ❄   Z e
M 5.00/6.50 🍷 1.75 – **53 rm**.

🏨 **Royal Yacht,** Weighbridge, ℰ 20511 – 🛗 📺 🚾 🍴🚾 ☜. 🔌 🅰🅴 *VISA*. ❄   Z c
M 7.00/10.00 and a la carte 🍷 2.75 – **45 rm** ⊆ 19.50/44.00.

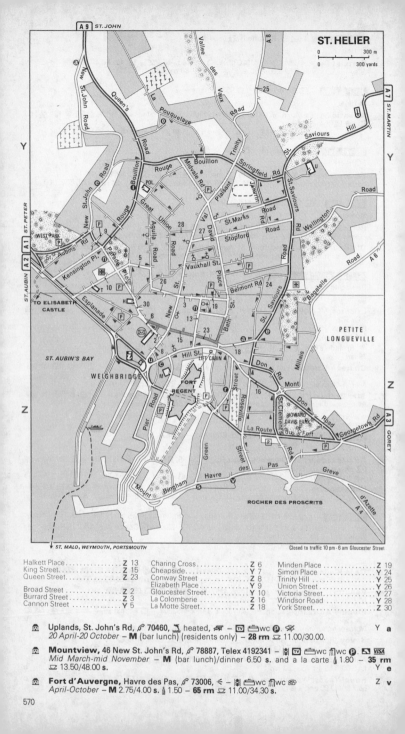

ST. HELIER

| | 0 | 300 m |
| | 0 | 300 yards |

Closed to traffic 10 pm - 6 am Gloucester Street

Halkett Place	Z 13
King Street	Z 15
Queen Street	Z 23
Broad Street	Z 2
Burrard Street	Z 3
Cannon Street	Y 5

Charing Cross	Z 6
Cheapside	Y 7
Conway Street	Z 8
Elizabeth Place	Y 9
Gloucester Street	Z 10
La Colomberie	Z 16
La Motte Street	Z 18

Minden Place	Z 19
Simon Place	Y 24
Trinity Hill	Y 25
Union Street	Y 26
Victoria Street	Y 27
Windsor Road	Y 28
York Street	Z 30

Uplands, St. John's Rd, ℰ 70460, ⊠ heated, ⇌ – TV ⊟wc P. ⌾
20 April-20 October – **M** (bar lunch) (residents only) – **28 rm** ⊇ 11.00/30.00.
Y **a**

Mountview, 46 New St. John's Rd, ℰ 78887, Telex 4192341 – 劇 TV ⊟wc ⃫wc P. ⟦⟧ VISA
Mid March-mid November – **M** (bar lunch)/dinner 6.50 s. and a la carte ⎸ 1.80 – **35 rm**
⊇ 13.50/48.00 s.
Y **e**

Fort d'Auvergne, Havre des Pas, ℰ 73006, ⩽ – 劇 ⊟wc ⃫wc ⟨⟩
April-October – **M** 2.75/4.00 s. ⎸ 1.50 – **65 rm** ⊇ 11.00/34.30 s.
Z **v**

🏠 **Millbrook House** ⌂, Rue de Trachy, W : 1 ¾ m. by A 1 ℰ 33036, 🍴 – ☕ ⌂wc 🛁wc 🅿.
⌂   by A 1   Y
   3 May-5 October – **M** (dinner only) 5.00 🍷 1.30 – **27 rm** ⊊ 17.95/35.90.

🏠 **Almorah,** 1 Almorah Cres., La Pougelaye., ℰ 21648, 🍴 – ⌂wc 🅿. ⌂   Y **o**
   April-October – **16 rm** ⊊ 11.00/31.00 **s.**

✕✕ **La Capannina,** 67 Halkett Pl., ℰ 34602, Italian rest. – 🔌 🅰🅴 ⓞ 𝗩𝗜𝗦𝗔   Z **n**
   closed Monday dinner and Sunday – **M** (booking essential) a la carte 8.60/12.00 🍷 1.95.

✕✕ **Mauro's,** 37 La Motte St., ℰ 20147 – 🔌 🅰🅴 𝗩𝗜𝗦𝗔   Z **a**
   closed Sunday – **M** 6.50/12.00 **s.** and a la carte 🍷 1.90.

✕ La Buca, The Parade, ℰ 34283, Italian rest.   Y **n**

ASTON-MARTIN, AUSTIN-ROVER. ROLLS ROYCE-   CITROEN 50 New St. ℰ 24541
BENTLEY 33-35 Lamotte St. ℰ 31341   NISSAN 1/2 Victoria St. ℰ 37357
AUSTIN-ROVER Havre des Pas ℰ 33233   PEUGEOT 17 Esplanade ℰ 33623

    St. Lawrence – pop. 3,845 – ✉ St. Lawrence – ✆ 0534 Jersey.
    See : German Military Underground Hospital★ *AC* Y.
    St Helier 3.

🏨 **Little Grove** ⌂, Rue de Haut, by A 11 ℰ 25321, ⌂ heated, 🍴 – 📺 🅿. 🔌 🅰🅴 ⓞ 𝗩𝗜𝗦𝗔
   M 6.50/8.00 **s.** and a la carte 🍷 1.75 – **14 rm** ⊊ 32.50/53.00 **s.**

    St. Martin – pop. 3,095 – ✉ St. Martin – ✆ 0534 Jersey.
    St. Helier 4.

🏠 **Le Relais de St. Martin,** ℰ 53271, ⌂, 🍴 – ⌂wc 🛁wc 🅿. ⌂
   closed January and weekdays November-April – **11 rm** ⊊ 11.55/31.00 **s.**

    St. Peter – pop. 3,713 – ✉ St. Peter – ✆ 0534 Jersey.
    Envir. : St. Ouen Manor★ *AC*, NW : 2 m.
    St. Helier 5.

🏨 **Mermaid,** Airport Rd, on B 36, ℰ 41255, Telex 4192249, ≤, ⌂ heated, 🍴 – 📺 🅿. 🏋. 🔌 🅰🅴
   ⓞ 𝗩𝗜𝗦𝗔
   M 6.00/7.00 and a la carte 🍷 2.20 – **68 rm** ⊊ 23.00/64.00.

🏨 **Greenhill Country,** Coin Varin, Mont de l'Ecole, on C 112 ℰ 81042, Telex 4192249, ⌂ heated
   – 📺 ⌂wc 🛁wc 🅿. 🔌 🅰🅴 ⓞ 𝗩𝗜𝗦𝗔. ⌂
   closed mid December-mid February – **M** 5.50/8.50 and a la carte 🍷 1.50 – **18 rm** ⊊ 25.00/82.00.

    St. Saviour – pop. 10,910 – ECD : Thursday – ✉ St. Saviour – ✆ 0534 Jersey.
    St. Helier 1.

🏨 **Longueville Manor,** Longueville Rd, on A 3 ℰ 25501, Telex 4192306, ⌂ heated, 🍴, park –
   ⌂ 🍽 rest 📺 ☎ 🅿. 🔌 🅰🅴 ⓞ 𝗩𝗜𝗦𝗔
   M 11.50/13.50 and a la carte 🍷 2.00 – **33 rm** ⊊ 40.00/105.00 **s.** – SB (weekends
   only)(November-March) 71.00 **s.**

PORSCHE Five Oaks ℰ 26156   RENAULT Bagot Rd ℰ 36471

SARK 🗺 P 33 and 🗺 – pop. 560 – ✆ 048 183.
See : La Coupée★★★ (isthmus) – Port du Moulin★★ – Creux Harbour★ – Happy Valley★ – Little
Sark★ – La Seigneurie★ (manor 18C, Residence of the Seigneur of Sark).
⛴ Shipping connections with the Continent : to France (Saint-Malo) (Condor : hydrofoil) summer
only – to Jersey (St. Helier) (Condor : hydrofoil) summer Monday/Saturday 1-2 daily (1 h 15 mn-2 h)
– to Guernsey (St. Peter Port) (Isle of Sark Shipping Co.) 1-6 daily (40 mn) – to Alderney (Condor :
hydrofoil) summer only 2 weekly (1 h 45 mn).
🗺 ℰ 2345.

🏠 **Petit Champ** ⌂, ℰ 2046, ≤ coast, Herm, Jetou and Guernsey, « Country house atmosphere », ⌂ heated, 🍴 – ⌂wc 🛁wc. 🔌 🅰🅴 ⓞ 𝗩𝗜𝗦𝗔. ⌂
   20 April-early October – **M** (booking essential to non-residents) 9.50/12.00 **s.** 🍷 2.00 – **16 rm**
   ⊊ (dinner included) 22.25/50.00 **s.**

🏠 **Stocks** ⌂, ℰ 2001, ⌂, 🍴 – 🛁wc. 🅰🅴. ⌂
   27 March-6 October – **M** 10.00 🍷 2.20 – **24 rm** ⊊ (dinner included) 19.50/55.00.

✕✕ **Aval du Creux** with rm, Harbour Hill, ℰ 2036, 🍴 – 🛁wc. ⌂
   May-September – **M** (booking essential) 6.50/9.00 and a la carte 🍷 2.50 – **7 rm** ⊊ (dinner included) 22.00/44.00.

This Guide is not a comprehensive list of all hotels and restaurants,
nor even of all good hotels and restaurants in Great Britain and Ireland.

Since our aim is to be of service to all motorists,
we must show establishments in all categories and so we have made a
selection of some in each.

Isle
of Man

Place with at least :

one hotel or restaurant	● Douglas
one pleasant hotel	🏠 , ✗ with rm
one quiet, secluded hotel	⊱
one restaurant with	✿, ✿✿, ✿✿✿, M
See this town for establishments located in its vicinity	

Localité offrant au moins :

une ressource hôtelière	● Douglas
un hôtel agréable	🏠 , ✗ with rm
un hôtel très tranquille, isolé	⊱
une bonne table à	✿, ✿✿, ✿✿✿, M
Localité groupant dans le texte les ressources de ses environs	

La località possiede come minimo :

una risorsa alberghiera	● Douglas
un albergo ameno	🏠 , ✗ with rm
un albergo molto tranquillo, isolato	⊱
un'ottima tavola con	✿, ✿✿, ✿✿✿, M
La località raggruppa nel suo testo le risorse dei dintorni	

Ort mit mindestens :

einem Hotel oder Restaurant	● Douglas
einem angenehmen Hotel	🏠 , ✗ with rm
einem sehr ruhigen und abgelegenen Hotel	⊱
einem Restaurant mit	✿, ✿✿, ✿✿✿, M
Ort mit Angaben über Hotels und Restaurants in seiner Umgebung	

ISLE OF MAN

ISLE OF MAN

Towns

BALLASALLA 402 G 21 – ✿ 0624.

Douglas 8.

✗✗ **La Rosette,** Main Rd, ℰ 822940
closed Monday lunch, Sunday and 2 weeks January – **M** a la carte 8.35/13.15 **t.** ⌀ 4.00.

CASTLETOWN 402 G 21 – pop. 3 ,141 – ECD : Thursday – ✿ 0624.

See : Rushen Castle★★ (13C) *AC* : Keep ❄★ – Port Erin (site★) W : 4 ½ m.

🏌 Fort Island ℰ 822201, E : 2 m.

🛈 Commissioner's Office, Parliament Sq. ℰ 823518.

Douglas 10.

🏨 **Castletown Golf Links** ⊱, Fort Island, E : 2 m. ℰ 822201, Telex 627636, ≤ sea and golf links, ⤫ heated, 🏌, ✗ – ⌂wc 🏳wc ☎ 🅟. 🅰 𝖵𝖨𝖲𝖠
April-October – **M** (bar lunch Monday to Saturday)/dinner 8.00 **t.** ⌀ 1.60 – **65 rm** ⌑ 24.00/47.50 **t.**

✗ **Bunters,** Parliament Sq., ℰ 824000 – 🅰 𝖵𝖨𝖲𝖠
closed lunch Saturday and Sunday – **M** 7.50 **t.** (dinner) and a la carte 9.10/12.40 **t.** ⌀ 2.50.

DOUGLAS 402 G 21 – pop. 19,944 – ECD : Thursday – 🕿 0624.

See : Manx Museum★★ – The Promenades★ – A 18 Road★★ From Douglas to Ramsey.

Envir. : Snaefell ☀★★★ (by electric railway from Laxey) *AC*, NE : 7 m. – Laxey (waterwheel★ : Lady Isabella) NE : 6 m. – St. John's (Tynwald Hill) NW : 8 m. – Peel : Castle★ (ruins 13C-16C) *AC*, NW : 11 ½ m.

🖍 Pulrose Park ℰ 5952, 1 m. from Douglas Pier – 🖍 Howstrake at Onchan ℰ 24299, N : 1 m.

✈ Ronaldsway Airport, ℰ 0624 (Castletown) 823311, SW : 7 m. – **Terminal** : Coach service from Lord St.

🚢 by Isle of Man Steam Packet Co. to Ardrossan : July-August 1 weekly (6 h) – to Belfast : July-September 1-2 weekly (4 h 30 mn) – to Dublin : June-September 1-3 weekly (4 h 30 mn) – to Fleetwood : June-September 2-3 weekly (3 h) – to Heysham summer 1-3 daily, winter 6 weekly (3 h 45 mn).

🛈 13 Victoria St. ℰ 74323 – Public Library, 10 Elm Tree Rd at Onchan ℰ 22311.

🏛 **Springfield Mansion House** ⤲, New Castletown Rd, SW : 2 m. on Airport road ℰ 21752, « Country house », 🚗 – 📺 🖭wc 🖬wc 🕿 🅿. 🔼 AE ⓞ *VISA*. ⤲
M (bar lunch)/dinner a la carte 7.40/9.40 **s.** 🍷 2.50 – **5 rm** ⚏ 28.00/44.00 **s.**

🏛 **Palace,** Central Promenade, ℰ 74521, Telex 627742, ≤, ☗ – 🛗 📺 🖭wc 🕿 🅿. 🔼 AE ⓞ *VISA*
M 5.75/7.75 **t.** and a la carte 🍷 3.75 – ⚏ 5.25 – **135 rm** 31.50/53.50 **t.**, **2 suites** 75.00/140.00 **st.** – SB (weekends only) 48.50 **st.**

🏠 **Sefton,** Harris Promenade, ℰ 26011, Telex 627519, ≤ – 🛗 📺 🖭wc 🕿 & 🅿. 🔼 AE ⓞ *VISA*. ⤲
M (carving rest.) a la carte 5.00/7.50 **st.** 🍷 2.75 – **80 rm** ⚏ 20.75/35.50 **st.**

🏠 **Empress,** Central Promenade, ℰ 27211 – 🛗 📺 🖭wc 🖬wc 🕿. 🔼 AE ⓞ *VISA*. ⤲
M *(closed Sunday dinner)* (dinner only and Sunday lunch) 🍷 3.00 – **94 rm** ⚏ (dinner included) 18.50/37.00 **s.**, **3 suites** (dinner included) 42.00 **s.**

AUSTIN-ROVER Westmoreland Rd ℰ 23481
BMW Castle Mona Av. ℰ 3380
CITROEN Kingswood Grove ℰ 24114
DAIHATSU Victoria Rd ℰ 5039
FIAT Station Rd ℰ 832021
FORD Douglas ℰ 3211
MERCEDES-BENZ Douglas Rd ℰ 822884
PEUGEOT-TALBOT Peel Rd ℰ 24519

RENAULT Peel Rd ℰ 3342
SAAB West St. ℰ 813350
TOYOTA Westmoreland Rd ℰ 5556
VAUXHALL-OPEL The Milestone, Peel Rd ℰ 3781
VOLVO New Castletown Rd ℰ 4683
YUGO Derby Rd, Kirk Michael ℰ 062 487 (Kirk Michael) 577

ONCHAN 402 G 21 – 🕿 0624 Douglas.

Douglas 1,5.

XXX **Boncomptes,** King Edward Rd, ℰ 75626, ≤ – 🅿. 🔼 ⓞ *VISA*
closed Saturday lunch, Sunday and first 2 weeks April – **M** 6.00 **t.** (lunch) and a la carte 10.90/14.10 **t.** 🍷 3.50.

Republic of Ireland

Prices quoted in this section of the guide are in " Punts "

Dans cette partie du guide, les prix sont indiqués en monnaie irlandaise " Punts "

In questa parte della guida, i prezzi sono indicati in lire irlandesi " Punts "

In diesem Teil des Führers sind die Preise in irländischer Währung " Punts " angegeben

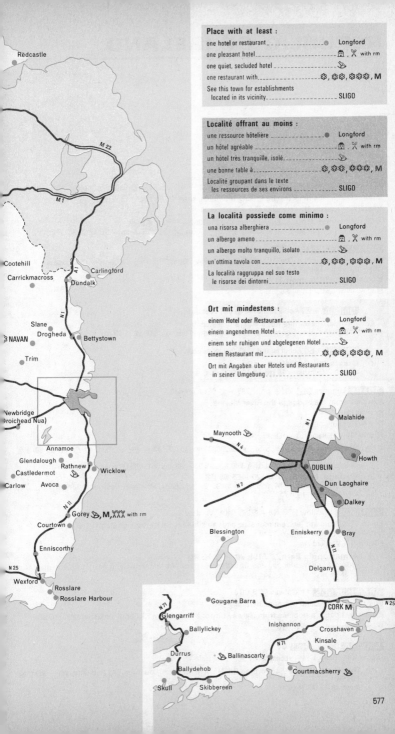

REPUBLIC OF IRELAND

Towns

ABBEYLEIX Laois **405** J 9 – pop. 1,402 – ECD : Wednesday – ✪ 0502 Portlaoise – 🏌.
Envir. : Dunamase Rock (castle★★ 13C-16C ruins), site★★, ❄★★ NE : 13 ½ m.
♦Dublin 64 – Kilkenny 21 – ♦Limerick 65 – ♦Tullamore 30.

🏛 **Hibernian House,** Lower Main St., ℰ 31252 – 🛏wc. 🔊 *VISA*. 🛠
 M 10.00 **t.** (dinner) and a la carte ⓐ 4.00 – **13 rm** 🖵 12.00/28.00 **st.** – SB 42.00/46.00 **st.**

ACHILL ISLAND Mayo **405** B 5 and 6.
See : Achill Sound★ – The Atlantic Drive★★★ SW : Coast Rd from Cloghmore to Dooega – Keel :
(the strand★) – Lough Keel★.
🏌 Achill Sound, Westport, in Keel.
🛈 ℰ Achill Sound 51 (June-August).

Dooagh – ✉ Achill Island – ✪ 098 Westport.

🏛 Atlantic, Slievemore Rd, ℰ 43113 – 🛏wc ℗
 Easter and June-September – **M** (dinner only) approx. 8.00 **st.** – **10 rm.**

Dugort – ✉ Achill Island – ✪ 098 Westport.

↑ **Gray's** 🍴, ℰ 43244, 🌳 – 🚿wc
 March-7 October – **15 rm** 🖵 10.00/22.00 **t.**

ADARE Limerick **405** F 10 – pop. 785 – ✪ 061 Limerick.
See : ≼★ from the bridge of the River Maigue.
🏌 ℰ 94204.
🛈 ℰ 94255 (June-August).
♦Dublin 131 – ♦Killarney 59 – ♦Limerick 10.

🏨 **Dunraven Arms,** Main St., ℰ 94209, Telex 70202, 🌳 – 🛏wc 🚿wc ☎ ℗. 🔊 *AE* ⓪ *VISA*.
 🛠
 M 8.25/15.00 **t.** and a la carte ⓐ 3.50 – 🖵 5.95 – **23 rm** 35.00/55.00 **st.**

✗ **Cottage,** Main St., ℰ 86520 – 🔊 ⓪ *VISA*
 May to October – **M** *(closed Sunday except Bank Holidays)* (restricted lunch) 7.95/20.00
 t. and a la carte ⓐ 3.75.

ANNAMOE Wicklow **405** N 8 – ✉ ✪ 0404 Wicklow.
Envir. : Glendalough (ancient monastic city★★ : site★★★, St. Kervin's Church★) and Upper Lake★ in
Glendalough Valley★★★ SW : 5 m.
♦Dublin 29 – Wexford 72.

✗✗ **Armstrong's Barn,** ℰ 5194, 🌳 – ℗. *AE* *VISA*
 closed Sunday, Monday and Christmas-Easter – **M** (dinner only) (booking essential) 18.50 **t.**
 ⓐ 4.00.

ARAN ISLANDS ★★ Galway **405** CD 8.
See : Inishmore Island (Kilronan harbour★).
Access by boat or aeroplane from Galway City or by boat from Kilkieran, or Fisherstreet (Clare).
 Hotels see : Galway.

ARDARA Donegal **405** G 3.
♦Dublin 188 – Donegal 24 – ♦Londonderry 58.

↑ **Bay View House** 🍴, Portnoo Rd, N : ¾ m. ℰ 45, ≼ Loughros Bay and hills, 🌳 – 🚿wc ℗
 AE. 🛠
 7 rm 🖵 12.00/24.00 **st.**

ATHLONE Westmeath **405** 17 – pop. 9,444 – ECD : Thursday – ✪ 0902.
Envir. : Clonmacnoise★★ (medieval ruins) SW : 8 m. – N : Lough Ree★.
☙ 17 Church St. ℰ 2866.
♦Dublin 75 – ♦Galway 57 – ♦Limerick 75 – Roscommon 20 – ♦Tullamore 24.

 🏨 Prince of Wales, Church St., ℰ 72626, Telex 25368 – 📺 🛏wc ☎ **𝐏**. 🎱 – **42 rm**.

 ✕✕ **Le Chateau,** Abbey Lane, ℰ 4517 – 🅰 𝗩𝗜𝗦𝗔
   April–mid October – **M** *(closed Sunday)* (dinner only)(booking essential) a la carte 8.75/17.25 **t.**
   🍷 3.50.

FORD Dublin Rd ℰ 75426

AVOCA Wicklow **405** N 9 – pop. 289 – ✪ 0402 Arklow.
See : Vale of Avoca★ from Arklow to Rathdrum on T 7.
♦Dublin 47 – ♦Waterford 72 – Wexford 55.

 🏨 **Vale View,** Kilcashel, N : 1 ¾ m. on T 7 ℰ 5236, ≤ – 📺 🛏wc ☎ **𝐏**. ✗
   10 rm.

BALLINA Mayo **405** E 5 – pop. 6,856 – ECD : Thursday – ✪ 096.
Envir. : Rosserk Abbey★ (Franciscan Friary 15C) N : 4 m. – Ballycastle (cliffs★) NW : 3 m. near Downpatrick Head★ NW : 18 m.
☐₉ ℰ 21050, E : 1 m. – **☐₉** Belmullet ℰ Belmullet 28.
☙ ℰ 21544 (July-August).
♦Dublin 150 – ♦Galway 73 – Roscommon 64 – ♦Sligo 37.

 🏨 **Downhill,** Sligo Rd, ℰ 21033, Telex 33796, 🔲, 🏊, squash – 📺 🛏wc 🛁wc ☎ **𝐏**. 🅰 🅰🅴
   ① 𝗩𝗜𝗦𝗔. ✗
   closed 14 to 26 December – **M** 11.00/18.00 **t.** and a la carte 🍷 8.50 – **54 rm** ⊊ 55.00/77.00 **t.** –
   SB (weekends only)(October-June) 110.00/132.00 **st.**

 🏛 Mount Falcon Castle 🦢, Foxford Rd, S : 4 m. on Foxford-Ballina rd (T 40/N 57) ℰ 21172,
   Telex 33149, ≤, « Country house atmosphere », 🦢, park, ✗ – 🛏wc **𝐏**
   11 rm.

AUSTIN-ROVER, RENAULT Lord Edward St. ℰ 21037

BALLINASCARTY Cork **405** F 12 – ✉ Clonakilty – ✪ 023 Bandon.
♦Dublin 188 – ♦Cork 27.

 🏨 **Ardnavaha House** 🦢, SE : 2 m. by L 63 ℰ 49135, ≤, 🔥 heated, 🦢, 🏊, park, ✗ – 🛏wc
   ☎ **𝐏**. 🅰 🅰🅴 ① 𝗩𝗜𝗦𝗔. ✗
   Easter–mid October – **M** 14.00/25.00 **t.** and a la carte – **36 rm** ⊊ 29.00/58.00 **t.**

BALLINASLOE Galway **405** H 8 – pop. 6,374 – ECD : Thursday – ✪ 0905.
☐₉ ℰ 2126.
☙ ℰ 2332 (July-August).
♦Dublin 91 – ♦Galway 41 – ♦Limerick 66 – Roscommon 36 – ♦Tullamore 34.

 🏨 Hayden's, Dunlo St., ℰ 42347, Telex 33147, 🏊 – 🛗 📺 🛏wc ☎ **𝐏**
   55 rm.

FORD Kilmartins ℰ 42204   RENAULT Brackernagh ℰ 42420
PEUGEOT Dunlo St. ℰ 42290

BALLYBOFEY Donegal **405** I 3 – pop. 2,928 – ECD : Wednesday – ✪ 074 Letterkenny.
☐₁₈ ℰ 93.
♦Dublin 148 – ♦Londonderry 30 – ♦Sligo 58.

 🏨 **Kee's,** Main St., Stranorlar, NE : ½ m. on N 15 ℰ 31018 – 📺 🛏wc ☎ **𝐏**. 🅰 🅰🅴 𝗩𝗜𝗦𝗔
   closed 24 to 27 December – **M** 6.50/11.50 **st.** and a la carte 🍷 3.00 – **26 rm** ⊊ 16.00/29.00 **st.** –
   SB 41.00/42.50 **st.**

 🏨 Jackson's, Glenfinn St., ℰ 49296, 🏊 – 📺 🛏wc 🛁wc ☎ **𝐏**
   44 rm.

BALLYCONNEELY Galway **405** B 7 – ✉ Connemara – ✪ 095 Clifden.
♦ Dublin 189 – ♦ Galway 54.

 🏡 **Erriseask House** 🦢, ℰ 21261, ≤, 🏊 – 🛁wc ☎ **𝐏**. ✗
   May–September – **M** (bar lunch)/dinner 12.50 **st.** 🍷 3.25 – **11 rm** ⊊ 18.00/34.00 **st.**

BALLYDEHOB Cork **405** D 13 – ✪ 028.
♦ Dublin 215 – ♦ Cork 61 – ♦ Killarney 58.

 ⌂ **Audley House** 🦢, Foilnanuck, S : 2 ¾ m. by Greenmount Rd ℰ 37179, ≤ Roaring Water
   Bay and Islands, 🏊 – 🛏wc **𝐏**. ① 𝗩𝗜𝗦𝗔
   May–mid September – **7 rm** ⊊ 14.50/29.00 **t.**

BALLYHEIGE Kerry **405** C 10 – ✪ 066.
- ♦ Dublin 187 – ♦ Killarney 33 – ♦ Limerick 67.

🏠 **White Sands,** ℰ 33102 – ➡wc ⋔wc ☎ 🅿 🔼 ⓞ 𝗩𝗜𝗦𝗔
   May-September – **M** 8.00/14.00 **st.** and a la carte ▮4.50 – **26 rm** ⌷ 18.00/36.00 **st.** – SB 44.00 **st.**

BALLYLICKEY Cork **405** D 12 – ✉ ✪ 027 Bantry.
♦ Dublin 216 – ♦ Cork 55 – ♦ Killarney 45.

🏠 **Sea View House** ⌂, ℰ 50462, ≼, 🌿 – ➡wc ⋔wc 🐾 🅿
   April-October – **M** (bar lunch)/dinner 15.50 **t.** and a la carte ▮5.00 – **10 rm** ⌷ 18.00/40.00 **t.** – SB (weekends only)(except July and August) 60.00/65.00 **st.**

✕✕ **Ballylickey House** ⌂ with rm, ℰ 50071, ≼, French rest., ⌙ heated, ⌇, 🌿, park – ➡wc 🐾 🅿 🔼 𝗔𝗘 𝗩𝗜𝗦𝗔 ⅍
   April-October – **M** *(closed Tuesday to non-residents)* a la carte 14.75/18.50 **t.** ▮6.00 – ⌷ 6.50 – **9 rm** 25.00/42.00 **t.**, **2 suites** 50.00/65.00 **t.**

BALLYLIFFIN Donegal **405** J 2 – pop. 260 – ✉ ✪ Clonmany.
Envir. : Carndonagh (Donagh Cross★) SE : 6 m. – Lough Naminn★ S : 6 m.
🛇 Lifford ℰ 19.
♦ Dublin 180 – Donegal 83 – ♦ Londonderry 35.

🏠 **Strand,** ℰ 7, 🌿 – 📺 ➡wc ⋔wc 🐾 🅿 🔼 𝗩𝗜𝗦𝗔 ⅍
   closed 24 to 26 December – **M** (bar lunch)/dinner 15.00 **t.** and a la carte ▮3.75 – **10 rm** ⌷ 22.00/32.00 **t.**

BALLYNAHINCH Galway **405** C 7 – ✪ 095 Clifden.
See : Lake★.
♦ Dublin 140 – ♦ Galway 41 – Westport 49.

🏛 **Ballynahinch Castle** ⌂, ℰ 21269, Telex 28809, ≼ Cranmore river, ⌇, 🌿, park, ✕ – ➡wc 🅿 🔼 𝗔𝗘 𝗩𝗜𝗦𝗔 ⅍
   April-October – **M** (lunch by arrangement) 10.55/17.50 **st.** ▮4.00 – **20 rm** ⌷ 40.00/78.00 **st.**

BALLYVAUGHAN Clare **405** E 8 – ✪ 065 Ennis.
Envir. : SW : Coast road L 54 from Ailladie to Fanore : Burren District (Burren limestone terraces★★) – Corcomroe Abbey★ (or Abbey of St. Maria de Petra Fertilis : 12C Cistercian ruins) NE : 6 m.
♦ Dublin 149 – Ennis 34 – ♦ Galway 29.

🏛 **Gregans Castle** ⌂, SW : 3 ¼ m. on T 69 ℰ 77005, Telex 70130, ≼ Countryside and Galway Bay, 🌿 – ➡wc 🅿 𝗩𝗜𝗦𝗔 ⅍
   Easter-October – **M** 17.50 **t.** (dinner) and a la carte ▮5.50 – **16 rm** ⌷ 30.00/55.00 **t.**
🏠 **Hylands,** – ➡wc ⋔wc ☎ 🅿
   M (bar lunch) – **14 rm.**

BANAGHER Offaly **405** I 8 – pop. 1,378.
See : ≼★ from the bridge of Shannon.
Envir. : Clonfert (St. Brendan's Cathedral : west door★ 12C, east windows★ 13C) NW : 4 ½ m. – Birr : Castle Demesne (arboretum★, gardens★, telescope of Lord Rosse) *AC*, SE : 8 m.
♦ Dublin 83 – ♦ Galway 54 – ♦ Limerick 56 – ♦ Tullamore 24.

↟ Brosna Lodge, Main St., ℰ 50, 🌿 – ➡wc 🅿 ⅍ – **12 rm.**

BANTRY Cork **405** D 12 – pop. 2,862 – ECD : Wednesday – ✪ 027.
See : Bantry Bay★★ – Bantry House (interior★★, ≼★) *AC*.
Envir. : Glengarrif (site★★★) NW : 8 m. – NE : Shehy Mountains★★.
🛇 Donemark ℰ 50579, on Glengariff Rd.
🛈 ℰ 50229 (July-August).
♦ Dublin 218 – ♦ Cork 57 – ♦ Killarney 48.

RENAULT Barrack St. ℰ 50092   VAUXHALL-OPEL The Square ℰ 50023

BARNA Galway **405** E 8 – ✪ 091 Galway.
♦ Dublin 135 – ♦ Galway 3.

✕ Ty Ar Mor, Sea Point, ℰ 69186, ≼, Seafood – 🅿

BETTYSTOWN Meath **405** N 6 – ✉ ✪ 041 Drogheda.
🛇 ℰ 27534.
♦ Dublin 28 – Drogheda 6.

✕✕ **Coastguard Inn,** ℰ 27115, ≼ – 🅿 🔼 𝗔𝗘 ⓞ 𝗩𝗜𝗦𝗔
   closed Sunday and Monday – **M** (dinner only) 16.00 **t.** and a la carte ▮7.00.

[BIRR] Offaly [405] I 8 – pop. 3,679 – ☎ 0509.
[i] ☎ 206 (June-August).
♦Dublin 87 – Athlone 28 – Kilkenny 49 – ♦Limerick 49.

🏨 County Arms, Railway Rd, ☎ 20191, 🌳, squash – [TV] 🛁wc ☎ [P]. 🚫🐕 – **18 rm**.

[BLARNEY] Cork [405] G 11 – pop. 1,980 – ✉ ☎ 021 Cork.
See : Castle★ 15C (top ※★, 112 steps) *AC*.
♦Dublin 167 – ♦Cork 6.

🏨 Blarney, ☎ 85281, 🌳 – [TV] 🛁wc 🚿wc ☎ ♿ [P]. 🏛 – **76 rm**.

[BLESSINGTON] Wicklow [405] M 8 – pop. 988 – ☎ 045 Naas.
Envir. : Lackan ≤★ SE : 4 ½ m. – SE : Poulaphuca Lake★ (reservoir).
♦Dublin 20.

🏨 Downshire House, Main St., ☎ 65199, 🌳, 🎾 – 🛁wc ☎ [P] – **25 rm**.

[BOYLE] Roscommon [405] H 16 – pop. 1,737 – ☎ 079.
See : Cistercian Abbey★ 12C – Envir. : NE : Lough Key★.
⛳9 Roscommon Rd.
[i] ☎ 145 (June-August).
♦Dublin 107 – Ballina 40 – ♦Galway 74 – Roscommon 26 – ♦Sligo 24.

🏨 **Forest Park,** Dublin Rd, E : ½ m. on T 3 ☎ 62229, 🌳 – [TV] 🛁wc ☎ [P]. [N] [AE] [VISA]. 🚫🐕
closed 24 to 26 December – **M** 7.50/13.00 **st.** and a la carte 🍷 4.00 – **12 rm** 🛏 18.00/40.00 **st.**

🏨 **Royal,** Bridge St., ☎ 62016 – 🛁wc ☎ [P]. [N] [AE] [D] [VISA]
closed 25 and 26 December – **M** 6.50/11.50 **t.** and a la carte 🍷 4.25 – **16 rm** 🛏 19.00/37.50 **t.** – SB (weekends only)(except summer and Bank Holidays) 45.00/50.00 **st.**

FORD Elphin St. ☎ 22

[BRAY] Wicklow [405] N 8 – pop. 22,853 – ECD : Wednesday – ☎ 01 Dublin.
⛳18 Woodbrook ☎ 824799, N : 1 m. – ⛳9 Ravenswell Rd ☎ 862484.
[i] ☎ 867128/9 (July-August).
♦Dublin 13 – Wicklow 20.

🏨 **Esplanade,** Sea Front, Strand Rd, ☎ 862056 – [P]. [N] [AE] [D] [VISA]. 🚫🐕
closed 25 to 30 December – **M** *(closed Sunday dinner)* 7.50/12.00 **t.** and a la carte 🍷 4.00 – **40 rm** 🛏 13.00/28.00 **t.** – SB 38.00 **st.**

🍴🍴 **Tree of Idleness,** Seafront, ☎ 863498, Greek-Cypriot rest. – [N] [AE] [D] [VISA]
closed Monday, 24 August-22 September and 22 to 30 December – **M** (dinner only) 11.50 **t.** and a la carte 🍷 3.75.

[BUNRATTY] Clare [405] F 9 – ✉ ☎ 061 Limerick.
See : Castle (Great Hall★) *AC* **– Folk Park★** *AC*.
♦Dublin 129 – Ennis 15 – ♦Limerick 8.

🏨 Fitzpatrick's Shannon Shamrock Inn, ☎ 61177, Telex 26214, [🏊], 🌳 – ▤ rest [TV] 🛁wc ☎ ♿ [P]. 🏛. [N] [AE] [D] [VISA]. 🚫🐕
closed Christmas Day – **M** approx. 5.50/12.50 **t.** and a la carte 🍷 3.50 – **103 rm**.

🍴🍴 **MacCloskey's,** Bunratty House Mews, ☎ 74082 – [P]. [N] [AE] [D] [VISA]
closed Sunday, Monday and 23 December-23 January – **M** (dinner only) 19.00 **t.**

[CAHERDANIEL] Kerry [405] B 12.
Envir. : Sheehan's Point ≤★★★ W : 5 m. – Staigue Fort★ (prehistoric stone fort : site★, ≤★) *AC*, **NE : 5 m.**
♦Dublin 238 – ♦Killarney 48.

[CAHER] Tipperary [405] I 10 – pop. 2,120 – ECD : Thursday – ☎ 052.
See : Castle★ (12C-15C) the most extensive medieval castle in Ireland.
⛳9 Cahir Park, ☎ 41474, S : 1 m.
[i] ☎ 41453 (July-August).
♦Dublin 112 – ♦Cork 49 – Kilkenny 41 – ♦Limerick 38 – ♦Waterford 39.

🍴🍴 Earl of Glengall, The Square, ☎ 41505.

FORD Dublin Rd ☎ 41432

[CAPPOQUIN] Waterford [405] I 11 – pop. 950 – ✉ Lismore – ☎ 058 Dungarvan.
♦Dublin 136 – ♦Cork 31 – ♦Waterford 40.

🏠 **Richmond House** 🌿, SE : ½ m. on N 72, ☎ 54278, 🌳, park – 🛁wc [P]. 🚫🐕
February-October – **9 rm** 🛏 12.00/24.00.

CARAGH LAKE Kerry 405 C 11 – 🕐 066 Tralee.

See : Lough Caragh★.

♦Dublin 212 – ♦Killarney 22 – Tralee 25.

🏛 **Caragh Lodge** ॐ, ℰ 69115, ≼, « Country house atmosphere, fine gardens », ॎ, park, ✂
– 🛏wc 🅿, 𝘝𝘐𝘚𝘈, ✂
April-September – **M** (dinner only) a la carte 12.00/17.00 t. 🍴 4.00 – **10 rm** 🍽 30.00/46.00 t.

🏛 **Ard-na-Sidhe** ॐ, ℰ 69105, ≼, « Country house atmosphere », ॎ, 🌳, park – 🛏wc 🅿
18 rm.

CARLINGFORD Louth 405 N 5 – pop. 631 – 🕐 042.

♦Dublin 66 – ♦Dundalk 13.

🏚 McKevitt's Village, Market Sq., ℰ 73116 – 📺 🛏wc 🚿wc. 🔼 𝘝𝘐𝘚𝘈. ✂
10 rm 🍽 16.00/32.00 st.

XX **Oscar's,** The Square, ℰ 73162 – 🅿. 🔼 ① 𝘝𝘐𝘚𝘈
closed Sunday dinner, Monday September-May and 24 to 26 December – **M** (dinner only and
Sunday lunch)/dinner 13.50 t. and a la carte 🍴 3.50.

CARLOW Carlow 405 L 9 – pop. 11,722 – ECD : Thursday – 🕐 0503.

🏌 Oak Park ℰ 31695.

🎫 ℰ 31554 (July-August).

♦Dublin 52 – Kilkenny 25 – ♦Tullamore 44 – Wexford 46.

🏨 Carlow Lodge, Kilkenny Rd, S : 2 m. on N 9 ℰ 42002, 🌳 – 🛏wc 🅿 🅿. ✂
10 rm.

BMW, SKODA, TOYOTA Dublin Rd ℰ 31572
CITROEN, HONDA, PEUGEOT, SAAB Tullow Rd ℰ
31391
FIAT, LANCIA Tullow Rd ℰ 31955

FORD Court Place ℰ 31665
OPEL, RENAULT Tullow Rd ℰ 31303
VW, AUDI, MAZDA, MERCEDES-BENZ Green Lane
ℰ 31047

CARRICKMACROSS Monaghan 405 L 6 – pop. 1,768 – ECD : Wednesday – 🕐 042.

🏌 Nuremore H. ℰ 61438.

♦Dublin 97 – ♦Dundalk 14.

🏨 **Nuremore** ॐ, SE : 1 m. on N 2 ℰ 61438, ≼, 🔼, 🏊, ॎ, 🌳, park, squash – 📺 🛏wc 🚿wc 🅿
🅿. 🏌. ✂
39 rm.

CARRICK-ON-SHANNON Leitrim 405 H 6 – pop. 2,037 – ECD : Wednesday – 🕐 078.

🏌 ℰ 157.

🎫 ℰ 20170 (June-September).

♦Dublin 97 – Ballina 50 – Roscommon 26 – ♦Sligo 34.

🏚 County, Bridge St., ℰ 20550 – 🛏wc 🚿wc 🅿 🅿. ✂ – **17 rm**.

AUSTIN-ROVER Cartober ℰ (078) 20080

CASHEL Tipperary 405 I 10 – pop. 2,436 – ECD : Wednesday – 🕐 062.

See : St. Patrick's Rock★★★ (or Rock of Cashel) : site and ecclesiastical ruins 12C-15C (✂★★) *AC* –
Hore Abbey★ ruins 13C – St. Dominick's Abbey★ ruins 13C.

Envir. : Holycross Abbey★★ (12C) *AC*, N : 9 m.

🎫 Town Hall ℰ 61333.

♦Dublin 101 – ♦Cork 60 – Kilkenny 34 – ♦Limerick 36 – ♦Waterford 44.

🏛 **Cashel Palace** ॐ, Main St., ℰ 61411, Telex 26938, « Former Archbishop's palace, gardens »
– 🕿 🅿. 🏌. 🔼 🄰🄴 ① 𝘝𝘐𝘚𝘈. ✂
M 25.00 t. (dinner) and a la carte 🍴 6.00 – 🍽 7.50 – **20 rm** 55.00/90.00 t. – SB (November-March)
65.00 st.

XX **Chez Hans,** Rockside, ℰ 61177, « Converted 19C church »
closed Sunday, Monday, 22 to 27 December and 3 to 22 January – **M** (dinner only) a la carte
15.50/20.00 t. 🍴 3.50.

DAIHATSU, TALBOT Ladyswell St. ℰ 61155

CASHEL BAY Galway 405 C 7 – 🕐 095 Clifden.

Envir. : SE : Kilkieran Peninsula★★.

♦Dublin 173 – Galway 41.

🏛 **Cashel House** ॐ, ℰ 21252, Telex 28812, ≼, « Country house set in attractive grounds »,
ॎ, 🌳, ✂ – 🛏wc 🅿. 🔼 🄰🄴 ① 𝘝𝘐𝘚𝘈
March-October – **M** 24.50/18.95 t. and a la carte 🍴 4.50 – **30 rm** 🍽 28.00/70.00 t.

🏛 **Zetland** ॐ, ℰ 31011, Telex 28853, ≼, ॎ, 🌳 – 🛏wc 🅿. 🔼 🄰🄴 ① 𝘝𝘐𝘚𝘈
5 April- 20 October – **M** (bar lunch)/dinner 24.00 t. and a la carte 🍴 5.00 – **16 rm** 🍽 25.00/75.00 t.
– SB (mid September-mid June) 75.00/100.00 st.

582

CASTLEBAR Mayo **405** E 6 – pop. 6 ,409 – ECD : Thursday – ✪ 094.

Envir. : Ballintuber Abbey★ (13C-15C) S : 7 m. – Pontoon (❄★, moraines★) NE : 10 m.

🏌 Rocklands ☎ 21649.

🏥 ☎ 21207 (July-August).

◆Dublin 152 – Ballina 25 – ◆Galway 48 – ◆Sligo 54.

🏨 **Breaffy House** (Best Western) ⏝, SE : 2 ¾ m. on T 39 ☎ 22033, ☛, park – ▮ ▥ ⌷wc ☎
🅿. 🎿. 🅰 AE ◑ *VISA*
closed Christmas – **M** 8.40/16.25 **t.** – **40 rm** ☲ 25.00/60.00 **t.**

CITROEN, TALBOT Breaffy Rd ☎ 21975   RENAULT Spencer St. ☎ 21355

CASTLEDERMOT Kildare **405** L 9 – pop. 805 – ✪ 0503 Carlow.

Envir. : Baltinglass (abbey ruins : scenery★) NE : 7 m.

◆Dublin 44 – Kilkenny 33 – Wexford 54.

🏨 Kilkea Castle (Best Western) ⏝, Kilkea, NW : 3 ½ m. ☎ 45156, Telex 25388, ≼, « 12C castle »,
🎿 heated, ⏉, ☛, park, ❊ – ⌷wc ☎ 🅿. 🎿. ❊ – **50 rm**.

CITROEN ☎ 44114

CAVAN Cavan **405** J 6 – pop. 3 ,240 – ✪ 049.

🏥 ☎ 31942 (June-September).

◆Dublin 71 – Drogheda 58 – Enniskillen 40.

🏨 Kilmore, Dublin Rd, E : 2 m. on N 3 ☎ 32288, Group Telex 33676 – ▥ ⌷wc ☎ 🎿 🅿. 🎿
40 rm.

🏠 Farnham Arms, ☎ 32577 – ▥ ⌷wc ☎ 🅿 – **30 rm**.

CHARLEVILLE (RATH LUIRC) Cork **405** F 12 – pop. 2 ,874 – ECD : Thursday – ✪ 063.

Envir. : Kilmallock (Dominican Friary ruins 13C, SS. Peter and Paul church 14C : scenery★) NE : 6 m.
– Kilfinnane (site★) E : 11 m.

🏌 ☎ 257.

◆Dublin 138 – ◆Cork 38 – ◆Killarney 57 – ◆Limerick 24.

🏠 Deerpark, Limerick Rd, N : ½ m. on N 20 ☎ 581, ☛ – ⌷wc ☎ 🅿 – **20 rm**.

FORD Limerick Rd ☎ 561

CLIFDEN Galway **405** B 7 – pop. 796 – ECD : Thursday – ✪ 095.

Envir. : E : Connemara★★ : The Twelve Pins★ (mountains), Lough Inagh★ – Cleggan (site★★) NW :
6 m. – Streamstown Bay★ NW : 2 m.

🏌 Connemara, Ballyconneely ☎ Ballyconneely 5, W : 8 m.

🏥 ☎ 103 (June-August).

◆Dublin 181 – Ballina 77 – ◆Galway 49.

🏨 **Abbeyglen House** ⏝, Sky Rd, W : ½ m. ☎ 21070, Telex 28366, ≼, 🎿 heated, ☛, ❊ – ▥
⌷wc ☎ 🅿. 🎿 🅰 AE ◑ *VISA*
closed last 3 weeks January – **M** 7.00/16.00 **t.** ▯ 6.00 – ☲ 6.00 – **40 rm** 42.00/54.00 **t.** – SB
(September-June) 80.00/90.00 **st.**

🏠 **Rock Glen Country House** ⏝, S : 1 ¼ m. by L 102 ☎ 21035 – ⌷wc 🅿. 🎿 🅰 AE ◑ *VISA*. ❊
March-October – **M** (bar lunch)/dinner 15.00 **t.** ▯ 4.00 – **30 rm** ☲ 24.00/45.00 – SB (weekdays
only) 73.00 **st.**

🏠 **Ardagh** ⏝, Ardbear Bay, S : 1 ¾ m. on L 102 ☎ 21384, ≼ Ardbear Bay, ⏉ – ⌷wc 🅿. 🎿
🅰 *VISA*. ❊
March-September – **M** (bar lunch)/dinner 13.50 **t.** ▯ 4.00 – **22 rm** ☲ 18.15/36.30 **t.** – SB (except
July and August) 66.00 **st.**

🏠 **Clifden Bay,** Main St., ☎ 21167 – ⌷wc. 🎿 🅰 AE ◑ *VISA*
May-15 October – **M** 10.00/15.00 ▯ 4.00 – **38 rm** ☲ 28.00/50.00 **t.** – SB 50.00/70.00 **st.**

CLONMEL Tipperary **405** I 10 – pop. 12 ,407 – ECD : Thursday – ✪ 052.

See : The Main Guard★ 1674.

Envir. : Ahenny (2 high crosses★) NE : 16 m. – S : Nire Valley★ (≼★★).

🏌 Lyreanearla, ☎ 21138.

🏥 ☎ 22960 (July-August).

◆Dublin 108 – ◆Cork 59 – Kilkenny 31 – ◆Limerick 48 – ◆Waterford 29.

🏨 **Clonmel Arms,** Sarsfield St., ☎ 21233, Telex 80263 – ▮ ▥ ⌷wc ▯wc ☎. 🎿. 🎿 🅰 AE ◑
VISA
M 8.00/13.00 **st.** and a la carte ▯ 3.50 – ☲ 6.00 – **33 rm** 23.00/38.00 **st.** – SB (weekends only)
55.00/58.00 **st.**

AUDI, MAZDA, MERCEDES-BENZ, VW Upper Irish-   FIAT Parnell St. ☎ 21615
town ☎ 22199   RENAULT Thomas St. ☎ 22430
CITROEN, NISSAN, RENAULT Dungarvon Rd ☎   SKODA, TOYOTA Cashel Rd ☎ 21652
22399

CONG Mayo 405 E 7 – pop. 213 – ✪ 094 Castlebar.

See : Ashford Castle (site ★).

Envir. : Ross Abbey★★, Franciscan Friary (tower ※★, 80 steps) SE : 9 m.

♦Dublin 160 – Ballina 49 – ♦Galway 28.

🏰 **Ashford Castle** 🦢, ℰ 71444, Telex 53749, ≼ Lough Corrib and countryside, « Tastefully converted castle », 🎏, 🏊, 🛥, park, ✖ – 🛗 TV ☎ ℗. 🔬. 🖾 AE ⓪ VISA. ⋘
April-December – **M** 15.00/29.00 t. and a la carte ₺ 6.00 – � 8.00 – **78 rm** 60.00/150.00 t., **5 suites** 175.00 t.

COOTEHILL Cavan 405 K 5 – pop. 1,554 – ECD : Tuesday – ✪ 049 Cavan.

Envir. : Bellamont Forest★ N : 1 ½ m.

♦Dublin 68 – ♦Dundalk 33.

🏠 **White Horse,** Market St., ℰ 52124 – ➩wc ⋔wc ☜ ℗. 🖾 VISA
M 7.50/11.75 t. and a la carte ₺ 4.50 – **30 rm** ⊒ 18.75/35.00 t. – SB (weekends only) 40.00 st.

CORK Cork 405 G 12 – pop. 136,344 – ✪ 021.

See : St. Patrick's Street★ YZ – St. Ann's Shandon Church★ 18C (steeple ※★ *AC*, 134 steps) Y A – University College★ 1845 X **U** – The Marina ≼★ X.

🏌 Little Island ℰ 953263, E : 5 m. by N 25 X – 🏌 Monkstown ℰ 841225, S : 7 m. by L 66 X.

✈ ℰ 965388, S : 4 m. by L 42 X – **Terminal :** Bus Station, Parnell Pl.

⚓ Shipping connections with the Continent : to France (Roscoff) (Brittany Ferries) – to France (Le Havre) (Irish Continental Line).

🛈 Cork City, Tourist House, Grand Parade ℰ 23251 – Cork Airport ℰ 964347 (July-August).

♦Dublin 154.

Plan opposite

🏰 **Jury's,** Washington St., ℰ 966377, Telex 26073, ⒣ heated, 🛥, squash – TV ☎ ℥ ℗. 🔬.
🖾 AE ⓪ VISA. ⋘   Z v
M a la carte approx. 16.65 t. ₺ 5.50 – ⊒ 6.00 – **140 rm** 55.00/65.00 t. – SB (weekends only) 74.00/85.00 st.

🏛 **Imperial,** South Mall, ℰ 965333, Telex 75126 – 🛗 TV ☎. 🔬. 🖾 AE ⓪ VISA. ⋘   Z n
closed 1 week at Christmas – **M** 12.00/16.00 t. and a la carte – **80 rm** ⊒ 40.00/70.00 t.

🏛 **Silver Springs,** Tivoli, E : 2 ½ m. on N 25 ℰ 507533, Telex 26111, 🛥, ✖ – 🛗 TV ☎ ℗. 🔬.
🖾 AE ⓪ VISA. ⋘   X c
closed 24 December - 4 January – **M** 9.00/13.50 t. – **72 rm** ⊒ 39.90/70.00 st.

🏛 **Arbutus Lodge,** Middle Glanmire Rd, Montenotte, ℰ 501237, Telex 75079, ≼, 🛥 – ▤ rest
TV ➩wc ⋔wc ☎ ℗. 🖾 AE ⓪ VISA. ⋘   Y a
closed 24 to 30 December – **M** *(closed Sunday)* 14.95/17.95 t. and a la carte ₺ 5.75 – **20 rm**
⊒ 36.50/66.00 st. – SB (weekends only) 60.00 st.

🏠 **Lotamore House** without rest., Tivoli, E : 3 ¼ m. on N 25 ℰ 822344, ≼, 🛥, park – TV ➩wc
☜ ℗. 🖾 AE VISA   X a
22 rm ⊒ 24.00/33.00 st.

XXX **Lovett's,** Churchyard Lane, off Well Rd, Douglas, ℰ 294909 – ℗. 🖾 AE ⓪ VISA   X s
closed Saturday lunch, Sunday and Bank Holidays – **M** 16.00/22.50 st. ₺ 4.50.

at Glounthaune E : 7 m. on N 25 – X – ✉ ✪ 021 Cork :

🏛 **Ashbourne House,** ℰ 353319, « Extensive gardens », ⒣ heated, ✖ – TV ➩wc ⋔wc ☜
℗. 🖾 AE ⓪ VISA
M 7.00/14.00 st. and a la carte ₺ 3.50 – **26 rm** ⊒ 25.00/44.00 st. – SB (weekends only) 63.00/65.00 st.

FIAT 24 Watercourse Rd ℰ 503228   OPEL 26 St. Patricks Quay ℰ 26657
FIAT 11 South Terr. ℰ 507344   RENAULT Tivoli ℰ 503397
FORD Dennehys Cross ℰ 42846   RENAULT ℰ 44655

COURTMACSHERRY Cork 405 F 13 – pop. 231 – ✉ ✪ 023 Bandon.

Envir. : Timoleague (Franciscan Abbey★ 16 C) W : 1 ½ m.

♦Dublin 190 – ♦Cork 29.

🏠 **Courtmacsherry** 🦢, ℰ 46198, ≼, 🛥, park, ✖ – ➩wc ℗
Easter-September – **M** (bar lunch Monday to Saturday)/dinner 12.00 t. ₺ 3.90 – **16 rm**
⊒ 15.50/34.00 t. – SB 55.00/60.50 st.

🏠 **Lislee House** 🦢, SW : 2 m. ℰ 40126, ≼, « Country house atmosphere », 🛥 – ➩wc ℗. ⋘
M (dinner only) – **7 rm**.

COURTOWN Wexford 405 N 10 – pop. 337 – ✪ 055 Gorey.

🏌 Courtown Harbour ℰ 21566.

♦Dublin 62 – ♦Waterford 59 – Wexford 42.

🏠 **Courtown,** ℰ 25108, 🖾 – ➩wc ⋔wc ℗. 🖾 AE ⓪ VISA. ⋘
Easter-October – **M** 7.00/14.30 st. – **28 rm** ⊒ 16.50/40.00 t. – SB 53.00/57.00 st.

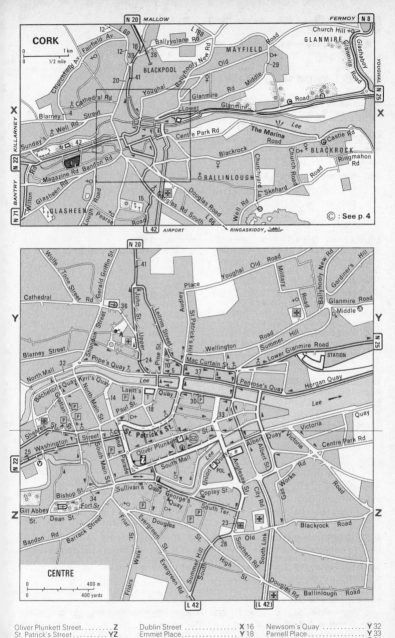

Oliver Plunkett Street	**Z**
St. Patrick's Street	**YZ**
Baker's Road	**X** 4
Camden Place	**Y** 5
Coburg Street	**Y** 10
Commons Road	**X** 12
Corn Market Street	**Y** 14
Curragh Road	**X** 15

Dublin Street	**X** 16
Emmet Place	**Y** 18
Great William O'Brien Street	**X** 20
Infirmary Road	**Y** 23
John Redmond Street	**Y** 24
Lancaster Quay	**Z** 25
Langford Row	**Z** 26
Lower Mayfield Road	**X** 29
Merchant's Quay	**Y** 30

Newsom's Quay	**Y** 32
Parnell Place	**Y** 33
Proby's Quay	**Z** 34
Roman Street	**Y** 36
St. Patrick's Quay	**Y** 37
Spring Lane	**X** 38
Thomas Davis Street	**X** 39
Watercourse Road	**X** 41
Western Road	**X** 42

CROSSHAVEN Cork 405 H 12 – pop. 1,419 – ✉ ❀ 021 Cork.

◆Dublin 173 – ◆Cork 12.

🏠 **Whispering Pines,** ✆ 831843, ≼, ≫ – ⌂wc 🅟 🔳 AE ⓞ VISA. ✻
closed Christmas – **M** (dinner only) 10.50 **st.** ⓗ 3.00 – **15 rm** ☲ 16.00/28.00 **st.** – SB 40.00/44.00 **st.**

DALKEY Dublin 405 N 8 – ❀ 01 Dublin.

◆Dublin 11.

XX **Guinea Pig,** 17-18 Railway Rd, ✆ 859055, Seafood – 🔳 AE ⓞ VISA
closed Sunday, 2 weeks Easter, 1 week August and 1 week early January – **M** (dinner only) (booking essential) 14.95 **t.** and a la carte ⓗ 4.00.

DELGANY Wicklow 405 N 8 – pop. 7,442 (inc. Greystones) – ✉ Bray – ❀ 01 Dublin.
🏌 ✆ 874645.

◆Dublin 19.

🏰 **Glenview** ≫, Glen of the Downs, NW : 2 m. on N 11 by L 164 ✆ 862896, Telex 30638, ≼, ≪, park – 🅟 🧖 AE VISA. ✻
M 9.00/18.00 **t.** ⓗ 5.75 – ☲ 6.00 – **23 rm** 25.50/44.00 **t.** – SB (weekends only) 47.50/50.00 **st.**

🏠 **Delgany Inn,** ✆ 875701 – ⌂wc ☜. AE VISA. ✻
M (closed Sunday) (bar lunch Monday to Saturday)/dinner 12.50 **t.** and a la carte ⓗ 5.00 – ☲ 4.00 – **10 rm** 12.00/24.00 **t.** – SB (weekends only) 41.00 **st.**

DINGLE Kerry 405 B 11 – pop. 1,358 – ECD : Thursday – ❀ 066.

See : Dingle Bay★ – Envir. : NE : Conair Pass ❆★ – Fahan : Belvedere (coast road) ≼★ SW : 7½ m. – Kilmakedar (church★ 12C), Gallarus Oratory★ 8C, NW : 5 m.

🛈 ✆ 51188 (July-August).

◆Dublin 216 – ◆Killarney 51 – ◆Limerick 95.

🏠 **Milltown House** ≫, W : ¾ m. ✆ 51372, ≼ – ⌂wc 🎋wc 🅟. ✻
Easter-September – **7 rm** ☲ 20.00 **st.**

🏠 **Alpine House,** Mail Rd, ✆ 51250, ≪ – 🎋wc 🅟. ✻
April-October – **15 rm** ☲ 21.00 **st.**

X **Half Door,** John St., ✆ 51600, Seafood – 🔳 AE ⓞ VISA
Mid March-mid November – **M** (closed Tuesday) a la carte 9.35/13.00 **st.** ⓗ 5.00.

X **Doyle's Seafood Bar,** 4 John St., ✆ 51174 – 🔳 AE ⓞ VISA
Mid March-mid November – **M** (closed Sunday) 15.00 **t.** and a la carte 10.70/13.50 **t.** ⓗ 5.00.

DONEGAL Donegal 405 H 4 – pop. 1,956 – ECD : Wednesday – ❀ 073.

See : Franciscan Priory (site★, ≼★).

🏌 Murvagh ✆ Ballintra 54, S : 8 m.

🛈 ✆ 21148 (June-August).

◆Dublin 164 – ◆Londonderry 48 – ◆Sligo 40.

🏰 **Hyland Central** (Best Western), The Diamond, ✆ 21027, Telex 40522, ≪ – 🕴 TV ⌂wc 🎋wc ☎ 🅟. 🔳 AE VISA. ✻
closed 3 days at Christmas – **M** 8.50/15.00 **t.** and a la carte ⓗ 3.75 – **57 rm** ☲ 26.00/42.00 **t.**

at St. Ernan's Island SW : 2¼ m. by T 18 – ✉ ❀ 073 Donegal :

XX **Ernan Park** ≫ with rm, ✆ 21065, ≼Donegal Bay, park – ⌂wc 🅟. 🔳 AE VISA. ✻
M (dinner only and Sunday lunch) 18.00 **st.** and a la carte ⓗ 3.35 – **12 rm** ☲ 18.00/50.00 **st.** – SB 70.00/75.00 **st.**

AUSTIN-ROVER Quay St. ✆ 073 21039
FORD The Glebe ✆ 073 21017
NISSAN Kerrykell ✆ 3
RENAULT ✆ 073 21117

DROGHEDA Louth 405 M 6 – pop. 23,247 – ECD : Wednesday – ❀ 041.

See : St. Lawrence's Gate ★ 13C – Envir. : Mellifont Abbey★★ (Cistercian ruins 1142) NW : 4½ m. – Monasterboice (3 tall crosses★★ 10C) NW : 5½ m. – Dowth Tumulus ❆★ W : 4 m. – Duleek (priory★ 12C ruins) SW : 5 m. – Newgrange Tumulus★ (prehistoric tomb) AC, SW : 7 m.

🏌 County Louth, Baltray ✆ 22327, E : 3 m.

🛈 ✆ 7070 (July-August).

◆Dublin 31 – ◆Dundalk 22 – ◆Tullamore 69.

🏰 Boyne Valley, SE : 1½ m. on T 1 ✆ 7737, ≪, park – TV ⌂wc 🎋wc 🅟. 🧖. ✻ – **20 rm**.

🏠 **Glenside,** Smithstown, SE : 3 m. on N 1 ✆ 29049, ≪ – TV ⌂wc 🎋wc ☎ 🅟. 🔳 AE ⓞ VISA
closed 18 to 31 December – **M** 7.50/12.00 **t.** and a la carte ⓗ 4.25 – **14 rm** ☲ 22.00/42.00 **t.** – SB (weekends only) 50.00/58.00 **st.**

FIAT, LANCIA North Rd ✆ 37920
FORD North Rd ✆ 31106
NISSAN North Rd ✆ 38566
PEUGEOT Palace St. ✆ 37303

DROICHEAD NUA = Newbridge.

♦Dublin 141 – ♦Sligo 8.

🏠 **Drumlease Glebe House** ⬙, NE : 2 ¼ m. *&* 64141, ≼, « Country house atmosphere », ⅃, ⬂, 🐎 – ▥wc **©**. **VISA**. ⬙
18 *March-September* – **M** (booking essential)(dinner only) 17.50 **t.** 🛉 4.50 – **8 rm** ⬚ 25.00/53.00 **t.**

DUBLIN Dublin **405** N 7 – pop. 528 ,882 – **©** 01.

See : National Gallery★★★ BY – Castle (State apartments★★★ *AC*) BY – Christ Church Cathedral★★ 12C BY – National Museum (Irish antiquities, Art and Industrial)★★ BY **M2** – Trinity College★ (Library★★) BY – National Museum (Zoological Collection)★ BY **M1** – Municipal Art Gallery★ BX **M3** – O'Connell Street★ (and the General Post Office) BXY – St. Stephen's Green★ BZ – St. Patrick's Cathedral (interior★) BZ – Phoenix Park (Zoological Gardens★) AY.

Envir. : St. Doolagh's Church★ 13C (open Saturday and Sunday, afternoon only) NE : 7 m. by L 87 AY.

🛆 Edmondstown, Rathfarnham *&* 907461, S : 3 m. by N 81 AZ – 🛆 Elm Park, Nutley House, Dunnybrook *&* 693438, S : 3 m. AZ – 🛆 Lower Churchtown Rd, Milltown *&* 977060, S : by T 43 AZ.

✈ *&* 379900, N : 5 ½ m. by N 1 AY – **Terminal** : Busaras (Central Bus Station) Store St.

⚓ to Liverpool (B & I Line) 1 nightly (8 h) – to Holyhead (B & I Line) 1-2 daily (3 h 30 mn) – to the Isle of Man : Douglas (Isle of Man Steam Packet Co.) June to September 1-3 weekly (4 h 30 mn).

🛈 14 Upper O'Connell St. *&* 747733 – Dublin Airport *&* 376387 and 375533.

♦Belfast 103 – ♦Cork 154 – ♦Londonderry 146.

Plans on following pages

🏨 **Berkeley Court,** Lansdowne Rd, Ballsbridge, *&* 601711, Telex 30554, ▨ – ▯ ▣ ☎ 🚗 **©**. 🛆, ⬛ ⚇ ⓘ **VISA**. ⬙   AZ **c**
M 15.00/18.00 **t.** and a la carte 🛉 5.00 – ⬚ 6.50 – **200 rm** 69.00/88.00 **t.**

🏨 **Westbury,** Grafton St., *&* 791122, Telex 91091 – ▯ ▤ rest ▣ ⌷wc ☎ **©**. 🛆   BY **z**
146 rm.

🏨 **Jury's,** Pembroke Rd, Ballsbridge, *&* 605000, Telex 25304, ⅃ heated, ▨ – ▯ ▣ ☎ 🖧 **©**. 🛆, ⬛ ⚇ **VISA**   AZ **c**
M 15.00/16.00 **t.** and a la carte 🛉 7.50 – ⬚ 7.50 – **300 rm** 63.00/82.50 **t.**

🏨 **Shelbourne** (T.H.F.), 27 St. Stephen's Green, *&* 766471, Telex 25184 – ▯ ▣ ☎. 🛆, ⬛ ⚇ ⓘ **VISA**   BZ **s**
M 18.00/21.00 **t.** and a la carte 🛉 6.40 – ⬚ 8.00 – **167 rm** 75.00/97.00 **t.**

🏨 **Blooms,** Anglesea St., *&* 715622, Telex 31688 – ▯ ▣ **©**. ⬛ ⚇ ⓘ **VISA**. ⬙   BY **e**
M (buffet lunch)/dinner 14.00 **t.** and a la carte 🛉 4.50 – **84 rm** 66.00/85.00 **t.**

🏨 **Tara Tower,** Merrion Rd, SE : 4 m. on T 44 *&* 694666 – ▯ ▣ ⌷wc 🖧 **©**. 🛆, ⬛ ⚇ **VISA**. ⬙   on T 44 AZ
M 7.85/9.10 **t.** and a la carte 🛉 3.15 – ⬚ 4.50 – **83 rm** 29.00/39.60 **t.** – SB (weekends only)(October-May) 39.00 **t.**

🏨 **Skylon,** Upper Drumcondra Rd, N : 2 ½ m. on N 1 *&* 379121, Group Telex 90790 – ▯ ▣ ⌷wc 🖧 **©**. 🛆. ⬙   AY **e**
M (coffee shop) – **88 rm.**

🏨 **Buswells,** 25-26 Molesworth St., *&* 764013, Telex 90622 – ▯ ▣ ⌷wc ☎. 🛆, ⬛ ⚇ ⓘ **VISA**. ⬙   BY **u**
M *(closed Saturday and Sunday)* a la carte 7.80/11.05 **st.** – ⬚ 6.00 – **70 rm** 37.00/54.00 **t.**

🏨 **Ashling,** Parkgate St., Kingsbridge, *&* 772324, Telex 32802 – ▯ ▣ ⌷wc 🖧 🚗 **©**. 🛆, ⬛ ⚇ ⓘ **VISA**. ⬙   AY **r**
closed 25 and 26 December – **M** 11.00/15.60 **st.** and a la carte 🛉 3.50 – **56 rm** ⬚ 36.00/54.00 **st.**

🏠 **Ariel House** without rest., 52 Lansdowne Rd, *&* 685512, 🐎 – ▣ ⌷wc ▥wc 🖧 **©**.   AZ **e**
15 rm ⬚ 25.00/50.00 **t.**

🏠 **Maples,** 79-81 Iona Rd, Glasnevin, *&* 728382 – ▥wc 🖧. ⬛ ⚇ ⓘ **VISA**. ⬙   AY **c**
M *(closed lunch Saturday and Bank Holidays and Sunday)* 7.50/15.00 **t.** and a la carte 🛉 3.25 – **25 rm** ⬚ 18.50/40.00 **t.**

🏠 **Kilronan House,** 70 Adelaide Rd, *&* 755266 – ⌷wc 🖧. ⬙   BZ **r**
closed 24 to 31 December – **11 rm** ⬚ 23.00/38.00 **t.**

🏠 **Egans House,** 7-9 Iona Park, Glasnevin, *&* 303611 – ⌷wc ▥wc 🖧 ⚇ **©**. ⬙   AY **a**
⬚ 4.60 – **24 rm** 13.00/27.00 **t.**

🏠 **Abrae Court,** 9 Zion Rd, Rathgar, *&* 979944 – ▥ **©**. ⬙   AZ **i**
10 rm ⬚ 15.00/24.00 **t.**

🏠 **St. Aidan's,** 32 Brighton Rd, Rathgar, *&* 970559 – ⌷wc ▥wc. ⬛ ⚇ ⓘ   AZ **r**
closed 23 December-1 January – **12 rm** ⬚ 15.00/30.00 **t.**

XXX Le Coq Hardi, 35 Pembroke Rd, *&* 689070 – **©**   AZ **n**

XXX **Patrick Guilbaud,** 46 St. James's Pl., St. James' St., off Lower Baggot St., *&* 764192, French rest. – **©**. ⬛ ⚇ ⓘ **VISA**   BZ **n**
closed Saturday lunch, Sunday, 24 to 28 December, 1 January and Bank Holidays – **M** 12.75 **t.** and a la carte.

XXX **Bailey,** 2-4 Duke St., *&* 770600 – ⬛ ⚇ ⓘ **VISA**   BY **a**
closed Saturday lunch, Sunday and Bank Holidays – **M** 12.50/14.95 **t.** and a la carte 🛉 5.95.

DUBLIN

Anne Street South .... **BY** 2
Dawson Street.............. **BY**
Duke Street .... **BY** 27
Grafton Street .... **BY**
Henry Street............... **BY**
Irish Life Mall Centre ..... **BY**
O'Connell Street........... **BXY**

Bath Avenue .... **AZ** 3
Belvidere Place .... **BX** 4
Benburb Street .... **AY** 5
Blessington Street .... **BX** 6
Botanic Road.............. **AY** 7
Brunswick Street North .... **BY** 8
Bull Alley .... **BY** 9
Chancery Street............ **BY** 13
Charlotte Street .... **BZ** 15
College Street............. **BY** 19

Denmark Street............ **BX** 23
D'Olier Street............. **BY** 24
Donnybrook Road .... **AZ** 25
Eglinton Road .... **AZ** 29
Essex Quay .... **BY** 30
Fitzgibbon Street.......... **BX** 31
Fitzwilliam Place .... **BZ** 32
Frederick Street North ..... **BX** 33
Gardiner Place .... **BX** 35
George's Quay............. **BY** 36
Golden Lane .... **BY** 39
Harrington Street.......... **BZ** 44
Infirmary Road............ **AY** 46
Kevin Street Upper .... **BZ** 47
Kildare Street .... **BYZ** 48
King Street South .... **AZ** 49
Macken Street............. **AZ** 50
Marlborough Street .... **BY** 53
Merchants Quay .... **BY** 56
Montague Street........... **BZ** 59
Morehampton Road........ **AZ** 60

Mountjoy Street .... **BX** 62
Nicholas Street .... **BY** 64
Parnell Square East .... **BX** 67
Parnell Square North ...... **BX** 68
Parnell Square West ...... **BX** 69
Rathmines Road Upper ... **AZ** 73
Ringsend Road .... **AZ** 75
Sandford Road .... **AZ** 77
Shelbourne Road .... **AZ** 79
Stephen Street .... **BY** 80
Tara Street .... **BY** 81
Terenure Road East .... **AZ** 83
Townsend Street .... **BY** 89
Victoria Quay............. **AZ** 92
Wellington Quay.......... **BY** 95
Westland Row............. **BY** 96
Westmoreland Street...... **BY** 97
Wexford Street .... **BZ** 99
Winetavern Street......... **BY** 100
Wolfe Tone Quay......... **AYZ** 102
Wood Quay .... **BY** 103

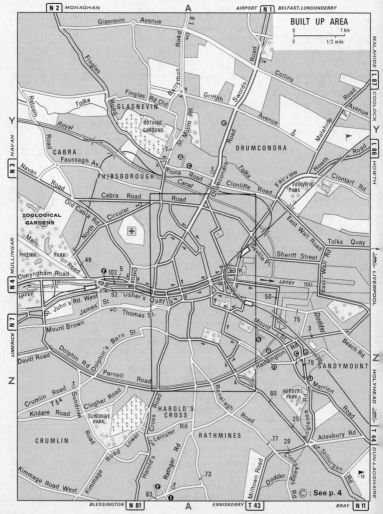

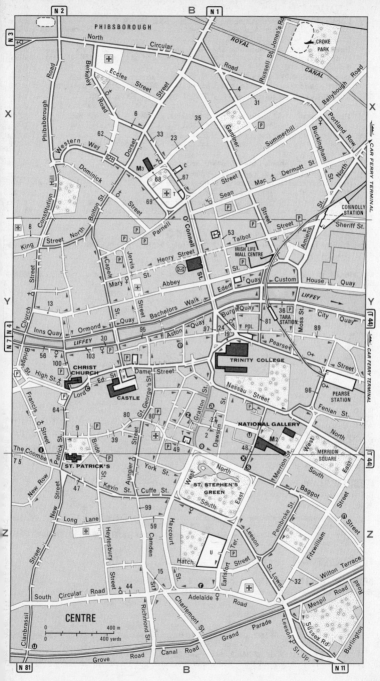

N 2 N 3

PHIBSBOROUGH

ROYAL

CROKE PARK

North

Circular

Russell St. Jones's Rd.

CANAL

Ballybough Road

Eccles Street

Berkeley Road

Street

4

31

Portland Row

X

Gardiner

Summerhill

Buckingham

X

CAR FERRY TERMINAL

Western Way

Dorset

62

33

23

35

Dominick

St.

Mac Dermott St.

North

Constitution Hill

Bolton St.

M3

68

67

c

Sean

CONNOLLY STATION

St.

69

Street

T

MacNorth

Sheriff St.

8

Parnell

53

Talbot

Amiens

King Street North

Jervis

O'Connell

IRISH LIFE MALL CENTRE

St.

Custom

House Quay

Capel

Henry Street

St.

Mary

Abbey

Eden

T Quay

LIFFEY

Y

13

St.

Quay

Bachelors Walk

Burgh Quay

City Quay

36 P

Y

T 44

Church Street

Ormond

Quay

95

Aston

97 24

TARA STATION

81

89

CAR FERRY TERMINAL

Inns Quay

LIFFEY

30

P

103

19

Pearse

Moss St.

T 44

56

100

T

Dame Street

TRINITY COLLEGE

CHRIST CHURCH

Lord

Ed. St.

H

St.St. George's

Gt.

Street

Nassau Street

96

PEARSE STATION

CASTLE

64

80

80

Gratton St.

NATIONAL GALLERY

Fenian St.

North

9

39

Street

Bride

2

2

Dawson St.

48

M2

West

MERRION SQUARE

The Coombe

Patrick St.

49

East

T 5

ST. PATRICK'S

York St.

West

North

South

Merrion St.

47

Kevin St.

Cuffe St.

ST. STEPHEN'S GREEN

Baggot

Aungier

South

East

Pembroke St.

Street

New Street

99

Leeson

Fitzwilliam

Street

Long Lane

59

Harcourt

U

32

Wilton Terrace

Heytesbury

Camden

Hatch

Earlsfort Street

St. Lower

15

St.

44

St.

Adelaide

Road

Mespil

Road

South Circular Road

Charlemont St.

Sussex Rd.

Clanbrassil

Richmond St.

Grand

Canal

Parade

Leeson St. Up.

Burlington

CENTRE

0   400 m

0   400 yards

Grove

Road

N 81

B

N 11

XX **Locks,** 1 Windsor Terr., Portobello, ☎ 752025 – [E] [AE] [D] VISA — BZ **u**
closed Saturday lunch, Sunday, 24 December-2 January and Bank Holidays – **M** 11.50 **t.** (lunch) and a la carte 15.50/20.50 **t.** 🍷 3.60.

XX **Park,** 26 Main Street, Blackrock, SE : 4 ½ m. on T 44 ☎ 886177 – [E] [AE] VISA — on T44 AZ
closed Saturday lunch, Sunday, 3 days at Christmas and Bank Holidays **M** (booking essential) 8.50/20.00 **t.** 🍷 2.60.

XX **Old Dublin,** 90-91 Francis St., ☎ 751173, Scandinavian rest. – [E] [AE] [D] VISA — BY **i**
closed Saturday lunch, Sunday and Bank Holidays – **M** 9.50/14.75 **t.** and a la carte 🍷 4.25.

XX **Lord Edward,** 23 Christchurch Pl., ☎ 752557, Seafood – [E] [AE] [D] VISA — BY **c**
closed Saturday lunch, Sunday and Bank Holidays – **M** a la carte 15.50/25.15 **t.** 🍷 4.25.

XX **Small Home,** 41-43 Shelbourne Rd, Ballsbridge, ☎ 608087 – [E] [AE] [D] VISA — AZ **u**
closed Saturday lunch and Sunday – **M** 10.50/14.95 **t.** and a la carte.

XX **Bentleys,** 46 Upper Baggot St., ☎ 682760 – [E] [AE] [D] VISA — AZ **a**
closed Monday dinner, Sunday, 2 weeks July and Bank Holidays – **M** a la carte 11.75/19.00 **t.** 🍷 3.95.

X Dobbin's, 15 Stephen's Lane, ☎ 764679, Bistro — AZ **s**

X **Mitchell's Cellars,** 21 Kildare St., ☎ 680367 – [E] [AE] VISA — BZ **x**
closed Saturday June-September, Sunday, 28-29 March, 23 December-2 January and Bank Holidays – **M** (lunch only) a la carte 8.00/8.95 **t.** 🍷 3.85.

X **Cafe de Paris** The Galleria, 6 St. Stephen's Green, ☎ 778499 – [E] VISA — BY **o**
closed lunch Sunday and Bank Holiday Mondays, 25-26 December and 1 January – **M** a la carte 9.55/13.25 **t.** 🍷 4.05.

at Dublin Airport N : 6 ½ m. by N 1 – AY – ✉ ☎ 01 Dublin :

🏨 **Dublin International** (T.H.F.), ☎ 379211, Telex 24612 – [TV] 🛁wc ☎ ♿ [P]. 🏃. [E] [AE] [D] VISA
M 12.75/11.00 **st.** and a la carte 🍷 4.25 – ☕ 6.00 – **195 rm** 57.00/69.50 **st.**

MICHELIN Branch, 4 Spilmak Pl., Bluebell Industrial Estate, Naas Rd, Dublin 12, ☎ **509096** by N7 AZ

AUSTIN-ROVER Temple Rd ☎ 885085
AUSTIN-ROVER, NISSAN 48-52 New St. ☎ 780033
AUSTIN-ROVER Northbrook Rd ☎ 970811
AUSTIN-ROVER-JAGUAR Richmond Rd ☎ 379162
BMW, ROLLS ROYCE-BENTLEY, SUZUKI, VOLVO Townsend St. ☎ 779177
BMW, MITSUBISHI Ballygall Rd East ☎ 342577
BMW, SKODA, TOYOTA Rathgar Av. ☎ 979456
CITROEN Buckingham St. ☎ 745821
FIAT Milltown Rd ☎ 698577
FIAT, LANCIA 56 Howth Rd ☎ 332301
FIAT Church Pl. ☎ 973999
FIAT North Rd ☎ 342977
FIAT, LANCIA 84 Prussia St. ☎ 791722
FIAT, LANCIA Herberton Rd ☎ 754216
FORD 172/175 Parnell St. ☎ 747831
FORD Naas Rd ☎ 505721
FORD Stillorgan Rd ☎ 886821
HONDA Upper Rathmines Rd ☎ 971227
MERCEDES-BENZ, TOYOTA 54 Glasnevin Hill ☎ 373771
NISSAN Howth Rd ☎ 314066
NISSAN Bluebell Av. ☎ 507887
OPEL Beach Rd ☎ 686011
OPEL 146 Cabra Rd ☎ 301222
OPEL Emmet Rd, Inchicore ☎ 755535
OPEL New Rd ☎ 592438
PEUGEOT North Rd ☎ 343033
PEUGEOT-TALBOT, CITROEN 23 Parkgate St. ☎ 710333
RENAULT 232 North Circular Rd, Grangegorman ☎ 300799
RENAULT 19 Conyngnam Rd ☎ 775677
RENAULT 27 Upper Drumcondra Rd ☎ 373706
RENAULT Newlands Cross ☎ 593751
RENAULT Merrion Rd ☎ 693911
RENAULT Crumlin Rd ☎ 752297
SKODA, TOYOTA Kilbarrack Rd ☎ 322701
TOYOTA Smithfield Market ☎ 721222
VW, AUDI, MAZDA, MERCEDES-BENZ 218/224 North Circular Rd ☎ 792011
VW, AUDI-NSU, MAZDA, MERCEDES-BENZ Ballybough Rd ☎ 723033
VW, AUDI-NSU, MAZDA, MERCEDES-BENZ Harolds Cross Rd ☎ 975757

DUNDALK Louth [405] M 5 – pop. 25 ,663 – ECD : Thursday – ☎ 042.

⛳18 Blackrock ☎ 35379, S : 3 m – [i] ☎ 35484 (July-August).

♦Dublin 53 – Drogheda 22.

🏨 **Ballymascanlon House** 🐦, N : 3 ½ m. by N 1 ☎ 71124, Group Telex 43735, [🏊], 🌳, park, 🎾, squash – [TV] 🛁wc 🚿wc ☎ [P]. 🏃. [E] [AE] [D] VISA. 🐕
closed 3 days at Christmas – **M** 7.00/12.00 **t.** and a la carte 🍷 4.00 – **36 rm** ☕ 28.00/46.00 **st.** – SB (weekends only) 50.00/63.00 **st.**

DUNDERRY Meath – see Navan.

DUNFANAGHY Donegal [405] I 2 – pop. 390 – ✉ ☎ 074 Letterkenny.

Envir. : Doe Castle★ 16 C ruins (site★, ≤ ★) SE : 7 ½ m. – SW : Bloody Foreland Head★.

⛳18 ☎ 074 (Letterkenny) 36238.

♦Dublin 172 – Donegal 54 – ♦Londonderry 43.

🏨 **Arnold's,** Main St., ☎ 36208, ≤, 🌳, 🎾 – 🛁wc [P]. [D] VISA. 🐕
Easter-October – **M** (bar lunch Monday to Saturday)/dinner 11.00 **t.** and a la carte 🍷 4.35 – **36 rm** ☕ 14.00/37.00 **t.** – SB (except Bank Holidays) 46.50/55.00 **st.**

🏠 **Carrig Rua,** Main St., ☎ 36133, ≤ – 🛁wc [P]. VISA
Easter-September – **M** 6.50/11.50 **t.** and a la carte 🍷 3.85 – **22 rm** ☕ 17.00/34.00 **t.** – SB 44.00/52.00 **st.**

at Port-na-Blagh E : 1 ½ m. on T 72 – ⊠ ☎ 074 Letterkenny :

🏨 Shandon ⌂, Marble Hill Strand, NE : 2 ½ m. ℰ 36137, ≤ bay and hills, ⌐, 🐟, ✕ – 📶 ⌂wc ⊕ ⊕
season – **55 rm**.

🏠 **Port-na-Blagh**, ℰ 36129, ≤ Sheephaven Bay and harbour, ⌐, 🐟, ✕ – ⌂wc ⊕
Easter-October – **M** a la carte lunch/dinner 13.00 t. ⓘ 4.50 – **59 rm** ☲ 16.00/42.00 t. – SB 46.00/55.00 t.

DUNGARVAN Waterford **405** J 11 – pop. 6,631 – ECD : Thursday – ☎ 058.

🏌 Ballinacourty, ℰ 41605.

🛈 ℰ 41741 (July-August).

♦Dublin 124 – ♦Cork 48 – ♦Killarney 90 – ♦Waterford 29.

✕ Seanachie, SW : 5 ½ m. by N 25, ℰ 46285 – ⊕.

☛ *To go a long way quickly, use **Michelin maps** at a scale of 1:1 000 000.*

DUN LAOGHAIRE Dublin **405** N 8 – pop. 54,496 – ☎ 01 Dublin.

See : Windsor Terrace ≤★ over Dublin Bay.

🏌 Eglinton Park ℰ 801055.

⛴ to Holyhead (Sealink) summer 2-4 daily; winter 2 daily (3 h 30 mn).

🛈 St. Michaels Wharf ℰ 805760, 806547 and 806984/5/6.

♦Dublin 9.

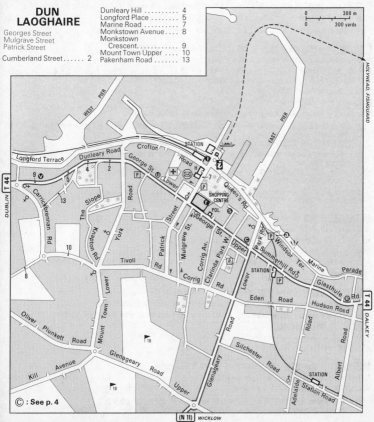

DUN LAOGHAIRE

Georges Street
Mulgrave Street
Patrick Street
Cumberland Street...... 2

Dunleary Hill	4
Longford Place	5
Marine Road	7
Monkstown Avenue	8
Monkstown Crescent	9
Mount Town Upper	10
Pakenham Road	13

ⓒ : See p. 4

XXX **na Mara,** 1 Harbour Rd, ℰ 806767, Seafood – ☒ AE ⓪ VISA   **i**
closed Sunday, Monday, Easter and Christmas – **M** 10.75/15.10 **t.** and a la carte ≬ 4.25.

XX **Digby's,** 5 Windsor Terr., ℰ 804600, ≤ – ☒ AE ⓪ VISA   **a**
closed lunch Saturday, Sunday June-August and Bank Holidays, Easter and 25-26 December
– **M** (restricted lunch) a la carte 14.75/18.75 **t.** ≬ 4.30.

XX **The Abbot of Monkstown,** Monkstown Cres., N : ¾ m. on T 44 ℰ 805174 – ☒ AE ⓪ VISA
closed Saturday lunch, Sunday, 26 to 30 December and Bank Holidays – **M** 14.00/18.00 **t.** and
a la carte ≬ 4.50.   **v**

X **Trudi's,** 107 Lower George's St., ℰ 805318, Bistro – AE ⓪ VISA   **u**
closed Sunday and Monday – **M** (dinner only) a la carte 11.10/14.80 **t.** ≬ 5.35.

X **Salty Dog,** 3a Haddington Terr. off Adelaide St., ℰ 808015, Indonesian rest. – ☒ AE ⓪
VISA   **s**
closed 25 December and 1 January – **M** 6.95/10.75 **t.** and a la carte ≬ 3.00.

X **Russell's,** 56 Glasthule Rd, Sandycove, ℰ 808878   **e**
closed Sunday – **M** (dinner only) a la carte 8.80/11.75 **t.** ≬ 3.00.

HONDA, OPEL Crofton Pl. ℰ 800341   RENAULT Rochestown Av. ℰ 852555
MITSUBISHI, TOYOTA Glasthule Rd ℰ 802991

DURRUS Cork 405 D 13 – ✉ – ☎ 027 Bantry.
♦Dublin 210 – ♦Cork 56 – ♦Killarney 53.

XX **Blairs Cove,** SW : 1 m. on L 56 ℰ 61127, « Converted barn », ☞ – P. ☒ AE ⓪ VISA
closed lunch Monday to Thursday mid October-Easter, Sunday Easter-15 October, January and
February – **M** (closed Sunday dinner mid October-Easter) (booking essential) 9.00/18.00 **t.**
≬ 4.25.

EMO Laois 405 K 8 – pop. 200 – ✉ ☎ 0502 Portlaoise.
♦Dublin 49 – ♦Limerick 74 – ♦Tullamore 20.

🏨 Montague, E : 1 ¾ m. on N 7 ℰ 26154, ☞ – ⌷wc ☎ Ꮕ P – **20 rm.**

ENNIS Clare 405 F 9 – pop. 6 ,223 – ECD : Thursday – ☎ 065.
See : Franciscan Friary★ (13C ruins).
Envir. : Tulla (site★, ancient church ※ ★★) E : 10 m. – Killone Abbey (site★) S : 4 m. – Dysert
O'Dea (site★) NW : 6 ½ m. – Kilmacduagh monastic ruins★ (site★) NE : 16 ½ m.
🛆 Drumbiggle Rd ℰ 21070.
🛄 Bank Pl. ℰ 21366.
♦Dublin 142 – ♦Galway 42 – ♦Limerick 22 – Roscommon 92 – ♦Tullamore 93.

🏨 **Old Ground** (T.H.F.), O'Connell St., ℰ 28127, Telex 28103, ☞ – 🖵 ⌷wc ☎ P. Ꮧ. ☒ AE
⓪ VISA
M 8.25/16.00 **st.** and a la carte ≬ 4.00 – 🖵 6.00 – **60 rm** 45.00/61.50 **st.**

🏠 **Auburn Lodge,** Galway Rd, N : 1 ½ m. on N 18 ℰ 21247, ☞, squash – 🖵 ⌷wc ☎ P. ☒
AE ⓪ VISA ※
closed 25 and 26 December – **M** 7.00/12.50 **t.** and a la carte ≬ 4.50 – **20 rm** 🖵 28.00/40.00 **t.** –
SB (weekends only)(October-June) 45.00/55.00 **st.**

DAIHATSU, TOYOTA Gort Rd ℰ 21904   RENAULT Tulla Rd ℰ 22758
FORD Lifford ℰ 21035   VW, AUDI, MAZDA Mill Rd ℰ 21505

ENNISCORTHY Wexford 405 M 10 – pop. 5 ,014 – ECD : Thursday – ☎ 054.
🛆 Bloomfield ℰ 33191.
♦Dublin 77 – Kilkenny 36 – ♦Waterford 36 – Wexford 14.

🏤 Murphy Floods, 24 Main St., Market Sq., ℰ 33413 – ⌷wc 🛆wc ☎. ☒ AE VISA
closed Christmas Day – **M** 6.50/10.00 **st.** and a la carte ≬ 3.40 – **22 rm** – SB 45.00/50.00 **st.**

FIAT Temple Shannon ℰ 33742   FORD Dublin Rd ℰ 33606

ENNISKERRY Wicklow 405 N 8 – pop. 1 ,179 – ☎ 01 Dublin.
See : Site★ – Powerscourt Demesne (gardens★★★, Araucaria Walk★) AC.
Envir. : Powerscourt Waterfall★ AC, S : 4 m. – Lough Tay★★ SW by T 43, T 61, L 161.
♦Dublin 17 – ♦Waterford 100.

🏨 Summerhill ☜, ℰ 867928, ☞ – 🖵 ⌷wc ☎ P
10 rm.

FAHAN Donegal 405 J 2 – ✉ Lifford – ☎ 077 Buncrana.
🛆 North West, Lisfannon, ℰ Buncrana 12.
♦Dublin 156 – ♦Londonderry 11 – ♦Sligo 95.

XX **St. John's,** ℰ 60289, « Lough-side setting » – P. ☒ AE ⓪ VISA
closed Monday, Good Friday and Christmas Day – **M** (dinner only) 14.50 **t.** and a la carte
≬ 3.25.

◆Dublin 125 – ◆Galway 36 – ◆Limerick 25.

🏠 **Smyth's Village** 🦢, 🅿️ 2, 🐿️, park, ✗ – 🚻wc ♿️wc ➋. 🆎
   April-October – **M** (lunch by arrangement)(booking essential) 4.00/7.00 🍷 4.00 – **12 rm**
   🛏️ 11.00/20.00 **t.**

GALWAY Galway 🗺️ E 8 – pop. 37,835 – ECD : Monday – ☎️ 091.

See : Lynch's Castle★ 16C – **Envir. :** NW : Lough Corrib★★★ – Claregalway (Franciscan Friary★
13C) NE : 7 m. – Abbeyknockmoy (Cistercian Monastery★ 12C ruins) NE : 18 m. – Tuam (St. Mary's
Cathedral : chancel arch★ 12C) NE : 20 m.

⛳ Blackrock, Salthill 🖉 21827, W : 3 m.

✈️ Carnmore Airport 🖉 55569, NE : 4 m.

🚢 to Aran Islands : Kilronan (Inishmore), Inishmaan and Inishere (C.I.E) 2-7 weekly.

🛈 Aras Failte, Eyre Sq. 🖉 63081.

◆Dublin 135 – ◆Limerick 64 – ◆Sligo 90.

🏨 Great Southern, Eyre Sq., 🖉 64041, Telex 28364, 🗺️ – 🛗 📺 ☎️. 🅰️
   120 rm

🏨 **Ardilaun House,** Taylor's Hill, 🖉 21433, Telex 28873, 🍴 – 🛗 📺 🚻wc ♿️wc ☎️ ➋. 🅰️ 🗺️
   🆎 🆅🆂🅰️. ✗
   closed 10 days at Christmas – **M** 8.00/16.00 **t.** and a la carte 🍷 3.50 – **72 rm** 🛏️ 26.00/52.00 **t.**

🏨 **Galway Ryan,** Dublin Rd, E : 1 ¼ m. on N 6 🖉 53181, Telex 28349, 🍴 – 🛗 🚻wc ☜ ➋. 🅰️
   🆎 🆅🆂🅰️. ✗
   closed 24 and 25 December – **M** (bar lunch)/dinner 11.00 **st.** and a la carte 🍷 3.75 – 🛏️ 5.25 –
   96 rm 30.00/60.00 **st.** – SB 45.00/80.50 **st.**

↑ **Adare House,** 9 Father Griffin Pl., Lower Salthill, 🖉 62638 – ➋. 🗺️ 🆎 ① 🆅🆂🅰️. ✗
   10 rm 🛏️ 10.00/22.00 **st.**

XX Casey's Westwood, Dangan Upper, Newcastle, NW : 1 ¾ m. on N 59 🖉 21442 – ➋
   M (restricted lunch).

   at Salthill SW : 2 m. – 📩 Salthill – ☎️ 091 Galway :

🏨 Warwick, 150 Lower Salthill, 🖉 21244 – 🚻wc ☜ ➋. ✗ – **50 rm**.

🏨 Anno Santo, Threadneedle Rd, 🖉 22110 – 🚻wc ☜ ➋. ✗ – **13 rm**.

🏨 **Rockbarton Park,** 5-7 Rockbarton Pk., 🖉 22018 – 🚻wc ♿️wc ☜ ➋. 🗺️ 🆎 ① 🆅🆂🅰️
   closed 23 December-1 January – **M** (bar lunch)/dinner 13.75 **st.** and a la carte 🍷 4.00 – **11 rm**
   🛏️ 14.85/36.30 **st.**

🏠 **Lochlurgain,** 22 Monksfield, Upper Salthill, 🖉 22884 – 🗺️ 🆎 🆅🆂🅰️. ✗
   Easter-September – **M** (bar lunch)/dinner 15.25 **st.** 🍷 3.75 – **19 rm** 🛏️ 16.85/39.90 **st.** – SB
   52.75/64.80 **st.**

NISSAN Headford Rd 🖉 65296   SKODA, TOYOTA Bohermore 🖉 63664
CITROEN, PEUGEOT, SAAB Spanish Par. 🖉 62167

GARRYVOE Cork 🗺️ H 12 – 📩 Castlemartyr – ☎️ 021 Cork.

◆Dublin 161 – ◆Cork 23 – ◆Waterford 62.

🏨 **Garryvoe,** Castlemartyr, 🖉 646718 – 🚻wc ♿️wc ☜ ➋. 🗺️ 🆎 ① 🆅🆂🅰️. ✗
   closed Christmas Day – **M** 9.00/15.00 **t.** and a la carte – 🛏️ 4.50 – **19 rm** 12.00/26.00 **t.**

GLENDALOUGH Wicklow 🗺️ MN 8 – ☎️ 0404.

See : Ancient monastic city★★ (site★★★, St. Kervin's Church★) and Upper Lake★ in Glendalough
Valley★★★.

◆Dublin 34 – Wexford 71.

🏠 **Royal,** 🖉 5135 – 🚻wc ➋. 🗺️ 🆅🆂🅰️. ✗
   Mid March-October – **M** 9.00/16.50 **t.** and a la carte 🍷 5.00 – **13 rm** 🛏️ 27.00/46.00 **t.** – SB
   45.00/50.00 **st.**

GLENGARRIFF Cork 🗺️ D 12 – pop. 159 – ☎️ 027.

See : Site★★★.

Envir. : S : Garinish Island (20 mn by boat *AC*) : Italian gardens★ – Martello Tower ✳️★★ *AC*.

⛳ 🖉 150, E : 1 m.

🛈 🖉 63084 (July-August).

◆Dublin 224 – ◆Cork 63 – ◆Killarney 37.

🏠 Casey's, 🖉 63010, 🍴 – 🚻wc ➋ – **20 rm**.

GLEN OF AHERLOW Tipperary 🗺️ H 10 – 📩 ☎️ 062 Tipperary.

See : Glen of Aherlow★ (statue of Christ the King★★).

◆Dublin 118 – Cahir 6 – Tipperary 9.

🏨 **Glen,** 🖉 56146, 🍴 – 🚻wc ☜ ➋. 🗺️ 🆎 🆅🆂🅰️. ✗
   M 7.50/12.50 **st.** and a la carte 🍷 4.00 – **24 rm** 🛏️ 19.00/37.20 **st.** – SB 43.00/47.00 **st.**

GLOUNTHAUNE Cork — see Cork.

GOREY Wexford 405 N 9 — pop. 2,588 — ECD : Wednesday — ☎ 055.
🛈 ✆ 21248 (July-August).
◆Dublin 58 — Waterford 55 — Wexford 38.

XXX **Marlfield House** ⊗ with rm, Courtown Rd, E : 1 m. ✆ 21124, Telex 80757, ≼, « Regency house and conservatory », ⚘, park — 📺 ⇌wc ☎ 📵. ⛽
closed mid November - mid December — **M** (booking essential) 16.00/19.50 **t.** and a la carte
🍴 4.50 — **12 rm** ⊏ 45.00/88.00 **t.**

GOUGANE BARRA Cork 405 D 12 — ⊠ ☎ 026 Ballingeary.
See : Lake (site★).
◆Dublin 206 — ◆Cork 45.

🏠 **Gougane Barra** ⊗, ✆ 47069, ≼ lough and mountains, 🔧 — ⇌wc 📵. 🔼 ① 🅥🅸🅢🅰. ⛽
April-September — **M** 11.00 **t.** (dinner) and a la carte 7.50/10.50 **t.** 🍴 5.00 — **29 rm** ⊏ 14.50/30.00 **t.**
— SB 45.10 **st.**

HOWTH Dublin 405 N 7 — ⊠ ☎ 01 Dublin.
See : Howth Summit ≼★★ — Cliff Walk ≼★★ — Harbour★ — St Mary's Abbey★ (ruins 13C, 15C),
site★ — Howth Gardens (rhododendrons★, site★, ≼★) AC.
🏌 Deer Park Hotel ✆ 322624.
◆Dublin 10.

🏠 **Howth Lodge** (Best Western), ✆ 390288, ≼ — 📺 ⇌wc 🍴wc ☎ 📵. 🔼. 🔼 🅰🅴 ① 🅥🅸🅢🅰. ⛽
closed Christmas Day — **M** (closed Sunday dinner) (buffet lunch Monday to Saturday)/dinner
14.00 **st.** and a la carte 🍴 4.00 — ⊏ 5.50 — **17 rm** 23.00/36.00 **st.** — SB (weekends only)(October-
April) 55.00/65.00 **st.**

XX **King Sitric,** Harbour Rd, East Pier, ✆ 325235, Seafood — 🔼 🅰🅴 ① 🅥🅸🅢🅰
closed Saturday lunch, Sunday, 1 week Easter, 10 days at Christmas and Bank Holidays — **M** a
la carte 16.95/20.80 **t.** 🍴 4.50.

INISHANNON Cork 405 G 12 — pop. 241 — ☎ 021 Cork.
🏌 Castlebernand, Bandon ✆ 41111, SW : 5 m.
◆Dublin 175 — ◆Cork 14 — ◆Killarney 46 — Bandon 4.5.

🏠 **Inishannon House,** S : ¾ m. on L 41 ✆ 75121, Telex 75398, 🔧, ⚘ — 📺 ⇌wc ☎ 📵. 🔼
🅰🅴 🅥🅸🅢🅰
closed 3 days at Christmas — **M** 8.95/14.95 **st.** and a la carte 🍴 3.95 — **13 rm** ⊏ 20.00/32.00 **st.**

FIAT, LANCIA ✆ 023 (Bandon) 41514   NISSAN, OPEL Irishtown ✆ 023 (Bandon) 41264
FORD 72 Main St. ✆ 023 (Bandon) 41522   RENAULT Clonakilty Rd ✆ 023 (Bandon) 41617

KANTURK Cork 405 F 11 — pop. 1,976 — ECD : Wednesday — ☎ 029.
◆Dublin 161 — ◆Cork 33 — ◆Killarney 31 — ◆Limerick 44.

🏠 **Assolas Country House** ⊗, E : 3 ¼ m. by L 38 on L 186 ✆ 50015, ≼, « Country house
atmosphere », 🔧, ⚘, park, ⛽ — ⇌wc 📵. ⛽
23 April-October — **M** (closed Sunday) (dinner only) 16.00 **t.** 🍴 3.95 — **7 rm** ⊏ 32.00/54.60 **t.**

AUDI, MAZDA ✆ 12

KELLS Kilkenny 405 K 10 — pop. 2,623.
See : Augustinian Priory★★ 14C.
Envir. : Kilree's Church (site★, round tower★) S : 2 m.
◆Dublin 86 — Kilkenny 9 — ◆Waterford 23.

Hotels and restaurant see : Kilkenny N : 9 m.

KENMARE Kerry 405 D 12 — pop. 1,123 — ECD : Thursday — ☎ 064 Killarney.
Envir. : Kenmare River Valley★★ E : by L 62.
🏌 ✆ 41291.
🛈 ✆ 41233 (July-August).
◆Dublin 210 — ◆Cork 58 — ◆Killarney 20.

🏛 ☎ **Park** ⊗, ✆ 41200, Telex 70005, ≼, « Antiques, paintings », ⚘, park, ⛽ — 🔲 ☎ 🔼 📵. 🔼
🅰🅴 ① 🅥🅸🅢🅰. ⛽
Easter-mid November and Christmas-New Year — **M** 13.80/26.50 **t.** and a la carte 🍴 7.00 —
50 rm ⊏ 54.00/128.00 **st.**, **6 suites** 146.00/175.00 **st.**
Spec. Veal sweetbreads with provençal tartlets, Selection of three fish with a herb mousse in a sea urchin sauce,
Selection of homemade ices with seasonal fruit.

X **Remy's House** with rm, Main St., ✆ 41589, French rest. — 📺 🍴wc ☎. 🔼 🅰🅴 ① 🅥🅸🅢🅰
Mid March-mid October — **M** (closed Tuesday) (dinner only) 7.50 **st.** and a la carte 🍴 3.00 —
2 rm ⊏ 14.00/22.00 **st.**

FORD Henry St. ✆ 41166   DATSUN Shelbourne St. ✆ 41355

KILLKENNY Kilkenny [405] K 10 – pop. 9,466 – ECD : Thursday – ☏ 056.

See : St. Canice's Cathedral★★ 13C – Grace's Castle (Courthouse)★ – Castle (park★, <★) – **Envir. :** Jerpoint Abbey★★ (ruins 12C-15C) SE : 12 m. – Callan (St. Mary's Church★ 13C-15C) SW : 13 m.

⛳18 Glendine ☎ 22125, N : 1 m. – [i] Rose Inn St. ☎ 21755.

♦Dublin 71 – ♦Cork 86 – ♦Killarney 115 – ♦Limerick 69 – ♦Tullamore 52 – ♦Waterford 29.

🏨 **Kilkenny,** College Rd, ☎ 62000, Telex 80177, 🏊, 🌳, 🎾 – [TV] 🛁wc 📞 [P]. 🏛. 💳 [VISA]
M 7.50/16.00 **st.** and a la carte 🍷3.50 – **60 rm** ☕38.75/58.00 **st.** – SB (weekends only) 72.00/75.00 **st.**

🏨 **Newpark,** Castlecomer Rd, N : ¾ m. on N 77 ☎ 22122, Telex 80080, 🌳, 🎾 – ▤ rest [TV] 🛁wc 🚿wc 📞 [P]. 🏛. 💳 [AE] ⓓ [VISA]. 🚫🐕
M 8.50/15.50 **t.** and a la carte 🍷4.75 – ☕ 6.00 – **43 rm** 26.50/42.00 **t.** – SB (weekends only)(except Bank Holidays) 52.00/55.00 **st.**

🏨 **Springhill Court,** Waterford Rd, S : 2 m. on N 10 ☎ 21122 – [TV] 🛁wc 🚿wc 📞 [P]. 💳 [AE] [VISA]. 🚫🐕
M 7.50/14.00 **st.** and a la carte 🍷3.50 – **44 rm** ☕ 24.20/40.00 **st.** – SB (weekends only) 55.00/60.00 **st.**

🍴🍴 **Lacken House** with rm, Dublin Rd, ☎ 61085, 🌳 – [P]. 🚫🐕
closed Sunday and Monday – **M** (dinner only) 14.50 **t.** and a la carte 🍷4.00 – **9 rm** ☕ 14.00/28.00 **t.** – SB 60.00 **st.**

at Knocktopher S : 13 m. on N 10 – ✉ ☏ 056 Kilkenny :

🍴🍴 **Knocktopher Abbey,** ☎ 28618, <, 🌳 – [P]. 💳 [VISA]
closed Sunday – **M** (dinner only) a la carte 10.25/16.50 **t.** 🍷3.75.

FORD Patrick St. ☎ 21016
OPEL Green St. ☎ 21304
RENAULT Irishtown ☎ 21494

KILLALOE Clare [405] G 9 – pop. 1,022 – ECD : Wednesday – ☏ 061.

See : Site★ – **Envir. :** N : Lough Derg Coast Road★★ (L 12) to Tuamgraney, Lough Derg★★★ (Holy Island : site★★) – Nenagh : Butler Castle (keep★ 13C) NE : 9 m.

♦Dublin 109 – Ennis 32 – ♦Limerick 13 – ♦Tullamore 58.

KILLARNEY Kerry [405] D 11 – pop. 7,693 – ECD : Thursday – ☏ 064.

Envir. : SW : Killarney District, Ring of Kerry : Lough Leane★★★, Muckross House (gardens★★★) – Muckross Abbey★ (ruins 13C), Tork Waterfall (Belvedere : <★★, 251 steps), Lady's View Belvedere★★ – Gap of Dunloe★★.

⛳18, ⛳18 Mahoney's Point ☎ 31034, W : 3 m. – [i] Town Hall ☎ 31633.

♦Dublin 189 – ♦Cork 54 – ♦Limerick 69 – ♦Waterford 112.

🏨 Europe 🐦, Fossa, W : 3 ½ m. on T 67 ☎ 31900, Telex 28213, < lake and mountains, 🏊, 🐟, 🌳, park – 🛗 📞 ♿ [P]. 🏛. 🚫🐕 – **175 rm**.

🏨 **Aghadoe Heights** 🐦, NW : 3 ½ m. by N 22 ☎ 31766, Telex 26942, < countryside, lake and mountains, 🌳, 🎾 – [TV] 📞 ♿ [P]. 🏛. 💳 [AE] ⓓ [VISA]
closed 1 to 20 January and 21 to 31 December – **M** 8.50/17.50 **t.** and a la carte 🍷4.00 – ☕ 6.50 – **55 rm** 22.00/63.50 **t.** – SB (weekends only) 60.00/87.50 **st.**

🏨 **Cahernane** 🐦, Muckross Rd, S : 1 m. on N 71 ☎ 31895, Telex 28123, <, 🐟, 🌳, 🎾 – 🛁wc 📞 [P]. 💳 [AE] ⓓ [VISA]. 🚫🐕
April-October – **M** (bar lunch)/dinner 17.50 **t.** and a la carte 🍷4.50 – **36 rm** ☕ 35.00/60.00 **t.**

🏨 Castlerosse (Best Western) 🐦, W : 2 m. on T 67 ☎ 31144, Telex 70010, < lake and mountains, ⛳, 🐟, 🌳, 🎾 – 🛁wc 📞 [P]. 🚫🐕 – **40 rm**.

🏨 **Linden House,** New Rd, ☎ 31379 – 🛁wc 🚿wc [P]. 🚫🐕
closed December and January – **M** *(closed Monday)* (dinner only) 10.00 **t.** and a la carte 🍷3.50 – **11 rm** ☕ 11.00/20.00 **t.**

⌂ **Carriglea Farmhouse** 🐦, Muckross Rd, S : 1 ½ m. on N 71 ☎ 31116, <, 🌳 – 🛁wc 🚿wc [P]. 🚫🐕
May to October – **9 rm** ☕ 23.00 **st.**

⌂ **Gardens,** Countess Rd, off Muckross Rd, ☎ 31147, 🌳 – 🛁wc 🚿wc [P]. 🚫🐕
16 March-October – **21 rm** ☕ 10.00/22.00 **st.**

⌂ **Loch Lein Farm** 🐦, Fossa, W : 4 m. on T 67 ☎ 31260, <, 🌳 – 🛁wc 🚿wc [P]. 🚫🐕
March-October – **12 rm** ☕ 9.50/25.00 **st.**

⌂ Castle Lodge, Muckross Rd, ☎ 31545 – 🚿wc [P]
16 rm.

⌂ **Kathleens Country House,** Madams Height, Tralee Rd, N : 2 m. on N 22 ☎ 32810, <, 🌳 – 🛁wc [P]. 🚫🐕
closed November and December – **10 rm** ☕ 25.00/30.00 **st.**

🍴 **Gaby's,** 17 High St., ☎ 32519, Seafood bistro – 💳 [AE] ⓓ [VISA]
Mid March-8 December – **M** *(closed Monday lunch and Sunday)* a la carte 16.00/21.00 **t.** 🍷5.00.

AUDI, MAZDA, MERCEDES-BENZ, VW Park Rd ☎ 31355
AUSTIN-ROVER, DATSUN Muckross Rd ☎ 31237
FORD New Rd ☎ 31087
RENAULT Ballycasheen ☎ 31416

KILLYBEGS Donegal 405 G 4 – pop. 1,570.

See : Fishing harbour★ – Carpet factory.

Envir. : NW : Glen Bay★★ – Glencolumbkille (site★★, folk village) NW : 14 m. – Portnoo (site★).

♦Dublin 181 – ♦Londonderry 65 – ♦Sligo 57.

KILTIMAGH Mayo 405 F 6 – pop. 1,145 – ECD : Monday – ✆ 094 Castlebar.

♦Dublin 140 – ♦Sligo 52.

🏠 **Westway,** James St., ℰ 81145 – ⌂wc ℗. 🅰 VISA
closed 23 December-3 January – **M** (closed Sunday and Bank Holidays) (bar lunch)/dinner a la carte 12.25/15.75 t. ⬧ 4.00 – **17 rm** ⊊ 15.00/30.00 t.

KINSALE Cork 405 G 12 – pop. 1,765 – ECD : Thursday – ✆ 021 Cork.

See : St. Multose's Church★ 12C.

🗌 Ringmanean, Belgooly ℰ 72197.

🗓 ℰ 72234 (July-August).

♦Dublin 178 – ♦Cork 17.

🏛 **Acton's** (T.H.F.), Pier Rd, ℰ 772135, Telex 75443, ≤, 🔟, 🚿 – 🕸 📺 ℗. 🔬. 🅰 AE ① VISA
closed January and February – **M** (carving lunch April-October only)/dinner 15.00 st. and a la carte ⬧ 4.00 – **55 rm** ⊊ 38.50/57.00 st.

⌂ **Old Presbytery,** Cork St., ℰ 772027 – 🚿
5 rm ⊊ 10.50/21.00 st.

XX **Billy Mackesy's Bawnleigh House,** N : 5 ½ m. on Old Cork Rd ℰ 771333 – ℗
closed Sunday, Monday, 18 August-2 September and 22 to 30 December – **M** (dinner only) 8.95 st. and a la carte ⬧ 4.50.

XX Blue Haven with rm, 3 Pearse St., ℰ 772209, Seafood – 🕸wc. 🚿 – **10 rm**.

XX **Vintage,** 50 Main St., ℰ 772502 – 🅰 AE ① VISA
closed Sunday, January and February – **M** (dinner only) 17.00 st. and a la carte ⬧ 5.50.

X **Man Friday,** Scilly, SE : ½ m. ℰ 772260 – 🅰 VISA
closed Sunday, 2 weeks January and 1 week November – **M** a la carte 12.70/16.95 st. ⬧ 5.40.

X Le Toucan, Milk Market, ℰ 772233.

X **Cottage Loft,** Castlepark, SW : 1 ¾m. by L 42 ℰ 772803, Seafood – ℗. 🅰 VISA
closed Monday – **M** (dinner only and Sunday lunch)/dinner a la carte 13.20/17.25 t. ⬧ 4.50.

KNOCKTOPHER Kilkenny – see Kilkenny.

LAHINCH Clare 405 D 9 – pop. 473 – ✆ 065.

Envir. : Cliffs of Moher★★★ (O'Brien's Tower 🚿★★ N : 1 h Rtn on foot) NW : 5 ½ m.

🗌₈, 🗌₈ ℰ Lahinch 3.

♦Dublin 162 – ♦Galway 49 – ♦Limerick 41.

🏛 Aberdeen Arms, ℰ 81100, Telex 70132 – ⌂wc ☎ ℗ – **48 rm**.

LEENANE Galway 405 C 7.

See : ≤★ on Killary Harbour★.

Exc. : SE : Joyces Country : by road L 100 from Leenane to Clonbur : Lough Nafooey★ – 🚿★ from the bridge on Lough Mask★★.

♦Dublin 173 – Ballina 56 – ♦Galway 41.

Hotels see : Clifden SW : 19 m.

LETTERFRACK Galway 405 C 7 – ✆ Moyard.

Envir. : Kylemore Abbey (site★★) and Kylemore Lake★, E : 4 m. – Renvyle (castle ≤★) NW : 5 m.

♦Dublin 189 – Ballina 69 – ♦Galway 57.

🏛 **Rosleague Manor** 🦢, W : 1 ½ m. on T 71 ℰ 7, ≤ Ballynakill harbour and Tully mountain, 🚿 – ⌂wc ℗. 🅰 VISA
Easter-October – **M** (bar lunch)/dinner 16.00 t. and a la carte ⬧ 5.00 – **15 rm** ⊊ 20.00/48.00 t. – SB (except July and August) 80.00/100.00 st.

LETTERKENNY Donegal 405 I 3 – pop. 6,444 – ECD : Monday – ✆ 074.

See : St. Eunan's Cathedral ≤★.

Envir. : Grianan of Aileach★ (stone fort) 🚿★★★ NE : 18 m. – Gartan Lake★ NW : 8 ½ m.

🗌₈ Barnhill ℰ 21150, NE : 1 m.

🗓 Derry Rd ℰ 21160.

♦Dublin 150 – ♦Londonderry 21 – ♦Sligo 72.

🏠 **Gallagher's,** 100 Upper Main St., ℰ 22066 – 📺 ⌂wc ☎ ℗. 🅰 AE ① VISA. 🚿
closed 25 to 30 December – **M** 8.00/12.50 st. and a la carte ⬧ 3.60 – **26 rm** ⊊ 15.00/36.00 st.

Envir. : Monasteranenagh Abbey★ (ruins 12C) S : 14 m. by N 20 Z.

Ballyclough ☞ 44083, S : 3 m. by N 20 Z.

Shannon Airport : ☞ 061 (Shannon) 61444, Telex 26222, W : 16 m. by N 18 Y – **Terminal :** Limerick Railway Station.

The Granary, Michael St. ☞ 317522.

◆Dublin 120 – ◆Cork 58.

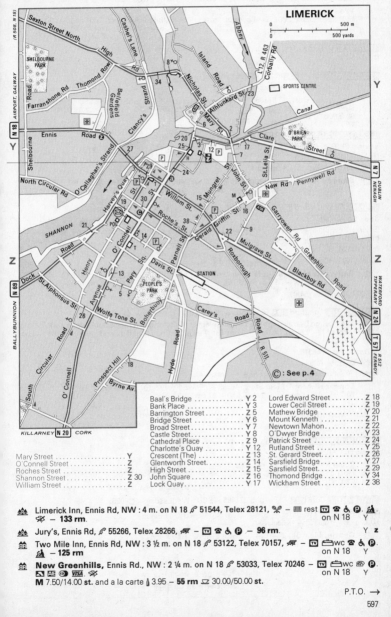

LIMERICK

Mary Street . . . . Y	
O'Connell Street . . . . Z	
Roches Street . . . . Z	
Shannon Street . . . . Z 30	
William Street . . . . Z	

Baal's Bridge . . . . Y 2		Lord Edward Street . . . . Z 18	
Bank Place . . . . Y 3		Lower Cecil Street . . . . Z 19	
Barrington Street . . . . Z 5		Mathew Bridge . . . . Y 20	
Bridge Street . . . . Y 6		Mount Kenneth . . . . Z 21	
Broad Street . . . . Y 7		Newtown Mahon . . . . Z 22	
Castle Street . . . . Y 8		O'Dwyer Bridge . . . . Y 23	
Cathedral Place . . . . Z 9		Patrick Street . . . . Y 24	
Charlotte's Quay . . . . Y 12		Rutland Street . . . . Y 25	
Crescent (The) . . . . Z 13		St. Gerard Street . . . . Z 26	
Glentworth Street . . . . Z 14		Sarsfield Bridge . . . . Y 27	
High Street . . . . Z 15		Sarsfield Street . . . . Y 29	
John Square . . . . Z 16		Thomond Bridge . . . . Y 34	
Lock Quay . . . . Y 17		Wickham Street . . . . Z 38	

🏨🏨 Limerick Inn, Ennis Rd, NW : 4 m. on N 18 ☞ 51544, Telex 28121, ✗ – ▤ rest 📺 ☎ & 🅿 △ ⛾ – **133 rm.** on N 18 Y

🏨🏨 Jury's, Ennis Rd, ☞ 55266, Telex 28266, 🚗 – 📺 ☎ & 🅿 – **96 rm.** Y z

🏨 Two Mile Inn, Ennis Rd, NW : 3 ½ m. on N 18 ☞ 53122, Telex 70157, 🚗 – 📺 ⇌wc ☎ & 🅿 △ – **125 rm.** on N 18 Y

🏨 **New Greenhills,** Ennis Rd., NW : 2 ¼ m. on N 18 ☞ 53033, Telex 70246 – 📺 ⇌wc ☎ 🅿 ▩ AE ⓞ VISA ✗ on N 18 Y
M 7.50/14.00 **st.** and a la carte ⓛ 3.95 – **55 rm** ⇌ 30.00/50.00 **st.**

P.T.O. →

🏛 **Limerick Ryan**, Ennis Rd, NW : 1 ¼ m. on N 18 ℰ 53922, Telex 26920 – 🕃 📺 ⛆wc 🕿 🅿 ♨.
⚘ – **181 rm**   on N 18   Y

🏛 **Cruise's Royal**, 4-7 O'Connell St., ℰ 44977, Telex 70088 – 🕃 📺 ⛆wc 🕿 ♨ 🔼 ⚑ AE
📇 ⚘   Z **a**
M 8.00/15.00 **t.** and a la carte ⋕ 3.95 – ⚌ 6.00 – **73 rm** 21.00/37.10 **t.**

🏛 **Royal George**, O'Connell St., ℰ 44566, Telex 26910 – 🕃 📺 ⛆wc ⚌. ♨. 🔼 AE ⓞ 📇 ⚘
closed Christmas Day – **M** 7.50/13.00 **st.** and a la carte ⋕ 3.85 – **60 rm** ⚌ 25.50/45.00 **st.**

Z **c**

AUSTIN-ROVER, SUZUKI, VOLVO   Coonagh Cross
ℰ 51577
BMW, NISSAN   Castle St. ℰ 43133
FORD   Lansdowne ℰ 52244
MAZDA, AUDI, MERCEDES-BENZ, PORSCHE, VW
Dublin Rd ℰ 46000

MITSUBISHI   Raheen ℰ 27277
OPEL, BEDFORD   Ennis Rd ℰ 53211
RENAULT   Dooradoyle ℰ 29311

LISCANNOR Clare 405 D 9 – 🕾 065 Lahinch.

♦Dublin 164 – ♦Galway 51 – ♦Limerick 43.

🏛 **Liscannor Golf**, ℰ 81186, ≤ Liscannor harbour, 🍴 – ⛆wc ⚌ 🅿 🔼 AE ⓞ 📇 ⚘
April-October – **M** (bar lunch)/dinner a la carte 6.75/9.50 **t.** – **26 rm** ⚌ 26.00/48.00 **t.** – SB 60.00/70.00 **st.**

LISDOONVARNA Clare 405 E 8 – pop. 607 – 🕾 065 Ennis.

Envir. : Cliffs of Moher★★★ (O' Brien's Tower ⚘★★ N : 1 h Rtn on foot) SW : 8 m.

🛈 ℰ 62 (July-September).

♦Dublin 167 – ♦Galway 39 – ♦Limerick 47.

🏨 **Sheedy's Spa View**, Sulphir Hill, ℰ 74026, 🍴, ⚘ – ⛆wc ⋔wc 🅿 🔼 📇 ⚘
15 March-October – **M** (bar lunch)/dinner 13.00 **t.** and a la carte ⋕ 6.50 – **10 rm** ⚌ 20.00/34.00 **t.**

LISMORE Waterford 405 I 11 – pop. 919 – ECD : Thursday – 🕾 058 Dungarvan.

See : Castle (site★).

Envir. : SE : Blackwater Valley★★ (from Lismore to the mouth, by a scenic road along the right bank of the River Blackwater).

🛅 ℰ 54026, N : 1 m.

♦Dublin 143 – ♦Cork 40 – ♦Killarney 74 – ♦Waterford 44.

🏨 **Ballyrafter House** 🦢, N : ¾ m. by T 30 on T 34 ℰ 54002, 🍴, park – ⛆wc 🅿 ⓞ ⚘
April-September – **M** (bar lunch)/dinner 12.00 **t.** ⋕ 4.25 – ⚌ 4.00 – **12 rm** 14.00/28.00 **t.**

TOYOTA   Lismore ℰ 54147

LONGFORD Longford 405 I 6 – pop. 3,998 – ECD : Thursday – 🕾 043.

Envir. : SE : Lough Derravaragh★ – Lough Owel★ – Multyfarnam (Franciscan College park : Stations of the Cross★) – Lough Lene★ – Fore (St. Feichin's Church and ruined priory 13C★) – Lough Ennell★.

🛅 Dublin Rd ℰ 46310.

🛈 ℰ 6566 (June-August).

♦Dublin 74 – Roscommon 19 – ♦Sligo 57 – ♦Tullamore 47.

🏨 **Longford Arms**, Main St., ℰ 46296 – ⛆wc ⋔wc ⚌ 🅿 ♨ 🔼 AE ⓞ 📇
M 7.95/14.95 **t.** and a la carte ⋕ 4.50 – **51 rm** ⚌ 22.75/45.50 **st.** – SB 50.00/60.00 **st.**

FORD   Dublin Rd ℰ 46421
MAZDA, VW, AUDI   Dublin Rd ℰ 46321
NISSAN   Drumlish ℰ 24104

RENAULT   Athlone Rd ℰ 46615
SKODA, TOYOTA   Lanesboro ℰ 21159
SKODA, TOYOTA   Athlone Rd ℰ 45621

LOUGH GOWNA Cavan 405 J 6 – pop. 125 – 🕾 043 Cavan.

♦Dublin 81 – ♦Tullamore 54.

🏨 **Robin Hill** 🦢, ℰ 83121, 🍴 – 🅿
closed Christmas Day – **M** (closed Monday to non-residents) (dinner only) – **5 rm** ⚌ 9.50/19.00 **st.**

MACROOM Cork 405 F 12 – pop. 2,495 – ECD : Wednesday – 🕾 026.

🛅 Lackadove ℰ 72.

♦Dublin 186 – ♦Cork 25 – ♦Killarney 30.

🏨 **Castle**, Main St., ℰ 41074 – ⛆wc ⋔wc 🕿 🔼 ⓞ 📇
M 6.00/8.00 **st.** and a la carte ⋕ 3.50 – **18 rm** ⚌ 14.00/28.00 **st.**

EUROPE on a single sheet

Michelin map no 920

MALAHIDE Dublin **405** N 7 – pop. 9,158 – ✪ 01 Dublin.
Envir. : Swords (St. Columba's Church : towers★) W : 2 ½ m. – Lusk (church : round towers★)
NW : 8 m.
ⓕ₉ ℰ 450245.
♦Dublin 9 – Drogheda 24.

XX **Johnny's,** 9 St. James's Terr., ℰ 450314 – 🅰 🆎 ⓪ *VISA*
closed Sunday, Monday, 1 week at Easter, September-mid October and 1 week at Christmas –
M (dinner only) 21.00 **st.** and a la carte ₤ 4.00.

MALLOW Cork **405** F 11 – pop. 6,572 – ECD : Wednesday – ✪ 022.
ⓕ₁₈ Balleyellis ℰ 21145, SE : 1 ½ m. from Mallow Bridge.
♦Dublin 149 – ♦Cork 21 – ♦Killarney 40 – ♦Limerick 41.

🏨 **Longueville House** ⟨⟩, W : 3 ½ m. by N 72 ℰ 27156, Telex 75498, ≤, « Georgian mansion
in extensive grounds », ⟨, 🌳, park – 🚻wc 🛆wc ℗. ⓪ *VISA*. ✿
Easter-October – **M** (booking essential)(bar lunch and Sunday and Monday dinner, residents only)/dinner 20.00 **st.** and a la carte ₤ 5.00 – **17 rm** ⇄ 35.50/71.00 **st.**

OPEL Buttevant ℰ 23338

MAYNOOTH Kildare **405** M 7 – pop. 3,388 – ECD : Wednesday – ✪ 01 Dublin.
♦Dublin 15.

XXX **Moyglare Manor** ⟨⟩ with rm, Moyglare, N : 2 m. ℰ 286351, Telex 90358, ≤, « Georgian
country house », 🌳, park – 🚻wc ☎ ℗. 🅰 🆎 ⓪ *VISA*. ✿
closed 25 and 26 December – **M** *(closed Saturday)* 13.95/26.00 **t.** and a la carte ₤ 4.95 – **11 rm**
⇄ 42.00/75.00 **st.**

MOUNTSHANNON Clare **405** G 9.
♦ Dublin 129 – ♦ Galway 45 – ♦ Limerick 30.

⌂ **Mountshannon,** Main St., ℰ 62, 🌳 – 🛆wc
Mid March-mid December – **11 rm** ⇄ 10.80/27.00 **st.**

MOYARD Galway **405** C 7.
♦Dublin 187 – ♦Galway 55.

🏨 Crocnaraw Country House ⟨⟩, ℰ 9, ≤, « Country house atmosphere », ⟨, 🌳, park –
🚻wc ℗. ✿
10 rm.

MOYCULLEN Galway **405** E 9 – pop. 228 – ✉ Rosscahill – ✪ 091 Galway.
♦Dublin 139 – ♦Galway 7.

☎ **Knockferry Lodge** ⟨⟩, Knockferry (on Lough Corrib), NE : 6 ½ m. ℰ 80122, ⟨ – 🚻wc
🛆wc ℗. 🆎 ⓪ *VISA*. ✿
Easter-mid October – **M** (booking essential)(bar lunch)/dinner 10.50 **t.** ₤ 3.25 – **12 rm**
⇄ 16.00/27.00 **t.**

XX **Drimcong House,** NW : 1 m. on N 59 ℰ 85115, « 17C estate house », 🌳 – ℗. 🅰 🆎 ⓪
VISA
closed Sunday, Monday, January and February – **M** (booking essential)(dinner only) 14.00
st. and a la carte ₤ 4.00.

MULLINGAR Westmeath **405** JK 7 – pop. 7,854 – ✪ 044.
Envir. : N : Lough Derravaragah★ – Lough Owel★ – Multyfarman (Franciscan College park: Stations
of the Cross★ – NE : Lough Lene★ – Fore (St. Feichin's Church and ruined priory 13C★)
– S : Lough Ennell.
♦ Dublin 49 – ♦ Drogheda 36.

🏨 **Greville Arms,** Pearse St., ℰ 48563, Telex 91880 – 📺 🚻wc 🛆wc ☎ ℗. 🅰. 🅰 🆎 ⓪ *VISA*
closed 25 and 26 December – **M** a la carte 8.40/17.15 **t.** ₤ 4.95 – **21 rm** ⇄ 15.00/42.00 – SB
33.00/35.00 **st.**

NAVAN Meath **405** L 7 – pop. 4,124 – ECD : Thursday – ✪ 046.
Envir. : Bective Abbey★ (12C ruins) S : 3 m.
ⓕ₁₈ Royal Tara, Bellinter Park ℰ 25244.
♦Dublin 30 – Drogheda 16 – ♦Dundalk 34.

at Dunderry SW : 5 ½ m. by N 51 on L 23 – ✉ ✪ 046 Navan :

XXX ✿ **Dunderry Lodge,** W : ¾ m. ℰ 31671, « Converted farm buildings » – ℗. 🅰 🆎 ⓪ *VISA*
closed Sunday, Monday, 27 March-1 April, 2 to 28 August and 24 December-3 January – **M**
(booking essential)(dinner only) 13.00 **t.** and a la carte ₤ 4.50
Spec. Terrine of two fish, sauce verte, Supreme of pigeon Empress Eugenie, Escalopes of turbot with champagne
and verbena (May-November).

FORD Dublin Rd ℰ 21212
PEUGEOT-TALBOT Castlemartin ℰ 21949

RENAULT Cannon Row ℰ 21312
TOYOTA Kells Rd ℰ 21336

NEWBAWN Wexford **405** L 10 – see New Ross.

[NEWBRIDGE] (DROICHEAD NUA) Kildare [405] L 8 – pop. 5,780 – ECD : Tuesday – ☎ 045 Naas.

Envir. : Kildare (St. Brigid's Cathedral★ 13C-19C and round tower★ 9C-10C) SW : 5 m. – Tully (National Stud★, Japanese gardens★ *AC*) SW : 6 m. via Kildare – Old Kilcullen (site★, ☀★).

⛳9 Cill-Dara, ✆ 045 (Kildare) 21433, Kildare Town, SW : 5 m. – ⛳18 Curragh ✆ 045 (Curragh) 41238, S : 3 m.

♦Dublin 28 – Kilkenny 57 – ♦Tullamore 36.

- Keadeen, Ballymany, SW : 1 m. on N 7 ✆ 31666, Telex 24326, 🌳 – [TV] ♿ [P]. 🏛 **36 rm**.

FIAT Moorefield ✆ 31725 — NISSAN, TOYOTA Dublin Rd ✆ 31281

[NEWMARKET-ON-FERGUS] Clare [405] F 7 – pop. 1,348 – ☎ 061 Shannon.

♦Dublin 136 – Ennis 8 – ♦Limerick 15.

- **Dromoland Castle** 🐎, NW : 1½ m. on T 11 ✆ 71144, Telex 26854, ←, « Converted castle », ⛳9, 🐟, 🌳, park, 🎾 – ☎ [P]. 🏛. [EN] [AE] [O] [VISA]. 🐕
  April-October – **M** 15.00/27.50 **t.** 🍷 8.00 – ☕ 9.00 – **67 rm** 72.00/120.00 **t.**

[NEWPORT] Mayo [405] D 6 – pop. 470 – ☎ 098.

See : St. Patrick's Church★, modern Irish-Romanesque style (site★).

Envir. : Burrishoole Abbey (site★) NW : 2 m.

♦Dublin 164 – Ballina 37 – ♦Galway 60.

- **Newport House** 🐎, ✆ 41222, Telex 53740, « Country house atmosphere, antiques », 🐟, 🌳, park – 🛁wc 🚿wc [P]. [AE] [O] [VISA]
  Mid March-September – **M** 13.00/18.00 **st.** and a la carte – **20 rm** ☕ 26.00/58.00 **st.**

[NEW ROSS] Wexford [405] L 10 – pop. 5,386 – ECD : Wednesday – ☎ 051.

Envir. : St. Mullins Monastery (site★) N : 9 m. – John F. Kennedy Memorial Park★ 1968 (arboretum, ←★) S : 7½ m. – SW : River Barrow Valley★.

⛳9 Tinneranny ✆ 21433.

[i] ✆ 21857 (July-August).

♦Dublin 88 – Kilkenny 27 – ♦Waterford 15 – Wexford 23.

- **Inishross House,** 96 Mary St., ✆ 21335 – [P]. 🐕
  6 rm ☕ 8.50/17.00 **st.**

at Newbawn E : 8 m. by N 25 and L 160 – ✉ ☎ 051 New Ross :

- 🍴🍴 **Cedar Lodge** with rm, Carrigbyrne, N : 1½ m. on N 25 ✆ 28386 – [TV] 🛁wc ☎ [P]. [EN] [VISA]
  M 10.50/15.50 **st.** and a la carte 🍷 3.75 – **13 rm** ☕ 27.50/40.00 **t.** – SB 70.00 **st.**

FIAT, LANCIA Rosebercon ✆ 21122 — FORD Waterford Rd ✆ 21403

[OUGHTERARD] Galway [405] E 7 – pop. 748 – ☎ 091 Galway.

See : The northern scenic road (cul-de-sac) ←★★ on Lough Corrib★★★.

Envir. : Aughnanure Castle★ (16C) SE : 3 m. – Leckavrea Mountain★ NW : 13 m. – Gortmore (←★★ S : on Kilkieran Bay, ←★ NW : on the Twelve Pins) SW : 16 m.

⛳9 Gurteeva ✆ 82131.

♦Dublin 149 – ♦Galway 17.

- **Currarevagh House** 🐎, NW : 4 m. ✆ 82313, ←, « Country house atmosphere », 🐟, 🌳, park, 🎾 – 🛁wc 🚿wc [P]. 🐕
  April-October – **M** (booking essential) 6.70/13.75 **t.** 🍷 3.50 – **15 rm** ☕ 26.00/52.00 **t.**
- **Sweeney's Oughterard House** 🐎, W : ½ m. on T 71 ✆ 82207, 🌳 – [lift] 🛁wc ☎ [P]. [EN] [AE] [O] [VISA]
  M a la carte 11.20/26.00 **st.** 🍷 4.30 – **21 rm** ☕ 27.00/72.00 **st.**

[PARKNASILLA] Kerry [405] C 12 – ☎ 064 Sneem.

⛳9 Parknasilla ✆ 45122.

♦Dublin 224 – ♦Cork 72 – ♦Killarney 34.

- **Great Southern** 🐎, ✆ 45122, Telex 26899, ← Kenmare river, bay and mountains, 🏊, ⛳9, 🐟, 🌳, park, 🎾 – ☎ [P]. 🏛. [EN] [AE] [O] [VISA]. 🐕
  22 March-3 November and Christmas – **M** 10.50/19.80 **t.** 🍷 4.70 – ☕ 5.50 – **57 rm** 62.50/101.50 – SB (April and October) 110.00 **st.**

[PORTLAOISE] Laois [405] K 8 – pop. 4,049 – ☎ 0502.

⛳18 Heath ✆ 26533, E : 4 m.

[i] ✆ 21178 (July-August).

♦ Dublin 54 – Kilkenny 31 – ♦Limerick 67.

- **Killeshin,** Dublin Rd, E : 1 m. on N 7 ✆ 21663, Telex 33272 – [TV] 🛁wc 🚿wc ☎ [P]. 🏛. [EN] [AE] [O] [VISA]. 🐕
  M 8.00/15.00 **t.** and a la carte 🍷 4.50 – **44 rm** ☕ 21.00/48.00 **t.** – SB 70.00/84.00 **st.**

[PORT NA BLAGH] Donegal [405] I 2 – see Dunfanaghy.

Envir. : Beltany Stone Circle★ (site★) from the road 10 mn on foot, S : 2 m.

♦Dublin 139 – Donegal 29 – ♦Londonderry 20 – ♦Sligo 69.

☆ **Central,** The Diamond, ✆ 45126 – 🏠wc. ⚡
closed 22 to 30 December – **M** (closed lunch Sunday and Bank Holidays) 6.00/10.50
st. and a la carte ♠ 3.10 – **10 rm** ⨧ 12.50/25.00 st.

RATH LUIRC = Charleville.

RATHMULLAN Donegal 405 J 2 – pop. 584 – ⊠ ✪ 074 Letterkenny.

Envir. : Mulroy Bay ★★ NW : 8 m. – Fanad Head ≤★ N : 20 m.

🏌 Otway, Saltpans ✆ Rathmullen 108.

♦Dublin 165 – ♦Londonderry 36 – ♦Sligo 87.

🏨 **Rathmullan House** ≫, N : ½ m. on L 77 ✆ 58188, ≤ Lough Swilly and hills, « Country
house atmosphere », ⚓, 🌴, park, ✗ – 🏠wc 🏠wc ⚡. 🔼 🅰🅴 ⓪ 𝑉𝐼𝑆𝐴. ⚡
Easter-8 October – **M** (restricted lunch) 9.00/15.00 t. ♠ 3.50 – ⨧ 2.00 – **20 rm** 15.00/56.00 t. –
SB 59.40/85.15 st.

🏠 **Fort Royal** ≫, N : 1 m. off L 77 ✆ 58100, ≤ Lough Swilly, 🏌, ⚓, 🌴, park, ✗, squash –
🏠wc ⚡. 🔼 🅰🅴 𝑉𝐼𝑆𝐴
April-September – **M** (bar lunch)/dinner 15.00 st. ♠ 4.00 – **20 rm** ⨧ 17.00/60.00 st. – SB
65.00/75.00 st.

RATHNEW Wicklow 405 N 8 – pop. 1 ,366 – ⊠ ✪ 0404 Wicklow.

♦Dublin 31 – ♦Waterford 82 – Wexford 65.

🏨 **Tinakilly House** ≫, ✆ 9274, ≤, « Victorian country house », 🌴, park – 🏠wc ⚡ ⚡. ♿.
🅰🅴 𝑉𝐼𝑆𝐴. ⚡
closed December and January – **M** 11.00/22.00 t. ♠ 4.00 – **10 rm** ⨧ 45.00/72.00 t.

🏨 **Hunter's,** N : ¾ m. on L 29 ✆ 4106, « Inn in attractive gardens », ⚓, 🌴 – 🏠wc ⚡. ⚡
17 rm.

REDCASTLE Donegal 405 K 2 – ⊠ ✪ Moville.

♦Dublin 162 – ♦Londonderry 17.

🏨 Redcastle, ✆ 243, ≤, 🏌, ⚓, park, ✗, squash – 📺 🏠wc ⚡ ⚡. ⚡ – **14 rm**.

RENVYLE Galway 405 C 7 – ⊠ Connemara – ✪ 095 Clifden.

♦ Dublin 196 – ♦ Galway 61.

🏨 **Renvyle House** ≫, ✆ 21122, Telex 28896, ≤ Atlantic Ocean, ⌇ heated, 🏌, ⚓, 🌴, park,
✗ – 🏠wc ☎ ⚡. 🔼 𝑉𝐼𝑆𝐴
Mid March-4 November and Christmas-New Year – **M** 8.00/14.50 t. ♠ 3.90 – **75 rm**
⨧ 19.50/39.50 t.

ROSAPENNA Donegal 405 I 2 – ✪ 074 Letterkenny.

♦ Dublin 216 – Donegal 52 – ♦ Londonderry 47.

🏨 **Rosapenna Golf,** Downings, ✆ 55301, ≤, 🏌, ✗ – 🏠wc ☎ ⚡. 🔼 🅰🅴 ⓪ 𝑉𝐼𝑆𝐴
Mid March-October – **M** (bar lunch)/dinner 14.50 t. ♠ 4.00 – **40 rm** ⨧ 26.00/45.00 t. – SB
60.00/70.00 st.

ROSCOMMON Roscommon 405 H 7 – pop. 1 , 673 – ECD : Thusrday – ✪ 0903.

🛈 ✆ 6356 (June-August).

♦Dublin 95 – ♦Galway 50 – ♦Sligo 51.

🏨 **Abbey,** ✆ 6015, 🌴 – 📺 🏠wc ☎ ♠ ⚡. 🔼 🅰🅴 ⓪ 𝑉𝐼𝑆𝐴. ⚡
M 9.50/16.00 t. and a la carte ♠ 4.50 – ⨧ 5.50 – **24 rm** 20.00/40.00 t. – SB (weekends
only)(except summer) 50.00/65.00 st.

ROSCREA Tipperary 405 I 9 – ✪ 0505.

♦Dublin 75 – ♦Limerick 45.

🏠 **Racket Hall,** Dublin Rd, E : 1 ¾ m. on N 7 ✆ 21748, 🌴 – 🏠wc ☎ ⚡. 🔼 🅰🅴 𝑉𝐼𝑆𝐴. ⚡
M 10.00/14.50 st. and a la carte – ⨧ 5.50 – **10 rm** 15.00/40.00 st. – SB 60.00/70.00 st.

ROSSES POINT Sligo 405 G 5 – see Sligo.

In this guide

a symbol or a character, printed in red or black, in **bold** or light
type, does not have the same meaning.
Pay particular attention to the explanatory pages (pp. 12 to 19).

ROSSLARE Wexford **405** M 11 – pop. 779 – ✪ 053.

ﬁ8 ℰ 32113.

♦Dublin 104 – ♦Waterford 50 – Wexford 12.

🏛 **Kelly's Strand,** Strand Rd., ℰ 32114, ⌛ heated, 🔲, 🚗, ⚗ , squash – 🎱 📺 ☎ ℗. ⚗
closed 7 December-21 February – **M** 9.00/15.90 t. 🍷 7.50 – **93 rm** ⊆ 26.00/49.90 t.

🏛 **Casey's Cedars,** Strand Rd., ℰ 32124, Telex 80237, 🚗 – 📺 ⌁wc 🕾 & ℗. ⚗. 🔃 AE ⦿
VISA.
closed January – **M** (booking essential in winter) 9.50/16.50 t. and a la carte 🍷 4.75 – **34 rm**
⊆ 9.00/52.00 t. – SB 64.00/81.00 t.

✗ **Le Gourmet,** Strand Rd, ℰ 32157, French rest.
Mid June-mid September – **M** a la carte 10.50/21.50 t. 🍷 5.00.

ROSSLARE HARBOUR Wexford **405** N 11 – pop. 777 – ✪ 053 Wexford.

⚓ Shipping connections with the Continent : to France (Cherbourg), (Le Havre) (Irish Continental
Line) – to Fishguard (Sealink) 1-2 daily (3 h 30 mn) – to Pembroke (B & I Line) 1-2 daily (4 h).
🛈 ℰ 33232.

♦Dublin 105 – ♦Waterford 51 – Wexford 13.

🏛 **Rosslare,** ℰ 33110, Telex 80772, ≼ – 📺 ⌁wc ☎ ℗. 🔃 AE VISA
closed Christmas Day – **M** 8.50/13.50 st. and a la carte 🍷 3.95 – ⊆ 4.50 – **25 rm** 13.50/38.00 st.
– SB (except Bank Holidays) 39.50/59.50 st.

🏛 **Tuskar House,** St. Martins Rd, ℰ 33363, ≼, 🚗 – ⌁wc 🕾 ℗. 🔃 AE ⦿ VISA. ⚗
M (bar lunch)/dinner a la carte 5.55/16.45 st. 🍷 3.95 – **15 rm** ⊆ 22.00/36.00 t.

ROSSNOWLAGH Donegal **405** H 4 – ✪ 072 Bundoran.

♦Dublin 157 – Donegal 9 – ♦Sligo 33.

🏛 **Sand House** ⟨S⟩, ℰ 51777, Telex 40460, ≼ bay, beach and mountains, ﬁ9, 🔃, ⚗ – ℗. 🔃
AE ⦿. ⚗
Easter-September – **M** 9.00/17.50 t. and a la carte 🍷 4.50 – **40 rm** ⊆ 25.00/60.00 t.

ST ERNAN'S ISLAND Donegal – see Donegal.

SALTHILL Galway **405** E 8 – see Galway.

SCHULL (SKULL) Cork **405** D 13 – pop. 502 – ✪ 028 Skibbereen.

Envir. : E : Roaringwater Bay★.

♦Dublin 226 – ♦Cork 65 – ♦Killarney 64.

✗ **Ard-na-Greine Inn** ⟨S⟩ with rm, SW : 1 ¾ m. by L 57 ℰ 28181, 🚗 – ⌁wc ℗. AE ⦿ VISA.
⚗
Mid April-September – **M** (booking essential) (bar lunch)/dinner 17.00 t. 🍷 4.50 – **7 rm**
⊆ 27.50/50.00 t.

✗ **Courtyard,** Main St., ℰ 28209 – 🔃 AE ⦿ VISA
closed Sunday, Monday to Thursday during October-May and February – **M** (booking essential)
(bar lunch)/dinner 16.00 t.

SHANAGARRY Cork **405** H 12 – ✉ ✪ 021 Cork.

♦Dublin 163 – ♦Cork 25 – ♦Waterford 64.

✗✗ **Ballymaloe House** ⟨S⟩ with rm, NW : 1 ¾ m. on L 35 ℰ 652531, Telex 75208, ≼, « Country
house atmosphere », ⌛ heated, 🚗, park, ⚗ – ⌁wc ⌁wc ☎ & ℗. 🔃 AE ⦿ VISA. ⚗
closed 24 to 26 December – **M** (buffet lunch)/dinner 19.50 t. 🍷 4.60 – ⊆ 4.50 – **30 rm**
24.50/54.00 s. – SB (weekends only) 73.20/110.00 st.

SHANNON AIRPORT Clare **405** F 9 – ✪ 061 Limerick.

ﬁ8 ℰ Shannon 61020.

✈ ℰ 61444, Telex 26222 – Terminal : Limerick Railway Station ℰ 42433.

🛈 ℰ 61664 and 61604.

♦Dublin 136 – Ennis 16 – ♦Limerick 15.

🏛 Shannon International, ℰ 61122, Telex 24018 – 📺 ☎ ℗ – **117 rm**.

SKIBBEREEN Cork **405** E 13 – pop. 2,130 – ✪ 028.

🛈 ℰ 21766.

♦Dublin 205 – ♦Cork 51 – ♦Killarney 68.

✗✗ **Mill House,** Rineen, E : 5 m. by L 60 on Union Hall rd ℰ 36299, 🚗 – ℗. 🔃 AE ⦿ VISA
closed Monday, 4 weeks January-February, November and 24 to 26 December – **M** (dinner
only)(booking essential) 15.00 t. 🍷 4.00.

SKULL = Schull.

SLANE Meath 405 M 6 – pop. 690 – ✪ 041 Drogheda.

See : Hill of Slane (site★, ⩽★).

◆Dublin 42 – Drogheda 8 – ◆Dundalk 26.

XX **Slane Castle,** W : 1 m. on N 51 ℘ 24207 – **P.** ☒ AE ⊙ VISA
closed Sunday dinner, Monday and Tuesday – **M** (dinner only and Sunday lunch) 12.50 **t.** and
a la carte ⌀ 3.25.

SLIEVERUE Waterford – see Waterford.

SLIGO Sligo 405 G 5 – pop. 17 ,232 – ✪ 071.

See : Sligo Abbey★ (13C ruins) – Court House★.

Envir. : E : Lough Gill★★★ (Innisfree★) Park's Castle (site★★), Lough Colgagh★★, Drumcliff (High
Cross) ⩽★ on Benbulbin Moutains N : 4 m. – Glencar Lough★ NE : 6 m. – Carrowmore (Megalithic
cemetery★) SW : 2 m.

🛅 Strandhill ℘ 78188, W : 8 m.

🛈 Aras Reddan, Temple St. ℘ 61201.

◆Dublin 133 – ◆Belfast 126 – ◆Dundalk 106 – ◆Londonderry 86.

🏛 **Sligo Park,** Pearse Rd, S : 1 m. on N 4 ℘ 60291, 🛋 – ☒ & **P.** 🏛 ☒ AE ⊙ VISA
M 8.00/12.00 **st.** and a la carte ⌀ 3.75 – ⫯ 5.00 – **60 rm** 30.00/42.00 **st.**

🏚 **Ballincar House** ⟳, Rosses Point Rd, NW : 2 ½ m. on L 16 ℘ 5362, ⩽, 🛋, %%, squash –
⌂wc �︙wc ⌾ **P.** ☒ AE VISA. %
closed 23 December-23 January – **M** 7.25/14.50 **t.** and a la carte ⌀ 4.00 – **20 rm** ⫯ 24.00/48.50 **t.**

at Strandhill W : 7 m. on L 132 – ✉ ✪ 071 Sligo :

XX **Knockmuldowney,** ℘ 68122, 🛋 – **P.** ☒ AE ⊙ VISA
Mid March-October – **M** (bar lunch residents only)(booking essential)/dinner
12.00 **t.** and a la carte ⌀ 3.40.

at Rosses Point NW : 5 m. on L 16 – ✉ ✪ 071 Sligo :

X **Moorings,** ℘ 77112, Seafood – **P.** ☒ AE ⊙ VISA
closed Saturday lunch, Sunday, 2 weeks October and last 2 weeks December – **M** (bar
lunch)/dinner a la carte 14.00/25.50 **t.** ⌀ 3.75.

AUSTIN-ROVER Bridge St. ℘ 2091
FIAT, LANCIA Ballinode ℘ 2188

FORD Bundoran Rd ℘ 2610
VW Ballisodare ℘ 67291

SPIDDLE Galway 405 E 8 – ✪ 091 Galway.

◆Dublin 143 – ◆Galway 11.

🏚 Bridge House, Main St., ℘ 83118, 🛋 – ⌂wc �︙wc **P.** %
14 rm.

🏚 **Park Lodge,** E : 1 ¾ m. on L 100 ℘ 83159 – ⌂wc �︙wc ☞ **P.** ☒ AE VISA. %
Easter and May-October – **M** 8.00/11.00 **st.** and a la carte ⌀ 4.25 – **25 rm** ⫯ 16.00/30.00 **t.**

STRANDHILL Sligo 405 G 5 – see Sligo.

TEMPLEGLENTAN Limerick 405 E 10 – ✪ 069 Newcastle West.

◆Dublin 154 – ◆Killarney 36 – ◆Limerick 33.

🏚 **Devon Inn,** on N 21 ℘ 62811, 🛋 – ☒ ⌂wc ☞ **P.** ☒ AE ⊙ VISA. %
M 10.00/11.50 **st.** and a la carte ⌀ 3.50 – **18 rm** ⫯ 17.00/30.00 **t.**

THURLES Tipperary 405 I 9 – pop. 7 ,352 – ✪ 0504.

See : Catholic Cathedral (interior)★.

🛅 Turtula ℘ 21983.

◆Dublin 93 – Kilkenny 29 – ◆Limerick 39.

🏚 **Hayes,** Liberty Sq., ℘ 22122 – ⌂wc **P.** 🏛 ☒ VISA
M 8.50/11.50 **st.** and a la carte ⌀ 3.50 – **38 rm** ⫯ 20.00/38.00 **st.**

TIPPERARY Tipperary 405 H 10 – pop. 4 ,984 – ECD : Wednesday – ✪ 062.

Envir. : S : Glen of Aherlow★ (statue of Christ the King ⩽★★).

🛅 Rathanny ℘ 51119, S : 1 m.

◆Dublin 113 – ◆Cork 57 – ◆Limerick 24 – ◆Waterford 53.

🏠 **Ach-na-Sheen House,** Waterford Rd, ℘ 51298 – ⌂wc **P.** VISA
closed mid December-January – **13 rm** ⫯ 10.00/24.00 **st.**

Une voiture bien équipée, possède à son bord
des **cartes Michelin** à jour.

TRALEE Kerry **405** C 11 – pop. 16,495 – ECD : Wednesday – ✆ 066.

🏌 Mount Hawke ✆ 51150.

🏛 32 The Mall ✆ 21288.

◆Dublin 185 – ◆Killarney 20 – ◆Limerick 64.

  🏨 Ballygarry House, SE : 1 ½ m. on N 21 ✆ 21233, 🐎 – 📺 ⛲wc ⫝̸wc ☎ 🅿
    16 rm.

  🏨 **Mount Brandon,** Princes St., ✆ 21311, Telex 28130 – 🛗 📺 ⛲wc ☎ 🅿. ⚖. 🔼 🅰🅴 ⓞ 𝚅𝙸𝚂𝙰.
    ✀
    closed 1 week at Christmas – **M** 7.95/12.50 **st.** and a la carte ⎱ 3.95 – ☲ 5.00 – **162 rm**
    25.50/40.85 **st.**

FIAT Ashe St. ✆ 21124
FORD Edward St. ✆ 21555

TOYOTA Denny St. ✆ 21688
VW The Market and Rock St. ✆ 21193

TRIM Meath **405** L 7 – pop. 2,144 – ECD : Thursday – ✆ 046.

🏌 ✆ 31463, SW : 2 ½ m.

◆Dublin 28 – Drogheda 25 – ◆Dundalk 43.

  🏛 Wellington Court, Summerhill Rd, ✆ 31516 – 📺 ⛲wc ☎ 🅿. ✀ – **18 rm**.

VIRGINIA Cavan **405** K 6 – pop. 657 – ✆ 049 Cavan.

Envir. : Kells : St. Columba's House★ 9C – St. Columba's Church : old tower★ 1783 – Churchyard
(high crosses★) SE : 11 m.

🏌 ✆ 35.

◆Dublin 52 – ◆Dundalk 39 – Roscommon 56 – ◆Tullamore 59.

  🏛 Park 🏌, ✆ 47235, ≼, 🏌, 🐎, 🐎, park, ✗ – ⛲wc ⫝̸wc ☎ 🅿
    27 rm.

WATERFORD Waterford **405** K 11 – pop. 38,473 – ✆ 051.

See : Franciscan ruins of the French Church★ 13C-16C (Grey Friars Street).

🏌 Newrath ✆ 74182.

🏛 41 The Quay ✆ 75788.

◆Dublin 96 – ◆Cork 73 – ◆Limerick 77.

  🏩 **Granville,** Meagher Quay, ✆ 55111, Telex 80188 – 🛗 📺 ☎. ⚖. 🔼 🅰🅴 ⓞ 𝚅𝙸𝚂𝙰. ✀
    closed 25 and 26 December – **M** 7.65/10.30 **st.** and a la carte ⎱ 4.85 – **60 rm** ☲ 26.00/56.00 **st.**
    – SB (weekends only) 62.50/65.00 **st.**

  🏛 Tower, The Mall, ✆ 75801, Telex 80699 – 🛗 📺 ⛲wc ☎. ⚖. ✀ – **82 rm**.

    at Slieverue N : 2 m. on N 25 – ✉ ✆ 051 Waterford :

  🏠 **Diamond Hill,** SW : ½ m. on N 25 ✆ 32855, 🐎 – ⫝̸wc 🅿. 𝚅𝙸𝚂𝙰. ✀
    closed 24 December-1 January – **10 rm** ☲ 15.00/28.00 **st.**

NISSAN, RENAULT 3 Michael St. ✆ 76181
OPEL Catherine St. ✆ 74988

TOYOTA William St. ✆ 74037

WATERVILLE Kerry **405** B 12 – pop. 478 – ✆ 0667.

Envir. : Sheehan's Point ≼★★★ S : 6 m. – Remains of Carhan House (birthplace of Daniel O'Connell)
N : 11 m. – Ballinskelligs (Augustinian Monastery ≼★) W : 9 m.

◆Dublin 238 – ◆Killarney 48.

  🏩 **Waterville Lake** 🏌, ✆ 4133, Telex 28246, ≼ Lough Currane, Atlantic and Countryside, 🔼,
    🏌, 🐎, 🐎, ✗ – 🛗 🅿. ⚖. 🔼 🅰🅴 ⓞ 𝚅𝙸𝚂𝙰. ✀
    May-September – **M** 10.00/20.00 **t.** and a la carte ⎱ 5.00 – ☲ 6.50 – **50 rm** 60.00/80.50 **t.**,
    8 suites 120.00 **t.**

  🏛 **Butler Arms,** ✆ 4144, Telex 26826, 🐎, 🐎, ✗ – ⛲wc ⫝̸wc 🅿. 🔼 🅰🅴 ⓞ 𝚅𝙸𝚂𝙰
    May-mid October – **M** (bar lunch)/dinner 17.00 **st.** ⎱ 5.00 – **34 rm** ☲ 15.00/42.00 **st.** – SB
    65.00/75.00 **st.**

  ✗ **Huntsman,** ✆ 4124, ≼, Seafood – 🔼 🅰🅴 ⓞ 𝚅𝙸𝚂𝙰
    Mid March-October – **M** 11.00/15.00 **t.** and a la carte ⎱ 4.00.

WESTPORT Mayo **405** D 6 – pop. 3,378 – ECD : Wednesday.

See : Westport House★ AC.

Envir. : Croagh Patrick Mountain★ (statue of St. Patrick ≼★, pilgrimage) SW : 6 m. – Roonah Quay
≼★ on Clare Island W : 15 m.

🏌 Carrowholly ✆ 547.

🏛 The Mall ✆ 098 (Newport) 25711.

◆Dublin 163 – ◆Galway 50 – ◆Sligo 65.

  ✗✗ **Ardmore,** The Quay, W : ½ m. on T 39 ✆ 25994, ≼ – 🅿. 🔼 🅰🅴 ⓞ 𝚅𝙸𝚂𝙰
    closed Sunday, 28 March, 1 week February, 2 weeks November and 24 to 26 December – **M**
    (dinner only and bar lunch April-October) a la carte 12.50/16.25 **t.** ⎱ 4.00.

WEXFORD Wexford 405 M 10 – pop. 11 ,417 – ECD : Thursday – ☺ 053.

Envir. : Johnstown Castle (the park-arboretum★) SW : 4 m.

🏌 Mulgannon ℘ 22238, SE : 1 m.

🛈 Crescent Quay ℘ 23111.

♦Dublin 88 – Kilkenny 49 – ♦Waterford 38.

🏛 **Talbot,** Trinity St., ℘ 22566, Telex 80658, 🔲, squash – 🛗 📺 🚻wc ☎ 🅿. 🏄. 🔲 🖭 ⓞ 𝘝𝘐𝘚𝘈. 🎿
  M 12.50/17.00 **t.** and a la carte 🍴 4.10 – 🖙 6.00 – **105 rm** 25.00/47.50 **t.**

🏛 **Ferrycarrig** 🐚, Ferrycarrig Bridge, NW : 2 ¾ m. on N 11 ℘ 22999, ≼, 🌺, 🍴 – 🛗 🚻wc 📶 🅿. 🔲 🖭 𝘝𝘐𝘚𝘈
  Easter-October – **M** (bar lunch Monday to Saturday)/dinner 12.00 **t.** and a la carte – 🖙 4.70 – **40 rm** 19.35/36.85 **t.**

🏛 **New Whites** (Best Western), George's St., ℘ 22311, Telex 80630 – 🛗 📺 🚻wc ☎ 🅿. 🔲 🖭 ⓞ 𝘝𝘐𝘚𝘈. 🎿
  closed Christmas Day – **M** (bar lunch)/dinner 12.50 **st.** and a la carte 🍴 5.50 – **64 rm** 🖙 30.25/44.00 **st.** – SB (weekends only)(October-May) 69.00 **st.**

⌂ **Whitford House,** New Line Rd, SW : 2 m. on L 159 ℘ 24244, 🔲, 🌺 – 🛗wc 🅿. 🖭 𝘝𝘐𝘚𝘈. 🎿
  closed 19 December-2 January – **20 rm** 🖙 15.00/33.00 **st.**

BEDFORD, OPEL Ferrybank ℘ 22107
FORD Ferrybank ℘ 23329
MITSUBISHI, VOLVO, SUZUKI ℘ 22998

RENAULT, SUBARU Redmond Rd ℘ 23133
TOYOTA Carriglawn, Newtown Rd ℘ 23788
VW, AUDI, MAZDA Drinagh ℘ 22377

WICKLOW Wicklow 405 N 9 – pop. 5 ,178 – ECD : Thursday – ☺ 0404.

Envir. : Ashford (Mount Usher or Walpole's Gardens★) *AC*, NW : 4 m.

🏌 Blainroe ℘ 2675, S : 3½ m.

🛈 ℘ 2904.

♦Dublin 33 – ♦Waterford 84 – Wexford 67.

🍴🍴 **Old Rectory** with rm, ℘ 2048, 🌺 – 🛗wc 📶 🅿. 🎿
  Easter-October – **M** (booking essential)(dinner only) 18.50 **st.** and a la carte 🍴 4.50 – **5 rm** 🖙 25.50/51.00 **st.** – SB (weekdays only) 75.00 **st.**

FIAT Bollarney ℘ 2212
FORD Whitegates ℘ 2331

VW, AUDI-NSU The Glebe ℘ 2126

YOUGHAL Cork 405 I 12 – pop. 5 ,870 – ECD : Wednesday – ☺ 024.

See : St. Mary's Collegiate Church★ 13C.

Envir. : Ardmore (site★, round tower★ 10C, cathedral ruins★ 12C, ≼★) E : 5 ½ m.

🏌 Knockaverry ℘ 2787.

🛈 ℘ 2390 (July-August).

♦Dublin 146 – ♦Cork 30 – ♦Waterford 47.

🍴 **Aherne's Seafood Bar,** 163 North Main St., ℘ 92424 – 🅿. 🔲 🖭 ⓞ 𝘝𝘐𝘚𝘈
  closed Sunday lunch, Monday except dinner July and August and 4 days at Christmas – **M** 8.00/16.00 **t.** and a la carte 🍴 4.25.

RENAULT North Abbey ℘ 2019

MAJOR
HOTEL GROUPS

**Abbreviations used in the Guide
and central reservation telephone
numbers**

PRINCIPALES
CHAINES HOTELIÈRES

**Abréviations utilisées dans nos
textes et centraux téléphoniques
de réservation**

PRINCIPALI
CATENE ALBERGHIERE

**Abbreviazioni utilizzate nei nostri testi
e centrali telefoniche di
prenotazione**

DIE WICHTIGSTEN
HOTELKETTEN

**Im Führer benutzte Abkürzungen der Hotel-
ketten und ihre Zentralen für telefonische
Reservierung**

ANCHOR HOTELS LTD	ANCHOR	0252 (Farnborough) 517517
BEST WESTERN HOTELS	BEST WESTERN	01 (London) 940 9766 041 (Glasgow) 204 1794
CREST HOTELS LTD	CREST	01 (London) 236 3242
DE VERE HOTELS PLC	DE VERE	0925 (Warrington) 35471
EMBASSY HOTELS	EMBASSY	01 (London) 581 3466
FORUM HOTELS	FORUM	01 (London) 491 7181
GOLDEN OAK INNS LTD	GOLDEN OAK	021 (Birmingham) 356 9177
GREENALL WHITLEY HOTELS	GREENALL WHITLEY	0925 (Warrington) 35471
INTER-CONTINENTAL HOTELS LTD	INTER-CON	01 (London) 491 7181
LADBROKE HOTELS	LADBROKE	01 (London) 734 6000
MOUNT CHARLOTTE HOTELS LTD	MT. CHARLOTTE	0532 (Leeds) 444866
NORFOLK CAPITAL HOTELS LTD	NORFOLK CAP.	01 (London) 589 7000
OSPREY HOTELS	OSPREY	041 (Glasgow) 552 7788
QUEENS MOAT HOUSES PLC	Q.M.H.	0904 (York) 256 74/5 0789 (Stratford upon Avon) 298677 0932 (Walton upon Thames) 231010
RANK HOTELS LTD	RANK	01 (London) 262 2893
STAKIS HOTELS	STAKIS	041 (Glasgow) 332 4343 and 01 (London) 222 4081
SWALLOW HOTELS PLC	SWALLOW	0783 (Sunderland) 294666
THISTLE HOTELS LTD	THISTLE	01 (London) 937 8033
TRUSTHOUSE FORTE (U.K.) LTD	T.H.F.	01 (London)567 3444

TRAFFIC SIGNS
A few important signs

SIGNALISATION ROUTIÈRE
Quelques signaux routiers importants

SEGNALETICA STRADALE
Alcuni segnali importanti

VERKEHRSZEICHEN
Die wichtigsten Straßenverkehrszeichen

Please note: The maximum speed limits in Great Britain are 70 mph (112 km/h) on motorways and dual carriageways and 60 mph (96 km/h) on all other roads, except where a lower speed limit is indicated.

N.B. N'oubliez pas qu'il existe des limitations de vitesse en Grande-Bretagne: 70 mph (112 km/h) sur routes à chaussée séparée et autoroutes, 60 mph (96 km/h) sur autres routes, sauf indication d'une vitesse inférieure.

N.B. In Gran Bretagna esistono dei limiti di velocità: 70 mph (112 km/h) sulle strade a doppia carreggiata e autostrade, 60 mph (96 km/h) sulle altre strade, salvo che sia indicata una velocità inferiore.

Zur Beachtung: In Großbritannien gelten folgende Geschwindigkeitsbegrenzungen: 70 mph (112 km/h) auf Autobahnen und Straßen mit getrennten Fahrbahnen, 60 mph (96 km/h) auf allen anderen Straßen, wenn keine niedrigere Geschwindigkeit angezeigt ist.

Warning signs — *Signaux d'avertissement*
Segnali di avvertimento — *Warnzeichen*

T junction
Jonction avec autre route
Confluenza con altra strada
Straßeneinmündung

Roundabout
Sens giratoire
Senso rotatorio
Kreisverkehr

Dual carriageway ends
Fin de chaussée à deux voies
Fine di doppia carreggiata
Ende der zweispurigen Fahrbahn

Change to opposite carriageway
Déviation sur chaussée opposée
Deviazione sulla carreggiata opposta
Überleitung auf Gegenfahrbahn

Distance to give way sign ahead
Cédez le passage à 50 yards
Dare la precedenza a 50 iarde
Vorfahrt gewähren in 50 yards Entfernung

REDUCE SPEED NOW
Ralentir maintenant
Rallentare subito
Geschwindigkeit verringern

Right-hand lane closed
Voie de droite barrée
Corsia di destra sbarrata
Rechte Fahrbahn gesperrt

Quayside or river bank
Débouché sur un quai ou une berge
Banchina o argine senza sponda
Ufer

Two-way traffic crosses one-way road
Voie à deux sens croisant voie à sens unique
Strada a due sensi che incrocia una strada a senso unico
Straße mit Gegenverkehr kreuzt Einbahnstraße

Level crossing with automatic half barriers ahead
Passage à niveau automatique
Passaggio a livello automatico con semi-barriere
Bahnübergang mit automatischen Halbschranken

Height limit
Hauteur limitée (en pieds et pouces)
Altezza limitata (piedi e pollici)
Maximale Höhe (in Fuß und Zoll)

Opening or swing bridge
Pont mobile
Ponte mobile
Bewegliche Brücke

607

Signs giving orders
Signaux de prescriptions absolues
Segnali di prescrizione (di divieto o d'obbligo)
Gebots- und Verbotszeichen

National speed limit applies
Fin de limitation de vitesse
Fine di limitazione di velocità
Ende der Geschwindigkeitsbeschränkung

School crossing patrol
Sortie d'école
Uscita di scolari
Achtung Schule

No stopping (« clearway »)

Arrêt interdit

Fermata vietata

Halteverbot

All vehicles prohibited
(plate gives details)
Circulation interdite à tous véhicules
(plaque donnant détails)
Divieto di transito a tutti i veicoli (la
placca sottostante fornisce dei dettagli)
Verkehrsverbot für Fahrzeuge aller Art
(näherer Hinweis auf Zusatzschild)

Give priority to vehicles from opposite
direction
Priorité aux véhicules venant de face
Dare la precedenza ai veicoli che proven-
gono dal senso opposto
Dem Gegenverkehr Vorrang gewähren

Voie à stationnement réglementé

Sosta regolamentata

Fahrbahn mit zeitlich begrenzter
Parkerlaubnis

Width limit
Largeur limitée (en pieds et pouces)
Larghezza limitata (piedi e pollici)
Breite begrenzt (in Fuß und Zoll)

End

Plate below sign at end of restriction
Fin d'interdiction
Fine del divieto posta sotto il segnale
Ende einer Beschränkung

Information signs
Signaux de simple indication
Segnali di indicazione
Hinweiszeichen

One-way street
Rue à sens unique
Via a senso unico
Einbahnstraße

No through road
Voie sans issue
Strada senza uscita
Sackgasse

Dual carriageway ahead

Accès à une chaussée à deux voies
Accesso ad una carreggiata a due corsie
Zufahrt zu einer zweispurigen Fahrbahn

Ring road
Voie de contournement
Strada di circonvallazione
Ringstraße

Warning signs on rural motorways
Signaux d'avertissement sur autoroutes
Segnali di avvertimento su autostrade
Warnzeichen auf Autobahnen

Maximum advised speed
Vitesse maximum conseillée
Velocità massima consigliata
Empfohlene Höchstgeschwindigkeit

1 Lane closed
1 voie barrée
1 Corsia sbarrata
1 Fahrstreifen gesperrt

Count-down markers at exit from motorway (or primary route if green-backed)
Balises situées sur autoroute ou route principale (fond vert) et annonçant une sortie
Segnali su autostrada o strade principali (fondo verde) annuncianti un'uscita
Hinweise auf Abfahrten an Autobahnen und Hauptverkehrsstraßen (grüner Grund)

End of restriction

Route libre

Strada libera

Straße frei

Direction to service area, with fuel, parking, cafeteria and restaurant facilities.

Indication d'aire de service avec carburant, parc à voitures, cafeteria et restaurant.

Indicazione di area di servizio con carburante, parcheggio, bar e ristorante

Hinweis auf Tankstelle, Parkplatz, Cafeteria und Restaurant

Warning signs on urban motorways
Signaux d'avertissement sur autoroutes urbaines
Segnali di avvertimento su autostrade urbane
Warnzeichen auf Stadtautobahnen

_1_   _2_   _3_

The insets show (flashing amber lights) (1) advised maximum speed, (2) lane to be used; (3) (flashing red lights), you must stop.

L'ensemble de ces panneaux indique : (1) la vitesse maximale conseillée, (2) la voie à utiliser (signaux lumineux jaunes) ; (3) l'arrêt obligatoire (signaux lumineux rouges).

L'insieme di questi segnali indica : (1) la velocità massima consigliata, (2) la corsia da imboccare (segnali luminosi gialli) ; (3) la fermata obbligatoria (segnali luminosi rossi).

Diese Schilder (mit blinkenden Ampeln) weisen hin auf : 1. die empfohlene Höchstgeschwindigkeit, 2. die zu befahrende Fahrbahn (gelbes Licht) und 3. Halt (rotes Licht).

In town — En ville
In città — in der Stadt

SIGNALISATION SHOWN ON OR ALONG KERBS	OTHER ROAD SIGNS
SIGNALISATION MATÉRIALISÉE SUR OU AU LONG DES TROTTOIRS	AUTRES PANNEAUX
SEGNALI TRACCIATI SOPRA O LUNGO I MARCIAPIEDI	ALTRI CARTELLI INDICATORI
ZEICHEN AUF ODER AN GEHWEGEN	ZUSÄTZLICHE VERKEHRSZEICHEN

No waiting during every working day
Stationnement interdit tous les jours ouvrables
Sosta vietata nei giorni feriali con indicazioni complementari
Parkverbot an Werktagen

Stationnement interdit de 8 h 30 à 18 h 30 du lundi au samedi
Sosta vietata da lunedì a sabato dalle 8,30 alle 18,30
Parkverbot Montag bis Samstag von 8.30 bis 18.30 Uhr

No loading or unloading during every working day

Livraisons interdites tous les jours ouvrables

Carico e scarico vietato nei giorni feriali con indicazioni complementari

Be- und Entladen verboten an allen Werktagen

No loading
Mon-Sat
8.30 am-6.30 pm

Livraisons interdites de 8 h 30 à 18 h 30 du lundi au samedi

Carico e scarico vietato da lunedi a sabato dalle 8,30 alle 18,30

Be- und Entladen verboten von Montag bis Samstag von 8.30 bis 18.30 Uhr

---

No waiting during every working day and additional times as indicated

Stationnement interdit tous les jours ouvrables plus autres périodes indiquées sur panneaux

Divieto di sosta tutti i giorni feriali e negli altri periodi indicati sul cartello

Parkverbot an Werktagen und den auf Zusatzschildern angegebenen Zeiten

At any time

Stationnement interdit en permanence

Divieto permanente di sosta

Parkverbot zu jeder Zeit

No loading or unloading during every working day and additional times as indicated

Livraisons interdites tous les jours ouvrables plus autres périodes indiquées sur panneaux

Divieto di carico e scarico tutti i giorni feriali e negli altri periodi indicati sul cartello

Be- und Entladen verboten an Werktagen und den auf Zusatzschildern angegebenen Zeiten

No loading
at any time

Livraisons interdites en permanence

Divieto permanente di carico e scarico

Be- und Entladeverbot zu jeder Zeit

No waiting during any other periods

Stationnement interdit à toute autre période

Sosta vietata in determinate ore

Parkverbot zu bestimmten Zeiten

Waiting
Limited
8 am-6 pm
20 minutes
in any hour

Stationnement limité à 20 mn de 8 h à 18 h

Sosta limitata a 20 mn dalle 8 alle 18

Höchstparkdauer 20 Min. in der Zeit von 8.00 bis 18.00 Uhr

No loading or unloading during any other periods

Livraisons interdites à toute autre période

Divieto di carico e scarico in determinate ore

Be- und Entladeverbot zu bestimmten Zeiten

No loading
Mon-Fri
8.00-9.30 am
4.30-6.30 pm

Livraisons interdites du lundi au vendredi de 8 h à 9 h 30 et de 16 h 30 à 18 h 30

Carico e scarico vietato da lunedi a venerdi dalle 8 alle 9,30 e dalle 16,30 alle 18,30

Be- und Entladeverbot Montag bis Freitag von 8.00 bis 9.30 und von 16.30 bis 18.30 Uhr

---

Remember : speed limit in Great Britain 70 mph and in Eire 60 mph.

Direction signs on the road network
Panneaux de direction sur le réseau routier
Cartelli direzionali sulla rete stradale
Richtungsschilder auf den Straßen

401 Michelin maps
402 Cartes Michelin
403 Carte Michelin
404 Michelin-Karten

Motorways and A (M) class roads
Sur autoroutes et routes classées A (M)
Sulle autostrade e strade classificate A (M)
Autobahn M und Schnellstraße A (M)

Primary routes

Apart from motorways, « Primary routes » provide the major road network linking towns of local and national traffic importance

Sur grands itinéraires routiers « Primary routes »

En complément du système autoroutier, les grands itinéraires constituent un réseau de routes recommandées reliant les villes selon leur importance dans le trafic national

Sui principali itinerari stradali (Primary routes)

I principali itinerari, unitamente alle autostrade, costituiscono una rete di strade consigliate che collegano le città secondo la loro importanza nel traffico nazionale

Empfohlene Fernverkehrsstraßen (Primary routes)

Sie bilden ein überregionales Straßennetz, das verkehrswichtige Orte verbindet ; sie ergänzen das Autobahnnetz

Other A class roads
Sur autres routes classées A
Sulle altre strade classificate A
Andere Straße der Kategorie A

B class roads
Sur routes classées B
Sulle strade classificate B
Straße der Kategorie B

Unclassified roads — Local direction sign
Sur routes non classées — Signalisation locale
Sulle strade non classificate — Segnaletica locale
Nicht klassifizierte Straßen — Örtliche Richtungsschilder

611

ADDRESSES OF SHIPPING COMPANIES AND THEIR PRINCIPAL AGENTS

ADRESSES DES COMPAGNIES DE NAVIGATION ET DE LEURS PRINCIPALES AGENCES

INDIRIZZI DELLE COMPAGNIE DI NAVIGAZIONE E DELLE LORO PRINCIPALI AGENZIE

ADRESSEN DER SCHIFFAHRTSGESELLSCHAFTEN UND IHRER WICHTIGSTEN AGENTUREN

BALTIC SHIPPING CO.

5 Mezhevoi Canal, Leningrad L35, USSR.

Agents : C.T.C. Lines (UK), 1-3 Lower Regent St., London, SW1Y 4NN, ✆ (01) 930 5833, Telex 917193.

Seannautic A/C, C.G. Hambrose Pl. 5, Oslo 1, ✆ 421051, Telex 76146.

Baltic Shipping Co, 35 Hertzen St., Leningrad 190000, U.S.S.R. ✆ 315.89.86, Telex 551.

Transtours, 49 Avenue de l'Opéra, 75067 Paris, France, ✆ (1) 42 61 58 28, Telex 230732

B & I LINE

16 Westmoreland St., Dublin 2, Eire, ✆ 724711, Telex 25651.

Agents : 155 Regent St., London, W1R 7FD, ✆ (01) 734 4681, Telex 23523.

42 Grand Par., Cork, Eire, ✆ (021) 273024, Telex 26137.

Reliance House, Water St., Liverpool, L2 8TP, ✆ (051) 227 3131, Telex 627839.

BRITISH RAIL see SEALINK and HOVERSPEED

BRITTANY FERRIES

BAI Brittany Ferries, Gare Maritime Roscoff, Port du Bloscon 29211, France, ✆ 98 61 22 11, Telex 940360.

Agents : Millbay Docks, Plymouth, PL1 3EW, Devon, ✆ (0752) 21321, Telex 45380.

The Brittany Centre, Wharf Rd, Portsmouth, PO2 8RU, Hampshire. ✆ (0705) 827701, Telex 86878.

Gare Maritime, 35400 St-Malo, France, ✆ 99 56 68 40, Telex 950487.

Tourist House, 42 Grand Parade, Cork, Eire, ✆ (021) 507666, Telex 75088.

Modesto Pineiro & Co., 27 Paseo de Pereda, Santander, Spain, ✆ (042) 214500, Telex 35913.

CALEDONIAN MACBRAYNE LTD.

Ferry Terminal, Gourock, PA19 1QP, Renfrewshire, Scotland, ✆ (0475) 34531, Telex 779318.

CHANNEL ISLAND FERRIES

Norman House, Albert Johnson Quay, Portsmouth, PO2 7AE, ✆ (0705) 864431.

Agents : Wharf Rd, Portsmouth, PO2 8RU, ✆ (0705) 819416.

New North Quay, St. Helier, Jersey, Channel Islands, ✆ (0543) 38300.

Piquet House, St. Peter Port, Guernsey, Channel Islands, ✆ (0481) 711111.

COMMODORE SHIPPING SERVICES AND CONDOR LTD.

Commodore House, Bulwer Av., St. Sampsons, Guernsey, Channel Islands, ✆ (0481) 46841, Telex 4191289.

Agents : Commodore Travel Ltd., 28 Conway St., St. Helier, Jersey, Channel Islands, ✆ (0534) 71263, Telex 419 2079.

Condor Ltd., Morvan Fils, 2 Place du Poids du Roi, 35402 St. Malo, France, ✆ 99 56 42 29, Telex 950486.

CORAS IOMPAIR EIREANN (CIE).

Ceannt Station, Galway, Eire, ✆ (091) 62141.

CUNARD LINE LTD.

South Western House, Canute Rd, Southampton, Hampshire, SO9 1ZA, ℰ (0703) 29933, Telex 477577.

Agents : 8 Berkeley St., London W1X 6NR, ℰ (01) 491 3930, Telex 295483.
555 Fifth Av., New York, NY 10017, USA, ℰ (212) 880 7500, Telex 220436.
American Express Co. Inc., 11 rue Scribe, Paris 75009, France, ℰ (1) 42 66 09 99, Telex 210718.

DFDS SEAWAYS

Sankt Annae Plads 30, DK-1295 Copenhagen K, Denmark, ℰ (01) 11 22 55, Telex 19416.
DFDS Seaways, Scandinavia House, Parkeston Quay, Harwich, CO12 4QG, ℰ (0255) 554681, Telex 987542.

Agents : DFDS Seaways Tyne Commission Quay, North Shields, NE29 6EE, Tyne and Wear, ℰ (0632) 575655, Telex 537285.
DFDS Seaways, Bruksgaten 1, S-21122 Malmo, Sweden, ℰ (040) 10 30 10, Telex 32888.
A/S Danske-Batene, Karl Johansgate 1, Oslo 1, Norway, ℰ 330700, Telex 18129.
Skandiahamnen, P.O. Box 8895, S-40272 Gothenburg 8, Sweden, ℰ (031) 54 03 00, Telex 20688.
D. Burger & Zoon B.V., PO Box 149, 3000 AC Rotterdam, ℰ 010 145044, Telex 21031.
DFDS, Jessenstrasse 4, 2000 Hamburg 50, West Germany, ℰ (040) 389030, Telex 2161759.

EMERAUDE FERRIES

Agents : Marine Management Ltd., 17a York St., St. Helier, Jersey, Channel Islands, ℰ (0534) 74458 and 74467, Telex 419 2029 MARMAN.
Emeraude Ferries, Albert Quay, St. Helier, Jersey, Channel Islands, ℰ (0534) 74458, Telex 4192311 SEACAR.
Gare Maritime du Naye, 35400 St-Malo, France, ℰ 99 81 61 46, Telex 950271.

FRED, OLSEN LINES

11 Conduit St., London W1R 0LS, ℰ (01) 491 3760, Telex 263670.

Agents : Fred Olsen Travel, 13 McCombies Court, Aberdeen, AB1 1AW, ℰ (0224) 646327, Telex 739958.
Consignataria Fred Olsen S.A., c/o Maestro Valle 22, Ciudad Jardin, P.O. Box 252, Las Palmas, Canary Islands, ℰ 232166, Telex 95020 NAFOL.
Consignataria Fred Olsen S.A., Calle Dr. Zerolo 14, Santa Cruz de Tenerife, ℰ 287250, Telex 92590 CMHN.
Joao, de Freitas Martins Lda, Avenida do Mar 15/16, Funchal, Madeira, ℰ 21106/07, Telex 72173 JFMART.
VCK-Zeereisen, P.O. Box 1418, De Ruyterkade 139, 1000 BK Amsterdam, Netherlands, ℰ (20) 262216, Telex 14561.

FRED OLSEN LINES KDS

Fergeterminaten, P.O. Box 82, 4600 Kristiansand, Norway, ℰ (042) 26500, Telex 21969.

Agent : Fred Olsen Lines, 11 Conduit St., London W1R OLS, ℰ 491 3760, Telex 263670.

HERM SEAWAY

Guernseybus Ltd., Picquet House, St. Peter Port, Guernsey, Channel Islands, ℰ (0481) 24677.

HOVERSPEED

International Hoverport, Ramsgate, Kent, CT12 5HS, ℰ (0843) 594881, Telex 96323. Reservations : General (0843) 595555, London (01) 554 7061, Birmingham (021) 236 2190, Manchester (061) 228 1321.

Agents : International Hoverport, Boulogne, France, ℰ 21 30 27 26, Telex 110008.
International Hoverport, Calais, France, ℰ 21 96 65 70, Telex 810856.

HOVERTRAVEL LTD.

Quay Road, Ryde, Isle of Wight, P033 2HB.

Agent : Clarence Pier, Southsea, Portsmouth, PO5 3AD, Hampshire, ℰ (0705) 829988.

IRISH CONTINENTAL LINE LTD.

19/21 Aston Quay, Dublin 2, Eire, ℰ (01) 774331, Telex 30355.

Agent : Transport et Voyages, 2 Rue de la Paix, 75002 Paris, France, ℰ (1) 42 61 58 04, Telex 042-230970 TOUVOYA.

ISLE OF MAN STEAM PACKET CO. LTD.

P.O. Box 5, Imperial Buildings, Douglas, Isle of Man, ℰ (0624) 23344, Telex 629414.

Agents : Caledonian MacBrayne Ltd., Buchanan Bus Station, Killermont St., Glasgow, Scotland, ℰ 041 (Glasgow) 332 4451, Telex 778177.
W.E. Williames & Co. Ltd., 35/39 Middlepath St., Belfast, Northern Ireland, ℰ (0232) 55411, Telex 747166.
B & I Line, 16 Westmoreland St., Dublin 2, Eire ℰ (01) 724711, Telex 002725651.
Queens Terr., Fleetwood, Lancashire, ℰ (039 17) 6263 (summer), ℰ 0624 (Douglas I.O.M.) 23344 (winter).
Sea Terminal, Heysham, Lancashire, LA3 2XF, ℰ (0524) 53802.

ISLE OF SARK SHIPPING CO. LTD.

White Rock, St. Peter Port, Guernsey, Channel Islands, ✆ (0481) 24059, Telex 419 1549.

ISLES OF SCILLY STEAMSHIP CO. LTD.

Hugh Town, St. Mary's, Isles of Scilly, TR21 OLJ, ✆ 0720 (Scillonia) 22357/8.

Agent : 16 Quay St., Penzance, TR18 4BD, Cornwall, ✆ (0736) 2009/4013.

LUNDY CO.

Lundy, Bristol Channel, via Bideford, Devon, EX29 2LY, ✆ 0271 (Woolacombe) 870870.

MERSEYSIDE PASSENGER TRANSPORT EXECUTIVE

24, Hatton Garden, Liverpool L3 2AN, Merseyside, ✆ (051) 227 5181.

NORFOLK LINE BV

Kranenburgweg 211, 2583 ER Scheveningen, Netherlands, ✆ (070) 514601, Telex 31515.

Agent : Atlas House, Southgates Rd, Great Yarmouth, Norfolk, ✆ (0493) 856133, Telex 97449.

NORTH SEA FERRIES LTD.

Noordzee Veerdiensten, Beneluxhaven, Europoort, P.O. Box 1123, 3180 AC Rozenburg Z.H., Netherlands, ✆ (01819) 62077, Telex 26571.

Agents : King George Dock, Hedon Rd, Hull, HU9 5QA, Humberside, ✆ (0482) 795141, Telex 52349.

Leopold II Dam (Havendam) B8380, Zeebrugge, Belgium, ✆ (050) 543430, Telex 81469.

NORWAY LINE

Postboks 4004, N5015 Bergen-Dreggen, Norway, ✆ 05-325969, Telex 40425 NLINE.

Agent : Tyne Commission Quay, North Shields, NE29 6EA, ✆ (0632) 585555, Telex 537275.

OLAU-LINE LTD.

Sheerness, Kent, ME12 1SN, ✆ (0795) 666666 and 663355, Telex 965605.

Agents : Olau-Line Terminal, Buitenhaven, Postbus 231, Vlissingen, Netherlands, ✆ (01184) 65400, Telex 37817.

ORKNEY ISLANDS SHIPPING CO. LTD.

4 Ayre Road, Kirkwall, Orkney Islands, Scotland, ✆ (0856) 2044.

ORWELL & HARWICH NAVIGATION CO. LTD.

The Quay, Harwich, Essex, ✆ (0255) 502004.

P & O FERRIES : ORKNEY & SHETLAND SERVICES

P.O. Box 5, P & O Ferry Terminal, Jamieson's Quay, Aberdeen, AB9 8DL, Scotland, ✆ (0224) 572615, Telex 73344.

Agents : Terminal Building, Scrabster, Caithness, KW14 7UJ, Scotland, ✆ (0847) 62052.
Harbour Street, Kirkwall, Orkney Islands, KW15 1LE, Scotland, ✆ (0856) 3330, Telex 75296.
Holmsgarth Terminal, Lerwick, Shetland Islands, ZE1 0PW, Scotland, ✆ (0595) 5252, Telex 75294.
Terminal Bldg., Stromness, Orkney Islands, KW16 3AA, Scotland, ✆ (0856) 850 655, Telex 75221.

POLISH OCEAN LINES

P.O. Box 265, 10 Lutego 24, 81-364 Gdynia, Poland, ✆ 20-19-01, Telex 054-231.

Agents : Gdynia America Shipping Lines (London) Ltd, 238 City Rd, London, EC1V 2QL, ✆ 01-251 3389, Telex 884477.
Riodan's Travel, 111 Lower Baggot St., Dublin 2, Eire, ✆ 62434, Telex 5163.
Hamburg Süd Reiseagentur GmbH, 59 Ostwest Strasse, P.O. Box 1661, 2, Hamburg 11, West Germany, ✆ 37051, Telex 21321629.
McLean Kennedy Ltd., 410 St. Nicholas St., P.O. Box 1086, Montreal H2Y 2P5, Canada, ✆ (514) 849 6111, Telex 05-25197.
HAL Zeereizen B.V., Postbus 791, Wilhelminakade 86, Rotterdam 3020, Netherlands, ✆ (010) 392213, Telex 288-76.
Franck and Tobiesen, 10 Strandagervg, Copenhagen DK 2900 Hellerup, Denmark, ✆ 13-02-55, Telex 275-15.

RED FUNNEL SERVICES

12 Bugle St., Southampton, SO9 4LJ, Hampshire, ✆ (0703) 26211.

Agents : Fountain Pier, West Cowes, Isle of Wight, ✆ (098 382) 292101 and 292704.

THE SALLY LINE LTD

54 Harbour Parade, Ramsgate, Kent, CT11 8LN ℘ (0843) 595522, Telex 96389.

Agents : 81 Piccadilly, London W1, ℘ (01) 409 0536 and 858 1127, Telex 291860.

Sally Viking Line, Dunkerque Port-Ouest, 59279 Loon Plage, France, ℘ (28) 68.43.44, Telex 130078.

SEALINK U.K. LTD. (British Rail)

Sealink UK Ltd., 163/203 Eversholt St., London, NW1 1BG, ℘ (01) 387 1234, Telex 269295 BRSLIN G.

SNCF, 88 Rue Saint-Lazare, 75436 Paris Cedex 09, France.

RTM Belgian Maritime Transport Authority, 30 Rue Belliard, B.1040 Brussels, Belgium, ℘ 230 0180, Telex 23851.

Zeeland Steamship Co., Hook of Holland, Netherlands, ℘ 47 39 44, Telex 31272 ZLDHK NL.

Agents : Sealink UK Ltd., Southern House, Lord Warden Square, Dover, CT17 9DH, Kent, ℘ (0304) 203203 Ext. 3187, Telex 96139.

Sealink UK Ltd., Fishguard Harbour, Dyfed, Wales, SA64 0BX, ℘ (0348) 872881, Telex 48167.

Sealink UK Ltd., Car Ferry Terminal, Folkestone Harbour, Kent, CT20, 1QH, ℘ (0303) 53949, Telex 965136.

Sealink UK Ltd., Parkeston Quay, Harwich, Essex, CO12 4SR, ℘ (025 55) 7022, Telex 98235.

Sealink UK Ltd., Sea Terminal, Heysham, Lancashire, LA3 2XF, ℘ (0524) 53802, Telex 65260 MANXL G.

Sealink UK Ltd., Car Ferry Booking Office, Lymington Pier, Lymington, Hampshire, SO4 8ZE, ℘ (0590) 73301.

Sealink UK Ltd., Newhaven Harbour, East Sussex, BN9 0BG, ℘ (0273) 514131, Telex 87151.

Sealink UK Ltd., Channel Islands Services, Norman House, Continental Ferry Terminal, Portsmouth, Hampshire, PO2 7AE, ℘ (0705) 811315, Telex 86636.

Sealink UK Ltd., Isle of Wight Ferry Services, P.O. Box 59, Portsmouth, Hampshire, PO1 2XB, ℘ (0705) 827744, Telex 86440.

Sealink UK Ltd., Car Ferry Office, The Slipway, Fishbourne Lane, Cowes, Isle of Wight, PO33 4EU, ℘ (0983) 882432.

Sealink UK Ltd., Weymouth Quay, Weymouth, Dorset, DT4 8DY, ℘ (030 57) 86363, Telex 41245.

Sealink UK Ltd., Car Ferry Office, The Slipway Quay Street, Yarmouth, Isle of Wight, PO41 0PB, ℘ (0983) 760213.

Sealink Travel Centre, Victoria Station, London SW1, ℘ (01) 834 3838/8511, Telex 22708.

Sealink (Scotland) Ltd., Stranraer Harbour, Dumfries and Galloway, DG9 8EJ, DG9 8EJ, ℘ (0776) 2262, Telex 778125.

Sealink UK Ltd., 24 Donegall Place., Belfast, BT1 5BH, Northern Ireland, ℘ (0232) 227525, Telex 748079.

Sealink UK Ltd., The Jetty, St Peter Port, Guernsey, Channel Islands, ℘ (0481) 24742, Telex 4191249.

Sealink UK Ltd., Wests Centre, St Helier, Jersey, Channel Islands, ℘ (0534) 77122, Telex 4192262.

Sealink Isle of Man, Sea Terminal, Douglas, Isle of Man, ℘ (0624) 24241.

Sealink UK Ltd., 15 Westmoreland St., Dublin 2, Eire, ℘ 714455, Telex 30847.

Manager British Rail, Rue de la Montagne 52, B-1000 Brussels, Belgium, ℘ 511 6685, Telex 23108 GB RAIL B .

Manager British Rail, Montergade 5, DK 1116 Kobenhavn K, Denmark, ℘ 12 64 60, Telex 15370.

Armement Naval SNCF, Gare Maritime BP 27, F-62201 Boulogne-sur-Mer, France, ℘ 21 30 25 11, Telex 110908.

Armement Naval SNCF, Terminal TNM, Gare Maritime, F-62100 Calais, France, ℘ 21 96 70 70, Telex 130086.

Agence Maritime Tellier, Gare Maritime, F-50100 Cherbourg, France, ℘ 33 53 24 27, Telex 170684.

Armement Naval SNCF, Gare Maritime BP 85, F-76203 Dieppe, France, ℘ 35 82 24 87, Telex 770924.

Armement Naval SNCF, 3 Rue Ambroise-Paré, 75010 Paris, France, ℘ 42 80 48 48, Telex 80549.

Manager British Rail, Boulevard de la Madeleine, F-75009 Paris, ℘ 42 66 90 53, Telex 210774.

Manager British Rail, Neue Mainzer Strasse 22, D-6000 Frankfurt/Main, Germany, ℘ 23.23.81, Telex 416421.

Manager British Rail, Via Pirelli 11, 20124 Milan, Italy, ℘ 655 683, Telex 310412.

Manager British Rail, Leidseplein 5, Amsterdam, Netherlands, ℘ 234 133, Telex 13395.

Manager British Rail, Centralbahnplatz 9, 4002 Basel, Switzerland, ℘ 23 14 04, Telex 62739.

SERVICE MARITIME CARTERET-JERSEY

BP 15, 50270 Barneville-Carteret, France, ✆ 33 53 87 21, Telex 170477.

Agent : CNTM Ltd., Gorey, Jersey, Channel Islands, ✆ (0534) 53737.

SHETLAND ISLANDS COUNCIL

Grantfield, Lerwick, Shetland, ZE1 ONT, ✆ (0595) 2024, Telex 75218.

SMYRIL LINE

P.O. Box 370, Jonas Broncksgoeta 25, 3800 Thorshavn, Faroe Islands, ✆ (042) 15900, Telex 81296.

Agent : P & O Ferries, Orkney & Shetland Services, P.O. Box 5, P & O Ferry Terminal, Aberdeen, AB9 8DL, Scotland, ✆ (0224) 572615, Telex 73344.

Ferdaskrivistofa Rikisins, Skogarhlid 6, Reykjavik, Iceland, ✆ (91) 25855, Telex 2049.

O.P. Travelagency, Radhuspladsen 16, 4 sal. 1550 Copenhagen, Denmark, ✆ (01) 120500, Telex 15799.

THOMAS & BEWS FERRIES

Ferry Office, John O'Groats, Caithness, Scotland, ✆ (095 581) 353 (summer).

Windieknap, Brough, Thurso, Caithness, Scotland, ✆ (084 785) 619 (winter).

TORBAY SEAWAY

Beacon Quay, Torquay, Devon, ✆ (0803) 211974.

TOWNSEND THORESEN

Agents : 127 Regent Street, London, W1R 8LB, ✆ (01) 734 4431, Telex 23802.

Main Reservation Centre, Enterprise Hse., Channel View Rd Dover, CT17 9TJ, Kent, ✆ (0304) 223000 Reservations : ✆ 203388.

Car Ferry House, Canute Road, Southampton, SO9 5GP, Hampshire, ✆ (0703) 34488.

Continental Ferry Port, Mile End, Portsmouth Hants, ✆ (0705) 827677 and 755521.

European House, The Docks, Felixstowe, IP11 8TS, Suffolk, ✆ (039 42) 78711, Telex 98236.

Cairnryan, Stranraer, Wigtownshire, Scotland, ✆ (058 12) 276 and 277.

Larne Harbour, Larne, Co. Antrim, Northern Ireland, ✆ (0574) 4321, Telex 747814.

Car Ferry Terminal, Doverlaan 7, B-8380 Zeebrugge, Belgium, ✆ (050) 54.50.50.

41 place d'Armes, 62226 Calais, France, ✆ 21 97 21 21, Telex 810750.

41 boulevard des Capucines, 75002 Paris, France, ✆ 42 61 51 75, Telex 210679.

Gare Maritime, 50101 Cherbourg, France, ✆ 33 44 20 13.

90 rue de Paris, 59000 Lille, ✆ 20 57 74 65, Telex 120311

Quai de Southampton, 76600 Le Havre, France, ✆ 35 21 36 50.

Leidsestraat 32, Amsterdam, Netherlands, ✆ (020) 223832, Telex 14601.

VEDETTES ARMORICAINES

Gare Maritime de la Bourse, B.P. 180, 35049 St-Malo, France, ✆ 99 56 48 88, Telex 950196 NAVIPAX.

Agents : Vedettes Armoricaines, Albert Pier, St. Helier, Jersey, ✆ 20361, Telex 4192131 NAVIEX.

Boutins Travel Bureau, Library Pl., St. Helier, Jersey, ✆ 21532/3/4, Telex 4192149.

12 rue Georges-Clemenceau, B.P. 24, 50400 Granville, France, ✆ 33 50 77 45, Telex 170449 F.

1er Bassin, Port de Commerce, BP 88, 29268 Brest, France, ✆ 98 44 44 04, Telex 940210 NAVIPAMF.

VEDETTES BLANCHES

Les Vedettes Blanches, Gare Maritime, 35400 St-Malo, France, ✆ 99 56 63 21.

Agent : Vedettes Blanches, Albert Quay, St. Helier, Jersey, ✆ (0534) 74458, Telex 4192311 SEACAR.

VEDETTES VERTES GRANVILLAISES

1-3 rue Le Campion, 50400 Granville, France, ✆ 33 50 16 36, Telex 170002.

Agent : Marine Management Ltd., Albert Quay, St. Helier, Jersey, ✆ (0534) 74458, Telex 4192311 SEACAR.

VIKING ISLAND FERRIES

Horries, Deerness, Orkney, KW17 2QL, ✆ (0856 74) 351 and 242, Telex 75519.

WESTERN FERRIES ARGYLL LTD.

16 Woodside Crescent, Glasgow, Scotland, G3 7UT, ✆ (041) 332 9766, Telex 77203 CLYDE-BUILT.

Agent : Hunters Quay, Dunoon, Argyll, Scotland, ✆ (0369) 4452.

MICHELIN

Consultez aussi les pages d'introduction (p. 2 à 48)

🏰	Grand luxe	XXXXX
🏨	Grand confort	XXXX
🏩	Très confortable	XXX
🏠	De bon confort	XX
🏠	Assez confortable	X
🏡	Simple mais convenable	
↑	Autre ressource hôtelière conseillée à prix modérés.	

❀❀❀	Une des meilleures tables : vaut le voyage
❀❀	Table excellente : mérite un détour
❀	Une très bonne table dans sa catégorie
M	Voir page 23
☕	Petit déjeuner

🏨...🏠	Hôtels agréables
XXX...X	Restaurants agréables
⇐	Vue exceptionnelle
⇐	Vue intéressante ou étendue
⚓	Hôtel très tranquille, isolé
⚓	Hôtel tranquille

⬛ ⬛	Piscine en plein air ou couverte
🌳 ✗	Jardin de repos - Tennis à l'hôtel
🎣 ⛳	Pêche ouverte aux clients de l'hôtel - Golf et nombre de trous

⬛ ⬛	Ascenseur - Air conditionné
TV	Télévision dans la chambre
⬛wc	Salle de bain et wc privés
⬛wc	Douche et wc privés
☎	Téléphone dans la chambre
☎	Téléphone direct
♿	Accessible aux handicapés physiques
🚗 Ⓟ	Garage - Parc à voitures
⬛	Salles de conférence
✗	Accès interdit aux chiens

☞ *Pour être inscrit au guide Michelin*
  - pas de piston,
  - pas de pot de vin !

MANUFA ... **MICHELIN**

Printed in France — 12-85-79

Photocomposition : S.C.I.A., La Chapelle d'Armentières - Impression : Tardy Quercy, Bourges n° 12602

MICHELIN

See also the explanatory pages (pp. 2 to 48)

Luxury	🏰🏰🏰🏰🏰
Top class comfort	🏨🏨🏨🏨
Very comfortable	🏨🏨🏨
Good average	🏨🏨
Quite comfortable	🏨
Modest comfort	
Other accommodation, at moderate prices.	

❀❀❀	Some of the best cuisine, worth a journey
❀❀	Excellent cooking, worth a detour
❀	An especially good restaurant in its class
M	See page 15
☕	Breakfast

Pleasant hotels	
Pleasant restaurants	
≤	Exceptional view
≤	Interesting or extensive view
⅀	Quiet and secluded hotel
⅀	Quiet hotel

Outdoor or indoor swimming pool	
Garden · Hotel tennis court	
Fishing available to hotel guests · Golf course and number of holes	

Lift · Air conditioning	
TV	Television in room
⇨wc	Private bathroom with toilet
⇨wc	Private shower with toilet
☏	External phone in room
☎	Direct dialling
♿	Accessible to the physically handicapped
🚗 ℗	Garage available · Car park
⚐	Business conference facilities
🐕	Dogs not allowed

☞ *Inclusion in the Michelin Guide cannot be achieved by pulling strings or by offering favours.*

With index of places

401 SCOTLAND

402 MIDLANDS - THE NORTH

403 WALES - WEST COUNTRY - MIDLANDS

404 SOUTH EAST - MIDLANDS - EAST ANGLIA

405 IRELAND

1/400 000 - 1 in : 6.30 miles

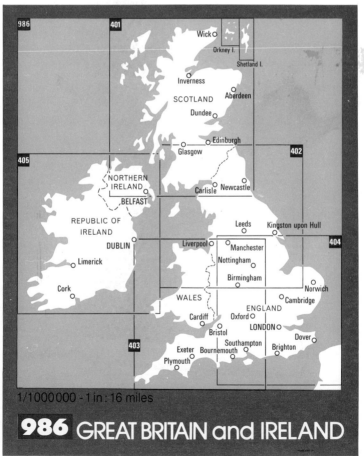

1/1 000 000 - 1 in : 16 miles

986 GREAT BRITAIN and IRELAND

619

Green
Tourist Guides
English editions

**ENGLAND: THE WEST COUNTRY - LONDON
SCOTLAND**

AUSTRIA - GERMANY - ITALY
PORTUGAL - ROME - SPAIN
SWITZERLAND

BRITTANY - CHATEAUX OF THE LOIRE
DORDOGNE - FRENCH RIVIERA - NORMANDY
PARIS - PROVENCE

CANADA - NEW ENGLAND - NEW YORK CITY